AMERICA

AMERICA

A NARRATIVE HISTORY

BRIEF THIRD EDITION

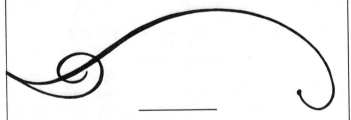

GEORGE BROWN TINDALL

DAVID E. SHI

W · W · NORTON & COMPANY · NEW YORK · LONDON

FOR BRUCE AND BLAIR

FOR

JASON AND JESSICA

The text of this book is composed in Caledonia, with the display set in
Torino Roman. Composition by New England Typographic Service, Inc.
Manufacturing by Courier, Westford. Book design by Antonina Krass.

Library of Congress Cataloging-in-Publication Data

Tindall, George Brown.
    America : a narrative history / George Brown Tindall ; David E. Shi.—
    Brief 3rd ed.
      p. cm.
    Includes index.
    ISBN 0-393-96295-4 (pbk)
      1. United States—History.   I. Shi, David E.   II. Title.
  E178.1.T55   1993   92-34788
  973—dc20   CIP

W. W. Norton & Company, Inc., 500 Fifth Avenue, New York, N. Y. 10110

W. W. Norton & Company Ltd., 10 Coptic Street, London WC1A 1PU

2   3   4   5   6   7   8   9   0

CONTENTS

List of Maps • xiii
Preface • xv

1. | DISCOVERY AND SETTLEMENT   1

PRE-COLUMBIAN INDIAN CIVILIZATIONS   1 • THE COLLISION OF
CULTURES   3 • SETTLING THE CHESAPEAKE   16 • SETTLING
NEW ENGLAND   20 • RENEWED SETTLEMENT   28
THRIVING COLONIES   35 • FURTHER READING   36

2. | COLONIAL WAYS OF LIFE   38

THE SHAPE OF EARLY AMERICA   38 • SOCIETY AND ECONOMY
IN THE SOUTHERN COLONIES   44 • SOCIETY AND ECONOMY
IN NEW ENGLAND   51 • SOCIETY AND ECONOMY IN
THE MIDDLE COLONIES   59 • COLONIAL CITIES   61
THE ENLIGHTENMENT   63 • THE GREAT AWAKENING   66
FURTHER READING   70

3. | THE IMPERIAL PERSPECTIVE   72

ENGLISH ADMINISTRATION OF THE COLONIES   72 • THE HABIT OF
SELF-GOVERNMENT   78 • TROUBLED NEIGHBORS   80
THE COLONIAL WARS   86 • FURTHER READING   91

4. | FROM EMPIRE TO INDEPENDENCE   93

THE HERITAGE OF WAR   93 • WESTERN LANDS   95 • GRENVILLE
AND THE STAMP ACT   96 • FANNING THE FLAMES   101
DISCONTENT ON THE FRONTIER   105 • A WORSENING CRISIS   106
SHIFTING AUTHORITY   112 • INDEPENDENCE   117 • FURTHER
READING   119

5. | THE AMERICAN REVOLUTION 121

1776: WASHINGTON'S NARROW ESCAPE 121 • AMERICAN SOCIETY AT
WAR 123 • 1777: SETBACKS FOR THE BRITISH 127 • 1778: BOTH
SIDES REGROUP 130 • THE WAR IN THE SOUTH 133
NEGOTIATIONS 138 • THE POLITICAL REVOLUTION 139
THE SOCIAL REVOLUTION 142 • EMERGENCE OF AN
AMERICAN CULTURE 148 • FURTHER READING 151

6. | SHAPING A FEDERAL UNION 152

THE CONFEDERATION 152 • ADOPTING THE CONSTITUTION 162
"A MORE PERFECT UNION" 173 • FURTHER READING 173

7. | THE FEDERALISTS: WASHINGTON AND ADAMS 175

A NEW GOVERNMENT 175 • HAMILTON'S VISION OF
AMERICA 178   THE REPUBLICAN ALTERNATIVE 183 • CRISES
FOREIGN AND DOMESTIC 185 • THE ADAMS YEARS 193 • FURTHER
READING 200

8. | REPUBLICANISM: JEFFERSON AND MADISON 202

JEFFERSON IN POWER 202 • DIVISIONS IN THE REPUBLICAN
PARTY 210 • WAR IN EUROPE 214 • THE WAR OF 1812 217
FURTHER READING 228

9. | NATIONALISM AND SECTIONALISM 229

ECONOMIC NATIONALISM 229 • "GOOD FEELINGS" 232
"A FIREBELL IN THE NIGHT" 237
JUDICIAL NATIONALISM 240
NATIONALIST DIPLOMACY 242 • ONE-PARTY POLITICS 244
FURTHER READING 250

10. | THE JACKSONIAN IMPULSE 252

SETTING THE STAGE 252 • NULLIFICATION 255 • INDIAN
POLICY 261 • THE BANK CONTROVERSY 264 • VAN BUREN AND
THE NEW PARTY SYSTEM 270 • ASSESSING THE JACKSON
YEARS 275 • FURTHER READING 277

11. | THE DYNAMICS OF GROWTH 278

AGRICULTURE AND THE NATIONAL ECONOMY 278 • TRANSPORTATION AND THE NATIONAL ECONOMY 280 • THE GROWTH OF INDUSTRY 286 • IMMIGRATION 292 • ORGANIZED LABOR 301 JACKSONIAN INEQUALITY 303 • FURTHER READING 304

12. | AN AMERICAN RENAISSANCE: RELIGION, ROMANTICISM, AND REFORM 306

RATIONAL RELIGION 306 • THE SECOND AWAKENING 308 ROMANTICISM IN AMERICA 313 • THE FLOWERING OF AMERICAN LITERATURE 316 • EDUCATION 321 • SOME MOVEMENTS FOR REFORM 323 • FURTHER READING 333

13. | MANIFEST DESTINY 335

THE TYLER YEARS 335 • MOVING WEST 337 • ANNEXING TEXAS 343 • POLK'S PRESIDENCY 347 • THE MEXICAN WAR 350 • FURTHER READING 357

14. | THE OLD SOUTH: AN AMERICAN TRAGEDY 359

MYTH, REALITY, AND THE OLD SOUTH 359 • WHITE SOCIETY IN THE SOUTH 364 • BLACK SOCIETY IN THE SOUTH 366 ANTISLAVERY MOVEMENTS 373 • FURTHER READING 381

15. | THE CRISIS OF UNION 383

SLAVERY IN THE TERRITORIES 383 • THE COMPROMISE OF 1850 387 • FOREIGN ADVENTURES 394 • THE KANSAS-NEBRASKA CRISIS 395 • THE DEEPENING SECTIONAL CRISIS 402 • THE CENTER COMES APART 409 • FURTHER READING 414

16. | THE WAR OF THE UNION 416

AN EPIC STRUGGLE 416 • A MODERN WAR 420 • THE WAR'S EARLY COURSE 423 • EMANCIPATION 432 • GOVERNMENT DURING THE WAR 434 • THE FALTERING CONFEDERACY 438 THE CONFEDERACY'S DEFEAT 444 • FURTHER READING 449

17. | RECONSTRUCTION: NORTH AND SOUTH   451

THE BATTLE OVER RECONSTRUCTION   451 • RECONSTRUCTING THE
SOUTH   460 • THE GRANT YEARS   471 • FURTHER READING   478

18. | NEW FRONTIERS: SOUTH AND WEST   480

THE NEW SOUTH   480 • THE NEW WEST   490 • FURTHER
READING   501

19. | BIG BUSINESS AND ORGANIZED LABOR   503

THE POST–CIVIL WAR ECONOMY   503 • ENTREPRENEURS   508
ADVANCES FOR LABOR   515 • FURTHER READING   528

20. | THE EMERGENCE OF MODERN AMERICA   530

AMERICA'S MOVE TO TOWN   530 • THE NEW IMMIGRATION   533
EDUCATION AND THE PROFESSIONS   541 • THEORIES OF SOCIAL
CHANGE   544 • REALISM IN FACT AND FICTION   545 • THE SOCIAL
GOSPEL   551 • EARLY EFFORTS AT URBAN REFORM   554 • FURTHER
READING   557

21. | GILDED AGE POLITICS AND AGRARIAN REVOLT   559

PARADOXICAL POLITICS   559 • CORRUPTION AND REFORM   562
THE PROBLEMS OF FARMERS   573 • AGRARIAN REVOLT   576
FURTHER READING   586

22. | THE COURSE OF EMPIRE   588

TOWARD THE NEW IMPERIALISM   588 • STEPS TO WORLD
POWER   591 • THE SPANISH-AMERICAN WAR   592 • IMPERIAL
RIVALRIES IN EAST ASIA   604 • AN AMERICAN ORIGINAL   606
ROOSEVELT'S FOREIGN POLICY   609 • FURTHER READING   613

23. | PROGRESSIVISM: ROOSEVELT, TAFT, AND WILSON   615

ELEMENTS OF REFORM   615 • THE FEATURES OF
PROGRESSIVISM   618 • ROOSEVELT'S PROGRESSIVISM   622
TOWARD A SECOND TERM   625 • FROM ROOSEVELT TO TAFT   627

WILSON'S PROGRESSIVISM   631   •   THE LIMITS OF
PROGRESSIVISM   641   •   FURTHER READING   642

24. | Wilson and the Great War   644

WILSON AND FOREIGN AFFAIRS   644   •   THE GREAT WAR AND
AMERICA   648   •   AMERICA'S ENTRY   656   •   "THE DECISIVE
POWER"   663   •   THE FIGHT FOR PEACE   667   •   LURCHING FROM
WAR TO PEACE   673   •   FURTHER READING   677

25. | Society and Culture Between the Wars   678

REACTION IN THE TWENTIES   678   •   SOCIAL TENSIONS   685   •   THE
CULTURE OF MODERNISM   691   •   CULTURE IN THE THIRTIES   696
FURTHER READING   701

26. | Republican Resurgence and Decline, 1920–1932   702

PROGRESSIVISM TRANSFORMED   702   •   "NORMALCY"   703   •   THE
NEW ERA   710   •   PRESIDENT HOOVER, THE ENGINEER   718
FURTHER READING   727

27. | Franklin D. Roosevelt and the New Deal   728

FROM HOOVERISM TO THE NEW DEAL   728   •   RECOVERY THROUGH
REGULATION   734   •   LAUNCHING THE SECOND NEW DEAL   741
SECOND-TERM SETBACKS AND INITIATIVES   749   •   THE LEGACY OF THE
NEW DEAL   754   •   FURTHER READING   757

28. | From Isolation to Global War   758

POSTWAR ISOLATIONISM   758   •   WAR CLOUDS   762   •   THE STORM IN
EUROPE   770   •   THE STORM IN THE PACIFIC   775   •   FURTHER
READING   780

29. | The World at War   781

AMERICA'S EARLY BATTLES   781   •   MOBILIZATION AT HOME   783
THE ALLIED DRIVE TOWARD BERLIN   790   •   LEAPFROGGING TO
TOKYO   796   •   A NEW AGE IS BORN   800   •   FURTHER READING   810

30. | THE FAIR DEAL AND CONTAINMENT 811

DEMOBILIZATION UNDER TRUMAN 811 • THE COLD WAR 816
HARRY GIVES 'EM HELL 823 • THE COLD WAR HEATS UP 828
FURTHER READING 836

31. | THROUGH THE PICTURE WINDOW: POSTWAR SOCIETY AND CULTURE, 1945–1960 838

PEOPLE OF PLENTY 838 • A CONFORMING CULTURE 844 •
CRACKS IN THE PICTURE WINDOW 848 • A PARADOXICAL ERA 855
FURTHER READING 856

32. | CONFLICT AND DEADLOCK: THE EISENHOWER YEARS 857

"TIME FOR A CHANGE" 857 • CIVIL RIGHTS IN THE FIFTIES 871
A SEASON OF TROUBLES 876 • ASSESSING THE EISENHOWER
YEARS 882 • FURTHER READING 883

33. | NEW FRONTIERS: KENNEDY AND JOHNSON 885

THE NEW FRONTIER 885 • FOREIGN FRONTIERS 893 • LYNDON
JOHNSON AND THE GREAT SOCIETY 897 • FROM CIVIL RIGHTS TO
BLACK POWER 902 • THE TRAGEDY OF VIETNAM 906 • SIXTIES
CRESCENDO 911 • FURTHER READING 913

34. | REBELLION AND REACTION IN THE SEVENTIES 915

THE ROOTS OF REBELLION 915 • NIXON AND VIETNAM 925
NIXON AND MIDDLE AMERICA 930 • NIXON TRIUMPHANT 934
WATERGATE 936 • AN UNELECTED PRESIDENT 940 • THE CARTER
INTERREGNUM 941 • FURTHER READING 947

35. | A NEW GILDED AGE 949

THE REAGAN RESTORATION 949 • REAGAN'S SECOND TERM 960
THE BUSH YEARS 972 • THE HOME FRONT 989 • THE SOCIAL
FABRIC IN THE 1990S 997 • FURTHER READING 1005

APPENDIX A1

THE DECLARATION OF INDEPENDENCE A1 • ARTICLES OF
CONFEDERATION A5 • THE CONSTITUTION OF THE UNITED
STATES A12 • PRESIDENTIAL ELECTIONS A30 • ADMISSION OF
STATES A38 • POPULATION OF THE UNITED STATES A39
IMMIGRATION TO THE UNITED STATES, FISCAL YEARS
1820–1990 A40 • IMMIGRATION BY REGION AND SELECTED
COUNTRY OF LAST RESIDENCE, FISCAL YEARS 1820–1989 A42
PRESIDENTS, VICE-PRESIDENTS, AND SECRETARIES OF STATE A49
CHRONOLOGY OF SIGNIFICANT EVENTS A54

ILLUSTRATION CREDITS A65

INDEX A69

MAPS

Columbus's Voyages 5
Early Virginia and Maryland 20
Early New England Settlements 22
Early Settlements in the South 30
Atlantic Trade Routes 53
Major Immigrant Groups in Colonial
  America 60
The French in North America 85
The Seven Years' War: Major
  Campaigns, 1754–1760 88
Lexington and Concord, April 19,
  1775 113
Major Campaigns in New York and
  New Jersey, 1776–1777 122
Major Campaigns of 1777: Saratoga
  and Philadelphia 129
Western Campaigns,
  1778–1779 132
Major Campaigns in the South,
  1778–1781 134
Yorktown, 1781 134
North America, 1783 139
The Old Northwest, 1785 155
Pinckney's Treaty, 1795 190
Election of 1800 199
Explorations of the Louisiana
  Purchase 208
The War of 1812: Major Northern
  Campaigns 221
The War of 1812: Major Southern
  Campaigns 224
The National Road, 1811–1838 232
Boundary Treaties, 1818–1819 236
The Missouri Compromise
  (1820) 239
Indian Removal, 1820–1840 263

Transportation West, about
  1840 282–283
The Mormon Trek, 1830–1851 312
The Webster-Ashburton Treaty,
  1842 337
Wagon Trails West 339
The Oregon Dispute,
  1818–1846 349
The Mexican War: Major
  Campaigns 355
Compromise of 1850 391
The Kansas-Nebraska Act,
  1854 399
Secession, 1860–1861 418
First Bull Run, July 21, 1861 419
Campaigns in the West, February-
  April 1862 425
The Peninsular Campaign,
  1862 428
Campaigns in Virginia & Maryland,
  1862 430
Campaigns in the East, 1863 439
Vicksburg, 1863 440
Battles near Chattanooga, 1863
  443
Grant in Virginia, 1864–1865 445
Sherman's Campaigns,
  1864–1865 446
Reconstruction, 1865–1877 470
Indian Wars, 1864–1890 493
Spanish-American War: The Pacific,
  1898 597
Spanish-American War: The
  Caribbean, 1898 598
U.S. Interests in the Caribbean 609
Europe at War 649

The Western Front, 1918   664
Europe after Versailles   669
The Tennessee Valley
    Authority   740
Aggression in Europe   766
Japanese Expansion before Pearl
    Harbor   776
War in Europe and Africa,
    1942–1945   792–793
The War in the Pacific,
    1942–1945   798–799

Occupation of Germany and
    Austria   822
The Korean War, 1950   830
The Korean War, 1950–1953   830
Postwar Alliances: The Far
    East   870
Postwar Alliances: Europe, North
    Africa, The Middle East   877
Vietnam, 1966   907
The Post Cold War West   979
The Gulf War, 1990–1991   985

PREFACE

The warm reception instructors have accorded the Brief Second edition of *America: A Narrative History* suggests that the book's purpose remains valid: to offer a succinct introductory narrative history of America—a narrative alive with character, augmented with analysis and social texture, and propelled by the energy of great events. The format continues to be unique in its field: *America* is designed to be read. Its single-column page remains uncluttered by distracting inserts, portfolios, or other interruptions to the story. It also remains the only text that students can purchase without breaking the bank and carry around without breaking the back.

Why a brief edition? We hope it meets the needs of those instructors who must cover the American past from its pre-Columbian roots to the present in one semester or less. It is also intended for those professors who prefer to assign students a brief text and rely more heavily on supplementary readings.

Smaller by one-third than the full Third Edition, the Brief *America* retains the character and appearance of its parent volume. The narrative is still strewn with colorful personalities and illuminating anecdotes, but its detail has been pared back throughout. Almost all the major subjects discussed in the full edition remain here, but most have been reduced in length and several sections have been reorganized.

The most salient theme of this new edition is embodied in a question posed over two hundred years ago by J. Hector St. John de Crèvecoeur, a transplanted French farmer: "What then is the American, this new man?" Crèvecoeur, who arrived in the colonies in 1759, married an American woman, and settled on a New York farm, went on to explain in *Letters from an American Farmer* that in America "individuals of all nations are melted into a new race of men, whose labors and posterity will one day cause great changes in the world." Fifty years later the transcendental philosopher-poet Ralph Waldo Emerson addressed the same point when he wrote in his journal that in America, this "asylum of all nations, the energy of Irish, Germans, Swedes, Poles and Cossacks, and all the European tribes—of the Africans and of the Polynesians, will construct a new race . . . as vigorous as the new Europe which came out of the smelting pot of the Dark Ages."

These statements express a shared truth: from its inception America has been an ambitious effort to create a pluralist society. The United States has welcomed more people from other places than any other country in history, and the process of absorbing such a multicultural population has given American life its roiling energy. The lofty social aim of American civilization is expressed in the official motto of the United States, *e pluribus unum*—"one out of many."

Yet the national motto has rarely described the reality. Americans have prided themselves on their ability to fashion what one New York mayor called a "gorgeous mosaic," an integration of different ethnic groups and cultural backgrounds. But in fact the United States has never become the mythic "melting pot" envisioned by Crèvecoeur, Emerson, and others. Instead, peoples from the four corners of the globe have converged to form a richly diverse—and often fractious, too often violent—society held tenuously together by a shared commitment to democratic principles, economic opportunity, religious freedom, and the rule of law.

From the Revolutionary era to the 1990s, the nation's politicians, preachers, and pundits have debated the effects of America's quest for unity through diversity. This quest forms a prominent thread running through the pages of this edition. It surfaces in discussions of the backgrounds and folkways of the colonists, in accounts of the waves of "new" immigration in the late nineteenth and late twentieth centuries and the nativist prejudices they aroused, in descriptions of the tangled skein of legislation affecting immigrants and refugees, and in data detailing recent trends in immigration and ethnic diversity. Few students, we suspect, realize that immigrants were responsible for one-third of the population growth of the United States in the 1980s, or that fully 80 percent of the newcomers were from Asia and Latin America.

To describe the remarkable "peopling of America," this edition of *America* highlights biography. From Anne Hutchinson and John Winthrop through Sojourner Truth, Mary Elizabeth

Lease, Amelia Earhart and Martin Luther King, Jr., brief biographies integrated throughout the narrative give students a more textured feel for the character and personality of key figures. And in fresh treatments of female slaves, women workers at the Lowell mills, women on the frontier and on the social fronts of foreign wars, this Brief Third Edition of *America* offers enhanced discussions of women's lives and their contributions to American history.

By its very nature a brief survey can neither exhaust the facts of history nor treat every fashion of theory or interpretation, whether old or new. It instead offers a tour of the house of history, so to speak, pointing out many doors, stopping to open a few, stepping inside some of them, and all the while hoping that readers will be enticed to explore further what is behind those doors and others.

Our collaboration on the Brief Third Edition and its parent version benefited greatly from the insights and suggestions of many people. The following scholars provided close readings of the full manuscript at various stages: Albert Broussard (Texas A & M University), Janet Coryell (Auburn University), Charles Eagles (University of Mississippi), Peter R. Knights (York University), Phillip L. Osborne (United States Air Force Academy), David Parker (Southwest Missouri State University), Malcolm Rohrbough (University of Iowa), and Daniel B. Thorp (Virginia Polytechnic Institute and State University). Copyeditors Debra Makay and Margie Brassil polished the manuscript. Kristin Prevallet showed remarkable energy in gathering material for illustrations, and Bonnie Hall helped with innumerable details. Linda Sellars (University of North Carolina) updated the bibliographies originally prepared by Gary Freeze (Erskine College) and revised for the second edition by David Parker. Steve Forman, our steadfast editor at W. W. Norton, remains a pillar of insight and patience. An accomplished wordsmith with a certain historical flourish himself, he pruned our prose without bruising our pride and in the process gave enhanced meaning to the term discretion. We are confident that this edition of *America* is the better for the assistance provided by all of these people.

—George B. Tindall
Chapel Hill, North Carolina

—David E. Shi
Davidson, North Carolina

1

DISCOVERY AND SETTLEMENT

The earliest Americans are lost in the mists of time, where legends abound. Some romancers have claimed that the continent's first human inhabitants came from the mythical lost continent of Atlantis; others believe that they drifted across from Asia, Africa, or Europe. The most plausible explanation is that nomadic people entered the New World from Siberia to Alaska, either by island-hopping across the Bering Strait or by traversing a fifty-mile land bridge (Beringia) exposed by receding waters during the Ice Ages. They arrived some 15,000–25,000 years ago, when people could still walk across. For thousands of years small bands of these Asian immigrants split off from one another and filtered southward from the desolate, frigid, and wind-swept Yukon, following migrating mammoths and giant bison toward warmer regions, eventually reaching the tip of South America and the Atlantic coast of North America.

Pre-Columbian Indian Civilizations

Once the ice sheets melted and the sea rose again, these migrants were cut off from the rest of humanity, except for the short-lived Viking settlements on Greenland (A.D. 985) and Newfoundland (A.D. 1001). Archeological digs add yearly to the fragments of knowledge about pre-Columbian America. The richest finds have been made in the high altitudes of Mexico and Peru, where the Olmecs, Mayas, Aztecs, Incas, and others built great empires and a monumental architecture, supported by large-scale agriculture and a far-flung commerce.

THE MAYAS, AZTECS, AND INCAS   By about 2000–1500 B.C. the nomadic Indian tradition began to give way in what is today Central

America to more permanent farming settlements. The more settled life in turn provided leisure for more complex cultures, for the cultivation of religion, crafts, art, science, civic administration—and organized warfare. A stratified social structure also developed. From about A.D. 300–900 this Middle American region reached its cultural peak, with great religious centers, gigantic pyramids, temple complexes, and ceremonial courts, all supported by the surrounding villages. The Mayas, living in present-day Yucatán, Guatemala, Belize, and western Honduras and El Salvador, were a warlike people who ruled a far-flung and loosely controlled empire. They built dozens of pyramids, devised a complex writing system based on hieroglyphs, and developed enough mathematics and astronomy to devise a calendar more accurate than that used by Columbus. Then, about A.D. 900, for reasons unknown, Mayan culture abruptly collapsed and the religious centers were abandoned.

The equally warlike Aztecs, who arrived from the northwest, founded the city of Tenochtitlán (now Mexico City) in 1325 and gradually extended their control over central Mexico. When the Spaniards invaded in 1519, the Aztec Empire under Montezuma II ruled over 5 million people who were held in fairly loose subjugation by a hereditary elite of warrior-priests. Their economy depended on agriculture, and their religious practices included human sacrifices to the sun god. (More than 5,000 people were supposedly sacrificed to celebrate the coronation of Montezuma II in 1502.) Farther south, Incas by the fifteenth century controlled an empire that stretched a thousand miles along the Andes mountains from Ecuador to Chile, connected by an elaborate system of roads and organized under an autocratic government which dominated community life as fully as any twentieth-century totalitarian state.

INDIAN CULTURES OF NORTH AMERICA   Of the hundreds of Indian tribes inhabiting the present-day United States, the ancestors of only a few such as the Pueblos, Creeks, and Iroquois ever approached the level of social organization or cultural sophistication achieved by the Mayas or Aztecs. North American tribes tended to be smaller, more scattered, and less settled. Most of them migrated with the seasons in search of food—fish, deer, rabbits, maize (corn), nuts, berries—and temperate locales. They built few permanent structures and tended to own land communally, although individuals were allowed to own the food they produced or gathered.

In the Ohio and Mississippi River valleys many tribes did

A wooden carving of a mother carrying a child, found in a Hopewell burial mound in southern Ohio.

develop a thriving village culture which, while still primarily dependent on hunting and gathering for subsistence, also cultivated squash, beans, and maize. But even the most developed Indian societies of the sixteenth century were ill-equipped to resist the dynamic European cultures invading their world. There were large and fatal gaps in Indian knowledge and technology. The Indians of Mexico, for example, had copper and bronze but no iron, except a few specimens of meteorites. They had domesticated dogs, turkeys, and llamas, but horses were unknown until the Spaniards arrived. When fighting erupted, arrows and tomahawks were seldom a match for guns.

But despite such disadvantages, the Indians resisted European invaders for centuries. They displayed an amazing capacity for adapting to changing circumstances, incorporating European technology and weaponry, forging new alliances, changing their own community structures, and in a surprising number of instances converting whites to their way of life. Many Spanish, English, and French settlers voluntarily joined Indian society or chose to stay after being captured. As a French colonist in America noted, "thousands of Europeans are Indians," yet "we have no examples of even one of those Aborigines having from choice become Europeans."

THE COLLISION OF CULTURES

The discovery of the New World coincided with the opening of the modern period in European history. Indeed the burst of energy with which Europe spread its power and culture around the world provided the epoch-making force of modern times. The expansion of Europe derived from, and in turn affected, the peculiar patterns and institutions which distinguished modern times from the medieval: the revival of learning and the rise of the inquiring spirit; the explosive growth of trade, towns, and modern corporations; the decline of feudalism and the rise of national states; the religious zeal generated by the Protestant Reformation and the Catholic Counter-Reformation; and on the darker side, some old sins—greed, conquest, racism, and slavery. By the fifteenth century these forces had combined to focus European eyes on new lands to conquer or settle and new peoples to convert, civilize, or exploit. They were especially attracted by the lure of Asia, a near-mythical land of spices, silks, jewels, and millions of "heathens" to be Christianized. Marco Polo had returned from the Orient bedazzled by a region where "sands sparkled and glittered with gems and precious ores." But equally valued were the spices—pepper, nutmeg, clove—so essential to the preserving of food, especially in southern Europe, where the warm and humid climate accelerated spoilage.

THE VOYAGES OF COLUMBUS   The Orient's mythic wealth caught the expansive vision of Christopher Columbus. Born in 1451, the son of an Italian weaver, Columbus took to the sea at an early age and made up for his lack of formal education by learning geography, navigation, and Latin. As a young man he went on voyages to England and Iceland, and during the 1480s he hatched a scheme to reach Asia by sailing west. Columbus turned to Spain for backing, and after years of disappointment, he finally won the support of Ferdinand and Isabella, the Spanish monarchs. The legend that the queen had to hock the crown jewels is as outrageous as the fable that Columbus had to prove the earth was round.

Columbus, a tall, robust, red-haired, and long-faced man with a ruddy complexion, prominent oval eyes, and huge nose, chartered one ship, the *Santa María*, and the Spanish city of Palos supplied two smaller caravels, the *Pinta* and *Niña*. From Palos this little squadron, with eighty-seven men, set sail on August 2, 1492, and headed by dead-reckoning westward for what Co-

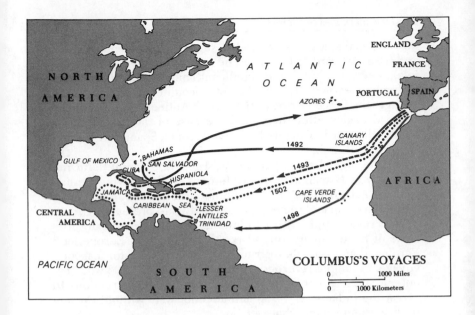

COLUMBUS'S VOYAGES

0   1000 Miles
0   1000 Kilometers

lumbus thought was Asia. The first leg of the journey went well,
thanks to a strong trade wind. But then the breeze lagged, the
days passed, and the crew began to grumble about their captain's
far-fetched plan. By October 10 talk of mutiny reached Columbus. He tried to rally flagging morale by reminding the crew
of the dazzling riches awaiting them. Yet skepticism remained
rife, and he finally promised that the expedition would turn back
if land were not sighted in three days.

Early on October 12, 1492, a lookout called out, "*Tierra!
Tierra!* [Land! Land!]." It was an island in the Bahamas that Columbus named San Salvador (Blessed Savior). According to Columbus's own reckoning he was near the Indies, so he called the
islanders "Indios,"—Indians. He described them as naked people, "very well made, of very handsome bodies and very good
faces." The Indians paddled out in dugout logs, which they
called *canoa*, and offered gifts of parrots and javelins to the
strangers. Their warm generosity and docile temperament led
Columbus to write in his journal that "they invite you to share
anything that they possess, and show as much love as if their
hearts went with it." Yet he added that "with 50 men they could
all be subjugated and compelled to do anything one wishes."

But at the moment Columbus was not interested in enslaving
"noble savages"; he was seeking the Orient and its fabled riches.
He therefore continued to search through the Bahamian Cays

down to Cuba, a place name that suggested Cipangua (Japan), and then eastward to the island he named Española (or Hispaniola), where he first found significant amounts of gold jewelry. Columbus learned of, but did not encounter until his second voyage, the fierce Caribs of the Lesser Antilles. The Caribbean Sea was named after them, and, because of their alleged bad habits, the word "Cannibal" derived from a Spanish version of their name (Caníbal).

On the night before Christmas, 1492, the *Santa María* ran aground off Hispaniola, and Columbus, still believing he had reached Asia, decided to return home. He left about forty men behind in camp and seized a dozen natives to present as gifts to Spain's royal couple. After Columbus finally reached Palos, the news of his discovery spread rapidly throughout Europe, and Ferdinand and Isabella instructed him to prepare for a second voyage. Columbus returned across the Atlantic in 1493 with seventeen ships and some 1,200 men, as well as instructions to "treat the Indians very well and affectionately without causing them any annoyance whatever."

Once back in the New World, Admiral Columbus discovered the camp in chaos. The unsupervised soldiers had run amok, raping native women, robbing Indian villages, and, as Columbus's son later added, "committing a thousand excesses for which they were mortally hated by the Indians." The Indians finally struck back and killed ten Spaniards. A furious Columbus immediately launched a wholesale attack on the Indian villages. The Spaniards, armed with crossbows, guns, and ferocious dogs, decimated the native defenders and loaded 500 of them onto ships bound for the slave market in Spain.

After two more voyages to the New World, Columbus finally returned to Spain in 1504, and two years later he died. To the end Columbus refused to believe that he had discovered anything other than outlying parts of the Orient. Ironically, the New World was named not for its discoverer but for one of the first to argue with conviction that it was indeed a New World rather than Asia. In 1501 Amerigo Vespucci, a Florentine merchant-turned-explorer, led a Portuguese expedition along South America's Atlantic coast. He reported that he had encountered lands making up what "we may rightly call a new world, because our ancestors had no knowledge of them, and it will be a matter wholly new to all those who hear about them." Vespucci's "new world" theories led European geographers to Latinize his first name and use it to label the new continent. "America" thus appeared for the first time on a printed map in 1507, along with a portrait of Vespucci.

THE GREAT BIOLOGICAL EXCHANGE The first European contacts with this New World began a remarkable diffusion of cultures, an exchange of such magnitude and rapidity as humanity had never known before. It was in fact more than a diffusion of cultures: it was a diffusion of distinctive biological systems. If anything, the plants and animals of the two worlds were more different than the people and their ways of life. Europeans, for instance, had never seen such creatures as the fearsome (if harmless) iguana, flying squirrels, catfish, rattlesnakes, or anything quite like several other species native to America: bison, cougars, armadillos, opossums, sloths, anacondas, electric eels, vampire bats, toucans, condors, or hummingbirds. Among the Indians' few domesticated animals they could recognize the dog and the duck, but turkeys, guinea pigs, llamas, and alpacas were all new. Nor did the Indians know of horses, cattle, pigs, sheep, goats, and (maybe) chickens, which soon arrived from Europe in abundance.

The transfer of plant life worked an even greater change, a revolution in the diets of both hemispheres. Before the discovery three main staples of the modern diet were unknown in the Old World: maize (corn), potatoes (sweet and white), and many kinds of beans (snap, kidney, lima beans, and others). When Columbus

An iguana drawn by John White, one of the earliest English settlers in America.

first sampled corn in Cuba, he declared it "most tasty boiled, roasted, or ground into flour." He returned to Spain with a handful of corn kernels, and within a few years corn was a staple crop throughout Europe. The white potato, although commonly called "Irish," actually migrated from South America to Europe and only reached North America with the Scotch-Irish immigrants of the 1700s. Other New World food plants were peanuts, squash, peppers, tomatoes, pumpkins, pineapples, papayas, avocadoes, cacao (the source of chocolate), and chicle (for chewing gum). Europeans in turn soon introduced rice, wheat, barley, oats, wine grapes, melons, coffee, olives, bananas, "Kentucky" bluegrass, daisies, and dandelions.

The beauty of the exchange was that the food plants were more complementary than competitive. They grew in different soils and climates, or in different seasons. Indian corn, it turned out, could flourish almost anywhere—high or low, hot or cold, wet or dry. It spread quickly throughout the world. Before the end of the 1500s American maize and sweet potatoes were staple crops in China. The green revolution exported from the Americas thus helped nourish a worldwide population explosion probably greater than any since the invention of agriculture, something like a fivefold increase between 1630 and 1950. Plants domesticated by American Indians now make up about a third of the world's food crops.

Europeans also adopted many Indian devices: canoes, snowshoes, moccasins, hammocks, kayaks, ponchos, dogsleds, toboggans, and parkas. The rubber ball and the game of lacrosse had Indian origins. New words entered European languages: *wigwam, teepee, papoose, succotash, tobacco, moose, skunk, opossum, woodchuck, chipmunk, tomahawk, hickory, pecan, raccoon,* and hundreds of others. And the aborigines left the map dotted with place names of Indian origin long after they were gone, from Miami to Yakima, from Penobscott to Yuma. There were still other New World contributions: tobacco and a number of drugs, including coca (for cocaine and novocaine), curare (a muscle relaxant), and cinchona bark (for quinine).

Unfortunately, the Europeans in exchange presented the Indians with illnesses they could not handle. Even minor diseases like measles turned killer in the bodies of Indians who had never encountered them and had built no immunity. Major infections like smallpox and typhus killed all the more speedily. The first contacts with some of Columbus's sailors devastated whole Indian communities. In the quarter century after Columbus colonized Hispaniola, the island's Indian population plummeted from 500,000 to 500. The epidemics spread rapidly into the interior, and some tribes lost 90–95 percent of their population within the first century of European colonization.

THE SPANISH EMPIRE Excited by Columbus's discoveries, professional explorers, mostly Italians, hired themselves out to look for that open sesame to riches, a western passage to the Orient. One after another of these men probed the shorelines of America during the early sixteenth century in the vain search for a passage to China, and in the process greatly increased European knowledge of the New World. The first to sight the North American continent was John Cabot, a Venetian sponsored by the English king, Henry VII. Cabot sailed across the North Atlantic in 1497. His landfall at what the king called "the newe founde lande" gave England the basis for later claim to all of North America. But during the early sixteenth century, the British became so preoccupied with internal divisions and conflicts with France that they failed to follow up Cabot's discoveries for several decades.

The New World thus was Spanish, except for Brazil, which was a Portuguese colony. The Caribbean Sea provided the funnel through which Spanish power entered the New World. After establishing colonies on Hispaniola and at Santo Domingo, which became the capital of the West Indies, the Spanish proceeded eastward to Puerto Rico (1508) and westward to Cuba (1511–1514). They were driven by very clear, if mixed, motives. Said one soldier: "We came here to serve God and the king, and also to get rich."

The great adventure of mainland conquest began in 1519, when Hernando Cortés and 600 men landed on the site of Vera Cruz, Mexico, which he founded. Cortés then set about a daring conquest of the Aztec Empire. The 200-mile march from Vera Cruz through difficult mountain passes to the Aztec capital of Tenochtitlán (Mexico City), and the subjugation of the Aztecs, was one of the most remarkable and tragic feats in human history.

Cortés had a few assets and made the most of them. An acute judge of character and a gifted diplomat as well as military leader, he landed in a region where the natives were still fighting off the spread of Aztec power and were ready to embrace new allies, especially those who possessed strange animals (horses) and powerful weapons. By a combination of threats and deception, Cortés was able to enter Tenochtitlán peacefully and to

In this 1599 woodcut, Cortés holds out his hand in friendship to the Aztec ruler Montezuma; Cortés would soon destroy Montezuma and enslave the Aztec nation.

make the emperor, Montezuma, his puppet. This state of affairs lasted until the spring of 1520, when the Aztecs rebelled and stoned Montezuma to death. The Spaniards lost about a third of their men as they fought their way out of the city. Their allies remained loyal, however, and Cortés gradually regrouped his forces; in 1521 he took the city again. Thereafter Cortés and his officers simply replaced the former Aztec overlords as rulers over the Indian empire.

In doing so they set the style for other conquistadors to follow, and within twenty years the Spanish had established an empire far larger than Rome's had ever been. Between 1522 and 1528 various lieutenants of Cortés conquered the remnants of Indian culture in Yucatán and Guatemala. In 1531 Francisco Pizarro led a band of soldiers down the Pacific coast from Panama toward Peru, where they attacked and subdued the Inca Empire. From Peru, conquistadors extended Spanish authority through Chile by about 1553, and to the north, in present-day Colombia, in 1536–1538.

SPANISH AMERICA The conquistadors transferred to America a system known as the *encomienda*, whereby favored officers took over entire Indian villages or groups of villages. They were called upon to protect and care for the villages and support missionary priests. In turn they could require tribute from the native villagers in the form of goods and labor. Spanish America therefore developed from the start a society of extremes: affluent European conquistadors, and subject native peoples who were held in poverty.

Those who remained, that is. By the mid-1500s Indians were nearly extinct in the West Indies, killed more by European diseases than by Spanish exploitation. To take their place the colonizers as early as 1503 began to import black slaves from Africa, a tragic practice that eventually would transport over 9 million people across the Atlantic in bondage. In all of Spain's New World empire, the Indian population dropped from about 50 million at the outset to 4 million in the seventeenth century, and slowly rose again to 7.5 million. Whites, who totaled no more than 100,000 in the mid-sixteenth century, numbered over 3 million by the end of the colonial period.

The Indians, however, did not always lack advocates. Catholic missionaries in many cases offered a sharp contrast to the conquistadors. They ventured into remote areas, often without weapons or protection, to spread the gospel—and often suffered martyrdom for their efforts. Where conquistadors sought to wrest gold, land, and labor from the Indians, the Spanish missionaries—as well as their French Jesuit and English Protestant counterparts of later years—wanted their souls, and they had a tremendous impact upon native American culture. At their worst the missionaries were bigots determined to rid "heathen" people of their native religions and many of their cultural practices. At their best, however, the missionaries were impassioned defenders of the Indians.

Although Spain's influence was strongest from Mexico southward, the "Spanish borderlands" of the southern United States from Florida to California preserve many reminders of Spanish presence. The earliest known exploration of Florida was made in 1513 by Juan Ponce de León, then governor of Puerto Rico. He sought the mythic fountain of youth but instead found alligators, swamps, and abundant wildlife. Meanwhile Spanish explorers skirted the Gulf coast from Florida to Vera Cruz, scouted the Atlantic coast from Cuba to Newfoundland, established a town at St. Augustine, Florida, and a mission at Santa Fe, New Mexico, and planted a short-lived colony on the Carolina coast. Spanish settlements along the Gulf coast and in California did not appear until the eighteenth century.

THE PROTESTANT REFORMATION   While Spain built her empire, a new movement flourished elsewhere in Europe, the Protestant Reformation, which would embitter national rivalries, and, by encouraging serious challenges to Catholic Spain's power, profoundly affect the course of early American history. When Columbus sailed in 1492, all of western Europe acknowledged the Catholic church and its pope in Rome. The unity of Christendom, however, began to crack in 1517, when Martin Luther, a German monk and theologian, launched his protest against abuses in the church and especially against the sale of indulgences for the remission of sins. Sinful people, Luther argued, could win salvation neither by good works nor through the mediation of the church, but only by faith in the redemptive power of Christ and through a direct relationship to God—the "priesthood of all believers." And the only true guide to the will of God was the Bible, not corrupt Catholic priests.

In Geneva the reform movement looked to John Calvin, a Frenchman who brought his adopted city under the sway of his stern beliefs. All people, he taught, were damned by Adam's original sin, but the sacrifice of Christ made possible redemption by faith. The gift of grace, however, was offered only to those who had been elected by God and thus predestined to salvation from the beginning of time. It was a hard doctrine requiring a rigid moral code, for the outward sign of having been "elected" for salvation was correct behavior. If this did not necessarily prove that one was saved, an immoral life clearly proved the opposite. This Calvinist doctrine provided the basis for the beliefs of the German Reformed and Dutch Reformed churches, the Presbyterians in Scotland, some of the Puritans in England, and the Huguenots in France.

THE REFORMATION IN ENGLAND   In England the Reformation, like so many other events, followed a unique course. There the rejection of papal authority occurred for purely political reasons. King Henry VIII (1509–1547), the second of the Tudor dynasty, requested an annulment of his marriage, which had not produced a male heir. When the pope refused, Henry severed the connection with Rome, named a new archbishop of Canterbury, who granted the annulment, and married the lively Anne Boleyn. In one of history's great ironies, she presented him not with the male heir he sought, but with a daughter, who as Elizabeth I

"Look here the Queen, whom no mishap can move." A 1563 woodcut portrait of Queen Elizabeth I.

would reign from 1558 to 1603 over one of England's greatest eras.

Elizabeth could not be a Catholic, for in the Catholic view she was illegitimate. During her reign, therefore, the Church of England became Protestant, but in its own way. The organizational structure, the bishops and archbishops, remained much the same, but the doctrine and practice changed: the Latin liturgy became, with some changes, the English *Book of Common Prayer*, the cult of saints was dropped, and the clergy were permitted to marry. For the sake of unity the "Elizabethan Settlement" allowed some latitude in theology and other matters, but this did not satisfy all. Some tried to enforce the letter of the law, stressing traditional practice. Many others, however, especially those under Calvinist influence from the Continent, wished to "purify" the Church of England of its Catholic remnants so that it more nearly fit their views of biblical authority. These so-called Puritans wanted to scrap the Anglican prayer book in favor of the Bible, simplify the rituals of worship, and strictly observe the sanctity of the Sabbath. Some Puritans would later despair of the effort to reform the Anglican church and would leave England to build their own churches and communities in America. Those who broke altogether with the Church of England were called Separatists.

CHALLENGES TO SPANISH EMPIRE The Spanish monopoly of the New World colonies remained intact throughout the sixteenth century, but not without challenge from national rivals spurred by the emotion unleashed by the Protestant Reformation and the lure of riches. The French were the first to pose a serious threat. In 1524 the French king sent an Italian named Giovanni da Verrazzano in search of a passage to Asia. Sighting land (probably at Cape Fear, North Carolina), Verrazzano ranged along the coast as far north as Maine, but it was not until a decade later that the French made their first colonization effort. On three voyages Jacques Cartier explored the Gulf of St. Lawrence and ventured up the St. Lawrence River as far as present-day Montréal. Near Québec he established a short-lived colony in 1542.

Thereafter, however, French interest in Canada waned, as they were preoccupied with the religious civil wars wracking their country. Not until the early seventeenth century, when the bold explorer Samuel de Champlain established new settlements in Acadia (Nova Scotia) and at Québec, did French colonization in Canada and America begin in earnest. Enterprising French traders negotiated with Indians for their fur pelts, and French Jesuit missionaries cultivated their souls. Those seeking profits frequently clashed with those promoting piety, as many Jesuits deplored the crass exploitation of the Indians. Unlike many English missionaries, the Jesuits were not determined to strip their converts of all vestiges of Indian culture. Instead they displayed considerable respect for native American values.

Acquiring furs and ministering to heathens took the French southward as well, and in 1673 Père Jacques Marquette, a Jesuit priest, took the first expedition down the Mississippi River. Nine years later Robert Cavalier, sieur de la Salle, did the same, but he ventured all the way to the Gulf of Mexico. There, at the river's delta, the French would establish a settlement called New Orleans in the early eighteenth century. The French thereby came to control not only Canada but also the major inland waterway in North America. But it was a deceptive control because the French monarchy never emphasized permanent settlement. Instead it viewed the region almost solely as a source for trade, and French America remained only sparsely populated.

From the mid-1500s forward, greater threats to Spanish power in the New World arose from the growing strength of the Dutch and English. The prosperous provinces of the Netherlands, which had passed by inheritance to the Spanish king, and which had become largely Protestant, rebelled against Spanish rule in 1567. A protracted, bloody struggle for independence was interrupted by a twelve-year truce, but Spain did not accept the independence of the Dutch republic until 1648.

Almost from the beginning of the revolt, Dutch privateers plundered Spanish ships. The Dutch raiders soon had their counterpart in England's Elizabethan "Sea Dogges": John Hawkins, Francis Drake, and others. While Elizabeth steered a tortuous course to avoid open war with Catholic Spain, she encouraged both Dutch and English sea captains to attack the Spanish. In 1577 Drake set out on his famous adventure around South America to raid Spanish towns along the Pacific. Three years later he returned in triumph. Elizabeth, who had secretly backed the voyage, shared a profit of 4,600 percent, and knighted Sir Francis.

THE ARMADA'S DEFEAT   Sporadic British piracy against the Spanish continued almost twenty years before circumstances provoked open war. In 1568 Elizabeth's Catholic cousin Mary, "Queen of Scots," ousted by Scottish Presbyterians in favor of her infant son, fled to England. Mary had a claim to the English throne by descent from Henry VII, and she soon became the focus for Spanish-Catholic intrigues to overthrow Elizabeth. Finally, after an abortive plot to kill Elizabeth and elevate Mary to the throne, the queen yielded to the demands of her ministers and had Mary beheaded in 1587.

In revenge, Spain's Philip II decided to crush Protestant England and began to gather his ill-fated Armada. But the ambitious enterprise quickly became a case of incompetence and mismanagement accompanied by bad luck. The heavy Spanish galleons could not cope with the smaller, faster English vessels commanded by Drake and others. The English harried the Spanish ships through the English Channel on their way to the Netherlands, where the Armada was to pick up invasion troops. But, caught up in a powerful "Protestant Wind," the storm-tossed Spanish fleet was swept into the North Sea, and what was left of it finally found its way home around the British Isles, leaving wreckage scattered on the shores of Scotland and Ireland.

Defeat of the Armada convinced the English that the Spanish navy was no longer invincible and cleared the way for English colonization of the Americas. England at the end of the sixteenth century entered the springtime of her power, filled with a youthful zest for the new worlds and wonders that were opening up before her.

ENGLISH EXPLORATIONS   English colonization in North America began in 1584 when Sir Walter Raleigh, eager "to seek new worlds for gold, for praise, for glory," sent an expedition to explore prospects for founding a colony in America. Sailing by way of the West Indies, they came to the Outer Banks of North Carolina and discovered Roanoke Island, where the soil seemed fruitful and the natives friendly. Three years later 117 settlers arrived, including women and children, under the leadership of Governor John White. After a month in Roanoke, White returned to England to get supplies, leaving behind his daughter, Eleanor, and her baby, Virginia Dare, the first English child born in the New World. White, however, was long delayed because of the war with Spain. When he finally returned in 1590, he found the village of "Ralegh" abandoned and pillaged.

No trace of the "lost colonists" was ever found. Hostile Indians or Spaniards may have destroyed the infant colony. The main body of colonists may have gone north to the southern shores of the Chesapeake Bay, where they lived for some years until killed by Indians. But not one of them was ever seen again, and there were no English settlers in North America when Queen Elizabeth died in 1603.

SETTLING THE CHESAPEAKE

With the death of Elizabeth, the Tudor line ended and the throne fell to her cousin James I, the son of the ill-fated Mary, Queen of Scots, and the first of the Stuarts. Their dynasty spanned most of the seventeenth century, a turbulent time of religious and political tensions, civil war, and foreign intrigues. During these eventful years in English history, all but one of the thirteen North American colonies and several more in the Caribbean had their start. They were quite diverse in geography, motives, and composition, a diversity that has since been a trademark and strength of American society.

In 1606, having made peace with Spain and thereby freeing up resources and men for colonization, James I chartered the Virginia Company with two divisions, the First Colony of London and the Second Colony of Plymouth. The stockholders expected a potential return from gold and products such as wine, citrus fruits, olive oil, pitch, tar, potash, and other forest products needed for naval stores. Many also still hoped to discover a passage to India. Few if any investors foresaw what the first English colony would become: a place to grow tobacco.

VIRGINIA   The London Company planted the first permanent colony in Virginia, named after Elizabeth I, the "Virgin Queen."

On May 6, 1607, three ships loaded with about one hundred men reached Chesapeake Bay after four storm-tossed weeks at sea. They chose a river with a northwest bent—in hope of a passage to Asia—and settled about forty miles from the sea to hide from marauding Spaniards. One of the settlers noted that they found "fair meadows and goodly, tall trees, with such fresh waters running through the woods as I was almost ravished with the first sight thereof." The river they called the James, and the colony, Jamestown. After building a fort, thatched huts, a storehouse, and a church, the sea-weary colonists then began planting, but most were either townsmen unfamiliar with farming or "gentlemen" adventurers who scorned manual labor. They had come to find gold, not to establish a farm settlement. Ignorant of woodlore, they did not know how to exploit the area's abundant game and fish. Supplies from England were undependable, and only firm leadership and their trade with the Indians, who taught the colonists to grow maize, enabled them to survive.

The Indians of the region were loosely organized under Powhatan, chief of the Pamunkey tribe, who had gained shaky control over some thirty tribes in the coastal area. Despite occasional clashes with the colonists, the Indians adopted a stance of watchful waiting. Powhatan apparently hoped for trade and alliance with newcomers who might serve his purposes, and he realized too late their plans to possess the country and subjugate the natives.

The colonists, as it happened, had more than a match for Powhatan in Captain John Smith, a swashbuckling soldier of fortune with rare powers of leadership and self-promotion. Smith had earlier fought as a mercenary with the Austrians in Hungary against the Turks. There, the story goes, he had beheaded three Turks in hand-to-hand challenges staged in front of a Turkish fortress, and the grateful Austrians awarded him the title of captain, a horse, a scimitar, and a coat of arms. Smith was then wounded, captured, and enslaved in Turkey, but he freed himself by killing his overseer. After fleeing across Russia and sailing in a pirate ship off the coast of Africa, the twenty-four-year-old Smith was "befriended by a gentlewoman" who facilitated his return to England in 1604.

The Virginia Company, understandably impressed by Smith's exploits, appointed him a member of the resident council to manage the new colony in America. It was a wise decision. With the colonists on the verge of starvation, Smith imposed strict discipline and forced all to labor, declaring that "he that will not work shall not eat." Smith also bargained with the Indians and

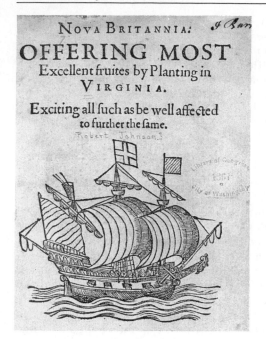

A 1609 handbill of
the Virginia Company
attempts to lure
settlers to Jamestown.

explored and mapped the Chesapeake region. Through his efforts, Jamestown survived, but Smith's dictatorial acts did not endear him to many of the colonists. One called him "ambitious, unworthy, and vainglorious."

John Smith's efforts to control the struggling colony abruptly ended when he suffered a gunpowder burn and sailed back to England in October 1609. The colony lapsed into anarchy and suffered the "starving time" of the winter of 1609-1610, during which most of the colonists, weakened by hunger, fell prey to disease. A relief party found only about sixty settlers still alive in May 1610. All poultry and livestock (including horses) had been eaten, and one man reportedly had dined on his wife.

For the next seven years the colony limped along until it gradually found a reason for being: tobacco. In 1612 John Rolfe had begun to experiment with the harsh Virginia tobacco, and by 1616 the weed had become an export staple. Meanwhile Rolfe had made another contribution to stability by marrying Pocahontas, the daughter of Powhatan. Distinguished Virginians still boast of their descent from the Indian "princess," who died of smallpox in London in 1620.

In 1618 officials in London initiated a series of reforms intended to shore up their struggling American colony. They first inaugurated a new headright policy. Anyone who bought a share in the company, or who could transport himself to Virginia, could have fifty acres, and fifty more for any servants he might send or bring. The following year, 1619, the company relaxed its tight legal code and promised that the settlers should have the "rights of Englishmen," including a representative assembly. On July 30, 1619, the first General Assembly of Virginia met in the Jamestown church and deliberated for five days, "sweating and stewing, and battling flies and mosquitoes." It was an eventful year in two other respects. During 1619 a ship arrived with ninety "young maidens," to be sold to likely husbands of their own choice for the cost of transportation (about 125 pounds of tobacco). And a Dutch man-of-war dropped off "20 Negars," the first blacks known to have reached English America.

Yet despite its successes the company again fell upon evil days. In 1622 Powhatan's brother led an uprising that killed 347 whites, including John Rolfe. Some 14,000 people had migrated to the colony since 1607, but the population in 1624 stood at a precarious 1,132. The king appointed a commission to investigate, and on its recommendation a court dissolved the company. In 1624 Virginia became a royal colony.

After 1622 relations with the Indians continued in a state of what the governor's council called "perpetual enmity" until the natives staged another concerted attack in 1644. The English suffered as many casualties as they had twenty-two years before, but they put down the uprising with such ferocity that nothing quite like it happened again.

MARYLAND   In 1634, ten years after Virginia became a royal colony, a neighboring settlement named Maryland appeared on the northern shores of Chesapeake Bay. It was the first so-called proprietary colony, granted not to a joint-stock company but to an individual, Lord Baltimore. Sir George Calvert, the first Lord Baltimore, had announced in 1625 his conversion to Catholicism and sought the colony as a refuge for English Catholics, who were subjected to discriminations at home. The charter for such a colony was finally issued in 1632, after his death.

His son, Cecilius Calvert, the second Lord Baltimore, actually founded the colony in 1634 at St. Mary's on a small stream near the mouth of the Potomac. Calvert brought along Catholic gentlemen as landholders, but a majority of the servants were Protestants. The charter gave Calvert power to make laws with the

EARLY VIRGINIA AND MARYLAND

Original grant to Lord Baltimore
- - - Present-day boundary of Maryland

consent of the freemen (all property holders). The first legislative assembly met in 1635 and later divided into two houses, with governor and council sitting separately. The charter also empowered the proprietor to grant manorial estates, and Maryland had some sixty before 1676, but the Lords Baltimore soon found that to draw settlers they had to offer farms. The colony was meant to rely on mixed farming, but its fortunes, like those of Virginia, soon came to depend on tobacco.

Settling New England

PLYMOUTH Meanwhile, far to the north of the Chesapeake, quite different colonies were taking shape. The Pilgrims who established Plymouth Colony were bent not on finding gold or making a fortune but on building a Christian commonwealth. They belonged to the most extreme and uncompromising sect of Puritans, the Separatists, who had severed all ties with the Church of England. Persecuted by James I and Anglican officials, they fled to Holland in 1607. The Calvinistic Dutch granted them asylum and toleration, but restricted them mainly to unskilled laboring jobs. After ten years in Leyden, the Pilgrims had wearied of such discrimination. Watching their children take on Dutch mores, drifting away to become sailors, soldiers, or worse, so that "their posterity would be in danger to degenerate and be corrupted," they longed for English ways and the English flag. If they could not have them at home, perhaps they might transplant them to the New World. King James would not promise outright toleration if they set up a colony, but he did agree to leave them alone.

The Leyden group secured a land patent from the Virginia Company, and in September 1620, 101 men, women, and children, led by William Bradford, crammed into the *Mayflower* for the transatlantic voyage. Only half of the voyagers were Pilgrim "Saints"—people recognized as having been elected by God for salvation; the rest were non-Pilgrim "Strangers"—ordinary settlers, hired hands, and indentured servants. They undertook the voyage, as Bradford asserted, "for the glorie of God, and advancements of the Christian faith and honour of our king & countrie." A stormy voyage led them in November to Cape Cod, far north of Virginia. Heading south, they encountered rough waters and turned back to seek safety at Provincetown. "Being thus arrived at safe harbor, and brought safe to land," Bradford wrote in his history, *Of Plymouth Plantation,* "they fell upon their knees and blessed the God of Heaven who had brought them over the vast and furious ocean." Exploring parties then scouted Cape Cod Bay and hit upon a place called Plymouth for their settlement. Since they were outside the jurisdiction of any organized government, forty-one of the Pilgrims entered into a formal agreement to abide by laws made by leaders of their own choosing—the Mayflower Compact of November 21, 1620. Later used as a model by other New England settlers, the compact helped establish the distinctive American tradition of consensual government.

The Pilgrims built and occupied their dwellings amid the winter snows, but many failed to see the arrival of spring. It "pleased God," Bradford noted, "to visit us with death daily, and with so general a disease that the living were scarce able to bury the dead." Nearly half the colonists died of exposure and disease, but friendly relations with the neighboring Indians proved their salvation. In the spring of 1621, the colonists met Squanto, who showed them how to grow maize. By autumn the Pilgrims had a bumper crop of corn, a flourishing fur trade, and a supply of lumber for shipment. To celebrate they held a harvest feast with the Indians, which later would be dubbed Thanksgiving.

Throughout its separate existence, until it was absorbed into Massachusetts in 1691, Plymouth Colony's government grew

EARLY NEW ENGLAND SETTLEMENTS

out of the Mayflower Compact, which was not a formal constitution but an agreement among members of a religious group who believed that God had made a covenant (or agreement) with people to provide a way to salvation. Thus the civil government evolved naturally out of the church government, and the members of each were initially identical.

JOHN WINTHROP AND THE BEGINNINGS OF MASSACHUSETTS BAY Plymouth Colony's population never rose above 7,000, and after ten years it was overshadowed by its larger neighbor, Massachusetts Bay Colony. It, too, was intended to be a holy commonwealth made up of religious folk bound together in the harmonious worship of God and pursuit of their "callings." And, like the Pilgrims, the Puritans who colonized Massachusetts Bay were primarily Congregationalists who wanted self-governing churches whose members would be limited to "visible saints," those who could demonstrate their receipt of the gift of God's grace. But unlike the Plymouth Separatists, the Puritans who settled Massachusetts were still hopeful that the Church of England could be reformed. Thus they were called Non-Separating Congregationalists.

In 1629 a group of Puritans and merchants convinced King Charles I to grant their newly formed Massachusetts Bay Company an area north of Plymouth Colony for settlement. Leaders of the company at first looked upon it mainly as a business venture, but a majority faction led by John Winthrop, a respected lawyer, resolved to use the colony as a refuge for persecuted Puritans and as an instrument for building a "wilderness Zion" in America. Winthrop was a courageous and committed leader who reflected the strengths and weaknesses of the Puritan movement. He remembered that as a youth he had been "very wild and dissolute, and as years came on my lusts grew stronger." But in 1606 he experienced an intense religious conversion and soon joined the Puritan movement, determined to rid the Church of England of its Catholic trappings and to lead a life of intense piety.

By 1629 Winthrop was forty years of age, had a large family, and found himself managing a floundering English estate that could not support his seven sons. Even more unsettling was the government's heightened persecution of Puritans and other dissenters. Hence he eagerly supported the idea of establishing a spiritual plantation in the New World, and he agreed to head up the enterprise. Winthrop shrewdly took advantage of a fateful omission in the charter for the Massachusetts Bay Company: the usual proviso that the company maintain its home office in England. Winthrop's group thus decided to take the charter with them, thereby transferring the entire government of the colony to Massachusetts Bay, where they hoped to ensure Puritan control.

In March 1630 the *Arbella*, with Governor John Winthrop and the charter aboard, embarked with six other ships for Massachusetts. In a sermon, "A Model of Christian Charity," delivered on board, Winthrop told his fellow Puritans "we must consider that we shall be a city upon a hill"—an exemplary beacon showing all people what a truly godly community could be. By the end of 1630 seventeen ships bearing 1,000 more colonists arrived. As settlers—Puritan and non-Puritan—poured into the region, Boston became the chief city and capital. The *Arbella* migrants proved but the vanguard of a massive movement, the Great Migration that carried some 40,000–50,000 English settlers to the

Gov. John Winthrop, who envisioned the Massachusetts Bay colony as "a city upon a hill."

New World over the next decade, fleeing persecution and economic depression at home.

The transfer of the Massachusetts charter, whereby an English trading company evolved into a provincial government, was a unique venture in colonization. Under this royal charter, power rested with the General Court, which elected the governor and assistants. The General Court consisted of shareholders, called freemen (those who had the "freedom of the company"), but of those who came, few besides Winthrop and his assistants had such status. This suited Winthrop and his friends, but soon other settlers demanded a share of political power. Rather than risk trouble, the inner group invited applications and finally admitted over one hundred additional freemen in 1631. They also stipulated that only official church members, a limited category, could become freemen.

At first the freemen had no power except to choose assistants, who in turn elected the governor and deputy governor. The procedure violated provisions of the charter, but Winthrop kept the document hidden and few knew of its exact provisions. Controversy simmered until 1634, when each town sent two delegates to Boston to confer on matters coming before the General Court. There they demanded to see the charter, which Winthrop reluctantly produced, and they read that the power to pass laws and levy taxes rested in the General Court. Winthrop argued that the body of freemen had grown too large, but when it met, the General Court responded by turning itself into a representative body with two or three deputies to represent each town. They also chose a new governor, and Winthrop did not resume the office until three years later. A final stage in the evolution of the government, a two-house legislature, came in 1644, with the deputies and assistants sitting apart and all decisions requiring a majority in each house.

Thus over a period of fourteen years, the Massachusetts Bay Company, a trading corporation, evolved into the governing body of a commonwealth. Membership in a Puritan church replaced the purchase of stock as a means of becoming a freeman, which was to say, a voter. The General Court, like Parliament, became a representative body of two houses, the House of Assistants corresponding roughly to the House of Lords, the House of Deputies to the House of Commons. The charter remained unchanged, but practice under the charter differed considerably from the original expectation.

ROGER WILLIAMS AND ANNE HUTCHINSON More by accident than design Massachusetts became the staging area for the rest of New England as new colonies grew out of religious quarrels within the fold. Puritanism created a volatile mixture: on the one hand the search for God's will could lead to a rigid orthodoxy; on the other hand it could lead troubled consciences to diverse, radical, or even bizarre convictions. Young Roger Williams, who arrived in 1631, was among the first to cause problems, precisely because he was the purest of Puritans, a Separatist troubled by the failure of the Massachusetts nonconformists to repudiate the Church of England entirely. He held a brief pastorate in Salem, then tried Separatist Plymouth. Governor Bradford found Williams to be gentle and kind in his personal relations and a charismatic speaker, but he "began to fall into strange opinions." A quarrel with the authorities over their treatment of Indians led Williams to return to Salem. There he continued to challenge the social and religious status quo. Williams's belief that a true church must have no relations either with the English government, the Anglican establishment, or with the unregenerate led him eventually to the absurdity that no true church was possible, unless perhaps consisting of his wife and himself—and he may have had doubts about her.

But eccentric as Williams's beliefs may have been to the authorities, they led him to establish principles that later generations would honor for other reasons. The purity of the church that he espoused required complete separation of church and state and freedom from coercion in matters of faith. Such views were too advanced even for the radical church of Salem, which finally removed him, whereupon Williams charged that the churches were "ulcered and gangrened." In 1635 a provoked General Court banished him to England. Aided by Indian friends, Williams and a few followers headed into the wilderness in the dead of winter and eventually were taken in by the Narragansetts. In the spring of 1636 Williams bought some land from the Indians and established the town of Providence at the head of Narragansett Bay, the first permanent settlement in Rhode Island, and the first in America to legislate freedom of religion.

Anne Hutchinson quarreled with the Puritan leaders for different reasons. Hutchinson was married to a prominent merchant and had given birth to thirteen children. Strong-willed and articulate she also worked as a healer and midwife and hosted meetings in her Boston home to discuss sermons. Soon, however, those discussions turned into forums for Hutchinson to provide her own commentaries on religious matters. She claimed to have had direct revelations from the Holy Spirit which convinced her that only two or three Puritan ministers actually preached the appropriate "covenant of grace." The others, she charged, were deluded and incompetent and were promoting a "covenant of works" which led people to believe that good conduct would ensure their salvation.

Hutchinson's beliefs were provocative for several reasons. Puritan theology affirmed the Calvinist doctrine that people could be saved only by God's grace rather than through their own willful actions. But Puritanism in practice also insisted that ministers were necessary to interpret God's will for the people. In challenging the very legitimacy of the ministerial community as well as the hard-earned assurances of salvation enjoyed by current church members, Hutchinson was undermining the stability of an already fragile social system. Moreover, her critics likened

Religious quarrels within the Puritan fold led to the founding of new colonies. Here a seventeenth-century cartoon shows wrangling sects tossing a Bible in a blanket.

her claim of direct revelations from the Holy Spirit to the Antinomian heresy, technically a belief that one is freed from obeying the moral law by one's own faith and by God's grace. What made the situation worse in such a male-dominated society, of course, was that a *woman* had the audacity to make such charges and assertions. Anne Hutchinson had both offended authority and sanctioned a disruptive individualism.

Hutchinson, again pregnant, was hauled before the General Court in 1637, and for two days she verbally sparred on equal terms with the presiding magistrates and testifying ministers. Her skillful deflections of the charges and her ability to cite chapter and verse defenses of her actions led an exasperated Governor Winthrop to explode: "We do not mean to discourse with those of your sex." He found Hutchinson to be "a woman of haughty and fierce carriage, of a nimble wit and active spirit, and a very voluble tongue." As the intense trial continued, an overwrought Hutchinson was eventually lured into convicting herself by claiming direct divine inspiration. Banished in 1638 as "a woman not fit for our society," she walked through the wilderness to Providence and then settled with her family and a few followers on an island near what is now Portsmouth. The arduous journey had taken a toll, however. Hutchinson grew sick and her baby was stillborn, leading her critics back in Massachusetts to assert that the "monstrous birth" was God's way of punishing her for her sins. Hutchinson's spirits never recovered. After her husband's death in 1642 she moved to Long Island, then under Dutch jurisdiction, and the following year she and five of her children were massacred during an Indian attack. Her fate, wrote an unusually vindictive Winthrop, was "a special manifestation of divine justice."

Thus the colony of Rhode Island, the smallest in America, grew up in Narragansett Bay as a refuge for dissenters who agreed that the state had no right to coerce religious belief. In 1640 they formed a confederation and in 1644 secured their first charter. Williams lived until 1683, an active and beloved citizen of the commonwealth he founded in a society which, during his lifetime at least, lived up to his principles of religious freedom and a government based on the consent of the people.

CONNECTICUT, NEW HAMPSHIRE, AND MAINE   Connecticut had a more orthodox beginning. It was founded by groups of Massachusetts Puritans seeking better lands and access to the fur trade farther west. In 1636 three entire church congregations trekked westward by the "Great Road," driving their hogs and cattle before them, and moved to the Connecticut River towns of Wethersfield, Windsor, and Hartford, which earlier arrivals had laid out the previous year.

Led by Thomas Hooker, they organized the self-governing colony of Connecticut in 1637 as a response to the danger of attack from the Pequot Indians, who lived east of the river. Before the end of the year the Pequots attacked Wethersfield, and the settlers, with help from Massachusetts, brutally responded by surprising and burning the chief Pequot town on the Mystic River and slaughtering some 400 men, women, and children; stragglers were sold into slavery.

In 1639 the Connecticut General Court adopted the "Fundamental Orders of Connecticut," a series of laws providing for a government like that of Massachusetts. Voting in the Connecticut Colony was not, however, limited to church members. New Haven had by then appeared within the later limits of Connecticut. A group of English Puritans, led by their minister, John Davenport, had migrated first to Massachusetts and then, seeking a place to establish themselves in commerce, to New Haven on Long Island Sound in 1638. The New Haven Colony became the most rigorously Puritan of all. Like all the other offshoots of Massachusetts, it too lacked a charter and maintained a self-governing independence until 1662, when it was absorbed into Connecticut under the terms of that colony's first charter.

To the north of Massachusetts, most of what is now New Hampshire and Maine was granted in 1622 by the Council for New England to Sir Ferdinando Gorges and Captain John Mason and their associates. In 1629 Mason and Gorges divided their territory at the Piscataqua River, Mason taking the southern part, which he named New Hampshire. In the 1630s Puritan immigrants began filtering in, and in 1638 the Reverend John Wheelwright, one of Anne Hutchinson's group, founded Exeter. Maine consisted of a few scattered and small settlements, mostly fishing stations, the chief of them being York.

RENEWED SETTLEMENT

Before 1640 English settlers in New England and around Chesapeake Bay had established two great beachheads on the Atlantic coast, separated by the Dutch colony of New Netherland. After 1640, however, the struggle between king and Parliament distracted attention from colonization, and migration dwindled to a trickle for more than twenty years. During the time of civil war and Oliver Cromwell's Puritan dictatorship, the struggling colonies were left pretty much alone, especially in New England, where English Puritans saw little need to intervene. Virginia and Maryland remained almost as independent from British authority as New England.

The Restoration of King Charles II in England in 1660 involved scarcely any changes in colonial governments, since little had occurred there under Cromwell. Emigration rapidly expanded the populations of Virginia and Maryland. Fears of reprisals against Puritan New England by the reestablishment of the Anglican Church as the official church proved unfounded, at least for the time being. Massachusetts gained reconfirmation of its charter in 1662, and Connecticut and Rhode Island received the first royal charters in 1662 and 1663. All three retained their status as self-governing corporations. New Haven disappeared as a separate entity and was absorbed into Connecticut.

SETTLING THE CAROLINAS The Restoration of Charles II, the Merry Monarch, opened a new season of enthusiasm for colonial expansion, directed mainly by royal favorites. Within twelve years the English had conquered New Netherland, had settled Carolina, and had very nearly filled out the shape of the colonies. In the middle region formerly claimed by the Dutch, four new colonies sprang into being: New York, New Jersey, Pennsylvania, and Delaware. Without exception the new colonies were proprietary, awarded by the king to "proprietors," men who had remained loyal during the civil war.

Carolina from the start comprised two widely separated areas of settlement. The northernmost part, long called Albemarle, remained a remote scattering of settlers along the shores of Albemarle Sound, isolated from Virginia by the Dismal Swamp and lacking easy access for ocean-going vessels. Albemarle had no governor until 1664, no assembly until 1665, and not even a town until a group of French Huguenots (Protestants) founded the village of Bath in 1704.

The eight Lords Proprietors to whom the king gave Carolina neglected Albemarle from the outset and focused on more promising sites to the south. Eager to find settlers who had already been seasoned in the colonies, they looked first to Barbados. The rise of large-scale sugar production in Barbados had persuaded small planters to try their luck elsewhere. Sir Anthony Ashley-Cooper finally spurred the enterprise by convincing his fellow proprietors to take on more of the financial burden of settlement. In 1669 three ships left London with about one hundred

VIRGINIA

James R.

APPALACHIAN MTS.

NORTH CAROLINA   Bath

ALBEMARLE
SOUND

ROANOKE
ISLAND

New Bern

SOUTH
CAROLINA   CAPE FEAR

Savannah R.

Ashley   *Cooper R.*   ATLANTIC OCEAN

GEORGIA   *R.*   Charles Town

Altamaha

ADDED   Port Royal
TO GEORGIA, 1763   Savannah

St. Mary's R.   **EARLY SETTLEMENTS
IN THE SOUTH**

0   200 Miles

0   200 Kilometers

FLORIDA   St. Augustine
(Spanish)   (Spanish)

GULF OF MEXICO

settlers recruited in England; they sailed first to Barbados to pick
up more settlers and then north to Bermuda. The expedition finally landed in America at a place several miles up the Ashley
River. There Charles Town remained from 1670 to 1680, when
it was moved across and downstream to Oyster Point, overlooking a fine harbor where, as proud Charlestonians later claimed,
the Ashley and Cooper Rivers "join to form the Atlantic Ocean."

The government rested on one of the most curious documents
of colonial history, the "Fundamental Constitutions of Carolina," drawn up by Lord Ashley-Cooper with the help of his secretary, the philosopher John Locke. Its cumbersome frame of
government and its provisions for an almost feudal social system
and an elaborate nobility had little effect in the colony except to
encourage a practice of large land grants, but from the beginning
smaller headrights were given to immigrants who paid their own
way. The provision that had greatest effect was a grant of religious toleration, designed to encourage immigration, which gave
South Carolina a distinctive degree of indulgence (extending
even to Jews and heathens) and ethnic pluralism.

Ambitious English planters from Barbados dominated the colony and soon organized a major trade in Indian slaves, whom the
Westo Indians obligingly drove to the coast for shipment to the

Caribbean. The first major export other than furs and slaves was cattle, and a true staple crop was not developed until the introduction of rice in the 1690s. Meanwhile the continuing Indian slave trade led to repeated troubles with the proprietors, who tried in vain to regulate Indian affairs and stabilize the colony. Ultimately the struggle provoked a rebellion against proprietary rule and an appeal to the crown to take charge. South Carolina became a separate royal colony in 1719. North Carolina remained under the proprietors' rule for ten more years, when they surrendered their governing rights to the crown.

NEW NETHERLAND BECOMES NEW YORK   Charles II resolved early to pluck out that old thorn in the side of the English colonies—New Netherland. The Dutch colony was older than New England and had been planted when the two Protestant powers enjoyed friendly relations in opposition to Catholic Spain. The Dutch East India Company (organized in 1620) had hired an English captain, Henry Hudson, to seek the elusive passage to the Orient. In 1609 Hudson had discovered Delaware Bay and had explored the river named for him to a point probably beyond Albany, where he and a group of Mohawks made merry with brandy. From that contact stemmed a lasting trade between the Dutch and Iroquois nations. In 1614 the Dutch established fur-trading posts on Manhattan Island and upriver at Fort Orange (later Albany). Ten years later a newly organized West India Company began permanent settlements. In 1626 Governor Peter Minuit purchased Manhattan Island from the Indians, and the new village of New Amsterdam became the capital of New Netherland.

Like the French, the Dutch were interested mainly in the fur trade and less in agricultural settlements. In 1629, however, the Dutch West India Company provided that any stockholder might obtain a large estate (a patroonship) if he peopled it with fifty adults within four years. The patroon supplied cattle, tools, and buildings. His tenants, in turn, paid him rent, used his grist mill, gave him first option on surplus crops, and submitted to a court he established. It amounted to transplanting the feudal manor into the New World and met with as little luck as similar efforts in Maryland and South Carolina. Volunteers for serfdom were hard to find when there was land to be had elsewhere, and most settlers took advantage of the company's provision that one could have as farms all the lands one could improve.

The colony's government was under the almost absolute control of a governor sent out by the company, subject to little check

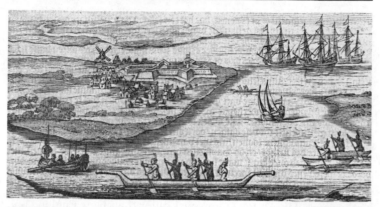

The earliest view of Fort New Amsterdam, at the southern tip of Manhattan, around 1636–1639.

from his council or from the directors back in Holland. The governors proved stubborn autocrats, either corrupt or inept, especially at Indian relations. They depended on a small professional garrison for defense, and the inhabitants (including a number of English on Long Island) betrayed almost total indifference in 1664 when Governor Peter Stuyvesant called them to arms against a threatening British fleet. Almost defenseless, old soldier Stuyvesant blustered and stomped about on his ornate silver leg, but he finally surrendered without firing a shot.

The plan of conquest had been hatched by Charles II's brother, James, the duke of York, later King James II. As lord high admiral and an investor in the African trade, the duke of York had already engaged in harassing Dutch shipping and Dutch forts in Africa. When he and his advisers counseled that New Netherland could easily be conquered, Charles II simply granted the region to his brother. The English transformed New Amsterdam into New York and Fort Orange into Albany, and they held the country thereafter, except for a brief Dutch reoccupation in 1673–1674. The Dutch, however, left a permanent imprint on the land and the language: the Dutch vernacular faded away, but places like Wall Street (the original wall provided protection against Indians) and Broadway (Breede Wegh) remained, along with family names like Rensselaer, Roosevelt, and Van Buren. The Dutch presence lingered in the Dutch Reformed church; in words like *boss, cooky, crib, snoop, stoop,* and *spook;* and in the legendary Santa Claus and Rip Van Winkle.

NEW JERSEY   Shortly after the conquest of New York, still in 1664, the duke of York granted his lands between the Hudson and the Delaware Rivers to Sir George Carteret and Lord John Berkeley and named the territory for Carteret's native island of Jersey. In East New Jersey, peopled at first by perhaps two hundred Dutch who had crossed the Hudson, new settlements gradually arose: disaffected Puritans from New Haven founded Newark, and a group of Scots founded Perth Amboy. In the west, which faced the Delaware, a scattering of Swedes, Finns, and Dutch remained, soon to be overwhelmed by swarms of English Quakers. In 1702 East and West Jersey were united as a royal colony.

PENNSYLVANIA AND DELAWARE   The Quaker sect, as the Society of Friends was called in ridicule, was the most influential of many radical groups that sprang from the turbulence of the English Civil War. Founded by George Fox about 1647, the Quakers carried further than any other group the doctrine of individual spiritual inspiration and interpretation—the "inner light," they called it. Discarding all formal sacraments and formal ministry, they refused deference to persons of rank, used the familiar "thee" and "thou" in addressing everyone, declined to take oaths because that was contrary to Scripture, and embraced simple living and pacifism. Quakers were subjected to intense persecution—often in their zeal they seemed to invite it—but never inflicted it on others. Their toleration extended to complete religious freedom for all, the equality of the sexes, and the full participation of women in religious affairs.

In 1673 George Fox returned from an American visit with the vision of a Quaker commonwealth in the New World and enticed others with his idea. The entrance of Quakers into the New Jersey proprietorships encouraged others to migrate, especially to the Delaware River side. And soon, across the river, arose Fox's "Holy Experiment," the Quaker Commonwealth, the colony of Pennsylvania. William Penn, the colony's founder, was born in 1644 and raised as a proper gentleman, but in 1667 he converted to Quakerism. "God took me by the hand," he later recalled, "and led me out of the pleasures, vanities and hopes of the world."

Upon his father's death, Penn inherited the friendship of the Stuarts and a substantial estate, including claim to a sizable loan his father had made to the crown. Whether in settlement of the claim or out of simple friendship, he received from Charles II in 1681 proprietary rights to a huge tract of land in America and

William Penn, the Quaker who founded the Pennsylvania colony in 1681.

named it, at the king's insistence, for his father: Pennsylvania (literally Penn Woods). Penn vigorously recruited settlers to his new colony, and religious dissenters from England and the Continent —Quakers, Mennonites, Amish, Moravians, Baptists—flocked to the region. Indian relations were good from the beginning because of the Quakers' friendliness and Penn's careful policy of purchasing land titles from the Indians.

Pennsylvania's government resembled that of other proprietary colonies, except that the councilors as well as the assembly were elected by the freemen (taxpayers and property owners) and the governor had no veto—although Penn as proprietor did. "Any government is free . . . where the laws rule and the people are a party to the laws," Penn wrote in the 1682 Frame of Government. He hoped to show that a government could run in accordance with Quaker principles, that it could maintain peace and order without oaths or wars, that religion could flourish without an established church and with absolute freedom of conscience.

In 1682 the duke of York also granted Penn the area of Delaware, another part of the Dutch territory. At first Delaware became part of Pennsylvania, but after 1701 the settlers were granted the right to choose their own assembly. From then until the American Revolution, Delaware had a separate assembly but had the same governor as Pennsylvania.

GEORGIA Georgia was the last of the British continental colonies to be established, half a century after Pennsylvania. In 1732 George II gave the land between the Savannah and Altamaha Rivers to the twenty-one trustees of Georgia. In two respects Georgia was unique among the colonies: it was set up as both a philanthropic experiment and a military buffer against Spanish Florida. General James E. Oglethorpe, who accompanied the first colonists as resident trustee, represented both concerns: as a soldier who organized the colony's defenses, and as a philanthropist who championed prison reform and sought a colonial refuge for the poor and persecuted.

In 1733 Oglethorpe and a band of 120 colonists founded Savannah near the mouth of the Savannah River. Soon thereafter they were joined by Protestant refugees from central Europe, who made the colony for a time more German than English. The addition of Scottish Highlanders, Portuguese Jews, Welsh, and others gave the early colony a cosmopolitan character much like that of South Carolina.

As a buffer against Spanish Florida the colony succeeded, but as a philanthropic experiment it failed. Efforts to develop silk and wine production floundered. Landholdings were limited to 500 acres, rum was prohibited, and the importation of slaves forbidden, partly to leave room for servants brought on charity, partly to ensure security. But the utopian rules soon collapsed. The regulations against rum and slavery were widely disregarded and finally abandoned. By 1759 all restrictions on landholding were removed.

In 1753 the trustees' charter expired and the province reverted to the crown. As a royal colony Georgia acquired for the first time an effective government. The province developed slowly over the next decade, but grew rapidly in population and wealth after 1763. Instead of wine and silk, Georgians exported rice, indigo, lumber, naval stores, beef, and pork, and carried on a lively trade with the West Indies. The colony, which got off to such a late start, had become a roaring success.

THRIVING COLONIES

After a late start and with little design, the English outstripped both the French and the Spanish in the New World. The lack of plan marked the genius of English colonization, for it gave free rein to a variety of human impulses. The centralized control imposed by the monarchs of Spain and France got their colonies off the mark more quickly but eventually brought their downfall because it hobbled innovation and responsiveness to new circumstances. The British acted by private investment and with a minimum of royal control. Not a single colony was begun at the direct initiative of the crown. In the English colonies poor immigrants had a much greater chance of getting at least a small parcel of land, and a degree of self-government made the English colonies more responsive to new challenges—if sometimes stalled by controversy.

Moreover, the compact pattern of English settlement contrasted sharply with the pattern of Spain's far-flung conquests or France's far-reaching trade routes to the interior by way of the St. Lawrence and Mississippi Rivers. Geography reinforced England's bent for concentrated occupation and settlement of its colonies. The rivers and bays indenting the coasts served as veins of communication along which colonies first sprang up, but no great river offered a highway to the far interior. About a hundred miles back in Georgia and the Carolinas, and nearer the coast to the north, the "fall line" of the rivers presented rocky rapids that marked the head of navigation and the end of the coastal plain. About a hundred miles beyond that, and farther back in Pennsylvania, stretched the rolling expanse of the Piedmont, literally the foothills. The final backdrop of English America was the Appalachian Mountain range running from New England to Georgia. For 150 years the western outreach of settlement stopped at the slopes of the mountains. To the east lay the wide expanse of ocean, which served as a highway for the transit of civilization from Europe to America, but also as a barrier beyond which civilization took to new paths in a new environment.

Further Reading

A fascinating study of pre-Columbian migration is Brian M. Fagan's *The Great Journey* (1987).° Fagan's *Kingdoms of Gold, Kingdoms of Jade: The Americas before Columbus* (1991) provides fascinating insights into pre-Columbian civilizations. On Columbus see Zvi Dor-Ner and William Scheller, *Columbus and the Age of Discovery* (1991). Several works explore the theme of cultural conflict. Among the best is James Axtell's *The Invasion Within* (1986).° Karen O. Kupperman's *Settling with the Indians: The Meeting of English and Indian Cultures in America, 1580–1640* (1980) stresses the racist nature of the conflict.

Alfred W. Crosby, Jr.'s *The Columbian Exchange* (1972)° discusses the biological aspects of the cultural collision. Crosby's *Ecological Imperialism: The Biological Expansion of Europe, 900–1900* (1986)° is a full exploration of the ecological side of European expansion. Equally illu-

° These books are available in paperback editions.

minating is Herman J. Viola and Carolyn Margolis, *Seeds of Change* (1991).°

The most comprehensive overviews of European exploration are two volumes by Samuel E. Morison, *The European Discovery of America: The Northern Voyages*, A.D. *500–1600* (1971), and *The Southern Voyages*, A.D. *1492–1616* (1974). James Lang's *Conquest and Commerce: Spain and England in the Americas* (1975) compares the Spanish and English processes of colonization. For the French experience, see William J. Eccles's *France in America* (1990)°. Three major studies detail Native American culture before and after European colonization: Inga Clendinnin, *Ambivalent Conquests: Maya and Spaniard in Yucatan, 1517–1570* (1989)°; James H. Merrell, *The Indians' New World: Catawbas and Their Neighbors from European Contact through the Era of Removal* (1989); Richard White, *The Middle Ground: Indians, Empires and Republics in the Great Lakes Region, 1650–1815* (1991).°

Several general interpretations handle the sweep of English settlement during the early colonial period. The first volume of Charles M. Andrews's *The Colonial Period of American History* (4 vols., 1934–1938) is detailed and comprehensive. Bernard Bailyn's multivolume work *The Peopling of British North America*, the first two volumes of which have appeared, *The Peopling of British North America: An Introduction* (1986)° and *Voyagers to the West: A Passage in the Peopling of America on the Eve of the Revolution* (1986),° represents a magisterial view of European migration.

Carl Bridenbaugh's *Jamestown, 1544–1699* (1980) traces the English experience on the Chesapeake. On the role of Captain John Smith, see Alden T. Vaughan's *American Genesis: Captain John Smith and the Founding of Virginia* (1975).°

Scholarship abounds on Puritanism. To learn about the English roots of the movement, see Charles H. George and Katherine George's *The Protestant Mind of the English Reformation, 1570–1640* (1961). A more recent analysis of Anglo-American Puritanism is Stephen Foster's *The Long Argument: English Puritanism and the Shaping of New England Culture, 1570–1700* (1991). The classic works of Perry Miller demonstrate how Puritan ideology evolved once transplanted to the New World; see especially *The New England Mind* (2 vols., 1939–1953)° and *Errand into the Wilderness* (1956).° The problem of translating idea into governance is treated elegantly in Edmund S. Morgan's *The Puritan Dilemma: The Story of John Winthrop* (1958).°

No comprehensive work explores the overall pattern of settlement in the Middle Colonies, yet good scholarship exists for each colony. Thomas J. Condon's *New York Beginnings: The Commercial Origins of New Netherlands* (1968) examines the Dutch connection. The influence of Quakers can be studied through Gary B. Nash's *Quakers and Politics: Pennsylvania, 1681–1726* (1968).

For an imaginative study of race and the settlement of South Carolina, see Peter Wood's *Black Majority: Negroes in Colonial South Carolina from 1670 through the Stono Rebellion* (1975).°

2

COLONIAL WAYS OF LIFE

THE SHAPE OF EARLY AMERICA

It is well to remember the prominent leaders and colorful figures of the colonial period—John Smith, Pocahontas, William Bradford, John Winthrop, Roger Williams, Anne Hutchinson, and others. But the process of carving a new civilization out of an abundant, yet menacing and violent frontier was largely the story of thousands of diverse folk engaged in the everyday tasks of building homes, planting crops, raising families, enforcing laws, and worshipping their God.

Those who colonized America during the seventeenth and eighteenth centuries were part of a massive pattern of social migration occurring throughout Europe and Africa. Everywhere, it seemed, people were on the move. They were migrating from farms to villages, from villages to cities, and from homelands to colonies. They moved for different reasons. Most were responding to powerful social and economic forces: rapid population growth, the rise of commercial agriculture, and the early stages of the Industrial Revolution. Others sought political security or religious freedom. Africans were moved to new lands against their will.

Migrants to America came from diverse locales—the streets of London and other cities in southern and central England, the farms of Yorkshire and the Scottish Highlands, the villages of Germany, Switzerland, and Protestant Ireland, and the savannas and jungles of west Africa. Most who came to America were young (over half were under twenty-five) and most were male. Almost half were indentured servants or slaves, and, during the eighteenth century, England transported some 50,000 convicted felons to the North American colonies. About a third of the settlers came with their families; most arrived alone. A very few were wealthy; more were impoverished. Most were of the "middling sort," neither very rich nor very poor. Whatever their status or ambition, however, this extraordinary mosaic of ordinary yet adventurous people was primarily responsible for creating America's enduring institutions and values.

BRITISH FOLKWAYS   The vast majority of early settlers came from Great Britain, called Albion by the ancient Greeks. In *Albion's Seed*, a pathbreaking study of the process of British-American cultural exchange, historian David Hackett Fischer isolated four mass migrations from distinct regions of Britain over the seventeenth and eighteenth centuries. The first involved some 20,000 Puritans who settled Massachusetts between 1629 and 1641, most of whom hailed from the East Anglian counties east of London. A generation later, a smaller group of wealthy royalist cavaliers and their indentured servants migrated from southern England (Kent to Devon) to Virginia. These English aristocrats, mostly Anglicans, were already accustomed to severe social inequalities and so had few qualms about the introduction of African slavery. The third migratory wave brought some 23,000 Quakers from the north midlands of England to the Delaware Valley colonies of West Jersey, Pennsylvania, and Delaware. They imported with them a social system distinctive for its sense of spiritual equality, suspicion of social hierarchy and powerful elites, and commitment to plain living and high thinking. The fourth and largest surge of colonization occurred between 1717–1775 and included hundreds of thousands of Celtic Britons and Scotch-Irish from northern Ireland, the Scottish lowlands, and the northern counties of England; these were mostly coarse, feisty, clannish folk who settled in the rugged backcountry along the Appalachian Mountains.

It was long assumed that the strenuous demands of the American frontier environment served as a great "melting pot" that stripped such immigrants of their native identities and melded them into homogeneous Americans. In the late eighteenth century, J. Hector St. John de Crèvecoeur, an articulate Frenchman who took up farming in Orange County, New York, sounded this theme when he wrote that the American was a European who, "leaving behind him all his ancient prejudices and manners, receives new ones from the new mode of life he has embraced. . . . Here individuals of all nations are melted into a new race of men, whose labors and posterity will one day cause great changes in the world." But it was not that simple. For all of the transforming effects of the New World, the persistence of disparate British ways of life was remarkable. Although most British settlers spoke a common language and shared the Protestant faith, they were in fact diverse people who carried with them—and retained— sharply different cultural attitudes and customs from their home regions. They spoke distinct dialects, cooked different foods, named and raised their children differently, adopted different educational philosophies and attitudes toward time, built their houses in quite different architectural styles, engaged in disparate games and forms of recreation, and organized their societies differently.

Echoes of these divergent regionally based folkways still resonate through American culture. Houses in New England still favor two styles brought from East Anglia: the "saltbox"—featuring two stories in front and one in back—and the one-and-a-half-story Cape Cod. People in the South prefer fried foods in part because their ancestors from southern and western England did so. And people in the hollows of Appalachia who manufacture "moonshine" are simply continuing a pattern of home distilling begun in the borderlands of northern Britain. Other examples of cultural continuity abound. The distinctive high-pitched nasal twine associated with the New England dialect, for instance, is a product not of the American environment but of the "Norfolk whine" still evident in England's East Anglia region. Likewise, the slow drawl associated with Virginia cavaliers replicates a dialect common in southern and western England, and the speech pattern common in Appalachia that pronounces *where* as *whar* and *there* as *thar* is a product of the Scottish and Irish borderlands. Terms common to the Appalachian back-country such as "hoosier," "redneck," and "cracker" were also imported from England rather than homegrown. But the British cultural legacy extends well beyond linguistics. In gender relations, religious practices, criminal propensities, and dozens of other ways, many Americans in the 1990s still reflect age-old British customs. Of course, such cultural continuity is not unique to British-Americans. Enduring folkways are also evident among the descendants of settlers from Africa, Europe, Latin America, the Middle East, and Asia. Americans thus constitute a mosaic rather than a homogeneous mass, and they share a diverse social and cultural heritage.

SEABOARD ECOLOGY   A cherished American legend asserts that those settling British America arrived to find a pristine environment, an unspoiled wilderness little touched by human activity. But that was not the case. For thousands of years, the pre-Columbian inhabitants of the eastern seaboard had modified their environment. Indian hunting practices over the centuries had produced what one scholar has called the "greatest known loss of wild species" in American history. In addition, the Indians had burned woods and undergrowth to provide cropland, to ease travel through hardwood forests, and to make way for grasses, berries, and other forage for the animals they hunted. This "slash and burn" agriculture had halted the normal forest succession and, especially in the southeast, created large stands of longleaf pines, still the most common source of timber in the region.

Equally important in shaping the ecosystem of America was the European attitude toward the environment. Where the native Americans tended to be migratory, considering land and animals as communal resources to be shared and consumed only as necessary, many European colonizers viewed natural resources as privately owned commodities. Settlers thus looked with disdain upon the subsistence level of Indian agriculture and quickly set about evicting Indians, clearing, fencing, improving, and selling land, growing surpluses, and trapping game for commercial use.

In many places—Plymouth, for instance, or St. Mary's, Maryland—settlers occupied the sites of former Indian towns, and maize, corn, beans, and squash quickly became colonial staples, along with new crops brought from Europe. In time a more dense population of humans and their domestic animals created a landscape of fields, meadows, fences, barns, and houses.

Such innovations radically altered the ecology of the New World environment. Cleared and grazed land is warmer and drier, more subject to flooding and erosion. Foraging cattle, sheep, horses, and pigs gradually changed the distribution of trees, shrubs, and grasses. Indians, far from being passive observers, contributed to the process of environmental change by trading furs for metal or glass trinkets. This decimated the populations of large mammals that had earlier been central to Indian culture. By 1750 such unintended consequences had changed markedly the physical environment from what it had been in 1600. New England, for example, by then had become a commercial success but essentially an agricultural waste land.

POPULATION GROWTH   England's first footholds in America were bought at a fearful price. The ocean crossing aboard crowded, disease-ridden ships was anything but pleasant, and the early settlements were even more threatening. But once the brutal seasoning time was past and the colony was on its feet, Virginia and its successors grew at a prodigious rate. After the last major Indian uprising in 1644, Virginia's population quadrupled from about 8,000 to 32,000 over the next thirty years, then more than doubled, to 75,000, by 1704. Throughout the mainland colonies, the yearly growth rate during the eighteenth century ran about 3 percent. In 1625 the English colonists numbered little more than 2,000 in Virginia and Plymouth together; by 1700 the population in the colonies was perhaps 250,000, and during the eighteenth century it doubled at least every twenty-five years. By 1750 the number of colonists had passed 1 million; by 1775 it stood at about 2.5 million. In 1700 the English at home outnumbered the colonists by about 20 to 1; by 1775, on the eve of the American Revolution, the ratio was about 3 to 1.

America's plentiful land beckoned immigrants and induced them to replenish the earth with large families. Where labor was scarce, children could lend a hand, and once grown, they could find new land for themselves if need be. Colonists tended, as a result, to marry and start new families at an earlier age than their European counterparts.

BIRTH AND DEATH RATES The initial scarcity of women in the colonies had significant social effects. Where in England the average age of women at marriage was twenty-five to twenty-six, in America it dropped to twenty or twenty-one. Men also married younger in the colonies than in the Old World. The birth rate rose accordingly, since those who married earlier had time for about two additional pregnancies during the childbearing years. Later a gradual reversion to a more even sex ratio brought the average age at marriage back toward the European norm. Even so, given the better economic prospects in the colonies, a greater proportion of American women married, and the birth rate remained much higher than in Europe. In eighteenth-century Virginia, Col. William Byrd of Westover asserted, matrimony thrived "so excellently" that an "Old Maid or an Old Bachelor are as scarce among us and reckoned as ominous as a Blazing Star." Early marriage remained common. The most "antique Virgin" Byrd knew was his twenty-year-old daughter.

Equally important in explaining rapid population growth in the New World was its much lower death rate. After the difficult first years of settlement, infants generally had a better chance to reach maturity, and adults had a better chance to reach old age than their counterparts in England and Europe. In seventeenth-

Mr. John Freake, and Mrs. Elizabeth Freake and Baby Mary. Elizabeth married John at age nineteen; Mary, born when Elizabeth was thirty-two, was the Freakes' eighth and last child.

century New England, apart from childhood mortality, men could expect to reach seventy and women nearly that age. This longevity resulted less from a more temperate climate than from the character of the settlements themselves. Since the land was more bountiful, famine seldom occurred after a settlement's first year, and while the winters were more severe than in England, firewood was plentiful. Being younger on the whole—the average age in the colonies in 1790 was sixteen!—Americans were less susceptible to disease than were Europeans. More widely scattered, they were also less exposed to disease. This began to change, of course, as population centers grew and trade and travel increased. By the mid-eighteenth century the colonies were beginning to experience levels of contagion much like those in Europe.

SOCIAL STATUS   The earliest settlers brought with them fixed ideas of social hierarchy and rank. People deferred to their "betters" almost without question. John Winthrop asserted it to be God's will that "in all times some must be rich, some poore, some high and eminent in power and dignitie, others meane and in subjection." But from Jamestown onward persons of "meane" birth like John Smith revealed rare qualities when confronted with the wilderness. The breadth of opportunity to be plucked from danger impelled settlers to shake off the sense of limitations that haunted the more crowded lands of Europe.

Discarding traditional attitudes about the role of women in society proved more difficult. Colonists brought to America deeply rooted convictions concerning the inferiority of women. God and nature, it was widely assumed, had stained women with original sin and made these "weaker vessels" smaller in stature, feebler in mind, and prone to both excited emotions and psychological dependency. Women were expected to be meek and model housewives. Their role in life was clear: to obey and serve their husbands, nurture their children, and maintain their households. As John Winthrop insisted, "A true wife accounts her subjection [as] her honor and freedom" and would find true contentment only "in subjection to her husband's authority." Such commonly held attitudes meant that most women were conditioned to accept their subordinate status in a male-dominated society. A Virginia woman explained that "one of my first resolutions I made after marriage was never to hold disputes with my husband." Both social custom and legal codes ensured that women remained deferential and powerless. They could not vote, preach, hold office, attend public schools or colleges, bring suits, make contracts, or own property except under extraordinary conditions.

Yet the New World environment did generate slight improvements in the status of women. The acute shortage of women in the early years made them more highly valued than in Europe, and the Puritan emphasis on well-ordered family life led to laws protecting wives from physical abuse and allowing for divorces. In addition, colonial laws gave wives greater control over property that they contributed to a marriage or that was left after a husband's death. But the central notion of female subordination and domesticity remained firmly entrenched in the New World. As a Massachusetts boy maintained in 1662, the superior aspect of life was "masculine and eternal; the feminine inferior and mortal."

SOCIETY AND ECONOMY IN THE SOUTHERN COLONIES

CROPS AND LAND   The southern colonies had one unique advantage—the climate, which enabled them to grow exotic staples (market crops) prized by the mother country. In Virginia by 1619, tobacco production had reached 20,000 pounds, and by 1688, it was up to 18 million pounds. Smoking had become the rage among Europeans, and Virginia planters took full advantage of the situation. As one of them stressed, "all our riches for the

An idyllic view of a tidewater plantation. Note the easy access to ocean-going vessels.

present do consist in tobacco." Tobacco, however, was only one of many cash crops being grown in the southern colonies. After 1690 rice became the staple in South Carolina. The southern woods also provided harvests of lumber and naval stores (tar, pitch, and turpentine). From their early leadership in the latter trade North Carolinians would later derive the nickname of Tar Heels.

In 1614 each of the Virginia Company's colonists received three acres, and this marked the beginning of a headright policy that provided every settler in the colony with a plot of land. When Virginia became a royal colony in 1624, the headright system continued to apply, administered by the governor and his council. Lord Baltimore adopted the same practice in Maryland, and successive proprietors in the other southern and middle colonies offered variations on the plan.

If one distinctive feature of the South's staple economy was a good market in England, another was a trend toward large-scale production. Those who planted tobacco discovered that it quickly exhausted the soil, thereby giving an advantage to the planter who had extra fields to rotate in beans and corn or to leave fallow. With the increase of the tobacco crop, moreover, a fall in prices meant that economies of scale might come into play —the large planter with lower cost per unit might still make a profit. Gradually he would extend his holdings along the river-fronts, and thereby secure the advantage of direct access to the ocean-going vessels that moved freely up and down the waterways of the Chesapeake. So easy was the access in fact that the Chesapeake colonies never required a city of any size as a center of commerce.

The plantation economy depended upon manual labor, and voluntary indentured servitude accounted for probably half the arrivals of white settlers in all the colonies outside New England. The name derived from the indenture, or contract, by which a person could agree to labor in return for transportation to the New World. Not all went voluntarily. The London underworld developed a flourishing trade in "kids" and "spirits" who were enticed or "spirited" into servitude. On occasion orphans were bound off to the New World, and from time to time the mother country sent convicts into colonial servitude, the first as early as 1617. Once the indenture had run its course, usually after four to seven years, the servant claimed the freedom dues set by law —some money, tools, clothing, food—and often took up land-owning.

SLAVERY   Slavery, long a dying institution in Europe, evolved in the Chesapeake after 1619, when a Dutch vessel dropped off twenty Africans in Jamestown. Some of the first were treated as indentured servants, with a limited term, and achieved freedom and landownership. They themselves sometimes acquired slaves and white indentured servants. But gradually, with rationalizations based on color difference or heathenism, the practice of perpetual black slavery became the custom and the law of the land.

As staple crops became established on the American continent, the demand for slaves grew, and as readily available lands diminished, Virginians were less eager to bring in indentured servants who would lay claim to land at the end of their service. Though British North America brought less than 5 percent of the total slave imports to the Western Hemisphere during the more than three centuries of that squalid traffic—400,000 out of some 9,500,000—it offered slaves better chances for survival, if few for human fulfillment. The natural increase of black immigrants in America approximated that of whites by the end of the colonial period, and over 20 percent of the American population was black. In South Carolina blacks were in the majority.

Slaves are so often lumped together as a social group that their great ethnic diversity is overlooked. They came from lands as remote from each other as Angola and Senegal, the west coast of Africa, and the area around the hump in between, and they spoke Mandingo, Ibo, Kongo, and countless other tongues. Herded up by ruthless traders, frequently branded with a company label, they were packed together in slave ships and subjected to a 4–6 week Atlantic passage so brutal that one in seven captives died en route. Once in America they were thrown indiscriminately together and treated like work animals. More than a few "saltwater" slaves rebelled against their new masters, resisting work orders, sabotaging crops and tools, or running away to the frontier. In a few cases there were crudely organized rebellions that were ruthlessly suppressed. "You would be surprised at their perseverance," noted one white planter. "They often die before they can be conquered." Those still alive when conquered frequently faced ghastly retribution. After capturing slaves who participated in the Stono uprising in South Carolina in 1739, enraged planters "Cutt off their heads and set them up at every Mile Post."

With the odds so heavily stacked against resistance, most slaves resigned themselves to the overwhelming authority of the

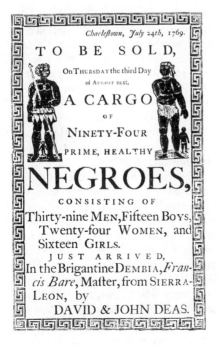

Advertisement for the sale of slaves—men, boys, women, and girls.

"peculiar institution." Yet in the process of being forced into lives of bondage, diverse blacks from diverse homelands forged a new identity as African-Americans, while at the same time leaving entwined in the fabric of American culture more strands of African heritage than historians and anthropologists can ever disentangle. Among them were new words that entered the language, such as "goober," "yam," "banana," and the names of the Coosaw, Peedee, and Wando Rivers. More important were African influences in music, folklore, and religious practices. On one level slaves used songs, stories, and sermons to distract them from their toil; on another level these conveyed coded messages of distaste for masters or overseers. Slave religion, a unique blend of African and Christian beliefs, was frequently practiced in secret. Its fundamental theme was deliverance: God, they believed, would eventually free them from slavery and open up the gates to the promised land. As one popular slave spiritual said:

> And it won't be long. And it won't be long,
> And it won't be long, Poor sinner suffer here.
> We'll soon be free.
> The Lord will call us home.

Africans also brought with them to America powerful kinship ties, and even though most colonies outlawed slave marriages, many masters realized that slaves would work harder and more reliably if allowed to form families. True, many couples were broken up when one partner was sold, but slave culture was remarkable for its powerful domestic ties. It was also remarkable for developing sex roles distinct from white society. Most slave women were by necessity field workers as well as wives and mothers responsible for household affairs. They worked in close proximity to black men, and in the process were treated more equally than most of their white counterparts.

Slavery and the growth of a multiracial South had economic, political, and cultural effects far into the future, and set America on the way to tragic conflicts. Questions about the beginnings of slavery still have a bearing on the present. Did a deep-rooted color prejudice lead to slavery, for instance, or did the existence of slavery produce the prejudice? Clearly slavery evolved because of the desire for a supply of controlled labor, and the English fell in with a trade established by the Portuguese and Spanish more than a century before—the very word "Negro" is Spanish for "black." But while the English often enslaved Indian cap-

The survival of African culture among American slaves is evident in this late-eighteenth-century painting of a South Carolina plantation. The musical instruments, pottery, and clothing are of African origin, probably Yoruba.

tives, they did not enslave white Europeans captured in wartime. Color was the crucial difference, or at least the crucial rationalization.

One historian has marshalled evidence that the seeds of slavery were already planted in Elizabethan attitudes. The English associated the color black with darkness and evil; they stamped the different appearance, behavior, and customs of Africans as representing "savagery." At the very least such perceptions could soothe the consciences of those who traded in human flesh. On the other hand most of the qualities imputed to blacks to justify slavery were the same qualities that the English assigned to their own poor to explain their status: their alleged bent for laziness, improvidence, treachery, and stupidity, among other shortcomings. Similar traits, moreover, were imputed by ancient Jews to the Canaanites and by the Mediterranean peoples of a later date to the Slavic captives sold among them. The names Canaanite and Slav both became synonymous with slavery—the latter lingers in our very word for it. Such expressions would seem to be the product of power relationships and not the other way around. Dominant peoples repeatedly assign ugly traits to those they bring into subjection.

THE GENTRY   By the early eighteenth century, Virginia and South Carolina were moving into the golden age of the Tidewater gentry, leaving the more isolated and rustic colony of North Carolina as "a valley of humiliation between two mountains of conceit." As the seventeenth century yielded to the eighteenth, the stately country seats in the Georgian, or "colonial," style began to emerge along the banks of the great rivers.

The new aristocracy patterned its provincial lifestyle after that of the English country gentleman. The great houses became centers of sumptuous living, and the planters relished their dominance over the region's social life. William Byrd remembered Virginia as a "place free from those 3 great Scourges of Mankind, Priests, Lawyers, and Physicians." In their zest for the good life the planters kept in touch with the latest refinements of London style and fashion, living on credit extended for the next year's crop and the years' beyond that, to such a degree that in the late colonial period Thomas Jefferson called the Chesapeake gentry "a species of property annexed to certain English mercantile houses." Dependence on outside capital remained a chronic southern problem lasting far beyond the colonial period.

RELIGION   Although Americans during the seventeenth century took religion more seriously than any time since, many of the colonists were not active communicants. One estimate holds that the proportion of church members to residents in the southern colonies was less than one in fifteen. There the tone of religious belief and practice was quite different from that in Puritan New England or Quaker Pennsylvania. Anglicanism predominated in the region, and it proved especially popular among the large landholders. As in England, colonial Anglicans were more conservative, rational, and formal in their forms of worship than their Puritan, Quaker, or Baptist counterparts. Anglicans tended to stress collective rituals over personal religious experience. Through most of the seventeenth century the Church of England was established (tax supported) only in Virginia and Maryland, but by the early eighteenth century it had become the established church throughout the South.

In the new environment, the Anglican church evolved into something quite unlike the state church of England. The scattered population and the absence of bishops in America made centralized control difficult. In practice therefore, if not in theory, the Anglican churches became as independent of any hierarchy as the Puritan congregations of New England. In Virginia ministerial salaries depended on the taxes paid in the parish, and after 1662 salaries fluctuated with the price of tobacco. Standards were often lax, and the Anglican clergy around the Chesapeake became notorious for its "sporting parsons," addicted to fox hunting, gambling, drunkenness, and worse. And few among the conscientious and upright Anglican ministers preached fire and brimstone sermons. Their congregations showed little toleration for being chastised from the pulpit. One minister lamented that the powerful planters removed any preacher who "had the courage and resolution to preach against any Vices taken into favor by the leading Men of his Parish."

SOCIETY AND ECONOMY IN NEW ENGLAND

TOWNSHIPS By contrast to the seaboard planters who transformed the English manor into the southern plantation, the Puritans transformed the English village into the New England town, although there were many varieties. Land policy in New England had a stronger social and religious purpose than elsewhere. The headright system of the Chesapeake never took root in New England. There were cases of large individual grants, but the standard practice was one of township grants to organized groups. A group of settlers, often gathered already into a congregation, would petition the General Court for a town, then divide the parcel according to a rough principle of equity—those who invested more or had larger families or greater status might receive more land—retaining some pasture and woodland in common and holding some for later arrivals. In some early cases the towns arranged each settler's land in separate strips after the medieval practice, but with time land was commonly divided into separate farms to which landholders would move, away from the central village.

ENTERPRISE New England farmers and their families led hard lives. Simply clearing the glacier-scoured soil of rocks might require sixty days of strenuous labor per acre. The growing season was short, and the harsh climate precluded any exotic staples. The crops were those familiar to the English countryside: wheat, barley, oats, some cattle, swine, and sheep.

With virgin forests ready for conversion into masts, lumber, and ships, and abundant fishing grounds that stretched northward to Newfoundland, it is little wonder that New Englanders turned to the sea for livelihood. New England's proximity to waters frequented by cod, mackerel, halibut, and other varieties of fish made it America's most important maritime center. Whales, too, abounded in New England waters and supplied oil for lighting and lubrication, as well as ambergris, a secretion used in perfumes.

New England's fisheries, unlike its farms, supplied a staple of export to Europe, while lesser grades of fish went to the West Indies as food for slaves. Fisheries encouraged the development of shipbuilding, and experience at seafaring spurred commerce. This in turn led to wider contacts in the Atlantic world and a degree of materialism and cosmopolitanism that clashed with the Puritan credo of plain living and high thinking. In 1714 an anxious Puritan deplored the "great extravagance that people are fallen into, far beyond their circumstances, in their purchases, buildings, families, expenses, apparel, generally in the whole way of living."

TRADE   But such laments failed to stop the material growth of the New England colonies. By the end of the seventeenth century, America had become part of a great North Atlantic commercial network, trading not only with the British Isles and the British West Indies, but also—and often illegally—with Spain, France, Portugal, Holland, and their colonies. Since they lacked the means to produce goods themselves, the colonists had to import manufactured goods from Britain and Europe. Their central economic problem was to find the means of paying for these imports —the eternal problem of the balance of trade.

The mechanism of trade in New England and the middle colonies differed from that in the South in two respects: the northern colonies were at a disadvantage in their lack of staples to exchange for English goods, but the abundance of their own shipping and mercantile enterprise worked in their favor. After 1660, in order to protect English agriculture and fisheries, the English government raised prohibitive duties (taxes) against certain major imports from the northern colonies: fish, flour, wheat, and meat, while leaving the door open to timber, furs, and whale oil. Consequently, in the early eighteenth century, New York and New England bought more from England than they sold there, incurring an unfavorable trade balance.

The northern colonies met the problem partly by using their own ships and merchants, thus avoiding the "invisible" charges for trade and transport, and by finding other markets for the staples excluded from England, thus acquiring goods or bullion to pay for imports from the mother country. American lumber and

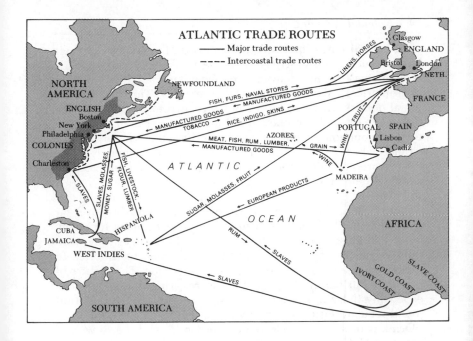

ATLANTIC TRADE ROUTES
——— Major trade routes
- - - - Intercoastal trade routes

fish therefore went to southern Europe, Madeira, and the Azores for money or in exchange for wine; lumber, rum, and provisions went to Newfoundland; and all of these and more went to the West Indies, which became the most important outlet of all. American merchants could sell fish, flour, corn, pork, beef, and horses to West Indian planters who specialized in sugarcane. In return they got money, sugar molasses, rum, indigo, and other products, much of which went eventually to England. This gave rise to the famous "triangular trade" (more a descriptive convenience than a rigid pattern) in which New Englanders shipped rum to the west coast of Africa and bartered for slaves, took the slaves on the "Middle Passage" to the West Indies, and returned home with various commodities including molasses, from which they manufactured rum. In another version they shipped provisions to the West Indies, carried sugar and molasses to England, and returned with manufactured goods from Europe.

The generally unfavorable balance of trade left the colonies with a chronic shortage of hard money, which drifted away to pay for imports and invisible charges. Various expedients met the currency shortage. Most of the colonies at one time or another issued bills of credit, on promise of payment in hard currency later (hence the dollar "bill"), and most set up land banks that issued paper money for loans to farmers on the security of their lands, which were mortgaged to the banks. Colonial farmers, recognizing that an inflation of paper money led to an inflation of crop prices, asked for more and more paper. Thus began in colonial politics what was to become a recurrent problem in later times, the issue of currency inflation. Wherever the issue arose, debtors commonly favored growth in the money supply, which would make it easier for them to settle accounts, whereas creditors favored a limited money supply, which would increase the value of their capital.

RELIGION   It has been said that in New England one was never far from the smell of fish and brimstone. The Puritans for many years had a bad press. By the standards of later ages they were judged prudes and bigots, but they had come to America to escape error, not to tolerate it in their New Zion. The picture of the dour Puritan, hostile to all pleasures, rings false. Puritans, especially those of the upper class, wore colorful clothing, enjoyed secular music, and imbibed prodigious quantities of rum. "Drink is in itself a good creature of God," said the Reverend Increase Mather, ". . . but the abuse of drink is from Satan." If found incapacitated by reason of strong drink, one was subject to arrest. A Salem man, for example, was tried for staggering into a house where he "eased his stomak in the Chimney." Repeated offenders were forced to wear the letter D in public.

Moderation in all things except piety was the Puritan guideline. This was true for sexual activity as well. Contrary to prevailing images of the Puritans as prudes, they were quite open in recognizing natural human desires. One minister emphasized that "the Use of the Marriage Bed" is "founded in man's Nature." Consequently, any unwillingness to engage in sexual intercourse on the part of husband or wife "Denies all reliefe in Wedlock unto Human necessity: and sends it for supply unto Beastiality. . ." Churches occasionally expelled members for failing to satisfy their partner's sexual needs. Sexual activity outside the bounds of marriage was strictly forbidden but, like most prohibitions, it seemed to provoke transgression. New England court records bulge with cases of adultery and fornication. In part the abundance of sexual offenses reflected the disproportionate number of men in the colonies. Many were unable to find a wife and were therefore tempted to satisfy their sexual desires outside of marriage.

The Puritans who settled Massachusetts, unlike the Separatists of Plymouth, proposed only to form a purified version of the Anglican church. They believed that they could remain loyal to the Church of England, the unity of church and state, and the principle of compulsory uniformity. But their remoteness from England led them very quickly to a congregational form of church government identical with that of the Pilgrim Separatists.

Certain aspects of the Puritan faith were pregnant with meaning for the future. In the Puritan version of Calvin's theology, God had voluntarily entered into a covenant, or contract, with people through which his creatures could secure salvation. By analogy, therefore, an assembly of true Christians could enter into a church covenant, a voluntary union for the common worship of God. From this it was a fairly short step to the idea of a voluntary union for purposes of government.

The covenant theory contained certain kernels of democracy in both church and state, but democracy was no part of Puritan political thought, which like so much else in Puritan belief began with original sin. Innate human depravity made governments necessary. "If people be governors," asked the Reverend John Cotton, "who shall be governed?" The Puritan was dedicated to seeking not the will of the people but the will of God. The ultimate source of authority resided in the Bible, but the Bible had to be known by right reason, which was best applied by those trained to the purpose. Hence, most Puritans deferred to an intellectual elite for a true knowledge of providential design. Church and state were but two aspects of the same unity, the purpose of which was to carry out God's will on earth. The New England way might thus be summarized in one historian's phrase as a kind of "dictatorship of the regenerate," or of those who had undergone the conversion experience required for church membership.

The church exercised a pervasive influence over the life of the town, but unlike the Church of England it technically had no political power. While Puritan New England has often been called a theocracy, the church technically was entirely separated from the state—except that town residents were taxed for its support. And if not all inhabitants were church members, they were to be present for church services. So complete was the apparent consensus of church member and nonmember alike that the closely knit communities of New England have been called peaceable kingdoms. Life in the small rural townships was intimate and essentially cooperative. Studies of Andover, Dedham, and Plymouth, Massachusetts, among other towns, suggest that, at least in the seventeenth century, family ties grew stronger and village life more cohesive than in the homeland.

DIVERSITY AND SOCIAL STRAINS   But such harmony was frequently short-lived. Increasing diversity and powerful disruptive forces combined to erode the idyllic consensual society envisioned by the founding settlers. Despite long-enduring myths, New England towns were not always pious, harmonious, static, and self-sufficient rural utopias populated by praying Puritans. Many communities were founded as centers of fishing, trade, and commerce rather than farming, religion, and morality, and the animating concerns of residents in such towns tended to be more entrepreneurial than spiritual. Interestingly enough, however, in Massachusetts seaport towns such as Gloucester and Marblehead, founded by diverse, contentious English immigrants on the make, community life grew more cohesive, settled, and religious in the midst of economic growth.

Nevertheless, among most of the godly communities in the backwoods, social strains and worldly pursuits increased as time passed, a consequence primarily of population pressure on the land and rising disparities of wealth. Initially, among the first settlers, fathers exercised strong patriarchal authority over their sons through their control of the land. They kept the sons in town, not letting them set up their own households or get title to their farmlands until they reached middle age. In New England as elsewhere the tendency was to subdivide the land among all the children. But by the eighteenth century, with land scarcer, the younger sons were either getting control of property early or else moving on. Often the younger male children were forced, with family help and blessings, to seek land elsewhere or find new kinds of work in the commercial cities along the coast or inland rivers. With the growing pressure on land in the settled regions, poverty and social tension increased in what had once seemed a country of unlimited opportunity.

Sectarian disputes and religious indifference were also on the rise in many communities. The emphasis on a direct accountability to God, which lay at the base of all Protestant theology, caused a persistent tension and led believers to challenge authority in the name of private conscience. Massachusetts repressed such heresy in the 1630s, but it resurfaced during the 1650s among Quakers and Baptists, and in 1659–1660 the colony hanged four Quakers who persisted in returning after they were expelled. These acts caused such revulsion—and an investigation by the crown—that they were not repeated, although heretics continued to face harassment and persecution.

More damaging to the Puritan utopia was the increasing diversity and worldliness of New England, which placed growing strains on church discipline. More and more children of the "visible saints" found themselves unable to testify that they had received the gift of God's grace. In 1662 an assembly of ministers at Boston accepted the "Half-Way Covenant," whereby baptized children of church members could be admitted to a "half-way" membership. Their own children could be baptized but such "half-way" members could neither vote nor take communion. A further blow to Puritan convention and control came with the Massachusetts royal charter of 1691, which required toleration of dissenters and based the right to vote on property rather than on church membership.

NEW ENGLAND WITCHCRAFT The strains accompanying Massachusetts's transition from Puritan utopia to royal colony reached an unhappy climax in the witchcraft hysteria at Salem Village (later Danvers) in 1692. Belief in witchcraft pervaded European and New England society in the seventeenth century. Indeed, prior to the dramatic episode in Salem, almost 300 New Englanders (mostly lower-class, middle-aged, marginal women—spinsters or widows) had been accused as witches, and more than thirty hanged.

Still, the Salem outbreak exceeded all precedents in its scope and intensity. The general upheaval in the colony's political, economic, social, and religious life was compounded in that locale by a conflict of values between a community rooted in the subsistence farm economy and the thriving port of Salem proper. Seething insecurities and family conflicts within the community apparently made many residents receptive to accusations by adolescent girls that they had been bewitched. The episode began when a few teenage girls became entranced listeners to voodoo stories told by Tituba, a West Indian slave, and began acting strangely—shouting, barking, groveling and twitching for no apparent reason. The town doctor concluded that they had been bewitched, and the girls pointed to Tituba and two white women as the culprits. Soon town dwellers were seized with panic as word spread that the devil was in their midst, wreaking havoc. At a hearing before the magistrates the "afflicted" girls rolled on the floor in convulsive fits as the three women were questioned by the magistrates. In the midst of this hysterical carnival, Tituba shocked her listeners by not only confessing to the charge but also divulging that many others in the community were performing the devil's work.

Four women being hanged as witches in seventeenth-century England. At Salem, nineteen people were hanged for witchcraft.

With that the crazed girls began pointing accusing fingers at dozens of residents, including several of the most respected members of the community. Within a few months the Salem jail overflowed with townspeople—men, women, and children—accused of practicing witchcraft. That the accusing girls were so readily believed illustrates how overwrought the community had become. Before the hysteria ran its course ten months later, nineteen people (including some men) had been hanged, one man—stubborn Giles Corey—pressed to death by heavy stones, and more than 100 others jailed. But as the net of accusation spread wider, extending far beyond the confines of Salem, colonial leaders began to worry that the witchhunts were out of control. When the afflicted girls charged Samuel Willard, the distinguished pastor of Boston's First Church and president of Harvard College, the stunned magistrates had seen enough. Shortly thereafter, the governor intervened when his own wife was accused of serving the devil. He disbanded the special court and ordered the remaining suspects released. A year after it had begun, the fratricidal event was finally over. Nearly everybody responsible for the Salem executions later recanted, and nothing quite like it happened in the colonies again. In Europe, however, witches were still being executed in the eighteenth century.

SOCIETY AND ECONOMY IN THE MIDDLE COLONIES

AN ECONOMIC MIX   Both geographically and culturally the middle colonies stood between New England and the South, blending their own influences with elements derived from the older regions on either side. In so doing they more completely reflected the diversity of colonial life and more fully foreshadowed the pluralism of the later American nation than the regions on either side. Their crops were those of New England but more bountiful, owing to better land and a longer growing season, and they developed surpluses of foodstuffs for exports to the plantations of the South and the West Indies: wheat, barley, and livestock. Three great rivers—the Hudson, Delaware, and Susquehanna —and their tributaries gave the middle colonies a unique access to their backcountry and to the fur trade of the interior, where New York and Pennsylvania long enjoyed friendly relations with the Indians. As a consequence the region's commerce rivaled that of New England, and indeed Philadelphia in time supplanted Boston as the largest city in the colonies.

Land policies followed the headright system of the South. In New York the early royal governors carried forward, in practice if not in name, the Dutch device of the patroonship, granting to influential favorites vast estates on Long Island and up the Hudson and Mohawk Valleys. These realms most nearly approached the Old World manor, self-contained domains farmed by tenants who paid fees to use the landlords' mills, warehouses, smokehouses, and wharfs. But with free land elsewhere, New York's population languished, and the new waves of immigrants sought the promised land of Pennsylvania.

AN ETHNIC MIX   In the makeup of their population the middle colonies stood apart from both the mostly English Puritan settlements and the biracial plantation colonies to the south. In New York and New Jersey, for instance, Dutch culture and language lingered for some time, along with the Dutch Reformed church. Up and down the Delaware River the few Swedes and Finns, the first settlers, were overwhelmed by the influx of English and Welsh Quakers, followed in turn by the Germans and Scotch-Irish.

The Germans came mainly from the Rhineland. Penn's brochures on the bounties of Pennsylvania circulated in German translation, and his promise of religious freedom brought an excited response from persecuted sects, especially the Mennon-

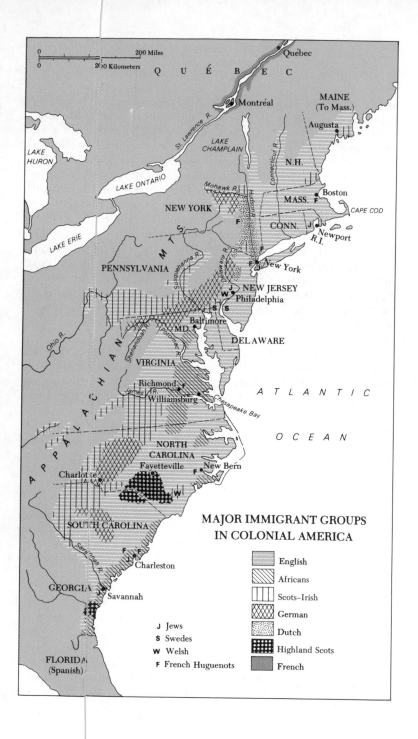

MAJOR IMMIGRANT GROUPS
IN COLONIAL AMERICA

English

Africans

Scots–Irish

German

Dutch

Highland Scots

French

J Jews

S Swedes

W Welsh

F French Huguenots

ites, whose beliefs resembled those of the Quakers. They were but the vanguard of a swelling migration in the eighteenth century which included Lutherans, Reformed Calvinists, Moravians, Dunkers, and others, a large proportion of whom paid their way as indentured servants or "redemptioners," as they were commonly called. West of Philadelphia these thrifty farmers and artisans created a belt of settlement in which the "Pennsylvania Dutch" (a corruption of Deutsch, meaning German) predominated.

The Scotch-Irish began to arrive later and moved still farther out in the backcountry. "Scotch-Irish" is an enduring misnomer for Ulster Scots, Presbyterians transplanted from Scotland to confiscated lands in northern Ireland to give that country a more Protestant tone. The Ulster plantation dated from 1607–1609, the years when Jamestown was fighting for survival. A century later the Ulster Scots, mostly Presbyterians, were on the move again, in flight from economic disaster and Anglican persecution. This time they looked mainly to Pennsylvania and the fertile valleys stretching southwestward into Virginia and Carolina. Unlike the more communal and pastoral Germans, they tended to settle in the wilderness areas, usually the western portions of the colonies, where they cleared the land, built rude log cabins, and lived by hunting and scratch farming. These "bold and indigent strangers," as one Pennsylvania official described them, were virulently anti-English and suspicious of all governments. Renowned for their piety and their acquisitiveness, they were said to keep "the Sabbath and everything else they could lay their hands on." This usually brought them into conflict with the Indians, toward whom they harbored an abiding hatred. From such rugged, hardheaded, and hardfisted people, however, would come many powerful leaders: John Calhoun, Andrew Jackson, Sam Houston, and Woodrow Wilson.

The Germans and Scotch-Irish became the most numerous of the non-English groups in the colonies, but others also enriched the diversity of population in New York and the Quaker colonies: French Huguenots, Irish, Welsh, Swiss, Jews, and others. By 1790 little more than half the populace, and perhaps fewer, could trace their origins to England.

COLONIAL CITIES

Since commerce was their chief reason for being, colonial cities hugged the coastline or, like Philadelphia, sprang up on rivers where ocean-going vessels could reach them. Never holding more than 10 percent of the colonial population, they exerted an influence in commerce, politics, and civilization generally out of proportion to their size. Five major port cities outdistanced the rest. By the end of the colonial period Philadelphia, with some 30,000 people, was the largest city in the colonies and second only to London in the British Empire; New York, with about 25,000, ranked second; Boston numbered 16,000; Charles Town, 12,000; and Newport, 11,000.

Merchants formed the upper crust of urban society and below them came a middle class of craftsmen, retailers, innkeepers, and small jobbers who met a variety of needs. At the bottom of the pecking order were sailors, unskilled workers, and some artisans. Such class stratification in the cities became more pronounced during the eighteenth century and after.

Problems created by urban growth are nothing new. Colonial cities had traffic problems which required not only paved streets and lighting but regulations to protect children and animals in the streets from reckless riders. Other regulations restrained citizens from creating public nuisances by tossing their garbage into the streets. Devastating fires led to preventive standards in building codes, restrictions on burning rubbish, and the organization of volunteer and finally professional fire companies. Crime and violence made necessary more police protection. And in cities the poor became more visible than in the countryside. Colonists brought with them the English principle of public responsibility for the needy. The number of Boston's poor receiving public assistance rose from 500 in 1700 to 4,000 in 1736; New York's from 250 in 1698 to 5,000 in the 1770s. Most of it went to "outdoor" relief in the form of money, food, clothing, and fuel, but almshouses also appeared in colonial cities.

THE URBAN WEB Communication within and between cities was difficult at first. On land people traveled initially by horse or by foot, and there was not a single hard-surfaced road during the entire colonial period, aside from city streets. Postal service through the seventeenth century was almost nonexistent—people entrusted letters to travelers or sea captains. During the eighteenth century, however, a postal system eventually extended the length of the Atlantic seaboard.

More reliable deliveries gave rise to newspapers in the eighteenth century. By 1745 twenty-two colonial newspapers had been started. An important landmark in the progress of freedom of the press was John Peter Zenger's trial for seditious libel for publishing criticisms of New York's governor in his paper, the *New York Weekly Journal*. Imprisoned for ten months and brought to trial in 1735, he was charged with fostering "an ill opinion of the government." The jury's function was only to determine whether the defendant had published the opinion, but the defense attorney startled the court with his claim that Zenger had published the truth—which the judge ruled an unacceptable defense. The jury, however, agreed with the assertion and found the editor not guilty. The libel law remained standing as before, but editors thereafter were emboldened to criticize officials more freely.

THE ENLIGHTENMENT

In the world of ideas a new fashion dazzled minds: the Enlightenment. During the seventeenth century Europe experienced a scientific revolution in which the prevailing notion of an earth-centered universe was overthrown by the new sun-centered system of Polish astronomer Nicolaus Copernicus. The revolution climaxed in 1687 when England's Sir Isaac Newton set forth his theory of gravitation. Newton had, in short, hit upon the design of a mechanistic universe moving in accordance with natural laws which could be grasped by human reason and explained by mathematics.

By analogy from Newton's view of the world as a machine one could reason that natural laws governed all things—the orbits of the planets and also the orbits of human relations: politics, economics, and society. Reason could make people aware, for instance, that the natural law of supply and demand governed economics or that natural rights to life, liberty, and property determined the limits and functions of government.

Much of enlightened thought could be reconciled with established beliefs—the idea of natural law existed in Christian theology, and religious people could reason that the world view of Copernicus and Newton simply showed forth the glory of God. Puritan leaders accepted Newtonian science from the start. Yet Deists carried the idea to its ultimate conclusion, reducing God to the position of a remote Creator, a master clockmaker who planned the universe and set it in motion. Evil in the world, one might reason further, resulted not from original sin so much as from an imperfect understanding of the laws of nature. People, the English philosopher John Locke argued in his *Essay on Human Understanding* (1690), reflected the impact of their environment, the human mind being a blank tablet at birth that gained knowledge through experience. Corrupt society therefore might corrupt the mind. The way to improve both society and human nature was by the application and improvement of Reason—which was the highest Virtue (enlightened thinkers often capitalized both words).

THE AMERICAN ENLIGHTENMENT However interpreted, such ideas profoundly affected the climate of thought in the eighteenth century. As a Connecticut minister recognized in 1788, "The present age is an enlightened one." The premises of Newtonian science and the Enlightenment, moreover, fitted the American experience. In the New World people no longer moved in the worn grooves of tradition that defined the roles of priest or peasant or noble. Much of their experience had already been with observation, experiment, and the need to think anew. America was therefore receptive to the new science. Anybody who pretended to a degree of learning revealed a curiosity about natural philosophy, and some carried it to considerable depth.

Benjamin Franklin epitomized the Enlightenment more than any other single person. Franklin rose from the ranks of the common folk and never lost the common touch, a gift that accounted for his success as a publisher. Born in Boston in 1706, Franklin was the son of a candle and soap maker. Apprenticed to his older brother, a printer, Franklin left home at the age of seventeen and

Benjamin Franklin, around age forty; he soon retired from business to devote himself to public service and the sciences.

relocated to Philadelphia. There, before he was twenty-four, he owned a print shop where he edited and published the *Pennsylvania Gazette*, and when he was twenty-seven he brought out *Poor Richard's Almanac*, full of homely maxims on success and happiness. Before he retired from business at the age of forty-two, Franklin, among other achievements, had founded a library, set up a fire company, helped start the academy that became the University of Pennsylvania, and organized a debating club that grew into the American Philosophical Society. After his early retirement he intended to devote himself to public affairs and the sciences.

The course of events allowed Franklin less and less time for science, but that remained his passion. His speculations extended widely to the fields of medicine, meteorology, geology, astronomy, and physics. He invented the Franklin stove, the lightning rod, and a glass harmonica for which Mozart and Beethoven composed. The triumph of this untutored genius further confirmed the Enlightenment trust in the powers of Nature.

EDUCATION IN THE COLONIES   The heights of abstract reasoning, of course, were remote from the everyday concerns of most colonists. For the colonists at large, education in the traditional ideas and manners of society—even literacy itself—remained primarily the responsibility of family and church, and one not always accepted.

Conditions in New England proved most favorable for the establishment of schools. The Puritan emphasis on Scripture reading, which all Protestants shared in some degree, implied an obligation to ensure literacy. In 1647 Massachusetts Bay required every town of fifty or more families to set up a grammar school (a Latin school that could prepare a student for college). Although the act was widely evaded, it set an example which the rest of New England emulated.

In Pennsylvania the Quakers never heeded William Penn's instructions to establish public schools, but did respect the usefulness of education and financed a number of private schools teaching practical as well as academic subjects. In the southern colonies efforts to establish schools were hampered by the more scattered populations, and in parts of the backcountry by indifference and neglect. Some of the wealthiest planters and merchants of the Tidewater sent their children to England or hired tutors, who in some cases would also serve the children of neighbors. In some places wealthy patrons or the people collectively managed to raise some kind of support for secondary academies.

THE GREAT AWAKENING

As a consequence of the new currents of learning and the Enlightenment, however, many people seemed to be drifting away from the old moorings of piety. Intellectually the educated classes were attracted to Deism and skepticism. And, so it was thought, if the Lord had allowed great Puritan and Quaker merchants of Boston and Philadelphia to prosper, the haunting fear arose that the devil had lured them into the vain pursuit of worldly gain. Meanwhile, out along the fringes of settlement there grew up a great backwater of the unchurched, people who had no minister to preach or administer sacraments or perform marriages, who fell, according to some, into a primitive and sinful life, little different from the "heathens" who lurked in the woods. An Anglican divine called the backcountry preachers in the Carolinas "ignorant wretches, who cannot write" and compared a Baptist communion service to "A Gang of frantic Lunatics broke out of Bedlam." By the 1730s the sense of falling-away had prepared the time for a revival of faith, the Great Awakening, a wave of evangelism that within a few years swept the colonies from one end to the other, America's first mass movement.

EDWARDS AND WHITEFIELD   In 1734–1735 a rehearsal for the event came in a remarkable spiritual revival that occurred in the congregation of Jonathan Edwards, a Congregationalist minister in Northampton, Massachusetts. One of America's most brilliant philosophers and theologians, Edwards entered Yale in 1716 at age thirteen and graduated valedictorian four years later. While a college student, he developed a mystical religious strain. "God's excellency, his wisdom, his purity and love," he wrote, "seemed to appear in everything; in the sun, moon and stars; in the clouds, and blue sky; in the grass, flowers, trees; in the water, and all nature; which used greatly to fix my mind."

In 1726 Edwards took charge of the Congregational church in Northampton and found the congregation's spirituality at low ebb. "Licentiousness for some years greatly prevailed among the youth of the town: there were many of them much addicted to night walking and frequenting the tavern, and lewd practices wherein some by their example exceedingly corrupted others." He was convinced that Christians had become too preoccupied with making and spending money and that religion had become too intellectual and in the process had lost its animating force. "Our people," he said, "do not so much need to have their heads stored as to have their hearts touched." He added that he considered it a "reasonable thing to endeavor to fright persons away

The Rev. Jonathan Edwards awoke many congregants to their plight in sermons such as "Sinners in the Hands of an Angry God."

from hell." His own vivid descriptions of the torments of hell and the delights of heaven helped rekindle spiritual fervor among his congregants. By 1735 he could report that "the town seemed to be full of the presence of God; it never was so full of love, nor of joy."

About the same time, William Tennent set up a "Log College" in Neshaminy, Pennsylvania, for the education of ministers to serve the Scotch-Irish Presbyterians around Philadelphia. The Log College specialized in turning out zealots who scorned complacency and proclaimed the need for revival. Among the most successful was Tennent's son Gilbert. Critics scorned these backwoods revivalists, branding them "half educated enthusiasts," but two of these rustic preachers later became presidents of Princeton.

The true catalyst of the Great Awakening, however, was a twenty-seven-year-old English minister, George Whitefield, whose reputation as a spellbinding evangelist in the Wesleyan revivals then underway in England preceded him to the colonies. Congregations were lifeless, he claimed, "because dead men preach to them." Too many ministers were "slothful shepherds and dumb dogs." To restore the fires of religious fervor to American congregations, Whitefield reawakened the notion of individual salvation. In the autumn of 1739 he arrived in Philadelphia, and late in that year preached to crowds of as many as 6,000 around Philadelphia. After visiting in Georgia, he made a triumphal procession northward to New England, drawing great crowds and releasing "Gales of Heavenly Wind" that dispersed sparks throughout the colonies.

Young and magnetic, possessed of a golden voice and a squinting left eye, Whitefield enthralled audiences with his unparalleled eloquence. Even the skeptical Benjamin Franklin, who went to see the show in Philadelphia, found himself so carried away that he emptied his pockets into the collection plate—perhaps the ultimate tribute to Whitefield's persuasiveness. The English revivalist stressed the need for individuals to experience a "new birth"—the need for a sudden and emotional moment of conversion and salvation—and the dangers of an unconverted ministry which had not experienced such rebirth. By the end of his sermon, one listener reported, the entire congregation was "in utmost Confusion, some crying out, some laughing, and Bliss still roaring to them to come to Christ, they answering, *I will, I will, I'm coming, I'm coming.*"

Jonathan Edwards heard Whitefield preach and was so moved by the experience that he wept through most of the sermon. Thereafter he took advantage of the commotion stirred up by Whitefield to spread his own revival gospel. The Awakening in New England reached its peak in 1741, when Edwards delivered his most famous sermon at Enfield, Massachusetts. Entitled "Sinners in the Hands of an Angry God," it represented a devout appeal to repentance. Edwards reminded the congregation of the reality of hell, the omnipotence of God's vision, and the certainty of his judgment. "The bow of God's wrath is bent," he declared, "and the arrow made ready on the string, and justice bends the arrow at your heart, and strains the bow, and it is nothing but the mere pleasure of God, and that of an angry God, without any promise or obligation at all, that keeps the arrow one moment from being made drunk with your blood." In a compelling metaphor, Edwards warned that God "holds you over the pit of hell, much as one holds a spider, or some loathsome insect, over the fire, abhors you, and is dreadfully provoked . . . he looks upon you as worthy of nothing else, but to be cast into the fire." But for all the terror of his theme, Edwards did not rant or engage in theatrics. Instead he delivered the carefully reasoned sermon in a soft, solemn voice and a calm manner. When he finished he had to wait several minutes for the congregation to quiet down before leading them in a closing hymn.

The message and technique of Edwards and Whitefield were infectious, and imitators sprang up everywhere, some of whom carried the fiery language and brimstone to extremes. Once unleashed, spiritual enthusiasm was hard to control, and in many ways the Awakening backfired on those who had intended it to bolster church discipline and social order. Some of the revivalists began to court those at the bottom of the social scale—laborers, seamen, servants, and farmers. The Reverend James Davenport, for instance, a fiery itinerant New England Congregationalist, set about shouting, raging, and stomping on the devil and beseeching his listeners to renounce the established clergy and become the agents of their own salvation. The churched and unchurched flocked to hear his mesmerizing sermons, and, seized by the terror and ecstasy, they groveled on the floor or lay unconscious on the benches, to the chagrin of more decorous churchgoers. One never knew, the more traditional clergymen warned, whence came these enthusiasms—perhaps they were delusions sent by the Devil to discredit the true faith. The radical revivalists, said one worried conservative, were breeding "anarchy, levelling, and dissolution."

PIETY AND REASON   Whatever their motive or method, the revivalists succeeded in awakening the piety of many Americans. Between 1740 and 1742 some 25,000–50,000 New Englanders, out of a total population of 300,000, joined churches. The Awakening spawned a proliferation of new religious groups and sects that helped undermine the notion of state-supported churches. Everywhere the revivals brought splits, especially in the more Calvinistic churches. Traditional clergymen found their position undermined as church members chose sides and either dismissed their ministers or deserted them. Many of the revivalists, or "New Lights," went over to the Baptists, and others flocked to Presbyterian or, later, Methodist groups, which in turn divided and subdivided into new sects.

By the middle of the eighteenth century, New England Puritanism had finally fragmented. The precarious balance in which the Founders had held the elements of piety and reason was shattered, and more and more Baptists, Presbyterians, Anglicans, and other denominations began establishing footholds in formerly Congregationalist Puritan communities. But the revival tradition paradoxically scored its most lasting victories along the chaotic frontiers of the middle and southern colonies. In the more sedate churches of Boston, moreover, Enlightened rationalism got the upper hand in a reaction against the excesses of revival emotion. Bostonian ministers like Charles Chauncey and Jonathan Mayhew assumed the lead in preaching a doctrine of calm rationality. Reassessing Calvinist theology, they found it too forbidding and irrational that people could be forever damned by predestination. The rationality of Newton and Locke, the idea of natural law, crept more and more into their sermons, and they embarked on the road to Unitarianism and Universalism.

In reaction to taunts that the "born-again" ministers lacked learning, the Awakening gave rise to the denominational colleges that became so characteristic of American higher education. The three colleges already in existence had grown earlier from religious motives: Harvard, founded in 1636, because the Puritans dreaded "to leave an illiterate ministry to the church when our present ministers shall lie in the dust"; the College of William and Mary, in 1693, to strengthen the Anglican ministry; and Yale College, in 1701, set up to serve the Puritans of Connecticut, who felt that Harvard was drifting from the strictest orthodoxy. The Presbyterian College of New Jersey, later Princeton University, was founded in 1746 as successor to William Tennent's Log College. In close succession came King's College (1754) in New York, later Columbia University, an Anglican institution; the College of Rhode Island (1764), later Brown University, Baptist; Queen's College (1766), later Rutgers, Dutch Reformed; and Congregationalist Dartmouth (1769), the outgrowth of an earlier school for Indians. Among the colonial colleges only the University of Pennsylvania, founded as the Philadelphia Academy in 1754, arose from a secular impulse.

The Great Awakening, like the Enlightenment, set in motion currents that still flow in American life. It implanted permanently in American culture evangelical principles and methods. Moreover, by weakening the status of the old-fashioned clergy and encouraging believers to exercise their own judgment, Awakeners thereby weakened habits of deference generally. The proliferation of denominations heightened the need for toleration of dissent. But in some respects the counterpoint between the Awakening and the Enlightenment, between the principles of piety and reason, led by different roads to similar ends. Both emphasized the power and right of individual choice and popular resistance to established authority, and both aroused millennial hopes that America would become the promised land in which people might attain to the perfection of piety or reason, if not of both. Such hopes had both social and political, as well as religious, implications. As the eighteenth century advanced, fewer and fewer people were willing to defer to the ruling social and political elite, and many such rebellious, if pious, folk would be transformed into Revolutionaries.

FURTHER READING

Scholarship in colonial social history is as active as in any historical field. The diversity of colonial societies may be seen in Jack P. Greene's

Pursuits of Happiness: The Social Development of the Early Modern British Colonies and the Formation of American Culture (1988)° and in David Hackett Fischer's *Albion's Seed: Four British Folkways in America* (1991).°

Studies of the New England town include Kenneth A. Lockridge's *A New England Town: The First One Hundred Years* (2nd ed., 1985)°; Philip J. Greven, Jr.'s *Four Generations: Population, Land, and Family in Colonial Andover, Massachusetts* (1970)°; and Paul S. Boyer and Stephen Nissenbaum's *Salem Possessed* (1974),° which connects the notorious witch trials to changes in community structure and economic base. Of the more recent works, see also Christine Heyrman, *Commerce and Culture* (1984)° and Stephen Innes's *Labor in a New Land; Economy and Society in Seventeenth-Century Springfield* (1983).°

For an interdisciplinary approach, see John Demos's *Entertaining Satan: Witchcraft and the Culture of Early New England* (1982).° Discussions of women in the New England colonies can be found in Laurel Ulrich's *Good Wives* (1982)°; Joy Buel and Richard Buel's *The Way of Duty* (1984)°; and Carol Karlsen's *The Devil in the Shape of a Woman: Witchcraft in Colonial New England* (1987).°

Allan Kulikoff's *Tobacco and Slaves: The Development of Southern Cultures in the Chesapeake Colonies, 1680–1800* (1986)° is a superb account of the relationship between economic, social, and cultural systems. Darrett B. Rutman and Anita H. Rutman's *A Place in Time* (2 vols., 1984)° is a study of community life in a Virginia county.

The best southern social history is intertwined with analysis of the origins of slavery. Begin with Edmund S. Morgan's *American Slavery, American Freedom: The Ordeal of Colonial Virginia* (1975).° More specific on the racial nature of the origins of slavery are Winthrop D. Jordan's *White over Black: American Attitudes toward the Negro* (1986)° and David B. Davis's *The Problem of Slavery in Western Culture* (1966).° On the interaction of black and white cultures, see Mechal Sobel's *The World They Made Together: Black and White Values in Eighteenth-Century Virginia* (1988).

For the role of Indians and settlers in shaping the New World's ecology, see William Cronon's fine work *Changes in the Land* (1983)° and Albert E. Cowdrey's *This Land, This South* (1983), and James Merrell, *The Indians' New World* (1989).

Henry F. May's *The Enlightenment in America* (1976)° examines intellectual trends in eighteenth-century America. Lawrence A. Cremin's *American Education: The Colonial Experience, 1607–1783* (1970) surveys educational developments.

On the Great Awakening see Edwin S. Gaustad's *The Great Awakening in New England* (1957) and Patricia U. Bonomi's *Under the Cope of Heaven* (1986).° The political impact of the new religious enthusiasm is shown in Rhys Isaac's *The Transformation of Virginia, 1740–1790* (1982).°

° These books are available in paperback editions.

3

THE IMPERIAL PERSPECTIVE

For the better part of the seventeenth century England remained too distracted by the struggle between Parliament and the Stuart kings to perfect either a colonial policy or effective agencies of imperial control. The English Civil War, which lasted from 1642 to 1649, was followed by Oliver Cromwell's Puritan Commonwealth and Protectorate, during which the colonies were given a respite from royal control. After the Restoration of Charles II and the Stuart dynasty in 1660, the British government slowly developed a plan of colonial administration. But by the end of the century it still lacked coherence and efficiency, leaving Americans accustomed to rather loose colonial reins.

ENGLISH ADMINISTRATION OF THE COLONIES

THE MERCANTILE SYSTEM   If the English government showed little passion for colonial administration, it had a lively interest in colonial trade, which had fallen largely to Dutch shipping during the English Civil War. To win back this trade, Cromwell, in 1651, convinced Parliament to adopt a Navigation Act which required that all goods imported into England or the colonies must arrive on English ships, and that the majority of each crew must be English.

On economic policy, if nothing else, Restoration England under Charles II took its cue from the mercantile system Cromwell had instituted. Mercantilism became in the seventeenth and eighteenth centuries the operative theory of all major European powers. In a world of national rivalries, the reasoning went, power and wealth went hand in hand. To be strong a state must be wealthy. Mercantilists assumed that the world's wealth, as reflected in the total stock of gold and silver, remained essentially fixed. All that changed was a nation's share of that stock, which it could increase only at the expense of its rivals. This meant limiting foreign imports and preserving a favorable balance of trade. To accomplish this the state should encourage manufacturers, providing subsidies and monopolies if need be, to develop and protect its own shipping, and exploit colonies as sources of raw materials and markets for its own finished goods.

The Navigation Act of 1660 added a new twist to Cromwell's act of 1651. Ships' crews now had to be not half but three-quarters English, and certain articles not produced by the mother country were to be shipped only to England or other English colonies. The list included tobacco, cotton, indigo dye, and sugar. Later, rice, naval stores, masts, copper, and furs were added. Not only did England (and the colonies) become the sole outlet for these colonial exports, but three years later the Navigation Act of 1663 sought to make England the funnel through which all colonial imports had to be routed. The act was sometimes called the Staple Act because it made England the staple (market or trade center) for goods sent to the colonies. Virtually all ships carrying goods from Europe to America had to dock in England, be offloaded, and pay a duty before proceeding. A third major act rounded out the trade system. The Navigation Act of 1673 (sometimes called the Plantation Duty Act) required that every captain loading enumerated articles in the colonies pay a duty or tax on the item.

ENFORCING THE NAVIGATION ACTS   The Navigation Acts supplied a convenient rationale for a colonial system to serve the economic needs of the mother country. Their enforcement in far-flung colonies, however, was another matter. During the reign of Charles II a bureaucracy of colonial administrators emerged, but it took shape slowly and in fact was never fully developed. In 1675 Charles II designated certain privy councilors the Lords of Trade and Plantations, whose name reflects the overall importance of economic factors. The Lords of Trade were to make the colonies abide by the mercantile system and to seek out ways to make them more profitable to the crown. To these ends they served as the clearinghouse for all colonial affairs, building up a staff of colonial experts. They also named colonial governors, wrote or reviewed the governors' instructions, and handled all reports and correspondence dealing with colonial affairs.

Between 1673 and 1679, British collectors of customs duties arrived in all the colonies, and with them appeared the first seeds

This view of eighteenth-century Boston shows the importance of shipping and its regulation in the colonies, especially Massachusetts Bay.

of colonial resentment. New England's expanding commercial interests counseled prudence and accommodation, but the Puritan leaders harbored a persistent distrust of Stuart intentions. Consequently, the Bay Colony not only ignored royal wishes; it tolerated violations of the Navigation Acts. This led the Lords of Trade to begin legal proceedings against the colonial charter in 1678. The issue remained in legal snarls for another six years, but eventually, in 1684, the Lords of Trade won a court decision annulling the Massachusetts charter. The Puritan utopia was fast becoming a lost cause.

THE DOMINION OF NEW ENGLAND   Temporarily, the Massachusetts government was placed in the hands of a special royal commission. Then in 1685 Charles II died, to be succeeded by his brother, the duke of York, as James II, the first Catholic sovereign since the death of Queen Mary in 1558. Plans long maturing in the Lords of Trade for a general reorganization of colonial government coincided with the autocratic notions of James II, who asserted his prerogatives more forcefully than his brother. The new king therefore readily approved a proposal to create a Dominion of New England and to place under its jurisdiction all colonies down through New Jersey. Something of the sort might have been in store for Pennsylvania and the southern colonies as well if the reign of James II had lasted longer. In that case the English colonies might have found themselves on the same tight leash as the colonies of Spain or France.

The Dominion was to have a government named by royal authority, a governor and council who would rule without any colonial assembly. The royal governor, Sir Edmond Andros, appeared in Boston in 1686 to establish his rule, which he soon extended over Connecticut and Rhode Island, and in 1688 over New York and the Jerseys. Andros was a soldier, accustomed to taking—and giving—orders. He seems to have been honest, efficient, and loyal to the crown, but tactless in circumstances that called for the utmost diplomacy—the uprooting of long-established institutions in the face of popular hostility.

King James II (1685–1688).

A rising resentment greeted his measures, especially in Massachusetts. Andros now levied taxes without consent of the General Court, and when residents protested against taxation without representation, he imprisoned or fined a number of them. Andros suppressed town governments, enforced the trade laws, and clamped down on smuggling. Most ominous of all, he and his lieutenants took over one of Boston's Puritan churches for Anglican worship. Puritan leaders believed, with good reason, that he proposed to break their power and authority.

But the Dominion was scarcely established before word arrived of the Glorious Revolution of 1688–1689. James II, like Andros in New England, had aroused resentment in England by his arbitrary measures and, what was more, by openly parading his Catholic faith. His second wife bore him a son, who was sure to be reared a Catholic, and this put the opposition on notice that James's system would survive him. In 1688, parliamentary leaders, their patience exhausted, invited James's Protestant daughter Mary and her husband, the Dutch leader, William of Orange, to assume the throne as joint monarchs. James II, his support dwindling, fled to France.

THE GLORIOUS REVOLUTION IN AMERICA When news reached Boston that William and Mary had landed in England, Boston staged its own Glorious Revolution, as bloodless as that in England. Andros and his councilors were arrested, and Massachusetts reverted to its former government, as did the other colonies that had been absorbed into the Dominion. All were permitted to retain their former status except Massachusetts and Plymouth, which, after some delay, were united under a new charter in 1691 as the royal colony of Massachusetts Bay.

The Glorious Revolution had significant long-term effects on American history. The Bill of Rights and Toleration Act, passed in England in 1689, limited the powers of rulers and affirmed a degree of freedom of worship for Christians. These acts influenced attitudes and the course of events in the colonies. And what was more significant for the future, the overthrow of James II set a precedent for revolution against the monarch. In defense of that action the English philosopher John Locke published his *Two Treatises on Government* (1690), which had an enormous impact on political thought in the colonies. While the *First Treatise* refuted theories of the divine right of kings, the more important *Second Treatise* set forth Locke's contract theory of government, which argued that people were endowed with natural rights to life, liberty, and property. When rulers violated these rights, the people had the right—in extreme cases—to overthrow the monarch and change their government.

In the American experience colonial governments, such as the Mayflower Compact and others, had actually grown out of contractual arrangements such as Locke described. The royal charters themselves also constituted a sort of contract between the crown and the settlers. Such precedents made Locke's writings especially appealing to colonial readers, and his philosophy probably had more influence in America than in England.

AN EMERGING COLONIAL SYSTEM   The accession of William and Mary to the English throne provoked a restatement and refinement of the Navigation Acts and the administrative system for regulating the American colonies. In 1696 two developments created at last the structure for a coherent colonial system. First, the Navigation Act of 1696 required colonial governors to enforce the Navigation Acts, allowed customs officials to use "writs of assistance" (general search warrants which did not have to specify the place to be searched), and ordered that accused violators be tried in Admiralty Courts, because colonial juries habitually refused to convict their peers. Admiralty cases were decided by judges whom the governors appointed.

Second, also in 1696, William III created the Board of Trade to take the place of the Lords of Trade and Plantations. Colonial officials were required to report to the Board, which continued through the remainder of the colonial period to make policy. Intended to ensure that the colonies served the mother country's economy, the Board oversaw the enforcement of the Navigation Acts, and recommended ways to limit manufacturing in the colonies and to encourage their production of raw materials.

From 1696 to 1725 the Board of Trade met regularly and worked vigorously toward subjecting the colonies to a more efficient royal control. After 1725, however, its energies and activities waned. The Board of Trade declined during the reign of the Hanoverian monarchs, George I (1714–1727) and George II (1727–1760), German princes who became English kings by virtue of their descent from James I. Under these monarchs, the cabinet (a kind of executive committee in the Privy Council) emerged as the central agency of administration. Robert Walpole, as first minister (1721–1742), deliberately followed a lenient policy toward the colonies, a policy which the philosopher Edmund Burke later called "a wise and salutary neglect." The Board became chiefly an agency of political patronage, studded with officials who took an interest mainly in their salaries.

THE HABIT OF SELF-GOVERNMENT

Government within the colonies, like colonial policy, evolved essentially without plan. In broad outline the governor, council, and assembly in each colony corresponded to the king, lords, and commons of the mother country. At the outset all the colonies except Georgia had begun as projects of trading companies or feudal proprietors holding charters from the crown, but eight colonies eventually relinquished or forfeited their charters and became royal provinces. Connecticut and Rhode Island were the last of the corporate colonies; they elected their own governors to the end of the colonial period. In the corporate and proprietary colonies, and in Massachusetts, the charter served as a rough equivalent to a written constitution. Rhode Island and Connecticut in fact kept their charters as state constitutions after independence. Over the years certain anomalies appeared, as colonial governments diverged from that of England. On the one hand the governors retained powers and prerogatives that the king had lost in the course of the seventeenth century. On the other hand the assemblies acquired powers, particularly with respect to appointments, that Parliament had yet to gain.

POWERS OF THE GOVERNORS   The crown never vetoed acts of Parliament after 1707, but the colonial governors still held an absolute veto over the assemblies, and the crown could disallow (in effect, veto) colonial legislation on advice of the Board of Trade. With respect to the assembly, the governor still had the power to determine when and where it would meet, to prorogue (adjourn or recess) sessions, and to dissolve the assembly for new elections or to postpone elections indefinitely. The crown, however, had pledged to summon Parliament every three years and call elections at least every seven, and could not prorogue sessions. The royal or proprietary governor, moreover, nominated for life appointment the members of his council (except in Massachusetts, where they were chosen by the lower house), and the council functioned as both the upper house of the legislature and the highest court of appeal within the colony. With respect to the judiciary, in all but the charter colonies the governor still held the prerogative of creating courts and of naming and dismissing judges, powers explicitly denied the king in England. The assemblies, however, generally made good their claim that courts should be created only by legislative authority, although the crown repeatedly disallowed acts to grant judges life tenure in order to make them more independent.

As chief executive the governor could appoint and remove officials, command the militia and naval forces, grant pardons, and, as his commission often put it, "execute everything which doth and of right ought to belong to the governor"—which might cover a multitude of powers. In these respects his authority resembled the crown's, for the king still exercised executive authority and had the power generally to name all administrative officials. This often served as a powerful means of royal influence in Parliament, since the king could appoint members or their friends to lucrative offices. And while the arrangement might seem to another age a breeding ground for corruption or tyranny, it was often viewed in the eighteenth century as a stabilizing influence, especially by the king's friends. But it was an influence less and less available to the governors. On the one hand colonial assemblies nibbled away at their power of appointment; on the other hand the authorities in England increasingly drew the control of colonial patronage into their own hands.

POWERS OF THE ASSEMBLIES Unlike the governor and council, appointed by either king or proprietor, the colonial assembly was elected. Whether called the House of Burgesses (Virginia), or Delegates (Maryland), or Representatives (Massachusetts), or simply Assembly, the lower houses were chosen by popular vote in counties or towns or, in South Carolina, parishes. Religious tests for voting were abandoned during the seventeenth century, and the chief restriction left was a property qualification, based on the notion that only men who held a "stake in society" could vote responsibly. Yet the property qualifications generally set low hurdles in the way of potential voters. Property holding was widespread, and a greater proportion of the population could vote in the colonies than anywhere else in the world of the eighteenth century. Women, children, and blacks were excluded— few then questioned this—and continued to be excluded for the most part into the twentieth century.

Colonial politics of the eighteenth century mirrored English politics of the seventeenth. In one case there had been a tug of war between king and Parliament, ending with the Parliament's supremacy, confirmed by the Glorious Revolution. In the other case colonial governors were still trying to wield prerogatives which the king had lost in England. The assemblies knew this; they also knew all the arguments for the "rights" and "liberties" of the people and their legislative bodies. A further anomaly in the situation was the undefined relationship of the colonies to Parliament. The colonies had been created by royal authority, yet Parliament on occasion passed laws which applied to the colonies and were tacitly accepted by the colonies.

By the early eighteenth century the assemblies, like Parliament, held two important strands of power. First, they held the power of the purse string in their right to vote on taxes and expenditures. Second, they held the power to initiate legislation and not merely, as in the early history of some colonies, the right to act on proposals from the governor and council. These powers they used to pull other strands of power into their hands when the chance presented itself. Governors were held on a tight leash by the assembly's control of salaries, his and others, which were voted annually and sometimes not at all.

Throughout the eighteenth century the assemblies expanded their power and influence, sometimes in conflict with the governors and sometimes in harmony with them. Often in the course of routine business, the assemblies passed laws and set precedents the collective significance of which neither they nor the imperial authorities fully recognized. Once established, however, these laws and practices became fixed principles, parts of the "constitution" of the colonies. Self-government in the colonies became first a habit, then a "right."

TROUBLED NEIGHBORS

Self-government was not the only institution that began as a habit during the colonial period. The claims of white settlers on Indian lands had their roots in the first English settlements, where relations between the colonists and Indians were at times cooperative and at times viciously hostile. Indian-white relations transformed the human and ecological landscape of colonial North America, roiled colonial politics, and disrupted or destroyed the fabric of Indian culture. Relations between European settlers and North American Indians were themselves agitated by the fluctuating balance of power in Europe. The French and the English each sought to use Indians to their advantage in fighting one another for control of New World territory.

DISPLACING THE INDIANS   The English invasion of North America would have been a different story, maybe a shorter and simpler story, had the English encountered greater Indian resistance. Instead, in the coastal regions they found scattered and mutually hostile tribes whom they subjected to a policy of divide and conquer. Some, perhaps most, of the Indians guessed at the settlers'

The Puritans and their Indian allies, the Narragansetts, mount a ferocious attack on the Pequots at Mystic, Connecticut (1637).

purpose quickly, like those, Powhatan told John Smith, "who do inform me your coming is not for trade, but to invade my people and possess my country." But tempted by trade goods or the promise of alliances, or intimidated by a show of force, most of the native Americans let matters drift until the English were too entrenched to push back into the sea.

During the first half of the seventeenth century the most severe tests of the colonists' will to prevail came with the Virginia troubles of 1622 and 1644 and Connecticut's Pequot War of 1637. In both colonies Indian leaders engaged in last-chance efforts to save their lands; in both they failed. For the Pequots the result was virtual extermination—Puritans killed Pequots with such savagery that they offended their allies, the Narragansetts, who had never seen such total war. In Virginia, according to a census taken in 1669, only eleven of twenty-eight tribes described by John Smith in 1608 and only about 2,000 of some 30,000 Indians remained in the colony. Indian resistance had been broken for the time.

Then in the mid-1670s both New England and Virginia went through another time of troubles: an Indian war in New England, and in Virginia a civil war masquerading as an Indian war. For a long time in New England the Indian fur trade had contributed to peaceful relations, but the growth of settlement and the decline of the animal population were reducing the eastern tribes to relative poverty. Colonial governments encroached repeatedly, forcing Indians to acknowledge English laws and customs, including Puritan codes of behavior, and to permit English arbitration of disputes. On occasion colonial justice imposed fines, whippings, and worse. At the same time Puritan missionaries reached out to the tribes and one, John Eliot, translated the Bible into the Algonquian language. By 1675 several thousand converts had settled in special "praying Indian" towns.

The spark that set New England ablaze was struck by the murder of Sassamon, a "praying Indian" who had attended Harvard, later strayed from the faith while serving King Philip of the Wampanoag tribe, and then returned to the Christian fold. When Plymouth tried and executed three Wampanoags for the murder of Sassamon, King Philip's tribesmen attacked.

Thus began "King Philip's War," which the land-hungry leaders of Connecticut and Massachusetts quickly enlarged by assaulting the peaceful Narragansetts at their chief refuge in Rhode Island—a massacre the Rhode Island authorities were helpless to prevent. From June to December 1675, Indian attacks ravaged the interior of Massachusetts and Plymouth, and guerrilla war continued through 1676. At one point Indians burned a town within twenty miles of Boston. Finally, depleted supplies and the casualty toll wore down Indian resistance. In August 1676 Philip himself was tracked down and killed. Sporadic fighting continued until 1678 in New Hampshire and Maine. Indians who survived the slaughter had to submit to colonial authority and accept confinement to ever-dwindling plots of land.

BACON'S REBELLION   The news from New England heightened tensions among settlers strung out into the interior of Virginia, and contributed to the tangled events thereafter known as Bacon's Rebellion. Depressed tobacco prices, rising taxes, and crowds of freed servants lusting for Indian lands provided the fuel for the rebellion. The discontent turned to violence in July 1675 when a petty squabble between a frontier planter and the Doeg Indians on the Potomac led to the murder of the planter's herdsman, and in turn retaliation by frontier militiamen who killed ten or more Doegs and, by mistake, fourteen Susquehannocks. Soon a force of Virginia and Maryland militiamen laid siege to the Susquehannocks and murdered in cold blood five chieftains who came out for a parley. The enraged Indian survivors then took their revenge on frontier settlements. Scattered attacks continued on down to the James, where Nathaniel Bacon's overseer was killed.

In May 1676 Nathaniel Bacon defied Governor William Berkeley's authority by assuming command of a group of frontier vigilantes. The tall, slender, black-haired, twenty-nine-year-old Bacon, a graduate of Cambridge University, had been in Virginia only two years, but he had been well set up by an English father relieved to get his vain, ambitious, and hot-tempered son out of the country. Later historians would praise Bacon as "The Torchbearer of the Revolution" and leader of the first struggle of common man versus aristocrat, of frontier versus tidewater. In part this was true. The rebellion was largely a battle of servants, small farmers, and even slaves against the wealthy planters and political leaders of Virginia. But Bacon was also the spoiled son of a rich squire, with a talent for trouble and an enthusiasm for punitive expeditions against peaceful Indians.

Bacon was early in the line of one lamentable American tradition. Indians, he declared, were "all alike," in that they were "wolves, tigers, and bears" who preyed upon "our harmless and innocent lambs," and therefore were fair game. After threatening to kill the governor and the assembly if they tried to intervene, Bacon began preparing for a total war against all Indians. To prevent any governmental interference, he ordered the governor arrested. Berkeley's forces resisted—but only feebly—and Bacon's men burned Jamestown in September 1676. But Bacon could not savor the victory long; he fell ill and died of swamp fever a month later.

Governor Berkeley quickly regained control and subdued the leaderless rebels. In the process he hanged twenty-three and confiscated several estates. When his men captured one of Bacon's closest lieutenants, Berkeley gleefully exclaimed: "I am more glad to see you than any man in Virginia. Mr. Drummond, you shall be hanged in half an hour." For such severity the king recalled Berkeley to England and a royal commission made treaties of pacification with the remaining Indians, some of whose descendants still live on tiny reservations guaranteed them in 1677. The fighting opened new lands to the colonists and confirmed the power of an inner group of established landholders who sat on the Virginia council.

NEW FRANCE AND LOUISIANA   Permanent French settlement in the New World began soon after the Jamestown landing, far away in Québec at Port Royal, Acadia (later Nova Scotia). While Acadia remained a remote outpost, New France expanded well beyond Québec, from which Champlain pushed his explorations into the Great Lakes as far as Lake Huron, and southward to the lake that still bears his name. There, in 1609, he joined a band of Huron and Ottawa allies in a fateful encounter, fired his gun into the ranks of their Iroquois foes, and thereby kindled a hatred which pursued New France to the end. Shortly afterward the Iroquois had a more friendly meeting with Henry Hudson near Albany, and soon acquired firearms from Dutch, and later English, traders. Thenceforth the Iroquois stood as a buffer against any French designs to move toward the English of the middle colonies, and as a constant menace on the flank of the French waterways to the interior.

From the Great Lakes French explorers moved southward. In 1673 Louis Joliet and Père Marquette, the Jesuit priest, ventured into Lake Michigan, and then journeyed down the Mississippi. Satisfied that the great river flowed to the Gulf of Mexico, they turned back for fear of meeting with Spaniards. Nine years later, in 1682, the daring explorer La Salle went all the way to the Gulf and named the country Louisiana after King Louis XIV. Actual settlement of the Louisiana country occurred later, when the French built several fortified towns, the most important of which was New Orleans, founded in 1718.

The French thus enjoyed access to the great water routes which led to the heartland of the continent. In the Illinois region scattered settlers began farming the fertile soil and courageous priests established missions at places such as Terre Haute (high land) and Des Moines (some monks). In the dense woods around the Great Lakes rugged French Canadians became adept trappers and traders. Unlike their English counterparts, many of these hardy *coureurs de bois* (runners of the woods) shed their Old World culture and adopted Indian ways of dress and living. Many of them married Indian women.

Yet French involvement in North America never approached that of the British. In part this was because the French-held areas

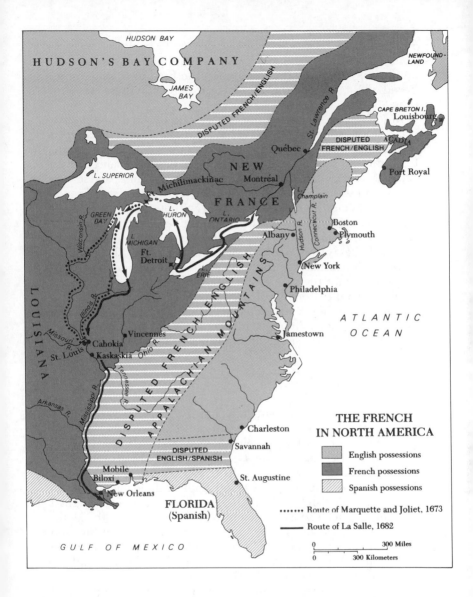

The French in North America

Legend:
- English possessions
- French possessions
- Spanish possessions
- .... Route of Marquette and Joliet, 1673
- —— Route of La Salle, 1682

were less enticing than the English seaboard settlements. Few Frenchmen were willing to challenge the interior's rugged terrain, fierce winters, and hostile Indians. In addition, the French government impeded colonization by refusing to allow French Protestants (Huguenots) to migrate. New France was to remain Roman Catholic. It also remained largely a howling wilderness,

home to a mobile population of traders, trappers, missionaries—
and, mainly, Indians. In 1750, when the English colonies numbered about 1.5 million, the French population was no more
than 80,000.

In some ways, however, the French had the edge on the British. Jesuit missionaries were far better financed and educated, as
well as more organized and tenacious, than their English Protestant counterparts. The French also offered European goods in
return for furs, encroached far less upon Indian lands, and so won
allies against the English, who came to possess the land. French
governors could mobilize for action without any worry about
quarreling assemblies or ethnic and religious diversity. The British may have had the greater number of colonists, but their separate colonies often worked at cross purposes. The middle
colonies, for instance, protected by the Iroquois buffer, could
afford to ignore the French threat—for a time at least. Whenever conflict threatened, colonial assemblies seized the opportunity to extract new concessions from their governors. Colonial
merchants, who built up a trade supplying foodstuffs to the
French, persisted in smuggling supplies even in wartime.

The Colonial Wars

For most of the seventeenth century the French and British
empires developed in relative isolation from each other, and for
most of that century the homelands remained at peace with each
other. After the Restoration, Charles II and James II pursued a
policy of friendship with Louis XIV. The Glorious Revolution of
1688, however, abruptly reversed English diplomacy. William
III, the new British king from the Dutch Republic, had fought a
running conflict against the ambitions of Louis XIV in the Netherlands and Germany. His ascent to the throne brought England
almost immediately into a Grand Coalition against Louis in the
War of the League of Augsburg, known in the colonies simply as
King William's War (1689–1697).

This was the first of four great European and intercolonial
wars over the next sixty-four years: the War of the Spanish Succession (Queen Anne's War, 1701–1713); the War of the Austrian Succession (King George's War, 1744–1748); and the
Seven Years' War (the French and Indian War, which lasted nine
years in America, 1754–1763). In all except the last, the battles
in America were but a sideshow to greater battles in Europe,

where British policy aimed to keep a balance of power against the French. The alliances shifted from one fight to the next, but Britain and France were pitted against each other every time.

So for much of the century after the great Indian conflicts of 1676, the colonies were embroiled in wars and rumors of wars. The effect on much of the population was devastating. The New England colonies, especially Massachusetts, suffered probably more than the rest, for they were closest to the centers of French population. The casualty rate for Massachusetts men exceeded that suffered by the Union in the Civil War. One result of such carnage was that Boston's population stagnated through the eighteenth century while Philadelphia and New York continued to grow, and the city had to struggle to support a large population of widows and orphans. Eventually, the economic impact of the four wars left increasing numbers of poor people in New England, and many of them would participate in the popular unrest leading to the revolutionary movement.

THE FRENCH AND INDIAN WAR   Of the four major wars involving the European powers and their New World colonies, the climactic conflict between Britain and France in North America was the French and Indian War. It began in 1754 after enterprising Virginians crossed the Appalachians into the upper Ohio Valley in order to trade with Indians and survey 200,000 acres granted them by King George. This infuriated the French, who saw such activity as a threat to their holdings, and they set about building a string of forts in the disputed area.

When news of these developments reached Williamsburg, the governor sent an emissary to warn off the French. An ambitious young officer in the Virginia militia, Major George Washington, volunteered for the mission. With a few companions, he made his way to Fort LeBoeuf and returned with a polite but firm French refusal. The governor then sent a small force to erect a fort at the strategic fork where the Allegheny and Monongahela Rivers meet to form the great Ohio. No sooner was it started than a larger French force appeared, ousted the Virginians, and proceeded to build Fort Duquesne on the same strategic site. Meanwhile Washington had been organizing a force of volunteers, and in the spring of 1754 he set out with an advance guard and a few Indian allies. Their clash with a French detachment marked the first bloodshed of a long—and finally decisive—war that reached far beyond America. Washington fell back with his prisoners and hastily constructed a stockade, Fort Necessity, which

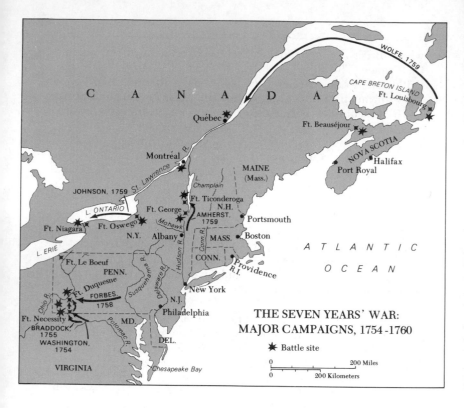

THE SEVEN YEARS' WAR:
MAJOR CAMPAIGNS, 1754-1760

✳ Battle site

0   200 Miles

0   200 Kilometers

soon fell under siege by a larger French force. On July 4, 1754, Washington surrendered and was permitted to withdraw with his survivors.

Back in London, the Board of Trade already had taken notice of the growing conflict in the Ohio backwoods and had called a meeting in Albany, New York, of commissioners from all the colonies as far south as Maryland to confer on precautions. The Albany Congress, which met during the summer of 1754, accomplished little. It is remembered mainly for the Plan of Union worked out by a committee under Benjamin Franklin. The plan called for a chief executive, appointed and supported by the crown, and a supreme assembly called the Grand Council, with forty-eight members chosen by the colonial assemblies. This federal body would oversee matters of defense, Indian relations, and trade and settlement in the west, and would levy taxes to support its programs. It must have been a good plan, Franklin reasoned, since the assemblies thought it gave too much power to the crown and the crown thought it gave too much to the colonies. At any rate the assemblies either rejected or ignored the plan.

In London the government decided to force a showdown with the French in America, but things went badly at first. In 1755 the British fleet failed to halt the landing of French reinforcements in Canada, but scored one success in Nova Scotia with the capture of a fort. The British buttressed their hold on the area by expelling most of its French population. Some 5,000–7,000 Acadians who refused to take an oath of allegiance were scattered through the colonies from Maine to Georgia. Impoverished and homeless, many of them desperately found their way to French Louisiana, where they became the "Cajuns" (a corruption of "Acadians") whose descendants still preserve the French language along the remote bayous.

A WORLD WAR   For two years war raged along the American-Canadian frontier without becoming the cause of war in Europe. In 1756, however, the colonial war merged with what became the Seven Years' War in Europe. There, Empress Maria Theresa of Austria, still brooding over the loss of territory in the last conflict, worked a diplomatic revolution by bringing Austria's old enemy, France, as well as Russia, into an alliance against Frederick the Great of Prussia. Britain, ever mindful of the European balance of power, now deserted Austria to ally with Frederick. The onset of war brought into office a new British government with the popular, eloquent William Pitt as war minister. Pitt's ability and assurance ("I know that I can save England and no one else can") instilled confidence at home and abroad. Pitt committed his main forces to the war for overseas empire while providing subsidies to Frederick, who was desperately fighting off attacks from three sides.

Soon the force of British sea power began to cut off French reinforcements and supplies to the New World—and the trading goods with which they bought Indian allies. Pitt improved the British forces, gave command to young men of ability, and carried the battle to the enemy. In 1758 the tide began to turn. Fort Louisbourg fell to the British. A new expedition marched against Fort Duquesne, and the outnumbered French chose discretion as the better part of valor, burned the fort and fled the scene. On the site arose the British Fort Pitt, and later, the city of Pittsburgh.

In 1759 the decisive battle occurred at Québec. Commanding the British expedition up the St. Lawrence was General James

The decisive British assault on Québec (1759).

Wolfe, a dedicated professional soldier who, at the age of thirty-three, had already spent more than half his life in military service. For two months Wolfe probed the defenses of Québec, seemingly impregnable on its fortified heights and manned by alert forces under General Louis Joseph de Montcalm. Finally Wolfe's troops found a path up the cliffs behind Québec. During the night of September 12–13, they scrambled up the sheer walls and emerged on the Plains of Abraham, athwart the main roads to the city. There, in a battle more like conventional European warfare than a frontier skirmish, the British forces allowed the French to advance within close range and then loosed two devastating volleys that ended French power in North America for all time. News of the victory was clouded by the word of Wolfe's—and Montcalm's—death in the battle.

The war dragged on until 1763, but the rest was a process of mopping up. Montréal, the last important vestige of French control in North America, fell in 1760, and while the frontiers remained active with scattered Indian raids, the French were whipped. In the South, where little significant action had occurred, the Cherokee nation flared into belated hostility, but General Jeffrey Amherst moved toward the mountains with a force of British regulars and provincials and broke Cherokee resistance in 1761. In the North, just as peace was signed, an Ottawa chief, Pontiac, attempted to unify all the Indians of the frontier and launched a series of attacks that were not finally suppressed until 1764, after the backwoods had been ablaze for ten years.

Just six weeks after the capture of Montréal in 1760, King George II died and his grandson ascended to the throne as George III. The new king resolved to take a more active role than his Hanoverian predecessors. He yearned for peace, which entailed forcing Pitt out of office. Pitt had wanted to carry the fight to the enemy by declaring war on Spain before the French could bring that other Bourbon monarchy into the conflict. He was forestalled, but Spain belatedly entered in 1761. During the next year the Spanish met the same fate as the French: in 1762 British forces took Manila in the Philippines and Havana in Cuba.

THE PEACE OF PARIS   The war culminated in the Peace of Paris of 1763. It ended French power in North America and all but eliminated it in India. In America, Britain took all of France's North American possessions east of the Mississippi River, several islands in the West Indies, and all of Spanish Florida, east and west. France ceded Louisiana to Spain in compensation for Spain's loss of the Floridas. This left France no territory on the continent of North America. British power reigned supreme over North America east of the Mississippi, but a fatal irony would pursue the British victory.

In gaining Canada the British government put in motion a train of events that would end twenty years later with the loss of the rest of British North America. France, humiliated in 1763, thirsted for revenge. In London, Benjamin Franklin, agent for the colony of Pennsylvania from 1764 to 1775, found the French minister inordinately curious about America and suspected him of wanting to ignite the coals of controversy. Less than three years after Franklin left London, and only fifteen years after the conquest of New France, he would be in Paris arranging an alliance on behalf of Britain's rebellious colonists.

FURTHER READING

For greater depth on the structure of colonial government and the global context of colonial development, see the fourth volume of Charles M. Andrews's *The Colonial Period of American History* (4 vols., 1934–1938). Lawrence H. Gipson's *The British Empire before the American Revolution* (15 vols., 1936–1970) places the British colonies in the context of European imperial politics. The economics motivating colonial policies are covered in John J. McCusker and Russell R. Menard's *The Economy of British America, 1607–1789* (1985).°

The effect of imperial policies on colonial politics is covered in Alison G. Olson's *Anglo-American Politics, 1600–1775* (1973). Jack P. Greene's *The Quest for Power* (1963)° describes the politics of the southern colonies, and Richard P. Johnson's *Adjustment to Empire* (1981) examines New England.

Richard Slotkin's *Regeneration through Violence* (1973)° links the colonists' treatment of Indians with later national character traits. Alden T. Vaughan defends the treatment of Indians by the Puritans in *New England Frontier: Puritans and Indians, 1620–1675* (1965).° Francis Jennings counters this thesis in *The Invasion of America* (1975).°

A good introduction to the imperial phase of the colonial conflicts is Howard H. Peckham's *The Colonial Wars, 1689–1762* (1964). More analytical is Douglas Leach's *Arms for Empire: A Military History of the British Colonies in North America* (1973). For insights into the complex role of Indians in the conflict, see Francis Jennings, *The Empire of Fortune: Crowns, Colonies and Tribes in the Seven Years War in America* (1990).°

° These books are available in paperback editions.

4

FROM EMPIRE TO INDEPENDENCE

THE HERITAGE OF WAR

Seldom if ever since the days of Elizabeth had England thrilled with such pride as in the closing years of the Great War for Empire. The victories of 1759 had delivered Canada and India to British control. In 1760 the young, vigorous George III ascended to the throne and confirmed once again the Hanoverian succession. And in 1763 the Peace of Paris confirmed the possession of a great new empire. The end of the French imperial domain in North America opened the prospect of future development of the sprawling region between the Appalachian Mountains and the Mississippi River and from the Gulf of Mexico to Hudson's Bay.

The American colonists shared in the euphoria of victory, but the moment of celebration was all too brief. It served to mask festering resentments and new problems that were the heritage of the war. Underneath the pride in the growing British Empire an American nationalism was maturing. For over a generation the colonists had essentially been allowed to govern themselves and were beginning to think and speak of themselves more as Americans than as English or British. With a great new land to exploit, they could look to the future with confidence.

The colonists had a new sense of importance after starting and fighting a vast world war with such success. Some harbored resentment, justified or not, at the haughty air of British soldiers and slights received at their hands, and many in the early stages of the war lost their awe of British soldiers who were at such a loss in frontier fighting. One Massachusetts soldier expressed some puzzlement that he should be expected to "stand still and be shot at" in the field rather than take cover. Many colonists were dismayed by the extremely sharp social distinctions between officers and men in the British army. The provincials, by contrast, presumed that by volunteering they had formed a contract with a particular American officer from their community.

In the aftermath of victory the British ministry faced a burden of new problems. How should they manage the defense and governance of the new possessions? What should be done with the western lands? How were they to pay an unprecedented debt built up during the war and bear the new burdens of greater administration and more far-flung defense? And—the thorniest problem of all, as it turned out—what role should the colonies play in all this? The problems were of a magnitude and complexity to challenge men of the greatest statesmanship and vision, but those qualities were rare among the ministers of George III. They were perhaps even more lacking in the king himself, who was justly described by his father as "half-witted."

In the British politics of the day nearly everybody called himself a Whig, even King George. "Whig" had been the name given to those who opposed James II, led the Glorious Revolution of 1688, and secured the Protestant Hanoverian succession in 1714. The Whigs were the champions of liberty and parliamentary supremacy, but with the passage of time Whiggism had drifted into complacency and leadership settled upon an aristo-

George III, at age thirty-three, the young king of a victorious empire.

cratic elite of the Whig gentry. This dominant group of land-holding families focused on the pursuit of personal power and local questions. In the absence of party organization, parliamentary politics hinged on factions bound together by personal loyalties, family connections, local interests, and on the pursuit of royal patronage. Throughout the 1760s the king turned first to one and then to another prime minister, and the government grew more and more unstable just as the new problems of empire required forceful solutions. Colonial policy remained marginal to the chief concerns of British politics. The result was first inconsistency and vacillation, followed by stubborn inflexibility.

WESTERN LANDS

No sooner was peace arranged in 1763 than events thrust the problem of America's western lands upon the British government in an acute form. The Indians of the Ohio region, unable to believe that their French friends were helpless and fearing the arrival of English settlers, grew restless and receptive to the warnings of Pontiac, chief of the Ottawa. In May 1763, the western tribes joined Pontiac's attempt to reopen frontier warfare, and within a few months wiped out every British post in the Ohio region except Detroit and Fort Pitt.

To secure peace, the ministers in London reasoned, further settlement of the western lands could wait another day. The immediate need was to stop Pontiac's warriors and pacify the Indians. In October the king signed the Royal Proclamation of 1763, which drew an imaginary line along the crest of the Appalachians beyond which settlers were forbidden to go and colonial governors were forbidden to authorize surveys or issue land grants. It also established the new British colonies of Quebec and East and West Florida, the last two consisting mainly of small settlements at St. Marks and St. Augustine respectively, peopled mainly by British garrisons.

But Pontiac did not agree to peace until 1766, and Britain's line did not long remain intact. During the turbulent decade that followed, hardy pioneers pushed on over the ridges. By 1770 the town of Pittsburgh had twenty log houses, and a small village had appeared on the site of Wheeling. Four years later Daniel Boone and a party of settlers cut the Wilderness Road through the Cumberland Gap in southwestern Virginia to the Kentucky River.

GRENVILLE AND THE STAMP ACT

As the Proclamation Line was being drafted in 1763, a new ministry in London began to grapple with the problems of imperial finances. The new chief minister, George Grenville, first lord of the treasury, was much like the king: industrious, honest, meticulous, and obtuse. Grenville assumed the need for redcoats to defend the frontier, although the colonies had been left mostly to their own devices before 1754. But on top of an already staggering debt he faced sharply rising costs for American defense.

With the large tax burden at home and a much lighter one in the colonies, Grenville reasoned that the Americans were obligated to share the cost of their own defense. He also learned that the American customs service was amazingly inefficient. Evasion and inefficiency, not to mention corruption, were rampant, and the service needed tightening. Grenville thus issued stern orders to colonial officials and set the navy to patrolling the coasts. Parliament agreed to set up a new vice-admiralty court in Halifax with jurisdiction over all the colonies. This court would have no juries of colonists sympathetic to smugglers. The old habits of salutary neglect in the enforcement of the Navigation Acts were coming to an end, causing no little annoyance to American shippers.

In 1764 Grenville also put through the Sugar Act, which cut the duty in half. This, he believed, would reduce the temptation to smuggle or to bribe customs officers. In addition the Sugar Act levied new duties on imports into the colonies of foreign textiles, wines, coffee, indigo, and sugar. The act, Grenville estimated, would bring in enough revenue to help defray "the necessary expenses of defending, protecting, and securing" the colonies. For the first time Parliament had adopted duties frankly designed to raise revenues in the colonies rather than just to regulate trade.

Another measure in Grenville's new colonial program that had an important impact on the colonies was the Currency Act of 1764. The colonies faced a chronic shortage of hard money, which kept going out to pay debts in England. To meet the shortage they issued their own paper money. British creditors, however, feared payment in such a depreciated currency. To alleviate their fears, Parliament in 1751 had forbidden the New England colonies to make their currency legal tender. Now Grenville extended the prohibition to all the colonies. The value of existing paper money soon plummeted, since nobody was obligated to accept it in payment of debts, even in the colonies. The deflationary impact of the Currency Act, combined with new duties and stricter enforcement, delivered a severe shock to a colonial economy already suffering a postwar slump.

THE STAMP ACT   Grenville's new design entailed one more key provision. Because the Sugar Act would defray only part of the cost of maintaining the 10,000 British troops to be stationed in the colonies, he proposed another measure to raise money in America, a stamp tax. Enacted on February 13, 1765, the Stamp Act created revenue stamps that must be fixed to printed matter and legal documents of all kinds: newspapers, pamphlets, almanacs, bonds, leases, deeds, licenses, insurance policies, ship clearances, college diplomas, even dice and playing cards. The requirement would go into effect on November 1, 1765.

In March 1765 Grenville put through the final measure of his new program, the Quartering Act. It required the colonies to supply British troops with provisions and to provide them barracks or submit to their use of inns and vacant buildings. It applied to all colonies, but affected mainly New York, headquarters of the British forces.

THE IDEOLOGICAL RESPONSE   The cumulative effect of Grenville's measures raised colonial suspicions to a fever pitch. Unwittingly this plodding minister of a plodding king had stirred up a storm of protest and set in motion a searching exploration of English traditions and imperial relations. By this time the radical ideas of the so-called "Real Whig" minority in England were being widely discussed in the colonies. These ideas drew upon the polemics of John Trenchard and Thomas Gordon, authors of *Cato's Letters* (1720–1723), and above all from the writings of John Locke, which justified the struggle by Parliament to preserve life, liberty, and property against royal tyranny.

Colonial critics of British policy also knew from their religious heritage and by what Patrick Henry called "the lamp of experience" that human nature is corruptible and lusts after power. The safeguard against abuses, in the view of those who, like Trenchard and Gordon, called themselves "Real Whigs," was not to rely on human goodness but to check power with power. The British Constitution had embodied these principles in a mixed government of kings, lords, and commons, each serving as a check on the others.

But in 1764 and 1765 many colonists insisted that the separation of powers was not working. Grenville had loosed upon them the very engines of tyranny from which Parliament had rescued England in the seventeenth century, and by imposition of that very Parliament! A standing army encouraged despots, and now with the French gone and Pontiac subdued, several thousand British soldiers remained in the colonies: to protect the colonists or to subdue them? It was beginning to seem clear that it was the latter. Among fundamental English rights were trial by jury and the presumption of innocence, but vice-admiralty courts excluded juries and put the burden of proof on the defendant. Most important, the English had the right to be taxed only by their elected representatives. Parliament claimed that privilege in England, and the colonial assemblies had long exercised it in America. Now, with the Stamp Act, Parliament was out to usurp the assemblies' power of the purse strings.

In a flood of colonial pamphlets, speeches, and resolutions, debate on the Stamp Tax turned mainly on the point expressed in a slogan familiar to all Americans: "no taxation without representation." Grenville had one of his subordinates prepare an answer which developed the ingenious theory of "virtual representation." If the colonies had no vote in Parliament, neither did most Englishmen who lived in boroughs that had developed since the last apportionment. Large cities, such as Manchester and Birmingham, had arisen that had no right to elect a member, while old boroughs with little or no population still returned members. Nevertheless, according to this theory, each member of Parliament represented the interests of the whole country and indeed the whole empire. To the colonists, however, virtual representation was nonsense, justified neither by logic nor by their own experience. James Otis, a popular leader in the Massachusetts assembly, went to the heart of the matter. If such considerable places as Manchester and Birmingham were not represented, he said, "they ought to be."

PROTEST IN THE COLONIES   The Stamp Act became the chief target of colonial protest: the Sugar Act affected mainly New England, but the Stamp Act burdened all colonists who did any kind of business. And it affected most of all the articulate elements in the community: merchants, planters, lawyers, printer-editors—all strategically placed to influence opinion.

Through the spring and summer of 1765 popular resentment against Grenville boiled over. The *Boston Gazette* directed a threatening couplet at the British minister:

In protest of the Stamp Act, which was to take effect the next day, the
Pennsylvania Journal *appeared with the skull and crossbones on its
masthead.*

To make us all Slaves, now you've lost Sir! the Hope,
You've but to go hang yourself.—We'll find the Rope.

Such anger found outlets in mass meetings, parades, bonfires,
and other demonstrations. North Carolina's royal governor reported the mobs to be composed of "gentlemen and planters."
Calling themselves Sons of Liberty, they met underneath "Liberty Trees"—in Boston a great elm, in Charleston a live oak. One
day in mid-August, nearly three months before the effective date
of the Stamp Act, an effigy of Boston's stamp agent swung from
the Liberty Tree and in the evening a mob carried it through the
streets, destroyed the stamp office, and used the wood to burn
the effigy. Somewhat later another mob sacked the home of the
lieutenant-governor and the local customs officer. The Boston
stamp agent, thoroughly shaken, resigned his commission, and
stamp agents throughout the colonies felt impelled to follow his
example.

The general revolt encouraged colonial unity, as colonists discovered that they had more in common with each other than
with London. In May 1765, long before the mobs went into action, the Virginia House of Burgesses had struck the first blow
against the Stamp Act in the Virginia Resolves, a series of resolutions inspired by young Patrick Henry's "torrents of sublime elo-

quence." Virginians, the burgesses declared, were entitled to all English rights, and the English could be taxed only by their own representatives. Virginians, moreover, had always been governed by laws passed with their own consent. Newspapers spread the resolutions throughout the colonies, along with even more radical statements that were kept out of the final version, and other assemblies hastened to copy Virginia's example. On June 8, 1765, the Massachusetts House of Representatives issued a circular letter inviting the various assemblies to send delegates to confer in New York on appeals for relief from the king and Parliament.

Nine responded, and on October 7 the Stamp Act Congress of twenty-seven delegates convened and issued expressions of colonial sentiment: a Declaration of the Rights and Grievances of the Colonies, a petition to the king for relief, and a petition to Parliament for repeal of the Stamp Act. The delegates argued that Parliament might have powers to legislate for the regulation of the empire, but it had no right to levy taxes, which were a free gift granted by the people through their representatives.

By November 1, its effective date, the Stamp Act was a dead letter. Business went on without the stamps. Newspapers appeared with the skull and crossbones in the corner where the stamp belonged. Colonial rebels were beginning to sense their power. After passage of the Sugar Act a movement had begun to boycott British goods. Now colonists adopted non-importation agreements to exert pressure on British merchants. Americans knew they had become a major market for British products. By shutting off imports they could exercise real leverage. Sage and sassafras took the place of tea, and homespun garments became the fashion as symbols of colonial defiance.

REPEAL OF THE ACT   The storm had scarcely broken before Grenville's ministry was out of office, dismissed not because of the colonial turmoil but because of tensions with the king over the distribution of lucrative government offices. In July 1765 the king installed a new minister, the marquis of Rockingham, leader of the "Rockingham Whigs," who sympathized with the colonists' views. Rockingham resolved to end the quarrel by repealing the Stamp Act, but he needed to move carefully in order to win a majority. Simple repeal was politically impossible without some affirmation of parliamentary authority over the colonies. When Parliament assembled early in 1766, William Pitt demanded that the Stamp Act be repealed "absolutely, totally, and immediately," but urged that Britain's authority over the colonies "be asserted in as strong terms as possible," except on the point of taxation. Rockingham steered a cautious course and seized upon the widespread but false impression that Pitt accepted the principle of "external" taxes or duties on trade but rejected "internal" taxes, such as the stamp tax, within the colonies.

In March 1766 Parliament passed the repeal, but at the same time passed the Declaratory Act, which asserted the full power of Parliament to make laws binding the colonies "in all cases whatsoever." It was a cunning evasion that made no concession with regard to taxes, but made no mention of them either. It left intact in the minds of many members the impression that a distinction had been drawn between "external" taxes on trade and "internal" taxes within the colonies, an impression that would have fateful consequences for the future. For the moment, however, the Declaratory Act seemed little more than a face-saving gesture. Amid the rejoicing and relief on both sides of the Atlantic there were no omens that the quarrel would be reopened within a year. To be sure, the Sugar Act remained on the books, but Rockingham reduced the molasses tax from three pence to one pence, less than the cost of a bribe.

FANNING THE FLAMES

The king continued to have his ministers play musical chairs. Rockingham fell for the same reasons as Grenville, a quarrel over appointments, and the king invited Pitt to form a ministry including the major factions of Parliament. Soon thereafter, however, Pitt slipped over the fine line between genius and madness, and he resigned in 1768. For a time in 1767 the guiding force in the ministry was Charles Townshend, chancellor of the Exchequer, whose "abilities were superior to those of all men," according to Horace Walpole, "and his judgment below that of any man." The witty but erratic Townshend took advantage of Pitt's absence to reopen the question of colonial taxation and seized upon the notion that "external" taxes were tolerable to the colonies—not that he believed it for a moment.

THE TOWNSHEND ACTS   In May and June 1767 Townshend put his plan through the House of Commons and in September he died, leaving a bitter legacy: the Townshend Acts. Their first objective was to bring the New York assembly to its senses. That body had defied the Quartering Act and refused to provide beds or supplies for the king's troops. Parliament, at Townshend's behest, suspended all acts of the New York assembly until it yielded. New York finally caved in, inadvertently confirming the suspicion that too much indulgence had encouraged colonial bad manners. Townshend followed up with the Revenue Act of 1767, which levied duties ("external taxes") on colonial imports of glass, lead, paints, paper, and tea. Third, he set up a board of Customs Commissioners at Boston, the colonial headquarters of smuggling. Finally, he reorganized the vice-admiralty courts, providing four in the continental colonies—at Halifax, Boston, Philadelphia, and Charleston.

The Townshend duties did increase government revenues, but the intangible costs were greater. The duties taxed goods exported from England, indirectly hurting British manufacturers, and had to be collected in colonial ports, increasing collection costs. More importantly, the new taxes accelerated colonial resistance. The Revenue Act of 1767 posed a more severe threat to colonial assemblies than Grenville's taxes, for Townshend proposed to apply the revenues to pay the salaries of governors and other officers and release them from financial dependence on the assemblies.

DICKINSON'S *LETTERS*   The Townshend Acts surprised the colonists and once again citizens resolved to resist, to boycott British goods, to wear homespun, to develop their own manufactures. Once again the colonial press spewed out expressions of protest, most notably the essays of John Dickinson, a Philadelphia lawyer who hoped to resolve the dispute by persuasion. Late in 1767 his twelve *Letters of a Pennsylvania Farmer* (as he chose to style himself) began to appear in the *Pennsylvania Chronicle*, from which they were copied in other papers and in pamphlet form. He argued that Parliament might regulate commerce and collect duties incidental to that purpose, but it had no right to levy taxes for revenue, whether they were internal or external. Dickinson used moderate language throughout. The colonists, he declared, should "speak at the same time the language of affliction and veneration" toward the mother country.

SAMUEL ADAMS AND THE SONS OF LIBERTY   But the affliction grew and the veneration waned. British ministers could neither conciliate moderates like Dickinson nor cope with firebrands like Boston's Samuel Adams, who was now emerging as the supreme genius of revolutionary agitation. Born in 1722, Adams, the son of moderately well-off and sternly pious parents, graduated from

Harvard and soon thereafter inherited the family brewery, which he proceeded to manage into bankruptcy. His distant cousin John Adams described Sam as a "universal good character," a "plain, simple, decent citizen, of middling stature, dress, and manners," who prided himself on his frugality and his distaste for ceremony and display. Politics, not profits, excited his passion, and he spent most of his time at mid-century and after debating political issues with sailors, roustabouts, and stevedores at local taverns. Adams insisted that Parliament had no right to legislate at all for the colonies, that Massachusetts must return to the spirit of its Puritan founders and defend itself from a new conspiracy against its liberties.

While other men tended their private affairs, Adams whipped up the Sons of Liberty, writing incendiary newspaper articles and letters, and organizing protests in the Boston pubs, town meeting, and the provincial assembly. A Tory opponent begrudgingly acknowledged Adams's intense commitment, noting that he "eats little, drinks little, thinks much, and is most decisive and indefatigable in the pursuit of his objects." The royal governor called him "the most dangerous man in Massachusetts." Early in 1768 Adams and James Otis formulated another Massachusetts Circular Letter, which the assembly dispatched to the other colonies. The letter restated the illegality of parliamentary taxation, warned that the new duties would be used to pay colonial officials, and invited the other colonies to join in a boycott of British goods.

In mid-May 1769 the Virginia assembly passed a new set of resolves reasserting its exclusive right to tax Virginians and calling upon the colonies to unite in protest. Virginia's governor promptly dissolved the assembly, but the members met independently, and adopted a new set of non-importation agreements. Once again, as with the Virginia Resolves against the Stamp Act, most of the other assemblies followed suit. One South Carolina planter urged his fellows: "Let us then, AT LAST, follow the example of our brother sufferers in the Northern Colonies, and encourage the making of our own manufactures. . . . Let us, Brother Planters, wear our old clothes as they will ever hang on us."

THE BOSTON MASSACRE   In Boston roving gangs enforced the boycott, intimidating Tory merchants and their customers. This led the governor to appeal for military support, and two British regiments sailed from Halifax. The presence of soldiers in Boston had been a constant provocation, and now tensions heightened, as

Paul Revere's engraving of the Boston Massacre.

surly crowds frequently heckled the "lobster backs." On March 5, 1770, in the square before the customs house, a mob of toughs began heaving taunts, snowballs, and oyster shells at the British sentry, whose call for help brought reinforcements. Then somebody rang the town firebell, drawing a larger crowd to the scene. At their head, or so the story goes, was Crispus Attucks, a runaway mulatto slave who had worked for some years on ships out of Boston. The riotous crowd began striking at the troops with sticks, and finally knocked one soldier down. He rose to his feet and fired into the crowd. Others fired too, and when the smoke cleared, five people lay dead or dying and eight more were wounded. The cause of resistance now had its first martyrs, and the first to die was Crispus Attucks. Governor Thomas Hutchinson, at the insistence of a mass meeting in Faneuil Hall, moved the soldiers out of town to avoid another incident. The troops involved in the shooting were indicted for murder but were defended by John Adams, who portrayed them as the victims of circumstance, provoked, he said, by a "motley rabble of saucy boys, negroes and mulattoes, Irish teagues and outlandish Jack tars." All were acquitted except two, who were convicted of manslaughter and branded on the thumb.

News of the Boston Massacre sent shock waves through the colonies. The incident, remembered one Bostonian, "created a resentment which emboldened the timid" and "determined the wavering." But late in April 1770 news arrived that Parliament had repealed all the Townshend duties save one. The cabinet, by a fateful vote of five to four, had advised keeping the tea tax as a token of parliamentary authority. Colonial diehards insisted that pressure should be kept on British merchants until Parliament gave in altogether, but the non-importation movement soon faded. Parliament, after all, had given up the substance of the taxes, with one exception, and much of the colonists' tea was smuggled in from Holland anyway.

For two years thereafter discontent simmered down and suspicions began to fade on both sides of the ocean. The Stamp Act was gone, as were all the Townshend duties except that on tea. Yet most of the hated innovations remained in effect: the Sugar Act, the Currency Act, the Quartering Act, the vice-admiralty courts, the Boards of Customs Commissioners. The redcoats had left Boston but they remained nearby, and the British navy still patrolled the coast. Each remained a source of irritation and the cause of occasional incidents. There was still tinder awaiting a spark, and colonial patriots remained alert to resist new tyrannies. As Sam Adams stressed, "Where there is a Spark of patriotick fire, we will enkindle it."

DISCONTENT ON THE FRONTIER

Through the years of agitation, parts of the backcountry had stirred with quarrels that had nothing to do with the Stamp and Townshend Acts. Rival land claims to the east of Lake Champlain pitted New York against New Hampshire, and the Green Mountain Boys led by Ethan Allen against both. Eventually the residents of the area would simply create their own state of Vermont in 1777, although not recognized as a member of the Union until 1791. In Pennsylvania a group of frontier ruffians took the law into their own hands. Outraged at the lack of frontier protection provided by the Quaker-influenced assembly during Pontiac's rebellion, a group called the "Paxton Boys" took revenge by massacring peaceful Conestoga Indians in Lancaster County, then threatened the so-called Moravian Indians, a group of Moravian converts near Bethlehem. When the Moravian Indians took refuge in Philadelphia, some 1,500 Paxton Boys marched on the capital, where Benjamin Franklin talked them into returning home by promising that more protection would be forthcoming.

Farther south, South Carolina frontier folk voiced similar complaints about the lack of settled government and the need for protection against horse thieves, cattle rustlers, and Indians. They organized societies called "Regulators" to administer vigilante justice in the region and refused to pay taxes until they gained effective government. In 1769 the assembly finally set up new circuit courts in the region and revised the taxes, but still did not respond to the backcountry's demand for representation.

In North Carolina the protest was less over the lack of government than over the abuses and extortion inflicted by government appointees from the eastern part of the colony. Farmers felt especially oppressed at the government's refusal either to issue paper money or to accept produce in payment of taxes, and in 1766 they organized to resist. Efforts of these "Regulators" to stop seizures of property and other court proceedings led to more disorders and a new law that made the rioters guilty of treason. In the spring of 1771 the royal governor and 1,200 militiamen defeated some 2,000 ill-organized Regulators in the Battle of Alamance. The pitched battle illustrated the growing tensions between backcountry settlers and the wealthy planters in the eastern part of the colony, tensions that would erupt again during and after the Revolution.

A Worsening Crisis

Two events in June 1772 broke the period of calm in the quarrels with the mother country. Near Providence, Rhode Island, a British schooner, the *Gaspee*, patrolling for smugglers, accidentally ran aground. Under cover of darkness a crowd from the town boarded the ship, removed the crew, and set fire to the vessel. A commission of inquiry was formed with authority to hold suspects, but no witnesses could be found. Four days after the burning, Massachusetts' governor, Thomas Hutchinson, told the provincial assembly that his salary thenceforth would come out of the customs revenues. Superior Court judges would be paid from the same source and would thereby no longer be dependent on the assembly for their income. The assembly feared that this portended "a despotic administration of government."

To keep the pot simmering, in November 1772 Sam Adams convinced the Boston Town Meeting to form a committee of correspondence, which issued a statement of rights and grievances and invited other towns to do the same. Committees of correspondence sprang up across Massachusetts and spread into other colonies. In March 1773 the Virginia assembly proposed the formation of such committees on an intercolonial basis, and a network of the committees spread across the colonies, keeping in touch, mobilizing public opinion, and keeping colonial resentments at a simmer. In unwitting tribute to their effectiveness, a loyalist called the committees "the foulest, subtlest, and most venomous serpent ever issued from the egg of sedition."

THE BOSTON TEA PARTY Lord North, who had replaced Townshend as chancellor of the Exchequer, soon brought colonial resentment from a simmer to a boil. In May 1773 he contrived a scheme to bail out the East India Company, which was foundering in a spell of bad business. The company had in its British warehouses some 17 million pounds of unsold tea. Under the Tea Act of 1773 the government would refund the British duty of twelve pence per pound on all tea shipped to the colonies and collect only the existing three pence duty payable at the colonial port. By this arrangement colonists could get tea more cheaply

Americans throwing the Cargoes of the Tea Ships into the River, at Boston, 1773.

than the English could, for less even than the black market Dutch tea. North, however, miscalculated in assuming that price alone would govern colonial reaction. And he erred even worse by permitting the East India Company to serve retailers directly through its own agents or consignees, bypassing the colonial wholesalers who had handled it before. Once that kind of monopoly was established, colonial merchants began to wonder, how soon would the precedent apply to other commodities?

The committees of correspondence, backed by colonial merchants, alerted people to the new danger. The government, they reported, was trying to purchase their loyalty and passivity with cheap tea. Before the end of the year large shipments of tea went out to major colonial ports. In New York and Philadelphia popular hostility forced company agents to resign. With no one to receive the tea, it went back to England. In Charleston it was unloaded into warehouses—and later sold to finance the Revolution. In Boston, however, Governor Hutchinson and Sam Adams resolved upon a test of will. The ships' captains, alarmed by the radical opposition, proposed to turn back, but Hutchinson refused permission until the tea was landed and the duty paid. On November 30, 1773, a group of colonial patriots disguised themselves as Mohawk Indians, boarded the three ships, and threw the 342 chests of tea overboard—cheered on by a crowd along the shore. Like those who had burned the *Gaspee*, they remained parties unknown—except to hundreds of Bostonians. One participant later testified that Sam Adams and John Hancock were there. "Sam Adams is in his glory," Governor Hutchinson muttered, and indeed he was.

Given a more tactful response from London, the Boston Tea Party might easily have undermined the radicals' credibility. Many people, especially merchants, abhorred the wanton destruction of property. A town meeting in Bristol, Massachusetts, condemned the action, and Benjamin Franklin called on his native city to pay for the drowned tea. British authorities, however, had reached the end of their patience. "The colonists must either submit or triumph," George III wrote to Lord North, and North hastened to make the king's judgment a self-fulfilling prophecy.

THE COERCIVE ACTS In April 1774 Parliament enacted four harsh measures designed by North to discipline Boston. The Boston Port Act closed the port from June 1, 1774, until the tea was paid for. An Act for the Impartial Administration of Justice let the governor transfer to England the trial of any official accused of

The Able Doctor, or America Swallowing the Bitter Draught. *This 1774 engraving shows Lord North, with the Boston Port Bill in his pocket, pouring tea down America's throat. America spits it back.*

committing an offense in the line of duty—no more redcoats would be tried on technicalities. A new Quartering Act directed local authorities to provide lodging for soldiers, in private homes if necessary. Finally, the Massachusetts Government Act made the colony's council and law-enforcement officers all appointive; sheriffs would select jurors and no town meeting could be held without the governor's consent, except for the annual election of town officers. In May, General Thomas Gage replaced Hutchinson as governor and assumed command of British forces.

Designed to isolate Boston and make an example of the colony, the actions instead hastened the development of colonial unity. "Your scheme yields no revenue," Edmund Burke warned North in Parliament; "it yields nothing but discontent, disorder, disobedience. . . ." At last, it seemed to colonists, their worst fears were confirmed. If these "Intolerable Acts," as the colonists labeled the Coercive Acts, were not resisted, they would eventually be applied to the other colonies. Further confirmation of British designs came with news of the Quebec Act, passed in June. It set up an unrepresentative government in the Canadian colony under an appointed governor and council and gave a privileged position to the Catholic church. The measure was actually designed to deal with the peculiar milieu of a British colony peopled mainly by French settlers unused to representative assemblies, but it seemed merely another indicator of tyrannical designs for the rest of the colonies. What was more, the act placed within the boundaries of Quebec the western lands north of the Ohio River, lands that Pennsylvania, Virginia, and Connecticut had long claimed.

Meanwhile colonists rallied to the cause of Boston, taking up collections and sending provisions. When the Virginia assembly met in May 1774, a young member of the Committee of Correspondence, Thomas Jefferson, proposed to set aside June 1; the effective date of the Boston Port Act, as a day of fasting and prayer in Virginia. The irate colonial governor thereupon dissolved the assembly, whose members retired to a nearby tavern and drew up a resolution for a "Continental Congress" to make representations on behalf of all the colonies. Similar calls were coming from Providence, New York, Philadelphia, and elsewhere, and in June the Massachusetts assembly suggested a meeting at Philadelphia. Shortly before George Washington left to represent Virginia at the meeting, he wrote to a friend that "the crisis is arrived when we must assert our rights, or submit to every imposition, that can be heaped upon us, till custom and use shall make us as tame and abject slaves, as the blacks we rule over with such arbitrary sway."

THE CONTINENTAL CONGRESS   On September 5, 1774, the First Continental Congress assembled in Philadelphia. The fifty-five delegates, elected by provincial congresses or irregular conventions, represented twelve continental colonies, all but Georgia, Quebec, Nova Scotia, and the Floridas. Peyton Randolph of Virginia was elected president and Charles Thomson, "the Sam Adams of Philadelphia," became secretary, but not a member. The Congress agreed to vote by colonies, although Patrick Henry urged the members to vote as individuals on the grounds that they were not Virginians or New Yorkers, but Americans. In effect the delegates functioned as a congress of ambassadors, gathered to join forces on common policies, and neither to govern nor to rebel but to adopt and issue a series of resolutions and protests.

The Congress endorsed the radical Suffolk Resolves, resolutions that declared the Intolerable Acts null and void, urged Massachusetts to arm for defense, and called for economic sanctions against British commerce. The Congress also adopted a Declaration of American Rights, which conceded only Parliament's right to regulate commerce and those matters that were strictly imperial affairs. It denied Parliament's authority with respect to internal colonial affairs and proclaimed the right of each assembly to determine the need for troops within its own province. In addition, Congress sent the king a petition for relief and issued addresses to the people of Great Britain and the colonies.

Finally, the Congress adopted the Continental Association of 1774, which recommended that every county, town, and city form committees to enforce a boycott on all British goods. In taking its stand Congress had adopted what later would be called the dominion theory of the British Empire, a theory long implicit in the assemblies' claim to independent authority but more recently formulated in two widely circulated pamphlets by James Wilson of Pennsylvania and Thomas Jefferson of Virginia. Each had argued that the colonies were not subject to Parliament but merely to the crown; each colony, like England itself, was a separate realm. Another congress was called for May 1775.

In London the king fumed. In November 1774 he wrote his prime minister that the "New England colonies are in a state of rebellion," and "blows must decide whether they are to be subject to this country or independent." Most members of Parliament agreed. Few were ready to comprehend, much less accept, the Congress's "liberal and expanded thought," as Jefferson called it. In the House of Lords, William Pitt did urge acceptance of the American view on taxation, however, and suggested a compromise under which the Continental Congress might vote a revenue for the crown. In the Commons, Edmund Burke, in a brilliant speech on conciliation, urged merely an acceptance of the American view on taxation as consonant with English principles. The real question, he argued, was "not whether you have the right to render your people miserable; but whether it is not your interest to make them happy."

But neither house was in a mood for such points. Instead, they declared Massachusetts in rebellion, forbade the New England colonies to trade with any nation outside the empire, and excluded New Englanders from the North Atlantic fisheries. Lord North's Conciliatory Resolution, adopted February 27, 1775, was as far as they would go. Under its terms, Parliament would levy taxes only to regulate trade and would grant to each colony the duties collected within its boundaries provided the colonies would contribute voluntarily to a quota for defense of the empire. It was a formula, Burke said, not for peace but for new quarrels.

SHIFTING AUTHORITY

Yet events were already moving beyond conciliation. All through the later months of 1774 and early 1775, the patriot defenders of American rights were seizing the initiative. The uncertain and unorganized Loyalists (or Tories), if they did not submit to non-importation agreements, found themselves confronted with tar and feathers. In October 1774 the Massachusetts House of Representatives, meeting in defiance of Governor Gage, restyled itself the provincial congress and named John Hancock head of a Committee of Safety with power to call up the militia. The militia, as much a social as a military organization in the past, now took to serious drill in formations, tactics, and marksmanship, and organized special units of Minute Men ready for quick mobilization. Everywhere royal officials were losing control as provincial congresses assumed authority and colonial militias organized and gathered arms and gunpowder. Still, British military officials remained smugly confident. Major John Pitcairn wrote home from Boston in March: "I am satisfied that one active campaign, a smart action, and burning two or three of their towns, will set everything to rights."

LEXINGTON AND CONCORD Pitcairn soon had his chance. On April 14, 1775, Gage received orders to suppress the "open rebellion," even at the risk of conflict. Leaders of the Massachusetts provincial congress, whom Gage was directed to arrest, were mostly beyond his reach, but he decided to seize Sam Adams and John Hancock in Lexington and destroy the militia's supply depot at Concord, about twenty miles away from his Boston headquarters. On the night of April 18, Lieutenant-Colonel Francis Smith and Major Pitcairn gathered 700 men on Boston Common and set out on a soggy route across the Cambridge marsh to Concord by way of Lexington. But local patriots got wind of the plan, and Boston's Committee of Safety sent silversmith Paul Revere and tanner William Dawes by separate routes on their famous ride to spread the alarm. Revere reached Lexington about midnight and alerted Hancock and Adams. Joined by Dawes and Dr. Samuel Prescott, who had been visiting in Lexington, he rode on toward Concord. A British patrol intercepted the trio, but Prescott slipped through with the warning.

At dawn on April 19, the British advance guard found Captain John Parker and about seventy Minute Men lined up on the dewy

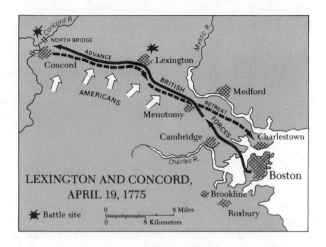

LEXINGTON AND CONCORD,
APRIL 19, 1775

Battle site

0   8 Miles
0   8 Kilometers

Lexington village green. Parker apparently intended only a silent protest, but Pitcairn rode onto the green, swung his sword, and brusquely yelled, "Disperse, you damned rebels! You dogs, run!" Parker then supposedly told his men, "Don't fire unless fired upon. But if they want a war let it begin here." He then ordered them to disperse. The Americans already had begun backing away when someone fired a single pistol shot, whereupon the British soldiers loosed a volley into the Minute Men, and then charged them with bayonets, leaving eight dead and ten wounded.

The British officers hastily reformed their men and proceeded to Concord. There the Americans had already carried off most of their valuable supplies, but the British destroyed what they could. In the meantime American patriots were swarming over the countryside, eager to wreak vengeance on the hated British troops. At Concord's North Bridge the growing American forces inflicted fourteen casualties on a British platoon, and about noon the exhausted redcoats began marching back to Boston.

By then, however, the road back had turned into a gauntlet of death as the embattled farmers from "every Middlesex village and farm" sniped at the redcoats from behind stone walls, trees, barns, and farmhouses, all the way back to Charlestown peninsula. By nightfall the redcoat survivors were safe under the protection of the fleet and army at Boston, having suffered over 250 killed or wounded; the Americans lost 93. A British official reported to London that the rebels, though untrained, had earned his respect: "Whoever looks upon them as an irregular mob will find himself much mistaken."

THE SPREADING CONFLICT   The war had started. When the Second
Continental Congress convened at Philadelphia on May 10,
1775, British-held Boston was under siege by the Massachusetts
militia. On the very day that Congress met, a force of "Green
Mountain Boys" under Ethan Allen of Vermont and Massachusetts volunteers under Benedict Arnold of Connecticut captured
strategic Fort Ticonderoga in New York. In a prodigious feat of
daring energy, the Americans then managed to transport 60 captured British cannon down rivers and over ridges to support the
siege of Boston.

The Continental Congress, with no legal authority and no resources, thus met amid reports of spreading warfare and had little choice but to assume the role of a revolutionary government.
The Congress accepted a request that it "adopt" the motley
army gathered around Boston and on June 15 named George
Washington to be general and commander-in-chief of a Continental Army. He accepted on the condition that he receive no
pay. To support the enterprise Congress resorted to a familiar colonial expedient, paper money, and voted to issue $2 million
with the colonies pledged to redemption in proportion to their
population.

On June 17, the very day that Washington was commissioned,
the colonial rebels and British troops engaged in their first major
fight, the Battle of Bunker Hill. While Congress deliberated,
both American and British forces in and around Boston had increased in strength. Militiamen from Rhode Island, Connecticut,
and New Hampshire joined in the siege. British reinforcements
included three major-generals—Sir William Howe, Sir Henry
Clinton, and John Burgoyne. On the day before the battle Americans began to fortify the high ground of Charlestown peninsula,
overlooking Boston. Breed's Hill was the battle location, nearer
to Boston than Bunker Hill, the site first chosen (and the source
of the battle's erroneous name).

The rebels were spoiling for a fight. As Joseph Warren, a dapper Boston physician put it, "The British say we don't fight; by
heavens, I hope I shall die up to my knees in blood!" He soon got
his wish. With civilians looking on from rooftops and church
steeples, Gage ordered a conventional frontal assault in the blistering heat, with 2,200 British troops moving in tight formation
through tall grass. Numerous fences obstructed the assault and
broke up the uniform lines. The Americans, pounded by naval
guns, watched from behind hastily built earthworks as the waves
of brightly uniformed British troops advanced up the hill. Ordered not to fire until they could "see the whites of their eyes,"

The Battle of Bunker Hill, and the burning of Charles Town.

the militiamen waited until the attackers came within fifteen to twenty paces, then loosed a shattering volley. Through the cloud of oily smoke, the Americans could see fallen bodies "as thick as sheep in a fold." The militiamen cheered as they watched the greatest soldiers in the world retreating in panic.

Within a half hour, however, the British had reformed and attacked again. Another sheet of flame and lead greeted them, and the vaunted redcoats retreated a second time. Still, the proud British generals were determined not to be humiliated by such ragtag rustics. On the third attempt, when the colonials began to run out of gunpowder, and were forced to throw stones, a bayonet charge ousted them. The British took the high ground, but at the cost of 1,054 casualties. Colonial losses were about 400. "A dear bought victory," recorded General Clinton; "another such would have ruined us."

While Boston remained under siege, the Continental Congress held to the dimming hope of a possible compromise. On July 5 and 6, 1775, the delegates issued two major documents: an appeal to the king, thereafter known as the Olive Branch Petition, and a Declaration of the Causes and Necessity of Taking Up Arms. The Olive Branch Petition, written by John Dickinson, professed continued loyalty to George III and begged him to restrain further hostilities pending a reconciliation. The Declaration, also largely Dickinson's work, traced the history of the controversy, denounced the British for the unprovoked assault at Lexington, and rejected independence but affirmed the colonists' purpose to fight for their rights rather than submit to slavery. "Our cause is just," he declared. "Our Union is perfect." Such impassioned rhetoric failed to impress the outraged king. On August 22 George III ordered the army at Boston to regard the colonists "as open and avowed enemies." The next day he issued a proclamation of rebellion.

As the fighting spread north into Canada and south into Virginia and the Carolinas, the Continental Congress assumed the functions of government. In July 1775 it appointed commissioners to negotiate peace treaties with Indian tribes and organized a Post Office Department with Benjamin Franklin as postmaster-general. In October it authorized formation of a navy, in November a marine corps. A committee began to explore the possibility of foreign aid. But the delegates continued to hold back from the seeming abyss of formal independence. Yet through late 1775 and early 1776 word came of one British action after another that proclaimed rebellion and war. In December 1775 Parliament declared the colonies closed to all commerce, and the king began hiring German mercenaries. Eventually almost 30,000 Germans served, about 17,000 of them from the region of Hesse-Kassel, and "Hessian" became the epithet applied to them all.

When Washington arrived outside of Boston to take charge of the American forces after the Battle of Bunker Hill, the military situation was stalemated, and so it remained through the winter, until early March 1776. At that time American forces occupied Dorchester Heights to the south of Boston, bringing the city under threat of bombardment with cannon and mortars. General William Howe, who had long since replaced Gage as British commander, reasoned that discretion was the better part of valor, and he retreated with his forces by water to Halifax, Nova Scotia. The last British troops, along with fearful American Loyalists, embarked from Boston on March 17, 1776. By that time British power had collapsed nearly everywhere, and the British faced not the suppression of a rebellion but the reconquest of a continent.

COMMON SENSE   In January 1776 Thomas Paine's pamphlet *Common Sense* was published anonymously in Philadelphia, transforming the revolutionary controversy. Born of Quaker parents,

Paine had distinguished himself in England chiefly as a drifter, a failure in marriage and business. At age thirty-seven he sailed for America with a letter of introduction from Benjamin Franklin and the purpose of setting up a school for young ladies. When that did not work out, he moved into the political controversy as a freelance writer and, with *Common Sense,* proved himself the consummate revolutionary rhetorician. Until his pamphlet appeared the squabble had been mainly with Parliament, but Paine directly attacked allegiance to the monarchy, the last frayed connection to Britain. The common sense of the matter, to Paine, was that King George III bore the responsibility for the malevolence toward the colonies. Americans should consult their own interests, abandon George III, and declare their independence: "The blood of the slain, the weeping voice of nature cries, 'TIS TIME TO PART."

INDEPENDENCE

Within three months, more than 100,000 copies of Paine's pamphlet were in circulation, an enormous number for the time. "*Common Sense* is working a powerful change in the minds of men," George Washington noted. One by one the provincial governments authorized their delegates in Congress to take the final step. On June 7, 1776, Richard Henry Lee of Virginia moved a resolution "that these United Colonies are, and of right

The Continental Congress votes Independence, July 2, 1776.

ought to be, free and independent states." Sam Adams immediately endorsed the idea: "We have no other alternative than independence, or the most ignominious and appalling servitude." But others balked. South Carolina and Pennsylvania initially opposed severing ties with England. After feverish lobbying by radical patriots, however, the dissenters changed their mind, and the resolution passed on July 2, a date that "will be the most memorable epoch in the history of America," John Adams wrote to his wife, Abigail. Reluctant American revolutionaries might "stamp and foam and curse," he added, "but all in vain. The decree has gone forth." The memorable date, however, became July 4, 1776, when Congress adopted the Declaration of Independence.

JEFFERSON'S *DECLARATION*   John Adams, a member of the committee appointed to draft the official declaration, coaxed a reluctant Thomas Jefferson to draft the document. "I am obnoxious, suspected, and unpopular," Adams explained: "You are much the otherwise." Jefferson's summary of the prevailing political sentiment was an eloquent restatement of John Locke's contract theory of government. In Jefferson's words, governments derived "their just Powers from the consent of the people," who were entitled to "alter or abolish" governments which denied their "unalienable rights" to "Life, Liberty, and the pursuit of Happiness." The appeal was no longer simply to "the rights of Englishmen" but to the broader "laws of Nature and Nature's God." Yet at the same time the Declaration implicitly supported the theory that the British Empire was a federation united only through the crown. Parliament, which had no proper authority over the colonies, was never mentioned by name. The enemy was a king who had "combined with others to subject us to a jurisdiction foreign to our constitution, and unacknowledged by our laws." The document set forth "a history of repeated injuries and usurpations, all having in direct object the establishment of an absolute Tyranny over these States." The "Representatives of the United States of America," therefore, declared the thirteen "United Colonies" to be "Free and Independent States." Upon signing the Declaration in an oversize script, John Hancock explained: "There, King George will be able to read that without his spectacles."

"WE ALWAYS HAD GOVERNED OURSELVES"   So it had come to this, thirteen years after Britain had won domination of all of North America. Historians have advanced numerous explanations of the revolutionary controversy: trade regulation, the restrictions on western lands, the tax controversy, the burden of debts to British merchants, the fear of an Anglican bishop, the growth of a national consciousness, the lack of representation in Parliament, ideologies of Whiggery and the Enlightenment, the evangelistic impulse, Scottish moral philosophy, the abrupt shift from a mercantile to an "imperial" policy after 1763, class conflict, revolutionary conspiracy.

Individually and collectively they are subject to challenge, but each contributed something to colonial grievances that rose to a climax in a gigantic failure of British statesmanship. A conflict between British sovereignty and American rights had come to a point of confrontation that adroit statesmanship might have avoided, sidestepped, or outflanked. Irresolution and vacillation in the British ministry finally gave way to the stubborn determination to force an issue long permitted to drift. The colonists saw these developments as the conspiracy of a corrupted oligarchy —and finally, they decided, of a despotic king—to impose an "absolute Tyranny."

Perhaps the last word on how the Revolution came about should belong to an obscure participant, Levi Preston, a Minute Man from Danvers, Massachusetts. Asked sixty-seven years after Lexington and Concord about British oppressions, he responded, as his young interviewer reported later: " 'What were they? Oppressions? I didn't feel them.' " When asked about the hated Stamp Act, he claimed that he " 'never saw one of those stamps,' " and was " 'certain I never paid a penny for one of them.' " Nor had he ever heard of John Locke or his theories. " 'We read only the Bible, the Catechism, Watts's Psalms and Hymns, and the Almanack." ' When his exasperated interviewer asked why, then, did he support the Revolution, Preston replied: " 'Young man, what we meant in going for those redcoats was this: we always had governed ourselves, and we always meant to. They didn't mean we should.' "

FURTHER READING

A superb narrative survey of the events leading to the Revolution is Edmund S. Morgan's *The Birth of the Republic, 1763–1789* (rev. ed., 1977).° For the perspective of Great Britain on the imperial conflict, see Ian Christie, *Crisis of Empire* (1966).°

° These books are available in paperback editions.

The intellectual foundations for revolt are traced in Bernard Bailyn's *The Ideological Origins of the American Revolution* (1967)° and in the opening chapters of Gordon S. Wood's *The Creation of the American Republic, 1776–1787* (1969).° Profiles of the revolutionary generation can be found in Pauline Maier's *The Old Revolutionaries: Political Lives in the Age of Samuel Adams* (1980).°

A number of books deal with specific events in the chain of crisis. Oliver M. Dickerson's *The Navigation Acts and the American Revolution* (1951) stresses the change from trade regulation to taxation in 1764. Edmund S. Morgan and Helen M. Morgan's *The Stamp Act Crisis* (rev. ed., 1962)° gives the colonial perspective on that crucial event. Also valuable are Hiller B. Zobel's *The Boston Massacre* (1970)° and Benjamin W. Labaree's *The Boston Tea Party* (1979).° Carl L. Becker's *The Declaration of Independence* (1922)° remains the best introduction to the framing of that document.

5 ✒

THE AMERICAN REVOLUTION

Few foreign observers thought the upstart American revolutionaries could win a war against the world's greatest empire, yet
that is what happened. The Americans lost most of the battles in
the revolutionary war, but eventually forced the British to sue
for peace and grant their independence. The surprising result
testified to the tenacity of the patriots and to the peculiar difficulties facing the British as they tried to conduct a demanding
campaign thousands of miles from home.

1776: WASHINGTON'S NARROW ESCAPE

On July 2, 1776, the day that Congress voted independence, British redcoats landed on Staten Island. They were the
vanguard of a gigantic effort to reconquer America and the first
elements of an enormous force that gathered around New York
Harbor over the next month. By mid-August General William
Howe, with the support of a fleet under his older brother, had
some 32,000 men at his disposal, including 9,000 German "Hessians"—the biggest single force ever mustered by the British in
the eighteenth century. Washington had expected the move and
transferred most of his men from Boston, but could muster only
about 19,000 Continentals and militiamen. With such a force
New York was indefensible, but Congress wanted it held, and
Washington had to expose his men to entrapments from which
they escaped more by luck and Howe's caution than by any strategic genius of the American commander. Washington was still
learning his trade, and the New York campaign afforded some
costly lessons.

FIGHTING IN NEW YORK AND NEW JERSEY The first conflicts took place on Long Island, where the Americans wanted to hold Brooklyn Heights, from which the city might be bombarded. In late August, however, Howe inflicted heavy losses and forced Washington to evacuate Long Island to reunite his dangerously divided forces. A timely rainstorm kept the British fleet out of the East River and made possible a nighttime withdrawal to Manhattan.

After their success on Long Island, the brothers Howe offered pardons to those revolutionaries who returned to British alle-

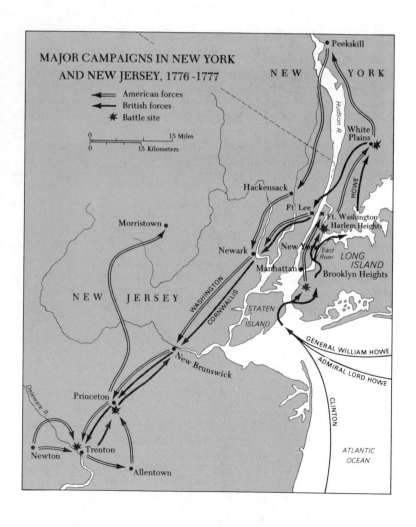

MAJOR CAMPAIGNS IN NEW YORK
AND NEW JERSEY, 1776 -1777

American forces
British forces
Battle site

0 _____ 15 Miles
0 _____ 15 Kilometers

giance and made vague promises of fair treatment—but only after all "extralegal" congresses and conventions were dissolved. Had Howe moved quickly, he could have penned Washington's army in lower Manhattan. But the main American force of 6,000 men was able to withdraw northward to the mainland and retreat slowly across New Jersey and over the Delaware River into Pennsylvania. In the retreating army marched a volunteer from England, Thomas Paine. Having opened an eventful year with his pamphlet *Common Sense*, he now composed *The American Crisis*, in which he exhorted Americans to fight on with the immortal line: "These are the times that try men's souls." The eloquent pamphlet, ordered read in the revolutionary army camps, helped restore shaken morale—as events would soon do more decisively.

General Howe, firmly—and comfortably—based in New York (which the British held throughout the war), followed conventional practice and settled down with his army to wait out the winter. But Washington was not yet ready to hibernate; instead he daringly seized the initiative. On Christmas night 1776, he slipped across the icy Delaware with 2,400 men and near dawn at Trenton surprised a garrison of 1,500 Hessians still befuddled from too much holiday rum. It was a total rout from which only 500 royal soldiers escaped death or capture. Washington's men suffered but six casualties, one of whom was Lt. James Monroe, the future president. At nearby Princeton, on January 3, the Americans repelled three regiments of redcoats, and finally took refuge in winter quarters at Morristown, in the hills of northern Jersey. The campaigns of 1776 had ended, after repeated defeats, with two minor, but uplifting victories. Howe had missed his great chance, indeed several chances, to bring the rebellion to a speedy end. Grumbled one British officer, the Americans had "become a formidable enemy."

AMERICAN SOCIETY AT WAR

DIVIDED LOYALTIES   Before the American victory at Trenton, New Jersey civilians had assumed that the rebellion was collapsing, and thousands hastened to sign an oath of allegiance to Britain. But the events at Trenton and Princeton reversed the outlook, and with the British withdrawal, New Jersey quickly reverted to insurgent control. Yet many colonists remained Tory in outlook. During or after the war roughly 100,000 of them, or more than 3 percent of the total population, left America. Opinion concerning the Revolution was about evenly divided three ways among Patriots or Whigs (as the revolutionaries called themselves), Tories (as Patriots called the Loyalists, recalling the die-hard royalists in England), and an indifferent middle swayed mostly by the better organized and more energetic radicals.

American Tories were concentrated mainly in the seaport cities, but they came from all walks of life. Almost all governors, judges, and other royal officials were loyal to Britain; colonial merchants might be tugged one way or the other, depending on how much they had benefited or suffered from mercantilist regulation; the great planters were swayed one way by dependence on British bounties, another by their debts to British merchants. In the backcountry of New York and the Carolinas many humble folk rallied to the crown. Where planter aristocrats tended to be Whig, as in North Carolina, backcountry farmers (many of them recently Regulators) leaned to the Tories.

The Revolution has ever since seemed to have been a fight between the Americans and the British, but the War for Independence was also very much a civil war that divided families and communities. The fratricidal hatred that often goes with civil war gave rise to some of the most bloodcurdling atrocities in the backcountries of New York and Pennsylvania, and in Georgia, where Tory Rangers and their Indian allies went marauding against frontier Whigs. Whigs responded in kind against the Loyalists.

MILITIA AND ARMY   American militiamen in the backcountry engaged in the kind of fighting that had become habitual when they were colonists. Dressed in hunting shirts and armed with muskets with long-grooved barrels, they preferred to ambush their opponents or engage them in hand-to-hand combat rather than fight in traditional formations. They also tended to kill unnecessarily and to torture prisoners. In general, they made for unreliable troops. To repel an attack, the militia somehow materialized; the danger past, it evaporated, for there were chores to do at home. They "come in, you cannot tell how," George Washington said in exasperation, "go, you cannot tell when, and act you cannot tell where, consume your provisions, exhaust your stores, and leave you at last at a critical moment." All too often the green troops would panic in a formal line of battle, and they were therefore usually placed in the front ranks in the hope that they would get off a shot or two before they fled. As General Nathanael Greene pointed out, the novice militiamen were hard pressed to "stand the shocking scenes of war, to

An American soldier, 1778. One report sent back to England claimed the "rebels are not the despicable rabble too many have supposed them to be."

march over dead men, to hear without concern the groans of the wounded."

The Continental Army, by contrast, was on the whole better trained and motivated. As one British officer commented, the American forces displayed "a sort of implacable ardor and revenge, which happily are a good deal unknown in the prosecution of war in general." True, many American troops were attracted by bounties of land or cash, and many deserted, but most of those who persevered were animated by genuine patriotic fervor and a thirst for adventure that enabled them to survive the horrors of combat and camp life. Washington's army, which fluctuated in size from 5,000 to 20,000, was populated mostly by poor native-born Americans or immigrants who had been indentured servants or convicts. Line regiments were organized state by state, and the states were supposed to keep them filled with volunteers, or conscripts if need be, but Washington could never be sure that his requisitions would be met.

PROBLEMS OF FINANCE AND SUPPLY   The same uncertainty beset the army and Congress in their quest for supplies. None of the states came through with more than a part of its share, and Congress reluctantly let army agents take supplies directly from farmers in return for certificates promising future payment. To pay for the war, Congress printed nearly $250 million in paper money, and the states issued about another $200 million. With goods scarce, prices in terms of paper dollars, or "Continentals," rose sharply. During the winter of 1777–1778 Washington's men would suffer terribly, less because of actual shortages than because farmers preferred to sell their produce for British gold and silver.

During the harsh winter at Morristown (1776–1777) Washington's army nearly disintegrated as enlistments expired and deserters fled the hardships of camp. Only about 1,000 soldiers stuck it out. With the spring thaw, however, recruits began arriving to claim the bounty of $20 and 100 acres of land offered by Congress to those who would enlist for three years or for the duration of the conflict, if less. With some 9,000 regulars, Washington began sparring and feinting with Howe in northern New Jersey. Howe had been making other plans, however, and so had other British officers.

BEHIND THE LINES Civilians saw their lives profoundly changed by the revolutionary war. Cities (Boston, New York, Philadelphia, Savannah, Charleston) were occupied by British forces, towns and villages were destroyed, crops and livestock confiscated, families disrupted, husbands and fathers killed or maimed. As in all wars, the families of soldiers suffered terrible anxiety and hardship. Sarah Hodgkins, a twenty-five-year-old mother of two living in Ipswich, Massachusetts, had a third child after her husband left to serve with the American forces after the battle of Lexington. In a letter to her husband, she expressed her loneliness: "I have got a Sweet Babe almost six months old but have got no father for it." She was understandably upset when her husband agreed to reenlist for three more years of service, but placed her trust in God. As she wrote her husband, "all I can do for you is commit you to God . . . for God is able to preserve us as ever and he will do it if we trust in him aright."

Not all civilians were so pious or patriotic. The inflationary spiral generated by a scarcity of consumer goods and the supplies needed for the military effort created new opportunities for quick profits and entrepreneurial chicanery. Many Americans saw in the Revolution a means of self-aggrandizement rather than self-sacrifice. Robert Morris, a prominent Philadelphia merchant who became treasurer of the Congress upon the condition that he could continue his private ventures, told a colleague that "there never has been so fair an opportunity for making a large fortune since I have been conversant in the world." Throughout the war years George Washington complained that "speculation, peculation, and an insatiable thirst for riches seems to have got the better of every other of Men."

Traders from Spain, France, and Holland replaced Great Britain as the source of consumer goods, and affluent Americans quickly abandoned notions of patriotic austerity.

The poor suffered most amid the disruptions and skyrocketing prices created by the war. A bushel of wheat that sold for less than a dollar in 1777 brought $80 two years later. Many consumers appealed to authorities to institute price controls so as to enable them to afford basic necessities. Others took more direct action. In Boston a throng of women paraded a merchant accused of hoarding through the streets while "a large concourse of men stood amazed." The shoemakers and leather tanners of Philadelphia expressed the frustrations of many among the "laboring poor" when they declared in 1779 that their efforts had always brought them a "bare living profit," regardless of "however industrious and attentive to business, however frugal in manner of living" they had been. Nevertheless, they had been "contented to live decently without acquiring wealth" because "our professions rendered us as useful and necessary members of the community." But they now saw themselves as victims of gouging merchants and retailers. No longer willing to defer quietly to such discrimination, they grabbed the opportunity afforded by the revolutionary crisis to claim new economic and political rights.

To revolutionary leaders such as John Adams, the "democratical" demands put forward by the laboring classes were as odious as British regulatory measures. The specter of unlearned mechanics and laborers exercising political power horrified him. The American people, he and others insisted, must accept social inequality as a fact of human existence and defer to the leadership of their betters. The "one thing" absolutely required of a new republic was "a decency, and respect, and veneration introduced for persons of authority."

1777: SETBACKS FOR THE BRITISH

Indecision, overconfidence, and poor communications plagued British planning for the campaigns of 1777. The profoundly confident General "Gentleman Johnny" Burgoyne, a charming mixture of poet, gambler, lover, and warrior, proposed to bisect the colonies by advancing southward from Quebec to the Hudson while another force moved eastward from Oswego down the Mohawk Valley. Howe had proposed a similar plan, combined with an attack on New England, and had he stuck to it, he might have cut the colonies in two and delivered them a disheartening blow. But he changed his mind and decided to move against the Patriot capital, Philadelphia, expecting that the Pennsylvania Tories would then rally to the crown and secure the colony.

Howe's plan succeeded, up to a point. Washington sensed Howe's purpose and withdrew most of his men from New Jersey to meet the new threat. At Brandywine Creek, south of Philadelphia, Howe pushed Washington's forces back on September 11, and eight days later the British occupied Philadelphia. But they found fewer Tories there than expected. Washington counterattacked against a British encampment at Germantown on October 4, but reinforcements from Philadelphia under General Lord Cornwallis arrived in time to repulse the Americans. Washington then retired into winter quarters at Valley Forge while Howe and his men remained in the relative comfort of Philadelphia, twenty miles away. To the north, meanwhile, Burgoyne was stumbling into disaster.

SARATOGA   After concluding his marching orders by declaring "This Army must not Retreat," Burgoyne moved southward toward Lake Champlain in 1777 with about 7,000 men, his mistress, and a baggage train that included some thirty carts filled with his personal trappings and a large supply of champagne. A powerful force on paper, the expedition was in fact much too cumbersome to be effective. Overloaded with excess equipment and heavy cannon, Burgoyne's forces had a difficult time traversing the heavily wooded and marshy terrain. And when they met the more mobile and seasoned Americans, the British suffered two serious reversals.

At Oriskany, New York, on August 6, 1777, a band of militia thwarted an ambush by Tories and Indians, and gained time for Benedict Arnold to bring a thousand Continentals to the relief of Fort Stanwix. The Indians, convinced they faced an even greater force than they actually did, deserted, and the Mohawk Valley was secured for the Patriot forces. To the east, at Bennington, Vermont (August 16), a body of New England militia repulsed a British foraging party with heavy losses. American reinforcements continued to gather, and after two sharp clashes, Burgoyne pulled back to Saratoga, where American forces under General Horatio Gates surrounded him. On October 17, 1777, Burgoyne, resplendent in his scarlet, gold, and white uniform, surrendered to the plain, blue-coated Gates. Most of Burgoyne's 5,700 soldiers were imprisoned in Virginia, but "Gentleman

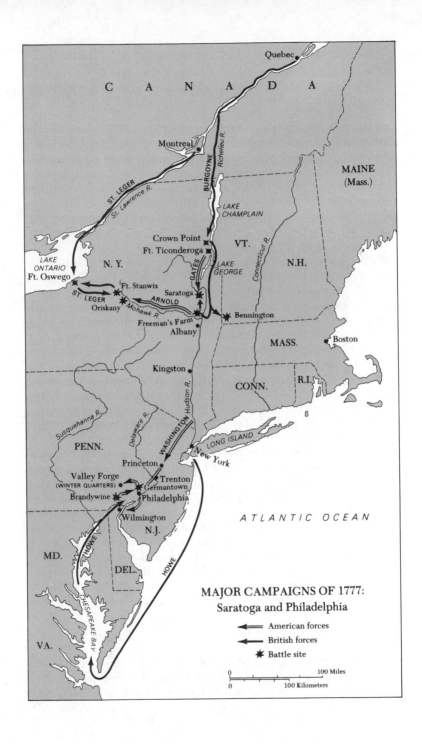

Quebec

C A N A D A

MAINE
(Mass.)

Montreal

ST. LEGER
St. Lawrence R.

BURGOYNE
Richelieu R.

LAKE
CHAMPLAIN

VT.

Crown Point
Ft. Ticonderoga

LAKE
ONTARIO
Ft. Oswego

N. Y.

GATES

LAKE
GEORGE

N.H.

Connecticut R.

ST. LEGER

Ft. Stanwix
ARNOLD

Saratoga

Oriskany

Mohawk R.

Freeman's Farm

Albany

Bennington

MASS.

Boston

Kingston

Hudson R.

CONN.

R.I.

Susquehanna R.

Delaware R.

WASHINGTON

LONG ISLAND

Princeton

New York

PENN.

Valley Forge
(WINTER QUARTERS)

Trenton
Germantown

Brandywine

Philadelphia

ATLANTIC OCEAN

Wilmington

N.J.

MD.

HOWE

DEL.

HOWE

MAJOR CAMPAIGNS OF 1777:
Saratoga and Philadelphia

VA.

CHESAPEAKE BAY

⟵⟵ American forces

⟵ British forces

★ Battle site

0   100 Miles

0   100 Kilometers

Johnny" himself was permitted to go home, where he received an icy reception. The victory at Saratoga proved critically important to the American cause.

ALLIANCE WITH FRANCE   On December 2, 1777, news of the American triumph reached London; two days later it reached Paris, where it was celebrated almost as if it were a French victory. Its impact on the French made the victory at Saratoga a decisive turning point of the war. In May 1776 the French had taken their first step toward aiding the colonists by sending fourteen ships with war supplies to America; most of the Continental Army's powder in the first years of the war came from this source. After Saratoga, the French saw their chance to strike a sharper blow at their hated enemy and entered into serious negotiations with the Americans. On February 6, 1778, France and America signed two treaties: a Treaty of Amity and Commerce, in which France recognized the United States and offered trade concessions, including important privileges to American shipping, and a Treaty of Alliance. Under the latter both agreed, first, that if France entered the war, both countries would fight until American independence was won; second, that neither would conclude a "truce or peace" without the consent of the other; and third, that each guaranteed the other's possessions in America "from the present time and forever against all other powers." France further bound herself to seek neither Canada nor other British possessions on the mainland of North America.

By June 1778 British vessels had fired on French ships and the two nations were at war. In 1779, after extracting French promises to help her get back territories taken by the British in the previous war, including Gibraltar, Spain entered the war as an ally of France, but not of the United States. The following year Britain declared war on the Dutch, who persisted in a profitable trade with the French and Americans. The embattled farmers at Concord had indeed fired the "shot heard round the world." Like Washington's encounter with the French in 1754, it was the start of another world war, and the fighting now spread to the Mediterranean, Africa, India, the West Indies, and the high seas.

1778: BOTH SIDES REGROUP

After Saratoga, Lord North knew that winning the war was unlikely, but the king refused to let him either resign or make peace. On March 16, 1778, the House of Commons adopted a program that in effect granted all the American demands prior to independence. Parliament repealed the Townshend tea duty, the Massachusetts Government Act, and the Prohibitory Act, which had closed the colonies to commerce. It then dispatched a peace commission, but its members did not reach Philadelphia until June, a month after Congress had ratified the French treaties. The Congress refused to begin any negotiations until independence was recognized or British forces withdrawn, neither of which the commissioners could promise.

Unbeknownst to the commissioners, the crown had already authorized the evacuation of Philadelphia, a withdrawal that further weakened what little bargaining power they had. After Saratoga, General Howe had resigned his command and Sir Henry Clinton had replaced him, with orders to pull out of Philadelphia, and if necessary, New York, but to keep Newport. In short, he was to take a defensive stance except in the South, where the government believed a latent Tory sentiment in the backcountry needed only the British presence for its release. The ministry was right up to a point, but the pro-British sentiment turned out once again, as in other theaters of war, to be weaker than it seemed.

For Washington's army at Valley Forge the winter of 1777–1778 had been a season of suffering far worse than the previous winter at Morristown. While the great diplomatic achievement was maturing in Paris, the American force, encamped in lice-infested log huts near Philadelphia, endured cold, hunger, and disease. Many deserted or resigned their commissions, leading Washington to warn Congress that unless substantial supplies were forthcoming, the army "must inevitably be reduced to one or other of these three things. Starve, dissolve, or disperse."

As winter drew to an end, the army's morale drew strength from congressional promises of extra pay and bonuses after the war and from news of the French alliance. Its fighting trim was sharpened by the Prussian von Steuben, who began to drill it in March. As General Clinton's forces withdrew eastward toward New York, Washington pursued them across New Jersey. On June 28, 1778, he engaged the British in an indecisive battle at Monmouth Court House. Clinton's forces then slipped away into New York while Washington took up a position at White Plains, north of the city. From that time on, the northern theater, scene of the major campaigns and battles in the first years of the war, settled into a long stalemate, interrupted by minor and mostly inconclusive engagements.

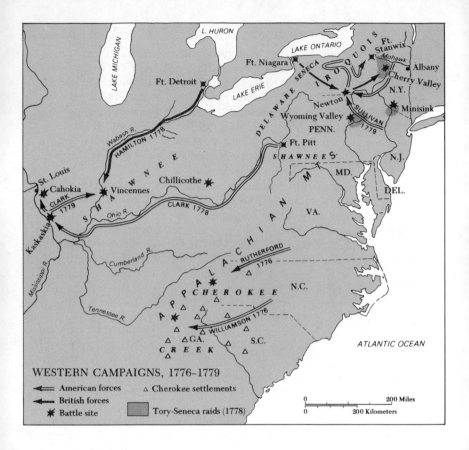

WESTERN CAMPAIGNS, 1776-1779

← American forces   △ Cherokee settlements
← British forces
✸ Battle site   ▧ Tory-Seneca raids (1778)

0   200 Miles
0   200 Kilometers

ACTIONS ON THE FRONTIER   The one major American success of
1778 occurred far from the New Jersey battlefields, out to the
west where the British at Forts Niagara and Detroit had set frontier Tories and Indians to raiding western settlements and had
offered to pay for American scalps. To end such attacks, young
George Rogers Clark took 175 frontiersmen and a flotilla of
flatboats down the Ohio River in early 1778, marched through
the woods, and on the evening of July 4 caught the British by
surprise. At the end of the year, Clark marched his men (almost
half French volunteers) through icy rivers and flooded prairies,
sometimes in water neck deep, and captured an astonished British garrison at Vincennes.

While Clark's captives traveled eastward, Tories and Iroquois
Indians in western Pennsylvania continued to terrorize frontier
settlements through the summer of 1778. In response Washington dispatched an expedition of 4,000 men to the area. At New-

town (now Elmira) the American force met and defeated the only serious opposition on August 29, 1779, and proceeded to carry out Washington's instruction that the Iroquois country be not "merely overrun but destroyed."

The American troops devastated about forty Seneca and Cayuga villages together with their orchards and food stores. So ruthless and complete was the destruction that large numbers of the Indians were thrown completely upon their British allies for scant supplies from Fort Niagara. The action broke the power of the Iroquois federation for all time, but it did not completely pacify the frontier. Sporadic encounters with various tribes of the region continued to the end of the war. By thus weakening the major Indian tribes along the frontier, the American Revolution, among its other results, cleared the way for rapid settlement of the trans-Appalachian West.

The War in the South

At the end of 1778 the focus of British action shifted suddenly to the south. The whole region from Virginia southward had been free from major action since 1776. Now the British would test King George's belief that a sleeping Tory power in the South needed only the presence of a few redcoats to awaken it. General Clinton took Savannah and Charleston, and rolled northward, gathering momentum from the Loyalist countryside. At this point, Congress, against Washington's advice, turned to the victor of Saratoga, Horatio Gates, to take command and sent him south. Charles Lord Cornwallis, dispatched with one of three columns to subdue the Carolina interior, surprised Gates's force at Camden, South Carolina, and routed his new army. The patriots retreated all the way to Hillsborough, North Carolina, 160 miles away.

THE CAROLINAS   Cornwallis had South Carolina just about under control, but his cavalry leaders Banastre Tarleton and Patrick Ferguson, who mobilized Tory militiamen, overreached themselves in their effort to subdue the Whigs. "Tarleton's Quarters" became bywords for savagery, because "Bloody Tarleton" ordered rebels killed after they surrendered. Ferguson sealed his own doom when he threatened to march over the mountains and hang the revolutionary leaders there. Instead the feisty "overmountain men" went after Ferguson and, allied with other backcountry Whigs, caught him and his Tories on Kings Mountain

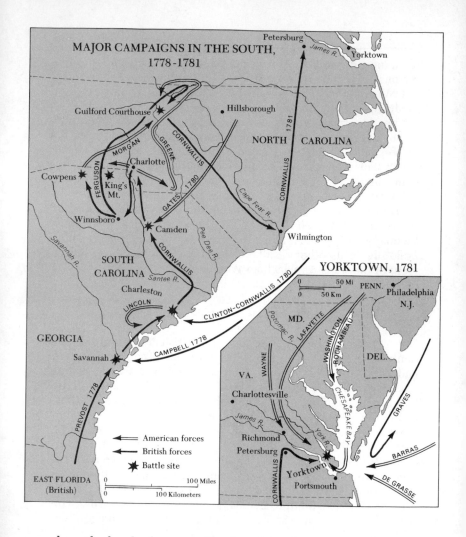

MAJOR CAMPAIGNS IN THE SOUTH,
1778-1781

Petersburg
James R. Yorktown
Guilford Courthouse
Hillsborough
NORTH CAROLINA
MORGAN
GREENE
CORNWALLIS
GATES 1780
Charlotte
Cowpens
Ferguson
King's Mt.
Winnsboro
Camden
CORNWALLIS
Cape Fear R.
CORNWALLIS 1781
Wilmington
SOUTH CAROLINA
Santee R.
Pee Dee R.
Savannah R.
Charleston
LINCOLN
CLINTON-CORNWALLIS 1780
CAMPBELL 1778
GEORGIA
Savannah
PREVOST 1778
EAST FLORIDA
(British)

American forces
British forces
★ Battle site

0   100 Miles
0   100 Kilometers

YORKTOWN, 1781

0   50 Mi
0   50 Km
PENN.
Philadelphia
N.J.
MD.
DEL.
VA.
WAYNE
LAFAYETTE
WASHINGTON
ROCHAMBEAU
Charlottesville
Potomac R.
CHESAPEAKE BAY
GRAVES
James R.
Richmond
Petersburg
BARRAS
CORNWALLIS
York R.
Yorktown
Portsmouth
DE GRASSE

along the border between North and South Carolina. There, on
October 7, 1780, they devastated his force. By then feelings
were so strong that American irregulars continued firing on
Tories trying to surrender and later slaughtered Tory prisoners.
Kings Mountain, an unaccustomed victory, is sometimes called
the turning point of the war in the South. By proving that the
British were not invincible, it emboldened small farmers to join
guerrilla bands under partisan leaders like Francis Marion, "the
Swamp Fox," and Thomas Sumter, "the Gamecock."

While the overmountain men were closing on Ferguson, Congress had chosen a new commander for the southern theater,
General Nathanael Greene, the "fighting Quaker" of Rhode Is-

land. A man of infinite patience, skilled at managing men and saving supplies, careful to avoid needless risks, he was well suited to a war of attrition against the British forces. He was also a selfless patriot who sold his own lands in order to provide supplies for his army. Greene shrewdly lured Cornwallis and his troops into chasing the Americans across the Carolinas, thus taxing British energies and supplies. Greene finally offered battle near Guilford Courthouse on March 15, 1781. After inflicting heavy losses, Greene prudently withdrew to fight another day, and Cornwallis was left in possession of the field, but at a cost of nearly 100 men killed and more than 400 wounded. In London, when the word arrived, a parliamentary leader moaned: "Another such victory and we are undone."

Cornwallis marched off toward the coast at Wilmington to lick his wounds and take on new supplies. Greene then resolved to go back into South Carolina in the hope of drawing Cornwallis after him or forcing the British to give up the state. There he joined forces with the guerrillas already active on the scene, and in a series of brilliant actions kept losing battles while winning the war: "We fight, get beat, rise, and fight again," he said. By September 1781 he had narrowed British control in the Deep South to Charleston and Savannah, although for more than a year longer Whigs and Tories slashed at each other "with savage fury" in the backcountry, where there was "nothing but murder and devastation in every quarter," Greene said.

Meanwhile Cornwallis had headed north away from Greene, reasoning that Virginia must be eliminated as a source of reinforcement before the Carolinas could be subdued. In May 1781 Cornwallis met up with Benedict Arnold, now a British general, who was engaged in a war of maneuver with American forces. Arnold, until September 1780, had been American commander at West Point. Overweening in ambition, lacking in moral scruples, and a reckless spender, he nursed a grudge over an official reprimand for his extravagances as commander of reoccupied Philadelphia. Traitors have a price, and Arnold soon found his. He crassly plotted to sell out the West Point garrison to the British, even suggesting how they might capture Washington himself. The American seizure of the British go-between, Major John André, ended Arnold's plot. Forewarned that his plan had been discovered, Arnold joined the British in New York while André was hanged as a spy.

YORKTOWN When Cornwallis linked up with Arnold at Petersburg, Virginia, their combined forces rose to 7,200, far more than the small American force they faced. British raiders struck deep into Virginia, and one sortie nearly captured Governor Jefferson and his legislature at Charlottesville. When American reinforcements arrived, Cornwallis moved back toward the coast. In a fatal miscalculation, he picked Yorktown as a defensible site. There seemed to be little reason to worry about a siege, with Washington's main land force attacking New York and the British navy in control of American waters.

To be sure, there was a small American navy, but it was no match for the British fleet. Most celebrated were the exploits of Captain John Paul Jones, who sailed east across the Atlantic in 1778 with his sloop *Ranger* and gave the British navy some bad moments in its home waters. In France, Benjamin Franklin got Jones an old ship which the captain named the *Bonhomme Richard* in honor of Franklin's Poor Richard. Off England's coast on September 23, 1779, Jones won a desperate battle with the British frigate *Serapis*, which he captured and occupied before his own ship sank. This was the occasion for his stirring and oft-repeated response to a British demand for surrender: "I have not yet begun to fight."

Such heroics were little more than nuisances to the British, but at a critical point, thanks to the French navy, the British lost control of the Chesapeake waters. For three years Washington had waited to get some military benefit from the French alliance. In 1780 the French finally landed a force of about 6,000 at Newport, but the French army under the comte de Rochambeau sat there for a year, blockaded by the British fleet. In 1781 the elements for combined action suddenly fell into place. As Cornwallis moved into Virginia in May, Washington persuaded Rochambeau to join forces for an attack on New York. The two armies linked up in July, but before they could strike at New York, word came from the West Indies that Admiral De Grasse was bound for the Chesapeake with his entire French fleet and some 3,000 soldiers. Washington and the combined American-French forces immediately set out toward Yorktown.

On August 30 De Grasse's fleet reached Yorktown, where his troops joined Lafayette's force already watching Cornwallis. On September 6, the day after a British fleet under Admiral Thomas Graves appeared, De Grasse gave battle and forced Graves to give up his effort to relieve Cornwallis, whose fate was quickly sealed. Graves departed four days later for repairs in New York. De Grasse then sent ships up the Chesapeake to ferry down Washington's 16,000 American and French forces, double the size of Cornwallis's army. The siege began on September 28. At one point during the attack Washington and his staff came under fire as they observed the action. A worried aide suggested to the commanding general that perhaps he should "step back a little." Washington tersely replied: "Colonel Cobb, if you are afraid, you have the liberty to step back."

On October 14 two major outposts guarding the left of the British line fell to French and American attackers, the latter led by Washington's aide Alexander Hamilton. A British counter-attack on October 16 failed to retake them, and later that day a squall forced Cornwallis to abandon a desperate plan to escape across the York River. On October 17, 1781, four years to the day after Saratoga, a red-coated drummer boy climbed atop the British parapet and began beating the call for a truce. Cornwallis sued for peace, and on October 19 the British force of almost 8,000 marched out, their colors cased, to the tune of "The World Turned Upside Down." Cornwallis himself claimed to be too "ill" to appear.

This French engraving shows Lord Cornwallis handing over his sword in surrender at Yorktown, October 19, 1781.

NEGOTIATIONS

Whatever lingering hopes of victory the British may have harbored vanished at Yorktown. "Oh God, it's all over," Lord North groaned at news of the surrender. On February 27, 1782, the House of Commons voted against continuing the war and on March 5 authorized the crown to make peace. On March 20 Lord North resigned and a new ministry was put together of the old friends of the Americans headed by the duke of Rockingham, who had brought about repeal of the Stamp Act. The new colonial minister, Lord Shelburne, became chief minister after Rockingham's death in September and directed the Paris negotiations with American commissioners appointed by the Continental Congress.

The American peace commissioners in Paris were John Adams, John Jay, minister to Spain, Benjamin Franklin, and Henry Laurens. Their difficult task was immediately complicated by the French commitment to Spain. Spain and the United States were both allied with France, but not with each other. America was bound by its alliance to fight on until the French made peace, and the French were bound to help the Spanish recover Gibraltar from England. Unable to deliver Gibraltar, or so the tough-minded Jay reasoned, the French might try to bargain off American land west of the Appalachians in its place. Fearful that the French were angling for a separate peace with the British, Jay persuaded Franklin to play the same game. Ignoring their instructions to consult fully with the French, they agreed to further talks with the British. On November 30, 1782, the talks produced a preliminary treaty with Great Britain. If it violated the spirit of the alliance, it did not violate the strict letter of the treaty with France, for the French minister was notified the day before it was signed, and final agreement still depended on a Franco-British settlement.

THE PEACE OF PARIS   Early in 1783 France and Spain gave up on Gibraltar and reached an armistice with Britain. The Peace of Paris was finally signed on September 3, 1783. In accord with the bargain already struck, Great Britain recognized the independence of the United States and agreed to a Mississippi River boundary to the west. Both the northern and southern borders left ambiguities that would require further definition. Florida, as it turned out, passed back to Spain. The British further granted Americans the "liberty" of fishing off Newfoundland and in the St. Lawrence Gulf, and the right to dry their catches on the un-

Claimed
by
Spain,
Russia,
and
England

HUDSON
BAY

UNEXPLORED

RUSSIANS

Claimed by
England and U.S.

Lake-of-the-Woods

Claimed by
England
and U.S.

NEWFOUND-
LAND

ST. PIERRE
& MIQUELON

MAGDALEN
IS. (France)

NOVA SCOTIA

Boston

New York

UNITED

STATES

LOUISIANA

Mississippi R.

St. Lawrence R.

PACIFIC
OCEAN

MEXICO

Claimed by U.S.
and Spain

Charleston
Savannah

ATLANTIC
OCEAN

FLORIDA

GULF OF MEXICO

CUBA

HISPANIOLA

BRITISH
HONDURAS

HAITI
(France)

NORTH AMERICA,
1783

CENTRAL AMERICA

CARIBBEAN SEA

England   United States

Spain

0   1000 Miles

0   1000 Kilometers

SOUTH AMERICA

settled coasts of Canada. On the matter of pre-revolutionary debts, the best the British could get was a promise that British merchants should "meet with no legal impediment" in seeking to collect them. And on the tender point of Loyalists whose property had been confiscated, the negotiators agreed that Congress would "earnestly recommend" to the states the restoration of confiscated property. Each of the last two points was little more than a face-saving gesture for the British.

THE POLITICAL REVOLUTION

REPUBLICAN IDEOLOGY The Americans had won their War for Independence. Had they undergone a political revolution as well? John Adams offered one answer: "The Revolution was effected before the war commenced. The Revolution was in the minds and hearts of the people. . . . This radical change in the principles, opinions, sentiments, and affections of the people, was the real American Revolution." A struggle for traditional English rights had become a fight for independence in which those rights found expression in governments that were new, yet deeply rooted in the colonial experience and in the prevailing viewpoints of Whiggery and the Enlightenment. Such ideas as the contract theory of government, the sovereignty of the people, the separation of powers, and natural rights found their way quickly, almost automatically, into the new frames of government that were devised while the fight went on—amid other urgent business.

The American Revolution was unique. Unlike France, the acute social observer Alexis de Tocqueville later said, the Americans did not have to "endure a democratic revolution." Not bound by a feudal tradition, Americans had been born free, and they saw their revolution as essentially a defense of their liberty and property against what seemed a tyrannical and corrupt government. Still, the revolutionary controversies forced Americans to formalize their attitudes into a cohesive ideology. Political thinking had to catch up with colonial institutions and practices, but once that process began it carried a momentum of its own.

The very idea of republican government—a balanced polity animated by civic virtue—was a far more radical departure in that day of kings and emperors than it would seem to later generations. Through the lens of republican thinking, Americans began to see themselves in a new light, no longer as the rustic provincials in a backwater of European culture but rather as the embodiment of the classical republican virtue so long praised by philosophers. As free citizens of a republic, Americans would cast off the aristocratic corruptions of the Old World and usher in a new reign of individual liberty and public virtue. Reality, of course, was bound to fall short of such millennial hopes, but the republican ideal served to focus and reinforce the new American vision of itself.

NEW STATE CONSTITUTIONS   At the onset of the fighting every colony experienced the departure of governors and other officials and usually the expulsion of Loyalists from the assemblies, which then assumed power as provincial "congresses" or "conventions." But they were acting as revolutionary bodies without any legal basis for the exercise of authority. In two of the states this presented little difficulty. Connecticut and Rhode Island, which had been virtually little republics as corporate colonies, simply purged their charters of any reference to colonial ties. Massachusetts followed their example until 1780.

In the other states the prevailing notions of social contract and popular sovereignty led to written constitutions which specified the framework and powers of government. One of the lessons of the Revolution, it seemed, had been that the vague body of law and precedent making up the unwritten British constitution was unreliable. Constitution making began even before independence. In May 1776 Congress advised the colonies to set up new governments "under the authority of the people."

The first state constitutions varied mainly in detail. They formed governments much like the colonial administrations, with elected governors and senates instead of appointed governors and councils. Generally they embodied, sometimes explicitly, a separation of powers as a safeguard against abuses, and most included a Bill of Rights which protected the time-honored rights of petition, freedom of speech, trial by jury, freedom from self-incrimination, and the like. Most tended to limit the powers of governors and increase the powers of the legislatures, which had led the people in their quarrels with the colonial governors. Pennsylvania went so far as to eliminate the governor and upper house of the legislature altogether. It had a twelve-man executive council and operated until 1790 with a unicameral legislature limited only by a house of "censors" who reviewed its work every five years.

THE ARTICLES OF CONFEDERATION   The central government, like the state governments, grew out of an extralegal revolutionary body. The Continental Congress exercised governmental powers by common consent and without any constitutional sanction before March 1781. Plans for a permanent frame of government were started very early, however, when on July 12, 1776, a committee headed by John Dickinson produced a draft constitution, the "Articles of Confederation and Perpetual Union." For more than a year Congress debated the articles in between more urgent matters and finally adopted them on November 15, 1777, subject to ratification by all the states.

When the Articles of Confederation took effect in March 1781, they did little more than legalize the status quo. Congress had a multitude of responsibilities but little authority to carry them out. It had full power over foreign affairs and questions of war and peace; it could decide disputes between the states; it had authority over coinage, postal service, and Indian affairs, and responsibility for the government of the western territories. But it had no power to enforce its resolutions and ordinances upon either states or individuals. And it had no power to levy taxes but had to rely on requisitions which state legislatures could ignore at their will.

The states, after their battles with Parliament, were in no mood for a strong central government. The Congress in fact had less power than the colonists had once accepted in Parliament, since it could not regulate interstate and foreign commerce. For certain important acts, moreover, a special majority was required. Nine states had to approve measures dealing with war, privateering, treaties, coinage, finances, or the army and navy. Amendments to the articles required unanimous ratification by the states. The Confederation had neither an executive nor a judicial branch; there was no administrative head of government (only the president of the Congress, chosen annually) and no federal courts.

Yet for all its weaknesses the Confederation government represented the most appropriate structure for the new nation. After all, the Revolution on the battlefields had yet to be won, and the statesmen did not have the luxury of engaging in prolonged and perhaps fratricidal debates over the distribution of power that proposals for other systems would have provoked. There would be time later for modifications.

The Social Revolution

On the general frame of government there was in America a consensus—the forms grew so naturally out of the experience and the ideas of the colonial period. On other issues raised by the Revolution, however, there was conflict among Americans. Just as the Great Awakening had created unforeseen social effects, the revolutionary turmoil allowed outlets for long pent-up frustrations among the lower ranks. What did the Revolution mean to those workers, servants, farmers, and freedmen who participated in the Stamp Act demonstrations, supported the boycotts, idolized Tom Paine, and fought with Washington and Greene?

To many among the laboring ranks, the Revolution was in part intended to remove, not reinforce, the traditional political and social advantages exercised by colonial elites. The more conservative Patriots would have been content to replace royal officials with the rich, the well-born, and the able, and let it go at that.

But more radical elements, in the apt phrase of one historian, raised the question not only of home rule, but of who shall rule at home.

EQUALITY AND ITS LIMITS   The spirit of equality spawned by the Revolution weakened old habits of deference. One Colonel Randolph of Virginia told of being in a tavern when a group of rough farmers entered, spitting and pulling off their muddy boots without regard to the sensibilities of the gentlemen present: "The spirit of independence was converted into equality," Randolph wrote, "and every one who bore arms, esteems himself upon a footing with his neighbors. . . . No doubt each of these men considers himself, in every respect, my equal." No doubt each did.

Participation in the army or militia activated and politicized people who had before taken little interest in politics. The large number of new political opportunities that opened up led more ordinary citizens into participation than ever before. The social base of the new legislatures was much broader than that of the old assemblies.

Men fighting for their liberty found it difficult to justify the denial to other men of the rights of suffrage and representation. The property qualifications for voting, which already admitted an overwhelming majority of white males, were lowered still further. In Pennsylvania, Delaware, North Carolina, Georgia, and Vermont, any taxpayer could vote, although commonly officeholders had to meet higher property requirements. In the state legislatures, new men often replaced older men, some of whom had been Loyalists. More often than not the newcomers were men of lesser property. Some states concentrated much power in a legislature chosen by a wide suffrage, but not even Pennsylvania went quite so far as universal manhood suffrage. Others, like New York and Maryland, took a more conservative stance.

New developments in land tenure that grew out of the Revolution extended the democratic trends of suffrage requirements. Confiscations during the war resulted in the seizure of Tory estates by all the state legislatures. These lands, however, were of small consequence in comparison to the unsettled lands that had formerly been at the disposal of crown and proprietors. Now in the hands of popular assemblies, much of this land went as bonuses to veterans of the war. Western lands, formerly closed by the Proclamation of 1763 and the Quebec Act of 1774, were soon thrown open for settlers.

Elizabeth Freeman, born in Africa around 1742, was sold as a slave to a Massachusetts family. She won her freedom by claiming in court that the "inherent liberty" of all applied to slaves as well.

THE PARADOX OF SLAVERY The revolutionary principles of liberty and equality, moreover, had clear implications for America's enslaved blacks. Jefferson's draft of the Declaration had indicted the king for having violated the "most sacred rights of life and liberty of a distant people" by encouraging the slave trade in the colonies, but the clause was struck out "in complaisance to South Carolina and Georgia." The clause was in fact inaccurate in completely ignoring the implication of American slaveholders and slavetraders in the traffic. After independence all the states except Georgia stopped the importation of slaves, although South Carolina later reopened it.

Black soldiers or sailors were present at most of the major battles, from Lexington to Yorktown; some were on the Loyalist side. Slaves who served in the cause of independence got their freedom and in some cases land bounties. But the British army, which freed probably tens of thousands, was a greater instrument of emancipation than the American forces. Most of the newly freed blacks found their way to Canada or to British colonies in the Caribbean.

In the northern states, which had fewer slaves than the southern, the doctrines of liberty led swiftly to emancipation for all either during the fighting or shortly afterward. South of Pennsylvania the potential consequences of emancipation were so staggering—South Carolina had a black majority—that whites refused to extend the principle of liberty to their slaves. Yet even there slaveholders like Washington, Jefferson, Patrick Henry, and others were troubled. On the slavery issue Jefferson sounded a note of foreboding in his *Notes on Virginia* (1785);

"Indeed I tremble for my country when I reflect that God is just; that his justice cannot sleep forever." But he, like many other white southerners, was riding the tiger and did not know how to dismount.

THE STATUS OF WOMEN   The logic of liberty applied to the status of women as much as to that of blacks, but wrought even less change in their condition. Women had remained essentially confined to the domestic sphere during the eighteenth century. They could not vote or preach or hold office. Few had access to formal education. Although in New England women could own property and execute contracts, in several colonies they could not legally own even their own clothes, and they had no legal rights over their children. Divorces were extremely difficult to obtain.

Yet the revolutionary ferment offered women new opportunities. They joined in prewar campaigns to boycott British goods —in fact their support was essential to success in that effort. The war also drew women at least temporarily into new roles. They plowed fields, kept shop, and melted down pots and pans to make shot. Women also served the armies in various ways, such as handling supplies and serving as spies or couriers. Wives often followed their husbands to camp, where they nursed the wounded and sick, cooked and washed for the able, and frequently buried the dead. On occasion women took their places in the firing line.

Early in the struggle, on March 31, 1776, Abigail Adams, one of the most learned, spirited, and principled women of the time,

Abigail Adams, in a portrait by Gilbert Stuart. She advised her husband, John: "Do not put such unlimited power into the hands of the Husbands."

wrote her husband, John: "In the new Code of Laws which I suppose it will be necessary for you to make I desire you would remember the Ladies. . . . Do not put such unlimited power into the hands of the Husbands." Since men were "Naturally Tyrannical," she stressed, "why then, not put it out of the power of the vicious and the Lawless to use us with cruelty and indignity. . . ." Otherwise, "the Ladies" would "foment a Rebellion, and will not hold ourselves bound by any Laws in which we have no voice, or Representation."

Husband John, who once recorded in his diary that Abigail was "a constant feast . . . prudent, modest, delicate, soft, sensible, obliging, and active," expressed surprise that women might be discontented, but he clearly knew the privileges enjoyed by males and was determined to retain them: "Depend upon it, we know better than to repeal our Masculine systems." The supposedly more liberal Thomas Jefferson was of one mind with Adams on this matter. When asked about women's voting rights, he replied that "the tender breasts of ladies were not formed for political convulsion."

The legal status of women thus did not benefit dramatically from the equalitarian doctrine unleashed by the Revolution. True, in Pennsylvania and parts of New England, divorces were easier to obtain after the Revolution. One Connecticut woman, for instance, brought suit against her husband on the grounds that he had "rendered her life miserable by frequent beating with brutal violence, almost constant intoxication and lascivious conduct with several lewd women." But married women in most of the new states still forfeited control of their own property to their husbands, and women gained no political rights. Although some limited advances were made in education, it was a slow process. The chief contribution of the Revolution seems to have been less in substantive gains for women than in a growing willingness on the part of a few spirited women, such as Abigail Adams, to challenge old assumptions.

FREEDOM OF RELIGION   The Revolution also set in motion a transition from the toleration of religious dissent to a complete freedom of religion in the separation of church and state. The Anglican church, established in five colonies and parts of two others, was especially vulnerable because of its association with the crown and because dissenters outnumbered Anglicans in all the states except Virginia. And all but Virginia removed tax support for the church before the fighting was over. In 1776, the Virginia Declaration of Rights guaranteed the free exercise of religion, and in 1786 the Virginia Statute of Religious Freedom (written by Thomas Jefferson) declared that "no man shall be compelled to frequent or support any religious worship, place or ministry whatsoever," that none should in any way suffer for his religious opinions and beliefs, "but that all men shall be free to profess and by argument to maintain, their opinions in matters of religion."

New England, with its Puritan heritage, was in less haste to end state tax support for the Congregational church, although the rules were already being relaxed enough by the 1720s to let Quakers and Baptists assign their tax support to their own churches. New Hampshire finally discontinued tax support for its churches in 1817, Connecticut in 1818, Maine in 1820, and Massachusetts in 1833. Certain religious requirements for office-holding lingered here and there on the law books: Massachusetts and Maryland required a declaration of Christian faith; Delaware had a Trinitarian test; New Jersey and the Carolinas held that officeholders must be Protestants. But in most cases these requirements disappeared before many more years.

In churches as well as in government the Revolution set off a period of constitution making, as some of the first national church bodies emerged. In 1784 the Methodists, who at first

The Congregational church developed a national body in the early nineteenth century, and Lemuel Haynes, depicted here, was its first black preacher.

were an offshoot of the Anglicans, came together in a general conference at Baltimore. The Anglican church, rechristened Episcopal, gathered in a series of meetings which by 1789 had united the various dioceses in a federal union; in 1789 the Presbyterians also held their first general assembly in Philadelphia. The following year, 1790, the Catholic church had its first bishop in the United States when John Carroll was named bishop of Baltimore. Other churches would follow in the process of organizing on a national basis.

EMERGENCE OF AN AMERICAN CULTURE

For all the weakness of the central government, the Revolution generated a budding sense of common nationality. The Revolution taught many Americans to think "continentally," as Alexander Hamilton put it. As early as the Stamp Act Congress of 1765, Christopher Gadsden, leader of the Charleston radicals, had said: "There ought to be no New England man, no New Yorker, known on the Continent; but all of us Americans." In the first Continental Congress Patrick Henry asserted that such a sense of identity had come to pass: "The distinctions between Virginians, Pennsylvanians, New Yorkers, and New Englanders are no more. I am not a Virginian but an American."

ARTS IN THE NEW NATION   The Revolution provided the first generation of native artists with inspirational subjects. It also filled them with high expectations that individual freedom would release creative energies and vitalize both commerce and the arts. At the Princeton commencement in 1771, two graduating seniors and budding young authors, Philip Freneau and Hugh Henry Brackenridge, presented "A Poem on the Rising Glory of America" in which they reviewed once again the westward transit of culture and foretold in America "the final stage . . . of high invention and wond'rous art, which not the ravages of time shall waste." The Revolution itself raised expectations yet higher. As David Ramsay put it in his *History of the American Revolution* (1789), the conflict with England "gave a spring to the active powers of the inhabitants, and set them on thinking, speaking and acting, in a line far beyond that to which they had been accustomed." The result was a sudden efflorescence of the arts.

If, as it happened, no American artist of the time quite measured up to the highest expectations, many of them chose patri-

Surrender of Lord Cornwallis. *John Trumbull completed his painting of the pivotal British surrender at Yorktown in 1794.*

otic themes and celebrated the new nation. Ironically, the best American painters of the time spent all or most of the Revolution in England, studying with Benjamin West of Pennsylvania and John Singleton Copley of Massachusetts, both of whom had set up shop in London before the outbreak of hostilities. Even John Trumbull, who had served in the siege of Boston and the Saratoga campaign, somehow managed a visit to London during the war before returning. Later he highlighted patriotic themes in numerous canvases celebrating scenes from the Revolution. Similarly, Charles Willson Peale, who fought at Trenton and Princeton and survived the winter at Valley Forge, produced a virtual portrait gallery of Revolutionary War figures. Over twenty-three years he painted George Washington seven times from life and produced in all sixty portraits of the general.

EDUCATION The most lasting effect of postwar nationalism may well have been its mark on education. The colonies had founded a total of nine colleges, but after the Revolution, eight more sprang up in the 1780s and six in the 1790s. Several of the revolutionary state constitutions provided for state universities. Georgia's was the first chartered, in 1785, but the University of North Carolina (chartered in 1789) was the first to open, in 1795.

Even more importantly, the Revolution provided the initial impetus for state-supported public school systems. Many of the founders believed that the survival of the new nation depended upon instilling in the public an appreciation for the fragility of republican government and its utter dependence on private and civic virtue. They came to look upon public schools as the best agencies for such moral and civic development. In such schools, as Pennsylvania's Benjamin Rush maintained, American children would not only become literate but would also learn to choose the public good over all private interests and concerns. Jefferson agreed that public education would serve as the very "keystone of our arch of government," and in 1779 he introduced his "Bill for the More General Diffusion of Knowledge" into the Virginia Assembly. It included an elaborate plan for the state to fund elementary schools for all free persons, and higher education for the talented, up through a state university. Several years later Samuel Adams proposed the same in Massachusetts. Yet almost every one of these schemes for public schools came to nought. Wealthy critics opposed spending tax money on schools that would mingle their sons "in a vulgar and suspicious communion" with the masses. The spread of public schools would have to wait for a more democratic climate.

MISSION   In a special sense American nationalism was the embodiment of an idea of mission. Many people, at least since the time of the Pilgrims, had thought America to be singled out for a special identity, a special mission. John Winthrop had referred to the Puritan commonwealth as representing a "city upon a hill," and to Jonathan Edwards, God had singled out America as "the glorious renovator of the world." Still later John Adams proclaimed the opening of America "a grand scheme and design in Providence for the illumination and the emancipation of the slavish part of mankind all over the earth." The mission had subtly changed, but it was still there. It was now a call to lead the way for all mankind toward liberty and equality. Meanwhile, however, Americans had to come to grips with more immediate problems created by their new nationhood.

FURTHER READING

The Revolutionary War is the subject of many good surveys. Don Higginbotham's *The War of American Independence* (1983)° and Robert Middlekauff's *The Glorious Cause: The American Revolution, 1763–1789* (1982)° are especially useful. Much good work has appeared recently on the social history of the Revolutionary War. See John W. Shy's *A People Numerous and Armed* (1976)°; Charles Royster's *A Revolutionary People at War* (1979)°; and Lawrence D. Cress's *Citizens in Arms* (1982).

Why some Americans remained loyal to the crown is the subject of Robert M. Calhoon's *The Loyalists in Revolutionary America, 1760–1781* (1973) and Mary Beth Norton's *The British-Americans* (1972).°

Efforts to trace the social effects of the Revolution include Jackson Turner Main's *The Social Structure of Revolutionary America* (1965); Rhys Isaac's *The Transformation of Virginia, 1740–1790* (1982)°; and Gary Nash's *The Urban Crucible* (1984).° A bold analysis of the Revolution's transforming implications is Gordon Wood's *The Radicalism of the American Revolution* (1992). One of the few community-level studies of Revolutionary change is Robert A. Gross's *The Minutemen and Their World* (1976).° Mary Beth Norton's *Liberty's Daughters* (1980)° and Linda K. Kerber's *Women of the Republic* (1980)° document the role women played in securing independence. Joy D. Buel and Richard Buel's *The Way of Duty* (1984)° shows the impact of the Revolution on one New England family. Gary Nash's *Forging Freedom: The Formation of Philadelphia's Black Community, 1720–1840* (1988)° traces the impact of the Revolution on urban blacks.

The standard introduction to the diplomacy of the Revolutionary era remains Samuel F. Bemis's *The Diplomacy of the American Revolution* (1935). Jonathan R. Dull's *A Diplomatic History of the American Revolution* (1985)° is especially useful in explaining European diplomacy.

° These books are available in paperback editions.

6 ⁂

SHAPING A FEDERAL UNION

Speaking to fellow graduates at the Harvard commencement in 1787, young John Quincy Adams lamented "this critical period" when the country was struggling to establish itself as a new nation. Historians thereafter used his phrase to designate the years when the United States operated under the Articles of Confederation, 1781–1787. The temptation for many has been to focus on the weaknesses of the Confederation and neglect the nation's major achievements during the so-called "critical period."

The Congress of the Confederation, to be sure, had little governmental authority. It could only request money from the states; it could make treaties with foreign countries but could not enforce them; it could borrow money but lacked the means to ensure repayment. The Congress was virtually helpless to cope with the postwar problems of diplomacy and depression, problems that would have challenged the resources of a much stronger government. It was not easy to find men of stature to serve in such a body and often hard to gather a quorum of those who did. Yet in spite of its handicaps the Confederation Congress somehow managed to keep afloat and to lay important foundations for the future. It concluded the Peace of Paris in 1783, created the first executive departments, and formulated principles of land distribution and territorial government that guided expansion all the way to the Pacific.

Throughout most of the War for Independence the Congress remained distrustful of executive power. It assigned administrative duties to its committees and thereby imposed a painful burden on conscientious members. At one time or another John

Adams, for instance, served on some eighty committees. In 1781, however, anticipating ratification of the Articles of Confederation, Congress began to set up three departments: Foreign Affairs, Finance, and War. Each was to have a single head responsible to Congress. For superintendent of finance Congress chose Robert Morris, a prominent Philadelphia merchant who brought a semblance of order to federal accounts. The other departments had less success and indeed lacked executive heads for long periods. The first secretary for foreign affairs, Robert R. Livingston, left the post in May 1783 and was not replaced by John Jay until the following summer. Given time and stability, however, Congress and the department heads might have evolved something like the parliamentary cabinet system. As it turned out, these agencies were the forerunners of the government departments established under the Constitution.

FINANCE As yet, however, there was neither president nor prime minister, only the presiding officer of Congress and its secretary, Charles Thomson, who served continuously from 1774 to 1789. The closest thing to an executive head of the Confederation was Robert Morris, who as superintendent of finance in the final years of the war became the most influential figure in the government, and who had ideas of making both himself and the Confederation more powerful. He envisioned a coherent program of taxation and debt management to make the government financially stable.

As the foundation of his plan, Morris secured in 1781 a congressional charter for the Bank of North America, which would hold federal deposits, lend money to the government, and issue bank notes that would provide a stable currency. But his program depended ultimately on a secure income for the Confederation government, and it proved impossible to win the unanimous approval of the states for the necessary amendments. Local interests and the fear of a central authority—a fear strengthened by the recent quarrels with king and Parliament—hobbled action. Consequently, the Confederation never did put its finances in order. The Continental currency quickly proved worthless, and it was never redeemed. The debt, domestic and foreign, grew from $11 million to $28 million as Congress paid off citizens' and soldiers' claims. Each year Congress ran a deficit on its operating expenses.

LAND POLICY The one source from which Congress might hope ultimately to draw an independent income was the sale of western lands, but throughout the Confederation period that income remained more a fleeting promise than an accomplished fact. The Confederation nevertheless dealt more effectively with the western lands than with anything else. There Congress had direct authority, at least on paper. Thinly populated by Indians, Frenchmen, and a growing number of American squatters, the region north of the Ohio River had long been the site of overlapping claims by colonies and speculators. In 1784 Virginia completed its cession of lands north of the Ohio, and by 1786 all states had abandoned their claims in the area except for a 120-mile strip along Lake Erie, which Connecticut held until 1800 as its "Western Reserve."

As early as 1779 Congress had decided not to treat the western lands as colonies. The delegates resolved instead that western lands ceded by the states "shall be . . . formed into distinct Republican states," equal in all respects to other states. Between 1784 and 1787 policies for western development emerged in three major ordinances of the Confederation Congress. These documents, which rank among its greatest achievements—and among the most important in American history—set precedents that the United States followed in its future expansion. Thomas Jefferson's inclination was to grant self-government to western territories from an early stage, when settlers would meet and choose their own officials. Under Jefferson's ordinance of 1784, when a territory's population equaled that of the smallest existing state, it would achieve full statehood.

In the Land Ordinance of 1785 the delegates outlined a plan of surveys and sales that eventually stamped a rectangular pattern on much of the nation's surface. Wherever Indian titles had been extinguished, the Northwest was to be surveyed into townships six miles square along east-west and north-south lines. Each township in turn was divided into thirty-six lots (or sections), each one-mile square (or 640 acres). The 640-acre sections were to be auctioned for no less than $1 per acre or $640 total. Such terms favored land speculators, of course, since few humble folk had that much money or were able to work that much land. In later years new land laws would make smaller lots available at lower prices, but in 1785 Congress confronted an empty treasury. In each township, however, Congress did reserve the income from the sixteenth section for the support of schools—a significant departure at a time when public schools were rare.

Spurred by the plans for land sales and settlement, Congress drafted a more specific frame of territorial government to replace Jefferson's ordinance of 1784. The new plan backed off from the commitment to early self-government. Because of the

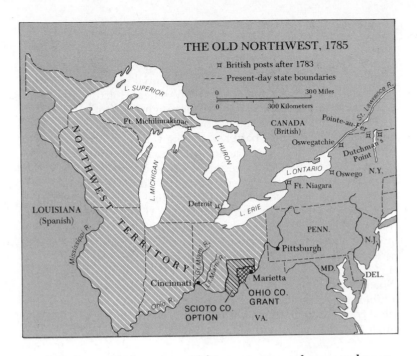

THE OLD NORTHWEST, 1785

¤ British posts after 1783
--- Present-day state boundaries

L. SUPERIOR

Ft. Michilimakinac

NORTHWEST TERRITORY

L. MICHIGAN

L. HURON

CANADA
(British)

Pointe-au-Fer

St. Lawrence R.

Oswegatchie

Dutchman's
Point

L. ONTARIO

¤ Oswego   N.Y.

¤ Ft. Niagara

Detroit

L. ERIE

LOUISIANA
(Spanish)

Mississippi R.

PENN.

Pittsburgh

N.J.

St. Marys R.

Gt. Miami R.

MD.

DEL.

Cincinnati

Marietta

OHIO CO.
GRANT

Ohio R.

SCIOTO CO.
OPTION

VA.

0   300 Miles
0   300 Kilometers

trouble that might be expected from squatters who were clamoring for free land, the Northwest Ordinance of 1787 required a period of colonial tutelage. At first the territory fell subject to a governor, a secretary, and three judges, all chosen by Congress. When any territory in the Northwest region had 5,000 free male adults it could choose an assembly, and Congress would name a governing council from names proposed by the assembly. The governor would have a veto and so would Congress. The resemblance to the old royal colonies is clear, but there were two significant differences. For one, the Ordinance anticipated statehood when any territory's population reached 60,000. For another, it included a bill of rights which guaranteed religious freedom, proportional representation, trial by jury, habeas corpus, and the application of common law. And finally, the Ordinance excluded slavery permanently from the Northwest. This proved a fateful decision. As the progress of emancipation in the existing states gradually freed all slaves above the Mason-Dixon line, the Ohio River boundary of the Old Northwest extended the line between freedom and slavery all the way to the Mississippi.

The lands south of the Ohio River followed a different process of development. Title to the western lands remained with Georgia, North Carolina, and Virginia for the time being, but settlement proceeded at a far more rapid pace during and after the Revolution, despite the Indians' fierce resentment of encroachments on their hunting grounds. Substantial population centers grew up in Kentucky and along the Watauga, Holston, and Cumberland Rivers, as far west as Nashborough (Nashville).

Indian claims were trampled by the new settlers. The Iroquois and Cherokees, badly battered during the Revolution, were in no position to resist encroachments. During the mid-1780s the Iroquois were forced to cede land in western New York and Pennsylvania, and the Cherokees gave up all claims in South Carolina, much of western North Carolina, and large portions of present-day Kentucky and Tennessee. At the same time, the major Ohio tribes gave up their claim to most of Ohio, except for a chunk bordering the western part of Lake Erie. The Creeks, pressed by Georgia to cede portions of their lands in 1784–1785, went to war in the summer of 1786 with covert aid from Spanish Florida. But when Spanish support lapsed, the Creek chief finally struck a bargain in 1791 that gave the Creeks favorable trade arrangements with the United States but did not restore the lost lands.

TRADE AND THE ECONOMY   In its economic life, as in planning westward expansion, the young nation dealt vigorously with the difficult problems created by war. Congress had little to do with achievements in the economy, but neither could it bear the blame for a depression that devastated the country for several years during the transition to independence, the result of the war and separation from the British Empire. In New England and much of the backcountry, fighting seldom interrupted the tempo of farming, and the producers of foodstuffs especially benefited from rising prices and wartime demands. The southern Tidewater suffered a loss of slave labor, much of it carried off by the British. Returns from indigo and naval stores declined with the loss of British bounties, but in the long run rice and tobacco profited from an enlarged foreign market for their products.

Merchants suffered far more wrenching adjustments during the Revolution than the farmers. Cut out of the British mercantile system, they had to find new outlets for their trade. Circumstances that impoverished some enriched those who financed privateers, supplied the armies on both sides, and hoarded precious goods while demand and prices soared. By the end of the war a strong sentiment for free trade had developed in both Britain and America. In the memorable year 1776, the Scottish economist Adam Smith published *The Wealth of Nations*, a classic manifesto against mercantilism. Some British statesmen embraced the new gospel of free trade, but the public and Parliament still clung to mercantilism for many years to come.

British trade with the United States resumed after 1783. American ships were allowed to deliver American products and return to the United States with British goods, but they could not carry British goods anywhere else. The pent-up demand for familiar goods created a vigorous market in exports to America, fueled by British credits and the hard money that had come into the new nation from foreign aid, the expenditures of foreign armies, or wartime trade and privateering. The result was a quick cycle of boom and bust, a buying spree followed by a money shortage and economic troubles that lasted several years.

In colonial days the chronic trade deficit with Britain had been offset by the influx of coins from trade with the West Indies. Now American ships found themselves legally excluded from the British West Indies. But the islands still demanded wheat, fish, lumber, and other products from the mainland, and American shippers had not lost their talent for smuggling; by 1787 their seaports were flourishing more than ever. By 1790 American commerce and exports had far outrun the trade of the colonies. American merchants had more ships than before the war. Farm exports were twice what they had been. Although most of the exports were the products of American forests, fields, and fisheries, during and after the war more Americans had turned to small-scale manufacturing— shoes, textiles, soap—mainly for domestic markets.

DIPLOMACY   The achievements of the flourishing young nation are more visible in hindsight than they were at the time. Until 1787 the shortcomings and failures of the Confederation remained far more apparent—and the advocates of a stronger central government were extremely vocal on the subject. In diplomacy, there remained the nagging problems of relations with Great Britain and Spain, both of which still kept military posts on United States soil and intrigued with Indians and white settlers in the West. The British, despite the peace treaty of 1783, held on to a string of forts along the northern frontier. From these they kept a hand in the fur trade and a degree of influence with the Indian tribes whom they were suspected of stirring up to make sporadic attacks on American settlers.

Another major irritant was the confiscation of Loyalist property. The peace treaty obligated Congress to stop confiscations, to guarantee immunity to Loyalists for twelve months during

John Adams, portrayed here while serving as United States ambassador to England.

which they could return and wind up their affairs, and to recommend that the states return confiscated property. Persecutions, even lynchings, of Loyalists still occurred until after the end of the war. Some Loyalists returned unmolested, however, and once again took up their lives in their former homes. By the end of 1787, moreover, all the states had rescinded those laws discriminating against former Tories that were in conflict with the peace treaty.

The British refused even to dispatch an ambassador to the new nation before 1791. As early as 1785, however, the United States took the initiative by sending over John Adams as ambassador to Great Britain. He was politely received by George III himself, but spent three years in futile efforts to settle disputes over the forts, debts, property rights of Loyalists, and trade concessions in the British West Indies.

With Spain the chief issues were the southern boundary and the right to navigate the Mississippi. According to the preliminary treaty with Britain, the United States claimed as its traditional boundary a line running eastward from the mouth of the Yazoo River. The American treaty with Britain had also specified the right to navigate the Mississippi River to its mouth, but the river was entirely within Spanish Louisiana in its lower reaches. The right to navigation assumed importance because of the growing settlements in Kentucky and Tennessee, but in 1784 Louisiana's Spanish governor closed the river to American commerce. He also began to intrigue with the Creeks, Choctaws, Chickasaws, and other Indians of the Southwest against the frontiersmen, and with the frontiersmen against the United States. In 1785 the Spanish government sent an ambassador to the United States who entered into lengthy but fruitless negotiations with John Jay, the secretary for foreign affairs. The issue of American access to the lower Mississippi remained unsettled for nearly another decade.

THE CONFEDERATION'S PROBLEMS   The problems of trans-Appalachian settlers, however, were of remote interest to most Americans. Of greater concern were protection for infant American industries and the currency shortage. Mechanics and artisans who were developing exports ranging from crude iron nails to the fine silver bowls of Paul Revere were frustrated by British policies excluding them from British markets. In retaliation, they sought from the states tariffs against foreign goods that competed with theirs. The country would be on its way to economic independence, they argued, if only the money that flowed into the country were invested in domestic manufactures instead of being paid out for foreign goods. Nearly all the states gave some preference to American goods, but the lack of consistency in their laws put them at cross purposes, and so urban mechanics along with merchants were drawn into the movement demanding a stronger central government in the interest of uniform regulation.

The shortage of cash gave rise also to more immediate demands for paper currency as legal tender, for postponement of tax and debt payments, and for laws to "stay" the foreclosure of mortgages. Farmers, who had profited during the war, found themselves squeezed by depressed crop prices and mounting debts while merchants sorted out and opened up their new trade routes. Creditors demanded hard money, but it was in short supply—and paper money was both scarce and virtually worthless after the depreciation of the Continental currency. The result was an outcry among debtor groups for relief, and around 1785 the demand for new paper money became the most divisive issue in state politics. In 1785–1786 seven states issued paper money. In spite of the cries of calamity at the time, the money served positively as a means of credit to hard-pressed farmers through state loans on farm mortgages. It was variously used to fund state debts and to pay off the claims of veterans.

SHAYS'S REBELLION   But many Americans—especially bankers and merchants—were horrified by such inflationary policies. Developments in Massachusetts provided the final proof (some said) that the country was poised on the brink of anarchy: Shays's Rebellion. After 1780 Massachusetts had remained in the grip of a rigidly conservative regime. Ever-larger poll and land taxes were levied to pay off a heavy debt, held mainly by wealthy creditors in Boston, and the taxes fell most heavily upon beleaguered farmers and the poor in general. When the legislature adjourned in 1786 without providing either paper money or any other relief from taxes and debts, three western counties erupted into spontaneous revolt. Armed bands closed the courts and prevented foreclosures, and a ragtag "army" of some 1,200 farmers led by Captain Daniel Shays, a destitute farmer and "brave and good" war veteran, advanced upon the federal arsenal at Springfield in January 1787.

A small militia force, however, scattered Shays's men with a single volley that left four dead. General Benjamin Lincoln, arriving soon after with reinforcements from Boston, routed the remaining Shaysites. The rebels nevertheless had a victory of sorts. The state legislature omitted direct taxes the following year, lowered court fees, and exempted clothing, household goods, and tools from the debt process. But a more important consequence was the impetus the rebellion gave to conservatism and nationalism.

Rumors, at times deliberately inflated, greatly exaggerated the extent of this pathetic rebellion of desperate men. Stories accusing them of seeking to pillage the wealthy horrified those whom New York's John Jay called the "better kind of people." The uprising seemed to provide an ominous example of even greater turmoil. "There are combustibles in every State," Washington wrote, "which a spark might set fire to." Panic set in among the republic's elite. New York's Gouverneur Morris was typically blunt: "The mob begin to think and reason. Poor reptiles! They bask in the sun and ere noon they will bite, depend upon it. The gentry begin to fear this." In a letter to Jefferson, Abigail Adams was equally anxious. She tarred the Shaysites as "Ignorant, wrestless, desperadoes, without conscience or principals . . . mobish insurgents [who] are for sapping the foundation" of the struggling young government. Jefferson disagreed. If Adams and others were overly critical of Shays's Rebellion, Jefferson was, if anything, too complacent. From his post in Paris, where one of history's great civil bloodbaths would soon occur, he wrote to a friend back home: "The tree of liberty must be refreshed from time to time with the blood of patriots and tyrants." Abigail Adams was so infuriated by Jefferson's position that she stopped corresponding with him for months.

CALLS FOR A STRONGER GOVERNMENT   Shays's Rebellion convinced many political leaders that the Articles of Confederation were incapable of providing an effective basis for the new republican government. Advocates of a stronger central authority already had gained momentum from the adversities of the times. Self-interest frequently led bankers, merchants, and mechanics to promote a stronger central government, and many public-spirited men saw it as the only alternative to anarchy. Gradually they were breaking down the ingrained fear of a tyrannical central authority with the evidence that tyranny might come from other quarters.

By the mid-1780s, in fact, several prominent political spokesmen had become convinced that the new state governments were being run by uneducated entrepreneurs pursuing selfish economic and petty political interests. Men of humble origins and parochial points of view were displacing the "wise and virtuous" from seats of power. And such inexperienced and frequently uncouth lawmakers were passing an avalanche of legislation merely to serve particular interest groups and constituents rather than the general welfare. They were printing excessive amounts of paper money and passing "stay" laws preventing judicial action against debtors. Such developments led many of the revolutionary leaders to revise their assessment of American character. "We have, probably," concluded George Washington in 1786, "had too good an opinion of human nature in forming our confederation." The following year James Madison reported to Jefferson that America was displaying "symptoms . . . truly alarming, which have tainted the faith of most orthodox republicans." People were stretching the meaning of liberty far beyond what he and others had envisioned. He found a "spirit of *locality*" rampant in the state legislatures that was destroying the "aggregate interests of the community." And he saw people taking the law and other people's property into their own hands.

For these reasons, well before the Shaysite rebellion in New England, nationalists were demanding a convention to revise the Articles of Confederation. Noah Webster, of dictionary fame, moaned in 1785 that "Our pretended union is but a name, and our confederation a cobweb." Animated by similar concerns, commissioners from Virginia and Maryland had met at Mount Vernon in March 1785 upon Washington's invitation to settle outstanding questions about the navigation of the Potomac and Chesapeake Bay. The delegates agreed on interstate cooperation, and at Madison's suggestion invited all thirteen states to send delegates for a general discussion of commercial problems.

Representatives from only five appeared at the Annapolis Convention in September 1786. Apparent failure was turned into success, however, by the alert New York delegate, Alexander Hamilton, who presented a resolution for still another convention in Philadelphia to consider all measures necessary "to render the constitution of the Federal Government adequate to the exigencies of the Union."

ADOPTING THE CONSTITUTION

THE CONSTITUTIONAL CONVENTION After stalling for several months, Congress on February 21, 1787, also passed a resolution endorsing a convention "for the sole and express purpose of revising the Articles of Confederation." By then five states had already named delegates; before the meeting six more states had acted. Rhode Island kept aloof throughout, leading critics to label it "Rogue Island." Twenty-nine delegates began work in Philadelphia on May 25. Altogether seventy-three men were elected by the state legislatures, fifty-five attended at one time or another, and after four months thirty-nine signed the Constitution they had drafted.

The document's durability and flexibility testify to the remarkable quality of the men who made it. Thomas Jefferson, who was still serving abroad as minister to France, later referred to the convention as "an assembly of demigods." The delegates were surprisingly young—forty-two was the average age. But they were even more surprisingly mature, audacious, and farsighted. Only two were small farmers. Most were planters, merchants, lawyers, judges, bankers—many of them widely read in history, law, and political philosophy, familiar with the writings of Locke and Montesquieu, and at the same time practical men of experience, tested in the fires of the Revolution. Twenty-one had worn uniforms in the conflict, seven had been state governors, and most of them had served in the Continental Congress. "Experience must be our only guide," insisted Pennsylvania's John Dickinson. "Reason may mislead us."

The magisterial Washington served as presiding officer but participated little in the debates. Eighty-one-year-old Benjamin Franklin, the oldest and most infirm delegate, also said little from the floor but did provide a wealth of experience, wit, and common sense. More active in the debates were the thirty-six-year-old James Madison, the ablest political philosopher in the group; Massachusetts's lanky, dapper Elbridge Gerry, a Harvard

James Madison was only thirty-six when he assumed a major role in the drafting of the Constitution. This miniature is by Charles Willson Peale (c. 1783).

graduate and merchant who earned the nickname "Old Grumbletonian" because, as John Adams once said, he "opposed everything he did not propose"; George Mason, the prickly author of the Virginia Bill of Rights and a planter and slaveholder who was burdened by gout, chronic indigestion, and a deep-rooted suspicion of all government; the witty, eloquent, and arrogant New York aristocrat, Gouverneur Morris; Marylander Luther Martin, the ardent spokesman for states' rights, whose speeches were made livelier by his frequent drunkenness; Scots-born James Wilson of Pennsylvania, one of the shrewdest lawyers in the new nation and next in importance at the convention only to Washington and Madison; and Roger Sherman of Connecticut, a self-trained lawyer adept at negotiating compromises. John Adams, like Jefferson, was serving abroad. Also conspicuously absent during most of the convention was thirty-two-year-old Alexander Hamilton, the staunch nationalist who regretfully went home when the two other New York delegates walked out because of their states'-rights principles.

The delegates spent four sweltering months fighting flies, the humidity, and each other. They worked earnestly and with a sense of urgency, five to six hours a day, six days a week, hammering out the compromises embedded in the Constitution. Their differences on political philosophy for the most part fell within a narrow range. On certain fundamentals they generally agreed: that government derived its just powers from the consent of the people, but that society must be protected from the tyranny of the majority; that the people at large must have a voice in their government, but that checks and balances must be provided to keep any one group from dominating power; that a stronger central authority was essential, but that all power was subject to abuse. They assumed with Madison that if people "were angels, no government would be necessary." Even the best of people were selfish by nature, they believed, and therefore government could not be founded upon a trust in good will and virtue. Yet by carefully checking power with power, the Founding Fathers hoped to devise institutions that could somehow constrain the inevitable sinfulness of individuals and channel some of it on behalf of the public good. Designing such a balanced government was not an easy process, as Washington recognized in July when he wrote to the departed Hamilton: "I almost despair of seeing a favourable issue to the proceedings of our Convention. . . ." But he and the others persevered, and the document they produced was as extraordinary as it was unexpected.

THE VIRGINIA AND NEW JERSEY PLANS   At the outset the delegates decided to meet behind closed doors in order to discourage outside pressures and theatrical speeches to the galleries. The secrecy of the proceedings was remarkably well kept, and knowledge of the debates comes mainly from Madison's extensive notes. Small of stature—barely over five feet tall—and frail in health, Madison was a shy, studious bachelor descended from wealthy, slave-owning Virginia planters. Crowds made him nervous, and he hated to use his high-pitched voice in public, much less in open debate.

But the Princeton graduate who had found the practice of law too "coarse and dry" possessed a keen, agile mind with a voracious appetite for learning. He proved to be the energizing force at the convention, persuading others by the convincing eloquence of his arguments. "Every person seems to acknowledge his greatness," wrote one delegate. Another commented that he possessed a "calm expression, blue eyes—and looked like a thinking man." Madison arrived in Philadelphia with trunks full of books and a head full of ideas, and he set about drafting the proposals that came to be called the "Virginia Plan," presented on May 29.

The Virginia plan called for separate legislative, executive, and judicial branches, and a truly national government whose laws would be binding upon individual citizens as well as upon states. Congress would be divided into two houses, a lower house chosen by popular vote and an upper house chosen by the lower house from nominees of the state legislatures. Congress could disallow state laws under the plan and would itself define the extent of its and the states' authority.

On June 15 William Paterson submitted the "New Jersey Plan," which kept the existing equal representation of states in a unicameral Congress, but gave the Congress power to levy taxes, regulate commerce, and name a plural executive (with no veto) and a Supreme Court. The different plans presented the convention with two major issues: whether to amend the Articles of Confederation or draft an entirely new document, and whether to apportion congressional representation by population or by states. On the first point the convention voted to work toward a national government as envisioned by the Virginians. Regarding the powers of this government there was little disagreement save in detail. Experience with the Articles had persuaded the delegates that an effective central government, as distinguished from a confederation, needed the power to levy taxes, to regulate commerce, to raise an army and navy, and to make laws binding upon individual citizens. The lessons of the 1780s suggested to them, moreover, that in the interest of order and uniformity the states must be denied certain powers: to issue money, to void contracts, to make treaties or wage war, to levy tariffs or export duties.

But furious disagreements then arose. The first clash in the convention involved the issue of representation, and it was solved by the "Great Compromise," sometimes called the "Connecticut Compromise," offered by Roger Sherman. The more populous states won apportionment by population in the House of Representatives; the states that sought to protect state power won equality in the Senate, but with the vote there by individuals and not by states.

An equally contentious struggle ensued between northern and southern delegates over slavery, an omen of future sectional controversies. Slavery, Madison's secretary noted, was a "distracting question" rather than a compelling moral dilemma. Few if any of the framers even considered the possibility of abolishing slavery in those states—mostly southern—where it was still legal. In this respect they reflected the prevailing attitudes of their time. Most agreed with South Carolina's canny John Rutledge, described by the French minister as "the proudest and most imperious man in the United States," when he asserted: "Religion and humanity [have] nothing to do with this [slavery] question. Interest alone is the governing principle of nations." The interest of southern delegates, with slaves so numerous in their states, dictated that slaves be counted as part of the population in determining the number of representatives. Northerners were happy enough to have slaves counted in deciding each state's share of direct taxes but not for purposes of representation. The delegates, with little dissent, agreed in a compromise to count three-fifths of the slaves as a basis for apportioning both representatives and direct taxes. In the final version, the framers carefully avoided the odious word "slavery," which did not appear in the Constitution until the Thirteenth Amendment (1865) abolished the "peculiar institution" by name.

If the delegates found the slavery issue distracting, they considered any discussion of the legal or political role of women under the new Constitution irrelevant. The Revolutionary rhetoric of liberty prompted a few women to demand political equality. "The men say we have no business" with politics, Eliza Wilkinson of South Carolina observed, "but I won't have it thought that because we are the weaker sex as to bodily strength we are capable of nothing more than domestic concerns. They won't even allow us liberty of thought, and that is all I want." Her plea, however, fell on deaf ears. There was never any formal discussion of women's rights at the convention. The new nationalism still defined politics and government as outside the realm of female endeavor.

THE SEPARATION OF POWERS   The details of governmental structure, while causing disagreement, occasioned far less trouble than the basic issues pitting the large and small states, the northern and southern states against each other. Existing state constitutions, several of which already separated powers among legislative, executive, and judicial branches, set an example which reinforced the convention's resolve to disperse power with checks and balances. Some delegates displayed a thumping disdain for any democratizing of the political system. Hamilton called the people "a great beast," and Massachusetts's Elbridge Gerry asserted that most of the nation's problems "flow from an excess of democracy." Roger Sherman likewise insisted that the people "should have as little to do as may be about the Government."

These elitist views were accommodated by the Constitution's mixed legislative system, which acknowledged the "genius of the people," as George Mason phrased it, but allowed direct popular choice of just one chamber of the Congress. The lower house was designed to be closest to the voters, who elected it every two years. The House of Representatives would be, according to Mason, "the grand repository of the democratic principle of the Government." Its members should "sympathize with their constituents, should think as they think, & feel as they feel; and for these purposes should even be residents among them."

The upper house, or Senate, its members elected by state legislatures, was at one remove from the voters. Staggered six-year terms further isolated senators from the passing fancies of public passion by preventing the choice of a majority of Senate seats in any given year.

The decision that a single person be made the chief executive caused "considerable pause," according to Madison. George Mason protested that this would create a "fetus of monarchy." Indeed, the president was to be an almost monarchical figure. Although subject to election every four years, the chief executive wielded powers that actually exceeded those of the British king. This was the sharpest departure from the recent experience in state government, where the office of governor had commonly been diluted because of the recent memory of struggles with the colonial executives. The president could veto acts of Congress, subject to being overridden by a two-thirds vote in each house, was commander-in-chief of the armed forces, and responsible for the execution of the laws. The chief executive could make treaties with the advice and consent of two-thirds of the Senate and appoint diplomats, judges, and other officers with the consent of a Senate majority.

But the president's powers were limited in certain key areas. The chief executive could neither declare war nor make peace; those powers were reserved for the Congress. In addition the Constitution required that the president report annually on the state of the nation. Unlike the British king, moreover, the president could be removed. "Shall any man be above Justice?" asked George Mason. "Above all, shall that man be above it who can commit the most extensive injustice?" No, answered the delegates, and they built into the Constitution the machinery for removing the president. The House could impeach (indict) the chief executive—and other civil officers—on charges of treason, bribery, or "other high crimes and misdemeanors"; the president could then be removed by the Senate with a two-thirds vote to convict. The presiding officer at the trial of a president would be the chief justice, since the usual presiding officer of the Senate (the vice president) would have a personal stake in the outcome.

The convention's nationalists—men like Madison, James Wilson, and Hamilton—wanted to strengthen the independence of the executive by entrusting the choice to popular election. At least in this instance the nationalists, often accused of being the aristocratic party, favored a bold new exercise in democracy. But an elected executive was still too far beyond the American experience. Besides, a national election would have created enormous problems of organization and voter qualification. Wilson suggested instead that the people of each state choose presidential electors equal to the number of their senators and representatives. Others proposed that the legislators make the choice. Finally, the convention voted to let the legislature decide the method in each state. Before long nearly all the states were choosing their electors by popular vote, and the electors were acting as agents of party will, casting their votes as they had pledged before the election. This method was contrary to the original expectation that the electors would deliberate and make their own choices.

On the third branch of government, the judiciary, there was surprisingly little debate. Both the Virginia and New Jersey plans had called for a Supreme Court, which the Constitution established, providing specifically for a chief justice of the United States and leaving up to Congress the number of other justices. The only major dispute was on courts "inferior" to the Supreme Court, and that too was left up to Congress. Although the Constitution nowhere authorized the courts to declare laws void when they conflicted with the Constitution, the power of judicial review was almost surely intended by the framers and was soon exercised in cases involving both state and federal laws. Article VI declared the federal constitution, federal laws, and treaties to be the "supreme law of the land," state laws or constitutions to the contrary notwithstanding.

While the Constitution extended vast new powers to the national government, the delegates' mistrust of unchecked power is apparent in repeated examples of countervailing forces: the separation of the three branches of government, the president's veto, the congressional power of impeachment and removal, the Senate's power over treaties and appointments, the courts' implied right of judicial review. In addition the new frame of government specifically forbade Congress to pass ex post facto laws (laws adopted after the event to make past deeds criminal). It also reserved to the states large areas of sovereignty—a reservation soon made explicit by the Tenth Amendment.

The most glaring defect of the Articles of Confederation, the rule of unanimity which defeated every effort to amend them, led the delegates to provide a less forbidding though still difficult method of amending the new Constitution. Amendments could be proposed either by two-thirds vote of each house or by a national convention specially called by two-thirds of the state legislatures. Amendments could be ratified by approval of three-fourths of the states acting through their legislatures or through special conventions. The national convention has never been used, however, and state conventions have been called only once—to ratify the repeal of the Eighteenth Amendment, which had enacted Prohibition.

THE FIGHT FOR RATIFICATION   The final article of the Constitution provided that it would become effective upon ratification by nine states (not quite the three-fourths majority required for amendment). The Congress submitted the convention's work to the states on September 28, 1787. In the ensuing political debate advocates of the new Constitution, who might properly have been called Nationalists because they preferred a strong central government, assumed the more reassuring name of Federalists. Opponents, who favored a more decentralized federal system, became Antifederalists. The Federalists were not only better prepared but better organized, and on the whole they represented the more articulate elements in the community. The Federalists were usually clustered in or near cities and tended to be more cosmopolitan, urbane, and well-educated. Antifederalists tended to be small farmers and frontiersmen who saw little to gain from the promotion of interstate commerce and much to lose from prohibitions on paper money and stay laws preventing the seizure of property for non-payment of debts. Many of them also feared that an expansive land policy was likely to favor speculators.

Historians have long debated what motivated the advocates of

Signing the Constitution, September 17, 1787. *Thomas Pritchard Rossiter's painting shows George Washington presiding over what Thomas Jefferson called "an assembly of demi-gods."*

the new Constitution. In 1913 Charles A. Beard's book *An Economic Interpretation of the Constitution* advanced the controversial thesis that the Philadelphia Convention was made up of men who had a selfish economic interest in the outcome. They held large amounts of depreciated government securities and otherwise stood to gain from the power and stability of the new order. In his view, then, the Constitution was an essentially economic document reflecting the self-interest of a powerful minority.

Beard's thesis provided a useful antidote to unquestioning hero worship, and it still contains a germ of truth, but he rested his argument too heavily on the claim that material self-interest predominated in the convention. Most of the delegates, according to evidence unavailable to Beard, had no compelling economic interests at stake. Many prominent nationalists, including the "Father of the Constitution," James Madison himself, had no western lands or bonds. Some opponents of the Constitution, on the other hand, held large blocks of bonds and securities. Economic interests certainly figured in the process of constitution making, but they functioned in a complex interplay of state, sectional, group, and individual interests which turned largely on how well people had fared under the Confederation.

But exaggerating the influence of selfish economic interests in shaping the Constitution obscures an important point. The most notable circumstance of the times was that, unlike so many later revolutions, the American Revolution led not to general chaos and class strife but to a remarkably orderly process of constitution making. From the 1760s through the 1780s there occurred a prolonged debate over the fundamental issues of government, which in its scope and depth—and in the durability of its outcome—is without parallel.

THE FEDERALIST Among the supreme legacies of that debate was *The Federalist*, a collection of essays originally published in New York newspapers between October 1787 and July 1788. Initiated by the eloquent and combative Alexander Hamilton, the eighty-five articles published under the name "Publius" included about thirty by James Madison, nearly fifty by Hamilton, and five by John Jay. Written in support of ratification, the essays defended the principle of a supreme national authority, but at the same time sought to reassure doubters that there was little reason to fear tyranny by the new government. In perhaps the most famous single essay, Number Ten, Madison argued that the country's very size and diversity would make it impossible for any single faction to form a majority that could dominate the government. This contradicted prevailing notions of republican government. Republics, the conventional wisdom of the times insisted, could work only in small, homogeneous countries like Switzerland and the Netherlands. In larger countries republican government would descend into anarchy and tyranny through the influence of factions. Quite the contrary, Madison argued. A republic with a balanced federal government could work in a large and diverse country better than in a smaller country. "Extend the sphere," he wrote, "and you take in a greater variety of parties and interests; you make it less probable that a majority of the whole will have a common motive to invade the rights of other citizens."

The Federalists did try to cultivate a belief that the new union would contribute to prosperity, in part to link their movement with the economic recovery already under way. The Antifederalists, however, highlighted the dangers of power. They noted the absence of a Bill of Rights protecting individuals and states, and they found the ratification process highly irregular, which it was —indeed illegal under the Articles of Confederation. Patrick Henry "smelt a rat" from the beginning. Not only did he refuse to attend the Constitutional Convention; he demanded later that it be investigated as a conspiracy. Maryland's Luther Martin, who had walked out of the Constitutional Convention, urged his state not to ratify by rejecting "those chains which are forged for it." The Antifederalist leaders—men like Martin, Patrick Henry and Richard Henry Lee of Virginia, George Clinton of New York, Sam Adams and Elbridge Gerry of Massachusetts—were often men whose careers and reputations had been established well before the Revolution. The Federalist leaders, on the other hand, were more likely to be younger men whose careers had begun in the Revolution and who had been "nationalized" in the fires of battle—men like Hamilton, Madison, and Jay.

The two groups disagreed, however, more over means than ends. Both sides for the most part agreed that a stronger national authority was needed, and that it required an independent income to function properly. Both were convinced that the people must erect safeguards against tyranny, even the tyranny of the majority. Once the new government had become an accomplished fact, few die-hards were left who wanted to undo the work of the Philadelphia convention.

THE DECISION OF THE STATES   Ratification gained momentum before the end of 1787, and several of the smaller states were among the first to act, apparently satisfied that they had gained all the safeguards they could hope for in equality of representation in the Senate. New Hampshire was the ninth to ratify, on June 21, 1788, and the Constitution could then be put into effect, but the union could hardly succeed without the approval of Virginia, the largest state, or New York, the third largest, which occupied a key position geographically. There was strong opposition in both states. In Virginia Patrick Henry became the chief spokesman of backcountry farmers who feared the powers of the new government, but wavering delegates were won over by a proposal that the convention should recommend a Bill of Rights. Virginia's convention ratified on June 25, 1788. In New York, Hamilton and the other Federalists delayed a vote in the hope that action by Virginia would persuade the delegates that the new framework would go into effect with or without New York. On July 26, 1788, they carried the day by the closest margin thus far, 30 to 27. North Carolina and Rhode Island remained the only holdouts, and North Carolina stubbornly withheld action until November 1789, when amendments composing a Bill of Rights were actually submitted by Congress. Rhode Island, true to form, continued to hold out and did not relent until May 29, 1790, by the closest margin of all—two votes.

The Confederation Congress began to draft plans for an orderly transfer of power. On September 13, 1788, it selected New York City as the seat of the new government and fixed the date for elections. On October 10, 1788, the Confederation

RATIFICATION OF THE CONSTITUTION

Order of Ratification	State	Date of Ratification
1	Delaware	December 7, 1787
2	Pennsylvania	December 12, 1787
3	New Jersey	December 18, 1787
4	Georgia	January 2,1788
5	Connecticut	January 9, 1788
6	Massachusetts	February 7, 1788
7	Maryland	April 28, 1788
8	South Carolina	May 23, 1788
9	New Hampshire	June 21, 1788
10	Virginia	June 25, 1788
11	New York	July 26, 1788
12	North Carolina	November 21, 1789
13	Rhode Island	May 29, 1790

Congress transacted its last business and passed into history. "Our constitution is in actual operation," the elderly Ben Franklin wrote to a friend; "everything appears to promise that it will last; but in this world nothing is certain but death and taxes." George Washington was even more uncertain about the future under the new plan of government. He had told a fellow delegate as the convention adjourned: "I do not expect the Constitution to last for more than twenty years."

"A More Perfect Union"

The Constitution has lasted much longer, of course, and in the process it has provided a model of republican government whose features have been repeatedly borrowed by other nations through the years. Yet what makes the American Constitution so distinctive is not its specific provisions but its remarkable harmony with the particular "genius of the people" it governs. The Constitution has been neither a static abstraction nor a "machine that would go of itself," as the poet James Russell Lowell would later assert. Instead it has provided a flexible system of government which presidents, legislators, judges, and the people have modified to accord with a fallible human nature and changing social, economic, and political circumstances. In this sense the Founding Fathers not only created "a more perfect Union" in 1787; they engineered a frame of government whose resilience has enabled later generations to continue to perfect their republican experiment.

Further Reading

A good overview of the Confederation period is Richard B. Morris's *The Forging of the Union, 1781–1789* (1987)°. Merrill Jensen's *The New Nation* (1981)° presents the "consensus" view that downplays the extent of crisis under the Confederation. Another useful analysis of this period is Richard Buel, Jr.'s *Securing the Revolution: Ideology in American Politics, 1789–1815* (1974).°

For a fine account of cultural change during the period, see Joseph J. Ellis's *After the Revolution: Profiles of American Culture* (1979)° and Oscar Handlin and Lilian Handlin's *A Restless People: America in Rebellion, 1770–1787* (1982).

Charles A. Beard's *An Economic Interpretation of the Constitution of the United States* (1913)° remained powerfully influential for more than a generation. For another view, see Forrest McDonald's *Novus Ordo Se-*

° These books are available in paperback editions.

clorum: The Intellectual Origins of the Constitution (1985). Other interpretations are found in *Essays on the Making of the Constitution* (2nd ed.,
1987),° edited by Leonard W. Levy. More recent studies include Edmund S. Morgan's *Inventing the People* (1988)° and Michael Kammen's
Sovereignty and Liberty (1988). On the Constitutional Convention, see
Christopher Collier and James Lincoln Collier, *Decision in Philadelphia*
(1987).° See also Richard B. Morris, *Witnesses at the Creation: Hamilton,
Madison, Jay, and the Constitution* (1986).°

For discussions of the problem of slavery in forming the Constitution,
see the relevant sections of Donald L. Robinson's *Slavery in the Structure
of American Politics, 1765–1820* (1970)° and James MacGregor Burns's
The Vineyard of Liberty: The American Experiment (1982).°

7

THE FEDERALISTS:
WASHINGTON AND ADAMS

A New Government

The new Congress of the United States opened with a whimper rather than a bang. On March 4, 1789, the appointed date of its first session in bustling New York City, only eight senators and thirteen representatives took their seats. A month passed before both chambers gathered a quorum. Only then could the temporary presiding officer of the Senate count the ballots and certify the foregone conclusion that George Washington, with sixty-nine votes, was the unanimous choice of the electoral college for president. John Adams, with thirty-four votes, the second-highest number, became vice-president.

Washington's journey from Mount Vernon, Virginia, to New York, where he was inaugurated on April 30, turned into a triumphal procession that confirmed the universal confidence he commanded and the excited expectancy with which the new experiment was awaited. But the fifty-seven-year-old Washington, tall and imposing, grown gray-haired, partly deaf, and almost toothless, himself confessed to feeling like "a culprit who is going to his place of execution," burdened with dread that so much was expected of him: "I face an ocean of difficulties." An awkward speaker, he shook visibly as he read his inaugural address. The new nation of 4 million Americans, however, required not brilliant oratory but firm leadership, and Washington possessed that in abundance.

GOVERNMENTAL STRUCTURE   Although opposed to the rule of monarchy, many Americans were not opposed to its trappings. In fact some suggested that Washington needed to assert his new authority as chief executive through his public presence as much as by his public policies. The president obliged them with a show of pomp and circumstance. He rode a gleaming white horse with a leopard skin saddlecloth, and on public occasions he appeared in a coach drawn by six cream-colored horses, escorted by liveried servants. Seven black slaves helped Martha Washington maintain the presidential mansion and serve the weekly formal dinners. Mixed emotions greeted the show of ceremony. Some members of Congress continued to fear that another president might make "that bold push for the throne" predicted by Patrick Henry.

More than matters of etiquette occupied the First Congress, of course. The president and the Congress had to create a government anew. Washington inherited but the shadow of a bureaucracy: a foreign office with John Jay at its head and two clerks; a Treasury Board with little or no treasury; a 300-pound secretary

Mary Varick's sampler celebrates George Washington's inauguration as president of the United States in 1789.

of war, Henry Knox, with a lightweight army of 672 officers and men, and no navy at all; a heavy federal debt and almost no federal revenue.

During the summer of 1789 Congress authorized executive departments corresponding in each case to those already formed under the Confederation. To head the Department of State Washington named Thomas Jefferson, recently back from his mission to France. Leadership of the Department of the Treasury went to Washington's wartime aide Alexander Hamilton, who had since become a prominent lawyer in New York. Tall, graceful Edmund Randolph, former governor of Virginia and owner of a 7,000-acre, debt-ridden plantation worked by 200 slaves, assumed the new position of attorney-general. Almost from the beginning Washington routinely called these men to sit as a group for discussion and advice on policy matters. This was the origin of the president's cabinet, an advisory body for which the constitution made no formal provision—except insofar as it provided for the heads of departments. The office of vice-president also took on what would become its typical character. "The Vice-Presidency," portly John Adams wrote his wife, Abigail, was the most "insignificant office . . . ever . . . contrived." As the first chief justice of the Supreme Court, Washington named John Jay, who served until 1795.

THE BILL OF RIGHTS   In the House of Representatives James Madison made a Bill of Rights one of the first items of business. The lack of protection for individual rights had been one of the Antifederalists' major objections to the Constitution. During the ratification debate, Madison and other Federalists had argued that the Constitution needed no enumeration of specific "rights" because, as Madison said, "everything not granted is reserved." But public anxiety about individual rights persisted, so in May 1789 Madison reluctantly drew the first eight amendments from the Virginia Bill of Rights, which George Mason had written in 1776. These all provided safeguards for certain fundamental individual rights: freedom of religion, speech, and the press; the right to bear arms and to be tried by a jury of peers; and the right to assemble and petition the government. The Ninth and Tenth Amendments declared that the enumeration of rights in the Constitution "shall not be construed to deny or disparage others retained by the people" and that "powers not delegated to the United States by the Constitution . . . are reserved to the States respectively, or to the people." The Bill of Rights became effective December 15, 1791.

HAMILTON'S VISION OF AMERICA

Revenue was the new government's most critical need, and Congress quickly enacted a tariff intended to raise revenue and protect America's new manufacturers from foreign competition. The tariff launched the effort to get the country on a sound financial basis. In finance, with all its broad implications for policy in general, it was thirty-four-year-old Alexander Hamilton who seized the initiative. The first secretary of the treasury was the protégé of the president. Born out of wedlock on a Caribbean island, deserted by a ne'er-do-well Scottish father, Hamilton was left an orphan at thirteen by the death of his mother. With the help of friends and relatives, he found his way at seventeen to New York, attended King's College (later Columbia University), entered the revolutionary agitations as speaker and pamphleteer, and joined the army, where he attracted Washington's attention. Hamilton distinguished himself at the siege of Yorktown, and he remained forever after a frustrated military genius, hungry for greater glory on the field of battle. He studied law, passed the bar examination, established a legal practice in New York, and became a self-made aristocrat, serving as collector of revenues and member of the Confederation Congress. An early convert to nationalism, he played a crucial part in promoting the Constitutional Convention and defending its work in the *Federalist Papers.*

The new government needed all of Hamilton's ambition and his brilliance. In a series of classic reports submitted to Congress

Alexander Hamilton in 1796.

in the two years from January 1790 to December 1791, he outlined his program for government finances and the economic development of the United States. The reports were soon adopted,
with some alterations in detail but little in substance. Less well-
received was the last of the series, the Report on Manufactures,
which outlined a neo-mercantilist program of protective tariffs
and other governmental aid to business.

ESTABLISHING THE PUBLIC CREDIT   Hamilton submitted the first
and most important of his reports to the House of Representatives in January 1790. This First Report on the Public Credit was
the cornerstone of the Hamiltonian program. It made two key
recommendations: first, funding of the federal debt at face value,
which meant that those citizens holding government securities
could exchange them for new interest-bearing bonds of the same
face value; and second, the federal government's assumption of
state debts from the Revolution to the amount of $21 million.
The funding scheme was controversial because many farmers
and soldiers in need of immediate money had sold their securities for a fraction of their value to speculators. Spokesmen for
these Americans argued that they should be reimbursed for their
losses; otherwise the speculators would gain a windfall. Hamilton sternly resisted. The speculators, he argued, had "paid what
the commodity was worth in the market, and took the risks."
Therefore, they should reap the benefits. In fact, Hamilton insisted, the government should do all it could to win over the financial community because it represented the bedrock of a
successful nation.

Hamilton's report echoed the one Robert Morris had urged
upon the Confederation a decade before, one which Hamilton
had strongly endorsed at the time. As Hamilton had written
Morris in 1781, a "national debt, if it is not excessive, will be to
us a great national blessing." Payment of the national debt, both
felt, would be not only a point of national honor and sound finance, ensuring the country's credit for the future; it would also
be an occasion to assert a national taxing power and thus instill
respect for the authority of the national government.

It was on this point, however, that Madison, who had been
Hamilton's close ally in the movement for a stronger government, broke with him. Their disagreement carried ominous
overtones of sectionalism. Madison did not question that the
debt should be paid, but was troubled that speculators and
"stock-jobbers" would become the chief beneficiaries. Also disturbing was the fact that northerners held most of the debt.
Madison's opposition touched off a vigorous debate which dead-

locked the whole question of debt funding and assumption through much of 1790.

The stalemate finally ended when Hamilton, Jefferson, and Madison reached an understanding. In return for northern votes in favor of locating the permanent national capital on the Potomac, Madison pledged to seek enough southern votes to pass the assumption bill, with the further arrangement that those states with smaller debts would get in effect outright grants from the federal government to equalize the difference. These arrangements secured enough votes to carry Hamilton's funding and assumption plans. The capital would be moved to Philadelphia for ten years, after which it would be settled at a new Federal City on the Potomac, the site to be chosen by the president. In August 1790 Congress finally passed the legislation for Hamilton's plan.

A NATIONAL BANK Through this vast program of funding and assumption Hamilton had called up from nowhere, as if by magic, a great sum of capital. As he put it in his original report, a national debt "answers most of the purposes of money." Transfers of government bonds, once the debt was properly funded, would be equivalent to monetary payments. This feature of the program was especially important in a country which had, from the first settlements, suffered a shortage of hard money. Having established the public credit, Hamilton moved on to a related measure essential to his vision of national greatness. He called for a national bank, which by issuance of banknotes (paper money) might provide a uniform currency, as well as a source of capital for the developing economy. Government bonds held by the bank would back up the currency. The national bank, chartered by Congress, would remain under governmental surveillance, but private investors would supply four-fifths of the $10 million capital and name twenty of the twenty-five directors; the government would purchase the other fifth of the capital and name five directors. Government bonds would be received in payment for three-fourths of the stock in the bank, and the other fourth would be payable in gold and silver.

Once again Madison rose to lead the opposition, arguing that he could find no basis in the Constitution for such a bank. That was enough to raise in President Washington's mind serious doubts as to the constitutionality of the measure, which Congress passed over Madison's objections. Before signing the bill into law, therefore, the president sought the advice of his cabinet and found an equal division of opinion. This resulted in the first great debate on constitutional interpretation. Should there be a strict or a broad construction of the document? Were the powers of Congress only those explicitly stated in the Constitution or were others implied? The argument turned chiefly on Article 1, Section 8, which authorized Congress to "make all laws which shall be necessary and proper for carrying into execution the foregoing Powers."

Such language left room for disagreement and led to a confrontation between Jefferson and Hamilton. Jefferson pointed to the Tenth Amendment, which reserved to the states and the people powers not delegated to Congress. A bank might be a convenient aid to Congress in collecting taxes and regulating the currency, but it was not, as Article l, Section 8, specified, *necessary*. Hamilton insisted that the power to charter corporations was included in the sovereignty of any government, whether or not expressly stated. The president accepted Hamilton's argument and signed the bill. By doing so, in Jefferson's words, he opened up "a boundless field of power" which in coming years would lead to a further broadening of implied powers with the approval of the Supreme Court.

ENCOURAGING MANUFACTURES Hamilton's imagination and his ambitions for the new country were not yet exhausted. On December 13, 1790, he submitted a Second Report on Public Credit, which included a proposal for an excise tax on alcoholic beverages to aid in raising revenue to cover the nation's debts. Six weeks later, the secretary proposed a national mint—which was established in 1792. And finally, on December 5, 1791, as the culmination of his basic reports, the Report of Manufactures proposed an extensive program of government aid to the development of manufacturing enterprises.

In the Report on Manufactures, Hamilton argued for the active encouragement of manufacturing to provide productive uses for the new capital he had created by his funding, assumption, and banking schemes. Multiple advantages would flow from the development of manufactures: the diversification of labor in a country given over too exclusively to farming; greater use of machinery; work for those not ordinarily employed, such as women and children; the promotion of immigration; a greater scope for the diversity of talents in business; and a better domestic market for the products of agriculture.

To secure his ends Hamilton advocated protective tariffs, "which in some cases might be put so high as to keep out foreign products altogether; restraints on the export of raw materials; bounties and premiums to encourage certain industries; induce-

ments to inventions and discoveries; and finally, the encouragement of internal improvements in transportation, the development of roads, canals, and navigable streams."

Some of his tariff proposals were enacted in 1792. Otherwise
the program was filed away—but not forgotten. It provided an
arsenal of arguments for the manufacturing spokesmen in years
to come. Hamilton denied that his scheme favored the northern
states. If, as seemed likely, the northern and middle states should
become the chief scenes of manufacturing, he claimed, they
would create robust markets for agricultural products, some of
which the southern states were peculiarly qualified to produce.
The nation as a whole would benefit, he argued, as commerce
between North and South increased, supplanting the trade
across the Atlantic.

HAMILTON'S ACHIEVEMENT   Largely owing to the skillful Hamilton, the Treasury Department began retiring the Revolutionary
War debt, enhanced the value of a "Continental" dollar, secured
the government's credit, and attracted foreign investment capital. Prosperity, so elusive in the 1780s, began to flourish once
again, although President Washington cautioned against attributing "to the Government what is due only to the goodness of
Providence."

Yet suspicions lingered that Hamilton had designed his program to promote a particular class and sectional interest, and
some even thought a personal interest. But such charges are
largely without foundation. There is no reason to believe that
Hamilton's conscious aim was to benefit either a section or a class
at the expense of the country. He was inclined toward a truly nationalist outlook, and he focused his energies on the rising power
of commercial capitalism. Tying the government closely to the
rich and the well-born, Hamilton believed, promoted the government's financial stability and guarded the public order
against the potential turbulence that always haunted him.

But many Americans then and since have interpreted such
views as elitist and self-serving. To be sure, Hamilton never understood the people of the small villages and farms, the people of
the frontier. They were foreign to his world, despite his own
humble beginnings. And they, along with the planters of the
South, would be at best only indirect beneficiaries of his programs. There were, in short, vast numbers of people who saw little gain from the Hamiltonian program and thus were drawn into
opposition. Indeed, Jefferson claimed that he and Hamilton
were "pitted against each other every day in the cabinet like two
fighting-cocks."

THE REPUBLICAN ALTERNATIVE

In this split over the Hamiltonian program lay the seeds of the first national political parties. Hamilton emerged as the embodiment of the party known as the Federalists; Madison and Jefferson assumed the leadership of those who took the name Republicans and thereby implied that the Federalists really aimed at a monarchy. Parties were slow in developing, or at least in being acknowledged as legitimate. All the political philosophers of the age deplored the spirit of party or faction. The concept of a loyal opposition, of a two-party system as a positive good, was yet to be formulated. Parties, or "factions," were bodies of men bent upon self-aggrandizement through the favor of the government. They smelled of corruption. As Jefferson once remarked, "If I could not go to Heaven but with a party I would not go there at all."

Neither side in the disagreement over national policy deliberately set out to create a party system. But there were important differences of both philosophy and self-interest that simply would not dissolve, and the strongly partisan and malicious newspapers of the day ensured that such differences were repeatedly accented for the reading public. The crux of the debate centered on the relative power of the federal government and the states. At the outset Madison assumed leadership of Hamilton's opponents in the Congress, and he argued that Hamilton was trampling upon states' rights in forging a consolidated central government. After the compromise which had assured the funding of state debts, Jefferson joined Madison in ever more resolute opposition to Hamilton's policies. They opposed his move to place an excise tax on whiskey, which would especially burden the trans-Appalachian farmers whose grain was the source of that liquid, his proposal for a national bank, and his report on manufactures. Against the last two both men raised constitutional objections. As these differences developed, the personal hostility between Jefferson and Hamilton festered, much to the distress of President Washington. In the process, Jefferson, the temperamentally shy and retiring secretary of state, emerged as the leader of the opposition to Hamilton's policies within the administration, while Madison continued to direct the opposition in Congress.

JEFFERSON'S AGRARIAN VIEW Thomas Jefferson, twelve years Hamilton's senior, was in most respects his opposite. In contrast to the self-made Hamilton, Jefferson was to the manor born, son of a successful surveyor and land speculator. Displaying little of Hamilton's ordered intensity, Jefferson instead conveyed an aristocratic carelessness and a breadth of cultivated interests that ranged perhaps more widely in science, the arts, and the humanities than those of any contemporary, even Franklin. Jefferson read or spoke seven languages. He was an architect of some distinction (Monticello, the Virginia Capitol, and the University of Virginia are monuments to his talent), a man who understood mathematics and engineering, an inventor, an agronomist. In his *Notes on Virginia* (1785) he displayed a knowledge of geography, paleontology, zoology, botany, and archeology. He collected paintings and sculpture, knew music and practiced the violin, although some said only Patrick Henry played it worse.

Philosophically, Hamilton and Jefferson had contrasting visions of the character of the Union in the first generation under the Constitution, and their opposite views defined certain fundamental issues of American life that still echo two centuries later. Hamilton foresaw a diversified capitalistic economy, agriculture balanced by commerce and industry, and was thus the better prophet. Jefferson feared the growth of crowded cities divided into a capitalistic aristocracy on the one hand and the depraved masses on the other. Hamilton feared anarchy and loved order; Jefferson feared tyranny and loved liberty.

Where Hamilton wanted a strong central government run by a wealthy elite actively encouraging capitalistic enterprise, Jeffer-

Thomas Jefferson, in a portrait by Rembrandt Peale (1800).

son desired a decentralized agrarian republic. "I am not a friend to a very energetic government," he once stressed; nor was he a friend of the financial and commercial elite. Jefferson's republic was to remain one in which small farmers predominated: "Those who labor in the earth," he wrote, "are the chosen people of God, if ever he had a chosen people, whose breasts He has made His peculiar deposit for genuine and substantial virtue." Jefferson, who spent several years in France, was the enlightened *philosophe*, the natural radical and reformer who attacked the aristocratic relics of entail and primogeniture in Virginia; opposed an established church; proposed an elaborate plan for public schools; prepared a more humane criminal code; and was instrumental in eliminating slavery from the Old Northwest, although he kept the slaves he had inherited. On his tomb were finally recorded his proudest achievements: author of the Declaration of Independence and the Virginia Statute of Religious Freedom, and founder of the University of Virginia.

CRISES FOREIGN AND DOMESTIC

As the disputes between Jefferson and Hamilton intensified, Washington proved ever more adept at transcending party differences and holding things together with his unmatched prestige. In 1792 he won unanimous reelection, and no sooner had his second term begun than problems of foreign relations leapt to center stage, brought there by the consequences of the French Revolution, which had begun during the first months of Washington's presidency. Americans followed the popular revolt against the French monarchy with almost universal sympathy, up to a point. By the spring of 1792, though, the hopeful experiment in liberty, equality, and fraternity had turned into a monster that plunged France into war with Austria and Prussia and began devouring its own children along with its enemies in the Terror of 1793–1794.

After the execution of King Louis XVI in January 1793, Great Britain joined with the monarchies of Spain and Holland in a war against the French Republic. For the next twenty-two years Britain and France were at war, with only a brief respite, until the final defeat of French forces under Napoleon in 1815. The war presented Washington, just beginning his second term, with an awkward problem. By the treaty of 1778 the United States was a perpetual ally of France, obligated to defend her possessions in the West Indies. But Americans wanted no part of the war; on this much Hamilton and Jefferson could agree. On April 22, 1793, Washington issued a neutrality proclamation that simply declared the United States "friendly and impartial toward the belligerent powers."

CITIZEN GENÊT At the same time, Washington accepted Jefferson's argument that the United States should recognize the new French government (becoming the first country to do so) and receive its new ambassador, Edmond Charles Genêt. Early in 1793 Genêt landed at Charleston, South Carolina, and made his way northward to New York. Along the way he brazenly began engaging in quite un-neutral activities. He outfitted privateers for use against the British royal navy and intrigued with frontiersmen and land speculators to launch an attack on Spanish Florida and Louisiana in retaliation for Spain's opposition to the French Revolution.

Genêt quickly became an embarrassment even to his Republican friends. "His conduct has been that of a madman," Madison charged. The cabinet finally agreed unanimously that he had to go, and in August 1793 Washington demanded his recall. Genêt's foolishness and the growing excesses of the French radicals were fast cooling American support for their revolution. To Hamilton's followers it began to resemble their worst nightmares of democratic anarchy and infidelity. The French made it hard even for Republicans to retain sympathy, but Jefferson and others swallowed hard and made excuses. Nor did the British make it easy for Federalists to rally to their side. Near the end of 1793 they announced Orders in Council under which they seized the cargoes of American ships with provisions for or produce from French islands in the Caribbean.

Despite the offenses by both sides, the French and British causes polarized American opinion and the two parties. In the contest, it seemed, one had to be either a Republican and support liberty, reason, and France or a Federalist and support order, faith, and Britain. And the division gave rise to some curious loyalties: slaveholding planters cheered Jacobin radicals who dispossessed their aristocratic counterparts in France, while Massachusetts shippers, who still profited from the British trade, kept quiet about British seizures of American ships. Boston, once a hotbed of revolution, became a bastion of Federalism.

JAY'S TREATY Early in 1794 Republican leaders in Congress were gaining support for commercial retaliation to bring the British to their senses, when the British gave Washington a timely opening

*John Jay, the first Chief Justice of
the United States.*

for a settlement. They repealed the Orders under which American ships were being seized, and on April 16, 1794, Washington named Chief Justice John Jay as a special envoy to Great Britain. Jay left with instructions to settle all major issues: to get the British out of their posts along the western frontier and to win reparations for the losses of American shippers, compensation for slaves carried away in 1783, and a commercial treaty which would legalize American commerce with the British West Indies.

The pro-British Jay, however, had little leverage with which to wring concessions from the British, and after seven months of negotiations he won only two pledges: the British promised to evacuate the northwest posts by 1796 and to pay damages for the seizures of American ships and cargoes in 1793–1794. In exchange for these gains, Jay conceded the British definition of neutral rights. He accepted the principles that provisions could not go in neutral ships to enemy ports, and that trade with enemy colonies prohibited in peacetime could not be opened in wartime (the "Rule of 1756"). Britain gained most-favored-nation treatment in American commerce and a promise that French privateers would not be outfitted in American ports. Jay also conceded that the long-standing American debts to British merchants would be adjudicated and paid by the American government. Perhaps most importantly, he failed to gain access for American shippers to the British West Indies.

Public outrage greeted the terms of the treaty. Even Federalist shippers, ready for settlement on almost any terms, criticized

Jay's failure to open up the British West Indies to American commerce. But much of the outcry came from disappointed Republican partisans who sought an escalation of conflict with hated England. Jay remarked that he could travel across the country by the light of his burning effigies. Yet the Senate debated the treaty in secret, and in the end moderation prevailed. Without a single vote to spare, Jay's Treaty won the necessary two-thirds majority on June 24, 1795. Washington hesitated but finally signed the treaty as the best he was likely to get and out of fear that refusal would throw the United States into the role of a French satellite.

THE FRONTIER STIRS   Other events also had an important bearing on Jay's Treaty, adding force to its settlement of the Canadian frontier. While Jay was haggling in London, frontier conflict with Indians was moving toward a temporary resolution. Washington had named General Wayne, known as "Mad Anthony," to head an expedition into the Northwest Territory, and in the fall of 1793 he marched into Indian country with some 2,600 men. On August 4, 1794, Indians representing eight tribes, led by the Miami and reinforced by some Canadian militia, attacked Wayne's force at the Battle of Fallen Timbers. The Americans repulsed them with heavy losses, after which American detachments destroyed their fields and villages. Dispersed and decimated, they finally agreed to the Treaty of Greenville, signed in August 1795. In the treaty, at the cost of a $10,000 annuity, the United States bought from twelve tribes the rights to the southeastern quarter of the Northwest Territory (now Ohio and Indiana) and enclaves at the sites of Vincennes, Detroit, and Chicago.

THE WHISKEY REBELLION   Wayne's forces were still mopping up after the Battle of Fallen Timbers when the administration resolved on another show of strength in the backcountry against the so-called Whiskey Rebellion. Hamilton's excise tax on strong drink, levied in 1791, had angered frontier farmers because it taxed their staple crop. Their grain was more easily transported to market in concentrated liquid form than in bulk. A pack horse, for example, could carry two bushels of unprocessed rye, but it could carry two barrels of whiskey representing twenty-four bushels of rye. Frontiersmen considered the tax another part of Hamilton's scheme to pick the pockets of the poor to enrich privileged speculators. All through the backcountry from Georgia to Pennsylvania and beyond, the tax provoked resistance and evasion. In the summer of 1794 the rumblings of discontent broke

Washington as commander-in-chief reviews the troops mobilized to quell the Whiskey Rebellion in 1794.

into open rebellion in Pennsylvania's four western counties where vigilantes, mostly of Scottish or Irish descent, organized to terrorize revenuers and taxpayers. One group, disguised as women, assaulted a revenue collector, cropped his hair, coated him with tar and feathers, and stole his horse. Other rebels robbed the mails, stopped court proceedings, and threatened an assault on Pittsburgh. On August 7, 1794, President Washington issued a proclamation ordering the rebels to disperse and go home, and calling out militiamen from Virginia, Maryland, Pennsylvania, and New Jersey. Getting no response from the "Whiskey Boys," he issued a proclamation on September 24 for suppression of the rebellion.

Under the command of Virginia's governor, Gen. Henry (Light-Horse Harry) Lee, 13,000 men, a force larger than any Washington had ever commanded in the Revolution, marched out from Harrisburg across the Alleghenies with Hamilton in their midst, itching to smite the insurgents. But the rebels vaporized like corn mash when heated. By dint of great effort and much marching the troops finally rounded up twenty barefoot, ragged prisoners whom they paraded down Market Street in

Philadelphia and clapped into prison. Some of the soldiers regretted not having cornered the rebels. As one of the militiamen explained, "We all lament that so few of the insurgents fell— such disorders can only be cured by copious bleedings." There was, in fact, little bleeding of any kind. One of the captured rebels died in prison. Two were convicted of treason and sentenced to be hanged, but Washington pardoned them on the grounds that one was a "simpleton" and the other "insane." The government had made its point in defense of the rule of law and federal authority. It thereby gained "reputation and strength," according to Hamilton, by suppressing a rebellion which, in Jefferson's words, "could never be found." But this came at the cost of creating or confirming new numbers of Republicans who scored heavily in the next Pennsylvania elections.

PINCKNEY'S TREATY While these stirring events were transpiring in the Keystone State, Spain was suffering some setbacks to its schemes to consolidate its control over Florida and the Louisiana territory. Spain had refused to recognize the legitimacy of America's southern boundary established by the Treaty of Paris

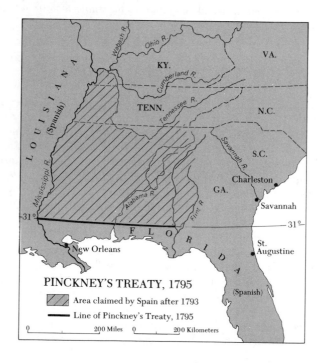

PINCKNEY'S TREATY, 1795

   Area claimed by Spain after 1793

   Line of Pinckney's Treaty, 1795

0   200 Miles   0   200 Kilometers

in 1783, and its agents thereafter sought to thwart American expansion southward. Spanish intrigues among the Creeks, Choctaws, Chickasaws, and Cherokees were keeping up the same turmoil the British fomented along the Ohio.

But for reasons growing out of the shifting balance of power in Europe, Spain decided in the mid-1790s to end its designs in America. This change of heart resulted in Pinckney's Treaty (1795), by which United States Minister Thomas Pinckney won acceptance of an American boundary at the Thirty-first Parallel; free navigation of the Mississippi; the right to deposit goods at New Orleans without having to pay customs duties for a period of three years (with promise of renewal); a commission to settle American claims against Spain; and a promise on each side to refrain from inciting Indian attacks on the other. Ratification of the Pinckney Treaty ran into no opposition at all.

Now that Jay and Pinckney had settled matters with Britain and Spain, and General Wayne in the Northwest had ended organized Indian resistance, a renewed surge of settlers headed for the West. New lands, ceded by the Indians in the Treaty of Greenville, revealed Congress once again divided on land policy. There were two basic viewpoints on the matter, one that the public domain should serve mainly as a source of revenue, the other that it was more important to accommodate settlers with low prices, even free land, and get the country settled. In the long run policy would evolve from the first toward the second viewpoint, but for the time being the government's need for revenue took priority.

Opinions on land policy, like other issues, separated Federalists from Republicans. Federalists involved in speculation might prefer lower land prices, but the more influential Federalists like Hamilton and Jay preferred to build the population of the eastern states first, lest the East lose political influence and a labor force important to the future growth of manufactures. Men of their persuasion favored high land prices to enrich the treasury, and the sale of relatively large parcels of land to speculators rather than small tracts to actual settlers. Jefferson and Madison were prepared reluctantly to go along with such a land policy for the sake of reducing the national debt, but Jefferson yearned for a plan by which the lands could be more readily settled. In any case, he suggested, frontiersmen would do as they had done before: "They will settle the lands in spite of everybody." The Daniel Boones of the West, always moving out beyond the settlers and surveyors, were already proving him right.

The Federalist land policy prevailed in the Land Act of 1796, which retained the 640-acre minimum size mandated by the Northwest Ordinance of 1787 while doubling the price per acre to $2 and requiring that the full amount be paid within a year. This was well beyond the means of most settlers and even many speculators. As a result, by 1800 government land offices had sold fewer than 50,000 acres. Continuing demands for cheaper land led to the Land Act of 1800, which reduced the minimum sale to 320 acres and spread the payments over four years. Thus with a down payment of $160 one could get a farm. The Land Act of 1804 further reduced the minimum parcel to 160 acres, which became the traditional homestead, and the price per acre went down to $1.64.

WASHINGTON'S FAREWELL   By 1796 President Washington had decided that two terms in office were enough. Tired of the political quarrels and the venom of the partisan press, he was ready to retire to Mount Vernon. He would leave behind a formidable record of achievement: the organization of a national government with demonstrated power, establishment of the national credit, the settlement of territory previously held by Britain and Spain, stabilization of the northwestern frontier, and the admission of three new states: Vermont (1791), Kentucky (1792), and Tennessee (1796). With the help of Jay and especially Hamilton, Washington set about preparing a valedictory address, using a draft prepared by Madison four years before.

Washington's Farewell Address, published in September 1796, focused on domestic policy, and particularly on the need for unity among Americans in backing their new government. Washington decried the "Baneful effects" of sectionalism and partisanship, while acknowledging a body of opinion that parties were "useful checks upon the administration of the government, and serve to keep alive the spirit of liberty."

In foreign relations, he asserted, America should show "good faith and justice toward all nations" and avoid either "an habitual hatred or an habitual fondness" for other countries. The United States should also "steer clear of permanent alliances with any portion of the foreign world." This statement drew little notice at the time, but it proved to be profoundly important in affecting American attitudes toward foreign policy for generations thereafter. Later spokesmen for an isolationist policy would distort Washington's position by claiming that he had opposed any "entangling alliances." On the contrary, Washington was not preaching isolationism; he was instead warning against any further permanent arrangements like that with France, still technically in effect. Washington recognized that "we may safely trust to temporary alliances for extraordinary emergencies."

THE ADAMS YEARS

With Washington out of the race, the United States in 1796 held its first partisan election for president. The logical choice of the Federalists would have been Washington's protégé Hamilton, the chief architect of their programs. But like many a later presidential candidate, Hamilton was not "available," however willing. His policies had left scars and made enemies. Nor did he suffer fools gladly, a common affliction of Federalist leaders, including the man on whom the choice fell. In Philadelphia a caucus of Federalist congressmen chose John Adams as heir apparent, with Thomas Pinckney of South Carolina, fresh from his triumph in Spain, as nominee for vice-president. As expected, the Republicans drafted Jefferson and added geographical balance to the ticket with Aaron Burr of New York.

The Providential Detection. *An anti-Republican cartoon shows the American eagle arriving just in time to stop Thomas Jefferson from burning the Constitution on the "Altar to Gallic Despotism."*

The rising strength of the Republicans, largely due to the smoldering resentment toward Jay's Treaty, very nearly swept Jefferson into office, and perhaps would have but for the public appeals of the French ambassador for Jefferson's election—an action that backfired. The Federalists won a majority among the electors, but Alexander Hamilton hatched an impulsive scheme that very nearly threw the election away after all. Between Hamilton and Adams there had been no love lost since the Revolution. As Abigail Adams warned her husband, Hamilton "is a man ambitious as Julius Caesar, a subtle intriguer. His abilities would make him dangerous if he was to espouse a wrong side, his thirst for fame is insatiable. I ever kept my Eye on him." Abigail was typically observant, for Hamilton indeed was plotting to thwart Adams's bid for the presidency. Thomas Pinckney, Hamilton thought, would be easier to influence than the strong-minded Adams. He therefore sought to have South Carolina Federalists withhold a few votes from Adams and bring Pinckney in first. The Carolinians cooperated, but New Englanders got wind of the scheme and dropped Pinckney. The upshot of Hamilton's intrigue was to cut Pinckney out of both offices and elect Jefferson as vice-president with sixty-eight votes, second to Adams's seventy-one.

Adams had behind him a distinguished career as a Massachusetts lawyer, a leader in the revolutionary movement and the Continental Congress, a diplomat in France, Holland, and Britain, and as vice-president. His political philosophy fell somewhere between Jefferson's and Hamilton's. He shared neither the one's faith in the common people nor the other's fondness for an aristocracy of "paper wealth." He favored the classic republican balance of aristocratic, democratic, and monarchical elements in government. At times, owing to his manner and appearance, his enemies portrayed him as a pompous ass. Indeed he was austere and aristocratic, but his fondness for titles and protocol arose from a reasoned purpose to exploit the public's "thirst for distinction." A man of powerful intellect, forthright convictions, and uncontrollable vanity, he was always haunted by the feeling that he was never properly appreciated—and he may have been right. On the overriding issue of his administration, war and peace, he kept his head when others about him were losing theirs—probably at the cost of his reelection.

WAR WITH FRANCE   Adams inherited from Washington his divided cabinet—there was as yet no precedent for changing personnel with each new administration. Adams also inherited a menacing quarrel with France, a by-product of Jay's Treaty. When Jay accepted the British position that food supplies and naval stores—as well as war matériel—bound for enemy ports were contraband subject to seizure, the French reasoned that American cargoes in the British trade were subject to the same interpretation. The French loosed their corsairs with even more devastating effect than the British had in 1793–1794. By the time of Adams's inauguration in 1797, the French had plundered some 300 American ships and had broken diplomatic relations with the United States.

Adams immediately acted to restore relations in the face of an outcry for war from the "High Federalists," including Secretary of State Timothy Pickering. Hamilton, however, agreed with Adams on this point and approved his last-ditch effort for a settlement. In October 1797 Charles C. Pinckney sailed for Paris with John Marshall (a Virginia Federalist) and Elbridge Gerry (a Massachusetts Republican) for further negotiations. After long, nagging delays, the three commissioners were accosted by three French counterparts (whom Adams labeled X, Y, and Z in his report to Congress), agents of Foreign Minister Talleyrand, a past master of the diplomatic shakedown. The three delicately let it be known that negotiations could begin only if there were a loan

A cartoon indicating the anti-French feeling generated by the XYZ Affair. The three American ministers at left reject the "Paris Monster's" demand for money.

to France of $12 million, a bribe of $250,000 to the five directors then heading the government, and suitable apologies for remarks recently made in Adams's message to Congress.

Such bribes were common eighteenth-century diplomatic practice—Washington himself had bribed a Creek chieftain, and ransomed American sailors from Algerian pirates at a cost of $100,000 each—but Talleyrand's price was high merely for a promise to negotiate. The answer, according to the commissioners' report, was "no, no, not a sixpence." When the XYZ Affair broke in Congress and the public press, this was translated into the more stirring slogan: "Millions for defense but not one cent for tribute." Expressions of hostility toward France rose to a crescendo—even the most partisan Republicans were hard put to make any more excuses—and many of them joined a chorus for war. An undeclared naval war in fact raged from 1798 to 1800, but Adams resisted a formal declaration of war. Congress, however, authorized the capture of armed French ships, suspended commerce with France, and renounced the alliance of 1778, which was already a dead letter.

Adams used the French crisis to strengthen American defenses. An American navy had ceased to exist at the end of the Revolution, but after Algerian pirates began to prey on American merchant vessels in the Mediterranean, Congress, in 1794, authorized the arming of six ships. Three of these—the *Constitution*, the *United States*, and the *Constellation*, were eventually completed in 1797. In 1798 Congress created a Department of the Navy and by the end of 1799 the number of naval ships had increased to thirty-three. By then American ships had captured eight French vessels and provided secure passage for American commerce.

While the naval war went on, a new army was established in 1798 as a 10,000-man force to serve three years. Adams called Washington from retirement to be its commander, agreeing to Washington's condition that he name his three chief subordinates. Washington sent in the names of Hamilton, Charles C. Pinckney, and Henry Knox. In the Revolutionary army the three had ranked in precisely the opposite order, but Washington insisted that Hamilton be his second in command. Adams relented, but resented the slight to his authority as commander-in-chief. The rift among the Federalists themselves thus widened further. Because of Washington's age, the choice meant that if the army ever took the field, Hamilton would be in command. But recruitment went slowly until late in 1799, by which time all fear of French invasion had been dispelled. Hamilton continued to dream of imperial glory, though, planning the seizure of Louisiana and the Floridas to keep them out of French hands, and even the invasion of South America, but these remained Hamilton's dreams.

By the fall of 1798, even before the naval war was fully under way, Talleyrand began to make peace overtures. Adams named three peace commissioners who arrived in Paris to find themselves confronting a new government under First Consul Napoleon Bonaparte. They sought two objectives: $20 million to pay for the American ships seized by the French, and the formal cancellation of the 1778 Treaty of Alliance. By the Convention of 1800, ratified in 1801, the French agreed only to terminate the alliance and the quasi-war.

THE WAR AT HOME   The real purpose of the French crisis all along, the more ardent Republicans suspected, was to create an excuse to put down domestic political opposition. The Alien and Sedition Acts of 1798 lent credence to their suspicions. These four measures, passed amid the wave of patriotic war fever, limited freedom of speech and the press, and the liberty of aliens. Proposed by Federalists in Congress, the legislation did not originate with Adams but had his blessing. Three of the four acts reflected native hostility to foreigners, especially the French and Irish, a large number of whom had become active Republicans and were suspected of revolutionary intent. The Naturalization Act changed from five to fourteen years the residence requirement for citizenship. The Alien Act empowered the president to expel "dangerous" aliens at his discretion. The Alien Enemies Act authorized the president in time of declared war to expel or imprison enemy aliens at will. Finally, the Sedition Act defined as a high misdemeanor any combination or conspiracy against legal measures of the government, including interference with federal officers and insurrection or riot. What is more, the law forbade writing, publishing, or speaking anything of "a false, scandalous and malicious" nature against the government or any of its officers.

The purpose of such laws was transparently partisan, designed to punish Republicans. To be sure, zealous Republican journalists were resorting to scandalous lies and misrepresentations. Just a few months before the new legislation took effect, for instance, a Republican editor characterized the president as the "old, querulous, bald, blind, crippled, toothless Adams." Such intemperate language was hardly grounds for clamping down on free speech, but it was a time when both sides seemed afflicted with paranoia. Of the ten convictions under the act, all were directed at Republicans and some for trivial matters. In the very first case a man was fined $100 for wishing out loud that the wad of a salute cannon might hit President Adams in his rear. The few convictions under the act only created martyrs to the cause of freedom of speech and the press, and exposed the vindictiveness of Federalist judges.

To offset the Alien and Sedition Acts, Jefferson and Madison brought forth drafts of what came to be known as the Kentucky and Virginia Resolutions. These passed the legislatures of the two states in November and December 1798. The resolutions, much alike in their arguments, denounced the Alien and Sedition Acts as unconstitutional and advanced the state compact theory. Since the Constitution arose as a compact among the states, the resolutions argued, it followed logically that the states retained the right to say when Congress had exceeded its powers. The states could "interpose" their judgment on acts of Congress and "nullify" them if necessary.

The doctrines of interposition and nullification, revised and edited by later theorists, were destined to be used for causes unforeseen by the authors of the Kentucky and Virginia Resolutions. At the time, it seems, both Jefferson and Madison intended the resolutions to serve chiefly as propaganda, the opening guns in the political campaign of 1800. Neither Kentucky nor Virginia took steps to nullify or interpose its authority against enforcement of the Alien and Sedition Acts. Instead, both called upon the other states to help them win a repeal in Congress. Jefferson counseled against any thought of violence, which was "not the kind of opposition the American people will permit." Alluding to the Federalists and a tax they had enacted in 1798 on houses, land, and slaves, he assured a fellow Virginian that "the reign of witches" would soon end, that it would be discredited by the arrival of the tax collector more than anything else. As Jefferson realized, the Alien and Sedition Acts touched comparatively few individuals, but the tax reached every property holder in the country. In eastern Pennsylvania the general discontent with the tax reached the stage of armed resistance and provoked Adams to dispatch army regulars and militia to enforce the law.

REPUBLICAN VICTORY   So as the presidential election of 1800 approached, grievances were mounting against Federalist policies: taxation to support an army that had little to do but chase Pennsylvania farmers, the Alien and Sedition Acts, the lingering fears of "monarchism," the hostilities aroused by Hamilton's pro-

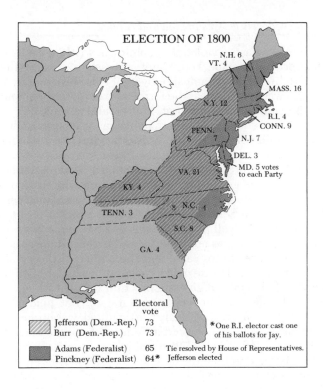

ELECTION OF 1800

N.H. 6
VT. 4
MASS. 16
N.Y. 12
R.I. 4
CONN. 9
PENN.
8   7
N.J. 7
DEL. 3
MD. 5 votes
to each Party
VA. 21
KY. 4
8 N.C. 4
TENN. 3
S.C. 8
GA. 4

Electoral
vote

Jefferson (Dem.-Rep.) 73
Burr (Dem.-Rep.) 73

Adams (Federalist) 65
Pinckney (Federalist) 64*

*One R.I. elector cast one
of his ballots for Jay.

Tie resolved by House of Representatives.
Jefferson elected

grams, the suppression of the Whiskey Rebellion, and Jay's
Treaty. When Adams decided for peace in 1800, he probably
doomed his one chance for reelection: a wave of patriotic war
fever with a united party behind him. His decision gained him
much goodwill among the people at large, but left the Hamiltonians unreconciled and his party divided.

In May 1800 the Federalists summoned enough unity to name
Adams as their candidate. But the Hamiltonians continued to
snipe at Adams and his policies, and soon after his renomination
Adams removed two of them from his cabinet. Hamilton struck
back with a pamphlet questioning Adams's fitness to be president, citing his "disgusting egotism." Intended for private distribution among Federalist leaders, the pamphlet reached the
hands of Aaron Burr, who put it in circulation.

Jefferson and Burr, as the Republican candidates, once again
represented the alliance of Virginia and New York. Jefferson,
perhaps even more than Adams, became the target of abuse. Unscrupulous opponents labeled him an atheist and a supporter of
the excesses of the French Revolution. His election, people were
told, would bring "dwellings in flames, hoary hairs bathed in

blood, female chastity violated . . . children writhing on the pike and halberd." Jefferson kept quiet, refused to answer the attacks, and directed the campaign by mail from his home at Monticello. He was portrayed as the farmers' friend, the champion of states' rights, frugal government, liberty, and peace.

Adams proved more popular than his party, whose candidates generally fared worse than the president, but the Republicans edged him out by seventy-three electoral votes to sixty-five. The decisive states were New York and South Carolina, either of which might have given the victory to Adams. But in New York Burr's organization won control of the legislature, which cast the electoral votes. In South Carolina, Charles Pinckney won over the legislature by well-placed promises of Republican patronage. Still, the result was not final, for Jefferson and Burr had tied with seventy-three votes each, and the choice of the president was thrown into the House of Representatives, where Federalist die-hards tried vainly to give the election to Burr. This was too much for Hamilton, who opposed Jefferson but held a much lower opinion of Burr. Eventually the deadlock was broken when a confidant of Jefferson assured a Federalist congressman from Delaware that Jefferson would refrain from wholesale removals of Federalists and uphold the new fiscal system. The representative resolved to vote for Jefferson, and several other Federalists agreed simply to cast blank ballots, permitting Jefferson to win without any of them actually having to vote for him.

Before the Federalists relinquished power to the Jeffersonian Republicans on March 4, 1801, their "lame duck" Congress passed the Judiciary Act of 1801. Intended to ensure Federalist control of the judicial system, this act provided that the next vacancy on the Supreme Court should not be filled, created sixteen Circuit Courts with a new judge for each, and increased the number of attorneys, clerks, and marshals. Before he left office Adams named John Marshall to the vacant office of Chief Justice and appointed Federalists to all the new positions, including forty-two justices of the peace for the new District of Columbia. The Federalists, defeated and destined never to regain national power, had in the words of Jefferson "retired into the judiciary as a stronghold."

Further Reading

The best introduction to the early Federalists remains John C. Miller's *The Federalist Era, 1789–1800* (1960).° More recent works analyze the ideological debates among the nation's first leaders. Joyce Appleby's *Capitalism and a New Social Order* (1984)° and Drew McCoy's *The Elusive Republic: Political Economy in Jeffersonian America* (1982)° trace the persistence and transformation of ideas first fostered during the Revolutionary crisis.

The 1790s may also be understood through the views and behavior of national leaders. Among recent studies of Alexander Hamilton are Forrest McDonald's *Alexander Hamilton: A Biography* (1979)° and Gerald Stourzh's *Alexander Hamilton and the Idea of Republican Government* (1970).° For the nation's first president, consult the two volumes by James T. Flexner, *George Washington and the New Nation, 1783–1793* (1970) and *George Washington: Anguish and Farewell, 1793–1799* (1972). The opposition viewpoint is the subject of Lance Banning's *The Jeffersonian Persuasion: Evolution of a Party Ideology* (1978).°

Federalist foreign policy is explored in Jerald A. Combs's *The Jay Treaty* (1970); William C. Stinchcombe's *The XYZ Affair* (1980); and Felix Gilbert's classic *To the Farewell Address: Ideas of Early American Foreign Policy* (1961).°

The treatment of Indians in the old Northwest is explored in Richard H. Kohn's *Eagle and Sword: The Federalists and the Creation of the Military Establishment in America, 1783–1802* (1975). For the Alien and Sedition Acts, consult James Morton Smith's *Freedom's Fetters: The Alien and Sedition Laws and American Civil Liberties* (1956) and Leonard W. Levy's *Legacy of Suppression: Freedom of Speech and Press in Early American History* (1960).

° These books are available in paperback editions.

8

REPUBLICANISM:
JEFFERSON AND MADISON

JEFFERSON IN POWER

On March 4, 1801, the soft-spoken, brilliant, and charming Thomas Jefferson became the first president to be inaugurated in the new Federal City, Washington, District of Columbia. The city was then an array of undistinguished buildings around two centers, Capitol Hill and the Executive Mansion. Between them lay a swampy wilderness full of stumps and mud holes. The Congress, having met in eight different towns since 1774, had at last found a permanent home, but as yet enjoyed few amenities. There were two places of amusement, one a racetrack, the other a theater filled with "tobacco smoke, whiskey breaths, and other stenches." Practically deserted much of the year, the town came to life only when Congress assembled.

Jefferson's inauguration befitted the surroundings. Tall and thin, with ill-fitting clothes, chiseled features, red hair, and a ruddy complexion, the new president left his lodgings and walked two blocks to the unfinished Capitol, entered the Senate chamber, took the oath from the recently appointed Chief Justice John Marshall, read his address in a barely audible voice, and returned to his boarding house for dinner. A tone of simplicity and conciliation ran through Jefferson's inaugural address. "We are all Republicans—we are all Federalists," he assured the nation. He then presented a ringing affirmation of republican government: "I know, indeed, that some honest men fear that a republican government cannot be strong; that this government is not strong enough. I believe this, on the contrary, the strongest government on earth. I believe it is the only one where every man . . . would meet invasions of the public order as his own personal concern."

The deliberate display of republican simplicity at Jefferson's inauguration typified the style of his administration. He took pains to avoid the monarchical trappings of his Federalist predecessors. Presidential messages went to Congress in writing lest they resemble the parliamentary speech from the throne. The practice also allowed Jefferson, a notoriously bad public speaker, to exploit his considerable skill as a writer. Jefferson, a widower, discarded the coach-and-six in which Washington and Adams had traveled to state occasions and rode about the city on horseback, often by himself. He also continued to attire himself in plain clothes. A Federalist senator, upon entering the White House, mistook Jefferson for "a servant." White House dinners were held around a circular table, so that none should take precedence. "When brought together in society, all are perfectly equal," Jefferson maintained. This infuriated several European diplomats accustomed to aristocratic formalities, and they boycotted White House affairs. But Jefferson had by no means ceased to be the Virginia gentleman, nor had he abandoned elegant manners or the good life. The cuisine of his French chef and the wines for his frequent dinners strained his budget to the point that he had to borrow money, and he left office with a debt which was to pursue him the rest of his life.

A watercolor of the president's house during Jefferson's term in office. Jefferson called it "big enough for two emperors, one pope, and the grand lama in the bargain."

Jefferson liked to think of his election as the "Revolution of 1800," but the margin had been close and the policies that he followed were more conciliatory than revolutionary. Perhaps the most revolutionary aspect of Jefferson's presidency was the orderly transfer of power in 1801, an uncommon event in the world of that day. Jefferson placed in policy-making positions men of his own party, and was the first president to pursue the role of party leader, cultivating congressional support at his dinner parties and otherwise. In the cabinet the leading fixtures were Secretary of State James Madison, a longtime neighbor and political ally, and Swiss-born Secretary of the Treasury Albert Gallatin, a Pennsylvania Republican whose financial skills had won him the respect of Federalists. In an effort to cultivate Federalist New England, Jefferson chose men from that region for the positions of attorney-general, secretary of war, and postmaster-general.

In lesser offices, however, Jefferson resisted the wholesale removal of Federalists, preferring to wait until vacancies appeared. But pressure from Republicans often forced him to yield and remove Federalists, trying as best he could to assign some other than partisan causes for the removals. In one area, however, he managed to remove the offices rather than the appointees. In 1802 Congress repealed the Judiciary Act of 1801, and so abolished the circuit judgeships and other offices to which Adams had made his "midnight appointments." A new judiciary act restored to six the number of Supreme Court justices, and set up six circuit courts, each headed by a justice.

MARBURY V. MADISON Adams's "midnight appointments" sparked the important case of *Marbury v. Madison* (1803), the first in which the Supreme Court asserted its right to declare an act of Congress unconstitutional. The case involved the appointment of one William Marbury as justice of the peace in the District of Columbia. Marbury's official letter of appointment, or commission, signed by President Adams two days before he left office, remained undelivered when Madison became secretary of state, and Jefferson directed him to withhold it. Marbury then sued for a court order (a writ of mandamus) directing Madison to deliver his commission. John Marshall, Jefferson's distant Virginia cousin with the gravelly voice, crystalline logic, and staunch Federalist views, wrote the Court's opinion. He held that Marbury was entitled to his commission, but he then denied that the Court had jurisdiction in the case. Section 13 of the Judiciary Act of 1789, which gave the Court original jurisdiction in mandamus proceedings, was unconstitutional, Marshall and the court ruled, because the Constitution specified that the Court should have original jurisdiction only in cases involving ambassadors or states. The Court, therefore, could issue no order in the case. With one bold stroke Marshall thus had chastised the Jeffersonians while avoiding an awkward confrontation with an administration that might have defied his order. At the same time, he established the precedent that the Court could declare a federal law invalid on the grounds that it violated provisions of the Constitution.

DOMESTIC REFORMS Jefferson's first term was a succession of triumphs in both domestic and foreign affairs. He did not set out to discard Hamilton's program. Under Treasury Secretary Gallatin's tutoring he learned to accept the national bank as an essential convenience. It was too late of course to undo Hamilton's funding and debt assumption operations, but none too soon, in the opinion of both Jefferson and Gallatin, to begin retiring the resultant federal debt. In 1802 Jefferson won the repeal of the whiskey tax and other Federalist excises, much to the relief of backwoods distillers and drinkers.

Without the excise taxes, frugality was all the more necessary to a government dependent for revenue chiefly on tariffs and the sale of western lands. Happily for Gallatin's treasury, both flourished. The European war brought a continually increasing traffic to American shipping and revenues to the Treasury. At the same

Cincinnati in 1800, twelve years after its founding. Though its population was only about 750, its inhabitants were already promoting Cincinnati as "the metropolis of the north-western territory."

time settlers flocked to the western lands, which were coming more and more within their reach. The admission of Ohio in 1803 increased the number of states to seventeen.

By the "wise and frugal government" promised in the inaugural, Jefferson and Gallatin reasoned, the United States could live within its income, like a prudent farmer. The basic formula was simple: cut back expenses on the military. A standing army was a menace to a free society anyway, and therefore should be kept to a minimum, with defense left to the militia. The navy, which the Federalists had already reduced after the quasi-war with France, ought to be reduced further. Coastal defense, Jefferson argued, should rely on fortifications and a "mosquito fleet" of small gunboats.

In 1807 Jefferson crowned his reforms by signing an act which outlawed the foreign slave trade as of January 1, 1808, the earliest date possible under the Constitution. At the time, South Carolina was the only state that still permitted the trade, but for years to come an illegal traffic in African slaves would continue. By one informal estimate perhaps 300,000 slaves were smuggled into southern states between 1808 and 1861.

THE BARBARY PIRATES   Issues of foreign relations intruded on Jefferson early in his term, when events in the Mediterranean gave him second thoughts about the need for a navy. On the Barbary Coast of North Africa, the rulers of Morocco, Algeria, Tunis, and Tripoli (now part of Libya) had for years promoted piracy and extortion. After the Revolution, American shipping in the Mediterranean became fair game, no longer protected by British payments of tribute. The new American government paid protection money too, first to Morocco in1786, then to the others in the 1790s. In May 1801, however, the pasha of Tripoli upped his demands and declared war on the United States. Jefferson thereupon sent warships to blockade Tripoli. A wearisome warfare dragged on until 1805, punctuated in 1804 by the notable exploit of Lt. Stephen Decatur, who slipped into Tripoli harbor by night and set fire to the frigate *Philadelphia*, which had been captured (along with its crew) after it ran aground. In 1805 the pasha settled for $60,000 ransom and released the *Philadelphia*'s crew (mostly British subjects), whom he had held hostage more than a year. It was still tribute, but less than the $300,000 the pasha had demanded, and much less than the cost of the war.

THE LOUISIANA PURCHASE   It was an inglorious end to a shabby affair, but well before it was over events elsewhere had conspired to produce the greatest single achievement of the Jefferson administration. The Louisiana Purchase of 1803 more than doubled the territory of the United States by bringing into its borders the entire Mississippi Valley west of the river itself. The French had settled Louisiana in the early eighteenth century, but after their defeat by England in the Seven Years' War, they had ceded the Louisiana territory to Spain. Soon after taking power in France in 1799, however, Napoleon Bonaparte forced the Spanish to return the territory and expressed his intention of creating a North American empire. When word of the deal reached Washington, Jefferson hastened Robert R. Livingston, the new minister to France, on his way to Paris. Spain in control of the Mississippi outlet was bad enough, but Napoleon in control could only mean serious trouble. Jefferson wrote Livingston: "The day that France takes possession of New Orleans . . . we must marry ourselves to the British fleet and nation," a sobering prospect for Jefferson.

Livingston had instructions to talk the French out of it, if it was not too late, and a series of long and frustrating negotiations began in January 1803. In April Napoleon's minister, Talleyrand, suddenly asked if the United States would like to buy the whole of Louisiana. Livingston, once he could regain his composure, snapped at the offer. Having failed to conquer the sugar-rich island of Santo Domingo, and eager to renew his struggle against England, Napoleon had apparently decided simply to cut his losses in the New World, turn a quick profit, please the Americans, and go back to reshaping the map of Europe.

By the treaty of cession, dated April 30, 1803, the United States paid about $15 million for the huge territory. In defining the boundaries of Louisiana, the treaty was vague. Its language could be stretched to provide a tenuous claim on Texas and a much stronger claim on West Florida, from Baton Rouge on the Mississippi past Mobile to the Perdido River on the east. When Livingston asked about the boundaries, Talleyrand responded: "I can give you no direction. You have made a noble bargain for yourselves, and I suppose you will make the most of it."

The turn of events had indeed presented Jefferson with a noble bargain, a great new "empire of liberty," but also with a constitutional dilemma. Nowhere did the Constitution mention the purchase of territory. By a strict construction, which Jefferson had professed, no such power existed. Jefferson at first thought to resolve the matter by amendment, but his advisers argued against delay lest Napoleon change his mind. The power to purchase territory, they reasoned, resided in the power to make treaties. Jefferson relented, trusting, he said, "that the good sense of our country will correct the evil of loose construction when it shall produce ill effects." New England Federalists boggled at the prospect of new states that would probably strengthen the Jeffersonian party, and in a reversal that foretokened many future reversals on constitutional issues, Federalists found themselves arguing strict construction of the Constitution while Republicans brushed aside such scruples.

In October 1803 the Senate ratified the treaty by an overwhelming vote of 26 to 6, and on December 20, 1803, American representatives took formal possession of Louisiana. The Spanish kept West Florida, but within a decade it would be ripe for the plucking. American settlers in 1810 staged a rebellion in Baton Rouge and proclaimed the Republic of West Florida, quickly annexed and occupied by the United States as far eastward as the Pearl River. In 1812 the state of Louisiana absorbed the region. The following year, with Spain itself a battlefield for French and British forces, American troops took over the rest of West Florida, now the Gulf coast of Mississippi and Alabama. The United States had truly made the most of a shrewd bargain.

EXPLORING THE CONTINENT   An amateur scientist long before he was president, Jefferson had nourished an active curiosity about the vast Louisiana country. In January 1803 he asked Congress for money to send an exploring expedition to the far northwest, beyond the Mississippi, in what was still foreign territory. Congress approved and Jefferson assigned as commanders Meriwether Lewis, the president's bow-legged private secretary, and another Virginian, tall, red-haired William Clark, the much younger brother of the Revolutionary hero George Rogers Clark.

In May 1804 the "Corps of Discovery," numbering nearly fifty, set out from St. Louis to ascend the Missouri River. Forced to live off the land, they quickly adapted themselves to a new environment. Local Indians introduced them to clothes made from deer hides and to new hunting techniques. Six months later, near the Mandan Sioux villages in what is now North Dakota, they built a fort and wintered there in relative comfort, sending back a barge loaded with plant and animal specimens such as the prairie dog, previously unknown to science, and the magpie, previously unknown in America. In the spring they added to the main party a French guide and his remarkable Shoshone wife, Sacajawea ("Canoe Launcher"), who proved an enormous help as interpreter with the Indians of the region, and set out once

EXPLORATIONS OF THE LOUISIANA PURCHASE

━━━━ Lewis and Clark, 1804-1806
╌╌╌╌ Pike, 1805-1806
──── Pike, 1806-1807

again upstream. At the head of the Missouri they took the north fork, thenceforth the Jefferson River, crossed the continental divide, braved attacks by grizzly bears, and in dugout canoes descended the Snake and Columbia Rivers to the Pacific. The following spring they headed back east by almost the same route, and after a swing through the Yellowstone country, returned to St. Louis in September 1806, having been gone nearly two and a half years. No longer was the Far West unknown country. Their reports of friendly Indians and abundant pelts attracted traders and trappers to the region and also gave the United States a claim to the Oregon country by right of discovery and exploration.

POLITICAL SCHEMES   Jefferson's policies, including the Louisiana Purchase, brought him almost solid support in the South and

West. Even New Englanders were moving to his side. By 1809 even John Quincy Adams, the son of the second president, would become a Republican. Die-hard Federalists read the handwriting on the wall. The acquisition of a vast new empire in the west would reduce New England to insignificance in political affairs, and along with it the Federalist cause. Under the leadership of Sen. Timothy Pickering, a group of bitter Massachusetts Federalists called the Essex Junto considered seceding from the Union, an idea that would simmer in New England for another decade.

Soon these New Englanders hatched a scheme to link New York with their secessionist fantasy. They contacted Vice-President Aaron Burr, who had long been on the outs with the Jeffersonians and who was, as ever, ready for conspiracies. Their plan depended on Burr's election as governor of New York, but in April 1804 Burr was overwhelmed by the regular Republican candidate. The extreme Federalists, it turned out, could not even hold members of their own party to their disunionist plan. Hamilton bitterly opposed the conspiracy, noting that Burr was "a dangerous man, and one who ought not to be trusted with the reins of government." When Hamilton's remarks appeared in the press, Burr's demand for an explanation led in 1804 to a duel in which Burr shot Hamilton through the heart. Hamilton went to his death, as his son had done in a similar affair the previous year, determined not to fire at his opponent. Burr had no such scruples. The death of Hamilton ended both Pickering's scheme and Burr's political career—but not his intrigues.

Meanwhile the presidential campaign of 1804 began in February when a Republican congressional caucus renominated Jefferson. Opposed by the Federalist Charles C. Pinckney, Jefferson won 162 of 176 electoral votes. He proudly noted in his second inaugural address that he had carried out the general policies announced in the first: "The suppression of unnecessary offices, of useless establishments and expenses, enabled us to discontinue our internal taxes. . . . What farmer, what mechanic, what laborer ever sees a tax-gatherer of the United States?"

Divisions in the Republican Party

RANDOLPH AND THE *TERTIUM QUID* "Never was there an administration more brilliant than that of Mr. Jefferson up to this period," asserted John Randolph of Roanoke after the 1804 election. "We were indeed in the full tide of successful experiment." But the Republican landslide had a disappointing sequel.

Freed from a strong opposition—Federalists made up only a quarter of the new Congress—the majority began to lose its cohesion. Cracks appeared in the Republican façade, signs of major fissures that would finally split the party. Ironically, John Randolph, a Jeffersonian mainstay in the first term, became the most conspicuous of the dissidents. A brilliant, witty, but erratic and unyielding Virginia planter-philosopher, given to fits of insanity in his later years, he was a powerful combination of principle, intelligence, wit, arrogance, and rancor. Famous for his venomous assaults delivered in a shrill soprano voice, the Virginia congressman flourished best in opposition. He once dismissed a rival as "a man of splendid abilities but utterly corrupt. Like a rotten mackeral by moonlight, he shines and stinks." Few of Randolph's colleagues had the stomach for his tongue-lashings.

Randolph became the crusty spokesman for a shifting group of "Old Republicans" whose adherence to party principles had rendered them more Jeffersonian than Jefferson himself. Their philosopher was John Taylor of Caroline, a Virginia planter-pamphleteer whose fine-spun theories reflected the continuing fear on the part of many that the national government was continuing to grow in power and scope at the expense of individual liberty and states' rights. Taylor's ideas had little effect at the time but delighted secessionists of later years. Neither Randolph nor Taylor could accept Jefferson's pragmatic gift for adjusting principle to circumstance, and they steadfastly defended states' rights against the intrusions of federal power. Said Randolph: "Asking one of the States to surrender part of her sovereignty is like asking a lady to surrender part of her chastity."

Randolph broke with Jefferson in 1806, when the president sought an appropriation of $2 million for a thinly disguised bribe to win French influence in persuading Spain to give up the Floridas. "I found I might co-operate or be an honest man—I have therefore opposed and will oppose them," Randolph pledged. Thereafter he resisted Jefferson's initiatives almost out of reflex. Randolph and his colleagues were sometimes called "Quids," or the *Tertium Quid* (the "third something"), and their dissents gave rise to talk of a third party, neither Republican nor Federalist. But they never got together, and their failure would typify the experience of almost all third-party movements thereafter.

THE BURR CONSPIRACY   If feisty John Randolph was sincerely committed to principle, opportunistic Aaron Burr was sincerely committed to himself. Born of a distinguished line of Puritans, including grandfather Jonathan Edwards, he cast off the family

Aaron Burr, the brilliant but erratic vice-president.

Calvinism to pursue money, power, and women. Burr was small and slight, with finely cut features and remarkably dark, piercing eyes. Rarely without a fine cigar or a grasping vision, he was a talented, witty, and charming man who was rumored to be the richest lawyer in New York. He boasted of never having lost a case. Sheer brilliance and shrewdness carried him to the vice-presidency, and he might have become heir-apparent to Jefferson, but a taste for intrigue was the tragic flaw in his character. Caught up in the dubious schemes of Federalist die-hards in 1800 and again in 1804, he ended his political career once and for all when he killed Hamilton. Indicted in New York and New Jersey for murder and heavily in debt, the vice-president fled first to Spanish-held Florida, then, once the furor subsided, he boldly returned to Washington in November to preside over the Senate. As long as he stayed out of New York, he was safe. Groused one senator: "We are indeed fallen on evil times."

But Burr focused his attention less on the Senate than on a cockeyed scheme to carve out a personal empire for himself in the West. The so-called Burr Conspiracy was hatched when Burr met with General James Wilkinson, an old friend with a tainted Revolutionary war record who was a spy for the Spanish and had a penchant for easy money, a taste for rum, and an eye for intrigue. Just what he and Burr were up to probably will never be known. The most likely explanation is that they sought to organize a secession of Louisiana and set up an independent republic. Earlier Burr had solicited British support for his scheme to separate "the western part of the United States in its whole extent."

Whatever the goal, Burr succeeded in having Wilkinson appointed governor of the Louisiana Territory, and in the summer of 1805 Burr himself sailed downriver from Pittsburgh on a lavishly outfitted flatboat, leaving behind a wake of rumors. By the summer of 1806 he was in Lexington, Kentucky, recruiting adventurers. Meanwhile, rumors began to reach Jefferson, and in November 1806 so did a letter from General Wilkinson warning of "a deep, dark, wicked, and wide-spread conspiracy." Wilkinson had apparently developed cold feet and now feigned ignorance of the whole affair.

In January 1807, as Burr neared Natchez with his motley crew, he learned that Wilkinson had betrayed him and that Jefferson had ordered his arrest. He cut out cross-country for Pensacola, disguised as a boatman, but was caught in Alabama and taken off to Richmond, Virginia, for a trial which, like the conspiracy, had a stellar cast. Charged with treason by the grand jury, Burr was brought for trial before Chief Justice Marshall. Events then revealed both Marshall and Jefferson at their partisan worst. Jefferson, determined to get a conviction at any cost, published relevant affidavits in advance and promised pardons to conspirators who helped to convict Burr. The Federalist Marshall in turn was so indiscreet as to attend a dinner given by the defense counsel at which Burr himself was present.

The case established two major constitutional precedents. First, on the grounds of executive privilege, Jefferson ignored a subpoena requiring him to appear in court with certain papers. He believed that the independence of the executive branch would be compromised if the president were subject to a court writ. The second major precedent was the rigid definition of treason. On this Marshall adopted the strictest of constructions. Treason under the Constitution, he concluded, consisted of "levying war against the United States or adhering to their enemies" and required "two witnesses to the same overt act" for conviction. Since the prosecution failed to produce two witnesses to an overt act of treason by Burr, the jury found him not guilty.

Whether or not Burr escaped his just deserts, Marshall's strict construction of the Constitution protected the United States, as the authors of the Constitution clearly intended, against the capricious judgments of "treason" that governments through the centuries have used to terrorize dissenters. As to Burr, with further charges pending, he skipped bail and took refuge in France, but returned unmolested in 1812 to practice law in New York. He survived to a virile old age. At age eighty, shortly before his death, he was divorced on grounds of adultery.

WAR IN EUROPE

Oppositionists of whatever stripe were more an annoyance than a threat to Jefferson. The more intractable problems of his second term were created by the renewal of the European war in 1803, which helped resolve the problem of Louisiana but put more strains on Jefferson's desire to avoid "entangling alliances" and the quarrels of Europe. In 1805 Napoleon's smashing defeat of Russian and Austrian forces made him the master of western Europe. The same year Lord Nelson's defeat of the French and Spanish fleets in the Battle of Trafalgar secured Britain's control of the seas. The war resolved itself into a battle of elephant and whale, Napoleon dominant on land, the British dominant on the water, neither able to strike a decisive blow at the other, and neither restrained by an appreciation of neutral rights or international law.

HARASSMENT BY BRITAIN AND FRANCE For two years after the renewal of hostilities, American shippers reaped the benefits, taking over trade with the French and Spanish West Indies. But in the case of the *Essex* (1805), a British prize court ruled that the practice of shipping French and Spanish goods through American ports while on their way elsewhere did not neutralize enemy goods. Such a practice violated the British rule of 1756 under which trade closed in time of peace remained closed in time of war. Goods shipped in violation of the rule, the British held, could be seized at any point under the doctrine of continuous voyage. After 1807 British interference with American shipping increased, not just to keep supplies from Napoleon's continent but also to hobble competition with British merchant ships.

In a series of Orders of Council adopted in 1806 and 1807, the British ministry set up a paper blockade of Europe. Vessels headed for continental ports had to get licenses and accept British inspection or be liable to seizure. Napoleon retaliated with his "Continental System," proclaimed in the Berlin Decree of 1806 and the Milan Decree of 1807. In the first he declared a blockade of the British Isles, and in the second, he ruled that neutral ships which complied with British regulations were subject to seizure when they reached continental ports. The situation presented American shippers with a dilemma. If they complied with the demands of one side they were subject to seizure by the other.

It was humiliating, but the prospects for profits were so great

Preparation for War to Defend Commerce. *In 1806 and 1807 American shipping was caught in the crossfire of war between Britain and France.*

that shippers ran the risk. Seamen faced a more dangerous risk: a renewal of the practice of impressment. The use of press gangs to kidnap men in British (and colonial) ports was a longstanding method of recruitment for the British navy. The seizure of British subjects from American vessels became a new source of recruits, justified on the principle that British subjects remained British subjects for life: "Once an Englishman, always an Englishman."

In the summer of 1807 the British *Leopard* accosted an American naval vessel, the *Chesapeake*, just outside territorial waters off Norfolk. After the *Chesapeake's* captain refused to be searched, the *Leopard* fired upon the American ship, killing three and wounding eighteen. The *Chesapeake*, caught unready for battle, was forced to strike its colors in surrender. A British search party seized four men, one of whom was later hanged for desertion from the British navy. Soon after the *Chesapeake* limped back into Norfolk, a Washington newspaper editorialized: "We have never, on any occasion, witnessed such a thirst for revenge. . . ." Public wrath was so aroused that Jefferson could have had war on the spot. But like Adams before him, he resisted the war fever and suffered politically as a result. One Federalist called Jefferson a "dish of skim milk curdling at the head of our nation."

THE EMBARGO   Jefferson resolved to channel public indignation into an effort at "peaceable coercion." In December 1807, in response to his request, Congress passed the Embargo Act, which stopped all export of American goods and prohibited American ships from clearing for foreign ports. It also effectively ended imports, since it was unprofitable for foreign ships to return from America empty. The constitutional basis of the embargo was the power to regulate commerce, which in this case Republicans interpreted broadly as the power to prohibit commerce.

Jefferson's embargo, however, failed from the beginning, for the public was unwilling to make the necessary sacrifices. Trade remained profitable despite the risks, and violating the embargo was almost laughably easy. Consequently, neither France nor Great Britain was significantly hurt by Jefferson's policy.

But Jefferson was. The embargo revived the languishing Federalist party in New England, which renewed the charge that Jefferson was in league with the French. The embargo, one New Englander said, was "like cutting one's throat to cure the nosebleed." At the same time, agriculture in the south and west suffered for want of outlets for grain, cotton, and tobacco. After fifteen months of ineffectiveness, Jefferson finally accepted failure and on March 1, 1809, repealed the embargo shortly before he relinquished the "splendid misery" of the presidency. In the election of 1808 the succession passed to another Virginian, Secretary of State James Madison.

THE DRIFT TO WAR   Madison was entangled in foreign affairs from the beginning. Still insisting on neutral rights and freedom of the seas, he pursued Jefferson's policy of "peaceful coercion" by different but equally ineffective means. In place of the embargo Congress had substituted the Non-Intercourse Act, which reopened trade with all countries except France and Great Britain and authorized the president to reopen trade with whichever of these gave up its restrictions. Non-intercourse proved as ineffective as the embargo. In the vain search for an alternative, Congress on May 1, 1810, reversed its ground and adopted a measure introduced by Nathaniel Macon of North Carolina, Macon's Bill No. 2, which reopened trade with the warring powers but provided that if either dropped its restrictions non-intercourse would be restored with the other.

Napoleon's foreign minister, the duc de Cadore, then informed the American minister in Paris that he had withdrawn the Berlin and Milan Decrees, but the carefully worded Cadore letter had strings attached: revocation of the decrees depended on withdrawal of the British Orders in Council. The strings were plain to see, but either Madison misunderstood or, more likely, went along in hope of putting pressure on the British. In response to the Cadore letter, he restored non-intercourse with the British. London refused to give in, but Madison clung to his policy despite Napoleon's continued seizure of American ships. The seemingly hopeless effort did indeed finally work. With more time, patience, or a transatlantic cable, Madison's policy would have been vindicated without resort to war. On June 16, 1812, the British foreign minister, facing economic crisis, revoked the Orders in Council. Britain preferred not to risk war with the United States on top of its war with Napoleon. But it was too late. On June 1 Madison had asked for war, and by mid-June the Congress concurred.

THE WAR OF 1812

CAUSES   The main cause of the war—the demand for neutral rights—seems clear enough. Neutral rights were the focus of Madison's war message and the salient reason for mounting public hostility toward the British. Yet the geographical distribution of the congressional vote for war raises a troubling question. Most votes for war came from the farm regions that stretched from Pennsylvania southward and westward. The maritime states of New York and New England, the region that bore the brunt of British attacks on American trade, voted against the declaration of war. One explanation for this seeming anomaly is simple enough. The farming regions were afflicted by the damage to their markets for grain, cotton, and tobacco, while New England shippers made profits in spite of British restrictions.

Other plausible explanations for the sectional vote, however, include frontier Indian attacks that were blamed on the British, western land hunger, and the desire for territory in British Canada and Spanish Florida. The constant pressure to open new lands repeatedly forced or persuaded Indians to sign treaties they did not always understand, causing stronger resentment among tribes that were losing more and more of their lands. It was an old story, dating from the Jamestown settlement, but one that took a new turn with the rise of a powerful Shawnee leader, Tecumseh.

According to General William Henry Harrison, governor of the Indiana Territory, Tecumseh was "one of those uncommon geniuses, which spring up occasionally to produce revolutions and overturn the order of things." Tecumseh recognized the consequences of Indian disunity and set out to form a confederation of tribes to defend Indian hunting grounds, insisting that no land cession was valid without the consent of all tribes since they held the land in common. By 1811 Tecumseh had matured his plans and headed south from the Indiana Territory to win the Creeks, Cherokees, Choctaws, and Chickasaws to his cause. His speeches were filled with emotion and anger. "The white race is a wicked race," he declared. "They seize your land; they corrupt your women." Only by driving them out "upon a trail of blood" would the Indians survive.

Governor Harrison gathered a force near Tecumseh's capital on the Tippecanoe River while the leader was away. On November 7, 1811, the Indians took the bait and attacked Harrison's encampment, although Tecumseh had warned against any fighting in his absence. The Shawnees were finally repulsed in a bloody engagement that left about a quarter of Harrison's men dead or wounded. Harrison then burned the Shawnee town and destroyed all its supplies. Tecumseh's dreams of an Indian confederacy went up in smoke, and Tecumseh himself fled to British protection in Canada.

Tecumseh, the Shawnee leader who tried to unite the tribes in defense of their lands. He was killed in 1813 at the Battle of the Thames.

The Battle of Tippecanoe reinforced suspicions that the British were inciting the Indians. To eliminate the Indian menace, frontiersmen reasoned, they needed to remove its foreign support. Conquest of Canada would thus accomplish a twofold purpose. It would end British influence among the Indians and open a new empire for land-hungry Americans. It was also the only place, in case of war, where the British were vulnerable to American attack. East Florida, still under the Spanish flag, posed a similar threat since Spain was either too weak or unwilling to prevent sporadic Indian attacks across the frontier. The British were also suspected of smuggling through Florida and intriguing with the Indians on the southwest border.

Such concerns helped generate a war fever. In the Congress that assembled in November 1811 a number of new, young members from southern and western districts began to clamor for war in defense of "national honor." Among them were Henry Clay of Kentucky, who became Speaker of the House, Richard M. Johnson of Kentucky, Felix Grundy of Tennessee, and John C. Calhoun of South Carolina. John Randolph of Roanoke christened these new "boys" the "War Hawks." After they entered the House, Randolph said, "We have heard but one word—like the whip-poor-will, but one eternal monotonous tone—Canada! Canada! Canada!"

PREPARATIONS   As it turned out, the War Hawks would get neither Canada nor Florida. For in June 1812 James Madison had carried into war a country that was ill-prepared both financially and militarily. The year before, despite earnest pleas from Treasury Secretary Gallatin, Congress had let the twenty-year charter of the Bank of the United States expire. A combination of strict-constructionist Republicans and Anglophobes, who feared the large British interest in the bank, caused its demise. Meanwhile, trade had collapsed and tariff revenues had declined. Loans were needed for about two-thirds of the war costs, but northeast opponents of the war were reluctant to lend money.

The military situation was almost as bad. War had been likely for nearly a decade, but Republican budgetary constraints had prevented preparations. When the war began the army numbered only 6,700 men, ill-trained, poorly equipped, and led by aging officers. One young Virginia officer named Winfield Scott, destined for military distinction, commented that most of the veteran commanders "had very generally slunk into either sloth, ignorance, or habits of intemperate drinking." The navy, on the other hand, was in comparatively good shape, with able officers and trained men whose seamanship had been tested in the fighting against France and Tripoli. Its ships were well outfitted and seaworthy—all sixteen of them. In the first year of the war the navy produced the only American victories in isolated duels with British vessels, but their effect was mainly an occasional lift to morale. Within a year the British had blockaded the coast, except for New England, where they hoped to cultivate antiwar feeling, and most of the little American fleet was bottled up in port.

THE WAR IN THE NORTH   The only place where the United States could effectively strike at the British was Canada. Madison's best hope was a quick attack on Quebec or Montréal to cut Canada's lifeline, the St. Lawrence River. Instead of striking directly at the lifeline, however, the administration opted for a three-pronged drive against Canada: along the Lake Champlain route toward Montreal, with General Henry Dearborn in command; along the Niagara River, with forces under General Stephen Van Rensselaer; and into Upper Canada (north of Lake Erie) from Detroit, where General William Hull and some 2,000 men arrived in early July 1812. In Detroit, the sickly and senile Hull procrastinated, while his position worsened and the news arrived that an American fort isolated at the head of Lake Huron had surrendered in mid-July. The British commander cleverly played upon Hull's worst fears. Gathering what redcoats he could to parade in view of Detroit's defenders, he announced that thousands of Indian allies were at the rear and that once fighting began he would be unable to control them. Fearing massacre, Hull, without consulting his officers and without a shot being fired, surrendered his entire force in August.

Along the Niagara front, General Van Rensselaer was more aggressive than Hull. On October 13 an advance party of 600 Americans crossed the Niagara River and worked their way up the bluffs on the Canadian side to occupy Queenstown Heights. The stage was set for a major victory, but the New York militia refused to reinforce Van Rensselaer's men, claiming that their military service did not obligate them to leave the country. They complacently remained on the New York side and watched their outnumbered countrymen fall to a superior force across the river.

On the third front, the old invasion route via Lake Champlain, the trumpet once more gave an uncertain sound. On November 19, 1812, the incompetent General Dearborn led his army north from Plattsburgh toward Montreal. He marched them up to the

LAKE SUPERIOR

Quebec

Ft. Michilimakinac

St. Lawrence R.

PREVOST,
AUG.-SEPT.
1814

Montreal

CANADA

Plattsburgh

Lake
Champlain

LAKE HURON

York
(Toronto)

LAKE ONTARIO

VT.

N.H.

MICHIGAN
TERRITORY

LAKE MICHIGAN

The Thames

BROCK,
JULY 1812

Ft. Niagara
Queenstown Heights
RENSSELAER
OCT. 1812

N.Y.

MASS.

Detroit

LAKE ERIE

Hudson R.

CONN.

Ft. Dearborn

Maumee R.

HARRISON,
OCT. 1813

HULL, AUG. 1812

PERRY,
SEPT. 1813

Presque Isle
(Erie)

Put-in-Bay

PENN.

Susquehanna R.

N.J.

INDIANA
TERRITORY

Wabash R.

OHIO

Pittsburgh

Ohio R.

MD.

Baltimore

BRITISH BLOCKADE

KY.

Ft. McHenry

Washington D.C.

DEL.

Chesapeake
Bay

VIRGINIA

Potomac R.

ROSS,
AUG. 1814

0   200 Miles
0   200 Kilometers

border, where the militia once again stood on its alleged constitutional rights and refused to cross, and then marched them
down again.

Madison's navy secretary now pushed vigorously for American
control of inland waters. At Presque Isle (Erie), Pennsylvania,
twenty-eight-year-old Commodore Oliver H. Perry, already a
fourteen-year veteran who had seen action against Tripoli, was
busy building ships from green timbers. By the end of the summer Perry set out in search of the British, whom he found at Lake
Erie's Put-in Bay on September 10, 1813. After completing the
preparations for battle, Perry told an aide: "This is the most important day of my life." It was indeed. Two British warships took
advantage of their superior weapons by pummeling the
Lawrence, Perry's flagship, at long distance. Blood flowed on the
deck so freely that the sailors slipped and fell as they wrestled
with the cannon. After four hours of intense shelling, none of the
Lawrence's guns was left working and 80 percent of the crew
were dead or wounded. The British expected the Americans to
turn tail, but Perry refused to quit. He transferred to another
vessel, carried the battle to the enemy, and finally accepted sur-

render of the entire British squadron. Hatless, begrimed, and bloodied, Perry sent General William Henry Harrison the long-awaited message: "We have met the enemy and they are ours."

More good news followed. At the Battle of the Thames (October 5), in Canadian territory east of Detroit, General Harrison eliminated British power in Upper Canada and released the Northwest from any further threat. In the course of the battle, Tecumseh fell and his persistent dream of Indian unity died with him.

THE WAR IN THE SOUTH   In the Southwest too the war flared up in 1813. On August 30 the Creeks attacked Fort Mims, on the Alabama River above Mobile, killing almost half the people in the fort. The news found Andrew Jackson home in bed in Nashville, recovering from a street brawl with Thomas Hart Benton, later a senator from Missouri. As major-general of the Tennessee militia, Jackson summoned about 2,000 volunteers and set out on a campaign which utterly crushed Creek resistance. The decisive battle occurred on March 27, 1814, at the Horseshoe Bend of the Tallapoosa River, in the heart of the upper Creek country. In the Treaty of Fort Jackson, signed that August, the Creeks ceded two-thirds of their lands to the United States, including part of Georgia and most of Alabama.

Four days after the Battle of Horseshoe Bend, Napoleon's empire collapsed. Now free to deal with America, the British developed a threefold plan of operations for 1814. They would launch a two-pronged invasion of America via Niagara and Lake Champlain to increase the clamor for peace in the Northeast, extend the naval blockade to New England, subjecting coastal towns to raids, and seize New Orleans to cut the Mississippi River, lifeline of the West. Uncertainties about the peace settlement in Europe, however, prevented the release of British veterans for a full-scale assault upon the New World. And after a generation of conflict, war weariness countered the British thirst for revenge against the former colonials. British plans were stymied also by the more resolute young commanders Madison had placed in charge of strategic areas by the summer of 1814.

The main British effort focused on the invasion via Lake Champlain. A land assault might have taken Plattsburgh and forced American troops out of their protected positions nearby, but England's army bogged down while its flotilla engaged an American naval squadron in a deadly battle on Lake Champlain. The battle ended in September 1814 with the entire British flotilla either destroyed or captured.

FIGHTING IN THE CHESAPEAKE Meanwhile, however, American forces suffered the most humiliating experience of the war, the capture and burning of Washington, D.C. With attention focused on the Canadian front, the Chesapeake Bay offered the British a number of inviting targets, including Baltimore, now the fourth-largest city in America. On the evening of August 24, 1814, the British marched unopposed into Washington, where British officers ate a meal in the White House intended for President and Mrs. Madison, who had hastily joined the other refugees in Virginia. The British then burned the White House, the Capitol, and all other government buildings except the Patent Office. A tornado the next day compounded the damage, but a violent thunderstorm dampened both the fires and the enthusiasm of the British forces, who left to prepare a new assault on Baltimore. One British newspaper editor expressed shameful regret at the army's actions: "The Cossacks spared Paris, but we spared not the Capital of America!"

The attack on Baltimore was a different story. With some 13,000 men, chiefly militia, American forces fortified the heights behind the city. About 1,000 men held Fort McHenry,

The Taking of the City of Washington in America. *An English cartoon depicts the taking of Washington, D.C., on August 24, 1814.*

on an island in the harbor. The British landed at North Point, where an advance group of American militia inflicted severe casualties. When the British finally came into sight of the city on September 13, they halted in the face of American defenses. All through the following night the British fleet bombarded Fort McHenry to no avail, and the invaders abandoned the attack on the city as too costly to risk. Francis Scott Key, a Washington lawyer, watched the siege from a vessel in the harbor. The sight of the flag still in place at dawn inspired him to draft the verses of "The Star Spangled Banner." Later revised and set to the tune of an English drinking song, it was immediately popular and eventually became the national anthem.

THE BATTLE OF NEW ORLEANS   The British failure at Baltimore followed by three days their failure on Lake Champlain, and their offensive against New Orleans had yet to run its course. Along the Gulf coast General Andrew Jackson had been busy shoring up the defenses of Mobile and New Orleans. In November 1814, without authorization, he invaded Spanish Florida and took Pen-

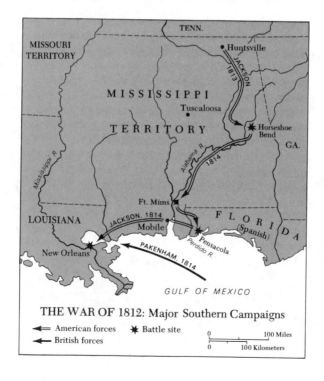

THE WAR OF 1812: Major Southern Campaigns

sacola, ending British intrigues there. Back in Louisiana by the end of November, he began to erect defenses on the approaches to New Orleans. But the British fleet, with some 7,500 European veterans under Gen. Sir Edwin Pakenham, cautiously took up positions on a level plain near the Mississippi just south of New Orleans.

Pakenham's painfully careful approach—he waited until all his artillery was available—gave Jackson time to build earthworks bolstered by cotton bales. It was an almost invulnerable position, but Pakenham, contemptuous of Jackson's motley array of frontier militiamen, Creole aristocrats, free blacks, and pirates, ordered a frontal assault at dawn on January 8, 1815. His redcoats emerged out of the morning fog and ran into a murderous hail of artillery shells and deadly rifle fire. Before the British withdrew about 2,000 had been killed or wounded, including Pakenham himself, whose body, pickled in a barrel of rum, was returned to the ship where his wife awaited news of the battle.

The Battle of New Orleans occurred after a peace treaty had already been signed, but this is not to say that it was an anticlimax or that it had no effect on the outcome of the war, for the treaty was yet to be ratified and the British might have exploited to advantage the possession of New Orleans had they won it. The battle assured ratification of the treaty as it stood, and both governments acted quickly.

THE TREATY OF GHENT AND THE HARTFORD CONVENTION   Peace efforts had begun in 1812, even before hostilities commenced, but negotiations bogged down after the fighting started. The British were stalling, awaiting news of smashing victories to strengthen their hand. Word of the American victory on Lake Champlain weakened the British resolve. Their will to fight was further eroded by a continuing power struggle in Europe, by the eagerness of British merchants to renew trade with America, and by the war-weariness of a tax-burdened public. The British finally decided that the war was not worth the cost. Envoys from both sides eventually agreed to end the fighting, return prisoners, restore previous boundaries, and to settle nothing else. The Treaty of Ghent was signed on Christmas Eve, 1814.

While the diplomats converged on a peace settlement, an entirely different kind of meeting took place in Hartford, Connecticut. An ill-fated affair, the Hartford Convention represented the climax of New England's disaffection with "Mr. Madison's war." New England had managed to keep aloof from the war and extract a profit from illegal trading and privateering. After the fall of Napoleon, however, the British extended their blockade to New England, occupied part of Maine, and conducted several raids along the coast. Even Boston seemed threatened. Instead of rallying to the American flag, however, Federalists in the Massachusetts legislature voted on October 5, 1814, to convene a meeting of New England states to plan independent action.

On December 15 the Hartford Convention assembled with delegates chosen by the legislatures of Massachusetts, Rhode Island, and Connecticut, two delegates from Vermont and one from New Hampshire: twenty-two in all. The convention included an extreme faction, Timothy Pickering's Essex Junto, who were prepared to secede from the Union, but it was controlled by a more moderate group led by Harrison Gray Otis, who sought only a protest against the war in language reminiscent of Madison's Virginia Resolutions of 1798. As the ultimate remedy for their grievances they proposed seven constitutional amendments designed to limit Republican influence, including the requirement of a two-thirds vote to declare war or admit new states, a prohibition on embargoes lasting more than sixty days, a one-term limit for the presidency, and a ban on successive presidents from the same state.

Their call for a later convention in Boston carried the unmistakable threat of secession if the demands were ignored. Yet the threat quickly evaporated. When messengers from Hartford reached Washington, they found the battered capital celebrating the good news from Ghent and New Orleans. The consequence was a fatal blow to the Federalist party, which never recovered from the stigma of disloyalty and narrow provincialism stamped on it by the Hartford Convention.

THE WAR'S AFTERMATH   For all the ineptitude with which the War of 1812 was fought, it generated an intense patriotic feeling. Despite the standoff with which it ended at Ghent, the American public felt victorious, thanks to Andrew Jackson and his men at New Orleans as well as the heroic exploits of American frigates in their duels with British ships. Remembered too were the vivid words of the dying Captain James Lawrence on the *Chesapeake*: "Don't give up the ship." Under Republican leadership the nation had survived a "Second War of Independence" against the greatest military power on earth and emerged with new symbols of nationhood and a new gallery of heroes.

The war revealed America's need for a more efficient system of internal transportation—roads, bridges, canals. Even more important, the conflict launched the United States toward eco-

We Owe Allegiance to No Crown. *The War of 1812 generated a new feeling of nationalism.*

nomic independence, as the interruption of trade encouraged the birth of American manufactures. This was a profound development, for the emergence of an American factory system would generate far-reaching social effects as well as economic growth. After forty years of independence, it dawned on the world that the new republic might not only survive but flourish.

As if to underline the point, Congress authorized a quick and decisive blow at the Barbary pirates. During the War of 1812 the dey of Algiers had renewed his plundering of American ships, claiming that he was getting too little tribute. On March 3, 1815, little more than two weeks after the Senate ratified the Peace of Ghent, Congress authorized a naval expedition against the Mediterranean pirates. On May 10 Captain Stephen Decatur sailed from New York with ten vessels. He first seized two Algerian ships and then sailed boldly into the harbor of Algiers. On June 30, 1815, the dey agreed to cease molesting American ships and to return all American prisoners. Decatur then forced similar concessions from Tunis and Tripoli. Piracy against American vessels was over.

One of the strangest results of the War of 1812 was a reversal of roles by the Republicans and Federalists. Out of the wartime experience the Republicans had learned some lessons in nationalism. The necessities of war had "Federalized" Madison, or "re-Federalized" the father of the Constitution. Perhaps, he reasoned, a peacetime army and navy would not be so bad after all. He also had come to see the value of a national bank and of higher tariffs to protect infant American industries from foreign competition. But while Madison was embracing such nationalistic measures, the Federalists were borrowing the Jeffersonian theory of states' rights and strict construction. It was the first great reversal of roles in constitutional interpretation. It would not be the last.

FURTHER READING

Marshall Smelser's *The Democratic Republic, 1801–1815* (1968) presents a fine overview of the Republican years. The standard modern biography of the third president is the multivolume work by Dumas Malone, *Jefferson and His Time* (6 vols., 1948–1981).° Merrill Peterson's *Thomas Jefferson and the New Nation* (1970)° is incisive.

A good introduction to the life of Jefferson's friend and successor is Ralph L. Ketcham's *James Madison* (1990).° Drew R. McCoy's *The Elusive Republic* (1982)° discusses the political economy of these years in the context of republicanism; Joyce Appleby's *Capitalism and a New Social Order* (1984)° deemphasizes the impact of republican ideology. The concept of judicial review and the courts can be studied in Richard E. Ellis's *The Jeffersonian Crisis* (1974).°

Burton Spivak's *Jefferson's English Crisis: Commerce, the Embargo, and the Republican Revolution* (1979) discusses Anglo-American relations during Jefferson's administration; Clifford L. Egan's *Neither Peace nor War* (1983) covers Franco-American relations. A review of the events that brought on war in 1812 is presented in Robert A. Rutland's *Madison's Alternatives: The Jeffersonian Republicans and the Coming of War, 1805–1812* (1975).

° These books are available in paperback editions.

9

NATIONALISM AND SECTIONALISM

Economic Nationalism

When did the United States become a nation? There is no easy answer to the question, for a sense of nationhood develops gradually and is always subject to cross-currents of localism, sectionalism, and class interest. Colonial Americans identified more closely with the local community and at most the province in which they resided than with any larger idea of empire or nation. The Revolution gave rise to a sense of nationhood, but Jefferson's "Revolution of 1800" revealed the countervailing forces of local and state interest. Jefferson himself, for instance, always spoke of Virginia as "my country."

Immediately after the War of 1812, however, there could no longer be any doubt that an American nation existed. An unusual economic prosperity after the war generated a sense of well-being and enhanced the prestige of the national government. The idea spread that the strength of the country was dependent on a more balanced economy of farming, commerce, and manufacturing and a more muscular military. President Madison, in his first annual message to Congress after the war, recommended several steps toward these ends: better fortifications, a standing army and a strong navy, a new national bank, effective protection of the new infant industries, a system of canals and roads for commercial and military use, and to top it off, a great national university. "The Republicans have out-Federalized Federalism," one observer remarked.

THE BANK OF THE UNITED STATES The trinity of economic nationalism—proposals for a second national bank, protective tariffs, and internal improvements—inspired the greatest controversies of the time. After the national bank expired in 1811, the country had fallen into a financial muddle. State-chartered banks mushroomed with little or no control, and their banknotes flooded the channels of commerce with money of uncertain value. Because hard money had been so short during the war, many state banks had suspended specie payments in redemption of their notes, thereby further depressing their value. And this was the money on which Americans depended. To remedy this situation, in 1816 Congress adopted over the protest of Old Republicans a provision for a new Bank of the United States. It was located in Philadelphia and modeled after Hamilton's bank. Once again the charter ran for twenty years, once again the government owned a fifth of the stock and named five of the twenty-five directors, and again the bank served as the government depository. Its banknotes were accepted in payments to the government. In return for its privileges the bank had to keep the government's funds without charge, lend the government $5 million on demand, and pay the government a cash bonus of $1.5 million.

The colorful and bitter debate on the bank set the pattern of regional alignment for most other economic issues. Missouri Senator Thomas Hart Benton predicted that the currency-short western towns would be at the mercy of such a centralized eastern bank. "They may be devoured by it any moment! They are in the jaws of the monster! A lump of butter in the mouth of a dog! One gulp, one swallow, and all is gone!" The debate was also noteworthy because of the leading roles played by the great triumvirate of John C. Calhoun of South Carolina, Henry Clay of Kentucky, and Daniel Webster of New Hampshire, later of Massachusetts. Calhoun, still in his youthful phase as a War Hawk nationalist, introduced the measure and pushed it through, justifying its constitutionality by the congressional power to regulate the currency. Clay, who had earlier opposed Hamilton's bank, now asserted that new circumstances had made the bank indispensable. Webster, on the other hand, led the opposition of the New England Federalists, who did not want Philadelphia to displace Boston as the nation's banking center. Later, after he moved from New Hampshire to Massachusetts, Webster would return to Congress as the champion of a much stronger national power, while events would carry Calhoun in the other direction.

A PROTECTIVE TARIFF   The shift of capital from commerce to manufactures, begun during Jefferson's embargo, had accelerated during the war. Peace in 1815 brought a sudden renewal of

The Union Manufactories of Maryland in Patapsco Falls, Baltimore County, c. 1815. *A textile mill begun during the embargo of 1807; by 1825 the Union Manufactories would employ over 600 people.*

cheap British imports and provoked a movement for the protection of infant industries. The self-interest of the manufacturers, who as yet had little political impact, was reinforced by a patriotic desire for economic independence from Britain.

The Tariff of 1816, the first intended more for the protection of industry against foreign competition than for revenue, easily passed Congress. The South and New England registered a majority of their votes against the bill, while the middle states and Old Northwest cast only five negative votes altogether. Led by Calhoun, the minority of southerners who voted for the tariff had hoped that the South might itself become a manufacturing center. But within a few years New England moved ahead of the South, and Calhoun turned against protection. The tariff then became a sectional issue, with manufacturers and food growers favoring higher tariffs, while planters and shipping interests favored lower duties.

INTERNAL IMPROVEMENTS   The third major economic issue of the time was internal improvements: the building of roads and the development of water transportation. The war had highlighted the shortcomings of existing facilities. Troop movements through the western wilderness had proved very difficult, and settlers found that unless they located near navigable waters, they were cut off from trade and limited to a frontier subsistence.

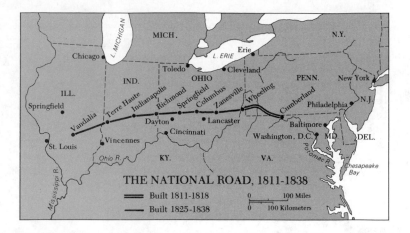

THE NATIONAL ROAD, 1811-1838

━━━ Built 1811-1818

━━ Built 1825-1838

The federal government had entered the field of internal improvements under Jefferson, who went along with some hesitation. In 1803, when Ohio became a state, Congress decreed that 5 percent of the proceeds from state land sales would go to building a National Road from the Atlantic coast into Ohio and beyond as the territory developed. In 1806 Jefferson authorized a survey, and construction of the National Road began in 1811. By 1818 it was open from Cumberland, Maryland, to Wheeling on the Ohio River. Construction stopped temporarily during the business panic of 1819, but by 1838 the road extended all the way to Vandalia, Illinois.

In 1817 Calhoun put through the House a bill to place in a fund for internal improvements the $1.5 million bonus the Bank of the United States had paid for its charter, as well as all future dividends on the government's bank stock. Once again opposition centered in New England and the South, which expected to gain least, and support came largely from the West, which badly needed good roads. On his last day in office Madison, bothered by its constitutionality, vetoed the bill. Internal improvements remained for another hundred years, with few exceptions, the responsibility of states and private enterprise.

"Good Feelings"

JAMES MONROE   As Madison approached the end of a turbulent tenure he, like Jefferson, turned to a fellow Virginian, another secretary of state, as his successor: James Monroe. At the outbreak of the Revolution, Monroe was just beginning college at William and Mary. He joined the army at age sixteen, was wounded at Trenton, and was a lieutenant-colonel when the war ended. Later he studied law with Jefferson and absorbed Jeffersonian principles at the master's feet.

Monroe never showed the depth in scholarship or political theory of his Republican predecessors, but what he lacked in intellect he made up in dedication to public service. His soul, Jefferson said, if turned inside out would be found spotless. Monroe served in the Virginia assembly, as governor, in the Confederation Congress and United States Senate, and as minister to Paris, London, and Madrid. Under Madison he had been secretary of state and twice had doubled as secretary of war. In the 1816 presidential election he overwhelmed his Federalist opponent, Rufus King of New York. Tall, rawboned Monroe, with his powdered wig, cocked hat, and knee-breeches, was the last of the revolutionary generation to serve in the White House and the last president to dress in the old style.

Firmly grounded in Republican principles, Monroe was never able to keep up with the onrush of the new nationalism. He accepted as accomplished fact the bank and the protective tariff, but during his tenure there was no further extension of economic nationalism. Indeed there was a minor setback. He permitted the National (or Cumberland) Road to be carried forward, but in his veto of the Cumberland Road Bill (1822), he denied the authority of Congress to collect tolls for its repair and maintenance. Like Jefferson and Madison, he also urged a constitutional amendment to remove all doubt about federal authority in the field of internal improvements.

James Monroe, portrayed as he entered the presidency in 1816.

Whatever his limitations, Monroe surrounded himself with some of the ablest young Republican leaders: John Quincy Adams became secretary of state, William Crawford of Georgia continued as secretary of the treasury, and John C. Calhoun headed the War Department. The new administration took power with America at peace and the economy flourishing. Soon after his 1817 inauguration Monroe embarked on a goodwill tour of New England. In Boston, lately a hotbed of wartime dissent, a Federalist paper commented on the president's visit under the heading "Era of Good Feelings." The label became a popular catch-phrase for Monroe's administration, and one that historians seized upon later. Like many a maxim, it conveys just enough truth to be sadly misleading. The collapse of the Federalist party did not mean that the Republicans grew more unified. They continued to suffer from rancorous internal tensions. Moreover, the social order began to show signs of increasing stratification as the nation experienced dramatic economic growth and rapid westward migration. Finally, a resurgence of sectionalism erupted just as the postwar prosperity collapsed in the Panic of 1819.

For two years, however, general harmony reigned, and even when the country's troubles revived, little of the blame fell on Monroe. In 1820 he was reelected without opposition, indeed without even a formal nomination. The Federalists were too weak to put up a candidate, and the Republicans did not bother to call a caucus. Monroe won all the electoral votes except for three abstentions and one vote from New Hampshire for John Quincy Adams.

IMPROVING RELATIONS WITH BRITAIN   Adding to the prevailing contentment after the war was a growing rapprochement with England. Trade relations with Britain were restored in 1815. The Peace of Ghent had left unsettled a number of minor disputes, but in the sequel two important compacts—the Rush-Bagot Agreement of 1817 and the Convention of 1818—removed several potential causes of irritation. In the first, effected by an exchange of notes between Acting Secretary of State Richard Rush and British Minister Charles Bagot, the threat of naval competition on the Great Lakes vanished with an arrangement to limit forces there to several revenue cutters. Although the exchange made no reference to the land boundary between the United States and Canada, its spirit gave rise to the tradition of an unfortified border, the longest in the world.

The Convention of 1818 covered three major points. The

northern limit of the Louisiana Purchase was settled by extending the national boundary along the Forty-ninth Parallel west from Lake of the Woods to the crest of the Rocky Mountains. West of that point the Oregon country would be open to joint U.S.-British occupation, but the boundary remained unsettled. The right of Americans to fish off Newfoundland and Labrador, granted in 1783, was acknowledged once again. But the problem remained of Britain's continuing exclusion of American ships from the West Indies in order to reserve that lucrative trade for British ships. The rapprochement with Britain therefore fell short of perfection.

JACKSON TAKES FLORIDA   The year 1819 was one of the more fateful years in American history, a time when a whole sequence of developments came into focus. Controversial efforts to expand American territory, a sharp financial panic, a tense debate over the extension of slavery, and several landmark Supreme Court cases combined to bring an unsettling end to the "Era of Good Feelings."

The aggressive new nationalism reached a climax with the acquisition of Florida. Spanish sovereignty over Florida was more a technicality than an actuality. The thinly held province had been a thorn in the side of the United States during the recent war, a center of British intrigue, a haven for Creek refugees who were beginning to take the name Seminole (runaway or separatist), and a harbor for runaway slaves and criminals.

Spain, once the dominant power of the Americas, was now a great nation in rapid decline, suffering from both internal and colonial revolt, and unable to enforce its obligations under the Pinckney Treaty of 1795 to pacify the frontiers. In 1816 American forces clashed with a group of escaped slaves who had taken over a British fort on the Appalachicola River. Seminoles were soon fighting white settlers in the area, and in 1817 Secretary of War Calhoun authorized a campaign against the Seminoles, summoning General Andrew Jackson from Nashville to take command. Jackson's orders allowed him to pursue the offenders into Spanish territory, but not to attack any Spanish post. A man of Jackson's tenacity naturally felt hobbled by such a restriction, since when it came to Spaniards or Indians, no white Tennessean —certainly not Andrew Jackson—was likely to bother with technicalities. Jackson pushed eastward through Florida, reinforced by Tennessee volunteers and a party of friendly Creeks, taking a Spanish post and skirmishing with the Seminoles. Jackson hanged two of their leaders without a trial. For two British

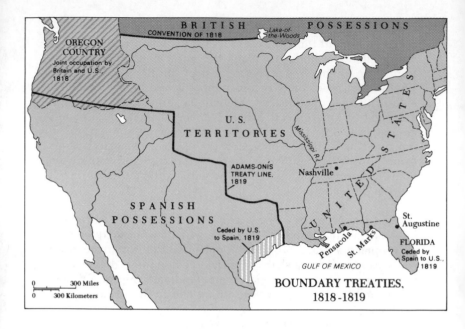

BOUNDARY TREATIES,
1818-1819

intriguers in the area, he convened a court-martial, during which it was revealed that they had befriended the Seminoles and had offered them military training. Jackson had one hanged and the other shot. The Florida panhandle was in American hands by the end of May 1818.

News of Jackson's exploits aroused anger in Madrid and concern in Washington. Spain demanded the return of its territory, reparations, and the punishment of Jackson, but Spain's impotence was plain for all to see. Monroe's cabinet at first prepared to disavow Jackson's action, especially his direct attack on Spanish posts. Calhoun, as secretary of war, wanted to discipline Jackson for disregard of orders—a stand that later caused bad blood between the two men—but privately confessed a certain pleasure at the outcome. In any case a man as popular as Jackson was almost invulnerable. And he had one important friend in Washington, Secretary of State John Quincy Adams, who realized that Jackson had strengthened his hand in negotiations already under way with the Spanish minister. American forces withdrew from Florida, but negotiations resumed with the knowledge that the United States could retake Florida at any time.

With Florida's fate a foregone conclusion, Adams cast his eye on a larger purpose, a final definition of the western boundary of the Louisiana Purchase and—his boldest stroke—extension of a boundary to the Pacific coast. In lengthy negotiations Adams gradually gave ground on claims to Texas, but stuck to his demand for a transcontinental line. Agreement finally came early in 1819. Spain ceded all of Florida to the United States in return for American assumption of private claims against Spain up to $5 million. The western boundary of the Louisiana Purchase would run along the Sabine River and then in stair-step fashion up to the Red River, along the Red, and up to the Arkansas River. From the source of the Arkansas it would go north to the Forty-second Parallel and thence west to the Pacific coast. Florida became a territory, and its first governor briefly was Andrew Jackson. In 1845 Florida finally achieved statehood.

"A FIREBELL IN THE NIGHT"

THE PANIC OF 1819 Adams's Transcontinental Treaty was a triumph of foreign policy and the climactic event of America's postwar nationalism. Even before it was signed in February 1819, however, two thunderclaps signaled the end of the brief "Era of Good Feelings" and gave warning of stormy weather ahead: the financial Panic of 1819 and the controversy over statehood for Missouri. The panic resulted from a sudden collapse of cotton prices in the English market, as British manufacturers turned away from American sources to cheaper East Indian cotton. The price collapse set off a decline in the demand for other American goods and suddenly revealed the fragility of the prosperity that followed the War of 1812.

Since 1815 much of the economic boom had been built on a shaky foundation. Businessmen, bankers, farmers, and land jobbers had caused a volatile expansion of credit, succumbing to the contagion of get-rich-quick fever that was sweeping the country. Even the directors of the Second Bank of the United States (B.U.S.) engaged in the same reckless extension of loans that state banks had pursued. In 1819, just as alert businessmen began to take alarm, a case of extensive fraud and embezzlement in the Baltimore branch came to light. The disclosure led to the resignation of the B.U.S. director. His replacement, Langdon Cheves, former congressman from South Carolina, established a sounder policy.

Cheves reduced salaries and other costs, postponed dividends, restrained the extension of credit, and presented for redemption the state banknotes that came in, thereby forcing the state-chartered banks to keep specie reserves. Cheves rescued the B.U.S.

from near-ruin, but only by putting heavy pressure on state banks. The state banks in turn put pressure on their debtors, who found it harder to renew old loans or get new ones. In 1823, his job completed, Cheves relinquished his position to Nicholas Biddle of Philadelphia. The Cheves policies were the result rather than the cause of the Panic, but hard-pressed debtors found it all the more difficult to meet their obligations. Hard times lasted about three years, and in the popular mind the bank deserved much of the blame. The Panic passed, but resentment of the national bank lingered, and it never fully regained the confidence of the South and the West.

THE MISSOURI COMPROMISE   Just as the Panic was breaking over the country, another cloud appeared on the horizon, the onset of a sectional controversy over slavery. By 1819 the country had an equal number of slave and free states, eleven of each. The line between them was defined by the southern and western boundaries of Pennsylvania and the Ohio River. Although slavery lingered in some places north of the line, it was on the way to extinction there. Beyond the Mississippi, however, no move had been made to extend the dividing line across the Louisiana Purchase territory, where slavery had existed from the days when France and Spain had colonized the area. At the time the Missouri Territory embraced all of the Louisiana Purchase except the state of Louisiana (1812) and the Arkansas Territory (1819). In the westward rush of population, the old French town of St. Louis became the funnel through which settlers pushed on beyond the Mississippi. These were largely settlers from the South who brought their slaves with them.

In February 1819, the House of Representatives confronted legislation enabling Missouri to draft a state constitution, its population having passed the minimum of 60,000. At that point Rep. James Tallmadge, Jr., a New York congressman, introduced a resolution prohibiting the further introduction of slaves into Missouri, which had some 10,000 in 1820, and providing freedom at age twenty-five for those born after the territory's admission as a state. After brief but fiery exchanges, the House passed the amendment on an almost strictly sectional vote and the Senate rejected it by a similar tally, but with several northerners joining in the opposition. With population at the time growing faster in the north, a political balance between the two sections could be held only in the Senate. In the House, slave states had 81 votes while free states had 105; a balance was unlikely to be restored ever again in the House.

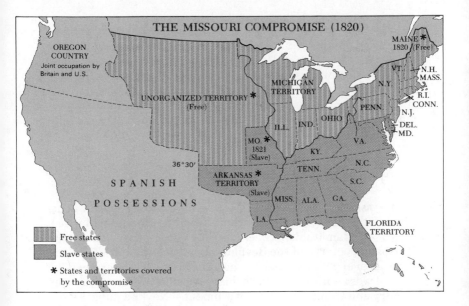

THE MISSOURI COMPROMISE (1820)

OREGON COUNTRY
Joint occupation by Britain and U.S.

UNORGANIZED TERRITORY *
(Free)

MICHIGAN TERRITORY

MAINE *
1820 (Free)

VT. N.H.
MASS.
N.Y. R.I.
CONN.
N.J.
PENN.
OHIO DEL.
ILL. IND. MD.
MO. *
1821
(Slave)
KY.
VA.
36° 30'
ARKANSAS *
TERRITORY
(Slave)
TENN.
N.C.
S.C.
MISS. ALA. GA.
LA.

SPANISH

POSSESSIONS

FLORIDA TERRITORY

Free states
Slave states
* States and territories covered by the compromise

Congress adjourned in March 1819, postponing further debate until the regular session in December. When the debate came, it was remarkable for the absence of moral argument, although repugnance to slavery and moral guilt about it were never far from the surface. The debate turned instead on the constitutional issue. Congress, several northerners asserted, was empowered to forbid slavery in Missouri as the Confederation Congress had done in the Northwest Territory. Southern leaders argued that under the Fifth Amendment, slaveholders could not be denied the right to carry their chattel into the territory, which would be deprivation of property without due process of law. Henry Clay and others expressed a view, which Jefferson and Madison now shared, that the expansion and dispersal of slavery would improve conditions for the slaves.

Maine's application for statehood made it easier to arrive at an agreement. Since colonial times Maine had been the northern province of Massachusetts. The Senate linked its request for separate statehood with Missouri's and voted to admit Maine as a free state and Missouri as a slave state, thus maintaining the balance in the Senate. An Illinois senator further extended the compromise by an amendment to exclude slavery from the rest of the Louisiana Purchase north of 36° 30', Missouri's southern border. Slavery thus would continue in the Arkansas Territory and in Missouri, and be excluded from the remainder of the area. Since most considered this the Great American Desert, unlikely ever to be settled, the arrangement seemed to be a victory for the slave states. On August 10, 1821, President Monroe proclaimed the admission of Missouri as the twenty-fourth state. For the time the controversy was settled. "But this momentous question," the aging Thomas Jefferson wrote to a friend after the first compromise, "like a firebell in the night awakened and filled me with terror. I considered it at once as the knell of the Union."

Judicial Nationalism

JOHN MARSHALL, CHIEF JUSTICE   Meanwhile nationalism still flourished in the Supreme Court, where Chief Justice John Marshall preserved Hamiltonian Federalism for yet another generation. Marshall, a veteran of the Revolution, was among those who had been forever nationalized by the experience. In later years he said: "I was confirmed in the habit of considering America as my country and Congress as my government." Never a judge before he became chief justice in 1801, he established the power of the Supreme Court by his force of mind and determination. During Marshall's early years on the Court (altogether he served thirty-four years) he affirmed the principle of judicial review of legislative acts. In *Marbury v. Madison* (1803) and *Fletcher v. Peck* (1810) the Court first struck down a federal law and then a state law as unconstitutional.

In the fateful year 1819 Marshall and the Court made two more decisions of major importance in checking the power of the states and expanding the power of the federal government: *Dartmouth College v. Woodward*, and *McCulloch v. Maryland*. The Dartmouth College case involved an attempt by the New Hampshire legislature to alter a charter granted the college by King George III in 1769 under which the governing body of trustees became a self-perpetuating board. In 1816 the state's Republican legislature, irritated by this residue of monarchical rule as well as by the fact that Federalists dominated the board of trustees, placed Dartmouth under the control of a new board named by the governor. The original trustees sued, lost in the state courts, but with Daniel Webster as their counsel gained a hearing before the Supreme Court. The charter, declared Marshall in speaking for the Court, was a valid contract which the legislature had violated, an act expressly forbidden by the Constitution. This decision implied a new and enlarged definition of contract which seemed to put private corporations beyond the reach of the states that chartered them. "If business is to prosper," Marshall explained, "men must have the assurance that contracts will be enforced."

Marshall's single most important interpretation of the constitutional system appeared in *McCulloch v. Maryland*. In the unanimous decision the Court upheld the "implied powers" of Congress to charter the Bank of the United States and denied the state of Maryland's attempt to tax the bank. In a lengthy opinion Marshall rejected Maryland's argument that the federal government was the creature of sovereign states. Instead, he insisted, it arose directly from the people acting through the conventions that ratified the Constitution. While sovereignty was divided be-

Deck Life on the *Paragon*, 1811–1812. *The* Paragon, *"a whole floating town," was the third steamboat operated on the Hudson by Robert Fulton and Robert R. Livingston. Fulton said the* Paragon *"beats everything on the globe, for made as you and I are we cannot tell what is in the moon."*

tween the states and the national government, the latter, "though limited in its powers, is supreme within its sphere of action."

The state's effort to tax the bank conflicted with the supreme law of the land. One great principle which "entirely pervades the constitution," Marshall wrote, was "that the constitution and the laws made in pursuance thereof are supreme: that they control the constitution and laws of the respective states, and cannot be controlled by them." The state tax therefore was unconstitutional for "the power to tax involves the power to destroy"— which was precisely what the legislatures of Maryland and several other states had in mind with respect to the bank.

Marshall's last great decision, *Gibbons v. Ogden* (1824), established national supremacy in regulating interstate commerce. In 1808 the New York legislature granted Aaron Ogden the exclusive ferry rights across the Hudson between New York and New Jersey. A competitor, Thomas Gibbons, protested the state's right to grant such a monopoly. On behalf of a unanimous Court, Marshall ruled that the monopoly granted by the state conflicted with the federal Coasting Act under which Gibbons operated. Congressional power to regulate commerce, the Court said, "like all others vested in Congress, is complete in itself, may be exercised to its utmost extent, and acknowledges no limitations other than are prescribed in the constitution." In striking down the monopoly created by the state, the nationalist Marshall had opened the way to extensive development of steamboat navigation and, soon afterward, steam railroads. Such judicial nationalism provided an important support for economic expansion.

NATIONALIST DIPLOMACY

THE NORTHWEST In foreign affairs, too, nationalism continued to be an effective force. Within two years after final approval of Adams's Transcontinental Treaty, the secretary of state was able to draw another important transcontinental line. In 1819 Spain had abandoned its claim to the Oregon country above the Forty-second Parallel. Russia, however, had claims along the Pacific coast as well, including trading outposts from Alaska as far south as California. In 1823 Secretary of State Adams contested "the right of Russia to any territorial establishment on this continent." The American government, he informed the Russian minister, assumed the principle "that the American continents are no longer subjects for any new European colonial establishments." The upshot of his protest was a treaty signed in 1824 whereby Russia, which had more pressing concerns in Europe, accepted the line of 54° 40' as the southern boundary of its claim. The Oregon Territory, to the south of the line, remained subject to joint occupation by the United States and Great Britain under their agreement of 1818.

THE MONROE DOCTRINE   Adams's disapproval of further colonization also had clear implications for Latin America. One consequence of the Napoleonic wars and French occupation of Spain and Portugal had been a series of wars of liberation in Latin America. Within little more than a decade after the flag of rebellion was first raised in 1811, Spain had lost its entire empire in the Americas. All that was left were the islands of Cuba, Puerto Rico, and Santo Domingo.

That Spain could not regain her empire seems clear enough in retrospect. The British navy would not permit it because Britain's trade with the area was too important. For a time after Napoleon's defeat, however, European rulers were determined to restore monarchical "legitimacy" everywhere. In 1822, when the allies met in the Congress of Verona, they authorized France to suppress the constitutionalist movement in Spain and restore the authority of the monarchy. In 1823 French troops crossed the Spanish border, put down the rebels, and restored King Ferdinand VII to absolute authority. Rumors began to circulate that France would also try to restore Ferdinand's "legitimate" power over Spain's American empire. Monroe and Secretary of War Calhoun were alarmed at the possibility, although John Quincy Adams took the more realistic view that such action was unlikely. British Foreign Minister George Canning was also worried about French and Spanish intentions, and he urged Anglo-American protection of Latin America. Monroe at first agreed, with the support of his sage advisors Jefferson and Madison.

Adams, however, urged upon Monroe and the cabinet the independent course of proclaiming a unilateral policy against the restoration of Spain's colonies. "It would be more candid," Adams said, "as well as more dignified, to avow our principles explicitly to Russia and France, than to come in as a cock-boat in the wake of the British man-of-war." Adams knew that the British navy would stop any action by a European power in Latin America. The British wanted, moreover, the United States to agree not to acquire any more Spanish territory, including Cuba, Texas, or California, and Adams preferred to avoid such a commitment.

Monroe incorporated the substance of Adams's views in his annual message to Congress on December 2, 1823. The Monroe Doctrine, as it was later called, comprised four major points: (1) that "the American continents. . . are henceforth not to be considered as subjects for future colonization by any European powers"; (2) the political system of European powers was different from that of the United States, which would "consider any attempt on their part to extend their system to any portion of this hemisphere as dangerous to our peace and safety"; (3) the United States would not interfere with existing European colonies; and (4) the United States would keep out of the internal affairs of European nations and their wars.

At the time the statement drew little attention either in the United States or abroad. Over the years, however, the Monroe Doctrine, not even so called until 1852, became one of the cherished principles of American foreign policy. But for the time being it slipped into obscurity for want of any occasion to invoke it. In spite of Adams's affirmation, the United States came in as a cock-boat in the wake of the British man-of-war after all, for the effectiveness of the doctrine depended on British naval supremacy. The doctrine had no standing in international law. It was merely a statement of intent by an American president to the Congress and did not even draw enough interest at the time for the European powers to renounce it.

ONE-PARTY POLITICS

Almost from the start of Monroe's second term the jockeying for the presidential succession in 1824 had begun. Three members of Monroe's cabinet were active candidates: Secretary of War John Calhoun, Secretary of the Treasury William Crawford, and Secretary of State John Quincy Adams. Henry Clay, longtime Speaker of the House, also thirsted after the office. And on the fringes of the Washington scene a new force appeared in the person of Andrew Jackson, the scourge of the British, Spaniards, and Seminoles, who was elected a senator from Tennessee in 1823. All were Republicans, for again no Federalist stood a chance, but they were competing in a new political world, complicated by the cross-currents of nationalism and sectionalism. With only one party there was in effect no party, for there existed no generally accepted method for choosing a "regular" candidate.

State legislatures were free to nominate candidates. Tennessee and Pennsylvania supported Jackson, and Calhoun agreed to serve as his running mate. (The 1824 election was the first to feature paired presidential and vice-presidential candidates.) Kentucky named Clay, Massachusetts dubbed Adams, and the amiable, hulking Crawford was selected by a poorly attended congressional caucus. Of the four candidates only two had clearly defined programs, and the outcome was an early lesson in the danger of being committed on the issues too soon. Crawford's friends emphasized his devotion to states' rights and strict construction. Clay, on the contrary, took his stand for the "American System": he favored the national bank, the protective tariff, and a national program of internal improvements to bind the country together and build its economy. Adams was close to Clay, openly dedicated to internal improvements but less strongly committed to the tariff. Jackson, where issues were concerned, carefully avoided commitment. His managers hoped that, by being all things to all voters, Jackson could capitalize on his popularity as the hero of New Orleans.

THE "CORRUPT BARGAIN" The outcome turned on personalities and sectional allegiance more than on issues. Adams, the only northern candidate, carried New England, the former bastion of Federalism, and most of New York's electoral votes. Clay took Kentucky, Ohio, and Missouri, while Crawford carried Virginia, Georgia, and Delaware. Jackson swept the Southeast, plus Illinois and Indiana, and with Calhoun's support the Carolinas, Pennsylvania, Maryland, and New Jersey.

The result in 1824 was inconclusive in both the electoral vote and the popular vote. In the electoral college Jackson had 99, Adams 84, Crawford 41, and Clay 37; in the popular vote the proportion ran about the same. Whatever might have been said about the outcome, it was a defeat for Clay's American System: New England and New York opposed him on internal improvements; the South and Southwest on the protective tariff. Sectionalism had defeated the national program, yet the advocate of the American System now assumed the role of president-maker, since the election was thrown into the House of Representatives, where Speaker Clay's influence was decisive. Clay had little trouble in choosing, since he regarded Jackson as unfit for the office. "I cannot believe," he muttered, "that killing 2,500 Englishmen at New Orleans qualifies for the various, difficult and complicated duties of the Chief Magistracy." He eventually threw his support to Adams. The final vote in the House, which was by state, carried Adams to victory with thirteen votes to Jackson's seven and Crawford's four.

It was a costly victory, for it united Adams's foes and crippled his administration before it got under way. There is no evidence that Adams entered into any bargain with Clay to win his support, but the charge was widely believed after Adams made Clay his secretary of state, the office from which three successive presidents had risen. A campaign to elect Jackson next time was launched almost immediately after the 1824 decisions. "The people have been cheated," Jackson growled. The Crawford people, including Martin Van Buren, the "Little Magician" of New York politics, soon moved into the Jackson camp.

JOHN QUINCY ADAMS'S PRESIDENCY   Short, plump, peppery John Quincy Adams was one of the ablest men, hardest workers, and finest intellects ever to enter the White House, but he lacked the common touch and the politician's gift for maneuver. He refused to play the game of patronage, believing that the presidency should be above partisan politics. His first annual message to Congress provided a grandiose blueprint for national development, set forth in such a blunt way that it became a political disaster. In the boldness and magnitude of its conception, the Adams plan outdid both Hamilton and Clay. The central government, the president asserted, should promote internal improvements, set up a national university, finance scientific explorations, build astronomical observatories, and create a new Department of the Interior.

John Quincy Adams, a president of great intellect but without the common touch.

To refrain from using broad federal powers, Adams maintained, "would be treachery to the most sacred of trusts." Officers of the government should not be "palsied by the will of our constituents. . . . ." Such provocative language obscured whatever grandeur of conception the message to Congress had. For a minority president to demean the sovereignty of the voter was tactless enough, but for the son of John Adams to cite the example "of the nations of Europe and of their rulers" was downright suicidal. At one fell swoop he had revived all the Republican suspicions of the Adamses.

Adams's presidential message hastened the emergence of a new party system. The minority who cast their lot with Adams and Clay were turning into National-Republicans; the opposition, the growing party of Jacksonians, were the Democratic-Republicans, who would eventually drop the name Republican and become Democrats.

Adams's headstrong plunge into nationalism and his refusal to play the game of politics condemned his administration to utter frustration. Congress ignored his domestic proposals, and in foreign affairs the triumphs he had scored as secretary of state had no sequels. The climactic effort to discredit Adams came on the tariff issue. The Panic of 1819 had given rise to action for a higher tariff in 1820, but the effort failed by one vote in the Senate. In 1824 the advocates of protection renewed the effort, with greater success. The Tariff of 1824 favored the Middle Atlantic and New England manufacturers with higher duties on woolens, cotton, iron, and other finished goods. Clay's Kentucky won a tariff on hemp, a fiber used for making rope, and a tariff on raw wool brought the wool-growing interests to the support of the measure. Additional revenues were provided by duties on sugar, molasses, coffee, and salt.

Three years later Jackson's supporters sought to advance their candidate through an awkward scheme hatched by Calhoun. The plan was to present a bill with such outrageously high tariffs on raw materials that the Eastern manufacturers would join the commercial interests there, and, with the votes of the agricultural South and Southwest, combine to defeat the measure. In the process Jackson men in the Northeast could take credit for supporting the tariff, and Jackson men, wherever it fitted their interests, could take credit for opposing it—while Jackson himself remained in the background. Virginia's John Randolph saw through the ruse. The bill, he asserted, "referred to manufactures of no sort of kind, but the manufacture of a President of the United States."

The measure served that purpose, but in the process Calhoun was hoist on his own petard. His tariff bill, to his chagrin, passed, thanks to the growing strength of manufacturing interests in New England and to several crucial amendments which exempted certain raw materials. Daniel Webster, now a senator from Massachusetts, explained that he was ready to deny all he had said before against the tariff because New England had built up her manufactures on the understanding that the protective tariff was a settled policy.

When the bill passed on May 11, 1828, it was Calhoun's turn to explain his newfound opposition to the gospel of protection, and nothing so well illustrates the flexibility of constitutional principles as the switch in positions by Webster and Calhoun. Back in South Carolina, Calhoun prepared the *South Carolina Exposition and Protest* (1828), which was issued anonymously along with a series of resolutions by the state legislature. In that document Calhoun set forth the right of a state to nullify an act of Congress which it found unconstitutional.

JACKSON SWEEPS IN   Thus far the stage was set for the election of 1828, which might more truly be called a revolution than that of 1800. But if the issues of the day had anything to do with the election, they were hardly visible in the campaign, in which politicians on both sides reached depths of scurrilousness that had not been plumbed since 1800. Jackson was denounced as a hot-tempered and ignorant barbarian, a participant in repeated duels and frontier brawls, a man whose fame rested on his reputation as a killer, and a man whom Thomas Jefferson himself had pronounced unfit because of his rash personality. In addition to that, his enemies dredged up the old story that Jackson had lived in adultery with his wife, Rachel, before they had been legally married. In fact they had been married for two years in the mistaken belief that her divorce from a former husband was final. Anxiety over this humiliation and her probable reception in Washington may have contributed to an illness from which Rachel died before her husband took office, a tragedy for which Jackson could never forgive his enemies.

The Jacksonians, however, got in their licks against Adams, condemning him as a man corrupted by foreigners in the courts of Europe. They called him a gambler and a spendthrift for having bought a billiard table and a chess set for the White House, and a puritanical hypocrite for despising the common people and warning Congress to ignore the will of its constituents. He had finally reached the presidency, the Jacksonians claimed, by a corrupt bargain with Henry Clay.

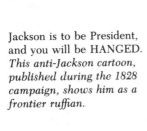

Jackson is to be President, and you will be HANGED. *This anti-Jackson cartoon, published during the 1828 campaign, shows him as a frontier ruffian.*

In the campaign of 1828 Jackson held most of the advantages. As a military hero he had some claim on patriotism. As a son of the West he was almost unbeatable there. As a planter and slave-holder he had the trust of southern planters. Debtors and local bankers who hated the national bank turned to Jackson. In addition his vagueness on the issues protected him from attack by various interest groups. Not least of all, Jackson benefited from a spirit of democracy in which the common folk were no longer satisfied to look to their betters for leadership, as they had done in the past. It had become politically fatal to be labeled an aristocrat.

Since the Revolution and especially since 1800, more and more states had been granting the vote to taxpaying white males. The traditional story of the broadening franchise has been that a surge of Jacksonian Democracy came out of the West like a great wave, supported mainly by small farmers, leading the way for the East. But there were other forces working in the older states toward a wider franchise: the revolutionary doctrine of equality and the feeling on the parts of the workers, artisans, and small merchants of the towns, as well as small farmers and landed grandees, that a democratic ballot provided a means to combat the rising commercial and manufacturing interests. After 1815 the new states of the West entered the Union with either white manhood suffrage or a low taxpaying requirement, and older states such as Connecticut (1818), Massachusetts (1821), and New York (1821) all abolished their property requirements.

Jackson embodied the ideal of this new, more democratic political world. A tall, sinewy frontiersman born into poverty in South Carolina, Jackson had scrambled his way up by will and tenacity. He grew to be proud, gritty, short-tempered, and a good hater. During the Revolution, when he was a young boy, his mother died, two of his brothers were killed by redcoats, and Jackson himself was wounded by a British officer's sabre. He would carry this scar for life, along with the conviction that it was not enough for a man to be right; he had to be tough as well. His toughness inspired his soldiers to nickname him "Old Hickory." During a duel with a man reputed to be the best shot in Tennessee, Jackson nevertheless let his opponent fire first. For his gallantry he received a bullet wedged next to his heart. But he straightened himself, patiently took aim, and killed his aghast foe. "I should have hit him," Jackson claimed, "if he had shot me through the brain." Even his opponents admired his courage and conviction. Daniel Webster once observed that Jackson "does what he thinks is right, and does it with all his might."

As a fighter, horse trader, land speculator, and frontier lawyer, Jackson symbolized the rugged new Western temperament. A fellow law student described him as a "most roaring, rollicking, game-cocking, horse-racing, card-playing, mischievous fellow." One of his campaign slogans announced: "Adams can write, Jackson can fight." He could write, too, but he once said that he had no respect for a man who could think of only one way to spell a word.

The 1828 returns revealed that Jackson had won by a comfortable margin. The electoral vote was 178 to 83. Adams won all of New England, except for one of Maine's nine electoral votes, and a scattering of votes in New York and Maryland. All the rest belonged to Jackson. A new, convulsive era in American politics was about to begin.

Further Reading

The standard overview of the Era of Good Feelings remains George Dangerfield's *The Awakening of American Nationalism, 1815–1828* (1965).° William H. Pease and Jane H. Pease's *The Web of Progress* (1987)° shows the emerging sectionalism through a look at two cities, Boston, Massachusetts, and Charleston, South Carolina.

For discussions of the American System, see Bray Hammond's *Banks and Politics in America from the Revolution to the Civil War* (1991)° and George R. Taylor's *The Transportation Revolution, 1815–1860* (1977).°

° These books are available in paperback editions.

For an overview of all the economic trends of the period, see Douglass C. North's *The Economic Growth of the United States, 1790–1860* (1961).°

On diplomatic relations after 1812, see Ernest R. May's *The Making of the Monroe Doctrine* (1975) and Dexter Perkins's *A History of the Monroe Doctrine* (1955).

Background on Andrew Jackson can be obtained from works cited in Chapter 10. The campaign that brought Jackson to the White House is analyzed in Robert V. Remini's *The Election of Andrew Jackson* (1963).°

10 ~~

THE JACKSONIAN IMPULSE

SETTING THE STAGE

INAUGURATION   On Inauguration Day, March 4, 1829, the new president, a sixty-two-year-old widower in poor health, plagued by a persistent cough and severe headaches, delivered his address in a voice so low that few in the crowd could hear it. It mattered little, for Jackson's advisers had eliminated anything that might give offense. On the major issues of the tariff, internal improvements, and the Bank of the United States, the new president remained vague. Only a few points foreshadowed policies that he would pursue: he favored retirement of the national debt, a proper regard for states' rights, a "just" policy toward Indians, and rotation in federal offices, which he pronounced "a leading principle in the republican creed"—a principle his enemies would dub the "spoils system."

After his speech Jackson mounted his horse and rode off to the White House, where a reception was scheduled for all who chose to come. The ensuing boisterous party evoked the climate of turmoil that seemed always to surround Jackson. The crowd pushed into the White House, surged through the rooms, jostled the waiters, broke dishes, leaped on the furniture—all in an effort to shake the president's hand or at least get a glimpse of him. To Supreme Court Justice Story, "the reign of 'King Mob' seemed triumphant."

APPOINTMENTS AND POLITICAL RIVALRIES   Democratic principles, Jackson believed, required that a man should serve a term in government, then return to the status of private citizen, for office-holders who stayed too long became corrupted by a sense of

All Creation Going to the White House. *The scene following Jackson's inauguration as president, according to satirist Robert Cruikshank.*

power. So he set about replacing Adams's appointees with his own supporters. But his use of the "spoils system" has been exaggerated. During his first year in office Jackson replaced only about 9 percent of the appointed officials in the federal government, and during his entire term fewer than 20 percent.

Jackson's administration was from the outset a house divided between the partisans of Secretary of State Martin Van Buren of New York and Vice-President Calhoun of South Carolina. Much of the political history of the next few years would turn upon the rivalry between the two, as each man jockeyed for position as Jackson's heir apparent. Van Buren held most of the advantages, foremost among them his skill at timing and tactics. As John Randolph put it, Van Buren always "rowed to his objective with muffled oars." Jackson, new to political administration, leaned heavily on him for advice and for help in soothing the ruffled feathers of rejected office seekers.

But Calhoun could not be taken lightly. He, too, expected to be Jackson's successor. A man of towering intellect, humorless outlook, and apostolic zeal, he was driven by a demonic sense of duty and animated by a brilliant interest in ideas. "There is no *relaxation* with him," a frazzled friend once wrote. Henry Clay perhaps described Calhoun best: "tall, careworn, with furrowed brow, haggard and intensely gazing, looking as if he were dissecting the last abstraction which sprung from a meta-physician's brain." Since returning from Washington to his plantation in South Carolina in 1825, Calhoun had nurtured his crops and his ardent love for his native region. And now as vice-president, he was determined to defend southern interests against the advance of northern industrialism and abolitionism.

THE EATON AFFAIR   In his battle for political power with Calhoun, Van Buren had luck as well as political skill on his side. Fate had quickly handed him a trump card: the succulent scandal of the Peggy Eaton affair. Peggy Eaton was a vivacious, pearl-skinned, auburn-haired Irish widow whose husband supposedly had committed suicide upon learning of her affair with Tennessee Senator Eaton. Her marriage to Eaton, three months before he entered the cabinet, had scarcely made an honest woman of her in the eyes of the proper ladies of Washington. Floride Calhoun, the vice-president's wife, pointedly snubbed her, and cabinet wives followed suit.

Peggy's plight reminded Jackson of the gossip that had pursued his wife, Rachel, and he pronounced Peggy "chaste as a virgin." But the cabinet members were unable to cure their wives of what Van Buren dubbed "the Eaton Malaria." Van Buren, however, was a widower, and therefore free to lavish on poor Peggy all the attention that Jackson thought was her due. Mrs. Eaton herself finally wilted under the chill, began to refuse invitations, and withdrew from society. The outraged Jackson came to link Calhoun with what he called a conspiracy against her and drew even closer to Van Buren.

INTERNAL IMPROVEMENTS   While capital society weathered the chilly winter of 1829–1830, Van Buren prepared some additional blows to Calhoun. It was easy to bring Jackson into opposition to internal improvements and thus to federal programs with which Calhoun had long been identified. In 1830 the Maysville Road Bill, passed by Congress, offered Jackson a happy chance for a dual thrust at both Calhoun and Clay. The bill authorized the government to buy stock in a road from Maysville to Clay's hometown of Lexington. The road lay entirely within the state of Kentucky, and though part of a larger scheme to link up with the National Road via Cincinnati, it could be viewed as a purely local undertaking. On that ground Jackson vetoed the bill, to widespread popular acclaim. Yet while Jackson continued to oppose federal aid to local projects, he supported projects such as the national road, as well as roadbuilding in the territories, and rivers and harbors bills, the "pork barrels" from which every congressman tried to pluck a morsel for his district. Even so, Jackson's attitude toward the Maysville Road set an important precedent, on the eve of the railroad age, for limiting federal initiative in internal improvements. Railroads would be built altogether by state and private capital at least until 1850.

NULLIFICATION

CALHOUN'S THEORY   There is a fine irony to Calhoun's plight in the Jackson administration, for Calhoun was now in midpassage from his early phase as a War Hawk nationalist to his later phase as a states'-rights sectionalist—and open to thrusts on both flanks. Conditions in his home state had brought on this change. Suffering from agricultural depression, South Carolina lost almost 70,000 people to emigration during the 1820s, and would lose nearly twice that number in the 1830s. Most South Carolinians blamed the protective tariff, which tended to raise the prices of manufactured goods and, insofar as it discouraged the sale of foreign goods in the United States, reduced the ability of British and French traders to acquire the American money with which to buy American cotton. This worsened problems of low cotton prices and exhausted lands. The South Carolinians' malaise was compounded by a growing reaction against the increasing criticism of slavery. Hardly had the country emerged from the Missouri controversy when Charleston was thrown into panic by the thwarted Denmark Vesey slave insurrection of 1822.

The unexpected passage of the Tariff of Abominations (1828)

John C. Calhoun. A War Hawk nationalist during the 1810s and 1820s, Calhoun was now becoming a states'-rights sectionalist.

left Calhoun no choice but to join the opposition or give up his home base. Calhoun's *South Carolina Exposition and Protest* (1828), written in opposition to that tariff, contained a fine-spun theory of nullification that stopped just short of secession from the Union. The unsigned statement accompanied resolutions of the South Carolina legislature against the tariff. Calhoun, however, had not entirely abandoned his earlier nationalism. His object was to preserve the Union by protecting the minority rights that the agricultural and slaveholding South claimed. The fine balance he struck between states' rights and central authority was actually not far removed from Jackson's own philosophy, but growing tension between the two men would complicate the issue. Jackson, in addition, was determined to draw the line at any defiance of federal law.

THE WEBSTER-HAYNE DEBATE   South Carolina had proclaimed its dislike for the tariff, but had postponed any action against its enforcement, awaiting with hope the election of 1828 in which Calhoun was the Jacksonian candidate for vice-president. The state anticipated a new tariff policy from the Jackson administration. There the issue stood until 1830, when the great Webster-Hayne debate sharpened the lines between states' rights and the Union. The immediate occasion for the debate, however, was the question of public lands.

The federal government still owned immense tracts of land, and the issue of their disposition elbowed its way again onto the center stage of sectional debate. Late in 1829 a Connecticut senator, fearing the continued drain of able-bodied men from New England, sought to restrict land sales in the West. When his resolution came before the Senate in January 1830, Missouri's Thomas Hart Benton, who for years had been calling for lower land prices, denounced it as a sectional attack designed to impede the settlement of the West so that the East might maintain its supply of cheap factory labor. Robert Y. Hayne of South Carolina took Benton's side. Hayne saw in the public-lands issue a chance to strengthen the alliance of South and West reflected in Jackson's election. Perhaps by supporting a policy of cheap lands in the West the southerners could win western support for lower tariffs. The government, said Hayne, endangered the Union by imposing a hardship upon one section to the benefit of another. The use of public lands as a source of revenue to the central government would create "a fund for corruption—fatal to the sovereignty and independence of the states."

Daniel Webster of Massachusetts rose to offer a dramatic defense of the East. Possessed of a thunderous voice and a theatrical flair, Webster was widely recognized as the nation's foremost orator and lawyer. His striking physical presence enhanced his rhetorical skills. Webster had the torso of a bull, and his huge head, with its jet-black hair, magisterial domed forehead, craggy brows overhanging deep-set, lustrous black eyes, and a mastiff's mouth, commanded attention. With the gallery hushed, the "God-like Daniel" began by denying that the East had ever sought to restrict development of the West. He then rebuked those southerners who "habitually speak of the Union in terms of indifference, or even of disparagement." Federal money derived from land sales, Webster argued, was not a source of corruption but a source of improvement. At this point the issue of western lands vanished from sight. Webster had adroitly shifted the ground of debate and lured Hayne into defending states' rights and upholding the doctrine of nullification, instead of pursuing coalition with the West.

Hayne took the bait. Young, handsome, and himself an accomplished speaker, Hayne launched into a defense of Calhoun's *South Carolina Exposition*, arguing that the union was created by a compact of the states, and the federal government could not be the judge of its own powers, else its powers would be unlimited. Rather, the states remained free to judge when the national government had overstepped the bounds of its constitutional authority. The right of state "interposition" was as "full and complete as it was before the Constitution was formed."

In rebuttal to the state-compact theory, Webster defined a nationalistic view of the Constitution. From the beginning, he asserted, the American Revolution had been a crusade of the united colonies rather than of each separately. True sovereignty resided in the people as a whole, for whom both federal and state governments acted as agents in their respective spheres. If a single state could nullify a law of the general government, then the Union would be a "rope of sand," a practical absurdity. Instead the Constitution had created a Supreme Court with the final jurisdiction on all questions of constitutionality. A state could neither nullify a federal law nor secede from the Union. The practical outcome of nullification would be a confrontation leading to civil war.

The Senate galleries and much of the country at large thrilled to Webster's eloquence. His closing statement has become justly famous: "Liberty and Union, now and forever, one and inseparable." In the practical world of coalition politics, Webster also had the better of the argument, for the Union and majority rule

The eloquent Massachusetts Sen. Daniel Webster stands to rebut the argument for nullification in the Webster-Hayne debate.

meant more to westerners, including Jackson, than the abstractions of state sovereignty and nullification. As for the public lands, the disputed resolution was soon defeated anyway. And whatever one might argue about the origins of the Union, its evolution would more and more validate Webster's position.

THE RIFT WITH CALHOUN   As yet, however, the enigmatic Jackson had not spoken out on the issue. Jackson, like Calhoun, was a slaveholder, albeit a westerner, and might be expected to sympathize with South Carolina, his native state. Soon all doubt was removed, at least on the point of nullification. On April 13, 1830, the Jefferson Day Dinner, honoring the birthday of the former president, was held in Washington. Jackson and Van Buren agreed that Jackson should present a toast that would indicate his opposition to nullification. When his turn came, Jackson rose, stood erect as a poplar, raised his glass, pointedly stared at Calhoun, and announced: "Our Union—it must be preserved!" Calhoun, who followed, trembled so that he spilled some of the amber fluid from his glass, but tried quickly to retrieve the situation with a toast to "The Union, next to our liberty most dear!" But Jackson had set off a bombshell that exploded the plans of the states'-righters.

Nearly a month afterward the final nail was driven into the coffin of Calhoun's presidential ambitions. On May 12, 1830, Jackson saw a letter confirming reports that in 1818 Calhoun, as secretary of war, had proposed to discipline Jackson for his reckless behavior during the Florida invasion. A tense correspondence between Jackson and Calhoun followed, and ended with a curt note from the president cutting it off. "Understanding you now," Jackson wrote, "no further communication with you on this subject is necessary."

As a result of the growing rift between the men, Jackson removed all Calhoun partisans from the cabinet. He then named Van Buren minister to London, pending Senate approval. In the fall of 1831 Jackson announced his readiness for one more term, with the idea of returning Van Buren from London in time for the New Yorker to succeed him as president in 1836. But in January 1832, when the Senate reconvened, Van Buren's enemies opposed his appointment as minister, and gave Calhoun, as vice-president, a chance to reject the nomination by a tie-breaking vote. "It will kill him [Van Buren], sir, kill him dead," Calhoun told Sen. Thomas Hart Benton. Benton disagreed: "You have broken a minister, and elected a Vice-President." So, it turned out, he had. Calhoun's vote against Van Buren provoked popular sympathy for the New Yorker, who would soon be nominated to succeed Calhoun as vice-president.

His presidential hopes blasted, Calhoun eagerly became the public leader of the nullificationists. These South Carolinians believed that, despite reductions supported by Jackson, tariff rates remained too high. By the end of 1831 Jackson was calling for further reductions to take the wind out of the nullificationists' sails, and the tariff of 1832 did cut revenues another $5 million, but mainly on unprotected items. Average tariff rates were about 25 percent, but rates on cottons, woolens, and iron remained up around 50 percent. South Carolinians labeled such high rates an "abomination."

THE SOUTH CAROLINA ORDINANCE   In the South Carolina state elections of October 1832, the advocates of nullification took the initiative in organization and agitation. A special legislative session in October called for the election of a state convention, which assembled at Columbia a month later and overwhelmingly adopted a nullification ordinance. This ordinance repudiated the tariff acts of 1828 and 1832 as unconstitutional and forbade collection of the duties in the state after February 1, 1833. The legislature also chose Robert Hayne as governor and elected Calhoun to succeed him as senator. Calhoun promptly resigned as vice-president in order to defend nullification on the Senate floor.

In the crisis South Carolina found itself standing alone. The Georgia legislature dismissed nullification as "rash and revolutionary." Alabama pronounced it "unsound in theory and dangerous in practice"; Mississippi stood "firmly resolved" to put down nullification. Jackson's response was measured and firm, but not rash—at least not in public. In private he threatened to hang Calhoun and all other traitors—and later expressed regret that he had failed to hang at least Calhoun. In his annual message on December 4, 1832, Jackson announced his firm intention to enforce the tariff, but once again urged Congress to lower the rates. On December 10 he followed up with his Nullification Proclamation, a document which characterized that doctrine as an "impractical absurdity." Jackson appealed to the people of his native state not to follow false leaders: "The laws of the United States must be executed. . . . Those who told you that you might peaceably prevent their execution, deceived you. . . . Their object is disunion. But be not deceived by names. Disunion by armed force is treason."

CLAY'S COMPROMISE Jackson sent General Winfield Scott to Charleston Harbor with reinforcements of federal soldiers. "In 40 days," the president announced, "I can have within the limits of South Carolina 50,000 men." A ship of war and seven revenue cutters appeared in the harbor, ready to enforce the tariff before ships had a chance to land their cargoes. The nullifiers mobilized the state militia while unionists in the state organized a volunteer force. In January 1833 the president requested from Congress a "Force Bill" authorizing him to use the army to compel compliance with federal law in South Carolina. At the same time he endorsed a bill in Congress which would have lowered duties to a maximum of 20 percent within two years.

When the Force Bill was introduced, Calhoun immediately rose in opposition, denying that either he or his state favored disunion. Indeed, Calhoun personally opposed the idea of secession. He did not want the South to leave the Union; he wanted the region to regain its political dominance of the Union. His comments to the Senate, wrote the future president, John Tyler of Virginia, were "warm—impassioned—burning." Passage of the bill eventually came to depend on the support of Henry Clay,who finally yielded to those urging him to save the day. On February 12, 1833, he introduced a plan to reduce the tariff gradually until 1842, by which time no rate would be more than

20 percent. South Carolina would have preferred a greater reduction, but Clay's plan got the nullifiers out of the corner into which they had painted themselves.

On March 1, 1833, the compromise tariff and the Force Bill passed Congress, and the next day Jackson signed both. The South Carolina Convention then met and rescinded its nullification ordinance, and in a face-saving gesture nullified the Force Bill, for which Jackson no longer had any need. Both sides were able to claim victory. Jackson had upheld the supremacy of the Union, and South Carolina had secured a reduction of the tariff. Calhoun, worn out by the controversy, returned to his plantation. "The struggle, so far from being over," he ominously wrote, "is not more than fairly commenced."

INDIAN POLICY

INDIAN REMOVAL   On Indian affairs Jackson's attitude was the typically western one, that Indians were barbaric impediments to white social progress. By the time of his election in 1828 he was convinced that a "just, humane, liberal policy toward Indians" dictated moving them onto the plains west of the Mississippi, an area fit mainly for horned toads and rattlesnakes. Congress agreed, and in 1830 it approved the Indian Removal Act. Thereafter some ninety-four removal treaties were negotiated, and by 1835 Jackson was able to announce that the policy had been carried out or was in process of completion for all but a handful of Indians.

Most of the northern tribes were too weak to resist the offers of Indian commissioners who, if necessary, used bribery and alcohol to woo the chiefs, and if sometimes the tribesmen rebelled, there was, on the whole, remarkably little resistance. In Illinois and Wisconsin Territory an armed clash known as the Black Hawk War sprang up from April to August 1832, when the Sauk and Fox under Chief Black Hawk sought to reoccupy some lands they had abandoned in the previous year. Facing famine and hostile Sioux west of the Mississippi, they were simply seeking a place to get in a corn crop. The Illinois militia mobilized to expel them, chased them into Wisconsin Territory, and massacred women and children as they tried to escape across the Mississippi. When Black Hawk surrendered he confessed that his "heart is dead, and no longer beats quick in his bosom. He is now a prisoner to the white men; they will do with him as they wish. But he can stand torture and is not afraid of death. He is no cow-

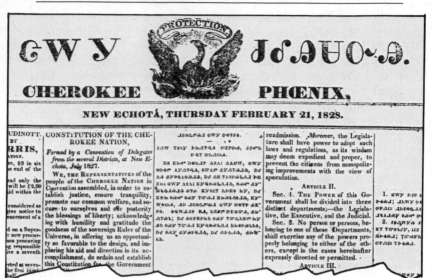

The first issue of the Cherokee Phoenix *published the Constitution of the Cherokee nation, which embraced "the lands solemnly guaranteed and reserved forever to the Cherokee Nation by the Treaties concluded with the United States."*

ard. Black Hawk is an Indian." The Black Hawk War came to be remembered later, however, less because of the atrocities inflicted on the Indians than because the participants included two native Kentuckians later to be pitted against each other: Lieutenant Jefferson Davis of the regular army and Captain Abraham Lincoln of the Illinois volunteers.

In the South two proud Indian nations, the Seminoles and Cherokees, also put up a stubborn resistance. The Seminoles were in fact a group of different tribes who had gravitated to Florida in the eighteenth century. They fought a protracted guerrilla war in the Everglades from 1835 to 1842, but most of the vigor went out of their resistance after 1837, when their leader Osceola was seized by treachery under a flag of truce and died a prisoner. After 1842 only a few hundred Seminoles remained, hiding out in the swamps. Most of the rest had been removed to the West.

THE TRAIL OF TEARS   The Cherokees had by the end of the eighteenth century fallen back into the mountains of northern Georgia and western North Carolina, onto land guaranteed to them in

1791 by treaty with the United States. In 1827 the Cherokees, relying on their treaty rights, adopted a constitution in which they said pointedly that they were not subject to any other state or nation. The next year Georgia responded with a law stipulating that after June 1, 1830, the authority of state law would extend over the Cherokees living within the boundaries of the state.

The discovery of gold in 1829 whetted the whites' appetite for Cherokee lands and brought bands of rough prospectors into the country. The Cherokees sought relief in the Supreme Court, but in *Cherokee Nation v. Georgia* (1831) John Marshall ruled that the Court lacked jurisdiction because the Cherokees were a "domestic dependent nation" rather than a foreign state in the

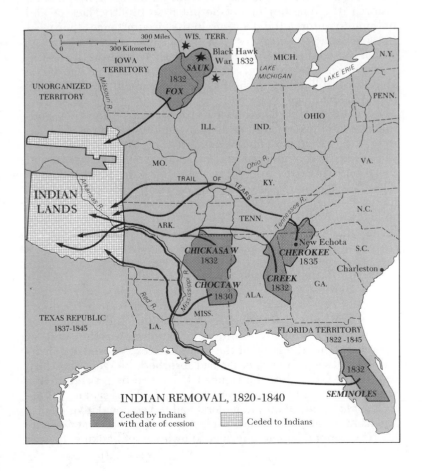

INDIAN REMOVAL, 1820-1840

Ceded by Indians with date of cession

Ceded to Indians

meaning of the Constitution. Marshall added, however, that the Cherokees had "an unquestionable right" to their lands until they wished to cede them to the United States.

In 1830 a Georgia law had required whites in the Cherokee territory to get licenses authorizing their residence there, and to take an oath of allegiance to the state. Two New England missionaries among the Indians refused and were sentenced to four years at hard labor. On appeal, their case reached the Supreme Court as *Worcester v. Georgia* (1832), and the court held that the Cherokee nation was "a distinct political community" within which Georgia law had no force. The Georgia law was therefore unconstitutional. Now Georgia faced down the Supreme Court with the tacit consent of the president. Jackson is supposed to have said privately: "Marshall has made his decision, now let him enforce it!" Whether or not he put it so bluntly, Jackson did nothing to enforce the decision. In the circumstances there was nothing for the Cherokees to do but give in and sign a treaty, which they did in 1835. They gave up their lands in the Southeast in exchange for lands in the Indian Territory west of Arkansas, $5 million from the federal government, and expenses for transportation.

By 1838 15,000 Cherokees had departed on the thousand-mile "trail of tears" westward, following the Choctaws, Chickasaws, Creeks, and Seminoles on a grueling journey marked by the cruelty and neglect of soldiers and private contractors, and scorn and pilferage by whites along the way. Four thousand Cherokees did not survive the trip. A few never left their homeland. They held out in their native mountains and acquired title to lands in North Carolina; thenceforth they were the "eastern band" of Cherokees.

The Bank Controversy

THE BANK'S OPPONENTS   The overriding national issue in the presidential campaign of 1832 was neither Jackson's Indian policy nor South Carolina's obsession with nullification. It was the question of rechartering the Bank of the United States, whose legal mandate would soon lapse. Jackson had absorbed the West's hostility toward the bank after the Panic of 1819, and he insisted that it was unconstitutional no matter what Marshall had said in *McCulloch v. Maryland*. Banks in general had fed a speculative mania, and Jackson, suspicious of all banks, preferred a hard-money policy. The general had no informed knowledge of banking; he was in fact blissfully ignorant of the subject. But he felt strongly that such a central bank was wrong, and his government "would never recharter that monster of corruption."

Under the management of Nicholas Biddle, the Second Bank of the United States had prospered and grown. The bank had facilitated business expansion and supplied a stable currency by forcing state banks to keep a specie reserve (gold or silver) behind their notes. But arrayed against the bank were powerful enemies: some of the state and local banks that had been forced to reduce their note issues, debtor groups that suffered from the reduction, and businessmen and speculators "on the make" who wanted easier credit. States'-rights groups questioned the bank's constitutionality. Financiers of New York's Wall Street resented the supremacy of the bank on Philadelphia's Chestnut Street. Many westerners and workingmen, like Jackson, felt that the bank was a powerful monopoly controlled by the wealthy few and that this was irreconcilable with a democracy. Biddle, born to wealth and social prestige, cultured, witty, and supremely self-confident, was an excellent banker but also a convenient symbol for those who saw the bank as the friend of capitalists.

BIDDLE'S RECHARTER EFFORT The bank's twenty-year charter would run through 1836, but Biddle could not afford the uncertainty of waiting until then for a renewal. He pondered whether to force the issue of recharter before the election of 1832 or after. On this point leaders of the National Republicans, especially Clay and Webster, argued that the time to move was before the election. Clay, already the candidate of the National Republicans, proposed to make the bank the central issue of the presidential canvas. Friends of the bank held a majority in Congress, and Jackson would risk loss of support in the election if he vetoed renewal. But they failed to grasp the depth of popular prejudice against the bank, and thereby they succeeded mainly in handing Jackson a charged issue on the eve of the election.

Both houses passed the recharter by comfortable margins, but without the two-thirds majority needed to override a veto. On July 10, 1832, Jackson vetoed the bill, sending it back to Congress with a ringing denunciation of monopoly and special privilege. The bill, he argued, demonstrated that many "of our rich men have not been content with equal protection and equal benefits, but have besought us to make them richer by act of Congress." An effort to overrule the veto failed in the Senate, where the vote of 22 to 19 for the bank fell far short of the needed two-thirds majority. The stage was set for a nationwide financial crisis. "This worthy President," fumed Biddle, "thinks that because he has scalped Indians and imprisoned judges, he is to have his way with the Bank. He is mistaken."

CAMPAIGN INNOVATIONS   The presidential campaign, as usual, began early, the nominations having been made before the bank veto, two in fact before the end of 1831. For the first time a third party entered the field. The Anti-Masonic party was, like the bank, the object of strong emotions then sweeping the new democracy. The group had grown out of popular hostility toward the Masonic order, a fraternal organization whose members were suspected of having kidnapped and murdered a New Yorker for revealing the "secrets" of his lodge. Opposition to a fraternal order was hardly the foundation on which to build a lasting party, but the Anti-Masonic party had three important "firsts" to its credit: in addition to being the first third party, it was the first party to hold a national nominating convention and

George Caleb Bingham's Verdict of the People *depicts the increasingly democratic politics of the early to mid–nineteenth century.*

the first to announce a platform, all of which it accomplished in September 1831 when it nominated William Wirt of Maryland for president.

The major parties followed its example by holding national conventions of their own. In December 1831 National Republican party delegates assembled in Baltimore to nominate Henry Clay for president. Jackson endorsed the idea of a nominating convention for the Democratic party (the name Republican was now formally dropped) to demonstrate popular support for its candidates. To that purpose the convention adopted the two-thirds rule for nomination (which prevailed until 1936), and then named Martin Van Buren as Jackson's running mate. The Democrats, unlike the other two parties, adopted no formal platform at their first convention, and relied substantially on hoopla and the president's personal popularity to carry their cause.

The outcome was an overwhelming endorsement of Jackson in the electoral college by 219 votes to 49 for Clay, and a less overwhelming but solid victory in the popular vote, 688,000 to 530,000. William Wirt carried only Vermont. South Carolina, preparing for nullification and unable to stomach either Jackson or Clay, delivered its eleven votes to the governor of Virginia.

REMOVAL OF GOVERNMENT DEPOSITS   Jackson viewed the election as a mandate to proceed further against the B.U.S., and he now resolved to remove all government deposits and distribute them to state banks. When Secretary of the Treasury McLane opposed removal of the government deposits and suggested a new and modified version of the bank, Jackson shook up his cabinet. He kicked McLane upstairs to head the State Department and replaced him with William J. Duane of Philadelphia. But by some oversight Jackson failed to explore Duane's views fully or advise him of his own expectations. Duane was antibank, but he was consistent in his convictions. Dubious about banks in general, he saw no merit in removing deposits from the central bank for deposit in countless state banks. Jackson might well have listened to Duane's warnings that such action would lead to speculative inflation, but the old general's combative instincts were too much aroused. He summarily dismissed Duane and moved Attorney-General Roger Taney to the Treasury, where the new secretary gladly complied with the president's wishes, which corresponded to his own views.

The procedure was to continue drawing on governmental accounts with Biddle's bank, and to deposit all new governmental receipts in state banks. By the end of 1833 there were twenty-three state banks that had the benefit of governmental deposits, "pet banks" as they came to be called. Jackson's headlong plunge into finance, it soon turned out, backfired. As so often happens with complex public issues, dissatisfaction had become focused on a symbol. In this case the symbol was the "Monster of Chestnut Street," which had been all along the one institution able to maintain some degree of order in the financial world. Jackson's action initially provoked a contraction of credit by Biddle's bank in order to shore up its defenses against the loss of deposits. By 1834 the tightness of credit was creating widespread complaints of business distress.

The contraction brought about by the bank war quickly gave way, however, to a speculative binge encouraged by the deposit of government funds in the pet banks. With the restraint of Biddle's bank removed, the state banks unleashed their wildcat tendencies, issuing banknotes without keeping sufficient gold reserves on hand. (The term "wildcat," used in this sense, originated in Michigan, where one of the fly-by-night banks featured a panther, or wildcat, on its worthless notes.) New banks mushroomed, blissfully printing banknotes to lend to speculators. Sales of public lands rose from 4 million acres in 1834 to 15 million in 1835 and to 20 million in 1836. At the same time the

The Downfall of Mother Bank. *In this pro-Jackson cartoon, the bank crumbles and Jackson's opponents flee in the face of the heroic president's removal of government deposits.*

states plunged heavily into debt to finance the building of roads and canals, inspired by the success of New York's Erie Canal. By 1837 total state indebtedness had soared to $170 million, a very large sum for this time.

FISCAL MEASURES Still the federal surplus continued to mount as the widespread speculation in public lands continued, and this set off an intense debate over how to deal with the growing surplus. Many westerners proposed simply to lower the price of land; southerners preferred to lower the tariff—but such action would now upset the compromise achieved in the tariff of 1833. Finally, in June 1836, a compromise allowed the government to distribute most of the surplus as loans to the states. To satisfy Jackson's concerns the funds were technically "deposits," but they were never demanded back. Distribution was to be in proportion to each state's representation in Congress.

About a month after passage of this Distribution Act Jackson's treasury secretary issued the Specie Circular of July 11, 1836. With that document the president belatedly applied his hard-money convictions to the sale of public lands. According to his order, the government after August 15 would accept only gold and silver in payment for lands. Doing so would supposedly "repress frauds," withhold support "from monopoly of the public lands in the hands of speculators and capitalists," and discourage the "ruinous extension" of banknotes and credit.

Irony dogged Jackson to the end on this matter. Since few actual settlers could get their hands on hard money, they were now left all the more at the mercy of speculators for land purchases. Both the distribution and the Specie Circular put many state banks in a precarious plight. The distribution reduced their deposits, or at least threw things into disarray by shifting them from bank to bank, and the increased demand for specie put an added strain on the supply of gold and silver. The distribution of the surplus and the Specie Circular combined suddenly to deflate the inflationary spiral, which had reached its greatest extent in 1836.

BOOM AND BUST But the boom and bust of the 1830s had causes larger even than Andrew Jackson, causes that were beyond his control. The inflation of mid-decade was rooted not solely in a sudden expansion of banknotes, as it seemed at the time, but also in an increase of gold and silver flowing in from England and France, and especially from Mexico, for investment and for the purchase of American cotton and other products.

Contrary to appearances, therefore, the specie reserves in American banks actually kept pace with the increase of banknotes, despite reckless behavior by some banks. But by 1836 a tighter British economy caused a decline in British investments abroad and in British demand for American cotton, just when the new western lands were creating a rapid increase in cotton supply. Fortunately for Jackson, the Panic of 1837 did not break until he was out of the White House and safely back at the Hermitage. His successor would serve as the scapegoat.

VAN BUREN AND THE NEW PARTY SYSTEM

THE WHIG COALITION   Before the economic crash, however, the Jacksonian Democrats reaped a political bonanza. Jackson had downed the dual monsters of nullification and the bank, and the people loved him for it. But by 1834 his opponents began to pull together a new coalition of diverse elements united chiefly by their hostility to Jackson. The imperious demeanor of that champion of democracy had given rise to the name of "King Andrew I." His followers therefore were "Tories," supporters of the king, and his opponents "Whigs," a name which linked them to the patriots of the American Revolution. This diverse coalition clustered around its center, the National Republican party of John Quincy Adams, Clay, and Webster. Into the combination streamed remnants of the Anti-Masons and Democrats who, for one reason or another, were alienated by Jackson's stands on the bank, Indian removal, hard money, or internal improvements. Of the forty-one Democrats in Congress who had voted to recharter the bank, twenty-eight had joined the Whigs by 1836.

Whiggery always had about it an atmosphere of social conservatism and superiority. The core Whigs were the supporters of Henry Clay, men whose vision was quickened by the vistas of his "American System." In the South the Whigs enjoyed the support of the urban banking and commercial interests, as well as their planter associates, owners of most of the slaves in the region. In the West, farmers who valued internal improvements joined the Whig ranks. Most states'-rights supporters eventually dropped away, and by the early 1840s the Whigs were becoming the party of nationalism, even in the South. Unlike the Democrats, who attracted Catholic immigrants from Germany and Ireland, Whig voters tended to be native-born and British-American evangelical Protestants—Presbyterians, Baptists, and Congregationalists—who were active in promoting social reforms such as abolitionism and temperance. Throughout their two decades of strength the Whigs were a national party, strong both North and South, and a cohesive force for Union.

THE ELECTION OF 1836 By the presidential election of 1836 a new two-party system was emerging out of the Jackson and anti-Jackson forces, a system that would remain in fairly even balance for twenty years. In May 1835, eighteen months before the election, the Democrats held their second national convention and nominated Jackson's handpicked successor, Vice-President Martin Van Buren. The Whig coalition, united chiefly in its opposition to Jackson, held no convention but adopted a strategy of multiple candidacies, hoping to throw the election into the House of Representatives. The result was a free-for-all reminiscent of 1824, except that this time one candidate stood apart from the rest. It was Van Buren against the field. The Whigs put up three favorite sons: Daniel Webster, named by the Massachusetts legislature; Hugh Lawson White, chosen by anti-Jackson Democrats in the Tennessee legislature; and William Henry Harrison of Indiana, nominated by a predominantly Anti-Masonic convention in Harrisburg, Pennsylvania. In the popular vote Van Buren outdistanced the entire Whig field, with 765,000 votes to 740,000 votes for the Whigs, most of which were cast for Harrison.

Martin Van Buren, the eighth president, was the first of Dutch ancestry and, at the age of fifty-five, the first born under the

Martin Van Buren, the "Little Magician."

Stars and Stripes. Son of a tavernkeeper in Kinderhook, New York, he had been schooled in a local academy, read law, and entered politics. Although he kept up a limited legal practice, he had been primarily a professional politician, so skilled in the arts of organization and manipulation that he was dubbed the "Little Magician." In 1824 he supported Crawford, then switched to Jackson in 1828, but continued to look to the Old Republicans of Virginia as the southern anchor of his support. After a brief tenure as governor of New York, Van Buren resigned to join the cabinet and, because of Jackson's support, became minister to London and then vice-president. Short and trim, Van Buren was also called the "Red Fox" for his long reddish sideburns, dominant forehead, and long, striking nose. His elegant attire, engaging personality, and constant political scheming gave further credence to his nicknames.

THE PANIC OF 1837   Van Buren owed much of his political success to having been in the right place at the right time. But once he had climbed to the top of the greasy pole, luck suddenly deserted him. Van Buren had inherited Jackson's favor and a good part of his following, but he also inherited a financial panic. An already precarious economy was tipped over into crisis by depression in England, which resulted in a drop in the price of cotton from 17 1/2 cents to 13 1/2 cents a pound, and caused English banks and investors to contract their activities in the New World and refuse extensions of loans. This was a particularly hard blow since much of America's economic expansion depended on European—and mainly English—capital. As creditors hastened to foreclose, the inflationary spiral went into reverse. States curtailed ambitious plans for roads and canals, and in many cases felt impelled to repudiate their debts. In the crunch a good many of the wildcat banks succumbed, and the government itself lost some $9 million it had deposited in pet banks.

The working classes, as always, were particularly hard hit during the economic slump, and they largely had to fend for themselves. By the fall of 1837 a third of the work force was jobless and those still fortunate enough to have jobs saw their wages cut by 30–50 percent within two years. At the same time, prices for food and clothing skyrocketed. As winter approached in late 1837, a journalist reported that in New York City there were 200,000 people "in utter and hopeless distress with no means of surviving the winter but those provided by charity." Indeed, there was no government aid, only that provided by churches and voluntary societies.

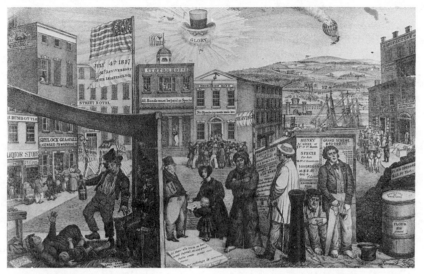

The Times. *This anti-Jacksonian cartoon depicts the effects of the depression of 1837: a panic at the bank, beggars in the street.*

Van Buren's advisers and supporters were inclined to blame speculators and bankers for the hard times. At the same time they expected the evildoers to get what they deserved in a healthy shakeout that would bring the economy back to stability. Van Buren did not believe that he or the government had any responsibility to rescue hard-pressed farmers or businessmen, or to provide public relief. But he did feel obliged to keep the government itself in a healthy financial situation. To that end he called a special session of Congress in September 1837, that quickly voted to postpone indefinitely the distribution of the surplus because of a probable upcoming deficit, and also approved an issue of Treasury notes to cover immediate expenses.

AN INDEPENDENT TREASURY   But Van Buren devoted most of his message to his idea that the government cease risking its deposits in shaky banks and set up an Independent Treasury. Under this plan the government would keep its funds in its own vaults and do business entirely in hard money. Van Buren observed that the republic's founders had "wisely judged that the less government interfered with private pursuits the better for the general prosperity." Webster's response typified the Whig reaction: "I feel . . . as if this could not be America when I see schemes of public policy proposed, having for their object the convenience of Gov-

ernment only, and leaving the people to shift for themselves."
The Whiggish approach, presumably, would have been some
kind of Hamiltonian program of government promotion of economic development, perhaps in the form of tariff or currency
legislation. Good Jacksonians disapproved of such programs, at
least when they were run from Washington.

Van Buren's Independent Treasury bill encountered stiff opposition from a combination of Whigs and conservative Democrats who feared deflation, and it took the "Red Fox" several
years of maneuvering to get what he wanted. Calhoun signaled a
return to the Democratic fold, after several years of flirting with
the Whigs, when he came out for the Independent Treasury. Van
Buren gained western support for the plan by backing a more liberal land policy. Congress finally passed the Independent Treasury on July 4, 1840. Although the Whigs repealed it in 1841, it
would be restored in 1846.

The protracted hassle over the Treasury was only one of several issues that kept Washington preoccupied through the Van
Buren years. Petitions asking Congress to abolish slavery and the
slave trade in the District of Columbia provoked tumultuous debate, especially in the House of Representatives. A dispute over
the Maine boundary kept British-American animosity at a simmer. But basic to the spreading malaise of the time was the depressed condition of the economy that lasted through Van
Buren's entire term. Fairly or not, the administration became the
target of growing discontent. The president won renomination
easily enough, but the general election was another matter.

THE "LOG CABIN AND HARD CIDER" CAMPAIGN   The Whigs got an
early start on their campaign when they met at Harrisburg, Pennsylvania, on December 4, 1839, to choose a candidate. Henry
Clay, the warm and personable legislative veteran who coupled
the ideas of a visionary with shrewd political savvy, expected
1840 to be his year. He was wrong. Although he led on the first
ballot, the convention preferred a Whiggish Jackson, as it were, a
military hero who could enter the race with few known political
convictions or enemies. So the delegates turned to William
Henry Harrison, victor at the battle of Tippecanoe while governor of the Indiana territory, and briefly a congressman and a senator from Ohio. To rally their states'-rights wing, the Whigs
chose for vice-president John Tyler of Virginia, Clay's close
friend.

The Whigs had no platform. That would have risked dividing a
coalition united chiefly by opposition to the Democrats. But

they had a slogan, "Tippecanoe and Tyler too," that went trip-
pingly on the tongue. And they soon had a rousing campaign
theme which a Democratic paper unwittingly supplied them
when it declared sardonically "that upon condition of his receiving a pension of $2,000 and a barrel of cider, General Harrison
would no doubt consent to withdraw his pretensions, and spend
his days in a log cabin on the banks of the Ohio." The Whigs
seized upon the cider and log cabin symbols to depict Harrison as
a simple man sprung from the people. Actually he sprang from
one of the first families of Virginia, was a college graduate, and
lived in a commodious Ohio farmhouse.

The campaign produced the largest turnout of any election up
to that time and left one lasting heritage in the American language, a usage now virtually worldwide. The expression "O.K."
was picked up as an abbreviation for "Old Kinderhook," an affectionate name for Van Buren, whose supporters organized
"O.K. Clubs" during the campaign. But the president was anything but O.K. to the Whigs. To them he symbolized the economic slump as well as aristocratic snobbery. "Van! Van! Is a
Used-up Man!" went one of their campaign slogans, and down he
went by the thumping margin of 234 electoral votes to 60.

ASSESSING THE JACKSON YEARS

The Jacksonian impulse had altered American politics permanently. Longstanding ambivalence about political parties had
been purged in the fires of political conflict, and mass political
parties had arrived to stay. They were now widely justified as a
positive good. By 1840 both parties were tightly organized down
to the precinct level, and the proportion of adult white males
who voted in the presidential election nearly tripled, from 27
percent in 1824 to 78 percent in 1840. That much is beyond dispute, but the phenomenon of Jackson, the great symbol for an
age, has inspired conflicts of interpretation as spirited as those
among his supporters and opponents at the time. Was he the
leader of a vast democratic movement that welled up in the West
and mobilized a farmer-laborer alliance to sweep the "Monster"
bank into the dustbin of history? Or was he essentially a frontier
nabob, an opportunist for whom the ideal of democracy provided effective political rhetoric?

Whatever else Jackson and his supporters had in mind, they
followed an ideal of republican virtue, of returning to the Jeffersonian vision of the Old Republic in which government would

Andrew Jackson in 1845. Jackson died shortly after this daguerrotype was taken.

leave people largely to their own devices. In the Jacksonian view the alliance of government and business always invited special favors and provided an eternal source of corruption. The central bank epitomized such evil. Good governmental policy, at the national level in particular, refrained from granting special privileges and let free competition regulate the economy.

In the bustling world of the nineteenth century, however, the idea of a return to agrarian simplicity represented a futile exercise in nostalgia. Instead, Jackson's laissez-faire policies actually opened the way for a host of aspiring entrepreneurs eager to replace the established economic elite with a new order of free enterprise capitalism. And in fact there was no great conflict in the Jacksonian mentality between the farmer or planter who delved in the soil and the independent speculator and entrepreneur who won his way by other means. Jackson himself was all these things. The Jacksonian mentality could not foresee the degree to which, in a growing country, unrestrained enterprise could lead to new economic combinations, centers of gigantic power largely independent of governmental regulation. But history is forever producing unintended consequences. Here the ultimate irony would be that the laissez-faire rationale for republican simplicity eventually became the justification for the growth of unregulated centers of economic power far greater than any ever wielded by Biddle's bank.

FURTHER READING

A useful survey of events covered in this chapter can be found in Harry L. Watson's *Liberty and Power: The Politics of Jacksonian America* (1990).° Edward Pessen's *Jacksonian America: Society, Personality, and Politics* (rev. ed., 1985)° provides a recent overview of differing interpretations of the period. An introduction to the development of political parties of the 1830s can be found in Richard P. McCormick's *The Second Party System* (1966).° For an outstanding analysis of women in New York City during the Jacksonian period, see Christine Stansell's *City of Women* (1986).° In *Chants Democratic* (1984)° Sean Wilentz analyzes the social basis of working-class politics.

The transformation of the economy during the Jacksonian era is the focus of Charles Sellers's *The Market Revolution: Jacksonian America, 1815–1846* (1992). The impact of the bank controversy is revealed in James R. Sharp's *The Jacksonians versus the Banks: Politics in the States after the Panic of 1837* (1970).

An outstanding book on the nullification issue is William W. Freehling's *Prelude to Civil War: The Nullification Controversy in South Carolina, 1816–1836* (1966).° John M. Belohlavek's *"Let the Eagle Soar!" The Foreign Policy of Andrew Jackson* (1985) provides a thorough study of Jacksonian diplomacy. Ronald N. Satz's *American Indian Policy in the Jacksonian Era* (1974) surveys that tragedy; Michael P. Rogin's *Fathers and Children: Andrew Jackson and the Subjugation of the American Indian* (1991)° is a psychological interpretation of Jackson's Indian policy. The question of rising inequality in American cities is treated in Edward Pessen's *Riches, Class, and Power before the Civil War* (1973).°

On the magisterial political leaders of the era, see Merrill Peterson's *The Great Triumverate: Webster, Clay, and Calhoun* (1988).° The best biography of Clay is Robert V. Remini, *Henry Clay, Statesman for the Union* (1991).

° These books are available in paperback editions.

11

THE DYNAMICS OF GROWTH

AGRICULTURE AND THE NATIONAL ECONOMY

During the decades following the end of the War of 1812, the American economy grew at a pace that generated profound social and political change. The first stage of industrialization brought with it an expansive commercial and urban outlook that by the end of the century would supplant the agrarian philosophy espoused by Thomas Jefferson and many others. "We are greatly, I was about to say fearfully, growing," John C. Calhoun told his congressional colleagues in 1816, and many other statesmen shared his ambivalent outlook. Would the Republic retain its virtue and cohesion amid the turmoil of commercial development? But in the brief period of good feelings after the War of 1812, such a troublesome question was easily brushed aside. Economic opportunities seemed available to free Americans everywhere, and nowhere more than in Calhoun's native South Carolina. The reason was cotton, the profitable new staple crop of the South, which was spreading from South Carolina and Georgia into the new lands of Mississippi and Alabama.

COTTON   Cotton had been in use from ancient times, but the proliferation of English textile mills during the late eighteenth century created a rapidly growing market for the fluffy staple. For many years cotton had remained rare and expensive because of the need for hand labor to separate the lint from the tenacious green seeds of most varieties. But that problem was solved in 1793 when Eli Whitney, a Yale graduate who went south to teach, devised a mechanism for removing the sticky seeds. The cotton gin enabled a person to separate fifty times as much cotton as could be done by hand.

By inventing the cotton gin, Whitney had unwittingly begun a revolution. Cotton production soared during the first half of the nineteenth century, and planters had found a new and profitable use for slavery. Indeed thereafter slavery became almost synonymous with the Cotton Kingdom in the popular view. Planters and their slaves migrated westward into Kentucky, Tennessee, Alabama, Mississippi, Louisiana, and Texas, and the cotton culture became a way of life that tied the Old Southwest to the coastal Southeast in a common interest.

Not the least of the cotton gin's revolutionary consequences was that cotton became a major export commodity for the United States. After Napoleon's defeat in 1815, European demand for cotton skyrocketed. From 1815 to 1819 American cotton exports averaged 39 percent of the value of all exports, and from the mid-1830s to 1860 they accounted for more than half the total. For the national economy as a whole during the first half of the century, cotton precipitated a phenomenal expansion. The South supplied the North both raw materials and markets for manufactures. Income from the North's role in handling the cotton trade then provided surpluses for capital investment.

FARMING THE WEST   The westward flow of planters and their slaves to Alabama and Mississippi during these flush times was paralleled by another migration through the Ohio Valley and the Great Lakes region, where the Indians had been steadily pushed. "Old America seems to be breaking up and moving westward," an English traveler observed in 1817. Family groups, stages, light wagons, riders on horseback made up "a scene of bustle and business, extending over three hundred miles, which is truly wonderful." By 1860 more than half the nation's expanded population resided in trans-Appalachia, and the restless movement had long since spilled across the Mississippi and touched the shores of the Pacific.

North of the expanding cotton belt in the Gulf states, the fertile woodland soils, riverside bottom lands, and black loam of the prairies drew farmers from the rocky land of New England and the leached, exhausted soils of the Southeast. The development of effective iron plows greatly eased the grueling job of breaking the soil. In 1819 a New York farmer developed an improved iron plow with parts that could be replaced separately without buying a whole new plow. Demand for plows grew so fast that the manufacturer could not supply the need. Further improvements would follow, including John Deere's steel plow (1837), which was better suited for breaking up the rock-hard soil of the Great Plains.

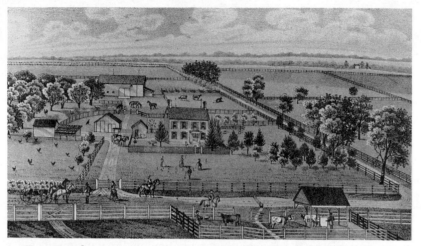

Farm Residence, Putnam County, Illinois. *Through the early decades of the nineteenth century migrants transformed midwestern plains to farmland.*

A new land law of 1820 reduced the minimum price per acre and the minimum plot from 160 to 80 acres. The settler could now buy a place for as little as $100, and over the years the proliferation of state banks made it possible to continue buying on credit. Even that was not enough for westerners who began a long—and eventually victorious—agitation for further relaxation of the land laws. They favored preemption—the right of squatters to purchase land at the minimum price—and graduation—the progressive reduction of the price on lands that did not sell.

Congress eventually responded with two acts. Under the Preemption Act of 1830, squatters could stake out claims ahead of the land surveys and later get 160 acres at the minimum price of $1.25 per acre. In effect the law recognized a practice enforced more often than not by frontier vigilantes. Under the Graduation Act of 1854, prices of unsold lands were to go down in stages until the lands could sell for 12 1/2 cents per acre after thirty years.

TRANSPORTATION AND THE NATIONAL ECONOMY

NEW ROADS   Crude pioneer life eventually gave way to staple farming for cash income, as markets for foodstuffs grew in both the South and the Old Northwest. Transportation improvements were beginning to spur the development of a national market. In 1795 the Wilderness Road, which followed the trail blazed by Daniel Boone twenty years before, was opened to wagon traffic, thereby easing the route through the Cumberland Gap in Kentucky. In the Deep South there were no such major highways. South Carolinians and Georgians pushed westward on whatever trails or rutted roads had appeared.

To the northeast public demand for graded and paved roads packed with crushed stones gathered momentum after completion of the Philadelphia-Lancaster Turnpike in 1794 (the term derives from a pole or pike at the tollgate, turned to admit the traffic). By 1821 there were some 4,000 miles of turnpikes, mainly connecting eastern cities, but western traffic could move along the Frederick Pike to Cumberland and thence along the National Road, completed to Wheeling on the Ohio in 1818, and to Vandalia, Illinois, by about mid-century.

WATER TRANSPORT   Once turnpike travelers had reached the Ohio River they could float westward in comparative comfort. At Pittsburgh, Wheeling, and other points, the emigrants could buy flatboats. At the destination the boat could be used again or sold for lumber. In the early 1820s an estimated 3,000 flatboats went down the Ohio every year, and for many years thereafter the flatboat remained the chief conveyance for heavy traffic downstream.

By the early 1820s the turnpike boom was giving way to new developments in water transportation: the river steamboat and the canal barge, which carried bulk commodities far more cheaply than did Conestoga wagons on the National Road. The first commercially successful steamboat appeared when Robert Fulton and Robert R. Livingston sent the *Clermont* up the Hudson to Albany in 1807. After that the use of steamboats spread rapidly to other eastern and western rivers.

By 1836, 361 steamboats were registered to navigate the western waters. During the next decade the shallow-draft, steam-powered ships that traveled *on* rather than *in* the water became the basis of the rivermen's boast that they were "so built that when the river is low and the sandbars come out for air, the first mate can tap a keg of beer and run the boat four miles on the suds." These boats ventured into far reaches of the Mississippi Valley, up such rivers as the Wabash, the Monongahela, the Cumberland, the Tennessee, the Missouri, and the Arkansas.

The durable flatboat still carried to market most of the western wheat, corn, flour, meal, port, whiskey, soap and candles

(the by-products of slaughterhouses), lead from Missouri, copper from Michigan, lumber from the Rockies, and ironwork from Pittsburgh. But the steamboat, by bringing cheaper and faster two-way traffic to the Mississippi Valley, created a continental market and an agricultural empire which became the new breadbasket of America. Along with the new farmers rushed promoters, speculators, retailers, and land-boomers. Villages at strategic trading points along the streams evolved into centers of commerce and urban life. The port of New Orleans grew in the 1830s and 1840s to lead all others in exports.

But by then the Erie Canal was drawing eastward much of the trade that once went down to the Gulf. In 1817 the New York legislature endorsed Governor De Witt Clinton's dream of a canal connecting the Hudson River with Lake Erie and authorized construction. Eight years later, in 1825, the canal was open for its entire 350 miles from Albany to Buffalo; branches soon

TRANSPORTATION WEST, about 1840

⊔⊔⊔⊔ Canals   ═══ Roads

〰 Navigable rivers

0   200 Miles

0   200 Kilometers

put most of the state within reach of the canal. The speedy success of the New York system inspired a mania for canals that lasted more than a decade and resulted in the completion of about 3,000 miles of waterways by 1837. But no canal ever matched the spectacular success of the Erie. It rendered the entire Great Lakes region an economic tributary to New York City, and had major economic and political consequences tying together the West and East while further isolating the Deep South. With the further development of canals spanning Ohio and Indiana from north to south, much of the upper Ohio Valley was also drawn within New York's economic sphere.

RAILROADS   The Panic of 1837 and the subsequent depression cooled the canal fever quickly. Some states that had borrowed heavily to finance canals were forced to repudiate their debts. Meanwhile a new and more versatile form of transportation was gaining on the canal: the railroad. In 1825, the year the Erie Canal was completed, the world's first commercial steam railway began operations in England, and soon the port cities of Baltimore, Charleston, and Boston were alive with schemes to penetrate the hinterlands by rail.

By 1840 American railroads, with a total of 3,328 miles, had outdistanced the canals by just two miles. Over the next twenty years, though, railroads grew nearly tenfold to cover 30,626 miles; more than a third of this total was built in the 1850s. But it was still not until the eve of the Civil War that railroads surpassed canals in total haulage: in 1859 they carried a little over 2 billion ton-miles compared to 1.6 billion on canals.

Travel on the early railroads was a chancy venture. Wood was used for fuel, and the sparks often caused fires along the way or damaged passengers' clothing. An English traveler, Harriet Martineau, reported seeing a lady's shawl ignited on one trip. She discovered in her own gown thirteen holes "and in my veil, with which I saved my eyes, more than could be counted." Creation of the "spark arrester" and the use of coal for fuel relieved but never eliminated the hazard. Different track widths often forced passengers to change trains until a standard gauge became national in 1882. Land travel, whether by stagecoach or train, was a jerky, bumpy, wearying ordeal.

Water travel, where available, offered far more comfort, but railroads gained supremacy over other forms of transport because of their economy, speed, and reliability. Early trains averaged ten miles an hour, doubling the speed of stagecoaches. Railroads provided indirect benefits by encouraging frontier settlement and boosting farming. During the antebellum period, the reduced shipping costs provided by the railroads aided the expansion of farming more than manufacturing, since manufacturers in the Northeast, especially New England, had better access to water transportation. The railroads' demand for iron and equipment of various kinds, however, did provide an enormous market for the industries that made these capital goods. And the ability of railroads to operate year round in all kinds of weather gave them an advantage in carrying finished goods too.

But the epic railroad boom had negative effects as well. By opening up new possibilities for quick and often shady profits, it helped to corrupt political life, and by opening up access to the trans-Appalachian west, it helped accelerate the decline of Indian culture. In addition, the railroad dramatically quickened the tempo and mobility of life. The noted writer Nathaniel Hawthorne spoke for many sensitive Americans when he charged that the locomotive "comes down upon you like fate, swift and inevitable." With its unsettling whistle it brought "the noisy world into the midst of our slumbrous peace."

OCEAN TRANSPORT   For ocean-going traffic the start of service on regular schedules was the most important change of the early 1800s. In the first week of 1818 ships of the New York-based Black Ball Line inaugurated a weekly transatlantic packet service between New York and Liverpool. With the business recovery in 1822 the packet business grew in a rush. By 1845 some fifty-two transatlantic lines ran square-riggers on schedule from New York, with three regular sailings per week. Many others ran in the coastwide trade, to Charleston, Savannah, New Orleans, and elsewhere.

The same year, 1845, witnessed a great innovation with the launching of the first clipper ship, the *Rainbow*. Built for speed, the sleek clippers were the nineteenth-century equivalent of the supersonic jetliner. They doubled the speed of the older merchant vessels, and trading companies rushed to purchase them. Long and lean, with taller masts and more sails, they cut dashing figures during their brief but colorful career, which lasted less than two decades. What provoked the clipper boom was the lure of Chinese tea, a drink long coveted in America but in scarce supply. The tea leaves were a perishable commodity that had to reach market quickly, and the new clippers made this possible. Even more important, the discovery of California gold in 1848 lured thousands of prospectors and entrepreneurs from the Atlantic seaboard. These new settlers generated an urgent demand for goods, and the clippers met the need. In 1854 the *Flying Cloud* took eighty-nine days and eight hours to get from New York to San Francisco, a speed that took steamships several decades to equal. But clippers, while fast, lacked ample cargo space, and after the Civil War they would give way to the larger steamship.

THE ROLE OF GOVERNMENT   The massive internal improvements of the antebellum era were the product of both state government and private initiatives, sometimes undertaken jointly and sometimes separately. After the Panic of 1837, however, the states left railroad development mainly to private corporations, the source of most railroad capital. Still, several southern and western states built their own lines, and most states granted generous tax concessions.

The federal government helped too, despite the constitutional scruples of some against direct involvement in internal improvements. The government bought stock in turnpike and canal companies, and after the success of the Erie, extended land grants to several western states for the support of canal projects. Congress provided for railroad surveys by government engineers, granted tracts of land, and reduced the tariff duties on iron used in railroad construction.

The Growth of Industry

While the South and West developed the agricultural basis for a national economy, the Northeast was laying the foundation for an industrial revolution. Technology in the form of the cotton gin, the harvester, and improvements in transportation had quickened agricultural development and to some extent decided its direction. But technology altered the economic landscape even more profoundly by giving rise to the factory system.

EARLY TEXTILE MANUFACTURES   At the end of the colonial period manufacturing remained in the household or handicraft stage of development, or at most the "putting-out" stage, in which the merchant capitalist would distribute raw material (say, leather patterns for shoes) to be worked up at a laborer's home, then collected and sold. Farmers themselves had to produce much of what they needed in the way of crude implements, shoes, and clothing. The transition from such production to the factory was slow, but one for which a base had been laid before 1815.

In the eighteenth century Great Britain had jumped out to a long head start in industrial production. Britain led the way in the development of iron smelting by coke (refined coal), the invention of the steam engine in 1705 and its improvement by James Watt in 1765, and a series of inventions that mechanized textile production. Britain also carefully guarded its hard-won secrets, forbidding the export of machines or descriptions of them, even preventing informed mechanics from leaving the country. But the secrets could not be kept. In 1789 Samuel Slater arrived in Rhode Island from England with the plan of a textile water frame in his head. He contracted with an enterprising merchant-manufacturer to build a mill in Pawtucket, and in this little mill, completed in 1790, nine children turned out a satisfactory cotton yarn.

Still, the beginnings of an American textile industry were slow and faltering until Jefferson's embargo in 1807 and the War of

New England Factory Village, 1830. *Mills and factories gradually transformed the New England landscape in the early nineteenth century.*

1812 restricted imports and encouraged New England merchant capitalists to switch their resources into manufacturing. New England, it happened, had one distinct advantage in that its ample water power stood near the coast where water transportation was also readily available. In 1813 a group of wealthy merchants known as the Boston Associates formed the Boston Manufacturing Company. At Waltham, Massachusetts, they built the first factory in which the processes of spinning and weaving by power machinery were brought under one roof, mechanizing every process from raw material to finished cloth. By 1815 New England textile mills numbered in the hundreds. The foundations of textile manufacture were laid, and they spurred the growth of garment trades and a machine-tool industry to build and service the mills.

TECHNOLOGY IN AMERICA Meanwhile American ingenuity was adding other bases for industrial growth. In 1804 Oliver Evans developed a high-pressure steam engine adapted to a variety of uses in ships and factories. Among the other outstanding American originals was Cyrus Hall McCormick of Virginia. McCormick invented a primitive grain reaper in 1834, a development as significant to the agricultural economy of the Old Northwest as the cotton gin was to the South. After tinkering with his machine for almost a decade, McCormick applied for a patent in 1841. Six years later he moved to Chicago and built a manufacturing plant for his reapers and mowers. Within a few years he had sold thousands of new machines, transforming the scale of American agriculture. With a hand-operated sickle a farmer could harvest a half acre of wheat a day; with a McCormick reaper two people could work twelve acres a day. McCormick's success attracted other manufacturers and inventors, and soon there were mechanical threshers to separate the grains of wheat from the straw. Farming remained, as it still is, a precarious vocation, subject to the whims of climate, the assault of insects, and the fluctuations of foreign markets, but by the 1850s it had become a major commercial activity. As the volume of agricultural products soared, prices dropped, income rose, and the standard of living for many farm families in the Old Northwest improved.

A spate of inventions in the 1840s foretokened future changes in American life. In 1844 Charles Goodyear patented a process for vulcanizing rubber which created the fabric for rainproof coats. In the same year the first intercity telegraph message was transmitted from Baltimore to Washington on the device Samuel F. Morse had invented back in 1832. The telegraph was slow to catch on at first, but seventeen years after that demonstration, with the completion of connections to San Francisco, an entire continent had been wired for instant communications. In 1846 Elias Howe invented the sewing machine, soon improved by Allen B. Wilson and Isaac Merritt Singer. The sewing machine, incidentally, was one invention that slowed the progress of the factory. Since it was adapted to use in the home, it gave the "putting-out" system a new lease on life in the clothing industry.

It is hard to exaggerate the importance of science and technology in changing the ways people lived by midcentury. To cite but a few examples: improved transportation and a spreading market economy combined with innovations in canning and refrigeration to provide people a more healthy and varied diet. Fruit and vegetables, heretofore only available during harvest season, could be shipped during much of the year. Scientific breeding of cattle helped make meat and milk more abundant.

Technological advances also helped improve living conditions: houses were larger, better heated, and better illuminated. Although working-class residences remained spartan, with few creature comforts, the affluent were able to afford indoor plumbing, central heating, gas lighting, bathtubs, iceboxes, and sewing machines. Even the lower classes were able to afford new coal-burning, cast-iron cooking stoves that facilitated more varied meals and improved heating. The first sewer systems began to help rid city streets of human and animal waste, while underground water lines enabled fire companies to use hydrants rather than bucket brigades. Machine-made clothes fit better and were cheaper than homespun; newspapers and magazines were more abundant and affordable, as were clocks and watches.

THE LOWELL SYSTEM Before the 1850s the factory system still had not become widespread. Handicraft and domestic production (putting-out) remained common, and as late as 1860 the United States was still preponderantly rural and agricultural. But modern industrialism made significant inroads, especially in New England. At Lowell, Massachusetts, along the Merrimack River, the Merrimack Manufacturing Company in 1822 developed a new plant similar to the Waltham mill. Lowell grew dramatically, and it soon provided the model for other mill towns in Massachusetts, New Hampshire, and Maine.

The chief features of the "Lowell System" were a large capital investment, the concentration of all processes in one plant under unified management, and specialization in a relatively coarse cloth requiring minimum skill by the workers. In the public mind, however, the system then and afterward was associated above all with the conscious attempt by the founders to establish an industrial center compatible with republican virtues. Jefferson and others had early on characterized urban-industrial development as being incompatible with a republican form of government rooted in self-reliant agrarianism, and early industrial developers were quite sensitive to such concerns.

Consequently, Lowell's founders insisted that they could design model factory centers and communities that would enhance rather than corrupt the social fabric. The drab, crowded, and wretched life of English mill-villages would be avoided by locating American mills in the countryside and then establishing an ambitious program of paternal supervision for the workers. The operatives were mostly young women from New England farm families who were increasingly without gainful employment and faced diminishing prospects for finding a husband. With so many men migrating westward, New England had been left with a surplus of women. Moreover, much of the household production previously carried out by the daughters had given way to "store bought" goods. Many women workers were also drawn to the mills by the chance to escape the routine of farm life, and to earn money to help the family or improve their own circumstances. As one female mill worker explained, she was working because of "a father's debts . . . to be paid, an aged mother to be supported,

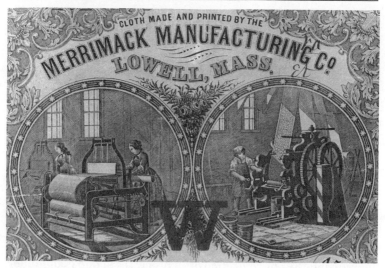

Textile mills at Lowell (1822), and elsewhere, transformed the nature of industrial work for women and men.

a brother's ambition to be aided." Another stressed in a letter to her parents the greater excitement and fellowship afforded by life in Lowell: "You may think me unkind but how can you blame me for wanting to stay here. I have but one life to live and I want to enjoy myself as well as I can."

A steady stream of single girls began flocking toward Lowell. To reassure concerned parents, the mill owners promised to provide the "Lowell girls" with good wages, tolerable work, comfortable housing, moral discipline, and a variety of educational and cultural opportunities. Such a carefully planned and supervised factory system would thereby bring together the benefits of both industrial capitalism and republican simplicity. Kentucky statesman Henry Clay asserted that the Lowell experiment "will tell whether the manufacturing system is compatible with the social virtues."

Initially visitors to Lowell praised the well-designed mills. The laborers appeared "healthy and happy." One appreciative worker, in fact, described the new community as demonstrating that "corporations should have souls, and should exercise a paternal influence over the lives of their operatives." Lowell was certainly paternalistic: the women workers lived in dormitories staffed by matronly supervisors, church attendance was mandatory, and temperance regulations and curfews were rigidly enforced. Despite the twelve-hour days and seventy-hour weeks, one woman operative described Lowell's community life as approaching "almost Arcadian simplicity." But like Arcadia, Lowell soon lost its innocence as it experienced mushrooming growth. By 1840 Lowell had thirty-two mills and factories in operation, and the blissful rural town had become a bustling, grimy, bleak industrial city.

Other factory centers began sprouting up across New England, displacing forests and farms and engulfing villages, filling the air with smoke, noise, and stench. As early as 1832, the writer Washington Irving lamented that the "march of mechanical invention is driving everything poetical before it." Between 1820 and 1840 the number of Americans engaged in manufactures increased eight-fold, and the number of city dwellers more than doubled.

Such booming growth transformed the experiment in industrial republicanism. By 1846 a concerned worker told those young farm women thinking about taking a job in a factory that they would do well not to leave their "homes in the country. It will be better for you to stay at home on your fathers' farms than to run the risk of being ruined in a manufacturing village." During the 1830s, as prices and wages dropped, relations between workers and managers rapidly deteriorated. A new generation of owners and foremen stressed efficiency and profit margins over community values. The machines and their operatives were worked at a faster pace, and workers organized strikes to protest deteriorating conditions. Visitors now noted the growing similarity between Lowell and the dismal factory towns of England immortalized in Charles Dickens's writings.

The "Lowell girls" drew attention less because they were typical than because they were special. An increasingly common pattern for industry was the family system, sometimes called the Rhode Island or Fall River system, which prevailed in textile manufactures outside of northern New England. Factories that relied on waterpower often rose in unpopulated areas, and part of their construction included tenements or mill villages which increasingly housed newly arrived foreign immigrants. Whole families might be hired, the men for heavy labor, the women and children for the lighter work. This system also promoted paternalism. Employers dominated the life of the mill villages, often setting rules of good behavior. Wages under the system are hard to establish, for employers often paid in goods from the company store. Working hours often ran from sunup to sunset, and longer in winter—a sixty-eight- to seventy-two-hour week. Such hours were common on the farms of the time, but in factories the work was more intense and offered no seasonal let-up. The labor of children, common on the farm, excited little censure from communities still close to the soil. Many considered the provision of gainful employment for the women and children of the lower orders as a community benefit.

INDUSTRY AND CITIES   In 1855 a journalist exclaimed that "the great phenomenon of the Age is the growth of cities." Using the census definition of "urban" as places with 8,000 inhabitants or more, the proportion of urban population grew from 3.3 percent in 1790 to 16.1 percent in 1860. New York outpaced all its competitors and the nation as a whole in its population growth. By 1860 it was the first American city to boast a population of more than a million, largely because of its superior harbor and its unique access to commerce afforded by the Erie Canal.

Pittsburgh, at the head of the Ohio, was already a center of iron production by 1800, and Cincinnati, at the mouth of the Little Miami, soon surpassed all other centers of meatpacking, with pork a specialty. Louisville, because it stood at the falls of the Ohio, became an important trade center. On the Great Lakes the leading cities also stood at important breaking points in water transportation: Buffalo, Cleveland, Detroit, Chicago, and Milwaukee. Chicago was especially well located to become a hub of both water and rail transportation on into the trans-Mississippi West. During the 1830s St. Louis tripled in size mainly because most of the trans-Mississippi grain and fur trade was funneled down the Missouri River. By 1860 St. Louis and Chicago were positioned to challenge Boston and Baltimore for third and fourth places.

IMMIGRATION

Amid all the new economic growth, one condition of American life carried over beyond the mid-nineteenth century: land remained plentiful and relatively cheap, while labor was scarce and relatively dear. A decline in the birth rate coinciding with the onset of industry and urbanization reinforced this condition. The United States in the nineteenth century remained a strong magnet to immigrants, offering them chances to take up farms in the country or jobs in the cities. Glowing reports from early arrivals who made good also reinforced romantic views of American economic opportunity and political and religious freedom. A

German immigrant in Missouri wrote home applauding the "absence of overbearing soldiers, haughty clergymen, and inquisitive tax collectors."

During the forty years from the outbreak of the Revolution until the end of the War of 1812 immigration had slowed to a trickle. The wars of the French Revolution and Napoleon restricted travel from Europe until 1815. Within a few years, however, packet lines had begun to cross the north Atlantic, and competing shippers who needed westbound payloads kept the transatlantic fares as low as $30 per person. The years from 1845 to 1854 saw the greatest proportionate influx of immigrants in American history, 2.4 million, or about 14.5 percent of the total population in 1845.

During the early 1800s most European immigrants entered the United States through the Port of New York. Ships would discharge passengers at wharves, and the newcomers would immediately have to fend for themselves in their alien environment. Before long thieves, thugs, and wily con-men began preying upon the new arrivals. The infectious diseases that many of the immigrants brought with them also aroused popular concern. By 1855 the problems associated with the immigrants' arrival in America provoked the New York state legislature to lease Castle Garden, at the southern tip of Manhattan, for use as an immigration receiving center. Inside the depot, clerks would record the names, nationalities, and destinations of the new arrivals, physicians would give them a cursory physical exam, and labor bureau representatives would assist them in seeking jobs.

THE IRISH   In 1860 America's population was 31 million, with more than one of every eight foreign born. The largest groups among them were 1.6 million Irish, 1.2 million Germans, and 588,000 British (mostly English). The Irish had a long-standing reason for migrating from their country: resentment of British rule, British landlords, British Protestantism, and British taxes. But what caused so many Irish to flee their homeland in the nineteenth century was the onset of a prolonged depression that brought immense social hardship. The most densely populated country in Europe, Ireland was so ravaged by the economic collapse that in rural areas the average age at death declined to nineteen. By the 1830s the number of Irish migrants to America was growing quickly, and after an epidemic of potato rot in 1845 brought a famine to rural Ireland that killed upwards of a million peasants, the flow of Irish immigrants to Canada and the United States rose to a flood.

In 1847, nearly 214,000 Irish emigrated to the United States and Canada aboard ships of the White Star Line and other companies. Thirty percent of these immigrants died on board, despite company promises of "unusually spacious, well lighted, ventilated, and warmed" steerage accommodations.

In 1847 Irish arrivals numbered above 100,000, and they stayed above that level for eight years, reaching a peak of 221,000 in 1851. By 1850 the Irish constituted 43 percent of the foreign-born population in the United States. Unlike the German immigrants, who were predominantly male, the Irish newcomers were more evenly apportioned by sex; in fact a slight majority of them were women, most of them single, young adults. Most of the Irish arrivals had been tenant farmers, but their rural sufferings left them little taste for farm work and little money to buy land in America. Great numbers of them hired on with construction gangs building the canals and railways—about 3,000 set to work on the Erie Canal as early as 1818. Others worked in iron foundries, steel mills, warehouses, and shipyards. Many Irish women found jobs as domestic servants, laundresses, or textile mill workers in New England. In 1845, the Irish constituted only 8 percent of the work force in the Lowell mills; by 1860 they made up 50 percent. Although there were substantial Irish communities in New Orleans, Vicksburg, and Memphis, relatively few immigrants during the Jacksonian era found their way into the South, where land was expensive and industries scarce. The widespread use of slaves also left few opportunities in the region for manual laborers.

Too poor to move inland, most of the destitute Irish congregated in the eastern cities, in or near their port of entry. By the 1850s the Irish made up over half the populations of Boston and of New York City, and they were almost as prominent in Philadelphia. They clustered in murky slums and around Catholic churches, both of which became familiar features of the urban scene. Irish newcomers crowded into filthy, poorly ventilated tenements, plagued by high rates of crime, infectious disease, prostitution, alcoholism, and infant mortality. The archbishop of New York City at mid-century described the Irish as "the poorest and most wretched population that can be found in the world."

But many enterprising Irish immigrants seized opportunities in their new environment to forge remarkable success stories. Twenty years after arriving in New York, Alexander T. Stewart became the owner of America's largest department store and thereafter accumulated vast real estate holdings in Manhattan. Michael Cudahy, who began work in a Milwaukee meat-packing business at age fourteen, became head of the Cudahy Packing Company and developed the process for the summer-curing of meats under refrigeration. Dublin-born Victor Herbert emerged as one of America's most revered composers, and Irish dancers and playwrights came to dominate the American stage. Irishmen were equally successful in the boxing arena and on the baseball diamond.

These accomplishments did little to quell the acute anti-Irish sentiments prevalent in nineteenth-century America. Irish immigrants confronted demeaning stereotypes and intense anti-Catholic prejudices. It was commonly assumed that the Irish were ignorant, filthy, clannish folk incapable of assimilation. George Templeton Strong, a prominent New York civic leader, expressed the contempt felt by many of his peers toward the Irish when he said: "Our Celtic fellow citizens are almost as remote from us in temperament and constitution as the Chinese." Even Theodore Parker, the esteemed minister and social reformer, dismissed the Irish as "the worst people in Europe to make colonists of." Many employers felt the same way, and "No Irish Need Apply" signs sprouted in every eastern city. But the Irish could be equally contemptuous of other groups, such as free blacks who competed with them for low-status jobs. In 1850 the *New York Tribune* expressed consternation at the fact that the Irish, having themselves escaped from "a galling, degrading bondage" in their homeland, typically voted against any proposal for equal rights for the "Negro." For their part, many blacks viewed the Irish with equal disdain.

Experienced at organized resistance to rent and tax collectors in their homeland, the Irish, after becoming naturalized citizens, formed powerful blocs of voters and found their way into American politics more quickly than any other immigrant group. Drawn mainly to the party of Jackson, they set a crucial pattern of identification with the Democrats that other ethnic groups by and large followed. In Jackson the Irish immigrants found a hero. Himself the son of Irish colonists, he was also popular for having defeated the hated British at New Orleans. In addition, the Irish loathing of aristocracy, which they associated with British rule, attracted them to the party claiming to represent "the common man." Although property requirements initially kept most Irish-Americans from voting, a New York state law extended the franchise in 1821, and five years later the state removed the property qualification altogether. The following year masses of Irish voters made the difference in the election between Jackson and John Quincy Adams. One newspaper expressed alarm at this new force in politics: "Every thing in the shape of an Irishman was drummed to the polls and their votes made to pass. . . . It was emphatically an Irish triumph. The foreigners have carried the day." Although women, blacks, and Indians still could not vote, these Irish newcomers were able to use the franchise to exert a remarkable political influence.

Perhaps the greatest collective achievement of the Irish immigrants was stimulating the growth of the Catholic Church in the United States. "In this country," wrote an Irish teacher in 1840, "the idea of Catholicity and Ireland is so blended in the minds of the American people, as to be in a manner inseparable." Years of persecution had instilled in Irish Catholics a fierce loyalty to the doctrines of the church, leading one Irish-American to proclaim that religion "overrides all other sovereigns, and has the supreme authority over all the affairs of the world." Such passionate attachment to Catholicism generated both community cohesion among Irish-Americans and fears of Romanism among American Protestants.

THE GERMANS AND OTHERS   During the eighteenth century, Germans had responded to William Penn's offer of free religious expression and cheap, fertile land by coming in large numbers to America. Consequently, when a new wave of German migration formed in the 1830s, there were still large enclaves of Germans in Pennsylvania and Ohio who had preserved their language and cultures, and in the Old World style had clustered in agricultural villages. The new German migration took on a markedly different cast. It peaked in 1854, just a few years after the crest of Irish arrivals, when 215,000 Germans disembarked in American ports. These migrants included a large number of learned, cultured professional people—doctors, lawyers, teachers, engineers—some of them refugees from the failed German revolution of 1830 and 1848. In addition to an array of political opinions ranging from laissez-faire conservatism to Marxism, the Germans at mid-century and after also brought with them a variety of religious preferences. A third of the new arrivals were Catholic, many were Protestants (usually Lutherans), and a significant number were Jewish, freethinking atheists, or agnostics.

Unlike the Irish, the Germans included fair numbers of independent farmers, skilled workers, and shopkeepers who arrived with some means to get themselves established in skilled labor or on the land. More so than the Irish, they migrated in families and groups rather than as individuals, and this clannish quality helped them better sustain elements of German language and culture in their New World environment. Among those who prospered in America were Ferdinand Schmacher, who began peddling oatmeal in glass jars in Ohio and eventually formed the Quaker Oats Company; Heinrich Steinweg, a piano-maker from Lower Saxony, who in America changed his name to Steinway and became famous for the quality of his pianos; and, Levi

Strauss, a Jewish tailor who followed the gold rushers to California and began making long-wearing work pants which later were dubbed blue jeans or Levi's. Major centers of German settlement developed in Missouri and southwestern Illinois (around St. Louis), in Texas (near San Antonio), in Ohio, and in Wisconsin (especially around Milwaukee). The larger German communities developed traditions of bounteous food, beer, and music along with German *Turnvereine* (gymnastic societies), sharpshooter clubs, fire engine companies, and kindergartens.

Among the British immigrants too were large numbers of professionals, independent farmers, and skilled workers. Two other groups that began to arrive in some number during the 1840s and 1850s were but the vanguard of greater numbers to come later. Annual arrivals from Scandinavia, most of them religious dissenters, did not exceed 1,000 until 1843, but by 1860 a total of 72,600 Scandinavians lived in America. The Norwegians and Swedes gravitated usually in family groups to Wisconsin and Minnesota, where the climate and woodlands reminded them of home.

By the 1850s the sudden development of California after the discovery of gold attracted Chinese who, like the Irish in the East, did the heavy work of construction. Infinitesimal in numbers until 1854, the Chinese in America numbered 35,500 by 1860. Most of the Chinese immigrants came from Kwangtung (Guangdong)° province, a region noted for its political turmoil, social violence, and economic hardships. The migrants to the United States were mostly married, illiterate men desperate for work. Single women did not travel abroad and married women usually stayed behind to raise their children. During the mid-nineteenth century, a laborer in south China might earn five dollars a month; in California, he could work for a railroad or a mine and make six times as much. After three or four years of such work, an immigrant could return to China with his savings and become a "big, very big gentleman."

Contrary to popular myth, the Chinese laborers in the United States were not "coolies." Technically, "coolies" were unfree workers who were kidnapped or pressed into service by force and shipped to foreign countries such as Peru and Cuba. The Chinese workers who arrived in the United States did so voluntarily. Some borrowed funds from friends or relatives for their

---

° The Wade-Giles transliterations are used in this text with the Pinyin transliterations, adopted by the Chinese government after Mao Tse-tung's (Mao Zedong's) death in 1976, given in parentheses.

passage; most used the services of brokers who charged a commission to be paid back with interest with their American wages.

NATIVISM   America had always been a land of immigrants, but the welcome accorded them had often been less than cordial. For many natives these waves of strangers in the land posed a threat of unknown tongues, mysterious customs, and, perhaps worst, feared religions. The greatest single group of newcomers were the Irish, most of whom were Catholic, and their numbers were swelled by the many German Catholics. This massive increase naturally aroused antagonisms which were rooted in the Protestant tradition of hostility to "popery" and were aggravated by job competition in the cities where immigrants gathered. A militant Protestantism growing out of the early nineteenth-century revivals heated up the climate of suspicion. There were fears of radicalism among the Germans and of voting blocs among the Irish, but above all hovered the menace of unfamiliar religious practices. Catholic authoritarianism was widely perceived as a threat to hard-won liberties, religious and political.

By the 1830s nativism was conspicuously on the rise. In 1834 a series of anti-Catholic sermons by the leading New England min-

Americans Shall Rule America. *This 1856 sketch satirizes Baltimore nativists out to bully German and Irish immigrants.*

ister of the era, revivalist and later abolitionist Lyman Beecher, aroused feelings to the extent that a mob attacked and burned a convent in Charlestown, Massachusetts. In 1844 armed clashes between Protestants and Catholics in Philadelphia ended with about twenty killed and one hundred injured. Sporadically, the nativist spirit took organized form in groups that proved their patriotism by hating foreigners and Catholics.

In July 1854 delegates from thirteen states gathered to form the American party, which had the trappings of a secret fraternal order. Members pledged never to vote for any foreign-born or Catholic candidate. When asked about the organization, they were to say "I know nothing," and in popular parlance the American party thus became the Know-Nothing party. For a season it seemed that the American party might achieve major-party status. In state and local campaigns during 1854 the Know-Nothings carried one election after another. In November they swept the Massachusetts legislature, winning all but two seats in the lower house. That fall they elected more than forty congressmen. For a while they threatened to control New England, New York, and Maryland, and showed strength elsewhere, but the movement subsided when slavery became the focal issue of the 1850s, only to be exploited again by the new Republican party.

The Know-Nothings demanded the exclusion of immigrants and Catholics from public office and extension of the period for naturalization from five to twenty-one years, but the party never gathered the political strength to effect such legislation. Nor did Congress act during the period to restrict immigration in any way.

IMMIGRANT LABOR   After 1840 waves of immigration became critical to the dynamics of growth. The increase in population contributed to economic growth and to demand, whether the newcomer took up farming or settled in a city. By meeting the demand for cheap, unskilled labor, immigrants made a twofold contribution: they moved into jobs vacated or bypassed by those who went into the factories, and they themselves made up a pool of labor from which in time factory workers were drawn.

In New England the large numbers of Irish workers, accustomed to hard treatment and willing to work for what natives considered low wages, spelled the end of the "Lowell girls." By 1860 immigrants made up more than half the labor force in New England mills. Even so, their price was generally higher than that of the women and children who worked to supplement family incomes, and the flood of immigration never rose fast enough to stop the long-term rise in wages. Factory labor thus continued to draw people from the countryside. Work in the cities offered higher real wages than work on the farm, which kept manufacturers alert for ways to cut their labor costs by improving machines. Labor costs also put a premium on mass production of low-priced goods for a mass market. Artisans who emphasized quality and craftsmanship for a custom trade found it hard to meet such competitive conditions. Many artisans in fact found that their skills were going out of style. Some took work as craftsmen in factories, while others went into small-scale manufacturing or shopkeeping, and some bought homesteads to practice their crafts in the West.

ORGANIZED LABOR

EARLY UNIONS   Few workers of the period belonged to unions, but in the 1820s and 1830s a growing fear that they were losing status led artisans of the major cities into intense activity in labor politics and unions. After the Revolution organizations of journeymen carpenters, masons, shipfitters, tailors, printers, and cordwainers (as shoemakers were called) became concerned with wages, hours, and working conditions and began to back up their demands with such devices as the strike and the closed shop (a requirement that all workers in a company be union members). These organizations were local, often largely social in purpose, and frequently lasted only for the duration of a dispute.

Early labor unions faced serious legal obstacles including prosecution as unlawful conspiracies. In 1806, for instance, Philadelphia shoemakers were found "guilty of a combination to raise their wages." The decision broke the union, and such precedents were used for many years to thwart labor organizations until the Massachusetts Supreme Court made a landmark ruling in the case of *Commonwealth v. Hunt* (1842). In this case the court ruled that forming a trade union was not in itself illegal, nor was a demand that employers hire only members of the union.

Until the 1820s labor organizations took the form of local trade unions, confined to one city and one craft. During the ten years from 1827 to 1837 organization on a larger scale began to take hold. In 1834 the National Trades' Union was set up in the effort to combine the local organizations. At the same time national craft unions were established by the shoemakers, printers, carpenters, and weavers, but all the national groups and most of the local ones vanished in the economic collapse of 1837.

The Shoemaker, *from* The Book of Trades, *1807. When boot- and shoemakers in Philadelphia went on strike in 1806, a court found them guilty of a "conspiracy to raise their wages."*

LABOR POLITICS   With the removal nearly everywhere of property qualifications for voting, labor politics flourished briefly in the 1830s. Working Men's parties appeared in New York, Boston, Philadelphia and about fifteen states. The Working Men's parties admitted many who were not workers by any strict definition, and their leaders were mainly reformers and small businessmen. These labor parties faded quickly for a variety of reasons: the inexperience of labor politicians that left the parties prey to manipulation by political professionals; the fact that some of their causes were espoused also by the major parties; and their vulnerability to attack on grounds of extreme radicalism. Additionally, they often splintered into warring factions, limiting their effectiveness.

Once the parties had faded, however, many of their supporters found their way into a radical wing of the Jacksonian Democrats, which became the Equal Rights party. In 1835 party members acquired the name "Locofocos" when their opponents from New York City's regular Democratic organization, Tammany Hall, turned off the gas lights at their meeting and the Equal Rights supporters produced candles, lighting them with the new friction matches known as Locofocos. The Locofocos soon faded as a separate group, but endured as a radical faction within the Democratic party.

Though the labor parties elected few candidates, they did succeed in drawing notice to their demands, many of which attracted the support of middle-class reformers. Above all they called for free public education and the abolition of imprison-ment for debt, causes that won widespread popular support. The labor parties and unions also actively promoted the ten-hour day. In 1836 President Jackson established the ten-hour day at the Philadelphia Navy Yard in response to a strike, and in 1840 Presi-dent Van Buren extended the limit to all government offices and projects. In private jobs the ten-hour day became increasingly common, although by no means universal, before 1860.

THE REVIVAL OF UNIONS   After the Panic of 1837 the nascent labor movement went into decline, but began to revive with improved business conditions in the early 1840s. Still, the unions of the time remained local, weak, and given to sporadic activity. Often they came and went with a single strike. The greatest single labor dispute before the Civil War came on February 22, 1860, when shoemakers at Lynn and Natick, Massachusetts, walked out for higher wages. Before the strike ended it had spread through New England, involving perhaps twenty-five towns and 20,000 workers. It stood out also as a strike the workers won. Most of the employers agreed to wage increases and some also agreed to rec-ognize the union as a bargaining agent.

This reflected the growing tendency of workers to view their unions as permanent. Workers sought union recognition and reg-ular collective bargaining agreements. They shared a growing sense of solidarity. In 1852 the National Typographical Union re-vived the effort to organize skilled crafts on a national scale. Others followed, and by 1860 about twenty such organizations had appeared, although none was strong enough as yet to do much more than hold national conventions and pass resolutions.

JACKSONIAN INEQUALITY

During the years before the Civil War, the United States had begun to develop a distinctive working class, and the gap be-tween rich and poor visibly widened. But the American myth of "rags to riches" endured. The legend had just enough basis in fact to make it plausible. John Jacob Astor, the wealthiest man in America, worth more than $20 million at his death in 1848, came of humble if not exactly destitute origins. But his and similar cases were more exceptional than common. Those who started with the handicap of poverty and ignorance seldom made it to the top. In 1828 the top 1 percent of New York's families (own-ing $34,000 or more) held 40 percent of the wealth, and the top

4 percent held 76 percent. Similar circumstances prevailed in Philadelphia, Boston, and other cities.

A supreme irony of the times was that the so-called "age of the common man," the "age of Jacksonian Democracy," seems actually to have been an age of increasing social stratification. Years before, in the late eighteenth century, slavery aside, American society probably approached equality more closely than any population its size anywhere else in the world. During the last half of the 1700s, social mobility was higher than either before or since. By the time popular egalitarianism caught up with reality, reality was moving back toward greater inequality.

Why this happened is difficult to say, except that the boundless wealth of the untapped frontier narrowed as the land was occupied and claims on various opportunities were staked out. Such developments took place in New England towns even before the end of the seventeenth century. But despite growing social distinctions, it seems likely that the white population of America, at least, was better off than the general run of European peoples. New frontiers, geographical and technological, raised the level of material well-being for all.

FURTHER READING

On economic development in the nation's early decades, see Stuart W. Bruchey's *Enterprise: The Dynamic Economy of a Free People* (1990)° and W. Elliot Brownlee's *Dynamics of Ascent: A History of the American Economy* (2nd ed., 1988). Older, yet still valuable, is Douglass C. North's *The Economic Growth of the United States, 1790–1860* (1961).° The resilient classic on transportation and economic growth is George R. Taylor's *The Transportation Revolution, 1815–1861* (1977).° On the infant railroad industry, see Albro Martin's *Railroad's Triumphant: The Growth, Rejection, and Rebirth of a Vital American Force* (1991).

Concurrent with transportation innovations was industrial growth. Thomas C. Cochran's *Frontiers of Change: Early Industrialism in America* (1981)° is a recent survey. The impact of technology is traced in David J. Jeremy's *Transatlantic Industrial Revolution: The Diffusion of Textile Technologies between Britain and America* (1981). Paul Johnson's *A Shopkeepers Millennium: Society and Revivals in Rochester, New York, 1815–1837* (1979)° studies the role religion played in the emerging industrial order.

Detailed case studies of working communities include Anthony F. C. Wallace's *Rockdale: The Growth of an American Village in the Early In-*

° These books are available in paperback editions.

dustrial Revolution (1980)°; Thomas Dublin's *Women at Work: The Transformation of Work and Community in Lowell, Massachusetts, 1826–1860* (1981)°; and Sean Wilentz's *Chants Democratic* (1984)° on New York City.

For introductions to urbanization, see Sam Bass Warner, Jr.'s *The Urban Wilderness* (1972) and Richard C. Wade's *The Urban Frontier* (1959). Studies of the origins of immigration include Oscar Handlin's classic *The Uprooted* (2nd ed., 1973)° and John Bodnar's *The Transplanted: A History of Immigrants in Urban America* (1985).° A thorough account of Chinese immigration can be found in Ronald Takaki, *Strangers from a Different Shore: A History of Asian Americans* (1990).°

12

AN AMERICAN RENAISSANCE: RELIGION, ROMANTICISM, AND REFORM

RATIONAL RELIGION

American thought and culture in the early nineteenth century remained rooted in Puritan piety and Enlightenment rationalism. Those ideas, most vividly set forth in Jefferson's Declaration of Independence, had in turn a universal application. America, it was widely believed, had a mission to stand as an example to the world, much as John Winthrop's "city upon a hill" had once stood as an example to errant humanity. The concept of America's unique mission still carried spiritual overtones, for the religious fervor quickened in the Great Awakening had reinforced the idea of providential national destiny. In turn the sense of high calling infused the national character with an element of perfectionism—and an element of impatience when reality fell short of expectations. The combination brought major reforms and advances in human rights. It also brought disappointments that could fester into cynicism and alienation.

DEISM   The currents of the Enlightenment and the Great Awakening, now mingling, now parting, flowed on into the nineteenth century and in different ways eroded the remnants of Calvinist orthodoxy. As time passed, the orthodox image of a just but stern God promising predestined hell-fire and damnation gave way to a more optimistic religious outlook. Enlightenment rationalism increasingly stressed mankind's inherent goodness rather than depravity, and it encouraged a belief in social progress and the promise of individual perfectibility.

Many leaders of the Revolutionary War era, like Jefferson and Franklin, became deists, even while nominally attached to churches. Deism, which arose in eighteenth-century Europe, simply carried the logic of Sir Isaac Newton's world machine to its logical conclusion. The God of the deist had planned the universe, built it, set it in motion, and then left it to its own devices. By the use of reason people might grasp the natural laws governing the universe.

Orthodox believers could hardly distinguish such doctrine from atheism, but Enlightenment rationalism soon began to make deep inroads into American Protestantism. The old Congregational churches around Boston proved most vulnerable. A strain of rationalism had run through Puritan belief all along in its stress on literacy and the need for "right reason" to interpret the Scriptures. Moreover, Boston's progress—some would say degeneration—from Puritanism to prosperity had persuaded many rising families that they were anything but sinners in the hands of an angry God. Drawn toward more consoling and less strenuous doctrines, some went back to the traditional rites of the Episcopal church. Others simply dropped or qualified their adherence to Calvinist theology while remaining in the Congregational churches.

UNITARIANISM AND UNIVERSALISM　By the end of the eighteenth century many New Englanders were drifting into Unitarianism, a belief emphasizing the oneness and benevolence of God, the inherent goodness of humankind, and the primacy of the individual's reason and conscience over established creeds and Scriptural literalism. Humans were not inherently depraved, Unitarianism stressed; people were capable of doing tremendous good and all were eligible for salvation. Boston was very much the center of the movement, and its notion of "rational religion" flourished chiefly within Congregational churches until controversy began to smoke them out. During the early nineteenth century more and more of these "liberal" churches accepted the name of Unitarian.

Boston's revered Unitarian minister William Ellery Channing emerged as the chief spokesman for the liberal position. "I am surer that my rational nature is from God," he said, "than that any book is an expression of his will." The American Unitarian Association, formed in 1826, included 125 churches (all but 5 of them in Massachusetts). Among them were 20 of the 25 oldest

Calvinist churches in the United States. That same year, when the Presbyterian minister Lyman Beecher moved to Boston, he lamented: "All the literary men of Massachusetts were Unitarian; all the trustees and professors of Harvard College were Unitarian, all the elite of wealth and fashion crowded Unitarian churches."

A parallel movement, Universalism, attracted a different social group: wage laborers and people of more humble means. Universalism stressed the salvation of all men and women, not just the predestined elect of the Calvinist doctrine. God, they taught, was too merciful to condemn anyone to eternal punishment; eventually all souls would come into harmony with God. "Thus, the Unitarians and Universalists were in fundamental agreement," wrote one historian of religion, "the Universalists holding that God was too good to damn man; the Unitarians insisting that man was too good to be damned."

The Second Awakening

For all the impact of rationalism, Americans remained a profoundly religious people—as they have ever since. There was, the perceptive French visitor Alexis de Tocqueville observed in the 1830s, "no country in the world where the Christian religion retains a greater influence over the souls of men than in America." Around 1800 fears that secularism was indeed taking root sparked a revival which soon grew into a Second Awakening.

FRONTIER REVIVALS   In its frontier phase, the Second Awakening, like the first, generated great excitement and strange manifestations. It gave birth, moreover, to a new ritual, the camp meeting, in which the fires of faith were repeatedly rekindled. Missionaries found ready audiences among lonely frontier folk hungry for spiritual meaning and a sense of community.

The Baptists embraced a simplicity of doctrine and organization that especially appealed to the common people of the frontier. Their theology was grounded in the authority of the Bible and the recognition of a person's innate depravity. But they replaced the Calvinist notion of predestination with the concept of universal redemption and highlighted the ritual of adult baptism. They also explicitly stressed the equality of all men and women before God, regardless of wealth, social standing, or educational training. Since each congregation was its own highest authority,

While Methodist preachers address the crowd at this revivalist camp meeting, a man in the foreground is overcome with religious ecstasy.

a frontier group could form a congregation and call a minister on their own. Sometimes whole congregations moved across the mountains as a body. As one historian and future president, Theodore Roosevelt, later described it: "Baptist preachers lived and worked exactly as their flocks. . . . they cleared the ground, split rails, planted corn, and raised hogs on equal terms with their parishioners."

But the Methodists, who shared with the Baptists an emphasis on salvation by free will but established a much more centralized organization, may have had the most effective recruiting method of all: the circuit rider who sought out people in the most remote areas with the message of salvation as a gift free for the taking. The system began with Francis Asbury, an aggressive, fervent, and utterly tireless British-born revivalist who scoured the trans-Appalachian frontier for lost souls, preaching some 25,000 sermons while defying hostile Indians and suffering through harsh winters. "When he came to America," a biographer wrote, "he rented no house, he hired no lodgings, he made no arrangements to board anywhere, but simply set out on the Long Road, and was traveling forty-five years later when death caught up with him." Asbury's mobile evangelism perfectly suited the frontier environment and the new democratic age.

Peter Cartwright emerged as the most successful Methodist "circuit rider," and this sturdy and fearless preacher grew justly famous for his highly charged sermons. He recalled stopping at a decaying Baptist church in frontier Kentucky: "While I was preaching, the power of God fell on the assembly, and there was an awful shaking among the dry bones. Several fell to the floor and cried for mercy. . . . I believe if I had opened the doors of the Church then, all of them would have joined the Methodist Church." Cartwright typified the Methodist disdain for an educated clergy, at one point arguing that it was "the illiterate Methodist preachers [who] actually set the world on fire." He may have been right, for by the 1840s the Methodists had grown into the largest Protestant denomination in the country.

The Great Revival spread quickly through the West and into more settled regions back east. Camp meetings were held typically in late summer or fall, when farm work slackened. People converged from far and wide, camping in wagons, tents, or crude shacks. Mass excitement swept up even the most skeptical onlookers, and infusions of the spirit provoked participants to strange manifestations. Some went into cataleptic trances; other contracted the "jerks," laughed the "holy laugh," babbled in unknown tongues, or got down on all fours and barked like dogs to "tree the Devil." But dwelling on the bizarre aspects of the camp meetings distorts a social institution that offered a meaningful outlet to an isolated people. This was especially true for women, for whom the camp meetings provided an alternative to the rigors and isolation of frontier domesticity. Camp meetings also brought a more settled community life through the churches they spawned, and they helped spread a more democratic faith among the frontier people.

FINNEY AND THE "BURNED-OVER DISTRICT" Regions swept by such revival fevers have been compared to forests devastated by fire. Western New York state achieved the name of the "Burned-Over District" long before 1821, when a "mighty baptism of the Holy Ghost" overwhelmed Charles Grandison Finney, a young lawyer in the town of Adams. The spirit went through him in "waves of liquid love," he remembered, and the next day he announced a new profession as a revivalist. In 1823 Finney was ordained and for the next decade he subjected the Burned-Over District to yet another scorching. In 1830, for instance, he preached his revival message for six months in Rochester, New York, and witnessed 100,000 conversions. Finney claimed to have converted "the great mass of the most influential people" in the community.

Finney became the greatest single exemplar of revivalism and, some would argue, the very inventor of professional evangelism. The saving of souls did not have to wait for a miracle, he argued, nor did it depend upon narrow doctrinal discussions; it could result from careful planning, advertising, showmanship, and, above all, emotion. He sought to arouse excitement, not for its own sake but to rivet attention on the Word. "New measures are necessary from time to time to awaken attention and bring the gospel to bear on the public mind." To those who challenged such calculated use of emotion Finney had a frank answer: "The results justify my methods."

Untrained in theology, Finney read the Bible and worked out his own theology of free will that was anything but Calvinist in its emphasis on the individual's ability to choose salvation. His gospel also combined faith and good works; one led to the other. "All sin consists in selfishness," he declared, "and all holiness or virtue, in disinterested benevolence." Regeneration therefore produced "a change from selfishness to benevolence, from having a supreme regard to one's own interest to an absorbing and controlling choice of the happiness and glory of God's Kingdom."

In 1835 Finney took the chair of theology at the new Oberlin College, founded by pious New Englanders in Ohio's Western Reserve. Later he served as its president. From the start Oberlin radiated a spirit of reform predicated on faith; it was the first college in America to admit either women or blacks, and it was a hotbed of antislavery activity. Finney himself, however, held that people must be reformed from within, and he cautioned against relying primarily on political action for moral ends.

THE MORMONS In addition to providing the scene of revivals, the Burned-Over District gave rise to several new religious departures, of which the most important was the Church of Jesus Christ of Latter Day Saints, or the Mormons. The founder, Joseph Smith, Jr., was the fourth child of wandering parents who finally settled in the village of Palmyra, New York. In 1820 young Smith (then fourteen) had a vision of "two Personages, whose brightness and glory defy all description." They identified themselves as the Savior and God the Father and cautioned him that all existing religious beliefs were false. About three years later, Smith claimed, an angel named Moroni led him to a hill where he found the Book of Mormon, a lost section of the Bible. It told the story of ancient Hebrews who had inhabited the New World and to whom Jesus had made an appearance.

On the basis of this revelation, Smith began forming his own church in 1830 and after a few years was gathering converts by the thousands. Mostly poor farmers, these religious seekers found in Mormonism the promise of a pure kingdom of Christ in America and an alternative to the social turmoil and the degrad-

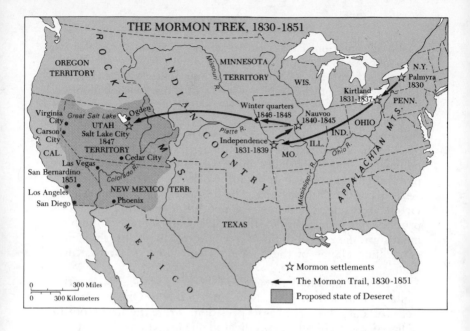

THE MORMON TREK, 1830-1851

OREGON TERRITORY

MINNESOTA TERRITORY

WIS.

N.Y.
Palmyra 1830

Kirtland 1831-1837

PENN.

Winter quarters 1846-1848

Nauvoo 1840-1845

OHIO

IND.

Virginia City
Great Salt Lake
Ogden
UTAH
Salt Lake City 1847
TERRITORY
Cedar City

Carson City

CAL.

Las Vegas

San Bernardino 1851

Los Angeles

San Diego

Colorado R.

NEW MEXICO TERR.

Phoenix

Platte R.
Independence 1831-1839

MO.

ILL.

Ohio R.

Mississippi R.

APPALACHIAN MTS.

TEXAS

MEXICO

ROCKY MTS.

INDIAN COUNTRY

Missouri R.

☆ Mormon settlements

← The Mormon Trail, 1830-1851

▨ Proposed state of Deseret

0 ___ 300 Miles

0 ___ 300 Kilometers

ing materialism of the era. From the outset the Mormon saints upset the "gentiles" with their close knit sense of community and their assurance of righteousness. Mormons rejected the notion of original sin staining the human race. They professed an optimistic creed stressing human goodness and the virtues of common folk.

In their search for a refuge from persecution, the Mormons moved from New York to Ohio, then to several places in Missouri, and finally in 1839 to Nauvoo, Illinois, where they settled for some five years. Nauvoo became a bustling city of 12,000 people, and Joseph Smith, "the Prophet," became the community's leading entrepreneur: he owned the hotel and general store, served as mayor and lieutenant general of the Nauvoo Legion, the city's 2,000-man militia, and was trustee for the church. At Nauvoo he codified the theocratic church organization, combining a hierarchical structure with the Protestant idea of the priesthood of all (male) believers. The charismatic Smith also practiced "plural marriage," much to the dismay of his first wife, Emma, who never accepted his argument that God sanctioned polygamy. In 1844 a crisis arose when dissidents accused Smith of justifying polygamy. The upshot was a schism in the church, a gathering movement among non-Mormons in the neighboring counties to attack Nauvoo, and the arrest of Smith and his brother Hyrum. On June 27, 1844, an anti-Mormon lynch mob stormed the feebly defended Nauvoo jail and shot both Joseph and Hyrum Smith.

In Brigham Young, successor to Joseph Smith, the Mormons found a leader who was strong-minded, intelligent, and decisive. He was also prolific, eventually marrying sixteen women and fathering fifty-seven children. After the murder of the founder, Young patched up an unsure peace with the neighbors by promising to leave Illinois. Before that year was out Young had chosen a new destination, sight unseen, from promotional literature on the West. It lay near the Great Salt Lake, guarded by mountains to the east and north, deserts to the west and south, yet itself fed by mountain streams of melted snow. Despite its isolation, moreover, it was close enough to the Oregon Trail for the saints to prosper by trade with passing gentiles.

Brigham Young trusted God, but made careful preparations— no wandering in the wilderness for the Mormon Moses. As a result, the epic Mormon trek was better organized and less arduous than most of the overland migrations of the time. By the fall of 1846 all 15,000 of the migrants had reached winter quarters on the Missouri River, where they paused until the first bands set out the next spring for the Promised Land. The first arrivals at Salt Lake in July 1847 found only "a broad and barren plain hemmed in by mountains . . . the paradise of the lizard, the cricket and the rattlesnake." But by the end of 1848 the Mormons had developed an efficient irrigation system and over the next decade, by cooperative labor, they brought about a spectacular greening of the desert. They organized at first their own State of Deseret (meaning "land of the honey bee," according to Young), but their independence was short-lived. Congress incorporated the Utah Territory, including the Mormon's Salt Lake settlement, into the United States in 1849. Nevertheless, with Brigham Young named the territorial governor, the new arrangement afforded the Mormons almost the same control.

ROMANTICISM IN AMERICA

The revival of piety during the early 1800s represented a widespread tendency in the western world to accentuate the stirrings of the spirit over the dry logic of reason. Another great victory of heart over head was the romantic movement in thought, literature, and the arts. By the 1780s a revolt was brewing in Europe against the well-ordered world of the Enlightened thinkers. Were there not, many wondered, more things in this world than reason and logic can box up and explain: moods, impressions, feelings; mysterious, unknown, and half-seen things? Americans took readily to the romantics' emphasis on individual freedom and the inspiring beauties of Nature.

TRANSCENDENTALISM The most intense expression of such thought in America was the Transcendentalist movement of New England, which drew its name from its emphasis on that realm of thought that transcended (or rose above) the limits of reason. American Transcendentalism was largely inspired by European thinkers such as Immanuel Kant and Samuel Taylor Coleridge, but it was rooted in New England Puritanism, to which it owed a pervasive moralism, and had a close affinity with the Quaker doctrine of the inner light. The inner light, a gift from God's grace, was transformed by Transcendentalists into intuition, a faculty of the human mind.

In 1836 an informal discussion group soon named the Transcendental Club began to meet in Boston and Concord. It drew at different times clergymen such as Theodore Parker and George Ripley; philosophical writers such as Henry David Thoreau, Bronson Alcott, and Orestes Brownson; and learned women like Margaret Fuller and Elizabeth and Sophia Peabody. Fuller edited the group's quarterly review, *The Dial* (1840–1844), before the duty fell to Ralph Waldo Emerson, soon to become the acknowledged high priest of transcendentalism.

EMERSON AND THOREAU More than any other person, Emerson spread the Transcendentalist gospel. Sprung from a line of New England ministers, he set out to be a Unitarian parson, then quit the "cold and cheerless"denomination before he was thirty because of growing doubts about its vitality. After travel to Europe, where he met England's great literary romantics, Emerson settled in Concord to take up the life of an essayist, poet, and popular speaker on the lecture circuit, preaching the good news of optimism, self-reliance, and the individual's unlimited potential. Having found reason "cold as a cucumber" and having discovered that the "ideal is truer than the actual," he was determined to *transcend* the limitations of inherited conventions and of Lockean rationalism in order to penetrate the inner recesses of the self. As he once suggested, Transcendentalism meant "a little beyond."

Emerson's young friend and Concord neighbor Henry David Thoreau practiced the introspective self-reliance that Emerson

Henry David Thoreau, author of the American classics Walden *and* "Civil Disobedience."

preached. "I like people who can do things," Emerson stressed, and Thoreau, fourteen years his junior, could do many things well—carpentry, masonry, painting, surveying, sailing, and gardening. Thoreau, Emerson noted, was "as ugly as sin, long-nosed, queer-mouthed" and possessed of "uncouth and somewhat rustic manners." But he displayed a sense of uncompromising integrity, outdoor vigor, and tart individuality that Emerson found captivating. Short and sinewy, Thoreau was an acknowledged master of the woodland arts and a probing thinker.

He was also a thoroughgoing individualist. "If a man does not keep pace with his companion," Thoreau wrote, "perhaps it is because he hears a different drummer." After graduating from Harvard, Thoreau settled down in Concord to eke out a living as a part-time surveyor and pencil-maker. But he yearned to be a writer and a philosophical naturalist, and he made almost daily escapes to the woods and fields to drink in the beauties of nature and reflect upon the mysteries of life. The contemporary scramble for wealth disgusted rather than tempted him. "The mass of men," he wrote, "lead lives of quiet desperation."

Determined himself to practice "plain living and high thinking," Thoreau boarded with the Emersons for a time and then embarked on an experiment in self-reliant simplicity. On July 4, 1845, he took to the woods to live in a cabin he had built on

Emerson's land beside Walden Pond. He wanted to see how far he could free himself from the complexities and hypocrisies of modern commercial life, and to devote his time to reflection and writing. His purpose was not to lead a hermit's life. He frequently walked the mile or so to town to dine with his friends, and he welcomed guests at his cabin. "I went to the woods because I wished to live deliberately," he wrote in *Walden, or Life in the Woods* (1854), ". . . and not, when I came to die, discover that I had not lived."

While Thoreau was at Walden Pond the Mexican War erupted. Believing it a corrupt attempt to advance the cause of slavery, he refused payment of his state poll tax as a gesture of opposition, for which he was put in jail (only for one night; an aunt paid the tax). Out of the incident grew the classic essay "Civil Disobedience" (1849), which was later to influence the passive-resistance movements of Mahatma Gandhi in India and Martin Luther King, Jr., in the American South. "If the law is of such a nature that it requires you to be an agent of unjustice to another," Thoreau wrote, "then, I say, break the law. Let your life be a counter friction to stop the machine."

The broadening ripples of influence more than a century after Thoreau's death show the impact a contemplative individual can have on the larger world of action. Although both he and Emerson lent their voices to worthy causes, they both shied away from organized reform or political activities. They prized their individual freedom and distrusted all institutions—even those promoting causes they deemed worthy. They primarily supplied the force of an animating idea: people must follow their consciences. In doing so they and other Transcendentalists inspired reform movements and were the quickening force for a generation of writers that produced the first great classic age of American literature.

THE FLOWERING OF AMERICAN LITERATURE

Ever since gaining independence, the United States had suffered from a cultural inferiority complex. The Old World continued to set the standards in philosophy, literature, and the fine arts. As a British critic sneered in 1819, the "Americans have no national literature." That may have been true, but during the Jacksonian era and after, American culture began to flower. Two New York writers, Washington Irving and James Fenimore Cooper, and four New England poets, Henry Wadsworth Longfellow, John Greenleaf Whittier, Oliver Wendell Holmes, Sr., and James Russell Lowell, began to achieve international distinction.

DICKINSON   A fifth poet, Emily Dickinson, the most original of the writers who contributed to the "New England Renaissance," lived as a recluse in Amherst, Massachusetts. Only two of her almost 1,800 poems had been published (anonymously) before her death in 1886, and the full corpus of her work remained unknown for years thereafter. Yet she possessed an imaginative power and inventive genius superior to her more famous male peers. Born in Amherst in 1830, the child of a prominent, stern father and gentle mother, she received a first-rate secondary education and then attended the new Mount Holyoke Female Seminary. Neither she nor her sister married, and they both lived out their lives in their parents' home.

Perhaps it was Emily's severe eye trouble during the 1860s that induced her solitary withdrawal from the larger society; perhaps it was the aching despair generated by her unrequited love for a married minister. Whatever the reason, her intense isolation led her to write about her own shifting psychic state. Her themes were elemental: life, death, fear, loneliness, Nature, and, above all, God, a "Force illegible," a "distant, stately lover."

HAWTHORNE   Nathaniel Hawthorne, the supreme artist of the New England group of fiction writers, never shared the sunny optimism of his Transcendentalist neighbors nor their belief in

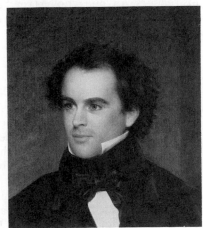

Nathaniel Hawthorne, author of The Scarlet Letter.

perfectionist reform. A sometime resident of Concord, but a native and longtime inhabitant of coastal Salem, he was haunted by the knowledge of evil bequeathed to him by his Puritan forebears—one of whom had been a judge at the Salem witchcraft trials. After graduating from Bowdoin, he worked for some time in obscurity in Salem, gradually began to place a few stories, and finally earned a degree of fame with his collection of *Twice-Told-Tales* (1837). In these, as in most of his later work, he presented powerful moral allegories. His central themes explored evil and its consequences: pride and selfishness, secret guilt, selfish egotism, the impossibility of rooting sin out of the human soul. His greatest novel, *The Scarlet Letter* (1850), explicitly pondered such burdens, focusing on the guilt felt by a woman and a minister who had committed adultery.

POE   Edgar Allan Poe, born in Boston but reared in Virginia, was arguably America's most inventive genius in the first half of the century, and many Europeans considered him the most important American writer of the time. As a poet he strove to design verses that would display the classic virtues of restraint, discipline, and unity. "The Raven" is a masterful example of his preoccupation with form as well as his interest in probing the dark recesses of the human soul. The tormented, hard-drinking, quarrelsome Poe was also a master of gothic horror in the short story and the inventor of the detective story. He judged prose by its ability to provoke emotional tension, and since he considered fear to be the most powerful emotion, he focused his efforts on making the grotesque and supernatural seem disturbingly real to his readers. Anyone who has read the "Tell-Tale Heart" or "The Pit and the Pendulum" can testify to his success.

MELVILLE   Although today considered one of America's greatest novelists, Herman Melville during his later years saw his literary reputation evaporate. Born in New York in 1819, he had only two years of formal schooling before he was forced to drop out because of his father's death. He then worked on a farm, as a bank messenger, and as a store clerk before shipping out as a seaman at age twenty. Some time later, after eighteen months aboard a whaler, he fetched up in the South Seas and jumped ship with a companion. After a month spent with a friendly tribe of cannibals in the valley of the Typees, he signed onto an Australian whaler, jumped ship again in Tahiti, was jailed for mutiny, obtained his release by signing on as a harpooner, and after landing in Hawaii, he finally returned to Boston as a seaman aboard a frigate of the United States Navy. An embroidered account of his exotic adventures, in *Typee* (1846), became an instant popular success, which he repeated in *Omoo* (1847), based on his stay in Tahiti.

Melville then produced a masterpiece in *Moby-Dick* (1851), a novel rich in action as well as symbolism. The story of Captain Ahab and his obsessive quest for the white whale that had caused the loss of his leg, *Moby-Dick* was aimed at two audiences. On one level it was a ripping good yarn of adventure on the high seas. But Ahab's single-minded mission to slay the evildoer turned the captain himself into a destructive monster who sacrificed his ship, his crew, and himself to his folly, leaving as the one survivor the narrator of the story. Unhappily, neither the larger reading public nor many of the critics at the time accepted the novel on either level, and after the Civil War Melville's career wound down into futility.

WHITMAN   The most provocative American writer during the antebellum period was Walt Whitman, a remarkably vibrant personality who disdained inherited social conventions and artistic traditions. There was something elemental in Whitman's character, something bountiful and generous and compelling—even his faults and inconsistencies were ample. Born on a Long Island farm, he moved with his family to Brooklyn and from the age of twelve worked mainly as a handyman and journalist, frequently taking the ferry across the river to booming, bustling Manhattan. The city fascinated him, and he gorged himself on the urban spectacle—shipyards, crowds, factories, shop windows.

From such material Whitman drew his editorial opinions and poetic inspiration, but he remained relatively obscure until the

Walt Whitman, in an 1866 photograph.

first edition of *Leaves of Grass* (1855) caught the eye and aroused the ire of readers. Emerson found it "the most extraordinary piece of wit and wisdom that America has yet contributed," but more conventional critics shuddered at Whitman's explicit sexual references and groused at his indifference to rhyme and meter as well as his buoyant egotism. The jaunty Whitman, however, refused to conform to genteel notions of art, and he spent most of his career working on his gargantuan collection of poems, *Leaves of Grass*, enlarging and reshaping it in successive editions. He identified the growth of the book with the growth of the country, which he celebrated in all its variety.

THE POPULAR PRESS   The flowering of American literature came at a time of massive expansion in the popular press. In 1847 Richard Hoe of New York invented the Hoe Rotary Press, which printed 20,000 sheets an hour. Like many technological advances, this was a mixed blessing. The high cost of such a press made it harder for someone of small means to break into publishing. On the other hand it expedited production of cheap "penny" newspapers as well as magazines and books—which were often cheap in more ways than one.

The *New York Sun*, in 1833 the first successful penny daily, and others like it, often ignored the merely important in favor of scandals and sensations, true or false. James Gordon Bennett, a native of Scotland, perfected this style in the *New York Herald*, which he founded in 1835. His innovations drew readers by the thousands: the first Wall Street column, the first society page (which satirized the well-to-do until it proved more gainful to show readers their names in print), pictorial news, telegraphic news, and great initiative in getting scoops. Eventually, however, the *Herald* suffered from dwelling so much on crime, sex, and depravity in general.

The chief beneficiary of a rising revulsion was the *New York Tribune*, founded as a Whig party organ in 1841. Horace Greeley, who became the most important journalist of the era, announced that it would be a cheap but decent paper avoiding the "matters which have been allowed to disgrace the columns of our leading Penny Papers." And despite occasional lapses, Greeley's "Great Moral Organ" typically amused its readers with wholesome human-interest stories. For a generation it was probably the most influential paper in the country. By 1860 its weekly edition had a national circulation of 200,000. The number of newspapers around the country grew from about 1,200 in 1833 to about 3,000 in 1860.

EDUCATION

EARLY PUBLIC SCHOOLS   Literacy in Jacksonian America was surprisingly widespread, given the condition of public education. In 1840, according to census data, some 78 percent of the total population and 91 percent of the white population could read and write. Since the colonial period, in fact, Americans had enjoyed the highest literacy rate in the Western world. Most children learned their letters from church or private schools, formal tutors, or from their families.

By the 1830s the demand for public schools was rising fast. Reformers argued that popular government depended upon a literate and informed electorate. With the lowering of barriers to the ballot box the argument carried all the more force. Workers wanted free schools to give their children an equal chance. Education, it was also argued, would be a means of social reform by improving manners and lessening crime and poverty. Horace Mann of Massachusetts stood out in the early drive for statewide school systems. Trained as a lawyer, Mann shepherded through the legislature in 1837 the creation of a state board of education, for which he then served as secretary. Mann went on to sponsor many reforms in Massachusetts, including the first state-supported training school for teachers, a state association of teachers, and a minimum school year of six months. Mann defended the school system as the way to social stability and equal economic opportunity. "Education then, beyond all other devices of human origin, is a great equalizer of the conditions of men—the balance wheel of the social machinery."

While the North made great strides in public education by 1850, the educational pattern in the South continued to reflect the region's aristocratic pretensions and rural isolation: the South had a higher percentage of college students than any other region, but a lower percentage of public school students. And the South had some 500,000 white illiterates, more than half the total number in the country.

Public school teachers were at first mostly men, often young men who did not regard teaching as a career but as a means of support while preparing for a career as a lawyer or preacher, or as part-time work during slack seasons on the farm. With the encouragement of educational reformers, however, teaching was beginning to be regarded as a profession. As the schools multiplied and the school term lengthened, women increasingly entered the field.

Most students going beyond the elementary grades went to private academies, often subsidized by church and public funds. Such schools, begun in colonial days, multiplied until there were more than 6,000 of them in 1850. Public high schools became well established in school systems only after the Civil War; in 1860 there were barely 300 in the whole country.

HIGHER EDUCATION   The postrevolutionary proliferation of colleges continued after 1800 with the spread of small church schools and state universities. Nine colleges had been founded in the colonial period, all of which survived; but not many of the fifty that sprang up between 1776 and 1800 lasted. Among those that did were Hampden-Sydney, Bowdoin, and Middlebury, all of which went on to long and fruitful careers. Of the seventy-eight colleges and universities in 1840, fully thirty-five had been founded after 1830, almost all as church schools. A postrevolutionary movement for state universities flourished in those southern states that had had no colonial university. Federal policy abetted the spread of universities into the West. When Congress granted statehood to Ohio in 1803, it set aside two townships for the support of a state university and kept up that policy in other new states.

The coexistence of state and religious schools, however, generated conflicts over funding and curriculum. Beset by the need for funds, as colleges usually were, denominational schools often competed with tax-supported schools. Regarding curricula, the Second Awakening led many of the church schools to emphasize theology at the expense of science and the humanities. On the other hand, America's development required broader access to education and programs geared to vocations. The University of Virginia, "Mr. Jefferson's University," founded in 1819 within sight of Monticello, introduced in 1826 a curriculum that reflected Jefferson's view that education ought to combine pure knowledge with "all the branches of science useful *to us*, and *at this day*." The model influenced the other new state universities of the South and West.

American colleges and universities during the nineteenth century were tiny when compared to today's institutions of higher learning. Most enrolled a hundred students or less, and the largest rarely had more than 600. Virtually all of these students were men. Elementary education for girls was generally accepted, but training beyond that level was not. Many men and women thought higher education unsuited to woman's destiny in life. Some, such as Abigail Adams, argued that education would make for better wives and mothers, but few were ready to demand equality on principle. Progress began with the academies, some of which taught boys and girls alike. Good "female seminaries" like those founded by Emma Willard at Troy, New York (1824), and Mary Lyon at Mount Holyoke, Massachusetts (1836), prepared the way for women's colleges.

The work in female seminaries usually differed from the courses in men's schools, giving more attention to the social amenities and such "embellishments" as music and art. Vassar, opened at Poughkeepsie, New York, in 1865, is usually credited with being the first women's college to give priority to conventional academic standards. Oberlin College in Ohio, founded in 1833, opened as both a biracial and a coeducational institution. Its first women students were admitted in 1837. In general, the West gave the greatest impetus to coeducation, with state universities in the lead. But once admitted, women students remained in a subordinate status. At Oberlin, for instance, they were expected to clean male students' rooms and were not allowed to speak in class or recite at graduation exercises. Coeducation did not mean immediate equality.

SOME MOVEMENTS FOR REFORM

Emerson spoke for his generation, as he so often did, when he asked: "What is man born for, but to be a Reformer, a Remaker of what man has made?" The urge to eradicate evil from nineteenth-century America had its roots in the widespread sense of mission, which in turn drew upon rising faith in the perfectibility of humankind. Belief in perfectibility had both evangelical and liberal bases. Transcendentalism, the spirit of which infected even those unfamiliar with its philosophical roots, offered a romantic faith in the individual and the belief that human intuition led to right thinking.

Such a perfectionist bent found outlet in a myriad of reform movements and activities during the Jacksonian era. Few areas of life escaped the concerns of the reformers, however trivial or weighty: observance of the Sabbath, dueling, crime and punishment, the hours and conditions of work, poverty, vice, care of the handicapped, pacifism, foreign missions, temperance, women's rights, the abolition of slavery. Some crusaders challenged a host of evils; other focused on pet causes. One Massachusetts reformer, for example, insisted that "a vegetable diet lies at the basis of all reforms." The greatest dietary reformer of the age, however, was Sylvester Graham, who started as a temperance speaker in 1830 and moved on to champion a natural diet of grains, vegetables, and fruits, and abstinence from alcohol, coffee, tea, tobacco, and many foods. The Graham cracker is one of the movement's legacies.

TEMPERANCE   The temperance crusade was perhaps the most widespread of all. The census of 1810 reported some 14,000 distilleries producing 25 million gallons of spirits each year. With a hard-drinking population of just over 7 million, the "alcoholic republic" was producing well over three gallons per year for every man, woman, and child, not counting beer, wine, and cider. And the census takers no doubt missed a few stills. William Cobbett, an English reformer who traveled in the United States, noted in 1819 that one could "go into hardly any man's house

The Way of Good & Evil. *Intemperance was one of the steps on the way of evil, leading to "everlasting punishment."*

without being asked to drink wine or spirits, even *in the morning.*"

The temperance movement rested on a number of arguments. First and foremost was the religious demand that "soldiers of the cross" lead blameless lives. Others stressed the economic implications of sottish workers. The dynamic new economy, with factories and railroads moving on strict schedules, made tippling by the labor force a far greater problem than it had been in a simple agrarian economy. Humanitarians emphasized the relations between drinking and poverty. Much of the movement's propaganda focused on the sufferings of innocent mothers and children. "Drink," said a pamphlet from the Sons of Temperance, "is the prolific source (directly or indirectly) of nearly all the ills that afflict the human family."

In 1826 a group of Boston ministers organized the American Society for the Promotion of Temperance. The society pursued its objectives through lecturers, press campaigns, a prize essay contest, and the formation of local and state societies. A favorite device was to ask each person who took the pledge to put by his signature a T for Total Abstinence. With that a new word entered the language: "teetotaler."

In 1833 the society called a national convention in Philadelphia, where the American Temperance Union was formed. The convention revealed internal tensions, however: Was the goal moderation or total abstinence, and if the latter, abstinence merely from ardent spirits or also from wine, cider, and beer? Should the movement work by persuasion or by legislation? Like nearly every movement of the day, temperance had a wing of perfectionists who rejected all compromises with Demon Rum, and they passed a resolution that the liquor traffic was morally wrong and ought to be prohibited by law. The union, at its spring convention in 1836, called for abstinence from all alcoholic beverages—a costly victory that caused moderates to abstain from the movement instead. Still, between 1830 and 1860 the temperance agitation drastically reduced Americans' per-capita consumption of alcohol.

PRISONS AND ASYLUMS   The sublime optimism of the Jacksonian age, the liberal belief that people are innately good and capable of improvement, brought major changes in the treatment of prisoners, the handicapped, and dependent children. Public institutions arose dedicated to the treatment and cure of social ills. If removed from society, it was believed, the needy and deviant could be made whole again. Unhappily, this ideal kept running up against the dictates of convenience and economy. The institutions had a way of turning into breeding grounds of brutality and neglect.

In the colonial period prisons were usually places for brief confinement before punishment, which was either death or some kind of pain or humiliation: whipping, mutilation, confinement in stocks, branding, and the like. A new attitude began to emerge after the Revolution, and gradually the idea of the penitentiary developed. It would be a place where the guilty experienced penitence and underwent rehabilitation, not just punishment.

An early model of the new system, widely copied, was the Auburn Penitentiary, commissioned by New York in 1816. The prisoners at Auburn had separate cells and gathered for meals and group labor. Discipline was severe. The men were marched out in lock step and never put face to face or allowed to talk. But prisoners were at least reasonably secure from abuse by other prisoners. The system, its advocates argued, had a beneficial effect on the prisoners and saved money since the workshops supplied prison needs and produced goods for sale at a profit. By 1840 there were twelve prisons of the Auburn type in the United States.

The reform impulse naturally found another outlet in the care of the insane. The Philadelphia Hospital (1752), one of the first in the country, had a provision in its charter that it should care for "lunaticks," but before 1800 few hospitals provided care for the mentally ill. There were in fact few hospitals of any kind. The insane were usually confined at home with hired keepers or in jails and almshouses. After 1815, however, public asylums that housed the disturbed separately from criminals began to appear. Early efforts led to such optimism that a committee reported to the Massachusetts legislature in 1832 that with the right treatment "insanity yields with more readiness than ordinary diseases." These high expectations gradually faded with experience.

The most important figure in arousing the public conscience to the plight of these unfortunates was Dorothea Lynde Dix. A pious, withdrawn, frail, almost saintly Boston schoolteacher, she was called upon to instruct a Sunday school class at the East Cambridge House of Correction in 1841. She found there a roomful of insane persons completely neglected, fed slop, and left without heat on a cold March day. In a report to the state legislature in 1843, Dix told of persons confined "in *cages, closets, cellars, stalls, pens! Chained, naked, beaten with rods, and lashed*

Dorothea Dix, one of the most influential of American reformers.

into obedience!" Wardens charged Dix with "slanderous lies," but she won the support of leading reformers as well as a large state appropriation for improving the treatment of the insane. From Massachusetts she carried her campaign throughout the country and abroad. By 1860 she had convinced twenty states to heed her advice and adopt similar programs to improve the state of prisons and asylums.

WOMEN'S RIGHTS   While Dorothea Dix stood out as an example of the opportunity reform gave middle-class women to enter public life, Catharine Beecher, a founder of women's schools in Connecticut and Ohio, published a guide prescribing the domestic sphere for women. *A Treatise on Domestic Economy* (1841) became the leading handbook of what historians have labeled the "cult of domesticity." While Beecher upheld high standards in women's education, she also accepted the prevailing view that "woman's sphere" was the home and argued that young women should be trained in the domestic arts of housework and child-rearing.

The official status of women during this period remained much as it had been in the colonial era. Legally, a woman was unable to vote, and, after marriage, denied legal control of her property and even of her children. A wife could not make a will, sign a contract, or bring suit in court without her husband's permission. Her legal status was thus like that of a minor, a slave, or a free Negro. Gradually, however, more and more women began to complain about their status. The organized movement for women's rights had its origins in 1840, when the American antislavery movement split over the question of women's right to participate. American women decided then that they needed to organize on behalf of their own emancipation too.

In 1848 two prominent moral reformers and advocates of women's rights, Lucretia Mott, a fifty-five-year-old Philadelphia Quaker, and Elizabeth Cady Stanton, a thirty-two-year-old graduate of Troy Seminary who refused to be merely "a household drudge," decided to call a convention to discuss "the social, civil, and religious condition and rights of women." The hastily organized Seneca Falls Convention, the first of its kind, issued on July 19, 1848, the Declaration of Sentiments, mainly the work of Mrs. Stanton, the wife of a prominent abolitionist and mother of seven. In a clever paraphrase of Jefferson's Declaration, the document proclaimed the self-evident truth that "all men and women are created equal," and the attendant resolutions said that all laws placing woman "in a position inferior to that of men, are contrary to the great precept of nature, and therefore of no force or authority." Such language was too strong for most of the thousand delegates, and only about a third of them signed it. Ruffled male editors lampooned the women activists as being "love-starved spinsters" and "petticoat rebels." Yet the Seneca Falls gathering represented an important first step in the evolving campaign for women's rights.

From 1850 until the Civil War the women's-rights leaders held annual conventions and carried on a program of organizing, lecturing, and petitioning. The movement had to struggle in the face of meager funds and antifeminist women and men. What success the movement had was due to the work of a few undaunted women who refused to be overawed by the odds against them. Susan B. Anthony, an ardent Quaker already active in temperance and anti-slavery groups, joined the crusade in the 1850s. At age seventeen she had angrily noted, "What an absurd notion that women have not intellectual and moral faculties sufficient for anything else but domestic concerns!" Unlike Stanton and Mott, Anthony was unmarried and therefore able to devote most of her attention to the women's crusade. As one observer put it, Mrs. Stanton "forged the thunderbolts and Miss Anthony hurled them." Both were young when the movement started and both lived into the twentieth century, focusing after the Civil War on demands for woman suffrage. While women did not win voting rights until much later, there were some legal gains. The state of Mississippi, seldom regarded as a hotbed of reform, was the first to grant married women control over their property in 1839; by the 1860s eleven more states had such laws.

Elizabeth Cady Stanton (left) and Susan B. Anthony. Mrs. Stanton "forged the thunderbolts and Miss Anthony hurled them."

Still, the only jobs open to educated women in any numbers were nursing and teaching, both of which extended the domestic roles of health care and nurturing into the world outside. Both brought relatively lower status and pay than "man's work" despite the skills, training, and responsibility involved. Yet if women could be teachers, Susan Anthony asked, why not lawyers or doctors or ministers or intellectuals? Why not indeed, replied a small band of hardy women who did carve out professional careers. Harriet Hunt of Boston was a teacher who, after nursing her sister through a serious illness, set up shop in 1835 as a self-taught physician and persisted in medical practice although twice rejected by Harvard Medical School. Voted into Geneva Medical College in western New York as a joke, Elizabeth Blackwell of Ohio had the last laugh when she finished at the head of her class in 1849. She founded the New York Infirmary for Women and Children and later had a long career as a professor of gynecology in the London School of Medicine for Women.

An intellectual prodigy among women of the time—the derisory term was "bluestocking"—was Margaret Fuller. A precocious child, she was force-fed education by a father who set her at Latin when she was six. (She would later claim that "I find no intellect comparable to my own" in America.) As a young adult she moved confidently in the literary circles of Boston and Concord, edited *The Dial* for two years, and became literary editor and critic for Horace Greeley's *New York Tribune*. From 1839 to 1844 she conducted "conversations" with the cultivated ladies of Boston. From this classroom-salon emerged many of the ideas that went into her pathbreaking book, *Woman in the Nineteenth Century* (1845), a plea for the removal of all intellectual and economic disabilities. Minds and souls were neither masculine nor feminine, she argued. Genius had no sex. "What woman needs," Fuller contended, "is not as a woman to act or rule, but as a nature to grow, as an intellect to discern, as a soul to live freely and unimpeded, to unfold such powers as were given her when we left our common home."

UTOPIAN COMMUNITIES   The pervasive climate of reform during the Jacksonian era and after also provoked a quest for utopia. "We are all a little mad here with numberless projects of social reform," Emerson wrote in 1840. Everyone, it seemed "has a draft of a new community in his pocket." Plans for new communities had long been an American passion, at least since the Puritans set out to build a Wilderness Zion. The visionary communes of the nineteenth century often had purely economic and social objectives, but those that were rooted in religion proved most durable.

Over a hundred utopian communities sprang up between 1800 and 1900. Among the most durable were the Shakers, officially the United Society of Believers in Christ's Second Appearing, founded by Ann Lee Stanley (Mother Ann), who reached New York state with eight followers in 1774. Believing religious fervor a sign of inspiration from the Holy Ghost, they had strange fits in which they saw visions and prophesied. These manifestations later evolved into a ritual dance—hence the name Shakers. Mother Ann claimed that God was genderless and that she was the female incarnation as Jesus had been the male. She preached celibacy to prepare Shakers for the perfection that was promised them. The church would first gather in the elect, and eventually in the spirit world convert and save all mankind.

Mother Ann died in 1784, but the group found new leaders. From the first community at Mount Lebanon, New York, the movement spread to new colonies in New England, and soon afterward into Ohio and Kentucky. By 1830 about twenty groups were flourishing. In Shaker communities all property was held in common, and strict celibacy was practiced. Men and women not only slept separately but also worked and ate separately. Governance of the colonies was concentrated in the hands of select elders chosen by the ministry. To outsiders this might seem almost despotic, but the Shakers emphasized equality of labor and reward, and members were free to leave at will. The superbly managed Shaker farms yielded a surplus for the market. They were among the leading sources of garden seed and medicinal herbs, and many of their manufactures, including clothing, household items, and especially furniture, were prized for their simple beauty. By the mid-twentieth century, however, few members remained alive; the Shakers had reached the peak of activity in the years 1830–1860.

John Humphrey Noyes, founder of the Oneida Community, was the son of a Vermont congressman. Educated at Dartmouth and then Yale Divinity School, he discovered true religion at one of Charles G. Finney's revivals and entered the ministry. He was forced out, however, when he concluded that with true conversion came perfection and a complete release from sin. In 1836 he gathered a group of a dozen or so "Perfectionists" around his home in Putney, Vermont. Ten years later Noyes announced a new doctrine of "complex marriage," which meant that every man in the community was married to every woman and vice versa. "In a holy community," he claimed, "there is no more reason why sexual intercourse should be restrained by law, than why eating and drinking should be." To outsiders such theology smacked of "free love" and Noyes was arrested. He fled to New York and in 1848 established the Oneida Community, which numbered more than 200 by 1851.

The communal group shared alike in the food, clothing, and shelter produced by their hard work. They eked out a living with farming and logging until the mid-1850s, when the inventor of a new steel trap joined the community. Oneida traps were soon known as the best money could buy. The community then branched out into sewing silk, canning fruits, and making silver tableware. Meanwhile, the community also carefully regulated its social life. Women enjoyed the same rights as men, and children were raised by the community as a whole, placed in a common nursery, supplied with toys and affection, and allowed to sleep until they awoke themselves. At age fourteen boys and girls were trained in sexual activity by elderly women. No one was forced to have sexual relations, but Noyes encouraged wide circulation in order to enhance community ties. In addition he insisted that only those who had embraced Christ as their Savior could participate. "Holiness," he stressed, "must go before free love." Noyes also practiced eugenics, pairing up "superior" mates in order to produce brighter and healthier offspring. (He named himself the most qualified male in nine instances, even though he was by then in his sixties). For well over a generation the passionate community prospered. In 1879, however, it faced a crisis when Noyes fled to Canada to avoid prosecution for adultery. The members then abandoned complex marriage, and in 1881 decided to convert into a joint-stock company, the Oneida Community, Ltd, which remains today a thriving flatware company.

In contrast to these religious communities, Robert Owen's New Harmony was based on a secular principle. A British capitalist who worried about the social effects of the factory system, Owen bought the town of Harmony, Indiana, from a group of communalists known as Rappites and promptly christened it New Harmony. In 1825 a varied group of about 900 colonists gathered in New Harmony and established a cooperative community based on the principles of Enlightenment rationalism and symmetry. Separate residences were to be built for the married, unmarried, and children. A complete school system, including nursery and university, was to be built along with a library, lecture halls, laboratories, and gymnasium. The high proportion of learned participants generated a certain intellectual electricity about the place. There were frequent lectures and social gatherings with music and dancing.

For a time it looked like a brilliant success, but New Harmony soon fell into discord. Leaders complained of "grumbling, carping, and murmuring" members, and others who had the "disease of laziness." The problem, it seems, was one common to most reform groups. Every idealist wanted his own patented plan put into practice. In 1827 Owen returned from a visit to England to find New Harmony insolvent. The following year he dissolved the project and sold or leased the lands on good terms, in many cases to the settlers.

Brook Farm was the most celebrated of all the utopian communities because it had the support of Emerson, Fuller, and countless other well-known literary figures of New England. George Ripley, a Unitarian minister and Transcendentalist, conceived of Brook Farm as a kind of early-day "think tank," combining high thinking and plain living. Nathaniel Hawthorne, a member, later memorialized its failure in his novel *The Blithedale Romance* (1852). He joined the community full of excitement at the prospect of living among articulate and interesting co-workers but soon grew tired of his assignment—shoveling manure—and he left the community after less than a year's residence. Soon after Hawthorne left Brook Farm he wrote that his life there was "an unnatural and unsuitable, and therefore an unreal one." But his disillusionment was exceptional rather than representative. Most Brook Farmers found considerable fulfillment in the new community. Said one: "We were happy, contented, well-off and care-free; doing a great work in the world, enthusiastic and faithful, we enjoyed every moment of every day." The place survived financially, however, mainly because of an excellent community school that drew tuition-paying students from outside. But when a new central building burned down on the day of its dedication in 1846, the community spirit expired in the embers.

Like Brook Farm, most of the utopian communities were short-lived. Such experiments, performed in relative isolation, had little effect on the larger society. Yet they did express the deeply engrained desire for perfectionism inherent in the American character, a desire that would continue to spawn such noble, if frequently naïve, experiments thereafter.

Among all the targets of reformers' wrath, however, one great evil would finally take precedence over the others—human bondage. The paradox of American slavery coupled with American freedom, of "the world's fairest hope linked with man's foulest crime," in Herman Melville's words, would inspire the climactic crusade of the age, abolitionism, one that would ultimately move to the center of the political stage and sweep the nation into an epic—and tragic—struggle.

FURTHER READING

Few single-volume works cover the diversity of early American reform and culture. Russel B. Nye's *Society and Culture in America, 1830–1860* (1974)° provides a wide-ranging survey. On reform itself, consult Ronald G. Walter's *American Reformers, 1815–1860* (1978).°

Sydney E. Ahlstrom's *A Religious History of the American People* (1972) provides a solid survey of antebellum religious movements and developments. Revivalist religion is discussed in Whitney R. Cross's *The Burned-Over District* (1950)° and John B. Boles's *The Great Revival* (1972).

Among the most recent books on the Mormons are Leonard J. Arrington's *Brigham Young: American Moses* (1985)° and Richard L. Bushman's *Joseph Smith and the Beginnings of Mormonism* (1988).°

The best introduction to transcendentalist thought are the writings of the Transcendentalists themselves collected in Perry Miller (ed.), *The Transcendentalists* (1950).° Also see Paul Boller's *American Transcendentalism, 1830–1860* (1974) and Robert D. Richardson, Jr.'s *Henry Thoreau: A Life of the Mind* (1986).° On Emerson see Mary Kupiec Cayton's *Emerson's Emergence: Self and Society in the Transformation of New England* (1991).

° These books are available in paperback editions.

Several good works describe various aspects of the antebellum reform movement. For temperance, see W. J. Rorabaugh's *The Alcoholic Republic: An American Tradition* (1979).° On prison reform and other humanitarian projects, see David J. Rothman's *The Discovery of the Asylum* (1971).° Lawrence A. Cremin's *American Education: The National Experience, 1783–1876* (1980) traces early school reform.

The literature of women's history is becoming both voluminous and diverse. A fine survey is Mary P. Ryan's *Womanhood in America* (3rd ed., 1983).° More particular to the antebellum period are Nancy F. Cott's *The Bonds of Womanhood: "Women's Sphere" in New England, 1780–1835* (1977)° and Suzanne Lebsock's *Free Women of Petersburg* (1984).°

Michael Fellman's *The Unbounded Frame: Freedom and Community in Nineteenth Century Utopianism* (1973) surveys the utopian movements.

13

MANIFEST DESTINY

The Tyler Years

When William Henry Harrison took office in 1841, elected like Jackson mainly on the strength of his military record and without committing himself on major issues, the Whig leaders expected him to be a tool in the hands of Webster and Clay. Webster became secretary of state, and while Clay preferred to stay in the Senate, his friends filled the cabinet. Within a few days of the inauguration signs of strain appeared between Harrison and Clay, whose disappointment at missing the nomination had made him peevish. But the quarrel never had a chance to develop, for Harrison served the shortest term of any president—after the longest inaugural address. At the inauguration, held on a chilling rainy day, he caught cold. The pleadings of office seekers in the following month filled his days and sapped his strength. On April 4, 1841, exactly one month after the inauguration, Harrison died of pneumonia.

John Tyler, the first vice-president to succeed on the death of a president, served practically all of Harrison's term. At age fifty-one the thin, fragile Virginia slaveholder already had a long career behind him as legislator, governor, congressman, and senator, and his positions on all the important issues had been forcefully stated and were widely known. Although a Whig, he favored a strict construction of the Constitution and was a stubborn defender of states' rights. When someone asked if he were a "nationalist," Tyler retorted that he had "no such word in my political vocabulary." Consequently, he ardently opposed Clay's American System—protective tariffs, a national bank, internal improvements at national expense. Once a Democrat, he had

335

broken with the party over Jackson's stand on nullification and his imperious use of executive authority. Thus Tyler, the states'-rights Whig, had been chosen to "balance" the ticket by the party leaders in 1840; no one expected that he would actually wield power. Acid-tongued John Quincy Adams said Tyler's proper title should be "vice-president acting as president." Other critics called the new president "His Accidency."

DOMESTIC AFFAIRS   Given more finesse on Clay's part, he might have bridged the policy divisions between himself and Tyler. But for once, driven by disappointment and ambition, the "Great Pacificator" lost his instinct for compromise. When Congress met in special session at the end of May 1841, Clay introduced a series of resolutions designed to supply the platform that the party had evaded in the previous election. The chief points were repeal of the Independent Treasury, establishment of a third Bank of the United States, distribution to the states of proceeds from public land sales, and a higher tariff. Clay then set out to push his program through Congress. Despite Tyler's known opposition, he remained optimistic. "Tyler dares not resist me. I will drive him before me," Clay predicted.

Tyler, it turned out, was not easily driven. Although he agreed to allow the repeal of the Independent Treasury and signed a higher tariff bill in 1842, Tyler vetoed Clay's bill for a new national bank. This provoked his entire cabinet, with the exception of Webster, to resign, an unprecedented action. Tyler replaced them with anti-Jackson Democrats who had become Whigs. Clay's leadership of the Whig party was now established beyond question, and Tyler was left in the position of a president without a party.

FOREIGN AFFAIRS   In foreign relations, meanwhile, developments of immense significance were taking place. A major issue between Britain and the United States involved the suppression of the African slave trade, which both countries had outlawed in 1808. In August 1841 the British prime minister asserted their right to patrol off the coast of Africa and search vessels flying the American flag to see if they carried slaves. But the American government remembered the impressments and seizures during the Napoleonic Wars and refused to accept such intrusions. Relations were further strained late in 1841 when American slaves on the *Creole*, bound from Hampton Roads to New Orleans, mutinied and sailed into Nassau, where the British set them free. Secretary of State Webster demanded that the slaves be returned as American property, but the British refused.

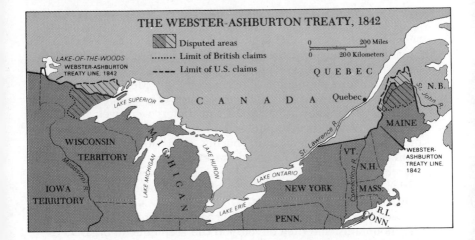

THE WEBSTER-ASHBURTON TREATY, 1842

Fortunately at this point a new British ministry decided to accept Webster's overtures for negotiations and sent Lord Ashburton to Washington. Ashburton was widely known to be friendly to Americans, and the talks proceeded smoothly. The negotiations settled the Maine boundary as well as other border disputes by accepting the existing line between the Connecticut and St. Lawrence rivers, and by compromising on the line between Lake Superior and the Lake-of-the-Woods. The Webster-Ashburton treaty (1842) also provided for joint patrols off Africa to repress the slave trade.

Moving West

In the 1840s the American people were no more stirred by the quarrels of Tyler and Clay over such issues as banking, tariffs, and distribution, important as they were, than students of history would be at a later date. What stirred the blood was the mounting evidence that more and more pioneers were hurdling the barriers of the "Great American Desert" and the Rocky Mountains, reaching out toward the Pacific coast. In 1845 editor John Louis O'Sullivan labeled this bumptious spirit of expansion. "Our manifest destiny," he wrote, "is to overspread the continent allotted by Providence for the free development of our yearly multiplying millions." At its best, this much-trumpeted notion of "Manifest Destiny" offered a moral justification for American expansion, a prescription for what an enlarged United States could and should be. At its worst, it was a cluster of flimsy rationalizations for naked greed and imperial ambition.

SPANNING THE ROCKIES   One of the first targets of this spirit of "manifest destiny" was Santa Fe, a remote outpost of the Spanish empire founded in the seventeenth century, the capital and trading center for a population of perhaps 60,000 Mexicans and Indians in New Mexico. In 1821 Mexico, newly independent from Spain, let it be known that American traders were welcome in Santa Fe. Word spread quickly and eastern merchants began making the long wagon train journey west along the Santa Fe Trail. The trade never involved more than one or two hundred merchants, but it was a profitable enterprise in which American goods were traded for Mexican gold, silver, and furs. But the Santa Fe traders had pioneered more than a new trail. They showed that heavy wagons could cross the plains and penetrate the mountains, and they developed the technique of organized caravans for mutual protection.

Beyond the mountains the Oregon country stretched from the Forty-second Parallel north to 54°40'. Between these parallels, Spain and Russia had given up their claims, leaving Great Britain and the United States as the only claimants. Under the Convention of 1818 the two countries had agreed to "joint occupation." Until the 1830s, however, joint occupation had been a legal technicality, because the only American presence was the occasional mountain man who wandered into the Pacific slope or the infrequent trading vessel from Boston, Salem, or New York.

But word of Oregon's fertile soil, temperate climate, and magnificent forests gradually spread, largely through the efforts of Methodist missionaries recently settled there. This enticed adventurous Americans, and by the late 1830s, a trickle of emigrants began flowing along the Oregon Trail. Soon "Oregon Fever" spread like a contagion. By 1843 the movement began to assume the proportions of mass migrations. That year about a thousand overlanders followed the trail westward from Independence, Missouri, along the Platte River into Wyoming, through South Pass down to Fort Bridger (abode of a celebrated mountain man, Jim Bridger), then down the Snake River to the Columbia and along the Columbia to their goal in the Willamette Valley. By 1845 there were about 5,000 settlers in the region.

The overland settlers traveled mostly in family groups, and they came from all over the United States. They usually left Missouri in late spring, and made the grueling 2,000-mile trek in about six months. Traveling in ox-drawn, canvas-covered wagons nicknamed "prairie schooners," they bounced and jostled their way across dusty or muddy trails and rugged mountains at the rate of about fifteen miles per day. The nerve-rasping fear of In-

WAGON TRAILS WEST

| 0 | 300 Miles |
| 0 | 300 Kilometers |

dian attack or contagious disease kept everyone on edge, and the never-ending routine of necessary chores and grinding physical labor took its toll on once buoyant spirits. This was especially true for women, whose labors went on day and night. The diary of one woman settler records with great poignancy the trail's wearying regimen: "I have done a washing. Stewed apples, made pies and a rice pudding, and mended our wagon cover. Rather tired." The next day brought more of the same: "baked biscuits, stewed berries, fried meat, boiled and mashed potatoes, and made tea for supper, afterward baked bread. Thus you see I have not much rest." Another complained that, unlike the men, who smoked and talked together after supper, "we *have no time for sociability*." All was "hurry scurry." There "is no rest in such a journey."

Such a difficult routine understandably provoked tensions within families and powerful nostalgic yearnings for home. Many a tired pioneer could identify with the following comment in a young girl's journal: "Poor Ma said only this morning, 'Oh, I wish we had never started.' " Another woman wondered "what had possessed my husband, anyway, that he should have thought of bringing us away out through this God forsaken country." Not a few turned back, but most continued on. And once in Oregon they immediately set about establishing stable communities. Noted one pioneer:

> Friday, October 27.—Arrived at Oregon City at the falls of the Willamette.
> Saturday, October 28.—Went to work.

EYEING CALIFORNIA   California was also becoming an alluring attraction for new settlers and entrepreneurs. It first felt the influence of European culture in 1769, when Spain grew concerned about Russian fur traders moving south along the Pacific coast from their base in Alaska. To thwart Russian intentions, Spain sent a naval expedition to explore and settle the region. The Spanish discovered San Francisco Bay and constructed *presidios* (military garrisons) at San Diego and Monterey. Even more importantly, Franciscan friars led by Junipero Serra established a mission at San Diego. Over the next fifty years Franciscans built twenty more missions, spaced a day's journey apart along the coast from San Diego to San Francisco. There they converted Indians to their faith and established thriving agricultural estates. As in Mexico, the Spanish monarchy awarded huge land grants in California to a few ex-soldiers and colonists, who turned the grants into profitable cattle ranches. The Indians were left with the least valuable land, and most of them subsisted as farmers or artisans serving the missions. By 1803, 40 percent of California's Indian population had embraced Catholicism. Friars encouraged the piety and diligence of these "Mission Indians" with whippings, causing some to flee the jurisdiction of the Church. Within three decades infectious diseases transmitted by European settlers decimated the Indian population, leaving only a third as many by 1833 as in 1803.

For all of its rich natural resources, California remained thinly populated by Indians and mission friars well into the nineteenth century. It was a simple, almost feudal, agrarian society, without schools, industry, or defenses. In 1821, when Mexico wrested its independence from Spain, Californians took comfort in the fact that Mexico City was so far away that it would exercise little effective control over its farthest state. During the next two decades, Californians, including many recent American arrivals, staged ten revolts against the governors dispatched to lord over them.

Yet Mexican rule did produce a dramatic change in California history. In 1824, Mexico passed a colonization act that granted hundreds of huge *rancho* estates to Mexican settlers. With free labor extracted from Indians, who were treated like slaves, these *rancheros* lived a life of self-indulgent luxury and ease, gambling, horse-racing, bull-baiting, and dancing. They soon cast covetous eyes on the vast estates controlled by the Franciscan missions, and in 1833–1834, they convinced the Mexican government to confiscate the California missions, exile the Franciscan friars, release the Indians from Church control, and make the mission lands available to new settlement. Within a few years some 700 huge new *rancho* grants of 4,500 to 50,000 acres were issued along the coast from San Diego to San Francisco. Organized like feudal estates, these California ranches resembled southern plantations, but the death rate for Indian workers was twice as high as that of slaves in the Deep South.

Few accounts of life in California, however, took note of the brutalities inflicted on the Indians. Instead they portrayed the region as a proverbial land of milk and honey, ripe for development. Such a natural paradise could not long remain a secret, and Americans had already been visiting the Pacific coast in search of profits and land. By the late 1820s American trappers wandered in from time to time, and American ships began to enter the "hide and tallow" trade. The *rancheros* produced cowhide and beef tallow in large quantity and both products enjoyed a brisk demand, cowhides mainly for shoes and the tallow chiefly for candles.

By the mid-1830s shippers began setting up agents on the scene to buy the hides and store them until a company ship arrived. One of these agents, John A. Sutter, had tried the Santa Fe trade first, then found his way to California. At the juncture of the Sacramento and American Rivers (later the site of Sacramento) he built an enormous enclosure that guarded an entire village of settlers and shops. Completed in 1843, the enclosure became the mecca for Americans bent on settling the Sacramento country. It stood at the end of what became the most traveled route through the Sierras, the California Trail, which forked off from the Oregon Trail and led through the mountains near Lake Tahoe. By 1846 there were perhaps 800 Americans in California, along with some 8,000–12,000 Californios of Spanish descent.

John Charles Frémont, the Pathfinder.

The premier press agent for California, and the Far West generally, was John Charles Frémont, "the Pathfinder." Frémont, born in Savannah, Georgia, and raised in the South, became the consummate explorer and romantic adventurer. Possessed of boundless energy and reckless courage, a relentless love of the outdoors and an exuberant, charismatic personality, he inspired both respect and awe. His densely curled black beard, high forehead, commanding nose, and piercing blue eyes added to his dash and bounce.

Frémont studied at the College of Charleston before being commissioned a second lieutenant in the United States Topographical Corps in 1838. In 1842 he mapped the Oregon Trail beyond South Pass—and met Christopher "Kit" Carson, one of the most knowledgeable of the mountain men. Carson became Frémont's frequent associate and the most famous frontiersman after Daniel Boone. In 1843–1844 Frémont, typically clad in deerskin shirt, blue army trousers, and moccasins, moved on to Oregon, then made a heroic sweep down the eastern slopes of the Sierras, headed southward through the central valley of California, bypassed the mountains in the south, and returned via Great Salt Lake. His reports on both expeditions, published together in 1845, gained a wide circulation and helped excite the interest of easterners.

Meanwhile, rumors flourished that the British and French were scheming to grab California, though neither government had such intentions. Political conditions in Mexico left the remote territory in near anarchy much of the time, as governors came and went in rapid succession. Amid the chaos a substantial number of Californians reasoned that they would be better off if they cut ties to Mexico altogether. Some favored an independent state, perhaps under French or British protection. A larger group admired the balance of central and local authority in the United States and felt their interests might best be served by American annexation. By the time the Americans were ready to fire the spark of rebellion in California, there was little will to resist.

ANNEXING TEXAS

AMERICAN SETTLEMENTS   America's lust for land was most clearly at work in the most accessible of all the Mexican borderlands, Texas. More Americans resided there than in all the other coveted regions combined. During the 1820s Texas was rapidly turning into an American province, for Mexico in 1823 began welcoming American settlers into the region as a means of stabilizing the border.

First and foremost among the promoters of Anglo-American settlement was Stephen F. Austin, a Missouri resident who gained from Mexico a huge land grant originally given to his father by Spanish authorities. Indeed before Spain finally granted Mexican independence he had started a colony on the lower Brazos River, and by 1824 more than 2,000 hardy souls had settled on his lands. Most of the newcomers were southern farmers drawn to rich new cotton lands selling for only a few cents an acre. As a young woman settler recalled, "I was a young thing then, but 5 months married, my husband . . . failed in Tennessee. . . . I ready to go anywhere . . . freely consented. . . . Texas fever rose then . . . there we must go. There without much reflection, we did go." By 1830 the coastal region of eastern Texas had approximately 20,000 white settlers and 1,000 Negro slaves brought in to work the cotton. The newcomers quickly outnumbered the 5,000 Mexicans in the area, and showed little interest in Catholicism or other aspects of Mexican culture.

At that point the Mexican government grew alarmed at the flood of strangers threatening to engulf the province, and it forbade further immigration. Mexican troops moved to the frontier to enforce the law. But illegal American immigrants crossed the long border as easily as illegal Mexican immigrants would later cross over in the other direction. By 1835 the American population had mushroomed to around 30,000, about ten times the number of Mexicans in Texas. Friction mounted in 1832 and 1833 as Americans organized conventions to demand greater representation and power from the Mexican government. Instead of granting the request, General Santa Anna, who had seized power in Mexico, dissolved the national congress late in 1834, abolished the federal system, and became dictator. Texans rose in rebellion, summoned a convention, and pledged to fight for the old Mexican constitution. On March 2, 1836, however, as Santa Anna approached with an army of conquest, the Texans declared their independence.

INDEPENDENCE FROM MEXICO   The Mexican army delivered its first blow at San Antonio, where it assaulted a small garrison of 188 Texans and American volunteers holed up in an abandoned mission, the Alamo. Among the most celebrated of the volunteers was Davy Crockett, the Tennessee frontiersman and soldier who had fought Indians under Jackson and then served as a congressman. He was indeed a colorful character, full of spunk and brag, and thoroughly expert at killing with his trusty rifle, "Old Betsy." As he once told his men, "Pierce the heart of the enemy as you would a feller that spit in your face, knocked down your wife, burnt up your houses, and called your dog a skunk! Cram his pesky carcass full of thunder and lightning like a stuffed sassidge . . . and bite his nose off into the bargain."

On February 23, 1836, Santa Anna demanded that the motley group of defenders surrender, only to be answered with a cannon shot. The 4,000 Mexicans then launched a series of frontal assaults. For twelve days they were repulsed with fearful losses. At one point, during a lull in the fighting, Colonel William B. Travis, the garrison commander from South Carolina, drew a line on the ground with his sword as he described their hopeless plight. "Those prepared to give their lives in freedom's cause," he said in a trembling voice, "come over to me." Every man crossed the line. The notorious slave smuggler, Indian fighter, and inventor of the Bowie knife, Colonel James Bowie, stricken with pneumonia, asked that his cot be carried over the line.

In the chilly, pre-dawn hours of March 6, the defenders of the Alamo were awakened by the sound of Mexican bugles playing the dreaded "Deguello" (no mercy to the defenders). Soon thereafter Santa Anna's men attacked from every side. They

Sam Houston, president of the Republic of Texas before it was annexed by the United States.

were twice repulsed, but on the third try, as the defenders ran low on ammunition, the Mexicans broke through the battered north wall and swarmed through the breach. Colonel Travis was killed by a bullet in the forehead. Davy Crockett and the other frontiersmen used their muskets as clubs, but they too were slain. Jim Bowie, his pistols emptied, his famous knife bloodied, and his body riddled by bullets, lay dead on his cot. Santa Anna ordered the wounded Americans put to death and their bodies burned with the rest. It was a complete victory, but a costly one. The defenders of the Alamo gave their lives at the cost of 1,544 Mexicans, and their heroic stand inspired the rest of Texas to fanatical resistance.

The commander-in-chief of the gathering Texas forces was Sam Houston, a flamboyant Tennessee frontiersman who had learned war under the tutelage of Andrew Jackson at Horseshoe Bend, had later represented the Nashville district in Congress, and had moved to Texas in 1833, only three years before. After the Mexican victory at the Alamo, Houston beat a strategic retreat eastward, gathering reinforcements as he went, including volunteers from the United States. Just west of the San Jacinto River he finally paused near the site of the city that later bore his name, and on April 21, 1836, surprised a Mexican encampment there. The 800 Texans and American volunteers charged, yelling "Remember the Alamo," and overwhelmed the Mexican force within fifteen minutes. They killed 630 while losing only 9, and they took Santa Anna prisoner. The Mexican dictator bought his freedom by signing a treaty recognizing Texan independence.

The Mexican Congress repudiated the treaty, but the war was at an end.

THE MOVE FOR ANNEXATION   Residents of the Lone Star Republic then drafted a constitution, made Houston their first president, and voted almost unanimously for annexation to the United States as soon as the opportunity arose. Houston's old friend Jackson was still the American president, but even Old Hickory could be discreet when delicacy demanded it. The addition of a new slave state at a time when Congress was beset with abolitionist petitions threatened a serious sectional quarrel that might endanger Van Buren's election. Worse than that, it raised the spectre of war with Mexico. Consequently, Jackson delayed recognition of the Texas Republic until his last day in office, and his successor, Van Buren, shied away from the issue of annexation during his entire term as president.

Rebuffed in Washington, Texans turned their thoughts to creating a separate country. Under President Mirabeau Bonaparte Lamar, elected in 1838, they began to talk of expanding to the Pacific as a new nation that would rival the United States. France and Britain extended recognition to the new country of Texas and began to develop trade relations. Texas supplied them an independent source of cotton, new markets, and promised also to become an obstacle to American expansion. The British, who had abolished slavery in their empire in 1833, hoped Texans might embrace abolition as the cost of guarantees against Mexico.

Many Texans, however, had never abandoned their hopes of annexation. Reports of growing British influence created anxieties in the United States government and among southern slaveholders, who became the chief advocates of annexation. The United States began secret negotiations with Texas in 1843, and in April John C. Calhoun, the new secretary of state, completed a treaty which went to the Senate for ratification.

Calhoun chose this moment also to send the British minister a letter instructing him on the blessings of slavery and stating that annexation of Texas was needed to foil the British abolitionists. Publication of the note fostered the claim that annexation was planned less in the national interest than to promote the expansion of slavery. It was so worded, one editor wrote Jackson, as to "drive off every northern man from the support of the measure." Sectional division, plus fear of a war with Mexico, contributed to the Senate's overwhelming rejection of the treaty. Solid Whig opposition contributed more than anything to its defeat.

POLK'S PRESIDENCY

THE ELECTION OF 1844   Prudent leaders in both political parties had hoped to keep the divisive issue of Texas out of the 1844 campaign. Clay and Van Buren, the leading candidates, had reached the same conclusion about Texas: when the treaty was submitted to the Senate, they both wrote letters opposing annexation because it would risk civil war. Whig party leaders showed no qualms about Clay's stance. The convention nominated him unanimously, and the Whig platform omitted any reference to Texas.

The Democratic convention was a different story. Van Buren's southern supporters, including Jackson, abandoned him because of his opposition to annexation. With the convention deadlocked, expansionist forces nominated James K. Polk of Tennessee. The party platform took an unequivocal stand favoring expansion, and to win support in the North and West as well as the South it linked the questions of Oregon and Texas: "Our title to the whole of the territory of Oregon is clear and unquestionable," the party proclaimed, and called for "the re-occupation of Oregon and the re-annexation of Texas."

The combination of southern and western expansionism constituted a winning strategy so popular that Clay began to hedge his statement on Texas. While he still believed the integrity of the Union to be the chief consideration, he had "no personal objection to the annexation of Texas" if it could be achieved "without dishonor, without war, with the common consent of the

James Knox Polk, in a daguerrotype by Mathew Brady.

Union, and upon just and fair terms." His explanation seemed clear enough, but prudence was no match for spread-eagle oratory and the emotional pull of Manifest Destiny. Clay's stand turned more votes to the Liberty party, an anti-slavery party begun by a group of abolitionists in 1840. In the western counties of New York the Liberty party drew enough votes away from the Whigs to give the state to Polk. With New York, Clay would have carried the election by seven electoral votes. Polk won a narrow plurality of 38,000 popular votes nationwide but a clear majority of the electoral college, 170 to 105. At forty-nine Polk was the youngest president up to that time.

Born near Charlotte, North Carolina, Polk moved to Tennessee as a young man. After studying mathematics and classics at the University of North Carolina, he became a successful lawyer and planter, entered politics early, served fourteen years in Congress (four as Speaker of the House) and two as governor of Tennessee. Young Hickory, as his partisans liked to call him, was a short, slender man with a shock of long, grizzled hair, probing gray eyes, and a seemingly permanent grimace on his face. He had none of Jackson's charisma, but shared his strong prejudices and his stubborn determination. Polk had a penchant for hard work and eighteen-hour days, which destroyed his health during four years in the White House. Single-mindedly committed to the tasks at hand, Polk was a poor diplomat but a formidable leader.

POLK'S PROGRAM In domestic affairs "Young Hickory" Polk hewed to the principles of the old hero, but he and the new Jacksonians subtly reflected the growing influence of the slaveholding South within the party. Abolitionism, Polk warned, could bring the dissolution of the Union, but his pro-slavery stance further fragmented public opinion. Antislavery northerners had already begun to drift away from the Democratic party, which was perceived to represent the slaveholding interest.

Polk's major objectives were reduction of the tariff, reestablishment of the Independent Treasury, settlement of the Oregon question, and the acquisition of California. He got them all. The Walker Tariff of 1846, in keeping with Democratic tradition, lowered the tariff, and in the same year Polk persuaded Congress to restore the Independent Treasury, which the Whigs had eliminated. Twice Polk vetoed internal improvement bills.

But Polk's chief concern remained geographical expansion. He privately vowed to acquire California, and New Mexico as well, preferably by purchase. The acquisition of Texas was already underway before Polk took office. President Tyler, taking Polk's election as a mandate to act, had asked Congress to accomplish annexation by joint resolution, which required only a simple majority in each house and avoided the two-thirds Senate vote needed to ratify a treaty. Congress had read the election returns too, and after a bitter debate over slavery, the resolution passed by votes of 27 to 25 in the Senate and 120 to 98 in the House. Tyler signed the resolution on March 1, 1845, offering to admit Texas to statehood. Texas voters ratified the action in October, and the new state formally entered the Union on December 29, 1845.

OREGON   Meanwhile the Oregon issue heated up as expansionists aggressively insisted that Polk abandon previous offers to settle on the Forty-ninth Parallel and stand by the platform pledge to take all of Oregon. Some expansionists were prepared

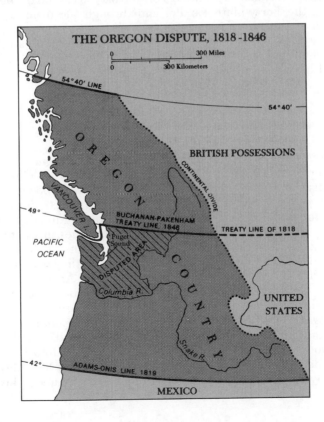

THE OREGON DISPUTE, 1818-1846

to risk war with Britain, even while relations with Mexico were simultaneously moving toward the breaking point. "Fifty-four forty or fight," they insisted. "All of Oregon or none." In his inaugural address Polk declared the American title to Oregon "clear and unquestionable," but privately he favored a prudent compromise. The British, however, refused his offer to extend the boundary along the Forty-ninth Parallel. Polk then withdrew the offer and renewed his claim to all of Oregon. In the annual message to Congress at the end of 1845, he asked for permission to give Britain a year's notice that joint occupation would be ended. To a hesitant congressman he avowed that "the only way to treat John Bull was to look him straight in the eye." After a long and bitter debate Congress adopted the resolution.

Fortunately for Polk the British government had no enthusiasm for war over that remote wilderness at the cost of profitable trade relations with the United States. In early June 1846 the British government submitted a draft treaty to extend the border along the Forty-ninth Parallel and through the main channel south of Vancouver Island. On June 18 the Senate ratified the treaty. Most of the country was satisfied. Southerners cared less about Oregon than Texas, and northern business interests valued British trade more than they valued Oregon. Besides, the country was already at war with Mexico.

The Mexican War

THE OUTBREAK OF WAR Relations with Mexico had gone from bad to worse. On March 6, 1845, two days after Polk took office, the Mexican ambassador broke off relations and left for home to protest the annexation of Texas. When an effort at negotiation failed, Polk focused his efforts on unilateral initiatives. Already his secretary of war was egging on American intrigues in California, telling the American consul in Monterey that "if the people should desire to unite their destiny with ours, they would be received as brethren." Meanwhile Polk ordered American troops under General Zachary Taylor to take up positions along the Rio Grande in the new state of Texas. These positions lay in territory that was doubly disputed: Mexico recognized neither the American annexation of Texas nor the Rio Grande boundary. Polk's intention was clear: he wanted to goad the Mexicans into a conflict in order to secure Texas and obtain California and New Mexico. As Ulysses S. Grant, then a young officer serving under Taylor, later admitted, "We were sent to provoke a fight, but it was essential that Mexico commence it."

After a final attempt to negotiate a settlement failed in March 1846, Polk resolved that he could achieve his purposes only by force, and he won the cabinet's approval of a war message to Congress. That very evening, May 9, the news arrived that Mexicans had attacked American soldiers north of the Rio Grande. Eleven Americans were killed, five wounded, and the remainder taken prisoner. Polk's provocative scheme had worked. "Hostilities may now be considered as commenced," wrote General Taylor.

In his war message Polk could now take the high ground that the war was a response to aggression, a recognition that war had been forced upon the United States. "The cup of forbearance had been exhausted" before the incident; now, he said, Mexico "has passed the boundary of the United States, has invaded our territory, and shed American blood upon the American soil." The House and Senate quickly passed the war resolution, and Polk signed the declaration of war on May 13, 1846.

OPPOSITION TO THE WAR   In the Mississippi Valley, where expansion fever ran high, the war was immensely popular. Likewise in New York, novelist Herman Melville reported that "people here are all in a state of delirium. . . . A military ardor pervades all ranks." Whig opinion, however, ranged from lukewarm to hostile. John Quincy Adams, who voted against participation, called it "a most unrighteous war." An obscure one-term congressman from Illinois named Abraham Lincoln, upon taking his seat in December 1847, began introducing "spot resolutions," calling on Polk to name the spot where American blood had been shed on American soil, implying that the troops may in fact have been in Mexico when fired upon. Once again, as in 1812, New England was a hotbed of opposition, largely in the belief that this war was the work of "Land-Jobbers and Slave-Jobbers." Some New Englanders were ready to separate from the slave states, and the Massachusetts legislature formally pronounced the conflict a war of conquest.

PREPARING FOR BATTLE   Both the United States and Mexico approached the war ill-prepared. The American military was especially small and inexperienced. At the outset of war the regular army numbered barely over 7,000 in contrast to the Mexican force of 32,000. Many of the Mexicans, however, were pressed into service or recruited from prisons and thus made less than enthusiastic fighters. Before the war ended the American force grew to 104,000, of whom about 31,000 were regular army troops and marines. The rest were six- and twelve-month volunteers.

Among the volunteers were sons of Henry Clay and Daniel Webster, but most came from coarser backgrounds. Volunteer militia companies, often filled with frontier toughs, made up as raunchy a crew as ever graced the American military—lacking uniforms, standard equipment, and discipline alike. Repeatedly, despite the best efforts of the commanding generals, these undisciplined forces ran out of control in plunder, rape, and murder. Nevertheless, these rough-and-tumble Americans consistently defeated larger Mexican forces, which had their own problems with training, discipline, and munitions. Mexican artillery pieces were generally obsolete, and the powder so faulty that American soldiers could often dodge cannon balls that fell short and bounced ineffectively along the ground.

The United States entered the war without even a tentative plan of action. One had to be worked out hastily, and politics complicated the task. What Polk wanted, Thomas Hart Benton wrote later, was "a small war, just large enough to require a treaty of peace, and not large enough to make military reputations, dangerous for the presidency." Winfield Scott, general-in-chief of the army, was both a Whig and politically ambitious. Polk nevertheless named him to take charge of the Rio Grande front, but when Scott quarreled with Polk's secretary of war, the exasperated president withdrew the appointment.

There now seemed a better choice. Zachary Taylor's men had scored two victories over Mexican forces north of the Rio Grande, and on May 18, 1846, they crossed over and occupied Matamoros, which a demoralized and bloodied Mexican army had abandoned. These quick victories brought Taylor instant popularity, and the president responded willingly to the demand that he be made overall commander for the conquest of Mexico. "Old Rough and Ready" Taylor, a bow-legged, squat, burly, and none-too-handsome man of sixty-one, seemed unlikely stuff from which to fashion a hero, but he had achieved Polk's main objective, the conquest of Mexico's northern provinces. Taylor was strikingly plain and unassuming. His uniform consisted of whatever he found handy at the moment. Outspoken and crusty, he became an immediate folk hero to his troops and to Americans back home, so much so that Polk began to see him as a political threat.

Zachary Taylor, "Old Rough and Ready." This daguerrotype was made around the time of the Mexican War.

ANNEXATION OF CALIFORNIA Along the Pacific coast, conquest began before definite news of the Mexican War arrived. Polk had long coveted the valuable Mexican territory along the Pacific coast and had first tried buying it, but to no avail. He then sought to engineer a Texas-style revolt against Mexican rule among the thousand or so American settlers in California. To that purpose, near the end of 1845 John C. Frémont brought out a band of sixty frontiersmen, including "Kit" Carson, ostensibly on another exploration of California and Oregon. In June 1846 Frémont and his men moved into the Sacramento Valley. Americans in the area fell upon Sonoma on June 14, proclaimed the independent "Republic of California," and hoisted the hastily designed Bear Flag, a California Grizzly and star painted on white cloth—a version of which became the state flag.

By the end of June Frémont had endorsed the Bear Flag Republic and set out for Monterey. Before he arrived, the commander of the Pacific Fleet, having heard of the outbreak of hostilities, sent a party ashore to raise the American flag and proclaim California a part of the United States. The Republic of California had lasted less than a month, and most Californians of whatever origin welcomed a change that promised order instead of the confusion of the unruly Bear Flaggers. Sporadic clashes with Mexicans continued until January 1847, when they finally capitulated. That same month, Colonel Stephen Kearny and 300 soldiers, having earlier captured Santa Fe, ousted the Mexican forces from southern California and occupied Los Angeles.

TAYLOR'S BATTLES   Both California and New Mexico had been taken before General Zachary Taylor fought his first major battle in northern Mexico. Having waited for more men and munitions, Taylor finally headed southward (in September 1846) toward the heart of Mexico. His first goal was the fortified city of Monterrey, which he took after a five-day siege. Polk, however, was growing increasingly unhappy with Taylor's popularity and with what he considered to be Taylor's excessive passivity.

But Polk's grand strategy was itself flawed. Having never seen the Mexican desert, he wrongly assumed that Taylor's men could live off the country and need not depend on resupply. Polk therefore misunderstood the general's reluctance to strike out across several hundred miles of barren land in front of Mexico City. On another point the president was simply duped. The old dictator Santa Anna, forced out in 1844, got word to Polk from his exile in Cuba that in return for the right considerations he could bring about a settlement of the war. Polk in turn assured the Mexican leader that Washington would pay well for any territory taken through such a settlement. In August 1846, after another overturn in the Mexican government, American forces allowed Santa Anna to return to his homeland. Soon he was again in command of the Mexican army and then was named president once more. But instead of carrying out his pledge to Polk to negotiate an end to the war, Santa Anna prepared to fight Taylor's army. Polk's intrigue had put the ablest Mexican general back in command of the enemy army.

In October 1846, Polk and his cabinet decided on a move against Mexico City from the south by way of Vera Cruz, which left Taylor's forces idle. Polk would have preferred a Democratic general to lead the new offensive, but for want of a better choice, he named Winfield Scott to the field command. Taylor, miffed at his reduction to a minor role and harboring a "violent disregard" for Scott's abilities, disobeyed orders and took the offensive himself.

Near the hacienda of Buena Vista, Santa Anna's large but illtrained army met Taylor's untested volunteers. The Mexican general invited the vastly outnumbered Americans to surrender. "Tell him to go to hell," Taylor replied. In the hard-fought Battle of Buena Vista (February 22–23, 1847), Taylor saw his son-inlaw, Colonel Jefferson Davis, the future president of the Confederacy, lead a regiment that broke up a Mexican cavalry charge. Neither side could claim victory on the strength of the outcome, but Taylor was convinced that only his lack of trained regular

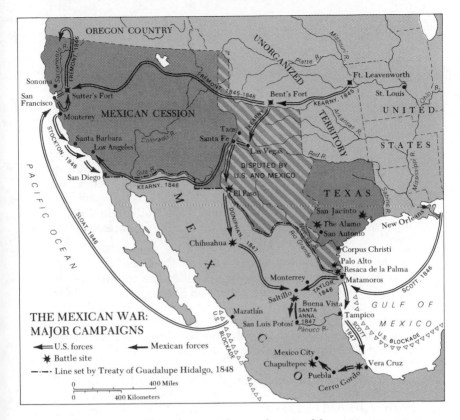

THE MEXICAN WAR:
MAJOR CAMPAIGNS

◄══ U.S. forces   ◄── Mexican forces
★ Battle site
─·─·─ Line set by Treaty of Guadalupe Hidalgo, 1848

0   400 Miles
0   400 Kilometers

troops prevented him from striking a decisive blow. At one point as he watched a Kentucky regiment in action, he exclaimed: "Hurrah for Old Kentuck! That's the way to do it. Give them hell, damn them." Buena Vista was the last major action on the northern front, and Taylor was granted leave to return home.

SCOTT'S TRIUMPH   Meanwhile, the long-planned southern assault on the enemy capital had begun on March 9, 1847, when Scott's army landed on the beaches south of Vera Cruz. It was the first major amphibious operation by American military forces and was carried out without loss. Vera Cruz surrendered on March 27 after a weeklong siege. Scott and some 14,000 soldiers then retraced the 260-mile route to Mexico City taken by Cortés more than 300 years before. It was a grueling march. A Kentucky officer reported: "My men are feeble . . . with diarrhea. They trudge along, curse the war." Santa Anna tried to set a trap for the Americans at the mountain pass of Cerro Gordo, but Scott's men did the trapping, taking more than 3,000 prisoners, large quantities of equipment and provisions, and the Mexican president's personal effects.

Thereafter Scott waited until reinforcements and new supplies arrived from the coast. After three months, with his numbers almost doubled, Scott and his army set out on August 7 through the mountain passes into the valley of Mexico, cutting his supply line to the coast. Scott directed a brilliant flanking operation around the lakes and marshes guarding the eastern approaches to Mexico City, then another around the Mexican defenses at San Antonio. On September 13, 1847, American forces entered Mexico City. At the National Palace a battalion of marines ran up the flag and occupied the "halls of Montezuma."

THE TREATY OF GUADALUPE HIDALGO   After the fall of the capital, Santa Anna resigned and a month later fled the country. By the treaty of Guadalupe Hidalgo, signed on February 2, 1848, Mexico gave up all claims to Texas above the Rio Grande and ceded California and New Mexico to the United States. In return the United States agreed to pay Mexico $15 million and assume the claims of American citizens against Mexico up to a total of $3 1/4 million.

A growing movement to annex all of Mexico had impelled Polk to hold out for more. But as Polk confided in his diary, rejecting the treaty would be too risky. If he rejected a treaty made in accord with his own original terms in order to gain more territory, "the probability is that Congress would not grant either men or money to prosecute the war." In that case he might eventually have to withdraw the army and lose everything. The treaty went to the Senate, which ratified it on March 10, 1848. By the end of July the last remaining American soldiers had boarded ship in Vera Cruz.

THE WAR'S LEGACIES   In almost seventeen months of conflict, the Mexican War had cost the United States 1,721 killed, 4,102 wounded, and far more—11,155—dead of disease. The military and naval expenditures had been $98 million. For this price, and payments made under the treaty, the United States acquired more than 500,000 square miles of territory (more than a million counting Texas), including the great Pacific harbors of San Diego, Monterey, and San Francisco, with uncounted millions in mineral wealth. Except for a small addition by the Gadsden Purchase in 1853, these annexations rounded out the continental

United States. Several important "firsts" are associated with the Mexican War: the first successful offensive war, the first major amphibious operation, and the nation's first war covered by correspondents. It was also the first significant combat experience for a group of junior officers who would later serve as leading generals during the Civil War: Robert E. Lee, Ulysses S. Grant, Thomas "Stonewall" Jackson, George B. McClellan, George Pickett, Braxton Bragg, George Meade, and others.

Initially, the victory in Mexico provoked a surge of national pride. American triumphs "must elevate the *true* self-respect of the American people," Walt Whitman exclaimed. Others were not so sure. Ralph Waldo Emerson rejected war "as a means of achieving America's destiny," but then accepted such forceful annexations of new territory with the explanation that "most of the great results of history are brought about by discreditable means." As the years passed the Mexican War somehow never became entrenched in the national legends. It was increasingly seen as a war of conquest provoked by a president bent on expansion. For a brief season, however, the glory of conquest did shed luster on the names of Zachary Taylor and Winfield Scott. Despite Polk's best efforts, he had manufactured the next, and last, two Whig candidates for president. One of them, Taylor, would replace him in the White House, with the storm of sectional conflict already on the horizon.

FURTHER READING

For background on Whig programs and ideas, see Glyndon Van Deusen's *The Jacksonian Era, 1828–1848* (1959),° and Daniel W. Howe's *The Political Culture of the American Whigs* (1984).°

Frederick Merk's *Manifest Destiny and Mission in American History* (1963)° remains a classic interpretation of the concept of Manifest Destiny. A more recent analysis of the economic motives behind expansion is Thomas R. Hietala's *Manifest Design: Anxious Aggrandizement in Late Jacksonian America* (1990).° Henry Nash Smith's *Virgin Land* (1950)° is an interpretation of the role of the West in the American imagination.

Ray A. Billington's *Westward to the Pacific* (1979),° John Mack Faragher's *Women and Men on the Overland Trail* (1979),° and John D. Unruh's *The Plains Across: The Overland Emigrants and the TransMississippi West, 1840–1860* (1979)° narrate well the story of pioneer movement. See also Patricia Limerick's insightful *The Legacy of Conquest* (1987).°

° These books are available in paperback editions.

California was the promised land for many, and Kevin Starr's *Americans and the California Dream, 1850–1915* (1973)° is a fine introduction. The controversy over annexation of Texas is analyzed in David M. Pletcher's *The Diplomacy of Annexation: Texas, Oregon, and the Mexican War* (1973) and Frederick Merk's *Slavery and the Annexation of Texas* (1972). On the perception of the Mexican War, see Robert W. Johannsen's *To the Halls of the Montezumas: The Mexican War in the American Imagination* (1988).°

14 ✌

THE OLD SOUTH:
AN AMERICAN TRAGEDY

Myth, Reality, and the Old South

SOUTHERN MYTHOLOGY Southerners, a North Carolina editor once wrote, are "a mythological people, created half out of dream and half out of slander, who live in a still legendary land." Indeed, most Americans, including southerners, carry in their minds an assorted cluster of myths about the South. But the main burden of southern mythology is carried in those especially pernicious images of the Old South set during the nineteenth-century sectional conflict: the idealized picture of a kindly old "massa" with his mint julep on the white-columned porch, happy "darkies" singing in fields perpetually in harvest, coquettish belles wooed by slender gallants underneath the moonlight and magnolias.

But there are other elements in the traditional myth. Off in the piney woods and erosion-gutted clay hills, away from the plantation elite, dwelt a depraved group known as the poor white trash: the crackers, hillbillies, sand-hillers, squatters, and the rag, tag, and bobtail. Somewhere in the myth the respectable small farmer so often praised by Jefferson and Jackson was lost from sight, perhaps neither romantic enough nor outrageous enough to fit in. He was absent too from the image of the Benighted South, in which the plantation myth simply appeared in reverse, as a pattern of corrupt opulence resting on human exploitation. Gentle old "massa" became the arrogant, haughty, imperious potentate, the very embodiment of sin, the central target of antislavery attack. He kept a slave mistress, and he bred his slaves

359

like cattle and sold them "down the river" to certain death in the sugar mills, separating families if that suited his purpose, while southern women suffered in silence the guilty knowledge of their men's infidelity. The "happy darkies" in this picture became an oppressed people longing for freedom, the victims of countless atrocities, forever seeking a chance to follow the North Star to freedom. The masses of the white folks were, once again, poor whites, relegated to ignorance and degeneracy by the slavocracy.

THE SOUTHERN CONDITION   Of course these pictures are overdrawn stereotypes, but myths die hard, partly because they have roots in reality. Efforts to get at what really set the Old South apart, generally turn on two lines of thought: the causal effects of environment (geography and climate), and the causal effects of human decisions and actions. The first approach suggests that the South's warm and humid climate fostered the growing of staple crops, and thus the plantation system and black slavery. These developments in turn brought sectional conflict and Civil War.

But while geography was and is a key determinant of southern life, explanations that involve human action are more persuasive. In the 1830s many observers located the origins of southern distinctiveness in the institution of slavery. The resolve of whites to

A slave family in the cotton fields near Savannah, Georgia.

maintain such a system in turn led to a sense of racial unity that muted class conflict among whites. But the biracial character of the population influenced other aspects of life. In shaping patterns of speech and folklore, of music and literature, black southerners immeasurably influenced and enriched the region's culture.

The South differed from other sections too in its high proportion of native population, both white and black. Despite a great diversity of origins in the colonial population, the South drew few immigrants after the Revolution. One reason was that the main shipping lines went to northern ports; another, that the prospect of competing with slave labor was unattractive to immigrants. After the Missouri Controversy of 1819–1821 the South became more and more a conscious minority, its population growth lagging behind that of other sections, its peculiar institution of slavery more and more an isolated and odious anachronism.

Other aspects differentiating the South included its architecture, its peculiar work ethic, its penchant for fighting, for guns, and for the military, and its country-gentleman ideal. One author, tongue in cheek, even suggested that the South was where the mule population was highest. The preponderance of farming remained a distinctive characteristic, whether pictured as the Jeffersonian yeoman living by the sweat of his brow or the lordly planter dispatching his slave gangs. But in the end what made the South distinctive was the popular assumption that it *was* distinctive.

AGRICULTURAL DIVERSITY   The focus in popular myth on King Cotton and the other cash crops such as rice and sugar cane has obscured the degree to which the South fed itself from its own fields. The upper South in many areas practiced general farming in much the same way as the Old Northwest. Cyrus McCormick first tested his harvester in the wheat fields of Virginia. Corn grew everywhere, but went less into the market than into local consumption by man and beast, as feed and fodder, as hoecake and grits. On many farms and plantations the rhythms of the growing season permitted the labor force to alternate attention between the staples and the food crops. Livestock added to the diversity of the farm economy. The South had in 1860 half of the nation's cattle, over 60 percent of the swine, nearly 45 percent of the horses, 52 percent of the oxen, nearly 90 percent of the mules, and nearly a third of the sheep, the last mostly in the upper South.

Yet the picture was hardly one of unbroken prosperity. The South's staple crops quickly exhausted the soil, and open row crops like tobacco, cotton, and corn left the bare ground in between subject to erosion. Much of eastern Virginia by 1800 had abandoned tobacco and in some places had turned to growing wheat for the northern market. The older farming lands had trouble competing with the newer soils farther west, but soon western lands too began to show wear and tear. So the Southeast and then the Southwest faced a growing sense of economic crisis as the nineteenth century advanced.

MANUFACTURING AND TRADE By 1840 many thoughtful southerners reasoned that by staking everything on agriculture the region had wasted chances in manufacturing and trade. After the War of 1812, as cotton growing swept everything before it, the South became increasingly dependent on northern manufacturing and trade. Cotton and tobacco were exported mainly in northern vessels. Southerners also relied on connections in the North for imported goods. The South became, economically if not formally, a kind of colonial dependency on the North.

There were two major explanations generally put forward at the time for the lag in southern industrial development. First, blacks were presumed unsuited to factory work, perhaps because they could not adjust to the discipline of work by the clock. Second, the ruling orders of the Old South were said to have developed a lordly disdain for commercial activity, because a certain aristocratic prestige derived from owning land and slaves, and from conspicuous consumption. But any argument that black

The Tredegar Iron Works in Richmond, Virginia.

labor was incompatible with industry simply flew in the face of the evidence, since factory owners bought or hired slave operatives for just about every kind of manufacture.

Nor should one take at face value the legendary indifference of aristocratic planters to profits and losses. More often than not the successful planter was a driving entrepreneur bent on maximizing profits. While the profitability of slavery has been a long-standing subject of controversy, in recent years economic historians, applying new statistical tools, have concluded that slaves on the average supplied a hefty 10 percent return on their cost. Slave ownership was, moreover, a reasonable speculation, for slave prices tended to move upward. By a strictly hardnosed and hardheaded calculation, investment in slaves and cotton lands was the most profitable investment available at the time in the South.

The notion that the South was economically backward emerged from the sectional quarrels of the times, in which southerners took a poorer-than-thou attitude, so to speak, in order to bolster their claims of northern exploitation. Antislavery elements also contributed to this notion by way of arguing the failure of a slave economy. It was true that in any economic comparison of the South with the North, the South usually came off second best. But in comparison with the rest of the world, the South as a whole was quite well off.

If an understanding of the Old South must begin with a knowledge of social myths, it must end with a sense of tragedy. White southerners had won short-term gains at the cost of both lagging development and moral isolation in the eyes of the world. The concentration on land and slaves, and the paucity of cities and immigrants, deprived the South of the dynamic bases of innovation. The slaveholding South hitched its wagon not to a star, but to the growing world (largely British) demand for cotton. In the piping times of the late 1850s, it seemed that prosperity would never end. The South, "safely entrenched behind her cotton bags . . . can defy the world—for the civilized world depends on the cotton of the South," boasted a Vicksburg newspaper in 1860. "No power on earth dares to make war upon it," added a South Carolinian. "Cotton is king." The only perceived threat to King Cotton was the growing antislavery sentiment in the North. The unperceived threat was an imminent slackening of the cotton market. The hey-day of expansion in British textiles ended by 1860, but by then the Deep South was locked into cotton production for generations to come.

WHITE SOCIETY IN THE SOUTH

THE PLANTERS   Although great plantations were relatively few in number, they set the tone of economic and social life in the South. What distinguished the plantation from the farm, in addition to its size, was the use of a large labor force managed by overseers to grow primarily staple crops (cotton, rice, tobacco, and sugar cane) for profit. A clear-cut distinction between management and labor set the planter apart from the small slaveholder, who often worked side by side with slaves at the same tasks.

If, to be called a planter, one had to own 20 slaves, the South in 1860 numbered only 46,274 planters. Fewer than 8,000 owned 50 or more slaves, and the owners of over 100 numbered 2,292. The census listed only 11 with 500 and just one with as many as 1,000 slaves. Yet this privileged elite tended to think of its class interest as synonymous with the interest of the entire South, and to perceive themselves as community leaders in much the fashion of the English gentry. The planter group, making up only 4 percent of the adult white males in the South, owned more than half the slaves, produced most of the cotton and tobacco and all of the sugar and rice. In a white population numbering just over 8 million in 1860, the total number of slaveholders was only 383,637. But assuming that each family numbered five people, the whites with some proprietary interest in slavery came to 1.9 million, or roughly one-fourth of the South's white population. While the preponderance of southern whites belonged to the small-farmer class, the presumptions of the planters were seldom challenged. Too many small farmers aspired to become planters themselves.

Often the planter did live in the splendor which legend attributed to him, with the wealth and leisure to cultivate the arts of hospitality, good manners, learning, and politics. More often the scene was less charming. Some of the mansions on closer inspection turned out to be modest houses with false fronts. The planter commonly had less leisure than legend would suggest, for he in fact managed a large enterprise. The mistress of the plantation, like the master, seldom led a life of idle leisure. She was called upon to supervise the domestic household in the same way the planter took care of the business, to see after food, linens, housecleaning, the care of the sick, and a hundred other details. The insightful Mary Boykin Chesnut, wife of a South

Carolina planter, complained in her illuminating diary that "there is no slave like a wife."

THE MIDDLE CLASS   Overseers on the largest plantations generally came from the middle class of small farmers or skilled workers, or were younger sons of planters. Most aspired to become slave-holders themselves, and sometimes rose to that status, but others were constantly on the move in search of better positions. Occasionally there were black overseers, but the highest management position to which a slave could aspire was usually that of driver or leader, placed in charge of a small group of slaves with the duty of getting them to work without creating dissension.

The most numerous white southerners were the yeoman farmers, those who lived with their families in modest two-room cabins rather than columned mansions. They raised a few hogs and chickens, grew some corn and cotton, and traded with neighbors more than with stores. The men in the family focused their energies on outdoor labors. Women also worked in the fields during harvest time, but most of their days were spent attending to domestic chores. As a Tennessee farmer explained, he and his father "did all kinds of farm work [while] my mother cooked, sewed, spun thread, wove clothes, and clothed the family of eleven children." Many of these "middling" farmers owned a handful of slaves, but most owned none. The most prosperous of these farm families generally lived in the mountain-sheltered valleys from the Shenandoah of Virginia down to northern Alabama, areas with rich soil but without ready access to markets, and so less suitable for staple crops or slave labor. But most of the South's small farms were located in the midst of the plantation economy.

In North Carolina in 1860, for instance, 70 percent of the farmers held less than 100 acres, and they were scattered throughout the state. These and other southern farmers were typically mobile folk, willing to pull up stakes and move west or southwest in pursuit of better land. They tended to be fiercely independent and suspicious of government authority, and they overwhelmingly identified with the party of Andrew Jackson and the spiritual fervor of evangelical Protestantism. Some southern farmers resented the planter elite because it controlled the most fertile land, the commodity markets, and the political machinery. Most of them, however, admired and envied the slaveholding aristocracy. And even though only a minority of the middle-class farmers owned slaves, most of them supported the slave system. They feared that the slaves, if freed, would compete with them for land, and they also enjoyed the status that racially-based slavery afforded them. Such sentiments were prevalent in the border states as well as the deep South. Kentucky, for example, held a popular referendum on the issue of slavery in 1849, and the voters, most of whom owned no slaves, resoundingly endorsed the "peculiar institution."

THE "POOR WHITES" But outside observers often had trouble telling yeomen apart from the true "poor whites," a degraded class crowded off into the hills, hollows, and pine barrens. Stereotyped views of southern society had prepared many travelers to see only planters and "poor whites," and many a small farmer living in rude comfort, his wealth concealed in cattle and swine off foraging in the woods, was mistaken for "white trash." The latter were characterized by a pronounced lankness and sallowness, given over to hunting and fishing, to hound dogs and moonshine whiskey. As one English traveler observed, they were "the most degraded race of human beings claiming an Anglo-Saxon origin that can be found on the face of the earth."

Speculation had it that they were descended from indentured servants or convicts transported to the colonies. But the problem was less heredity than environment, the consequence of infections and dietary deficiencies which gave rise to a trilogy of "lazy diseases": hookworm, malaria, and pellagra, all of which produced an overpowering lethargy. Many poor Southerners—white and black—displayed a morbid craving to chew clay, from which they got the name "dirt eaters"; the cause was a dietary deficiency, although a folklore grew up about the nutritional and medicinal qualities of certain clays. Around 1900 modern medicine discovered the causes and cures for these diseases and by 1930 they had practically disappeared, taking with them many stereotypes of poor whites.

BLACK SOCIETY IN THE SOUTH

"FREE PERSONS OF COLOR" In the Old South, free Negroes, or "free persons of color," occupied an uncertain status, balanced somewhere between slavery and freedom, subject to legal restrictions not imposed on whites. In the seventeenth century a few blacks had been freed on the same basis as indentured servants. Over the years some slaves were able to purchase their freedom, while some gained freedom as a reward for service in

American wars. Others were simply freed by conscientious masters, either in their wills, as in the case of George Washington, or during their lifetimes, as in the case of John Randolph.

The free persons of color included a large number of mulattoes, people of mixed white and black ancestry. In urban centers like Charleston and especially New Orleans, "colored" society became virtually a third caste, a new people who occupied a status somewhere between black and white. Some of them built substantial fortunes and even became slaveholders. In Louisiana a mulatto bought an estate with ninety-one slaves for $250,000.

William Ellison, a freed slave of partial white ancestry who lived in Stateburg, South Carolina, prospered as a cotton-gin maker. In 1816, at the age of twenty-six, he purchased his own freedom from his white master (who may have been his father). By the start of the Civil War he had become the wealthiest free black in South Carolina, owner of a thriving business, an 800-acre plantation, and some sixty slaves. He was so indifferent to the plight of his fellows of African descent that he commonly sold his slaves' female babies because he believed they were unprofitable in his business. Like other successful mulattoes, Ellison distanced himself from the slaves and displayed a snobbish preoccupation with graduations of color. As a member of Charleston's "brown aristocracy," he looked down upon black people. During the Civil War Ellison supported the Confederacy.

But such cases were rare. Free blacks more often were skilled artisans (blacksmiths, carpenters, cobblers), farmers, or common laborers. The increase in their numbers slowed as legislatures put more and more restrictions on the right to free slaves, but by 1860 there were 262,000 free blacks in the slave states, a little over half the national total of 488,000. They were most numerous in the upper South.

THE TRADE IN SLAVES   The slaves languished at the bottom of the social hierarchy. From the first census in 1790 to the eighth in 1860 their numbers had grown from 698,000 to almost 4 million. The rise in the slave population occurred mainly through a natural increase, the rate of which was very close to that of whites at the time. When the African slave trade was outlawed in 1808, it seemed to many a step toward the extinction of slavery, but the expansion of the cotton belt, with its voracious appetite for workers, soon increased the demand for slaves. And shutting off the import of slaves only added to the value of those already present. Prices for prime fieldhands ranged between $300 and

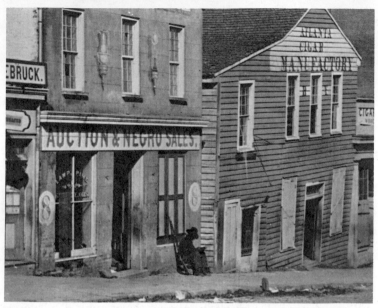

The offices of Pine, Birch & Co., dealers in slaves, Alexandria, Virginia.

$400 in the 1790s, up to $1,000–$1,300 in the 1830s, peaked just before the onset of depression in 1837, and rose again in the great prosperity of the 1850s to $1,500–$2,000. Slaves with special skills cost even more.

The rise in slave value tempered some of the harsher features of the peculiar institution. "Massa was purty good," one ex-slave recalled later. "He treated us jus' 'bout like you would a good mule." Some owners hired wage laborers, often Irish immigrants, for ditching and other dangerous work rather than risk the lives of the more valuable slaves.

The end of the foreign slave trade gave rise to a flourishing domestic trade, with slaves moving mainly from the used-up lands of the Southeast into the booming new country of the Southwest. Many slaves moved south and west with their owners, but there also developed an organized business with brokers, slave pens, and auctioneers. Every town of any size had public auctioneers and dealers willing to buy and sell slaves— along with other merchandise—or handle sales on a commission. The worst aspect of the slave trade was its breakup of families. Many such sales are matters of record, and although the total number is controversial, it took only a few to have a damaging effect on the morale of all.

PLANTATION SLAVERY   More than half of all slaves in 1860 worked on plantations, and most of those were fieldhands. The preferred jobs were those of household servants and skilled workers, including blacksmiths, carpenters, and coopers. Housing for the fieldhands was usually in simple one- or two-room wooden shacks with dirt floors, some without windows. Based on detailed records from eleven plantations in the lower South, scholars have calculated that more then half of all slave babies died in the first year of life, a mortality rate more then twice that of white infants.

To some extent, chiefly in the rice and tobacco belts, work was parceled out by the task. But more commonly fieldhands worked long hours from dawn to dusk, or "from kin [see] to kaint." The slave codes adopted in each state concerned themselves mainly with the owner's interests and subjected the slaves not only to his governance but to surveillance by patrols of county militiamen, who struck fear into the slave quarters by abusing slaves found at large without a good explanation. Evidence suggests that a majority of both planters and small farmers used the whip, which the slave codes authorized. The difference between a good owner and a bad one, according to one ex-slave, was the difference between one who did not "whip too much" and one who "whipped till he bloodied you and blistered you."

A slave's ultimate recourse was rebellion or flight, but most recognized the futility of such measures with whites wielding most of the power and weapons. In the nineteenth century only three slave insurrections drew much notice, and two of those were betrayed before they got under way. Only the Nat Turner insurrection of 1831 in rural Virginia got beyond the planning stage. Turner, a black overseer, was also a religious exhorter who professed a divine mission in leading the movement. The revolt began when a small group killed Turner's master's household and set off down the road repeating the process at other farmhouses, where other slaves joined the marauders. Before it ended at least fifty-five whites had been killed. Eventually trials resulted in seventeen hangings and seven deportations. The Virginia militia, for its part, killed large numbers of slaves indiscriminately in the process of putting down the rebels.

There were very few Nat Turners, however. Slaves more often retaliated against oppression by malingering or by outright sabotage, though there were constraints even on such protests. Slaves would likely eat better on a prosperous plantation than on one they had reduced to poverty, and the shrewdest slaveholders knew that they would more likely benefit by holding out rewards than by inflicting pain. Plantations based on the profit motive

Sale of Slaves and Stock.

The Negroes and Stock listed below, are a Prime Lot, and belong to the ESTATE OF THE LATE LUTHER McGOWAN, and will be sold on Monday, Sept. 22nd, 1852, at the Fair Grounds, in Savannah, Georgia, at 1:00 P. M. The Negroes will be taken to the grounds two days previous to the Sale, so that they may be inspected by prospective buyers.

On account of the low prices listed below, they will be sold for cash only, and must be taken into custody within two hours after sale.

No.	Name.	Age.	Remarks.	Price.
1	Lunesta	27	Prime Rice Planter,	$1,275.00
2	Violet	16	Housework and Nursemaid,	900.00
3	Lizzie	30	Rice, Unsound,	300.00
4	Minda	27	Cotton, Prime Woman,	1,200.00
5	Adam	28	Cotton, Prime Young Man,	1,100.00
6	Abel	41	Rice Hand, Eyesight Poor,	675.00
7	Tanney	22	Prime Cotton Hand,	950.00
8	Flementina	39	Good Cook, Stiff Knee,	400.00
9	Lanney	34	Prime Cottom Man,	1,000.00
10	Sally	10	Handy in Kitchen,	675.00
11	Maccabey	35	Prime Man, Fair Carpenter,	980.00
12	Dorcas Judy	25	Seamstress, Handy in House,	800.00
13	Happy	60	Blacksmith.	575.00
14	Mowden	15	Prime Cotton Boy,	700.00
15	Bills	21	Handy with Mules,	900.00
16	Theopolis	39	Rice Hand, Gets Fits,	575.00
17	Coolidge	29	Rice Hand and Blacksmith,	1,275.00
18	Bessie	69	Infirm, Sews,	250.00
19	Infant	1	Strong Likely Boy	400.00
20	Samson	41	Prime Man, Good with Stock,	975.00
21	Callie May	27	Prime Woman, Rice,	1,000.00
22	Honey	14	Prime Girl, Hearing Poor,	850.00
23	Angelina	16	Prime Girl, House or Field,	1,000.00
24	Virgil	21	Prime Field Hand,	1,100.00
25	Tom	40	Rice Hand, Lame Leg,	750.00
26	Noble	11	Handy Boy,	900.00
27	Judge Lesh	55	Prime Blacksmith,	800.00
28	Booster	43	Fair Mason, Unsound,	600.00
29	Big Kate	37	Housekeeper and Nurse,	950.00
30	Melie Ann	19	Housework, Smart Yellow Girl,	1,250.00
31	Deacon	26	Prime Rice Hand,	1,000.00
32	Coming	19	Prime Cotton Hand,	1,000.00
33	Mabel	47	Prime Cotton Hand,	800.00
34	Uncle Tim	60	Fair Hand with Mules,	600.00
35	Abe	27	Prime Cotton Hand,	1,000.00
36	Tennes	29	Prime Rice Hand and Cocahman,	1,250.00

There will also be offered at this sale, twenty head of Horses and Mules with harness, along with thirty head of Prime Cattle. Slaves will be sold separate, or in lots, as best suits the purchaser. Sale will be held rain or shine.

Announcement of a "Sale of Slaves and Stock," with prices, and the implication that families may be broken up.

fostered between slaves and owners mutual dependency as well as natural antagonism. And in an agrarian society where personal relations counted for much, blacks could win concessions which moderated the harshness of slavery, permitting them a certain degree of individual and community development.

FORGING THE SLAVE COMMUNITY   To generalize about slavery is to miss elements of diversity from place to place and from time to time. The experience could be as varied as people are. Slaves were victims, but to stop with so obvious a perception would be to miss an important story of endurance and achievement. If ever there was a melting pot in American history, the most effective may have been that in which Africans from a variety of ethnic, linguistic, and tribal origins fused into a new community and a new culture as African-Americans.

Members of the slave community were bound together in helping and protecting one another, which in turn created a sense of cohesion and pride. Slave culture incorporated many African survivals, especially in areas where whites were few. Among the Gullah blacks of the South Carolina and Georgia coast more than 4,000 words are still in use from the languages of twenty-one African tribes. Elements of African cultures thus not only have survived but have interacted with other cultures with which they came in contact.

SLAVE RELIGION AND FOLKLORE   Among the most important manifestations of slave culture was the slaves' religion, a mixture of African and Christian elements. Most Africans brought with them a concept of a Creator, or Supreme God, whom they could recognize in Jehovah, and lesser gods whom they might identify with Christ, the Holy Ghost, and the saints, thereby reconciling their earlier beliefs with the new Christian religion. Alongside the church they also retained African beliefs in spirits, voodoo, magical spells and herbs, and conjuring (the practice of healing and warding off evil spirits). Belief in magic is in fact a common human response to conditions of danger or helplessness.

Slaves, however, found greater comfort in the church. There they could find both balm for the soul and release for their emotions, and they brought with them from Africa a demonstrative spirituality. They sang, danced, shouted, and prayed with great gusto and emotion. Masters sought to instill lessons of humility and obedience, but blacks could identify their plight with that of the Israelites in Egypt. And the ultimate hope of a better world gave solace in this one. Some owners openly encouraged religious meetings among their slaves, but those who were denied the open use of "praise houses" held "bush meetings" in secret. The preachers and exhorters who sprang up in the slave world commonly won the acceptance of the owners if only because efforts to get rid of them proved futile. The peculiar cadences of their exhortations, chants, and spirituals have influenced a music of great rhythmic complexity, forms of dance and body language, spirituals and secular songs, and folk tales.

THE SLAVE FAMILY   Slave marriages had no legal status, but slaveowners generally seem to have accepted marriage as a stabilizing influence on the plantation. Sometimes they performed marriages themselves or had a minister celebrate a formal wedding with all the trimmings. A common practice was the "broomstick wedding," in which the couple was married by simply jumping over a broomstick, a custom of uncertain origin. But whatever the formalities, the norm for the slave community as for the white was the nuclear family of parents and children, with the father regarded as head of the family. Slaves also displayed a lively awareness of the extended family of cousins. Most slave children were socialized into their culture through the nuclear family, which afforded some degree of independence from white influence.

Several generations of a family raised in slavery. Plantation of J. J. Smith, Beaufort, South Carolina, 1862.

Slaves were not always allowed to realize this norm. In some cases the matter of family arrangements was ignored or left entirely up to the slaves on the assumption that black females were simply promiscuous—a convenient rationalization for sexual exploitation, to which the presence of many mulattoes attested. The census of 1860 reported 412,000 persons of mixed ancestry in the United States, or about 10 percent of the Negro population, probably a drastic undercount. That planters and their sons took sexual advantage of female slaves was widely admitted, and sometimes clumsily defended on the grounds that the practice protected the chastity of white women. "Like the patriarchs of old," wrote Mary Boykin Chesnut, "our men live all in one house with their wives and concubines." And, she observed, "any lady is ready to tell you who is the father of all the mulatto children in everybody's household but her own."

ANTISLAVERY MOVEMENTS

EARLY OPPOSITION TO SLAVERY   Scattered criticism of slavery developed in the North and the South in the decades after the Revolution, but the emancipation movement accelerated with the formation of the American Colonization Society in 1817. The society proposed to re-settle freed slaves in Africa. Its supporters included such prominent figures as James Madison, James Monroe, Henry Clay, John Marshall, and Daniel Webster, and it appealed to diverse opinions. Some backed it as an antislavery group, while others saw it as a way to bolster slavery by getting rid of potentially troublesome free Negroes. Articulate elements of the free black community denounced it from the start. A group of free blacks in Philadelphia, for example, stressed in 1817 that they had "no wish to separate from our present homes for any purpose whatever." America, they insisted, was now their native land.

Nevertheless, in 1821 agents of the society acquired from local chieftains in West Africa a parcel of land which became the nucleus of a new country. In 1822 the first freed slaves arrived there, and twenty-five years later the society relinquished control to the independent republic of Liberia. But given its uncertain purpose, the colonization movement received but meager support from either antislavery or proslavery elements. By 1860 only about 15,000 blacks had migrated to Africa, approximately 12,000 with the help of the Colonization Society. The number was infinitesimal compared to the number of slave births.

FROM GRADUALISM TO ABOLITIONISM   Meanwhile in the early 1830s the antislavery movement took a new departure. Three dramatic events marked its transition from favoring gradualism to demanding the immediate end of slavery. In 1829 a pamphlet appeared in Boston: *Walker's Appeal . . . to the Colored Citizens of the World*. Its author, David Walker, born a free Negro in North Carolina, sold secondhand clothes in Boston. In the pamphlet Walker preached insurrection and violence as a proper response to the wrongs that blacks suffered. He warned whites: "We must and shall be free . . . in spite of you. . . . And woe, woe, will it be to you if we have to obtain our freedom by fighting." Over the next few years Walker circulated the pamphlet widely among blacks and white sympathizers. Southerners demanded his arrest, but Massachusetts officials replied that he had broken no law.

Two other major events followed in close sequence during 1831. On January 1, William Lloyd Garrison began publication in Boston of a new antislavery newspaper, *The Liberator*. Garrison, who rose from poverty in Newburyport, Massachusetts, had been apprenticed to a newspaperman and had edited a number of antislavery papers, but he grew impatient with the prevailing strategy of moderation. In the first issue of his new paper he renounced "the popular but pernicious doctrine of gradual emancipation" and vowed: "I *will be* as harsh as truth, and as uncompromising as justice. On this subject, I do not wish to think, to speak, or write, with moderation."

Garrison's combative language provoked outraged retorts from slaveholders, who publicized the paper more than his own

William Lloyd Garrison.

supporters did. In the South, literate blacks would more likely encounter Garrison's ideas being criticized in the local papers than in what few copies of *The Liberator* found their way to them. Slaveholders' outrage mounted higher after the Nat Turner insurrection in August 1831. Garrison, they assumed, bore a large part of the responsibility for the affair, but there is no evidence that Nat Turner had ever heard of him, and Garrison said that he had not a single subscriber in the South at the time. What is more, however violent his language, Garrison was a pacifist, opposed to the use of physical violence.

THE AMERICAN ANTI-SLAVERY SOCIETY In 1832 Garrison and his followers set up the New England Anti-Slavery Society. A year later two wealthy New York merchants, Arthur and Lewis Tappan, founded a similar group in their state and then took the lead in starting a national society with the help of Garrison and others. They hoped to build on the publicity gained by the British antislavery movement, which in 1833 had induced Parliament to end slavery, with compensation to slaveholders, throughout the British Empire.

The American Anti-Slavery Society conceded the right of each state to legislate its domestic institutions, but set a goal of convincing fellow citizens "that Slaveholding is a heinous crime in the sight of God, and that the duty, safety, and best interests of all concerned, require its *immediate abandonment*, without expatriation." The society went beyond the issue of emancipation to argue that blacks should "share an equality with the whites, of civil and religious privileges." The group issued a barrage of propaganda for its cause, including periodicals, tracts, agents, lecturers, organizers, and fund-raisers.

THE MOVEMENT SPLITS As the antislavery movement spread, debates over tactics intensified. The Garrisonians, mainly New Englanders, were radicals who felt that American society had been corrupted from top to bottom and needed universal reform. Garrison embraced just about every important reform movement of the day: antislavery, temperance, pacifism, and women's rights. Deeply affected by the perfectionism of the times, he refused to compromise principle for expediency, to sacrifice one reform for another. Abolition was not enough. He opposed colonization of freed slaves and stood for equal rights. He broke with the organized church, which to his mind was in league with slavery. The federal government was all the more so. The Constitution, he said, was "a covenant with death and an agreement with hell." Garrison therefore refused to vote. He was, however, prepared to collaborate with those who did or with those who disagreed with him on other matters.

Other reformers saw American society as fundamentally sound and concentrated their attention on purging it of slavery. Most of these abolitionists were evangelical Christians, and they promoted pragmatic political organization as the best instrument of reform. Garrison struck them as an impractical fanatic—as he was.

A showdown came in 1840 on the issue of women's rights. Women had joined the abolition movement from the start, but quietly and largely in groups without men. The activities of the Grimké sisters brought the issue of women's rights to center stage. Sarah and Angelina Grimké, daughters of a prominent slaveowning family in South Carolina, had broken with their parents and moved north to embrace Quakerism, antislavery, and feminism. They set out speaking to women in New England and slowly widened their audiences to "promiscuous assemblies" of both men and women. Such unseemly behavior inspired male leaders to chastise the Grimké sisters and other women activists for engaging in unfeminine activity. The chairman of the Connecticut Anti-Slavery Society declared: "No woman will speak or vote where I am a moderator. It is enough for women to rule at home." He refused to "submit to PETTICOAT GOVERNMENT." Catharine Beecher reminded the activist sisters that women occupied "a subordinate relation in society to the other sex" and should therefore limit their activities to the "domestic and social circle." Angelina Grimké stoutly rejected such conventional arguments. "It is a woman's right," she insisted, "to have a voice in all laws and regulations by which she is to be governed, whether in church or in state."

This debate over the role of women in the antislavery movement crackled and simmered until it finally exploded in 1840. At the American Anti-Slavery Society's annual meeting the Garrisonians insisted on the right of women to participate equally in the organization, and they carried their point. They did not commit the group to women's rights in any other way, however. Contrary opinion, mainly from the Tappans' New York group, ranged from outright antifeminism to simple fear of scattering shots on too many reforms. The New Yorkers broke away to form the American and Foreign Anti-Slavery Society.

BLACK ANTISLAVERY White male antislavery activists also balked at granting full recognition to black abolitionists of either sex.

Often blindly patronizing, white leaders expected free blacks to take a back seat in the movement. Not all blacks were easily put down, and most became exasperated at whites' tendency to value purity over results, to strike a moral posture at the expense of action. But despite the invitation to form separate black groups, black leaders were active in the white societies from the beginning. Three attended the organizational meeting of the American Anti-Slavery Society in 1833, and some became outstanding agents for the movement, notably the former slaves who could speak from firsthand experience.

Among the black abolitionists one of the most effective was Sojourner Truth. Born in New York State in 1797, Isabella Baumfree renamed herself in 1843 after experiencing a mystical conversation with God, who told her "to travel up and down the land" preaching the sins of slavery. She did just that, crisscrossing the country during the 1840s and 1850s, exhorting audiences to support abolitionism and women's rights. Having been a slave until she fled to freedom in 1827, Sojourner Truth was able to speak with added conviction and knowledge about the evils of the "peculiar institution" and the inequality of women. As she told a gathering of the Ohio Women's Rights Convention in 1851, "I have plowed, and planted, and gathered into barns, and no man could head me—and ar'n't I a woman? I have borne thirteen chilern, and seen em mos' all sold off into slavery, and when I cried out with a mother's grief, none but Jesus heard—and ar'n't I a woman?" Through such compelling testimony, So-

Frederick Douglass (left) *and Sojourner Truth* (right) *were both leading abolitionists.*

journer Truth demonstrated the powerful intersection of abolitionism and women's rights agitation, and in the process she
displayed and tapped the distinctive energies that women
brought to reformist causes. "If the first woman God ever made
was strong enough to turn the world upside down all alone," she
concluded her address to the Ohio gathering, "these women together ought to be able to turn it back, and get it right side up
again!"

An equally gifted black abolitionist was Frederick Douglass of
Maryland. Blessed with an imposing frame and a simple eloquence, he became the best known black man in America. "I appear before the immense assembly this evening as a thief and a
robber," he told a Massachusetts group in 1842. "I stole this
head, these limbs, this body from my master, and ran off with
them." Fearful of capture after publishing his *Narrative of the
Life of Frederick Douglass* (1845), he left for an extended lecture
tour of the British Isles and returned two years later with enough
money to purchase his freedom. He then started an abolitionist
newspaper for blacks in Rochester, New York.

Douglass's *Narrative* was but the best known among a hundred
or more such accounts. Escapees often made it out on their own
—Douglass borrowed a pass from a free black seaman—but
many were aided by the Underground Railroad, which grew in
legend into a vast system to conceal runaways and spirit them to
freedom, often over the Canadian border. Actually, there seems
to have been more spontaneity than system about the matter,
and blacks contributed more than was credited in the legend. Experience had conditioned escapees to distrust whites. One esca-
pee recalled later: "We did not dare ask [for food], except when
we found a slave's or a free colored person's house remote from
any other, and then we were never refused, if they had food to
give." A few intrepid black refugees actually ventured back into
slave states to organize escapes. Harriet Tubman, the most celebrated liberator, went back nineteen times.

REACTIONS TO ANTISLAVERY Even the road north, many blacks
found to their dismay, did not lead to the Promised Land. North
of slavery, they encountered much of the discrimination and segregation that freed slaves would later encounter in the southern
states. When Prudence Crandall of Connecticut admitted a black
girl to her private school in 1833, she lost most of her white
pupils. She held out in the face of insults, vandalism, and a law
that made her action illegal, but closed the school after eighteen
months and left the state. Garrison, Douglass, and other aboli-

tionists had to face down hostile crowds who disliked blacks or found antislavery agitation bad for business. In 1837 an Illinois mob killed the antislavery editor Elijah P. Lovejoy, giving the movement a martyr to both abolition and freedom of the press.

In the 1830s abolitionism took a political turn, focusing at first on Congress. One shrewd strategy was to deluge Congress with petitions calling for the abolition of slavery in the nation's capital, the District of Columbia. Most such petitions were presented by former President John Quincy Adams, elected to the House from Massachusetts in 1830. In 1836, however, the House adopted a rule to lay abolition petitions automatically on the table, in effect ignoring them. Adams, "Old Man Eloquent," stubbornly fought this "Gag Rule" as a violation of the First Amendment and hounded its supporters until the Gag Rule was finally repealed in 1844.

Meanwhile, in 1840, the year of the schism in the antislavery movement, a small group of abolitionists called a convention in Albany, New York, and launched the Liberty party, with James G. Birney, one-time slaveholder from Alabama and Kentucky, as its candidate for president. In the 1840 election Birney polled only 7,000 votes, but in 1844 his total rose to 60,000, and from that time forth an antislavery party contested every national election until Abraham Lincoln won the presidency in 1860.

THE DEFENSE OF SLAVERY   Birney was but one among a number of southerners propelled north during the 1830s by the South's growing hostility to emancipationist ideas. Antislavery in the upper South had its last stand in 1831–1832 when the Virginia legislature debated a plan of gradual emancipation and colonization, then rejected it by a vote of 73 to 58. Thereafter, southern partisans worked out an elaborate intellectual defense of slavery, presenting it as a positive good.

The biblical argument in favor of slavery became one of the most powerful. The evangelical churches, which had widely condemned slavery at one time, gradually turned proslavery, at least in the South. Ministers of all denominations joined in the argument. Had not the patriarchs of the Old Testament held bondsmen? Had not Noah, upon awakening from a drunken stupor, cursed Canaan, son of Ham, from whom the Negroes were descended? Had not Saint Paul advised servants to obey their masters and told a fugitive servant to return to his master? And had not Jesus remained silent on the subject, at least so far as the Gospels reported his words? In 1843–1844 disputes over slavery split two great denominations along sectional lines and led to the formation of the Southern Baptist Convention and the Methodist Episcopal Church, South. Presbyterians, the only other major denomination to split, did not divide until the Civil War.

Another, and more fundamental, feature of the proslavery argument developed a theory of the intrinsic inferiority of Negroes. Stereotyping the poor and powerless as inferior is an old and seemingly ineradicable human habit. There was in fact a theory championed by a physician from Mobile, Alabama, that blacks were the product of a separate creation, but this challenged orthodox faith in the biblical account of creation and was generally rejected.

Other arguments took a more "practical" view of slavery. Not only was slavery profitable, it was a matter of social necessity. Jefferson, for instance, in his *Notes On Virginia* (1785), had argued that emancipated slaves and whites could not live together without risk of race war growing out of the recollection of past injuries. What is more, it seemed clear that blacks could not be expected to work if freed. They were too shiftless and improvident, the argument went. White workmen, on the other hand, feared their competition.

In 1856 William J. Grayson of Charleston published a lengthy poem, *The Hireling and the Slave*, which defended slavery as being better for the worker than the "wage slavery" of northern industry. George Fitzhugh of Virginia developed the same argument, among others, in two books: *Sociology for the South; or, The Failure of a Free Society* (1854) and *Cannibals All! or, Slaves Without Masters* (1857). Few if any socialists ever waxed more eloquent over the evils of industrial capitalism than these proslavery theorists. The factory system had brought abuses and neglect far worse than those of slavery, they contended. Slavery, Fitzhugh argued, was the truest form of socialism, for it provided security for the workers in sickness and old age, whereas workers in the North were exploited for profit and then cast aside. Men were not born equal, he insisted: "it would be far nearer the truth to say that some were born with saddles on their backs, and others booted and spurred to ride them—and the riding does them good." Fitzhugh argued for an organic, hierarchical society, much like the family, in which each had a place with both rights and obligations. John C. Calhoun endorsed slavery with the more popular argument that it freed masters from drudgery to pursue higher things, and thus made possible a Greek democracy—or what one historian has more aptly tagged a "Herrenvolk [master race] democracy."

Within one generation such ideas had triumphed in the white South over the postrevolutionary apology for slavery as an evil bequeathed by the forefathers. Opponents of the orthodox faith in slavery as a positive good were either silenced or exiled. Freedom of thought in the Old South had become a victim of the nation's growing obsession with slavery.

FURTHER READING

Contrasting analyses of the plantation system in the South are Eugene D. Genovese's *The World the Slaveholders Made* (1969)° and Gavin Wright's *The Political Economy of the Cotton South* (1978).°
Other works on southern culture and society include Bertram Wyatt-Brown's *Southern Honor* (1982)°; Catherine Clinton's *Plantation Mistress* (1982)°; Suzanne Lebsock's *Free Women of Petersburg* (1984)°; and Theodore Rosengarten's *Tombee: Portrait of a Cotton Planter* (1987).° William J. Cooper, Jr.'s *Liberty and Slavery* (1983)° and Robert F. Durden's *The Self-Inflicted Wound* (1985) cover southern politics of the era.
The historiography of slavery and racism includes an impressive array of exciting and controversial scholarship. A provocative discussion of the psychology of black slavery can be found in Stanley M. Elkin's *Slavery: A Problem in American Intellectual Life* (3rd ed., 1976).° More recent scholarship emphasizes the self-generative, dynamic character of black society under slavery. John W. Blassingame's *The Slave Community: Plantation Life in the Antebellum South* (rev. ed., 1979)°; Eugene D. Genovese's *Roll, Jordon, Roll: The World the Slaves Made* (1974)°; and Herbert G. Gutman's *The Black Family in Slavery and Freedom, 1750–1925* (1976)° all stress the theme of a persisting and identifiable slave culture.
On the question of slavery's profitability, see Robert W. Fogel and Stanley L. Engerman's *Time on the Cross: The Economics of Negro Slavery* (2 vols., 1974)° and Herbert G. Gutman's *Slavery and the Numbers Game* (1975).
Other recent works on slavery include Elizabeth Fox-Genovese's *Within the Plantation Household: Black and White Women of the Old South* (1988).° Lawrence W. Levine's *Black Culture and Black Consciousness: Afro-American Folk Thought from Slavery to Freedom* (1977)°; Albert J. Raboteau's *Slave Religion: The "Invisible Institution" in the Antebellum South* (1978)°; and Joel Williamson's *The Crucible of Race* (1985).° A vivid account of a female slave who was exploited by her master is Melton A. McLaurin's *Celia: A Slave* (1991).
Useful surveys of abolitionism include Ronald G. Walter's *The Antislavery Appeal* (1976)° and James B. Stewart's *Holy Warriors: The Aboli-*

° These books are available in paperback editions.

tionists and American Slavery (1976).° For textured insights into the tension between feminism and abolitionism, see Dorothy Sterling's *Ahead of Her Time: Abby Kelley and the Politics of Antislavery* (1991).

Surveys of black history for the period include John B. Boles's *Black Southerners, 1619–1869* (1983)°; Leon F. Litwack's *North of Slavery: The Negro in the Free States, 1790–1860* (1965)°; and Ira Berlin's *Slaves without Masters* (1974),° on southern free blacks. William McFeeley's *Frederick Douglass* (1990)° is a superb biography of the most eminent black abolitionist.

For the proslavery argument as it developed in the South, see William J. Cooper's *The South and the Politics of Slavery, 1828–1856* (1978)°; James Oakes's *The Ruling Race: A History of American Slaveholders* (1982)°; and *Slavery Defended* (1963), edited by Eric L. McKitrick, the last a collection of proslavery writings.

15

THE CRISIS OF UNION

SLAVERY IN THE TERRITORIES

John C. Calhoun and Ralph Waldo Emerson had little else in common, but both men sensed in the Mexican War the omens of a greater disaster. Mexico was "the forbidden fruit; the penalty of eating it would be to subject our institutions to political death," Calhoun warned. "The United States will conquer Mexico," Emerson conceded, "but it will be as the man swallows the arsenic . . . Mexico will poison us." Wars, as both men knew, have a way of breeding new wars, often in unforeseen ways. Indeed, America's winning of the Southwest gave rise in turn to quarrels over newly acquired lands. These quarrels set in motion a series of disputes that would culminate in a crisis of union.

THE WILMOT PROVISO The Mexican War was less than three months old when the seeds of a new conflict began to sprout. On August 8, 1846, a freshman Democrat from Pennsylvania, David Wilmot, stood up in the House of Representatives to discuss Polk's request for $2 million to expedite negotiations with Mexico. He favored expansion, Wilmot explained, even the annexation of Texas as a slave state. But slavery had come to an end in Mexico, and if free soil should be acquired, "God forbid that we should be the means of planting this institution upon it." Drawing upon the words of the Northwest Ordinance, he offered a fateful amendment to Polk's appropriations bill: in lands acquired from Mexico, "neither slavery nor involuntary servitude shall ever exist in any part of said territory."

Within ten minutes an otherwise obscure congressman had immortalized his name. The Wilmot Proviso, although never a law, politicized slavery once and for all. For a generation, since the Missouri Controversy of 1819–1821, the issue had been lurking in the wings, kept there most of the time by politicians who feared its disruptive force. But for the two decades following Wilmot's proposal the question would never be far from center stage.

The first flurry of excitement, however, passed quickly. The House adopted the Wilmot Proviso, but the Senate refused to concur and Congress adjourned without giving Polk his $2 million. When Congress reconvened in December 1846 Polk prevailed on Wilmot to withhold his amendment, but by then others were ready to take up the cause. When a New York congressman revived the proviso he signaled a revolt by the Van Burenites in concert with the antislavery forces of the North. Once again the House approved the amendment; again the Senate refused. In March the House finally gave in, but in one form or another Wilmot's idea kept cropping up. Abraham Lincoln later recalled that during one term as congressman, 1847–1849, he voted for it "as good as forty times."

John C. Calhoun meanwhile devised a thesis to counter the proviso, and he set it before the Senate in four resolutions on February 19, 1847. The Calhoun Resolutions, which never came to a vote, argued that since the territories were the common possession of the states, Congress had no right to prevent any citizen from taking slaves into them. To do so would violate the Fifth Amendment, which forbade Congress to deprive any person of life, liberty, or property without due process of law, and slaves were property. Thus by a clever stroke of logic Calhoun took the basic guarantee of liberty, the Bill of Rights, and turned it into a basic guarantee of slavery. The irony was not lost on his critics, but the point became established southern dogma—echoed by his colleagues and formally endorsed by the Virginia legislature.

Senator Thomas Hart Benton of Missouri, himself a slaveholder but also a Jacksonian nationalist, found in Calhoun's resolutions a set of abstractions "leading to no result." Wilmot and Calhoun between them, he said, had fashioned a pair of shears. Neither blade alone would cut very well, but joined together they could sever the ties of union. Within another year Benton was complaining that the slavery issue had become like the plague of frogs in Pharaoh's Egypt, with "this black question, forever on the table, on the nuptial couch, everywhere."

POPULAR SOVEREIGNTY Many others, like Benton, refused to be polarized, seeking to bypass the brewing conflict. President Polk was among the first to suggest extending the Missouri Compromise dividing free and slave territory at latitude 36°30' all the way to the Pacific. Senator Lewis Cass of Michigan, an ardent Whig expansionist, suggested that the citizens of a territory "regulate their own internal concerns" like the citizens of a state. Such an approach would combine the merits of expediency and democracy. It would take the issue out of the national arena and put it in the hands of those directly affected.

Popular sovereignty, or squatter sovereignty, as the idea was also called, had much to commend it. Without directly challenging the slaveholders' access to the new lands, it promised to open them quickly to non-slaveholding farmers who would almost surely dominate the territories. With this tacit understanding the idea prospered in Cass's Old Northwest, where Stephen A. Douglas of Illinois and other prominent Democrats soon endorsed it.

When the Mexican War ended in 1848, the question of bondage in the new territories was no longer hypothetical—unless one reasoned, as many did, that their arid climate excluded plantation crops and therefore excluded slavery. For Calhoun that was beside the point since the right to carry slaves into the territories was the South's outer defense line, not to be yielded without opening the way to further assaults. In fact there is little reason in retrospect to credit the argument that slavery had reached its natural limits of expansion. Slavery had been adapted to occupations other than plantation agriculture. Besides, on irrigated lands, cotton later became a staple crop of the Southwest.

Nobody doubted that Oregon would become free soil, but it too was drawn into the growing controversy. Territorial status, pending since 1846, was delayed because its provisional government had excluded slavery. To concede that provision would imply an authority drawn from the powers of Congress, since a territory was created by Congress. After much wrangling, an exhausted Congress let Oregon organize without slavery, but postponed decision on the Southwest territories. Polk signed the bill on the principle that Oregon was north of 36°30'.

Polk had promised to serve only one term, and having reached his major goals, he refused to run again in 1848. At the Democratic convention Lewis Cass, the author of squatter sovereignty, won nomination, but the platform simply denied the power of Congress to interfere with slavery in the states and criticized all efforts to bring the question before Congress. The Whigs devised an even more artful shift. Once again, as in 1840, they passed over Clay, their party leader, for a general, Zachary Taylor, whose popularity had grown since the Battle of Buena Vista. A legal resident of Louisiana and owner of more than a hundred slaves, he was an apolitical figure who had never voted in a national election. Once again, as in 1840, the party adopted no platform at all.

THE FREE-SOIL COALITION But the antislavery impulse was not easily squelched. Wilmot had raised a standard to which a broad coalition could rally. People who shied away from the abolitionism of Garrison could readily endorse the exclusion of slavery from all the territories. By doing so, moreover, one could strike a blow for liberty without caring about slavery itself, or about the slaves. One might simply want free soil for white farmers, while keeping the unwelcome blacks far away in the South, where they belonged. Free soil in the new territories, therefore, rather than abolition in the South itself, became the rallying point—and also the name of a new party.

Three major groups entered the free-soil coalition: rebellious Democrats, antislavery Whigs, and members of the antislavery Liberty party. Disaffection among the Democrats centered in New York, where the Van Burenites seized on the free-soil issue as a moral imperative. Free-soil principles among the Whigs centered in Massachusetts where a group of "conscience" Whigs battled the "cotton" Whigs. The latter, according to the fiery Massachusetts reformer and future senator Charles Sumner, belonged to a coalition of northern businessmen and southern planters, "the lords of the lash and the lords of the loom." Conscience Whigs rejected the slaveholding nominee of their party, Zachary Taylor.

In August 1848 these groups—Van Buren Democrats, Conscience Whigs, and Liberty party followers—organized the Free Soil party in a convention at Buffalo. Its presidential nomination went to Martin Van Buren. The Free Soil party platform pledged the government to abolish slavery whenever such action became constitutional, but the party's main principle was the Wilmot Proviso and it entered the campaign with the catchy slogan of "free soil, free speech, free labor, and free men."

Its impact on the election was mixed. The Free Soilers split the Democratic vote enough to throw New York to Taylor, and the Whig vote enough to give Ohio to Cass, but Van Buren's total of 291,000 votes was far below the popular totals of 1,361,000 for Taylor and 1,222,000 for Cass. Taylor won with 163 to 127 electoral votes, and both major parties retained a national following.

TOWARD STATEHOOD FOR CALIFORNIA   Meanwhile a new dimension had been introduced into the question of the territories. On January 24, 1848, gold was discovered in the California territory. The word spread quickly, and Polk's confirmation of the discovery in his last annual message, on December 5, 1848, turned the gold-fever into a worldwide contagion. During 1849 more than 80,000 persons reached California, with 55,000 going overland and the rest by way of Panama or Cape Horn. The influx quickly reduced the Mexicans there to a minority, and sporadic conflicts with the Indians of the Sierra Nevada foothills decimated the native peoples.

Meanwhile, the new president did not remain an enigma for long. Born in Virginia and raised in Kentucky, Zachary Taylor had been a soldier most of his adult life. Constantly on the move, he had acquired a home in Louisiana and a plantation in Mississippi. Southern Whigs had rallied to his support, expecting him to uphold the cause of slavery. Instead they had turned up a southern man with Union principles, who had no more use for Calhoun's proslavery abstractions than Jackson had for his nullification doctrine. Honest, forthright, and decisive, "Old Rough and Ready" had the direct mind of the soldier he was. Slavery should be upheld where it existed, he felt, but he had little patience with abstract theories about slavery in territories where it probably could not exist. Why not make the California and New Mexico territories, acquired from Mexico, into states immediately, he reasoned, and bypass the whole issue?

But the Californians, in need of organized government, were already ahead of him. By December 1849, without consulting Congress, California organized a free-state government. New Mexico responded more slowly, but by June 1850 Americans there had adopted another free-state constitution. In Taylor's annual message on December 4, 1849, he endorsed immediate statehood for California and enjoined Congress to avoid injecting slavery into the issue.

THE COMPROMISE OF 1850

THE GREAT DEBATE   The spotlight thus fell on the Senate, where the Compromise of 1850, one of the great dramas of American politics, was enacted by a stellar cast: the great triumvirate of Clay, Calhoun, and Webster, with support from William H. Seward, Stephen A. Douglas, Jefferson Davis, and Thomas Hart

Benton. Seventy-three-year-old Henry Clay once again took the role of the "great Pacificator," which he had played in the Missouri and nullification controversies. In January 1850 he presented a package of eight resolutions which solved all the disputed issues. He proposed to (1) admit California as a free state, (2) organize the remainder of the Southwest without restriction as to slavery, (3) deny Texas its extreme claim to a Rio Grande boundary up to its source, (4) compensate Texas for this by assuming the Texas debt, (5) uphold slavery in the District of Columbia, but (6) abolish the slave trade across its boundaries, (7) adopt a more effective fugitive slave act, and (8) deny congressional authority to interfere with the interstate slave trade. His proposals, in substance, became the Compromise of 1850, but only after a prolonged debate, the most celebrated, if not the greatest, in the annals of Congress—and the final great debate for Calhoun, Clay, and Webster.

On February 5–6 Clay, haggard in appearance and faltering in speech, summoned all his eloquence in defending the settlement. In the interest of "peace, concord and harmony" he called for an end to "passion, passion—party, party—and intemperance." Otherwise, continued sectional bickering would lead to a "furious, bloody, implacable, exterminating" civil war. To avoid such a catastrophe, he stressed, California should be admitted on the terms that its own people had approved. The debate continued sporadically through February, with Sam Houston rising to support Clay's compromise, Jefferson Davis defending the slavery cause on every point, and none endorsing President Taylor's straightforward plan.

Then on March 4, Calhoun, desperately ill with tuberculosis, from which he would die in a few weeks, dramatically left his sickbed to sit in the Senate chamber, a gaunt, heavy-lidded figure swathed in flannels. A colleague read his defiant remarks. "I have, Senators, believed from the first that the agitation of the subject of slavery would, if not prevented by some timely and effective measure, end in disunion," wrote Calhoun. Neither Clay's compromise nor Taylor's efforts would serve the Union. The South needed but an acceptance of its rights: equality in the territories, the return of fugitive slaves, and some guarantee of "an equilibrium between the sections."

Three days later Calhoun returned to hear Daniel Webster. The "godlike Daniel," long since acknowledged the supreme orator in an age of superb oratory, no longer possessed the thunderous voice of his youth nor did his shrinking frame project its once magisterial aura, but he remained a formidable presence.

Daniel Webster, in a daguerreotype made around the time of the 1850 Compromise.

His weathered face was lined with worry and sorrow as he addressed the hushed Senate. He chose as his central theme the preservation of the Union, as he had done twenty years earlier in the classic debate with Hayne: "I wish to speak today, not as a Massachusetts man, not as a Northern man, but as an American . . . I speak today for the preservation of the Union." The extent of slavery was already determined, he insisted, by the Northwest Ordinance, by the Missouri Compromise, and in the new lands by the law of nature. Both sections, to be sure, had legitimate grievances: on the one hand the excesses of "infernal fanatics and abolitionists" in the North; and on the other hand southern efforts to expand slavery. But instead of threatening secession, he asked, let people "enjoy the fresh air of liberty and union."

The March 7 speech was a supreme gesture of conciliation, and Webster had knowingly brought down a storm upon his head. New England abolitionists lambasted this new "Benedict Arnold" for not aggressively supporting the free-soil cause and for endorsing the new fugitive slave law. On March 11 William H. Seward, freshman Whig senator from New York, gave the antislavery reply to Webster. Compromise with slavery, he argued, was "radically wrong and essentially vicious." There was "a higher law than the Constitution" which demanded the abolition of slavery.

In mid-April a select Committee of Thirteen bundled Clay's suggestions into one comprehensive bill, which the committee reported to the Senate early in May. The measure was quickly dubbed the "Omnibus bill" because it resembled the vehicle that carried many riders. Taylor continued to oppose Clay's compromise, and their feud threatened to split the Whig party wide open. Another crisis loomed when word came near the end of June that a convention in New Mexico was applying for statehood, with Taylor's support, and with boundaries that conflicted with the Texas claim to the east bank of the Rio Grande.

TOWARD A COMPROMISE On July 4, 1850, friends of the Union staged a grand rally at the base of the unfinished Washington Monument. Taylor attended the ceremonies in the hot sun. Back at the White House he quenched his thirst with iced water and milk, ate some cherries or cucumbers, and was soon stricken with cholera morbus (gastroenteritis). Five days later he was dead. The outcome of the sectional quarrel, had he lived, probably would have been different, whether for better or worse one cannot know.

Taylor's sudden death, however, strengthened the chances of compromise. The soldier in the White House was followed by a politician, Millard Fillmore. The son of a poor farmer in upper New York, Fillmore had come up through the school of hard knocks. Largely self-educated, he had made his own way as a lawyer and then as a candidate in the rough-and-tumble world of New York politics. Experience had taught him caution, which some thought was indecision, but he had made up his mind to support Clay's compromise and had so informed Taylor. It was a strange switch. Taylor, the Louisiana slaveholder, who had nevertheless stoutly opposed the expansion of slavery, was ready to make war on his native region if it pressed the issue; Fillmore, whom southerners thought was antislavery, was ready to make peace.

At this point young Senator Stephen A. Douglas of Illinois, a rising star of the Democratic party, rescued Clay's faltering compromise. Short and stocky, brash and brilliant, Douglas was known affectionately as the "Little Giant." His strategy was in fact the same one that Clay had used to pass the Missouri Compromise thirty years before. Reasoning that nearly everybody objected to one or another provision of the Omnibus, Douglas worked on the principle of breaking it up into six (later five) separate measures. Few members were prepared to vote for all of them, but from different elements Douglas hoped to mobilize a majority for each.

It worked. Thomas Hart Benton noted that the separate items were like "cats and dogs that had been tied together by their tails for months, scratching and biting, but being loose again, every one of them ran off to his own hole and was quiet." In early Sep-

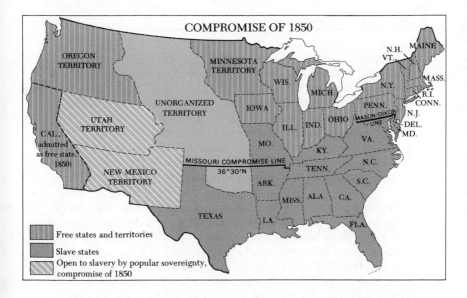

COMPROMISE OF 1850

OREGON TERRITORY

MINNESOTA TERRITORY

WIS.

MICH.

N.H.
VT.

MAINE

N.Y.

MASS.
R.I.
CONN.

UNORGANIZED TERRITORY

IOWA

PENN.

N.J.

UTAH TERRITORY

ILL. IND. OHIO MASON-DIXON LINE

DEL.
MD.

CAL. (admitted as free state, 1850)

MO.

VA.

KY.

MISSOURI COMPROMISE LINE 36°30'N

NEW MEXICO TERRITORY

ARK.

TENN.

N.C.

S.C.

TEXAS

MISS. ALA. GA.

LA.

FLA.

Free states and territories

Slave states

Open to slavery by popular sovereignty, compromise of 1850

tember 1850 the main bills passed, and on September 20 Fillmore signed the last of the five measures into law. The Union had muddled through, and the settlement went down in history as the Compromise of 1850. For the time it defused an explosive situation and settled each of the major points at issue.

First, California entered the Union as a free state, ending forever the old balance of free and slave states. Second, the Texas and New Mexico Act made New Mexico a territory and set the Texas boundary at its present location. In return for giving up its claims east of the Rio Grande Texas was paid $10 million. Third, the Utah Act set up another territory. The territorial act in each case omitted reference to slavery except to give the territorial legislature authority over "all rightful subjects of legislation" with provision for appeal to federal courts. For the sake of agreement the deliberate ambiguity of the statement was its merit. Northern congressmen could assume that territorial legislatures might act to exclude slavery on the unstated principle of popular sovereignty. Southern congressmen assumed that they could not do so.

Fourth, a new Fugitive Slave Act put the matter of retrieving runaways wholly under federal jurisdiction and stacked the cards in favor of slave-catchers. Fifth, as a gesture to antislavery forces the slave trade, but not slavery itself, was abolished in the District of Columbia.

Millard Fillmore's message to Congress in December 1850 pronounced the measures "a final settlement." Still, doubts lingered that either North or South could be reconciled to the measures permanently. In the South the disputes of 1846–1850 had transformed the abstract doctrine of secession into a movement animated by such "fire-eaters" as Robert Barnwell Rhett of South Carolina, William L. Yancey of Alabama, and Edmund Ruffin of Virginia. In their view slavery must expand into the territories or it would wither and die—and southern culture would die along with it. They refused to view the matter as settled, and they would do all in their power to see it returned to the center stage of political debate.

THE FUGITIVE SLAVE LAW   Northern abolitionists were equally determined to keep the issue of slavery's evils in the forefront of public concerns. Southern intransigence in demanding the Fugitive Slave Law had presented abolitionists a new focus for agitation and one that was far more charged with emotion. The law offered a strong temptation to kidnap free Negroes by denying alleged fugitives a jury trial and by providing a fee of $10 for each fugitive delivered to federal authorities. "This filthy enactment was made in the nineteenth century, by people who could read and write," Ralph Waldo Emerson marveled in his journal. He advised neighbors to break it "on the earliest occasion." The occasion soon arose in many places. Within a month of the law's enactment claims were filed in New York, Philadelphia, Harrisburg, Detroit, and other cities. Trouble followed. In Detroit only military force stopped the rescue of an alleged fugitive by an outraged mob in October 1850.

There were relatively few such incidents, however. In the first six years of the fugitive act only three runaways were forcibly rescued from the slave-catchers. On the other hand probably fewer than 200 were returned to bondage during the same years. More than that were rescued by stealth, often through the Underground Railroad. Still, the Fugitive Slave Act had tremendous effect in widening and deepening the antislavery impulse in the North.

UNCLE TOM'S CABIN AND THE 1852 ELECTION   Antislavery forces found their most persuasive appeal not in opposition to the Fugitive Slave Act but in the fictional drama of Harriet Beecher Stowe's *Uncle Tom's Cabin* (1851), a combination of unlikely saints and sinners, stereotypes and melodramatic escapades—and a smashing commercial success. Slavery, seen through Mrs. Stowe's eyes, subjected its victims either to callous brutality or, at the hands of indulgent masters, to the indignity of extravagant

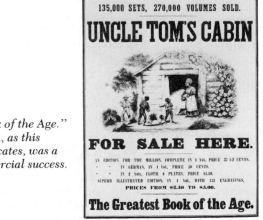

135,000 SETS, 270,000 VOLUMES SOLD.

UNCLE TOM'S CABIN

FOR SALE HERE.

AN EDITION FOR THE MILLION, COMPLETE IN 1 Vol, PRICE 37 1-2 CENTS.
" " IN GERMAN, IN 1 Vol, PRICE 50 CENTS.
" " IN 2 Vols, CLOTH, 6 PLATES, PRICE $1.50.
SUPERB ILLUSTRATED EDITION, IN 1 Vol, WITH 153 ENGRAVINGS,
PRICES FROM $2.50 TO $5.00.

The Greatest Book of the Age.

"The Greatest Book of the Age." Uncle Tom's Cabin, *as this advertisement indicates, was a tremendous commercial success.*

ineptitude and bankruptcy. It took time for the novel to work its effect on public opinion, however. The country was enjoying a surge of prosperity, and the course of the presidential campaign in 1852 reflected a common desire to lay sectional quarrels to rest.

The Democrats, despite a fight over the nomination, had some success in papering over the divisions within their party. As their nominee for president they turned finally to Franklin Pierce of New Hampshire, a personable veteran of the Mexican War with little political experience. Soon they had a catchy slogan to aim at the Whigs: "We Polked you in 1844, we shall Pierce you in 1852." The platform pledged the Democrats to "abide by and adhere to a faithful execution of the acts known as the Compromise measures . . ." Pierce rallied both the Southern Rights men and the Van Burenite Democrats. The Free Soilers, as a consequence, mustered only half as many votes as they had totaled in 1848.

The Whigs were less fortunate. They repudiated the lackluster Fillmore, who had faithfully supported the Compromise, and tried to exploit martial glory by finally choosing Winfield Scott, the hero of Mexico City, a native of Virginia backed mainly by northern Whigs. The convention dutifully endorsed the Compromise of 1850, but with some opposition from the North. Scott, an able field commander but politically inept, had gained a reputation for antislavery and nativism, alienating German and Irish ethnic voters. In the end Scott carried only four states. The popular vote was closer: 1.6 million to 1.4 million.

Pierce, an undistinguished but sincere, boyishly handsome figure, a former congressman, senator, and brigadier in Mexico, was, like Polk, touted as another "Young Hickory." But he turned out to be made of more pliable stuff, unable to dominate the warring factions of his party, trying to be all things to all people, but looking more and more like a "Northern man with Southern principles."

FOREIGN ADVENTURES

CUBA Foreign diversions now distracted attention from domestic quarrels. Cuba, one of Spain's earliest and one of its last possessions in the New World, had long been an object of American desire, especially to southerners determined to expand slavery into new areas. In 1854 the Pierce administration instructed Pierre Soulé, the American minister in Madrid, to offer $130 million for Cuba, which Spain peremptorily spurned. Soulé then joined the American ministers to France and Britain in drafting the Ostend Manifesto. It declared that if Spain, "actuated by stubborn pride and a false sense of honor refused to sell," then the United States "shall be justified in wresting it from Spain." Publication of the supposedly confidential dispatch left the administration no choice but to disavow what northern opinion widely regarded as a "slaveholders' plot."

DIPLOMATIC GAINS IN THE PACIFIC In the Pacific, however, American diplomacy scored some important achievements. In 1844 China, still reeling from its defeat by Britain in the Opium War, signed an agreement with the United States that opened four ports, including Shanghai, to American trade. A later treaty opened eleven more ports and granted Americans the right to travel and trade throughout China. China quickly became a special concern of American Protestant missionaries as well. About fifty were already there by 1855, and for nearly a century, China remained far and away the most active mission field for Americans.

Japan meanwhile had remained for two centuries closed to American trade. Moreover, American whalers wrecked on the shores of Japan had been forbidden to leave the country. Mainly in their interest President Fillmore entrusted a special Japanese expedition to Commodore Matthew C. Perry, who arrived in Tokyo on July 8, 1853. Commodore Perry sought to impress— and intimidate—the Japanese with American military and technological superiority. He demonstrated the cannon on his steamships and presented the Japanese with gifts of rifles, pistols, telegraph instruments, and a working miniature locomotive. For their part the Japanese presented Perry with silk and ornate furnishings. While the Americans paraded their warships, the Japanese offered a performance of *sumo* wrestlers. Negotiations followed, and Japan eventually agreed to an American consulate, promised good treatment to castaways, and permitted visits in certain ports for supplies and repairs. Broad commercial relations began after the first envoy, Townsend Harris, negotiated the Harris Convention of 1858, which opened five Japanese ports to American trade. Japan continued to ban emigration but found the law increasingly difficult to enforce, and by the 1880s the government abandoned efforts to prevent Japanese from seeking work abroad.

The Kansas-Nebraska Crisis

American commercial interests in Asia were in part responsible for the growing interest in constructing a transcontinental railroad line linking the eastern seaboard with the Pacific coast. But other powerful motives were at work as well. Railroad developers and land speculators also promoted this transportation link, as did slaveholders who were eager to expand the area open to slavery. During the 1850s the idea of building a transcontinental railroad, though a great national goal, spawned sectional rivalries in still another quarter and reopened the slavery issue.

DOUGLAS'S PROPOSAL In 1852 and 1853 Congress debated and dropped several likely proposals for the route of the rail line. For various reasons, including terrain, climate, and sectional interest, Secretary of War Jefferson Davis favored a southern route and encouraged what became known as the Gadsden Purchase, a barren stretch of land in present New Mexico and Arizona. In December 1853, at a cost of $10 million, the United States acquired the area from Mexico as a likely route for a Pacific railroad.

But midwestern spokesmen had other ideas concerning the path of the railroad. Since 1845, Illinois Senator Stephen A. Douglas and others had offered bills for a new territory in the lands west of Missouri and Iowa, bearing the Indian name Nebraska. In January 1854, as chairman of the committee on territories, Douglas put forward yet another Nebraska bill. Unlike the

Sen. Stephen A. Douglas (D-Ill.)

others this one included the entire unorganized portion of the Louisiana Purchase to the Canadian border. At this point fateful connections began to transform his proposal from a railroad bill to a proslavery bill. To carry his point Douglas needed the support of southerners, and to win that support he needed to make some concession on slavery in the new territories. This he did by writing popular sovereignty into the bill, allowing territories to decide the issue themselves.

It was a clever dodge, since the Missouri Compromise would still exclude slaves until the territorial government had made a decision, preventing slaveholders from getting established before a decision was reached. Southerners quickly spotted the barrier, and Douglas as quickly made two more concessions. He supported an amendment for repeal of the Missouri Compromise insofar as it excluded slavery north of 36°30', and then agreed to organize two territories, Kansas, west of Missouri; and Nebraska, west of Iowa and Minnesota.

Douglas's motives are unclear. Railroads were surely foremost in his mind, but he was influenced also by the desire to win support for his bill in the South, by the hope that popular sovereignty would quiet the slavery issue and open the Great Plains, or by a chance to split the Whigs. But he had blundered, thus damaging his presidential chances and setting his country on the road to civil war. He had failed to appreciate the depth of antislavery feelings. Douglas himself preferred that the territories become free. Their climate and geography excluded plantation agriculture, he reasoned, and he could not comprehend how people could get so wrought up over abstract rights. Yet he had in fact opened the possibility that slavery might gain a foothold in Kansas.

Douglas's move to repeal the Missouri Compromise was less than a week old before six antislavery congressmen published a protest, the "Appeal of the Independent Democrats." Their moral indignation quickly spread among those who opposed Douglas. Across the North editorials, sermons, speeches, and petitions denounced Douglas's bill as a conspiracy to extend slavery. What had been radical opinion was fast becoming the common view of people in the North. But Douglas had the votes and, once committed, forced the issue with tireless energy. President Pierce impulsively added his support, and the bill passed in May 1854 by 37 to 14 in the Senate and 113 to 100 in the House.

Very well, many in the North reasoned, if the Missouri Compromise was not a sacred pledge, then neither was the Fugitive Slave Act. On June 2, 1854, Boston witnessed the most dramatic demonstration against the act. After several attempts had failed to rescue a fugitive named Anthony Burns from being returned south, a force of soldiers and marines marched him to a waiting ship through streets lined with people shouting "Kidnappers!" past buildings draped in black, while church bells tolled across the city. Burns was the last fugitive slave to be returned from Boston, and was himself soon freed through purchase by Boston's black community.

THE EMERGENCE OF THE REPUBLICAN PARTY What John C. Calhoun had called the cords holding the Union together had already begun to part. The national church organizations of Baptists and Methodists, for instance, had split over slavery by 1845. The national parties, which had created mutual interests transcending sectional issues, were beginning to unravel under the strain. The Democrats managed to postpone disruption for yet a while, but their congressional delegation lost heavily in the North, enhancing the influence of the southern wing.

The strain of the Kansas-Nebraska Act, however, soon destroyed the Whig party. Southern Whigs now tended to abstain from voting while Northern Whigs moved toward two new parties. One was the new American (Know-Nothing) party, which had raised the banner of native Americanism and the hope of serving the patriotic cause of Union. More Northern Whigs joined with independent Democrats and Free Soilers in spontaneous antislavery coalitions with a confusing array of names,

including "anti-Nebraska," "Fusion," and "People's party."
These coalitions finally converged in 1854 on the name "Republican," evoking the memory of Jefferson.

"BLEEDING" KANSAS   After passage of the Kansas-Nebraska Act,
attention swung to the plains of Kansas, where opposing elements gathered to stage a rehearsal for civil war. All agreed that
Nebraska would be free, but Kansas soon exposed the potential
for mischief in Douglas's concept of popular sovereignty. The
ambiguity of the law, useful to Douglas in getting it passed, only
added to the chaos. The people of Kansas were "perfectly free to
form and regulate their domestic institutions in their own way,
subject only to the Constitution." That in itself was subject to
conflicting interpretations, but the law failed to specify the time
of decision, adding to each side's sense of urgency about getting
control of the territory.

The settlement of Kansas therefore differed from the usual pioneering efforts. Groups sprang up North and South to hurry
right-minded settlers westward. The first and best known was
the New England Emigrant Aid Society. Southern efforts of the
same kind centered in Missouri, a slave state, which was separated from Kansas only by a surveyor's line. When Kansas's first
governor arrived in October 1854, he found several thousand
settlers already in place. He ordered a census and scheduled an
election for a territorial legislature in March 1855. On election
day, several thousand "Border Ruffians" crossed over from Missouri, illegally cast proslavery votes, and pledged to kill every
"God-damned abolitionist in the Territory." The governor denounced the vote as a fraud, but did nothing to alter the results.
The new legislature expelled the few antislavery members,
adopted a drastic slave code, and made it a capital offense to aid a
fugitive slave.

Free-state advocates rejected this "bogus" government and
quickly formed their own. In October 1855 a constitutional convention, the product of an election of dubious legality, met in
Topeka, drafted a state constitution excluding both slavery and
free Negroes from Kansas, and applied for admission to the
Union. By March 1856 a free-state "governor" and "legislature"
were functioning in Topeka. Thus the territory had two illegal
governments vying for recognition and control. But the prospect
of getting any government to command general authority in
Kansas seemed dim, and both sides began to arm. Once armed
they began to fight. In May 1856, 700 proslavery thugs entered
the free-state town of Lawrence and smashed newspaper

THE KANSAS-NEBRASKA ACT, 1854

Free states and territories

Slave states

Open to slavery by popular sovereignty, Compromise of 1850

Open to slavery by popular sovereignty, Kansas-Nebraska Act, 1854

BLEEDING KANSAS

presses, set fire to the free-state governor's home, stole property, and destroyed the Free State Hotel.

The "sack of Lawrence" left just one casualty, but the incident aroused a fanatical Kansas free-soiler named John Brown, who had a history of mental instability. A companion described him as a man "impressed with the idea that God had raised him up on purpose to break the jaws of the wicked." Two days after the sack of Lawrence, Brown, the father of twenty children, set out with his four sons and three other men toward Pottawatomie Creek, site of a proslavery settlement, where they dragged five men from their houses and hacked them to death in front of their screaming wives and children, ostensibly as revenge for the deaths of free-state men.

The Pottawatomie Massacre (May 24–25, 1856) set off a running guerrilla war in the territory that lasted through the fall. On August 30, Missouri ruffians raided the free-state settlement at Ossawatomie. They looted the houses, burned them to the ground, and shot John Brown's son Frederick through the heart. The elder Brown, who barely escaped, looked back at the site being devastated by "Satan's legions," and muttered, "God sees it." He then swore to his surviving sons and followers: "I have only a short time to live—only one death to die, and I will die fighting for this cause." Altogether, by the end of 1856 Kansas lost about 200 killed and $2 million in property destroyed during the territorial civil war.

VIOLENCE IN THE SENATE   Violence in Kansas spilled over into the Congress itself. On May 22, 1856, the day after the sack of Lawrence and two days before Brown's Pottawatomie Massacre, a sudden flash of savagery on the Senate floor electrified the whole country. Just two days earlier Senator Charles Sumner of Massachusetts had finished an inflammatory speech in which he described the treatment of Kansas as "the rape of a virgin territory," and blamed it on the South's "depraved longing for a new slave State." Sumner made Senator Andrew P. Butler of South Carolina a special target of his censure. He charged that Butler was a liar and implied that he kept a slave mistress. Sumner also teased him about a speech impediment caused by a stroke.

Sumner's rudeness might well have backfired, had it not been for Preston S. Brooks, a fiery-tempered South Carolina congressman. For two days Brooks brooded over the insults to his uncle, Senator Butler. Knowing that Sumner would refuse a challenge to a duel, he finally confronted Sumner at his Senate desk on May 22, accused him of libel against South Carolina and Butler, and began beating him about the head with a cane while stunned senators, including Douglas, looked on. Sumner, struggling to rise, wrenched the desk from the floor and collapsed. "Towards the last he bellowed like a calf," a gloating Brooks reported. "I wore my cane out completely but saved the head which is gold."

Brooks had satisfied his rage but in the process had created a martyr for the antislavery cause. Like so many other men in those years, he betrayed the zealot's gift for snatching defeat from the jaws of victory. For two and a half years Sumner's empty seat was a solemn reminder of the violence done to him. Some thought the senator was feigning injury, others that he really was physically disabled. In fact, although his injuries were bad enough, including two gashes to the skull, he seems to have suffered psychosomatic shock that left him incapable of functioning adequately. When the House censured Brooks, he resigned, but was triumphantly reelected. His admirers showered him with new canes.

SECTIONAL POLITICS   Within the span of five days in May 1856 "Bleeding Kansas," "Bleeding Sumner," and "Bully Brooks" had set the tone for another presidential year. The major parties could no longer evade the slavery issue. Already in February it had split the hopeful American party wide open. Southern delegates, with help from New York, killed a resolution to restore the Missouri Compromise, and nominated Millard Fillmore for president. Later, what was left of the Whig party endorsed Fillmore as well.

At its first national convention the new Republican party followed the Whig tradition by seeking out a military hero, John C. Frémont, the "Pathfinder" and leader in the conquest of California. The Republican platform owed much to the Whigs too. It favored a transcontinental railroad and, in general, more internal improvements. It condemned the repeal of the Missouri Compromise and the Democratic policy of expansion. The campaign slogan echoed that of the Free Soilers: "Free soil, free speech, and Frémont." It was the first time a major party platform had taken a stand against slavery.

The Democrats, meeting two weeks earlier in June, had rejected Pierce, the hapless victim of so much turmoil. They also spurned Douglas because of the damage done by his Kansas-Nebraska Act. The party therefore turned to its old wheelhorse, James Buchanan of Pennsylvania, who had long sought the nomination. The platform endorsed the Kansas-Nebraska Act and urged Congress not to interfere with slavery in either states or territories. The party reached out to its newly acquired Irish and German Catholic voters by condemning nativism and endorsing religious liberty.

The campaign of 1856 resolved itself into two sectional campaigns. The "Black Republicans" had few southern supporters, and only a handful in the border states, where fears of disunion held many Whigs in line. Buchanan thus went to the country as the candidate of the only remaining national party. Frémont swept the northernmost states, with 114 electoral votes, but Buchanan added five free states to his southern majority for a total of 174.

Few presidents before Buchanan had a broader experience in politics and diplomacy. He had been over twenty years in Congress, minister to Russia and Britain, and Polk's secretary of state in between. His long quest for the presidency had been built on a southern alliance, and his political debts reinforced his belief that saving the Union depended on concessions to the South. Republicans belittled him as another "doughface" like Pierce, a northerner lacking the backbone to stand up to the southerners who dominated the Democratic majorities in Congress. His choice of four slave-state and only three free-state men for his cabinet seemed to them another bad omen.

THE DEEPENING SECTIONAL CRISIS

THE DRED SCOTT CASE   During Buchanan's first six months in office he encountered three crises in succession: the Dred Scott decision, new troubles in Kansas, and a business panic. On March 6, 1857, two days after the inauguration, the Supreme Court rendered a decision in the long-pending case of *Dred Scott v. Sandford*. Dred Scott, born a slave in Virginia about 1800, had been taken to St. Louis in 1830 and sold to an army surgeon, who took him as body servant to Illinois, then to the Wisconsin Territory (later Minnesota), and finally returned him to St. Louis in 1838. After his master's death in 1843 Scott apparently tried to buy his freedom. In 1846, with help from white abolitionist friends, he brought suit in Missouri courts claiming that residence in Illinois and Wisconsin Territory had made him free. A jury decided in his favor, reaffirming the widespread notion that "once free, forever free." But the state supreme court ruled against him, arguing that a slave state did not have to honor freedom granted to slaves by free states. When the case rose on ap-

Dred Scott (left) and Chief Justice Robert B. Taney (right). The Supreme Court's decision on Dred Scott's suit for freedom fanned the flames of discord.

peal to the Supreme Court, the country anxiously awaited its opinion on the issue of whether freedom once granted could be lost by returning to a slave state. Each of the eight justices filed a separate opinion, except one who concurred with Chief Justice Roger Taney. By different lines of reasoning seven justices ruled that Scott reverted to slave status upon his return to Missouri. The aging Taney ruled that Scott lacked standing in court because he lacked citizenship. At the time the Constitution was adopted, Taney added, Negroes "had for more than a century been regarded as . . . so far inferior, that they had no rights which the white man was bound to respect."

To further clarify the definition of Scott's status, Taney moved to a second major question. He argued that the Missouri Compromise, by ruling that certain new territories were to exclude slaves, had deprived citizens of property in slaves, an action "not warranted by the constitution." The Supreme Court had declared an act of Congress unconstitutional for the first time since *Marbury v. Madison* (1803). Congress had repealed the Missouri Compromise in the Kansas-Nebraska Act three years earlier, but the decision now challenged the concept of popular sovereignty. If Congress itself could not exclude slavery from a territory, then presumably neither could a territorial government created by act of Congress.

Proslavery elements, of course, greeted the court's opinion with glee. But many northerners denounced Taney's ruling. Little wonder that Republicans protested: the Court had declared their free-soil program unconstitutional. It had also reinforced the suspicion that the slavocracy was hatching a conspiracy. Were not all but one of the justices who joined Taney southerners? And had not Buchanan chatted with the chief justice at the inauguration and then urged the people to accept the early decision as a final settlement, "Whatever this may be?"

And what of Dred Scott? Ironically, his owner, now a widow, married a prominent Massachusetts abolitionist, who saw to it that the slave and his family were freed in 1857. A year later Scott died of tuberculosis.

THE LECOMPTON CONSTITUTION   Out in Kansas, meanwhile, the struggle continued through 1857. The contested politics in the territory now resulted in an antislavery legislature and a proslavery constitutional convention. The convention, meeting at Lecompton, drew up a constitution under which Kansas would become a slave state. A referendum on the document was set for December 21, 1857, with rules and officials chosen by the convention.

Although Kansas had only about 200 slaves at the time, free-state men boycotted the election, claiming that it too was rigged. At this point President Buchanan took a fateful step. Influenced by southern advisers and politically dependent upon southern congressmen, he decided to support the action of the proslavery Lecompton Convention. The election went according to form: 6,226 votes for the constitution with slavery, 569 for the constitution without slavery. Meanwhile, the acting governor had convened the antislavery legislature, which called for another election to vote the Lecompton Constitution up or down. The result on January 4, 1858, was overwhelming: 10,226 against the constitution, 138 for the constitution with slavery, 24 for the constitution without slavery.

The combined results suggested a clear majority against slavery, but Buchanan stuck to his support of the Lecompton Constitution, driving another wedge into the Democratic party. Senator Douglas, up for reelection, could not afford to run as a champion of Lecompton. He broke dramatically with the president in a tense confrontation, but Buchanan persisted in trying to drive Lecompton "naked" through the Congress. In the Senate, administration forces held firm, and in March 1858 Lecompton was passed. In the House, enough anti-Lecompton Democrats combined to put through an amendment for a new and carefully supervised popular vote in Kansas. Enough senators went along to pass the House bill. Southerners were confident the vote would favor slavery, because to reject slavery the voters would have to reject the constitution, which would postpone statehood until the population reached 90,000. On August 2, 1858, Kansas voters nevertheless rejected Lecompton by 11,300 to 1,788. With that vote Kansas, now firmly in the hands of its antislavery legislature, largely ended its role in the sectional controversy.

THE PANIC OF 1857   The third crisis of Buchanan's first half-year in office, a financial panic, broke in August 1857. It was brought on by a reduction in Europe's demand for American grain, a surge in manufacturing which outran the growth of markets, and the continued weakness and confusion of the state banknote system. Failure of the Ohio Life Insurance and Trust Company precipitated the panic, which brought on a depression from which the country did not emerge until 1859.

Everything in those years seemed to get drawn into the vortex of sectional conflict, and business troubles were no exception. Northern businessmen tended to blame the depression on the Democratic Tariff of 1857, which had put rates at their lowest level since 1816. The agricultural South weathered the crisis better than the North. Cotton prices fell, but slowly, and world markets for cotton quickly recovered. The result was an exalted notion of King Cotton's importance to the world, and apparent confirmation of the growing argument that the southern system was superior to the free-labor system of the North.

DOUGLAS VS. LINCOLN Amid the recriminations over Dred Scott, Kansas, and the depression, the center could not hold. The Lecompton battle put severe strains on the most substantial cord of Union left, the Democratic party. To many, Douglas seemed the best hope, one of the few remaining Democratic leaders with support in both sections. But now Douglas was being whipsawed between the extremes. Kansas-Nebraska had cast him in the role of "doughface." His opposition to Lecompton, the fraudulent fruit of popular sovereignty, however, had alienated him from Buchanan's southern junta. But for all his flexibility and opportunism, Douglas had convinced himself that popular sovereignty was a point of principle, a bulwark of democracy and local self-government. In 1858 he faced reelection to the Senate against the opposition of both Buchanan Democrats and Republicans. The year 1860 would give him a chance for the presidency, but first he had to secure his home base in Illinois.

To oppose him, Illinois Republicans named Abraham Lincoln of Springfield, the lanky, raw-boned former Whig state legislator and one-term congressman, a moderately prosperous small-town lawyer. Lincoln's early life had been the hardscrabble existence of the frontier farm. Born in a Kentucky log cabin in 1809, raised on frontier farms in Indiana and Illinois, the young Lincoln had the wit and will to rise above his coarse beginnings. With less than twelve months of sporadic schooling he learned to read, studied such books as came to hand, and eventually developed a prose style as lean and muscular as the man himself. He worked at various farm tasks, operated a ferry, and made two trips down to New Orleans as a flatboatman. Striking out on his own, he managed a general store in New Salem, Illinois, learned surveying, served in the Black Hawk War (1832), won election to the legislature in 1834 at the age of twenty-five, read law, and was admitted to the bar in 1836. As a Whig regular, he adhered to the economic philosophy of Henry Clay. He stayed in the legislature until 1842, and in 1846 won a term in Congress. After a single term he retired from active politics to cultivate his law practice.

In 1854 the Kansas-Nebraska debate drew Lincoln back into the political arena. At first he held back from the rapidly growing Republican party, but in 1856 he joined them, getting over 100 votes for their vice-presidential nomination. By 1858 he was the obvious Republican choice to oppose Douglas himself for the Senate, and Douglas knew he was up against a formidable foe. Lincoln resorted to the classic ploy of the underdog: he challenged the favorite to a debate. Douglas had little relish for drawing attention to his opponent, but agreed to meet him in seven sites around the state. The legendary Lincoln-Douglas debates took place that fall.

The two men could not have presented a more striking contrast in appearance. Lincoln was well over six feet tall, sinewy, and craggy-featured, with a singularly long neck, and deep-set, brooding, even melancholy eyes. A fellow lawyer described him as "the ungodliest figure I ever saw." Unassuming in manner, dressed in homely, well-worn clothes and walking with a shambling gait, he lightened his essentially serious demeanor with a refreshing sense of humor. To sympathetic observers he conveyed an air of simplicity, sincerity, and common sense. Douglas, on the other hand, was short, rotund, bulb-nosed, stern, and cocky, attired in the finest custom-tailored suits and possessed of supreme self-confidence. A man of considerable abilities and even greater ambition, he strutted to the platform with the pugnacious air of a predestined champion.

At the time and since, much attention focused on the second debate, at Freeport, where Lincoln asked Douglas how he could reconcile popular sovereignty with the Dred Scott ruling that citizens had the right to carry slaves into any territory. Douglas's answer, thenceforth known as the Freeport Doctrine, was to state the obvious. Whatever the Supreme Court might say about slavery, it could not exist anywhere unless supported by local police regulations. Thus, if settlers did not want slavery, they simply should refuse to adopt a local code protecting it.

Douglas then tried to set some traps of his own. He sought to pin on Lincoln the stigma of advocating racial equality. Lincoln handled the volatile question with caution. There was, he asserted, a "physical difference between the white and black races," and it would "forever forbid the two races living together on terms of social and political equality." He simply favored the containment of slavery where it existed so that "the public mind shall rest in the belief that it is in the course of ultimate extinction." But the basic difference between the two men, Lincoln insisted, lay in Douglas's professed indifference to the moral question of slavery.

If Lincoln had the better of the argument, at least in the long view, Douglas had the better of the election, which he won on a vote by the Illinois legislature. Across the nation the elections recorded one loss after another for Buchanan Democrats. The administration had lost control of the House.

JOHN BROWN'S RAID The gradual return of prosperity in 1859 offered hope that the political storms of the 1850s might yet pass. But the sectional issue still haunted the public mind, and like sheet lightning on the horizon, it warned that a storm was still brewing. In October 1859 John Brown once again surfaced, this time in the East. Since the Pottawatomie Massacre in 1856 he had led a furtive existence, engaging in fundraising, recruiting, and occasional bushwhacking. His commitment to abolish the "wicked curse of slavery," meanwhile, had intensified to a fever pitch.

Finally, on October 16, 1859, Brown was ready for his supreme gesture. From a Maryland farm he crossed the Potomac with nineteen men, including five blacks, and occupied the federal arsenal in Harper's Ferry, Virginia (now West Virginia). He apparently intended to arm the Maryland slaves he assumed would flock to his cause, set up a black stronghold in the mountains of western Virginia, and provide a nucleus of support for slave insurrections across the South.

What Brown actually did was to take the arsenal by surprise, seize a few hostages, and hole up in the fire-engine house. There

John Brown.

he and his band were quickly surrounded by militiamen and town residents. The next morning Brown sent his son Watson and another supporter out under a white flag, but the enraged crowd shot them both. Intermittent shooting then broke out, and another Brown son was wounded. He begged his father to kill him and end his suffering, but the righteous Brown, befuddled and distraught by the unexpected collapse of his glorious insurrection, lashed out: "If you must die, die like a man." A few minutes later the son was dead.

That night Lieutenant-Colonel Robert E. Lee, U.S. Cavalry, arrived with his aide, Lieutenant J. E. B. Stuart, and a force of marines. The following morning, on October 18, Stuart and his troops broke down the barricaded doors and rushed into the fire-engine room. A young lieutenant found Brown kneeling with his rifle cocked, but before the pious patriarch could fire, the marine used the hilt of his sword to beat Brown unconscious. By then the siege was over. Altogether Brown's men killed four people (including one marine) and wounded nine. Of their own force, ten died (including two of Brown's sons), five escaped, and seven were captured.

Brown was quickly tried for treason, convicted on October 31, and sentenced to be hanged on December 2, 1859. "Let them hang me," Brown exulted. "I am worth inconceivably more to hang than for any other purpose." He was never more right. If Brown had failed in his purpose—whatever it was—he had become a martyr for the antislavery cause, and he had set off panic throughout the slaveholding South. At his sentencing he delivered one of the classic American speeches: "Now, if it is deemed necessary that I should forfeit my life for the furtherance of the ends of justice, and mingle my blood further with the blood of my children and with the blood of millions in this slave country whose rights are disregarded by wicked, cruel, and unjust enactments, I say, let it be done."

When Brown, still unflinching, met his end, northern sympathizers held solemn observances. Prominent Republicans, including Lincoln and Seward, repudiated Brown's attempted coup, but the discovery of Brown's correspondence revealed that he had enjoyed support among prominent antislavery leaders who defended his deeds. "That new saint," Emerson predicted, ". . . will make the gallows glorious as the Cross." Garrison, the lifelong pacifist, now wished "success to every slave insurrection at the South and in every slave country."

By far the gravest aftereffect of Brown's raid was to leave southerners in no mood to distinguish between John Brown and the Republican party. Southern defenders of the status quo now merged those who would contain slavery with those who would drown it in blood. All through the fall and winter of 1859–1860 rumors of conspiracy and insurrection swept the region. Every northern visitor, commercial traveler, or schoolteacher came under suspicion, and many were driven out. "We regard every man in our midst an enemy to the institutions of the South," said an Atlanta editor, "who does not boldly declare that he believes African slavery to be a social, moral, and political blessing."

THE CENTER COMES APART

THE DEMOCRATS DIVIDE Amid emotional hysteria the nation approached a presidential election destined to be the most fateful in its history. The Democrats had settled on Charleston, South Carolina, as the site for their 1860 convention. Charleston in April, with the azaleas and dogwoods ablaze, was perhaps the most enticing city in the United States, but the worst conceivable place for such a meeting, except perhaps Boston. It was a hotbed of extremist sentiment, and the port city lacked adequate accommodations. South Carolina itself had chosen a remarkably moderate delegation, but the extreme southern-rights men held the upper hand in the delegations from the Gulf states.

Douglas supporters preferred to stand by the platform of 1856, which simply promised congressional noninterference with slavery. Southern firebrands, however, now demanded a federal code protecting slavery in the territories. Buchanan supporters, hoping to stop Douglas, encouraged the strategy. The platform debate reached a heady climax when the Alabama fire-eater William L. Yancey informed the northern Democrats that they had erred by failing to defend slavery as a positive good. An Ohio senator offered a blunt reply: "Gentlemen of the South," he declared, "you mistake us—you mistake us. We will not do it."

When the southern planks lost, Alabama's delegation walked out of the convention, followed by the other Gulf states, Georgia, South Carolina, and parts of the delegations from Arkansas and Delaware. The convention then decided to leave the overwrought atmosphere of Charleston and reassemble in Baltimore on June 18. The Baltimore convention finally nominated Douglas on the 1856 platform. The Charleston seceders met first in Richmond, then in Baltimore, where they adopted the slave-code platform defeated in Charleston, and named Vice-President John C. Breckinridge of Kentucky for president. Another cord of union had snapped: the last remaining national party.

LINCOLN'S ELECTION   The Republicans meanwhile gathered in Chicago, where everything suddenly came together for "Honest Abe" Lincoln, "the Railsplitter," the uncommon common man. Lincoln had suddenly emerged in the national view during his senatorial campaign two years before and had since taken a stance designed to make him available for the nomination. He was strong enough on the containment of slavery to satisfy the abolitionists, yet moderate enough to seem less threatening than they were.

Lincoln won the Republican nomination on the third ballot. The party platform foreshadowed future policy better than most. It denounced John Brown's raid as "among the gravest of crimes," and affirmed that each state should "order and control its own domestic institutions." The party repeated its resistance to the extension of slavery, and in an effort to gain broader support, endorsed a higher protective tariff for manufacturers, free homesteads for farmers, and internal improvements, including a Pacific railroad. With this platform Republicans made a strong appeal to eastern businessmen, western farmers, and the large immigrant population.

Both major conventions revealed that opinion tended to become more radical in the upper North and deep South. Attitude

Abraham Lincoln, Republican candidate for president, June, 1860.

seemed to follow latitude. In the border states a sense of moderation aroused the diehard Whigs there to make one more try at reconciliation. Meeting in Baltimore a week before the Republicans met in Chicago, they reorganized into the Constitutional Union party and named John Bell of Tennessee for president. Their platform simply called for the preservation of the Constitution and the Union.

Of the four candidates not one was able to command a national following, and the campaign resolved into a choice between Lincoln and Douglas in the North, Breckinridge and Bell in the South. One consequence of these separate campaigns was that each section gained a false impression of the other. The South never learned to distinguish Lincoln from the radicals; the North failed to gauge the force of southern intransigence—and in this Lincoln was among the worst. He stubbornly refused to offer the South assurances or to explain his position on slavery, which he insisted was a matter of public record. The one man who tried to break through the veil that was falling between the sections was Douglas, who tried to mount a national campaign. Only forty-seven, but already weakened by excessive drink, ill-health, and disappointments, he wore himself out in one final glorious campaign. Down through the hostile areas of Tennessee, Georgia, and Alabama he carried appeals on behalf of the Union. "I do not believe that every Breckinridge man is a disunionist," he said, "but I do believe that every disunionist is a Breckinridge man."

By midnight of November 6, however, Lincoln's victory was clear. In the final count he had about 39 percent of the total popular vote, but a clear majority with 180 votes in the electoral college. He carried all eighteen free states by a wide margin. Among all the candidates, only Douglas had electoral votes from both slave and free states, but his total of 12 was but a pitiful remnant of Democratic Unionism. He ran last. Bell took Virginia, Kentucky, and Tennessee, and Breckinridge swept the other slave states to come in second with 72.

SECESSION OF THE DEEP SOUTH   Soon after the election the South Carolina legislature, which had assembled to choose the state's electors, set a special election for December 6 to choose delegates to a convention. In Charleston on December 20, 1860, the convention unanimously voted an Ordinance of Secession, declaring the state's ratification of the Constitution repealed and the union with other states dissolved. By February 1, 1861, six more states had declared themselves out of the Union. On February 4, a convention of those seven states met in Montgomery, Alabama, and on February 7, they adopted a provisional constitution for the Confederate States of America. Two days later they elected Jefferson Davis its president. He was inaugurated February 18, with Alexander Stephens of Georgia as vice-president.

In all seven states of the southernmost tier a solid majority had voted for secessionist convention delegates, but their combined vote would not have been a majority of the presidential vote in November. What happened, it seemed, was what often happens in revolutionary situations: a determined and decisive minority acted quickly in an emotionally charged climate and carried its program against a confused and indecisive opposition. Trying to decide if a majority of southern whites actually favored secession probably is beside the point—a majority were vulnerable to the decisive action of the secessionists.

Southern Unionists lamented this situation, noting that the "fire-eaters" rather than true statesmen were in control. "Webster and Clay are gone," mourned one Louisianan, "and God has given us over to fools and mad men." Others predicted that secession, instead of conserving traditional southern society, would in fact accelerate its demise. Alexander Stephens had warned in 1860: "Revolutions are much easier started than controlled, and the men who begin them, even for the best purposes and objects, seldom end them."

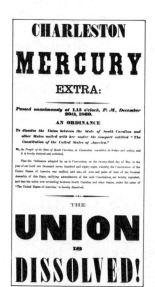

A handbill announcing South Carolina's secession from the Union.

BUCHANAN'S WAITING GAME   History is full of might-have-beens. A bold stroke, even a bold statement, by the lame-duck president at this point might have defused the crisis, but there was no Jacksonian will in Buchanan. As Ulysses S. Grant recognized, Buchanan was a "granny of an Executive." Besides, a bold stroke might simply have hastened the conflict. No bold stroke came from Lincoln either, nor would he consult with the administration during the long months before his inauguration on March 4, 1861. He inclined all too strongly to the belief that secession was just another bluff, and kept his public silence. Buchanan followed his natural bent, the policy on which he had built a career: make concessions, seek a compromise to mollify the South. In his annual message on December 3, 1860, Buchanan made a forthright argument that secession was illegal, but that he lacked authority to coerce a state. "Seldom have we known so strong an argument come to so lame and impotent a conclusion," the *Cincinnati Enquirer* editorialized. There was, however, a hidden weapon in the president's reaffirmation of a duty to "take care that the laws be faithfully executed" insofar as he was able. If the president could enforce the law upon all citizens, he would have no need to "coerce" a state. Indeed Buchanan's position became the policy of the Lincoln administration, which fought a war on the theory that individuals but not states as such were in rebellion.

Buchanan held firmly to his resolve, with some slight stiffening by the end of December 1860, when secession became a fact, but he refused to assert federal power provocatively. On the day after Christmas the small garrison at Charleston's Fort Moultrie had been moved into the nearly completed Fort Sumter by Major Robert Anderson, a Kentucky Unionist. Anderson's move, designed to achieve both disengagement and greater security, struck South Carolina authorities as provocative, a violation of an earlier "gentleman's agreement" that the administration would make no changes in its arrangements. Commissioners of the newly "independent" state peremptorily demanded withdrawal of all federal forces, but they had overplayed their hand. Buchanan's cabinet, with only one southerner left, insisted it would be a gross violation of duty, perhaps grounds for impeachment, for the president to yield. His backbone thus stiffened, he sharply rejected the South Carolina ultimatum to withdraw: "This I cannot do: This I will not do." His nearest approach to coercion was to dispatch a steamer, *Star of the West*, to Fort Sumter with reinforcements and provisions. As the ship approached Charleston Harbor, Carolina batteries at Fort Moultrie and

Morris Island opened fire and drove it away on January 9. It was in fact an act of war, but Buchanan chose to ignore the challenge. He decided instead to hunker down and ride out the remaining weeks of his term, hoping against hope that one of several compromise efforts would yet prove fruitful.

LAST EFFORTS AT COMPROMISE   Forlorn efforts at compromise continued in Congress until dawn of Lincoln's inauguration day. On December 18 Sen. John J. Crittenden of Kentucky had proposed a series of resolutions which recognized slavery in the territories south of 36° 30' and guaranteed to maintain slavery where it already existed. The fight for a compromise was carried to the floor of each house, and subjected to intensive but inconclusive debate during January and February.

Meanwhile a Peace Conference met in a Washington hotel in February 1861. Twenty-one states sent delegates and former president John Tyler presided, but the convention's proposal, substantially the same as the Crittenden Compromise, failed to win the support of either house of Congress. The only compromise proposal that met with any success was a constitutional amendment to guarantee slavery where it existed. Many Republicans, including Lincoln, were prepared to go that far to save the Union, but they were unwilling to repudiate their stand against slavery in the territories. As it happened, after passing the House the amendment passed the Senate without a vote to spare, by 24 to 12, on the dawn of inauguration day. It would have become the Thirteenth Amendment, with the first use of the word "slavery" in the Constitution, but the states never ratified it. When a Thirteenth Amendment was ratified in 1865, it did not guarantee slavery—it abolished slavery.

Further Reading

Surveys of the coming of the Civil War include Allan Nevins's *Ordeal of the Union* (2 vols., 1947); David M. Potter's *The Impending Crisis, 1848–1861* (1976)°; and James M. McPherson's *Battle Cry of Freedom: The Civil War Era* (1989).° Interpretive essays can be studied in Eric Foner's *Politics and Ideology in the Age of the Civil War* (1980)° and Joel H. Silbey's *The Partisan Imperative* (1987).°

Numerous works discuss the political crises of the 1850s. Holman Hamilton's *Prologue to Conflict: The Crisis and Compromise of 1850*

° These books are available in paperback editions.

(1964) probes that crucial dispute. Michael F. Holt's *The Political Crisis of the 1850s* (1978)° traces the demise of the Whigs. Kenneth Stampp's *America in 1857* (1990) examines in detail that crucial year. Eric Foner provides an excellent introduction to how events and ideas combined in the formation of a new political party in *Free Soil, Free Labor, Free Men: The Ideology of the Republican Party before the Civil War* (1970).° The best study of the Republican party is William E. Gienapp's *The Origins of the Republican Party, 1852–1856* (1988).°

On the issue of popular sovereignty, see James A. Rawley's *Race and Politics: "Bleeding Kansas" and the Coming of the Civil War* (1969). For an excellent analysis of the critical Dred Scot case, see Don E. Fehrenbacher's *Slavery, Law, and Politics* (1981).° The growing alienation of southerners from national trends is explored in William Freehling's *The Road to Disunion* (1990).

Harry V. Jaffa's *Crisis of the House Divided* (1959)° details the Lincoln–Douglas debates, and Richard N. Current's *Lincoln and the First Shot* (1963)° treats the Fort Sumter controversy.

16

THE WAR OF THE UNION

An Epic Struggle

Shrouded in an ever-thickening mist of gallant images and larger-than-life mythology, the Union triumph in the Civil War has acquired the mantle of inevitability. The North was destined to win, was it not? The Confederacy's fight for independence, on the other hand, has taken on the aura of a romantic lost cause, doomed from the start by the region's sparse industrial development, smaller pool of able-bodied men, paucity of capital resources and warships, and spotty transportation network. But in 1861 the military situation was by no means so clear-cut. For all of the South's obvious disadvantages, it initially enjoyed a captive labor force, superior officers, the prospects of foreign assistance, and the benefits of fighting a defensive campaign on familiar territory. Jefferson Davis and other Confederate leaders were genuinely confident that their cause would prevail on the battlefields. It is important to remember that this epochal event was endowed from the start not with inevitability but with uncertainty, and its outcome was decided as much by human decisions and human willpower as by physical resources.

END OF THE WAITING GAME   In his inaugural address on March 4, 1861, Lincoln reassured southerners that he had no intention of interfering with "slavery in the States where it exists." But secession was another matter. He insisted that the "Union of these States is perpetual," and he promised to hold areas belonging to the government. Still, he pledged that the federal government would use force only if attacked.

But the momentum of secession took control of events. The

day after the inauguration word arrived from Charleston that time was running out for the federal garrison at Fort Sumter. The commander, Major Robert Anderson, a Kentuckian with a Georgian wife, had enough supplies for only a month, and the fort was being surrounded by a Confederate "ring of fire." On April 4, 1861, Lincoln decided to resupply Anderson's garrison. A week later the dashing Confederate General Pierre G. T. Beauregard, who had taught artillery to Anderson at West Point, demanded that his former student surrender Sumter. Anderson refused, and just before dawn on April 12, Confederate batteries began shelling the fort. After more than thirty hours, Anderson, his ammunition exhausted, surrendered.

The guns of Charleston thus signaled the end of the tense waiting game. On April 15 Lincoln called upon the loyal states to supply 75,000 militiamen. Volunteers in both the North and the South soon crowded recruiting stations, and huge new armies began to take shape. On April 19 Lincoln proclaimed a blockade of southern ports which, as the Supreme Court later ruled, confirmed the existence of a state of war.

TAKING SIDES   Lincoln's proclamation led four upper South states to join the Confederacy—Virginia, Arkansas, Tennessee, and North Carolina. Each had areas (mainly in the mountains) where both slaves and secessionists were scarce and where Union sentiment ran strong. In fact, Unionists in western Virginia, bolstered by a Union army from Ohio under General George B. McClellan, formed a new state. In 1863 Congress admitted West Virginia with a state constitution that provided for emancipation of the few slaves there.

Of the other slave states, Delaware remained firmly in the Union, but Maryland, Kentucky, and Missouri went through bitter struggles for control. The secession of Maryland posed a special threat, since it would have encircled Washington with Confederate states. To hold the state Lincoln took drastic measures: he suspended the writ of habeas corpus (under which judges could require arresting officers to produce their prisoners and justify their arrest) and jailed pro-Confederate leaders. The fall elections ended the threat of Maryland's secession by returning a solidly Unionist majority in the state.

Kentucky, native state of both Lincoln and Jefferson Davis, was torn by divided loyalties. The state legislature proclaimed its "neutrality" in the conflict, but that only lasted until September 3, 1861, when a Confederate force captured several towns. General Ulysses S. Grant then moved troops into Paducah. Thereaf-

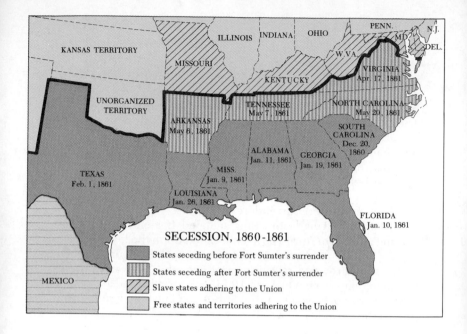

SECESSION, 1860-1861

- ◼ States seceding before Fort Sumter's surrender
- ◫ States seceding after Fort Sumter's surrender
- ◿ Slave states adhering to the Union
- ◻ Free states and territories adhering to the Union

ter, Kentucky for the most part remained with the Union. It joined the Confederacy, some have said, only after the war.

In Missouri, Unionists had a numerical advantage, but secessionist sympathies were strong and a Confederate militia began to gather near St. Louis. On May 10, 1861, Unionist forces surprised and disarmed the militia at its camp. They finally broke the back of Confederate resistance in Missouri at the battle of Pea Ridge (March 6–8, 1862), just over the state line in Arkansas. Nevertheless, border warfare continued in Missouri, pitting rival bands of gunslingers who kept up the feuding and banditry for years after the war ended.

Robert E. Lee epitomized the agonizing choice facing many border-state residents. Son of "Light-horse Harry" Lee, a Revolutionary War hero, and married to a descendant of Martha Washington, Lee had graduated second in his class from West Point and had served in the United States Army for thirty years. Now a colonel and master of Arlington, an elegant estate facing Washington across the Potomac, he was summoned by Lincoln's seventy-five-year-old general-in-chief, Winfield Scott, another Virginian, and offered command of the new Federal forces. After a sleepless night pacing the floor, he told Scott he could not go against his "country," meaning Virginia. Although Lee failed to "see the good of secession," he could not "raise my hand against my birthplace, my home, my children." Lee resigned his commission, retired to his estate, and soon answered a call to the Virginia—later the Confederate—service.

BULL RUN   The actual outbreak of war injected a sudden urgency of meaning into the commonplace routine of everyday life. Visions of gallantry flashed through young minds as they eagerly left farms, factories, shops, and families to don blue or gray. Caught up in the frothy excitement of military preparation, neither side recognized how deadly earnest the other was; both predicted an easy and quick victory.

Nowhere was this naive optimism more clearly displayed than at the first battle at Bull Run. An impatient public pressured both Lincoln and Davis to strike quickly and decisively. Davis responded by allowing the battle-hungry General Beauregard to hurry his main forces in Virginia to Manassas Junction, about twenty-five miles west of Washington. Lincoln decided that General Irvin McDowell's hastily assembled army of some 30,000 might overrun the outnumbered Confederates and quickly march on to Richmond, the Confederate capital. With buoyant assumptions of victory, Johnny Reb and Billy Yank thus breezily stumbled into an entangling web of horror. The mood was so breezy in fact that hundreds of civilians rode out from Washington to picnic and watch the entertaining spectacle of a one-battle war.

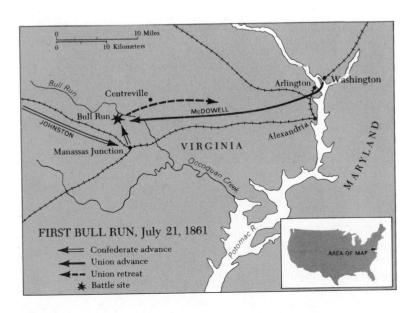

FIRST BULL RUN, July 21, 1861

◄═══ Confederate advance
◄─── Union advance
◄--- Union retreat
★ Battle site

It was a dry summer day on July 21, 1861, when McDowell's forces encountered Beauregard's army dug in behind a meandering, log-strewn little stream called Bull Run. The two generals, who had been classmates at West Point, adopted markedly similar plans—each would try to turn the other's left flank. The Federals almost achieved their purpose early in the afternoon, but reinforcements led by General Joseph E. Johnston poured in to check the Union offensive. Amid the fury, a South Carolina general rallied his men by pointing to Thomas Jackson's brigade of Virginians: "Look at Jackson standing there like a damned stone wall." It was true, and Jackson was called "Stonewall" thereafter.

Their attack blunted, the exhausted northern troops eventually broke, and their confused and frantic retreat turned into a panic as fleeing soldiers and terrified civilians clogged the Washington road. Lincoln read a gloomy dispatch from the front: "The day is lost. Save Washington and the remnants of this army. The routed troops will not re-form." Fortunately for the Federals, the Confederates were about as disorganized and demoralized by victory as the Yankees were by defeat, and they failed to give chase. It would have been futile anyway, for the next day a summer downpour turned roads into quagmires.

A MODERN WAR

Bull Run was a sobering experience for both sides. Much of the romance—the splendid uniforms, bright flags, fervent songs —gave way to the agonizing realization that this would be a long, mean, and costly struggle in which many—far too many— would die. *Harper's Weekly* bluntly warned: "From the fearful day at Bull Run dates war. Not polite war . . . but war that breaks hearts and blights homes." The sobering defeat "will teach us in the first place . . . that this war must be prosecuted on scientific principles."

Indeed, the Civil War was thereafter conducted on "scientific" principles. It was in many respects the first modern war. First of all, its scope was tremendous. One out of every twelve adult American males served in the war, and few families were unaffected by the event. Over 630,000 men were killed or died of disease, more than in all other American wars combined. Almost any stomach or head wound proved fatal, and gangrene was rampant. Of the survivors, 50,000 returned home with one or more limbs amputated. The Civil War was not tidy and self-contained; it was a total war, fought not solely by professional armies but by and against whole societies. As Nathaniel Hawthorne recognized in 1862, "There is no remoteness of life and thought, no hermetically sealed seclusion, except, possibly, that of the grave, into which the disturbing influences of this war do not penetrate."

THE REALITY OF MODERN WAR The Civil War was also a modern war in the sense that much of the killing was distant, impersonal, and mechanical. Hand-to-hand combat was the exception rather than the rule. The increasing use of rifled cannons and muskets meant that the carnage occurred mostly at long distance rather than face to face. Either attacking infantrymen were decimated by minie balls or grape shot, or the defenders simply broke and ran. One general observed that the glittering bayonets were "rarely reddened with blood. The day of the bayonet is passed." Combatants armed with rifles frequently never got close enough to see each other. As a participant in the ferocious Union assault on Port Hudson in 1864 remembered, "Many men in the regiment never laid eyes on a Rebel during the whole action."

The Civil War was thus greatly affected by industrial and scientific developments. This first of modern wars brought into use devices and techniques never before used on such a scale:

Civil War firearms. *The Spencer repeating carbine (top), with its continuous firing capability, brought a new technology to war.*

railroad transport, rifled artillery, repeating rifles, ironclad ships, the telegraph, observation balloons, the Gatling gun (a rudimentary machine-gun), trenches, and wire entanglements.

WOMEN AND THE WAR   The Civil War was also modern in that its impact penetrated well behind the front lines. While men fought and suffered, women worked, sorrowed, and sacrificed. A Mississippi woman saw her husband and all five sons join the Confederate army at the same time. A North Carolina mother lost seven sons in the fighting; another lost four, all at Gettysburg. The colossal carnage created a generation of widows, spinsters, and wives of disabled husbands. Women who suffered such grieving losses or who witnessed death on a horrifying scale while serving as nurses were permanently altered by the experience. So, too, were those who had to take over the duties of men gone off to war. The circumstances of war thrust women into new public roles during the conflict. Women became farmers or plantation managers, clerks, munitions plant workers, and schoolteachers. Said one Georgia woman whose husband was killed in 1863, leaving her to direct three plantations and over a hundred slaves alone, "this cruel war imposes strange duties on us all." She added, however, that "I am willing to stand my lot."

Julia Ward Howe, the women's suffrage activist who composed the "Battle Hymn of the Republic," later observed that many women who were transformed by the war experience in one way or another refused to revert to their "chimney corner life of the fifties." Clara Barton, the tireless nurse, likewise saw in the Civil War an opportunity to end her desperate search for "something to do that *was* something." She claimed that the Civil War accelerated by fifty years the involvement of women in traditionally male vocations. This was saying too much, for after the conflict ended most women reverted to their traditional domestic roles, but many did not or could not, and as such the war did mark a significant change in women's status.

THE DRAFT   As the war gained momentum, each side eventually found it necessary to institute a draft in order to replenish the devastated ranks. The Confederates adopted conscription first. By an act of April 16, 1862, all male white citizens, aged eighteen to thirty-five, were declared members of the Confederate army for three years. Five months later the upper age was raised to forty-five, and in 1864 the limits were further extended to cover all from seventeen to fifty. One could escape the draft by providing a substitute not of draft age or by paying $500. Those with key civilian jobs were also given exemptions. That planters with twenty or more slaves were also exempted led to bitter complaints in the South about "a rich man's war and a poor man's fight."

The North did not mandate a draft until March 1863, when men aged twenty to forty-five were conscripted. As in the South, those unwilling to serve could find substitutes or pay a fee of $300. Eventually the draft in the North produced 46,000 conscripts and 116,000 substitutes, or about 6 percent of the Union armies.

Widespread opposition limited enforcement of the draft acts in both North and South. In New York City draft riots erupted in July 1863, and angry mobs focused their resentment on blacks, lynching Negroes and burning a Negro orphanage. Seventy-four persons were killed and $2 million in property destroyed before soldiers recalled from Gettysburg could restore order.

THE WAR'S EARLY COURSE

The battle of Bull Run demonstrated that the war would not be decided with one sudden stroke. General Winfield Scott, the crusty veteran, had predicted as much, and now Lincoln fell back upon the three-pronged strategy which Scott had long before proposed. It called first for the Army of the Potomac to defend Washington and exert constant pressure on the Confederate capital at Richmond. At the same time, the navy would blockade the southern coast and thereby dry up the Confederacy's access to foreign goods and weapons. The final component of the plan was intended to divide the Confederacy by invading along the main water routes: the Mississippi, Tennessee, and Cumberland Rivers. This so-called Anaconda strategy would slowly entwine and crush the southern resistance.

The Confederate strategy was simpler. If the Union forces could be stalemated, Davis and others hoped, then the British or French might be convinced to join their cause, or perhaps public sentiment in the North would force Lincoln to seek a negotiated settlement. So, at the same time that armies were forming in the South, Confederate diplomats were seeking assistance in London and Paris, and Confederate sympathizers in the North were urging an end to the North's war effort.

NAVAL ACTIONS   After Bull Run and for the rest of 1861 and early 1862 the most important military actions involved naval war and blockade. The one great threat to the Union navy proved to be short-lived. The Confederates in Norfolk had fashioned an iron-clad ship from an abandoned Union steam frigate, the *Merrimack*. Rechristened the *Virginia*, it ventured out on March 8, 1862, and wrought havoc among the Union ships at the entrance to Chesapeake Bay. But as luck would have it, a new Union iron-clad, the *Monitor*, arrived from New York in time to engage the *Virginia* on the next day. They fought to a draw and the *Virginia* returned to port, where the Confederates destroyed it when they had to give up Norfolk soon afterward.

Gradually, the northern "anaconda" tightened its grip on the South. At Fortress Monroe, Virginia, Union forces held the tip of the peninsula between the James and the York rivers. The navy extended its bases down the Carolina coast in the late summer and fall of 1862. In the Gulf of Mexico, Flag Officer David Farragut's ships forced open the lower Mississippi and surprised New Orleans in the spring of 1862. The city surrendered on May 1, and Farragut's forces then moved on to take Baton Rouge in the same way.

ACTIONS IN THE WEST   Except for the amphibious thrusts in the Chesapeake and along the southern coast, little happened in the Eastern Theater (east of the Appalachians) before May 1862. The Western Theater (from the mountains to the Mississippi), on the other hand, flared up with several clashes and an important penetration of the Confederate states. In western Kentucky, Confederate General Albert Sidney Johnston, a strapping Texan whom Davis considered the South's best general, had perhaps 40,000 men stretched over some 150 miles. Early in 1862 the relentlessly aggressive Ulysses S. Grant made the first thrust against the weak center of Johnston's overextended lines. Moving out of Cairo and Paducah with a gunboat flotilla, he swung southward up the Tennessee River toward Fort Henry. After a pounding from the Union gunboats, the fort fell on February 6. Grant then moved overland to attack Fort Donelson, and on February 16 captured its 12,000 men. Grant's blunt demand of "immediate and unconditional surrender," and his quick success sent a thrill through the dispirited North.

Ulysses S. "Unconditional Surrender" Grant had not only opened a water route to Nashville but also forced the Confederates thereafter to give up their foothold in Kentucky. The short, slouching, disheveled Grant was now a national hero. But not for long.

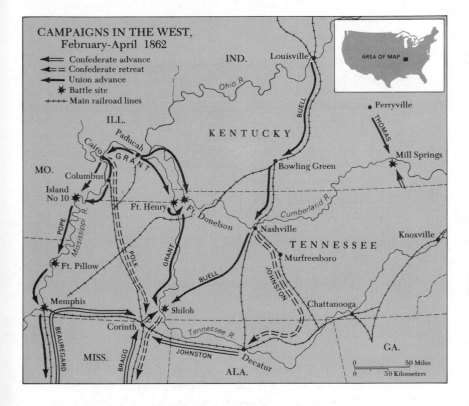

SHILOH   As he moved his forces southward along the Tennessee
River during the early spring of 1862, Grant made a costly mistake. While planning his attack on Corinth, Mississippi, he clumsily placed his troops on a rolling plateau between two creeks
flowing into the Tennessee and failed to set up defensive
trenches. General A. S. Johnston shrewdly recognized Grant's
oversight, and on the morning of April 6, the tall and confident
Johnston ordered an attack on the vulnerable Federals, urging
his men to be "worthy of your race and lineage; worthy of the
women of the South." The Confederates struck suddenly at Shiloh, a log church in the center of the Union camp. There amid
flowering dogwoods, peach trees, and honeysuckle, they found
most of Grant's troops still sleeping or groggily eating breakfast.
Some died in their bedrolls. Reported one Union officer: "The
Rebels are out there thicker than fleas on a dog's back." After a
day of bloody carnage and confusion, Grant's men were pinned
against the river. But under the cover of gunboats and artillery at
nearby Pittsburg Landing, Grant and the brilliant, falcon-eyed

general from Ohio, William Tecumseh Sherman, superbly rallied their troops. Reinforcements arrived that night during a torrential rainstorm, and the next day Grant took the offensive. The Confederates withdrew to Corinth, leaving the Union army too battered to pursue.

Shiloh was the costliest battle in American history up to that point, although worse was yet to come. "The scenes on this field," Sherman sadly noted, "would have cured anybody of war." Combined casualties of nearly 25,000 exceeded the total dead and wounded of the Revolution, the War of 1812, and the Mexican War combined. Among the dead was General A. S. Johnston, who bled to death when a minie ball severed an artery in his leg. The Union, too, lost for a while the leadership of its finest general. Grant had blundered badly. Some critics charged that he had been drinking and called upon Lincoln to replace him. But the president declined: "I can't spare this man; he fights." Grant's superior, hulking, balding, puffy-eyed General Henry Halleck, however, was not as forgiving. He relieved Grant of his command for several months, and as a result the Union thrust southward ground to a halt.

MCCLELLAN'S PENINSULAR CAMPAIGN The Eastern Theater remained fairly quiet for nine months after Bull Run. After the Union defeat, Lincoln had replaced McDowell with the brilliant, if theatrical and hesitant, General George B. McClellan. Stonewall Jackson's classmate at West Point, McClellan had served in the army as a captain before resigning and becoming president of a railroad. After the firing on Fort Sumter, he was named a major general overseeing forces in Ohio, Indiana, and Illinois. Now, as head of the Army of the Potomac, he set about establishing a rigid training regimen, determined to build a powerful, well-trained army that would be ready for its next battle. On the surface, the wide-shouldered and broad-chested McClellan exuded confidence and poise, as well as a certain flair for parade-ground showmanship. His troops adored him. Yet for all of McClellan's organizational ability and dramatic flair, his paralyzing caution would prove crippling.

Time passed and McClellan kept building his forces to meet the superior numbers he always claimed were facing him. Lincoln initially gave McClellan his complete support, but the "Young Napoleon" grew more and more enamored of himself and openly contemptuous of the backwoods president. Lincoln, however, refused to respond in kind. "Never mind," he once said after enduring another affront by his general. "I will hold McClellan's horse if he will only bring us success."

But as the weeks passed McClellan brought only more requests for troops and equipment. After nine months of such agonizing preparation, Lincoln and much of the public had grown understandably impatient. The exasperated president, convinced that his general "has got the slows," finally ordered McClellan to begin forward movement by Washington's Birthday, February 22, 1862. McClellan brashly predicted: "I will be in Richmond in ten days." He planned to attack the Confederate capital by the side door, so to speak, up the neck of land between the York and James Rivers, at the tip of which Union forces already held Fortress Monroe.

In mid-March 1862 McClellan's army finally embarked, and before the end of May his advance units sighted the church stee-

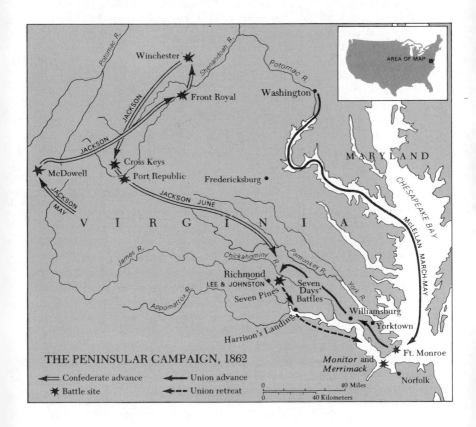

THE PENINSULAR CAMPAIGN, 1862

ples in Richmond. On May 31 Confederate General Joseph E. Johnston struck at Union forces isolated by floodwaters on the south bank of the Chickahominy River. In the battle of Seven Pines (Fair Oaks), only the arrival of reinforcements prevented a disastrous Union defeat. Both sides took heavy casualties, and Johnston was severely wounded.

At this point the fifty-five-year-old Robert E. Lee assumed command of the Army of Northern Virginia. Tall, erect, and wide-shouldered, Lee was a reticent Christian gentleman in private, but a slashing, daring leader in uniform. He believed duty to be the "sublimest word in our language." Unlike Johnston, he enjoyed Davis's trust and was adept at forging a galaxy of superb field commanders: Stonewall Jackson, the fearless, pious mathematics professor from the Virginia Military Institute; James Longstreet, Lee's deliberate but tireless "war horse"; sharp-tongued, tenacious D. H. Hill, the former engineering professor at Davidson College; Ambrose P. Hill, the consummate fighter who challenged one commander to a duel, feuded with Jackson, and kept secret his own mortal disease; and, J. E. B. Stuart, the incurably romantic and recklessly courageous young cavalryman who once said: "All I ask of fate is that I may be killed leading a cavalry charge."

Once in command, Lee quickly decided to hit the Union forces hard, north of the Chickahominy River on June 26, 1862, leaving only a token force in Richmond. But heavy losses prevented the Confederates from sustaining their momentum. Lee launched a final desperate attack at Malvern Hill (July 1), where the Confederates were riddled by artillery and gunboats in the James. As D. H. Hill observed, "It was not war, it was murder." This week of intense fighting, lumped together as the Seven Days' Battles, had failed to dislodge the Union forces. McClellan was still near Richmond.

On July 9 Lincoln visited the front, where McClellan sternly lectured him on the correct strategy to follow. Such insubordination was ample reason to remove the cocky general. Instead Lincoln returned to Washington and on July 11 called Henry Halleck from the west to take charge as general-in-chief, a post that McClellan had temporarily vacated. Thus began what would become a frustrating search on Lincoln's part for a capable and consistent military leader.

SECOND BATTLE OF MANASSAS The new high command ordered McClellan to return to Washington and join the defending forces there, now under bombastic John Pope, for a new assault against

Richmond. As McClellan's Army of the Potomac pulled out, Lee moved northward to strike Pope before the Union forces could be joined. Once again he adopted an audacious strategy. Dividing his forces, he sent Jackson's famous "foot cavalry" on a sweep around Pope's right flank to attack his supply lines. At Second Bull Run (or Second Manassas), fought on almost exactly the same site as the earlier battle, the Confederates thoroughly confused Pope. J. E. B. Stuart's horsemen raided his headquarters, taking Pope's dress uniform, and his strategy book, which outlined the position of his units. Pope then exhausted his own men frantically trying to find the elusive Jackson. By the time they made contact with what they thought were only Jackson's forces, Lee's main army had joined in. The trap was baited, and the Union army was lured in. On August 30, 1862, as Pope's troops engaged Jackson's line, there came a crushing surprise attack on the Federal flank. James Longstreet's corps of 30,000 Confederates, screaming the Rebel yell "like demons emerging from the earth," drove the Union forces from the field. One New York regiment lost 124 of its 490 men, the highest percentage of deaths in any battle of the war. In the next few days the whipped Union forces pulled back into fortifications around Washington, where McClellan once again took command and reorganized. He displayed his unflagging egotism in a letter to his wife: "Again I have been called upon to save the country." The disgraced Pope was dispatched to Minnesota to fight Indians.

ANTIETAM Lee gave his new adversary little time to prepare. Still on the offensive, determined to move the battlefield out of the South and perhaps thereby gain foreign recognition of the Confederacy, he led his troops into western Maryland in September 1862 and headed for Pennsylvania. As luck would have it, however, Lee's bold strategy was uncovered when a Union soldier picked up a bundle of cigars and discovered a secret order from Lee wrapped around them. The paper revealed that Lee had again divided his army, sending Jackson off to take Harper's Ferry. McClellan boasted upon seeing the captured document: "Here is a paper with which, if I cannot whip Bobby Lee, I will be willing to go home." But instead of leaping at his unexpected opportunity, he again delayed for sixteen crucial hours, still worried—as always—about enemy strength, and Lee was thereby able to reassemble most of his tired army behind Antietam Creek. Still, McClellan was optimistic, and Lincoln, too, relished the chance for a truly decisive blow: "God bless you

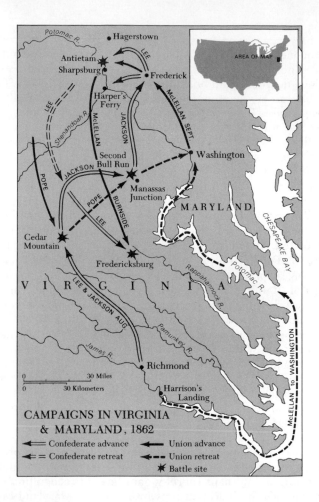

Map labels:
Potomac R.
Hagerstown
Antietam
Sharpsburg
LEE
Frederick
Harper's Ferry
McLELLAN
JACKSON
McLELLAN SEPT
Shenandoah R.
LEE
Second Bull Run
Washington
JACKSON
POPE
Manassas Junction
MARYLAND
POPE
LEE
BURNSIDE
Cedar Mountain
Fredericksburg
VIRGINIA
Rappahannock R.
Potomac R.
CHESAPEAKE BAY
LEE & JACKSON AUG
Pamunkey R.
James R.
Richmond
Harrison's Landing
McLELLAN to WASHINGTON

0   30 Miles
0   30 Kilometers

AREA OF MAP

CAMPAIGNS IN VIRGINIA & MARYLAND, 1862

⟵ Confederate advance   ⟵ Union advance
⟵= Confederate retreat   ⟵--- Union retreat
✳ Battle site

and all with you," he wired McClellan. "Destroy the rebel army
if possible."

On September 17, 1862, McClellan's forces attacked, and the
furious Battle of Antietam (Sharpsburg) began. Just as the Confederate lines seemed ready to break, A. P. Hill's division arrived
from Harper's Ferry, having marched sixteen hot, dusty miles to
the battlefield. Bone-weary and foot-sore, they nevertheless
plunged immediately into the fray, battering the Union's left
flank. It was a ghastly scene. "No tongue can tell, no mind conceive, no pen portray the horrible sights I witnessed this morning," a Pennsylvania soldier reported. Still outnumbered more
than two to one, the Confederates were able to force a standoff in
the bloodiest single day of the Civil War, a day participants
thought would never end.

But in the late afternoon McClellan backed off, letting Lee slip away across the Potomac. Lincoln was disgusted by McClellan's failure to follow up and gain a truly decisive victory, and he fired off the following tart message to the general: "I have just read your dispatch about sore-tongued and fatigued horses. Will you pardon me for asking what the horses of your army have done . . . that fatigues anything?" Later the president sent his commander a one-sentence letter: "If you don't want to use the army, I should like to borrow it for a while." Failing to receive a satisfactory answer, Lincoln removed McClellan and assigned him to recruiting duty in New Jersey. Never again would he command troops.

FREDERICKSBURG Lee's invasion had failed, and with it failed the Confederacy's hopes of foreign recognition. But the war was far from over. In his search for a fighting general Lincoln now made the worst choice of all. He turned to Ambrose E. Burnside, a handsome, personable, modest figure whose main achievement to that time had been to grow his famous side-whiskers. Burnside had twice before turned down the job on the grounds that he felt unfit for so large a command.

But if the White House wanted him to fight, Burnside would fight even in the face of the oncoming winter. On a cold December 13, 1862, he sent his men across the icy Rappahannock River to face Lee's forces, well entrenched behind a stone wall and on high ground just west of Fredericksburg on Marye's Heights in Virginia. Watching the massive Union army approaching, an aide asked Stonewall Jackson his intentions. "We will give them the bayonet," he replied. But few Federals ever got close enough for such hand-to-hand fighting. Blessed with a clear field of fire, Confederate artillery and muskets chewed up the valorous blue ranks as they crossed a mile of open bottomland outside the town.

Six times the courageous but suicidal assaults melted under the murderous fire coming from protected Confederate positions above and below them. It was, as a Federal general said, "a great slaughter pen." The scene was both awful and awe-inspiring, prompting Lee to remark: "It is well that war is so terrible —we should grow too fond of it." After seeing his men suffer more than 12,000 casualties, twice as many as the Confederates, Burnside wept as he gave the order to withdraw, and his battered forces sullenly limped back across the river. A northern reporter aptly summarized the battle: "It can hardly be in human nature for men to show more valor, or generals to manifest less judgment."

The year 1862 ended with forces in the East deadlocked and the Federal advance in the West stalled since mid-year. Union morale reached a low ebb. Northern Democrats were calling for a negotiated peace, while the so-called Radical Republicans were pushing Lincoln to prosecute the war even more forcefully. Several even questioned the president's competence.

But in the midst of such second-guessing and carping, the deeper currents of the war were in fact turning in favor of the Union: in a lengthening war its superior resources began to tell on the morale of the Confederacy. In both the Eastern and Western Theaters the Confederate counterattack had been repulsed. And while the armies clashed, Lincoln by a stroke of a pen had changed the conflict from a war for the Union into a revolutionary struggle for abolition. On January 1, 1863, he signed the Emancipation Proclamation.

EMANCIPATION

The Emancipation Proclamation was the product of long and painful deliberation. Lincoln had always insisted that the purpose of the conflict was to restore the Union, not to free the slaves. The prolonged war forced the issue. Fugitive slaves began to turn up in Union army camps, and generals did not know whether to declare them free or not. Some put these "contrabands" to work building fortifications, others liberated those who belonged to Confederate owners, thus risking upsetting

Former slaves, or "contrabands," on a farm in Cumberland Landing, Virginia, 1862.

border-state slaveholders. Lincoln himself edged toward emancipation. As the war ground on, he finally decided that complete emancipation was required for several reasons: slave labor bolstered the Confederate cause, sagging morale in the North needed the lift of a transcendent moral ideal, and public opinion was swinging that way as the war continued. Proclaiming a war on slavery, moreover, would end forever any chance that France or Britain would support the Confederacy.

The time to act finally came after Antietam. It was a dubious victory, but it did force Lee's withdrawal from the North. On September 22, 1862, Lincoln issued a preliminary Emancipation Proclamation which warned that on January 1, 1863, all slaves in Confederate states or areas still under active rebellion would be "thenceforward and forever free."

REACTIONS TO EMANCIPATION   The proclamation, with few exceptions, freed only those slaves still under Confederate control, as cynics noted then and later. But critics missed a point that slaves readily grasped. "In a document proclaiming liberty," wrote a black historian, "the unfree never bother to read the fine print." Word of Lincoln's proclamation spread quickly into slave quarters. One South Carolina ex-slave remembered the scene on his plantation: "Some were sorry, some hurt, but a few were silent and glad." Some actively claimed their freedom. One spectacular instance was that of the black river pilot Robert Smalls, who one night in May 1862 took over a small Confederate gunboat and sailed his family through Charleston harbor out to the blockading Union fleet. Later he served in the Union navy and eventually became a congressman.

BLACKS IN THE MILITARY   Lincoln's Emancipation Proclamation reaffirmed the policy that blacks could enroll in the armed services and sparked efforts to organize new all-black units. By mid-1863 black soldiers were involved in significant combat both in the Eastern and in the Western Theaters. Lincoln reported that several of his commanders believed that "the use of colored troops constitutes the heaviest blow yet dealt to the rebels."

Altogether, between 180,000 and 200,000 black Americans served in the Union army, providing around 10 percent of its total. Some 38,000 gave their lives. Blacks accounted for about a fourth of all enlistments in the navy, and of these, almost 3,000 died. Black women also served in the war. Harriet Tubman and Susie King, for instance, were nurses along with their more famous white counterpart Clara Barton.

As the war entered its final months, freedom emerged more

fully as a legal reality. The Thirteenth Amendment, which abolished slavery, was ratified by three-fourths of the states and became part of the Constitution on December 18, 1865, thus removing any lingering doubts about the legality of emancipation. By then, in fact, slavery remained only in the border states of Kentucky and Delaware.

GOVERNMENT DURING THE WAR

Striking the shackles from 3.5 million slaves was a monumental social and economic revolution. But an even broader revolution developed as political power shifted from South to North after secession. Before the war, southern congressmen had been able to frustrate the designs of both Free Soil and Whiggery. But once the secessionists abandoned Congress to the Republicans, a dramatic change occurred. A new protective tariff, a transcontinental railroad to run through Omaha to Sacramento, a homestead act, which granted free homesteads of 160 acres to settlers who occupied the land for 5 years—all acts that had been stalled by sectional controversy—were adopted before the end of 1862. That year also saw the passage of the Morrill Land Grant Act, which provided federal aid to state colleges of "agricultural and mechanic arts." The National Banking Act, which created a uniform system of banking and banknote currency, followed in 1863. This last act helped the Union address a critical problem: how to finance the war.

UNION FINANCES Congress had three options for solving this problem: higher taxes, printing paper money, and borrowing. The higher taxes came chiefly in the form of the Morrill Tariff and excise taxes, which fell on manufacturers and nearly every profession. On top of the excises came an income tax, and to collect these revenues Congress created the Bureau of Internal Revenue.

But tax revenues trickled in so slowly that Congress in 1862 ordered the printing of paper money. Eventually $450 million in "greenbacks" were printed, enough to pay the bills but not unleash the kind of runaway inflation that burdened the Confederacy after Jefferson Davis allowed the unlimited issue of paper money.

Still, paper money and taxes provided only about two-thirds of the money to finance the war. The rest came chiefly from the sale of bonds. After October 1862 a Philadelphia banker named

Jay Cooke mobilized a nationwide network of agents and propaganda for the sale of government war bonds. It worked well, and over $2 billion was raised in the process. All wars provide new opportunities for quick profits, and the Civil War was no different. Many American entrepreneurs reaped quick riches from war contracts. Several cut corners in the process, providing shoddy goods, paying bribes and kickbacks, or in some cases, not delivering supplies at all. Not all wartime fortunes, however, were made dishonestly, and their long-run importance was in promoting the capital accumulation with which American businessmen fueled the phenomenal postwar expansion of the national economy.

CONFEDERATE FINANCES Confederate finances were a disaster from the start. Tariffs were tried, but imports were low and therefore raised little revenue. In April 1863 the Confederate Congress passed a measure which, like the Union's excises, taxed nearly everything. A 10 percent tax on all agricultural products, however, did more to outrage farmers and planters than to supply the army. Enforcement was so lax and evasion so easy that the taxes produced only negligible income.

The last resort, the printing press, was in fact resorted to early. Beginning in February 1861 the new Confederate government began an extended inflationary binge for which the only cure was more of the same. Altogether the Confederacy turned out more than $1 billion in paper money, forcing prices up geometrically. By March 1864 a wild turkey sold in a Richmond market for $100, flour went for $425 a barrel, and bacon for $10 a pound. Those living on fixed incomes were caught in a merciless squeeze.

CONFEDERATE DIPLOMACY Civil wars often mushroom into international conflicts. The foundation of Confederate diplomacy in fact was the hope of help from foreign governments in the form of supplies, formal recognition, or perhaps even armed intervention. The Confederates indulged the pathetic hope that diplomatic recognition would prove decisive, when in fact it more likely would have followed decisive victory in the field, which never came.

The first Confederate emissaries to England and France took hope when the British foreign minister received them informally after their arrival in London in May 1861. In Paris, France's Napoleon III even promised them that he would recognize the Confederacy if England would lead the way. But when the agents returned to London, the government refused to see them, partly because of Union pressures and partly out of British self-interest.

Confederate negotiators were far more successful at getting supplies than gaining recognition. The most spectacular feat was the procurement of raiding ships. Although British law prohibited the sale of warships to belligerents, a southern agent contrived to have the ships built and then, on trial runs, to escape and be outfitted with guns. In all, eighteen such ships were activated and saw action in the Atlantic, Pacific, and Indian Oceans, where they sank hundreds of Yankee ships and sparked terror in the rest.

UNION POLITICS AND CIVIL LIBERTIES   On the homefronts during the Civil War there was no moratorium on partisan politics, North or South. Within his own party Lincoln faced a Radical wing composed mainly of prewar abolitionists. Led by House members such as Thaddeus Stevens and George Julian, and senators such as Charles Sumner, Benjamin Wade, and Zachariah Chandler, they formed a Joint Committee on the Conduct of the War which increasingly pressured Lincoln to emancipate the slaves, confiscate southern plantations, and prosecute the war more vigorously. Yet the majority of Republicans supported the president, and the party was virtually united on economic matters.

The Democratic party was devastated by the loss of its southern wing as well as by the death of its leader, Stephen A. Douglas, in June 1861. By and large, northern Democrats supported a war for the "Union as it was" before 1860, giving reluctant support to war policies but opposing wartime constraints on civil liberties and the new economic legislation. "War Democrats" like Senator Andrew Johnson from Tennessee and Secretary of War Edwin Stanton fully supported Lincoln's policies, however, while a Peace Wing of the party preferred a negotiated end to the fighting, even at the risk of the Union. An extreme fringe among the Peace Democrats even flirted with outright disloyalty. The "Copperheads," as they were called, organized secret societies, mostly in Ohio, Indiana, and Illinois, states with many transplanted southerners, some of whom were pro-Confederate.

Such open sympathy for the enemy provoked Lincoln to crack down hard. Early in the war he assumed certain emergency powers such as the suspension of the writ of habeas corpus and the right to invoke martial law. When critics charged that this violated the Constitution, Lincoln's congressional supporters pushed through the Habeas Corpus Act of 1863, which authorized the suspension of the writ. Some 14,000 arrests of Confederate sympathizers resulted.

In the mid-term elections of 1862, the Democrats exploited growing war weariness and resentment of Lincoln's war measures to gain a startling recovery, though not actual control of Congress. When asked his reaction to the election results, Lincoln replied that he felt somewhat "like the boy in Kentucky who stubbed his toe while running to see his sweetheart. The boy said he was too big to cry, and far too badly hurt to laugh." But the political situation made Lincoln even more perplexed as time passed. At their 1864 national convention the Democrats called for an immediate armistice and named General McClellan as their candidate, but he distanced himself from the peace platform by declaring that the two sides must agree on reunion before the fighting should stop.

Radical Republicans, who still regarded Lincoln as being too soft on the traitorous southerners, tried to thwart Lincoln's renomination, but he outmaneuvered them at every turn. In a shrewd move he named as his vice-presidential running mate Andrew Johnson, a War Democrat from Tennessee, and called their ticket the "National Union" so as to minimize partisanship. As the war ground on through 1864, with Grant taking heavy losses in Virginia, Lincoln fully expected to lose the election. But key military victories in August and September turned the tide. McClellan carried only New Jersey, Delaware, and Kentucky.

CONFEDERATE POLITICS Unlike Lincoln, Jefferson Davis never had to contest a presidential election. Both he and his vice-president, Alexander Stephens, were elected for a six-year term. But discontent flourished in the South as events went from bad to worse. A bread riot in Richmond in April 1863, for example, ended only when Davis himself persuaded the mob (mostly women) to disperse. After the congressional elections of 1863, about a third of the Confederacy's legislators were openly hostile toward the administration. Although parties as such did not figure in the elections, it was noteworthy that many ex-Whigs and other opponents of secession were chosen.

Davis, like Lincoln, had to contend with dissenters. Especially troublesome were those committed to states' rights who had supported secession but steadfastly opposed the centralizing tendencies of the government in Richmond. Georgia and North Carolina were strongholds of such sentiment. They challenged, among other things, the legality of conscription, taxes on farm produce, and above all the suspension of habeas corpus. Vice-

Jefferson Davis, president of the Confederacy.

President Stephens himself carried on a running battle with Davis, accusing the president of trying to establish a "military despotism." Such internal bickering did not alone cause the Confederacy's defeat, but certainly contributed to it.

THE FALTERING CONFEDERACY

In 1863 the hinge of fate began to close the door on the brief career of the Confederacy. After the Union disaster at Fredericksburg, Lincoln's frustrating search for a capable general turned to one of Burnside's disgruntled lieutenants, Joseph E. Hooker, a handsome, ruddy-faced, hard-drinking character whose pugnacity had earned him the nickname "Fighting Joe." As he planned a new spring campaign, Hooker brashly announced: "May God have mercy on General Lee, for I will have none." But he was no more able to deliver the goods than Burnside. Hooker failed his test at Chancellorsville in May 1863.

CHANCELLORSVILLE   With a force of perhaps 130,000, the largest Union army yet gathered, and a brilliant plan, Hooker suffered a loss of control, perhaps a failure of nerve, at the critical juncture. Lee, with perhaps half that number, staged what became a textbook classic of daring and maneuver. Hooker's plan was to leave his base, opposite Fredericksburg, on a sweeping movement upstream across the Rappahannock and Rapidan, and flank Lee's position. A large diversionary force was to cross the Rappahannock below the town. Initially all went well, but Lee sniffed out the ruse. He moved his main force to meet Hooker and dispatched Stuart's cavalry to disrupt the Union lines of communications. Hooker suddenly lost sight of his opponents and was caught by surprise when rebel skirmishers fired on his advance columns. He then ordered his troops to pull back to the Chancellorsville crossroads. "I just lost faith in Joe Hooker," he later admitted, and Lee quickly took advantage of his opponent's failure of nerve. He divided his army again, sending Jackson with more than half the men on a long march to hit the enemy's exposed right flank.

On May 2, just about suppertime, Jackson surprised Hooker's right flank at the edge of a densely wooded area called the Wil-

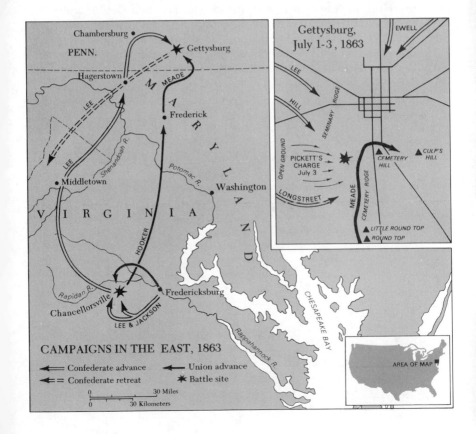

Gettysburg, July 1-3, 1863

EWELL

LEE

HILL

SEMINARY RIDGE

OPEN GROUND

PICKETT'S CHARGE July 3

LONGSTREET

MEADE CEMETERY RIDGE

CEMETERY HILL

▲ CULP'S HILL

▲ LITTLE ROUND TOP
▲ ROUND TOP

Chambersburg ●

PENN.

● Gettysburg

Hagerstown

MEADE

M
A
R
Y
L
A
N
D

Shenandoah R.

LEE

LEE

● Middletown

Potomac R.

● Frederick

Washington

V I R G I N I A

HOOKER

Rapidan R.

Chancellorsville

LEE & JACKSON

● Fredericksburg

Rappahannock R.

CHESAPEAKE BAY

CAMPAIGNS IN THE EAST, 1863

◄━ Confederate advance   ◄━ Union advance
◄= Confederate retreat   ✳ Battle site

0   30 Miles
0   30 Kilometers

AREA OF MAP

derness. The Confederates slammed into the Union lines with such furor that the defenders panicked and ran. The thick undergrowth made troop movements more chaotic than usual, and the fighting died out in confusion as darkness fell. The next day was Lee's, however, as his troops forced Hooker's army to recross the Rappahannock. It was the peak of Lee's career, but Chancellorsville was his last significant victory, and his costliest: the South suffered some 12,000 casualties and more than 1,600 killed, among them Stonewall Jackson, mistakenly shot by his own men in the confused fighting. "I have lost my right arm," lamented Lee.

VICKSBURG   While Lee held the Federals at bay in the East, they had resumed a torturous advance in the West. Since the previous fall, Grant, his command now restored, had been groping his way down the Mississippi River toward Vicksburg, which along with Port Hudson, Louisiana, was one of the last two Confederate strongholds on the Mississippi. Located on a bluff 200 feet above the river, Vicksburg had withstood naval attacks and a downriver expedition led by the steely Sherman. For months Grant tried to discover a way to penetrate the city's heavily fortified defenses.

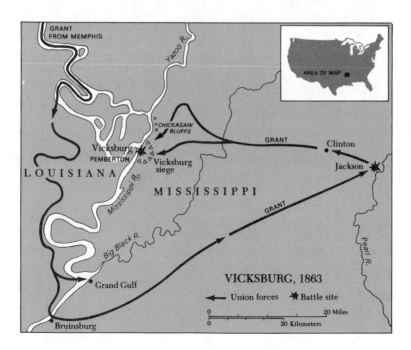

The terrain complicated his task: Vicksburg was surrounded by bayous and marshes that made travel and resupply almost impossible. In May he finally decided to pin the 30,000 Confederates in Vicksburg and wear them down or starve them out.

GETTYSBURG The plight of besieged Vicksburg put the Confederate high command in a quandary. Lee proposed a diversion. If he could win a great victory on northern soil, he reasoned, he might do more than just relieve the pressure on Vicksburg; he might bring an end to the war. In June 1863 he moved his forces into the Shenandoah Valley and headed north across Maryland.

Hooker followed, keeping his forces between Lee and Washington. But, demoralized by defeat at Chancellorsville, Hooker resigned his post and was replaced on June 28 by Major-General George G. Meade, an aristocratic Philadelphian distinctive for his bravery. Neither side chose Gettysburg, Pennsylvania, as the site for the climactic battle, but a Confederate foraging party entered the town in search of shoes and encountered units of Union cavalry on June 30. The main forces then quickly converged there. On July 1, a hot, steamy day, the Confederates pushed the Federals out of the town, but into stronger positions on high ground to the south. Meade hastened reinforcements to the new lines along the heights. On July 2 Lee, hampered by a lack of information because of the inexcusable absence of Stuart's cavalry, ordered assaults at both the extreme left and the extreme right flanks of Meade's army. The Confederates fought fiercely. Longstreet declared that his corps's assault was "the best three hours' fighting ever done by any troops on any battle-field." But the Federals, who outnumbered their attackers almost two to one, fought just as bravely—and the assaults were repulsed.

The next day Lee staked everything on one final attack on the Union center at Cemetery Ridge. Confederate cannon pounded the northern lines, but with less effect than intended. About 2 P.M. General George E. Pickett's division emerged from the woods west of Cemetery Ridge and began their advance across rising open ground commanded by Union artillery. It was as hopeless and as terribly majestic as Burnside's assault at Fredericksburg. At a distance of 700 yards the Federal artillery homed in on the advancing Virginians. Those who avoided the canister and grape shot were then devastated by a wall of musket fire. Said one southern officer, the attackers "seemed to melt away in the blue musketry smoke which now covered the hill. Nothing but stragglers came back." Of the 14,000 attackers, barely half returned, leading Lee to mutter: "All this has been my fault."

Harvest of Death. *T. H. O'Sullivan's grim photograph of the dead at Gettysburg.*

With nothing left to do but retreat, on July 4 Lee's dejected and mangled army began to slog south in a driving rain that "washed the blood from the grass." They left about a third of their number behind on the ground. They also had failed in all their purposes, not the least being to relieve the pressure on Vicksburg. On that same day the entire Confederate garrison at Vicksburg surrendered. The Confederacy was now irrevocably split, and had Meade aggressively pursued Lee he might have delivered the final blow before the boys in gray could get back across the flooded Potomac.

CHATTANOOGA   The third great Union victory of 1863 occurred in fighting around Chattanooga, the railhead of eastern Tennessee and gateway to northern Georgia. On September 9 a Union army led by General William Rosecrans took Chattanooga and then rashly pursued General Braxton Bragg's forces into Georgia, where the two sides clashed at Chickamauga (an old Cherokee word ironically meaning "river of death"). The battle (September 19–20) had the makings of a Union disaster, since it was one of the few times when the Confederates had a numerical advantage (about 70,000 to 56,000). On the second day Bragg smashed the Federal right, and only the stubborn stand on the left under Virginia Unionist George H. Thomas (thenceforth known as the "Rock of Chickamauga") prevented a general rout. The battered Union forces fell back to Chattanooga, while Bragg cut the railroad and held the city virtually under siege.

Rosecrans seemed stunned and immobilized, but Lincoln urged him to hang on: "If we can hold Chattanooga, and East Tennessee, I think rebellion must dwindle and die." The president then dispatched Joe Hooker with reinforcements from Virginia, and Grant and Sherman arrived with more fresh troops from the west. Grant, given overall command of the West on October 16, pushed through the rings of Confederate troops around the city and opened up a supply route in the process. He then replaced Rosecrans with George Thomas. On November 24 the Federals broke out of the city. Hooker's forces took Lookout Mountain in what was mainly a feat of mountaineering. The next day Grant ordered Thomas's troops forward to positions at the foot of Missionary Ridge. But the men did not stop there. Still fuming because the Confederates had jeered them at Chickamauga, they charged toward the crest without orders. One of his

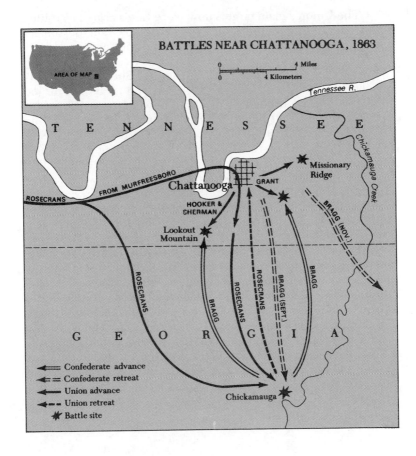

BATTLES NEAR CHATTANOOGA, 1863

aides explained to Grant: "When those fellows get started all hell can't stop them." The attackers could have been decimated, but the Confederates were unable to lower their big guns enough to hit the scrambling Yankees, and, despite Bragg's "cursing like a sailor," his men fled as Thomas's troops reached the summit.

After the Federal victory, as the Union forces consolidated their control of East Tennessee, already full of Unionist sympathizers, Jefferson Davis reluctantly replaced Bragg with Joseph Johnston. Lincoln, on the other hand, had finally found the general he had been searching for in vain for almost three years. In March 1864 Grant was brought to Washington and made general-in-chief.

THE CONFEDERACY'S DEFEAT

The Union's main targets now were Lee's army in Virginia and General Joseph Johnston's in Georgia. Grant personally would accompany Meade, who retained direct command over the Army of the Potomac; operations in the West were entrusted to Grant's long-time lieutenant, William T. Sherman. As Sherman later wrote, Grant "was to go for Lee, and I was to go for Joe Johnston." Grant brought with him a new strategy. Where his predecessors had all hoped for the climactic single battle, he adopted a war of attrition. He would attack, attack, attack, keeping the pressure on the Confederates, grinding down their numbers, and taking away their initiative and will to fight. Victory, he had decided, would come to the side "which never counted its dead." Grant ordered his commanders to wage total war, confiscating or destroying any and all civilian property of military use. It was a brutal, costly, but ultimately effective plan.

GRANT'S PURSUIT OF LEE In May 1864 the Army of the Potomac, numbering about 115,000 to Lee's 65,000, moved south across the Rappahannock into the Wilderness, where Hooker had earlier come to grief in the Battle of Chancellorsville. In the Battle of the Wilderness (May 5–6) the armies fought blindly through the tangled brush and vines, the horror and agony of the wounded heightened by crackling brush fires. Grant's men suffered heavier casualties than Lee's, but the Confederates were running out of replacements. Always before, Lee's adversaries had retreated to lick their wounds, but Grant slid off to the left and continued his relentless advance southward, now toward Spotsylvania Court House.

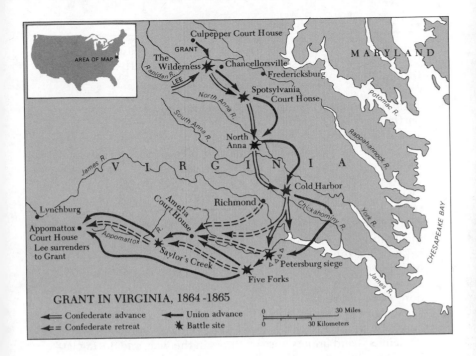

Culpepper Court House

GRANT

The Wilderness · Chancellorsville

Rapidan R. · Fredericksburg

LEE

MARYLAND

North Anna R.

Spotsylvania Court House

South Anna R.

North Anna

VIRGINIA

James R.

Lynchburg

Amelia Court House · Richmond

Cold Harbor

Chickahominy R.

Appomattox Court House
Lee surrenders to Grant

Appomattox R.

Saylor's Creek

Five Forks

Petersburg siege

York R.

Rappahannock R.

Potomac R.

CHESAPEAKE BAY

James R.

GRANT IN VIRGINIA, 1864-1865

⬅ Confederate advance   ⬅ Union advance
⬅= Confederate retreat   ✶ Battle site

0 — 30 Miles
0 — 30 Kilometers

There the armies settled down for five days of carnage, May 8–12, in which the Federals failed to break the Confederate center, the "Bloody Angle." Before it was over, Grant sent word to Washington: "I propose to fight it out along this line if it takes all summer." But he soon changed his mind, slid off to his left and kept moving. Along the Chickahominy, the two sides clashed again at Cold Harbor (June 1–3). In twenty minutes, 7,000 attacking Federals were killed or wounded. Many of them predicted as much. After the failed assault, Confederates retrieved a diary from a dead Massachusetts soldier. The final entry read: "June 3, 1864, Cold Harbor, Virginia. I was killed." Battered and again repulsed, Grant soon had his men moving again, headed for Petersburg, the junction of railroads into Richmond from the south. "I shall take no backward steps," he declared.

Lee's army dug in around the town while Grant laid siege. For nine months the two forces faced each other down while Grant kept trying to break the railroad arteries that were Lee's lifeline. His men were generously supplied by vessels moving up the James River while Lee's forces, beset by hunger, cold, and desertion, wasted away in their muddy trenches. Petersburg had become Lee's prison, while disasters piled up for the Confederacy elsewhere. "From the summer of 1862," wrote a Confederate veteran, "the war became a war of wholesale devastation. From the spring of 1864, it seemed to have become nearly a war of extermination."

SHERMAN'S MARCH   While Grant was chasing Lee in Virginia, the battle-hardened Sherman was relentlessly pursuing Joe Johnston's army through north Georgia toward Atlanta. Sherman was, wrote the poet Walt Whitman, "a bit of stern open air made up in the image of a man." Tightly-strung, profane, and plagued by fits of depression, Sherman was one of the few generals to appreciate the concept of total war. Where Sherman loved a toe-to-toe fight, Johnston was a master of retreat and evasion, determined not to risk a single life until the perfect conditions for fighting were obtained. An impatient President Davis finally exploded at Johnston's retreat and replaced him with the towering, blond-bearded Texan John B. Hood, who did not know the meaning of retreat or evasion. As Lee once noted, he was "all lion, none of the fox." Having had an arm crippled by a ball at Gettysburg and most of one leg shot off at Chickamauga, Hood had to be strapped to his horse. But he remained one of the most tenacious—and impetuous—fighters in the war, and during late July 1864, "the gallant Hood's" army struck three times from his

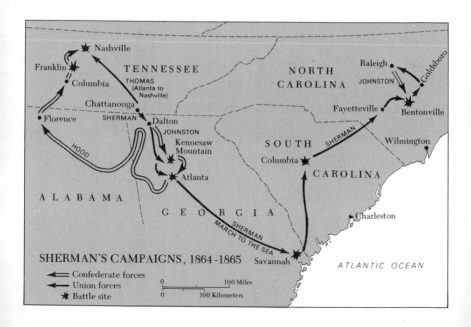

SHERMAN'S CAMPAIGNS, 1864-1865

base at Atlanta, each time fighting desperately but meeting a bloody rebuff. Sherman then circled the city and cut off the rail lines, forcing Hood to evacuate on September 1. Sherman's letter to the Atlanta mayor demanding the surrender of the city reflected his military philosophy: "War is cruelty, and you cannot refine it, and those who brought war into our country deserve all the curses and maledictions a people can pour out."

Sherman now resolved to make all of "Georgia howl," as his army embarked on its devastating march southeast through central Georgia. Hood went in the other direction, cutting through northern Alabama and into Tennessee in the hope of luring Sherman away from the undefended deep South. But Sherman refused to take the bait, although he did dispatch George Thomas with 30,000 men to keep watch on Hood. They did more than observe, however. In the Battle of Franklin (November 30) Hood sent his army across two miles of open Tennessee ground. Six waves of gray crashed against the Union lines but never broke through. "It is impossible to exaggerate the fierce energy with which the Confederate soldiers . . . threw themselves against the works," recalled a Union colonel. They fought "with what seemed the very madness of despair." A Confederate soldier described the ghastly scene: "We looked over the battlefield, O, my God! What did we see! It was the grand holocaust of death. . . . The dead were piled the one on the other all over the ground. I never was so horrified and appalled in my life." One dead general had been hit by forty-nine bullets. A month later, on December 27, Hood suffered another devastating defeat at Nashville that effectively ended Confederate activity in Tennessee.

During all this, Sherman and the main Union force were marching triumphantly through Georgia, pioneering the modern practice of total war against the enemy's resources and will to resist. "War is war," Sherman bluntly declared, "not a popularity contest." On November 15, 1864, his men burned much of Atlanta and then spread out over a front twenty to sixty miles wide and headed south, living off the land and destroying any crops, livestock, or supplies that might serve Confederate forces. Bands of stragglers and deserters from both armies joined in looting along the flanks. When, after a month, Sherman's army approached Savannah, they had cut a swath of desolation 250 miles long. Sherman's purpose was clear. He would keep the pressure on "until they are not only ruined, exhausted, but humbled in pride and spirit." Too often, however, his foraging men displayed a wanton brutality that shocked even those they were ostensibly liberating. A Georgia slave reported that he saw Union soldiers "cut the hams off a live pig or ox and go off leavin' the animal groanin'."

On December 21 Sherman rode into Savannah, and three days later he offered the city as a Christmas gift to Lincoln. But Sherman paused only long enough to resupply his forces, who then moved on across the river into that "hell-hole of secession," South Carolina. There his men wrought even greater destruction. More than a dozen towns were torched, including the state capital at Columbia, captured on February 17, 1865. That same day the Confederates defending Charleston abandoned the city and pulled north to join an army Joe Johnston was desperately trying to form.

APPOMATTOX During this final season of the Confederacy, Grant kept pushing, probing, and battering the Petersburg defenses. News of Sherman's devastating sweep through Dixie only added to the Confederacy's gloom and the impulse to desert. Under siege for almost ten months, their lines around Petersburg were becoming woefully thin, and Lee decided to sneak away and try to join Johnston's forces in North Carolina. In Richmond President Davis, exhausted but still defiant, gathered what papers and treasure he could carry and escaped by train, only to be captured in Georgia on May 10 by Union cavalry.

Robert E. Lee. *Mathew Brady took this photograph in Richmond eleven days after Lee's surrender at Appomattox.*

By then the Confederacy was already dead. Lee pulled his shrunken army out of the trenches around Petersburg with Grant's men in hot pursuit, but he soon found his escape route cut by General Philip Sheridan's cavalry. Although his men shouted their willingness to keep fighting, Lee decided it was senseless to waste any more lives. On April 9 (Palm Sunday), 1865, he donned a crisp dress uniform and met the mud-spattered Grant in the parlor of the McLean home at Appomattox to tender his surrender. Grant, at Lee's request, let the Confederate officers keep their side arms and permitted soldiers to keep their own horses and mules. Three days later the Confederate troops formed ranks for the last time as they prepared for the formal surrender. Deeply moved by the sight of such solemn splendor, Joshua Chamberlain, the Union general in charge, ordered his men to salute their foes as they paraded past. His Confederate counterpart signaled his troops to do likewise. General Chamberlain remembered that there was not a sound—no trumpets or drums, no cheers or jeers, simply "an awed stillness . . . as if it were the passing of the dead." On April 18 Johnston surrendered his forces to Sherman near Durham, North Carolina.

The debate over why the North won and the South lost the Civil War will probably never end, but Lee's own explanation of the Confederate defeat retains an enduring legitimacy: "After four years of arduous service marked by unsurpassed courage and fortitude, the Army of Northern Virginia has been compelled to yield to overwhelming numbers and resources."

BITTERSWEET VICTORY In Charleston the first occupation troops to arrive in February 1865 were black units, several of whose members had been slaves in the city in 1860. On April 14, 1865, the War Department staged a massive victory celebration at Fort Sumter on the fourth anniversary of its fall. At noon Major Anderson ran up the flag he had lowered previously, while gaily decorated ships and all the forts in the harbor sounded a salute.

The same day President Lincoln spent the afternoon discussing postwar policy with his cabinet. That night he and his wife went to Ford's Theater.

FURTHER READING

For a magisterial illustrated overview of the Civil War, see Geoffrey Ward, *The Civil War: An Illustrated History* (1990). The most comprehensive treatment of the Civil War period is Allan Nevins's *The War* for the Union (4 vols., 1959–1971). The best concise overview is James M. McPherson's *Battle Cry of Freedom: The Civil War Era* (1988).° *The Image of War, 1861–1865* (6 vols., 1981–88), edited by William C. Davis, is a stunning collection of photographs.

The Civil War period features a number of firsthand accounts. Among the better are *Mary Chesnut's Civil War* (1981),° edited by C. Vann Woodward, and *The Children of Pride* (1972; abridged ed., 1984),° edited by Robert M. Myers. The life of the common soldier is well treated by Bell I. Wiley in *The Life of Johnny Reb* (1971)° and *The Life of Billy Yank* (1971).° Soldiering under fire is graphically evoked in Gerald E. Linderman's *Embattled Courage: The Experience of Combat in the American Civil War* (1989),° and Reid Mitchell, *Civil War Soldiers: Their Expectations and Their Experiences* (1989).°

For emphasis on the South, turn to Emory M. Thomas's *The Confederate Nation, 1861–1865* (1981).° Shelby Foote's *The Civil War* (3 vols., 1958–1974)° gives the most thorough treatment of the military conflict from the southern perspective. A more analytical approach is contained in Gabor S. Boritt, ed., *Why the Confederacy Lost* (1992).°

Treatments of northern politics during the war include David H. Donald's *Charles Sumner and the Coming of the Civil War* (1989)° and Harold M. Hyman's *A More Perfect Union* (1973).

Works dealing with northern military strategy include Stephen W. Sears's *Landscape Turned Red: The Battle of Antietam* (1988)° and T. Harry Williams's *Lincoln and His Generals* (1952).° The views of northern intellectuals on the war are the subject of George M. Fredrickson's fine work *The Inner Civil War* (1968).° The war's devastating effects are splendidly assessed in Charles Royster's *The Destructive War* (1991).

How the emancipated slave fared during the war is treated in Benjamin Quarles's *The Negro in the Civil War* (1953)° and Ira Berlin et al., eds., *Freedom: A Documentary History of Emancipation, 1861–1867* (2 vols., 1986–1991. The career of the black soldier is found in Joseph T. Glatthaar's *Forged in Battle: The Civil War Alliance of Black Soldiers and White Officers* (1991).° Willie Lee Rose's *Rehearsal for Reconstruction: The Port Royal Experiment* (1964) traces the short-lived experiment in black autonomy. For insights into the war's effects on women, see George C. Rable, *Civil Wars: Women and the Crisis of Southern Nationalism* (1989).°

° These books are available in paperback editions.

17

RECONSTRUCTION:
NORTH AND SOUTH

THE BATTLE OVER RECONSTRUCTION

In the spring of 1865 the wearying war was over. At the frightful cost of 620,000 lives and the destruction of the southern economy and much of its landscape, American nationalism emerged triumphant, and some 4 million slaves emerged free. But peace had come only on the battlefields. "Cannon conquer," recognized a northern editor, "but they do not necessarily convert." Now the North faced the imposing task of "reconstructing" a ravaged and resentful South. A few northerners thought the task relatively simple. The poet and professor James Russell Lowell wrote a friend in April 1865: "I worry a little about reconstruction, but am inclined to think that matters will very much settle themselves." He was wrong. A tangle of difficult issues confronted northern politicians. Should the Confederate leaders be tried for treason? How were new governments to be formed? How and at whose expense was the South's economy to be rebuilt? What was to be done with the freed slaves? Were they to be given land? social equality? education? voting rights? Such complex questions required careful planning, but policymakers did not have the luxury of time or the benefits of consensus.

LINCOLN'S PLAN AND CONGRESS'S RESPONSE   The problem of reconstruction arose early in the Civil War, as Union forces advanced into the South and were forced to create new local governments. Lincoln in 1862 named military governors for Tennessee, Arkansas, and Louisiana, and by the end of the following year he had formulated a plan for regular civilian governments in those states and any others that might be liberated from the Confederacy.

Acting under his pardon power, President Lincoln issued in December 1863 a Proclamation of Amnesty and Reconstruction under which any Rebel state could form a Union government whenever a number equal to 10 percent of those who had voted in 1860 took an oath of allegiance to the Constitution and Union and received a presidential pardon. Participants also had to swear support for laws and proclamations dealing with emancipation. Excluded from the pardon, however, were certain groups: civil, diplomatic, and high military officers of the Confederacy; judges, congressmen, and military officers of the United States who had left their posts to aid the rebellion; and those accused of failure to treat captured Negro soldiers and their officers as prisoners of war.

Under this plan loyal governments appeared in Tennessee, Arkansas, and Louisiana, but Congress refused to recognize them. In the absence of any specific provisions for reconstruction in the Constitution, politicians disagreed as to where authority properly rested. Lincoln claimed the right to direct reconstruction under the presidential pardon power, and also under the Constitutional obligation to guarantee each state a republican form of government.

A few conservative and most moderate Republicans supported Lincoln's program of immediate restoration. A small but influential group known as Radical Republicans, however, desired to see a sweeping transformation of southern society that would include making the freedmen full-fledged citizens. The Radicals were talented, earnest, and frequently colorful men who maintained that Congress, not the president, should supervise the reconstruction program. To this end they helped pass in 1864 the Wade-Davis Bill, sponsored by Senator Benjamin Wade of Ohio and Representative Winter Davis of Maryland, which proposed much more stringent requirements than Lincoln had. In contrast to Lincoln's 10 percent plan, the Wade-Davis Bill required that a majority of white male citizens declare their allegiance and that only those who swore an "ironclad" oath that they had always remained loyal to the Union could vote or serve in the state constitutional conventions. The conventions, moreover, would have to abolish slavery. deny political rights to high-ranking civil and military officers of the Confederacy, and repudiate war debts. Passed during the closing days of the 1864 session, the bill went unsigned by Lincoln, and this "pocket veto" provoked the bill's sponsors to issue the Wade-Davis Manifesto, a blistering statement that accused the president of usurping power and attempting to use readmitted states to ensure his reelection.

By early 1865 Lincoln and the Radical Republicans were embroiled in an increasingly heated debate about the direction of reconstruction policy. A few Radicals argued that what the freedmen needed most was land. But the several proposals for land confiscation and distribution never materialized. Even most dedicated abolitionists shrank from the measures of land reform that might have given the freedmen more self-support and independence. Citizenship and legal rights were one thing, wholesale confiscation quite another. Instead of land or material help the freedmen more often received age-old advice: work hard and lead sober, honest, and frugal lives. Frederick Douglass, the black abolitionist, suggested that after the war the former slave was left "free from the individual master but a slave of society. He had neither money, property, nor friends. He was free from the old plantation, but he had nothing but the dusty road under his feet. . . . He was turned loose, naked, hungry, and destitute to the open sky." According to a former Confederate general, recently freed blacks had "nothing but freedom."

In March 1865 Congress did establish within the War Department the Bureau of Refugees, Freedmen, and Abandoned Lands, to provide "such issues of provisions, clothing, and fuel" as might be needed to relieve "destitute and suffering refugees and freedmen and their wives and children." The Freedmen's Bureau would also take over abandoned and confiscated land for rental in forty-acre tracts to "loyal refugees and freedmen," who might buy the land at a fair price within three years. But such lands were limited, and by the end of 1865 all confiscated lands were returned to the original owners. Bureau agents were also entrusted with negotiating labor contracts (something new for both freedmen and planters), providing medical care, and setting up schools.

This was as far as Congress would go. Beyond such temporary measures of relief, no program of reconstruction ever incorporated much more than basic constitutional and legal rights for freedmen. These were important in themselves, of course, but their scope was uncertain, to be settled more by the course of events than by any clear-cut commitment to equality.

Lincoln issued his final statement on reconstruction in his last public address, on April 11, 1865. Speaking from the White

House balcony, he dismissed the theoretical question of whether the Confederate states had technically remained in the Union as "good for nothing at all—a mere pernicious abstraction." These states were simply "out of their proper practical relation with the Union," and the object was to get them "into their proper practical relation" as quickly as possible. At a cabinet meeting on April 14, Lincoln proposed to get state governments in operation before Congress met in December. He worried that Congress might push through a harsher reconstruction program. Lincoln wanted "no persecution, no bloody work," no dramatic restructuring of southern social and economic life.

That evening Lincoln went to Ford's Theater and his rendezvous with death. Shot in the head by John Wilkes Booth, a crazed actor and Confederate zealot, the president died the next morning. Pursued into Virginia, Booth was trapped and shot in a burning barn. His last words were: "Tell mother I die for my country. I thought I did for the best." Three collaborators were tried and hanged, along with Mrs. Mary Surratt, at whose boarding house they had plotted. Three others received life sentences, including a Maryland doctor who set the leg Booth had broken when he jumped from Lincoln's box onto the stage. The doctor achieved lasting fame by making common a once obscure expression. His name was Mudd.

JOHNSON'S PLAN Lincoln's death suddenly elevated to the White House Andrew Johnson of Tennessee, a man whose state remained in legal limbo and whose party affiliation was unclear. He was a War Democrat who had been put on the Union ticket in 1864 as a gesture of unity. Of humble origins like Lincoln, Johnson had moved as a youth from his birthplace in Raleigh, North Carolina, to Greenville, Tennessee, where he became proprietor of a tailor shop. Self-educated with the help of his wife, he had made himself into an effective, salty orator, and he won election as mayor, congressman, governor, and senator, then as military governor of Tennessee before he became vice-president. In the process Johnson had become an advocate of the small farmers against the large planters. He also shared the racial attitudes of most white yeomen. "Damn the negroes," he exclaimed to a friend during the war, "I am fighting those traitorous aristocrats, their masters." Scrupulously honest but often tactless, Johnson was tenacious and unyielding in defending his principles. After visiting the White House, the English writer Charles Dickens noted that the stern Johnson displayed great commitment but no "genial sunlight."

Andrew Johnson.

Some of the Radicals at first thought Johnson, unlike Lincoln, to be one of them—an illusion created by Johnson's gift for strong language. He had, for example, asserted that treason "must be made infamous and traitors must be impoverished." Such vindictive language made Ben Wade giddy with admiration for the new president. "Johnson, we have faith in you," he pledged. "By the gods, there will be no trouble now in running this government." But Wade would soon find him as untrustworthy as Lincoln, if for different reasons. Johnson's very loyalty to the Union sprang from a strict adherence to the Constitution. Given to dogmatic abstractions that were alien to Lincoln's temperament, he nevertheless arrived by a different route at similar objectives. The states should be brought back into their proper relation to the Union, not by ignoring as a pernicious abstraction the theoretical question of their status, but because the states and the Union were indestructible. By May 1865 he was arguing that "there is no such thing as reconstruction. Those states have not gone out of the Union. Therefore reconstruction is unnecessary."

Johnson's plan to restore the Union thus closely resembled Lincoln's. A new Proclamation of Amnesty (May 29, 1865) added to the list of those Lincoln had excluded from pardon everybody with taxable property worth more than $20,000. These wealthy planters and merchants were the people Johnson believed had led the South into secession. But those in the excluded groups might make special applications for presidential pardon, and before the year was out Johnson had issued some 13,000 such pardons.

In each of the Rebel states not already organized by Lincoln, Johnson named a native Unionist provisional governor with authority to call a convention elected by loyal voters. Lincoln's 10 percent requirement was omitted. Johnson called upon the conventions to invalidate the secession ordinances, abolish slavery, and repudiate all debts incurred to aid the Confederacy. Each state, moreover, was to ratify the Thirteenth Amendment, which ended slavery. Like Lincoln, Johnson endorsed a limited black suffrage. He reminded the provisional governor of Mississippi, for example, that the state conventions might "with perfect safety" extend suffrage to those blacks with education or with military service so as to "disarm the adversary"—the adversary being "radicals who are wild upon Negro franchise."

The state conventions for the most part met Johnson's requirements. But a northern visitor found in the South "an utter absence of national feeling . . . and a desire to preserve slavery . . . as much and as long as possible." Southern whites accepted the situation because they thought so little had changed after all. Emboldened by Johnson's indulgence, they ignored his advice to move cautiously in restoring their political and social traditions. Suggestions of Negro suffrage were scarcely raised in the conventions, and promptly squelched when they were.

SOUTHERN INTRANSIGENCE When Congress met in December 1865, for the first time since the end of the war, it had only to recognize the new state governments functioning in the South. But there was the rub: the new governments were remarkably like the old. Among the new members presenting themselves to Congress were Georgia's Alexander H. Stephens, late vice-president of the Confederacy, four Confederate generals, eight colonels, six cabinet members, and a host of lesser Rebels. The Congress forthwith denied seats to all members from the eleven former Confederate states. It was too much to expect, after four bloody years, that Unionists would welcome ex-Confederates back like prodigal sons.

Furthermore, the new southern legislatures, in passing repressive Black Codes regulating the freedom of blacks, baldly revealed that they intended to preserve the trappings of slavery as nearly as possible. As one southerner stressed, the "ex-slave was not a free man; he was a free Negro," and the Black Codes were intended to highlight the distinction. They extended to blacks certain new rights, but also insisted that the freedmen be set aside as a separate caste subject to special restraints. The details of the Black Codes varied from state to state, but some

According to a former Confederate general, recently freed blacks had "nothing but freedom."

provisions were common. Existing black marriages, including common-law marriages, were recognized, and testimony of blacks was accepted in legal cases involving them—in six states in all cases. Blacks could hold property. They could sue and be sued in the courts. On the other hand blacks in Mississippi could not own farm lands, and in South Carolina they could not own city lots. Blacks were required to enter into annual labor contracts, with provision for punishment in case of violation. Dependent children were subject to compulsory apprenticeship and corporal punishment by masters. Vagrant blacks were punished with severe fines and could be sold into private service if unable to pay. To many people it indeed seemed that slavery was on the way back in another guise.

THE RADICALS   Faced with such evidence of southern intransigence, moderate Republicans drifted more and more toward the Radical camp. Having excluded southern members, the new Congress set up a Joint Committee on Reconstruction, with nine members from the House and six from the Senate, to gather evidence and submit proposals. As a parade of witnesses testified to the Rebels' impenitence, initiative on the committee fell to determined Radicals: Ben Wade of Ohio, George W. Julian of Indiana, Henry Wilson of Massachusetts—and most conspicuously of all, Thaddeus Stevens of Pennsylvania and Charles Sumner of Massachusetts. Stevens, a crusty old bachelor with a chiseled face, thin, stern lips, and brooding eyes, was the domineering floor leader in the House. Driven by a genuine, if at times fanatical, idealism, he angrily insisted that the "whole fabric of southern society *must* be changed."

Sumner, Stevens's counterpart in the Senate, agreed. Now recovered from "Bully" Brooks's 1856 assault, Sumner was determined to see the South *reconstructed* rather than simply restored. This put him at odds with Johnson. After visiting the White House in December 1865, Sumner found the president "harsh, petulant, and unreasonable." He was especially disheartened by Johnson's "prejudice, ignorance, and perversity" regarding the treatment of blacks. Sumner and other Radicals now grew determined to take matters into their own hands. He argued that "Massachusetts could govern Georgia better than Georgia could govern herself." The southern plantations, seedbeds of aristocratic pretension and secession, he later added, "must be broken up, and the freedmen must have the pieces."

Most of these Radical Republicans had long been connected with the antislavery cause, and they approached the question of black rights with a sincere humanitarian impulse. Few, however, could escape the bitterness bred by the long and bloody war or remain unaware of the partisan advantage that would come to the Republican party from "Negro suffrage." But they reasoned that their party, after all, could best guarantee the fruits of victory and that granting suffrage could best guarantee black rights. Stevens reflected the mixed motives of the Radicals when he proclaimed: "I am for negro suffrage in every rebel state. If it be just, it should not be denied; if it be necessary, it should be adopted; if it be a punishment to traitors, they deserve it."

The growing conflict of opinion over reconstruction policy brought about an inversion in constitutional reasoning. Secessionists—and Johnson—were now arguing that their states had in fact remained in the Union, and some Radicals were contriving arguments that they had left the Union after all. Stevens argued that the Confederate states had indeed seceded and were now conquered provinces, subject to the absolute will of the victors. Sumner maintained that the southern states, by their acts of secession, had in effect committed suicide and reverted to the status of unorganized territories subject to the will of Congress. But most congressmen embraced the "forfeited rights theory," which held that the states continued to exist, but by the acts of secession and war had forfeited "all civil and political rights under the constitution." And Congress was the proper authority

Two leading Radicals: Charles Sumner (left) and Rep. Thaddeus Stevens.

to determine conditions under which such rights might be restored.

JOHNSON'S BATTLE WITH CONGRESS   A long year of political battling remained, however, before this idea triumphed. By the end of 1865 Radical views had gained only a slight majority in Congress, insufficient to override presidential vetoes. But the critical year 1866 saw the gradual waning of Johnson's power and influence, much of this self-induced. Johnson first challenged Congress in February, when he vetoed a bill to extend the life of the Freedmen's Bureau. For the moment Johnson's prestige remained sufficiently intact that the Senate upheld his veto.

Three days after the veto, however, Johnson undermined his already weakening prestige by launching an intemperate assault on Radical leaders during an impromptu speech on Washington's Birthday. From that point forward moderate Republicans backed away from the president, and Radical Republicans went on the offensive. Johnson was now "an alien enemy of a foreign state," Stevens declared.

In mid-March 1866 Congress passed the Civil Rights Act. A direct response to the Black Codes, this bill declared that "all persons born in the United States . . . excluding Indians not taxed," were citizens entitled to "full and equal benefit of all laws." The grant of citizenship to native-born blacks, Johnson claimed, went beyond anything formerly held to be within the scope of federal power. It would, moreover, "foment discord among the races."

He vetoed the measure, but this time, in April 1866, Congress overrode the presidential veto. Then in July it enacted a revised Freedmen's Bureau Bill, again overturning a veto. From that point on Johnson's support steadily eroded.

THE FOURTEENTH AMENDMENT   To remove all doubt about the validity of the new Civil Rights Act, the Joint Committee recommended a new constitutional amendment which passed Congress in June 1866, and was ratified in July 1868. The Fourteenth Amendment, however, went far beyond the Civil Rights Act, and it would have significant and unforeseen effects long thereafter. In the first section it asserted four principles: it reaffirmed state and federal citizenship for all persons—regardless of race—born or naturalized in the United States, it forbade any state (the word "state" was important in later litigation) to abridge the "privileges and immunities" of citizens; to deprive any person (again an important term) of life, liberty, or property without "due process of law"; or to deny any person "the equal protection of the laws." The amendment also voided all Confederate debts.

Johnson's home state was among the first to ratify. In Tennessee, which had harbored probably more Unionists than any other Confederate state, the government had fallen under Radical control. But the rest of the South steadfastly resisted the Radical challenge to Johnson's program. In May and July bloody race riots in Memphis and New Orleans added fuel to the flames. Both incidents amounted to indiscriminate massacres of blacks by local police and white mobs. The rioting, Radicals argued, was the natural fruit of Johnson's policy.

Reconstructing the South

THE TRIUMPH OF CONGRESSIONAL RECONSTRUCTION   As 1866 drew to an end, the upcoming congressional elections promised to be a referendum on the growing split between Johnson and the Radicals. Johnson embarked on a speaking tour of the Midwest, a "swing around the circle," which provoked undignified shouting contests between the president and his audiences. Subjected to attacks on his integrity, Johnson responded in kind. In Cleveland he described the Radicals as "factious, domineering, tyrannical" men. Once, while Johnson was speaking from an observation car, the engineer mistakenly pulled the train out of the station, making the president appear quite the fool. Such incidents tended to

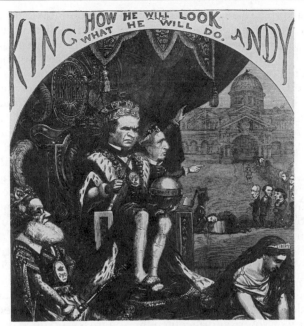

This cartoon appeared at the time of the 1866 congressional elections. It shows "King Andy I" approving the execution of Radical leaders in Congress.

confirm his image as a "ludicrous boor," which Radical papers eagerly projected. When the election returns came in, the Republicans had well over a two-thirds majority in each house, a comfortable margin with which to override any presidential vetoes.

The Congress actually enacted a new program even before new members took office. On March 2, 1867, two days before the old Congress expired, it passed three basic laws of congressional reconstruction over Johnson's vetoes: the Military Reconstruction Act, the Command of the Army Act, and the Tenure of Office Act.

The first of the three acts prescribed conditions under which new southern state governments should be formed. The other two sought to block obstruction by the president. The Army Act required that all orders from the president, as commander-in-chief, go through the headquarters of the general of the army, then Ulysses S. Grant. The Radicals trusted Grant, who was already leaning their way. The Tenure of Office Act required the consent of the Senate for the president to remove any office-holder whose appointment the Senate had to confirm in the first place. In large measure it was intended to retain Secretary of War Edwin M. Stanton, the one Radical sympathizer in Johnson's cabinet. The Military Reconstruction Act, often hailed or denounced as the triumphant victory of "Radical" Reconstruction, actually fell short of a thoroughgoing transformation. Diluted by moderate Republicans, the Military Reconstruction Act boiled down to little more than a requirement that southern states accept black suffrage and ratify the Fourteenth Amendment.

Tennessee, which had ratified the Fourteenth Amendment, was exempted from the application of the act. The other ten states were divided into five military districts, and the commanding officer of each was authorized to keep order and protect the "rights of persons and property." The Johnson governments remained intact for the time being, but new constitutions were to be framed "in conformity with the Constitution of the United States," in conventions elected by male citizens twenty-one and older "of whatever race, color, or previous condition." Each state constitution had to provide the same universal male suffrage. Then, once the constitution was ratified by a majority of voters and accepted by Congress, and once the state legislature had ratified the Fourteenth Amendment, and once the amendment became part of the Constitution, any given state would be entitled to representation in Congress. Persons excluded from officeholding by the proposed amendment were also excluded from participation in the process. Before the end of 1867 new elections had been held in all the states but Texas.

Having clipped the president's wings, the Republican Congress moved a year later to safeguard its program from possible interference by the Supreme Court. On March 27, 1868, Congress simply removed the power of the Supreme Court to review cases arising under the Military Reconstruction Act, which Congress clearly had the constitutional right to do under its power to define the Court's appellate jurisdiction. The Court accepted this curtailment of its authority on the same day it affirmed the notion of an "indestructible Union" in *Texas v. White* (1869). In that case it also acknowledged the right of Congress to reframe state governments, thus endorsing the Radical point of view.

THE IMPEACHMENT AND TRIAL OF JOHNSON (1868) Congress's move to restrain the Supreme Court preceded by just two days the trial of the president in the Senate on an impeachment brought in by the House. Johnson, though hostile to the congressional program, had gone through the motions required of him. He continued, however, to pardon former Confederates in wholesale lots and transferred several of the district military commanders who had displayed Radical sympathies. Nevertheless a lengthy investigation by the House Judiciary Committee, extending through most of the year 1867, failed to convince the House that grounds for impeachment existed.

Johnson himself provided the occasion for impeachment when he deliberately violated the Tenure of Office Act in order to test its constitutionality. Secretary of War Stanton had become a thorn in the president's side, refusing to resign despite his disagreements with Johnson's reconstruction policy. On August 12, 1867, during a Congressional recess, Johnson suspended Stanton and named General Grant in his place. When the Senate refused to confirm Johnson's action, however, Grant returned the office to Stanton. On February 24, 1868, the House voted impeachment.

Of the eleven articles of impeachment, eight focused on the charge that Johnson had unlawfully removed Stanton and had failed to give the Senate the name of a successor. Article 9 accused the president of issuing orders in violation of the Army Act. The last two articles in effect charged him with criticizing Congress by "inflammatory and scandalous harangues." Article 11 also accused Johnson of "unlawfully devising and contriving" to violate the Reconstruction Acts, contrary to his obligation to execute the laws. At the very least, Johnson had tried to obstruct Congress's will while observing the letter of the law.

The Senate trial opened on March 5, 1868, and continued until May 26, with Chief Justice Salmon P. Chase presiding. On May 16 enough Republican senators joined their pro-Johnson colleagues to prevent conviction by the narrowest of margins— one vote. These Republicans had broken ranks with their party largely because they feared the consequences of removing a president essentially for political rather than criminal reasons, and they opposed the economic and social agenda of the Radicals. Impeachment of Johnson was in the end a great political mistake, for the failure to remove the president damaged Radical morale and support. Nevertheless the Radical cause did gain something. To blunt the opposition, Johnson agreed not to obstruct the process of Reconstruction, and thereafter Radical Reconstruction began in earnest.

REPUBLICAN RULE IN THE SOUTH In June 1868 Congress agreed that seven states had met the conditions for readmission, all but

Virginia, Mississippi, and Texas. Congress rescinded Georgia's admission, however, when the state legislature expelled twenty-eight black members and seated some former Confederate leaders. The military commander of Georgia then forced the legislature to reseat the black members and remove the Confederates, and the state was compelled to ratify the Fifteenth Amendment before being admitted in July 1870. Mississippi, Texas, and Virginia had returned earlier in 1870, under the added requirement that they too ratify the Fifteenth Amendment. This amendment, ratified in 1870, forbade the states to deny any citizen the vote on grounds of race, color, or previous condition of servitude.

Long before the new governments were established, partisan Republican groups began to spring up in the South, promoted by the Union League, an organization founded in 1862 to rally support for the Union. League representatives enrolled blacks and loyal whites as members, initiated them into the secrets and rituals of the order, and instructed them "in their rights and duties." These Union Leagues became a powerful source of Republican political strength in the South and as a result drew the ire of unreconstructed whites.

BLACKS IN SOUTHERN POLITICS The new role of blacks in politics caused the most controversy, then and afterward. If largely illiterate and inexperienced in the rudiments of politics, they were little different from millions of whites enfranchised in the age of Jackson or immigrants herded to the polls by political bosses in New York and other cities after the war. Some freedmen frankly confessed their disadvantages. Beverly Nash, a black delegate in the South Carolina convention of 1868, told his colleagues: "I believe, my friends and fellow-citizens, we are not prepared for this suffrage. But we can learn. Give a man tools and let him commence to use them, and in time he will learn a trade. So it is with voting."

Several hundred black delegates participated in the statewide political conventions. Most had been selected by local political meetings or by churches, fraternal societies, Union Leagues, and black army units, although a few simply appointed themselves. "Some bring credentials," explained a North Carolina black leader, "others had as much as they could to bring themselves, having to escape from their homes stealthily at night" to avoid white assaults. The black delegates "ranged all colors and apparently all conditions," but free mulattoes from the cities played the most prominent roles. At Louisiana's Republican state con-

A lithograph depicting five of the major black political figures of the Reconstruction period: Revels (top left) and Bruce (center) served in the U.S. Senate, Rainey (bottom left), Lynch (bottom right), and Rapier (top right) in the House of Representatives.

vention, for instance, nineteen of the twenty black delegates had been born free.

By 1867, however, former slaves began to gain political influence, and this led to debates that revealed emerging tensions within the black community. Some southern blacks resented the presence of northern brethren while others complained that few ex-slaves were represented in leadership positions. Northern blacks and the southern free black elite, most of whom were urban dwellers, tended to oppose efforts to confiscate and redistribute land to the rural freedmen, and many insisted that political equality did not mean social equality. As an Alabama black leader stressed, "We do not ask that the ignorant and degraded shall be put on a social equality with the refined and intelligent." In general, however, unity rather than dissension prevailed, and blacks focused on common concerns such as full equality under the law.

Brought suddenly into politics in times that tried the most skilled of statesmen, many blacks nevertheless served with distinction. Yet the derisive label "black Reconstruction" used by later critics exaggerates black political influence, which was limited mainly to voting, and overlooks the large numbers of white Republicans, especially in the mountain areas of the upper South. Only one of the new conventions, South Carolina's, had a black majority, 76 to 41. Louisiana's was evenly divided racially, and in only two other conventions were more than 20 percent of the members black: Florida's, with 40 percent, and Virginia's, with 24 percent. The Texas convention was only 10 percent black, and North Carolina's, 11 percent—but that did not stop a white newspaper from calling it a body consisting of "baboons, monkeys, mules . . . and other jackasses."

In the new state governments, any black participation was a novelty. Although some 600 blacks—most of them former slaves —served as state legislators, no black man was ever elected governor and few served as judges, although in Louisiana, Pinckney B. S. Pinchback, a northern black and former Union soldier, won the office of lieutenant-governor and served as acting governor when the white governor was indicted for corruption. Several blacks were elected lieutenant-governors, state treasurers, or secretaries of state. There were two black senators in Congress, Hiram Revels and Blanche K. Bruce, both from Mississippi, and fourteen black members of the House during Reconstruction. Among these were some of the ablest congressmen of the time.

It is also true, though, that a number of black politicians were more concerned with promoting their own interests than helping the black masses and that many black voters were manipulated by the Union Leagues. Recent studies suggest that blacks also differed among themselves over political and economic issues. In several southern communities, light-skinned Negroes who were free before the war, and tended to be educated and relatively prosperous, dominated black politics and clashed frequently with the darker, poorer freedmen.

CARPETBAGGERS AND SCALAWAGS   The top positions in southern state governments went for the most part to white Republicans, whom the opposition soon labeled "carpetbaggers" and "scalawags," depending on their place of birth. Northern opportunists who allegedly came south with all their belongings in carpetbags to reap political spoils were more often than not Union veterans who had arrived as early as 1865 or 1866, drawn south by the hope of economic opportunity. Others were lawyers, businessmen, editors, teachers, social workers, or preachers who came on missionary endeavors.

The "scalawags," or southern white Republicans, were even more reviled and misrepresented. A Nashville editor called them the "merest trash that could be collected in a civilized community, of no personal credit or social responsibility." Most "scalawags" had opposed secession, forming a Unionist majority in many mountain counties as far south as Georgia and Alabama, and especially in the hills of eastern Tennessee. Though many were indeed crass opportunists who indulged in corruption at the public's expense, several were quite distinguished figures. They included former Confederate general James A. Longstreet, who decided after Appomattox that the Old South must change its ways. To that end, he became a successful cotton broker in New Orleans, joined the Republican party, and supported the Radical reconstruction program. Others were former Whigs who found the Republican party's expansive industrial and commercial program in keeping with Henry Clay's earlier "American System."

THE REPUBLICAN RECORD The new state constitutions were objectionable to adherents of the old order more because of their origin than because of their content, excepting their provisions for black suffrage and civil rights. Otherwise the documents were in keeping with other state constitutions of the day, their provisions often drawn from the basic laws of northern states. Most remained in effect for some years after the end of Radical control, and later constitutions incorporated many of their features. Conspicuous among Radical innovations were such steps toward greater democracy as requiring universal manhood suffrage, reapportioning legislatures more nearly according to population, and making more state offices elective.

Given the hostile circumstances in which the Radical governments arose and operated, they made a surprisingly good record. In most of the South they established the first state school systems, however inadequate and ill-supported at first. Some 600,000 black pupils were in schools by 1877. State governments under the Radicals also gave more attention than ever before to poor relief and to public institutions for the disadvantaged and handicapped: orphanages, asylums, institutions for the deaf, dumb, and blind of both races. Public roads, bridges, and buildings were repaired or rebuilt. Blacks achieved new rights and opportunities that would never again be taken away, at least in principle: equality before the law, and the right to own property, carry on business, enter professions, attend schools, and learn to read and write.

Yet several of these Republican regimes also practiced systematic corruption. In Louisiana, the carpetbag governor acknowledged the situation: "Why," he said, "down here everybody is demoralized. Corruption is the fashion." Public money and public credit were often voted to privately owned corporations, especially railroads, under conditions which invited influence-peddling. Contracts were let at absurd prices and public officials took their cut. Taxes and public debt rose in every state. Still, the figures of taxation and debt hardly constitute an unqualified indictment of Radical governments, since they then faced unusual and inflated costs for the physical reconstruction of public works in the South. Corruption was not invented by the Radical regimes, nor did it die with them. In Mississippi, the Republican governments of Reconstruction were quite honest compared to their Democratic successors.

WHITE TERROR   The case of Mississippi suggests that whites were hostile to Republican regimes less because of their corruption than their inclusion of blacks. Most white southerners remained unreconstructed, so conditioned by slavery that they were unable to conceive of blacks as citizens or even free agents. In some places hostility to the new regimes took the form of white terror. The prototype of terrorist groups was the Ku Klux Klan, first organized in 1866 by some young men of Pulaski, Tennessee, as a social club with the costumes, secret ritual, and mumbo-jumbo common to fraternal groups. At first a group of pranksters, they soon began to intimidate blacks and white Republicans, and the KKK spread rapidly across the South in answer to the Union League. Klansmen rode about the countryside hiding under masks and robes, spreading horrendous rumors, harassing assertive blacks, and occasionally running amok in violence and destruction.

In Mississippi Klansmen mutilated a black Republican leader in front of his family. Three white "scalawag" Republicans were murdered in Georgia in 1870. That same year, an armed mob of whites assaulted a Republican political rally in Alabama, killing four blacks and wounding fifty-four. In South Carolina the Klan was especially active. Virtually the entire white male population of York County joined the Klan, and they were responsible for eleven murders and hundreds of whippings. In 1871 some 500 masked men laid siege to the Union County jail and eventually lynched eight black prisoners. Although most Klansmen were poor farmers and tradesmen, middle-class whites—planters, merchants, bankers, lawyers, doctors, even ministers—also joined the group and participated in its brutalities.

This Thomas Nast cartoon chides the Ku Klux Klan and the White League for promoting conditions "worse than slavery" for southern blacks after the Civil War.

Congress struck back with three Enforcement Acts (1870–1871) to protect black voters. The first of these measures levied penalties on persons who interfered with any citizen's right to vote. A second placed the election of congressmen under surveillance by federal election supervisors and marshals. The third (the Ku Klux Klan Act) outlawed the characteristic activities of the Klan—forming conspiracies, wearing disguises, resisting officers, and intimidating officials. President Grant, in October 1871, singled out nine counties in upcountry South Carolina as an example, and pursued mass prosecutions which brought an abrupt halt to Klan terrorism. The program of federal enforcement broke the back of the Klan, whose activities declined steadily as recalcitrant southerners resorted to more subtle methods of racial intimidation.

CONSERVATIVE RESURGENCE The Klan in fact could not take credit for the overthrow of Republican control in any state. Perhaps its most important effect was to weaken Negro and Republican morale in the South and strengthen in the North a growing weariness with the whole "southern question." Americans had other

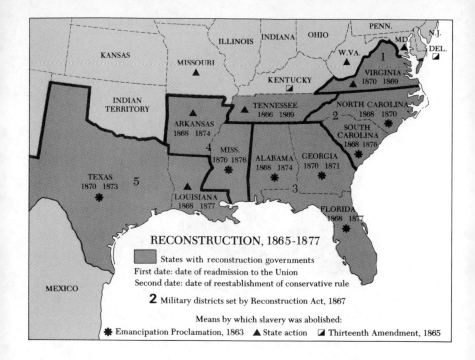

RECONSTRUCTION, 1865-1877

States with reconstruction governments
First date: date of readmission to the Union
Second date: date of reestablishment of conservative rule

2 Military districts set by Reconstruction Act, 1867

Means by which slavery was abolished:
✳ Emancipation Proclamation, 1863 ▲ State action ◨ Thirteenth Amendment, 1865

fish to fry anyway. Western expansion, Indian wars, industrial development, and political controversy over the tariff and the currency distracted attention from southern outrages. Republican control in the South gradually loosened as "Conservative" parties—Democrats used that name to mollify former Whigs—mobilized the white vote. Scalawags, and many carpetbaggers, drifted away from the Radical ranks under pressure from their white neighbors. Few of them had joined the Republicans out of concern for Negro rights in the first place. And where persuasion failed to work, Democrats were willing to use chicanery. As one enthusiastic Democrat boasted, "the white and black Republicans may outvote us, but we can outcount them."

Such factors led to the collapse of Republican control in Virginia and Tennessee as early as 1869, in Georgia and North Carolina in 1870. Reconstruction lasted longest in the Deep South states with the heaviest black population, where whites abandoned Klan hoods for barefaced intimidation in paramilitary groups like the Mississippi Rifle Club and the South Carolina Red Shirts. By 1876 Radical regimes survived only in Louisiana, South Carolina, and Florida, and these all collapsed after the elections of that year.

THE GRANT YEARS

GRANT'S ELECTION   Ulysses S. Grant, who presided during this period of upheaval, brought to the presidency less political experience than any man who had ever occupied the office, except perhaps Zachary Taylor, and arguably less political judgment than any other. But in 1868 the rank-and-file voter could be expected to support "the Lion of Vicksburg" because of his brilliant record as a war leader. Both parties wooed him, but his falling-out with President Johnson pushed him toward the Republicans and built trust in him among the Radicals. They were, as Thad Stevens said, ready to "let him into the church." Impeachment proceedings were still in progress when the Republicans gathered in Chicago and named Grant their unanimous choice. The platform endorsed Radical Reconstruction, cautiously defending black suffrage as a necessity in the South but a matter each northern state should settle for itself. It also urged payment of the nation's war debt in gold rather than in the new "greenback" paper currency printed during the war. More important than the platform were the great expectations of a soldier-president and his slogan: "Let us have peace."

The Democrats took an opposite position on both Reconstruction and the debt. The Republican Congress, the platform charged, had "subjected ten states, in the time of profound peace, to military despotism and Negro supremacy." As to the

President Ulysses S. Grant.

public debt, the party endorsed Representative George H. Pendleton's "Ohio idea" that since most bonds had been bought with depreciated greenbacks, they should be paid off in greenbacks unless they specified payment in gold. With no conspicuously available candidate in sight, the convention turned to Horatio Seymour, war governor of New York and chairman of the convention. The Democrats made a closer race than expected, attesting to the strength of traditional party loyalties. While Grant swept the electoral college by 214 to 80, his popular majority was only 307,000 out of a total of over 5.7 million votes. More than 500,000 black voters accounted for Grant's margin of victory.

Grant had proven himself a great leader in the war, but in the White House he seemed blind to the political forces and influence peddlers around him. Shy and withdrawn, he was uncomfortable around intellectuals and impatient with idealists. Grant preferred watching horse races to reading about complex issues. Although personally honest, he was dazzled by men of wealth and unaccountably loyal to greedy subordinates who betrayed his trust. In the formulation of policy he passively followed the lead of Congress. This approach endeared him at first to party leaders, but it left him at last ineffective and caused others to grow disillusioned with his leadership. At the outset Grant consulted nobody on his cabinet appointments. Some of his choices indulged personal whims; others simply reflected bad judgment. Secretary of State Hamilton Fish of New York turned out to be a fortunate exception; he masterfully guided foreign policy throughout the Grant presidency.

THE GOVERNMENT DEBT   Financial issues dominated the political agenda during Grant's presidency. After the war the Treasury had assumed that the $400 million worth of greenbacks issued during the conflict would be retired from circulation. Congress in 1866 granted the Treasury discretion gradually to do just that. Many agrarian and debtor groups resisted this contraction, believing that a larger money supply would mean rising farm prices and easier-to-pay debts. They were joined by a large number of Radicals who thought a combination of high tariffs and inflation would generate more rapid economic growth. In 1868 "soft money" supporters in Congress halted the retirement of greenbacks, leaving $356 million outstanding. There matters stood when Grant took office.

The "sound" or "hard" money advocates, mostly bankers, merchants, and other creditors, claimed that Grant's election was a mandate to save the country from the Democrats' "Ohio idea." Quite influential in Republican circles, they also had the benefit of a deeply ingrained popular assumption that hard money was morally preferable to paper currency. Grant agreed, and in his inaugural address he endorsed payment of the national debt in gold as a point of national honor.

REFORM AND SCANDAL The "money question" confused Grant, but that was the least of his worries. Within less than a year of his election Grant was adrift in a cesspool of scandal. In the summer of 1869 two brilliant, if crass, young railroad entrepreneurs, the crafty Jay Gould and the flamboyant Jim Fisk, connived with the president's brother-in-law to corner the gold market. Grant apparently smelled a rat from the start, but was seen in public with the speculators. As the rumor spread on Wall Street, gold rose from $132 to $163 an ounce. Finally, on "Black Friday," September 24, 1869, Grant ordered the Treasury to sell a large quantity of gold and the bubble burst. Fisk got out by repudiating his agreements and hiring thugs to intimidate his creditors. "Nothing is lost save honor," he said.

The plot to corner the gold market was only the first of several scandals that rocked the Grant administration. In 1872 the public first learned about the financial buccaneering of the Crédit Mobilier, a construction company which had milked the Union Pacific Railroad for exorbitant fees to line the pockets of insiders who controlled both firms. Rank-and-file Union Pacific shareholders were left holding the bag. This chicanery had transpired before Grant's election in 1868, but it touched a number of prominent Republicans who had been given shares of Crédit Mobilier stock in exchange for favorable votes. Of thirteen Congressmen involved, only two were censured.

Even more odious disclosures soon followed, and some involved the president's cabinet. Grant's secretary of war, it turned out, had accepted bribes from Indian traders at army posts in the West. He was impeached, but resigned in time to elude senate trial. Post-office contracts, it was revealed, went to carriers who offered the highest kickbacks. In St. Louis a "Whiskey Ring" bribed tax collectors to bilk the government of millions in revenue. Grant's private secretary was enmeshed in that scheme, taking large sums of money and other valuables in return for inside information. There is no evidence that Grant himself participated in any of the fraud, but his poor choice of associates earned him widespread censure.

Long before Grant's first term ended, a reaction against the

The People's Handwriting on the Wall. *An 1872 engraving comments on the corruption engulfing Grant.*

Radical Reconstruction measures, and against incompetence and corruption in the administration, had incited mutiny within the Republican ranks. Open revolt broke out first in Missouri, where Carl Schurz, a German immigrant and war hero, led a group which elected a governor with Democratic help in 1870 and sent Schurz to the Senate. In 1872 the Liberal Republicans (as they called themselves) held a clamorous national convention in Cincinnati, which produced a compromise platform condemning the party's "vindictive" southern policy and favoring civil service reform, but which remained silent on the protective tariff. The delegates stampeded toward an anomalous presidential candidate: Horace Greeley, editor of the *New York Tribune*, a strong protectionist and quixotic reformer. During his long journalistic career he had promoted vegetarianism, brown bread, free-thinking, socialism, and spiritualism. His image as a visionary eccentric was complemented by his open hostility to Democrats, whose support the Liberals needed. One reporter suggested that there had been "too much brains and not enough whiskey" at the convention. The Democrats nevertheless swallowed the pill and gave their nomination to Greeley as the only hope of beating Grant.

The result of the 1872 election was a foregone conclusion. Republican regulars duly endorsed Radical Reconstruction and the protective tariff. Grant still had seven carpetbag states in his pocket, generous support from business and banking interests, and the stalwart support of the Radicals. Above all he still evoked the glory of Vicksburg and Appomattox. Greeley, despite an exhausting tour of the country—still unusual for a presidential candidate—carried only six southern and border states and none in the North. Devastated by his crushing defeat and the simultaneous death of his wife, Greeley entered a mental sanitarium and died three weeks later.

PANIC AND REDEMPTION A paralyzing economic panic followed close upon the public scandal besetting the Grant administration. Contraction of the money supply brought about by the Treasury's postwar withdrawal of greenbacks and the reckless overexpansion of the railroads into sparsely settled areas helped precipitate a financial crisis. During 1873 some twenty-five strapped railroads defaulted on their interest payments. Caught short, the prominent investment firm of Jay Cooke and Company went bankrupt on September 18, 1873. The ensuing stampede of selling forced the stock market to close for ten days. The Panic of 1873 set off a depression that lasted for six years, the longest and most severe that Americans had yet suffered, marked by widespread bankruptcies, chronic unemployment, and a drastic slowdown in railroad building.

Hard times and corruption hurt Republicans in the midterm elections of 1874, allowing the Democrats to win control of the House of Representatives and gain in the Senate. The new Democratic House immediately launched inquiries into the Grant scandals and unearthed further evidence of corruption in high places. The panic meanwhile focused attention once more on greenback currency. Since greenbacks were valued less than gold, they had become the chief circulating medium. Most people spent greenbacks first and held their gold or used it to settle foreign accounts, which drained much gold out of the country. To relieve this deflationary spiral and stimulate business, therefore, the Treasury reissued $26 million in greenbacks previously withdrawn.

For a time the advocates of paper money were riding high. But Grant vetoed an attempt to issue more greenbacks in 1874, and in his annual message he called for their gradual withdrawal. In January, before the Republicans gave up control of the House, Congress obliged the president by passing the Resumption Act of 1875. The resumption of paying gold to customers who turned

in their greenbacks began on January 1, 1879, after the Treasury
had built a gold reserve for the purpose and reduced the value of
greenbacks in circulation. This act infuriated those promoting an
inflationary monetary policy and provoked the formation of the
National Greenback party. The much debated "money question" would remain one of the most divisive issues in American
politics until the end of the century.

THE COMPROMISE OF 1877   Grant yearned to run again in 1876,
but the recent scandals precluded any challenge to the two-term
tradition. James G. Blaine of Maine, former Speaker of the
House, emerged as the Republican front-runner, but he too bore
the taint of scandal. Letters in the possession of James Mulligan
of Boston linked Blaine to some dubious railroad dealings. Newspapers soon published these "Mulligan Letters," and Blaine's
candidacy was dealt a body blow.

The Republican convention in Cincinnati therefore eliminated
Blaine and several other hopefuls in favor of Ohio's favorite son,
Rutherford B. Hayes. Three times governor of Ohio, and an ad-
vocate of hard money, Hayes had a sterling character and had
been a civil service reformer. But his chief virtue, as Henry
Adams put it, was "that he is obnoxious to no one."

The Democratic convention in St. Louis was abnormally harmonious from the start. The nomination went on the second ballot to Samuel J. Tilden, millionaire corporation lawyer and
reform governor of New York, who had directed a campaign to
overthrow first the corrupt Tweed Ring in New York City and
then another ring in Albany which had bilked the state of millions.

The campaign generated no burning issues. Both candidates
favored the trend toward restoring conservative rule in the
South. During one of the most corrupt elections ever, both candidates favored civil service reform. In the absence of strong differences, Democrats waved the Republicans' dirty linen. In
response, Republicans waved the bloody shirt, which is to say
that they engaged in verbal assaults on former Confederates and
the spirit of Rebellion, linking the Democratic party with Secession and with the outrages committed against black and white
Republicans in the South. As one Republican speaker insisted,
"Every man that tried to destroy this nation was a Democrat. . . .
The man that assassinated Abraham Lincoln was a Democrat. . . .
Soldiers, every scar you have on your heroic bodies was given
you by a Democrat!"

Early election returns pointed to a Tilden victory, but the Republicans refused to concede. As it fell out, Tilden had 184 electoral votes, just one short of a majority, but Republicans claimed nineteen doubtful votes from Florida, Louisiana, and South Carolina, while Democrats laid a counterclaim to one of Oregon's three votes. The Republicans had clearly carried Oregon, but the outcome in the South was less certain, and given the fraud and intimidation perpetrated on both sides, nobody will ever know the truth of the matter. In all three of the disputed southern states, rival canvassing boards sent in different returns. The Constitution offered no guidance in this unprecedented situation. Even if Congress were empowered to sort things out, the Democratic House and the Republican Senate proved unable to reach an agreement.

The impasse dragged on for months, and there was even talk of public violence. Finally, on January 29, 1877, the two houses decided to set up a special Electoral Commission. It had fifteen members, five each from the House, the Senate, and the Supreme Court. Members were so chosen as to have seven from each major party, with Justice Joseph P. Bradley, a nominal Republican, as the swing man. The decision on each contested state went by a vote of 8 to 7, along party lines, in favor of Hayes. After much debate and threat of filibuster by Democrats, the House voted on March 2 to accept the report and declare the Republican Hayes elected by an electoral vote of 185 to 184.

Critical to this outcome was the defection of southern Democrats who had made several informal agreements with the Republicans. On February 26, 1877, a bargain was struck between prominent Ohio Republicans and powerful southern Democrats. The Republicans promised that, if elected, Hayes would withdraw federal troops from Louisiana and South Carolina, letting the Republican governments there collapse. In return the Democrats pledged to withdraw their opposition to Hayes, to accept in good faith the Reconstruction amendments, and to refrain from partisan reprisals against Republicans in the South.

With this agreement in hand, southern Democrats could justify deserting Tilden. This so-called Compromise of 1877 brought a final "redemption" from the "Radicals" and a return to "home rule," which actually meant rule by native white Democrats. Other, more informal promises bolstered the secret agreement. Hayes's friends pledged more support for Mississippi levees and other internal improvements, including federal subsidy for a transcontinental railroad along a southern route. Southerners extracted a further promise that Hayes would name a white southerner as postmaster-general, the cabinet position with the most patronage jobs at hand. In return, southerners would let Republicans make James A. Garfield Speaker of the new House.

THE END OF RECONSTRUCTION After Hayes took office, most of these promises were either renounced or forgotten. In April 1877, Hayes withdrew federal troops from the state houses in Louisiana and South Carolina, and the Republican governments there soon collapsed—along with much of Hayes's claim to legitimacy. Hayes chose a Tennessean as postmaster-general. But after southern Democrats failed to permit the choice of Garfield as Speaker, Hayes expressed doubt about any further subsidy for railroad building, and none was voted.

As to southern promises regarding the civil rights of blacks, only a few Democratic leaders remembered them for long. Over the next three decades those rights crumbled under the pressure of white rule in the South and the force of Supreme Court decisions narrowing the application of the Fourteenth and Fifteenth amendments. The Compromise of 1877, viewed in the light of its consequences, might justly bear the label which one historian gave it: "The betrayal of the Negro." But "betrayal" implies that a promise was made in the first place, and Reconstruction never offered more than an uncertain commitment to racial equality before the law. Yet it left an enduring legacy, the Thirteenth, Fourteenth, and Fifteenth Amendments—not dead but dormant, waiting to be warmed back into life. If Reconstruction did not provide social equality or substantial economic opportunities for blacks, it did create the opportunity for future transformation. It was a revolution, sighed North Carolina Governor Jonathan Worth, and "nobody can anticipate the action of revolutions."

FURTHER READING

Reconstruction has long been "a dark and bloody ground" of conflicting interpretations. The best survey of the period is Eric Foner's *Reconstruction: America's Unfinished Revolution, 1862–1877* (1988).°
More specialized works give closer scrutiny to the aims of the principal political figures. Eric L. McKitrick's *Andrew Johnson and Reconstruction* (1988)° and LaWanda Cox and John H. Cox's *Politics, Principle, and Prejudice, 1865–1866* (1963) criticize Johnson's policies. Why Johnson

° These books are available in paperback editions.

was impeached is detailed in Michael Les Benedict's *The Impeachment and Trial of Andrew Johnson* (1973).°
On the aims and motives of the Radical Republicans, see Herman Belz's *Reconstructing the Union* (1969). The ideology of the Radicals is explored in Michael Les Benedict's *A Compromise of Principle: Congressional Republicans and Reconstruction* (1974).
The intransigence of southern white attitudes is examined in Michael Perman's *Reunion without Compromise* (1973).° Allen W. Trelease's *White Terror* (1971)° covers the various organizations that practiced vigilante tactics, chiefly the Ku Klux Klan. See also George C. Rable's *But There Was No Peace: The Role of Violence in the Politics of Reconstruction* (1984).° The "carpetbaggers" are explained in Richard N. Current's *Those Terrible Carpetbaggers: A Reinterpretation* (1989).° The difficulties former planters had in adjusting to the new labor system are documented in James L. Roark's *Masters without Slaves* (1977).° Recent books on southern politics during Reconstruction include Michael Perman's *The Road to Redemption* (1984)° and Dan T. Carter's *When the War Was Over* (1985).°
Numerous works have appeared on the freedmen's experience in the South. Start with Leon F. Litwack's *Been in the Storm So Long* (1979).° Joel Williamson's *The Crucible of Race* (1984)° analyzes white attitudes toward blacks in the South. See also Howard N. Rabinowitz, ed., *Southern Black Leaders of the Reconstruction Era* (1982).° The role of the Freedman's Bureau is explored in William S. McFeely's *Yankee Stepfather: General O. O. Howard and the Freedmen* (1968).°
The political maneuvers of the election of 1876 and the resultant crisis and compromise are explained in C. Vann Woodward's *Reunion and Reaction* (1951)° and William Gillette's *Retreat from Reconstruction, 1869–1879* (1979).°

18

NEW FRONTIERS:
SOUTH AND WEST

By the 1870s most Americans had grown tired of the complicated and controversial process of "reconstructing" the South.
Many were eager to exploit two new frontiers, the New South
and the New West. In both regions the distinctive American entrepreneurial and pioneering spirit—brash, aggressive, and persistent—went to work, and as a result, the South and West by the
end of the century were regions transformed.

THE NEW SOUTH

A FRESH VISION   After the Civil War many southerners looked
back wistfully to the plantation life that had characterized their
region before the firing on Fort Sumter. A few prominent
spokesmen, however, insisted that the postwar South must liberate itself from such paralyzing nostalgia and create a new society
of small farms, thriving industries, and bustling cities. The major
prophet of this "New South" was Henry W. Grady, the thirty-
six-year-old editor of the *Atlanta Constitution*. During the 1880s,
Grady set forth the vision that inspired a generation of southerners: "The Old South rested everything on slavery and agriculture, unconscious that these could neither give nor maintain
healthy growth. The New South presents a perfect democracy
. . . a social system compact and closely knitted, less splendid on
the surface, but stronger at the core—a hundred farms for every
plantation, fifty homes for every palace—and a diversified industry that meets the complex need of this complex age."
   It was a compelling vision, and other advocates of this New

South Creed soon emerged. In the aftermath of the Civil War these men, and their Yankee patrons, preached the gospel of industry with evangelical fervor. The Confederacy, they reasoned, had lost because it relied too much on King Cotton. In the future the South must follow the North's example and industrialize. From that central belief flowed certain implications: that a more diversified and efficient agriculture would be a foundation for economic growth, that more widespread education, especially vocational training, would promote material success. By the late 1870s, with Reconstruction over and the panic of 1873 forgotten, a mood of progress permeated the editorials and the speeches of the day.

ECONOMIC GROWTH   The first and chief fruit of the New South movement was an expansion of the area's textile production that began in the 1880s and overtook the older New England industry by the 1920s. From 1880 to 1900 the number of cotton mills in the South grew from 161 to 400, and the number of mill workers (among whom women and children outnumbered the men) increased fivefold.

Tobacco growth also increased significantly. Leading the way was the Duke family, whose road to success started at a farm near Durham, North Carolina. At the end of the Civil War, the story goes, old Washington Duke had fifty cents obtained from a Yankee soldier in exchange for a souvenir Confederate five-dollar bill. He took a load of tobacco, and with the help of his three

White Oak Cotton Mills, Greensboro, North Carolina. *These women are measuring, sewing, and finishing denim.*

sons, beat it out with hickory sticks, stuffed it in bags, hitched up two mules to his wagon, and set out across the state, selling bright leaf as he went. Success followed quickly. By 1872 the Dukes had a factory producing 125,000 pounds of tobacco annually, and Washington Duke prepared to settle down and enjoy success.

His son Buck (James Buchanan Duke), however, had the same drive that animated the Carnegies and Rockefellers of that day. Buck Duke recognized early that the tobacco industry was "half smoke and half ballyhoo," so he poured large sums into advertising schemes. Duke also squeezed competitors by underselling them in their own markets, and by cornering the supply of ingredients. Eventually his competitors were ready to take the hint that they join forces, and in 1890 Duke brought most of them into the American Tobacco Company, which controlled nine-tenths of the nation's cigarette production. In 1911 the Supreme Court found the company in violation of the anti-trust laws and ordered it broken up, but by then Duke had found new worlds to conquer in hydroelectric power and aluminum.

Systematic use of other natural resources brought into the New South that area along the Appalachian mountain chain from West Virginia to Alabama. Coal production in the South (including West Virginia) grew from 4.6 million tons in 1875 to 49.3 million tons by 1900. At the southern end of the mountains, Birmingham, Alabama, sprang up during the 1870s as a major steel producing center and soon tagged itself the "Pittsburgh of the South."

Industrial growth created a need for housing, and after 1870 lumbering became a thriving industry in the South. By the turn of the century it had surpassed textiles in value. Tree cutting seemed to know no bounds, despite the ecological devastation it caused. In time the industry would be saved only by the warm climate, which fostered quick renewal, and the rise of scientific forestry.

Two forces that would impel an even greater industrial revolution were already on the southern horizon at the turn of the century: petroleum in the Southwest and hydroelectric power in the Southeast. In 1901 the Spindletop oil gusher in Texas brought a huge bonanza. Electrical power proved equally profitable, and local powerplants dotted the South by the 1890s. Richmond, Virginia, had the nation's first electric streetcar system in 1888, and Columbia, South Carolina, boasted the first electrically powered cotton mill in 1894. The greatest advance would begin in 1905 when Buck Duke's Southern Power Company set out to electrify entire river valleys in the Carolinas.

AGRICULTURE, OLD AND NEW At the turn of the century, however, most of the South remained undeveloped, at least by northeastern standards. Despite the optimistic rhetoric of New South spokesmen, the typical southerner was less apt to be tending a loom or forge than, as the saying went, facing the eastern end of a westbound mule. King Cotton survived the Civil War and expanded over new acreage even as its export markets leveled off. Louisiana cane sugar, probably the most war-devastated of all crops, also flourished again by the 1890s.

The majority of southern farmers were not flourishing, however. Sharecropping and tenancy grew increasingly prevalent in the aftermath of emancipation. By 1890 most southern farms were worked by people who did not own the land. Tenancy rates in the deep South belied the rosy rhetoric of New South prophets: South Carolina, 61%; Georgia, 60%; Alabama, 58%; Mississippi, 62%; and Louisiana, 58%.

How did the system work? The sharecropper, who had nothing to offer the landowner but his labor, tilled the land in return for supplies and a share of the crop, generally about half. The tenant farmer, hardly better off, might have his own mule, a plow, and credit with the country store. He was entitled to claim a larger share, commonly three-fourths of the cash crop and two-thirds of the subsistence crop, which was mainly corn. The system was horribly inefficient, for the tenant lacked incentive to care for the land and the owner had little chance to supervise the work. In addition the system bred a morbid suspicion on both sides, and the folklore of the rural South was replete with tales of

Black sharecroppers, ca. 1880–1890.

tenants who remained stubbornly shiftless and improvident, and landlords who kept books with crooked pencils.

The crop lien system was equally flawed. At best, it supplied credit where cash was scarce. Country merchants furnished supplies in return for liens (or mortgages) on farmers' crops. To a few tenants and small farmers who seized the chance, such credit offered a way out, but to most it offered only a hopeless cycle of perennial debt. The merchant, who assumed great risks, generally charged interest which ranged, according to one journalist, "from 24 percent to grand larceny." The merchant, like the planter (often the same man), demanded a cash crop that could be readily sold at harvest time. Thus, for all the New South ballyhoo about diversification, the routines of tenancy and sharecropping were geared to a staple crop, usually cotton. The resulting stagnation of rural life held millions, white and black, in bondage to privation and ignorance.

THE BOURBON REDEEMERS   In politics, despite the South's formal democracy, habits of deference still prevailed. After Reconstruction ended in 1877, a planter-merchant elite, collectively known as Bourbons, dominated southern politics. Like the French Bourbons, the royal family which, Napoleon once said, forgot nothing and learned nothing in the ordeal of revolution, the southern Bourbons were said to have forgotten nothing and learned nothing in the ordeal of Civil War.

The word functioned mainly as a hateful epithet, and few could glory in it. Bourbon came to signify the leaders of the Democratic party, whether they were real reactionaries or, more commonly, champions of an industrial New South who, if they had forgotten nothing, had at least learned something. They may have worshipped at the shrine of the old order, but they embraced a new order of economic development.

These Bourbons of the New South perfected a political alliance with northeastern conservatives and an economic alliance with northeastern capitalists. They generally pursued a policy of laissez-faire, except for the tax exemptions and other favors they offered to business. They avoided political initiatives, making the transition from Republican rule to Bourbon rule less abrupt than is often assumed. The Bourbons' favorable disposition toward the railroads was not unlike that of the Radicals. And despite their reputation for honesty, Bourbon officeholders were occasionally caught with their fingers in the till.

Being basically antigovernment, the Bourbons made a cardinal virtue of cutting state spending, which spelled austerity for public services, including the school systems started during Reconstruction. In 1871 the South Atlantic states were spending $10.27 per pupil; by 1880 the figure was down to $6.00 and in 1890 it still stood at only $7.63. Illiteracy rates at the time ran at about 12 percent of the white population and 50 percent of the black population.

The Bourbons' urge to economize led them to adopt the degrading system of convict leasing. The destruction of prisons and the poverty of state treasuries combined with the demand for cheap labor on the railroads, in the mines, and in lumber camps, to make the leasing of convict labor a way for southern states to avoid expenses and even bring in revenue. The burden of detaining criminals grew after the war because freedmen, who as slaves had been subject to the discipline of masters, were now subject to the criminal law. Convict leasing, in the absence of state supervision, allowed inefficiency, neglect, and disregard for human life to proliferate.

The Bourbons scaled down not only state expenditures but also the public debt, and by a simple means—they repudiated a vast amount of the bonds that had been issued by the Radical state regimes. The corruption and extravagance of Radical rule were commonly advanced as justification for the process, but repudiation did not stop with Reconstruction debts. Altogether nine states repudiated more than half of what they owed to bondholders and various creditors.

There are elements of diversity in the Bourbon record, however. These scrimping regimes did respond to the demand for commissions to regulate the rates charged by railroads for commercial transport. They established boards of agriculture, boards of public health, agricultural experiment stations, agricultural and mechanical colleges, teacher training schools and women's colleges, even state colleges for African Americans. Nor will any simplistic interpretation encompass the variety of Bourbon leaders. The Democratic party was then a mongrel coalition which threw Old Whigs, Unionists, secessionists, businessmen, small farmers, hillbillies, planters, and even some Republicans together in alliance against the Reconstruction Radicals. Democrats therefore, even those who willy-nilly bore the Bourbon label, often marched to different drummers, and the Bourbon regimes never achieved complete unity in philosophy or government.

Perhaps the ultimate paradox of the Bourbons' rule was that these paragons of white supremacy tolerated a lingering black voice in politics and showed no haste about raising legal barriers of racial separation. Blacks sat in the state legislature of South Carolina until 1900, and of Georgia and Virginia until 1890; some of these black representatives were Democrats. The South sent black congressmen to Washington in every election down to 1900 except one, though they always represented gerrymandered districts into which most of the state's black voters had been thrown. Under the Bourbons the disfranchisement of black voters remained inconsistent, a local matter brought about mainly by fraud and intimidation, though it occurred enough to ensure white control of the southern states.

A like flexibility applied to other areas of race relations. The color line was drawn less strictly than it would be in the twentieth-century South. In some places, to be sure, racial segregation appeared before the end of Reconstruction, especially in schools, churches, hotels and rooming houses, and private social relations. In places of public accommodation such as trains, depots, theaters, and soda fountains, however, segregation was more sporadic.

DISFRANCHISING BLACKS During the 1890s the attitudes of patrician benevolence that permitted such moderation eroded swiftly. One reason for this was that despite signs of progress, many whites embraced a radical racism that held that blacks, loosed from the restraints of slavery, were "retrogressing" toward bestiality, especially the younger ones born after emancipation.

Another reason was political. The rise of Populism, a farm-based protest movement that culminated in the creation of a third political party in the 1890s, divided the white vote to such an extent that in some places the black vote became the balance of power. Some Populists courted black votes. The Bourbons' response was to revive the race issue, which they exploited with seasoned finesse, all the while controlling for their ticket a good part of the black vote in plantation areas. Nevertheless the Bourbons soon argued that the black vote be eliminated completely from southern elections. It was imperative, the Louisiana governor told the state legislature in 1894, that "the mass of ignorance, vice and venality without any proprietary interest in the State" be denied the vote. Some farm leaders hoped that disfranchisement of blacks would make it possible for whites to divide politically without raising the specter of "Negro domination."

But since the Fifteenth Amendment made it illegal to disfranchise blacks as such, racists accomplished their purpose indirectly with devices such as poll taxes, head taxes, and literacy tests. Some opposed such devices because they also ensnared poor whites, and this led to the creation of loopholes through which some whites could slip.

Mississippi led the way to near-total disfranchisement of blacks. The state called a constitutional convention in 1890 for the express purpose of changing the suffrage provisions of the old Radical constitution of 1868. The resulting Mississippi plan set the pattern that seven more states would follow over the next twenty years. First, a residence requirement—two years in the state, one year in the election district—struck at those tenant farmers who were in the habit of moving yearly in search of a better chance. Second, voters were disqualified if convicted of certain crimes, many of them petty. Third, all taxes, including a poll tax, had to be paid by February 1 of election year, which left plenty of time to lose the receipt before the fall vote. This proviso fell most heavily on the poor, most of whom were black. Fourth and finally, all voters had to be literate. The alternative, designed as a loophole for whites otherwise disqualified, was an "understanding" clause. The voter, if unable to read the constitution, could qualify by "understanding" it—to the satisfaction of the registrar. Fraud was thus institutionalized rather than eliminated by "legal" disfranchisement.

In other states, variations on the Mississippi plan added a few flourishes. In 1898 Louisiana invented the "grandfather clause," which allowed illiterates to qualify if their fathers or grandfathers had been eligible to vote on January 1, 1867, when blacks were still excluded. By 1910 Georgia, North Carolina, Virginia, Alabama, and Oklahoma had all adopted the grandfather clause. Every southern state, moreover, adopted a statewide Democratic primary between 1896 and 1915, which became the only meaningful election outside isolated areas of Republican strength. With minor exceptions, the Democratic primaries excluded black voters altogether. The effectiveness of these measures can be seen in a few sample figures: Louisiana in 1896 had 130,000 black voters registered, and in 1900, 5,320. Alabama in 1900 had 121,159 literate black males over twenty-one, according to the census; only 3,742 were registered to vote.

SEGREGATION SPREADS   What came to be called "Jim Crow" segregation followed hard on disfranchisement and in some states came first. The symbolic target at first was the railway train. In the 1880s it was still common practice for American trains to have first- and second-class cars, which afforded a degree of racial segregation by the difference in cost. In 1885, nevertheless, novelist George Washington Cable noted that in South Carolina blacks "ride in first class cars as a right" and "their presence excites no comment." From 1875 to 1883, in fact, any racial segregation violated a federal Civil Rights Act, which forbade discrimination in places of public accommodation. But in 1883 the Supreme Court ruled on seven *Civil Rights Cases* involving discrimination against blacks by corporations or individuals. The Court held, with only one dissent, that the force of federal law could not extend to individual action because the Fourteenth Amendment, which provided that "no State" could deny citizens the equal protection of the laws, stood as a prohibition only against state, not individual, action.

This left as an open question the validity of state laws *requiring* separate public facilities under the rubric of "separate but equal," a slogan popular with the New South prophets. In 1888 Mississippi required railway passengers, under penalty of law, to occupy the car set aside for their race. When Louisiana followed suit in 1890, the law was challenged in the case of *Plessy v. Ferguson*, which the Supreme Court decided in 1896. The test case originated in New Orleans when Homer Plessy, an octoroon (a person of one-eighth black ancestry), refused to leave a white car when asked to do so. He was convicted, and the case rose on appeal to the Supreme Court. The Court ruled that segregation laws "have been generally, if not universally recognized as within the competency of state legislatures in the exercise of their police power."

Very soon the principle of statutory segregation extended into every area of southern life, including street railways, hotels, restaurants, hospitals, recreations, sports, and employment. If an activity was overlooked by the laws, it was not overlooked in custom and practice. The editor of the *Richmond Times* expressed the prevailing view in 1900: "It is necessary that this principle be applied in every relation of Southern life. God Almighty drew the color line and it cannot be obliterated. The negro must stay on his side of the line and the white man must stay on his side, and the sooner both races recognize this fact and accept it, the better it will be for both."

Violence accompanied the Jim Crow laws. From 1890 to 1899 lynchings in the United States averaged 187 per year, 82 percent of which occurred in the South; from 1900 to 1909 they averaged 93 per year, 92 percent in the South. Whites constituted 32 percent of the victims during the first period, only 11 percent in the latter. A young Episcopal priest in Montgomery remarked that extremists had proceeded "from an undiscriminating attack upon the Negro's ballot to a like attack upon his schools, his labor, his life."

WASHINGTON AND DU BOIS   A few brave souls, black and white, spoke out against such attitudes, but by and large blacks had to accommodate them as best they could. Some blacks even began to make a virtue of necessity, and their chief spokesman was Booker T. Washington, the black prophet of the New South creed. Born in Virginia of a slave mother and a white father, Washington had fought extreme adversity to get an education at Hampton Institute, one of the postwar missionary schools, and then, in 1881, to build at Tuskegee, Alabama, a leading college for blacks. Washington argued that black Americans should not antagonize whites by demanding social or political equality; instead they should concentrate on establishing an economic base for their advancement. In his speech at the Atlanta Cotton States and International Exposition in 1895, which propelled him to fame and was later labeled the "Atlanta Compromise," Washington advised fellow blacks to begin "at the bottom of life" and stress their opportunities rather than their grievances: "Cast down your bucket where you are—cast it down in making friends . . . of the people of all races by whom we are surrounded. Cast it down in agriculture, mechanics, in commerce, in domestic service, and in the professions." He conspicuously omitted politics and let fall an oblique endorsement of segrega-

Booker T. Washington.

W. E. B. Du Bois.

tion: "In all things that are purely social we can be as separate as the five fingers, yet one as the hand in all things essential to mutual progress."

Some people bitterly criticized Washington in his lifetime and after for making a bad bargain: the sacrifice of broad education and of civil rights for the dubious acceptance of white conservatives. W.E.B. Du Bois led blacks in this criticism of Washington. A native of Great Barrington, Massachusetts, the son of free blacks, Du Bois once said defiantly that he was born "with a flood of Negro blood, a strain of French, a bit of Dutch, but thank God! no 'Anglo-Saxon.'" Du Bois first experienced southern racial practices as an undergraduate at Fisk University in Nashville. Later he earned a Ph.D. in history from Harvard and afterwards attended the University of Berlin. In addition to an active career in racial protest, he left a distinguished record as a teacher and scholar. Trim and dapper in appearance, sporting a goatee, cane, and gloves, he possessed a combative, fiery spirit. Not long after he began his teaching career at Atlanta University in 1897, he began to assault Washington's accommodationist philosophy of black progress and put forward his own program of "ceaseless agitation."

Washington, Du Bois argued, preached "a gospel of Work and Money to such an extent" that it overshadowed "the higher aims of life." The education of blacks, he maintained, should not be merely vocational but should nurture leaders willing to challenge segregation and discrimination through social protest and political action. He believed in work, "but work is not necessarily education. Education is the development of power and ideal." He demanded that disfranchisement and legalized segregation cease and that the laws of the land be enforced. And he provided the formula for attaining such goals: "By voting where we may vote, by persistent, unceasing agitation, by hammering at the truth, by sacrifice and work." Du Bois minced no words in criticizing Washington's "Atlanta Compromise" philosophy: "We refuse to surrender the leadership of this race to cowards and trucklers."

The New West

For vast reaches of western America the great epics of Civil War and Reconstruction were remote events hardly touching the lives of Indians, trappers, miners, cowboys, traders, and Mormons scattered through the plains and mountains. There the march of Manifest Destiny continued its inexorable course, energized by a lust for land and a passion for profits. On one level, the settlement of the West beyond the Mississippi constitutes a colorful drama of determined pioneers overcoming all obstacles to secure their visions of freedom and opportunity amid the region's awesome vastness. Of course, this romantic vision of western history has long gripped the American imagination. But on another level, the colonization of the Far West involved shortsighted greed and irresponsible behavior, a story of reckless exploitation that nearly exterminated the culture of Native Americans, scarred the land, and decimated its wild animals. The history of the West seen from this prespective is not a grand success story but a tale of hardship, frustration, and failure. Both images of the process of western settlement are accurate in some respects, and it is now our task to strike the appropriate balance.

In the second tier of trans-Mississippi states—Iowa, Kansas, Nebraska—and in western Minnesota, the last frontier of farmers pressed out onto the Great Plains. From California the miners' frontier scattered enclaves east through the mountains at one new strike after another. From Texas the nomadic cowboys migrated northward into the plains and across the Rockies into the Great Basin. Now there were two frontiers of settlement, east and west, and even a third on the south; in another generation there would be none. After one great final rush the occupation of the continent would be complete, less than three centuries after the first English beachhead at Jamestown.

As settlement moved west, the environment gradually altered. The Great Plains were arid, and the scarcity of water and timber rendered obsolete the axe, the log cabin, the rail fence, and the usual methods of tilling the soil. For a long time the region had been called the Great American Desert, a barrier to cross on the way to the Pacific, unfit for human habitation and therefore, to white Americans, the perfect refuge for Indians. But that pattern changed in the last half of the nineteenth century as a result of new finds of gold, silver, and other minerals, completion of transcontinental railroads, destruction of the buffalo, the rise of the range-cattle industry, and the dawning realization that the arid region need not be a sterile desert. With the use of what water was available, techniques of dry farming and irrigation could make the land fruitful after all.

MINING THE WEST   The miners' frontier was in fact not so much a frontier as a scattering of settlements in parts unsuitable for farming, such as steep mountainsides, remote highlands, and barren deserts. The California miners of '49 set the typical pattern in which the disorderly rush of prospectors was quickly followed by the arrival of the campfollowers, a motley array of saloonkeepers, prostitutes, card sharps, hustlers, and assorted desperadoes, out to mine the miners. An era of lawlessness eventually gave place to vigilante rule and, finally, to a stable community and more subtle forms of exploitation.

The drama of the 1849 gold rush was reenacted time and again in the following three decades. Though the California fever had passed by 1851, and no big strikes were made for seven years, new finds in Colorado and Nevada revived hopes for riches. While nearly 100,000 early rushers were crowding around Pike's Peak in Colorado, miners discovered the Comstock Lode at Gold Hill, Nevada. The lode produced gold and silver, and within twenty years had yielded more than $300 million from shafts that reached hundreds of feet into the mountainside. In both Arizona and Montana, the most important mineral proved to be neither gold nor silver, but copper.

The growing demand for orderly government in the West led to the hasty creation of new territories, and eventually the admission of a host of new states. In 1861 Nevada became a territory and in 1864 the state of Nevada was admitted in time to give its three electoral votes to Lincoln. After Colorado was admitted in 1876, however, no new states entered for over a decade because of the party divisions in Congress. Democrats were reluctant to create states out of territories that were heavily Republican. After the sweeping Republican victory of 1888, however, Congress admitted the Dakotas, Montana, and Washington in 1889, and Idaho and Wyoming in 1890, completing a tier of states from coast to coast. Utah entered in 1896 (after the Mormons abandoned the practice of polygamy), Oklahoma in 1907, and in 1912 Arizona and New Mexico finally rounded out the forty-eight continental states.

THE INDIAN WARS As the frontier pressed in from east and west, relentless greed and duplicity pursued the Indians into what was supposed to be their last refuge. Mounted on horses that were a legacy of the Spaniards, perhaps 250,000 Indians in the Great Plains and mountain regions lived mainly off the buffalo herds that provided food and, from their hides, clothing and shelter. No sooner was Andrew Jackson's removal policy complete than the onrush of white migration in the 1840s began to crowd the Indians' land. From the early 1860s until the late 1870s the frontier was ablaze with Indian wars, and intermittent outbreaks continued through the 1880s.

INDIAN WARS,
1864-1890

0 ___ 300 Miles
0 ___ 300 Kilometers

In Colorado, where chiefs of the Cheyennes and Arapahos accepted a treaty banishing them westward, protesting braves began sporadic raids on the trains and mining camps. In 1864 the territorial governor persuaded most of the warring Indians to gather at Fort Lyon on Sand Creek, where they were promised protection. Despite this promise, Colonel J.M. Chivington's militia fell upon an Indian camp that was flying a white flag of truce, and slaughtered 450 peaceful Indians—men, women, and children. One general called it the "foulest and most unjustifiable crime in the annals of America."

With other scattered battles erupting, in 1865 a congressional committee began to gather evidence on the grisly Indian wars and massacres. Its 1867 *Report on the Condition of the Indian Tribes* led to an act to establish an Indian Peace Commission charged with removing the causes of Indian wars in general. Congress decided this was best accomplished at the expense of the Indians, by persuading them to take up life on out-of-the-way reservations. This solution, in short, was to continue the persistent encroachment on Indian hunting grounds.

In October 1867 a conference at Medicine Creek Lodge, Kansas, ended with the Kiowa, Comanche, Arapahos, and

Cheyennes reluctantly accepting lands in western Oklahoma. The following spring the Sioux agreed to settle within the Black Hills reservation in Dakota Territory. But Indian resistance in the southern Plains continued until the Red River War of 1874-1875. In a winter campaign of relentless pursuit, Gen. Philip Sheridan, the hard-charging Civil War cavalryman, scattered the Indians and finally brought them to terms in the spring of 1875.

By then trouble was brewing once again in the north. In 1874, General George A. Custer led an exploring expedition into the Black Hills, accompanied by gold seekers who began to find what they were after. Miners were soon filtering into the Sioux hunting grounds despite promises that the army would keep them out. The army had done little to protect the Indian lands, but when ordered to move against wandering bands of Sioux hunting on the range according to their treaty rights, the army moved vigorously. After several indecisive encounters, Custer found the main encampment of Sioux and their Cheyenne allies on the Little Big Horn River. Separated from the main body of his men, Custer and 200 soldiers were surrounded by 2,500 warriors and annihilated.

Instead of following up their victory, the Indians threw away their advantage in celebration and renewed hunting. The army regained the offensive, and the Sioux were forced to give up their hunting grounds and the gold fields in return for payments. In response to the peace commission that imposed this settlement, Chief Spotted Tail said: "Tell your people that since the Great Father promised that we should never be removed, we

Chief Joseph of the Nez Perce tribe.

Geronimo, a chief of the
Chiricahua Apaches.

have been moved five times. . . . I think you had better put the
Indians on wheels and you can run them about wherever you
wish."

In the Rockies and westward the same story of hopeless resistance was repeated. In Idaho the peaceful Nez Perces finally refused to surrender lands along the Salmon River. Chief Joseph
tried to avoid war, but when some unruly braves started a fight,
he directed a masterful campaign against overwhelming odds,
one of the most spectacular feats in the history of Indian warfare.
After a 1,500-mile retreat through mountains and plains, he was
finally caught thirty miles short of the Canadian border, and exiled to Oklahoma. A generation of Indian wars virtually ended in
1886 with the capture of Geronimo, a chief of the Chiricahua
Apaches, who had fought encroachments in the Southwest for
fifteen years.

Over the long run the collapse of Indian resistance resulted as
much from the killing off of the buffalo herds on which they subsisted as from direct suppression. White hunters felled buffaloes
for sport, sometimes firing from train windows for the joy of seeing the large animals die. In the 1870s a systematic slaughter of
the buffalo served the demand of fashionable easterners for buffalo robes and overcoats. By the mid-1880s the herds were near
extinction.

Most frontier folk had little tolerance for moralizing on the Indian question, but Easterners who were far removed from frontier dangers took a different view. The slaughter of the Indian
wars was immensely unpopular. In his annual message of 1877

President Hayes echoed the protest: "Many, if not most, of our Indian wars have had their origin in broken promises and acts of injustice on our part." Statesmen and churchmen spoke out against mistreatment of Indians, but the most effective voice was a woman's. Helen Hunt Jackson, a novelist and poet, focused attention on the Indian cause in *A Century of Dishonor* (1881), a book which aroused public indignation and calls for new legislation.

INDIAN POLICY   As a result of such outcries, Indian policy gradually became more benevolent. Well-intentioned reformers sought to "Americanize" the Indians by dealing with them as individuals rather than as tribes. The fruition of reform efforts came in the Dawes Severalty Act of 1887, which proposed to introduce the Indians to individual land ownership and agriculture. The Dawes Act permitted the president to divide the lands of any tribe and grant 160 acres to each head of family and lesser amounts to others. To protect the Indian's property, the government held it in trust for twenty-five years, after which the owner won full title and became a citizen. In 1901 citizenship was extended to the Five Civilized Tribes of Oklahoma, and in 1924 to all Indians.

But the more it changed, the more Indian policy remained the same. Despite the best of intentions, the Dawes Act struck a double blow at the Indians. It created new chances for more land spoliation, and it disrupted what remained of the traditional cultures. Those lands not distributed to Indian families were sold, while others were lost to land sharks because of the Indians' inexperience with private ownership, or simply their powerlessness in the face of fraud. Between 1887 and 1934 Indians lost an estimated 86 million of their 130 million acres. Most of what remained was unsuited to agriculture.

CATTLE AND COWBOYS   While the West was being taken from the Indians, cattle entered the grasslands where the buffalo had roamed, and the cowboy enjoyed his brief heyday, fading then into the folklore of the Wild West. From colonial times, especially in the South, cattle raising had been a common enterprise just beyond the fringe of settlement. In many cases the early slaves took care of the livestock. Later, in the West, black cowboys were still a common sight, although they were lost from view in the novels and "horse operas" which pictured a lily white frontier. Much of the romance of the open-range cattle industry derived from its Mexican roots. The Texas longhorns and the cowboys' horses had in large part descended from stock brought over by the Spaniards, and many of the industry's trappings had been worked out in Mexico first: the cowboy's saddle, his chaps (*chaparejos*) to protect the legs, his spurs, and his lariat. For many years wild cattle competed with the buffalo in the Spanish borderlands. Natural selection and contact with "Anglo" scrub cattle produced the Texas longhorns: lean and rangy, they were noted more for speed and endurance than for providing a choice steak. They had little value, moreover, because the largest markets for beef were too far away. At the end of the Civil War, perhaps as many as 5 million head roamed the grasslands of Texas, still neglected—but not for long. In the upper Mississippi valley, where herds had been depleted by the war, cattle prices ranged from $30 to $50 a head, while the Texas cattle could be had just for the effort of rounding them up.

Cattle drives after the Civil War took on a scale far greater than before. In 1866 a large herd set out for Sedalia, Missouri, the western terminus of the Missouri-Pacific Railroad. But that route proved unsuitable because it was subject to raids by postwar bushwhackers, obstructed by woodlands, and opposed by Arkansas and Missouri farmers. New opportunities arose as railroads pushed farther west where cattle could be driven through relatively vacant lands. Joseph G. McCoy, an Illinois livestock dealer, realized the possibilities and encouraged railroad executives to run a line from the prairies to Chicago, the meat-packing center.

The Kansas Pacific Railroad liked McCoy's vision, and with its help he made Abilene, Kansas, the western terminus of a new line. In September 1867, the first shipment of Texas cattle went to Chicago. As the railroads moved west, so did the cowtowns and the trails.

The flush times of the cowtowns soon passed, however, and many reverted to sleepy villages. The long cattle drives played out because they were economically unsound. The dangers of the trail, the wear and tear on men and cattle, the charges levied on drives that crossed Indian Territory, and the advance of farms across the trails combined to persuade cattlemen that they could best function near the railroads. As railroads spread out into Texas and the Plains, the cattle business spread with them over the High Plains as far as Montana and on into Canada.

In the absence of laws governing the open range, cattlemen at first worked out their own arrangements when rights and uses conflicted. But in 1873 Joseph Glidden, an Illinois farmer, invented the first effective barbed-wire, which ranchers used to fence off their claims at relatively low cost. Five years later an eastern promoter, John W. "Bet-a-Million" Gates, one of the early agents for Glidden, gave a persuasive demonstration of the barbed-wire in San Antonio. Skeptical cattlemen discovered that their meanest longhorns shied away from the fence which, as Gates put it, was light as air, stronger than whiskey, and cheaper than dirt. Orders poured in, and Gates eventually put together a virtual monopoly in the American Steel and Wire Company. The coming of barbed-wire was the crucial factor in ending the open, free range. Thereafter the cowboy settled into a more sedentary existence.

FARMERS AND THE LAND Among the legendary figures of the West, the sodbusters projected an unromantic image in contrast to the cowboys, the cavalry, and the Indians. After 1860, on paper at least, the land laws offered favorable terms to the farmer. Under the Homestead Act of 1862 a farmer could either realize the old dream of free land simply by staking out a claim and living on it for five years, or buy the land at $1.25 an acre after six months. But the land legislation of earlier days was predicated upon an entirely different environment from that of the Plains, and the laws never completely adjusted to the fact that much of the land was suited only for cattle. Cattlemen were forced to garner land by gradual acquisition from homesteaders or land grant railroads.

The unchangeable fact of aridity, rather than land laws, shaped institutions in the New West. Where farming was impossible the cattlemen simply established dominance by control of the water, regardless of the laws. Belated legislative efforts to develop irrigable lands finally achieved a major success when the Newlands Reclamation Act (after the aptly named Sen. Francis G. Newlands of Nevada) of 1901 set up the Bureau of Reclamation. The proceeds of public land sales in sixteen states became a fund for irrigation works, and the Reclamation Bureau set about building such major projects as Boulder (later Hoover) Dam on the Nevada-Arizona line, Roosevelt Dam in Arizona, Elephant Butte Dam in Idaho, and Arrowrock Dam in New Mexico.

But the stubborn problem of water remained, rendering much of the West's land useless for field crops. The area in which rainfall averaged ten to twenty inches per year was marginal, but with the techniques of "dry farming," it could support such crops as sorghums, kaffir corn, and Turkey wheat. Certain varieties of spring and winter wheat grew at the times of greatest rainfall. The eastern Plains from Minnesota and North Dakota down to Texas emerged as the wheat belt, the new breadbasket of the nation, and behind wheat the corn belt and corn-hog combination edged westward.

The lands of the New West, as on previous frontiers, passed to their ultimate owners more often from private hands than directly from the government. Much of the 274 million acres claimed under the Homestead Act passed quickly to cattlemen or speculators, and thence to settlers. The land-grant railroads got some 200 million acres of the public domain in the twenty years from 1851 to 1871, and sold much of this land to build population and traffic along the lines. The New West of cattlemen and farmers was in fact largely the product of the railroads.

The first arrivals on the sod-house frontier faced a grim struggle with danger, adversity, and monotony. Farmers and their families fought a constant battle with the elements: grasshoppers, tornadoes, hailstorms, droughts, prairie fires, and blizzards. The virgin land itself, although fertile, resisted planting. The heavy sod broke plows and wearied backs. Since wood was almost non-existent on the prairies, pioneer families came to rely on dried dung (buffalo chips) for fuel.

Such grueling conditions generated significant changes in family roles. The fight for survival made husbands and wives more equal partners than their eastern counterparts. Prairie life also allowed women more independence than could be had by

The Shores family. *Black homesteaders near Westerville, Nebraska, in 1887.*

those living domestic lives back east. One woman declared that she insisted on leaving out the phrasing about "obeying" her husband from their marriage vows. "I had served my time of tutelage to my parents as all children are supposed to. I was a woman now and capable of being the other half of the head of the family." Similar examples of strong-willed femininity abound. Explained one Kansas woman: "The outstanding fact is that the environment was such as to bring out and develop the dominant qualities of individual character. Kansas women of that day learned at an early age to depend on themselves—to do whatever work there was to be done, and to face danger when it must be faced, as calmly as they were able." Their goal, she added, was to carve out a new world, to "develop from wild prairie to comfortable homes."

Indeed, as the railroads arrived from Chicago bearing lumber from the wooded regions to the north, farm families could leave their dugouts or sod homes and build frame houses. New machinery helped open fresh opportunities for farmers. In 1868 James Oliver of Indiana made a successful chilled-iron plow. With further improvements his "sod buster" was ready for mass production by 1878, easing the task of breaking the shallow but tough grass roots of the Plains. Improvements and new inventions lightened the burden of labor but added to the capital outlay of the farmer.

To get a start on a family homestead required a minimum investment of $1,000. And while the overall value of farm lands and farm products increased in the late nineteenth century, the small farmer did not keep up with the march of progress. His numbers grew, but decreased in proportion to the population at large. Wheat, like cotton in the antebellum period, provided the great export crop which evened America's balance of payments and spurred economic growth. But for a variety of reasons few small farmers prospered. And by the decade of the 1890s many were in open revolt against the "system" that thwarted their efforts and denied their dreams.

"THE FRONTIER HAS GONE" American life reached an important juncture in the last decade of the nineteenth century. After the 1890 population count, the superintendent of the census noted that he could no longer locate a continuous frontier line beyond which population thinned out to less than two per square mile. This fact inspired the historian Frederick Jackson Turner to develop the influential frontier thesis, first outlined in his paper "The Significance of the Frontier in American History," delivered to the American Historical Association in 1893. "The existence of an area of free land," Turner wrote, "its continuous recession, and the advance of American settlement westward, explain American development." The frontier had shaped the national character in striking ways. It was

> to the frontier [that] the American intellect owes its striking characteristics. That coarseness and strength combined with acuteness and acquisitiveness; that practical, inventive turn of mind, quick to find expedients; that masterful grasp of material things, lacking in the artistic but powerful to effect great ends; that restless, nervous energy; that dominant individualism, working for good and for evil, and with all that buoyancy and exuberance which comes with freedom—these are traits of the frontier, or traits called out elsewhere because of the existence of the frontier.

But, Turner ominously concluded in 1893, "the frontier has gone and with its going has closed the first period of American history."

Turner's "frontier thesis" guided several generations of scholars and students in their understanding of the distinctive characteristics of American history. His view of the frontier as the westward-moving source of America's democratic politics, open society, unfettered economy, and rugged individualism, far removed from the corruptions of urban life, gripped the popular imagination as well. But it left much out of the story. Turner's description of the frontier experience exaggerated the homogenizing effect of the physical environment and virtually ignored the roles of women, blacks, Indians, Mormons, Hispanics, and Asians in shaping the diverse human geography of the western United States. Turner also implied that the West would be fundamentally different after 1890 because the frontier experience was essentially over. But in many respects that region has retained the qualities associated with the rush for land, gold, timber, and water rights during the post–Civil War decades. The mining frontier, as one historian has recently written, "set a mood that has never disappeared from the West: the attitude of extractive industry—get in, get rich, get out."

FURTHER READING

The concept of the "New South" is explored in Paul M. Gaston's *The New South Creed: A Study in Southern Mythmaking* (1970).° C. Vann Woodward's *Origins of the New South, 1877–1913* (1951)° is a classic.

° These books are available in paperback editions.

A splendid survey of industrialization in the South is James C. Cobb's *Industrialization and Southern Society, 1877–1984* (1984). Scholarship on the textile industry, which formed the heart of New South aspirations, includes Patrick J. Hearden's *Independence and Empire: The New South's Cotton Mill Campaigns, 1865–1901* (1982)° and Jacquelyn D. Hall et. al., *Like a Family: The Making of a Southern Cotton Mill World* (1987).° For developments in the tobacco industry, consult Nannie M. Tilley's *The R. J. Reynolds Tobacco Company* (1985).

C. Vann Woodward's *The Strange Career of Jim Crow* (3rd ed., 1974)° remains the standard on southern race relations in this period. Some of Woodward's points are challenged in Howard N. Rabinowitz's *Race Relations in the Urban South, 1865–1890* (1978)° and Joel Williamson's *A Rage for Order* (1986).° The attitudes of the two principal black leaders are described in Louis R. Harlan's two-volume biography *Booker T. Washington: The Making of a Black Leader, 1865–1901* (1972, 1983)° and Elliott M. Rudwick's *W. E. B. Du Bois: Propagandist of Negro Protest* (1960).° J. Morgan Kousser's *The Shaping of Southern Politics: Suffrage Restriction and Establishment of the One-Party South, 1880–1910* (1974)° handles disfranchisement.

Several good books discuss developments in southern agriculture. Roger L. Ransom and Richard Sutch's *One Kind of Freedom: The Economic Consequences of Emancipation* (1977)° and Jonathan M. Wiener's *Social Origins of the New South: Alabama, 1860–1885* (1978)° examine the origins of sharecropping.

A concise overview of western history is Richard White's *"It's Your Misfortune and None of My Own": A New History of the American West* (1991).° A provocative interpretive synthesis is Patricia Limerick's *The Legacy of Conquest* (1988).°

The classic work on the "Great American Desert" is Walter Prescott Webb's *The Great Plains* (1931).° Much recent scholarship examines life among the western cowboys. See especially David Dary's *Cowboy Culture: A Saga of Five Centuries* (1989).°

The sodbusters also have their scholars. Gilbert C. Fite's *The Farmer's Frontier, 1865–1900* (1987)° and Allan G. Bogue's *From Prairie to Corn Belt* (1963) detail the harsh Great Plains life. The views of important participants are analyzed in Joanna L. Stratton's *Pioneer Women: Voices from the Kansas Frontier* (1981).°

The best introduction to the history of the Plains Indians remains Wilcomb E. Washburn's *The Indian in America* (1975).° The Indian conflict with encroaching whites is explored in Dee Brown's *Bury My Heart at Wounded Knee* (1971)° and two books by Robert M. Utley, *The Last Days of the Sioux Nation* (1963)° and *The Indian Frontier of the American West, 1846–1890* (1984).°

19

BIG BUSINESS AND
ORGANIZED LABOR

The Post–Civil War Economy

America's rise as an industrial giant and agricultural cornu-copia in the late nineteenth century is a fact of towering visibil-ity. Between 1869 and 1899 the nation's population nearly trebled, farm production more than doubled, and the value of manufactures grew sixfold (in constant prices). Within three generations after the Civil War, the nation that had long been a predominantly rural society dependent upon household produc-tion, governed by the requirements of the land and the rhythms of the seasons, burst forth as the world's preeminent economic power. The United States would soon become a highly struc-tured, increasingly centralized, urban-industrial society buf-feted by the imperatives of mass production, mass consumption, and time-clock efficiency. Bigness became the prevailing stan-dard of corporate life, and social tensions worsened with the scale of business enterprise. The industrial revolution "controls us all," recognized Yale University sociologist William Graham Sumner, "because we are all in it."

BUILDING THE TRANSCONTINENTAL RAILROADS   The key to this eco-nomic explosion was the dramatic growth of railroads. They were the first big business, the first magnet for the great financial markets, and the first industry to develop a large-scale manage-ment bureaucracy. The railroads opened the West, connected raw materials to factories and markets, and in so doing created a national market for the nation's goods and produce. At the same time they were themselves gigantic markets for iron, steel, lumber, and other capital goods.

The renewal of railroad building after the Civil War increased the total mileage from 30,600 in 1862 to 53,000 in 1870 and 94,000 by 1880. During the 1880s, the greatest decade of railroad building, mileage leaped to 167,000 and then grew to 199,000 by 1900. Most of this construction filled out the network east of the Mississippi, but the most spectacular exploits were the transcontinental lines built across the plains and mountains. Running through sparsely settled lands, they served the national purpose of binding the country together, and so received generous government aid. In addition to federal land grants the railroads received financial aid in the form of loans and tax breaks from federal, state, and local governments.

Before the Civil War, sectional differences over routes held up the start of a transcontinental line. Secession finally permitted passage of the Pacific Railway Bill, which Lincoln signed into law in 1862. The act authorized a line along a north-central route, to be built by the Union Pacific railroad westward from Omaha and the Central Pacific railroad eastward from Sacramento. As amended in 1864, the act donated to these two corporations huge tracts of adjoining land and loans from $16,000 to $48,000 per mile, depending on the difficulty of the terrain.

Both roads began construction during the war, but most of the work was done after 1865. The Union Pacific pushed across the Plains at a rapid pace, avoiding the Rockies by going through Evans Pass in Wyoming. The work crews, with large numbers of ex-soldiers and Irish immigrants as laborers, had to cope with bad roads, water shortages, rugged weather, and Indian attacks. Construction was hasty and much of it so flimsy that it had to be redone later, but the Union Pacific made its rendezvous with the Central Pacific.

The Central Pacific was organized by the Sacramento shopkeepers who made an indelible imprint on their state as the California "Big Four": Charles Crocker, Mark Hopkins, Collis P. Huntington, and Leland Stanford, who was elected governor in 1862. To build their rail lines they relied heavily on Chinese recently arrived from the region around Canton on the southeast coast of China. Made destitute by the mid-century economic and political collapse in south China, and lured first by the California gold rush and then by railroad jobs, thousands of Chinese migrated to America, raising their numbers in the United States from 7,500 in 1850 to 105,000 in 1880. Most of these "coolie" laborers were single males intent upon accumulating money and then returning to their homeland, where they could then afford to marry and buy a parcel of land. Their temporary status and dream of a good life back in China apparently made them more willing than American laborers to endure the dangerous working conditions and low pay of railroad work. Charles Crocker explained: "We can't get enough white labor to build this railroad, and build it we must, so we're forced to hire them." He failed to mention the economic benefit to the railroad of paying the Chinese one-third less than Americans. By 1867 the Central Pacific Railroad's 12,000 Chinese laborers represented 90 percent of its entire work force.

Clearing trees, handling explosives and operating power drills, and working in snow drifts was dangerous work, and many Chinese died on the job. Fifty-seven miles east of Sacramento, the construction crews encountered the towering Sierras, but they were eventually able to cut through to more level country in Nevada. The Union Pacific had built 1,086 miles to the Central Pacific's 689 when the race ended on the salt plains of Utah near Ogden, at Promontory. There, on May 10, 1869, Leland Stanford drove a gold spike which symbolized the road's completion.

It was twelve years before the next transcontinental was completed, when the Atchison, Topeka and Santa Fe made contact with the Southern Pacific in southern California. These transcon-

The celebration after the last spike was driven at Promontory, Utah, on May 10, 1869, completing the first transcontinental railroad.

tinentals soon sprouted numerous trunk lines that in turn encouraged the building of other transcontinentals. The result was a massive and continuous railroad building boom that lasted into the early 1890s and in turn stimulated the rest of the economy.

FINANCING THE RAILROADS The building of both the Union Pacific and Central Pacific generated shameless profiteering through construction companies, controlled by insiders, which overcharged the railroad companies. The Crédit Mobilier Company, according to a congressional investigation, bought congressmen like sacks of potatoes and charged the Union Pacific $94 million for construction that cost at most $44 million.

Eastern rail lines engaged in similar acts of financial buccaneering, which centered first on the Erie Railroad, the favorite prey of manipulators. Prince of the railroad "robber barons" was Jay Gould, a secretive trickster who developed the fine art of buying up run-down railroads, making cosmetic improvements, and selling out at a profit, meanwhile using corporate treasuries for personal speculation and judicious bribes. Nearly every enterprise he touched was either compromised or ruined, while Gould built a fortune that amounted to $100 million upon his death.

Few railroad fortunes were built in those free-wheeling times by purely ethical methods, but compared to such as Gould, most railroad entrepreneurs were giants of honesty. They at least took some interest in the welfare of their companies, if not always in that of the public. Cornelius Vanderbilt, called "Commodore" by virtue of his early exploits in steamboating, stands out among the railroad barons. Already rich before the Civil War, he decided to give up the hazards of wartime shipping and move his money into land transport. His great achievement was consolidating separate trunk lines into a single powerful rail network led by the New York Central. After the Commodore's death in 1877, his son William Henry extended the Vanderbilt lines to include more than 13,000 miles in the Northeast. This consolidation trend was nationwide. About two-thirds of the nation's railroad mileage fell under the control of only seven major groups by 1900.

ADVANCES IN MANUFACTURING The story of manufacturing after the Civil War shows much the same pattern of expansion and merger in both old and new industries. The Patent Office, which had recorded only 276 inventions during its first decade of existence, the 1790s, registered 234,956 in the decade of the 1890s.

And whether or not necessity was the mother of invention, invention was the mother of new industries—and new departures in old ones. The list of innovations after the Civil War can be extended indefinitely: barbed-wire, farm implements, the air brake for trains, steam turbines, gas distribution and electrical devices, the typewriter, vacuum cleaner, and countless others. Before the end of the century the internal combustion engine and the motion picture were laying foundations for new industries of the twentieth century.

These technological advances altered the lives of ordinary people far more than politics or intellectual developments. In no field was this more true than in the applications of electricity to communications and power. Few if any inventions of the times could rival the importance of the telephone, which Alexander Graham Bell patented in 1876 and demonstrated at the Philadelphia Centennial Exposition the same year. To promote the new device the inventor and his supporters formed the Bell Telephone Association, out of which grew in 1879 the National Bell Telephone Company. Its stiffest competition came from Western Union which, after turning down a chance to buy Bell's "toy," employed Thomas Edison to develop an improved version. Edison's telephone, with its separate transmitter and receiver, became the prototype of the modern instrument.

EDISON'S INVENTIONS   In the rise of electrical industries the name of Thomas Alva Edison stands above those of other inventors. He started his career at an early age selling papers and candies on trains, soon learned telegraphy, and began making improvements in that and other areas. In 1876 Edison went full-time into the "invention business." He invented the phonograph in 1877, the first successful incandescent light bulb in 1879, and altogether in his New Jersey factories, created or perfected hundreds of new devices and processes including the storage battery, dictaphone, mimeograph, dynamo, electric transmission, and the motion picture. In 1882, with the backing of the financier J.P. Morgan, the Edison Electric Illuminating Company began to supply current to eighty-five customers in New York City, beginning the great electric utility industry. A number of companies making light bulbs merged into the Edison General Electric Company in 1888. Financially secure, Edison retired from business to devote full time once again to invention.

The use of direct current limited Edison's lighting system to a radius of about two miles. To get more distance required an alternating current, which could be transmitted at high voltage

Thomas Edison in his laboratory.

and then stepped down by transformers. George Westinghouse, inventor of the air brake, developed the first alternating-current system in 1886 and manufactured the equipment through the Westinghouse Electric Company. Edison considered the new method too dangerous, but just as Edison's instrument supplanted Bell's first telephone, the Westinghouse system won the "Battle of the Currents," and the Edison companies had to switch over. After the invention of the alternating-current motor in 1888, Westinghouse acquired and improved the motor, which worked a revolution by enabling factories to disperse widely. Capable now of using electricity as a power source, they no longer had to cluster around waterfalls and coal supplies.

ENTREPRENEURS

Edison and Westinghouse were rare examples of inventors with the luck and foresight to get rich from the industries they created. Most of the architects of industrial growth—the great captains of industry—were not inventors but pure entrepreneurs, men skilled mainly in organizing and promoting industry. Three stand out both for their achievements and for their special contributions: John D. Rockefeller, Andrew Carnegie, and J. Pierpont Morgan.

ROCKEFELLER AND THE OIL TRUST   Born in New York state, the son of a pious, uncompromising mother and a carousing, conniving father, John D. Rockefeller learned early the lessons of hard work and shrewd dealing. He moved as a youth to Cleveland, where railroad and ship connections provided a strategic location for servicing the newly discovered oil fields of western Pennsylvania. In economic importance the Pennsylvania oil rush of the 1860s far outweighed the California gold rush of just ten years before. Well before the end of the Civil War, derricks checkered the area around Titusville, and refineries sprang up in Pittsburgh and Cleveland. Of the two cities, Cleveland had the edge in transportation, and John D. Rockefeller made the most of the fast-growing commercial city's advantages. His desire for personal advancement and material gain was obsessive. He started as a bookkeeper, but before age twenty-one was already a partner in a wholesale house. While other young men were going off to fight the Civil War, Rockefeller moved aggressively into the oil business. In 1862 he backed a refinery started by his friend, Samuel Andrews, with whom Rockefeller then formed a partnership. The firm expanded, and in 1870, Rockefeller incorporated his various interests as the Standard Oil Company of Ohio, capitalized at $1 million.

Rockefeller's refinery was already the nation's largest, but as he put it, "the butcher, the baker, and the candlestick maker began to refine oil." As a result, "the price went down and down until the trade was ruined." Rockefeller resolved to bring order out of chaos, which is to say he decided to weed out the competition. He did so largely by putting a premium on efficiency and hard work, but soon he hatched another competitive scheme. In 1872 the inscrutable Rockefeller acquired the South Improvement Company, which he made the marketing agent for a large percentage of his oil shipments. By controlling this traffic, he gained clout with the railroads, which gave him large rebates (refunds) on the standard freight rates in order to keep his business. In some cases they even gave him information on competitors' shipments. Rockefeller then approached his Cleveland competitors and offered to buy them out at his own price. Most of them saw the wisdom of this course. By 1879 Standard Oil had come to control 90–95 percent of the oil refining in the country.

John D. Rockefeller, whose Standard Oil Company dominated the oil business.

Much of Rockefeller's success was based on his determination to "pay nobody a profit." Instead of depending on the products or services of other firms, Standard undertook to make its own barrels, cans, and whatever else it needed. Economists label this vertical integration. The company kept large amounts of cash reserves to make it independent of banks in case of a crisis. Rockefeller also set out to control his transportation needs. With Standard owning most of the pipelines leading to railroads, as well as the tank cars and the oil-storage facilities, it was able to dissuade the railroads from servicing eastern competitors. Those competitors who insisted on holding out then faced a giant marketing organization capable of driving them to the wall with price wars.

Eventually, in order to consolidate scattered business interests under a more efficient control, Rockefeller and his advisers resorted to the legal device of the trust. Long established in law to enable one or more people to manage property belonging to others, such as children or the mentally incompetent, the trust now was used for another purpose—centralized control of business across state lines. In 1882 all of the thirty-seven stockholders in various Standard Oil enterprises conveyed their stock to nine trustees, getting "trust certificates" in return. The nine trustees were thus empowered to give central direction to all the Standard companies.

The original plan, never fully carried out, was to organize a

Standard Oil Company in each state in which the trust did business. But the trust device, widely copied in the 1880s, proved legally vulnerable to prosecution under state laws against monopoly or restraint of trade. In 1892 the Supreme Court of Ohio ordered the Standard Oil Trust dissolved. For a while the company managed to unify control by the simple device of interlocking directorates, through which the board of directors of one company was made identical or nearly so to the boards of the others. Gradually, however, Rockefeller took to the idea of the holding company: a company that controlled other companies by holding all or at least a majority of their stock. In 1899 Rockefeller brought his empire under the direction of the Standard Oil Company of New Jersey, a holding company. Though less vulnerable to prosecution under state law, some holding companies, as we will see, proved vulnerable to the Sherman Antitrust Act of 1890. Meanwhile the term "trust" had become so fixed in the public mind that it was used to describe large combinations under holding companies as well.

CARNEGIE'S GOSPEL OF WEALTH   Andrew Carnegie, like Rockefeller, experienced the untypical rise from poverty to riches that came to be known in those days as "the typical American success story." Born in Scotland, the son of a weaver who fell upon hard times, he migrated with his family to Allegheny, Pennsylvania in 1848. Then thirteen, he started out as a bobbin boy and engine tender in a textile mill at wages of $1.20 per week. At fourteen he was getting $2.50 per week as a telegraph messenger. He worked hard, arriving early and staying late, and soon won promotion to telegrapher. In 1853 he became personal secretary and telegrapher to the district superintendent of the Pennsylvania Railroad. When the superintendent became the president of the line, Carnegie took his place and the pace of his career accelerated. During the Civil War, Carnegie went to Washington, where he developed a military telegraph system and personally helped evacuate the wounded from Bull Run.

Carnegie kept on moving—from telegraphy to railroading to bridge building, then to iron and steel making, and investments. In 1865 he quit the railroad to devote full time to his own interests. These were mainly in iron and bridge building, but the versatile entrepreneur also made money in oil and sold railroad bonds in Europe. In his *Autobiography* Carnegie recalled his growing determination to allow "nothing to interfere for a moment with my business career." He kept his pledge. In 1872 he netted $150,000 on a trip during which he also met Sir Henry

*Andrew Carnegie, apostle of
"The Gospel of Wealth."*

Bessemer, inventor of a new process of steel making. The process dazzled Carnegie, and he returned to America a converted prophet of steel, exclaiming to a friend: "The day of iron has passed!" The next year Carnegie resolved to concentrate on steel, or as he put it, to put all his eggs in one basket and then watch the basket. As competitors arose, Carnegie picked them off one by one.

Carnegie was never a technical expert on steel. He was a promoter, salesman, and organizer with a gift for finding and using men of expert ability. He always insisted on up-to-date machinery and equipment, and shrewdly used times of recession to expand more cheaply. In much of this Carnegie was a typical businessman of the time, if abler and luckier than most. But he stands out from the lot as a thinker who publicized a philosophy for big business, a conservative rationale that became deeply implanted in the conventional wisdom of Americans. Carnegie argued that however harsh their methods at times, the captains of industry were on the whole public benefactors.

Carnegie's best remembered essay was "The Gospel of Wealth," published in 1889. In this basic statement of his philosophy Carnegie drew upon the ideas of the English naturalist, Charles Darwin, and especially on the social implications of Darwinism elaborated by Herbert Spencer, who had invented the phrase "survival of the fittest." In the evolution of society, Carnegie argued, the contrast between the millionaire and the laborer measures the distance society has come. "Not evil, but good, has come to the race from the accumulation of wealth by those who have the ability and energy that produces it." The process had been costly in many ways, but the law of competition was "best for the race, because it insures the survival of the fittest in every department."

Carnegie then delivered a sermon on the proper uses of wealth. The best way to dispense a fortune was to administer it during one's lifetime for the public good: "The man who dies rich dies disgraced." One should first set an example of humble living—in Carnegie's case this included owning a castle in Scotland as well as enjoying an annual income of $40 million—and provide for his dependents, then consider the rest a trust fund for the public good. One should avoid alms-giving, for the "pauper is a social leper." Instead the wealthy should provide means for people to help themselves by supporting universities, libraries, hospitals, parks, halls for meetings and concerts, swimming baths, and church buildings—in that order. To his credit, Carnegie devoted his wealth to many such benefactions and to the cause of world peace. He spent some $60 million on public libraries and another $60 million on higher education. Rockefeller too gave many gifts, mainly to education and medicine, but partly because he was persuaded it would make for good public relations.

Carnegie's gospel of wealth fit perfectly the late nineteenth century's worship of success and respect for the self-made man. The popularity of such attitudes was shown by the market for inspirational literature touting the ancient verities of thrift, integrity, and hard work. Among the sages of that school none was better known than Horatio Alger, whose very name became a byword for vocational success. A Unitarian minister in New York, he wrote novels for boys with titles like *Ragged Dick* (1867), *Luck and Pluck* (1869), and *Tattered Tom* (1871).

J.P. MORGAN, THE FINANCIER J. Pierpont Morgan, who was born to wealth and increased it enormously, was about as far from being a Horatio Alger hero as one could get. Morgan's father was a partner in a London banking house, and his wealth enabled him to send young Pierpont to boarding school in Switzerland and Germany. After a brief apprenticeship, Morgan in 1857 began work in a New York firm that represented his father's bank, and in 1860 he set himself up as its New York agent under the name of J. Pierpont Morgan and Company. This firm, under various names, channeled much European capital into the country and grew into a financial power in its own right.

As an investment banker, Morgan bought corporate stocks and

bonds wholesale and then sold them at a profit, much as other merchants would market, say, hardware, but on a larger scale. The growth of large corporations put Morgan's and other investment firms in an increasingly strategic position in the economy. Morgan realized that railroads were the key to the times, and he picked up and reorganized one line after another. After the Panic of 1893, when hard times gutted the net worth of many railroads, Morgan took over the Erie, Philadelphia and Reading, the Northern Pacific, and organized the Southern Railway; he already had a hand in the Vanderbilt and Pennsylvania lines. Since the investment business depended on the general good health of client companies, investment bankers became involved in the operation of their clients' firms, demanding places on boards of directors and helping to shape their fiscal dealings. By these means bankers could influence company policies. Eventually people were speaking of the "money trust," the greatest trust of all, with its hand in all kinds of other enterprises.

Morgan's crowning triumph was the consolidation of the steel industry. In 1901 he bought out Carnegie's huge steel and iron holdings. Carnegie set his own price, which came to nearly $500 million, of which Carnegie's personal share was nearly $300 million. After closing the deal, Morgan told the steel king, "Mr. Carnegie, I want to congratulate you on being the richest man in the world." In rapid succession Morgan added other steel mills.

J. Pierpont Morgan. *This is the famous portrait by the photographer Edward Steichen, done in 1903.*

Altogether the new United States Steel Corporation, a holding company for these varied interests, was capitalized at $1.4 billion, a total that was heavily watered (well above the company's actual assets) but was soon made solid by large profits. The new giant was a marvel of the new century, the first billion-dollar corporation, the climactic event in that age of corporate consolidation. By 1904 there were some 318 industrial trusts in the United States, capitalized at over $7 billion, with nearly 5,300 distinct plants.

ADVANCES FOR LABOR

SOCIAL TRENDS   Accompanying the spread of these industrial combinations was a rising standard of living for most people. If the rich were still getting richer, a lot of other people were at least becoming better off. The continuing demand for unskilled or semi-skilled workers meanwhile was filled by new groups entering the workforce at the bottom: immigrants above all, but also growing numbers of women and children. Because of a long-term decline in prices and the cost of living, real wages and earnings in manufacturing went up about 50 percent between 1860 and 1890, and another 37 percent from 1890 to 1914. By latter-day standards, however, working conditions then were dreary indeed. At the turn of the century the average hourly wage in manufacturing was 21 cents, and average annual earnings were $490. The average work week was 59 hours, which amounted to nearly six ten-hour days, but that was only an average. Most steelworkers put in a twelve-hour day, and as late as the 1920s, a great many worked a seven-day or 84-hour week.

Moreover, although wages were steadily rising, working and living conditions remained precarious. In the crowded tenements of immigrant neighborhoods in the major cities the death rates ran substantially higher than in the countryside. Factories often maintained poor health and safety conditions. In 1913, for instance, there were some 25,000 factory fatalities and some 700,000 injuries that required at least four weeks' disability— more than half the number of American casualties in World War I. In this new industrial world ever-larger numbers of people were dependent on the machinery and factories of owners whom they seldom if ever saw. In the simpler world of small shops, workers and employers could enter into close personal relationships; the larger corporation, on the other hand, was likely run by a bureaucracy in which ownership was separate from management. Much of the social history of the modern world in fact turns on the transition from a world of personal relationships to one of impersonal and contractual relationships.

DISORGANIZED PROTEST   In these circumstances it was far more difficult for workers to organize for mutual benefit than for a few captains of industry to organize for personal profit. Civic officials and business leaders respected property rights more than the rights of labor. Among workers recently removed from an agrarian world, the idea of durable unions was slow to take hold. Immigrant workers represented diverse and frequently antagonistic cultures and spoke many tongues. Many if not most saw their jobs as transient, the first rung on the ladder to success. They hoped to move on to a homestead, or to return with their earnings to the old farms of their European homelands. With or without unions, though, workers often staged impromptu strikes protesting long working hours and wage cuts. But impromptu action often led to violence, and three violent incidents of the 1870s colored much of the public's view of labor unions thereafter.

The decade's early years saw a reign of terror in the eastern Pennsylvania coal fields, attributed to an Irish group called the Molly Maguires. Taking their name from an Irish patriot who had directed violent resistance against the British, the group aimed to right perceived wrongs against Irish workers by such methods as intimidation, beatings, and killings. Their terrorism reached its peak in 1874–1875. At trials in 1876, twenty-four of the Molly Maguires were convicted, and the next year twenty of them were hanged. The trials also resulted in a wage reduction in the mines.

THE RAILROAD STRIKE OF 1877   Far more significant, because more widespread, was the Great Railroad Strike of 1877, the first major national strike. It grew out of the combustible atmosphere of an economic depression and spread like wildfire across hundreds of cities and towns from New York to California, leaving a scarred landscape of physical destruction and personal violence. By its end over a hundred people had been killed, millions of dollars in property had been destroyed, and federal troops had been mobilized to restore law and order. For many people it raised the specter of a European-style social revolution led by workers, like the short-lived Paris Commune of 1871 when disgruntled mobs chanted "Bread or Blood."

Equally disturbing was the presence of many women among the protesters. A Baltimore journalist noted that the "singular part of the disturbances is the very active part taken by the women, who are the wives and mothers of the firemen [coal stokers]. They look famished and wild, and declare for starvation rather than have their people work for the reduced wages." Such intense commitment suggested to many observers the dawning of a new era of social strife. As a Pittsburgh newspaper warned, "This may be the beginning of a great civil war in this country between labor and capital."

Wage cuts caused the Great Strike. After the Panic of 1873 the major rail lines in the East had cut wages, and then in the summer of 1877 they made another 10 percent cut. This provoked most of the railroad workers at Martinsburg, West Virginia, to walk off the job and block the tracks. Without organized direction, however, their movement degenerated into a mob that burned and plundered railroad property.

Walkouts and sympathy demonstrations spread spontaneously in the July heat from Cumberland, Maryland, to Chicago and San Francisco. The greatest outbreak began at Pittsburgh on July 19,

The Devastation Wrought by the Railroad Strike of 1877. *Railroad workers in Pittsburgh reacted violently to wage cuts.*

when the Pennsylvania Railroad put on "double-headers" (long trains pulled by two locomotives) in order to reduce crews. Public sympathy for the strikers was so great at first that local militiamen, called out to suppress them, instead joined the protesters. But militiamen from Philadelphia dispersed one crowd at the cost of 26 lives, then found themselves besieged in the railroad's roundhouse, where they disbanded and shot their way out.

Looting, rioting, and burning went on for another day until the frenzy subsided. A reporter described the scene of one conflagration as "the most horrible ever witnessed, except in the carnage of war. There were fifty miles of hot rails, ten tracks side by side, with as many miles of ties turned into glowing coals and tons on tons of iron car skeletons and wheels almost at white heat." Public opinion, sympathetic at first, tended to blame the strikers for the violence. Eventually the strikers, lacking organized bargaining power, had no choice but to drift back to work. Everywhere the walkouts failed, but the Great Railroad Strike's effects were enduring. It demonstrated to workers their potential strength and the need for tighter organization. "The railroad strike of 1877," labor leader Samuel Gompers later recalled, "was the tocsin that sounded a ringing message of hope for us all."

TOWARD PERMANENT UNIONS   Meanwhile efforts to build a permanent union movement had begun to bear fruit. Earlier efforts, in the 1830s and 1840s, had largely been dominated by reformers with schemes that ranged from free homesteads to utopian socialism. But the 1850s witnessed the beginning of "job-conscious" unions in certain skilled trades. By 1860 there were about twenty such unions, and during the Civil War, because of the demand for labor, these craft unions grew in strength and numbers.

There was no overall federation of these groups until August 1866, when the first National Labor Union convened in Baltimore. Essentially the NLU comprised delegates from labor and reform groups more interested in political and social change than in bargaining with employers. The groups espoused such ideas as the eight-hour day, workers' cooperatives, paper money, and equal rights for women and blacks. But the organization lost momentum after the death of its president in 1869, and by 1872 it had entirely collapsed. The National Labor Union, however, was not a total failure. It was influential in persuading Congress to enact an eight-hour day for federal employees and to repeal the

1864 Contract Labor Law, which allowed employers to bind immigrant laborers by paying for their passage from Europe.

THE KNIGHTS OF LABOR Before the National Labor Union collapsed, another labor group of national standing was emerging, the Noble and Holy Order of the Knights of Labor. The name betokened a tendency to copy the forms of fraternal orders and to evoke the aura of medieval guilds. The founder of the Knights of Labor, Uriah S. Stephens, a Philadelphia tailor, was a habitual "joiner" involved with several secret orders, including the Masons. Secrecy, he felt, along with a semi-religious ritual, would protect members against retaliation and at the same time create a sense of solidarity.

The Knights of Labor, started in 1869, at first grew slowly, but during the years of depression after 1873, as other unions collapsed, it spread more rapidly. In 1878 its first General Assembly established a national organization. Its preamble and platform endorsed producers' and consumers' cooperatives, hoping to replace the wage-labor system with worker-owned factories. The Knights also called for free homesteads, bureaus of labor statistics, elimination of convict-labor competition, the eight-hour day, and the acceptance of greenbacks as currency in order to enlarge the money supply and ease credit. One plank in the platform, far ahead of the times, called for equal pay for equal work by both sexes.

Throughout their existence the Knights emphasized reform measures and preferred boycotts to strikes as a way to put pressure on employers. They also had a liberal membership policy, welcoming all who had ever worked for wages except lawyers, doctors, bankers, and those who sold liquor. Theoretically it was one big union of all workers regardless of race, color, creed, or sex, skilled and unskilled. Each local assembly was to be formed on such a basis, but in practice some local and district assemblies were organized on a craft basis, such as the telegraphers and cigarmakers. Above these stood the General Assembly, a General Executive Board, and at the head of the organization a Grand Master Workman.

Stephens was the first elected to this office, but in 1879 he gave way to Terence V. Powderly, the thirty-year-old mayor of Scranton, Pennsylvania. In many ways Powderly was unsuited to the new job. At once mayor, head of the Knights, county health officer, and part-owner and manager of a grocery store, he had too many irons in the fire. He was physically frail, sensitive to criticism, and indecisive at critical moments. Powderly was temperamentally opposed to strikes, and when they did occur, did not always back up the locals. Yet the Knights ironically owed their greatest growth to strikes that occurred under his leadership.

In the mid-1880s the Knights enjoyed a meteoric rise. In 1884 a successful strike against wage cuts in the Union Pacific shops at Denver led many railroad workers to form new assemblies. Then, in 1885, the Knights scored a startling victory over Jay Gould. Late the previous year and early in 1885 Gould had cut wages on the Missouri, Kansas, and Texas and Wabash roads. A spontaneous strike on these lines in February 1885 spread to Gould's Missouri-Pacific, and as organizers from the Knights of Labor moved in, Gould restored the wage cuts. In June another strike on the Wabash against the firing of union members brought another victory. These successes allowed the Knights to grow rapidly from about 100,000 members to more than 700,000 in 1886.

But the Knights peaked in 1886 and then went into rapid decline. Jay Gould, taken by surprise in 1885, set a trap for the Knights in 1886. He spoke favorably of unions, expressing his wish that all railroad workers were organized, but in February 1886 he provoked another strike by firing a foreman in the Texas-Pacific shops. When the Knights struck, Gould refused arbitration and hired Pinkerton agents to harass strikers and keep the trains running. On May 4 the Knights had to call off the strike. The organization was further damaged by an incident in Chicago's Haymarket Square that very night, with which the Knights had little to do but which provoked widespread revulsion against labor groups in general.

THE HAYMARKET AFFAIR   The Haymarket Affair grew indirectly out of agitation for the eight-hour day. On May 3, 1886, Chicago's International Harvester plant was the site of an unfortunate clash between strikers and policemen in which one striker was killed. Leaders of a minuscule anarchist movement in Chicago scheduled an open meeting the following night at Haymarket Square to protest the killing. Under a light drizzle the crowd listened to lengthy speeches promoting socialism and anarchism, and was beginning to break up when a group of policemen arrived and called upon the activists to disperse. At that point someone threw a bomb at the police, killing one and wounding others. The police responded by firing into the crowd. In a trial marked by prejudice and hysteria, seven anarchist leaders were sentenced to death despite the lack of any evidence linking them to the bomb-thrower, whose identity was never established. Of the seven, two were reprieved and some years later pardoned, one committed suicide in prison, but four were hanged. The episode helped stamp in anxious American minds the stereotype of bearded and swarthy alien anarchists and labor radicals. All but one of the group were German-speaking, but that one held a membership card in the Knights of Labor.

Despite his best efforts, Powderly could never dissociate in the public mind the Knights from the anarchists. He clung to leadership until 1893, but after that the union evaporated and by the turn of the century it was but a memory. A number of problems accounted for the Knights' decline: a leadership devoted more to reform than to pragmatic organization, the failure of the Knights' cooperative enterprises, and a preoccupation with politics rather than negotiations with management.

The Knights nevertheless attained some lasting achievements, among them the creation of the Federal Bureau of Labor Statistics and the Foran Act of 1885, which penalized employers who imported contract laborers from abroad. The Knights also spread the idea of unionism and initiated a new type of union organization: the industrial union, an industry-wide union of the skilled and unskilled.

GOMPERS AND THE AFL   The craft unions opposed the industrial unionism of the Knights. They organized workers who shared special skills, such as typographers or cigarmakers. Leaders of the crafts feared that joining with the unskilled would mean a loss of their separate craft identities and a loss of the bargaining power held by skilled workers. In the summer of 1886 delegates

Samuel Gompers, head of the American Federation of Labor.

from craft unions met at Columbus, Ohio, and organized the American Federation of Labor (AFL). In structure it differed from the Knights in that it was a federation of national craft organizations, each of which retained a large degree of autonomy and exercised greater leverage against management. Samuel Gompers served as president of the AFL from its start until his death in 1924.

Born in London of Dutch-Jewish ancestry, Gompers came to the United States as a teenager, joined the Cigarmakers Union in 1864, and became president of his New York local in 1877. This background was significant. The Cigarmakers tended to be the intellectuals of the labor movement; to relieve the tedium of their task, they hired young men to read aloud as they worked, and debated such weighty topics as socialism and Darwinism. But Gompers and other leaders of the union focused on concrete economic gains, avoiding involvement with utopian ideas or politics. "At no time in my life," Gompers once admitted, "have I ever worked out a definitely articulated economic theory." Adolph Strasser, head of the Cigarmakers, put it more strongly: "We have no ultimate ends," he told a Senate hearing. "We are going on from day to day. We are fighting only for immediate objects—objects that can be realized in a few years."

Such job-consciousness became the policy of the AFL under Gompers, whose lifetime concern was the effectiveness of the federation. Gompers hired organizers to spread unionism, and worked as a diplomat to prevent overlapping unions and to settle jurisdictional disputes. The federation represented workers in matters of national legislation and acted as a sounding board for their cause. On occasion it exercised its power to request dues from members for the support of strikes. Gompers, it turned out, was temperamentally more fitted than Powderly for the rough-and-tumble world of unionism. He had a thick hide, liked to talk and drink with the boys in the back room, and advocated using the strike to achieve labor's objectives. His preference, though, was to achieve these objectives through agreements with management which included provisos for union recognition in the form of closed shops (which could hire only union members) or union-preference shops (which could hire others only if no union members were available).

The AFL at first grew slowly, but by 1890 it had already surpassed the Knights of Labor in membership. By the turn of the century it claimed 500,000 members in affiliated unions; in 1914, on the eve of World War I, it had 2 million, and in 1920, reached a peak of 4 million. But even then the AFL embraced less than 15 percent of the nonagricultural workers, and all unions, including the unaffiliated railroad brotherhoods, accounted for little more than 18 percent of these workers. Organized labor's strongholds were in transportation and the building trades. Most of the larger manufacturing industries, including textiles, tobacco, and packing houses, remained almost untouched.

THE HOMESTEAD STRIKE   Two violent incidents in the 1890s scarred the emerging industrial union movement and set it back for forty years to come—the Homestead Steel Strike of 1892 and the Pullman Strike of 1894. The Amalgamated Association of Iron and Steel Workers, founded in 1876, had by 1891 a membership of more than 24,000 and was probably the largest craft union at that time. But it excluded the unskilled and had failed to organize the larger steel plants. The Homestead Works at Pittsburgh was an important exception. There the union had enjoyed friendly relations with the Carnegie company until H.C. Frick became its president in 1889. A showdown was delayed, however, until 1892, when the union contract came up for renewal. Andrew Carnegie, who had expressed sympathy for unions in the past, had gone to Scotland and left matters in the hands of Frick. Carnegie, however, knew what was afoot: a cost-cutting reduction in the number of workers through the use of laborsaving devices, and a deliberate attempt to smash the union.

As negotiations dragged on, the company announced it would deal with workers as individuals unless an agreement was reached by June 29. A strike, or more properly a lockout of unionists, began on that date. Even before the negotiations ended, Frick had begun barricading the plant and hired as plant guards 300 Pinkerton detectives whose specialty was union-busting. But on the morning of July 6, 1892, when the Pinkertons came up the Monongahela River on barges, discharged union workers were waiting behind iron breastworks on shore. Who fired the first shot remains unknown, but a battle erupted in which nine workers and seven Pinkertons died. In the end, the Pinkertons surrendered and marched away, to the taunts of crowds in the street. Six days later 8,000 state militiamen appeared at the plant. The strike dragged on until November, but by then the union was dead at Homestead. Its cause was not helped when on July 23 an anarchist shot and wounded Frick.

THE PULLMAN STRIKE   The Pullman Strike of 1894 involved a dispute at the "model" town of Pullman, Illinois, just outside Chicago, which housed workers of the Pullman Palace Car Company in neat brick homes nestled on grassy lots along shaded streets. The town's idyllic appearance, however, was deceptive. Employees were required to live there, pay rents and utility costs higher than in nearby towns, and buy their goods from company stores. With the onset of the depression in 1893 George Pullman laid off 3,000 of 5,800 employees, and cut wages 25–40 percent, but not his rents and other charges. When Pullman fired three members of a grievance committee, a strike began on May 11, 1894.

During this tense period the Pullman workers had been joining the American Railway Union, founded the previous year by Eugene V. Debs. The tall, gangly Debs was a charismatic man who led by example and by the electric force of his convictions. A child of working-class immigrants, he quit school in 1869 at age fourteen in order to go to work for an Indiana railroad. There he soon "learned of the hardships of the rail in snow, sleet, and hail, of the ceaseless danger that lurks along the iron highway, the uncertainty of employment, scant wages and altogether trying lot of the workingman, so that from my very boyhood I was made to feel the wrongs of labor." He felt them so deeply that he eagerly accepted an invitation to start a local of the railroad brotherhood, a craft union of skilled workers.

Eugene V. Debs, founder of the American Railway Union and later candidate for president as head of the Socialist Party of America.

Still, it was not until the Haymarket bombing that Debs came to see an inevitable conflict between labor and management. By the early 1890s he had become a tireless spokesman for labor radicalism, and he launched a crusade to organize *all* railway workers—skilled or unskilled—into the American Railway Union. His earnest appeal generated a tremendous response, and soon he was in charge of a powerful new labor organization. He quickly turned his attention to the Pullman controversy.

After Pullman refused Debs's plea for arbitration, the union workers in June 1894 stopped handling Pullman cars and by the end of July had tied up most of the railroads in the Midwest. The rail owners then brought strikebreakers from Canada and elsewhere, instructing them to connect mail cars to Pullman cars so that interference with Pullman cars also meant interference with the federal mail. Attorney-General Richard Olney, a former railroad attorney, swore in 3,400 special deputies to keep the trains running, and when clashes occurred between these and some of the strikers, lawless elements ignored Debs's plea for an orderly boycott and repeated some of the violent scenes of the 1877 strike. Finally, on July 3, 1894, President Grover Cleveland answered an appeal from the railroads that he send federal troops into the Chicago area, where the strike was centered. Illinois Governor John Peter Altgeld issued a vigorous protest, insisting that the state could keep order, but Cleveland claimed authority and a duty to ensure delivery of the mails. "If it takes every dollar in the Treasury and every soldier in the United States to deliver a postal card in Chicago," he vowed, "that postal card should be delivered."

As strikers clashed with troops and burned hundreds of cars, the federal district court granted an injunction forbidding any interference with the mails or any combination to restrain interstate commerce. On July 13 the union called off the strike, and on the same day the district court cited Debs for violating the injunction and sentenced him to six months in jail. The Supreme Court upheld the decree in the case of *In re Debs* (1894) on broad grounds of national sovereignty: "The strong arm of the national government may be put forth to brush away all obstructions to the freedom of interstate commerce or the transportation of the mails." Debs served his term, during which time he read deeply in socialist literature, and he emerged to devote the rest of his life to that cause.

SOCIALISM AND THE UNIONS   The major American unions, for the most part, never allied themselves with the socialists, as many

European labor movements did. But socialist ideas had been abroad in the country at least since the time Robert Owen visited America in the 1820s. The movement gained little notice before the rise of Daniel DeLeon in the 1890s as the dominant figure in the Socialist Labor party. A native of the Dutch West Indies, De-Leon had studied law and lectured for some years at Columbia University. He proposed to organize industrial unions with a socialist purpose, and to build a political party that would abolish the state once it gained power. His ideas seem to have influenced Lenin, leader of Russia's Bolshevik revolution of 1917, but DeLeon preached revolution at the ballot box, not by violence.

Yet Debs was more successful at building a socialist movement in America. To many, DeLeon seemed doctrinaire and inflexible. Debs, however, built his new party by following a method now traditional in the United States: he formed a coalition, one that embraced viewpoints ranging from moderate reform to doctrinaire Marxism. In 1897 Debs organized the Social Democratic party from the remnants of the American Railway Union, and he received over 4,000 votes as its candidate for president in 1900. In 1901 his followers joined a number of secessionists from De-Leon's party, led by Morris Hillquit of New York, to set up the Socialist Party of America. In 1904 Debs polled over 400,000 votes as the party's candidate for president and more than doubled that to almost 900,000 votes in 1912, or 6 percent of the popular vote.

By 1912 the party seemed well on the way to becoming a permanent fixture in American politics. Thirty-three cities had Socialist mayors. The party sponsored five English daily newspapers, eight foreign-language dailies, and a number of weeklies and monthlies. Its support was not confined to urban workers and intellectuals. In the Southwest the party built a sizable grass-roots following among farmers and tenants. But the party reached its peak in 1912. During World War I it was wracked by disagreements over America's participation, and was split thereafter. The Great Depression of the 1930s served only to interrupt, not halt, its decline.

THE WOBBLIES   During the years of Socialist party growth there emerged a parallel effort to revive industrial unionism, led by the Industrial Workers of the World (IWW), dubbed the Wobblies. The chief base for this group was the Western Federation of Miners, organized at Butte, Montana, in 1893. Over the next decade the Western Federation was the storm-center of violent confrontation with unyielding bosses who mobilized private armies against it in Colorado, Idaho, and elsewhere. In June 1905 the founding convention of the IWW drew a variety of people who opposed the AFL's philosophy. Debs participated, although many of his comrades preferred to work within the AFL. DeLeon was of course happy at this chance to strike back at craft unionism. A radical manifesto issued from the meetings, arguing that the IWW "must be founded on the class struggle, and its general administration must be conducted in harmony with the recognition of the irrepressible conflict between the capitalist class and the working class."

But the IWW waged class war better than it articulated class ideology. Like the Knights of Labor, it was designed to be "One Big Union," including all workers, skilled or unskilled. Its roots were in the mining and lumber camps of the West, where unstable conditions of employment created a large number of nomadic workers, to whom neither the AFL's pragmatic approach nor the socialists' political appeal held much attraction. The revolutionary goal of the Wobblies was an idea labeled syndicalism by its French supporters: the ultimate destruction of the state and its replacement by one big Union. How it would govern remained vague.

Like other radical groups the IWW was split by sectarian disputes. Because of policy disagreements all the major founders withdrew, first the Western Federation of Miners, then Debs, then DeLeon. William D. "Big Bill" Haywood of the Western Federation remained, however, and as its leader he held the group together. Although since embellished in myth, Haywood was indeed an imposing figure. Well over six feet tall, handsome, broad-shouldered, one-eyed, and rippling with muscles, he commanded the attention and respect of his listeners. This thirty-six-year-old hardrock miner, union organizer, and Socialist from Salt Lake City had nothing but disdain for the AFL and its conservative labor philosophy. He called Samuel Gompers "a squat specimen of humanity" with "small, snapping eyes, a hard cruel mouth," and "a personality vain, conceited, petulant, and vindictive." Instead of following Gompers's advice to organize only skilled workers, Haywood promoted the concept of one all-inclusive union whose credo would be the promotion of a socialism "with its working clothes on."

But Haywood and the Wobblies were reaching out to the fringe elements of least power and influence, chiefly the migratory workers of the West and the ethnic groups of the East. Always ambivalent about diluting their revolutionary principles, they heaped scorn on the usual labor agreements, even when they participated in them. They engaged in spectacular battles with corporate America but scored few victories. The largest was a textile strike at Lawrence, Massachusetts, in 1912; the strikers won wage raises, overtime pay, and other benefits. But the next year a strike of silk workers at Paterson, New Jersey, ended in disaster, and the IWW entered a rapid decline.

The fading of the movement was accelerated by the hysterical opposition it engendered. The *Los Angeles Times*, for instance, declared that "I.W.W. stands for I won't work, and I want whiskey. . . . The average Wobbly, it must be remembered, is a sort of half wild animal." Many of the authorities treated them as such. Bragged one sheriff, "When a Wobbly comes to town, I just knock him over the head with a night stick and throw him in the river. When he comes up he beats it out of town."

Branded as anarchists, bums, and criminals, the Wobblies were effectively destroyed during World War I, when most of their leaders were jailed for their militant opposition to the war. Big Bill Haywood fled to the Soviet Union, where he married a Russian woman, died in 1928, and was honored by burial in the Kremlin wall. But the IWW, decried as a haven for alien ideas, was actually an American original, born of the rough-and-tumble world of western miners and migrants. The Wobblies left behind a rich folklore of nomadic working folk and a gallery of heroic agitators such as Elizabeth Gurley Flynn, a dark-haired Irish girl who at age eighteen, ardent and pregnant, chained herself to a lamppost to impede her arrest during a strike. The movement also bequeathed martyrs like the Swedish songster and labor organizer Joe Hill, framed (so the faithful assumed) for murder and executed by a Utah firing squad. His last words were written to Haywood: "Goodbye, Bill. I die like a true blue rebel. Don't waste any time mourning. Organize." Such intensity of conviction and devotion to a cause ensured that the IWW's ideal of a classless society did not die.

Further Reading

Two fine surveys of the Gilded Age are Robert H. Wiebe's *The Search for Order, 1877–1920* (1966)° and John A. Garraty's *The New Commonwealth, 1877–1890* (1968).° A succinct overview of economic development after the Civil War is Glenn Porter's *The Rise of Big Busi-*

° These books are available in paperback editions.

ness (rev. ed. 1992).° An important organizational synthesis is Olivier Zunz's *Making America Corporate, 1870–1920* (1990).°

Scholarship on the growth of railroads includes George R. Taylor and Irene D. Neu's *The American Railroad Network, 1861–1890* (1956) and Robert W. Fogel's *Railroads and American Economic Growth* (1964).° The best recent overview is Albro Martin's, *Railroads Triumphant: The Growth, Rejection, and Rebirth of a Vital American Force* (1991).° On entrepreneurship in the iron and steel sector, see Peter Temin's *Iron and Steel in Nineteenth Century America: An Economic Inquiry* (1964). Harold Livesay's *Andrew Carnegie and the Rise of Big Business* (1975)° treats the titan of the steel mills. Maury Klein's *The Life and Legend of Jay Gould* (1986) is sympathetic.

Nathan Rosenberg's *Technology and American Economic Growth* (1972)° documents the growth of invention during the period. Robert V. Bruce's *Bell: Alexander Graham Bell and the Conquest of Solitude* (1990)° stresses the social impact of technology. A discussion of one justification for business growth is Richard Hofstadter's *Social Darwinism in American Thought* (rev. ed., 1955).°

Much of the recent scholarship on labor in the Gilded Age stresses the traditional values and the culture of work which the laborers brought to the factory. Herbert G. Gutman's *Work, Culture, and Society in Industrializing America* (1976)° best introduces these themes. For an insightful overview of the impact of labor and farm movements on the larger political and social scene, see Nell Painter's *Standing at Armageddon, The United States, 1877–1919* (1989).° David Montgomery, in *The Fall of the House of Labor* (1989),° interprets labor-management conflict over work organization.

Gerald N. Grob's *Workers and Utopias* (1961) examines the difference in outlook between the Knights of Labor and the American Federation of Labor. To trace the rise of socialism among organized workers, see Nick Salvatore's *Eugene V. Debs: Citizen and Socialist* (1982).° For insights into one of the era's most violent labor disputes, see Paul Krause, *The Battle for Homestead, 1880–1892* (1992).

20

THE EMERGENCE OF
MODERN AMERICA

AMERICA'S MOVE TO TOWN

The novelist Henry James remarked in 1866 that the "dreadful chill of change" was in the air. Some Americans found the whirlwind of accelerating social change invigorating; others found it profoundly disturbing. Whatever their reaction, all Americans were buffeted to some degree by the effects of what people began to call the claims of modernity.

EXPLOSIVE URBAN GROWTH   The animating center of this process of modernization was the bustling metropolis. Between 1860 and 1910 population in towns of 2,500 or more grew from 6 million to 44 million, or from 20 to 46 percent of the nation's total population. After 1920 more than half the nation's population would be living in urban areas. Thus, despite the rapid settlement of the frontier after the Civil War, the flow of population toward the cities was greater than toward the prairies.

Much of the westward migration in fact was itself an urban movement, spawning new towns near the mining digs or at the railheads. The Pacific coast boasted a greater urban proportion of the population than anywhere else; its major concentrations were first around San Francisco Bay and then in Los Angeles, which became a boom town after the arrival of the Southern Pacific and Santa Fe Railroads in the 1880s. Seattle also grew quickly, first as the terminus of three transcontinental railroad lines, and by the end of the century, as the staging area for the Alaska gold rush. Minneapolis, St. Paul, Omaha, Kansas City, and

Denver were no longer the mere villages they had been in 1860. The South, too, produced new cities: Durham and Birmingham, which were centers of tobacco and iron manufactures, and Houston, which handled cotton and cattle, and soon, oil. The industrial explosion powered the growth of new cities during this period. Factories brought huge concentrations of labor, and both required the proliferation of services that became synonymous with city life.

The cities expanded both vertically and horizontally to absorb their huge populations. In either case transportation innovations played an important role: the elevator, the streetcar, and before the end of the century, the first automobiles. In 1889 the Otis Elevator Company installed the first electric elevator, which made possible the erection of taller buildings. Before the Civil War few structures had gone higher than three or four stories. Another support for the vertical city came from the engineers who developed cast-iron and steel-frame construction during the 1800s.

Before the 1890s the chief sources of urban transport were either animals or steam. Horse- and mule-drawn streetcars had appeared in antebellum cities, but they were slow and cumbersome, and cleaning up after the animals added to the cost. In 1873 San Francisco became the first city to use cable cars which clamped onto a moving underground cable driven by a central power source. Some cities used steam-powered commuter trains or elevated tracks, but by the 1890s electric trolleys were replacing these. Mass transportation received an added boost when around the turn of the century subway systems began to function in Boston, New York, and Philadelphia.

The spread of mass transit made it possible for large numbers of people to become commuters, and a growing middle class (working people often could not afford even the nickel fare) retreated to quieter tree-lined "streetcar suburbs" whence they could travel into the central city for business or entertainment. The pattern of urban growth often became a sprawl, however, since it took place usually without plan, in the interest of a fast buck, and without thought to the need for parks and public services. But some developers had the wit to look ahead. New York in the early 1850s had set up a park commission which hired Frederick Law Olmsted as superintendent to plan Central Park. By 1870, six years before its official completion, as many as 100,000 people a day visited the 840-acre park. Olmsted later planned parks and even new subdivisions in San Francisco, Brooklyn, Chicago, and other cities.

Pedestrians, horse-drawn carts, trolleys, and electric trains all made their way between Brooklyn and Manhattan over the Brooklyn Bridge, completed in 1883.

CITY PROBLEMS AND POLITICS   Although housing conditions in the mill villages of the New South could be bad indeed, workers in the big cities often had no choice other than crowded tenements, most of which were poorly designed. In 1900 Manhattan's 42,700 tenements housed almost 1.6 million people, an average of 34 residents per building. Before the day of high-rise apartments this represented an extremely high density, and such unregulated urban growth created immense problems of health and morale.

The sheer size of these cities helped create a new politics. Since individuals could hardly provide for themselves such necessary services as transit, paving, water, sewers, street lighting and cleaning, and fire and police protection, they came increasingly to rely on city government support. These services as well as many city problems were handled by local political bosses who traded in patronage favors and graft. Big-city political machines were not altogether sinister in their effects: they provided food and money for the poor, fixed problems at city hall, and generally helped immigrants in their adjustment to a new life. One ward boss in Boston said: "There's got to be in every ward somebody that any bloke can come to—no matter what he's done—and get help. Help, you understand, none of your law and justice, but help." In return the political professionals felt entitled to some reward for having done the grubby work of the local organization.

But whatever the problems of the cities, the wonder of their glittering new arc and electric lights, their streetcars, telephones, vaudeville shows and other amusements, newspapers and magazines, and a thousand other attractions exerted a magnetic lure on the farm youths. The new cities threw into stark contrast the frustration of unending toil and the isolation and loneliness of country life. In times of rural depression thousands left for the cities in search of the opportunity and personal freedom that Horatio Alger and other writers of success literature dangled before their eyes.

Indeed, one of the most persistent subjects of American literature during this period was the rural youth migrating to the city. Where Alger's heroes almost always succeeded, however, a few fictional characters confronted the grinding reality of modern city life. In Theodore Dreiser's *Sister Carrie*, for instance, Carrie Meeber leaves her country village and travels to Chicago, attracted by the beguiling image of the city's throbbing activity and dazzling material opportunities. But once in the city she abruptly discovers that its life is not all excitement and fun. "Amid all the maze, uproar, and novelty," Dreiser wrote, "she felt cold reality taking her by the hand."

THE NEW IMMIGRATION

AMERICA'S PULL Newcomers to the cities arrived not only from the surrounding rural areas but from Europe and Asia as well. They gathered in American cities to live with others of like language, customs, and religion, and because they lacked the means to go west and take up farms. Though cities of the South and West (excepting the Far West) drew their populations mainly from the native-born of their regions, American cities as a whole drew more residents from abroad. During the peak decade of immigration, 1900–1910, 41 percent of the urban newcomers arrived from abroad.

This nation of immigrants continued to draw new inhabitants

Steerage Deck of the S.S. *Pennland,* 1893. *These immigrants are about to arrive at New York's Ellis Island.*

for much the same reasons as always, and from much the same strata of society. Immigrants came in flight from famine, cholera, or the lack of economic opportunity in their native lands. They fled racial, religious, and political persecution, and compulsory military service.

Yet more immigrants probably were pulled by America's promise than were pushed out by conditions at home. American industries, seeking cheap labor, kept recruiters abroad and at American ports. Railroads, eager to sell land and build up the traffic on their lines, distributed tempting propaganda in a medley of languages. Many of the western and southern states set up official bureaus and agents to attract immigrants. Under the Contract Labor Law of 1864 the federal government itself encouraged immigration by allowing companies to recruit foreign workers by paying for their passage.

After the Civil War the tide of immigration rose from just under 3 million in the 1870s to more than 5 million in the 1880s, then fell to a little over 3.5 million in the depression decade of the 1890s, and rose to its high-water mark of 8.8 million in the first decade of the new century.

A NEW WAVE During the 1880s the continuing search for cheap labor combined with renewed persecutions in eastern Europe to bring a noticeable change in the source of immigration, one fraught with meaning for American social history. Before 1880 immigrants were mainly of Germanic and Celtic origin, hailing from northern and western Europe. But by the 1870s there were signs of a change. The proportion of Latin, Slavic, and Jewish people from southern and eastern Europe rose sharply. After 1890 these groups made up a majority of the newcomers, and by the first decade of the new century they formed 70 percent of the immigrants to this country. Among these new immigrants were Italians, Hungarians, Czechs, Slovaks, Poles, Serbs, Croats, Russians, Rumanians, and Greeks—all people of markedly different cultural and language stocks from those of western Europe, and most followers of different religions, including Judaism and Catholicism.

ELLIS ISLAND As the number of immigrants passing through the Port of New York soared during the late nineteenth century, the state-run Castle Garden receiving center became rife with corruption. Money-changers cheated new arrivals, railroad agents overcharged them for tickets, and baggage-handlers engaged in blackmail. With reports of these abuses filling the newspapers, Congress ordered an investigation of Castle Garden that resulted in the closure of the facility in 1890. Thereafter the federal government's new Bureau of Immigration took over the business of admitting newcomers to New York City.

To launch this effort, Congress funded the construction of a new reception center on a tiny island off the New Jersey coast, a mile south of Manhattan and some 1,300 feet from the Statue of Liberty. The statue, unveiled in 1886, was a centennial gift from the French government commemorating the Franco-American alliance during the Revolutionary War. But it soon came to be viewed as a symbol of hope for immigrants passing under "Lady Liberty." In the base of the statue, workers had chiseled the poet Emma Lazarus's tribute to the promise of new life in America:

> Give me your tired, your poor,
> Your huddled masses yearning to breathe free,
> The wretched refuse of your teeming shore.
> Send these, the homeless, tempest-tossed to me,
> I lift my lamp beside the golden door!

In 1892 Ellis Island (named after its late-eighteenth-century owner, Samuel Ellis) opened its doors to the "huddled masses"

Immigrants, with identification papers, newly arrived at Ellis Island.

Immigrants waiting in the Registry Room for further inspections.

of the world, and before 1954, when it closed, some twelve million people first touched American soil there. Forty percent of Americans today have ancestors who passed through Ellis Island. In 1907, the center's busiest year, more than a million new arrivals filtered through the cavernous Great Hall, an average of about 5,000 per day; in one day alone immigration officials processed some 11,750 arrivals. These were the immigrants who arrived crammed into the steerage compartments of ship hulls. Those immigrants who could afford first- and second-class cabins did not have to visit Ellis Island; they were examined onboard ship, and most of them simply walked down the gangway onto the docks in lower Manhattan.

The first Ellis Island Immigration Station—a 400-foot-long barn-like structure made of Georgia pine—burned to the ground in 1897. In its place rose a majestic structure, a 220,000 square-foot Main Building made of fireproof red brick and limestone. Four graceful copper-plated domes towered above the massive roof, giving the building the appearance of a European palace. The enormous dimensions of the Great Hall, with its arching two-story ceiling, must have awed the new arrivals as they sat on benches waiting to be processed.

The prevailing atmosphere at Ellis Island was not comforting. Its bureaucratic purpose was to process immigrants, not welcome them. An army of inspectors, doctors, nurses, and public officials questioned, examined, and documented the newcomers. Inspectors had a list of probing questions: Have you money, relatives, or a job in the United States? Are you a polygamist? An anarchist? Doctors and nurses poked and prodded, searching for any sign of debilitating handicap or infectious disease. All the while, the immigrant worried: "Will they let me in?" Although some who were sick or lame were detained for days or weeks, the vast majority of immigrants received stamps of approval and were on their way after three or four hours. Only two percent of the newcomers were denied entry altogether, usually because they were criminals, strikebreakers, anarchists, or carriers of some "loathsome or dangerous contagious disease," such as tuberculosis or trachoma, a contagious eye disease resulting in blindness. These luckless folk were then returned to their places of origin, with the steamship companies picking up the tab.

Between 1892 and 1954, 70 percent of all European immigrants circulated through Ellis Island. (Others landed at Boston, Philadelphia, Baltimore, New Orleans, and Galveston.) Among the arrivals at Ellis Island were many youngsters who would distinguish themselves in their new country: songwriter Irving Berlin (Russia), football legend Knute Rockne (Norway), Supreme Court justice Felix Frankfurter (Austria), singer Al Jolson (Lithuania), and comedian Bob Hope (England). But many others found America's opportunities harder to grasp.

MAKING THEIR WAY Disembarking finally from the ferry onto American soil in Manhattan or New Jersey, the immigrants felt exhilaration, exhaustion, and usually a desperate need for work. Many were greeted by family and friends who had come over before; others by representatives of the many immigrant aid societies or by hiring agents offering jobs in mines, mills, and sweatshops. Since most knew little if any English and nothing about American employment practices, the immigrants were easy subjects for exploitation. In exchange for providing arrivals with a bit of whiskey and a job, obliging hiring agents claimed a healthy percentage of their wages. Among Italians and Greeks these agents were known as *padrones,* and they came to dominate the labor market in New York. Other contractors provided train tickets for immigrants to travel inland to jobs in cities such as Buffalo, Pittsburgh, Cleveland, Chicago, Milwaukee, Cincinnati, and St. Louis. Eager to retain a sense of community and to sustain skills they may have brought with them, the members of ethnic groups tended to cluster in particular vocations. Poles, Hungarians, Slovaks, Bohemians, and Italians used to the pick and shovel flocked to coal mines, just as the Irish, Cornish, and Welsh had done at mid-century; Slavs and Poles comfortable with muscle work gravitated to the steel mills; Greeks preferred working in textile mills; Russian and Polish Jews peopled the needle trades or pushcart markets of New York. The vast majority of women immigrants found work as domestic servants. Others worked in textile mills or urban "sweatshops." A few determined peasants uprooted from their agricultural heritage made their way west and were able to find work on farms or even a parcel of land for themselves.

Most of the immigrants, however, settled in the teeming cities. Strangers in a new land, they naturally gravitated to neighborhoods populated by their own kind. These immigrant enclaves —nicknamed Little Italy, Little Hungary, Chinatown, and so on—served as crucial transitional communities between the newcomers' Old World past and their New World future. By 1920 Chicago had some seventeen separate Little Italy colonies scattered across the city representing various home provinces. In such kinship communities the immigrants could practice their religions and native customs, converse in their native tongue, and fill an aching loneliness. But they paid a price for such community solidarity. When the "new immigrants" moved into an area, older residents typically moved out, taking with them whatever social prestige and political influence they had achieved. The quality of living conditions quickly deteriorated as housing and sanitation codes went unenforced.

As the number of new arrivals mushroomed during the last quarter of the nineteenth century, cities grew so cramped and land so scarce that designers were forced to build upward. The result was the "dumbbell" tenement house. These structures, usually six to eight stories in height and jammed tightly against one another, came to line street after street. They derived their name from the fact that housing codes required a two-foot wide air shaft between buildings, giving the structure the appearance of a dumbbell when viewed from overhead. Twenty-four to thirty-two families would cram into each building, meaning that some city blocks housed almost 4,000 people. The tiny air shaft provided little ventilation; instead, it proved to be a fire hazard, fueling and conveying the flames from building to building. The early tenements were poorly heated and had water closets outside in the yard or alley for communal use. By the end of the century they would feature two toilets on each floor, available to all comers. Shoehorned into such quarters, families had no privacy, free space, or sunshine; children had few places to play except in the city streets; infectious diseases and noxious odors were rampant. Not surprisingly, the mortality rate for urban immigrants was much higher than that of the general population. In one Chicago ethnic ghetto at the end of the century, three babies of every five died before their first birthday.

THE NATIVIST RESPONSE Many Americans of longer standing saw the new immigration as a threat, and the undercurrent of nativism so often present in American culture surfaced during the late nineteenth century, mainly in anti-Catholic and anti-Semitic sentiments. But more than religious prejudice underlay hostility toward the latest newcomers. Cultural differences confirmed in the minds of nativists the assumption that the Nordic peoples of the old immigration were superior to the Slavic and Latin peoples of the new immigration. Many of the new immigrants were illiterate, and more appeared so because they could not speak English. Some resorted to crime in order to survive in the new land, and political and social radicals turned up among these immigrant groups in sufficient numbers to encourage nativists to blame labor disputes on alien elements.

A resurgence of nativism in the 1880s led to the creation of the

American Protective Association, operated mainly in Protestant strongholds of the upper Mississippi Valley. The movement grew slowly from its start in 1887 until 1893, when keen leaders took advantage of a severe depression to draw large numbers of the frustrated to its ranks. The APA soon vanished with the return of prosperity, but while it lasted it promoted restricted immigration, more stringent naturalization requirements, refusal to employ aliens or Catholics, and the teaching of only the "American" language in the schools.

IMMIGRATION RESTRICTION   The movement to restrict immigration had mixed success beyond the exclusion of certain individuals deemed "undesirable." In 1891 Representative Henry Cabot Lodge of Massachusetts took up the cause of excluding illiterates —a measure that would have affected much of the new immigration, even though the language of literacy did not have to be English. Several times during the next twenty-five years Congress passed bills embodying the restriction, but they were vetoed by Presidents Cleveland, Taft, and Wilson. In 1917, however, Congress overrode Wilson's veto.

Proponents of immigration restriction during the late nineteenth century did succeed in excluding the Chinese, who were victims of everything the European immigrants suffered and color prejudice as well. By 1880 there were some 75,000 Chinese in California, about one-ninth of the state's population. Railroad owners found them hard-working and submissive. "They prove nearly equal to white men in the amount of labor they perform," one owner wrote, "and are much more reliable. No danger of strikes among them." Many white workers resented the Chinese for accepting lower wages, but their greater sin, a New York editor stressed, was perpetuating "those disgusting habits of thrift, industry, and self-denial."

Exclusion of the Chinese began in 1880, when the urgent need for railway labor had ebbed. A new treaty with China permitted the United States to "regulate, limit, and suspend" Chinese immigration, and in 1882 President Chester Arthur signed a bill authorizing a ten-year suspension. The Chinese Exclusion Act was made permanent in 1904. By then, prejudice against Japanese immigrants was simmering as well.

The West Coast counterpart to Ellis Island was the Immigration Station on rugged Angel Island, six miles offshore from San Francisco. Opened in 1910, it served as a processing center for tens of thousands of Asian immigrants, most of them Chinese. Although the Chinese Exclusion Act had sharply reduced the flow

The slogan of the
Workingmen's party was
"The Chinese Must Go!"

of Chinese immigrants, it did not stop the influx completely. Those arrivals who could claim a Chinese-American parent were allowed to enter, as were certain officials, teachers, merchants, and students. The powerful prejudice the Chinese immigrants encountered helps explain why over 30 percent of the arrivals at Angel Island were denied entry. Those who appealed such denials were housed in prison-like barracks for weeks or months. One of the detainees scratched a moving poem on the wall:

> This place is called an island of
> immortals,
> When, in fact, this mountainous wilderness
> is a prison.
> Once you see the open net, why throw
> yourself in?
> It is only because of empty pockets.
> I can do nothing else.

EDUCATION AND THE PROFESSIONS

THE SPREAD OF SCHOOLS   The spread of public education, spurred partly by the determination to "Americanize" immigrant children, helped quicken the emergence of a new America after the Civil War. By the 1870s, America's commitment to public education was well nigh universal. In 1870 there were 7 million pupils in public schools; by 1920 the number had tripled. Despite such progress, educational leaders all too often had to struggle against a pattern of political appointments, corruption, and incompetence in the public schools.

The spread of secondary schools accounted for much of the increased enrollment in public schools. In antebellum America private academies prepared those who intended to enter college. At the beginning of the Civil War there were only about 100 public high schools in the whole country, but in the next decades their number grew rapidly to about 800 in 1880 and 6,000 at the turn of the century.

HIGHER EDUCATION   American colleges as this time sought to instill discipline, morality, and a curriculum heavy on mathematics and the classics (and in church schools, theology), along with ethics and rhetoric. History, modern languages and literature, and some science courses were tolerated, although laboratory work would likely be limited to a professor's demonstration in class. The college teacher was all too apt to be a young man seeking temporary refuge, or a broken-down preacher seeking safe harbor. In 1871 one writer called the typical professor "nondescript, a jack of all trades, equally ready to teach surveying and Latin eloquence, and thankful if his quarter's salary is not docked to whitewash the college fence."

Nevertheless the increasing demand for higher learning drove the college student population up from 52,000 in 1870, to 157,000 in 1890, and to 600,000 in 1920. During the same years the number of institutions rose from 563 to about 1,000. To accommodate the diverse needs of these growing numbers, colleges moved away from rigidly prescribed courses toward an elective system. The new approach allowed students to favor their strong points and colleges to expand their scope. But as Henry Cabot Lodge complained, it also allowed students to "escape without learning anything at all by a judicious selection of unrelated subjects taken up only because they were easy or because the burden imposed by those who taught them was light."

Women's access to higher education improved markedly in this period. Before the Civil War a few colleges had already gone coeducational, and state universities in the West were commonly open to women from the start. But colleges in the South and East fell in line very slowly. Of the women's colleges, Vassar (1865) was the first to teach by the same standards as the best of the men's colleges. In 1875 two more excellent women's schools appeared in Massachusetts: Wellesley and Smith, the latter being the first to set the same admission requirements as men's colleges. Thereafter the older women's colleges rushed to upgrade their standards in the same way.

The dominant new trend in American higher education after the Civil War was the rise of the graduate school. Heretofore, most professors had a knowledge more broad than deep. With some notable exceptions they engaged in little research, nor were they expected to advance the frontiers of knowledge. Gradually, however, more and more American scholars studied at German universities, where training was more systematic and focused. After the Civil War the German system became the basis for the modern American graduate university. By the 1890s the Ph.D. was fast becoming the ticket of admission to the guild of professors.

THE RISE OF PROFESSIONALISM The Ph.D. revolution, moreover, was but one aspect of a growing emphasis on professionalism, with its imposition of uniform standards, licensing of practitioners, and accreditation of professional schools. The number of professional schools grew rapidly in fields such as theology, law, medicine, dentistry, pharmacy, and veterinary medicine.

Along with advanced schooling went a movement for licensing practitioners in certain fields. During the second half of the nineteenth century, the first state licensing laws were enacted for dentistry, pharmacy, veterinary medicine, accounting, and architecture. Such licensing benefited the public by certifying competence in a given field, but it also benefited members of the profession by limiting competition.

A Red Sox home game, 1897. Professional baseball became a major attraction in the late nineteenth century.

THEORIES OF SOCIAL CHANGE

Every field of thought in the postbellum years felt the impact of Charles Darwin's *On the Origin of Species* (1859), which argued that existing species, including humanity itself, had evolved through a long process of "natural selection" from less complex forms of life. Those species that adapted to survival by reason of quickness, shrewdness, or other advantages reproduced their kind, while others died away. The idea of species evolution shocked those of conventional religious views by contradicting a literal interpretation of the creation stories in Genesis. Heated arguments arose among scientists and clergymen. Some of the faithful rejected Darwin's doctrine, while others found their faith severely shaken. Most of the faithful, however, eventually came to reconcile science and religion, viewing evolution as a natural process designed by God.

SOCIAL DARWINISM   Though Darwin's theory applied only to biological phenomena, other thinkers drew broader inferences from it. The temptation to apply evolutionary theory to the social world proved irresistible. Darwin's fellow Englishman Herbert Spencer became the first major prophet of what came to be called Social Darwinism, and he exerted an important influence on American thought. Spencer argued that human society and institutions, like organisms, passed through the process of natural selection, which resulted in what he called the "survival of the fittest."

If, as Spencer believed, society naturally evolved for the better, then individual freedom was inviolable, and any governmental interference with the process of social evolution was a serious mistake. Social Darwinism thus implied a hands-off governmental policy; it decried the regulation of business, the proposals for a graduated income tax, sanitation and housing regulations, and even protection against medical quacks. Such initiatives, no matter how well intended, would only impede progress by contributing to the survival of the unfit. The only acceptable charity was voluntary, and even that was of dubious value. Spencer warned that "fostering the good-for-nothing at the expense of the good, is an extreme cruelty."

For Spencer and his many supporters, accumulated wealth was the best evidence of evolutionary fitness. Successful businessmen and corporations were the engines of progress. If small businesses were crowded out by trusts and monopolies, that too was part of the evolutionary process. As John D. Rockefeller told his Baptist Sunday school class: "The growth of a large business is merely a survival of the fittest."

The ideas of Darwin and Spencer were quickly popularized in America. Their most powerful advocate was William Graham Sumner, a professor at Yale who preached the gospel of natural selection to his classes and in writings such as *What Social Classes Owe to Each Other* and "The Absurd Effort to Make the World Over."

REFORM DARWINISM   The influence of Darwin and Spencer over the American mind did not go without challenge. Reform found its major philosopher in an obscure civil servant, Lester Frank Ward, who had fought his way up from poverty and never lost his empathy for the underdog. Ward's book *Dynamic Sociology* (1883) singled out one product of evolution that Spencer and others had neglected, the human brain. Humans, unlike animals, had a mind that could plan for and shape the future. Far from being the helpless pawn of powerful evolutionary forces, Ward argued, humanity could actively shape the process of evolution. The competition extolled by Sumner, Spencer, and other Social Darwinists was in fact highly wasteful, and so was the natural competitive process: plant or cattle breeding, for instance, could actually improve on the results of natural selection.

Ward's Reform Darwinism challenged Sumner's conservative Social Darwinism, holding that cooperation, not competition, would better promote progress. Government could become the agency of progress by striving to ameliorate poverty, which impeded the development of the mind, and to promote the education of the masses. "Intelligence, far more than necessity," Ward wrote, "is the mother of invention," and "the influence of knowledge as a social factor, like that of wealth, is proportional to the extent of its distribution." Intellect, rightly informed by science, could plan successfully. In the benevolent "sociocracy" of the future, Ward argued, legislatures would function mainly to sanction decisions worked out in the sociological laboratory.

REALISM IN FACT AND FICTION

HISTORY AND THE SOCIAL SCIENCES   The pervasive effect of Darwinism in late nineteenth-century American intellectual circles was comparable to the effect of romanticism in the first part of the century. Like the earlier reaction against the Enlightenment's praise of reason, the trend in social thought now was to turn against abstract logic and toward concrete reality. The revolt had two salient features: its emphasis on history, on looking to the past for explanations, and its interest in investigating contemporary reality broadly through a variety of the social sciences. Oliver Wendell Holmes, Jr., in *The Common Law* (1881), expressed the first feature succinctly: "The life of the law has not been logic, it has been experience," Holmes explained. And experience was history. "The law embodies the story of a nation's development through many centuries," Holmes wrote, "and it cannot be dealt with as if it contained only the axioms and corollaries of a book of mathematics."

In the milieu of Darwinism, the study of history flourished. The historian, like the biologist, studied the process of development, but in the origins and the evolution of society. Under the influence of German scholarship, and the new emphasis on science, history aspired to become "scientific." This meant examining documents and manuscripts critically, using external and internal evidence to determine validity and relevancy. The ideal of the scientific historian was to reproduce history with perfect objectivity, a noble if unreachable goal.

PRAGMATISM   Around the turn of the century the evolutionary idea found expression in a philosophical principle set forth in mature form by William James in his book *Pragmatism: A New Name for Some Old Ways of Thinking*. James, a professor of philosophy and psychology at Harvard, was concerned, like Lester Frank Ward, with the role of ideas in the process of evolution. Truth, to James, arose from the testing of new ideas, the value of which lay in their practical consequences. Similarly, scientists could test the validity of their ideas in the laboratory, and judge their import by their applications. Pragmatism thus reflected a quality often looked upon as genuinely American: the inventive, experimental spirit focusing on tangible results.

John Dewey, who would become the chief philosopher of pragmatism after James, preferred the term "instrumentalism," by which he meant that ideas were instruments of practical use, especially for promoting social reform. Dewey, unlike James, threw himself into movements for the rights of labor and women, the promotion of peace, and the reform of education. He believed that education was the process through which society would gradually progress toward greater social equality and harmony. Dewey became the prophet of what was later labeled "progressive education," which emphasized the teaching of history, geography, and science in order to enlarge the child's personal experience. Dewey also pointed out that social conditions had so changed that schools now had to find ways to inculcate values once derived from participation in family and community activities.

THE LOCAL COLORISTS   American literature in this period also sought new ways to capture concrete reality, present and past. What came to be called the local color movement expressed the nostalgia of a people for places where old values and folkways survived. Sarah Orne Jewett depicted the down-easters of her native Maine most enduringly in the stories and sketches collected in *The Country of the Pointed Firs* (1896). Jewett's creative glance was always backward and affectionate, as she identified more with her forebears than her peers. She looked upon her parents' "generation as the one to which I really belong—I who was brought up with grandfathers and granduncles and aunts for my best playmates." She told another writer that her head was always full of old women and old houses, and when the two came together the result was a richly textured fiction marked by the essential dignity of a bygone day.

This local color impulse was not limited to New England. Once the passions of war and Reconstruction were spent, the South became for many northern readers an inexhaustible gallery of quaint types and picturesque settings. George Washington Cable exploited the local color of the quaint Louisiana Creoles and Cajuns in *Old Creole Days* (1879), *The Grandissimes* (1880), and other books. Joel Chandler Harris, a white newsman and columnist, wove authentic African-American folk tales into the unforgettable stories of Uncle Remus.

CLEMENS, HOWELLS, AND JAMES   The best of the local colorists could find universal truths in local life, but Samuel Langhorne Clemens (Mark Twain) transcended them all. A native of Missouri, Clemens was forced to work from the time he was twelve, becoming first a printer and then a Mississippi riverboat pilot. When the Civil War shut down the river traffic, he briefly joined a Confederate militia company, then left with his brother for Nevada, where he wrote for a local newspaper. He moved on to California in 1864 and first gained widespread notice with his tall tale of the gold country, "The Celebrated Jumping Frog of Calaveras County" (1865). With the success of *Roughing It* (1871), an account of his western years, he moved to Hartford, Connecticut, and was able to set up as a full-time author and hilarious lecturer.

Clemens was the first significant American writer born and

*Samuel Langhorne Clemens,
or Mark Twain.*

raised west of the Appalachians. His early writings accentuated
his western background, but for his greatest books he drew heavily upon his boyhood in the border slave state of Missouri and the
tall-tale tradition of southwestern humor. In *The Adventures of
Tom Sawyer* (1876) he evoked the prewar Hannibal, Missouri,
where his own boyhood was cut so short. Its story of childhood
adventures is firmly etched on the American memory. *Life on the
Mississippi* (1882), based on articles written eight years before,
drew upon what Clemens remembered as his happiest days as a
young riverboat pilot before the war. His pseudonym "Mark
Twain" was in fact derived from a phrase that referred to the
depth of the river.

Clemens's masterpiece, *The Adventures of Huckleberry Finn*
(1884), created unforgettable characters in Huck Finn, his shiftless father, the runaway slave Jim, the Widow Douglas, the
"King," and the "Duke." Huck Finn embodied the instinct of
every red-blooded American boy to "light out for the territory"
whenever polite society set out to civilize him. Huck's effort to
help his friend Jim escape bondage expressed well the moral dilemmas imposed on everyone by slavery. Many years later another great American writer, Ernest Hemingway, would claim
that "All modern literature comes from one book by Mark
Twain, called *Huckleberry Finn.*"

One of Clemens's foremost supporters was his close friend

William Dean Howells. During the half century after the Civil War, Howells dominated the American literary scene. As editor of the influential *Atlantic Monthly* and later a columnist and critic for *Harper's Monthly,* Howells preached and practiced the new doctrine of realism, a literary rebellion against romantic idealism which sought to portray with scientific accuracy the contemporary social scene. He wrote that realism "was nothing more or less than the truthful treatment of . . . the motives, the impulses, the principles that shape the life of actual men and women."

To this end Howells wrote novels, plays, travel books, criticism, essays, biography, and autobiography. Amid the varied output of a long and productive life, *The Rise of Silas Lapham* (1885) stands out as his most famous novel. In it Howells presented a sympathetic portrayal of a newly rich manufacturer from the West, and one of the earliest fictional treatments of an American businessman.

The third major literary figure of the times, Henry James, moved in a world far different from those of Clemens or Howells. Brother of the pragmatist philosopher William James, and son of wealthy parents, Henry spent most of his adult life as a voluntary expatriate in London, where he produced elegant novels that for the first time explored the international society of Americans in Europe. In works such as *Portrait of a Lady* (1881), *The Ambassadors* (1903), and *The Golden Bowl* (1904), James explored the tensions that developed between direct, innocent, and idealistic Americans (most often young women) and sophisticated, devious Europeans. Unlike Clemens, James typically wrote of the cosmopolitan upper class, and his stories turned less on plot than on moral dilemmas. His intense exploration of the inner selves of his characters brought him the title of "father of the psychological novel."

LITERARY NATURALISM Realism grew into a powerful literary movement during the 1880s, but during the 1890s it took on a new character in the writings of the naturalists. This group of younger writers sought to integrate scientific determinism into literature. Having grown up in the era of Darwin and Spencer, they viewed humankind as prey to natural forces and internal drives without control or full knowledge of them. Frank Norris thus pictured in *McTeague* (1899) the descent of a San Francisco dentist and his wife into madness, driven by greed, violence, and lust. Stephen Crane in *Maggie: A Girl of the Streets* (1893) and *The Red Badge of Courage* (1895) portrayed people caught up in situations beyond their control. *Maggie* depicted a girl driven to prostitution and death amid scenes so grim and sordid that Crane had to finance publication himself. *The Red Badge of Courage*, his masterpiece, told the story of a young man going through his baptism of fire in the Civil War, and evoked fear, nobility, and courage amid the ungovernable carnage of war.

Two of the naturalists achieved a degree of popular success: Jack London and Theodore Dreiser. London, of California, was both a professed socialist and a believer in the German philosopher Friedrich Nietzsche's doctrine of the superman. In adventure stories like *Call of the Wild* (1903) and *The Sea Wolf* (1904) he celebrated the triumph of brute force and the will to survive.

Theodore Dreiser did not celebrate the overwhelming power of social and biological forces; he dissected them for the reader. The result was powerfully disturbing to readers accustomed to more genteel fare. Dreiser shocked the public probably more than the others with protagonists who sinned without remorse and without punishment. *Sister Carrie* (1900), for example, showed Carrie Meeber surviving illicit lovers and going on to success on the stage.

SOCIAL CRITICISM Behind their dogma of determinism several of the naturalists harbored intense outrage at human misery. Their indignation was shared by an increasing number of journalists and social critics who addressed themselves more directly to protest and reform. One of the most influential of these reformers was Henry George, a journalist who vowed to seek out the cause of poverty in the midst of the industrial progress he saw around him. The basic problem, George reasoned, was the unearned increment in wealth that came to those who owned the land. He wrote down the fruit of his thought in *Progress and Poverty* (1879), a thick, rambling, and difficult book whose earnest moralism and sympathetic tone helped it sell about 2 million copies in several languages.

George held that everyone had a basic right to the use of the land since it was provided by nature to all. Nobody had a right to the increasing value that accrued from the land, since that was created by the community, not by its owner. Labor and capital, on the other hand, did have a just claim on the wealth they produced. He proposed simply to tax the unearned increment in the value of the land, or the rent. George's "single-tax" idea was intended to free capital and labor from paying tribute for the land, and to put to use lands previously held out of production by speculators. George's idea provoked much discussion and actually affected local tax policy here and there, but his influence on the thinking of the day came less from his "single-tax" panacea than from the paradox he posed in his title *Progress and Poverty,* and his plea for social cooperation and equality.

The journalist and free-lance writer Henry Demarest Lloyd, son of a minister, addressed himself to what many found a more vital issue than Henry George's, not the monopoly in land but industrial monopoly. His best known book, *Wealth Against Commonwealth* (1894), drew on more than a decade of studying the Standard Oil Company. Lloyd, like George and Lester Frank Ward, saw the key to social progress in cooperation rather than competition. Economic activities in their cooperative aspects demonstrated a civilizing process. The cooperative principle should be applied "to all toils in which private sovereignty has become through monopoly a despotism over the public." Where monopoly had developed, it should be transferred to public operation in the public interest. In 1903, just before his death, Lloyd joined the Socialist party.

Thorstein Veblen brought to his social criticism a background of formal training in economics and a purpose of making economics more an evolutionary or historical science. By all accounts he taught miserably, even inaudibly, and seldom held a job for long, but he wrote brilliantly. In his best known work, *The Theory of the Leisure Class* (1899), he examined the pecuniary values of the affluent and introduced phrases that have since become commonplace in our language: "conspicuous consumption" and "conspicuous leisure." With the advent of industrial society, Veblen argued, the showy display of money and property became the conventional basis of status. For the upper classes, moreover, it became necessary to spend time casually as evidence of the ability to afford a life of leisure.

THE SOCIAL GOSPEL

While novelists, journalists, and commentators were writing about the rising social tensions and injustices of late nineteenth-century America, more and more people were addressing these problems through direct social action. Some reformers focused on legislative solutions to social problems; others stressed philanthropy or organized charity. A few militants promoted socialism or anarchism. Whatever the method or approach, however, social reformers were on the march at the turn of the century, and their activities gave to American life a new urgency and energy.

RISE OF THE INSTITUTIONAL CHURCH The churches responded slowly to the mounting social criticism, for American Protestantism had become one of the main props of the established order. The Reverend Henry Ward Beecher, for instance, pastor of the fashionable Plymouth Congregational Church in Brooklyn, preached material success, Social Darwinism, and the unworthiness of the poor.

As the middle classes moved out to the streetcar suburbs, their churches followed. In the years 1868–1888, for instance, seventeen Protestant churches abandoned the areas below Fourteenth Street in Manhattan. In the center of Chicago 60,000 residents had no church, Protestant or Catholic. Where churches became prosperous they fell easily under the spell of complacent respectability and do-nothing Social Darwinism. Some prominent clergymen expressed open disdain for the lower classes. De Witt Talmage, an outspoken Presbyterian minister in Brooklyn, stressed that he wanted no working men stinking up his church. "If you are going to kill the church thus with bad smells, I will have nothing to do with this work of evangelization." Not surprisingly, more and more working-class people felt out of place in churches where affluence was both worshipped and flaunted.

But gradually some religious leaders realized that Protestantism was in danger of losing its working class constituency unless

A Salvation Army group in Flint, Michigan, 1894.

it reached out to the urban poor. Two organizations were created expressly for that purpose. The Young Men's Christian Association had entered the United States from England in the 1850s and grew rapidly after 1870; the Salvation Army, founded in London in 1876, entered the United States four years later. Individual urban churches also began to develop institutional features that were more social than strictly religious in function. Church buildings acquired gymnasiums, libraries, lecture rooms, and other facilities in an effort to attract working-class people back to organized religion.

RELIGIOUS REFORMERS Some church reformers who feared that Christianity was becoming irrelevant to the needs and aspirations of the working poor began preaching what came to be called the social gospel. One of the earliest, Washington Gladden of Columbus, Ohio, managed to profess the social gospel from the pulpit of a middle-class Congregational church. The new gospel in fact expressed the social conscience of the middle class. Gladden maintained that true Christianity resided not in rituals, dogmas, or even in the mystical experience of God, but in the principle that "Thou shalt love thy neighbor as thyself." Christian law should therefore govern the workplace, with laborer and employer united in serving each other's interest. The "law of greed and strife," he insisted, "is not a natural law; it is unnatural; it is a crime against nature; the law of brotherhood is the only natural law." He thus argued for labor's right to organize, supported maximum-hours laws and factory inspections, and endorsed anti-trust legislation.

THE CATHOLIC CHURCH In the post-Civil War years Catholic social thought was initially quite conservative. Papal decrees declared erroneous such current ideas as progress, liberalism, rationalism, and socialism, and warned American Catholics against supporting the new social movements. The Vatican's outlook altered drastically in 1891 when Pope Leo XIII issued his encyclical, *Rerum novarum* ("Of Modern Things"). This new expression of Catholic social doctrine upheld private property as a natural right but condemned capitalism where it had imposed poverty and degradation on workers. It also affirmed the right of Catholics to join labor unions and socialist movements insofar as these were not antireligious. But American Catholics for the most part remained isolated from organized reform movements until the twentieth century, though they themselves were among the most abused victims of urban slums.

EARLY EFFORTS AT URBAN REFORM

THE SETTLEMENT HOUSE MOVEMENT   While preachers of the social gospel dispensed inspiration, other dedicated reformers attacked the problems of the slums from residential and community centers called settlement houses. By 1900 perhaps a hundred settlement houses existed in America, some of the best known being Jane Addams's and Ellen Starr's Hull House in Chicago and Lillian Wald's Henry Street Settlement in New York.

The settlement houses were staffed mainly by idealistic middle-class young people, a majority of them college-trained women who had few other outlets for meaningful work. Settlement workers sought to broaden the horizons and improve the lives of slum dwellers in diverse ways. At Hull House, for instance, workers sought to draw the neighborhood children into clubs, kindergartens, and a nursery, which served the infant children of working mothers. Settlement houses were also meant to provide workingmen an alternative to the saloon as a place of recreation, and an alternative to the political boss as a source of social services. Their programs gradually expanded to include health clinics, lectures, music and art studios, employment bureaus, men's clubs, training in skills such as bookbinding, gymnasiums, and savings banks. Addams and other settlement house leaders realized, however, that the spreading slums made their work as effective as bailing out the ocean with a teaspoon. They therefore spoke out and organized political support for housing laws, public playgrounds, juvenile courts, mothers' pensions,

Jane Addams.

workmen's compensation laws, and legislation against child labor. Julia Lathrop, another Hull House staffer, was appointed in 1912 the first head of the federal Children's Bureau, an agency designed to scrutinize the use and abuse of child labor.

THE WOMEN'S SUFFRAGE MOVEMENT   Settlement house workers, insofar as they were paid, of course made up but a fraction of all gainfully employed women. With rapid population growth in the late nineteenth century the number of employed women steadily increased, as did their percentage of the labor force. The greatest leaps forward came in the decades of the 1880s and the 1900s, both of which were also peak decades of immigration, a correlation which can be explained by the immigrants' need for income. The number of employed women doubled from 1880 to 1900 and then doubled again by 1910. Through all those years domestic work remained the largest category of employment for women; teaching and nursing also remained among the leading fields. The main change was that clerical work (bookkeeping, stenographic work, and the like) and sales jobs became increasingly available to women.

These changes in occupational status had little connection with the women's rights movement, which increasingly focused on the issue of suffrage. Immediately after the Civil War, Susan B. Anthony, a seasoned veteran of the movement though still in her forties, demanded that the Fourteenth Amendment include a guarantee of the vote for women as well as black males. She made little impression on the defenders of masculine prerogative, however, who continued to insist that women belonged solely in the home. "Their mission is at home, by their blandishments and their love to assuage the passions of men as they come in from the battle of life . . ." said a New Jersey senator. "It will be a sorry day for this country when those vestal fires of love and piety are put out."

In 1869 the unity of the women's movement disintegrated in a manner reminiscent of the antislavery rift three decades before. The question once again was whether the movement should concentrate on one overriding issue or broaden its focus. Anthony and Elizabeth Cady Stanton founded the National Woman Suffrage Association to promote a woman suffrage amendment to the Constitution, but they looked upon suffrage as but one among many feminist causes to be promoted as well. Later that same year, Lucy Stone, Julia Ward Howe, and other leaders formed the American Woman Suffrage Association, which focused single-mindedly on the vote as the first and basic reform. The long struggle for state legislation on the suffrage issue fo-

Carrie Chapman Catt, a leader in the women's suffrage movement.

cused the women's cause ever more on the primary objective of the vote. In 1890, after three years of negotiation, the rival groups united as the National American Woman Suffrage Association, with Elizabeth Cady Stanton as president for two years, followed by Susan B. Anthony until 1900. The work thereafter was carried on by a new generation led by Anna Howard Shaw and Carrie Chapman Catt. Over the years the movement slogged its way to some local and some partial victories, as a few states granted woman suffrage in school board or municipal elections. In 1869 the Territory of Wyoming granted full suffrage to women, and after 1890 retained woman suffrage as a state. Three other western states soon followed suit, but not until New York acted in 1917 did a state east of the Mississippi adopt universal suffrage.

Despite the focus on the vote, women did not confine their public work to that issue. In 1866 a Young Women's Christian Association, a parallel to the YMCA, appeared in Boston and spread elsewhere. The New England Women's Club, started in 1868 by Julia Ward Howe and others, was an early example of the women's clubs that then proliferated to the extent that a General Federation of Women's Clubs tied them together in 1890. Many women's clubs confined themselves to "literary" and social activities, but others became deeply involved in charities and reform. The New York Consumers League, formed in 1890, and the National Consumers League, formed nine years later, sought to make the buying public, chiefly women, better aware of degrading labor conditions.

GROWTH OF THE WELFARE STATE   Even without the support of voting women in most places, the states groped toward rudimentary measures to regulate big business and labor conditions in the public interest. By the end of the century nearly every state had provided for the regulation of railroads, if not always effectively, and had moved to supervise banks and insurance companies. Between 1887 and 1897, by one count, the states and territories passed more than 1,600 laws relating to conditions of work that limited the hours of labor, provided special protection for women, limited or forbade child labor, required regular wage payments in cash, called for factory inspections, and outlawed blacklisting or the importation of "Pinkerton men." Still, the effect of the effort was limited by poor enforcement and by conservative judges who ruled that the Constitution protected employers from many such attempts at state regulation.

As the turn of the century neared, opinion in the country stood poised between conservative rigidities and a growing sense that new occasions impose new personal and governmental responsibilities. The last two decades of the nineteenth century had already seen a slow erosion of laissez-faire, free market values, that had found their most secure home in the courts. There emerged instead a concept of the general-welfare state that called upon the government to act on behalf of the whole society rather than allow rugged individualism to run rampant. The conflict between this notion and laissez-faire values spilled over into the new century, but by the mid-twentieth century, after the Progressive Movement and the New Deal, the nation would be firmly committed to the premises of the general-welfare state.

FURTHER READING

Recent surveys of urbanization include Eric H. Monkkonen's *America Becomes Urban* (1988)° and Charles N. Glaab and A. Theodore Brown's *A History of Urban America* (3rd ed., 1983).° Urban politics is treated in John M. Allswang's *Bosses, Machines, and Urban Voters* (rev. ed., 1986).° Sam Bass Warner examines how space and distance changed urban configurations in *Streetcar Suburbs: The Process of Growth in Boston, 1870–1900* (2nd ed., 1978).°

Immigration has an extensive scholarship. Start with Leonard Din-

° These books are available in paperback editions.

nerstein and David M. Reimers's *Ethnic Americans: A History of Immigration and Assimilation* (2nd ed., 1982)° and Alan M. Kraut's *The Huddled Masses* (1982).° John Higham's *Strangers in the Land: Patterns of American Nativism* (1955)° remains a classic. The best survey of Asian immigrants is Ronald Takaki's *Strangers from a Different Shore: A History of Asian Americans* (1989).°

For trends in higher education, consult Laurence Veysey's *The Emergence of the American University* (1965).° Helen Horowitz's *Alma Mater* (1984) offers fascinating insights about the first women's colleges. Burton J. Bledstein's *The Culture of Professionalism: The Middle Class and the Development of Higher Education in America* (1976)° is particularly insightful.

Morton White and Lucia White's *The Intellectual versus the City* (1962)° surveys the insights of the Gilded Age's leading thinkers. The best study of America's most influential philosopher is Robert B. Westbrook's *John Dewey and American Democracy* (1992).° Richard Hofstadter's *Social Darwinism in American Thought* (rev. ed., 1955)° and Cynthia E. Russett's *Darwin in America* (1976)° examine the impact of the theory of evolution. Robert Bannister's *Social Darwinism* (1979) revises views of that idea. Alan Trachtenberg's *The Incorporation of America* (1982)° surveys cultural developments. Larzer Ziff's *The American 1890s: The Lost Generation* (1966)° discusses the key writers during that crucial decade. John L. Thomas's *Alternative America: Henry George, Edward Bellamy, Henry Demarest Lloyd, and the Adversary Tradition* (1983) provides the best introduction to the social critics of the Gilded Age. Jane Addams's *Twenty Years at Hull House* (1910)° remains the classic account of the settlement house movement. See also Allen Davis's *Spearheads for Reform: The Social Settlements and the Progressive Movement* (1967).° A revealing new study of the social gospel is Susan Curtis's *A Consuming Faith: The Social Gospel and Modern American Culture* (1992).

Eleanor Flexner's *Century of Struggle: The Women's Rights Movement in the United States* (rev. ed., 1975)° provides a good introduction to the condition of women in the Gilded Age. For the subject of working women, see Alice Kessler-Harris's *Out to Work* (1983).°

An important profession is analyzed in Paul Starr's *The Social Transformation of American Medicine* (1982).° Gunther P. Barth discusses the emergence of a new urban culture in *City People: The Rise of Modern City Culture in Nineteenth Century America* (1980).° The rise of the consumer culture is traced in Daniel Horowitz's *The Morality of Spending* (1985).

21

GILDED AGE POLITICS AND AGRARIAN REVOLT

PARADOXICAL POLITICS

In 1873 Mark Twain and Charles Dudley Warner created an enduring label for the three decades after the Civil War when they collaborated on a novel entitled *The Gilded Age*. The book depicted an age of widespread political corruption, personal greed, and social vulgarity. Perspectives on the times would eventually change, but generations of political scientists and historians have since reinforced the two novelists' judgment. As a young college graduate in 1879 Woodrow Wilson described the state of the American political system: "No leaders, no principles; no principles, no parties." His contemporary, the Harvard historian Henry Adams, shared his view. "The period," he groused, "was poor in purpose and barren in results." Indeed, the real movers and shakers of the Gilded Age were not the men who sat in the White House or the Congress but the captains of industry who flung railroads across the continent and decorated its cities with their plumed smokestacks and gaudy mansions.

On the national issues of the day the major parties pursued for the most part a policy of evasion. Only the tariff provoked clear-cut divisions between protectionist Republicans and low-tariff Democrats, but there were individual exceptions even on that. On questions of the currency, regulation of big business, farm problems, civil service reform, and immigration, one would be hard put to distinguish between the parties. Said one British observer, the two American parties were no more different than "Tweedledee and Tweedledum."

The Bosses of the Senate. *This 1889 cartoon bitingly portrays the alliance between big business and politics in this period.*

The primary reason for the muddled politics of this period was the even division between the parties. From 1869 to 1913, from Grant to Taft, Republicans monopolized the White House except during the two nonconsecutive terms of Grover Cleveland, but Republican domination was more apparent than real. Between 1872 and 1896 no president won a majority of the popular vote. And while Republicans usually controlled the Senate, Democrats usually controlled the House. Only during 1881–1883 and 1889–1891 did a Republican president have a Republican Congress. And only between 1893 and 1895 did a Democratic president enjoy a Democratic Congress.

Deferential presidents also contributed to the political stalemate. No chief executive between Lincoln and Theodore Roosevelt could be described as a "strong" president. Though reasonably effective and honest men, none seriously challenged the prevailing view that the formulation of public policy belonged to Congress. Senator John Sherman of Ohio expressed the widely held notion that the legislative branch should be primary in a republic: "The President should merely obey and enforce the laws." At the same time the almost equal strength of the parties in Congress worked against any vigorous new departures there, since most bills required bipartisan support to pass both houses.

Under such static conditions, the parties became machines for seeking office and dispensing patronage in the form of government jobs and contracts. An alliance of business and politics was characteristic of the period. This alliance was not necessarily corrupt, since many a politician favored business interests out of conviction. Nor was the public as sensitive to conflicts of interest as it would be later. James G. Blaine of Maine, for example, and many of his supporters, saw nothing wrong in his accepting stock from an Arkansas railroad after helping it win a land grant from Congress. Railroad passes, free entertainment, and a host of other favors were freely accepted by politicians, editors, and other leaders in positions to influence public opinion.

POLITICS AND THE VOTERS   But if observers considered this a time of political mediocrity in which the parties refused to face up to such "real issues" as the growth of an unregulated economy and its attendant social injustices, it is nonetheless clear that the voters of the time thought more was at stake. Voter turnout during the Gilded Age was commonly about 70–80 percent, even in the South, where the disfranchisement of blacks was not yet complete. (By contrast, the turnout for the 1988 presidential election was barely 50 percent.) How was it then that leaders who failed to face up to the real issues presided over the most highly organized and politically active electorate in American history?

The answer is partly that the politicians and the voters deeply believed that they *were* dealing with crucial issues: the tariff, monopolies, the currency, civil service reform, and immigration. But what most motivated party loyalties and voter turnout in these years were intense cultural conflicts among ethnic and religious groups. The Republican party attracted mainly Protestants of British descent. Their native seat was New England, and their other strongholds were New York and the upper Middle West, both of which were seeded with Yankee stock. Legitimate heirs to the abolitionist tradition, Republicans drew to their ranks a host of reformers and moralists, spiritual descendants of the perfectionists who populated the revivals and the reform movements of the antebellum years. The party's heritage of anti-Catholic nativism would also make a comeback in the 1880s. And the Republicans could also rely on the votes of blacks and Union veterans of the Civil War.

The Democrats, by contrast, tended to be a heterogeneous, often unruly coalition embracing southern whites, immigrants and Catholics of any origin, Jews, freethinkers, skeptics, and all those repelled by the "party of morality." As one Chicago Democrat explained, "A Republican is a man who wants you t' go t' church every Sunday. A Democrat says if a man wants to have a glass of beer on Sunday he can have it."

In the Midwest especially, tensions over religious and social issues, such as Sunday closing laws and liquor prohibition, created sharp political allegiances. Republicans pressed nativist causes, calling for restrictions on immigration and on the employment of foreigners, and greater emphasis on the teaching of the "American" language in the schools. Prohibitionism revived along with nativism in the 1880s. Among the immigrants who crowded into the growing cities were numbers of hard-drinking Irish, beer-drinking Germans, and wine-drinking Italians. Republicans increasingly saw saloons as the central social evil around which all others revolved, including vice, crime, political corruption, and neglect of families, and they associated these ethnic groups with the problem.

CORRUPTION AND REFORM

While grassroots Republicans and Democrats differed over ethnic and cultural issues, their party leaders spent much of their time arguing over the so-called "spoils" of office. Each party had its share of corrupt officials willing to buy and sell government appointments or congressional votes, yet each also witnessed the emergence of factions promoting honesty in government. This struggle for clean government soon became one of the foremost issues of the day.

HAYES AND CIVIL SERVICE REFORM   In the aftermath of Reconstruction, Rutherford B. Hayes admirably embodied the "party of morality." Hayes brought to the White House in 1877 a new style of uprightness that contrasted with the graft and corruption of the Grant administration. The son of an Ohio farmer, Hayes became one of the early Republicans, was wounded four times in the Civil War, and was promoted to major-general. Elected governor of Ohio in 1867, he served three terms. Honest and respectable, competent and dignified, he lived in modest style with his wife, who was nicknamed "Lemonade Lucy" because of her refusal to serve alcohol at White House functions.

Yet Hayes's tenure as president was besmirched by the manner of his defeat of Tilden in the 1876–1877 election. Snide references to him as "His Fraudulence" dogged his steps and denied him any chance at a second term, which he renounced from the beginning. Hayes's own party was split between so-called Stalwarts and Half-Breeds, led respectively by Senators Roscoe Conkling of New York and James G. Blaine of Maine. The difference between these Republican factions was murkier than that between the parties. The Stalwarts generally supported Grant, a Radical southern policy, and the spoils system. The Half-Breeds took a contrary view on the first two and were even vaguely touched by the sentiment for civil service reform.

But for the most part, the Stalwart and Half-Breed factions were loose alliances designed to advance the careers of Conkling and Blaine. The two men could not abide one another. Blaine once referred to Conkling as displaying a "majestic, supereminent, overpowering, turkey-gobbler strut." He was right. Tall and lordly, with a pointed beard, thick, auburn hair, and up-turned jaw and nose, Conkling was distinctive for his good looks, fine clothes, and arrogant manner. He dressed and lived flamboyantly, sporting pastel bow ties, silk scarves, moon-colored vests, and patent leather shoes. Yet for all his sartorial splendor and glamorous facade, he was always the ruthless power broker. Conkling viewed politics as a brute struggle for power, and its arena was no place for faint hearts. Politics "is a rotten business," he declared. "Nothing counts except to win."

Hayes thought otherwise, and he aligned himself with the growing public discontent over the corruption and jobbery that had prevailed under Grant. In promoting the cause of civil service reform, he issued an Executive Order in June 1877 which declared that those already in office would be dismissed only for the good of the government and not for political reasons. His cabinet tried to carry out the new policy. Secretary of the Treasury John Sherman showed Hayes evidence that both Collector Chester A. Arthur and Naval Officer Alonzo Cornell were guilty of "laxity" and of using the New York Customs House for political management on behalf of Conkling's organization. Hayes removed Arthur and Cornell, and thereby won Conkling's lasting hatred.

For all his efforts to clean house, Hayes retained a limited vision of government's role. On the economic issues of the day he held to a conservative line that would guide his successors for the rest of the century. His solution to labor troubles, demonstrated during the Great Railroad Strike of 1877, was to send in troops and break the strike. A financial conservative, he denied the demands of farmers and debtors for an expansion of the currency by vetoing the Bland-Allison Act. Passed over his veto, the bill enacted a limited expansion of silver currency through the government's purchase for coinage of $2–$4 million worth of silver per month.

GARFIELD AND ARTHUR   With Hayes unavailable for a second term, the Republicans were forced to look elsewhere in 1880. The Stalwarts, led by Conkling, brought Grant forward for a third time, still a strong contender despite the tarnish of his administration's scandals. For two days the Republican convention in Chicago was deadlocked, with Grant leading but strongly challenged by Blaine and John Sherman. On the thirty-fifth ballot, Wisconsin suddenly switched sixteen votes to former House Speaker (now Senator-elect) James A. Garfield, Sherman's campaign manager. Garfield rose to protest but was ruled out of order, and on the next ballot the convention stampeded to the dark-horse candidate. As a sop to the losing faction the convention tapped Chester A. Arthur, of Custom House notoriety, for vice-president.

The Democrats named Winfield Scott Hancock, a Union commander at Gettysburg, to counterbalance the Republicans' Brigadier-General Garfield and thus ward off "bloody-shirt" attacks on their party as the vehicle of secession. The election turned out to be the closest of the century. Garfield eked out a plurality of only 39,000 votes with 48.5 percent of the vote, but with a comfortable margin of 214 to 155 in the electoral college.

An Ohio native, Garfield had distinguished himself at Shiloh and Chickamauga during the Civil War, and was mustered out as a general when he entered Congress in 1863. Noted for his oratory and parliamentary skills, he became one of the outstanding leaders in the House and eventually its Speaker.

On July 2, 1881, President Garfield was leaving on a vacation in New England when, as he walked through the Baltimore and Potomac railroad station, a deranged office seeker named Charles Guiteau shot him in the back. "I am a Stalwart," Guiteau shouted to the arresting officers. "Arthur is now President of the United States." Guiteau's announcement would prove crippling to the Stalwarts, and his attack fatal to Garfield, who died after a two-month struggle. Garfield had been president for a little over six months.

One of the chief henchmen of Stalwart leader Roscoe Conkling was now president. Little in Chester Arthur's past suggested that he would rise above spoils politics. A native of Vermont and a Phi Beta Kappa graduate of Union College, he had made a political career in appointive offices, most notably as New York's col-

Chester A. Arthur.

lector of customs from 1871 to 1878. But Arthur, a wealthy, handsome widower who loved fine wines and sported a lavish wardrobe and billowing sideburns, demonstrated surprising leadership qualities as president. He began by distancing himself from Conkling and the Stalwarts and establishing a genuine independence, almost a necessity after Guiteau's announcement. As Arthur noted, "For the vice-presidency I was indebted to Mr. Conkling, but for the presidency of the United States my debt is to the Almighty."

Most startling of all was Arthur's emergence as something of a civil service and tariff reformer. Stalwarts had every reason to expect him to oppose such changes, but instead he allied himself with the reformers. While the assassin Guiteau had unwittingly added a certain urgency to the public support of reform, the defeat of a reform bill in 1882 sponsored by "Gentleman George" Pendleton, Democratic senator from Ohio, aroused public opinion further. As a result the Pendleton Civil Service Act finally passed in January 1883, setting up a three-member Civil Service Commission independent from the regular cabinet departments, the first such federal agency established on a permanent basis. About 14 percent of all government jobs came under the category of "classified services," in which new appointments had to be made on the basis of competitive examinations rather than political connections. What was more, the president could enlarge the list of classified services at his discretion, as many later did.

Meanwhile the tariff continued to be the most controversial

political issue. The high protective tariff, a heritage of the Civil War, had by the early 1880s raised revenues to the point that the government actually enjoyed a surplus that drew money into the Treasury and out of circulation, impeding economic growth. Some argued that lower tariff rates would reduce prices and the cost of living, and at the same time leave more money in circulation. In 1882 Arthur named a special commission to study the problem. The Tariff Commission recommended a 20–25 percent rate reduction, which gained Arthur's support, but Congress's effort to enact the proposal was marred by logrolling to further local interests. The result was the "Mongrel Tariff" of 1883, so called because of its diverse percentages for different commodities. Overall the tariff provided for a slight rate reduction, but it actually hiked the duty on some articles.

SCURRILOUS CAMPAIGN   When the 1884 election came around, Arthur's record might have commended him to the voters, but it did not set well with the leaders of his party. The Republicans dumped Arthur and turned to the majestic Senator James G. Blaine of Maine, leader of the Half-Breeds. Blaine was the consummate politician. He never forgot a name or a face, he inspired the party faithful with his oratory, and at the same time he knew how to wheel and deal in the backrooms.

Back in 1876 Blaine had been nominated for the presidency by a Republican official who, in an eloquent flight of oratory, had announced: "Like an armed warrior, like a plumed knight, James G. Blaine marched down the halls of American Congress and threw his shining lance full and fair against the brazen forehead of the defamers of his country and maligners of his honor." To his followers in 1884 Blaine remained the plumed knight, with a strikingly long, pale face, animated by dark eyes and anchored in a silvery beard. But Democratic newspapers portrayed him as the plumed knave who, as was clear from the evidence in the "Mulligan letters," had sold his soul to the railroads. Even Roscoe Conkling, certainly no pillar of integrity himself, refused to campaign for the tainted Blaine, explaining that "I don't engage in criminal practice."

During the campaign more letters surfaced with disclosures embarrassing to Blaine. For the reform element of the Republican party, this was too much, and many bolted the ticket. Party regulars scorned the idealists as "goo-goo"—the "good-government" crowd who ignored partisan realities—and one editor jokingly tagged them Mugwumps, after an Indian word meaning a great chieftain. To the regulars, in what soon became a stale joke, Mugwumps were unreliable Republicans who had their "mugs" on one side of the fence and their "wumps" on the other.

The rise of the Mugwumps, however, influenced the Democrats to nominate Stephen Grover Cleveland as a reform candidate. Cleveland had a rapid rise from obscurity to prominence. One of many children in the family of a New York Presbyterian minister, he had been forced by his father's death to go to work at an early age. He got a job as clerk in a law office, read law, passed the bar examination, became an assistant state attorney-general in New York in 1863 and later sheriff of Erie County. Elected mayor of Buffalo in 1881, Cleveland first attracted national attention for effectively battling graft and corruption in that city. In 1882 the Democrats elected him governor, and he continued to build a reform record by fighting New York's Tammany Hall organization. Cleveland saw the corruption of government by the rich and powerful as a constant danger, and as mayor and as governor he repeatedly vetoed what he considered special-privilege bills serving selfish interests.

A short, stocky, 250-pound man with a droopy mustache, Cleveland seemed the stolid opposite of Blaine. He possessed little charisma, but impressed the public with something that was more important that year, a stubborn integrity. Austere and at times seemingly self-righteous and haughty, he inspired respect rather than affection. Cleveland was a crusader against government and corporate corruption, and as such he drew to him many of those making up the growing chorus of reformers. One supporter said: "We love him for the enemies he has made."

Then the *Buffalo Evening Telegraph* revealed some of bachelor Cleveland's escapades during the early 1870s with a tall, attractive Buffalo widow, Maria Halpin, who managed the cloak department in a department store. Mrs. Halpin had named Cleveland as the father of a boy born to her in 1874. Cleveland took responsibility and provided financial help when the child was placed in an orphanage. When supporters asked Cleveland what to say about the affair, he answered with typical candor: "Tell the truth." The respective personal escapades of Blaine and Cleveland provided the 1884 campaign with some of the most colorful battle cries in American political history. "Blaine, Blaine, James G. Blaine, the continental liar from the state of Maine," Democrats chanted. Republicans countered with "Ma, ma, where's my pa? Gone to the White House, ha, ha, ha!"

Near the end of the campaign Blaine and his supporters committed two fateful blunders. At New York's fashionable Delmon-

Another Voice for Cleveland. *This 1884 cartoon attacks "Grover the Good" for allegedly fathering an illegitimate child.*

ico's restaurant Blaine attended a lavish fundraising dinner with a clutch of millionaire bigwigs. Cartoons and accounts of this "Belshazzar's Feast" festooned the opposition press for days to come. Even more volatile was an incident earlier the same day. When a member of a delegation of Protestant ministers visiting Republican headquarters in New York insolently referred to the Democrats as the party of "rum, Romanism, and rebellion," a Cleveland campaign worker heard the remark and rushed back to his headquarters. Blaine, who was present, let it pass and perhaps failed to catch the implied insult to Irish Catholics—a fatal oversight, since he had always cultivated Irish-American support with his anti-British talk and public reminders that his mother was Catholic. Democrats spread word that he had let the insult pass, even that he had made it himself.

The two incidents may have tipped the election. The electoral vote in Cleveland's favor stood at 219 to 182, but the popular vote ran far closer; Cleveland's plurality was fewer than 30,000 votes.

CLEVELAND AND THE SPECIAL INTERESTS For all Cleveland's hostility to the spoils system and politics as usual, he represented no sharp break with the conservative policies of his Republican predecessors, except in opposing governmental favors to business. He held to a strictly limited view of government's role in both economic and social matters, a rigid philosophy illustrated by his 1887 veto of a bill to aid drought-stricken farmers. Back to Congress it went with a lecture on the need to limit the powers and functions of government—"though the people support the government, the government should not support the people," Cleveland asserted.

For a man who took such high ground philosophically, Cleveland had a mixed record on the civil service. He harbored good intentions, but he also had a hungry party with its first president since Buchanan. Before his inauguration he repeated his support for the Pendleton Act, and he pledged not to remove able workers on partisan grounds. But party pressures gradually forced Cleveland's hand. To a friend he remarked: "The damned everlasting clatter for office continues . . . and makes me feel like resigning." When he left office about two-thirds of the federal officeholders were Democrats, but at the same time Cleveland had almost doubled the classified civil service list. He thereby satisfied neither Mugwumps nor spoilsmen; indeed he managed to antagonize both.

Cleveland incurred the wrath of many Union veterans by his firm stand against expanded pensions. Congress had passed the first general Civil War pension law in 1862 to provide for veterans disabled in service and for the widows, orphans, and dependents of veterans. By 1882 the Grand Army of the Republic, an organization of Union veterans and a powerful pressure group, was trying to get pensions paid for any disability, no matter how it was incurred. Meanwhile many veterans enjoyed such benefits by having private pension bills put through by an obliging congressman or senator. Insofar as time permitted, Cleveland examined such bills critically and vetoed the dubious ones. Although he signed more than any of his predecessors, he also vetoed more. The issue climaxed in January 1887 when Cleveland vetoed a new Dependent Pension bill containing more liberal benefits and qualifications. Cleveland argued that it would become a refuge for frauds rather than a "roll of honor."

About the middle of his term Cleveland set out after new special interests by advocating an important new policy, railroad regulation. Since the late 1860s state after state had adopted regulatory laws, and from the early 1870s Congress had debated federal legislation to regulate the rates charged by railroads. In 1886 a Supreme Court decision finally spurred action. In the case of *Wabash Railroad v. Illinois* the Court ruled that a state could not regulate rates on interstate traffic. Cleveland urged in his annual message in December that since this "important field of control and regulation [has] thus been left entirely unoccupied," Congress should act.

It did, and in February 1887 Cleveland signed into law an act creating the Interstate Commerce Commission (ICC), the first such independent federal regulatory commission. The law required that all freight and passenger rates be "reasonable and just," and it empowered the ICC to investigate carriers and prosecute violators. Railroads were also forbidden to grant secret rebates, discriminate against persons, places, and commodities, or enter into pools (agreements to fix rates). The commission's actual powers, however, proved to be weak when first tested in the courts. If creating the ICC seemed to conflict with Cleveland's fear of big government, it accorded with his wariness of big business. The Interstate Commerce Act, to his mind, was a legitimate exercise of sovereign power. To Jay Gould and other railroad owners, it was a means of defusing growing public outrage while not truly hurting corporations. "Let it go," Gould advised, "or we will get a worse dose next season."

Cleveland's most dramatic challenge to special interests came in his efforts to spur tariff reform. Having decided that the rates were too high and included many inequities, Cleveland sought to dramatize the issue near the end of 1887 by devoting his entire annual message to the subject. He did so in full knowledge that he was walking onto a political minefield on the eve of an election year. "What is the use of being elected if you don't stand for something?" he asked skeptical advisors.

Cleveland's message noted that tariff revenues had bolstered the federal surplus, making the Treasury "a hoarding place for money needlessly withdrawn from trade and the people's use." It pushed up prices for everybody and benefited only a few politically powerful manufacturing interests. The wise solution was to spur Congress to look at the more than 4,000 items on the tariff list with an eye to eliminating as many as possible and lowering all the remaining duties.

The House soon passed a bill calling for modest reductions from an average level of about 47 percent of the value of imported goods to about 40 percent. But the bill stalled in the Republican Senate and finally died a lingering death in committee. If Cleveland's tariff proposal accomplished his purpose of drawing party lines more firmly, it also confirmed the fears of his advisers. The election of 1888 for the first time in years highlighted a sharp difference between the major parties on an issue of substance.

Cleveland was inevitably the nominee of his party, whose platform endorsed "the views expressed by the President in his last message to Congress." The Republicans passed up old warhorses like Blaine and Sherman and turned to the obscure Benjamin Harrison, who had all the attributes of availability. Grandson of a former president, a flourishing lawyer in Indiana, the diminutive Harrison resided in a pivotal state, boasted a good war record, and had little in his political record to offend any voter. The Republican platform picked up the gauntlet thrown down by Cleveland, accepted the protective tariff as the chief issue, and promised generous pensions to veterans.

The campaign thus became the first waged mainly on the tariff issue. As insurance against tariff reduction, manufacturers obligingly larded Harrison's campaign fund, which was used to denounce Cleveland's un-American "free-trade" stance and his pension vetoes.

On the eve of the election Cleveland suffered a devastating blow from a dirty campaign trick. Posing as an English immigrant and using the false name "Charles F. Murchison," a California Republican had written British Minister Sir Lionel Sackville-West and asked his advice on how to vote. Sackville-West hinted in reply that he should vote for Cleveland. Published two weeks before the election, the "Murchison letter" aroused a storm of protest against foreign intervention and further linked Cleveland to British free-traders.

Still, the outcome in 1888 was very close. Cleveland won the popular vote by 5,538,000 to 5,447,000, but that was poor comfort. The distribution was such that Harrison, with the key states of Indiana and New York on his side, carried the electoral college by 233 to 168. For the first time since John Quincy Adams's election in 1824, the country had not only a minority president, but one who lacked even a plurality in the popular vote.

REPUBLICAN REFORM UNDER HARRISON Harrison became a competent and earnest figurehead, overshadowed by his secretary of state, James G. Blaine. His first step was to reward those responsible for his victory. He owed a heavy debt to the old-soldier vote, which he discharged by naming the head of the veterans' group to the office of pension commissioner. "God help the surplus," the new commissioner reportedly exclaimed, and proceeded to approve pensions with such abandon that the secretary of the interior removed him six months and several million dollars later. In 1890 Congress passed, and Harrison signed, the Dependent Pension Act, substantially the same measure that Cleveland had vetoed three years earlier. Any veteran unable to make a living by manual labor for whatever reason was granted a monthly pension. The pension rolls almost doubled by 1893, as did the program's costs.

During the first two years of Harrison's term, the Republicans controlled the presidency and both houses of Congress for the only time in the twenty years between 1875 and 1895. They made the most of their clout. During 1890 several significant pieces of legislation made their way to the White House for Harrison's signature. In addition to the Dependent Pension Act, Congress and the president approved the Sherman Antitrust Act, the Sherman Silver Purchase Act, the McKinley Tariff, and the admission of the last of the "omnibus states," Idaho and Wyoming, which followed the admission of the Dakotas, Montana, and Washington in 1889.

Both parties had pledged themselves to do something about the growing power of trusts and monopolies. The Sherman Antitrust Act, named for Sen. John Sherman, chairman of the committee that drafted it, forbade contracts, combinations, or conspiracies in restraint of trade or in the effort to establish monopolies in interstate or foreign commerce. A broad consensus put the law through, but its passage turned out to be largely symbolic. During the next decade successive administrations expended little effort on the act's enforcement. From 1890 to 1901 the Justice Department instituted only eighteen antitrust suits, and four of those were against labor unions.

Congress meanwhile debated currency legislation against the backdrop of growing distress in the farm regions of the West and South. Hard-pressed farmers were now agitating to inflate the currency by an increased coinage of silver. Their purpose was to raise commodity prices, making it easier for farmers to earn the money with which to pay their debts. The silverite forces were also strengthened, especially in the Senate, by members from those new states that had silver-mining interests. Congress thus passed the Sherman Silver Purchase Act of 1890, replacing the Bland-Allison Act of 1878. It required the Treasury to purchase 4.5 million ounces of silver each month and to issue in payment Treasury notes redeemable in either gold or silver. The act, however, fell far short of satisfying the demands of the silverites. Although it approximately doubled the amount of silver purchased, that was still too little to have much inflationary impact on the economy. The stage was thus set for the currency issue to eclipse all others during the financial panic that swept the country three years later.

Republicans took their victory over Cleveland as a mandate not just to maintain the protective tariff but to raise it. Yet the mandate was less than clear, in view of Cleveland's plurality, and passage of the new tariff remained doubtful until its backers struck their bargain with western silverites. Piloted through by the prominent Ohio senator William McKinley, the McKinley Tariff of 1890 raised duties on manufactured goods to an average of about 49.5 percent, the highest to that time.

The absence of a public consensus for higher tariffs became clearly visible in the 1890 elections. The November congressional election returns suggested that the voters had repudiated the Republican-sponsored McKinley tariff with a landslide of Democratic votes. In the new House, Democrats outnumbered Republicans by almost a three to one margin; in the Senate, the Republican majority was reduced to eight. One of the election casualties was McKinley himself. But there was more to the election than the tariff. Voters reacted also against the baldly partisan measures of the Harrison administration and its extravagant expenditures on pensions and other programs.

The large Democratic vote in 1890 may have also been a reaction to Republican efforts on a local level to legislate against alcohol and government-supported Catholic schools. With the politics of righteousness, Republicans were playing a losing game, arousing wets (antiprohibitionists) on the Democratic side. In 1889 Wisconsin Republicans compounded their party's problems by pushing through a law that struck at parochial schools, thus turning large numbers of outraged Catholic immigrants into Democratic activists. In 1890 the Democrats swept state after state.

THE PROBLEMS OF FARMERS

The 1890 election returns reflected more than a reaction against the Republican tariff, spoils politics, extravagance, and moralizing. The returns revealed a deep-seated unrest in the farming communities of the South and West that was beginning to find voice in the new People's party, a grassroots movement destined to have a fundamental impact on American politics and social thought.

ECONOMIC CONDITIONS   For some time farmers had been subject to worsening economic and social conditions. The source of their problem was a long-term decline in commodity prices from 1870 to 1898, the product of domestic overproduction and growing international competition for world markets. Considerations of abstract economic forces, however, puzzled many farmers. How could one speak of overproduction when so many remained in need? Instead, many assumed, there must be a screw loose somewhere in the system.

The railroads and the middlemen who handled the farmers' products became convenient targets. Farmers felt victimized by the high railroad rates which prevailed in farm regions that had no alternative forms of transportation. Individual farmers could not get the rebates the industrial shippers could extract from railroads, nor could they exert the political influence wielded by the railroad lobbies. In other ways farmers found themselves with little bargaining power either as buyers or sellers. When they went to sell wheat or cotton, the buyer set the price; when they went to buy a plow point, the seller set the price.

During the late nineteenth century farmers suffered from a long-term decline in the prices of farm commodities, including cotton. Domestic overproduction and international competition were among the causes.

High tariffs operated to the farmers' disadvantage because they protected manufacturers against foreign competition, allowing them to raise the prices of factory goods on which farmers depended. Farmers, however, had to sell their wheat, cotton, and other staples in foreign markets, where competition lowered prices. Tariffs inflicted a double blow on farmers because insofar as they hampered imports, they indirectly hampered exports by making it harder for foreign buyers to get the necessary American currency or exchange to purchase American crops.

Debt, too, had been a perennial agricultural problem. After the Civil War farmers grew ever more enmeshed in debt: western farmers in mortgages to cover the costs of land and machinery, southern farmers in crop liens to the local merchant. As commodity prices dropped, the debt burden grew because farmers had to cultivate more wheat or cotton to raise the same amount of money. By growing more they furthered the vicious cycle of surpluses and price declines.

AN INADEQUATE CURRENCY Currency deflation was yet another target of discontented farmers because it raised the cost of borrowing money: a tight money supply caused bankers to hike interest rates on loans. Ultimately, the festering farm discontent focused on the currency issue, magnifying this grievance out of proportion to all others. The basic problem with the nation's money supply in the late nineteenth century was that it lacked the flexibility to grow along with America's expanding economy. From 1865 to 1890 the amount of currency in circulation per capita decreased about ten percent.

Metallic currency dated from the Mint Act of 1792, which authorized free and unlimited coinage of silver and gold at a ratio of 15:1. The ratio meant that the amount of precious metal in a silver dollar weighed fifteen times as much as that in a gold dollar. This reflected the relative values of silver and gold at the time. The phrase "free and unlimited coinage" simply meant that owners of precious metals could have any quantity of their gold or silver coined free, except for a nominal fee to cover costs. A fixed ratio of values, however, could not reflect fluctuations in the market value of the metals. When gold rose to a market value higher than that reflected in the official ratio, owners ceased to present it for coinage. The country was actually on a silver standard until 1837, when Congress changed the ratio to 16:1, which soon reversed the situation. Silver became more valuable in the open market than in coinage, and the country drifted to a gold standard. This state of affairs prevailed until 1873, when

Congress passed a general revision of the coinage laws and, without fanfare, dropped the then-unused provision for the coinage of silver.

This occurred, however, just when silver production began to increase, reducing its market value through the growth in supply. Under the old laws this would have induced owners of silver to present it at the mint for coinage. Soon advocates of currency inflation began to denounce the "crime of '73," which they had scarcely noticed at the time. Gradually suspicion grew that bankers and merchants had conspired in 1873 to ensure a scarcity of money. But the silverites had little more legislative success than the advocates of greenback inflation. The Bland-Allison Act of 1878 and the Sherman Silver Purchase Act of 1890 provided for some silver coinage, but too little in each case to offset the overall contraction of the currency.

AGRARIAN REVOLT

Frustrated by the unwillingness of Congress to meet their demands and ease their plight, disgruntled farmers began to organize after the Civil War. Like so many of their counterparts laboring in urban factories, they realized that social change could be provoked only by demonstrations of power, and power lay in numbers. But unlike labor unions, farm organizations faced a more complex array of economic variables affecting their livelihood. They had to deal with more than just management; bankers, middlemen, railroad and grain elevator operators, and the world market all played a role in affecting the agricultural sector. So too did the unpredictable forces of nature: droughts, blizzards, insects, erosion. Other important obstacles to collective action by farmers included the deeply ingrained tradition of rugged individualism and physical isolation. American farmers had long prided themselves on their self-reliant hardihood, and many balked at sacrificing their independence. Consequently, farm activists discovered that it was often difficult to develop and maintain a cohesive organization. But for all the difficulties, they persevered, and the results were dramatic, if not completely successful.

THE GRANGER MOVEMENT   When the Department of Agriculture sent Oliver H. Kelley, a former Minnesota farmer and post office clerk, on a tour of the postbellum South in 1866, it was the farmers' isolation that most impressed him. Resolving to do something about it, Kelley in 1867 founded the Patrons of Husbandry, better known as the Grange (an old word for granary). In the next few years the Grange mushroomed, reaching a membership as high as 1.5 million by 1874. The Grange started out as a social and educational response to the farmers' isolation, but as it grew it began to promote farmer-owned cooperatives for buying and selling. Soon the Grange became indirectly involved in politics through independent third parties, especially in the Midwest, during the early 1870s.

The Grangers' chief political goal was state regulation of the rates charged by railroads and warehouses. In five states they brought about the passage of "Granger Laws," which provoked court challenges. In a key case involving warehouse regulation, *Munn v. Illinois* (1877), the high court affirmed that the state under its "police powers" had the right to regulate property where that property was clothed with a public interest.

The Granger movement gradually declined (but never vanished) as members' energies were drawn off into cooperatives, many of which failed, and into political action. Out of the independent political movements of the time there grew, in 1875, a party known as the Greenback party, which favored expansion of the currency with more paper money. In the 1878 midterm elections it polled over 1 million votes and elected fifteen congressmen. But in 1880 the party's fortunes declined, and it disintegrated after 1884.

FARMERS' ALLIANCES As the Granger movement waned, another farm organization grew in size and significance: the Farmers' Alliance. In county after county in the South and Midwest, farmers rushed to join the Alliance movement, which promised to address the hardships created by chronic indebtedness, declining prices, and devastating droughts. Many isolated, struggling farmers and their families were attracted also by the sense of community provided by the Alliances, whose gatherings often resembled spiritual camp meetings.

The Alliance movement was attractive to women and men alike. Alliances welcomed rural white women and men over sixteen years old who displayed a "good moral character," believed in God, and demonstrated "industrious habits." One North Carolina woman in 1891 expressed her appreciation for the "grand opportunities" the Alliance provided women to liberate themselves from traditional domesticity. "Drudgery, fashion and gossip," she declared, "are no longer the bounds of woman's sphere." One of the Alliance publications made the point explicitly: "The Alliance has come to redeem woman from her en-slaved condition, and place her in her proper sphere." In the eyes of some agrarian radicals that new sphere entailed greater self-reliance and political, social, and educational equality. Not all Alliance groups, however, embraced such an agenda. As one Alliance official harrumphed, "I think that the ladies are best suited to home affairs." Nevertheless, overall the number of women in the Alliance movement increased rapidly, and many assumed key leadership roles.

By 1890 there were two major groups: the northwestern Alliance, organized in 1880, was never effective and by the late 1880s was mostly a paper organization; the southern Alliance proved the more militant, effective, radical, and ultimately the more national in scope of the two. The southern group, started in 1877 in Texas, grew into the Grand State Alliance in 1879. In 1886 Dr. Charles W. Macune became its leader and dazzled members with a glittering vision of large-scale farm cooperatives, whereby farmers would band together to handle the warehousing and marketing of their crops, avoiding the much-despised middlemen. The cooperative ideal drew new converts rapidly to the organization. By absorbing existing farm groups and organizing new locals, the Alliance swept the cotton belt and established strong positions in Kansas and the Dakotas.

After Reconstruction ended, many black families (called "Exodusters") left the South to farm in Kansas. They laid the groundwork for later organizations like the Colored Farmers Alliance.

By 1890 it had members from New York to California numbering about 1.5 million. A parallel Colored Farmers Alliance, centered in the Deep South, claimed over 1 million members.

The Alliance economic program was much more elaborate than that of the Grange, but Alliance agencies and exchanges soon went the way of the Granger cooperatives, victims of discrimination by wholesalers, manufacturers, railroads, and bankers, but above all victims of inexperienced management and overextended credit. As the cooperatives struggled to survive, many southern Alliancemen threw their support to a subtreasury plan that would allow farmers to store their crops in new government warehouses and secure government loans for up to 80 percent of their crops' value at 1 percent interest. Besides credit, the plan allowed farmers to hold their crops for a good price, since they would not have to sell immediately at harvest time to pay off debts. The plan also promoted inflation, because loans to farmers would be made in new legal-tender notes. The plan went before Congress in 1890 but was never adopted. Its defeat as well as setbacks to other proposals convinced many farm leaders that they needed more political power to secure railroad regulation, currency inflation, state departments of agriculture, antitrust laws, and farm credit.

In 1890 Alliance members plunged headlong into politics. In the West, where hard times had descended after the blizzards of 1887, farmers were ready for third-party action, and locally they began calling themselves the "people's party," or, more commonly, Populists. In the South, however, white Alliancemen hesitated to bolt the Democratic party, seeking instead to influence or control it. Both approaches gained startling success. Independent parties under various names upset the political balance in western states, almost electing a governor under the banner of the Populist party in Kansas, and taking control of one house of the legislature there and both houses in Nebraska. In South Dakota and Minnesota they gained a balance of power in the legislatures, while Kansas and South Dakota sent Populists to the Senate.

The Populists produced colorful leaders, especially in Kansas, where Mary Elizabeth Lease advised farmers "to raise less corn and more hell." Born in Pennsylvania to parents who were political exiles from Ireland, she eventually migrated to Kansas, taught school, raised a family, and finally failed at farming in the mid-1880s. She then studied law for a time, "pinning sheets of notes above her wash tub," and through strenuous effort became one of the state's first female lawyers. At the same time, she took up public speaking on behalf of various causes ranging from Irish nationalism to temperance to women's suffrage. By the end of the 1880s she had joined the Alliance as well as the Knights of Labor, and soon applied her natural gifts as a fiery speaker to the cause of free silver. A tall, proud, and imposing woman, Lease drew excited and attentive audiences. "The people are at bay," she warned in 1894, "let the bloodhounds of money beware."

"Sockless" Jerry Simpson was an equally colorful farm leader. Born in Canada Simpson eventually moved to Kansas, where he tried and failed at farming and cattle-raising. Simpson's difficulties led him to the Alliance movement, and in 1890 he campaigned for Congress. A shrewd, witty, and intelligent man with huge, calloused hands and pale blue eyes, Simpson effectively simplified the complex economic and political issues of the day. "Man must have access to the land," he maintained, "or he is a slave." He warned Republicans whose policies he blamed for so many farmers losing their lands, "You can't put this movement down by sneers or by ridicule, for its foundation was laid as far back as the foundation of the world. It is a struggle between the robbers and the robbed." His Republican opponent for Congress, a wealthy railroad lawyer, conducted his campaign from a private rail car, and this gave Simpson a perfect foil. Simpson dismissed him as an indulgent pawn of the corporations whose "soft white hands" and "silk hosiery" betrayed his true priorities. His outraged opponent thereupon shouted that it was better to have silk socks than none at all, providing Simpson with an endearing nickname.

"Sockless" Jerry Simpson won a seat in Congress, and so, too, did many other farmers' advocates. In the South the Alliance won equal if not greater success by forcing the Democrats to nominate candidates pledged to their program. In 1890 the southern states elected four pro-Alliance governors, seven pro-Alliance legislatures, forty-four pro-Alliance congressmen, and several senators. Among the most respected of the southern Alliancemen was Tom Watson of Georgia. The son of prosperous slaveholders who lost everything during and after the Civil War, he attended Mercer University for two years before running out of funds, and eventually became a successful lawyer and charismatic orator on behalf of the Alliance cause. He took the lead in appealing to black tenants and sharecroppers to join with their white counterparts in ousting the Bourbon white political elite. "You are kept apart," he told black and white farmers, "that you may be separately fleeced of your earnings."

THE POPULIST PARTY   As economic conditions worsened, many insurgents began promoting the formation of a new national political party. In May 1891 delegates from farm, labor, and reform organizations met in Cincinnati to discuss the creation of a People's party. Few southerners attended, but many endorsed the third-party idea after their failure to win over the Democratic party to the subtreasury plan. In February 1892 a larger meeting at St. Louis proposed a national convention of the People's party at Omaha on July 4 to adopt a platform and choose national candidates. The stirring platform, written by Ignatius Donnelly of Minnesota, typified the apocalyptic, almost paranoid, style that increasingly characterized both the farmers' movement and its opponents:

> We meet in the midst of a nation brought to the verge of moral, political, and material ruin. Corruption dominates the ballot-box, the Legislatures, the Congress, and touches even the ermine of the bench. The newspapers are largely subsidized or muzzled, public opinion silenced, business prostrated, homes covered with mortgages, labor impoverished, and the land concentrating in the hands of the capitalists. . . . A vast conspiracy against mankind has been organized. . . . If not met and overthrown at once it forebodes terrible social convulsions . . . or the establishment of an absolute despotism.

The platform itself focused on issues of finance, transportation, and land. Its financial program demanded the subtreasury plan, free and unlimited coinage of silver at the 16:1 ratio, an increase in the amount of money in circulation, and a graduated income tax. As to transportation, the government should nationalize the railroads, and the telephone and telegraph systems as well. It should also reclaim from railroads and other corporations lands "in excess of their actual needs," and forbid land ownership by aliens. Finally, the platform endorsed the eight-hour day and immigration restriction laws. The party took these positions to win support from the urban workers, whom Populists looked upon as fellow "producers."

The party's platform turned out to be more exciting than its candidate, Iowa's James B. Weaver. Though an able and prudent man, Weaver carried the stigma of his defeat on the Greenback ticket twelve years before. To balance Weaver, a former Union general, the party named a former Confederate general for vice-president.

The Populist party was the startling new feature of the 1892 campaign, but for the major parties the contest was simply a repetition of 1888, with Grover Cleveland the Democratic candidate and Benjamin Harrison the Republican, and with the tariff the chief issue between them. The outcome, however, was different. Both major candidates polled over 5 million votes, but Cleveland carried a plurality of the popular votes and a majority of the electoral college. Weaver gained over 1 million votes, and carried Colorado, Kansas, Nevada, and Idaho, for a total of twenty-two electoral votes.

THE DEPRESSION OF 1893 Cleveland's second administration came to grief early amid one of the most devastating business panics in history, set off just before he took office by the failure of the Philadelphia and Reading Railroad and a panic on Wall Street. By 1894 the economy had reached bottom. That year some 750,000 workers went out on strike; millions found themselves unemployed; railroad construction workers, laid off in the West, began tramping east and, to the dismay of alarmists who sniffed revolution in the air, talked of marching on Washington. Few of them made it to the capital. One group that did was "Coxey's Army," led by Jacob S. Coxey, a wealthy Ohio quarry owner turned Populist who demanded that the federal government provide unemployed people with meaningful work. Coxey, his wife, and their son, Legal Tender Coxey, rode in a carriage ahead of some 400 hardy protesters who finally straggled into Washington. There Coxey was arrested for walking on the grass, but his army as well as the growing political strength of Populism struck fear into the hearts of many Americans. Critics portrayed Populists as "hayseed socialists" whose election would endanger property rights.

In this anxious climate the 1894 Congressional elections took place. The elections amounted to a severe setback for Democrats, who paid politically for the economic downturn, and the Republicans were the chief beneficiaries. The Populists emerged with six senators and seven representatives. They had polled 1.5 million votes for their congressional candidates and still expected the festering discontent to carry them to national power in 1896.

SILVERITES VS. GOLDBUGS The course of events, however, would dash that hope. In the mid-1890s events conspired to focus all agitations on the currency issue. One of the causes of the 1893 depression had been the failure of a major British bank, which led many British investors to unload their American investments in return for gold. Soon after Cleveland's inauguration the gold reserve fell below $100 million. To plug this drain on the Treasury the president sought repeal of the Sherman Silver Purchase Act in order to stop the issuance of silver notes redeemable in gold. Cleveland won the act's repeal in 1893, but at the cost of irreparable division in his own party. One embittered silver Democrat labeled the president a "Benedict Arnold."

Western silver interests raised the agitation for silver coinage to a crescendo, which presented a strategic dilemma for Populists: should the party promote the long list of varied reforms it had originally advocated, or should it try to ride the silver issue into power? The latter seemed the practical choice. Consequently the Populist leaders decided, over the protest of more radical members, to hold their 1896 convention last, confident that the two major parties would at best straddle the silver issue and that the Populists would then reap a harvest of bolting silverite Republicans and Democrats.

THE ELECTION OF 1896   Contrary to these expectations the major parties took clear and opposing positions on the currency issue. The Republicans, as expected, chose handsome William McKinley on a gold-standard platform. McKinley had a magisterial appearance. His high forehead, sharply cut mouth, and Roman nose looked presidential, and then, as now, looks were important in national politics. On the Democratic side the pro-silver forces gathered in force to wrest control of the party from Cleveland and the fiscal conservatives. A reporter covering the convention recognized the shift of power: "All the silverites need is a Moses. They have the principle, they have the grit . . . and they have the howl and the hustle." They also soon had their Moses, who emerged this time not from the bullrushes but from the Nebraska plains.

In William Jennings Bryan the silver Democrats found a crusading, charismatic leader. The son of a judge who was a fervent Baptist, Bryan was a two-term congressman from Nebraska who had been defeated in the senatorial race in 1894. He had distinguished himself mainly with an exhausting three-hour speech he gave against Cleveland's repeal of the Sherman Silver Purchase Act. That speech had endeared him to silverites and had nourished his ambition for higher office. At the 1896 convention the self-assured Bryan shrewdly drew upon his strength as a superb orator and delivered a galvanizing speech that had most of the 20,000 delegates on their feet and many in tears.

Bryan began by admitting his relative youth and inexperience, but claimed he nevertheless felt compelled to make his views

William Jennings Bryan, whose "Cross of Gold" speech at the 1896 Democratic convention roused the delegates and secured him the party's presidential nomination.

known, for he was "clad in the armor of a righteous cause." Much like a revivalist at a camp meeting, he drew the audience with the emotion of his appeal. When he paused or drew a sharp point they would shout encouragement or amen in unison. With righteous indignation and fervent eloquence, Bryan spoke for silver and the new West, for the "hardy pioneers" and against the "financial magnates" of the urban East. "Burn down your cities and leave our farms [untouched]," he predicted, "and your cities will spring up again as if by magic; but destroy our farms and the grass will grow in the streets of every city in the country." The people of the plains and the South had tried to gain a hearing, he noted, but they had been rebuffed by entrenched interests. Now they must act. "We beg no longer; we entreat no more; we petition no more. We defy them!" He then directly challenged Republicans as well as Cleveland and the gold Democrats with a compelling metaphor: "You shall not press down upon the brow of labor this crown of thorns. You shall not crucify mankind upon a cross of gold!"

The next day the heroic Bryan was nominated on the fifth ballot, and in the process the Democratic party was fractured beyond repair. Groused one Cleveland supporter, "For the first time, I can understand the scenes of the French Revolution."

Disappointed gold Democrats walked out of the convention and nominated their own candidate, who then announced: "Fellow Democrats, I will not consider it any great fault if you decide to cast your vote for William McKinley."

When the Populists met in St. Louis two weeks later they faced an impossible choice. "If we fuse [with the Democrats]," one Populist recognized, "all the silver men we have will leave us for the more powerful Democrats." But if they named their own candidate they would divide the silver vote with Bryan and give the election to McKinley. "Sockless" Jerry Simpson advised merger: "I care not for party names; it is substance we are after, and we have it in William J. Bryan." In the end the delegates agreed. They named Bryan, but chose their own vice-presidential candidate, Georgia's Tom Watson, and invited the Democrats to drop their vice-presidential nominee—an action which Bryan refused to countenance.

The thirty-six-year-old Bryan launched a whirlwind campaign. He crisscrossed the country, exploiting his spellbinding eloquence and radiating honesty, sincerity, and energy. McKinley, meanwhile, conducted a "front-porch campaign," receiving selected delegations of supporters at his home in Canton, Ohio, and giving only prepared responses. His campaign manager, Mark Hanna, shrewdly portrayed Bryan as a radical whose "communistic spirit" would ruin the capitalist system. Many observers agreed with the portrait. The editor of the *New York Tribune* denounced Bryan as a "wretched rattle-pated boy, posing in vapid vanity and mouthing resounding rottenness." A factory owner told his employees: "Men, vote as you please, but if Bryan is elected . . . the whistle will not blow Wednesday morning."

By preying upon such fears Hanna raised a huge campaign chest and financed an army of Republican speakers who stumped the country in support of McKinley. The Democratic-Populist-Silverite candidates were overwhelmed. McKinley won the popular vote by 7.1 million to 6.5 million and the electoral college by 271 to 176. Bryan carried most of the West and the South below the border states, but neither the Populists nor Bryan ever made inroads into the metropolitan centers east of the Mississippi and north of the Ohio and Potomac. Urban workers simply saw little to gain from the inflation promoted by Bryan and the silverites. Moreover, in the critical midwestern battleground, from Minnesota and Iowa eastward to Ohio, Bryan carried not a single state. Many ethnic voters, normally drawn to the Democrats, were repelled by Bryan's evangelical style. Farmers in the

East and Midwest, moreover, were hurting less than farmers in the wheat and cotton belts. There was less tenancy and a greater diversity of crops in those farm regions, and the prospering farmers therefore saw little attraction in agrarian radicalism.

A NEW ERA   The election of 1896 proved a climactic political struggle between rural and metropolitan America, and metropolitan America won. Anticipating Bryan's defeat and the collapse of the Populist vision, Mark Hanna telegraphed McKinley on election night, "God's in his Heaven, all's right with the world!"

The values of urban-industrial America had indeed taken firm hold of the political system. As its first important act the McKinley administration called a special session of Congress to raise the tariff again. The Dingley Tariff of 1897 became the highest to that time. By 1897 prosperity was returning, helped along by inflation of the currency, which bore out the arguments of greenbackers and silverites. But the inflation came, in one of history's many ironies, not from silver but from a new flood of gold onto the market and into the mints. During the 1880s and 1890s new discoveries of gold in South Africa, Canada, and Alaska led to spectacular new gold rushes, a return to the gold standard, and an end to the free silver movement. To compound the irony, most of the Populist platform, which seemed so radical in 1892, would nevertheless take effect within two decades.

Amid the new prosperity, the old issues of tariffs and currency were now swallowed up by a dispute that ushered in a new era. "The Spanish War finished us," said the old Populist Tom Watson. "The blare of the bugle drowned the voice of the Reformer."

FURTHER READING

Useful overviews of the Gilded Age include John A. Garraty's *The New Commonwealth, 1877–1890* (1968),° and Morton Keller's *Affairs of State: Public Life in Nineteenth Century America* (1977).°

Scholars have made effective use of an ethnocultural approach to study Gilded Age politics. See the seminal works of Paul Kleppner, *The Cross of Culture: A Social Analysis of Midwestern Politics, 1850–1900* (1970) and *The Third Electoral System, 1853–1892* (1979), as well as Richard J. Jensen's *The Winning of the Midwest: Social and Political Conflicts, 1888–1896* (1971).

Scholars have also examined various Gilded Age issues and interest groups. Gerald W. McFarland's *Mugwumps, Morals, and Politics, 1884–1920* (1975) examines the issue of civil service reform. Tom E. Terrill's *The Tariff, Politics, and American Foreign Policy, 1874–1901* (1973) lends clarity to that complex issue. The finances of the Gilded Age are covered in Walter T. K. Nugent's *Money and American Society, 1865–1880* (1968). The waning of popular interest in politics is examined in Michael McGerr, *The Decline of Politics: The American North, 1865–1928* (1988).°

One of the most controversial works on Populism is Lawrence Goodwyn's *The Populist Moment* (1978).° Goodwyn's emphasis on the cooperative nature of agrarian protest contradicts the interpretations in John D. Hicks's *The Populist Revolt* (1931), which portrays agrarians as forerunners of liberal reform, and Richard Hofstadter's *The Age of Reform* (1955),° which focuses on their reactionary strain. For an outstanding biography and history of southern Populism, see C. Vann Woodward's *Tom Watson, Agrarian Rebel* (1938).° A splendid local study of the impact and nature of Populism is Stephen Hahn's, *The Roots of Southern Populism: Yeoman Farmers and the Transformation of the Georgia Upcountry* (1983).°

° These books are available in paperback editions.

22

THE COURSE OF EMPIRE

Toward the New Imperialism

Throughout most of the late nineteenth century Americans displayed what one senator called "only a languid interest" in foreign affairs. Indeed, the overriding concerns of the time were industrial development, western settlement, and domestic politics. Compared to these, foreign relations simply were not important to the vast majority of Americans. After the Civil War an isolationist mood swept across the United States, as the country basked in its geographic advantages: wide oceans as buffers on either side, the British navy situated between America and the powers of Europe, and militarily weak neighbors in the Western Hemisphere.

EXPANSION IN THE PACIFIC Yet the spirit of Manifest Destiny remained alive, if muted, in the decades after Appomattox, and a few key figures sought to lead the United States out of its isolationist shell. For such expansionists Asia especially offered an alluring temptation. Andrew Johnson's secretary of state, William H. Seward, believed that the United States must inevitably exercise commercial domination "on the Pacific ocean, and its islands and continents." Eager for American manufacturers to capture Asian markets, Seward believed the United States first had to remove all foreign interests from the northern Pacific coast and gain access to that region's valuable ports. To that end he cast covetous eyes on the British Crown Colony of British Columbia, sandwiched between Russia's possessions in Alaska and Washington Territory. Late in 1866, while encouraging annexation sentiment among the British Columbians, Seward learned of Russia's desire to sell Alaska, which for them had become an unprofitable possession. He leapt at the offer, and in March 1867 the United States bought Alaska for $7.2 million, less than 2 cents an acre. "Seward's folly" of buying the Alaskan "icebox" proved in time to be the biggest bargain for the United States, economically and strategically, since the Louisiana Purchase.

Seward bought Alaska in part because he feared the British would buy it, and in part because he knew of the territory's rich mineral deposits, fisheries, and bountiful forests. He also hoped, however, that its purchase by the United States would convince the British Columbians to request annexation as well. For a while that seemed a real possibility, but in 1870 British Columbia decided instead to join the new Confederation of Canada.

SAMOA AND HAWAII   Seward's successors at the State Department never completely lost sight of his expansionist vision, and the Pacific Ocean remained the major field of overseas activity. During the post-Civil War years the United States sought coaling stations and trading posts in this area, and it laid claim to various small islands and coral atolls of the mid-Pacific. Among these islands two inhabited groups occupied especially strategic positions: Samoa and Hawaii (also known as the Sandwich Islands).

American interest in these islands gradually deepened as commercial activity in the Pacific increased, and in 1878 the Samoans signed a treaty with the United States which granted a naval base at Pago Pago. The following year the German and British governments worked out similar arrangements on other islands of the Samoan group.

In Hawaii the Americans had more nearly a clear field. The islands, a united kingdom since 1795, hosted a sizable settlement of American missionaries and planters, and had long been a popular way-station for whalers and traders. They were also strategically more important than Samoa to the United States, since their occupation by another major power might have posed a threat to American sugar interests and even to defense of the continent.

In 1875 the Hawaiians signed a reciprocal trade agreement under which their sugar entered the United States duty free. Twelve years later it was amended to grant the United States exclusive right to a fortified naval base at Pearl Harbor, near Honolulu. These agreements resulted in a boom in sugar growing, and American settlers in Hawaii came to have a dominant position economically. In 1887 the Americans forced Hawaii's king to grant a constitutional government, which they dominated.

Queen Liliuokalani.

Hawaii's political climate changed sharply when the king's sister, Queen Liliuokalani, ascended the throne in 1891 and began efforts to reclaim power. Shortly before that the McKinley Tariff had destroyed Hawaii's favored position in the sugar trade by putting the sugar of all countries on the free list and granting growers in the United States a two-cent bounty. The resultant discontent in Hawaii led the white population to stage a revolt early in 1893. A committee of public safety seized power, and the American minister brought in marines to support the coup. As he cheerfully reported to Washington, "The Hawaiian pear is now fully ripe, and this is the golden hour for the United States to pluck it." Within a month a committee of the new American-dominated government turned up in Washington and, in February 1893, signed an annexation treaty.

This occurred just weeks before President Harrison left office, however, and Democratic senators blocked ratification. President Cleveland withdrew the treaty and sent a special commissioner to investigate. He withdrew the American marines and reported that Americans on the islands had acted improperly. Most Hawaiians opposed annexation, said the commissioner, who thought the revolution had been engineered mainly by sugar planters hoping to get the new domestic sugar bounty by annexation to the United States. Cleveland therefore proposed to restore the queen in return for amnesty to the revolutionists. The provisional government refused and on July 4, 1894, proclaimed the Republic of Hawaii, which had in its constitution a standing provision for American annexation, presumably after

Cleveland yielded to a president whose sensibilities were less easily offended.

STEPS TO WORLD POWER

The antebellum spirit of expansionism thus had neither died out with the 1850s nor gone completely dormant. It would return full blown in the 1890s with the addition of some new flourishes. European powers from about 1870 on set an example with a new surge of imperialism in Africa and Asia, where they seized territory, established colonies and protectorates, and began a systematic program of economic exploitation and Christian evangelism. Above all, the new imperialism was economic, a quest for markets and raw materials, and to more than one observer the European example seemed to address a new aspect of the American experience. The closing of America's frontier was brought forcefully to public attention by the census of 1890 and by historian Frederick Jackson Turner's classic 1893 essay on the significance of the frontier. Many thought this signaled the end of America's constantly growing domestic market and a need to seek markets overseas.

Most Americans became increasingly aware of world markets as developments in transportation and communication quickened the pace of commerce and diplomacy. From the first, agricultural exports had been the basis of American economic growth. Now the conviction grew that American manufactures had matured to the point that they could outsell foreign goods in the world market. But should the expansion of markets lead to territorial expansion as well? Or to intervention in the internal affairs of other countries? On such points Americans disagreed, but a small yet growing and vocal group of public officials was ready to entertain the idea of overseas possessions. They were led by senators Albert J. Beveridge of Indiana and Henry Cabot Lodge of Massachusetts, Theodore Roosevelt, and not least of all, Captain Alfred Thayer Mahan.

NAVAL POWER During the 1880s Captain Mahan, a graduate of Annapolis, became a leading advocate of sea power and western imperialism. In 1890 he published *The Influence of Sea Power upon History, 1660–1783*, in which he argued that national greatness and prosperity flowed from sea power. To Mahan, economic development called for a big navy, a strong merchant marine, foreign commerce, colonies, and naval bases. Mahan expounded on America's destiny to control the Caribbean, build an isthmian canal, and spread Western civilization in the Pacific. His ideas were widely circulated in popular journals and within the American government. Even before Mahan's writings became influential a gradual expansion of the navy had begun. In 1880 the nation had fewer than a hundred sea-going vessels, many of them rusting or rotting at the docks. By 1896 eleven powerful new battleships had been built or authorized.

RACIAL THOUGHT Meanwhile certain intellectual currents of the day worked to bolster the new surge of Manifest Destiny. Applications of the Darwinian idea of natural selection to society and politics afforded a handy argument for imperialism. Among nations as among individuals, expansionists claimed, the fittest survive and prevail. John Fiske, the historian and popular lecturer on Darwinism, developed racial corollaries from Darwin's idea. In *American Political Ideas* (1885) he stressed the superior character of "Anglo-Saxon" institutions and peoples. The English "race," he argued, was destined to dominate the globe: in the institutions, traditions, language, even in the blood of the world's peoples.

Josiah Strong, a Congregationalist minister, added the sanction of religion to American imperialism. In his book *Our Country: Its Possible Future and Its Present Crisis* (1885), Strong asserted that "Anglo-Saxons" embodied two great ideas: civil liberty and "a pure spiritual Christianity." The Anglo-Saxon was "divinely commissioned to be, in a peculiar sense, his brother's keeper." Expansion to establish foreign missions also found favor in both Protestant and Catholic churches.

These religious, intellectual, and economic factors combined to provide a potent rationale for an expansionist foreign policy. The *Washington Post* made the point explicitly in 1898:

> A new consciousness seems to have come upon us—the consciousness of strength—and with it a new appetite, the yearning to show our strength. . . . We are face to face with a strange destiny. The taste of Empire is in the mouth of the people even as the taste of blood in the jungle.

THE SPANISH-AMERICAN WAR

"CUBA LIBRE" Animated by such aggressive expansionism, the United States suddenly in 1898 and 1899 thrust its newly developed power to the far reaches of the Pacific. The occasion for this explosion of imperialism lay neither in the Pacific nor in the quest for bases and trade, but to the south in Cuba. The chief motive was a sense of outrage at another country's imperialism. Throughout the second half of the nineteenth century, Cubans had repeatedly revolted against Spanish rule, only to be ruthlessly put down. All the while American investments in Cuba, mainly in sugar and mining, were steadily rising. The United States in fact traded more with Cuba than Spain did. Their growing economic interest in their island neighbor made more and more Americans sympathetic to the ideal of Cuban independence. When insurrection broke out again on February 24, 1895, public feeling in the United States sided with the rebels, and many Americans extended help to the Cuban Revolutionary party, which organized the revolt and waged an effective propaganda campaign from headquarters in New York.

The insurrectionists' strategy was to use guerrilla warfare to damage Spain's economic interests on the island, which in turn would excite the concern of American investors. The strategy dictated hit-and-run attacks on trains, railways, and plantations. Such tactics forced people either into the insurgent forces or into garrisoned towns, which in turn might be cut off from food supplies. Revolutionary propaganda of course presented the effort in a different light, and Americans were more than ready to look upon the insurrection in the light of their own War of Independence.

The strategies needed to counter guerrilla warfare nearly always cast their practitioners in a bad light. In 1896 Spanish general Valeriano Weyler adopted a policy of gathering Cubans behind Spanish lines, often in detention (*reconcentrado*) centers so that no one could join the insurrections by night and appear peaceful by day. In some of these centers poor food and unsanitary conditions soon brought a heavy toll of disease and death. The American press promptly christened the Spanish commander "Butcher" Weyler.

Events in Cuba supplied exciting copy for the popular press. Chance had it that William Randolph Hearst's *New York Journal* and Joseph Pulitzer's *New York World* were at the time locked in a monumental struggle for circulation. "It was a battle of gigantic proportions," one journalist wrote, "in which the sufferings of Cuba merely chanced to furnish some of the most convenient ammunition." The sensationalism practiced by both papers came to be called "yellow journalism," and Hearst emerged as the undisputed champion. His *Journal* excelled at invective against "Weyler the brute, the devastator of haciendas, the destroyer of men."

PRESSURE FOR WAR   American neutrality toward events in Cuba changed sharply when McKinley entered office. His platform had endorsed Cuban independence, as well as American control of Hawaii and of an isthmian canal. In October 1897 a new Spanish commander liberalized the reconcentration system, and in November, Spain offered Cuba autonomy in return for peace. What the Cubans might once have welcomed, however, they now rejected as they sensed their growing power. Spain was impaled on the horns of a dilemma, unable to end the war and unready to give up Cuba.

Early in 1898 events moved rapidly to arouse opinion against Spain. On February 9, Hearst's *New York Journal* released the text of a letter from Spanish Minister Depuy de Lôme to a friend in Havana. In the letter, which had been stolen from the post office by a Cuban spy, de Lôme called President McKinley "weak and a bidder for the admiration of the crowd." This was hardly more extreme than what McKinley's assistant secretary of the navy, Theodore Roosevelt, had said about him. As early as 1895 Roosevelt had written: "This country needs a war," and he had since become increasingly frustrated by McKinley's refusal to declare one. The "white-livered" president, Roosevelt groused, had "no more backbone than a chocolate eclair." But that comment had remained private. De Lôme's had not, and he resigned to prevent further embarrassment to his government.

Six days later, during the night of February 15, 1898, the American battleship *Maine* exploded in Havana harbor and sank with a loss of 260 men, most of whom died in their hammocks. Those eager for a war with Spain now demanded an immediate declaration. Roosevelt called the sinking "an act of dirty treachery on the part of the Spaniards." A naval court of inquiry reported in March that an external mine had set off an explosion in the ship's magazine. Lacking hard evidence, the court made no effort to fix the blame, but the yellow press had no need of evidence. The *New York Journal* gleefully reported: "The Whole Country Thrills with War Fever." The jingoistic outcry against Spain reached a crescendo in the words "Remember the Maine! To Hell with Spain!" Few jingoes wrestled with the obvious fact that the Spanish government was determined to *avoid* a confrontation with the United States and therefore had nothing to gain from sinking the *Maine*. What actually happened, whether accidentally or deliberately, remains a mystery.

McKinley, under the mounting pressure of public excitement, tried to maintain a steady course. The president, a Civil War veteran, told an aide, "I have been through one war. I have seen the dead piled up, and I do not want to see another." But the frazzled president, besieged by demands that he take a forceful stand, had so much trouble sleeping that he required sedatives. He was increasingly swayed by the weight of outraged public opinion and by militants in his own party such as Roosevelt and Lodge. As one congressman remarked, McKinley "keeps his ear to the ground so close that he gets it full of grasshoppers much of the time." On March 9, 1898, the begrudgingly militant president pushed through Congress a $50-million defense appropriation. Still, he sought to avoid war, as did most business spokesmen. Such caution infuriated Roosevelt. "We will have this war for the freedom of Cuba," he fumed on March 26, "in spite of the timidity of the commercial interests."

The Spanish government, sensing the growing militancy in the United States, announced a unilateral cease fire in early April 1898. On April 10, the Spanish minister gave the State Department a message that amounted to a surrender: the United States should indicate the nature and duration of the armistice; Cuba would have an autonomous government; and the two countries would submit the question of the *Maine* to arbitration. The United States minister to Spain then cabled from Madrid: "I

An American cartoon depicts the sinking of the Maine *in Havana Harbor. The uproar created by the incident and its coverage in the "yellow press" edged McKinley toward war.*

hope nothing will now be done to humiliate Spain, as I am satisfied that the present government is going . . . as fast and as far as it can." McKinley, he predicted, could win a settlement by August 1 on any terms, including either Cuban independence or cession of Cuba to the United States.

But the message came too late. The following day McKinley sent Congress his war message. He asked for the power to use armed forces in Cuba to abate a nuisance off the United States' shores and to protect American property and trade. Back to the president on April 20 came a joint resolution of Congress, which went beyond endorsing the use of the armed forces: it declared Cuba independent and demanded withdrawal of Spanish forces. The Teller Amendment, added on the Senate floor, disclaimed any American designs on Cuban territory. McKinley signed the resolution and sent a copy to the Spanish government. On April 22 the president announced a blockade of Cuba, under international law an act of war. Rather than give in to an ultimatum, the Spanish government declared war on April 24. Congress then, determined to be first, declared war the next day but made it retroactive to April 21, 1898.

Why such a rush into war after the American minister had predicted that Spain would cave in before the summer was out? No one knows for sure, but it seems apparent that too much momentum and popular pressure had already built up for a confidential message to change the course of events. Also, leaders of the business community, which tolerates uncertainty poorly, were demanding a quick resolution of the problem. Many lacked faith in the willingness or ability of the Spanish government to carry out a moderate policy in the face of a hostile public opinion. Still, it is fair to ask why McKinley did not take a stand for peace, knowing what he did. He might have defied Congress and public opinion, but in the end he deemed the political risk too high. The Democrats were likely to adopt the popular cause of Cuban independence. The ultimate blame for war, if blame must be levied, belongs to the American people for letting themselves be whipped up into such a hostile frenzy.

DEWEY TAKES MANILA   The war itself lasted only four months. The American victory marked the end of Spain's once-great New World empire, which had begun with Columbus, and the emergence of the United States as a world power. But if American participation saved many lives by ending the insurrection in Cuba, it also led to American involvement in another insurrection, in the Philippines, and it created a host of commitments in the Caribbean and the Pacific that would haunt American policymakers during the twentieth century.

The war was barely under way before the navy produced a quick, spectacular victory in an unexpected quarter—Manila Bay. While public attention was fixed on Cuba, Roosevelt focused on the Philippines. As assistant secretary of the navy, he had Commodore George Dewey appointed commander of the small Asiatic squadron, and ordered him to engage Spain's ships in the Philippines in case of war. President McKinley had approved those orders.

Arriving late on April 30, 1898, Dewey's squadron destroyed or captured all the Spanish warships in Manila Bay. Dewey, without an occupation force, was now in awkward possession of Manila Bay. Promised reinforcements, he stayed while foreign

warships, including a powerful German force, loomed about the scene like watchful vultures. Army troops finally arrived, and with the help of Filipino insurrectionists under Emilio Aguinaldo, Dewey's forces liberated Manila from Spanish control on August 13.

THE CUBAN CAMPAIGN   While these events transpired halfway around the world, the war reached a quick climax closer to home, which was surprising because America was ill-prepared for war. The navy was fit, but the army could muster only an ill-assorted guard of 28,000 regulars and about 100,000 militiamen. The armed forces suffered badly from both inexperience and maladministration, with the result that far more American troops died from disease than from enemy action. The United States' salvation was that Spanish forces were even worse off, their morale infinitely so.

An invasion force of some 17,000 American troops was hastily assembled at Tampa. One significant element of that force was the so-called "Rough Riders," best remembered because Lieutenant-Colonel Theodore Roosevelt was second in command. Eager to get "in on the fun," and "to act up to my preachings," Roosevelt had quit the Navy Department after war was declared,

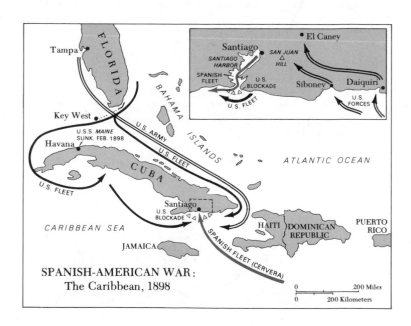

SPANISH-AMERICAN WAR:
The Caribbean, 1898

Lieutenant-Colonel Theodore Roosevelt posing with his "Rough Riders" after the battle of San Juan, 1898.

ordered a custom-fitted, fawn-colored uniform with yellow trim from Brooks Brothers, grabbed a dozen pair of spectacles, and rushed to help organize a colorful volunteer regiment of Ivy League athletes, leathery ex-convicts, Indians, and southwestern deadshots. Faced with this motley force as they began training in Texas, Roosevelt wrote Lodge: "More than ever I fail to get the relations of this regiment and the universe straight."

The major land action of the Cuban campaign occurred on July 1. While a much larger American force attacked Spanish positions at San Juan Hill, a smaller unit, including the dismounted Rough Riders—most of whose horses were still in Florida—and two crack black regiments, seized the enemy position atop nearby Kettle Hill. In the midst of the fray, Roosevelt felt the joy "when the wolf rises in the heart" and satisfied his bloodlust by seeing a Spaniard he shot double up "neatly as a jackrabbit." He later claimed that he "would rather have led that charge than served three terms in the U.S. Senate." A friend wrote to Roosevelt's wife that her husband was "revelling in victory and gore."

The two battles put American forces atop heights from which they could bring the Spanish fleet under siege. On July 3 the Spanish ships made a gallant run for it, but the aging vessels were little match for the newer American fleet. The casualties were one-sided: 474 Spanish were killed and wounded and 1,750 were taken prisoner, while only one American was killed and one wounded. Santiago, port for the Spanish fleet, surrendered with a garrison of 24,000 on July 17. On July 25, an American force also moved into the Spanish-held island of Puerto Rico.

The next day the Spanish government sued for peace. After discussions lasting two weeks, negotiators signed an armistice on August 12, 1898, less than four months after the war's start and the day before Americans entered Manila. The peace protocol specified that Spain should give up Cuba, and that the United States should annex Puerto Rico and should occupy the city, bay, and harbor of Manila pending disposition of the Philippines.

And so the "splendid little war," as the future secretary of state, John Hay, called it in a letter to his friend Roosevelt, officially ended. It was splendid only in the sense that its cost was relatively slight. Among more than 274,000 Americans who served during the war and the ensuing demobilization, 5,462 died, but only 379 in battle. Most succumbed to malaria, typhoid, dysentery, or yellow fever. At such a cost the United States was launched onto the world stage as a great power, with all the benefits—and burdens—of that new status.

THE DEBATE OVER ANNEXATION The United States and Spain signed the Treaty of Paris on December 10, 1898. Disposition of the Philippines posed the key question, indeed one of the biggest decisions to face United States foreign policy to that time, and one that caught the country unprepared for sober reflection. McKinley, who claimed that at first he himself could not locate the Philippines on a map within two thousand miles, gave ambiguous signals to the peace commission, which itself was divided.

· There had been no demand for annexation of the Philippines or other Spanish possessions before the war, but Dewey's victory quickly kindled expansionist fever. Businessmen began thinking of the commercial possibilities not so much in the islands as in the nearby continent of Asia, such as oil for the lamps of China and textiles for its teeming millions. "If this be commercialism," cried Senator Mark Hanna, then "for God's sake let us have commercialism." Other Americans supported annexation literally for God's sake. Missionary societies yearned to save the "little brown brother." It was neither the first nor the last time that Americans would get caught up in fantasies of saving Asian souls or getting rich there. McKinley pondered the alternatives and later explained his reasoning to a group of Methodists:

And one night late it came to me this way—I don't know how it was, but it came: (1) that we could not give them [the Philippines] back to Spain—that would be cowardly and dishonorable; (2) that we could not turn them over to France or Germany—our commercial rivals in the Orient—that would be bad business and discreditable; (3) that we could not leave them to themselves—they were unfit for self-government—and they would soon have anarchy and misrule over there worse than Spain's was; and (4) that there was nothing left for us to do but to take them all, and to educate the Filipinos, and uplift and civilize and Christianize them, and by God's grace do the very best we could by them, as our fellowmen for whom Christ also died. And then I went to bed, and went to sleep and slept soundly.

So although these Filipino candidates for conversion were already largely Catholic, the word went forth to take the Philippines for the sake of their souls. Spanish negotiators raised the delicate point that American forces had no claim by right of conquest, and had even taken Manila after the armistice. American negotiators finally offered the Spanish $20 million as compensation for possession of the Philippines as well as Puerto Rico in the Caribbean and Guam in the Pacific.

"Well, I Hardly Know Which to Take First." *At the end of the nineteenth century it seemed that Uncle Sam had developed a considerable appetite for foreign territory.*

Meanwhile Americans had taken other giant steps in the Pacific. Hawaiian annexation, promised in McKinley's platform, failed to get a two-thirds majority in the Senate, but the Spanish-American war demonstrated the islands' strategic importance all the more. The administration therefore moved to annex Hawaii, like Texas, by joint congressional resolution. The resolution passed on July 7, 1898, in the midst of the war. The United States also laid claim to Wake Island (1898), which would be a vital link in a future trans-Pacific cable line.

The Treaty of Paris had yet to be ratified in the Senate, where most Democrats and Populists, and some Republicans, opposed it. Anti-imperialists argued that acquisition of the Philippines would undermine American democracy. They appealed to traditional isolationism, American principles of self-government, the inconsistency of liberating Cuba and annexing the Philippines, the involvement in foreign entanglements that would undermine the logic of the Monroe Doctrine, and the danger that the Philippines would become an Achilles heel, expensive if not impossible to defend. The prospect of incorporating so many alien peoples into American life was not the least of some people's worries. "Bananas and self-government cannot grow on the same piece of land," one senator claimed.

The opposition may have been strong enough to kill the treaty had not William Jennings Bryan influenced the vote for approval. A formal end to the war, he argued, would open the way for the future independence of Cuba and the Philippines. Ratification finally came on February 6, 1899.

By this time Americans had already clashed with Filipino insurrectionists near Manila. The Filipino rebel leader, Emilio Aguinaldo, had been in exile until Commodore Dewey brought him back to Luzon to make trouble for the Spanish. Since Aguinaldo's forces were almost in control of the islands outside Manila, what followed over the next two years was largely an American war of conquest. Organized Filipino resistance collapsed by the end of 1899, but even after the capture of Aguinaldo in March 1901, sporadic guerrilla action lasted until mid-1902. It was a sordid little war, marked by massacre and torture on both sides. American forces soon displayed the same callous outlook that had animated the Spanish in Cuba. One American colonel boasted that he and his men "would rawhide these bullet-headed Asians until they yell for mercy." They must be pacified, he added, in order to make way for the "bandwagon of Anglo-Saxon progress and decency."

Against the backdrop of this nasty guerrilla war the great de-

Emilio Aguinaldo (seated third from right) and other leaders of the Filipino insurgents.

bate over annexation continued. The treaty debates inspired a number of anti-imperialist groups which united in October 1899 as the American Anti-Imperialist League. The league attracted members representing many shades of opinion; the main thing they had in common was that most belonged to an older generation. Andrew Carnegie footed the bills, but on imperialism at least, labor leader Samuel Gompers was in agreement with him. The usually soft-spoken philosopher William James exploded in opposition: "God damn the United States for its vile conduct in the Philippine Isles!" The selfish proponents of imperialism, he declared, had caused the nation to "puke up its ancient soul."

ORGANIZING THE NEW ACQUISITIONS Such criticism, however, did not faze the expansionists. Senator Beveridge boasted in 1900: "The Philippines are ours forever. And just beyond the Philippines are China's illimitable markets. We will not retreat from either. . . . The power that rules the Pacific is the power that rules the world. That power will forever be the American Republic."

In the Philippines, McKinley quickly moved toward setting up a civil government. On July 4, 1901, military government ended, and under an act of Congress, Judge William Howard Taft became the civil governor. The Philippine Government Act, passed by Congress on July 1, 1902, made the Philippine Islands an "unorganized territory" and made the inhabitants citizens of the Philippines. In 1934 the Tydings-McDuffie Act offered independence after a tutelary period of ten more years. Independence finally took effect on July 4, 1946.

Puerto Rico had been acquired in part to serve as an American outpost guarding the approaches to the Caribbean and any future isthmian canal. In 1900 the Foraker Act established a civil government on the island. Residents of the island were citizens of Puerto Rico but not of the United States until 1917, when they were granted United States citizenship. In 1952 Puerto Rico became a commonwealth with its own constitution and elected officials, a unique status. Like a state, Puerto Rico is free to change its constitution insofar as it does not conflict with the United States Constitution.

American authorities soon learned that liberated Cuba posed problems at least as irksome as those in the new possessions. After the American forces had restored order, started schools, and improved sanitary conditions, they began turning over the reins of power to the Cubans. The Platt Amendment to an army appropriation bill passed by Congress in March 1901, however, sharply restricted the new government's independence. The amendment required Cuba never to impair its independence by treaty with a third power, to maintain its debt within the government's power to repay out of ordinary revenues, and to acknowledge the right of the United States to intervene for the preservation of Cuban independence and the maintenance of "a government adequate for the protection of life, property, and individual liberty." Finally, Cuba was called upon to sell or lease to the United States lands to be used for coaling or naval stations—a proviso that eventuated in an American naval base at Guantanamo Bay, which remains in existence.

IMPERIAL RIVALRIES IN EAST ASIA

CHINA AND THE "OPEN DOOR" During the 1890s not only the United States but also Japan emerged as a world power. Commodore Matthew Perry's voyage of 1853–1854 had opened Japan to Western ways, and the island nation began modernization in earnest after the 1860s. Flexing its new muscles, Japan engaged China's stagnant empire in the Sino-Japanese War (1894–1895) and, as a result, acquired the island of Taiwan (renamed Formosa). China's weakness, demonstrated in the war, led Russia, England, France, and Germany to renew their scramble for "spheres of influence" on that remaining frontier of imperialist expansion.

The bright prospect of American trade with China dimmed with the possibility that these competing powers would carve up China and erect tariff barriers in their own spheres of influence. The British had much to lose in a tariff war though, for they already enjoyed substantial trade with China. Fearful of such a development, the British suggested in 1899 that the United States join them in preserving China's commercial and territorial integrity.

The State Department agreed that something must be done, but Secretary of State John Hay preferred to act alone rather than in concert with the British. In its origins and content, then, what came to be known as the Open Door Policy was reminiscent of the Monroe Doctrine. In both cases the United States proclaimed unilaterally a hands-off policy that the British had earlier proposed as a joint statement. The policy outlined in Hay's Open Door Note, dispatched on September 6, 1899, to London, Berlin, and St. Petersburg, and a little later to Tokyo, Rome, and Paris, proposed to keep China open to trade with all countries on an equal basis. As it turned out, none except Britain accepted Hay's principles, but none rejected them either. Consequently, on March 20, 1900, Hay blandly announced that all powers had accepted the policy.

Soon after that a new crisis arose. In June 1900 a group of Chinese nationalists known to the Western world as Boxers rose in rebellion against foreign encroachments on China, laying siege to foreign embassies in Peking. The British, Germans, Russians, Japanese, and Americans quickly mounted a military expedition to relieve the embassy compound. Hay, fearful that the intervention might become an excuse to dismember China, seized the chance to further refine his Open Door Policy. The United States, he declared in a circular letter of July 3, 1900, sought a solution which would "preserve Chinese territorial and administrative integrity" as well as "equal and impartial trade with all parts of the Chinese Empire." On August 14 the expedition reached Peking and broke the Boxer Rebellion.

The Open Door Policy, if rooted in the self-interest of American businessmen eager to exploit the markets of China, also tapped the deep-seated sympathies of those who opposed imperialism, especially as it endorsed China's territorial integrity. But it had little more legal standing than a pious affirmation. When the Japanese, concerned about Russian pressure in Manchuria, asked Hay how he intended to enforce the policy, Hay replied that the United States was "not prepared" to do so. So it would remain for forty years, a hollow but dangerous commitment, until continued Japanese expansion would bring war with America in 1941.

AN AMERICAN ORIGINAL

ROOSEVELT'S RISE   In the fall elections of 1898 Republicans benefited from the euphoria of military victory and increased their majority in Congress. That hardly amounted to a mandate for imperialism, however, since the election preceded most of the debates on the issue. In 1900 the Democrats turned once again to Bryan, who sought to make imperialism the "paramount issue" of the campaign. The Democratic platform condemned the Philippine involvement as "an unnecessary war" that had "placed the United States, previously known . . . throughout the world as the champion of freedom, in the false and un-American position of crushing with military force the efforts of our former allies to

TR on the stump.

achieve liberty and self-government." The Republicans welcomed the issue. They renominated McKinley, and named as his running mate Theodore Roosevelt, who had been elected governor of New York after his role in the Spanish-American War. The trouble with Bryan's idea of a solemn referendum on imperialism was the near impossibility of making any presidential contest so simple. Bryan himself complicated his message by insisting once again on free silver, and the tariff became an issue again too. The Republicans' biggest advantage was probably the return to prosperity, which they were fully ready to take credit for. So those who opposed imperialism but also opposed free silver or tariff reduction faced a bewildering choice.

The outcome was a victory for McKinley greater than his last, by 7.2 million to 6.4 million in the popular vote and by 292 to 155 in the electoral vote. There had been no clear-cut referendum on annexations, but the question was settled nonetheless, although it would take yet another year and a half to subdue the Filipino rebels. The job would be finished, however, under the direction of another president.

On September 6, 1901, while McKinley attended a reception at the Pan-American Exposition in Buffalo, a fanatical anarchist named Leon Czolgosz approached him with a gun and fired at point-blank range. McKinley died six days later, suddenly elevating Theodore Roosevelt to the White House. "Now look," Mark Hanna erupted, "that damned cowboy is President of the United States!"

Six weeks short of his forty-third birthday, Roosevelt was the youngest man ever to take charge of the White House, but he brought to it more experience in public affairs than most and more vitality than any. Born in 1858, the son of a wealthy New York merchant and a Georgia belle, Roosevelt grew up in Manhattan in cultured comfort, visited Europe as a child, spoke German fluently, and graduated Phi Beta Kappa from Harvard in 1880. A sickly, scrawny boy, he built himself up by sheer force of will into a uniquely blended physical and intellectual athlete who became a lifelong preacher and practitioner of the "strenuous life." Boxer, wrestler, and hardy outdoorsman, he was also an omnivorous reader, renowned historian and essayist, and outspoken moralist.

After Harvard, Roosevelt read law briefly and within two years of graduation won election to the New York legislature. That same year he published *The Naval War of 1812*, the first of a number of historical, biographical, and other writings to flow from his pen. He seemingly had the world at his feet—and then disaster struck. In 1884 his beloved mother, only forty-eight years old, died. Eleven hours later, in the same house, his twenty-two-year-old wife died in his arms, soon after giving birth to their only child. That night Roosevelt drew a large cross over the entry in his diary: "The light has gone out of my life." The double funeral was so wrenching that the officiating minister wept throughout his prayer.

Roosevelt was understandably devastated by this "strange and terrible fate," and in an attempt to heal his psychic wounds he sold the family house and moved west to take up the cattle business on the Dakota frontier. Adorned in a custom-fitting buckskin shirt, silver spurs, and alligator boots, he told a relative he was "having a glorious time here." The blue-blooded New Yorker came to relish hunting, leading roundups, capturing outlaws, fighting Indians—and reading Tolstoy by the campfire. Although his western career was brief, he never quite got over being a cowboy.

Back in New York the charming, earnest Roosevelt ran for mayor, and later served six years as civil service commissioner and two years as New York City's police commissioner. In the latter capacity he loved to don a black cloak and broad-brimmed hat and patrol the streets at midnight. When he came upon a sleeping policeman, Roosevelt would rap the man with his nightstick. Such devotion to duty led McKinley to appoint him assistant secretary of the navy in 1897, and Roosevelt did all he could to promote the war with Spain over Cuba. "A just war," he insisted, "is in the long run far better for a man's soul than the most prosperous peace."

As a public servant Roosevelt quickly developed a reputation as a prodigious worker renowned for his pristine integrity and infectious sense of humor. Indeed, Teddy Roosevelt was an American original of seismic magnitude. His glittering spectacles and glistening teeth, along with his captivating grin and overflowing gusto, were a godsend to the cartoonists, who added another trademark when he pronounced the adage: "Speak softly, and carry a big stick."

Along with his boundless energy went an unshakable righteousness and a tendency to cast every issue in moral and patriotic terms. He saw the presidency as his "bully pulpit," and he was eager to preach fist-smacking sermons on the virtues of righteousness, honesty, civic duty, and the strenuous life to his national flock. But appearances were deceiving with TR. The boundless energy left a false impression of impulsiveness, and the talk of morality actually cloaked a cautious pragmatism. Roosevelt could get carried away on occasion, but as he said of his foreign policy steps, this was likely to happen only when "I am assured that I shall be able eventually to carry out my will by force."

ROOSEVELT'S FOREIGN POLICY

BUILDING THE PANAMA CANAL After the Spanish-American War the United States became more deeply involved than ever in the Caribbean area, where one issue overshadowed every other: the Panama Canal. The narrow isthmus of Panama had excited dreams of an interoceanic canal ever since Balboa's crossing in 1513. After America's victory over Spain, Secretary of State Hay commenced talks with the British ambassador to gain their consent to an American plan to build a canal. These negotiations led to the Hay-Pauncefote Treaty of November 1901, in which Britain gave its consent to the American plan.

Other obstacles remained, however. From 1881 to 1887 a French company had spent nearly $300 million and sacrificed some 20,000 lives to dig less than a third of a canal through Panama. The company now offered to sell its holdings to the United

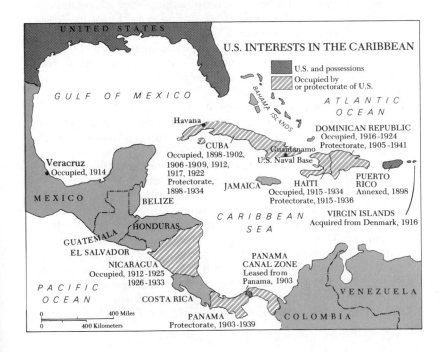

U.S. INTERESTS IN THE CARIBBEAN

States. Meanwhile Secretary Hay had opened negotiations with Ambassador Thomas Herrán of Colombia to build a canal across Panama, which was then a reluctant province of Colombia. In return for a Canal Zone six miles wide, the United States agreed to pay $10 million in cash and a rental fee of $250,000 a year. The United States Senate ratified the Hay-Herrán Treaty in 1903, but the Colombian Senate held out for $25 million in cash. Incensed by the "foolish and homicidal corruptionists at Bogotá," Theodore Roosevelt flew into a rage punctuated by references to "dagoes" and "contemptible little creatures."

Meanwhile in Panama itself, Colombia's rejection of the treaty heightened the desire for independence. Recognizing this development, an employee of the French canal company then hatched a plot in collusion with the company's representative, Philippe Bunau-Varilla. He visited Roosevelt and Hay and, apparently with inside information, informed the Panamanian rebels that the U.S.S. *Nashville* would call at Colón in Panama on November 2, 1903.

An army of some 500 Panamanians revolted against Colombian rule the next day. Colombian troops, who could scarcely penetrate the overland jungle, found American ships athwart the sea lanes. On November 4 the rebel commander addressed his victorious forces. "The world is astounded at our heroism. President Roosevelt has made good." A few days later the Roosevelt administration indeed made good on its collusion with the revolutionaries by recognizing Panama's independence, and on November 18 Roosevelt and the new Panamanian ambassador, who happened to be Bunau-Varilla, signed a treaty extending the Canal Zone from six to ten miles in width. For $10 million down and $250,000 a year the United States received "in perpetuity the use, occupation and control" of the zone. "I took Panama," Roosevelt would later boast.

In essence he had, but by needlessly offending Latin American sensibilities, Roosevelt had committed one of the greatest blunders in American foreign policy. Colombia eventually got its $25 million from the Harding administration, but only after America's interest in Colombian oil had lubricated the wheels of diplomacy. There was no apology, but the payment was made to remove "all misunderstandings growing out of the political events in Panama, November, 1903." The canal itself opened on August 15, 1914, less than two weeks after the outbreak of World War I in Europe. It was a tribute to American engineering and a boon to American commerce and the Panamanian economy.

The World's Constable. *TR, shown here as the world's
policeman, wields the "big stick" symbolizing his
approach to diplomacy.*

THE ROOSEVELT COROLLARY   Even without the canal the United
States would have been concerned with the stability of the Caribbean area, and particularly with the activities of any hostile
power in the region. A prime excuse for intervention in those
days was to force the collection of debts owed to foreigners. In
1904 a crisis over the Dominican Republic's debts gave Roosevelt an opportunity to formulate American policy. In his annual
address to Congress in 1904 he set forth what came to be known
as the Roosevelt Corollary to the Monroe Doctrine: the principle, in short, was that since the Monroe Doctrine enjoined European intervention in the region, the United States was justified in
intervening first to forestall the actions of outsiders. Roosevelt
suggested that the United States could exercise an "international
police power" in its own sphere of influence. As put into practice by mutual agreement with the Dominican Republic in 1905,
the Roosevelt Corollary called for the United States to install and
protect a collector of customs who would apply a portion of his
revenues to debt payments. The principle, applied peaceably in
1905, became the basis for more forcible interventions later.

THE RUSSO-JAPANESE WAR   In East Asia, meanwhile, the Open
Door policy received a serious challenge when tensions between
Russia and Japan flared into a fight over China and Korea. On
February 8, 1904, war broke out when the Japanese launched a
surprise attack that devastated the Russian fleet. They then oc-

cupied Korea and drove the Russians back into Manchuria. But neither side could score a knockout blow, and neither relished a prolonged war. When the Japanese signaled President Roosevelt that they would welcome a negotiated settlement, he agreed to sponsor a peace conference in Portsmouth, New Hampshire. In the Treaty of Portsmouth, signed on September 5, 1905, the concessions all went to the Japanese. Russia acknowledged Japan's "predominant political, military, and economic interests in Korea" (Japan would annex the kingdom in 1910), and both powers agreed to evacuate Manchuria.

AMERICA'S RELATIONS WITH JAPAN   Japan's show of strength in the war with Russia raised doubts about the security of the Philippines. During the Portsmouth talks Roosevelt sent Secretary of War William Howard Taft to meet with the Japanese foreign minister in Tokyo, and the two men arrived at the Taft-Katsura Agreement of July 29, 1905, in which the United States accepted Japanese control of Korea and Japan disavowed any designs on the Philippines. The understanding was reinforced by the Root-Takahira Agreement on November 30, 1908, negotiated by Secretary of State Elihu Root and the Japanese ambassador. In it both sides endorsed the status quo, promised to respect the other's possessions, and reinforced the Open Door Policy by supporting "the independence and integrity of China" and "the principle of equal opportunity for commerce and industry in China."

Behind the diplomatic facade of goodwill, however, lay simmering mutual distrust. For many Americans the Russian threat in East Asia now gave way to distrust of Japan's "yellow peril" (a term coined by Germany's Kaiser Wilhelm II). Racial animosities on the West Coast helped sour relations with Japan. In October 1906 the San Francisco school board ordered students of Chinese, Japanese, and Korean descent to attend a separate public school. The Japanese government sharply protested this show of prejudice, and President Roosevelt managed to talk the school board into changing its mind. For its part Japan then agreed to limit sharply its issuance of passports to the United States. This "Gentleman's Agreement" of 1907, the precise terms of which have never been revealed, halted the influx of Japanese immigrants and brought some respite in racial agitations in California.

THE UNITED STATES AND EUROPE   During these years of expansionism abroad the United States was looking mainly westward and southward. Toward Europe's affairs the fixed policy was, as Admiral Mahan affirmed it should be, abstention. To Roosevelt, however, total abstention from European affairs was an improper stance for a newly arrived world power. While he was moving toward mediation of the Russo-Japanese War in 1905, another dangerous crisis began heating up in Morocco, where the Germans and French fought for control. Roosevelt felt that the United States had something at stake in preventing the outbreak of a major war. At the kaiser's behest he talked the French and British into attending an international conference at Algeciras, Spain, with American delegates present. Roosevelt then maneuvered the Germans into accepting his lead. The Act of Algeciras, signed on April 7, 1906, affirmed the independence of Morocco and guaranteed an open door for trade there. Roosevelt received the Nobel Peace Prize in 1906 for his work at Portsmouth and Algeciras. For all his bellicosity on other occasions, he had earned it.

Before Roosevelt left the White House in March 1909, he celebrated America's rise to world power with one great flourish. In December 1907 he sent the United States Navy, by then second only to the British fleet, on a grand tour around the world. At every port of call the "Great White Fleet" set off rousing celebrations. It was the first such display of American naval might in the Pacific, and many feared the reaction of the Japanese, for whose benefit Roosevelt had in fact staged the show. They need not have worried, for in Japan the flotilla got the greatest welcome of all. Thousands of schoolchildren turned out waving tiny American flags and singing "The Star Spangled Banner" in English. The triumphal procession continued home by way of the Mediterranean, and steamed back into American waters in February 1909, just in time to close out Roosevelt's presidency on a note of success. But that note would not resonate for long. In time the mixed consequences of Roosevelt's policies in Latin America and Asia would catch up to the United States.

FURTHER READING

A concise survey of Gilded Age diplomacy is Robert L. Beisner's *From the Old Diplomacy to the New, 1865–1900* (2nd ed., 1986).° William Appleman Williams's *The Tragedy of American Diplomacy* (2nd ed.,

° These books are available in paperback editions.

1972)° advances most clearly the economic interpretation. A useful interpretive synthesis is Michael Hunt's *Ideology and U.S. Foreign Policy* (1987).°

For background to the events of the 1890s, see Walter LaFeber's *The New Empire: An Interpretation of American Expansion, 1860–1898* (1963).° The dispute over American policy concerning Hawaii is covered in Thomas J. Osborne's *"Empire Can Wait": American Opposition to Hawaiian Annexation, 1893–1898* (1981).

David F. Trask's lengthy *The War with Spain in 1898* (1981) is the comprehensive volume on that conflict. Frank Freidel's *The Splendid Little War* (1958) shows what the war was like for those who fought it. For the war's aftermath in the Philippines, see Stuart C. Miller's *"Benevolent Assimilation": American Conquest of the Philippines, 1899–1903* (1984).° Robert L. Beisner's *Twelve against Empire: The Anti-Imperialists, 1898–1900* (1968)° handles the debate over annexation.

A good introduction to American interest in China is Michael H. Hunt's *The Making of a Special Relationship* (1983).° For the immediate consequences of the Open Door, see Warren I. Cohen's *America's Response to China* (2nd ed., 1980).°

The role of Theodore Roosevelt in foreign policy both before and during his time as president is treated in Howard K. Beale's *Theodore Roosevelt and the Rise of America to World Power* (1956).° See also Richard Turk, *The Ambiguous Relationship: Theodore Roosevelt and Alfred Thayer Mahan* (1987).

For American policy in the Caribbean and Central America, see Walter LaFeber's *Inevitable Revolutions* (1983)° and Bruce J. Calder's *The Impact of Intervention* (1984).° David McCullough's *The Path between the Seas: The Creation of the Panama Canal, 1870–1914* (1978)° presents the fullest account of how the United States secured the Panama Canal.

23

PROGRESSIVISM: ROOSEVELT, TAFT, AND WILSON

ELEMENTS OF REFORM

Theodore Roosevelt's emergence as a national leader coincided roughly with the onset of what historians have labeled the Progressive Era (1900–1917). The rise of the so-called Progressive movement had many causes, the most powerful of which was the devastating depression of the 1890s and its attendant social unrest. The depression brought hard times to the cities and provoked both the fears and consciences of the rapidly growing middle- and upper-middle-classes. By the turn of the century so many activists were at work seeking to diagnose and heal the worst sores on the body politic that people began to speak of a "Progressive age," an era of fermenting idealism and constructive social, economic, and political change.

Progressivism was a reform movement so varied and comprehensive it almost defies definition. Political progressives saw themselves as engaged in a democratic crusade against the abuses of urban political bosses and corporate robber barons. Their goals were greater democracy, honest government, more effective regulation of business, and greater social justice for the masses. One paradox in the movement was that it contained an element of conservatism. In some cases the regulation of business turned out actually to be regulation proposed *by* businessmen, who preferred the stability afforded by a regulated market to the chaos and uncertainty of unrestrained competition.

The Kansas editor William Allen White hinted at another paradox in the movement when he called progressivism just populism that had "shaved its whiskers, washed its shirt, put on a derby, and moved up into the middle class." As White suggested, urban business and professional leaders brought to progressivism a certain respectability that the Populists had lacked. They also brought a more businesslike, efficient approach to reform. While one strand in the complex fabric of progressivism retained the resonant appeal of agrarian democracy and its antitrust traditions, a new emphasis on efficiency and tighter organization soon gained ascendancy. Even farm groups replaced their loose, grassroots structures with more centralized and bureaucratic forms of organization. In so doing, they and other progressives may have been trying to find a new sense of identity, no longer derived from the local community, in business and professional groups.

It should be clear, then, that the Progressive movement represented the common spirit of an age rather than a single organized group or party. What reformers shared was a common assumption that the complex social ills and tensions generated by the urban-industrial revolution required new responses, responses that frequently entailed expanding the scope of local, state, and federal government authority.

The "real heart of the movement," declared one reformer, was "to use the government as an agency of human welfare." Governments were now called upon to extend a broad range of direct services: schools, good roads (a movement propelled first by cyclists and then by automobilists), conservation, public health and welfare, care of the handicapped, farm loans and demonstration agents, among other things. Such initiatives represented the first tentative steps toward what would become known during the 1930s and after as the welfare-state.

ANTECEDENTS TO PROGRESSIVISM Populism was indisputably one of the key currents feeding the mainstream of progressivism. The Populist platform of 1892 outlined many reforms that would be accomplished in the Progressive era. After the collapse of the farmers' movement in the aftermath of Bryan's defeats in 1896 and 1900, the focus of the reform spirit increasingly shifted to cities, where middle-class reformers had for years attacked the problems of political bossism and urban development.

The Mugwumps, those gentlemen reformers who had fought the spoils system and promoted a civil service based on merit, supplied the Progressive movement with an important element of its thinking, the good-government ideal. Over the years their ranks had been supplemented and the good-government outlook broadened by leaders who confronted such new urban problems as crime, vice, and the efficient provision of gas, electricity, water, sewers, mass transit, and garbage collection.

Finally, another significant force in fostering the spirit of progressivism was the growing prominence of socialist doctrines and their critiques of living and working conditions. The Socialist party of the time, small but earnest and vocal, can be considered the left wing of progressivism. Still, most progressives found socialist remedies unacceptable, and the main progressive reform impulse grew in part from a desire to counter the growing appeal of socialist doctrines.

THE MUCKRAKERS   Also important in stimulating reform activity were those social critics who publicized festering problems. The writers who thrived on exposing scandal got their name when Theodore Roosevelt compared them to a character in John Bunyan's *Pilgrim's Progress*: "A man that could look no way but downwards with a muckrake in his hands." The "muckrakers" (and TR was no mean muckraker himself) "are often indispensable to . . . society," Roosevelt said, "but only if they know when to stop raking the muck."

Henry Demarest Lloyd is sometimes cited as the first of the muckrakers for his critical examination of the Standard Oil Company and other monopolies, *Wealth Against Commonwealth* (1894). Lloyd exposed the growth of corporate giants responsible to none but themselves, able to corrupt if not control governments. Lincoln Steffens likewise revealed the prevalence of municipal corruption in a series of articles later collected into a book, *The Shame of the Cities* (1904). The chief outlets for these social critics were the popular middle-class magazines that began to flourish in the 1890s, such as *The Arena* and *McClure's Magazine*.

Without the muckrakers, progressivism surely would never have achieved the popular support it had. In feeding a growing public appetite for facts about the new urban industrial society, the muckrakers demonstrated one of the salient features of the Progressive movement, and one of its central failures. The progressives were stronger on diagnosis than on remedy, thereby reflecting a naïve faith in the power of democracy. Let the people know, expose corruption, and bring government close to the people, they assumed, and the correction of evils would follow automatically. The cure for the ills of democracy was, to progressive reformers, simply a more enlightened democracy.

THE FEATURES OF PROGRESSIVISM

DEMOCRACY   The most important reform with which the progressives tried to democratize government was the direct primary, whereby candidates would be nominated by the vote of all party members, rather than by a few political bosses. After South Carolina adopted the first statewide primary in 1896 the concept spread within two decades to nearly every state.

The primary was but one expression of a broad movement for greater public participation in the political process. In 1898 South Dakota became the first state to adopt the initiative and referendum, procedures that allowed voters to enact laws directly. If a designated number of voters petitioned to have a measure put on the ballot (the initiative), the electorate could then vote it up or down (the referendum). In 1910 Oregon instituted the recall, whereby public officials could be removed by petition and vote. By 1920 nearly twenty states had adopted the initiative and referendum and nearly a dozen the recall. The direct election of senators by the people, rather than by the state legislatures, was another progressive political reform. The popular election of senators required a constitutional amendment, and by 1912 the Senate finally agreed to the Seventeenth Amendment, which was ratified by the states in 1913.

EFFICIENCY   A second major theme of progressivism was the "gospel of efficiency." In the business world at the turn of the century and after, Frederick W. Taylor, the original "efficiency expert," developed an array of new scientific management techniques designed to cut costs and enhance productivity. In government, efficiency demanded the reorganization of agencies to prevent overlapping, to establish clear lines of authority, and to fix responsibility.

Two new ideas for making municipal government more efficient gained headway in the first decade of the new century. The commission system was first adopted by Galveston, Texas, in 1901, when local government there collapsed in the aftermath of a devastating hurricane that killed 6,000 people and destroyed half the town. It placed ultimate authority in a board composed of elected administrative heads of city departments—commissioners of sanitation, police, utilities, and so on. By 1914 over 400 towns and small cities across the country had adopted the commission system. The more durable idea, however, was the city-manager plan, under which a professional administrator ran the government in accordance with policies set by the elected council and mayor. Staunton, Virginia, first adopted the plan in 1908. By 1914 the National Association of City Managers heralded the arrival of a new profession.

In the more complex age of the early twentieth century it was apparent that many functions of government and business now required greater expertise. This principle's most ardent disciple was progressive governor Robert M. ("Fighting Bob") La Follette of Wisconsin (1901–1906), who established a Legislative Reference Bureau staffed by professors and specialists to provide research, advice, and help in the drafting of legislation designed to curb the power of special interests and promote social justice. This "Wisconsin Idea" of efficient government was widely publicized and copied. La Follette also worked for such reforms as the direct primary, stronger railroad regulation, the conservation of natural resources, and workmen's compensation.

Born in a log cabin and educated at the University of Wisconsin, the short, muscular La Follette possessed an abiding faith in grassroots democracy, in the power and judgment of the people. He was more enlightened about modern trends than William Jennings Bryan, and equally intense, sincere, and determined. He was also Bryan's equal as an orator; La Follette could talk for hours without taxing himself or his listeners.

Counterparts to La Follette appeared as progressive governors in other states. As counsel to a legislative committee in New York, Charles Evans Hughes became a national figure by uncovering spectacular insurance frauds, and won the governorship in 1906. Hiram Johnson was elected governor of California in 1910 on the promise of reining in the railroads.

REGULATION Of all the problems facing American society at the turn of the century, one engaged a greater diversity of reformers and elicited more controversial solutions than any other: the regulation of giant corporations, which became a third major theme of progressivism. Some progressives advocated a policy of trust-busting in the belief that restoring old-fashioned competition would best prevent economic abuses. The Sherman Antitrust Act of 1890 had aimed for this, but the act turned out to be a paper tiger.

Efforts to restore the competition of small firms proved unworkable in part because breaking up large combinations was complex and difficult. Consequently, the main thrust of progressive reform over the years was toward regulation, rather than dissolution, of big businesses. To some extent regulation and "stabilization" won acceptance among businessmen who, whatever respect they paid to competition in principle, preferred not to face it in practice. In the long run, regulation posed the problem raised in the old maxim: Who will guard the guards? Regulatory agencies often came under the influence or control of those they were supposed to regulate. Railroad executives, for instance, generally had more intimate knowledge of the intricate details involved in their business, giving them the advantage over the outsiders who might be appointed to the Interstate Commerce Commission.

SOCIAL JUSTICE   A fourth important feature of the progressive spirit was the impulse toward social justice, which motivated diverse actions from private charities to campaigns against child labor and liquor. The settlement house movement of the late nineteenth century had spawned a corps of social workers and genteel reformers devoted to the uplift of slum dwellers. But with time it became apparent that social evils extended beyond

Addie Laird, 12 years old. Spinner in a Cotton Mill, Vermont, 1910. *Photograph by Lewis Hine.*

the reach of private charities and demanded governmental intervention.

Labor legislation was perhaps the most significant reform to emerge from the drive for social justice. The National Child Labor Committee, organized in 1904, led a movement for state laws banning the still widespread employment of young children. Within ten years the committee helped foster new laws in most states banning the labor of underage children (the minimum age varied from twelve to sixteen) and limiting the working hours of older children. Closely linked with the child-labor reform movement was a concerted effort to regulate the hours of work for women. Spearheaded by Florence Kelley, the head of the National Consumers League, this progressive crusade promoted the passage of state laws addressing the distinctive hardships that long working hours imposed on women who were wives and mothers.

The Supreme Court pursued a curiously erratic course in ruling on such state labor laws. In *Lochner v. New York* (1905), the Court voided a ten-hour-day law because it violated workers' "liberty of contract" to accept any terms they chose. Then in *Muller v. Oregon* (1908), the high court upheld a ten-hour law for women largely on the basis of sociological data that attorney Louis D. Brandeis presented regarding the adverse effects of long hours on the health and morals of women. In *Bunting v. Oregon* (1917), the Court accepted a ten-hour day for both men and women, but held out for twenty more years against state minimum-wage laws.

Legislation to protect workers against accidents gained momentum from disasters like the 1911 fire at the Triangle Shirtwaist Company in New York in which 146 people, mostly young women, died for want of adequate exits. The victims either were trapped on the three upper floors of a ten-story building or plunged to the street below. Stricter building codes and factory inspection acts followed.

For many activists the cause of prohibition absorbed the yearnings for reform. The Women's Christian Temperance Union had been battling booze since 1874, but the most successful political action followed the formation in 1893 of the Anti-Saloon League, an organization which pioneered the strategy of the single-issue pressure group. In 1913 the Anti-Saloon League endorsed a prohibition amendment to the Constitution, adopted by Congress that year. By the time it was ratified six years later, state and local action already had dried up areas occupied by nearly three-fourths of the nation's population.

ROOSEVELT'S PROGRESSIVISM

Theodore Roosevelt brought to the White House in 1901 not only his inexhaustible energy but also an expansive vision of the presidency that was admirably suited to the cause of progressive reform. In one of his first addresses to Congress, he stressed the need for a new political approach. When the Constitution was first drafted, he explained, the nation's social and economic conditions were quite unlike those at the dawn of the twentieth century. "The conditions are now wholly different and wholly different action is called for."

More than any other president since Lincoln, Roosevelt possessed an activist bent. His was the politics of pure energy. Still, his initial approach to reform was cautious. He sought to avoid the extremes of socialism on the one hand and laissez-faire individualism on the other. A skilled political maneuverer, he cultivated party leaders in Congress and steered away from such meat-grinder issues as the tariff and regulation of the banks. And when he did approach the explosive issue of the trusts, he always took care to reassure the business community. For him, politics was the art of the possible. Unlike the more radical progressives and the doctrinaire "lunatic fringe," as he called them, he would take half a loaf rather than none at all.

THE TRUSTS Caution characterized Roosevelt's first annual message, delivered in December 1901, but he felt impelled to take up the trust problem in the belief that it might be even more risky to ignore it. The message carefully balanced arguments on both sides of the question. Roosevelt endorsed the "sincere conviction that combination and concentration should be, not prohibited, but supervised and within reasonable limits controlled." In August 1902, he proposed a "square deal" for all, calling for enforcement of existing antitrust laws and stricter controls on big business.

From the outset, however, Roosevelt believed that wholesale trust-busting was too much like trying to unscramble eggs. Effective regulation, he insisted, was better than a futile effort to restore small business, which might be achieved only at a cost to the efficiencies of scale gained in larger operations. Roosevelt nevertheless soon acquired a reputation as a "trust-buster."

Because Congress balked at regulatory legislation, Roosevelt sought to force the issue by a more vigorous prosecution of the Sherman Antitrust Act (1890). He chose his target carefully. In

No Lack of Big Game. *A 1905 cartoon shows TR going after the trusts.*

the case against the Sugar Trust (*United States v. E.C. Knight and Company*, 1895) the Supreme Court had declared manufacturing a strictly intrastate activity. Most railroads, however, were beyond question engaged in interstate commerce and thus subject to federal authority. Consequently, in February 1902 Roosevelt moved against the Northern Securities Company, a holding company controlling the Great Northern and Northern Pacific railroads. When Roosevelt attacked the new trust, J. P. Morgan invited him to "send your man to my man and they can fix it up." The president refused, and in 1904 the Supreme Court ordered the combination dissolved in *U.S. v. Northern Securities Company*. Roosevelt continued to use his executive powers to enforce the Sherman Act, but he avoided conflict in Congress by drawing back from further proposals for antitrust legislation. Altogether his administration brought about twenty-five antitrust suits.

THE 1902 COAL STRIKE Support for Roosevelt's use of the "big stick" against corporations was strengthened by the stubbornness of mine owners in the anthracite coal strike of 1902. On May 12 the United Mine Workers (UMW) walked off the job in West Virginia and Pennsylvania. They demanded a 20 percent wage increase, a reduction in daily hours from ten to nine, and formal management recognition of their union. The operators dug in their heels against concessions and shut down the mines in an effort to starve out the miners. As one of them asserted, "The miners don't suffer—why, they can't even speak English."

Facing the real prospect of a coal shortage, Roosevelt called the parties to a conference at the White House. The mine owners, led by George F. Baer, president of the Reading Railroad, attended but refused even to speak to the UMW leaders. This outraged Roosevelt, who expressed his irritation at the "extraordinary stupidity and temper" of the "wooden-headed" owners. The boiling president also confessed a temptation to grab Baer "by the seat of his breeches" and "chuck him out" a White House window.

After the conference ended in an impasse, Roosevelt threatened to take over the mines and run them with the army. When a congressman questioned the constitutionality of such a move, an exasperated Roosevelt grabbed the man by the shoulders and roared: "To hell with the Constitution when the people want coal!" Such a comment and others like it over the years led Joe Cannon, the crusty House Speaker, to note: "Roosevelt's got no more respect for the Constitution than a tomcat has for a marriage license." Militarizing the mines would indeed have been an act of dubious legality, but the owners feared that Roosevelt might actually do it and that public opinion would support him.

The coal strike ended in October 1902 with an agreement to submit the issues to an arbitration commission named by the president. The agreement enhanced the prestige of both Roosevelt and the union's leader, although it produced only a partial victory for the miners. By the arbitrators' decision of March 1903, the miners won only a 10 percent wage increase and a nine-hour day, but no union recognition.

AN EXPANDING STATE   In 1903 Congress strengthened both antitrust enforcement and governmental regulation by creating the Department of Commerce and Labor and by passing the Elkins Act, which made it illegal for corporations to take as well as to give rebates. The Bureau of Corporations, a new federal agency within the new department, had no direct regulatory powers but it did have a mandate to study and report on the activities of interstate corporations. Its findings could lead to antitrust suits, but its purpose was rather to help corporations correct malpractices and avoid the need for lawsuits. Many companies cooperated, but others held back. When Standard Oil refused to turn over records, the government brought an antitrust suit that resulted in its dissolution in 1911. The Supreme Court ordered the American Tobacco Company broken up at the same time.

TOWARD A SECOND TERM

Roosevelt's policies built a coalition of progressive- and conservative-minded voters that assured his election in his own right in 1904. The Democrats, having twice lost with Bryan, turned to Alton B. Parker who, as chief justice of New York's state supreme court, had upheld labor's right to the closed shop and the state's right to limit hours of work. Despite Parker's liberal record, party leaders presented him as a safe conservative, and his acceptance of the gold standard as "firmly and irrevocably established" bolstered such a view. Yet the effort to portray their candidate as more conservative than Roosevelt proved a futile gesture for the party that had twice nominated Bryan. Despite Roosevelt's trust-busting, most businessmen, according to the *New York Sun*, preferred the "impulsive candidate of the party of conservatism to the conservative candidate of the party which the business interests regard as permanently and dangerously impulsive." Even J. P. Morgan and E. H. Harriman contributed handsomely to Roosevelt's campaign chest.

An invincible popularity and the sheer force of his personality swept Roosevelt to an impressive victory by a popular margin of 7.6 million to 5.1 million. Parker carried only the Solid South of the former Confederacy and two border states: Kentucky and Maryland. It was a great personal triumph for Roosevelt. Amid the excitement of election night he announced that he would not run again, a statement he later had reason to regret.

LEGISLATIVE LEADERSHIP Elected in his own right, Roosevelt approached his second term with heightened confidence and a stronger commitment to progressive reform. In December 1905 he devoted most of his annual message to the need for greater regulation and control of business. This understandably irked his corporate contributors. Said steel baron Henry Frick, "We bought the son of a bitch and then he did not stay put." The independent Roosevelt took aim at the railroads first.

Roosevelt asked Congress to extend the authority of the Interstate Commerce Commission (ICC) and give it effective control over railroad rates. He had to mobilize all the pressure and influence at his disposal to push through the bill introduced by Representative Peter Hepburn of Iowa. Enacted on June 29, 1906, the Hepburn Act for the first time gave the ICC power to set maximum freight rates. The commission no longer had to go to court to enforce its decisions. In other ways too the Hepburn Act enlarged the mandate of the ICC, whose regulatory reach now extended beyond railroads to pipelines, freight companies, sleeping-car companies, bridges, and ferries.

On the very day after passage of the Hepburn Act, a growing movement for the regulation of meat-packers, food processors, and makers of drugs and patent medicines reached fruition. Discontent with abuses in these fields had grown rapidly as a result of the muckrakers' disclosures. The chief chemist of the Agriculture Department, for example, supplied telling evidence of harmful additives used in the preparation of "embalmed meat" and other food products. Others disclosed dangerous ingredients in patent medicines.

Perhaps the most telling blow against such abuses was struck by Upton Sinclair's novel *The Jungle* (1906), which graphically portrayed the filthy conditions in Chicago's meatpacking industry. In the storage rooms, Sinclair wrote, "a man could run his hand over these piles of meat and sweep off handfuls of the dried dung of rats. These rats were nuisances, and the packers would put poisoned bread out for them, they would die, and then rats, bread, and meat would go into the hoppers together." Roosevelt read *The Jungle*—and reacted quickly. He sent two federal agents to Chicago to investigate, and their report confirmed all that Sinclair had said. Soon he and the Congress were hammering out a bill to address the problem.

The Meat Inspection Act of June 30, 1906, required federal inspection of meats destined for interstate commerce and empowered officials in the Agriculture Department to impose sanitary standards. The Pure Food and Drug Act, enacted the same day, placed restrictions on the makers of prepared foods and patent medicines, and forbade the manufacture, sale, or transportation of adulterated, misbranded, or harmful foods, drugs, and liquors.

With the achievements of 1903 and 1906, Theodore Roosevelt's campaign for regulatory legislation reached its chief goals and in the process moved the federal government a great distance from the laissez-faire policies that had prevailed before the turn of the century.

CONSERVATION One of the most enduring legacies of the Roosevelt years was the president's energetic support for the budding conservation movement. Concern for protecting the environment grew with the rising awareness that the frontier was being

Gifford Pinchot, chief of the Forestry Service under Roosevelt.

exhausted by the end of the nineteenth century. As early as 1872 Yellowstone National Park had been set aside as a public reserve, and in 1881, Congress had created a Division of Forestry in the Department of Agriculture. Roosevelt, an ardent hiker, camper, hunter, and bird watcher, was determined to halt the unchecked destruction of the nation's natural resources and wonders by providing a barrier of federal regulation and protection. His appointment of Gifford Pinchot as chief forester resulted in vigorous new scientific management of public lands. Roosevelt added fifty federal wildlife refuges, approved five new national parks, and initiated the system of designating national monuments, such as the Grand Canyon. He also used the Forest Reserve Act (1891) to exclude from settlement or harvest some 172 million acres of timberland. Lumbermen were irate, but Roosevelt held firm, bristling, "I hate a man who would skin the land."

FROM ROOSEVELT TO TAFT

Toward the end of his second term, Roosevelt crowed: "I have had a great time as president." But he was ready to move on, and he held to his 1904 decision not to run again. Instead he sought to have his secretary of war, William Howard Taft, replace him, and the Republican convention ratified the choice on its first ballot in 1908. The Democrats, whose conservative strategy had backfired in 1904, decided to give William Jennings Bryan one more chance. Still vigorous at forty-eight, Bryan retained a faithful following, but once again it was not enough. In the end the voters opted for Roosevelt's chosen successor, leaving Bryan only the southern states plus Nebraska, Colorado, and Nevada. The real surprise of the election was the strong showing of the Socialist party candidate, labor hero Eugene V. Debs. He attracted over 400,000 votes, illustrating the mounting intensity of working-class unrest.

Born to a prominent Cincinnati family, Taft boasted more experience in public service than any president since Van Buren. After graduating second in his class at Yale, he progressed through appointive offices, from assistant prosecutor, tax collector, and judge in Ohio, to solicitor in the Justice Department, federal judge, governor-general in the Philippines, and secretary of war. The presidency was the only elective office he ever held. Later he would be appointed Chief Justice of the Supreme Court (1921–1930), a job more suited to his reserved temperament.

Weighing in at over 325 pounds, Taft was a jovial slab of a man who loved playing golf or poker but detested politics. "Politics, when I am in it," he admitted, "makes me sick." Taft never felt comfortable in the White House. He once observed that whenever someone said "Mr. President," he looked around for Roosevelt. The political dynamo in the family was his wife, Nellie, who had wanted the presidency more than he. One of the major tragedies of Taft's presidency was that Helen "Nellie" Taft suffered a debilitating stroke soon after they entered the White House, and for most of his term, she remained unable to serve as his political adviser.

TARIFF REFORM   Once a student of the Social Darwinist, William Graham Sumner, Taft had absorbed the laissez-faire views of his mentor and had since differed with orthodox Republican protectionism. Contrary to TR's advice, he had promised a tariff reduction during the campaign, and true to his word, he called a special session of Congress on March 15, 1909, eleven days after his inauguration. But if, in pressing an issue that TR had skirted, Taft seemed bolder, he proved less adroit in shepherding legislation.

A reduced tariff passed the House with surprising ease. But before the Senate passed the bill it made more than 800 changes, most of which raised rates. Outraged by such obvious catering to special interests, a group of ten progressive Republicans joined the Democrats in an unsuccessful effort to defeat the bill. Taft at first agreed with them, but then, fearful of a party split, he backed the majority and agreed to an imperfect bill. He only made matters worse by calling the tariff the best "that the Republican party ever passed."

Taft lacked TR's charisma and his love of a grand battle, as well as his gift for political maneuvering and public relations. As one Republican congressman recognized, the president was "a well-meaning man who was born with two left feet." Temperamentally conservative, inhibited by scruples about interfering too much with the legislative process, Taft drifted into the orbit of the Republican Old Guard and quickly alienated the progressive wing of his party, whom he tagged "assistant Democrats."

BALLINGER AND PINCHOT   In 1910 Taft's policies drove the wedge deeper between the Republican factions. What came to be known as the Ballinger-Pinchot controversy made Taft appear to be a less reliable custodian of TR's conservation policies than he actually was. The controversy arose after Taft's secretary of the interior, Richard A. Ballinger, turned over coal-rich government lands in Alaska to a group of investor friends. Apparently without Ballinger's knowledge, this group had already agreed to sell part of the lands to a mining syndicate. When Chief of Forestry Pinchot revealed the scam, Taft fired him for insubordination. A joint congressional investigation later exonerated Ballinger from all charges of fraud or corruption, but conservationist suspicions created such pressures that he resigned in 1911.

In firing Pinchot, Taft acted on the strictly legal view which his training had taught him to value. But the unsavory circumstances surrounding the incident tarnished Taft's public image. He had been elected to carry out the Roosevelt policies, his opponents said, and he *was* carrying them out—"on a stretcher." And it did not take long for Roosevelt, who was in Europe after completing an African safari ("Let every lion do his duty," J. P. Morgan had wished when TR left for Africa), to learn of Taft's apparent change of principles.

Events had conspired to cast Taft in a conservative role at a time when progressive sentiment was riding high. The result was a sharp setback for the president in the congressional elections of 1910, first by the widespread defeat of pro-Taft candidates in the Republican primaries, then by the election of a Democratic majority in the House and of enough Democrats in the Senate that progressive Republicans could wield the balance of power.

TAFT AND ROOSEVELT   In June 1910 Roosevelt had returned from his travels abroad. As news accounts highlighted the Taft "betrayal," his followers urged him to take action. After hesitating for several months, Roosevelt again entered the political arena, having concluded that Taft had "sold the Square Deal down the river." At a speech in Kansas in August 1910, he gave a catchy name to his latest principles, the "New Nationalism," declaring that he intended to put the national interest above any "sectional or personal advantage." Roosevelt then issued a stirring call for an array of new federal regulatory laws and new measures of direct democracy, including the old Populist demands for the initiative, recall, and referendum. His purpose was not to revolutionize American life but to save it from the threat of revolution. "What I have advocated," he explained a few days later, "is not wild radicalism. It is the highest and wisest kind of conservatism."

Thereafter, Roosevelt intensified his criticism of the administration. Equally critical of Taft was Senator Robert La Follette of Wisconsin, who in 1911 helped organize the National Progressive Republican League and soon became its leading candidate for the Republican party nomination. Sensing Taft's weakness, Roosevelt officially threw his hat in the ring in February 1912. Even though many of La Follette's supporters thereupon rushed to embrace the ex-president, the Wisconsin idealist stubbornly refused to give way to TR. He felt that Roosevelt was not genuinely committed to the sweeping reforms necessary for a truly progressive America.

The rebuke implicit in Roosevelt's decision to run against Taft, his chosen successor, was in many ways undeserved. During Taft's first year in office one political tempest after another left his image irreparably damaged. The three years of solid achievement that followed could not restore its luster or reunite his divided party. Taft had at least attempted tariff reform, which TR had never dared, and in the end his administration set aside more public lands in four years than TR's had in nearly eight, and brought more antitrust suits, by a score of eighty to twenty-five. Taft's reform record was further extended by the establishment of the Bureau of Mines and the Federal Children's Bureau (1912). He also supported both the Sixteenth Amendment (1913), which authorized a federal income tax, and the Seventeenth Amendment (1913), which provided for the popular election of senators.

Despite this record, Roosevelt now hastened Taft's demise. Brusquely pushing aside La Follette's claim to the "progressive" Republican mantle, Roosevelt won most of the Republican primaries in 1912, even in Taft's Ohio. But such popular support was no match for Taft's advantages as president and party leader. The Old Guard's control of the convention machinery ensured their triumph, and the Taft forces proceeded to nominate their man by the same "steamroller" tactics that had nominated TR in 1904. Outraged at such "naked theft," the Roosevelt delegates issued a call for a Progressive party convention, which assembled in Chicago on August 5. The new third-party supporters were a curious mixture of Social Gospel clergymen and laymen, college presidents, professors, journalists, liberal businessmen, and social workers. TR told the group he felt "fit as a bull moose" in accepting their nomination. Now it was the Democrats' turn.

WILSON'S PROGRESSIVISM

WILSON'S RISE   The emergence of Thomas Woodrow Wilson as the Democratic nominee in 1912 climaxed a political rise even more rapid than that of Cleveland. In 1910, before his election as governor of New Jersey, Wilson had been president of Princeton University, but had never run for public office. Born in Staunton, Virginia in 1856, the son of a "noble-saintly mother" and a stern Presbyterian minister, he had grown up in Georgia and the Carolinas during the Civil War and Reconstruction. But he himself was from the beginning a reconstructed southerner. As he once stressed, "*because* I love the South, I rejoice in the failure of the Confederacy."

Young Wilson, tall, slender, and a bit awkward, with a long, sharply chiseled face, inherited his father's unquestioning piety, once declaring that "so far as religion is concerned, argument is adjourned." His father also stressed the importance of rhetorical skills: "Learn to think on your feet," he told his son. "Shoot your words straight at the target. Don't mumble and fumble."

Young Wilson soaked up such advice. He also developed a consuming ambition to "serve" mankind. Driven by a sense of destiny and duty, as well as by a certain moral fastidiousness, he was resolute, humane, rigid, and self-exacting to a fault. Indeed, Wilson nurtured a righteous commitment to principle. When a friend once insisted that there were two sides to every question, Wilson replied: "Yes, a right side and a wrong side." Although he would prove to be an adept compromiser, his fits of tenacious inflexibility would prove to be his Achilles heel.

After college at Princeton and law school at the University of Virginia, Wilson went on to the new Johns Hopkins University in Baltimore, where he studied history and political science. Wilson's dissertation, *Congressional Government*, published in 1885, argued that the president, like the British prime minister, should be the leader of party government, as active in directing legislation as in the administration and enforcement of laws. In calling for a strong presidency Wilson expressed views closer to those of Roosevelt than those of Taft. He likewise shared Roosevelt's belief that politicians should promote the general welfare rather than narrow special interests. And, like Roosevelt, he was critical of big business, organized labor, socialists, and radical agrarianism.

After teaching at Princeton for twelve years, Wilson was unanimously elected president of the university in 1902. In that position he showed the first evidence of reform views. "We are not put into this world to sit still and know," he stressed in his inaugural address. "We are put into it to act." And act he did. At Princeton he revamped the curriculum, expanded and improved the faculty, introduced the tutorial system, raised admissions standards, and attacked the boisterous and snobbish eating clubs.

His success at Princeton began to attract outside attention. In 1910 New Jersey's Democratic boss offered Wilson his support for the gubernatorial nomination, and Wilson accepted. The party leaders sought a respectable candidate to ward off progressive challengers, but they discovered too late that the supposedly innocent schoolmaster actually had an iron will of his own. He also had a developing political philosophy. "We are not in the same America as we were ten years ago," he acknowledged in one speech. Elected as a reform candidate, Governor Wilson promoted progressive measures and pushed them through the legislature. He pressured New Jersey lawmakers to enact a workmen's compensation law, a corrupt-practices law, measures to regulate public utilities, and ballot reforms. Such strong leadership in a state known as the "home of the trusts" for its lenient corporation laws brought Wilson to national attention.

THE ELECTION OF 1912 In the spring of 1911 a group of southerners resident in New York opened a Wilson presidential campaign headquarters, and Wilson set forth on strenuous tours into all regions of the country, denouncing special privilege and political bossism. But by convention time, despite a fast start, the Wilson campaign seemed headed for defeat. House Speaker Bennett Champ Clark of Missouri seemed destined to win the nomination. On the fourteenth ballot, however, Bryan, having decided that party conservatives were behind Clark, went over to Wilson; others followed and Wilson captured the nomination.

Democratic candidate Woodrow Wilson speaking from a train platform during the election of 1912.

No sooner did the campaign open than Roosevelt's candidacy almost ended. While stepping into a car in Milwaukee, he was shot by a crazed fanatic. The bullet went through his overcoat, spectacles case, folded speech, then fractured a rib before lodging just below his right lung. Jolted, he reeled backward, coughed, and then righted himself. "Stand back, don't hurt the man," he yelled at the crowd as it mobbed the attacker. Roosevelt then demanded that he be driven to the auditorium to deliver his speech. His dramatic sense unhampered, he showed the audience his blood-stained shirt and punctured text and vowed: "It takes more than this to kill a bull moose." He apologized for his halting delivery, but, bullet and all, he gave his speech.

Roosevelt was soon shooting verbal bullets at Taft and Wilson. He called Taft a "fathead" with "brains less than those of a guinea pig." Taft, deeply wounded by the sharp rhetoric of his "closest friend," fought back, branding TR a "demagogue" and "a dangerous egotist." But it quickly became clear that in a three-man race Taft was out of the running. "There are so many people in the country who don't like me," he lamented.

After the initial name-calling, the campaign settled down to a running debate over the competing ideologies of the two front-runners: Roosevelt's "New Nationalism" and Wilson's "New Freedom." The fuzzy ideas that Roosevelt fashioned into his New Nationalism had first been presented systematically in *The*

Promise of American Life (1909), a widely influential book by Herbert Croly, a New York journalist. Its central point was often summarized in a useful catch-phrase: Hamiltonian means to achieve Jeffersonian ends, meaning that the times required progressives to give up Jeffersonian prejudices against big government and use it to achieve democratic ends in the public interest.

The old nationalism had been used "by the sinister . . . special interests," TR claimed. His New Nationalism would enable government to achieve social justice, and more specifically to effect such reforms as graduated income and inheritance taxes, workmen's compensation for disabling injuries or illnesses, regulation of the labor of women and children, and a stronger Bureau of Corporations. These and more went into the platform of his Progressive party, which called for a federal trade commission with sweeping authority over business, and a tariff commission to set rates on a "scientific basis."

Before the end of his administration, Wilson would be swept into the current of such new nationalism too, but initially he adhered to the decentralizing antitrust traditions of his party. Before the start of the campaign Wilson conferred with Louis D. Brandeis, a progressive lawyer from Boston who focused Wilson's thought much as Croly had focused Roosevelt's. Brandeis's design for the New Freedom differed from Roosevelt's New Nationalism in its belief that the federal government should restore competition rather than regulate monopolies. This required eliminating *all* trusts, lowering tariffs, and breaking up the concentration of financial power on Wall Street. Brandeis and Wilson also dreamed of turning over most social programs to the states and cities. In this sense they saw the vigorous expansion of federal power as only a temporary necessity, not a permanent condition. Having restored competition and the diffusion of power and programs, the national government would revert to its aloof heritage. Roosevelt, who was convinced that both corporate concentration as well as an expanding federal government were permanent developments, dismissed the New Freedom as mere nostalgia.

The Republican schism opened the way for Woodrow Wilson to win by 435 electoral votes to 88 for Roosevelt and 8 for Taft. The Republican Taft and the former Republican Roosevelt were now private citizens. Taft took his loss with grace. When Yale offered him the Kent Chair of Constitutional Law, the rotund ex-president accepted, noting, however, that a "Sofa of Law" might be more appropriate. During the 1920s Chief Justice Taft served on the Supreme Court with distinction. Even his liberal jurist associates afforded him the highest respect. "It's very difficult for me to understand," Louis Brandeis later wrote, "why a man who is so good as Chief Justice . . . could have been so bad as President."

The 1912 election was significant in a number of respects. First, it was a high-water mark for progressivism. The two leading candidates debated the basic issues in a campaign unique for its focus on vital alternatives and for its high philosophical tone. Taft, too, despite his temperament and associations, showed his own progressive instincts. And the Socialist party, the left wing of progressivism, polled over 900,000 votes for Eugene V. Debs, about 6 percent of the total vote, its highest proportion ever.

Second, the election brought the Democrats back into effective national power for the first time since the Civil War. For two years during the second Cleveland administration, 1893–1895, they had held the White House and majorities in both houses of Congress, but they quickly fell out of power during the most severe depression in American history to that time. Now they had their chance again.

Third, Wilson's election brought southerners back into the orbit of national and international affairs in a significant way for the first time since the Civil War. Five of Wilson's ten cabinet members were born in the South, and William Jennings Bryan, the secretary of state, was an idol of the southern masses. At the president's right hand, and one of the most influential members of the Wilson circle, served Colonel Edward M. House of Texas. On Capitol Hill southerners, by virtue of their seniority, held most committee chairmanships. As a result, much of the progressive legislation of the Wilson era would bear the names of the southerners who guided the bills through Congress.

WILSONIAN REFORM   Wilson's 1913 inaugural address vividly expressed the ideals of social justice that inspired many progressives. "We have been proud of our industrial achievements," he observed, "but we have not hitherto stopped thoughtfully enough to count the human cost." He promised specifically a lower tariff and a new banking system. "This is not a day of triumph; it is a day of dedication. Here muster, not the forces of party, but the forces of humanity."

Whereas Roosevelt had been a strong president by force of personality, Wilson became a strong president by force of conviction. The president, he argued, must become the dynamic voice in national affairs. Wilson courted popular support, but he also courted members of Congress through personal contacts, invitations to the White House, and visits to the Capitol. He used the patronage power to reward friends and punish enemies. Though he might have acted through a bi-partisan progressive coalition, he chose instead, as he had argued the president should in *Congressional Government*, to rely on party loyalty.

THE TARIFF   The new president's leadership met its first test on the issue of tariff reform. Wilson summoned Congress into special session on April 7, 1913, and the day after it convened he went before it in person—the first president to do so since John Adams. "The object of the tariff duties henceforth laid must be effective competition," Wilson declared. Congress now acted vigorously on tariff reductions. Only four Democrats bolted the party line, as the bill passed the House easily.

The crunch came in the Senate, the traditional graveyard of tariff reform. Swarms of lobbyists got so thick in Washington, Wilson noted, that "a brick couldn't be thrown without hitting one of them." But Wilson turned the tables with a public statement that focused the spotlight on the "industrious and insidious" tariff lobby. In the end Louisiana's two "sugar senators" were the only Democrats to vote against the bill, which the president signed on October 3. The Underwood-Simmons Tariff of 1913 reduced the overall average duty from about 37 to about 29 percent. The act lowered tariffs but raised internal revenues with the first income tax levied under the newly ratified Sixteenth Amendment.

THE FEDERAL RESERVE ACT   Before the new tariff had cleared the Senate, the administration proposed the first major banking and currency reform since the Civil War. The need for a change had been acknowledged since the brief financial panic of 1907, which threatened to bring on widespread bank failures. The panic revealed what the Populists had long ago pointed out: that the nation's financial fate was determined by huge New York banks and that there was no reliable way to regulate the nation's money supply. Wilson and his advisors wanted a more flexible and decentralized financial system that would expand or contract to meet the nation's fluctuating credit needs.

The Federal Reserve Act, signed into law two days before Christmas 1913, created a new banking system with twelve regional Federal Reserve Banks, each owned by member banks in its district. All national banks became members; state banks could join if they wished. Each member bank had to subscribe 6 percent of its capital to the Federal Reserve Bank and deposit a

Reading the Death Warrant.
*Wilson's plan for banking and
currency reform spells the
death of the "Money Trust,"
according to this cartoon.*

portion of its reserve there, the amount depending on the size of the community.

These "bankers' banks" dealt chiefly with their members and not at all with individuals. Along with other banking functions, the chief service to member banks was to take over their outstanding loans in exchange for Federal Reserve Notes (paper currency), which member banks might then use to make further loans. This arrangement made it possible to expand both the money supply and bank credit in times of high business activity, or as the level of borrowing increased. A Federal Reserve Board exercised general supervision over the activities of the member banks and adjusted interest rates to fight inflation or stimulate business. It is hard to exaggerate the significance of the passage of the Federal Reserve Act. Through Wilson's skillful leadership, the Congress took a major step in providing the nation with a sound, yet flexible currency system and at the same time helped decentralize the money supply.

ANTITRUST LAWS   The next major issue confronting Wilson, after tariffs and banking, concerned the antitrust laws. In his campaign Wilson had made trust-busting the central focus of the New Freedom, for the concentration of economic power had continued to grow despite the Sherman Act and the Bureau of Corporations. During the summer of 1914, Wilson decided to make a strong Federal Trade Commission the cornerstone of his anti-

Mr. Wilson Taking Charge of the School. *A cartoon depicting the professorial president taking on big business.*

trust program. Created in September 1914, the five-member commission replaced Roosevelt's Bureau of Corporations and assumed new powers to define "unfair trade practices" and to issue "cease and desist" orders when it found evidence of unfair competition.

Having embraced the Brandeis principle of "controlled competition," Wilson seemed to lose interest in the antitrust bill drafted by Henry D. Clayton (D-Ala.) of the House Judiciary Committee. The Clayton Antitrust Act, passed in October 1914, outlawed such practices as price discrimination (charging different customers different prices for the same goods), "tying" agreements that limited the right of dealers to handle the products of competing manufacturers, and corporations' acquisition of stock in competing corporations. In every case, however, conservative forces in the Senate qualified these provisions by tacking on the weakening phrase "where the effect may be to substantially lessen competition" or words of similar effect. In accordance with the president's recommendation, however, corporate officials were made personally responsible for any violations.

Agrarian reformers, in alliance with organized labor, won a stipulation in the Clayton Act that declared farm and labor organizations not to be, per se, unlawful combinations in restraint of trade. Injunctions in labor disputes, moreover, were not to be handed down by federal courts unless "necessary to prevent irreparable injury to property." Hailed by Samuel Gompers as labor's "Magna Charta," these provisions were little more than pious affirmations, as later court decisions would demonstrate. Wilson himself remarked that the act did little more than affirm the right of unions to exist by forbidding their dissolution for being in restraint of trade.

Administration of the antitrust laws generally proved disappointing to the more vehement progressives under Wilson. The Justice Department offered help and advice to businessmen interested in arranging matters so as to avoid antitrust prosecutions. The appointment of conservative men to the Interstate Commerce Commission and the Federal Reserve won plaudits from the business world and profoundly disappointed progressives.

SOCIAL JUSTICE   Wilson had in fact never been a strong progressive of the social-justice persuasion. He had carried out his promises to lower the tariff, reorganize the banking system, and strengthen the antitrust laws, but was not inclined to go much further. The New Freedom was now complete, he wrote late in 1914; the future would be "a time of healing because a time of just dealing."

The sweep of events and the pressures of more far-reaching progressives pushed Wilson beyond where he intended to go on some points. Yet Wilson retained several social blind spots. Although he endorsed state action for women's suffrage, he declined to support a suffrage amendment because his party platform had not. He had cultivated the support of black voters, but let members of his cabinet extend Jim Crow practices in the federal government. He withheld support from federal child labor legislation because he regarded it a state matter, and he opposed a bill providing federal loans for strapped farmers on the ground that it was "unwise and unjustifiable to extend the credit of the government to a single class of the community."

PROGRESSIVE RESURGENCE   The need to weld a winning coalition in 1916 pushed Wilson back on the road of reform. Progressive Democrats were restless, and after war broke out in Europe in August 1914, further divisions arose over defense and foreign policy. At the same time, the Republicans were repairing their own rift. The Progressive party showed little staying power in the 1914 midterm election and Roosevelt showed little will to preserve it. Most observers recognized that Wilson could shape a majority only by courting progressives of all parties. In January 1916 Wilson scored points with them when he nominated Louis D. Brandeis to the Supreme Court. Conservatives waged a vigorous battle against Brandeis, but Senate progressives rallied to win confirmation of the social-justice champion as the first Jewish member of the Supreme Court.

Wilson meanwhile began to embrace a broad program of farm and labor reforms he earlier had spurned. On the issue of federal farm credit, he reversed himself abruptly, supporting early in 1916 a proposal to set up land banks to sponsor farm loans. With this boost the Federal Farm Loan Act became law in July 1916. Under the control of a Federal Farm Loan Board, twelve Federal Land Banks, each with a minimum capital of $750,000, paralleled the Federal Reserve Banks and offered low-interest loans to farmers.

The dream of cheap rural credits, sponsored by a generation of

Louis D. Brandeis.

Populists, had come to fruition. Democrats never embraced the Populist subtreasury plan, but made a small step in that direction with the Warehouse Act of 1916. This measure authorized federal licensing of private warehouses; federal backing made their receipts for stored produce more acceptable to local bankers as collateral for short-term loans. Other concessions to farm demands included the Smith-Lever Act of 1914 and the Smith-Hughes Act of 1917, both of which passed with little controversy. The first provided federal grants-in-aid for farm demonstration agents under the supervision of land-grant colleges to show farmers new planting techniques, fertilizers, and equipment. The second measure funded agricultural and mechanical education in the high schools.

The progressive resurgence of 1916 broke the logjam on labor reforms as well. Advocates of child-labor legislation persuaded Wilson to overcome doubts of its constitutionality and sign the Keating-Owen Child Labor Act, which excluded from interstate commerce goods manufactured by children under fourteen. But the Supreme Court soon ruled it unconstitutional on the grounds that regulation of interstate commerce could not extend to the conditions of labor. Another important accomplishment was the Adamson Act of 1916, which mandated the eight-hour day for railroad workers.

In Wilson's first term progressive government reached its zenith. A creative time, the age of progressivism at the beginning of the twentieth century set a framework within which American politics and society would still function, by and large, near the end of the century. Progressivism had conquered the old dictum that the government is best which governs least, whatever political rhetoric might be heard to the contrary, and left the more extreme doctrines of limited government as dead as Grover Cleveland. Progressivism, an amalgam of agrarian, business, governmental, and social reform, amounted in the end to a movement for active government on behalf of the public interest.

THE LIMITS OF PROGRESSIVISM

Like all great historic movements, progressivism contained elements of paradox and irony. Despite all the talk of greater democracy at the turn of the century, it was also the age of disfranchisement for southern blacks and xenophobic reactions to "new" immigrants. The initiative and referendum, supposedly democratic reforms, proved subject to manipulation by well-financed publicity campaigns. And much of the public policy of the time came to be formulated by experts and members of appointed boards, not by broad segments of the population. There is a fine irony in the fact that the drive to increase the political role of ordinary people moved parallel with efforts to strengthen executive leadershp and exalt expertise. This age of much-ballyhooed efficiency and bureaucracy, in business as well as government, generated a situation in which more and more key decisions were made by faceless policy-makers.

Progressivism was largely a middle-class movement in which the poor and unorganized had little influence. The supreme irony was that a movement so dedicated to the democratic rhetoric should experience so steady a decline in voter participation. In 1912, the year of the Bull Moose campaign, voting dropped off by almost 7 percent. The new politics of issues and charismatic leaders proved to be less effective in turning out voters than party organizations and bosses had been. And by 1916 the optimism of an age that looked to infinite progress was already confronted by a vast slaughter. Europe had stumbled into war, and America would soon be drawn in. The twentieth century, which had dawned with such bright hopes, held in store episodes of unparalleled horror.

FURTHER READING

A good introduction to the topic of Progressivism can be found in Arthur S. Link and Richard L. McCormick's *Progressivism* (1983).° George E. Mowry's *The Era of Theodore Roosevelt, 1900–1912* (1958)° and Arthur S. Link's *Woodrow Wilson and the Progressive Era, 1910–1917* (1954)° remain useful.

Progressivism has been interpreted in many ways. Robert H. Wiebe's *The Search for Order, 1877–1920* (1967)° presents the organizational model for reform. Richard Hofstadter's *The Age of Reform: From Bryan to FDR* (1955)° examines the consensus as the basis of reform. Gabriel Kolko sees reform as a means of social control in *The Triumph of Conservatism* (1963).° Dewey W. Grantham's *Southern Progressivism* (1983)° shows the distinctiveness of reform in that region.

Edmund Morris's *The Rise of Theodore Roosevelt* (1979)° is a favorable account. Also helpful is John M. Blum's *The Republican Roosevelt* (2nd ed., 1977).° For the Taft years, see Paolo E. Coletta's *The Presidency of William Howard Taft* (1973). Arthur S. Link's multivolume biography *Wilson* (1947–1965)—particularly *The New Freedom* (1956)

° These books are available in paperback editions.

—is the place to start on that president. John Milton Cooper, Jr., compares Wilson and Roosevelt in *The Warrior and the Priest* (1983).°

The evolution of government policy toward business is examined in Martin J. Sklar's *The Corporate Reconstruction of American Capitalism, 1890–1916* (1988).° Roy Lubove's *The Progressives and the Slums* (1962) and Jack M. Holl's *Juvenile Reform in the Progressive Era* (1971) examine the problem of urban decay.

Other issues are covered in David M. Kennedy's *Birth Control in America: The Career of Margaret Sanger* (1970),° David J. Rothman's *Conscience and Convenience: The Asylum and Its Alternatives in Progressive America* (1980),° and John Ettling's *The Germ of Laziness: Rockefeller Philanthropy and Public Health in the New South* (1981).

On other aspects of the Progressive impulse, see James H. Timberlake's *Prohibition and the Progressive Movement, 1900–1920* (1963) and Ruth Rosen's *The Lost Sisterhood* (1982),° on prostitution. Samuel P. Hays's *Conservation and the Gospel of Efficiency: The Progressive Conservation Movement, 1890–1920* (1959)° covers conservation and the Ballinger-Pinchot controversy.

The central role played by women in the Progressive movement is described in Paula Baker's, *Gender and the Transformation of Politics: Public and Private Life in New York, 1870–1930* (1989); Nancy Cott's, *The Grounding of Modern Feminism* (1987)°; and Rosalind Rosenberg's *Beyond Separate Spheres: Intellectual Roots of Modern Feminism* (1982).°

Labor studies include Stephen Meyer III's *The Five Dollar Day: Labor Management and Social Control in the Ford Motor Company, 1908–1921* (1981)° and Tamara K. Hareven's *Family Time and Industrial Time: The Relationship between the Family and Work in a New England Industrial Community* (1982).°

24 ᨆ

WILSON AND THE
GREAT WAR

WILSON AND FOREIGN AFFAIRS

When Woodrow Wilson was sworn in as president of the
United States in March 1913, the former historian brought to the
office little background in the study or conduct of foreign relations. Wilson admitted as much when he remarked just before
taking office that it "would be an irony of fate if my administration had to deal chiefly with foreign affairs." But events in Latin
America and Europe were to make the irony all too real. From
1914 on, foreign relations increasingly preoccupied Wilson's
attention.

Although lacking in international experience, Wilson did not
lack ideas or convictions in this area. Both he and his secretary of
state, William Jennings Bryan, believed that America had been
called to promote democracy and moral progress in the world.
"When properly directed," Wilson maintained in 1914, "there
is no people not fitted for self-government." How to promote
such democratic idealism and self-determination abroad, however, remained a thorny issue, as Wilson soon discovered in responding to rapidly changing events in Mexico.

INTERVENTION IN MEXICO   For most of the thirty-five years from
1876 to 1911 President Porfirio Díaz had dominated Mexico. As
military dictator he had suppressed opposition and showered
favors on his followers and on foreign investors, who piled up
holdings in Mexican mines, petroleum, railroads, and agriculture. But eventually the dictator's hold slipped, and in 1910

popular resentment boiled over in revolt. By May 1911 revolutionary armies had occupied Mexico City and Díaz had fled.

The leader of the rebellion, Francisco I. Madero, a charismatic dreamer, proved unable to manage the tough customers drawn to the revolt by the scramble for power. In February 1913 General Victoriano Huerta assumed power, and Madero was murdered soon afterward. Wilson challenged the legitimacy of Huerta's violent coup. "I will not recognize a government of butchers," he stressed privately. At the same time he obliquely expressed sympathy with a new revolutionary movement led by Venustiano Carranza and began to put diplomatic pressure on Huerta. "I am going to teach the South American republics to elect good men," he vowed to a visiting British diplomat.

Early in 1914 Wilson removed an embargo on arms to Mexico in order to help Carranza's forces, and he stationed warships off Veracruz to halt foreign arms shipments to Huerta. On April 9, 1914, several American sailors, gathering supplies ashore at Tampico, strayed into a restricted area and were arrested. The local commander quickly released them and sent an apology to the American naval commander. There the incident might have ended, but the naval commander demanded a salute to the American flag. Wilson backed him up and won from Congress authority to use force to bring Huerta to terms. Before the Tampico incident could be resolved, Wilson sent a naval force to Veracruz. American marines and sailors went ashore on April 21, 1914, and they forcibly occupied the town at a cost of nineteen killed. The Mexicans lost at least two hundred killed.

General Victoriano Huerta, whose seizure of power in Mexico in 1913 aroused Wilson's opposition.

In Mexico the American occupation aroused the opposition of all factions, and Huerta tried to rally support against foreign invasion. At this juncture Wilson accepted a mediation offer by the ABC powers (Argentina, Brazil, and Chile). In June 1914 they proposed withdrawal of United States forces, the removal of Huerta, and installation of a provisional government. Huerta refused, but the moral effect of the proposal, his isolation abroad, and the growing strength of his foes forced him to leave office in July. In August the Carranzistas entered Mexico City, and in November the Americans left Veracruz. Wilson's "missionary diplomacy" seemed to have worked. "With the retirement of Huerta," one editor predicted, "prospects are bright for the triumph of President Wilson's moral-suasion peace policy." Finally, in October 1915 the United States and several Latin American governments recognized Carranza as president of Mexico.

Still, the troubles south of the border continued. No sooner had the Carranzistas taken power than they began to squabble among themselves for the spoils of office. The most incendiary confrontation occurred between Carranza and his foremost general, Pancho Villa, a moody, violent former bandit who shrewdly claimed to represent "the people" behind the revolution. Such a public stance attracted Wilson's sympathy, and he initially threw American support behind Villa. This turned out to be a colossal blunder. As fighting erupted in 1915 the Villistas suffered several serious defeats. The Wilson administration, confused and frantic, thereupon shifted its stance to that of strict neutrality, with the president announcing that the Mexicans should be allowed to determine their own fate without outside interference.

Critics, however, charged that Wilson was a bungler and a coward. The always militant Theodore Roosevelt, for example, attacked the president's earlier support of the revolution and called for American military intervention to restore order. Responding to such pressure, Wilson in June 1915 warned the two Mexican factions to stop fighting or risk the involvement of American troops. Villa then requested an armistice, but Carranza, sensing his military dominance, rejected Wilson's right to intrude in Mexico's affairs. This led Wilson to grumble that he had "never known a man more impossible to deal with on human principles than this man Carranza."

By the fall of 1915, however, relations between Carranza and Wilson improved, as the United States formally recognized his claim as the *de facto* leader of the Mexican nation. This enraged Villa, and his naturally violent tendencies now came to the fore. In January 1916 Villa's men stopped a train and murdered six-

The Veracruz incident in April 1914 provoked this comment on Wilson's policy in Mexico.

teen American mining engineers in a deliberate attempt to provoke American intervention, discredit Carranza, and build himself up as an opponent of the "Gringos." On March 9 Villa's band of renegades entered Columbus, New Mexico, burned the town, and killed seventeen Americans.

Outraged, Wilson asked Carranza to allow American forces to pursue the attackers into Mexico. Carranza agreed, but grew understandably alarmed when Wilson sent General John J. Pershing and a force of some 11,000 men deep inside Mexico. For nearly a year Pershing's troops chased Villa through northern Mexico but, missing their catch, they returned home in January 1917. Carranza then pressed his own war against the bandits and put through a new liberal constitution in 1917. Mexico was by then well on the way to a more orderly government, but almost in spite of Wilson's actions rather than because of them.

PROBLEMS IN THE CARIBBEAN   In the Caribbean Wilson found it as hard to act on his ideals as in Mexico. During President Taft's term (1909–1913) refinements of Roosevelt's interventionist policy had earned from its opponents the less exalted—if fairly accurate—title of "dollar diplomacy." The policy so tagged had its origin in China in 1909, when President Taft personally cabled the Chinese government on behalf of American investors interested in an international consortium to finance railroad lines in China. In Latin America "dollar diplomacy" worked differently and with somewhat more success. The idea was to encourage American bankers to help prop up the finances of shaky Caribbean governments.

One of the first applications of Wilsonian idealism to foreign policy came when the president renounced dollar diplomacy. The government, he declared, was not supporting any "special groups or interests." Despite Wilson's public stand against using American force to back up American investments, however, he kept the marines in Nicaragua, where they had sent by Taft in 1912, to prevent renewed civil war. There they would stay almost continuously through 1933. Then in July 1915 he dispatched more marines to Haiti after two successive revolutions and subsequent disorders. The American forces stayed until 1934. Disorders in the Dominican Republic brought American marines to the country in 1916, where they remained until 1924. The presence of American military force in the region only worsened the already prevalent irritation at "Yankee imperialism."

THE GREAT WAR AND AMERICA

Problems in Mexico and Central America loomed larger in Wilson's thinking than the gathering storm in Europe. When the thunderbolt of war struck Europe in the summer of 1914 it came to most Americans, one North Carolinian wrote, "as lightning out of a clear sky." Whatever the troubles in Mexico, whatever disorders and interventions agitated other countries, it seemed unreal that civilized Europe could descend into such an orgy of destruction. But the assassination of Austrian Archduke Franz Ferdinand by a Serbian nationalist, Austria-Hungary's determination to punish Serbia, and Russia's mobilization in sympathy with her Slavic brothers in Serbia suddenly triggered a conflict between a European system of alliances: the Triple Alliance or Central Powers (Germany, Austria-Hungary, and Italy) and the Triple Entente (France, Great Britain, and Russia). When Russia refused to stop its mobilization, Germany, which backed Austria-Hungary, declared war on Russia on August 1, 1914, and on Russia's ally France two days later. Germany then invaded Belgium to get at France, which brought Great Britain into the war on August 4. Japan, eager to seize German holdings in the Pa-

EUROPE AT WAR

- ██ Central Powers (Triple Alliance)
- ░░ Allied Powers (Triple Entente)
- ▓▓ Neutral countries

ATLANTIC OCEAN

IRELAND

NORTH SEA

NORWAY

SWEDEN

DENMARK

GREAT BRITAIN

BALTIC SEA

St. Petersburg

Memel

London

Dover Strait

NETH.

BELG.

Berlin

Danzig

GERMANY

RUSSIA

Paris

LUX.

Vienna

FRANCE

SWITZ.

AUSTRIA-HUNGARY

ROMANIA

BLACK SEA

PORTUGAL

SPAIN

ITALY

MONTE-NEGRO

ALBANIA

SERBIA

BULGARIA

SPANISH MOROCCO

MEDITERRANEAN SEA

GREECE

TURKEY (Ottoman Empire)

NORTH AFRICA

cific, declared war on August 23, and Turkey entered on the side of the Central Powers a week later. Italy stayed out, however, and struck a bargain under which it joined the Allied Powers in 1915.

AMERICA'S INITIAL REACTIONS The initial shock in the United States was followed by gratitude that an ocean stood between America and the battlefields. "Our isolated position and freedom from entangling alliances," said the *Literary Digest*, "inspire our press with cheering assurance that we are in no peril of being drawn into the European quarrel." In August 1914 President Wilson urged the American people to be "neutral in thought as well as in action."

That was more easily said than done, not least for Wilson himself. Americans might want to stay out, but most of them cared deeply which side won. In the 1910 U.S. population of 92 million, more than 32 million were "hyphenated Americans," first- or second-generation immigrants who retained close ties to their old countries. Among the more than 13 million from the countries at war, the 8 million German-Americans were by far the largest group, and the 4 million Irish-Americans harbored a deep-rooted enmity to Britain. These groups instinctively leaned toward the Central Powers.

Old-line Americans, largely of British origin, were sympathetic to the Allies. If, as has been said, Britain and the United States were divided by a common language, they were united by ties of culture and tradition. Americans identified also with France, which had contributed to American culture and ideas, and to independence itself. Britain and France, if not their ally Russia, seemed the custodians of liberal democracy, while Germany more and more seemed the embodiment of autocracy and militarism. If not a direct threat to the United States, Germany would pose at least a potential threat if it destroyed the balance of power in Europe. High officers of the United States government were pro-British in thought from the outset. Robert Lansing, first counselor of the State Department, Walter Hines Page, ambassador to London, and Colonel Edward House, Wilson's closest adviser, saw in German militarism a potential danger to America.

What effects the propaganda of the warring powers had on American opinion is unclear. The Germans and the British were most active, but German propaganda, which played on American dislike of Russian autocracy and Russian anti-Semitism, fell mainly upon barren ground. Only German- and Irish-Americans responded to a "hate England" theme. From the outset the British had one supreme advantage in this area. Once they had cut the direct telegraph cable from Germany early in the war, nearly all news from the battle fronts had to clear through London.

A STRAINED NEUTRALITY   At first the war brought a slump in American exports and the threat of a depression, but by the spring of 1915 the Allies' demand for supplies generated a wartime boom. The Allies bought so much that they soon needed loans to continue their purchases. Early in the war Secretary of State Bryan argued that loans to any warring nation were "inconsistent with the true spirit of neutrality." Technically he was correct, but Wilson, for all his public professions of neutrality, was in fact determined to aid Great Britain. By October 1914 he quietly began approving credits to sustain trade with the Allies. American investors would advance over $2 billion to the Allies before the United States entered the war, and only $27 million to Germany.

The administration nevertheless clung to its official stance of neutrality through two and a half years of warfare in Europe, and tried to uphold the traditions of "freedom of the seas" which had guided American policy since the Napoleonic Wars. Trade on the high seas assumed a new importance as the German drive through Belgium and toward Paris finally ground down into the stalemate of trench warfare. In a war of attrition survival depended on access to supplies, and in such a war British naval power counted for a great deal. With the German fleet outnumbered and bottled up almost from the outset, the war in many ways assumed the pattern that in 1812 had led America into war with Britain.

In November 1914 the British declared the whole North Sea a war zone and sowed it with mines. Four months later they further announced that they would seize ships carrying goods of presumed enemy destination, ownership, or origin. British policies of search and seizure caused extended delays in shipping, sometimes running into months. Britain also ordered its ships to stop vessels carrying German goods via neutral ports. When the State Department protested, Britain reminded the United States that this was the same doctrine of continuous voyage on which the United States had acted in the 1860s to keep British goods out of the Confederacy.

NEUTRAL RIGHTS AND SUBMARINES   British actions, which included blacklisting companies that traded with the enemy and censoring the mails, raised some old issues of neutral rights, but the German reaction introduced an entirely new question. In the face of the British blockade, only German submarines could venture out to harass the enemy. On February 4, 1915, in response to the "illegal" British blockade, the German government proclaimed a war zone around the British Isles. Enemy merchant ships in those waters were liable to sinking by submarines, the Germans declared. Since the British sometimes flew neutral flags as a ruse, neutral ships in the zone would also be in danger. U-boat (*Unterseeboot*) warfare violated the established international procedure of stopping enemy vessels on the high seas and providing for the safety of passengers and crews, since the chief advantage was in surprise.

The United States pronounced the German policy "an indefensible violation of neutral rights" and warned that Germany would be held to "strict accountability" for any destruction of American lives and property. The administration asked the British to give up flying neutral flags and its blockade of foodstuffs in return for German renunciation of submarine warfare, but nothing came of the effort. On March 28, 1915, one American drowned when the Germans sank a British steamer in the Irish Sea. The following May an American tanker went down with a loss of two lives. The administration was divided on the proper course of action. Bryan wanted to warn American citizens that they entered the war zone at their own risk; his counselor, Robert Lansing, and Colonel House wanted to threaten a possible break in diplomatic relations with Germany.

As Wilson pondered the alternatives, the sinking of the majestic British liner *Lusitania* provoked a crisis. On May 7, 1915, a German U-boat torpedoed the *Lusitania*, which exploded and sank within eighteen minutes. Before the ship's departure from New York, bound for Liverpool, the German Embassy had published warnings in the American press against travel to the war zone, but among the 1,198 persons lost were 128 Americans.

The American public was outraged. It was an act of piracy, Theodore Roosevelt declared. In an effort to quiet the uproar Wilson stressed: "There is such a thing as a man being too proud to fight. There is such a thing as a nation being so right that it does not need to convince others by force that it is right." Wilson's previous demand for "strict accountability," however, forced him to make a strong response. On May 13 Bryan reluctantly signed a note demanding that the Germans abandon unrestricted submarine warfare, disavow the sinking, and pay reparations. The Germans responded that the passenger ship had been armed (which it was not) and carried a secret cargo of small

Americans were outraged when a German torpedo sank the Lusitania *on May 7, 1915.*

arms and ammunition (which it did). A second note on June 9 repeated American demands in stronger terms. Bryan, unwilling to risk war on the issue, resigned in protest and joined the peace movement as a private citizen. His successor, Robert Lansing, signed the note.

In response to the uproar over the *Lusitania*, the German government had secretly ordered U-boat captains to avoid sinking large passenger vessels. When, despite the order, two American lives were lost in the sinking of the British liner *Arabic*, bound for New York, the German ambassador demanded and got from Berlin a public assurance, which he delivered on September 1, 1915: "Liners will not be sunk by our submarines without warning and without safety of the lives of non-combatants, provided that the liners do not try to escape or offer resistance." With this "Arabic pledge" Wilson's resolute stand seemed to have won a victory for his policy.

THE DEBATE OVER PREPAREDNESS   The *Lusitania* incident, and more generally the quarrels over neutral commerce, contributed to a growing demand for a stronger American army and navy. After the *Lusitania* sinking the outcry from preparedness advocates grew into a clamor, and Theodore Roosevelt stood at the forefront of the movement. As journalist William Allen White recognized, "Social and industrial justice no longer interested Colonel Roosevelt. He had a war, a war greater than he ever realized it would be, to engage his talents."

In his annual message in December 1915 Wilson alerted Congress to his plans for war preparedness. The response was far from unanimous. Progressives and pacifists, and a broad-based antiwar sentiment running through the rural South and West, awakened the traditional American suspicion of standing armies, which dated back to the colonial period. Jane Addams and suffragist Carrie Chapman Catt organized a Women's Peace party. Bryan, La Follette, and other leaders also lent their voices to the peace movement.

Wilson eventually accepted a compromise between advocates of an expanded force under federal control and advocates of a traditional citizen army. The National Defense Act of June 3, 1916, expanded the regular army from 90,000 to 175,000 and permitted a gradual enlargement to 223,000. It also authorized a National Guard of 440,000. The bill for an increased navy had less trouble because of the general feeling expressed by Secretary Josephus Daniels that there was "no danger of militarism from a relatively strong navy such as would come from a big standing army." The Naval Construction Act of August 1916 authorized between $500–600 million for a three-year building program.

Forced to relent on preparedness, progressive opponents determined that the financial burden should rest on the wealthy. The income tax became their weapon. Supported by a groundswell of popular support, they wrote into the Revenue Act of 1916 changes that included doubling the basic income tax from 1 to 2 percent. The new taxes on wealth amounted to the most clear-cut victory of radical progressives in the entire Wilson period, a victory that Wilson supported in preparation for the election of 1916.

THE ELECTION OF 1916 Republicans started that year hoping to regain their normal electoral majority, and Roosevelt started out hoping to be their leader again. But in 1912 he had committed the deadly sin of bolting his party and, what was more, he now expressed a bellicosity on war issues that would scare off voters. Needing somebody who would draw Bull Moose progressives back into the fold, the regulars turned to Justice Charles Evans Hughes, who had made a progressive record as governor of New York from 1907 to 1910. On the Supreme Court since then, he had neither endorsed a candidate in 1912 nor spoken out on foreign policy.

Peace with Honor. *Wilson's neutral policies proved popular in the 1916 campaign.*

The Democrats, as expected, chose Wilson once again, and in their platform endorsed a program of social legislation, neutrality, and reasonable preparedness. The party further commended women's suffrage to the states, denounced groups that placed the interests of other countries above those of the United States, and pledged support for a postwar League of Nations to enforce peace with collective security measures against aggressors. The Democrats found their most popular issue, however, in Wilson's commitment to neutrality. The peace theme, refined into the slogan "He kept us out of war," became the rallying cry of the campaign, one that had the merit of taking credit without making any promises for the future.

In the end Wilson's twin pledges of peace and progressivism, a unique combination of issues forged in the legislative and diplomatic crucibles of 1916, brought victory. The final vote showed a Democratic sweep of the Far West and South, enough for victory in the electoral college by 277 to 254, and in the popular vote by 9 million to 8.5 million. Wilson also carried many social-justice progressives who in 1912 had supported the Bull Moose campaign.

LAST EFFORTS FOR PEACE   Immediately after the election Wilson began to plan another peace move, but before he was ready the German government announced on December 12 its readiness to discuss peace terms. Six days later Wilson sent identical notes to the belligerent powers, asking each to state its war aims. The Germans responded promptly that they would state theirs only to a conference of the belligerents at a neutral site. In January 1917 the Allies made it plain that they intended to exact reparations, break up the Austro-Hungarian and Ottoman Empires, and destroy German power. Wilson then decided to make one more appeal, in the hope that public opinion would force the hands of the warring governments. Speaking before the Senate on January 22, 1917, he asserted the right of the United States to share in laying the foundations for a lasting peace. This would have to be a "peace without victory," for only a "peace among equals" could endure.

Although Wilson did not know it, he was already too late. Exactly two weeks before he spoke, German leaders had decided to wage unrestricted submarine warfare. Faced with weakening resources in a war of attrition, the Germans took the calculated risk of provoking American anger in the hope of scoring a quick knockout. On January 31, 1917, Germany announced the new policy, effective the next day: all vessels in the war zone, belligerent or neutral, would be sunk without warning. "Freedom of the seas," said the *Brooklyn Eagle*, "will now be enjoyed by icebergs and fish."

On February 3, 1917, Wilson informed a joint session of Congress that the United States had broken diplomatic relations with the German government. He added that he still did not believe the Germans would do what they said they felt at liberty to do— only overt acts would persuade him that they actually intended to sink neutral ships. In case of such acts, he would take measures to protect American seamen and citizens.

Then, on March 1, news of the Zimmermann Telegram broke in the American press. The British had intercepted and decoded an important message from German Foreign Secretary Arthur Zimmermann to his minister in Mexico. The note instructed the envoy to offer an alliance and financial aid to Mexico in case of war between the United States and Germany. In return for diversionary action against the United States, Mexico would recover "the lost territory in Texas, New Mexico, and Arizona." All this was contingent on war with the United States, but an electrified public read in it an aggressive intent. Later in March another bombshell burst when a revolution overthrew Russia's czarist government and established the provisional government of a Russian Republic. The fall of the czarist autocracy allowed Americans the illusion that all the major Allied powers were now fighting for constitutional democracy. Not until November 1917 was this illusion shattered when the Bolsheviks seized power in Russia.

AMERICA'S ENTRY

The overt acts of war Wilson awaited came in March 1917 when German submarines sank five American merchant vessels. On March 20 Wilson's cabinet unanimously endorsed a declaration of war, and the following day the president called a special session of Congress. When it met on April 2, Wilson asked Congress to recognize the war that Imperial Germany was already waging against the United States, then turned to a discussion of the issues. The German government had revealed itself as a natural foe of liberty, and, Wilson argued, "The world must be made safe for democracy." The war resolution passed the Senate by a vote of 82 to 6 on April 4. The House concurred, 373 to 50, and Wilson signed the measure on April 6. It was Good Friday.

How had it come to this, less than three years after Wilson's proclamation of neutrality? Prominent among the various explanations of America's entrance into the war are the effects of British propaganda and America's deep involvement in trade with the Allies, which some observers then and later credited to the intrigues of war profiteers and munitions makers. Some Americans thought German domination of Europe would be a threat to American security, especially if it meant the destruction or capture of the British navy. Whatever the influence of such factors, they likely would not have been decisive without the issue of submarine warfare. This issue need not have become decisive, either, since such neutrals as Norway, Sweden, and Denmark took relatively heavier losses and yet stayed out of the war. But once Wilson had taken a stand for the traditional rights of neutrals and noncombatants, he was to some extent at the mercy of decisions by the German high command. Wilson was then led step by step into a war over what to a later generation would seem a rather quaint, if noble, set of principles.

AMERICA'S EARLY ROLE   The scope of America's role in the European land war remained unclear for a time. Few on either side of the Atlantic expected more from the United States than a token military effort.

Within a month of America's declaration of war, the British and French requested money with which to buy supplies, a request Congress had already anticipated in the Liberty Loan Act of April 24, which added $5 billion to the national debt in "Liberty Bonds." Of this amount, $3 billion could be loaned to the Allied powers. The United States was also willing to furnish naval support, credits, supplies, and munitions. But to raise and train a large army, equip it, and send it across a submarine-infested ocean seemed out of the question. The United States did agree to send a token force to bolster Anglo-French morale, and on June 26, 1917, the first American contingent, about 14,500 men commanded by General John J. Pershing, began to disembark on the French coast. After reaching Paris, Pershing decided that the war-weary Allies would be unable to mount an offensive by themselves. He therefore requested that Wilson send a million American troops by the following spring, and the president obliged.

When the United States entered the war the combined strength of the regular army and National Guard was only 379,000; at the end it would be 3.7 million. The need for such large numbers of troops converted Wilson to the idea of conscription. Under the Selective Service Act of May 18, 1917, all

A Liberty Loan poster with an "honor roll" of ethnic Americans.

men aged twenty-one to thirty (later, from eighteen to forty-five) had to register for service. In the course of the war about 2 million Americans crossed the Atlantic and about 1.4 million saw some combat.

MOBILIZING A NATION   Such a total war required complete economic mobilization and more regulation of industry than most progressives had imagined. Still, a lingering lack of coordination among public and private officials made wartime mobilization less efficient than it should have been. It was not the Wilson administration's finest hour.

In August 1916 Congress had created a Council of National Defense, which in turn set up more wartime agencies. The United States Shipping Board, organized in January 1917, within two years had more than forty steel and ninety wooden ships coming off the ways monthly. In August 1917 Congress created both a Food Administration, headed by Herbert Hoover, a future president, and a Fuel Administration. Hoover, a mining engineer and former head of the Commission for Relief in Belgium, had the responsibility of raising production while reducing civilian use of foodstuffs. "Food will win the war" was the slogan. Hoover directed a propaganda campaign which "Hooverized" the country with "Wheatless Mondays," "Meatless Tuesdays," "Porkless Thursdays," the planting of victory gardens, and the use of leftovers. The Fuel Administration introduced the country to Daylight Saving Time and "heatless Mondays."

The War Industries Board (WIB) was established in July 1917, and it soon became the most important of all the mobilization agencies. Wilson summoned Bernard Baruch, a brilliant Wall Street investor, to head the board, giving him a virtual dictatorship over the economy. The WIB could allocate raw materials, tell manufacturers what to produce, order construction of new plants, and, with presidential approval, fix prices.

With the high wartime demand for labor, the closing off of foreign immigration, and the movement of 4 million men from the labor force into the armed services, women, blacks, and other ethnic minorities were encouraged to enter industries and agricultural activities heretofore dominated by white males. Northern businesses sent recruiting agents into the Deep South to find workers for their factories and mills, and over 400,000 southern blacks began the "Great Migration" northward during the war years, a mass movement that continued unabated through the 1920s. Mexican-Americans followed the same migratory pattern. Recruiting agents and newspaper editors portrayed the North as the "land of promise" for southern blacks suffering from their region's depressed agricultural economy and rising racial intimidation and violence. The African-American newspaper *Chicago Defender* exclaimed: "To die from the bite of frost is far more glorious than at the hands of a mob." By 1930 the number of African-Americans living in the North had tripled from what it had been in 1910.

But the newcomers were not always welcomed above the Mason-Dixon line. Many native white workers resented the new arrivals, and racial tensions sparked riots in cities across the country. In 1917 over forty African-Americans and nine whites were killed during a riot over employment in a defense plant in East St. Louis. Two years later the toll of a Chicago race riot was nearly as high, with twenty-three black and fifteen white deaths. In these and other incidents of racial violence the pattern was the same. Whites angered by the influx of blacks into their communities would seize upon an incident to rampage through black neighborhoods, killing, burning, and looting, while white police-men turned the other way or actively encouraged the hooligan-ism.

American intervention in World War I also had a significant impact on women. Initially, women supported the war effort in traditional ways. They helped organize war-bond and war-relief drives, conserved food stuffs and war-related materials, sup-ported the Red Cross, and joined the Army nurse corps. But as the scope of the war widened, both government and industry sought to mobilize women workers for service on farms, loading docks, and railway crews, as well as in armaments industries, ma-chine shops, steel and lumber mills, and chemical plants. Many women leaders saw such opportunities as a real breakthrough. "At last, after centuries of disabilities and discrimination," said a speaker at a Women's Trade Union League meeting in 1917, "women are coming into the labor and festival of life on equal terms with men." A black woman who exchanged her job as a live-in servant for work in a factory declared: "I'll never work in nobody's kitchen but my own any more. No indeed, that's the one thing that makes me stick to this job."

Women taking the place of male workers on the Great Northern Railway, Great Falls, Montana, 1918.

In fact, however, war-generated changes in female employment were limited and brief. About a million women participated in "war work," but most of them were young single women already working outside the home. Most returned to their previous jobs once the war ended. In fact, male-dominated unions encouraged women to revert to their stereotypical domestic roles after the war ended. The Central Federated Union of New York baldly insisted that "the same patriotism which induced women to enter industry during the war should induce them to vacate their positions after the war." The anticipated gains of women in the work force failed to materialize. In fact, by 1920 the 8.5 million working women made up a smaller percentage of the labor force than they had in 1910. Still, one tangible result of women's contributions to the war effort was Woodrow Wilson's decision to endorse female suffrage. In the fall of 1918 he told the Senate that giving women the vote was "vital to the winning of the war."

The wartime emergency placed organized labor in a position to make solid advances in employment and wages, despite the rise in consumer prices. A newly created United States Employment Service placed some 4 million workers in war-related jobs. Labor unions benefited from expanded employment, the increased demand for labor, and government policies favorable to collective bargaining. From 1913 to 1918 the AFL membership increased by 37 percent.

The government sought to mobilize more than economic life: the progressive gospel of efficiency suggested mobilizing public opinion as well. On April 14, 1917, eight days after the declaration of war, Wilson established the Committee on Public Information. Its executive director, George Creel, a Denver newsman, sold Wilson on the idea that the best approach to influencing public opinion was "expression, not repression"— propaganda instead of censorship. Creel's purpose was to organize a propaganda machine that would carry word of the Allies' war aims to the people, and above all to the enemy, where it might encourage the forces of moderation. Creel pumped propaganda into Germany that accentuated Wilson's idealism, the size of the American war effort, and offers of an easy peace if the German people would rebel against their government.

CIVIL LIBERTIES The bitter irony in Creel's "expression, not repression" policy was that the one led to the other. By arousing public opinion to such a frenzy, the war effort channeled the zeal of progressivism into grotesque campaigns of "Americanism" and witch-hunting. Wilson had foreseen such consequences. "Once lead this people into war," he told an editor, "and they'll forget there even was such a thing as tolerance." Popular prejudice equated anything German with disloyalty. Schools even dropped German language courses.

While mobs hunted spies and chased rumors, the federal government stalked bigger game, with results often as absurd. The Espionage and Sedition Acts of 1917 and 1918 effectively outlawed criticism of government leaders and war policies. These laws led to more than 1,500 prosecutions and 1,000 convictions. According to one law professor: "It became criminal to advocate heavier taxation instead of bond issues, to state that conscription was unconstitutional though the Supreme Court had not yet held it valid, to say that the sinking of merchant vessels was legal, to urge that a referendum should have preceded our declaration of war, to say that war was contrary to the teachings of Christ."

The impact of these acts fell with most severity upon radicals. In Chicago over 100 leaders of the Industrial Workers of the World went on trial for opposing the war effort. All were found guilty, and the IWW never fully recovered from the blow. The same fate befell the Socialist party. Eugene V. Debs, who had polled over 900,000 votes as the socialist candidate for president in 1912, ardently opposed American intervention, declaring that "I am opposed to every war but one; I am for that war heart and soul, and that is the world-wide revolution." He repeatedly urged men to refuse to serve in the military, even though he knew he could be prosecuted for such remarks under the Espionage Act. "I would a thousand times rather be a free soul in jail than a sycophant and a coward in the streets." He received his wish. Debs was arrested and eventually sentenced to twenty years in prison for encouraging draft resistance. In 1920, still in jail, he polled nearly 1 million votes for president.

In an important decision just after the war the Supreme Court upheld the Espionage and Sedition Acts. *Schenck v. United States* (1919) sustained the conviction of a man for circulating antidraft leaflets among members of the armed forces. In this case Justice Oliver Wendell Holmes observed: "Free speech would not protect a man in falsely shouting fire in a theater, and causing a panic." The act applied where there was "a clear and present danger" that free speech in wartime might create evils Congress had a right to prevent.

"THE DECISIVE POWER"

American troops played little more than a token role in the fighting until the end of 1917 when the Allied position turned desperate. In October the Italian lines collapsed in the face of the Austrian offensive. In November the Bolshevik Revolution overthrew the infant Russian Republic, and four months later Lenin's new Soviet government dropped out of the war. With the Central Powers now free to concentrate their forces on the Western Front, the American war effort became a "race for France" to restore the balance of strength in that arena. By March 1918 American troops had assumed responsibility for only 4.5 miles of the Western front. Anticipating a major German offensive, French Premier Georges Clemenceau appealed to the Americans to accelerate their mobilization: "A terrible blow is imminent," he predicted to an American journalist. "Tell your Americans to come quickly."

THE WESTERN FRONT   The turning point in the western campaign came on July 15, 1918, in the Second Battle of the Marne. On

A gun crew firing on entrenched German positions, 1918.

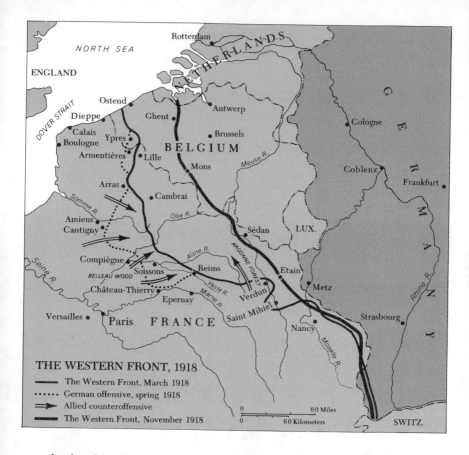

THE WESTERN FRONT, 1918
——— The Western Front, March 1918
•••••• German offensive, spring 1918
⇒ Allied counteroffensive
━━━ The Western Front, November 1918

0 _____ 60 Miles
0 _____ 60 Kilometers

both sides of Rheims the Germans commenced their push against the French lines. Within three days they had shot their bolt, and the Allies, mainly with American troops, took the offensive.

Soon the British, French, and American forces began to roll the German front back into Belgium. On September 12, an army of more than 500,000 staged the first strictly American offensive of the war, aimed at German forces at St. Mihiel. Within three days the Germans had pulled back. Two weeks later the great Meuse-Argonne offensive employed American divisions in a drive toward the rail center at Sedan, which supplied the entire German front. The largest American action of the war, it cost 117,000 American casualties, including 26,000 dead. Through October and early November the battle raged. By the first week of November the Americans were at the outskirts of Sedan and had cut the railroad. All along the front from Sedan to Flanders the Germans were in retreat. "America," wrote a German commander, "thus became the decisive power in the war."

THE FOURTEEN POINTS The approaching end of the war brought the question of war aims to the point of decision. Neither the Allies nor the Central Powers, despite Wilson's prodding, had stated openly what they hoped to gain through the bloodletting. Wilson insisted that the Americans had no selfish ends. "We desire no conquest, no dominion," he stressed in his war message. Unfortunately for his purpose, the Bolsheviks later published copies of secret treaties in which the Allies had promised territorial gains in order to win Italy, Rumania, and Greece to their side. When an Interallied Conference in Paris late in 1917 failed to agree on a statement of aims, Colonel House advised Wilson to formulate his own.

With advice from a panel of experts, Wilson drew up a statement that would comprise the famous Fourteen Points. These he delivered to a joint session of Congress on January 8, 1918, "as the only possible program" for peace. The first five points called for open diplomacy, freedom of the seas, removal of trade barriers, armaments reduction, and an impartial adjustment of colonial claims based on the interests of the populations involved. Most of the remainder called on the Central Powers to evacuate occupied lands and endorsed self-determination for various nationalities. Point 14, the capstone in Wilson's thinking, championed a general association of nations to guarantee the independence and territorial integrity of all countries, great and small.

Wilson sincerely believed in the Fourteen Points, but they also served important political purposes. One of their aims was to keep Russia in the war by a more liberal statement of purposes —a vain hope, as it turned out. Another was to reassure the Allied peoples that they were involved in a noble cause. A third was to drive a wedge between the governments of the Central Powers and their peoples by the offer of a reasonable peace. But the chaos into which central Europe descended in 1918, as both Germany and Austria-Hungary verged on starvation and experienced socialist uprisings, took matters out of Wilson's hands.

On September 29, 1918, German general Erich Ludendorff advised his government to seek the best peace terms possible. On October 3, a new chancellor made the first German overtures for peace on the basis of the Fourteen Points. The Allies, after a month of diplomatic fencing, accepted the Fourteen

Members of the U.S. 369th Infantry Regiment, which was awarded the Croix de Guerre for bravery at the battle of Meuse-Argonne.

Points as a basis of peace but with two significant reservations: they reserved the right to discuss freedom of the seas further, and they demanded reparations for war damages.

Meanwhile German morale plummeted, culminating in a naval mutiny. Germany's allies, Bulgaria, Turkey, and Austria-Hungary, dropped out of the war during the early fall of 1918. On November 9 the kaiser, head of the German Empire, abdicated and a German Republic was proclaimed. Two days later, on November 11, 1918, at 5:00 A.M., an armistice was signed, ceasing the hostilities. Under the armistice the Germans agreed to evacuate occupied territories, pull back behind the Rhine, and surrender their navy, railroad equipment, and other materials. The Germans were assured that the Fourteen Points would be the basis for the peace conference.

INTERVENTION IN RUSSIA   When the war broke out in 1914, Czarist Russia was one of the Allied Powers. By 1917 the Russians had suffered some 5.5 million casualties, there were widespread food and ammunition shortages, and the government was in shambles. It finally succumbed in November 1917 to a revolution led by Vladimir Lenin and his Bolshevik party, which promised the Russian people "Peace, Land, and Bread."

With German troops then deep in Russian territory, and with armies of "White" Russians organizing to resist the Bolsheviks, Lenin concluded a separate peace with the Germans in the Treaty of Brest-Litovsk (March 3, 1918). In an effort to protect stockpiled Allied supplies and encourage the counter-revolutionary Russian "Whites" in prosecuting a civil war against the "Reds," fourteen Allied nations sent troops into eastern Russia. On August 2, 1918, some 8,000 Americans joined the expedition and remained on Russian soil until April 1920.

The Allied intervention in Russia was a colossal failure. The Bolsheviks were able to consolidate their power, defeat the "Whites," and withdraw from World War I. The Russians therefore did not participate in the peace settlement. Even more importantly, Lenin and the Soviets never forgave the West for attempting to thwart their revolution.

THE FIGHT FOR PEACE

WILSON'S ROLE Wilson made a fateful decision to attend in person the Paris peace conference, which convened on January 18, 1919, and would last almost six months. A president had never left the country for so long a time, but doing so dramatized all the more Wilson's desire to ensure his goal of a lasting peace. From one viewpoint it was a shrewd move, for his prestige and determination made a difference in Paris. But he lost touch with developments at home, where his political coalition was already unraveling under the pressures of wartime discontent. Western farmers complained about the government's control of wheat prices, while Eastern businessmen chafed at revenue policies designed, according to the *New York Sun*, "to pay for the war out of taxes raised north of the Mason and Dixon Line." Labor, despite real gains, groused about inflation and the problems of reconversion to a peacetime economy.

In the midterm elections of 1918, Wilson made matters worse with a partisan appeal for a Democratic Congress to ensure support of his foreign policies. Republicans, who for the most part had supported his war measures, took affront. So too did many voters. In elections held a week before the Armistice, the Democrats lost control of both houses of Congress. With an opposition majority in the new Congress, Wilson further weakened his standing by failing to include a single prominent Republican in the American delegation headed for Paris and the treaty negotiations. Humorist Will Rogers joked that Wilson was telling the Republicans, "I tell you what, we will split 50–50. I will go and you fellows can stay." Former President Taft suggested that Wilson's real intention in going to Paris was "to hog the whole show."

When Wilson reached Europe in December 1918, enthusiastic demonstrations greeted him in Paris. At the conference table, however, Wilson had to deal with some tough-minded statesmen. The Paris conference comprised a body of delegates from all countries that had declared war or broken diplomatic relations with Germany. But it was dominated by the Big Four: the prime ministers of Britain, France, and Italy, and the president of the United States. David Lloyd George of England was a gifted politician fresh from electoral victory on the slogan "Hang the Kaiser." Italy's Vittorio Orlando was there to pick up the spoils promised in the secret Treaty of London (1915). French Premier Georges Clemenceau, a stern realist, insisted on severe measures to weaken Germany and guarantee French security. He scorned Wilson's idealism. "God gave us the ten commandments and we broke them," he sneered. "Wilson gave us the Fourteen Points —we shall see."

THE LEAGUE OF NATIONS Wilson carried the point that his cherished League of Nations must come first in the conference and in the treaty. Whatever compromises he might have to make, whatever mistakes might result, Wilson believed that such a permanent peace agency would maintain international stability.

Wilson presided over the commission set up to work out a charter for the League. Article X of the charter, which he called "the heart of the League," pledged members to consult on military and economic sanctions against aggressors. The use of arms would be a last resort. The League structure allowed each member an equal voice in the Assembly; the Big Five (Britain, France, Italy, Japan, and the United States) and four other rotating members would make up the Council.

On February 14, 1919, Wilson delivered the finished draft of the League charter and departed the next day for a month-long visit home. Already he faced rumblings of opposition. Republican senator Henry Cabot Lodge, chairman of the Foreign Relations Committee, claimed that the League was unacceptable "in the form now proposed." His statement of March 4 bore the signatures of thirty-nine Republican senators or senators-elect, more than enough to block ratification.

TERRITORY AND REPARATIONS Back in Paris, Wilson found it politic to seek amendments to meet the objections at home. These provided that any member nation could withdraw from the League on two years' notice, that domestic affairs remained outside League jurisdiction, and that regional understandings like the Monroe Doctrine would remain undisturbed. All these went pretty much without saying, but the French exploited Wilson's discomfort to press for territorial concessions and reparations from Germany. Wilson clashed sharply with Clemenceau, but after the president threatened to leave the conference they agreed that the Allies would occupy a demilitarized German Rhineland for fifteen years, and that the League of Nations would administer Germany's Saar Basin. France could use Saar coal mines for fifteen years, after which the region's voters would determine their status.

In other territorial matters Wilson had to compromise his principle of national self-determination. There was in fact no way to make boundaries correspond to ethnic divisions, because the folk wanderings of centuries had left mixed populations scat-

tered through central Europe. In some areas, moreover, national self-determination yielded to other interests such as trade and defense. The result was a reorganized map of central Europe in which portions of the former Austro-Hungarian Empire became independent, most notably Czechoslovakia and Yugoslavia, and portions became attached to Poland, Rumania, and Italy. Ethnic and nationalist tensions continued, and would contribute to the crisis that culminated in World War II.

The discussion of reparations (financial compensation to the victors) began after the French felt they had already given up a great deal in territorial matters. Britain and France both sought reparations, and the French wanted enough to cripple Germany's economy. Discussions of the issue were among the longest and most bitter at the conference. Despite a pre-Armistice agreement that Germany would be liable only for civilian damages, Clemenceau and Lloyd George proposed reparations for the entire cost of the war. On this point Wilson made perhaps his most fateful concessions. He agreed to a clause in the treaty by which Germany accepted responsibility for starting the war and for its entire costs. The "war guilt" clause offended all Germans and provided a source of persistent bitterness. In 1921 a Reparations Commission estimated that Germany owed the victors $33 billion.

On May 7, 1919, the victorious powers presented the treaty to the German delegates, who returned three weeks later with 443 pages of criticism protesting that the terms violated the Fourteen Points. A few small changes were made, but when the Germans still refused to sign, Marshal Ferdinand Foch prepared to move his army across the Rhine. On June 28 the Germans gave in and signed the treaty at Versailles.

WILSON'S LOSS AT HOME Wilson returned home with the Versailles Treaty on July 8, 1919. Two days later he called on the Senate to accept "this great duty." The force of Wilson's idealism struck deep, and he returned amid a great clamor of popular support. A third of the state legislatures had endorsed the League, as had thirty-three of forty-eight governors.

Lodge, however, harbored serious reservations. He did not wish the United States to withdraw from world affairs, but he doubted that the Paris negotiators could make "mankind suddenly virtuous by a statute or written constitution." A partisan Republican who nourished an intense dislike for Wilson, Lodge relished a fight. "I never thought I could hate a man as I hate Wilson," he confessed. Lodge knew the undercurrents already stirring up opposition to the treaty: the resentment felt by German, Italian, and Irish groups, the disappointment of liberals at Wilson's compromises on reparations and boundaries, the distractions of demobilization and resulting domestic problems, and the revival of isolationism. Lodge's close friend, Theodore Roosevelt, still a popular figure, lambasted the League, noting that he keenly distrusted a "man who cares for other nations as much as his own."

Others agreed. In the Senate a group of "irreconcilables," fourteen Republicans and two Democrats, opposed American participation in the League on any terms. They were mainly western or midwestern progressives who stood on principle. The irreconcilables would be useful to Lodge's purpose, but he belonged to a larger group of "reservationists" who were ready to compromise with Wilson, but insisted on limiting American involvement in the League and its actions. Wilson of course said that he had already amended the covenant to these ends, pointing out that with a veto in the League Council the United States could not be obligated to do anything against its will.

Lodge, who set more store by the old balance of power than by the new idea of collective security, offered a set of amendments, or reservations. Wilson responded by agreeing to interpretive reservations, but to nothing that would reopen the negotiations. He especially opposed the amendments weakening Article X, which provided for collective action by the signatory governments against aggression.

By September, with momentum for the treaty slackening, Wilson decided to go directly to the people. Bold appeals to public opinion had helped get the New Freedom through Congress—why not the treaty? Against the advice of doctors and friends he set forth on a swing through the Midwest to the West Coast, pounding out speeches on his typewriter between stops. In all he traveled 8,000 miles in twenty-two days, gave thirty-two major addresses, refuted his opponents, and voiced dire warnings.

For a while Wilson seemed to be regaining the initiative, but then his body rebelled. On October 2 he suffered a severe stroke and paralysis on his left side, leaving him an invalid for the rest of his life. For more than seven months his protective wife kept him isolated from all but the most essential business. The illness intensified his stubbornness. He might have done better to have stayed in the White House and secured the best compromise possible, but now he refused to yield anything. As he scoffed to an aide, "Let Lodge compromise."

Between November 7 and 19, the Senate adopted fourteen of Lodge's reservations to the Versailles Treaty, most having to do with the League. Wilson refused to make any compromises or concessions. As a result the Wilsonians found themselves thrown into an unlikely combination with irreconcilables who opposed the treaty under any circumstances. The Senate vote on the treaty with reservations was 39 for and 55 against. On the question of taking the treaty without reservations, irreconcilables and reservationists combined to defeat ratification again, with 38 for and 53 against.

In the face of strong public criticism, however, the Senate voted to reconsider. But the stricken Wilson remained adamant: "Either we should enter the league fearlessly . . . or we should retire as gracefully as possible from the great concert of powers by which the world was saved." On March 19, 1920, twenty-one Democrats deserted Wilson and joined the reservationists, but the treaty once again fell short of a two-thirds majority by a vote of 49 yeas and 35 nays. The real winners were the smallest of the three groups in the Senate, neither the Wilsonians nor the reservationists but the irreconcilables.

Wilson still hoped that he could make the next presidential election a "solemn referendum" on the League of Nations. He deluded himself, as Bryan had in 1900, for presidential elections are determined by many issues. When Congress declared the war at an end by joint resolution on May 20, 1920, Wilson vetoed the action; it was not until after he left office, on July 2,

Three Senators Refuse the Lady a Seat. *Americans reacted against the Senate's defeat of the Versailles peace treaty.*

1921, that a joint resolution officially ended the state of war with Germany and Austria-Hungary. Peace treaties with Germany, Austria, and Hungary were ratified on October 18, 1921, but by then Warren Gamaliel Harding was president of the United States.

LURCHING FROM WAR TO PEACE

The Versailles Treaty, for all the time it took in the Senate, was but one issue clamoring for public attention in the turbulent period after the war. On the domestic scene Wilson's leadership was missing. He had been preoccupied by the war and the League, and once broken by his illness became strangely grim and peevish. His rudderless administration floundered through rough waters its last two years.

Demobilization proceeded without plan, indeed without much sense that a plan was needed once the war ended. The War Industries Board closed shop on January 1, 1919, and the sudden cancellation of war contracts left workers and businessmen to cope with reconversion on their own. By April 1919, the armed forces were discharging about 4,000 men daily, and within a year the process was nearly complete.

THE SPANISH FLU Amid the initial confusion of postwar life many Americans confronted a virulent menace that produced far more casualties than the war itself. It became known as the Spanish flu and its contagion spread across the globe. Erupting in the spring of 1918 and lasting a year, the pandemic killed more than 22 million people, twice as many as the number who had died in World War I. In the United States alone the flu accounted for over 500,000 deaths, five times the number of combat deaths in France. "Never before," a writer in *Science* magazine observed in 1919, had there been "a catastrophe at once so sudden, so devastating and so universal."

American servicemen returning from France brought the flu with them, and it raced through the congested army camps and naval bases. At Fort Riley, Kansas, 522 soldiers contracted the virus and were hospitalized during one week in March 1918. Still, no one seemed alarmed, for the flu remained a common if severe ailment. But then the hospitalized men started dying by the dozens, and it became obvious that this was no ordinary flu virus. Most surprising was the fact that this flu epidemic exacted an unusually high toll among young adults rather than among children and the elderly. In fact, 43,000 American servicemen died of influenza in 1918.

By September 1918 the epidemic had spread into the civilian population. In that month alone 10,000 Americans died from the disease. Municipal health officers began fining people for spitting on the sidewalks or for sneezing without a handkerchief. Millions of people began wearing surgical masks to work. Phone booths were locked up, as were other public facilities such as dance halls, pool rooms, and theaters. Even churches and saloons in many communities were declared off limits. Still, the death toll rose. From September 1918 to June 1919 a quarter of the population had contracted the illness.

Yet by the spring of 1919 the pandemic had run its course. It ended as suddenly—and as inexplicably—as it had begun. Although another outbreak occurred in the winter of 1920, the population had grown more resistant to its assaults. No disease, plague, war, famine, or natural catastrophe in world history killed so many people in such a short time.

THE ECONOMIC TRANSITION   An unforeseen postwar boom eased the country over the difficult economic transition from war to peace. The boom fed on markets renewed by pent-up demand and wartime savings, and on overseas trade left open because German and British shippers had been weakened by wartime damage. Both farmers and businessmen benefited. A record $2-billion cotton crop resulted from a happy mix of high prices and high production in 1919. Reports from the southern countryside marveled at the unaccustomed wealth to be found among tenants and sharecroppers, but a drop in farm prices in 1920 and a general business slump in 1921 ended the euphoria.

The problems of postwar readjustment were worsened by general labor unrest. Prices continued to rise steeply after the war, and discontented workers, released from wartime constraints, were more willing to strike for their demands. In 1919, more than 4 million workers went out in thousands of disputes, and after a general strike in Seattle, public opinion began to turn hostile.

The most celebrated postwar labor dispute was the Boston Police Strike, which inadvertently launched a presidential career. On September 9, 1919, most of Boston's police force went out on strike, demanding recognition of their union. Governor Calvin Coolidge mobilized the National Guard to arrest looters and restore order. After four days the strikers were ready to return, but the police commissioner fired them all. When Samuel

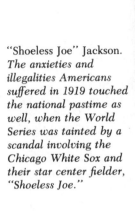

"Shoeless Joe" Jackson. *The anxieties and illegalities Americans suffered in 1919 touched the national pastime as well, when the World Series was tainted by a scandal involving the Chicago White Sox and their star center fielder, "Shoeless Joe."*

Gompers appealed that they be reinstated, Coolidge responded in words that suddenly turned him into a national figure: "There is no right to strike against the public safety by anybody, anywhere, anytime."

RACIAL FRICTION   The summer of 1919 also brought a season of race riots, North and South. Whites invaded the black section of Longview, Texas, in search of a teacher who had allegedly accused a white woman of a liaison with a black man. They burned shops and houses and ran several blacks out of town. A week later in Washington, D.C., reports of attacks on white women aroused white mobs, and for four days gangs of white and black rioters waged race war in the streets until soldiers and driving rains ended the fighting. These were but preliminaries to the Chicago riot of late July in which 38 people were killed and 537 injured. The climactic disorders of the summer occurred in the rural area around Elaine, Arkansas, where black tenant farmers tried to organize a union. According to official reports 5 whites and 25 blacks were killed in the violence, but whites told one reporter in the area that more than 100 blacks died. Altogether twenty-five race riots took place in 1919, and more threatened.

THE RED SCARE   Public reaction to the wave of strikes and riots was influenced by the impact of Russia's Bolshevik Revolution. A minority of radicals thought America's domestic turbulence, like that in Russia, was the first scene in a drama of revolution. A much larger public was persuaded that they might be right. After all, Lenin's tiny faction in Russia had exploited confusion to impose its will. Wartime hysteria against all things German was thus readily transformed into a postwar Red Scare.

Fears of revolution might have remained latent except for the actions of a lunatic fringe. In April 1919 the post office intercepted nearly forty bombs addressed to various prominent citizens. One slipped through and blew off the hands of a Georgia senator's maid. In June another destroyed the front of Attorney-General A. Mitchell Palmer's house in Washington. Such random violence led many Americans to see Red on all sides and to condone attacks on all minorities in retaliation.

Soon the government itself was promoting witch-hunts. Attorney-General Palmer, a Pennsylvania Quaker and once a progressive congressman with pro-labor leanings, harbored a bitter distrust of aliens and a strong desire for the presidency. In June 1919 the Justice Department decided to deport radical aliens, and Palmer set up as the head of the department's new General Intelligence Division the young J. Edgar Hoover, who began to collect an index file on radicals. Raids began on November 7, 1919, when agents swooped down on the Union of Russian Workers in twelve cities. Many of those arrested were deported without a court hearing. On January 2, 1920, police raids in dozens of cities swept up some 6,000 suspects, many taken from their homes without search warrants. About half of those seized were kept in custody. That same month the New York legislature expelled five duly elected Socialist members.

Basking in popular approval, Palmer continued to warn of the Red menace, but like other fads and alarms, the ugly mood of intolerance passed. By the summer of 1920 the Red Scare had begun to evaporate. Communist revolutions in Europe died out, leaving Bolshevism isolated in Russia; bombings tapered off; the strike wave and race riots receded. The attorney-general and his mimics began to seem more threatening to civil liberties than a handful of radicals were to the social order. By September 1920, when a bomb explosion at the corner of Broad and Wall Streets in New York killed thirty-eight people, Americans were ready to take it for what it was, the work of a crazed mind and not the start of a revolution. The Red Scare nevertheless left a lasting mark on American life. Part of its legacy was the continuing crusade for

"100 percent Americanism" and restrictions on immigration. It also left a stigma on labor unions and contributed to the anti-union open-shop campaign—the "American Plan," its sponsors called it. But for many thoughtful Americans the chief residue of the Great War and its disordered aftermath was a profound disillusionment.

FURTHER READING

A thorough overview of events covered in this chapter is Robert H. Ferrell's *Woodrow Wilson and World War I, 1917–1921* (1985).° Different interpretations of why the United States entered the First World War appear in George F. Kennan's *American Diplomacy, 1900–1950* (1951)° and William Appleman Williams's *The Tragedy of American Diplomacy* (rev. ed., 1972).°

A number of scholars concentrate on the neutrality issue. Arthur S. Link, Wilson's biographer, is sympathetic to the ideals of the president in *Woodrow Wilson: Revolution, War, and Peace* (1979).° For a more critical view, see Ross Gregory's *The Origins of American Intervention in the First World War* (1971).°

Edward M. Coffman's *The War to End All Wars: The American Military Experience in World War I* (1968)° is a detailed presentation of America's military involvement. David M. Kennedy's *Over Here: The First World War and American Society* (1980)° surveys the impact of the war on the home front. On the Great Migration, see Neil Fligstein, *Going North: Migration of Blacks and Whites from the South, 1900–1950* (1981) and James R. Grossman, *Land of Hope: Chicago, Black Southerners, and the Great Migration* (1990).° Maurine Weiner Greenwald's *Women, War, and Work* (1980)° and Barbara Steinson's *American Women's Activism in World War I* (1982) discuss the role of women.

The tensions of the immediate postwar years are chronicled in Robert K. Murray's *Red Scare: A Study of National Hysteria, 1919–1920* (1955)° and William Tuttle, Jr.'s *Race Riot: Chicago and the Red Summer of 1919* (1970).° Labor tensions are examined in David E. Brody's *Labor in Crisis: The Steel Strike of 1919* (1987)° and Francis Russell's *A City in Terror: 1919, the Boston Police Strike* (1975).

How American diplomacy fared in the making of peace has received considerable attention. See Arno J. Mayer's *Politics and Diplomacy in Peacemaking: Containment and Counterrevolution at Versailles, 1918–1919* (1967) and N. Gordon Levin, Jr.'s *Woodrow Wilson and World Politics: America's Response to War and Revolution* (1968).° The treaty controversy is handled in Thomas A. Bailey's *Woodrow Wilson and the Great Betrayal* (1945).

° These books are available in paperback editions.

25

SOCIETY AND CULTURE BETWEEN THE WARS

REACTION IN THE TWENTIES

The "Roaring Twenties" were supposedly years of prosperity, frivolity, and loosening morals. They were that for some Americans, yet for others, the period provoked despair and doubt. The war's unprecedented carnage hastened a growing challenge in modern thought to the old values of progress, faith, reason, and optimism. As novelist F. Scott Fitzgerald observed in 1920, "here was a new generation . . . grown up to find all Gods dead, all wars fought, all faiths in man shaken." Such aching disillusionment among what came to be called the "lost generation" was not as widespread as Fitzgerald or others have suggested, but it was a prominent feature of postwar intellectual and social life. Equally visible—and even more potent—was a contrasting mood of defiance against the changes transforming national life. Most Americans remained firmly tied to the old values of church, home, family, farm, and small business, but in the 1920s these ties took on a defensive quality. This mood found expression in a growing tendency to connect American nationalism with nativism, Anglo-Saxon racism, and militant Protestantism.

NATIVISM   The foreign connections of so many radicals strengthened the suspicion that sedition was chiefly foreign-made. That radicalism went hand in hand with crime seemed confirmed by the most celebrated case of the times, which involved two Italian-born anarchists, Nicola Sacco and Bartolomeo Vanzetti. Arrested on May 5, 1920, for a robbery and murder in South Braintree, Massachusetts, they were tried by a judge who privately referred to the defendants as "anarchist bastards." The question of the two men's guilt remains in doubt, and the belief persists that they were sentenced more for their beliefs and their ethnic origins than for any crime they had committed. The case became a great radical and liberal cause of the 1920s, but despite pleas for mercy and world-wide demonstrations on behalf of the two men, Sacco and Vanzetti were sent to the electric chair on August 23, 1927.

The surging postwar nativism brought an end to three centuries of unlimited European immigration dating back to the first colonial settlements. Congress, alarmed at the influx of new foreigners after 1919, passed the Emergency Immigration Act of 1921, which restricted new European arrivals each year to 3 percent of the foreign-born of any nationality as shown in the 1910 census. A new quota law in 1924 reduced the number to 2 percent based on the 1890 census, which included fewer of the "new" immigrants from southern and eastern Europe. This law set a permanent limitation, which became effective in 1929, of slightly over 150,000 immigrants per year based on the "national origins" of the American people as of 1920. In signing the law, President Coolidge pledged: "America must be kept American."

However inexact the quotas, the obvious purpose was to tilt the balance in favor of the old immigration from northern and western Europe, which was assigned about 85 percent of the total. The law completely excluded people from East Asia. Yet it left the gate open to new arrivals from Western Hemisphere countries, so that an ironic consequence was a great increase in the Hispanic Catholic population. People of Latin American descent (chiefly Mexicans, Puerto Ricans, and Cubans) became the fastest growing ethnic minority in the country.

THE KLAN During the postwar years the nativist tradition took on a new form, a revived Ku Klux Klan modeled on the group founded during Reconstruction, but now devoted to "100 percent Americanism" rather than the old Confederacy, and restricted in membership to native-born white Protestants. The new Klan was determined to protect its warped notion of the American way of life not only from Negroes, but also from Roman Catholics, Jews, and immigrants. America was no melting pot, its founder, the failed Methodist minister William J. Simmons, warned: "It is a garbage can! . . . When the hordes of

In 1925 the Ku Klux Klan staged a 40,000-man parade down Pennsylvania Avenue in Washington, D.C.

aliens walk to the ballot box and their votes outnumber yours, then that alien horde has got you by the throat." In going nativist, the Klan had spread far outside the South. Its appeal reached areas as widely scattered as Oregon and Maine, flourishing mainly among the uprooted and insecure native newcomers to the cities and towns. The spooky robes, flaming crosses, kneeling recruits, and occult liturgies brought drama into the dreary routine of a thousand communities.

For all its own exotic ritual, the Klan represented a visceral and vicious reflex against the strange and exotic, against shifting moral standards, the declining influence of churches, and the social permissiveness of cities and colleges. In the Southwest the Klan became more than anything else a moral crusade. "It is going to drive the bootleggers forever out of this land," declared a Texan. "It is going to bring clean moving pictures . . . clean literature . . . break up roadside parking . . . enforce the laws . . .protect homes." All these things it set out to achieve by intimidation and floggings. Estimates of its peak membership, probably inflated, range from 3 million to 8 million, but the Klan's influence decayed as quickly as its numbers grew. For one thing, the Klan suffered from a decline in nativist excitement after passage of the 1924 immigration law. For another, it suffered recurrent factional quarrels and schisms. And perhaps most damaging was the tarnishing of its moral pretensions by the violence it perpetrated.

FUNDAMENTALISM   While the Klan saw a threat mainly in the alien menace, many adherents of the old-time religion saw threats from modernism in the churches: new ideas that the Bible should be studied in the light of modern scholarship (the "higher criticism"), or that it could be reconciled with the theory of evolution. Fearing that such "modernist" notions had infected schools and even pulpits, fundamentalism, grounded in a literal interpretation of the Bible, took on a new militancy.

Among the rural fundamentalist leaders only William Jennings Bryan, the political progressive, had the following, prestige, and eloquence to make the movement a popular crusade. By 1920, Bryan was showing signs of age: paunchy, balding, his face lined with deepening creases, he had lost his commanding physical presence. But he remained as silvery-tongued as ever. In 1921 Bryan sparked a drive for laws to prohibit the teaching of evolution. He denounced Darwin with the same zeal he had once directed against McKinley. Anti-evolution bills began to appear in legislatures in the Midwest and South, but the only victories came in the South—and there were few of those. Some officials took direct action without legislation. Governor Miriam "Ma" Ferguson of Texas ordered textbooks upholding Darwinism eliminated from state schools. "I am a Christian mother . . . " she declared, "and I am not going to let that kind of rot go into Texas schoolbooks."

The climax came in Tennessee, where in 1925 the legislature outlawed the teaching of evolution in public schools and colleges. A young teacher at a high school in Dayton, Tennessee, John T. Scopes, accepted an offer from the American Civil Liberties Union to defend a test case. It soon was a case heard round the world. Before the opening day of the "monkey trial" on July 10, 1925, the streets of Dayton swarmed with "holy rollers," publicity hounds, curiosity-seekers, professional evangelists and professional atheists, hot-dog and soda-pop hucksters, and a miscellany of reporters. The scene struck H. L. Mencken, the prominent Baltimore columnist and satirist, as "genuinely fabulous. I have stored up enough material to last me twenty years."

The two stars of the show were Bryan, who led the prosecution

Clarence Darrow (right) shaking hands with John Scopes at the start of the notorious "monkey trial" in Dayton, Tennessee, 1925.

of Scopes for teaching evolution in violation of Tennessee law, and Clarence Darrow, renowned Chicago trial lawyer and confessed agnostic, who defended Scopes by challenging the anti-evolution law. The trial quickly became a debate between fundamentalism and modernism. When the judge (a practicing evangelist) damaged Darrow's case by ruling out scientific testimony on evolution, most observers assumed the trial was over. But the defense rebounded by calling Bryan as an expert witness on biblical interpretation. Darrow, who had once supported Bryan, now relentlessly entrapped the elderly statesman in literal-minded interpretations and exposed Bryan's ignorance of biblical history and scholarship. Bryan insisted that a "great fish" actually swallowed Jonah, that Joshua literally made the sun stand still, that the world was created in 4004 B.C.—all, according to Darrow, "fool ideas that no intelligent Christian on earth believes." It was a bitter scene. At one point the two men, their patience exhausted in the broiling summer heat, lunged at one another, shaking their fists, leading the judge to adjourn the court.

The next day the testimony ended. The only issue before the court, the judge ruled, was whether Scopes had in fact taught evolution. He was found guilty, but the Tennessee Supreme Court, while upholding the law, overruled the $100 fine on a legal technicality. The chief prosecutor accepted the higher court's advice against "prolonging the life of this bizarre case" and dropped the issue. With more prescience than he knew, Bryan had described the trial as a "duel to the death." A few days after it closed he died suddenly of a heart condition aggravated by heat and fatigue. After Dayton, the fundamentalists—their fury spent for the moment—went dormant.

PROHIBITION Prohibition offered another example of reforming zeal channeled into a drive for moral righteousness and conformity. American moralists had been campaigning against excessive drink since the eighteenth century. Around 1900, however, the leading temperance organizations, the Women's Christian Temperance Union and the Anti-Saloon League, had converted from efforts to reform individuals to a campaign for legal prohibition. By the 1910s the Anti-Saloon League had become one of the most effective pressure groups in American history, mobilizing Protestant churches behind its single-minded battle to elect "dry" candidates.

The 1916 elections finally produced two-thirds majorities in both houses of Congress for a prohibition amendment to the Constitution. Soon the wartime spirit of sacrifice, the need to use grain for food, and wartime hostility to German-American brewers transformed the cause virtually into a test of patriotism. On December 18, 1917, Congress passed and sent to the states the Eighteenth Amendment, which, one year after ratification on January 16, 1919, banned nationwide the manufacture, sale, or transport of intoxicating liquors.

But determined Americans kept drinking. Congress never supplied adequate enforcement, if such were indeed possible given the public thirst, the spotty support of local officials, and the profits to be made in bootlegging. In Detroit the liquor industry was second in size only to automobiles. Speakeasies, hip flasks, and cocktail parties were among the social innovations of the prohibition era, along with increased drinking by women.

It would be too much to say that prohibition gave rise to organized crime, for organized vice, gambling, and extortion had long been practiced, and often tied in with the saloons. But prohibition supplied ruthless and flamboyant criminals, such as Al Capone, an enormous new source of income, while the automobile and the submachine gun provided greater mobility and firepower. Gangland leaders showed remarkable gifts for exploiting loopholes in the law, when they did not simply buy up policemen and politicians.

Capone was by far the most celebrated criminal of the 1920s.

Al Capone in 1929.

In 1927 he pocketed $60 million from his bootlegging, prostitution, and gambling empire, and he took pains to flaunt his wealth as well as his open disregard for legal authorities. The son of Italian immigrants, "Scarface" Capone rapidly worked his way up from nightclub bouncer to syndicated crime boss. He wore expensive suits and silk pajamas, rode in a custom-upholstered and bullet-proof Cadillac, surrounded himself with an entourage of bodyguards, lavishly supported city charities, and always insisted that he was merely providing the public with the goods and services they demanded. "I've given people light pleasures," he once complained, "and all I get is abuse." He neglected to say that he had also bludgeoned to death several conspiring police lieutenants and ordered the execution of dozens of his criminal competitors. Law-enforcement officials began to smash his bootlegging operations in 1929, but were unable to pin anything on Capone until a Treasury agent infiltrated his gang and uncovered evidence to nail him later that year for tax-evasion. He was sentenced to eleven years in prison.

In the light of the illegal activities of Capone and other organized crime members, it came as no great surprise in 1931 when a commission reported evidence that enforcement of prohibition had broken down. Still, the commission voted to extend prohibition, and President Hoover chose to stand by what he called the "experiment, noble in motive and far-reaching in purpose."

SOCIAL TENSIONS

In many ways the defensive temper of the 1920s and the repressive movements to which it gave rise seem the dominant trends of the decade, but they arose in part as reactions to social and intellectual currents that seemed about to sweep America away from its old moorings. During those years a new cosmopolitan, urban America confronted an old provincial, small town and farm America, and cultural conflict reached new levels of tension.

The smart set of the sophisticated metropolis developed an active disdain for the old-fashioned values of the hinterlands. Sinclair Lewis's novel *Main Street* (1920) caricatured the stifling life of the prairie town, depicting a "savorless people, gulping tasteless food, and sitting afterward, coatless and thoughtless, in rocking chairs prickly with inane decorations, listening to mechanical music, saying mechanical things about the excellence of Ford automobiles, and viewing themselves as the greatest race in the world." The banality of small-town life became a pervasive theme in much of the literature of the time, and the heartland responded with counter-images of alien cities infested with vice, crime, corruption, and foreigners.

THE NEW MORALITY   Much of the shock to traditionalists came from the changes in manners and morals evidenced first among young people, and especially on the college campuses. In *This Side of Paradise* (1920), a novel of student life at Princeton, F. Scott Fitzgerald wrote of "the great current American phenomenon, the 'petting party.' " None of the Victorian mothers, he said, "had any idea how casually their daughters were accustomed to be kissed." From such novels, and from magazines and movies, many Americans learned about the cities' wild parties, bathtub gin, promiscuity, and speakeasies.

Sex came to be discussed with surprising frankness. Much of the talk derived from a spreading awareness of Dr. Sigmund Freud, the Viennese father of psychoanalysis. When in 1909 Freud visited Clark University in Massachusetts, he was surprised to find himself so well known "even in prudish America." By the 1920s his ideas had begun to percolate into the popular awareness, and the talk spread in society and literature about libido, inhibitions, Oedipus complexes, sublimation, and repression. The writer Sherwood Anderson recalled in his memoirs:

"Freud had been discovered at the time and all the young intellectuals were busy analyzing each other and everyone they met."

Freudian themes also penetrated popular culture. Radio singers during the 1920s belted out songs with titles like "Hot Lips," "I Need Lovin'," and "Burning Kisses." Movie ads promised kisses on screen "where heart, and soul, and sense in concert move, and the blood is lava, and the pulse is ablaze." The new jazz music percolating in New Orleans, Memphis, and Chicago blended African and European musical traditions into a distinctive brew characterized by improvisation, "blue notes," and polyrhythms. Its leading performers included King Oliver, Jelly Roll Morton, and the great Louis Armstrong. Jazz's syncopated rhythms were immensely popular among young blacks and whites and gave rise to carefree dance steps such as the Charleston and Black Bottom.

In 1919 women's skirts were typically six inches above the ground; by 1927 they were at the knees, and the "flapper," with her bobbed hair, rolled stockings, cigarettes, lipstick, and sensuous dancing, was providing a shocking new model of feminism. The name derived from the way female rebels allowed their galoshes to "flap" about their ankles. Conservative moralists saw the flappers as just another sign of a degenerating society. Others saw in the "new woman" an expression of rugged American individualism. "By sheer force of violence," explained the *New York Times* in 1929, the flapper has "established the feminine right to equal representation in such hitherto masculine fields of endeavor as smoking and drinking, swearing, petting, and upsetting the community peace."

But by 1930 or so the thrill of rebellion was waning; the revolution against Victorian morality had run its course. Its extreme expressions in time aroused doubts that the indulgence of lust equaled liberation. And the much-discussed revolution in morals was also greatly exaggerated. The twenties "roared" for only a small proportion of the population. F. Scott Fitzgerald reminded Americans in 1931 that the "jazz age" was jazzy only for the "upper tenth of [the] nation." Still, some new folkways had come to stay. In the late 1930s a survey disclosed that among college women almost one-half (47 percent) had had sexual relations before marriage, but of these three-quarters had had them only with their future spouses.

THE WOMEN'S MOVEMENT   At the same time that many women were embracing new sexual mores, all women were being liber-

Margaret Sanger (left) *founded the American Birth Control League and in 1916 opened the first public clinic for counseling on contraception.*

ated politically. The suffrage movement, which had been in the doldrums since 1896, sprang back to life in the second decade of the new century. In 1912 Alice Paul, a Quaker social worker, returned from an apprenticeship with the militant suffragists of England, to become chair of the National American Woman Suffrage Association's Congressional Committee. By 1917 Paul and her followers were engaged in picketing the White House and deliberately inviting arrest, after which they went on hunger strikes in prison.

In 1915 Carrie Chapman Catt once again became head of the National Suffrage Association and through her gift for organization spurred the final campaigns for voting rights. For several years President Wilson had evaded the issue of a suffrage amendment, but he supported a plank in the 1916 Democratic platform endorsing state action for woman suffrage. He addressed the National Suffrage Organization that year, and thereafter he worked closely with its leaders. On June 4, 1919, the Senate finally adopted the Nineteenth Amendment by a bare two-thirds majority, and after an agonizing fourteen months, the states finally ratified the women's suffrage amendment on August 21, 1920, the climactic achievement of the Progressive Era.

Women thereafter entered politics in growing numbers, but this did not usher in any basic political change or any sudden release of women from deeply embedded social customs and legal discrimination. The new women voters tended to vote like men on most issues. What was more, the suffrage victory left the broader women's movement prey to a letdown that lasted for a generation. A few years after the triumph, Catt wrote that suffragists were disappointed "because they miss the exaltation, the thrill of expectancy, the vision which stimulated them in the suffrage campaign. They find none of these appeals to their aspiration in the party of their choice."

One group, however, wanted to advance equality yet further. Alice Paul set a new goal, first introduced in Congress in 1923: an Equal Rights Amendment that would eliminate any remaining legal distinctions between the sexes—including the special legislation for the protection of working women put on the books in the previous fifty or so years. Women activists who had been caught up in the social-justice movement considered this a sacrifice of gains painfully accomplished. It would be another fifty years before Alice Paul would see Congress adopt her amendment in 1972; she did not live, however, to see it fall short of ratification.

Alice Paul organized this march for women's suffrage in 1913. Held in Washington, D.C., the march preceded Wilson's inauguration by one day.

The sharp increase in the number of women in the workforce during World War I proved ephemeral, but in the longer view a steady increase in the numbers of employed women occurred in the 1920s and, surprisingly, continued through the depression decade of the 1930s. Still these women remained concentrated in traditional occupations: domestics, office workers, teachers, clerks, salespeople, dressmakers, milliners, and seamstresses. In manufacturing they were found mainly in related work, such as textiles or garment making. On the eve of World War II women's work was little more diversified than it had been at the turn of the century, but by 1940 it would be on the eve of a great transformation.

THE "NEW NEGRO" The discriminations that have befallen blacks and women display many parallels, and the loosening of restraints for both have frequently coincided. The most significant development in African-American life during these years was known as the Great Migration. The movement of blacks from the South northward began in 1915–1916 when war industries were depleting the ranks of common labor leaving openings for blacks. Competition for jobs from foreign immigrants was prevented first by the war and then by postwar legal restrictions on immigration. Altogether, between 1910 and 1920 the Southeast lost some 323,000 blacks, or 5 percent of the 1920 native black population, and by 1930 had lost another 615,000 or 8 percent of the native black population. With the migration north, a slow but steady growth in black political influence set in. African Americans were freer to speak and act in a northern setting, and they gained political leverage by concentrating in large cities located in states with many electoral votes.

Along with political activity came a bristling spirit of protest among blacks, a spirit that received cultural expression in a literary and artistic movement labeled the "Harlem Renaissance." Claude McKay, a Jamaican immigrant, was the first significant writer of the movement, which sought to rediscover black folk culture. Poems collected in McKay's *Harlem Shadows* (1922) expressed defiance in such titles as "If We Must Die" and "To the White Fiends." Other emergent black writers included Langston Hughes, Zora Neale Hurston, Countee Cullen, and James Weldon Johnson. Perhaps the greatest single creation of the time was Jean Toomer's novel *Cane*, which portrayed the lives of simple blacks in rural Georgia and the sophisticated inhabitants of Washington's African-American middle class.

The spirit of the "New Negro" also found outlet in what came

Marcus Garvey, founder of the
United Negro Improvement
Association and a leading spokesman for "Negro nationalism"
in the 1920s.

to be called "Negro nationalism," which exalted blackness, black cultural expression, and, at its most extreme, black exclusiveness. The leading spokesman for such views was the flamboyant Marcus Garvey, who in 1916 brought to New York the United Negro Improvement Association, which he had started in his native Jamaica two years before. His organization grew rapidly under the strains of the postwar years. Racial bias, he charged, was so ingrained in whites that it was futile to appeal to their sense of justice. The only hope for blacks was to flee America and build their own republic in Africa. Garvey, the "Black Moses," quickly enlisted half a million members in his association, and claimed as many as 6 million by 1923. As one of his followers remarked, Garvey gave "my people backbone where they had wishbone." At the peak of his popularity, however, Garvey was convicted of mail fraud. He was imprisoned in 1925 and remained so until President Coolidge pardoned and deported him to Jamaica in 1927. Garvey died in obscurity in London in 1940, but the memory of his movement kept alive an undercurrent of racial pride that would reemerge later under the slogan of "black power."

Even more influential in promoting black rights was a new organization, the National Association for the Advancement of Colored People (NAACP). Founded in 1910, it was led by northern white liberals and black leaders such as W. E. B. Du Bois.

Although most progressives shunned the NAACP, the new group took seriously the progressive idea that the solution to social problems began with educating the people, and it planned an active press bureau to accomplish this. Its main strategy, however, was legal action aimed at enforcing the Fourteenth and Fifteenth Amendments. One early victory came with *Guinn v. United States* (1915), in which the Supreme Court struck down Oklahoma's grandfather clause, which had been part of the state's attempt to disenfranchise blacks.

In 1919 the NAACP launched a campaign against lynching, still a common atrocity in many parts of the country. An anti-lynching bill making mob murder a federal offense passed the House in 1922, but lost to a filibuster by southern senators. Yet the continued agitation of the issue did help reduce lynchings, which fell off to a third of what they had been the previous decade.

During the 1930s, the NAACP's legal campaign gathered momentum. An important precedent arose from the celebrated Scottsboro case of 1931, in which nine black youths were convicted of raping two young white women while riding a freight train in Alabama. The Supreme Court overturned their conviction in *Norris v. Alabama* (1935), because systematic exclusion of blacks from Alabama juries had denied the defendants equal protection of the law—a principle that had significant and widespread impact on state courts.

THE CULTURE OF MODERNISM

Changes in the realms of science and social thought were perhaps even more dramatic than those affecting women and blacks in the interwar years. As the twentieth century advanced, the easy faith in progress and reform expressed by progressives fell victim to a series of frustrations and disasters, including the Great War, the failure of the League of Nations, Woodrow Wilson's physical and political collapse, and the failure of prohibition. Deeper still, startling new findings in physics further shook prevailing assumptions of order and certainty.

SCIENCE AND SOCIAL THOUGHT Physicists of the early twentieth century altered the image of the cosmos in ways that seemed almost a conspiracy against common sense. The conventional wisdom since Sir Isaac Newton held the universe to be governed by laws which the scientific method could ultimately uncover. A world of such certain order bolstered hopes of infinite progress in human knowledge.

This world of order and certainty had begun to fray at the turn of the century when Albert Einstein, a young German physicist working in the Swiss patent office, concluded that space, time, and mass were not absolutes but relative to the location and motion of the observer. Isaac Newton's eighteenth-century mechanics, according to Einstein's relativity theories, worked well enough at relatively slow speeds, but the more nearly one approached the velocity of light (about 186,000 miles per second) the more all measuring devices would change accordingly, so that yardsticks would become shorter, clocks and heartbeats would slow down, even the aging process would ebb.

Certainty dissolved the farther one reached out into the universe, and the farther one reached down into the minute world of the atom. The discovery of radioactivity in the 1890s showed that atoms were not irreducible units of matter but that some of them emitted particles of energy. This meant, Einstein noted, that mass and energy were not separate phenomena but interchangeable. Meanwhile Max Planck in Berlin had discovered that electromagnetic emissions of energy, whether as electricity or light, came in little bundles which he called quanta. The development of quantum theory suggested that atoms were far more complex than once believed and, as German physicist Werner Heisenberg stated in his uncertainty principle in 1927, ultimately indescribable. One could never know both the position and the velocity of an electron, Heisenberg concluded, because the very process of observation would inevitably affect the behavior of the particle, altering its position and velocity.

Heisenberg's thesis meant that human knowledge had limits. "The physicist thus finds himself in a world from which the bottom has dropped clean out," a Harvard mathematician wrote in 1929. He had to "give up his most cherished convictions and faith. The world is not a world of reason, understandable by the intellect of man, but as we penetrate ever deeper, the very law of cause and effect, which we had thought to be a formula to which we could force God Himself to subscribe, ceases to have any meaning." Hard for the public to grasp, such findings proved too troubling even for Einstein, who spent much of the rest of his life in quest of an explanation that would unify the relativity and quantum theories. "I shall never believe that God plays dice with the world," Einstein asserted.

Just as Enlightenment thinkers drew on Newton's laws of gravitation two centuries before to formulate their views on the laws governing society, the ideas of relativity and uncertainty in the twentieth century provoked people to deny the relevance of absolute values in any sphere of society, which undermined the concepts of personal responsibility and absolute standards. Anthropologists aided the process by transforming the word "culture," which had before meant refinement, into a term for the whole system of ideas, folkways, and institutions within which any group lived. Even the most primitive groups had cultures and, all things being relative, one culture should not impose its value judgments on another. Two anthropologists, Ruth Benedict and Margaret Mead, were especially effective in spreading this viewpoint.

MODERNIST LITERATURE   The cluster of scientific ideas associated with Darwin and Einstein helped inspire a revolution in the minds of many intellectuals and creative artists during the early twentieth century. Some observers now count this new modernism as ranking with the Enlightenment or Romanticism in its sweep and significance. The modernist movement sought to explore and even celebrate the irrational as an essential part of human nature. It viewed the universe not as rational and orderly but as turbulent and unpredictable, and it embraced uncertainty as a desirable condition. The early twentieth-century modernists also rejected the genteel tradition's restrained, polite, and detached perspective. In the various arts such concerns resulted in abstract painting, which sought to represent the artist's inner mood rather than an external object, atonal music, free verse in poetry, stream-of-consciousness narrative, and interior monologues in stories and novels. Writers dramatized their separation from the past. They showed an intense concern with new forms in language in an effort to violate expectations and shock their audiences.

This search for the new did not begin with World War I; it emerged around the turn of the century and was centered in America's first major artistic bohemias: Chicago's South Side and New York's Greenwich Village. In 1913 the Armory Show in New York, which then toured Chicago, Philadelphia, and Boston, shocked traditionalists with its display of the latest in experimental and nonrepresentational art, including Pablo Picasso's Cubist work.

By 1914, "Everyone was cooking up some sort of revolution," recalled one literary editor. To be "modern," to attack conventional art and morality, was the animating purpose of the ongoing "little renaissance" in the arts. In Chicago, Harriet Monroe provided a sounding board for modern experimentalists in *Poetry: A Magazine of Verse*. A poet of some local renown, and already past fifty when she started *Poetry* in 1912, she found her vocation as patron to a renaissance. Within a few years she had spotlighted a dozen and more major figures: Carl Sandburg, Vachel Lindsay, Elinor Wylie, Edna St. Vincent Millay, Robinson Jeffers, and the imagists Amy Lowell, Conrad Aiken, and William Carlos Williams. To her eternal regret Harriet Monroe "missed" Edgar Lee Masters, a Chicago lawyer and author of *Spoon River Anthology* (1915), a collection of poetic epitaphs for midwestern types. She also missed Sherwood Anderson, whose stories of midwestern characters in *Winesburg, Ohio* (1919), offered a prose parallel to *Spoon River*.

The chief American prophets of modernism lived neither in Chicago nor New York, but were emigrés in Europe: Ezra Pound and T. S. Eliot in London, and Gertrude Stein in Paris. All were deeply concerned with creating new and often difficult styles of expression. Pound, as foreign editor for *Poetry*, served as the conduit through which many American poets achieved publication in America and Britain. At the same time he became the leader of the Imagist movement, a revolt against the ornamental verbosity of Victorian poetry in favor of the concrete image.

Pound's brilliant protégé was the St. Louis–born, Harvard graduate, T. S. Eliot, who in 1915 contributed to *Poetry* his first major poem, "The Love Song of J. Alfred Prufrock," the musings of an ineffectual man who "after tea and cakes and ices" could never find "the strength to force the moment to its crisis." Eliot went to Oxford in 1913 and soon decided to make England his home and poetry his career. Skeptical of the Western notion of social progress through scientific advance and horrified by the slaughter of the Great War, he rejected the nineteenth century's "cheerfulness, optimism, and hopefulness." He rejected as well the traditional notion of poetry as the representation of a beautiful world. The modern poet, he insisted, must "be able to see beneath both beauty and ugliness; to see the boredom, and the horror and the glory." Eliot's "The Waste Land" (1922) made few concessions to readers in its obscure allusions, its juxtaposition of unexpected metaphors, its deep sense of postwar disillusionment and melancholy, and its suggestion of a burnt-out civilization. But it became for an alienated younger generation almost the touchstone of the modern temper.

Gertrude Stein, another voluntary exile, settled in Paris in 1903, and became an early champion and collector of modern art. Long regarded as no more than the literary eccentric who wrote "Rose is a rose is a rose is a rose," she would later be recognized as one of the chief originators of the modernist prose style. But she was long known chiefly through her influence on such 1920s expatriates as Sherwood Anderson and Ernest Hemingway, whom she told: "All of you young people who served in the war, you are the lost generation."

The earliest chronicler of that generation, F. Scott Fitzgerald, blazed up brilliantly and then quickly flickered out, like all the tinseled, carefree, sad young people of his novels. Successful and famous at age twenty-four with *This Side of Paradise* (1920), he, along with his wife, Zelda, experienced and depicted the "greatest, gaudiest spree in history," and then both had their crack-up during the Great Depression. What gave depth to the best of his work was what a character in *The Great Gatsby* (1925), his finest novel, called "a sense of the fundamental decencies" amid all the surface gaiety—and almost always a sense of impending doom.

Hemingway suffered even more from a psychic wound inflicted by an uncaring world. For him literature was a means of defense, a way to strike back, and in the process find a meaning

Frankie "Half Pint" Jackson and His Band at the Sunset Cafe, Chicago, 1920s. *Jazz emerged during this period as an especially American expression of the modernist spirit. Black artists bent musical conventions to give fuller reign to improvisation.*

for himself rather than accept one imposed by society. Hemingway's first novel, *The Sun Also Rises* (1926), pictures a desperate search for life by a group of American expatriates, chasing about frantically from the bistros of Paris to the bullrings of Spain. Young Jake Barnes, emasculated by a war wound, explains his postwar outlook toward the world: "I did not care what it was all about. All I wanted to know was how to live in it." Hemingway's second novel, *A Farewell to Arms* (1929), is based on his own experience as a volunteer in the ambulance corps in northern Italy during World War I. It pursues the love affair of a driver and a nurse who abandon the war for Switzerland, where the young woman dies in childbirth. Hundreds of writers tried to imitate Hemingway's terse style, but few had his gift, which lay less in what he had to say than in the way he said it.

CULTURE IN THE THIRTIES

THE RETURN OF SOCIAL SIGNIFICANCE   In the aftermath of World War I, many of the most prominent young writers and intellectuals turned inward, divorcing themselves from societal concerns. As one of them explained in 1919, the "great problems of the world—social, political, economic, theological—do not concern me in the slightest. . . . What concerns me alone is myself, and the interests of a few close friends." In view of the celebrated—if exaggerated—alienation of writers caught in the materialistic world of the 1920s, one might have expected the onset of the Great Depression in 1929 to deepen the despair. Instead it brought a renewed sense of militancy and affirmation, as if people could no longer afford the art-for-art's-sake affectations of the 1920s. Said one writer early in 1932: "I enjoy the period thoroughly. The breakdown of our cult of business success and optimism, the miraculous disappearance of our famous American complacency, all this is having a tonic effect."

In the early 1930s the "tonic effect" of commitment sometimes took the form of allegiance to revolution. For a time leftist politics and rhetoric made significant inroads in literary circles. By the summer of 1932 even the "golden boy" of the lost generation, F. Scott Fitzgerald, was saying that "to bring on the revolution, it may be necessary to work within the Communist party." But few remained Party followers for long. Writers being a notoriously independent lot, most rebelled at demands to hew to a shifting Party line. And many abandoned Communism upon

A migrant family on their way west to California.

learning that Soviet leader Joseph Stalin practiced tyranny and terror more efficient and bloody than anything under the czars.

Among the writers who addressed themes of immediate social significance two novelists deserve special notice: John Steinbeck and Richard Wright. The single piece of fiction that best captured the ordeal of the depression, Steinbeck's *The Grapes of Wrath* (1939), avoided political formula to treat workers as people. Steinbeck had taken the trouble to travel with displaced "Okies" driven from the Oklahoma Dust Bowl by bankers and farm combines to pursue the illusion of jobs in the fields of California's Central Valley. The story focused on the Joad family as they made their painful journey west from Oklahoma. Met chiefly with contempt and rejection, Ma Joad strove to keep hope alive and at the end, even as the family was breaking up under the pressure, she grasped at a broader loyalty: "Use 'ta be the fambly was fust. It ain't so now. It's anybody. Worse off we get, the more we got to do."

Perhaps the supreme genius among the new young novelists emerging in the thirties was Richard Wright, a black writer born on a plantation near Natchez, Mississippi. The son of a matriarch whose husband deserted the family, Wright grew up in the course of moving from town to town, ended his formal schooling with the ninth grade (as valedictorian of his class), worked in Memphis, and greedily devoured books he borrowed on a white friend's library card, all the while saving up to go north. In Chi-

Richard Wright, author of Native Son *and* Black Boy.

cago, where he arrived on the eve of the depression, the Federal Writers' Project gave him a chance to perfect his talent, and his period as a Communist from 1934 to 1944 gave him an intellectual framework, Marxism, which did not, however, overpower his fierce independence. His autobiographical *Black Boy* (1945) revealed in its rebellion against racial injustice his ties to the South, for, he wrote, "there had been slowly instilled into my personality and consciousness, black though I was, the culture of the South."

Native Son (1940), Wright's masterpiece, was set in the Chicago he had come to know before moving on to New York. It was the story of Bigger Thomas, a product of the black ghetto, a man hemmed in and finally impelled to murder by forces beyond his control. "They wouldn't let me live and I killed," he says unrepentently at the end. Somehow Wright managed to sublimate into literary power his bitterness and rage at what he called "The Ethics of Living Jim Crow."

THE SOUTHERN RENAISSANCE In different ways southern whites had shared the same tragic past as the black writers. Out of the memory and the consciousness of change the best writers among them nurtured a renaissance that burgeoned into one of the most notable literary growths since the flowering of New England a century before. There was little reason to expect it in 1920 when H. L. Mencken published his essay "The Sahara of the Bozart," which described the southern cultural landscape as a barren wasteland: "It would be impossible in all history to match so complete a drying-up of civilization."

What Mencken's essay had missed was that the South had reached a historical watershed. It stood between two worlds: the dying world of tradition and the modern, commercial world struggling to be born. The resultant conflict of values, felt more intensely in the South than in the North, aroused the Ku Klux Klan and fundamentalist furies, but had quite another effect on many of the South's most promising young writers. With remarkable speed after 1920, Mencken's cultural Sahara turned into a forest populated with nests of singing birds. "One may reasonably argue," wrote one critic in 1930, "that the South is the literary land of promise today."

Just the previous year two vital figures had emerged: Thomas Wolfe, with *Look Homeward, Angel,* and William Faulkner, with *Sartoris* and *The Sound and the Fury.* Fame rushed in first on Wolfe and his native Asheville, North Carolina, which became a classic example of the scandalized community. "Against the Victorian morality and the Bourbon aristocracy of the South," Wolfe had "turned in all his fury," a friend wrote. The reaction was a common response to the works of the southern renaissance, created by authors who had outgrown their "provincial" hometowns and looked back from new perspectives acquired in travel and education.

Yet Wolfe never completely severed his roots in the South. *Look Homeward, Angel,* his first novel, remained his most successful; it was the lyrical and searching biography of Eugene Gant's (actually Wolfe's) youth in Altamont (Asheville) and his college days in Pulpit Hill (Chapel Hill). It established him as "the giant among American writers of sensitive youth fiction."

Faulkner's achievement, more than Wolfe's, was rooted in the world that produced him. Born and raised near Oxford, Mississippi, Faulkner passed the postwar decade in, what seemed to fellow townsmen, an aimless drifting. He briefly attended classes at the University of Mississippi, worked at odd jobs, went to New Orleans, shipped out briefly for Europe, and after knocking around the Gulf Coast, returned to Oxford.

There, in writing *Sartoris* (1929), he began to discover that his "own little postage stamp of native soil was worth writing about" and that he "would never live long enough to exhaust it." In this book a postwar wasteland stood out the more starkly against a legend of past glory in the Sartoris family. With *Sartoris* and the creation of his mythical land of Yoknapatawpha, Faulkner kindled a blaze of creative energy. Next, as he put it, he wrote his

William Faulkner.

gut into *The Sound and the Fury*, again the story of a demoralized family. Faulkner's creative frenzy continued through the writing of *As I Lay Dying* (1930) and *Light in August* (1932). He began to fill in the early history of Yoknapatawpha and the conflict between tradition and the modern world with *Absalom! Absalom!* (1936).

Most critics at first missed Faulkner's obscure and rankling genius. Some viewed him as the leader in a "cult of cruelty." Others attacked his obscure prose, the slow unfolding of meaning, convoluted syntax, and runaway rhetoric of his novels. Not until the mid-twentieth century did critics generally begin to grasp that Faulkner, in composing his mythical history of Yoknapatawpha, had become also—certainly among Americans—the most skillful creator of modernist style in the novel during the first half of the twentieth century.

THE REDISCOVERY OF AMERICA In the 1930s America experienced what *Fortune* magazine called "a sort of cultural revolution." Americans learned that, like it or not, they had a culture and had had one all along—it had simply been overlooked. Now Americans tried to make up for lost time by tracking the culture down, recording, restoring, and celebrating it. They became intrigued with American art of all kinds, and particularly that least influenced by Europe: primitive, folk, or as it was called most often, "popular" art. American writers and artists turned their attention to their homeland. And so the two decades of the 1920s and 1930s, times of unusually creative vitality, began with disillusionment and flight to Europe, but ended with the rediscovery of America.

FURTHER READING

For a standard survey of the interwar period, start with William E. Leuchtenburg's *The Perils of Prosperity, 1914–1932* (1958).° The best single introduction to the culture of the 1920s is Loren Baritz's *The Culture of the Twenties* (1970).°

John Higham's *Strangers in the Land: Patterns of American Nativism, 1860-1925* (1955)° details the story of immigration restriction. For analysis of the more extreme nativist measures, see David M. Chalmers's *Hooded Americanism: The History of the Ku Klux Klan* (1987).° On Prohibition see Norman H. Clark's *Deliver Us from Evil* (1976).° Humbert S. Nelli's *The Business of Crime* (1976)° examines those who profited from bootlegging, including Al Capone. The best treatment of the Sacco and Vanzetti case is Paul Avrich's *Sacco and Vanzetti: The Anarchist Background* (1991).°

Other social groups also receive scholarly treatment. See Charles F. Kellogg's *NAACP* (1967)° for his analysis of the pioneering court cases against racial discrimination. Nathan I. Huggins's *Harlem Renaissance* (1971)° and Houston Baker's *Modernism and the Harlem Renaissance* (1987)° cover the cultural impact of the Great Migration. See also Judith Stein's *The World of Marcus Garvey* (1991).° Women's suffrage is treated extensively in Eleanor Flexner's *Century of Struggle: The Women's Rights Movement in the United States* (rev. ed., 1975).° Paula S. Fass's *The Damned and the Beautiful: American Youth in the 1920s* (1977)° describes the social attitudes of youth in general.

Stuart Ewen looks at the effect of mass advertising in *Captains of Consciousness* (1976).° Motion pictures are the subject of Robert Sklar's *Movie-Made America* (1976)° and Lary May's *Screening out the Past* (1980).° Much of the theoretical basis for the chapter's discussion of "modernism" comes from Daniel J. Singal's *The War Within: From Victorian to Modernist Thought in the South, 1919–1945* (1982).° Alfred Kazin's *On Native Grounds* (1942)° is an excellent introduction to the literature of the period.

° These books are available in paperback editions.

26

REPUBLICAN RESURGENCE AND DECLINE, 1920–1932

PROGRESSIVISM TRANSFORMED

The progressive coalition that reelected Woodrow Wilson in 1916 proved to be quite fragile, and by 1920 it had fragmented. It began to show signs of fissure during the war when radicals and others grew disaffected with America's involvement. After the war Wilson's support continued to erode. Organized labor resented the administration's unsympathetic attitude toward the strikes of 1919–1920, and farmers complained that wartime price controls had discriminated against them. Some intellectuals grew disillusioned with mass democracy because of popular support for prohibition and religious fundamentalism. Many among the middle class, meanwhile, lost interest in political activism and channeled their energies into building a new business civilization based upon mass production and mass consumption, greater leisure, and the introduction of labor-saving electrical appliances in the home. Moreover, progressivism's final triumphs at the national level were already pretty much foregone conclusions before the war's end: the Eighteenth Amendment, which imposed national prohibition, was ratified in 1919, and the Nineteenth Amendment, which extended women's suffrage to the entire country, became law a year later.

Progressivism, however, did not completely disappear in the 1920s. Reformers dominated Congress during much of the decade even while the White House was in conservative hands. The progressive impulse for "good government" and extended public services remained strong, especially at the state and local levels, where movements for good roads, education, public health, and social welfare all gained momentum during the decade. The progressive impulse for reform, however, was largely transformed into the drive for moral righteousness and conformity led by the Ku Klux Klan and the fundamentalist and prohibitionist movements.

"NORMALCY"

HARDING'S ELECTION   Amid the postwar confusion, another presidential season approached. Most Americans now seemed weary of idealistic crusades and suspicious of leaders sounding the trumpet of reform. In speaking of Wilson's fall from favor, one observer explained: "The moralist unquestionably secures wide popular support—but he also wearies his audience." Wilson himself recognized this fact. "It is only once in a generation," he remarked, "that a people can be lifted above material things. That is why conservative government is in the saddle two-thirds of the time."

When the Republicans met in Chicago in June 1920, the Old Guard was ready to reclaim its conservative heritage. The regulars found their man in Ohio senator Warren Gamaliel Harding, who had set the tone of his campaign when he told a Boston audience: "America's present need is not heroics, but healing; not nostrums, but normalcy; not revolution, but restoration; not agitation, but adjustment; not surgery, but serenity; not the dramatic, but the dispassionate; not experiment, but equipoise, not submergence in internationality, but sustainment in triumphant nationality." His prose was clumsy, but Harding caught the mood of the times—a longing for "normalcy" and contentment with the status quo. So too did his running mate, Massachusetts governor Calvin Coolidge, who had gained national attention with his stern opposition to the Boston Police Strike.

Harding's promise of a "return to normalcy" reflected his own conservative values and folksy personality. The son of an Ohio farmer, he described himself as not an intellectual or a crusader but "just a plain fellow" who was "old-fashioned and even reactionary in matters of faith and morals." But such a description suggests a certain puritan regimen that Harding never practiced. Far from being an old-fashioned moralist in his personal life, he drank bootleg liquor in the midst of Prohibition, smoked and chewed tobacco, relished weekly poker games, and actively

Warren Harding "bloviating" on the stump.

sought sexual satisfaction from women other than his austere and matronly wife, whom he called "Duchess." But the general public was unaware of Harding's self-indulgence and weak character. Instead the voters saw him as a handsome, charming, gregarious, and loveable politician. A man of self-confessed limitations in vision, leadership, and intellectual power, he once admitted that "I cannot hope to be one of the great presidents, but perhaps I may be remembered as one of the best loved."

The Democrats hoped that Harding would not be president at all. James Cox, former newsman and former governor of Ohio, won the nomination of an increasingly fragmented party on the forty-fourth ballot. For vice-president the convention named Franklin D. Roosevelt, who as assistant secretary of the navy occupied the same position his Republican cousin Teddy had held before him.

The Democrats' fate was sealed by the breakup of the Wilsonian coalition and the conservative postwar mood. In the words of journalist William Allen White, Americans in 1920 were "tired of issues, sick at heart of ideals, and weary of being noble." The country voted overwhelmingly for Harding's promised "return to normalcy." Harding got 16 million votes to 9 million for Cox, who carried no state outside the Solid South. In the minority again, the Democrats had returned to normalcy too.

EARLY APPOINTMENTS AND POLICY   Harding in office had much in common with Ulysses Grant. His cabinet, like Grant's, mixed some of the best men in the party with some of the worst. Charles Evans Hughes became a distinguished secretary of state. Herbert Hoover in the Commerce Department, Andrew W. Mellon in Treasury, and Henry A. Wallace in Agriculture were also efficient and forceful figures. Of the others, Secretary of the Interior Albert B. Fall landed in prison and Attorney-General Harry M. Daugherty only narrowly escaped prosecution. Many lesser offices went to members of the soon notorious "Ohio Gang," headed by Daugherty, a group of Harding's old Ohio friends with whom the president met regularly for poker games lubricated by illegal liquor.

Until he became president, Harding had loved politics. He was the complete party hack, "bloviating" (a verb of his own making, which meant speaking with gaseous eloquence) on the stump, jollying it up in the clubhouse and cloakroom, hobnobbing with the great and near-great in Washington. As president, however, Harding was simply in over his head, and self-doubt overwhelmed him. "I don't think I'm big enough for the Presidency," he confided to a friend. Alice Roosevelt Longworth, Theodore Roosevelt's oldest daughter, recognized Harding's limitations. "Harding wasn't a bad man," she noted. "He was just a slob."

Harding and his friends set about dismantling or neutralizing as many of the social and economic components of progressivism as they could. Harding's four appointments to the Supreme Court were all conservatives, including Chief Justice William Howard Taft, who announced that he had been "appointed to reverse a few decisions." During the 1920s the Taft Court struck down a federal child-labor law and a minimum wage law for women, issued numerous injunctions against striking unions, and passed rulings limiting the powers of federal regulatory agencies.

The Harding administration established a pro-business tone reminiscent of the McKinley White House. Big business, whipping-boy of many progressives, had won renewed respectability by expanding production during the war and by initiating a "New Era" of prosperity after the postwar slump in 1921. To sustain economic growth, Secretary of the Treasury Mellon vigorously promoted a policy of spending cuts and tax reduction. Mellon insisted that tax cuts should go mainly to the rich, on the Hamiltonian principle that wealth in the hands of the few would promote the general welfare through increased capital investment.

In Congress a group of western Republicans and southern Democrats fought a dogged battle to preserve the progressive principle built into wartime taxes, but Mellon, in office through the 1920s, eventually won out. At his behest Congress first repealed the wartime excess-profits tax and lowered the maximum rate on personal income from 65 to 50 percent. Subsequent revenue acts eventually lowered the maximum rate to 20 percent. The Revenue Act of 1926 extended further benefits to high-income groups by lowering estate taxes and repealing the gift tax. Much of the money released to wealthy people by these acts seems unfortunately to have fueled the speculative excess of the late 1920s as much as it boosted consumer spending and entrepreneurial activity. Mellon, however, did balance the federal budget for a time. Governmental expenditures fell, as did the national debt.

In addition to tax cuts, Mellon favored the time-honored Republican policy of high tariffs. So too did spokesmen for several emerging new industries. Wartime innovations in chemical and metal processing revived the argument for protection of infant industries from foreign competition. The Fordney-McCumber Tariff of 1922 dramatically increased rates on chemical and metal products as a safeguard against the revival of German industries that had previously commanded the field. To please the farmers, the new act further extended the duties on imported farm products.

Higher tariffs, however, had unexpected consequences. During the war the United States had been transformed from a debtor to a creditor nation. In former years foreign capital had flowed into the United States, playing an important role in fueling economic expansion. But the private and public credits given the Allies during the war had reversed the pattern. Mellon now insisted that the European powers must repay all that they had borrowed during the war. The tariff walls erected against imports, however, made it all the harder for other nations to sell in the United States and thereby acquire the dollars with which to repay their war debts. For nearly a decade further extensions of American loans and investments sent more dollars abroad, postponing the reckoning.

Rounding out the Republican economic program was a more lenient attitude toward government regulation of corporations. Neither Harding nor his successor Coolidge could dissolve the regulatory agencies created by progressivism, but by naming commissioners who looked askance at regulation, they rendered these agencies ineffective. Harding named advocates of big business to the Interstate Commerce Commission, the Federal Reserve Board, and the Federal Trade Commission. One senator characterized the new appointments as "the nullification of federal law by a process of boring from within." Senator Henry Cabot Lodge agreed, noting: "We have torn up Wilsonism by the roots."

A CORRUPT ADMINISTRATION Republican conservatives such as Lodge, Mellon, Coolidge, and Hoover were at least operating out of philosophical conviction. The crass members of Harding's "Ohio Gang," however, used White House connections to line their own pockets. In 1923 Harding learned that the head of the Veterans Bureau was systematically looting medical and hospital supplies. The corrupt administrator resigned and fled to Europe. Harding's general counsel then committed suicide. Not long afterward a close crony of Attorney-General Daugherty also shot himself. The man held no federal appointment, but he had set up an office in the Justice Department from which he peddled influence for a fee. Daugherty himself was implicated in the fraudulent handling of German assets seized after the war. When this was discovered, he refused to testify on the ground that he might incriminate himself. Twice brought to court, he was never indicted; the lack of evidence possibly resulted from his destruction of pertinent records. These were but the most visible among many scandals that touched the Justice Department, the Prohibition Bureau, and other agencies under Harding.

But one major scandal rose above all others. Teapot Dome, like the Watergate break-in fifty years later, became the catchword for an era of government corruption. An oil deposit on federal land in Wyoming, Teapot Dome had been set aside as a reserve to be administered by the Interior Department under Albert B. Fall. He proceeded to let private companies exploit the deposits, arguing that these contracts were in the government's interest. It was harder for Fall to explain, however, why he acted in secret, without allowing competitive bids.

Suspicion grew when Fall's own standard of living suddenly grew lavish. It turned out that he had taken loans of about $400,000 (which came in "a little black bag") from oil executives. For the rest of his life Fall insisted that the loans were unrelated to the leases, and that he had contrived a good deal for the government, but at best the circumstances revealed his fatal blindness to impropriety.

Harding himself was spared the humiliation of public disgrace. How much he knew of the scandals remains unclear, but he knew enough to become visibly troubled. "My God, this is a hell of a job!" he confided to a journalist. "I have no trouble with my en-

emies, I can take care of my enemies all right. But my damn
friends, my God-damn friends . . . they're the ones that keep me
walking the floor nights!" In June 1923 Harding left on what
would be his last journey, a western speaking tour and a trip to
the Alaska territory. Sailing to Alaska, he asked Commerce Secretary Herbert Hoover: "If you knew of a great scandal in our
administration, would you for the good of the country and the
party expose it publicly or would you bury it?" Hoover replied
quickly: "Publish it, and at least get credit for integrity on your
side."

But little time was left to Harding. Back in Seattle he suffered a
heart attack, recovered briefly, then died in a San Francisco
hotel. Not since the death of Lincoln had there been such an outpouring of grief for a "beloved President," for the kindly, ordinary man with the face of a Roman senator, the man who found it
in his heart (as Wilson had not) to pardon the former Socialist
candidate Eugene Debs and receive him at the White House. As
the funeral train moved toward Washington, then back to Ohio,
millions stood by the tracks to honor their lost leader.

Eventually, however, grief yielded to scorn and contempt. For
nearly a decade after Harding's death, scandalous revelations
concerning administrative officials were paraded before congressional committees and then courts. Harding's affairs with
several mistresses also came to light. As a result of such amorous
detours and corrupt associates, Harding's foreshortened administration came to be widely viewed as one of the worst in American history. More recently, however, scholars have suggested
that the scandals obscured several real accomplishments. Some
historians credit Harding with leading the nation out of the turmoil of the postwar years and creating the foundation for the
decade's remarkable economic boom. They also stress that he
was a hard-working president who played a far more forceful
role in shaping administrative economic and foreign policies
than previously believed. Still, even Harding's foremost scholarly defender admits that he lacked good judgment and "probably should never have been president."

"SILENT CAL" The news of Harding's death came when Vice-
President Calvin Coolidge was visiting his father in the mountain
village of Plymouth, Vermont, his birthplace. There at 2:47 on
the morning of August 3, 1923, by the light of a kerosene lamp,
Colonel John Coolidge administered the oath of office to his son.
The rustic simplicity of Plymouth, the very name itself, evoked
just the image of traditional roots and solid integrity that the

Calvin Coolidge dresses up for the photographers.

country would long for amid the slimy wake of the Harding scandals.

Coolidge brought to the White House a clear conviction that the presidency should revert to its passive stance of the Gilded Age, and defer to the leadership of Congress. One editor observed that Coolidge "aspired to become the least President the country ever had; he attained his desire." Coolidge insisted on twelve hours of sleep and an afternoon nap. H. L. Mencken asserted that Coolidge's really notable talent was that "he slept more than any other president, whether by day or by night. Nero fiddled, but Coolidge only snored."

But Americans took to their hearts the unflappability of "Silent Cal," his long midday naps, and the pictures of him fishing, pitching hay, and wearing Indian bonnets while primly clad in business suit and necktie. His pinched facial expression and dry personality provoked affectionate satire. One wit, commenting on Coolidge's seemingly dour facial expression, suggested that he must have been weaned on a pickle. Another popular story reported that a dinner guest had bet Coolidge she could make him say three words. "You lose," he replied. But the image of "Silent Cal" has been overdrawn: he may have been a man of few words, but he was not as bland or as dry as critics claimed.

As Herbert Hoover once stressed, Coolidge was a "real conservative, probably the equal of Benjamin Harrison. He was a fundamentalist in religion, in the economic and social order, and in fishing, too." (He used live worms for bait). Even more than Harding, Coolidge embraced the orthodox creed of business. "The chief business of the American people is business," he intoned. "The man who works there worships there." Where Harding had sought to balance the interests of labor, agriculture, and industry, Coolidge focused on industrial development at the expense of the other two areas. He sought to unleash the free enterprise system and even more than Harding he sought to end government regulation. His pro-business stance led the *Wall Street Journal* to exult: "Never before, here or anywhere else, has a government been so completely fused with business."

THE 1924 ELECTION Coolidge successfully distanced himself from the Harding scandals and put in charge of the prosecutions two lawyers of undoubted integrity. Coolidge also quietly took control of the Republican party machinery and seized the initiative in the campaign for the 1924 nomination, which he won with only token opposition.

The Coolidge luck held as the Democrats fell victim to continuing internal dissensions, which were enough to prompt Will Rogers's classic statement: "I am a member of no organized political party. I am a Democrat." The party's divisions reflected the deep alienation growing up between the new urban culture of the twenties and the more traditional hinterland, a gap that the Democratic party could not bridge. It took 103 ballots to bestow the party's tarnished nomination on John W. Davis, a Wall Street lawyer from West Virginia who could hardly outdo Coolidge in conservatism.

While the Democrats fumbled, a new farm-labor coalition was mobilizing a third-party effort. Meeting in Cleveland on July 4, 1924, farm and labor groups reorganized the Progressive party and nominated Wisconsin senator Robert M. La Follette for president. La Follette also won the support of the Socialist party and the American Federation of Labor.

In the campaign Coolidge chose to focus on La Follette, whom he called a dangerous radical who would turn America into a "communistic and socialistic state." The country preferred to "keep cool with Coolidge," who swept both the popular and electoral votes by decisive majorities. Davis took only the Solid South, and La Follette carried only his native Wisconsin.

The New Era

Businessmen interpreted the Coolidge victory as a vindication of their leadership, and Coolidge saw in the surging prosperity of the time a confirmation of his philosophy. In fact the prosperity and technological achievements of the time had much to do with Coolidge's victory over the Democrats and Progressives. Those in the large middle class who before had formed an important part of the progressive coalition were now absorbed instead in the new corporate and consumer world created by advances in communications, transportation, and business organization. As more and more commentators stressed, the United States seemed to be entering a "new era" of advanced capitalism.

A GROWING CONSUMER CULTURE The American economy was markedly changing during the 1920s. A new consumption ethic began to replace the production ethic of the nineteenth century as dramatic increases in productive efficiency flooded the marketplace with new consumer delights. Goods once available only to the affluent were now made accessible to the working classes: hand cameras, wristwatches, cigarette lighters, vacuum cleaners, washing machines. But such a cornucopia of enticing new goods threatened to produce economic havoc unless people abandoned traditional notions of frugality. Hence, business leaders, salesmen, and public relations experts began a concerted effort to eradicate what was left of the original Protestant ethic's emphasis on plain living. "People may ruin themselves by saving instead of spending," warned one economist. A newspaper editorial was even more blunt. It insisted that the American's "first importance to his country is no longer that of citizen but that of consumer. Consumption is a new necessity."

The public had to be taught the joys of consumerism, and New York's Madison Avenue, the home of the new industry of mass advertising, was happy to oblige. By portraying impulse buying as a therapeutic measure to help self-esteem, the advertising industry shrewdly helped undermine notions of simple living. In his popular novel, *Babbitt*, Sinclair Lewis recognized advertising's impact upon middle-class life: "These standard advertised wares—toothpastes, socks, tires, cameras, instantaneous hot water heaters—were the symbols and proofs of excellence."

Inventions in communications and transportation, such as motion pictures, radio, telephones, and automobiles, not only brought transformations in society but also ignited the decade's economic boom. By 1905 the first movie house opened in Philadelphia, and within three years there were nearly 10,000 nationwide. During the next decade Hollywood became the center of movie production, grinding out serials, features, westerns, and the timeless two-reel comedies of Mack Sennett's Keystone

A farm family gathered around the radio, Hood River County, Oregon, 1925.

Studios, where slapstick comedians, most notably Charlie Chaplin, perfected their art into a powerful form of social criticism. By the mid-1930s every large American city and most small towns had theatres, and movies replaced oratory as the chief mass entertainment, growing into a multi-million dollar industry.

Radio broadcasting had an even more spectacular growth. The first radio commercial aired in 1922. By the end of that year there were over 500 stations and some 3 million receivers in action. In 1927 Congress established a Federal Radio Commission to regulate the industry; in 1934 it became the Federal Communications Commission, with authority over other forms of communication as well.

AIRPLANES, AUTOMOBILES, AND THE ECONOMY Advances in transportation were equally startling. Wilbur and Orville Wright of Dayton, Ohio, owners of a bicycle shop, built and flew the first airplane at Kitty Hawk, North Carolina, on December 17, 1903, but the use of planes advanced slowly until the outbreak of war in 1914. An American aircraft industry developed during the war but foundered in the postwar demobilization. In 1925 the government began to subsidize the industry through airmail contracts and, the following year, started a program of federal aid to air transport and navigation, including funds for constructing airports.

Aviation received a psychological boost in May 1927 when Charles A. Lindbergh, Jr., flew the first transatlantic solo flight from New York to Paris in thirty-three hours and thirty minutes. The drama of the deed, which won him a prize of $25,000, was heightened by the fact that he had flown blindly through a dense fog for part of the way, and had at times dropped to within ten feet of the water, before sighting the Irish coast and regaining his bearings. The New York City parade honoring Lindbergh surpassed even the celebration of the Armistice in its scope.

Four years later New York City honored another pioneering American aviator—Amelia Earhart. In 1931 she became the first woman to fly solo across the Atlantic Ocean. Born in Kansas in 1897, she made her first solo flight in 1921. Soon thereafter she bought her own plane and began working as a barnstorming stunt pilot at air shows across the country. A tall, thin, grey-eyed young woman with short, tousled blond hair and a "boyish" smile, she looked remarkably like Lindbergh, and after her first transatlantic flight in 1928, as a passenger with two male pilots, reporters dubbed her "Lady Lindy," the "First Lady of the Air." She became aviation editor of *Cosmopolitan* and vice-president of an airline company. Newly emancipated American women looked to the radiant Earhart as an inspiring example of female leadership and courage. Earhart's popularity soared after her own transatlantic solo flight from Newfoundland to Northern Ireland. The fifteen-hour feat led Congress to award her the Distinguished Flying Cross, and she was named Outstanding American Woman of the Year.

Caught up in the fervor of the time for such dramatic exploits, Earhart began preparing in 1935 for "just one more long flight." Two years later she and a male navigator left Miami, Florida, and headed east on a round-the-world flight. The trip went smoothly until July 2, 1937, when they attempted the most difficult leg: from New Guinea to a tiny atoll in the Pacific 2,556 miles away. A Coast Guard vessel anchored near the island picked up weakening signals indicating that Earhart's plane was losing fuel. The plane disappeared, and despite extensive searches, no trace of it or the pilots was ever found. It remains the most perplexing and intriguing mystery in aviation history.

The accomplishments of Earhart and Lindbergh helped catapult the aviation industry into prominence. By 1930 there were forty-three American airline companies in operation. But the most significant transportation development of the time was the automobile. The first motor car had been manufactured for sale in 1895, but in 1900 the census did not even give the infant industry a separate listing. The founding of the Ford Motor Company in 1903 revolutionized the industry. Ford's reliable Model T (the celebrated "tin lizzie") appeared in 1908 at a price

of $850 (in 1924 it would sell for $290). Ford aimed "to democratize the automobile. When I'm through everybody will be able
to afford one, and about everyone will have one." He was right.
In 1916 the number of cars manufactured passed 1 million; by
1920 more than 8 million were registered, and in 1929 more
than 23 million. The production of automobiles consumed large
portions of the nation's steel, rubber, glass, and textile output,
among other materials. It gave rise to a gigantic market for oil
products just as the Spindletop gusher (1901) in Texas heralded
the opening of vast southwestern oilfields. It quickened the
movement for good roads, introduced efficient, mass-production assembly-line techniques to other industries, speeded
transportation, encouraged the sprawl of suburbs, and sparked
real-estate booms in California and Florida.

STABILIZING THE ECONOMY   The efficiency craze, which had been
a prominent feature of the progressive impulse, was now power-
ing the wheels of mass production and consumption during the
1920s, and had become a cardinal belief of Republican leaders.
Herbert Hoover, who served as secretary of commerce through
the Harding-Coolidge years, was himself an engineer who had
made a fortune in far-flung mining operations in Australia,
China, Russia, and elsewhere. During World War I he was a brilliant manager of the Belgian relief program and the Food Administration. When young Franklin D. Roosevelt met Hoover in
1919, he labeled him "a wonder." Roosevelt then added with
what would become prophetic irony: "I wish we could make him
President of the United States. There could not be a better one."
    Hoover had developed a concrete social and political philoso-
phy which he set forth in his book *American Individualism*
(1922). The book's central idea might best be called "cooperative individualism," or in one of his favorite terms, "association-
alism." Hoover prescribed a kind of middle way between the
regulatory and trust-busting traditions, a way of voluntary cooperation.
    As Harding's and Coolidge's dynamic secretary of commerce,
Hoover transformed the trifling Commerce Department into the
most active agency of two Republican administrations. During a
period of governmental retrenchment, he promoted expansion.
Hoover sought out new markets for business and sponsored more
than a thousand conferences on product design, production, and
distribution. He also continued the wartime emphasis on stan-
dardization of everything from automobile tires and paving
bricks to bedsprings and toilet paper.

Most of all Hoover endorsed the burgeoning trade-association movement. The organization of business trade associations became his favorite instrument for "stabilization" to avoid the waste inherent in competition. Through such associations executives in a given field would gather and disseminate information on everything: sales, purchases, shipments, production, and prices. This information allowed them to lay plans with more confidence, the advantages of which included predictable costs, prices, and markets, as well as more stable employment and wages. Sometimes abuses crept in as trade associations skirted the edge of legality by engaging in price-fixing and other monopoly practices, but the Supreme Court in 1925 held the practice of sharing information as such to be within the law.

THE BUSINESS OF FARMING During the Harding and Coolidge administrations, agriculture remained a weak point in the economy, in many ways as weak as it had been during the 1890s when cities flourished and agriculture languished. For a brief time after the war the farmers' hopes soared on wings of prosperity. The wartime boom lasted into 1920, and then commodity prices collapsed as European farmers began to resume high levels of production. Low prices persisted into 1923, especially in the wheat and corn belts, and after that improvement was spotty. A bumper cotton crop in 1926 resulted only in a price collapse and an early taste of depression in much of the South, where foreclosures and bankruptcies spread.

Yet in some ways farmers shared the business outlook of the so-called New Era. Many farms, like corporations, were getting

While industry boomed, agriculture remained weak in the 1920s.

larger, more efficient, and more mechanized. By 1930 about 13 percent of all farmers had tractors, and the proportion rose even higher on the western Plains. Better plows and other machines were part of the mechanization process which accompanied improved crops, fertilizers, and animal breeding.

Farm organizations of the 1920s moved away from the proposed alliance with urban labor that marked the Populist era and toward a new view of farmers as profit-conscious businessmen. During the postwar farm depression the idea of marketing cooperatives emerged as the farmer's equivalent to the businessman's trade-association movement. Farm groups formed regional commodity-marketing associations that enabled them to negotiate ironclad contracts with producers for the delivery of their crops over a period of years. These associations also brought order to the marketing of farm products, requiring uniform standards and grades, efficient handling and advertising, and a businesslike organization with professional technicians and executives.

But if concern with marketing co-ops and other businesslike approaches drew farmers ever farther away from Populist traditions, farm problems still invited political solutions. The most effective political response to the crisis of the early 1920s was the formation of the Farm Bloc, a congressional coalition of western Republicans and southern Democrats that put through an impressive, if fairly moderate, program of legislation from 1921 to 1923. During that period the Farm Bloc passed bills exempting farm cooperatives from antitrust laws and creating new credit banks which could lend to cooperative producing and marketing associations.

In the spring of 1924 a new panacea appeared when Senator Charles L. McNary of Oregon and Representative Gilbert N. Haugen of Iowa introduced a bill to secure "equality for agriculture in the benefits of the protective tariff." Complex as it would have been in operation, it was simple in conception: in short, the McNary-Haugen plan sought to dump American farm surpluses on the world market in order to raise commodity prices in the home market. The goal was to achieve "parity"—that is, to raise domestic farm prices to a point where farmers would have the same purchasing power relative to other prices that they had enjoyed between 1909 and 1914, a time viewed in retrospect as a golden age of American agriculture.

A McNary-Haugen bill finally passed both houses of Congress in 1927 and again a year later, only to be vetoed both times by President Coolidge. He criticized the measure as an unsound effort at price-fixing, and as un-American and unconstitutional to boot. He was partially right, but in a broader sense McNary-Haugenism did not fail. The debates over the bill catapulted the farm problem into the arena of national debate and defined it as a problem of crop surpluses. The evolution of the McNary-Haugen plan, moreover, revived the political alliance between the South and West, a coalition that became in the next decade a dominant influence on national farm policy. That policy would follow a different procedure, but its chief focus would be on surpluses and its goal would be "parity."

SETBACKS FOR UNIONS   Urban workers shared more than farmers in the affluence of the times. Their annual per-capita earnings rose between 1921 and 1928 from an average of $1,171 to $1,408. Without a matching rise in living costs, this meant a gain of about 20 percent in real wages. The benefits of this rise, however, were distributed unevenly. Miners and textile workers actually suffered a decline in real wages. In these and other trades the introduction of new production methods and machines eliminated jobs. Still, most workers witnessed a rise in their standard of living during the Coolidge years. "A workman is far better paid in America than anywhere else in the world," a French visitor wrote in 1927, "and his standard of living is enormously higher."

Organized labor, however, did no better than organized agriculture in the 1920s. In fact, unions suffered a setback after the growth years of the war. The Red Scare and strikes of 1919 left the uneasy impression that unions and subversion were linked, an idea promoted by the enemies of unions. The brief postwar depression of 1921 further weakened the unions, and they felt the severe impact of open-shop associations that proliferated across the country after the war, led by chambers of commerce and other business groups. While the open shop in theory implied only the right of employers to hire whom they pleased, in practice it frequently meant discrimination against unionists and refusal to recognize unions even in shops where most of the workers were members.

Nor were employers always above the use of strong-arm methods, such as requiring "yellow-dog" contracts that forced workers to agree to stay out of unions, using labor spies, exchanging blacklists, and resorting to intimidation and coercion. Some employers tried to kill the unions with kindness. They introduced programs of "industrial democracy" guided by company unions, or various schemes of "welfare capitalism" such as profit-sharing, bonuses, pensions, health programs, recreational activities, and the like. The benefits of such programs were often considerable. The combined result of prosperity, propaganda, welfare capitalism, and active hostility was a decline in union membership from about 5 million in 1920 to 3.5 million in 1929.

PRESIDENT HOOVER, THE ENGINEER

HOOVER VS. SMITH   On August 2, 1927, while on vacation in the Black Hills of South Dakota, President Coolidge passed out to reporters slips of paper with the curious statement: "I do not choose to run for President in 1928." Exactly what he meant puzzled observers then and has since. Apparently he at least half hoped for a convention draft, but his statement cleared the way for Herbert Hoover to mount an active campaign for the Republican nomination. Well before the June 1928 Republican convention in Kansas City, Hoover was too far in the lead to be stopped. The platform took credit for prosperity, debt and tax reduction, and the protective tariff that had been in operation since 1922 ("as vital to American agriculture as it is to manufacturing"). It rejected the McNary-Haugen program, but promised a farm board to manage surpluses more efficiently.

The Democratic nomination was as quickly decided, because Governor Alfred E. Smith of New York faced no effective opposition. The Democratic party had had its fill of factionalism in 1924, and all remained fairly harmonious until Smith revealed in his acceptance speech a desire to liberalize Prohibition. Hoover by contrast had pronounced the outlawing of alcoholic beverages "a great social and economic experiment, noble in motive and far-reaching in purpose," and he called for improved enforcement.

The two candidates projected sharply different images that obscured the similarity of their platforms. Hoover was the Quaker son of middle America, the successful engineer and businessman, the architect of Republican prosperity, while Smith was the prototype of those things which rural–small-town America distrusted: the son of Irish immigrants, Catholic, a critic of prohibition, and a Tammanyite with an East Side New York twang. Outside the large cities such qualities were handicaps he could scarcely surmount for all his affability and wit.

In the election Hoover won in the third consecutive Republican landslide, with 21 million popular votes to Smith's 15 million, and an even more top-heavy electoral majority of 444 to 87. Hoover even cracked the Solid South, leaving Smith only a hard core of six Deep South states plus Massachusetts and Rhode Island. The election was above all a vindication of Republican prosperity, but the shattering defeat of the Democrats concealed a major realignment in the making. Smith had nearly doubled the vote for the Democratic candidate of four years before. Smith's image, though a handicap in the hinterlands, swung big cities back into the Democratic column. In the farm states of the West there were signs that some disgruntled farmers had switched over to the Democrats. A coalition of urban workers and unhappy farmers was in the making.

HOOVER IN CONTROL The milestone year of 1929 dawned with high hopes. Business seemed solid, incomes were rising, and the chief architect of Republican prosperity was about to enter the White House. "I have no fears for the future of our country," Hoover told his inauguration audience. "It is bright with hope."

Forgotten in the rush of later events would be Hoover's credentials as a progressive and humanitarian president. Over the objection of Treasury Secretary Mellon, he announced a plan for

"I have no fears for the future of our country," Herbert Hoover told his audience at his inauguration in 1929.

tax reductions in the low-income brackets. He shunned corrupt patronage practices, and he refused to countenance "red hunts" or interference with peaceful picketing of the White House. He also defended his wife's right to invite prominent blacks to the White House, and he sought more money for all-black Howard University.

Hoover also showed greater sympathy than Coolidge for the struggling agricultural sector. To open up glutted markets he proposed higher tariffs on imported farm products. After fourteen months of struggle with competing interests, however, Hoover settled for a general upward revision on manufactures as well as farm goods. The Hawley-Smoot Tariff of June 1930 carried duties to an all-time high. Average rates went from about 32 to 40 percent. More than 1,000 economists petitioned Hoover to veto the bill because, they predicted, it would raise prices to consumers, damage the export trade, and thus hurt farmers, promote inefficiency, and provoke foreign reprisals. Events proved them right, but Hoover felt that he had to go along with his party in an election year. This proved to be a disastrous mistake, for it only exacerbated the growing economic depression.

THE ECONOMY OUT OF CONTROL   Depression? Most Americans had come to assume during the 1920s that there would never be another depression. This misguided optimism proved to be an important factor in generating the economic free-fall after 1929. Throughout the 1920s the idea grew that American business had entered a New Era of *permanent* growth. Such naïve talk helped promote an array of foolhardy get-rich-quick schemes. Speculative mania fueled the Florida real-estate boom, which got under way when the combination of Coolidge prosperity and Henry Ford's "tin lizzies" made Florida an accessible playground.

The Florida real-estate boom collapsed in 1926, but the stock market took up the slack. Until 1927 stock values had risen with profits, but then they began to soar on wings of fanciful speculation. Mellon's tax reductions had released money which, with the help of aggressive brokerage houses, found its way to Wall Street. One could now buy stock on margin—that is, make a small down payment (usually 10 percent) and borrow the rest from a broker who held the stock as security against a down market. If the stock price fell and the buyer failed to provide more cash, the broker could sell the stock to cover his loan.

Gamblers in the market ignored warning signs. By 1927 residential construction and automobile sales were catching up to demand, business inventories rose, and the rate of consumer spending slowed. By mid-1929 production, employment, and other gauges of economic activity were declining. Still the stock market rose, driven by excessive confidence and perennial greed. By 1929 the market had become a fantasy world. Conservative financiers and brokers who counseled caution went unheeded. The president worried too and sought to discourage speculation, but to no avail. On September 4, stock prices wavered, and the next day they dropped. The Great Bull Market staggered on into October, trending downward but with enough good days to keep hope alive. On October 22 the president of the National City Bank told reporters: "I know of nothing fundamentally wrong with the stock market or with the underlying business and credit structure."

THE CRASH AND ITS CAUSES   The next day prices crumbled, and the day after that a wild scramble to unload stocks lasted until word arrived that leading bankers had formed a pool to stabilize prices. For the rest of the week prices steadied, but after a weekend to think the situation over stockholders began to unload their portfolios. On Tuesday, October 29, the most devastating single day in the market's history to that point, the index dropped another 43 points, almost 13 percent. The plunge in prices fed on itself as brokers sold the shares they held for buyers who failed to come up with more cash. During October the value of stocks on the New York Exchange fell by an average of 37 percent.

The first impulse of business and government leaders was to express hope. According to President Hoover, "the fundamental business of the country" was sound. John D. Rockefeller issued his first public statement in decades, admitting that "my son and I have for some days been purchasing sound common stocks." Some speculators who got out of the market went back in for bargains but found themselves caught in a slow, tedious erosion of values. By March 1, 1933, the value of stocks on the New York Exchange was less than 20 percent of the value at the market's peak.

Caution was now the watchword for consumers and businessmen. Buyers held out for lower prices, orders fell off, wages fell or ceased altogether, and the decline in purchasing power brought further cutbacks in business. From 1929 to 1932 Americans' personal incomes declined by more than half, from $82 million to $40 million. Unemployment continued to rise exponentially, from 1.6 million in 1929 to 12.8 million in 1933, from 3 percent to 25 percent of the labor force. And farmers, already in trouble, faced catastrophe as commodity prices fell by half. More than 9,000 banks closed during the period, factories and mines shut down, entire towns were abandoned, and thousands of farms sold for debt.

The crash had revealed the fundamental business of the country to be unsound. Most harmful to the economy had been the ability of business during the boom years to maintain prices and take profits while holding down wages and the cost of raw materials, with the result that about one-third of the nation's personal income went to only 5 percent of the population. By plowing profits back into expansion, business brought on a growing imbalance between rising productivity and declining purchasing power. As the demand for goods declined, the rate of investment in new plants and equipment began to decline. For a time the softness of purchasing power was concealed by greater use of installment buying, and the deflationary effects of high tariffs were concealed by the volume of loans and investments abroad, which supported foreign demand for American goods. But the flow of American capital abroad began to dry up when the stock market became a more attractive investment. Swollen profits and dividends enticed the rich into market speculation. When trouble came, the bloated corporate structure collapsed.

Governmental policies also contributed to the debacle. Mellon's tax reductions brought oversaving, which helped diminish consumer demand. The growing money supply fed the fever of speculation by lowering interest rates. Hostility toward unions discouraged collective bargaining and may have worsened the prevalent imbalances in income. High tariffs discouraged foreign trade. Lax enforcement of antitrust laws encouraged concentration, monopoly, and high prices.

HOOVER'S EFFORTS AT RECOVERY   Not only did the policies of public officials help bring on economic collapse, but few public leaders acknowledged the severity of the crisis: all that was needed, they thought, was a slight correction of the market. Those who held to the theory of laissez-faire thought the economy would cure itself. The best policy, Mellon advised, would be to "liquidate labor, liquidate stocks, liquidate the farmers, liquidate real estate." Doing so would "purge the rottenness out of the system." Hoover, however, was unwilling to sit by and let events take their course. In fact he did more than any previous president in such dire economic circumstances. Still, his own philosophy, now hardened into dogma, set strict limits to governmental action, and he refused to set it aside even to meet an emergency.

Hoover believed that the country's main need was confidence. In speech after speech he exhorted the public to keep up hope, and he asked businessmen to keep the mills and shops open, maintain wage levels, and spread the work to avoid layoffs—in short to let the shock fall on corporate profits rather than on purchasing power. In return union leaders, who had little choice, agreed to refrain from wage demands and strikes.

While reassuring the American public, Hoover also accelerated the building of public works in order to provide jobs, but state and local cutbacks more than offset federal spending. At Hoover's demand the Federal Reserve returned to an easier credit policy, and Congress passed a modest tax reduction to put more purchasing power in people's pockets. The high Hawley-Smoot Tariff, proposed at first to help farmers, brought reprisals abroad, devastating foreign trade.

As always, depression hurt the party in power, and the floundering president was easy game. Near the city dumps and along railroad tracks, the dispossessed huddled in shacks of tarpaper and galvanized iron, in old packing boxes and abandoned cars. These squalid settlements were labeled "Hoovervilles." A "Hoover blanket" was a newspaper, a "Hoover flag" an empty

"Hoovervilles" of tarpaper shacks sprang up around the country as the depression set in.

pocket turned inside out. Such derisive labels reflected the quick erosion of Hoover's political support. In November 1930 the Democrats gained their first national victory since 1916, winning a majority in the House and enough gains in the Senate to control it in coalition with western agrarians.

In the first half of 1931 economic indicators rose, renewing hope for an upswing. Then, as recovery beckoned, another shock jolted public confidence. In May 1931 the failure of Austria's largest bank triggered a financial panic in central Europe. On June 20, to halt the domino effect of spreading defaults, President Hoover proposed a one-year moratorium on both reparations and war-debt payments. In July the major European nations accepted the moratorium and later also a temporary "standstill" on settlement of private obligations between banks. The general shortage of exchange drove Europeans to withdraw their gold from American banks and dump their American securities. One European nation after another abandoned the gold standard and devalued its currency. All these foreign developments worsened the collapse of the American economy, which slid into the third bitter winter of depression.

CONGRESSIONAL INITIATIVES   With a new Congress in session, demands for federal action impelled Hoover to stretch his philosophy to its limits. He was ready now to use governmental resources at least to shore up the financial institutions. In January 1932 the new Congress set up the Reconstruction Finance Corporation (RFC) with $500 million (and authority to borrow $2 billion more) for emergency loans to banks, life insurance companies, building and loan societies, farm mortgage associations, and railroads. The RFC staved off some bankruptcies, but Hoover's critics charged that it favored business at the expense of workers. The RFC nevertheless remained a key agency through the decade and during World War II.

Further help to the financial structure came with the Glass-Steagall Act of February 1932, which eased the availability of commercial loans. It also released about $750 million in gold formerly used to back Federal Reserve Notes, countering the effect of foreign withdrawals and domestic hoarding of gold at the same time that it enlarged the supply of credit. For homeowners the Federal Home Loan Bank Act of July 1932 created with Hoover's blessing a series of discount banks for home mortgages. They provided savings and loan associations a service much like that which the Federal Reserve System provided to commercial banks.

All these measures reflected a dubious "trickle-down" theory, Hoover's critics argued. If government could help banks and railroads, asked New York's senator Robert G. Wagner, "is there any reason why we should not likewise extend a helping hand to that forlorn American, in every village and every city of the United States, who has been without wages since 1929?" By 1932 members of Congress were filling the hoppers with bills for federal relief for individuals. At that point Hoover might have pleaded "dire necessity," taken the leadership of the relief movement, and salvaged his political fortunes.

Instead he held back and only grudgingly edged toward federal relief. On July 21, 1932, Hoover signed the Emergency Relief and Construction Act, which avoided a direct federal dole (cash payments to individuals) but gave the RFC $300 million for relief loans to the states, authorized loans of up to $1.5 billion for state and local government construction projects, and appropriated $322 million for federal public works projects.

Relief for farmers had long since been abandoned. In mid-1931 the government quit buying surpluses and helplessly watched prices slide. In 1919 wheat had fetched $2.16 a bushel; by 1932 it had sunk to 38 cents. Cotton had reached a high of 41.75 cents a pound in 1919; before the 1932 harvest it went to 4.6 cents. Other farm prices declined comparably. Between 1930 and 1934 nearly a million farms passed from their owners to the mortgage holders.

FARMERS AND VETERANS IN PROTEST Faced with total loss, some desperate farmers began to defy the law. Angry mobs stopped foreclosures and threatened to lynch judges. In Nebraska farmers burned corn to keep warm; dairy farmers dumped milk into roadside ditches in an effort to raise prices. Like voluntary efforts to reduce acreage, the strikes generally failed, but they vividly dramatized the farmers' frustration and anger.

Fears of organized disorder arose when unemployed World War I veterans converged on Washington in the spring of 1932. The "Bonus Expeditionary Force" grew quickly to more than 15,000. Their purpose was to get immediate payment of the cash bonus to war veterans that Congress had voted in 1924. The House approved a bonus bill, but when the Senate voted it down in June most of the veterans went home. The rest, having no place to go, camped in vacant government buildings and in a shantytown within sight of the Capitol.

The chief of the Washington police gave the squatters a friendly welcome and won their trust, but a fearful White House fretted. Eager to disperse the destitute veterans, Hoover convinced Congress to vote funds to buy their tickets home. More left, but others stayed even after Congress adjourned, hoping at least to meet with the embattled president. Late in July the administration ordered the shantytown razed. In the ensuing melee, one policeman panicked, fired into the crowd, and killed two veterans. The Secretary of War then dispatched about 700 soldiers under General Douglas MacArthur, aided by junior officers Dwight D. Eisenhower and George S. Patton, Jr. The soldiers easily drove out the unarmed veterans and their families, and they then burned the shacks. MacArthur self-righteously explained in his report that when dealing with "riotous elements" a show of "obvious strength gains a moral ascendancy." Among the evicted was a New Jersey veteran who had received the Distinguished Service Cross for a wartime exploit that had saved the life of George Patton. The one fatality—from tear gas—was an eleven-week-old boy, born in one of the shanties.

General MacArthur, already prone to flights of Caesarean fantasy, said the "mob," spurred by "the essence of revolution," was about to seize control of the government. The administration insisted that the Bonus Army consisted mainly of Communists and criminals, but neither a grand jury nor the Veterans Administration could find evidence to support the charge. One observer wrote before the incident: "There is about the lot of them an atmosphere of hopelessness, of utter despair, though not of desperation. . . . they have no enthusiasm whatever and no stomach for fighting."

Their mood, and the mood of the country, was much like that of Hoover himself. He worked hard, but took no joy from his labors. "I am so tired," he sometimes sighed, "that every bone in my body aches." Presidential news conferences were more strained and less frequent. When friends urged Hoover to seize the reins of leadership, he replied, "I can't be a Theodore Roosevelt," or "I have no Wilsonian qualities." His gloom and growing sense of futility were conveyed to the country. In a mood more despairing than rebellious, people waited to see what another presidential campaign would bring forth.

Further Reading

The most recent synthesis of events immediately following the First World War is Ellis W. Hawley's *The Great War and the Search for a Modern Order: A History of the American People and Their Institutions, 1917–1933* (rev. ed., 1991).°

For an introduction to Harding, see Francis Russell's *The Shadow of Blooming Grove: Warren G. Harding in His Times* (1968). A more favorable account is Robert K. Murray's *Harding Era: Warren G. Harding and His Administration* (1969). On Coolidge, see Donald R. McCoy's *Calvin Coolidge: The Silent President* (1988).° Studies on Hoover include Joan Hoff Wilson's *Herbert Hoover: Forgotten Progressive* (1975)° and George Nash's multivolume *The Life of Herbert Hoover* (1983–).

Other works on politics include Burl Noggle's *Teapot Dome: Oil and Politics in the 1920s* (1962)° and David Burner's *The Politics of Provincialism: The Democratic Party in Transition, 1918–1932* (1968).° William H. Chafe's *The American Woman: Her Changing Social, Economic, and Political Roles* (1972)° is a good introduction to the achievement of suffrage.

An overview of the depression is found in C. P. Kindleberger's *The World in Depression* (rev. ed., 1986).° John Kenneth Galbraith details the fall of the stock market in *The Great Crash, 1929* (1955).° Another interpretation is given in Peter Temin's *Did Monetary Forces Cause the Great Depression?* (1976).° John A. Garraty's *Unemployment in History: Economic Thought and Public Policy* (1978) explores what the nation thought about its plight. Firsthand accounts of the Great Depression can be found in Tom E. Terrill and Jerrold Hirsch's *Such As Us* (1978),° Studs Terkel's *Hard Times* (1970),° and Robert S. McElvaine's *Down and Out in the Great Depression* (1983).°

° These books are available in paperback editions.

27 ✎

FRANKLIN D. ROOSEVELT
AND THE NEW DEAL

FROM HOOVERISM TO THE NEW DEAL

FDR'S ELECTION   On June 14, 1932, while the Bonus Army was still encamped in Washington, Republicans gathered in Chicago to renominate Hoover. The delegates went through the motions in a mood of defeat. The Democrats, in contrast, converged on Chicago late in June confident that they would nominate the next president. New York governor Franklin D. Roosevelt already had lined up most of the delegates, but he still faced an uphill battle for a two-thirds majority. Among the favorite sons only House Speaker John Nance Garner of Texas had any serious chance, but he released his delegates after the third ballot and Roosevelt went over the top. Garner's reward was the vice presidency, an office he later pronounced "not worth a pitcher of warm spit."

In a bold gesture, Roosevelt appeared before the convention in person to accept the nomination instead of awaiting formal notification. He told the expectant delegates: "I pledge you, I pledge myself to a new deal for the American people." What the New Deal would be in practice Roosevelt had little idea as yet, but he was much more flexible and willing to experiment than Hoover. What was more, his ebullient personality communicated joy and hope—as did his campaign song: "Happy Days Are Here Again."

Roosevelt was strengthened also by his background and experience. Born in New York in 1882, the only child of a wealthy patrician father and an imperious mother, and a distant cousin of

Theodore Roosevelt, he had the advantage of a refined education at prestigious Groton School and Harvard, topped off by the Columbia Law School. Tall, handsome, and athletic, he seemed destined for great achievement. In 1912 he backed Woodrow Wilson, and for both of Wilson's terms served as his assistant secretary of the navy. Then, in 1920, largely on the strength of his name, he gained the vice-presidential nomination. Political defeat was followed by personal crisis when in 1921 he contracted polio, which left him permanently crippled, unable to stand or walk without braces. But his prolonged struggle with this handicap, eased immeasurably by the untiring efforts of his wife, Eleanor, transformed the once snobbish young aristocrat into one of the century's most outgoing political figures. Justice Oliver Wendell Holmes, Jr., later summed up his qualities: "A second-class intellect—but a first-class temperament."

For seven years Roosevelt fought his way back to health and in 1928 ran for governor of New York and won. Reelected by a whopping majority of 700,000 in 1930, he became the Democratic front runner for the presidency in 1932. Behind the public facade of a cheery and self-confident politician, Roosevelt was also a shrewd and at times crass manipulator of people and power. Obsessed with gaining the highest office in the land, he was willing to subordinate and utilize all else in his life—family, health, staff, friends—to that end. Roosevelt occasionally inflated his own accomplishments and took credit for those of others, but his own strengths and achievements were considerable. A born leader, he had a talent for surrounding himself with capable people and getting the most out of them. Most important, however, was his bulldog determination to succeed, to overcome all obstacles, to triumph over despair and adversity, and in the process achieve greatness.

Partly to dispel doubts about his health, Roosevelt set forth on a grueling campaign speaking tour in 1932. He sought to pin responsibility for the depression on Hoover and the Republicans, and to attract interest in his promised New Deal. Like Hoover, Roosevelt made the requisite pledge to balance the budget, but he left open the loophole that he would incur deficits to prevent starvation. He was evasive on the tariff, and on farm policy he offered several options pleasing to farmers but ambiguous enough not to alarm city-dwellers. He did come out unequivocally for strict regulation of utilities, and he consistently stood by his party's pledge to repeal the Prohibition Amendment. He also announced that a mature economy would require more imaginative national planning. "The country needs, and, unless I mistake

Governor Franklin D. Roosevelt, the Democratic nominee, campaigning in Topeka, Kansas. Roosevelt's confidence inspired voters.

its temper, the country demands bold, persistent experimentation." What came across to voters, however, was less the content of his speeches than the confidence and irrepressible buoyancy of the man.

The dour Hoover, by contrast, had no confidence. He could turn a neat phrase, but many elegant passages suffered from the pedestrian manner of his delivery. Democrats, he argued, ignored the international causes of the depression. Roosevelt's reckless proposals, Hoover warned, "would destroy the very foundations of our American system." But few were listening. Mired in the persistent depression, the country wanted a new course, a new leadership, a new deal.

Not a few thoughtful voters took a dim view of both candidates. Those who believed only a truly radical departure would suffice went over to the Socialist Norman Thomas, who polled 882,000 votes, and some went on to support the Communist candidate, who won 103,000 votes. The wonder is that a desperate people did not turn in greater numbers to such radical alternatives. Instead they swept Roosevelt into office by a whopping margin.

THE INAUGURATION   For the last time the country waited four long months, until March 4, for a new president and Congress to take office. The Twentieth Amendment, ratified on February 6, 1933, provided that the president would take office thereafter on January 20 and the newly elected Congress on January 3. Amid spreading destitution and misery, unemployment continued to rise during the bleak winter of 1932–1933, and panic struck the banking system. Depositors played it safe by taking their cash out and squirreling it away. When the Hoover administration left office, four-fifths of the nation's banks were closed and the country was on the brink of economic paralysis.

The profound crisis of confidence that prevailed when Roosevelt took the oath of office on March 4, 1933, was tempered by a mood of expectancy. The new president exploited both with a spirit of assurance that conveyed a new sense of vigorous action. First, he asserted a "firm belief that the only thing we have to fear is fear itself." He would not merely exhort, he promised: "This nation asks for action, and action now!" It was exactly what a distraught nation wanted to hear. One citizen wrote Roosevelt that the speech was "the finest thing this side of heaven. It seemed to give the people, as well as myself, a new hold on life."

It was Roosevelt's willingness to act, to be decisive, to experiment with new programs and policies, that set his presidency apart from most others. Nevertheless, for all his energy and daring, Roosevelt brought to the White House no concrete agenda or long-range plan. He was a pragmatist rather than an ideologue. As he once explained, "Take a method and try it. If it fails admit it frankly and try another." The new president compared himself to a football quarterback: he could not call the next play until he knew the results of the previous one. Roosevelt's "New Deal," therefore, would take the form of a series of trial-and-error actions. And soon Roosevelt was in action on more than a dozen fronts.

STRENGTHENING THE MONETARY SYSTEM   The first order of business for the new administration was to unclog the channels of finance. On his second day in office, Roosevelt called for a special session of Congress, and he then declared a four-day banking holiday. It took Congress only seven hours to pass the Emergency Banking Relief Act, which permitted sound banks to reopen under approval from the Treasury, and provided managers for those still in trouble. On March 12, 1933, in the first of his radio "fireside chats," the president told his audience that it was safer to "keep your money in a reopened bank than under the mattress." The following day, deposits in reopened banks exceeded with-drawals, and by March 15 banks controlling nine-tenths of the nation's banking resources were once again open. In rapid or-der Roosevelt next slashed military pensions and government payrolls and then urged Congress to pass the Twenty-first Amendment, which the states ratified on December 5, ending prohibition.

The measures of March 1933 were but the beginning of an av-alanche of executive and legislative action. During the session from March 9 to June 16, the so-called Hundred Days, Congress passed over a dozen of Roosevelt's major proposals, legislation whose scope was unprecedented in American history. Said one dizzied legislator, Roosevelt's New Deal "reads like the first chapter of Genesis."

With the banking crisis over, there still remained an acute debt problem for farmers and homeowners and a lingering dis-trust of the banks, which might yet be aroused again. On March 27, by executive decree, Roosevelt reorganized all farm credit agencies into the Farm Credit Administration (FCA). Congress confirmed that action and authorized the extensive refinancing of farm mortgages at lower interest rates. The Home Owner's Loan Act (June 13) provided a similar service to city-dwellers through the new Home Owner's Loan Corporation (HOLC)—something which, incidentally, Hoover had vainly urged on Congress in 1931. The Glass-Steagall Banking Act (June 16) fur-ther shored up confidence in the banking system by creating the Federal Deposit Insurance Corporation (FDIC) to guarantee bank deposits of up to $5,000. It also required commercial banks to separate themselves from investment brokerages.

Roosevelt and Congress then turned their attention to tight-ening the regulation of Wall Street. The Federal Securities Act (May 27) required that new stock and bond issues register with the Federal Trade Commission and later with the Securities and Exchange Commission (SEC), a new agency created on June 6, 1934, to regulate the stock and bond markets.

Throughout 1933 Roosevelt tinkered with devaluation of the currency as a way to raise stock and commodity prices and ease the debt burden on strapped investors and farmers. On April 19 the government achieved this by officially abandoning the gold standard, which infuriated fiscal conservatives. One fumed that Roosevelt's decision "can't be defended except as mob rule." Yet the consequent decline in the value of the dollar increased the prices of commodities and stocks at home.

RELIEF MEASURES   Another urgent priority in 1933 was relieving the widespread personal distress caused by the depression. As Roosevelt once remarked, the "test of our progress is not whether we add to the abundance of those who have much. It is whether we provide enough for those who have too little." Congress took a first step toward such relief with the creation in March of the Civilian Conservation Corps (CCC), which was designed to provide useful jobs for young men aged eighteen to twenty-five. Beginning in April 1933 nearly 3 million men took to the woods to work at a variety of jobs in forests, parks, recreational areas, and soil conservation projects at the nominal pay of thirty dollars per month. Directed by army officers and foresters, they worked under a semi-military discipline and provided perhaps the most direct analogue of war in the whole New Deal.

The Federal Emergency Relief Administration (FERA), created on May 12, 1933, addressed the broader problems of human distress. Harry L. Hopkins, a tireless social worker from Iowa who had earlier directed Roosevelt's state relief program in New York, headed the new effort and became the second most powerful figure in the administration. He pushed the FERA with a boundless nervous energy, spending $5 million within two hours of taking office. FERA funds supported state construction of over 5,000 public buildings and 7,000 bridges, organized adult literacy programs, financed college education for poor students, and set up day-care centers for low-income families. The agency also provided direct cash payments to the chronically unemployed.

The first large-scale experiment with federal work relief, which put people directly on the government payroll at competitive wages, came with the formation of the Civil Works Administration (CWA). Created in November 1933, when it had become apparent that the state-sponsored programs under the FERA would not prevent widespread privation, the CWA provided federal jobs and wages to those unable to find work that winter. It was hastily conceived and implemented, and many of its projects were "make-work" jobs such as leaf-raking and ditch-digging. During its four-month existence, however, it put to work over 4 million people and spent over $900 million (mostly in wages) for a variety of useful projects, from making highway repairs to constructing or improving over 1,000 airports and 40,000 schools, to providing 50,000 teaching jobs that helped keep rural schools open. The CWA, unlike the FERA, which financed state projects, was a wholly federal operation. As the numbers it employed soared, the program's costs skyrocketed to over a billion dollars. Roosevelt balked at such high expenditures and, feeling the CWA had served its purpose of helping many unemployed people weather the winter, he ordered the agency dissolved in the spring of 1934. By April some 4 million workers were again unemployed.

Roosevelt, however, continued to favor work relief over direct cash payment to individuals; he thought the dole was "a narcotic, a subtle destroyer of the human spirit." In 1935 he asked Congress for an array of new federal job programs, and it responded by passing a $4.8 billion bill providing work relief for the jobless. To manage these programs, Roosevelt created the Works Progress Administration (WPA), headed by Harry L. Hopkins, to replace the Federal Emergency Relief Administration. Hopkins was told to provide millions of jobs quickly, and as a result some jobs appeared to be make-work or mere "leaning on shovels." But before the WPA died during World War II, it left permanent monuments on the landscape in the form of buildings, bridges, hard-surfaced roads, airports, and schools.

The WPA also employed a wide range of talents in the Federal Theatre Project, the Federal Art Project, and the Federal Writers' Project. Talented writers such as Ralph Ellison, John Cheever, and Saul Bellow found work writing travel guides to the United States, and Orson Welles directed Federal Theatre productions. The National Youth Administration (NYA), under the WPA, provided part-time employment to students, set up technical training programs, and aided jobless youth. Twenty-seven year-old Lyndon Johnson was director of an NYA program in Texas, and Richard Nixon, a penniless Duke University law student, found work through the local NYA at thirty-five cents an hour. Although the WPA took care of only about 3 million out of some 10 million jobless at any one time, in all it helped some 9 million clients weather desperate times before it expired in 1943.

RECOVERY THROUGH REGULATION

In addition to rescuing the banks and providing relief for the unemployed, Roosevelt and his advisors sought to promote the recovery of the agricultural and industrial sectors of the economy. Roosevelt's so-called "brain trust" of university-trained experts, lawyers, and professors initially felt that the trend toward economic concentration was inevitable. They also believed that the mistakes of the 1920s showed that the only way to operate an integrated economy at full capacity and in the public interest was through stringent regulation and organized central planning, not through trust-busting. The success of centralized economic planning on a national scale during World War I reinforced such ideas. New farm and recovery programs sprang from their beliefs and experiences.

AGRICULTURAL RECOVERY: THE AAA   The Agricultural Adjustment Act, signed into law on May 12, 1933, provided a plan to compensate farmers for voluntary cutbacks in production. The money for the benefit payments made to farmers would result from a tax levied on the "middlemen," the businesses that processed farm products for sale, such as cotton gins, flour mills, and meat-packing plants.

By the time Congress acted, the growing season was already advanced, and the prospect of another bumper cotton crop created an urgent problem. The AAA reluctantly resolved to sponsor a plow-under program. To destroy a growing crop was a "shocking commentary on our civilization," Agriculture Secretary Henry A. Wallace lamented. "I could tolerate it only as a cleaning up of the wreckage from the old days of unbalanced production." In addition to promoting the plowing under of ripening crops, the AAA encouraged farmers to destroy young livestock as a means of raising prices. Critics thereafter labeled Wallace the "assassin of little pigs." As a complement to the AAA, Roosevelt created in October 1933 the Commodity Credit Corporation (another CCC!), which extended loans based on the value of cotton and other crops kept in storage and off the market. In principle, if not in form, it was a revival of the old Farmers' Alliance-Populist sub-treasury plan.

For a while these farm measures worked. By the end of 1934 Wallace could report significant declines in wheat, cotton, and corn production and a simultaneous increase in commodity prices. Farm income increased by 58 percent between 1932 and 1935. The AAA, however, was only partially responsible for such gains. The devastating drought that settled over the plains states between 1932 and 1935 played a major role in reducing production and creating the epic "Dust Bowl" migrations so poignantly evoked in John Steinbeck's *Grapes of Wrath*. Many of these migrant families had actually been driven off the land by AAA benefit programs that encouraged large farmers to take the lands worked by tenants and sharecroppers out of cultivation

The Great Blow of 1934. *Severe drought and soil erosion created conditions for the dust storms that plagued the Middle West in the mid-1930s. This photograph is by Dorothea Lange.*

first. These displaced farmers joined a migratory stream rushing from the South and Midwest toward California, buoyed by currents of hope and desperation. One couple claimed they had heard "how much money a man could make out there and we wanted to go."

Although frequently lumped together as "Okies," the Dust Bowl refugees were actually from cotton-belt communities in Arkansas, Texas, and Missouri, as well as Oklahoma. During the 1930s and 1940s some 800,00 people left those four states and headed toward the West. Not all were farmers; many were professionals, white-collar workers, retailers, and farm implement salesmen whose jobs had been tied to the health of the agricultural sector. Ninety-five percent of the Dust Bowl migrants were white, and most were young adults in their twenties and thirties who relocated with spouses and children. Some traveled on trains or buses, others hopped a freight or hitched a ride; most rode in their own cars, the trip taking four to five days on average.

Most of the Dust Bowl migrants who had come from cities gravitated to California's urban areas—Los Angeles, San Diego, or San Francisco. Half of the newcomers, however, moved into the San Joaquin Valley, the agricultural heartland of the state. There they discovered that California was no paradise. Only a few of the migrants could afford to buy land. Most (men and women) found themselves competing with local Hispanics and Asians for seasonal work as pickers in the cotton fields or orchards of large corporate farms. Living in tents or crude cabins and frequently on the move, they suffered from exposure and from poor sanitation. They also felt the sting of social prejudice. Steinbeck explained that "Okie us'ta mean you was from Oklahoma. Now it means you're a dirty son-of-a-bitch. Okie means you're scum. Don't mean nothing in itself, it's the way they say it." Such hostility drove a third of the "Okies" to return to their home states. Most of the farm workers who stayed tended to fall back upon their old folkways rather than assimilate themselves into their new surroundings. These gritty "plain folk" brought with them their own prejudices against blacks and ethnic minorities as well as a potent tradition of evangelical Protestantism and a distinctive style of music variously labeled "country," "hillbilly," or "cowboy." This "Okie" subculture remains a vivid part of California society today.

Although it created unexpected problems, the AAA achieved real successes in boosting the overall farm economy. Then, on January 6, 1936, the Supreme Court in *United States v. Butler* (1936) ruled the AAA's processing tax unconstitutional because farm production was intrastate and thus beyond the reach of federal power. The administration hastily devised a new plan to achieve crop reduction indirectly in the Soil Conservation and Domestic Allotment Act (1936), which it pushed through Congress in six weeks. The new act omitted processing taxes and acreage quotas, but provided benefit payments to farmers who engaged in soil conservation practices and cut back on soil-depleting staple crops.

The act was an almost unqualified success as an engineering and educational project because it went far to heal the scars of erosion and the plague of dust storms. But soil conservation nevertheless failed as a device for limiting production. With their worst lands taken out of production, farmers cultivated their fertile acres more intensively. In response, Congress passed the second Agricultural Adjustment Act (February 16, 1938), which reestablished the earlier programs but left out the processing taxes. Benefit payments would now come from general funds. Increasingly, federal farm programs came to dominate the nation's agricultural economy. As the novelist William Faulkner recognized, "Our economy is not agricultural any longer. Our economy is the federal government. We no longer farm in Mississippi cotton fields. We farm now in Washington corridors and Congressional committee rooms."

INDUSTRIAL RECOVERY: THE NRA   For industry, the New Deal counterpart to the AAA was the National Industrial Recovery Act (NIRA), passed in June 1933. The NIRA had two major components. One part created the Public Works Administration (PWA) with $3.3 billion for public buildings, highway programs, flood control, bridges, tunnels, and aircraft carriers. The purpose was to "prime the pump" of business with new expenditures and provide jobs for the unemployed. Under the direction of Interior Secretary Harold L. Ickes, the PWA indirectly served the purpose of work relief, although Ickes directed it toward well planned permanent improvements rather than the provision of hasty make-work jobs, and he used private contractors rather than placing workers directly on the government payroll. PWA workers built Virginia's Skyline Drive, New York's Triborough Bridge, the Overseas Highway from Miami to Key West, and Chicago's subway system.

The more controversial and ambitious part of the NIRA created the National Recovery Administration (NRA), headed by General Hugh S. Johnson. Its purposes were essentially twofold: first, to stabilize business with codes of "fair" competitive practice, and second, to generate more purchasing power by providing jobs, defining labor standards, and raising wages. The NRA also enlisted trade union hopes for protection of basic hour and wage standards and raised liberal hopes for comprehensive planning.

In each industry, committees representing management, labor, and government drew up the fair practice codes. The labor standards were quite progressive. Every code set a forty-hour week and minimum weekly wages of $13 ($12 in the South, where living costs were considered lower), which more than doubled earnings in some cases. Child labor under the age of sixteen was also prohibited.

As the drafting of other codes governing particular industries began to drag, the NRA launched a crusade to whip up popular support for its efforts. The public responded, proudly displaying the NRA symbol of compliance, the "Blue Eagle," on signs and in stores. Some 2 million employers signed a much-publicized pledge affirming their support for the NRA codes.

For a time the NRA worked, perhaps because a new air of confidence had overcome the depression blues and the downward spiral of wages and prices had ended. But as soon as recovery began, the honeymoon was over. Charges mounted that the larger companies dominated the code negotiations, that they used the codes to stifle competition by dividing up markets and entrenching their own positions, and that price-fixing robbed small producers of the chance to compete. The NRA wage codes also excluded agricultural workers and domestics—occupations involving three out of every four employed blacks. The effort to develop codes for every industry in the nation proved an administrative nightmare, and the daily annoyances of code enforcement inspired growing hostility among businessmen.

By 1935 the NRA had developed more critics than friends. When it died in May 1935, struck down by the Supreme Court as unconstitutional, few mourned. Yet, while generally deemed a failure, the NRA experiment left an enduring mark. With dramatic suddenness, the codes had set new standards, such as the forty-hour week and the end of child labor, from which it proved hard for management to retreat. The NRA's endorsement of collective bargaining also spurred union growth.

REGIONAL PLANNING: THE TVA   The wide-ranging philosophy of the New Deal embraced more than the restrictive approaches of the NRA. The creation of the Tennessee Valley Authority (TVA) was a truly bold venture, the product neither of a single imagination nor of a single concept, but of an unfolding progression of purposes. In 1916 the government started power and nitrate plants at Muscle Shoals, Alabama, to strengthen national defense. New objectives unfolded in succession: the plants could produce nitrate fertilizers as well as nitrate explosives, promote general industrial development, and provide cheap public power to be used as a "yardstick" for private utility rates. Water-power development led in turn to improved flood control, and to conservation of soil and forests to prevent silting. The chain of connections led ultimately to the concept of overall planning for an entire watershed, which included a total drainage area in the southeast of 41,000 square miles overlapping seven states.

Through the 1920s Nebraska senator George W. Norris had fought off efforts to sell the Alabama project to private developers, but he never marshaled sufficient support for his goal of a federal project to provide electricity for the public. In 1932,

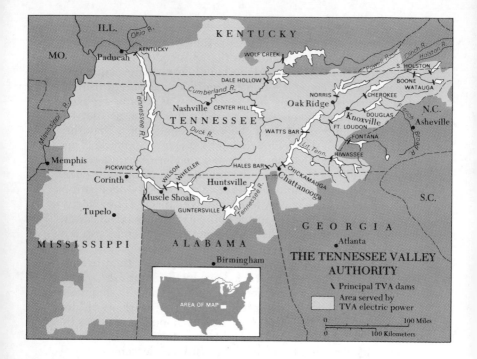

The Tennessee Valley Authority map showing principal TVA dams and area served by TVA electric power. States shown include Kentucky, Tennessee, Alabama, Mississippi, Georgia, and portions of Illinois, Missouri, North Carolina, and South Carolina. Cities labeled include Paducah, Nashville, Knoxville, Oak Ridge, Memphis, Chattanooga, Huntsville, Muscle Shoals, Corinth, Tupelo, Birmingham, Atlanta, and Asheville. Dams labeled include Wolf Creek, Dale Hollow, Center Hill, Norris, Cherokee, Douglas, Boone, Watauga, S. Holston, Fontana, Hiwassee, Chickamauga, Hales Bar, Watts Bar, Fort Loudon, Guntersville, Wheeler, Wilson, Pickwick, and Kentucky.

however, Norris won the new president's support for a vast enlargement of the Muscle Shoals project.

On May 18, 1933, Congress created the TVA as a multipurpose public corporation. By 1936 the TVA board had six dams completed or under way, and a master plan to build nine high dams on the Tennessee River, which would create the "Great Lakes of the South," and other dams on the tributaries. The agency, moreover, opened the rivers for navigation, fostered soil conservation and forestry, experimented with fertilizers, drew new industry to the region, and sent cheap power pulsating through the valley.

TVA's success at generating greater power consumption and lower rates awakened private utilities to the mass consumer markets. It also transported farmers of the valley from the age of kerosene to the age of electricity. "The women went around turning the switches on and off," reported a Farm Bureau man who witnessed the transition. "The light and wonder in their eyes was brighter than that from the lamps." Through loans of more than $321 million to rural cooperatives, the Rural Electrification Administration (REA) paved the way to the electrification of the nation's farms.

LAUNCHING THE SECOND NEW DEAL

During Roosevelt's first year in office his programs and his personal charms aroused massive support. The president's travels and speeches, his twice-weekly press conferences, and his "fireside chats" over the radio generated vitality and warmth from a once-remote White House. In the congressional elections of 1934 the Democrats actually increased their strength in both House and Senate, an almost unprecedented midterm victory for the party in power. When it was over only seven Republican governors remained in office throughout the country.

Criticism of the New Deal during 1933 was muted or reduced to helpless carping. But as the sense of crisis passed, the spirit of unity relaxed. The depression's downward slide had been halted, but prosperity remained elusive. Even more unsettling to some was the dramatic growth of executive power. In August 1934 a group of conservative businessmen and politicians, including Al Smith and John W. Davis, two previous Democratic presidential candidates, formed the American Liberty League to oppose New Deal measures as violations of personal and property rights.

THUNDER ON THE LEFT More potent threats to Roosevelt came from the hucksters of social nostrums, old and new. The most flamboyant of the group by far was Louisiana's "Kingfish," Senator Huey P. Long, Jr. A short, strutting man, Long sported pink suits and pastel-colored shirts, red ties, and two-toned shoes. He seemed like a clown to some observers and loved to make people think he was a country bumpkin. But underneath all the carefully designed hoopla was a shrewd lawyer and consummate politician. First as Louisiana governor, then as political boss of the state, Long had delivered to its citizens tax favors, roads, schools, free textbooks, charity hospitals, and generally better public services. That he had become a sort of state dictator in the process, using bribery, physical intimidation, and blackmail to achieve his ends, seemed irrelevant to many of his ardent supporters.

In 1933 Long joined Roosevelt in Washington as a Democratic senator. He initially supported the New Deal but quickly grew suspicious of the NRA's collusion with Big Business. He also had grown jealous of Roosevelt's mushrooming popularity, having himself developed aspirations for the Oval Office. Promoting himself as a radical egalitarian, a true, if self-indulgent friend of

The "Kingfish," Huey Long of Louisiana.

the people, Long had his own plan for dealing with the Great Depression.

Long's Share Our Wealth program was tantalizingly generous and simple. In one version he proposed to confiscate large personal fortunes, guarantee every family a cash grant of $5,000, every worker an annual income of $2,500, provide pensions to the aged, reduce working hours, pay veterans' bonuses, and assure a college education for every qualified student. It did not matter to him that his figures failed to add up or that his program offered little to promote an economic recovery. As he told a group of distressed Iowa farmers, "Maybe somebody says I don't understand it. Well, you don't have to. Just shut your damn eyes and believe it. That's all." Whether he had a workable plan or not, by early 1935 the charismatic Long was claiming a file of 7.5 million supporters. He was also successful in arousing the concern and ire of the Roosevelt administration. Interior Secretary Harold Ickes growled that Long suffered from "halitosis of the intellect."

Another popular social scheme was hatched by a California doctor, Francis E. Townsend. Outraged by the sight of three haggard old women raking through garbage cans in Long Beach, Townsend proposed government pensions for the aged. In January 1934 he began promoting the Townsend Plan of paying $200 a month to every citizen over sixty who retired from employment and promised to spend the money within the month. The plan had the lure of providing both security for the aged and job openings for the young. As the Townsend Clubs grew, critics noted that the cost of his program for 9 percent of the population would be more than half the national income. "I'm not in the least interested in the cost of the plan," Townsend blandly told a House committee.

A third huckster of panaceas, Father Charles E. Coughlin, the "radio priest" of Royal Oak, Michigan, founded the National Union for Social Justice in 1934. In broadcasts over the CBS network, he specialized in schemes for the coinage of silver and in attacks on bankers that carried growing overtones of anti-Semitism.

Coughlin, Townsend, and Long drew support largely from lower-middle-class Americans thwarted by the depression. Of the three, Long had the widest following. A 1935 canvass by the Democratic National Committee showed that he could draw 5–6 million votes as a third-party candidate for president in 1936, perhaps enough to undermine Roosevelt's chances of reelection.

Beset by pressures from both ends of the political spectrum, Roosevelt hesitated for months before deciding to "steal the thunder" from the left with new programs of reform and social security. Political pressures impelled Roosevelt, but so did the growing influence within the administration of Justice Brandeis and Felix Frankfurter. These advisers urged Roosevelt to be less cozy with big business and to push for restored competition and heavy taxes on large corporations.

LIGHTNING FROM THE COURT   A series of Supreme Court decisions finally galvanized the president into action. On May 27, 1935, the Court killed the National Industrial Recovery Act by unanimous vote. In *Schechter Poultry Corporation v. United States*, quickly tagged the "sick chicken" case, the defendants had been convicted of selling an "unfit chicken" and violating other NRA code provisions. The high court ruled that Congress had delegated too much power to the executive when it granted the code-making authority, and had exceeded its power under the commerce clause by regulating intrastate commerce. The poultry in question, the Court decided, had "come to permanent rest within the state," although it earlier had been moved across state lines. In a press conference soon afterward, Roosevelt fumed: "We have been relegated to the horse-and-buggy definition of interstate commerce." The same line of reasoning, he warned, might endanger other New Deal programs.

LEGISLATIVE ACHIEVEMENTS OF THE SECOND NEW DEAL   To rescue his program Roosevelt in June 1935 ended the stalemate in Congress and launched the so-called Second New Deal with demands for several pieces of "must" legislation, most of which were already pending. During the next two months Congress passed another cluster of significant—and quite controversial—legislation.

The National Labor Relations Act, often called the Wagner Act for its sponsor, New York senator Robert Wagner, gave workers the right to bargain through unions of their own choice and prohibited employers from interfering with union activities. A National Labor Relations Board of five members could supervise plant elections and certify unions as bargaining agents where a majority of the workers approved. The board could also investigate the actions of employers and issue "cease and desist" orders against specified unfair practices. The Wagner Act salvaged most of the labor guarantees included in the National Industrial Recovery Act, and under its protection, union activities quickly intensified.

The Social Security Act of 1935, Roosevelt announced, was the New Deal's "cornerstone" and "supreme achievement." Indeed, it has proven to be the most significant and far-reaching of all the New Deal initiatives. The concept was by no means new. Progressives during the early 1900s had proposed a federal system of social security for the aged, indigent, handicapped, and unemployed. Other nations had already enacted such programs, but the United States remained steadfast to its tradition of individual self-reliance. The Great Depression, however, revived the idea, and Roosevelt masterfully guided the legislation through Congress.

The Social Security Act included three major provisions. Its centerpiece was the creation of a pension fund for retired people over 65 and their survivors. Beginning in 1937 workers and employers contributed payroll taxes to establish the fund. Benefit payments started in 1940 and averaged $22 per month, a quite modest sum even for those depressed times. Roosevelt knew this, and stressed that the pension program was not intended to guarantee a comfortable retirement; it was designed to supplement other sources of income and protect the elderly from some of the "hazards and vicissitudes of life." Only later did American voters and politicians come to perceive Social Security as the *primary* source of retirement income for most of the aged. Today the average monthly payment is $850.

The Social Security Act also set up a shared federal-state unemployment insurance program, financed by a payroll tax on

"Yes, You Remembered Me."
*The social legislation of the
Second New Deal prompted this
depiction of FDR as the friend
of "The Forgotten Man."*

employers. In addition, the new legislation committed the national government to a broad range of social welfare activities based on the assumption that "unemployables"—people who were unable to work—would remain a state responsibility while the national government would provide work relief for the able-bodied. To that end the law inaugurated federal grants-in-aid for three state-administered public assistance programs—old age assistance, aid for dependent children, aid for the blind—and further aid for maternal, child welfare, and public health services.

Relatively speaking the new federal program was quite conservative. It was the only government pension program in the world financed by taxes on the earnings of current workers. Most other countries funded such programs out of general revenues. The Social Security payroll tax was also a regressive tax in that it entailed a single fixed rate for all, regardless of income level. It thus hurt the poor more than the rich, and it also hurt Roosevelt's efforts to revive the economy by removing from circulation a significant amount of money. In addition, the Social Security system initially excluded many of those classes of workers who needed it the most: farm workers, maids, and the self-employed.

Roosevelt recognized and regretted such limitations, but he knew that they were necessary compromises in order to see the Social Security Act through Congress and to enable it to withstand court challenges. As he replied to an aide who criticized funding the pension program through employee contributions, "I guess you're right on the economics, but those taxes were never a problem of economics. They are politics all the way through. We put those payroll contributions there so as to give the contributors a moral, legal, and political right to collect their pensions and their unemployment benefits. With those taxes in there, no damn politician can ever scrap my social security program."

The last of the major laws passed during this period was the Revenue Act of 1935, sometimes called the Wealth Tax Act, but popularly known as the "Soak-the-Rich" tax. The Revenue Act raised tax rates on incomes above $50,000. Estate and gift taxes also rose, as did the corporate tax on all but small corporations— those with less than $50,000 annual income. By "soaking" the rich, Roosevelt stole much of the thunder from the left, as he claimed, although the results fell short of the promise. The new tax law failed to increase federal revenue significantly, nor did it result in a significant redistribution of income.

Still, the prevailing view was that Roosevelt had moved in a radical direction. Newspaper editor William Randolph Hearst growled that the Wealth Tax was "essentially Communism. This bastard proposal should be ascribed to a composite personality which might be labeled Stalin Delano Roosevelt." But the extent of the new departure taken by the Second New Deal is easy to exaggerate. Such measures as Social Security, utility regulation, and higher taxes on the wealthy had long been in the works in Congress and had already been adopted by most other industrial nations. Roosevelt himself stressed that he had no love for socialism. "I am fighting Communism. . . . I want to save our system, the capitalistic system." Yet he added that to save it from revolutionary turmoil required a more equal "distribution of wealth."

THE ELECTION OF 1936 Whatever economic or philosophical judgment might be passed on the New Deal program, Roosevelt's political instincts were acute. Businessmen fumed over his tax and spending policies. The wealthy resented their loss of status and the growing power of government and labor. They railed against the New Deal and Roosevelt, whom they called "a traitor to his own class." Visitors at the home of J. P. Morgan, Jr., were cautioned not to mention Roosevelt's name lest it raise his blood pressure. But the conservative coalition of business and wealth, by its incoherent rage, made a perfect foil for the confident president, and the voting public rushed to his side. As Roosevelt recognized, businessmen "are unanimous in their hatred for me—and I welcome their hatred."

Another key element in Roosevelt's unprecedented popularity was his wife, Anna Eleanor Roosevelt, who had increasingly become an enormous political asset and would prove to be one of the most influential and revered women leaders of her time. She had lost both parents by age ten and had been a shy, withdrawn youth, utterly aware that her peers deemed her plain and even ugly. "I was a solemn child, without beauty," she recalled. "I seemed like a little old woman entirely lacking in the spontaneous joy and mirth of youth." But Eleanor grew into a tall, willowy, outgoing woman, and in the White House she became a more public figure than any previous First Lady.

Eleanor channeled her energies into social service. As a teen she had volunteered in a New York settlement house, and she remained ardently concerned about issues of human welfare and rights for women and blacks. As her secretary recalled, Eleanor Roosevelt "lived to be kind." Compassionate without being maudlin, more stoical than sentimental, she exuded warmth and sincerity, and she challenged the complacency of the affluent. "No woman," observed a friend, "has ever so comforted the distressed or so distressed the comfortable."

One of Eleanor Roosevelt's key functions was to keep the president from being isolated from the public. She served, he said, as his "eyes and ears," as well as his conscience, and she relished

Eleanor Roosevelt and Civil Rights Leader A. Philip Randolph. *The 1936 election marked the first time black voters cast a majority of their votes for a Democratic president.*

traveling around the country, representing him and the New Deal, defying local segregation ordinances, supporting women's causes, highlighting the plight of unemployed youth, and imploring Americans to live up to their equalitarian and humanitarian ideals. She was especially forceful in prodding officials to ease racial discrimination in federal programs. A Maine fisherman described her uniquely endearing qualities: "She ain't stuck up, she ain't dressed up, and she ain't afraid to talk." Eleanor Roosevelt also became her husband's most visible and effective liaison with many liberal groups, bringing labor leaders, women activists, and black spokesmen into the White House after hours, and serving to deflect criticism of the president by taking progressive stands and running political risks he himself dared not. He was the politician, she once remarked, she was the agitator.

The popularity of Eleanor and Franklin Roosevelt, and the New Deal, impelled the Republican convention in 1936 to avoid candidates too closely identified with the "hate-Roosevelt" contingent. The party chose Governor Alfred M. Landon of Kansas, a former Bull Moose Progressive. A fiscal conservative, Landon had nevertheless endorsed many New Deal programs. He was probably more liberal than most of his backers, and clearly more so than the party's platform, which accused the New Deal of usurping power.

Landon started the campaign on a moderate note, arguing that a Republican president could achieve the objectives of the New Deal more efficiently. As the campaign progressed, however, his statements grew more and more conservative. Before the end, Republican party leaders even tried to make an issue of the Social Security program, which they denounced as dangerous "regimentation."

Such appeals carried little weight. The Republicans hoped that the followers of Long, Coughlin, Townsend, and other dissidents would combine to draw enough votes away from Roosevelt to throw the election to them. But that possibility faded when an assassin, the son-in-law of a Louisiana judge whom Long had sought to remove, gunned down the "Kingfish" in September 1935. Coughlin, Townsend, and a remnant of the Long movement did support Representative William Lemke of North Dakota on a Union party ticket, but it was a forlorn effort that polled only 882,000 votes.

In 1936 Roosevelt forged a new electoral coalition that would affect national politics for years to come. While holding the support of most traditional Democrats North and South, FDR made strong gains among beneficiaries of the AAA farm program in the

West. In the northern cities he held on to the ethnic groups helped by New Deal welfare measures and afforded greater recognition in government appointments. Middle-class voters, whose property had been saved by New Deal measures, flocked to Roosevelt's support, along with intellectuals stirred by the ferment of new governmental ideas. The revived labor movement threw its support to Roosevelt, and in the most profound new departure of all, black voters for the first time cast the majority of their ballots for a Democratic president. "My friends, go home and turn Lincoln's picture to the wall," a black Pittsburgh journalist told black Republicans. "That debt has been paid in full."

In his acceptance speech to the Democratic convention Roosevelt dropped efforts to reassure corporate leaders. As the Americans of 1776 had sought freedom from political autocracy, he noted, the Americans of 1936 sought freedom from the "economic royalists." Roosevelt campaigned with tremendous buoyancy, and wound up carrying every state except Maine and Vermont, with a popular vote of 27.7 million to Landon's 16.7 million. Democrats would also dominate Republicans in the new Congress, by 77 to 19 in the Senate and 328 to 107 in the House.

SECOND-TERM SETBACKS AND INITIATIVES

As former presidents Jefferson and Jackson had found (and Lyndon Johnson, Richard Nixon, and Ronald Reagan would later discover), some malevolent fate often seems to await presidents who win such big victories, and the victorious Roosevelt found himself deluged in a sea of troubles during the next year. His second inaugural address, delivered on January 20, 1937, suggested that he was ready to move toward even more controversial reforms. The challenge to American democracy, he maintained, was that millions of citizens "at this very moment are denied the greater part of what the very lowest standards of today call the necessities of life. . . . I see one-third of a nation ill-housed, ill-clad, ill-nourished." The election of 1936 had been a mandate for even more extensive reforms, he argued, and the overwhelming Democratic majorities in Congress ensured their passage. But one major roadblock stood in the way: the Supreme Court.

THE COURT-PACKING PLAN By the end of the 1936 term the Court had ruled against New Deal laws in seven of the nine major cases it reviewed. Suits against the Social Security and Wagner Labor Relations Acts were also pending. Given the established trend of rulings, the Second New Deal seemed in danger of being nullified like the first.

For that reason, Roosevelt resolved to change the Court's philosophy by enlarging it, a move for which there was ample precedent and power. Congress, not the Constitution, determined the size of the Court, which at different times had numbered six, seven, nine, and ten justices, and in 1937 numbered nine. On February 5 Roosevelt sent his plan to Congress, without having consulted congressional leaders. He wanted to create up to fifty new federal judges including six new Supreme Court justices, and to diminish the power of the judges who had served ten or more years or reached the age of seventy.

But the "court-packing" maneuver, as opponents quickly tagged it, backfired. It was a shade too contrived, much too brazen, and far too political. By implying that some judges were impaired by senility, it affronted the elder statesmen of Congress and the Court, especially Justice Louis D. Brandeis, who was both the oldest and the most liberal of the Supreme Court judges. It also ran headlong into a deep-rooted veneration of the courts and aroused fears that another president might use the precedent for quite different purposes.

As it turned out, unforeseen events blunted Roosevelt's drive to change the Court. A sequence of Court decisions during the spring of 1937 reversed previous judgments in order to uphold the Wagner Act and the Social Security Act. A conservative justice resigned, and Roosevelt named to the vacancy one of the most consistent New Dealers, Senator Hugo Black of Alabama.

Roosevelt later claimed he had lost the battle but won the war. The Court had reversed itself on important New Deal legislation, and Roosevelt was able to appoint justices in harmony with the New Deal. But it was a costly victory that sowed dissension in his party and blighted Roosevelt's own prestige. For the first time Democrats in large numbers deserted the "champ," and the Republican opposition found a powerful issue. During the first eight months of 1937 the momentum of Roosevelt's great 1936 victory was lost.

A NEW DIRECTION FOR LABOR   Rebellions meanwhile erupted on other fronts. Under the impetus of the New Deal the labor movement stirred anew. John L. Lewis rebuilt the United Mine Workers from 150,000 members to 500,000 within a year. Spurred by the mine workers' example, Sidney Hillman of the

Amalgamated Clothing Workers and David Dubinsky of the International Ladies Garment Workers joined Lewis in promoting a campaign to organize workers in the mass-production industries. As leaders of some of the few industrial unions in the American Federation of Labor (AFL), they found the smaller, more restrictive, craft unions, whose membership was limited to workers in a single skilled trade, to be obstacles to organizing the basic industries.

In 1934 these leaders persuaded the AFL and its president William Green to charter industrial unions in the unorganized industries. But Green and other craft unionists saw these "federal" unions as temporary pools from which to draw members into the crafts. Lewis and the industrial unionists saw them as a chance to organize on a massive scale. In 1935, with passage of the Wagner Act, action began in earnest. The industrial unionists formed a Committee for Industrial Organization (CIO), and craft unionists began to fear submergence by the mass unions. Jurisdictional disputes spread among the unions, and in 1936 the AFL expelled the CIO unions, which then formed a permanent structure called after 1938 the Congress of Industrial Organizations. The rivalry spurred both groups to greater unionizing efforts.

The CIO's major organizing drives in automobiles and steel began in 1936, but they were thwarted by management's use of blacklisting, private detectives, labor spies, vigilante groups, and intimidation. Early in 1937 automobile workers spontaneously adopted a new technique, the "sit-down strike," in which workers refused to leave the shop until employers granted the right to collective bargaining. Many employers and much of the public saw in such revolutionary tactics a threat to property rights, an alarming gesture of contempt for authority, and further evidence of the New Deal's evil influence. Union leaders, fearing a public opinion backlash, frowned on the tactic, but it brought the first union victory in a major industry. In February 1937 General Motors recognized the United Automobile Workers as the bargaining agent for its employees. The following month, United States Steel capitulated to the Steel Workers Organizing Committee (later the United Steelworkers of America), granting it recognition, a 10 percent wage hike, and a forty-hour week.

Having captured two giants of heavy industry, the CIO went on in the next few years to organize much of industrial America: rubber, oil, electronics, and a good part of the textile industry, in which unionists had to fight protracted struggles to organize scattered plants. The laggard pace in textiles denied the CIO a major victory in the South comparable to its swift conquest of autos and steel in the North, but even down south a labor movement appeared that was at last something more than a vehicle for sporadic revolt.

A SLUMPING ECONOMY   Beset by the divisive effects of the Court fight and the sit-down strikes, Roosevelt in the fall of 1937 also faced a renewed depression. The years 1935 and 1936 had been marked by steady economic improvement, and by the spring of 1937 output had moved above the 1929 level. Then in the late summer the economy suddenly slid into a deep business slump, which the press called a "recession" to distinguish it from the "depression." By the end of the year an additional two million people had been thrown out of work; grim scenes of the earlier depression reappeared.

The prosperity of early 1937 had been achieved largely through governmental spending. But in June 1937 Roosevelt, worried about mounting deficits and rising inflation, ordered sharp cuts in federal spending. At the same time, the Treasury began to reduce disposable income by collecting $2 billion in Social Security taxes from employee paychecks. Private spending could not fill the gap left by reductions in government spending, and business still lacked the faith to risk large investments. The result was the slump of 1937.

In 1937, the "American Way" was out of reach for many. Photograph by Margaret Bourke-White.

The recession brought to a head a fierce debate within the administration. One group, led by Treasury Secretary Henry Morgenthau, Jr., favored less spending and a balanced budget. The other group, which included Harry Hopkins and Harold Ickes, argued for renewed spending and stricter enforcement of antitrust laws.

ECONOMIC POLICY AND LATE REFORMS   Roosevelt eventually endorsed the ideas of the spenders and antitrusters. On April 14, 1938, he asked Congress to adopt a large-scale spending program, and Congress voted almost $4 billion mainly for public works. In a short time the increase in spending reversed the economy's decline, but the recession and Roosevelt's reluctance to adopt massive spending forestalled the achievement of full recovery by the end of the decade. Only the crisis of World War II would return the American economy to full production and full employment.

The 1937 recession helped further erode Roosevelt's prestige and dissipate the mandate of the 1936 elections. Only a few major new reforms were enacted in 1937 and 1938 for the benefit of the "ill-housed, ill-fed, and ill-clad." They included the Wagner-Steagall National Housing Act, the Bankhead-Jones Farm Tenant Act, and the Fair Labor Standards Act.

The Housing Act set up the United States Housing Authority (USHA) in the Department of the Interior, which extended long-term loans to local agencies willing to assume part of the cost for slum clearance and public housing. The agency also subsidized rents for low-income residents.

Congress in 1937 also passed the Farm Tenant Act, administered by a new agency, the Farm Security Administration (FSA). The program made available loans to prevent marginal farmers from sinking into tenancy. It also offered loans to tenants for the purchase of their own farms. But the idea of small homesteads by the late 1930s was, as a tenant spokesman warned, "an economic anachronism, doomed to failure." American mythology still exalted the family farm, but in reality the ever-larger agricultural unit predominated. In the end the FSA proved to be little more than another relief operation which tided a few farmers over difficult times. A more effective answer to the problem, sadly, awaited mobilization for war, which took many tenants off into the military services or defense industries, broadened their horizons, and taught them new skills.

The Fair Labor Standards Act of 1938 applied to employees in enterprises that operated in or affected interstate commerce. It

The Farm Tenant Act (1937) and the Agricultural Adjustment Act (1938), among the last major reforms of the New Deal era, addressed the problem of rural poverty, which had worsened in the mid-1930s.

set a minimum wage of 40 cents an hour and a maximum work-week of forty hours, to be put into effect over several years. The act also prohibited child labor under the age of sixteen, and in hazardous occupations under eighteen. Southern congressmen howled in opposition to the bill because it would have the effect of raising wages in their region and thus increasing employers' expenses. They also feared that higher wage levels would make their region less attractive to northern industries that were considering relocation. A Democratic senator from Georgia denounced the bill as "the wildest dream that was ever presented to the American Congress." It was, he added, a sign of "bureaucracy run mad" under Roosevelt.

THE LEGACY OF THE NEW DEAL

SETBACKS FOR THE PRESIDENT   Although critics were unable to defeat the Fair Labor Standards Act, their stiff resistance revealed that an effective opposition was emerging within the president's own party, especially in the southern wing. Southern Democrats were at best uneasy bedfellows with organized labor and blacks, and more and more of them drifted toward closer cooperation with conservative Republicans. By the end of 1937 a formidable anti-New Deal bloc had developed.

In 1938 the bi-partisan conservative opposition stymied a bill granting Roosevelt authority to reorganize the executive branch amid cries that it would lead to dictatorship. The House also set up a Committee on Un-American Activities chaired by Martin Dies of Texas. Dies launched a crusade against Communists, and soon he began to brand New Dealers as Red Dupes. "Stalin baited his hook with a 'progressive' worm," Dies wrote in 1940, "and New Deal suckers swallowed bait, hook, line, and sinker."

As the political season of 1938 advanced, Roosevelt unfolded a new idea as momentous as his Court-packing plan—a proposal to reshape the Democratic party in the image of the New Deal. In June he announced his purpose to campaign in Democratic primaries as the party leader, "charged with the responsibility of carrying out the definitely liberal declaration of principles set forth in the 1936 Democratic platform." The effort ended in a standoff. Administration defeats in efforts to unseat conservative Democratic senators in Georgia, South Carolina, and Maryland broke the spell of presidential invincibility, or what was left of it. As in the Court fight, Roosevelt had risked his prestige while handing his adversaries persuasive issues. His opponents tagged his intervention in the primaries an attempted "purge"; the word evoked visions of Adolf Hitler and Josef Stalin, tyrants who had purged their Nazi and Communist parties in blood.

The elections of November 1938 handed the administration another setback, a result partly of the friction among Democrats. Their majority in the House fell from 229 to 93, in the Senate from 56 to 42. The margins remained large, but the president headed an increasingly divided party. In his State of the Union message in January 1939 Roosevelt for the first time proposed no new reforms, but spoke of the need "to *preserve* our reforms." Roosevelt did manage, however, to put through his plan to reorganize the executive branch. Under the Administrative Reorganization Act of 1939 the president could "reduce, coordinate, consolidate, and reorganize" the agencies of government. With that Roosevelt's domestic innovations feebly ended.

A HALF-WAY REVOLUTION   The New Deal had lost momentum, but it had wrought several enduring changes. By the end of the 1930s the power of the national government was vastly enlarged over what it had been in 1932, and hope had been restored to people who had grown fatalistic. But the New Deal entailed more than just bigger government and revived public confidence. It also constituted a significant change from the older liberalism embodied in the progressivism of Theodore Roosevelt and Woodrow Wilson. Those earlier reformers, despite their sharp differences, had assumed that the function of progressive government in the American republic was to ensure through aggressive regulation that the people had equal opportunity to pursue their notions of happiness.

Franklin Roosevelt and the New Dealers, however, went beyond this regulatory-state concept by insisting that the government should not simply *respond* to social crises but take positive steps to avoid them. Even more important, the New Deal's various welfare and benefit programs conferred on government the responsibility to ensure a minimum level of well-being for all Americans. The New Deal had established minimum standards for labor conditions and public welfare and helped middle-class Americans hold on to their savings, their homes, and their farms. The protection afforded by deposit insurance, unemployment pay, and Social Security pensions would come to be universally accepted as a safeguard against future depressions. The old progressive formulation of regulation versus trust-busting had finally been superseded by the rise of the "broker state," a government that mediated among major interest groups. Government's role was to act as an honest broker protecting a variety of interests, not just business but workers, farmers, consumers, small business, and the unemployed.

In implementing his domestic program, Roosevelt had steered a zigzag course between the extremes of laissez-faire capitalism and socialism. The first New Deal had experimented for a time with a managed economy under the NRA, but had abandoned that experiment for a turn toward enforcing competition and priming the economy with increased government spending. This finally produced full employment during World War II.

Roosevelt himself, impatient with theory, was indeed a pragmatist in developing policy: he kept what worked and discarded what did not. The result was, paradoxically, both profoundly revolutionary and profoundly conservative. Roosevelt sharply increased the regulatory functions of the federal government and laid the foundation for what would become an expanding welfare state. But his initiatives fell far short of socialism; they left the basic capitalistic structure in place. In the process of such bold experimentation and dynamic preservation, the New Deal represented a "half-way revolution" that permanently altered the social and political agenda.

FURTHER READING

A sound introduction to the decade of the New Deal is William E. Leuchtenburg's *Franklin D. Roosevelt and the New Deal, 1932–1940* (1963)° Paul Conkin's *The New Deal* (2nd ed., 1975)° is more critical. Sidney Baldwin's *Poverty and Politics: The Rise and Decline of the Farm Security Administration* (1969) looks at agricultural reforms. Michael E. Parrish's *Securities Regulation and the New Deal* (1970)° and Ellis W. Hawley's *The New Deal and the Problem of Monopoly* (1966)° analyze government attempts to forestall another market crash. Bernard Bellush's *The Failure of the NRA* (1976)° studies government relations with business.

The New Deal can also be understood by studying its chief proponents. Frank Freidel's *Franklin D. Roosevelt* (4 vols., 1952–1973)° and Arthur M. Schlesinger, Jr.'s *The Age of Roosevelt* (1957)° are multivolume, detailed works. James MacGregor Burns's *Roosevelt: The Lion and the Fox* (1956)° offers an astute political analysis. On Eleanor Roosevelt, see Lois Scharf's *Eleanor Roosevelt: First Lady of American Liberalism* (1987).°

For scholarship about the various groups involved in the New Deal, consult Lois Scharf's *To Work and to Wed* (1985)° and Susan Ware's *Beyond Suffrage: Women in the New Deal* (1981)°; Nancy J. Weiss's *Farewell to the Party of Lincoln* (1983)° and Harvard Sitkoff's *A New Deal for Blacks* (1978),° on blacks; and John M. Allswang's *A House of All Peoples: Ethnic Politics in Chicago, 1890–1936* (1971), on immigrants. Works on the critics of the New Deal include William Ivy Hair's *The Kingfish and His Realm: The Life and Times of Huey Long* (1991)° and Alan Brinkley's *Voices of Protest: Huey Long, Father Coughlin, and the Great Depression* (1982).° For radical leftist reactions to reform, see Harvey Klehr's *The Heyday of American Communism* (1984).

One interest group that was both supportive and critical of New Deal policies was organized labor. See Sidney Finc's *Sit-down: The General Motors Strike of 1936–1937* (1969) and Jerold S. Auerbach's *Labor and Liberty: The La Follette Committee and the New Deal* (1966).°

How Roosevelt dealt with the South is handled in Frank Freidel's *FDR and the South* (1965). How southern farmers fared is examined in David E. Conrad's *The Forgotten Farmers: The Story of the Sharecroppers in the New Deal* (1965). Dan T. Carter provides an insightful analysis of the influence of reform on race relations in the 1930s in his *Scottsboro: A Tragedy of the American South* (1969).°

For the cultural impact of the New Deal, consult Richard H. Pells's *Radical Visions and American Dreams: Cultural and Social Thought in the Depression Years* (1973)° and Richard D. McKinzie's *The New Deal for Artists* (1973).°

°These books are available in paperback edition.

28

FROM ISOLATION TO
GLOBAL WAR

Postwar Isolationism

THE LEAGUE AND THE UNITED STATES   In the late 1930s the winds of war swept across Asia and Europe, abruptly shifting the direction of American politics from domestic to foreign affairs. Another Democratic president had to turn his attention from social and economic reform to military preparedness and war. But between Woodrow Wilson and Franklin Roosevelt lay two decades of relative isolation from foreign entanglements. The postwar mood of 1920 set the pattern. The voters expressed their resistance to international commitments, and President-elect Harding lost little time in disposing of American membership in the League of Nations. The spirit of isolation found other expressions as well: the higher tariff walls, the Red Scare, the rage for "100 percent Americanism," and tight immigration laws by which the nation all but shut the door to any more newcomers.

The United States may have felt the urge to leave a wicked world to its own devices, but it could hardly stop the world and get off. American business, despite the tariff walls, now had worldwide connections. Investments and loans abroad put in circulation the dollars that purchased American exports. Overseas possessions, moreover, directly involved the country in world affairs, especially in the Pacific. Even the League of Nations was too great an organization entirely to ignore. After 1924 the United States gradually entered into joint efforts with the League on such matters as policing the international trade in drugs and arms, and on a variety of economic, cultural, and technical conferences.

WAR DEBTS AND REPARATIONS Probably nothing did more to heighten American isolationism during the 1920s and 1930s— or anti-American feeling in Europe—than the war-debt tangle. When in 1917 the Allies had begun to exhaust private credit in the United States, the American government advanced them funds first for the war effort and then for postwar reconstruction. To Americans the repayment of the war debts seemed a simple matter of obligation, but Europeans commonly had a different perception.

The French and British insisted that they could pay America only as they collected reparations from Germany. Twice during the 1920s the resulting·strain on Germany brought the structure of international payments to the verge of collapse, and both times the Reparations Commission called in private American bankers to work out rescue plans.

The whole structure finally did collapse during the Great Depression. In 1931 President Hoover negotiated a moratorium on both German reparations and Allied payment of war debts. At the end of 1932, after Hoover's debt moratorium ended, most of the European countries defaulted on their war debts to the United States. In retaliation, Congress passed the Johnson Debt Default Act of 1934, which prohibited private loans to any such government.

ATTEMPTS AT DISARMAMENT Yet, for all the isolationist sentiment of the time, Wilsonian idealism persisted during the 1920s and after. A lingering doubt, tinged with guilt, haunted many Americans about their rejection of the League. Before long the Harding administration hit upon a happy substitute—disarmament. The conviction had grown after World War I that the armaments race had caused the war, and that arms limitation would bring lasting peace. The United States had no intention of maintaining a large army, but under the naval building program begun in 1916 it had constructed a fleet second only to that of Britain.

Neither the British nor the Americans relished a naval armaments race, but both shared a common concern about the alarming growth of Japanese power. Since 1914 Japanese-American relations had grown increasingly strained, as the United States objected to continued Japanese encroachments in Asia. During World War I Japan had quickly taken China's Shantung Peninsula and the islands of Micronesia from its enemy, Germany. In 1917, after the United States entered the war, Viscount Kikujiro Ishii visited Washington to secure American recognition of Japan's expanded position in Asia, dropping hints that Germany had several times tried to get Japan to quit the war. To forestall the loss of an ally in the war, Secretary of State Robert Lansing signed an ambiguous agreement saying that "Japan has special interests in China." Americans were unhappy with the Lansing-Ishii Agreement, but it was viewed as the only way to keep Japan in the war.

After the war ended Japanese-American relations grew more tense. To address the problem, President Harding invited countries to an armaments conference at which Pacific and East Asian affairs would also be discussed. The Washington Armaments Conference of November 1921 opened with a surprise announcement by the American secretary of state, Charles Evans Hughes, who told the delegates that "the way to disarm is to disarm." He then offered concrete suggestions that ultimately became the basis of agreement. It was one of the most dramatic moments in American diplomatic history. In less than fifteen minutes, one electrified reporter said, Hughes had destroyed more tonnage "than all the admirals of the world have sunk in a cycle of centuries."

Delegates from the United States, Britain, Japan, France, and Italy signed a Five-Power Naval Treaty incorporating Hughes's plan for tonnage limits and a naval holiday of ten years during which no capital ships (battleships and aircraft carriers) would be built. These powers also agreed to refrain from further fortification of their Pacific possessions. The agreement in effect partitioned the world: United States naval power became supreme in the Western Hemisphere, Japanese power in the western Pacific, British power from the North Sea to Singapore.

Two other major agreements were concluded at the Washington Conference. With the Four-Power Treaty, the United States, Britain, Japan, and France agreed to respect each other's possessions in the Pacific and to refer any disputes or any outside threat to consultation. The Nine-Power Treaty for the first time formally pledged the signers to support the Open Door and the territorial integrity of China. The powers, in addition to those signing the Five-Power Treaty, were China, Belgium, Portugal, and the Netherlands.

With these agreements in hand, Harding's supporters could boast of a brilliant diplomatic stroke which relieved American taxpayers of the need to pay for an enlarged navy, and which defused potential conflicts in the Pacific. Yet the agreements were uniformly without obligation and without teeth. The signers of the Four-Power Treaty agreed only to consult, not to help each other. The formal endorsement of the Open Door in the Nine-Power Treaty was just as ineffective, for the United States remained unwilling to uphold the principle with anything but pious affirmation. Moreover, the naval disarmament treaty set limits only on capital ships; the race to build cruisers, destroyers, submarines, and other smaller craft continued.

THE KELLOGG-BRIAND PACT   In the midst of such wishful thinking, the fanciful ideal of simply abolishing war altogether seized the American imagination. Peace societies thrived, and the glorious vision of ending war by the stroke of a pen culminated in the signing of the Kellogg-Briand Pact in 1928. This unique treaty originated when French Foreign Minister Aristide Briand proposed to Coolidge's secretary of state, Frank B. Kellogg, an agreement that the two countries would never go to war with each other.

The Pact of Paris (its official name), signed on August 27, 1928, solemnly declared that the signatories "condemn recourse to war . . . and renounce it as an instrument of national policy." Eventually sixty-two powers joined the pact, but all explicitly or tacitly reserved "self-defense" as an escape hatch. The United States Senate included a reservation declaring the Monroe Doctrine necessary to America's self-defense, and then ratified the agreement by a vote of 85 to 1. A Virginia senator who voted for "this worthless, but perfectly harmless peace treaty" wrote a friend that he feared it would "confuse the minds of many good people who think that peace may be secured by polite professions of neighborly and brotherly love."

Indeed, the treaty proved to be the grandest illusion in an age of illusions. Its impotence surfaced in 1930 when war broke out in Manchuria, where Russian forces quickly put down a Chinese effort to regain control of the Chinese Eastern Railway. When Hoover's secretary of state, Henry L. Stimson, called the Soviet Union's attention to the Pact of Paris, the Soviet foreign minister noted that the United States had not yet recognized the Soviet government and scorned the presumption of Stimson's communication.

THE "GOOD NEIGHBOR" POLICY   In Latin America the spirit of peace and noninvolvement helped allay resentments against the United States, which had freely intervened in the Caribbean during the first two decades of the century. In 1924 American forces left the Dominican Republic after an eight-year occupation. The marines left Nicaragua a year later, but returned in 1926 with the outbreak of disorder and civil war. In 1927 the Coolidge administration negotiated an agreement for American-supervised elections, but one rebel leader, César Augusto Sandino, held out and the marines stayed until 1933. The unhappy legacies of this intervention were public bitterness toward the United States and a Nicaraguan National Guard, created to keep order after the marines left, but used in 1936 to set up the dictatorship of Anastasio Somoza. These legacies continue to have their effects down to the present day.

The troubles in Nicaragua increased strains with Mexico. Relations were already threatened by repeated Mexican threats to take over American oil properties. In 1928, however, the American ambassador to Mexico so pleased the Mexicans by his gestures of friendship that he was able to get an agreement protecting American economic rights. Expropriation did in fact occur in 1938, but the Mexican government agreed to reimburse American owners.

In 1928 President-elect Hoover improved America's image in Latin America by permitting publication of a memorandum which denied that the Monroe Doctrine justified American intervention in Latin America. It stopped short of repudiating intervention on any grounds, but that fine point hardly blunted the celebration in Latin America. Although Hoover never endorsed this so-called Clark Memorandum, he never ordered intervention in the area. Before he left office, steps had already been taken to withdraw American forces from Nicaragua and Haiti.

Franklin D. Roosevelt likewise embraced "the policy of the good neighbor" and soon advanced it in practice. In December 1933 at the seventh Pan-American Conference, the United States supported a resolution which affirmed: "No state has the right to intervene in the international or external affairs of another." Under Roosevelt the marines completed their withdrawals from Nicaragua and Haiti, and in 1934 the president negotiated with Cuba a treaty that abrogated the Platt Amendment (1901), which had given America a formal right to intervene in Cuba.

WAR CLOUDS

JAPANESE INCURSIONS IN CHINA The lessening of irritants in the Western Hemisphere proved an exception in an otherwise dismal world scene, as war clouds darkened over Europe and Asia. Actual conflict erupted first in Asia, where unsettled social and political conditions in China had attracted foreign encroachments since before the turn of the century. After the overthrow of the last imperial dynasty in 1911, the Kuomintang (or National

Party) under Dr. Sun Yat-sen and, later, Chiang Kai-shek, extended its power from a southern base around Canton to take Peking in 1928 and set up a new capital in Nanking. But when the new government tried to extend its power to the north in Manchuria it ran into the vested interest of the Russians and Japanese there. Chinese nationalist aspirations convinced the Japanese that their own extensive rights in Manchuria, including the South Manchurian Railway, were in danger.

Japanese occupation of Manchuria began with the Mukden Incident of September 18, 1931, an explosion that destroyed a section of railway track near that city. The Japanese "Kwantung Army," based in Manchuria to guard the railway, blamed the incident on the Chinese and used it as a pretext to begin its occupation, which it extended during the winter of 1931–1932 to all of Manchuria, including the Russian sphere of influence. In 1932 the Japanese converted Manchuria into the puppet empire of "Manchukuo." The Manchuria Incident, as the Japanese called their undeclared war, flagrantly violated the Nine-Power Treaty, the Kellogg-Briand Pact, and Japan's pledges as a member of the League of Nations. But when China asked the League and the United States for help, neither obliged. President Hoover refused to invoke either military or economic sanctions.

In January 1932, Japan's indiscriminate bombing of civilians in Shanghai, China's great port city, aroused Western indignation, but provoked no action. When the League of Nations condemned Japanese aggression in February 1933, Japan withdrew from the League. Thereafter hostilities in Manchuria gradually subsided and ended with a truce. An uneasy peace settled upon East Asia for four years, during which Japan's military leaders further extended their political sway at home.

ITALY AND GERMANY   The rise of the Japanese militarists paralleled the rise of warlike dictators in Italy and Germany. In 1922 Benito Mussolini had seized power in Italy after organizing the Fascist movement, which was based on a composite faith in nationalism and socialism. The party's program, and above all Mussolini's promise to restore order in a country fragmented by dissension, enjoyed a wide appeal. Once in power, Mussolini largely abandoned the socialist part of his platform and gradually suppressed all opposition. By 1925 he wielded dictatorial power as Il Duce (the leader).

There was always something ludicrous about the strutting Mussolini. Italy, after all, afforded but a limited power base in the total European picture. But Germany was another matter,

Mussolini and Hitler.

and most Americans were not amused, even at the beginning, by Il Duce's counterpart, Adolf Hitler. Hitler's National Socialist (Nazi) party duplicated the major features of Italian Fascism, including the ancient Roman salute. Hitler capitalized on the weakness of Germany's postwar government, especially in the face of world depression, and on festering German resentment toward the Versailles treaty. Named chancellor on January 30, 1933, Hitler moved swiftly to intimidate the opposition, won dictatorial powers by March, and in 1934 assumed the title of *Reichsfuhrer* (national leader) with absolute powers. The Nazi police state cranked up the engines of tyranny, persecuting Jews, whom Hitler blamed for all Germany's troubles, and rearming in defiance of the Versailles Treaty. Hitler flouted international agreements, pulled Germany out of the League of Nations in October 1933, and frankly proclaimed that he meant to extend control over all German-speaking peoples. Despite one provocation after another the European democracies seemed to lack the will to resist.

RUSSIAN RECOGNITION   Isolationism grew even more potent during the early 1930s, but one significant exception to American insularity was Roosevelt's decision to favor official recognition of Soviet Russia. By 1933 the reasons for American refusal to recognize the Bolshevik regime had grown stale. Seen as an expansive market, Russia stirred fantasies of an American trade boom, much as China had at the turn of the century. Japanese expansionism in Asia, moreover, gave Russia and the United States a common foreign policy concern. Given an opening by the shift of opinion, Roosevelt invited the Soviet commissar for foreign affairs to visit Washington. After nine days of talks, a formal exchange of notes on November 16, 1933, signaled the renewal of diplomatic relations. The Soviet commissar promised that his country would abstain from propaganda in the United States, extend religious freedom to Americans in the USSR, and reopen the question of pre-revolutionary debts to the United States.

THE MARCH OF AGGRESSION   After 1932 a catastrophic chain of events in Asia and Europe sent the world hurtling toward disaster. In 1934 Japan renounced the Five-Power Naval Treaty. The next year Mussolini commenced Italy's conquest of Ethiopia. That same year a referendum in Germany's Saar Basin, held in accordance with the Versailles Treaty, delivered that coal-rich region into the hands of Hitler. In 1936 Hitler reoccupied the Rhineland with armed forces, in violation of the Versailles Treaty but without any forceful response from the French. The year 1936 also brought the Spanish Civil War, which began with an uprising of the Spanish armed forces in Morocco, led by General Francisco Franco, against the democratically elected Spanish Republic. Over the next three years Franco established a fascist dictatorship with help from Hitler and Mussolini while the Western democracies left the Spanish Republic to its fate. On July 7, 1937, Japanese and Chinese troops clashed at the Marco Polo Bridge near Peking, and the incident quickly developed into a full-scale war. It was the beginning of World War II in Asia, two years before war erupted in Europe. That same year Japan joined Germany and Italy in establishing an alliance known as the Rome-Berlin-Tokyo "Axis."

By 1938 the peace of Europe trembled in the balance. Having rebuilt German military force, Hitler forced the *Anschluss* (union) of Austria with Germany in March 1938. Six months later Germany took the mountainous Sudetenland, largely German in population, which had been given to Czechoslovakia at the Versailles Peace Conference in 1919 because of its strategic importance to that new nation's defense. Hitler's latest aggression came shortly after the conference at Munich, where Britain and France sought to appease Hitler by agreeing to abandon Czechoslovakia, a country that had probably the second-strongest army

AGGRESSION IN EUROPE

← Aggressive moves

▨ Axis Powers

in central Europe. After promising that the Sudetenland would
be his last territorial demand, Hitler in March 1939 brazenly
broke his pledge by occupying the remainder of Czechoslovakia.
In quick succession the Spanish Republic finally collapsed on
March 28, and Mussolini seized the kingdom of Albania on April
7. Finally, on September 1, 1939, Hitler launched his conquest
of Poland. A few days before, he had reached a nonaggression
pact with Russia. Having deserted Czechoslovakia, Britain and
France now honored their commitment to go to war if Poland
were invaded.

DEGREES OF NEUTRALITY   During these years of deepening crisis,
the Western democracies seemed paralyzed, hoping in vain that
each concession would appease the appetites of fascist dictators.
The American response was to retreat more deeply into isolation. A Senate inquiry into the origins of American involvement
in World War I reinforced the desire to stay out of Europe's con-

flicts. Under Senator Gerald P. Nye of North Dakota, a progressive Republican, the committee sat from 1934 to 1937 and concluded that bankers and munitions makers had made scandalous profits from the war. Although Nye never showed that greed for profit had actually impelled Wilson into war, he did insist that Uncle Sam had been duped by the "merchants of death." If the United States wanted to remain neutral in the current crisis, therefore, it would have to keep Americans out of war zones, keep belligerent vessels out of American ports, embargo arms shipments, and set quotas on the export of contraband. Such ideas became official policy as war enveloped Asia and Europe.

Like generals who are said to be always preparing for the last war, Congress occupied itself with keeping out of the last war. Neutrality laws of the 1930s moved the United States back toward complete isolation from the quarrels of Europe. But while Americans wanted to keep out of war, their sympathies were more strongly than ever with the Western democracies, and the triumph of fascist aggression aroused growing fears for national security.

On August 31, 1935, President Roosevelt signed the first in what would become a series of annual neutrality acts. The Neutrality Act of 1935 forbade the sale of arms and munitions to all belligerents whenever the president proclaimed that a state of war existed. Americans who traveled on belligerent ships thereafter did so at their own risk. Roosevelt would have preferred discretionary authority to levy an embargo only against aggressors, but he reluctantly accepted the act because it was to be effective for only six months, and for the time being met "the need of the existing situation." That is, it would likely be enforced against Italy, which was then threatening war with Ethiopia.

On October 3, 1935, Italy invaded Ethiopia and the president invoked the Neutrality Act. When Congress reconvened in January 1936, it fell into a three-cornered debate among the advocates of mandatory embargoes, flexible embargoes aimed only at aggressors, and traditional neutrality. After six weeks Congress simply extended the arms embargo and added a provision forbidding loans to belligerents.

Then in July 1936, while Italian troops mopped up the last resistance in Ethiopia, the Spanish Civil War broke out. Roosevelt now became more isolationist than some of the isolationists. Although the Spanish Civil War involved a fascist uprising against a recognized, democratic government, Roosevelt accepted the French and British position that only nonintervention would localize the fight. There existed, moreover, a strong bloc of pro-

Franco Catholics in America who feared that the liberal Spanish Republic was influenced by the Communists and was a threat to the Church. Intrigues by Spanish Communists did prove divisive, and the Soviet Union did supply aid to the Republic, but nothing like the quantity of German and Italian aid to Franco.

Roosevelt asked for a "moral embargo" on the arms trade, and he encouraged Congress to extend the neutrality laws to cover civil wars. Congress did so in January 1937 with only one dissenting vote. The Western democracies then stood witness while German and Italian soldiers, planes, and armaments supported Franco's overthrow of Spanish democracy.

In the spring of 1937 American isolationism reached a peak. A Gallup poll found that 94 percent of its respondents preferred efforts to keep out of war over efforts to prevent war. That same spring Congress passed yet another neutrality law, which continued restraints on arms sales and loans, forbade Americans to travel on belligerent ships, and forbade the arming of American merchant ships trading with belligerents. The new law also empowered the president to require that goods other than arms or munitions exported to belligerents be placed on a cash-and-carry basis. This was an ingenious scheme to preserve a profitable trade without running the risk of war.

The new law had its first test on July 7, 1937, when Japanese and Chinese forces clashed at the Marco Polo Bridge. Since neither side declared war, Roosevelt was able to avoid invoking the neutrality law, which would have favored the Japanese, since China had greater need of arms but few means to get supplies past the Japanese Navy. A flourishing trade in munitions to China flowed around the world as ships carried American arms across the Atlantic to England, where they were reloaded on British ships bound for Hong Kong. Roosevelt, by inaction, had challenged strict isolationism.

He soon ventured a step further. In Chicago on October 5, 1937, Roosevelt denounced the "reign of terror and international lawlessness" in which 10 percent of the world's population threatened the peace of the other 90 percent. He called for a quarantine against nations "creating a state of international anarchy and instability from which there is no escape through mere isolation or neutrality." On the whole, public reaction to the speech was mixed, but the president nevertheless quickly backed off from its implications and refused to spell out any specific program for dealing with aggression.

The continuing Japanese war against China brought public

outrage and protests from Secretary of State Cordell Hull. In July 1938, after nearly a year of war in China, the State Department notified domestic aircraft manufacturers and exporters that it opposed sales to those guilty of attacks on civilian populations. To have imposed an outright embargo would have violated a commercial treaty of 1911 with Japan, but after another year, on July 26, 1939, the United States gave six-months' notice of the termination of the treaty—thus clearing the way for an embargo on war materials.

By then Hitler had brought Europe into war. After the German occupation of Czechoslovakia, Roosevelt no longer pretended impartiality in the impending struggle. He urged Congress to repeal the embargo and permit the United States to sell arms on a cash-and-carry basis to Britain and France, but to no avail. "You haven't got the votes," Vice-President Garner told him, "and that's all there is to it." When the Germans attacked Poland on September 1, 1939, Roosevelt proclaimed neutrality, but in a radio talk stressed that he did not, like Wilson, ask Americans to remain neutral in thought because "even a neutral has a right to take account of the facts."

Roosevelt summoned Congress into special session on September 21 and asked it again to amend the Neutrality Act. "I regret the Congress passed the Act," he confessed. "I regret equally that I signed the Act." This time he got what he wanted by winning the support of conservative Democrats. Under the Neutrality Act of 1939 the Allies could buy for cash and take away in their own ships arms or anything else they wanted. American ships, on the other hand, were excluded from belligerent ports and from specified war zones. Roosevelt then designated as a war zone the Baltic Sea and the waters around Great Britain and Ireland from Norway south to the coast of Spain. One unexpected effect of this move was to relieve Hitler of any inhibitions against using unrestricted submarine warfare to blockade Britain.

American attitudes continued to vacillate. When the war crisis first developed, an isolationist policy prevailed. Once the great democracies of western Europe faced war, American public opinion, appalled at Hitler's tyranny, came to support measures short of war to help their cause. For a time it seemed possible that the Western Hemisphere could remain insulated from the war. After Hitler overran Poland in less than a month, the war settled into an unreal stalemate that began to be called the "Phony War." What lay ahead, it seemed, was a long war of attrition—much like World War I—in which Britain and France would have the resources to outlast Hitler. The illusion lasted from October 1939 through the winter of 1940.

THE STORM IN EUROPE

BLITZKRIEG   In the spring of 1940 the winter's long *Sitzkrieg* suddenly erupted into *Blitzkrieg*—lightning war. At dawn on April 9, without warning, Nazi troops entered Denmark and disembarked along the Norwegian coast. Denmark fell in a day, Norway within a few weeks. On May 10 Hitler unleashed his dive bombers and panzer tank divisions on neutral Belgium and the Netherlands. On May 21 German forces moving down the valley of the Some reached the English Channel, cutting off a British force sent to help the Belgians and French. A desperate evacuation from the beaches at Dunkirk enlisted every available boat from warship to tug. Some 338,000 men, about a third of them French, escaped to England. Having outflanked France's heavily fortified defense perimeter, the Maginot Line, the German forces rushed ahead, cutting the French armies to pieces and spreading panic by strafing refugees in a deliberate policy of terror. On June 10 Mussolini entered the war. "I need only a few thousand dead to enable me to take my seat . . . at the peace table," Il Duce said. Speaking at the University of Virginia the same day, Roosevelt grimly ad libbed: "The hand that held the dagger has plunged it into the back of France." On June 14 the swastika flew over Paris.

AMERICA'S GROWING INVOLVEMENT   Britain now stood alone, but in Parliament Prime Minister Winston Churchill breathed defiance. "We shall go on to the end," he pledged; "we shall never surrender." Despite such grim resolution, America itself seemed suddenly vulnerable as Hitler unleashed his air force against Britain. President Roosevelt, who in his annual budget had requested $1.9 billion for defense, now asked for more, and called for the production of 50,000 combat planes a year. By October 1940 Congress had voted more than $17 billion for defense. In response to Churchill's appeal for American military supplies, the War and Navy Departments began releasing stocks of arms, planes, and munitions to the British.

The summer of 1940 brought the desperate Battle of Britain, in which the Royal Air Force finally forced the Germans to give up plans to invade the British Isles. Submarine warfare mean-

St. Paul's Cathedral looms above the destruction wrought by German bombs during the Blitz. Churchill's response: "We shall never surrender."

while strained the resources of the battered Royal Navy. To relieve the pressure, Churchill urgently requested the transfer of American destroyers, and secret negotiations led to an executive agreement under which fifty "overaged" destroyers went to the British in return for ninety-nine-year leases on naval and air bases in Newfoundland, Bermuda, and other islands in the Caribbean. Two weeks later, on September 16, 1940, Congress adopted the first peacetime conscription in American history. All men aged twenty-one to thirty-five were required to register for a year's military service within the United States.

The new state of affairs prompted vigorous debate between "internationalists" who believed national security demanded aid to Britain and isolationists who charged that Roosevelt was drawing the United States into a needless war. In May 1940 the nonpartisan Committee to Defend America by Aiding the Allies was organized, drawing its strongest support from the East and West Coasts and the South. Two months later, isolationists formed the America First Committee. The group included the historian Charles A. Beard, Herbert Hoover, and the celebrated aviator, Charles A. Lindbergh. Before the end of 1941 the committee had about 450 chapters around the country, but probably two-thirds of its members lived within a 300-mile radius of Chicago. The isolationists argued that a Nazi victory, while distasteful, would pose no threat to national security.

A THIRD TERM FOR FDR   In the midst of these profound developments the quadrennial presidential campaign came due. Isolationist sentiment was strongest in the Republican party, yet their nominee took a different stance. Wendell L. Willkie was a former Democrat who had voted for Roosevelt in 1932. An Indiana farm boy whose disheveled charm inspired strong loyalty, he openly supported aid to the Allies.

The Nazi victory also ensured another nomination for Roosevelt. The president cultivated party unity behind his foreign policy and kept a sphinx-like silence about his intentions. The world crisis reconciled southern conservatives to the man whose foreign policy at least they supported. At the July convention in Chicago Roosevelt won nomination for a third term with only token opposition. For his new running mate, Roosevelt tapped his Secretary of Agriculture, Henry Wallace, a devoted supporter who would appeal to farm voters.

Through the summer Roosevelt assumed the role of a man above the political fray, busy rather with urgent matters of defense and diplomacy. Willkie inspired a more intense personal devotion than any Republican candidate since Theodore Roosevelt, but he had trouble positioning himself since there was little on which he disagreed with Roosevelt. Most New Deal programs were too popular, in any case, to oppose head-on.

Like Landon in 1936, Willkie was reduced to attacking New Deal red tape, and promising to run the programs better. A widespread reluctance to violate the tradition against a presidential third term strengthened his argument that new blood was needed in the White House. In the end, however, as his campaign languished, he switched to an attack on Roosevelt's conduct of foreign policy. In October he warned: "If you re-elect him you may expect war in April, 1941." To this Roosevelt responded, "I have said this before, but I shall say it again and again and again: Your boys are not going to be sent into any foreign wars." Three days before the election he declared in Buffalo that "this country is not going to war." Neither man distinguished himself with such hollow claims, since each knew the risk of the all-out aid to Britain, which they both supported.

Roosevelt won the election by a comfortable margin of 27 million votes to Willkie's 22 million, and a wider margin of 449 to 82 in the electoral college. Though the popular vote was closer than any presidential election since 1916, the dangerous world situation convinced a majority of voters to back the Democrats' slogan: "Don't switch horses in the middle of the stream."

THE ARSENAL OF DEMOCRACY Bolstered by the mandate for an unprecedented third term, Roosevelt moved quickly to provide greater aid to Britain. Soon after the election, Churchill informed him that British credit was fast running out. Since direct American loans would arouse memories of earlier war-debt defaults—the Johnson Act of 1934 forbade such loans anyway—the president created an ingenious device to bypass that issue and yet supply British needs: the "lend-lease" program.

In a fireside chat on December 29, 1940, Roosevelt told the nation that it must become "the great arsenal of democracy" because of the threat of Britain's fall. In his annual message to Congress on January 6, 1941, he warned that only the British navy stood between America and the peril of attack. Greater efforts to bolster British defenses were therefore in order. At the end of the speech he defined the Four Freedoms for which the democracies fought: freedom of speech, freedom of worship, freedom from want, and freedom from fear. The Lend-Lease Bill, introduced in Congress on January 10, authorized the president to sell, transfer, exchange, lend, lease, or otherwise dispose of arms and other equipment and supplies to "any country whose defense the President deems vital to the defense of the United States."

For two months a bitter debate over the bill raged in Congress and around the country. Isolationists saw it as the point of no return. "The lend-lease-give program," claimed Senator Burton K. Wheeler, "is the New Deal's triple A foreign policy; it will plow under every fourth American boy." Roosevelt pronounced this "the rottenest thing that has been said in public life in my generation." Administration supporters denied that lend-lease would lead to American involvement in the war, but it did indeed increase the risk. On March 11, 1941, lend-lease became law, and Britain and China were the first beneficiaries.

While the nation debated, the war intensified. In October 1940, as the presidential campaign approached its climax, Mussolini launched attacks on Greece and, from Italian Libya, assaulted the British in Egypt. But his forces had to fall back in both cases, and in the spring of 1941 Hitler came to his aid. German forces under General Erwin Rommel joined the Italians in Libya, forcing the British, whose resources had been drained to help Greece, to withdraw into Egypt.

In April 1941 lightning attacks by Nazi panzer divisions overwhelmed Yugoslavia and Greece, and by the end of May, airborne forces subdued the Greek island of Crete, putting Hitler in a position to menace the entire Middle East. With Hungary, Rumania, and Bulgaria forced into the Axis fold, Hitler controlled nearly all of Europe. Then, on June 22, 1941, he suddenly fell upon Russia, his ally, hoping to eliminate the potential threat on his rear with another lightning stroke. The Nazis moved on a 2,000-mile front from the Arctic to the Black Sea with seeming invincibility until, after four months, the Russian soldiers and civilians rallied in front of Leningrad, Moscow, and Sevastopol. During the winter of 1941–1942 Hitler began to learn the bitter lesson the Russians had taught Napoleon in 1812.

Winston Churchill had already decided to provide British support to Russia in case of such an attack. Roosevelt adopted the same policy, offering American aid two days after the German invasion. Stalinist Russia, so long as it held out, ensured Britain's survival. American aid was now indispensable to Europe's defense, and the logic of lend-lease led to deeper American involvement. To deliver aid to Britain, goods had to be maneuvered through the U-boat "wolfpacks" in the North Atlantic. So on April 11, 1941, Roosevelt informed Churchill that the United States Navy would extend its patrol areas in the North Atlantic nearly all the way to Iceland.

In August 1941 Roosevelt and Churchill held a secret rendezvous in Newfoundland. There they drew up a statement of principles known as the Atlantic Charter. In effect it amounted to a joint declaration of war aims, its eight points a mixture of the idealistic goals of the New Deal and Wilson's Fourteen Points. It called for the self-determination of all peoples, equal access to raw materials, economic cooperation, freedom of the seas, and a new system of collective security. The Soviet Union later endorsed the statement.

Having entered into a joint statement of war aims with the anti-Axis powers, the United States soon became involved in shooting incidents in the North Atlantic. As early as May 21, 1941, in fact, a German U-boat had sunk an American freighter off the coast of Brazil, in retaliation for which Roosevelt froze all German and Italian assets and closed down German and Italian consulates. On September 4 came the first attack on an American warship, when a German submarine fired two torpedoes at a destroyer. A week later the president ordered American ships to "shoot on sight" any German or Italian raiders ("rattlesnakes of the Atlantic") that ventured into American defensive waters. Five days later the United States Navy announced it would convoy merchant ships all the way to Iceland.

Further attacks in October hastened Congress into making changes in the neutrality act already requested by the president. On November 17 the legislation was in effect repealed through removal of the bans on arming merchant vessels and allowing them to enter combat zones and belligerent ports. Step by step the United States was giving up neutrality and embarking on naval warfare against Germany. Still, the American people hoped to avoid taking the final step into all-out war. The decision for war would come in an unexpected quarter—the Pacific.

The Storm in the Pacific

JAPANESE AGGRESSION   After the Nazi victories in the spring of 1940, America's relations with Japan also took a turn for the worse. Japanese militarists, bogged down in the vastness of China, now eyed new temptations: French Indochina, the Dutch East Indies, British Malaya, and Burma. They could thereby incorporate into their "Greater East Asia Co-Prosperity Sphere" the oil, rubber, and other strategic materials that the crowded homeland lacked. As it was, they depended on the United States for important supplies, including 80 percent of their oil. During the summer of 1940 Japan forced the helpless French government at Vichy to permit the construction of Japanese airfields in northern Indochina and sever the rail line into South China, thus cutting off Western supplies to the Chinese. The United States responded with a loan to China and the Export Control Act of July 2, 1940, which authorized the president to restrict the export of arms and other strategic materials to Japan. Gradually Roosevelt extended embargoes on aviation gas, scrap iron, and other supplies to Japan.

On September 27, 1940, the Tokyo government signed a Tripartite Pact with Germany and Italy, by which each pledged to declare war on any nation that attacked any of them. The Germans hoped to persuade Japan to enter Siberia when their forces entered Russia from the West. The Soviet presence in Siberia did inhibit the Japanese impulse to move southward into Indochina, but on April 13, 1941, while the Nazis were sweeping through the Balkans, Japan signed a nonaggression pact with Russia and, once the Nazis invaded Russia in June, the Japanese were freed of any threat from the north.

They first moved southward on July 25, 1941, when Japan announced that it was assuming a protectorate over all of French Indochina. The next day Roosevelt took three steps: he froze all Japanese assets in the United States; he restricted exports of oil

JAPANESE EXPANSION
BEFORE PEARL HARBOR

▮ Territory under Japanese
control, Dec. 7, 1941

Dates indicate year of
acquisition or occupation

Map labels:

U.S.S.R.

KAMCHATKA PEN.
(U.S.S.R.)

MONGOLIA

Lupin

Khabarousk

SAKHALIN,
1905

KURILE
ISLANDS,
1875

Harbin

MANCHURIA
1932

Vladivostok

Mukden

KWEISUI, 1937

PEKING
1937

KOREA
PROTECTORATE,
1905
ANNEXED, 1910

C H I N A

Yenan

PORT ARTHUR
1905
SHANTUNG
PEN. 1905

KAIFENG
1938

Tokyo

JAPAN

HANKOW, 1938

ICHANG, 1940

Chungking

Nanking

SHANGHAI,
1937

NACHANG, 1939

HANGCHOW,
1937

RYUKYU
ISLANDS,
1879

BONIN IS.,
1876

AMOY, 1938

PESCADORES,
1895

SWATOW, 1939

CANTON, 1938

FORMOSA (TAIWAN),
1895

VOLCANO IS.
1891

PACIFIC
OCEAN

MARCUS, 1899

BURMA

Hanoi

Hong Kong

KWANGCHOW (Fr.), 1940

HAINAN, 1939

THAI–
LAND

FRENCH
INDOCHINA,
1940

PHILIPPINE
ISLANDS
(U.S.)

GUAM (U.S.)

MARIANA
ISLANDS

MICRONESIA

OCCUPIED, 1914, MANDATED, 1922

MARSHALL
ISLANDS

Saigon

BRITISH
MALAYA

CAROLINE ISLANDS

Singapore

DUTCH EAST INDIES

0   1000 Miles
0   1000 Kilometers

to Japan; and he took the armed forces of the Philippines into the
Army of the United States and put their commander, General
Douglas MacArthur, in charge of all American forces in the Far
East. By September the oil restrictions had tightened into an embargo. Forced by the embargo to secure oil supplies elsewhere,
the Japanese army and navy began to plan attacks on the Dutch
and British colonies in southeast Asia.

Actions by both sides put the United States and Japan on the
path to a war neither wanted. In his regular talks with the Japanese ambassador, Secretary of State Cordell Hull insisted that
Japanese withdrawal from Indochina and China was the price of
renewed trade. A more flexible position might have strengthened the moderates in Japan. Premier Konoye, however, while
known as a man of liberal principles who preferred peace, caved
in to pressures from the militants. Perhaps he had no choice.

The Japanese warloads, for their part, seriously misjudged the
United States. The desperate wish of Americans to stay out of
war might still have enabled the Japanese to conquer the British
and Dutch colonies before an American decision to act. But the

warlords decided that they dared not leave the American navy intact and the Philippines untouched on the flank of their new lifeline to the south.

TRAGEDY AT PEARL HARBOR   Thus a tragedy began to unfold with a fatal certainty mostly out of sight of the American people, whose attention was focused on the war in the Atlantic. Late in August 1941 Premier Konoye proposed a personal meeting with President Roosevelt. Hull advised Roosevelt not to meet unless agreement on fundamentals could be reached in advance. Soon afterward, on September 6, an imperial conference approved preparations for an attack on Hawaii and gave Premier Konoye six more weeks to reach a settlement. The Japanese emperor's clear displeasure with the risk of an attack afforded the premier one last chance to pursue a compromise, but the presence of Japanese troops in China remained a stumbling block. In October Konoye urged War Minister Hideki Tojo to consider withdrawal while saving face by keeping some troops in North China. Tojo refused. Faced with this rebuff, and Tojo's threat to resign and bring down the cabinet, Konoye himself resigned on October 15; Tojo became premier the next day. The war party was now in complete control.

On the very day that Tojo became premier, a special Japanese envoy conferred with Hull and Roosevelt in Washington. His arrival was largely a cover for Japan's war plans, although neither he nor Japan's ambassador to the United States knew that. On November 20 they presented Tojo's final proposal to Hull. Japan would occupy no more territory if the United States would cut off aid to China, restore trade with Japan, and help the Japanese get supplies from the Dutch Indies. In that case Japan would pull out of southern Indochina immediately and abandon the remainder once peace had been established with China—presumably on Japanese terms. Tojo expected the United States to refuse such demands. On November 26 Hull repeated the demand that Japan withdraw altogether from China. That same day a Japanese naval force began heading silently across the North Pacific toward Pearl Harbor, Hawaii.

Washington already knew that war was imminent. Reports of Japanese troop transports moving south from Formosa prompted Washington to send warnings to Pearl Harbor and Manila, and to the British government. The massive movements southward clearly signaled attacks on the British and the Dutch. American leaders had every reason to expect war in the southwest Pacific, but none expected that Japan would commit most of its carriers to another attack 5,000 miles away at Pearl Harbor.

On the morning of December 7, 1941, American cryptanalysts decoded the last part of a Japanese message breaking off the negotiations. Tojo instructed Japan's ambassador to deliver the message at 1:00 P.M. EST (7:30 A.M. in Honolulu), about a half hour before the blow fell, but delays held up delivery until more than an hour later than schedule. The War Department sent out an alert at noon that something was about to happen, but the message, which went by commercial wire because radio contacts were broken, arrived in Hawaii eight and a half hours later. Even so, the decoded Japanese message did not mention Pearl Harbor specifically, and American military leaders there would probably have assumed the attack was to come in southeast Asia.

It was still a sleepy Sunday morning when the first Japanese planes roared down the west coast and the central valley of Oahu to begin their assault. At 7:53 A.M. the flight commander sounded the cry "Tora! Tora! Tora!" (Tiger! Tiger! Tiger!), the signal that the attackers had taken the American navy by surprise. For nearly two hours the Japanese planes kept up their fierce attack on an unready Pacific fleet. Of the eight battleships in Pearl Harbor, three were sunk and the others were badly battered. Altogether nineteen ships were sunk or disabled. At the airfields on the island the Japanese destroyed about 150 planes. Before it was over the raid had killed more than 2,400 American servicemen and civilians. The surprise attack fulfilled the dreams of its planners, but it fell short of total success in two ways. The Japanese ignored shore installations and oil tanks, without which the surviving ships might have been forced back to the West Coast, and they missed the American aircraft carriers which had fortuitously left port a few days earlier. In the naval war to come, these carriers would be decisive.

Later the same day (December 8 in the western Pacific) Japanese forces began assaults on the Philippines, Guam, and Midway, and on British forces in Hong Kong and the Malay Peninsula. With one stroke the Japanese had silenced America's debate on neutrality, and a suddenly unified and vengeful nation resolutely prepared for the struggle. A Michigan man recalled his reactions to the Japanese attack: "First it was indignation, then it turned to anger, and by the time one went to work the following morning it was determination: 'They can't do that to us.' " The day after the attack President Roosevelt told Congress that December seventh "will live in infamy," and he asked for a declaration of war. It was approved unanimously, with the sole exception of Representative Jeanette Rankin, who was unable in conscience to vote for war in 1917 or 1941. On December 11

The Attack on Pearl Harbor. (Above) *The view from a Japanese fighter plane shows American battleships in vulnerable positions.* (Below) *The view from an American airfield shows the destruction and confusion brought on by the surprise attack.*

Germany and Italy declared war on the United States. The separate wars in Asia and Europe had become one global war—and American isolationism was cast aside.

FURTHER READING

Robert Dallek's *Franklin D. Roosevelt and American Foreign Policy, 1932–1945* (1979)° covers the foreign policy of the 1930s. A number of revisionists stress the economic base of foreign policy; see William Appleman Williams's *The Tragedy of American Diplomacy* (rev. ed., 1972)° and Joan Hoff-Wilson's *American Business and Foreign Policy, 1920–1933* (1971).

Other scholars have concentrated on diplomatic issues of the 1920s. Thomas H. Buckley's *The United States and the Washington Conference, 1921–1922* (1970) examines disarmament. For a study of the Kellogg-Briand Pact, see Robert H. Ferrell's *Peace in Their Time: The Origins of the Kellogg-Briand Pact* (1968).°

For American relations in the Far East during the period, see Akira Iriye's *After Imperialism: The Search for a New Order in the Far East, 1921–1933* (1965). For relations with Latin America, see David Green's *The Containment of Latin America* (1971) and Walter LaFeber's *Inevitable Revolutions* (1983).°

Bruce M. Russett's *No Clear and Present Danger* (1972)° provides a critical account of America's eventual entry into World War II. For another interpretation of Roosevelt's diplomacy see Robert A. Divine's *The Reluctant Belligerent* (2nd ed., 1979).° A more recent analysis is Waldo Heinrich's *Threshold of War: Franklin D. Roosevelt and American Entry into World War II* (1988).

On Pearl Harbor, see Gordon W. Prange's *At Dawn We Slept: The Untold Story of Pearl Harbor* (1981)° and John Toland's *Infamy* (1982).°

° These books are available in paperback editions.

29

THE WORLD AT WAR

The Japanese attack on Pearl Harbor ended a tense period of un-easy neutrality for the United States. Even more importantly, of course, it launched America into an epochal world event that would ultimately transform the nation's social and economic landscape as well as its position in international affairs. In early December 1941, however, few Americans envisioned such seis-mic consequences. For the moment all attention was focused on halting the Japanese advance and mobilizing the whole nation for war.

AMERICA'S EARLY BATTLES

SETBACKS IN THE PACIFIC   For months after Pearl Harbor the news from the Pacific was "all bad," as President Roosevelt frankly confessed. A string of Allied outposts fell to the enemy in the three months after December 1941: Guam, Wake Island, the Gilbert Islands, Hong Kong, Singapore, and Java. The Japanese capture of Rangoon in March 1942 cut off the Burma Road, the main supply route to China.

In the Philippines, where General MacArthur abandoned Manila on December 27, the main American forces, outmanned and outgunned, held out tenaciously on Bataan Peninsula until April 9, and then on the fortified island of Corregidor. MacAr-thur himself slipped away in March, when he was ordered to Australia to take command of Allied forces in the Southwest Pa-cific. By May 6, when American forces surrendered Corregidor, Japan controlled a new empire that stretched from Burma east-ward through the Dutch Indies and on out to Wake Island and the Gilberts.

If the Japanese had stopped there, they might have consolidated an almost impregnable empire with the resources they had seized. But the Japanese navy succumbed to what one of its admirals later called "victory disease." The Supreme Command grew ever more greedy and decided to push on into the South Pacific, isolate Australia, and strike again at Hawaii. The aim was to draw out and destroy the American navy before the productive power of the United States could be brought to bear on the war effort.

CORAL SEA AND MIDWAY   Japanese advances were finally halted in two decisive naval battles, the first of which started the day after Corregidor fell. The Battle of the Coral Sea (May 7–8, 1942) stopped a fleet convoying Japanese troop transports toward the southern coast of New Guinea. Planes from the *Lexington* and *Yorktown* sank one Japanese carrier, damaged another, and destroyed smaller ships. American losses were greater, and included the carrier *Lexington*, but the Japanese transports had to abandon their designs on Australia.

Less than a month after the Coral Sea engagement Admiral Isoruku Yamamoto, the Japanese naval commander, decided to force a showdown in the central Pacific. With nearly every capital ship under his personal command, he headed for Midway Island, from which he hoped to render Pearl Harbor helpless. This time it was the Japanese who were the victims of surprise. American cryptanalysts had by then broken their naval code, and Admiral Chester Nimitz, commander of the central Pacific, knew their plan of attack. He reinforced Midway with planes and the carriers *Enterprise*, *Hornet*, and *Yorktown*.

The first Japanese foray against Midway, on June 4, severely damaged the American installation on the island, but at the cost of about a third of the Japanese planes. Before another attack could be mounted, American torpedo planes and dive bombers had caught three of the four Japanese carriers in the process of servicing their planes. Dive bombers sank three of them during the first assault. Later the Japanese lost another carrier, but not before its planes disabled the *Yorktown*. The only other major American loss was a destroyer. The Japanese defeat was the turning point of the Pacific war, a loss they were never able to surmount.

SETBACKS IN THE ATLANTIC   Early Allied setbacks in the Pacific were matched by losses in the Atlantic. Since the *Blitzkrieg* of 1940 German submarine "wolfpacks" had wreaked havoc in the

North Atlantic. In January 1942, after an ominous lull, German U-boats suddenly appeared off American shores and began to sink coastal shipping, much of it tankers. From January through June 1942 nearly 400 ships were lost in American waters before effective countermeasures brought the problem under control. The naval command hastened the building of small escort vessels, meanwhile pressing into patrol service all kinds of surface craft and planes, some of them civilian. During the second half of 1942 these efforts reduced losses to a negligible number.

Mobilization at Home

The Pearl Harbor attack ended not only the long debate between isolation and intervention but also the long depression of the 1930s. The war effort required all of America's huge productive capacity and full employment of the workforce. For 1942 alone the government ordered 60,000 planes, 45,000 tanks, and 8,000,000 tons of merchant shipping, and the next year's goals were even higher. Soon after Pearl Harbor, Winston Churchill recalled that someone had compared the United States to a gigantic boiler: "Once the fire is lighted under it, there is no limit to the power it can generate."

Mobilization was in fact already farther along than preparedness had been in 1916–1917. The draft had been in effect for more than a year, and the army had grown to more than 1.4 million men by June 30, 1941. Congress quickly extended the term of military service to last until six months after the war's end. Men between eighteen and forty-five became subject to service. Altogether more than 15 million American men and women served in the armed forces during the war.

ECONOMIC CONVERSION The economy too was already partially mobilized by lend-lease and defense efforts. Congress authorized the president to reshuffle government agencies and to allot materials and facilities as needed for defense, with penalties for those who failed to comply. The War Production Board (WPB), created in January 1942, directed industrial conversion to war production. For a year the WPB oversaw a wild scramble of manufacturers for available supplies. The Office of Scientific Research and Development mobilized thousands of scientists to create and modify radar, sonar, the proximity fuse, the bazooka, and the many other innovations which contributed to the war effort.

The pressure of wartime needs and the stimulus of government spending doubled the gross national product between 1940 and 1945. Government expenditures during the war years soared. The total was about 10 times what America spent in World War I, and 100 times the expenditures during the Civil War. The massive infusion of government capital into the economy also encouraged greater centralization and consolidation in private industry. The larger companies tended to win the most government contracts, and the more they won the larger they became. Conversely, those without government contracts withered and died. In 1942 alone 300,000 businesses shut down.

FINANCING THE WAR   To cover the war's huge cost the president preferred taxes to borrowing, but Congress, dominated by fiscal conservatives, feared taxes more than deficits and refused to go more than halfway with Roosevelt's fiscal prudence. The government covered about 45 percent of its 1939–1946 costs with tax revenues; the rest was borrowed from the public. War-bond drives induced citizens to put aside more than $150 billion in bonds. Financial institutions picked up most of the rest of the government's debt. In all, the national debt grew by the end of the war to $260 billion, about six times its size at the time of Pearl Harbor.

America's basic economic problem during the war years was no longer finding jobs but finding workers for the booming shipyards, aircraft factories, and powder mills. Millions of people were brought fully into the economic system who before had lived on its margin. Stubborn poverty did not disappear, but for most of those who stayed home the war spelled neither severe hardship nor suffering, but a better life than ever before, despite shortages and rationing. Labor unions benefited directly from the dramatic growth of the civilian workforce. Union membership increased significantly during the war years, from about 11 million to 15 million.

ECONOMIC CONTROLS   Increased incomes and spending during the war raised up the specter of inflation. Some of the available money went into taxes and war bonds, but even so, more was sent chasing after civilian goods just as production was converting to war needs. Such consumer durables as cars, washing machines, and non-defense housing in fact ceased to be produced at all. Only strict restraints would keep prices on other items from soaring out of sight. In April 1941 Roosevelt had created the Office of Price Administration (OPA), and the following year Congress authorized it to set price ceilings. With prices frozen, goods had to be allocated through rationing, which began with tires in December 1941 and was gradually extended to other scarce items such as sugar, coffee, and gasoline. Wages and farm prices at first were not controlled, however, and this complicated matters. War prosperity offered farmers a chance to redress the balance from two decades of distress, and farm-state congressmen raised both floors and ceilings on farm prices. Higher food prices reinforced worker demands for higher wages. To relieve this inflationary pressure, in October 1942, the president won new authority to control wages and farm prices. Both business and workers chafed at the new controls, and on occasion the government was forced to seize industries threatened by strike. The coal mines and railroads were both nationalized for a short time in 1943. Despite these problems, the government's program to stabilize the economy succeeded. By the end of the war consumer prices had risen about 31 percent, a far better record than the World War I rise of 62 percent.

To bolster the economic controls, the conservation of resources was paramount. As one popular slogan had it, "Use it up, wear it out, make it do or do without." The public collected scrap metal and grew their own food in backyard "Victory gardens." In June 1942, when the war plants faced a rubber shortage, Roosevelt asked citizens to turn in "old tires, old rubber raincoats, old garden hoses, rubber shoes, bathing caps, gloves —whatever you have that is made of rubber."

SOCIAL EFFECTS: WOMEN   The war proved to be an important watershed in the changing status of women. From 1910 to 1940 the proportion of women working had barely altered, but at a time when millions of men were going into military service the demand for labor shook up old prejudices about sex roles in the workplace—and in the military. Nearly 200,000 women went into the Women's Army Corps (WAC) and the navy's equivalent, Women Accepted for Volunteer Emergency Service (WAVES). Lesser numbers joined the Marine Corps, the Coast Guard, and the Army Air Force.

Even more significant were the 6 million women who entered the workforce during the war, an increase in general of over 50 percent and in manufacturing alone of some 110 percent. By 1944 over a third of all American women were in the labor force. Old barriers fell overnight as women put on slacks, gloves, goggles, hairnets, and hardhats to become toolmakers, machinists, riveters, crane operators, lumberjacks, stevedores, blacksmiths,

Women workers assembling the tail section of the B17F bomber (the Flying Fortress) at the Douglas Aircraft plant in Long Beach, California, 1942.

and railroad workers. Desperate for laborers, the government launched an intense publicity campaign to draw women into traditional male jobs. "Do your part, free a man for service," one ad pleaded. "Rosie the Riveter," a beautiful model dressed in overalls, served as the cover-girl for the campaign.

One striking feature of the wartime economy was the larger proportion of older, married women in the workforce. In 1940 about 15 percent of married women went into gainful employment; by 1945 it was 24 percent. In the workforce as a whole, married women for the first time outnumbered single women. There were many vocal opponents to this new trend. One disgruntled legislator asked what would happen to traditional domestic tasks if married women worked in factories: "Who will do the cooking, the washing, the mending, the humble homey tasks to which every woman has devoted herself; who will rear and nurture the children?" Many women, however, were eager to get away from the grinding routine of domestic life. One woman welder remembered that her wartime job "was the first time I had a chance to get out of the kitchen and work in industry and make a few bucks. This was something I had never dreamed would happen." And it was something that many women did not want to relinquish after the war.

SOCIAL EFFECTS: BLACKS   The most volatile issue ignited by the war was that of black participation in the defense effort. From the start black leaders demanded full recognition in the armed forces and defense industries. Eventually about a million African Americans served in the armed forces, in every branch and every theater. But most served in segregated units that mirrored the society from which they came. Every army camp had its separate facilities and its periodic racial "incidents." The most important departure from this pattern came in a 1940 decision to give up segregation in officer candidate schools, except those for air force cadets. A separate flight school at Tuskegee, Alabama, trained about 600 black pilots, many of whom distinguished themselves in combat.

War industries were even less accessible to black influence and pressure, although government policy in theory opposed discrimination. In February 1941, A. Philip Randolph, the resolute head of the Brotherhood of Sleeping Car Porters, organized a March on Washington Movement to demand an end to discrimination in defense industries. The administration, alarmed at the prospect of a mass descent on Washington, struck a bargain. The Randolph group called off its march in return for an executive order prohibiting discrimination in defense work and training programs by requiring a nondiscrimination clause in defense contracts. About two million blacks were working in war plants

Members of the 99th Fighter Group of the U.S. Army Air Force, a unit of black pilots famous for their skill and bravery.

by the end of 1944. The demand for black labor revived migration out of the South, which had lagged during the Depression, and large numbers of southern blacks now headed for the Far West as well as the North. States with the highest proportionate increases of black population in the 1940s were, in order, California, Michigan, Oregon, Washington, Utah, Colorado, Wisconsin, Illinois, and New York.

Blacks quickly broadened their drive for wartime participation into a more inclusive and open challenge to all kinds of discrimination, including racial segregation itself. Membership in the NAACP soared during the war from 50,000 to 450,000. Blacks could look forward to greater political participation after the Supreme Court, in *Smith v. Allwright* (1944), struck down Texas's white primary on the grounds that Democratic primaries were part of the election process and thus subject to the Fifteenth Amendment.

Growing black militancy aroused antagonism from some whites. Racial violence did not approach the level of that in World War I, but rising tensions on a hot summer afternoon in Detroit sparked two days of fighting in 1943, until federal troops arrived on the second evening to stop it. Twenty-five blacks and nine whites had been killed.

SOCIAL EFFECTS: JAPANESE-AMERICANS   The record on civil liberties during World War II was on the whole better than that during World War I, if only because there was virtually no opposition to the war effort after the attack on Pearl Harbor. Neither German-Americans nor Italian-Americans faced the harassments meted out to their counterparts in the previous war; few had much sympathy for Hitler or Mussolini. The shameful exception to an otherwise improved record was the treatment given to Americans of Japanese descent. Few, if any, were disloyal, but all were victims of fear and racial prejudice.

This was especially the case in the months following the attack on Pearl Harbor. One California barbershop offered "free shaves for Japs" but noted that it was "not responsible for accidents." Others were even blunter. Idaho's governor declared: "A good solution to the Jap problem would be to send them all back to Japan, then sink the island. They live like rats, breed like rats, and act like rats." Such attitudes were regrettably widespread, and the government finally succumbed to demands that it force all Japanese, citizens or not, into "War Relocation Camps" in the interior. More than 100,000 were eventually removed from their homes and businesses in this sorry episode. As one

Young Japanese-Americans awaiting baggage inspection upon arrival at a "war relocation camp" in Turlock, California, 1942. Photograph by Dorothea Lange.

Japanese-American poignantly complained, "What really hurts most is the constant reference to us evacuees as 'Japs.' 'Japs' are the guys we are fighting. We're on this side and we want to help. Why won't America let us?" Not until 1983 did the government finally acknowledge the injustice of the internment policy. Five years later, Congress voted to give $20,000 and an apology to the 60,000 former internees who were still living.

DOMESTIC CONSERVATISM   In domestic politics a growing conservatism marked the wartime period. Discontent with price controls, labor shortages, rationing, and a hundred other petty vexations spread, and the 1942 congressional elections registered a national swing against the New Deal. Republicans gained forty-six seats in the House and nine in the Senate, chiefly in the Midwest farm areas. Democratic losses outside the South strengthened the southern delegation's position within the party, and the delegation itself was becoming increasingly conservative. A coalition of Republican and Democratic conservatives gutted "nonessential" New Deal agencies. In 1943 Congress abolished the Work Projects Administration, the National Youth Administration, and the Civilian Conservation Corps.

Organized labor, despite substantial gains during the war, was also vulnerable to the conservative trend. In the spring of 1943, when John L. Lewis led the coal miners out on strike, widespread public resentment prompted Congress to pass the Smith-Connally War Labor Disputes Act, which authorized the government to seize plants useful to the war, required pre-strike votes, and forbade unions to make political contributions. The intended effect of the act was somewhat blunted by the tendency of unionists to vote routinely for strikes as a bargaining ploy. In 1943 a dozen states adopted laws variously restricting picketing and other union activities, and in 1944 Arkansas and Florida started a wave of state "right-to-work" laws that outlawed the closed shop.

THE ALLIED DRIVE TOWARD BERLIN

In mid-1942 the "home front" began to get news from the war fronts that some of the lines were holding at last. By midyear a fleet of American air and sea subchasers was ending six months of happy hunting for U-boats off the Atlantic coast. This was all the more important because war plans called for the defeat of Germany first.

WAR AIMS AND STRATEGY There were many reasons for the priority of defeating Hitler: Nazi forces in western Europe and the Atlantic posed a more direct threat to the Western Hemisphere; German war potential exceeded Japan's, and German science was more likely to come up with some devastating new weapon. Lose in the Atlantic, General George Marshall grimly predicted, and you lose everywhere. Hitler's attack on Russia in June 1941 strengthened the argument. Yet Japanese attacks involved Americans directly in the Pacific war from the start, and as a consequence, during the first year of fighting more Americans went to the Pacific than across the Atlantic.

The Pearl Harbor attack brought Prime Minister Churchill quickly to Washington for lengthy talks about a common war plan that affirmed the priority of first winning the war against Germany. Agreement on war aims, however, did not bring agreement on strategy, and when Roosevelt and Churchill met at the White House again in June 1942, they could not agree on where to hit first. American strategists wanted to strike directly across the English Channel before the end of 1942. With vivid memories of the last war, the British feared a mass bloodletting in trench warfare if they struck prematurely. The Russians, bearing the brunt of the German attack in the East, insisted that the Western Allies must do something to relieve the pressure. Finally, the Americans accepted Churchill's proposal to invade French North Africa.

THE NORTH AFRICA CAMPAIGN   It was not only the Russians who needed a diversion, but also the strapped British forces defending Egypt against German and Italian invaders from Libya. On November 8, 1942, Anglo-American forces under the command of General Dwight D. Eisenhower landed in Morocco and Algeria. Completely surprised, French forces under the Vichy government (which collaborated with the Germans) had little will to resist.

Farther east the tide had turned and British forces were pushing German armies back across Libya. Before spring, the Germans were caught in a gigantic pincers. By April the British had linked up with American forces. Hammered from all sides, unable to retreat across the Mediterranean, an army of 275,000 Germans surrendered on May 13, 1943, leaving all of North Africa in Allied hands.

While this battle of Tunisia was still unfolding, in January 1943, Roosevelt, Churchill, and the Combined Chiefs of Staff met at Casablanca. Stalin declined to leave beleaguered Russia for the meeting but continued to press for the opening of a second front in western Europe. The Anglo-American planners, however, decided to postpone the cross-Channel invasion further and to carry out Churchill's scheme to attack what he called the "soft underbelly of the Axis" by invading Sicily and then Italy. They also authorized an American offensive in the Pacific islands. Top priority, however, went to an antisubmarine campaign in the Atlantic.

Before leaving Casablanca, Roosevelt announced, with Churchill's endorsement, that the war would end only with the "unconditional surrender" of all enemies. This was designed to reassure Stalin that the Western Allies would not negotiate separately with the enemy. The West desperately needed Soviet cooperation in defeating Germany, and Roosevelt and Churchill were eager to reassure Stalin of their good intentions.

The announcement also reflected Roosevelt's determination to see that "every person in Germany should realize that this time Germany is a defeated nation." This dictum was later criti-

WAR IN EUROPE AND AFRICA, 1942-1945

Axis Powers at outbreak of war

Maximum extent of Axis military power

Allies

Neutral countries

Allied offensives

--- Heaviest Allied aerial bombing

.... Inside limit of German U-boat operations

cized for having stiffened enemy resistance, but it probably had little effect; in fact neither the Italian nor Japanese surrender would be totally unconditional. But the decision did have one unexpected result: it virtually assured eventual Soviet control of eastern Europe because it required Russian armies to pursue Hitler's forces all the way to Germany. And as they liberated the countries of eastern Europe, the Russians were determined to remain in control.

SICILY AND ITALY   After the Allied victory in the North African campaign, on July 10, 1943, about 250,000 British and American troops landed on Sicily, scoring a complete surprise. General George Patton led his Seventh Army ashore on the southwest coast, and after a fierce battle at the beachhead, the Americans moved swiftly across the island to take Palermo twelve days later. The entire island was in Allied hands by August 17, although some 40,000 Germans escaped to the mainland.

The German-Italian collapse in Sicily ended Mussolini's twenty years of Fascist rule. On July 25, 1943, Italy's king notified the dictator of his dismissal as premier. A new regime startled the Allies when it offered not only to surrender but to switch sides in the war. Unfortunately, mutual suspicions prolonged talks until September 3, while the Germans poured reinforcements into Italy and seized key points. In the confusion the Italian army disintegrated, although most of the navy escaped to Allied ports. A few army units later joined the Allied effort, and many of the soldiers joined bands of partisans who fought behind the German lines. Mussolini, plucked from imprisonment by a daring German airborne raid, became head of a shadowy puppet government in northern Italy.

The Allied assault on the Italian mainland therefore did not turn into an easy victory. The main landing at Salerno on September 9 encountered heavy German resistance. The Americans, joined by British troops, nevertheless secured beachheads within a week and by October 1 were in Naples. Rome was the next objective, but mountainous country stood in the way. Fighting stalled through the winter of 1943–1944 in some of the most miserable, muddy, and frigid conditions of the war. After a five-month siege the Americans finally took Rome on June 4, 1944. Yet they enjoyed only a brief moment of glory, for the long-awaited cross-Channel landing in France began two days later.

STRATEGIC BOMBING OF EUROPE   Behind the long-postponed landings on the Normandy beaches lay months of preparation. While waiting, the United States Army Air Force and the Royal Air Force (RAF) carried the battle into Hitler's "Fortress Europe." By 1943 American strategic bombers were full-fledged partners of the RAF in the effort to pound Germany into submission. Yet despite the widespread damage it caused, the strategic air offensive ultimately failed to cut severely into German production or, as later studies found, to break civilian morale. German war production in fact increased until the last few weeks of the war, and German fighter planes downed more and more Allied bombers. By the end of 1943, however, new jettisonable gas tanks permitted Allied escort fighters to fly as far as Berlin and back. Thereafter, heavy losses of both planes and pilots forced the German Luftwaffe to conserve its strength and cease challenging every Allied mission.

With air supremacy assured, the Allies were free to concentrate on their primary urban and industrial targets, and when the time came, to provide cover for the Normandy landings. On April 14, 1944, General Eisenhower assumed control of the Strategic Air Forces for use in the Normandy landings, less than two months away. On D-Day he told the troops: "If you see fighting aircraft over you, they will be ours."

THE TEHERAN MEETING By the summer of 1943 the build-up of American forces in Britain, combined with successes in the Battle of the Atlantic and the strategic bombing of Europe, finally brought Churchill around on the cross-Channel invasion. Late in November he and Roosevelt met with Stalin in Teheran, Iran, to coordinate plans for the cross-Channel invasion and a Russian offensive. After Churchill and Roosevelt assured Stalin that a cross-Channel invasion was finally coming, the Russian premier in return promised to enter the war against Japan after Germany's defeat. The Allied leaders also agreed to begin plans for an international organization and for the occupation of postwar Germany.

Earlier in November 1943, while on the way to the Teheran meeting with Stalin, Churchill and Roosevelt had met with China's Generalissimo Chiang Kai-shek in Cairo, Egypt. The resultant Declaration of Cairo affirmed that war against Japan would continue until Japan's unconditional surrender, that all Chinese territories taken by Japan would be restored to China, and that "in due course Korea shall become free and independent."

D-DAY AND AFTER In January 1944 General Eisenhower arrived in London to take command at Supreme Headquarters, Allied

Gen. Dwight D. Eisenhower instructing paratroopers just before they board their airplanes to launch the D-Day assault.

Expeditionary Forces (SHAEF). Already battle-tested in North Africa and the Mediterranean, he now faced the supreme test of Operation "Overlord," the cross-Channel assault on Hitler's "Atlantic Wall." D-Day fell on June 6, 1944. At dawn the invasion fleet of some 4,000 ships began to pour out their cargoes of troops and supplies along sixty miles of Normandy beaches.

Having surprised the Germans, the Allies within two weeks had landed a million men and seized a beachhead sixty miles wide and five to fifteen miles deep. They quickly contrived manmade harbors, and during July the Allies edged inland through the Norman marshes and hedgerows, then fanned out westward into Brittany and eastward toward Paris. Meanwhile a joint American-French invasion force landed on the French Mediterranean coast, took Marseilles and Toulon, and raced up the Rhône Valley. German resistance in France collapsed. By mid-September 1944 most of France and Belgium were cleared of enemy forces.

LEAPFROGGING TO TOKYO

Even in the Pacific, relegated to lower priority, Allied forces had brought the war within reach of the enemy homeland by the end of 1944. The war's first American offensive in fact had been in the southwest Pacific. There the Japanese, stopped at Coral Sea and Midway, had thrust into the southern Solomons, and were building an airstrip on Guadalcanal from which they could attack transportation routes to Australia. On August 7, 1942, two months before the North Africa landings, the First Marine Division landed on Guadalcanal.

This provoked a savage Japanese response. Reinforcements poured in, and the opposing navies challenged each other in a confusing series of night battles that battered both badly. But while the Americans suffered heavy losses, they so devastated the Japanese carrier groups that the Japanese navy remained on the defensive for the rest of the war. The marines, helped by reinforcements, finally cleared the steaming jungles of Japanese six months later.

MACARTHUR IN NEW GUINEA Meanwhile American and Australian forces under General MacArthur had begun to push the Japanese out of their positions on New Guinea's north coast. These costly battles, fought through some of the hottest, most humid and mosquito-infested swamps in the world, secured the eastern tip of New Guinea by the end of January 1943.

At this stage American war planners made a critical decision. MacArthur proposed to advance westward along the northern coast of New Guinea toward the Philippines and ultimately Tokyo. Admiral Chester Nimitz argued for a sweep through the islands of the central Pacific toward Formosa and China. The Combined Chiefs of Staff agreed to MacArthur's plan, but they also ordered Nimitz to undertake his sweep in order to protect MacArthur's northern flank.

A new tactic expedited the movement. During the air Battle of the Bismarck Sea (March 2–3, 1943), American bombers sank eight Japanese troopships and ten warships bringing reinforcements. Thereafter the Japanese dared not risk sending transports to points under siege, making it possible to use the tactic of neutralizing Japanese strongholds with air and sea power, and moving on, leaving them to die on the vine. Some called it "leapfrogging," and Premier Tojo later acknowledged the strategy as a major cause of Allied victory. By the end of 1943 MacArthur's forces controlled the northern coast of New Guinea.

NIMITZ IN THE CENTRAL PACIFIC Admiral Nimitz's advance through the central Pacific had as its first target Tarawa in the Gilbert islands. Tarawa was one of the most heavily protected islands in the Pacific. There nearly 1,000 American soldiers, sailors, and marines lost their lives rooting out 4,000 Japanese who refused to surrender. The Gilberts provided airfields from

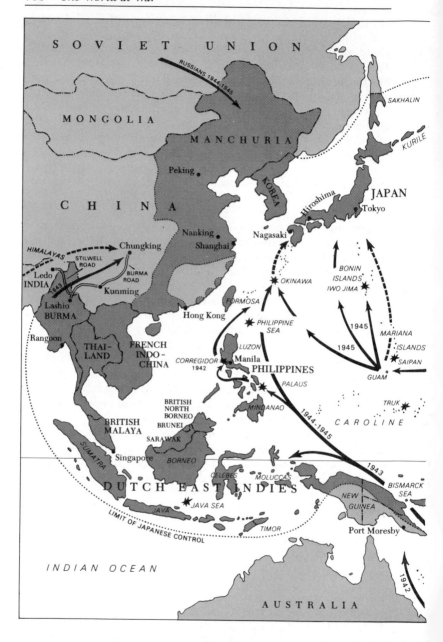

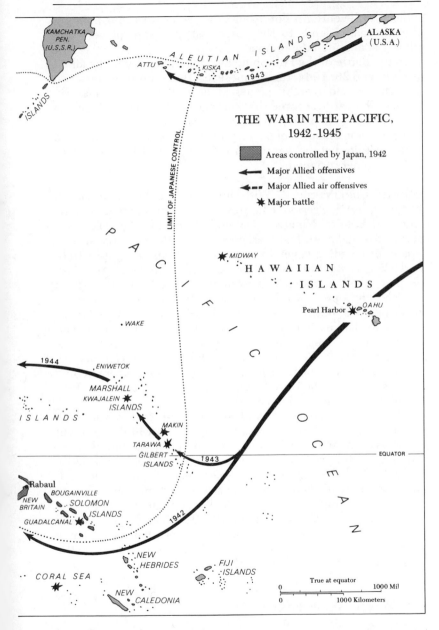

KAMCHATKA PEN. (U.S.S.R.)

ALEUTIAN ISLANDS

ALASKA (U.S.A.)

ATTU KISKA 1943

ISLANDS

LIMIT OF JAPANESE CONTROL

THE WAR IN THE PACIFIC, 1942–1945

Areas controlled by Japan, 1942

Major Allied offensives

Major Allied air offensives

★ Major battle

P A C I F I C

MIDWAY

H A W A I I A N ISLANDS

WAKE

Pearl Harbor OAHU

1944 ENIWETOK

MARSHALL KWAJALEIN ISLANDS

ISLANDS

MAKIN

TARAWA

GILBERT 1943 ISLANDS

EQUATOR

O C E A N

Rabaul BOUGAINVILLE NEW SOLOMON BRITAIN ISLANDS GUADALCANAL

1942

NEW HEBRIDES FIJI ISLANDS

CORAL SEA

NEW CALEDONIA

True at equator

0   1000 Mil
0   1000 Kilometers

which the Seventh Air Force began softening up strong points in the Marshall Islands to the northwest. Japanese planes completely abandoned the region.

In the Battle of the Philippine Sea, fought mostly in the air on June 19 and 20, 1944, the Japanese lost three more carriers, two submarines, and over 300 planes, at the cost of only 17 American planes. The battle secured the Marianas, and soon B-29 bombers were winging their way to the first systematic bombing of the Japanese homeland. Defeat in the Marianas finally convinced General Tojo that the war was lost. On July 18, 1944, he and his entire cabinet resigned.

THE BATTLE OF LEYTE GULF   With New Guinea and the Marianas all but conquered, President Roosevelt met with General MacArthur and Admiral Nimitz in Honolulu to decide the next major step. Previous plans had marked China as the essential springboard for invading Japan, but a Japanese offensive in April 1944 had taken most of the south China airfields from which American air power had operated. This strengthened MacArthur's opinion that the Philippines would provide a safer staging area. He also had a personal desire to recapture the islands he and his American troops had earlier defended. Sentimental and political considerations, as well as military, tipped the decision his way. MacArthur made his move into the Philippines on October 20, 1944, landing first on the island of Leyte. Wading ashore behind the first landings, he issued an emotional announcement: "People of the Philippines: I have returned."

The Japanese, knowing that loss of the Philippines would cut them off from the essential resources of the East Indies, brought in fleets from three directions. The three encounters that resulted on October 25 came to be known collectively as the Battle of Leyte Gulf, the largest naval engagement in history. The Japanese lost most of their remaining sea power and the ability to protect the Philippines. The battle also brought the first of the suicide attacks by Japanese pilots. The "Kamikaze" units, named for the "Divine Wind" that centuries before had saved Japan from Mongol invasion, were able to inflict severe damage on the American navy until the end of the war.

A NEW AGE IS BORN

ROOSEVELT'S FOURTH TERM   In 1944, war or no war, the calendar dictated another presidential election. This time the Republicans turned to the former crime-fighter and New York governor,

Thomas E. Dewey, as their candidate. Once again no Democratic challenger rose high enough to contest Roosevelt, but a fight did develop over the second spot on the ticket. Vice-President Henry Wallace had aggravated both southern conservatives and northern city bosses who feared his ties with labor, so Roosevelt finally chose the relatively unknown Missouri senator Harry S Truman.

Dewey ran under the same handicap as Landon and Willkie before him. He did not propose to dismantle Roosevelt's programs, but argued that it was time for younger men to replace the tired old leaders of the New Deal. The problem was that, even though considerably younger than Roosevelt, Dewey showed few signs of vitality. Though blessed with a silky voice and a stylish wardrobe, he was ill at ease in public, stiff, formal, seemingly arrogant, and worst of all—dull. "How can we be expected to vote for a man who looks like the bridegroom on a wedding cake?" one Washington veteran asked. Roosevelt betrayed decided signs of illness and exhaustion, but nevertheless carried the contest to the opposition. On November 7, 1945, he was once again elected, this time by a popular margin of 25.6 million to 22 million and an electoral vote of 432 to 99.

CONVERGING FRONTS   The war was not going as well; final victory remained elusive.   After the quick sweep across France, the Allies lost momentum in the fall of 1944 and settled down to slugging it out on the frontiers of Germany. The armies fought along this line all winter.

Then the Germans sprang a surprise in the rugged Ardennes Forest, where the Allied line was thinnest. On December 16, 1944, they advanced along a fifty-mile bulge in Belgium and Luxembourg before they stalled at Bastogne, hence the name: Battle of the Bulge. Reinforced by the Allies just before it was surrounded, Bastogne held out for six days against all the Germans could bring against it. On December 22 General "Tony" McAuliffe gave his memorable answer to the German demand for surrender: "Nuts." His situation remained desperate until the next day when the clouds lifted, allowing Allied airpower to hit the Germans and drop in supplies. On December 26 Bastogne was relieved, but it would be mid-January 1945 before the previous lines were restored.

Germany's sudden thrust upset Eisenhower's timetable and made continued coordination with the Soviet army even more crucial. The Nazi counterattack in the West had weakened their defense of the eastern front, and in January 1945 the Russians began their final offensive. The western offensives started in

February, and by early March Allied forces were pouring across the Rhine. By this time the Russian offensive had also reached Germany itself.

YALTA AND THE POSTWAR WORLD   As the final offensives got under way, the Big Three leaders met again in early February 1945 at Yalta, a resort in southern Russia. While the focus at Teheran in 1943 had been on wartime strategy, it was now on the shape of the postwar world. Two aims loomed large in Roosevelt's thinking. One was the need to ensure that the Soviet Union join the war against Japan. The other was based on the lessons he drew from the previous world war. Chief among the mistakes to be remedied were the failure of the United States to join the League of Nations and the failure of the Allies to maintain a united front in negotiations with the German aggressors.

The Yalta meeting thus began by calling for a conference on world organization to be held in the United States. The conferees also decided that substantive decisions in the Security Council would require the agreement of its five permanent members: the United States, Britain, Russia, France, and China.

The Yalta Conference, February 1945. *Stalin* (right), *FDR* (center), *and Churchill* (left) *confer on the shape of the postwar world.*

GERMANY AND EASTERN EUROPE With Hitler's "Thousand-Year Reich" stumbling to its doom, the leaders at Yalta had to make arrangements for the postwar governance of Germany. The war map dictated the basic pattern of occupation zones: Russia would control the east and the Western Allies would control the rich industrial areas of the west. Berlin, isolated within the Russian zone, would be jointly occupied. Churchill and Roosevelt insisted that liberated France receive a zone along its border and also in Berlin. Austria was similarly divided, with Vienna, like Berlin, under joint occupation within the Russian zone. Russian demands for reparations of $20 billion to the Allies, half of which would go to Russia, were referred to a Reparations Commission. The commission never reached agreement, although the Russians made off with untold amounts of machinery and equipment from their occupation zone.

With respect to eastern Europe, where Russian forces were advancing on a broad front, there was little the Western Allies could do to influence events. Churchill urged that the Western Allies try to beat the Russian forces to Berlin in order to gain more leverage for the postwar negotiations, but Roosevelt was inhibited by his wish to win Russian cooperation in the continuing fight against Japan and in the effort to build the proposed United Nations organization. General Eisenhower also advised against such a bold move, fearing an open split with the Russians that would delay Germany's surrender.

Poland then became the main focus of Western concern. Britain and France had gone to war in 1939 to defend Poland, and now, six years later, the course of the war had ironically left Poland's fate in the hands of the Russians. Events had long foreshadowed the outcome. When Russian forces reentered Poland in 1944, the Soviets placed civil administration under a puppet regime in Lublin. The Soviets refused to recognize the legitimacy of Poland's government-in-exile in London, formed by officials who had fled the country following Hitler's invasion in September 1939. With Soviet troops at the gates of Warsaw, the underground resistance in the city rose against the Nazi occupiers. The underground, however, supported Poland's government-in-exile in London. The Russians then stopped their offensive for two months while the Nazis in Warsaw wiped out thousands of Poles, potential rivals to the Lublin puppet government.

Hope that postwar cooperation could survive such events was a triumph of optimism over experience. The Western Allies found at Yalta that they could do no more than acquiesce or stall. On the Soviet proposal to expand the Lublin Committee into a provisional government together with representatives of the London Poles, they acquiesced. On the issue of Poland's boundaries, they stalled. The Russians proposed to keep eastern Poland, offering land taken from Germany as compensation. Roosevelt and Churchill accepted the proposal, but considered Poland's new western boundary at the Oder-Western Neisse Rivers only provisional. But the peace conference at which Poland's western boundary was to be settled never took place because of later disagreements. The presence of the London Poles in the provisional government only lent a tone of legitimacy to a regime dominated by the Communists, who soon ousted their rivals.

The Big Three also promised to sponsor free elections, democratic governments, and constitutional safeguards of freedom throughout the rest of Europe. The Yalta Declaration of Liberated Europe reaffirmed faith in the principles of the Atlantic Charter and the United Nations, but in the end it made little difference. It may have postponed Communist takeovers in eastern Europe for a few years, but before long Communist members of coalition governments had their hands on the levers of power and purged the opposition. Russia, twice invaded by Germany in the twentieth century, was determined to create buffer states between it and the Germans.

YALTA'S LEGACY Critics later attacked the Yalta agreements for "giving" eastern Europe over to Soviet domination. Some argued that Roosevelt's declining health caused him to buckle under Stalin's insistent demands. But the course of the war shaped the actions at Yalta, not personal diplomacy. The Red Army had the upper hand in eastern Europe. Perhaps the most bitterly criticized of the Yalta understandings was a secret agreement on the Far East, not made public until after the war. The Joint Chiefs of Staff still estimated that Japan could hold out for eighteen months after the defeat of Germany. Costly campaigns thus lay ahead and the atomic bomb was still an expensive and untested gamble.

So Roosevelt felt that he had no choice but to accept Stalin's demands on postwar arrangements in the Far East, subject technically to later agreement by Chiang Kai-shek. Stalin wanted continued Russian control of Outer Mongolia through its puppet People's Republic there, acquisition of the Kurile Islands from Japan, and recovery of rights and territory lost after the Russo-Japanese War in 1905. Stalin in return promised to enter the war against Japan two or three months after the German defeat, to recognize Chinese sovereignty over Manchuria, and to conclude a treaty of friendship and alliance with the Chinese Nationalists.

Later Roosevelt's concessions would appear in a different light, but given their geographical advantages in Asia as in eastern Europe, the Soviets were in a position to get what they wanted in any case.

THE THIRD REICH COLLAPSES The collapse of Nazi resistance was imminent, but President Roosevelt did not live to join the celebrations. All through 1944 his health had been declining, and on April 12, 1945, while he was drafting a speech, a cerebral hemorrhage brought sudden death.

Hitler's Germany collapsed less than a month later. The Allied armies rolled up almost unopposed to the Elbe River, where they met advanced detachments of Russians on April 25. Three days later Italian partisans captured and brutally killed Mussolini and his mistress as they tried to flee. In Berlin, which was under siege by the Russians, Hitler married his mistress, Eva Braun, in an underground bunker on the last day of April, just before killing her and himself. On May 2 Berlin fell to the Russians. That same day German forces in Italy surrendered. On May 7 the Germans signed an unconditional surrender in Allied headquarters at Rheims. So ended the Thousand-Year Reich, little more than twelve years after its Führer had come to power.

U.S. troops encounter surviving inmates at the Nazi concentration camp at Wobbelin, May 1945.

Massive victory celebrations on V-E Day, May 8, 1945, were tempered by the tragedies that had engulfed the world: mourning for the lost president and the death and mutilation of untold millions. Most shocking was the revelation of the Nazi Holocaust, scarcely believable until the Allied armies discovered the death camps in which Nazis had sought to apply their "final solution" to the Jewish "problem": the wholesale extermination of some 6 million Jews along with more than 1 million others who had incurred Nazi contempt for one reason or another.

During the war, reports from Red Cross and underground sources had amassed growing evidence of Germany's systematic genocide against European Jews. Stories appeared in major American newspapers as early as 1942, but they were nearly always buried on inside pages. And reports of such horror seemed beyond belief. American government officials, even some Jewish leaders, dragged their feet on the question for fear that relief for Jewish refugees might stir latent anti-Semitism at home. Finally, Roosevelt set up a War Refugees Board in 1944, but with few resources at its disposal. It nevertheless managed to rescue about 200,000 European Jews and some 20,000 others. But more might have been done. The Allies rejected the bombing of rail lines into the largest death camp, Auschwitz in Poland, although American planes hit industries five miles away. Moreover, few refugees were accepted into the United States. The Allied handling of the tragic affair was inept at best and disgraceful at worst.

A GRINDING WAR The sobering thought that the defeat of Japan remained to be accomplished cast a further pall over the victory celebrations. American forces continued to penetrate and disrupt the Japanese Empire in the early months of 1945, but at heavy cost. Stubborn Japanese resistance slowed the reconquest of the Philippines. On February 19, 1945, marine assault forces invaded Iwo Jima, a speck of volcanic rock 750 miles from Tokyo. The island was needed to provide the fighter escort for bombers over Japan and as a landing strip for disabled B-29s. It took nearly six weeks to secure Iwo Jima from defenders hiding in an underground labyrinth, and the cost was high: more than 20,000 American casualties, including 7,000 dead.

The fight for Okinawa, beginning on Easter Sunday, April 1, was even bloodier. Okinawa was large enough to afford a staging area for invasion of the Japanese islands, and it took the largest amphibious operation of the Pacific war, involving some 300,000 troops, to capture the island. Desperate Japanese counterattacks inflicted heavy losses on land, by air, and by sea. Kamikaze planes attacked by the hundreds. The fight for Okinawa raged until late June, when the bloody attrition destroyed any further Japanese ability to resist. The fighting brought nearly 50,000 American casualties. The Japanese lost an estimated 140,000 dead. Casualties included about 42,000 Okinawans. The campaign was significant mainly for wearing down the remaining Japanese defenses. Now American ships could freely roam the coastline of Japan, shelling targets ashore. American planes bombed at will and mined the waters of the Inland Sea. Tokyo and other major cities were devastated by firestorms ignited by incendiary bombs, made all the worse by the prevalence of wooden structures in earthquake-prone Japan. Still, it seemed that ahead lay further beachheads and more bitter fighting against the same suicidal fury that had made Okinawa so costly a conquest. But as the irony of timing would have it, Okinawa was never needed as a staging area. When resistance on the island collapsed, the Japanese emperor instructed the new premier to seek peace terms. Washington had picked this up by decoding Japanese messages that suggested either an effort to avoid unconditional surrender or perhaps just a stall.

THE ATOMIC BOMB   By the summer of 1945, however, news of a new weapon had changed all strategic calculations: President Truman had just learned of the first successful test-firing of an atomic bomb, the result of several years of intensive work. In October 1939, Albert Einstein had alerted President Roosevelt to German research on nuclear fission. In 1940 the president diverted some army and navy funds into research that grew ultimately into the $2 billion top-secret Manhattan Project, involving over 120,000 workers. A group of physicists under Dr. J. Robert Oppenheimer worked out the scientific and technical problems of bomb construction in a laboratory at Los Alamos, New Mexico. On July 16, 1945, the first atomic fireball rose from the New Mexico desert. This was obviously not a conventional weapon. The test explosion broke windows 125 miles away and a blind woman saw the flash. The awestruck Oppenheimer said later that in the observation bunker, "A few people laughed, a few people cried, most people were silent. There floated through my mind a line from the Bhagavad-Gita . . .: 'I am become death, the shatterer of worlds.' " After learning of the successful test, Truman wrote in his diary: "We have discovered the most terrible bomb in the history of the world."

How to use this awful weapon posed unique problems. Some scientists favored a demonstration in a remote area, but this was vetoed because only two bombs were available, and even those

might misfire. The choice of targets received more consideration. Four Japanese cities had been reserved from conventional
bombing as potential targets for the new weapon. After Secretary of War Henry Stimson eliminated Kyoto, Japan's ancient
capital and repository of many national and religious treasures,
priority went to Hiroshima, center of war industries, headquarters of the Second General Army, and command center for
the homeland's defenses. This met Truman's guidelines. He had
written that, even though "the Japs are savages, ruthless, merciless, and fanatic," only military personnel and installations
rather than "women and children" should be targeted. He had
no idea that the bomb would destroy virtually an entire city.

On July 25, 1945, President Truman, then at the Big Three
Conference in Potsdam, Germany, ordered the bomb dropped if
Japan did not surrender before August 3. The next day the heads
of the American, British, and Chinese governments issued the
Potsdam Declaration demanding that Japan surrender or face
"prompt and utter destruction." The deadline passed, and at
9:15 A.M. on a warm August 6, 1945, a B-29, the *Enola Gay*,
dropped an atomic bomb over Hiroshima. A sudden flash wiped
out four square miles of the city, wrecked the defense headquarters, destroyed most of the Second General Army, and killed
more than 60,000 people. Even those who appeared unhurt

*Nagasaki, Japan, one month after U.S. forces dropped an atomic bomb on
the city.*

began mysteriously to sicken and die, the first victims of a deadly radiation that blighted lives and the environment for years to come. In the United States, Americans greeted the first news with elation: it promised a quick end to the long nightmare of war. Only later would the awareness dawn that it marked the start of a more enduring nightmare, the atomic age.

Three days later Russia hastened to enter the war, and a few hours after that, about noon on August 9, a second atomic bomb exploded over the port city of Nagasaki, killing 36,000 more. That night the emperor urged his cabinet to accept the inevitable and surrender on the sole condition that he remain as sovereign. The next day the United States government, to facilitate surrender and an orderly transition, announced its willingness to let him keep the throne, but under the authority of an Allied supreme commander. Frantic exchanges ended with Japanese acceptance on August 14, 1945, when the emperor himself broke precedent to record a radio message announcing the surrender to his people. Even then a last-ditch palace revolt had to be squashed. On September 2, 1945, General MacArthur and other allied representatives accepted Japan's formal surrender on board the battleship *Missouri*.

THE FINAL LEDGER Thus ended the most deadly conflict in human history. No effort to tabulate a ledger of death and destruction can ever take the full measure of the war's suffering, nor hope to be more than a rough guess as to the numbers involved. One estimate has it that 70 million in all fought in the war, at a cost of some 45 million military and civilian dead. Material costs were also enormous, perhaps $1 trillion in military expenditures and twice that in property losses. The Soviet Union suffered the greatest losses of all, over 6 million military deaths, over 10 million civilians dead, and at least 25 million left homeless. World War II was more costly for the United States than any other of the country's foreign wars: 294,000 battle deaths and 114,000 other deaths. But in proportion to population, the United States suffered a far smaller loss than any of the major allies or enemies, and American territory escaped the devastation inflicted on so many other parts of the world.

The war's end opened a new era for the United States. It accelerated the growth of American power while devastating all other world powers, leaving the United States economically and militarily the strongest nation on earth. But Russia, despite its human and material losses, emerged from the war with much new territory and enhanced influence, making it the greatest power on the whole Eurasian land mass. Just a little over a century after the

French observer Alexis de Tocqueville predicted that western Europe would come to be overshadowed by the power of the United States and Russia, his prophecy had come to pass.

FURTHER READING

Russell F. Weigley's *The American Way of War: A History of United States Military Strategy and Policy* (1973)° provides a scholarly assessment of strategy and tactics. Gordon Wright's *The Ordeal of Total War, 1939–1945* (1968)° surveys the European conflict in its entirety, while Charles B. MacDonald's *The Mighty Endeavor: American Armed Forces in the European Theatre in World War II* (1969) concentrates on American involvement. On Eisenhower's generalship, see David Eisenhower's *Eisenhower: At War* (1986). Roosevelt's wartime leadership is analyzed in Eric Larrabee's *Commander in Chief* (1988).°

For the war in the Far East, see John Toland's *The Rising Sun: The Decline and Fall of the Japanese Empire, 1936–1945* (1970),° Ronald H. Spector's *Eagle against the Sun* (1984),° and John Dower's award-winning *War Without Mercy: Race and Power in the Pacific War* (1986).° Dan van der Vat's *The Pacific Campaign: The U.S.-Japanese Naval War, 1941–45* (1991) analyzes the greatest sea war in history.

Overviews of the war's impact on the home front include Richard R. Lingeman's *Don't You Know There's a War On?* (1970) and John Morton Blum's *V Was for Victory: Politics and American Culture during World War II* (1976).° *"The Good War"* (1984),° edited by Studs Terkel, contains many fascinating reminiscences of the war years. See also Harold G. Vatter's *The U.S. Economy in World War II* (1988).° Susan M. Hartmann's *The Home Front and Beyond* (1983)° and Karen Anderson's *Wartime Women* (1981) treat the new working environment for women. Neil Wynn looks at the participation of blacks in *The Afro-American and the Second World War* (1976). The story of the oppression of Japanese-Americans is told in Peter Irons's *Justice at War* (1983).°

A sound introduction to American diplomacy During the conflict can be found in Gaddis Smith's *American Diplomacy During the Second World War, 1941–1945* (2nd ed., 1985).° An introduction to the issues and events that led to the deployment of atomic weapons is traced by Herbert Feis in *The Atomic Bomb and the End of World War II* (1966).° Also helpful are Gregg Herken's *The Winning Weapon* (1980)° and Martin J. Sherwin's *A World Destroyed: The Atomic Bomb and the Grand Alliance* (1975).° Gar Alperovitz's *Atomic Diplomacy: Hiroshima and Potsdam* (new ed., 1985)° details how the bomb helped shape American postwar policy. Paul S. Boyer's *By the Bomb's Early Light* (1985)° shows the bomb's impact on American cultural and intellectual life.

Martin Gilbert's *Auschwitz and the Allies* (1981)° and David S. Wyman's *The Abandonment of the Jews* (1984)° discuss the Allies and the Holocaust.

° These books are available in paperback editions.

30

THE FAIR DEAL
AND CONTAINMENT

DEMOBILIZATION UNDER TRUMAN

TRUMAN'S UNEASY START "Who the hell is Harry Truman?" Roosevelt's chief-of-staff asked the president in the summer of 1944. The question was on more lips when, after less than twelve weeks as vice-president, Harry Truman took the presidential oath on April 12, 1945. Clearly he was not Franklin Roosevelt and that was one of the burdens he would bear. Roosevelt, a journalist wrote years later, "looked imperial, and he acted that way, and he talked that way. Harry Truman, for God's sake—looked and acted and talked like—well, like a failed haberdasher"—which he was.

In their origins Roosevelt and Truman arose from different worlds. For Truman there had been no inherited wealth, no early contact with the great and near-great, no European travel, no Groton, no Harvard—indeed, no college at all. Born in 1884 in western Missouri, Truman had pioneer grandparents from Kentucky and a Southern Baptist background. He grew up in Independence, outside of Kansas City. Too nearsighted to join in the activities of other boys, Truman became bookish and introverted. After high school, however, he spent a few years working in Kansas City banks and grew into an outgoing young man.

During World War I Truman served in France as captain of an artillery battery. Afterward, he and a partner went into the clothing business, but it failed during the recession of 1922 and Truman then entered politics. Elected county judge in 1922, he was defeated in 1924 and elected once again in 1926. In 1934

Missouri sent him to the United States Senate, where he remained fairly obscure until he became chairman of the committee to investigate corruption in defense industries.

Something about Harry Truman evoked the spirit of Andrew Jackson: his decisiveness, his feisty character, his family loyalty. But that was a side of the man that the American people came to know only as he settled into the job. On his first full day as president, as the war in Asia ground on, he remained awestruck. "Boys, if you ever pray, pray for me now," he told a group of reporters. "I don't know whether you fellows ever had a load of hay fall on you, but when they told me yesterday what had happened, I felt like the moon, the stars and all the planets had fallen on me."

Truman's accession heartened the party bosses who had helped engineer his nomination as Roosevelt's vice-president. But as one newsman put it, the men who put Truman in "knew what they wanted but did not know what they were getting." What they were getting was a man who favored much of the New Deal and was even prepared to extend it, but at the same time was uneasy with many of the most ardent New Deal reformers. Within ninety days he had replaced much of the Roosevelt cabinet with his own choices. These included fewer Missourians and "cronies" than his detractors claimed, but on the whole his cabinet was more conservative in outlook and included enough mediocrities to lend credence to the criticism. Truman suffered the further handicap of seeming to be a caretaker for the remainder of Roosevelt's term. Few expected him to run on his own in 1948.

Truman gave one significant clue to his domestic policies on September 6, 1945, when he sent Congress a comprehensive peacetime program which in effect proposed to continue and enlarge the New Deal. Its twenty-one points included expansion of unemployment insurance, a higher minimum wage, a permanent Fair Employment Practices Commission, slum clearance and low-rent housing projects, regional development of the nation's river valleys, and a public works program. "Not even President Roosevelt asked for so much at one sitting," charged the House Republican leader. "It's just a plain case of out-dealing the New Deal." Beset by other problems, Truman failed to set priorities among his demands, and his new domestic proposals soon were mired down in disputes over the transition to a peacetime economy.

CONVERTING TO PEACE The raucous celebrations that greeted Japan's surrender signaled the habitual American response to victory: a rapid demobilization and a return to more carefree pursuits. The president and Congress were besieged by demands for bringing the boys home. By 1947 the total armed forces were down to 3 million from a wartime high of almost 12 million. In his memoirs Truman termed this "the most remarkable demobilization in the history of the world, or 'disintegration' if you want to call it that." By early 1950 the army had fallen to 600,000 personnel.

The veterans returned to schools, new jobs, wives, and babies. Population growth, which had dropped off sharply in the Depression decade, now soared: the birth rate per 1,000 of total population grew from 19.4 in 1940 to above 24 per annum by 1946, and did not begin to show a decline until the 1960s. Americans born during this postwar period composed what came to be known as the baby-boom generation.

The end of the war, with its sudden demobilization and reconversion to a peacetime economy, brought sharp dislocations but not the postwar depression that many feared. The economic impact of demobilization was cushioned by numerous shock-absorbers: unemployment pay and other Social Security benefits; the Servicemen's Readjustment Act of 1944, known as the "GI Bill of Rights," under which $13 billion was spent for veterans on education, vocational training, medical treatment, unemployment insurance, and loans for building houses or going into business; and most important, the pent-up demand for consumer

The Eldridge General Store, Fayette County, Illinois. *Postwar America quickly demobilized, turning its attention to the pursuit of abundance.*

goods that was fueled by wartime incomes. Instead of sinking into depression after the war, the economy enjoyed a spurt of private investment in new industrial plants and equipment.

CONTROLLING INFLATION   The economic problem facing Truman was not depression but inflation. Released from wartime restraints, the demands of businesses for higher prices and of workers for higher wages alike conspired to frustrate Truman's efforts to "continue stabilization of the economy." Truman endorsed "reasonable" demands for wage increases, which he thought businesses could absorb without raising prices, and which he considered necessary to sustain purchasing power. Management, however, did not agree. Within six weeks of war's end, corporations confronted a wave of union demands for higher wages and better benefits, and a series of strikes followed in the automotive, steel, mine, petroleum, and railroad industries. Truman, miffed at what he considered to be excessive union demands, including a 30 percent wage boost, responded forcefully, using powers granted the chief executive during wartime to seize the mines and threaten to draft striking railroad workers into the armed forces. In a staff meeting, Truman asked what organized labor "wanted to do—run the country?"

Into 1946 the wartime Office of Price Administration maintained some restraint on price increases while gradually ending the rationing of most goods, and Truman asked for a one-year renewal of its powers. But during the late winter and spring of 1946 business lobbyists mounted a massive campaign against price controls and Truman allowed them to end. Congress finally extended controls in July, but by then the cost of living had already risen by 6 percent. After the 1946 congressional elections Truman gave up the battle against inflationary prices, ending all controls except on rents, sugar, and rice.

PARTISAN CONFLICT   As congressional elections approached in the fall of 1946, discontent ran high, most of it directed against the administration. Truman caught the blame for labor problems from both sides. A speaker at the CIO national convention tagged Truman "the No. 1 strikebreaker," while much of the public, angry at striking unions, blamed the White House for the strikes. In September 1946 Truman fired Henry A. Wallace as secretary of commerce in a disagreement over foreign policy, thus offending the Democratic left. At the same time, Republicans charged that Communists had infiltrated the government. Critics of the administration had a field day coining slogans. "To err is Truman" was credited to the wife of Senator Robert Taft.

But most effective was the simple "Had enough?" attributed to a Boston ad agency: their message was that the Democrats had simply been in power too long. In the end, Republicans won majorities in both houses of Congress for the first time since 1928.

With momentum building up against organized labor, the new Congress quickly passed the Taft-Hartley Act of 1947, which banned the closed shop (in which nonunion workers could not be hired) but permitted a union shop (in which workers newly hired were required to join the union), except where banned by state law. The legislation included provisions against "unfair" union practices such as "featherbedding" (pay for work not done), refusal to bargain in good faith, and contributing to political campaigns. Unions' political action committees were allowed to function only on a voluntary basis, and union leaders had to take oaths that they were not members of the Communist party. Employers were permitted to sue unions for breaking contracts and to speak freely during union campaigns. The act forbade strikes by federal employees, and imposed a "cooling-off" period of eighty days on any strike that the president found to be dangerous to the national health or safety.

Truman vetoed the bill, which unions called the "slave-labor act." This restored his credit with labor and brought many unionists who had gone over to the Republicans in 1946 back to the Democratic fold. But the bill passed over Truman's veto and, as it turned out, had a less than ruinous effect on unions. Its most severe impact probably was on the CIO's "Operation Dixie," a drive to win for unions a more secure foothold in the South. By 1954 fifteen states, mainly in the South, had used the Taft-

"To the Rescue!" Labor is being pulled under by the Taft-Hartley law as Congress, which passed the bill over Truman's veto, makes sure there is no rescue.

Hartley Act's authority to pass "right-to-work" laws forbidding the union shop.

Truman clashed with the Republicans on other domestic issues, including a tax reduction measure passed by Congress but vetoed by the president on the principle that in times of high production and employment the federal debt should be reduced. In 1948, however, Congress finally managed to override his veto of a $5-billion tax cut at a time when government debt still ran high.

These conflicts between Truman and Congress obscured the high degree of bipartisan cooperation marking matters of governmental reorganization and foreign policy. After a postwar congressional investigation into the Pearl Harbor disaster made plain a fatal lack of coordination among the armed forces and intelligence services, a bipartisan majority in Congress set out to correct this problem by passing the National Security Act in July 1947. It created a national military establishment, headed by a secretary of defense with subcabinet departments of army, navy, and air force, and a new National Security Council (NSC) which included the president, heads of the defense departments, and the secretary of state, among others. The act made permanent the Joint Chiefs of Staff, which had been a wartime innovation, and established the Central Intelligence Agency (CIA), to coordinate intelligence gathering abroad. There was at the time no intention to have the CIA engage in covert actions, nor any purpose that it engage in domestic activities. But the act included two gigantic loopholes which would in time allow the CIA to engage in both: authority to perform "such other functions and duties related to intelligence" as the NSC might direct, and responsibility for "protecting intelligence sources and methods."

Congress also adopted the Presidential Succession Act of 1947, which inserted the Speaker of the House and the president pro tempore of the Senate ahead of the secretary of state, on the principle that the presidency should first go to elected rather than appointed officers. Congress itself took the initiative in adopting the Twenty-second Amendment, ratified in 1951, which limited presidents after Truman to two terms—a belated slap at Roosevelt.

THE COLD WAR

BUILDING THE U.N. The hope that the wartime alliance would carry over into the postwar world proved but another great illusion. The pragmatic Roosevelt had shared no such illusion. He expected that the Great Powers in the postwar world would have spheres of influence, but felt he had to temper such *Realpolitik* with an organization "which would satisfy widespread demand in the United States for new idealistic or universalist arrangements for assuring the peace."

On April 25, 1945, two weeks after Roosevelt's death and two weeks before the German surrender, delegates from fifty nations at war with the Axis met in San Francisco to draw up the charter of the United Nations. These fifty—and Poland—became charter members, with the provision that additional members could be admitted by a two-thirds vote of the General Assembly. This body, one of the two major agencies set up by the charter, included delegates from all member nations and was to meet annually in regular session to approve the budget, receive annual reports from U.N. agencies, and choose members of the Security Council and other bodies. The Security Council, the other major charter agency, would remain in permanent session and had "primary responsibility for the maintenance of international peace and security." Its eleven members included six elected for two-year terms and five permanent members: the United States, Russia, Britain, France, and China. Each permanent member could veto any question of substance, though not of procedure. The Security Council might investigate any dispute, recommend settlement or reference to another U.N. body—the International Court of Justice at the Hague—and take measures including a resort to military force. The United States Senate, in sharp contrast to the reception it gave the League of Nations, ratified the U.N. charter by a vote of 89 to 2.

DIFFERENCES WITH THE SOVIETS   There were signs of trouble in the grand alliance as early as the spring of 1945 as Russia moved to set up compliant governments in eastern Europe, violating the Yalta promises of democratic elections. On February 1 the Polish Committee of National Liberation, a puppet group already claiming the status of provisional government, moved from Lublin to Warsaw. In March the Soviets installed a puppet premier in Rumania. Protests at such actions led to Russian counterprotests that the British and Americans were negotiating German surrender in Italy "behind the back of the Soviet Union." A few days before his death, Roosevelt responded to Stalin: "I cannot avoid a feeling of resentment toward your informers . . . for such vile misrepresentations."

Such was the atmosphere when Truman entered the White House. A few days before the San Francisco conference, he gave Soviet Foreign Minister Vyacheslav Mikhaylovich Molotov a dressing down in Washington on the Polish situation. "I have never been talked to like that in my life," Molotov protested. "Carry out your agreements," Truman snapped, "and you won't get talked to like that." On May 12, 1945, four days after victory in Europe, Winston Churchill sent Truman a telegram: "What is to happen about Europe? An iron curtain is drawn down upon [the Russian] front. We do not know what is going on behind [it]. . . . Surely it is vital now to come to an understanding with Russia, or see where we are with her, before we weaken our armies mortally." Nevertheless, as a gesture of goodwill, and over Churchill's protest, the American forces withdrew from the occupation zone assigned to Russia at Yalta. Americans still hoped that the Yalta agreements would be carried out, and were even more eager to have Russian help against Japan.

Although the Russians admitted British and American observers to their sectors of eastern Europe, there was little the Western powers could have done to prevent Russian control of the region even if they had kept up their military strength. The presence of Soviet armed forces frustrated the efforts of non-Communists to gain political influence. Opposition leaders were either exiled, silenced, executed, or imprisoned.

Secretary of State James F. Byrnes, who took office in June 1945, struggled on through 1946 with the problems of postwar settlements. In early 1947, the Council of Foreign Ministers finally produced treaties for Italy, Hungary, Rumania, Bulgaria, and Finland. The treaties in effect confirmed Russian control over eastern Europe, which in Russian eyes seemed but a parallel to American control in Japan and Western control over most of Germany and all of Italy. The Yalta guarantees of democracy in eastern Europe had turned out much like the Open Door Policy in China, little more than pious rhetoric sugar-coating the realities of power.

Byrnes's impulse to brandish the atomic bomb only added to the irritations, intimidating no one. As early as April 1945, he had suggested to Truman that possession of the new weapon "might well put us in a position to dictate our own terms at the end of the war." And after becoming secretary of state, he tried on several occasions to threaten Russian diplomats with America's growing arsenal of nuclear weapons. But they paid little notice, and such attempts at intimidation were soon dropped.

The United States still enjoyed exclusive possession of atomic weapons and, together with Britain and Canada (partners in developing the atomic bomb), proposed in 1946 to internationalize the control of atomic energy. Under the plan presented to the

U.N. Atomic Energy Commission, an International Atomic Development Authority would have a monopoly of atomic explosives and atomic energy. The Russians, fearing Western domination of the agency, proposed instead simply to outlaw the manufacture and use of atomic bombs, with enforcement vested in the Security Council and thus subject to a veto. Later they conceded the right of international inspection, but still refused to give up the veto. The American government rejected the arrangement, which it considered a compromise of international control.

CONTAINMENT　By the beginning of 1947 relations with the Soviet Union had become more troubled. The year before, Stalin had already pronounced international peace impossible "under the present capitalistic development of the world economy." His statement impelled George F. Kennan, counselor of the American Embassy in Moscow, to send an 8,000-word dispatch in which he sketched the roots of Soviet policy and warned that the Soviet Union was "committed fanatically to the belief that it is desirable and necessary that the internal harmony of our society be disrupted, our traditional way of life be destroyed, the international authority of our state be broken, if Soviet power is to be secure."

More than a year later, by then back at the State Department in Washington, Kennan spelled out his ideas for a proper response to the Soviets in a July 1947 article published anonymously in *Foreign Affairs*. He advocated "a long-term, patient but firm and vigilant containment of Russian expansive tendencies." Americans, he added, could hope for a long-term moderation of Soviet ideology and policy, so that in time tensions with the West would lessen. There was a strong possibility "that Soviet power, like the capitalistic world of its conception, bears within it the seeds of its own decay, and that the sprouting of those seeds is well advanced."

Kennan's containment strategy lay behind the new departure in foreign policy that America's political leaders had already decided to take. Containment reflected a growing fear that Russian aims reached beyond eastern Europe, posing dangers in the eastern Mediterranean, the Middle East, and western Europe itself. The USSR was indeed looking for a breakthrough into the Mediterranean, long important to Russia for purposes of trade and defense. After the war the USSR began to press Turkey for territorial concessions and the right to build naval bases on the Bosporus, an important gateway between the Black Sea and the

Mediterranean. In August 1946 civil war broke out in neighboring Greece between a British-backed government and a Communist-led faction that held the northern part of Greece. In February 1947 the British ambassador informed the American government that the British could no longer bear the economic and military burden of aiding Greece and suggested that the United States assume the responsibility. Truman agreed, and on March 12, 1947, he asked Congress for $400 million in economic and military aid to both Greece and Turkey.

THE TRUMAN DOCTRINE AND THE MARSHALL PLAN In his speech to Congress the president announced what quickly became known as the Truman Doctrine. Although intended as a response to a specific crisis, its rhetoric was dangerously universal. "I believe," Truman declared, "that it must be the policy of the United States to support free peoples who are resisting attempted subjugation by armed minorities or by outside pressures." In May 1947, Congress passed the Greek-Turkish aid bill, and by 1950 had spent $659 million on the program. Turkey achieved economic stability, and Greece defeated the Communist insurrection in October 1949.

But such immediate gains were offset by long-term problems. The Truman Doctrine marked the beginning of a contest which stock market whiz turned government adviser Bernard Baruch labeled "a cold war." Greece and Turkey were but the front lines of an ideological struggle for world power and influence between East and West. That struggle quickly focused on western Europe, where wartime damage had devastated factory production, and a severe drought in 1947, followed by a harsh winter, destroyed crops. Europe had become, in Winston Churchill's words, "a rubble heap, a charnel house, a breeding ground of pestilence and hate." Amid the chaos the Communist parties of France and Italy were flourishing.

In the spring of 1947, the State Department reported to George C. Marshall, who had replaced Byrnes as secretary of state in January, that the United States had underestimated the extent of wartime damage in Europe. Only a program of massive aid could rescue western Europe from disaster and possible Communist subversion. Late in May, George Kennan developed a plan that Secretary Marshall presented at the Harvard Commencement on June 5. Taking Kennan's lead, Marshall avoided the ideological overtones of the Truman Doctrine. "Our policy," he pledged, "is directed not against country or doctrine, but against hunger, poverty, desperation, and chaos." Marshall offered comprehensive economic aid to all European countries, including Russia. On June 27 the foreign ministers of France, Britain, and Russia met in London to discuss Marshall's overture. Molotov arrived with eighty advisers, but during the talks got word from Moscow to withdraw from this "imperialist" scheme. Two weeks later a meeting of delegates from western Europe formed a Committee of European Economic Cooperation (CEEC), which had a plan ready by September.

In December 1947 Truman submitted his proposal for the European Recovery Program to Congress. Two months later, a Communist coup d'état in Czechoslovakia ended the last remaining coalition government in eastern Europe. The seizure of power in Prague assured congressional passage of the Marshall Plan, which from 1948 until 1951 poured $13 billion into European recovery.

DIVIDING GERMANY   The breakdown of the wartime alliance left the problem of postwar Germany unsettled. The German economy had stagnated, requiring the American army to carry a staggering burden of relief. Slowly, occupation zones evolved into functioning governments. In 1948 the British, French, and Americans merged their zones, and the West Germans were then invited to elect delegates to a federal constitutional convention.

Soviet reactions to the Marshall Plan and the unification of West Germany were sharp and quickly focused on Berlin, situated deep in the Soviet occupation zone. In April 1948 the Russians began to restrict the flow of traffic into West Berlin; on June 23 they stopped all traffic. The blockade was designed to leave the allies no choice but to give up either Berlin or the plan to unify West Germany. But the American commander in Germany proposed to stand firm. "If we mean . . . to hold Europe against communism," he told his superiors at the Pentagon, "we must not budge."

Truman agreed, and after considering the use of armed convoys to supply West Berlin, he opted for a massive airlift. At the time this seemed an enormous and perhaps impossible task. By quick work, however, the allied air forces brought in planes from around the world and by October 1948 were flying in nearly 5,000 tons of food and coal a day. Altogether, from June 1948 to mid-May 1949, the Berlin Airlift provided more than 1.5 million tons of supplies, or well over a half ton for each of the 2.2 million West Berliners.

Finally, on May 12, 1949, after extended talks, the Russians

OCCUPATION OF GERMANY AND AUSTRIA

French zone British zone U.S. zone Soviet zone

lifted the blockade. That same May, West Germany adopted a constitution, and before the end of the year, the German Federal Republic had a functioning government. At the end of May 1949, a German "Democratic" Republic arose in the Soviet-dominated eastern zone, dividing Germany into two independent states.

BUILDING NATO   As relations between the Soviets and western Europe chilled, transatlantic unity ripened into an outright military alliance. By March 1948 Britain, France, and the "Benelux" countries (Belgium, the Netherlands, and Luxembourg) had signed a fifty-year treaty of alliance and economic cooperation, the Brussels Pact. That June the Senate passed a resolution authorizing the administration to develop a collective defense pact. On April 4, 1949, diplomats signed the North Atlantic Treaty in Washington. Twelve nations were represented: the five Brussels Pact countries plus the United States, Canada, Denmark, Iceland, Italy, Norway, and Portugal. Greece and Turkey joined the

NATO, a hopeful sign for the West.

alliance in 1952, West Germany in 1955, and Spain in 1982. The treaty pledged that an attack against any one of the signers would be considered an attack against all, and provided for a council of the North Atlantic Treaty Organization (NATO), which could establish other necessary agencies. In September 1950 the council decided to create an integrated defense force for western Europe. Five years later the Warsaw Treaty Organization appeared as the eastern European counterpart to NATO.

One other foreign-policy decision with long-term consequences occurred during the eventful year 1948. Late in 1947 the U.N. General Assembly voted to partition Palestine into Jewish and Arab states. Despite fierce Arab opposition, Jewish leaders proclaimed the independence of the new state of Israel on May 14, 1948. President Truman, who had been in close touch with Jewish leaders, ordered immediate recognition of the new state—the United States became the first nation so to act. The neighboring Arab states reacted by going to war against Israel, which, however, held its own. U.N. mediators gradually worked out truce agreements with Israel's Arab neighbors that restored an uneasy peace by May 11, 1949, when Israel was admitted as a member of the United Nations. But the hard feelings and intermittent warfare between Israel and the Arab states have festered ever since, complicating American foreign policy, which has tried to maintain friendship with both sides while insisting on the legitimacy of the Israeli nation.

HARRY GIVES 'EM HELL

SHAPING THE FAIR DEAL   The determination Truman projected in foreign affairs did not alter his lackluster image on the domestic front. By early 1948, after three years in the White House, Truman had yet to shake the impression that he was not up to the job. Rather than go with a loser, New Deal stalwarts and party regulars tried to draft General Eisenhower as their presidential candidate for 1948, but in vain. The Democratic party seemed about to fragment: southern conservatives as well as the party's liberal wing had problems with Truman.

Unknown to all these groups, Truman had a game plan for 1948. His advisers knew that to win he needed the midwestern and western farm belts, and happily he enjoyed fairly strong support among farmers. In metropolitan areas the trick was to carry the labor and the black vote, which Truman wooed by working closely with unions and pressing the cause of civil rights. Truman's advisers counted on the Solid South to stay in the Democratic column. With the South and West, Truman could afford to lose some New Deal strongholds in the East and still win. This strategy erred chiefly in underrating the rebellion that would take four Deep South states out of Truman's camp.

What provoked the southern defection was Truman's forthright support of civil rights—a politically advantageous issue now that so many blacks had migrated to northern cities in states with large electoral votes. Truman's motivations in embracing the issue were complex. When in 1946 he appointed the President's Committee on Civil Rights—a panel of distinguished citizens, black and white, North and South—he acted not only in response to the pressures of black organizations but apparently also out of outrage at several recent attacks on blacks. The committee's report, *To Secure These Rights* (1947), touched on virtually every category of racial discrimination and called for the "elimination of segregation based on race, color, creed, or national origin, from American life."

Like other presidents, Truman used his State of the Union message in January 1948 to set the agenda for an election year. The speech offered something to nearly every group the Democrats hoped to win over. The first goal, Truman remarked, was "to secure fully the essential human rights of our citizens" and promised a special message later on civil rights. "To protect human resources," he asked for federal aid to education, increased and extended unemployment and retirement benefits, a comprehensive system of health insurance, more federal support for housing, and extension of rent controls. The requests mounted: for more rural electrification, a higher minimum wage, and much more. As one senator put it, the speech "raised all the ghosts of the old New Deal. . . ." On February 2 Congress received Truman's message on civil rights, which called for a broad range of actions, none of which he seriously hoped to get out of Congress. On July 26, 1948, however, he did ban racial discrimination in hiring federal employees, and four days later ordered an end to segregation in the armed forces. This last act was truly significant since it involved the nation's largest single organization.

THE 1948 ELECTION   The Republican majority in Congress for the most part spurned the Truman program, an action it would later regret. Scenting victory in November, Republican delegates again nominated Thomas Dewey, former New York governor. The platform endorsed most of the New Deal reforms as an accomplished fact and approved the administration's bipartisan foreign policy, but as Landon had in 1936, Dewey promised to run things more efficiently.

In July a glum Democratic convention gathered in Philadelphia, expecting to do little more than go through the motions, only to find itself doubly surprised: first by the battle over the civil rights plank, and then by Truman's acceptance speech. To keep from stirring southern hostility, the administration sought a platform plank that opposed discrimination only in general

*The opening of the 1948 Democratic National
Convention is marked by demonstrations against
racial segregation, led by A. Philip Randolph (left).*

terms. Activists, however, sponsored a plank that called on Congress for specific action and commended Truman "for his courageous stand on the issue of civil rights." Speaking last in favor of the change, Minneapolis Mayor Hubert H. Humphrey electrified the delegates and set off a ten-minute demonstration: "The time has arrived for the Democratic party to get out of the shadow of states' rights and walk forthrightly into the bright sunshine of human rights." Segregationist delegates from Alabama and Mississippi walked, instead, out of the convention.

After the convention had nominated Truman, the president appeared on the rostrum during the wee hours of the morning to give his acceptance speech. It was a rousing, combative address, unlike most of his earlier speeches, which he usually read in a flat drone. Near the end he dropped a bombshell. On July 26, he would call Congress back into session "to get the laws the people need."

On July 17 a group of rebellious southerners, miffed by the party's civil rights plank, met in Birmingham, Alabama, and nominated South Carolina governor J. Strom Thurmond on a States' Rights Democratic ticket, quickly dubbed the "Dixiecrat" ticket. The Dixiecrats sought to draw enough electoral votes to preclude a majority for either major party, throwing the election into the House, where they might strike a sectional bargain like that of 1877. A few days later, on July 23, the left wing of the Democratic party gathered in Philadelphia to name Henry A. Wallace on a Progressive party ticket. These splits in the Democratic ranks seemed to spell the final blow to Truman. The special session of Congress petered out in futility.

But Truman, undaunted, set out on a 31,000-mile "whistle stop" train tour during which he castigated the "do-nothing" Eightieth Congress, provoking cries from his audiences: "Pour it on, Harry!" and "Give 'em hell, Harry." And Harry would respond: "I don't give 'em hell. I just tell the truth and they think it's hell." Dewey, in contrast, ran a restrained campaign designed to avoid controversy. By so doing he may have snatched defeat from the jaws of victory.

To the end the polls and the pundits predicted a sure win for Dewey, and most speculation centered on his cabinet choices. But on election day Truman chalked up the biggest upset in American history, taking 24 million votes (49.5 percent) to Dewey's 22 million (45.1 percent) and winning a thumping 303 to 189 margin in the electoral college. Thurmond and Wallace each got more than a million votes, but the revolt of right and left

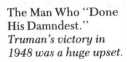

The Man Who "Done His Damndest." *Truman's victory in 1948 was a huge upset.*

worked to Truman's advantage. The Dixiecrat rebellion reassured black voters who had questioned the Democrats' commitment to civil rights, while the Progressive movement, which had received support from the Communist party, made it hard to tag Truman as "soft on Communism." Thurmond carried four Deep South states, and his success started a momentous disruption of the Democratic Solid South. But Truman's victory also carried Democratic majorities into Congress.

The outcome seemed a vindication for the New Deal and a mandate for liberalism, and Truman so regarded it. His State of the Union message repeated substantially the agenda he had set forth a year previously. "Every segment of our population and every individual," he stressed, "has a right to expect from his government a fair deal." Whether deliberately or not, he had invented a tag, the "Fair Deal," to set off his program from the New Deal.

The president won some of his Fair Deal proposals, but they were mainly extensions or enlargements of New Deal programs already in place: a higher minimum wage, bringing more people under Social Security, extension of rent controls, farm price supports, a sizable slum-clearance and public housing program, and more money for the TVA, rural electrification, and farm housing. Despite Democratic majorities in Congress, however, the conservative coalition was able to resist any drastic new departures in domestic policy. Congress balked at civil rights bills, national health insurance, federal aid to education, and a plan to provide subsidies that would hold up farm incomes rather than farm prices. Congress also turned down Truman's demand for repeal of the Taft-Hartley Act.

THE COLD WAR HEATS UP

Global concerns, never far from center stage in the postwar world, plagued Truman's second term as they had his first. In his inaugural address he called for foreign policy to rest on four pillars: the United Nations, the Marshall Plan, NATO, and a "bold new plan" for technical assistance to underdeveloped parts of the world, a sort of global Marshall Plan that came to be known simply as "Point Four." This program to aid the postwar world began in 1950 with a modest outlay of $35 million. But it never accomplished its goals, in part because other international problems soon diverted Truman's attention.

"LOSING" CHINA AND THE BOMB   One of the most intractable problems, the China tangle, was fast coming unraveled in 1949. The Chinese Nationalists (Kuomintang) of Chiang Kai-shek had been fighting Mao Tse-tung° and the Communists since the 1920s. The outbreak of war with Japan in 1937 halted the civil war, and Roosevelt, and Stalin as well, believed that the Nationalists would organize China after the war.

The commanders of American forces in China during World War II, however, concluded that Chiang's government had become hopelessly corrupt, tyrannical, and inefficient. United States' policy during and immediately after the war was to promote peace between the factions in China. But when the civil war resumed in 1945, American forces nevertheless ferried nationalist armies back into the eastern and northern provinces as the Japanese withdrew.

It soon became a losing fight for the Nationalists, as the Communists radicalized the land-hungry peasantry. By late 1948 the Communists were in Peking and heading southward. A year later they had taken the port city of Canton, and the Nationalist government had fled to the island of Formosa, which it renamed Taiwan.

From 1945 through 1949 the United States had funneled some $2 billion in aid to the Nationalists, to no avail. Administration critics asked bitterly: "Who lost China?" and a State Department report blamed Chiang for his failure to hold the support of the Chinese people. In fact it is hard to imagine how the United

---

°The traditional spellings are used in this text. After Mao's death the Chinese government adopted the "Pinyin" transliterations that are widely used today: Mao Tse-tung became Mao Zedong; and Peking became Beijing.

States government could have prevented the outcome short of military intervention, which would have been very risky, quite costly, and exceedingly unpopular. The United States continued to recognize the Nationalist government on Taiwan as the rightful government of China, delaying formal relations with Red China for thirty years. In an effort to shore up friendly regimes in Asia, the United States in February 1950 recognized the French-supported regime of Emperor Bao Dai in Vietnam and shortly afterward extended aid to the French in their battle against Ho Chi Minh's Vietnamese guerrillas.

As the Communists secured control in China, American intelligence in September 1949 found evidence that the Soviets had set off an atomic explosion. The discovery of the Russian bomb provoked an intense reappraisal of the strategic balance in the world, causing Truman in 1950 to order the construction of a hydrogen bomb, a weapon far more powerful than the Hiroshima bomb, lest the Russians make one first. Another result was a National Security Council recommendation for rebuilding conventional military forces to provide options other than nuclear war. This represented a major departure from America's time-honored aversion to keeping large standing armies in peacetime, and was an expensive proposition. But the American public was growing more receptive to the nation's world role, and an invasion of South Korea by Communist forces from the north clinched the issue for most.

WAR IN KOREA The Japanese had occupied Korea during World War II, and after their defeat and withdrawal, the victorious allies faced the difficult task of creating a new nation. Complicating that task was the fact that Russian troops had advanced into northern Korea and had accepted the surrender of Japanese forces above the 38th parallel, while American forces did the same south of the line. The Soviets quickly organized a Korean government along Stalinist lines while the Americans set up a Western-style regime in the south.

Like the division of Germany, the division of Korea at the Thirty-eighth Parallel in 1945 began as a temporary expedient and ended as a permanent fact. With the onset of the Cold War, it became clear that Soviet-American agreement on unification was no more likely in Korea than in Germany. By the end of 1948, separate regimes had appeared in the two sectors and occupation forces had withdrawn. American leaders then inadvertently may have given false impressions to the Communists. General MacArthur and Secretary of State Dean Acheson omit-

THE KOREAN WAR,
1950

CHINA
MANCHURIA

Vladivostok
U.S.S.R.

Yalu R.

• Chosan

NORTH
KOREA

SEA OF JAPAN

Pyongyang

NORTH KOREAN OFFENSIVE,
JUNE-SEPT. 1950

38°

Inchon • Seoul

SOUTH
KOREA

YELLOW SEA

U.N. POSITION
SEPT. 1950

• Pusan

KOREA STRAIT

0   100 Miles
0   100 Kilometers

THE KOREAN WAR,
1950-1953

CHINA
MANCHURIA

Vladivostok
U.S.S.R.

CHINESE ATTACK NOV. 1950

Yalu R.

• Chosan

FARTHEST
U.N. ADVANCE,
NOV. 1950

NORTH
KOREA

SEA OF JAPAN

Pyongyang

Panmunjom
• Chorwon

TRUCE LINE,
JULY 27, 1953

Inchon •   Seoul

YELLOW
SEA

38°

U.N. RETREAT,
JAN. 1951

MacARTHUR SEPT. 15, 1950

U.N.
FORCES

SOUTH
KOREA

U.N. POSITION
SEPT. 1950

• Pusan

KOREA STRAIT

ted both Korea and Formosa (Taiwan) from an America defense perimeter that included the Philippines and Japan. The weakened state of the demobilizing American military contributed to the impression that South Korea was vulnerable.

For whatever reasons, North Korean forces crossed the boundary on June 25, 1950, and swept down the peninsula. President Truman responded decisively. Korea might have been outside America's defense perimeter, but its southern tip was dangerously close to United States–occupied Japan. Besides, American policy remained subject to what might be called the "Munich syndrome," or what MacArthur called "history's clear lesson . . . that appeasement but begets new and bloodier war." Failure to act, Truman reasoned, would embolden Communist leaders "to override nations closer to our own shores."

An emergency meeting of the U.N. Security Council quickly censured the North Korean "breach of peace." The Soviet delegate, who held a veto power, was at the time boycotting the council because it would not seat Communist China in place of Nationalist China. On June 27, its first resolution having been ignored, the Security Council called on U.N. members to "furnish such assistance to the Republic of Korea as may be necessary to repel the armed attack and to restore international peace and security in the area." Truman ordered American air, naval, and ground forces into action. Eventually American forces numbered over 350,000 while the South Koreans contributed 400,000. In all, some fourteen other U.N. members sent in military units totaling about 50,000 men. Later, when the U.N. voted a unified command, it put General MacArthur in charge. The war remained chiefly an American affair, and one that set a precedent of profound consequence: war by order of the president rather than by vote of Congress. It had the sanction of the U.N. Security Council, to be sure, and could technically be considered a "police action," not a war. And other presidents had ordered American troops into action without a declaration of war, but never on such a scale.

For three months things went badly indeed for the South Korean and U.N. forces. By September they were barely hanging on to the Pusan perimeter in the southeast corner of Korea. Then, in a brilliant ploy, on September 15, 1950, MacArthur landed a new force to the North Korean rear at Inchon. Synchronized with a breakout from Pusan, the sudden blow stampeded the enemy back across the border.

At this point MacArthur convinced Truman to allow him to push on and seek to reunify Korea. The Russian delegate was back in the Security Council, wielding his veto, so on October 7 the United States got approval for this course from the U.N. General Assembly, where the veto did not apply. American forces had already crossed the boundary into North Korea by October 1, and now continued northward against minimal resistance. President Truman, concerned over broad hints of Communist Chinese intervention, flew out to Wake Island for a conference with General MacArthur on October 15. There the general discounted chances that the Red Army would act, but if it did, he confidently predicted, "there would be the greatest slaughter."

That same day Peking announced that China "cannot stand idly by." On October 26, U.N. units reached the Yalu River border with China. MacArthur predicted total victory by Christmas, but on the night of November 25, thousands of Chinese "volunteers" counterattacked, and massive "human wave" attacks, with the support of tanks and planes, turned the tables on the U.N. forces, sending them into a desperate retreat just at the onset of winter. It had become "an entirely new war," MacArthur concluded. Soon he was reporting that the war dragged on because the administration refused to let him blockade China and use Taiwanese Nationalists to invade the mainland. MacArthur seemed to have forgotten altogether his one-time reluctance to bog down the country in a major war on the Asian mainland.

Truman opposed leading the United States into the "gigantic booby trap" of war with China, and the U.N. forces soon rallied. By January 1951, U.N. troops under General Matthew Ridgway finally secured their lines below Seoul, and then launched a counterattack that in some places carried them back across the Thirty-eighth Parallel in March. When Truman seized the chance and offered negotiations to restore the boundary, MacArthur undermined the move by issuing an ultimatum for China to make peace or be attacked. Truman decided then that he had no choice but to accept MacArthur's policy or fire him. Civilian control of the military was at stake, Truman later asserted, and he did not let it remain at stake very long. The Joint Chiefs of Staff all backed the decision, and on April 11, 1951, the president removed MacArthur from all his commands and replaced him with Ridgway.

Truman's action set off an uproar across the country, and a tumultuous reception greeted MacArthur upon his return home for the first time since 1937. MacArthur's dramatic speech to a joint session of Congress provided the climactic event. "Once war is forced upon us," he maintained, "there is no alternative than to apply every available means to bring it to a swift end." A Senate investigation brought out the administration's arguments, best summarized by General Omar Bradley, chairman of the Joint Chiefs of Staff. The MacArthur strategy "would involve

"The Heat Is On."
*Truman's firing of Mac-
Arthur was unpopular
with the American public.*

us in the wrong war at the wrong place at the wrong time and with the wrong enemy." Americans, nurtured on classic western showdowns in which good always triumphed over evil, found the logic of limited war hard to take, but also found Bradley's logic persuasive.

On June 24, 1951, the Soviet representative at the United Nations proposed a cease-fire and armistice along the Thirty-eighth Parallel; a few days later Secretary of State Acheson accepted in principle, with the consent of the U.N. China and North Korea responded favorably—at the time General Ridgway's "meat-grinder" offensive was inflicting severe losses—and truce talks started at Panmunjom on July 10, 1951, only to drag out for another two years while the fighting continued. The chief snags were prisoner exchanges and the insistence of South Korea's president on unification. By the time a truce was finally reached on July 27, 1953, Truman had relinquished the White House to Dwight D. Eisenhower. The truce line followed the front at that time, mostly a little north of the Thirty-eighth Parallel, with a demilitarized zone of four kilometers separating the forces; repatriation of prisoners would be voluntary, supervised by a neutral commission. No final peace conference ever took place, and Korea, like Germany, remained divided. The war had cost the United States more than 33,000 deaths and 103,000 wounded and missing. South Korean casualties, all told, were about 1 million, and North Korean and Chinese casualties, an estimated 1.5 million.

ANOTHER RED SCARE In calculating the costs of the Korean War one must add in the far-reaching consequences of the second Red Scare, which had grown since 1945 as the domestic counterpart to the Cold War abroad and reached a crescendo during the Korean conflict. Since 1938, a House Committee on Un-American Activities had kept up a barrage of accusations about subversives in government. On March 21, 1947, just nine days after the president announced the Truman Doctrine, he signed an executive order setting up procedures for an employee loyalty program in the federal government. Designed partly to protect the president's political flank, it failed to do so, mainly because of disclosures of earlier Communist penetrations into government that were few in number but sensational in character.

Perhaps the single case most damaging to the administration involved Alger Hiss, president of the Carnegie Endowment for International Peace, who had served in several government departments, including the State Department. Whittaker Chambers, a former Soviet agent and later an editor of *Time* magazine, told the House Un-American Activities Committee in 1948 that Hiss had given him secret documents ten years earlier, when Chambers worked for the Soviets. Hiss sued for libel, and Chambers produced microfilms of the State Department documents he claimed Hiss had passed on to him. Before a federal grand jury Hiss denied the accusation, whereupon he was indicted for perjury and, after one mistrial, convicted in January 1950.

Most damaging to the administration was the fact that President Truman, taking at face value the many testimonials to Hiss's integrity, called the charges against him a "red herring." Secretary of State Dean Acheson compounded the damage when, meaning to express compassion, he said: "I do not intend to turn my back on Alger Hiss." The Hiss affair had another political consequence: it raised to national prominence a young California congressman, Richard M. Nixon, who doggedly insisted on pursuing the case and then exploited an anticommunist stance to win election to the Senate in 1950.

More cases surfaced. In 1950, the government disclosed the existence of a British-American spy network that had fed information about the development of the atomic bomb to Russia. These disclosures led to the arrest of, among others, Julius and Ethel Rosenberg. The Rosenbergs, convicted of espionage in wartime, were executed in 1953.

MCCARTHY'S WITCH-HUNT   Such revelations encouraged politicians to exploit public fears. If a man of such respectability as Hiss were guilty, many wondered, who then could be trusted? Early in 1950 the hitherto obscure Republican senator from Wisconsin, Joseph R. McCarthy, suddenly surfaced as the shrewdest and most ruthless exploiter of such anxieties. He took up the cause, or at least the pose, of anticommunism with a vengeance. He began with a speech at Wheeling, West Virginia, on February 9, 1950, in which he claimed that the State Department was infested with Communists and that he held in his hand a list of their names. Later there was confusion as to whether he had said 205, 81, 57, or "a lot" of names, and even whether the sheet of paper carried a list. But such confusion always pursued McCarthy's charges.

A special Senate committee looked into the matter and pronounced McCarthy's charges "a fraud and a hoax." McCarthy then turned, in what became his common tactic, to other

Senator Joseph McCarthy.

charges, other names. McCarthy never uncovered a single Communist agent in government. But with the United States at war with Korean Communists in mid-1950, he continued to mobilize true believers. Republicans encouraged him to keep up the game. By 1951 he was riding so high as to list Generals George C. Marshall and Dwight D. Eisenhower among the disloyal. He kept up his campaign without successful challenge until the end of the Korean War.

Under the influence of the anticommunist hysteria the Congress in 1950 passed the McCarran Internal Security Act over President Truman's veto. The act required Communist and Communist-front organizations to register with the attorney-general. Aliens who had belonged to totalitarian parties were barred from admission to the United States, a provision that, ironically, also discouraged any temptation for lapsed Communists to defect to the United States.

ASSESSING THE COLD WAR   In retrospect the onset of the Cold War takes on an appearance of terrible inevitability. America's preference for international principles, such as self-determination and democracy, conflicted with Stalin's preference for international spheres of influence. Russia, after all, had suffered two German invasions in the first half of the twentieth century, and Soviet leaders wanted tame buffer states on their borders for protection. The people of eastern Europe, as usual, were caught in the middle. But the Communists themselves held to a universal principle: world revolution. And since the time of President Monroe, Americans had bristled at the thought of foreign intervention in their own sphere of influence, the Western Hemisphere.

If international conditions set the stage for the Cold War, the actions of political leaders and thinkers set events in motion. President Truman may have erred in suggesting that the United

States must intervene anywhere in the world to stop the tide of Communist aggression. His loyalty program, following on the heels of the Truman Doctrine, may have spurred on the anticommunist hysteria of the times.

The years after World War II were unlike any other postwar era in American history. Having taken on global burdens, the nation had become, if not a "garrison state," at least a country committed to a major and permanent national military establishment. By 1952 this newly entrenched sector of the government included the National Security Council, the Central Intelligence Agency, and the enormous National Security Agency, entrusted with the monitoring of media and communications for foreign intelligence. The policy initiatives of the Truman years had led the country to abandon its longstanding aversion to peacetime alliances. It was a far cry from the world of 1796, when George Washington in his Farewell Address warned his countrymen against "those overgrown military establishments which . . . are inauspicious to liberty" and advised his country "to steer clear of permanent alliances with any portion of the foreign world." But, then, Washington had warned only against participation in the "ordinary" combinations and collisions of Europe, and surely the postwar years had seen extraordinary events.

FURTHER READING

The Cold War, like Reconstruction, is an area of American history still hotly debated by scholars. Traditional interpretations by Herbert Feis in *From Trust to Terror: The Onset of the Cold War, 1945-1950* (1970) and John L. Gaddis in *The United States and the Origins of the Cold War, 1941-1947* (1972)° can be balanced with the revisionists Walter LaFeber in *America, Russia, and the Cold War, 1945-1980* (1981)° and Gabriel Kolko in *The Limits of Power: The World and United States Foreign Policy, 1945-1954* (1972). The most recent—and best— overview of the Cold War is Melvin Leffler's *A Preponderance of Power: The Truman Administration and the Cold War* (1991).°

For the Truman administration's reliance on the atomic bomb monopoly, see Michael Mandelbaum's *The Nuclear Question: The United States and Nuclear Weapons, 1946-1976* (1979)° and Daniel Yergin's *Shattered Peace: The Origins of the Cold War and the National Security State* (1977).°

° These books are available in paperback editions.

The domestic policies of the Fair Deal receive analysis in William C. Berman's *The Politics of Civil Rights in the Truman Administration* (1970) and Maeva Marcus's *Truman and the Steel Seizure* (1977).°

For an introduction to the tensions in Asia, see Akira Iriye's *The Cold War in Asia* (1974). For the Korean conflict, see Callum A. MacDonald's *Korea: The War Before Vietnam* (1987).° The high command perspective is shown in William Manchester's *American Caesar: Douglas MacArthur, 1880–1960* (1978).°

The anti-Communist syndrome which helped produce McCarthy is surveyed in David Caute's *The Great Fear: The Anti-Communist Purge under Truman and Eisenhower* (1978).° Thomas C. Reeve's *The Life and Times of Joe McCarthy* (1982)° covers McCarthy himself.

31 ⟋⟍

THROUGH THE PICTURE WINDOW:
POSTWAR SOCIETY AND CULTURE,
1945–1960

Americans emerged from World War II elated, justifiably proud
of their military strength and industrial might. As the editors of
Fortune magazine proclaimed in 1946, "this is a dream era, this is
what everyone was waiting through the blackouts for. The Great
American Boom is on." So it was, from babies to Buicks to Admiral television sets. An American public that had known deprivation and sacrifice for the last decade and a half began to enjoy
unprecedented prosperity. The postwar era enjoyed tremendous economic growth and seeming social contentment. Yet in
the midst of such rising affluence and optimism, many social
critics, writers, and artists expressed a growing sense of unease.
Was postwar American society becoming too complacent, too
conformist, too materialistic? These questions reflected the perennial tension in American life between idealism and materialism, a tension that arrived with the first settlers and remains with
us today. Americans have always struggled to accumulate goods
and cultivate goodness. During the postwar era the nation tried
to do both, and for a while, at least, it appeared to succeed.

PEOPLE OF PLENTY

The dominant feature of post-World War II American society was
its remarkable prosperity. After a surprisingly brief postwar recession, the economy soared to record heights. The gross national product (GNP) nearly doubled between 1945 and 1960,

and the 1960s witnessed an even more spectacular expansion of the economy. By 1970 the gap between living standards in the United States and the rest of the world had become a chasm: with 6 percent of the world's population, Americans produced and consumed two-thirds of the world's goods.

Such abundance generated a mood of giddy optimism. During the 1950s government officials assured the citizenry that they should not fear another economic collapse. The leading economists of the postwar era were likewise agreed that with the New Deal safeguards built into the economy there need be no more dramatic downturns. They and others led the public to believe that perpetual economic growth was possible, desirable, and, in fact, essential. The expectation of unending plenty thus became the reigning assumption of social thought in the two decades after 1945.

Several factors contributed to this sustained economic surge. The massive federal expenditures for military needs during World War II, which had catapulted the economy out of the Depression, continued to drive the postwar economy, thanks to the tensions generated by the Cold War and the increase in defense spending provoked by the Korean conflict. Military-related research also helped spawn the new glamor industries of the postwar era: chemicals, electronics, and aviation.

Most of the other major industrial nations of the world—England, France, Germany, Japan, Russia—had been physically devastated during the war, which meant that American manufacturers enjoyed a virtual monopoly in international trade. In addition, the widespread use of new and more efficient machinery and computers led to a 35 percent jump in the productivity of American workers between 1945 and 1955.

The major catalyst in promoting economic expansion after 1945 was the unleashing of pent-up consumer demand. During the war Americans had postponed purchases of such major items as cars and houses, and in the process had saved over $150 billion. Now they were eager to buy. Likewise, many young adults who had delayed having a family were also intent upon making up for lost time. The United States after World War II experienced both a purchasing frenzy and a population explosion.

The return of some fifteen million soldiers to private life helped generate a postwar "baby boom," which peaked in 1957. Between 1946 and 1964 America's total population grew by almost 40 million, a whopping 30 percent increase. Such a dramatic growth rate had a host of reverberating effects. Indeed, much of America's social history since the 1940s has been the story of the unusually large baby-boom generation and its progress through the stages of life. One initial effect of the baby boom was to create a massive demand for diapers, baby food, toys, medicines, schools, books, teachers, and housing. Another was the growth of new suburban communities as the burgeoning population moved from the cities into the countryside.

AN EXPANDING CONSUMER CULTURE   American factories soon adjusted to new consumer demands. Native and foreign observers alike marveled at the widespread abundance generated by America's prolific industrial plant. In 1950 almost 37 percent of American homes were deemed substandard; in 1970 only 9 percent. The proportion of homeowners in the population increased by 50 percent between 1945 and 1960. And those new homes were increasingly filled with the latest electrical appliances— refrigerators, washing machines, sewing machines, vacuum cleaners, freezers, and mixers.

By far the most popular new household product was the television set. In 1946 there were only 7,000 primitive black-and-white sets in the country; by 1960 there were 50 million high-quality sets. Nine out of ten homes had one, and by 1970, 38 percent owned new color sets. *TV Guide* was the fastest growing new periodical of the 1950s, and the new television culture had a transforming effect on the patterns of daily living. Time previously devoted to reading, visiting, playing, or movie-

"I Love Lucy," starring Lucille Ball (right), was one of the most popular television series in the 1950s.

going was now spent in front of the "electronic hearth." Television, one social commentator recognized in 1950, "is even upsetting the established patterns of courtship and the marketing of beer." Said one housewife: "Until we got that TV set, I thought my husband had forgotten how to neck."

What differentiated the affluence of the post-World War II era from earlier periods of prosperity was its ever-widening dispersion. Although pockets of rural and urban poverty persisted, destined to explode in the 1960s, during the 1950s few noticed such exceptions to the prevailing prosperity. After being sworn in as head of the AFL-CIO in 1955, George Meany proclaimed that "American labor never had it so good."

To perpetuate such prosperity, economists repeated the basic marketing strategy of the 1920s: the public must be taught to consume more and expect more. Experts knew that people had more money than ever before. The average American had twice as much *real* income in 1955 as in the rosy days of the late 1920s before the Crash. Still, many adults who had undergone the severities of the Depression and the rationing required for the war effort had to be weaned from a decade and a half of imposed frugality in order to nourish the consumer culture. A motivational researcher told a business group that the fundamental challenge facing the modern capitalist economy was to demonstrate to the consumer that "the hedonistic approach to life is a moral, not an immoral one."

Advertising became a more crucial component of the consumer culture than ever before. TV advertising expenditures increased 1,000 percent during the 1950s. Such startling results led the president of the National Broadcasting Company (NBC) to claim in 1956 that the primary reason for the postwar economic boom was that "advertising has created an American frame of mind that makes people want more things, better things and newer things."

Paying for such "things" was no problem; the age of the credit card had arrived. Between 1945 and 1957, consumer credit soared 800 percent. Where families in other industrialized nations were typically saving 10 to 20 percent of their income, American families by the 1960s were saving only 5 percent. "Never before have so many owed so much to so many," *Newsweek* announced in 1953. "Time has swept away the Puritan conception of immorality in debt and godliness in thrift."

This consumer revolution had far-reaching cultural effects. Shopping, for instance, became a major recreational activity. In 1945 there were only eight shopping centers in the entire country; by 1960 there were almost 4,000. Much as life in a medieval town revolved around the cathedral, life in postwar suburban America seemed to center on the new giant shopping centers and malls. Playwright Arthur Miller addressed this phenomenon in *The Price*:

> Because you see the main thing today is—shopping. Years ago a person, if he was unhappy, didn't know what to do with himself—he'd go to church, start a revolution—*something*. Today you're unhappy? Can't figure it out? What is the salvation? Go shopping.

Young Americans especially participated in this shopping culture. By the late 1950s the baby boom generation was entering its teens, and the disproportionate number of affluent adolescents generated a vast new specialized market for goods ranging from transistor radios, hula hoops, and rock-and-roll records to cameras, surfboards, *Seventeen* magazine, and Pat Boone movies. Most teenagers had far more discretionary income than previous generations. Teens in the postwar era knew nothing of depressions or rationing; they were immersed in abundance from an early age and took the notion of carefree consumption for granted.

THE CRABGRASS FRONTIER The population increase of the 1950s and 1960s was an urban as well as a suburban phenomenon. Dramatic new technological advances in agricultural production reduced the need for manual laborers and thereby accelerated the flight from the farm in the postwar years: 20 million Americans left the land for the city between 1940 and 1970. Much of the urban population growth occurred in the South, the Southwest, and the West, in an arc that stretched from the Carolinas down through Texas and into California, diverse states that by the 1970s were being lumped together into the "Sunbelt." The dispersion of air conditioning throughout these warm regions dramatically enhanced their attraction to northerners. But the Northeast remained the most densely populated area; by the early 1960s, 20 percent of the national population lived in the corridor that stretched from Boston to Norfolk, Virginia.

While more concentrated in cities, Americans were simultaneously spreading out within metropolitan areas. In 1950 the Census Bureau redefined the term "urban" to include suburbs as well as central cities. During the 1950s suburbs grew six times faster than cities. By 1970 more Americans lived in suburbs (76 million) than in central cities (64 million). "Suburbia," proclaimed the *Christian Century* in 1955, "is now a dominant social group in American life."

William Levitt, a brassy New York developer, led the suburban revolution. In 1947, on 1,200 acres of flat Long Island farmland, he built 10,600 houses which were immediately sold and inhabited by more than 40,000 people—mostly adults under thirty-five and their children. "Everyone is so young," one Levittowner noted, "that sometimes it's hard to remember how to get along with older people."

Within a few years there were similar Levittowns in Pennsylvania and New Jersey, and other developers soon followed suit around the country. The federal government aggressively fostered this suburban revolution. "If it weren't for the government," a San Francisco developer explained, "the boom would end overnight." By insuring loans for up to 95 percent of the value of a house, the Federal Housing Administration made it easy for a builder to borrow money to construct low-cost homes. Veterans were given added benefits. A veteran could buy a Levitt house with no down payment and monthly installments of $56.

Expanded automobile production and highway construction also facilitated the rush to the suburbs as more and more people were able to commute longer distances to work. Car production soared from 2 million in 1946 to 8 million in 1955, and a "car culture" soon emerged. As one commentator observed, the proliferation of automobiles "changed our dress, manners, social customs, vacation habits, the shape of our cities, consumer purchasing patterns, and common tastes." Widespread car owner-

Moving Day, 1953. *A new subdivision opens its doors.*

ship also necessitated an improved road network. Local and state governments built many new roads, but the guiding force was the federal government. In 1947 Congress authorized the construction of 37,000 miles of highways, and nine years later it funded 42,000 additional miles of interstate freeways.

Such new roads provided access to the suburbs, and Americans—mostly young middle-class white Americans—rushed to take advantage of the new living spaces. Motives for moving to the suburbs were numerous. The availability of more spacious homes, as well as greater security and better educational opportunities for children, all played a role. Racial considerations were also a factor. After World War II blacks migrated in record numbers from the rural South into the cities of the North and Midwest. And as they moved in, white residents moved out. Those engaged in "white flight" were usually eager to maintain residential segregation in their new suburban communities. Contracts for homes in Levittown, Long Island, for example, specifically excluded "members of other than the Caucasian race." Such discrimination, whether explicit or implicit, was widespread; the nation's suburban population in 1970 was 95 percent white.

A Conforming Culture

As evidenced in many of the new look-alike suburbs sprouting up across the land, much of middle-class American social life during the two decades after the end of World War II exhibited an increasingly homogenized character. Fears generated by the Cold War initially played a key role in encouraging orthodoxy. But suburban life itself encouraged uniformity. In new communities of strangers people quickly felt a need for companionship and a sense of belonging. "Nobody wants people around who criticize and sit off by themselves and don't take part," observed one resident. Changes in corporate life also played an important socializing role. "Conformity," predicted an editor in 1954, "may very well become the central social problem of this age."

CORPORATE LIFE   During World War II big business grew bigger. The government relaxed anti-trust activity, and huge defense contracts tended to promote corporate concentration and consolidation. In 1940, for example, 100 companies were responsible for 30 percent of all manufacturing output; three years later they were providing 70 percent. In such huge companies as well as in similarly large government agencies and universities, the working atmosphere began to take on a distinctive new cast. The traditional notion of the hard-working, strong-minded individual advancing by dint of competitive ability and creative initiative gave way to a new managerial personality and an ethic of collective cooperation and achievement.

WOMAN'S "PLACE" Increasing conformity in middle-class business and corporate life was mirrored in the middle-class home. A special issue of *Life* magazine in 1956 featured the "ideal" middle-class woman, a thirty-two-year-old "pretty and popular" suburban housewife, mother of four, who had married at age 16. Described as an excellent wife, mother, hostess, volunteer, and "home manager" who made her own clothes, she hosted dozens of dinner parties each year, sang in the church choir, worked with the PTA and Campfire Girls, and was devoted to her husband. "In her daily round," *Life* reported, "she attends club or charity meetings, drives the children to school, does the weekly grocery shopping, makes ceramics, and is planning to study French." She also exercised on a trampoline in order "to keep her size 12 figure."

Life's ideal of the American middle-class woman was symptomatic of a veritable cult of feminine domesticity that witnessed a dramatic revival in the postwar era. The soaring birth rate reinforced the deeply embedded notion that a woman's place was in the home as tender of the hearth and guardian of the children. "Of all the accomplishments of the American woman," the *Life* cover story proclaimed, "the one she brings off with the most spectacular success is having babies."

So even though millions of women had responded to intense wartime appeals and joined "Rosie the Riveter" in the traditionally male workforce, afterwards they were encouraged—and even forced—to turn their jobs over to the returning veterans and resume their full-time commitment to home and family. An article in *House Beautiful* in 1945, entitled "Home Should Be Even More Wonderful Than He Remembers It," lectured women on their postwar responsibilities. The ex-serviceman was "head man again. . . . Your part in the remaking of this man is to fit his home to him, understanding why he wants it this way, forgetting your own preferences." Women were also to forget any thoughts of continuing their own careers in the workplace. "Back to the kitchen" was the repeated refrain after 1945.

Throughout the postwar era, educators, politicians, ministers,

The Ideal Woman. *A 1956* Life *magazine cover story pronounced the ideal woman a "pretty and popular" suburban housewife who "attends club or charity meetings, drives the children to school, does the weekly grocery shopping, makes ceramics, and is planning to study French."*

advertisers, and other commentators exalted the cult of domesticity and castigated the few feminists who were encouraging women to broaden their horizons beyond crib and kitchen. Even a liberal politician and self-styled progressive intellectual such as Adlai Stevenson preached a similar doctrine. He reminded Smith College graduates in 1955 that their heroic purpose in life was to "influence man and boy" in the "humble role of housewife."

RELIGIOUS REVIVAL   Another illustration of the conformist tendencies of middle-class life during the 1950s was the spiraling growth of membership in social institutions. Americans, even more than usual, became joiners; they joined civic clubs, garden clubs, bridge clubs, car pools, and babysitting groups.

They also joined churches and synagogues in record numbers. The postwar era witnessed a massive renewal of religious participation, and the Cold War was a strong impetus behind the awakening. "Since Communists are anti-God," FBI director J. Edgar Hoover advised, "encourage your child to be active in the church." Many American parents heeded his warning. In 1940 less than half of the adult population belonged to institutionalized churches; by 1960 over 65 percent were official communicants. Bible sales soared, and books, movies, and songs with religious themes were stunning commercial successes. Hollywood glamor girl Jane Russell, hitherto noted more for her buxom bosom and sultry smile than her spiritual intensity, was one of many celebrities who promoted the religious revival. "I Love God," she confessed. "And when you get to know him, he's a livin' doll."

President Eisenhower also repeatedly promoted a patriotic crusade to bring Americans back to God. "Recognition of the Supreme Being," he declared, "is the first, the most basic, expression of Americanism. Without God, there could be no American form of government, nor an American way of life." Not to be outdone in professing piety, Congress in 1954 added the phrase "one nation under God" to the pledge of allegiance. The following year it made the statement "In God We Trust" mandatory on all American currency.

The prevailing tone of the popular religious revival during the 1950s was upbeat and soothing. Many ministers assumed that people were not interested in "fire-and-brimstone" harangues from the pulpit; they did not want their consciences overly burdened with a sense of personal sin or social guilt over such issues as segregation or inner-city poverty. Instead they wanted to be reassured that their own comfortable way of life was indeed God's will. As the Protestant Council of New York City explained to its corps of radio and television speakers, their addresses "should project love, joy, courage, hope, faith, trust in God, good will. Generally avoid condemnation, criticism, controversy. In a very real sense we are 'selling' religion, the good news of the Gospel."

By far the best salesman of this gospel of reassuring "good news" was the Reverend Norman Vincent Peale, the impresario of "positive thinking" and feel-good theology. No speaker was more in demand during the 1950s, and no writer was more widely read. Peale's book *The Power of Positive Thinking* (1952) was a phenomenal bestseller throughout the decade—and for good reason. It offered a simple "how to" course in personal happiness. "Flush out all depressing, negative, and tired thoughts," Peale advised. "Start thinking faith, enthusiasm, and joy." By following this simple formula for success, he pledged, the reader could become "a more popular, esteemed, and well-liked individual."

Peale's message of psychological security and material success was powerfully reassuring, and many Americans stood in need of reassurance. That tranquilizers were the fastest growing new medication suggested the anxiety accompanying America's much-trumpeted affluence. Many Americans were profoundly anxious about the meaning of their lives and of life in general in the nuclear age. Peale offered them peace of mind and peace of soul, assuring them that everything was fine and for the best as long as they believed in God, the American Way, and themselves. "Stop worrying and start living" was his simple credo.

NEO-ORTHODOXY   But was it too simple? The "positive thinking" psychology promoted by Peale and other feel-good ministers struck some members of the religious community as shallow and dangerously misleading. These spokesmen for "neo-orthodox" theology charged that such consoling religiosity lacked genuine conviction and commitment.

The towering leader of the "neo-orthodox" movement was Reinhold Niebuhr (1892–1970). A brilliant preacher-professor at New York's Union Theological Seminary, Niebuhr repeatedly lashed out at the "undue complacency and conformity" settling over American life in the postwar era. He found the popular religion of self-assurance and the psychology of material success promoted by Peale and his followers woefully inadequate prescriptions for the ills of modern society. "They cannot be taken seriously by responsible religious or secular people," he warned in 1955, "because they do not come to terms with the basic collective problems of our atomic age, and because the peace which they seek to inculcate is rather too simple and neat." True peace, Niebuhr insisted, entailed the reality of pain, a pain "caused by love and responsibility" for the well-being of the entire human race, rather than to be solely concerned with one's tortured self. Self-love, he reminded smug Americans, was the very basis of sin.

CRACKS IN THE PICTURE WINDOW

Niebuhr was one of many impassioned disturbers of the peace who challenged the moral complacency and social conformity that he and others claimed had come to characterize American social life during the 1950s and early 1960s. As the philosopher and editor Joseph Wood Krutch recognized in 1960, "the gap between those who find the spirit of the age congenial and those who do not seems to have grown wider and wider."

THE LONELY CROWD   The criticism of postwar American life and values began in the early 1950s and quickly gathered momentum among intellectuals, theologians, novelists, playwrights, poets, and artists. Social scientists, too, attacked the prevailing optimism of the time. In *The Affluent Society* (1958), for example, economist John K. Galbraith warned that sustained economic growth would not necessarily solve chronic social problems. He reminded readers that for all of America's vaunted postwar prosperity, the nation had yet to confront, much less eradicate, the chronic poverty plaguing the nation's inner cities and rural hamlets.

Postwar cultural critics also questioned the supposed bliss offered by middle-class suburban life. John Keats, in *The Crack in the Picture Window* (1956), launched the most savage assault on life in the huge new suburban developments. He ridiculed Levittown and other such mass-produced communities as having been "conceived in error, nurtured in greed, corroding everything they touch." In these rows of "identical boxes spreading like gangrene," commuter fathers were always at work and "mothers were always delivering children, obstetrically once and by car forever after." Locked into a deadly routine, hounded by financial insecurity, and engulfed by mass mediocrity, suburbanites, he concluded, were living in a "homogeneous, postwar Hell."

Social critics repeatedly cited the huge modern corporation as an equally important source of regimentation in American life. The most comprehensive and provocative analysis of the docile new corporate character was David Riesman's *The Lonely Crowd* (1950). Riesman, a social psychologist, detected a fundamental shift in the dominant American personality from what he called the "inner-directed" to the "other-directed" type. Inner-directed people, Riesman argued, possessed a deeply internalized set of basic values implanted by strong-minded parents or other elders. This core set of fixed principles, analogous to the traditional Protestant ethic of piety, diligence, and thrift, acted, in his words, like an internal gyroscope. The inner-directed person was kept on a steady course by the built-in stabilizer of fixed values.

Such an assured, self-reliant personality, Riesman claimed, had been dominant in American life throughout the nineteenth century. But during the mid-twentieth century a new, other-directed personality had displaced it. In the huge, hierarchical corporations that abounded in postwar America employees who could win friends and influence people thrived; rugged individualists indifferent to personal popularity did not. The other directed people who adapted to this corporate culture had few internal convictions and standards; they did not follow their conscience so much as adapt to the prevailing standards of the moment. They were more concerned with being well-liked than being independent.

Riesman amassed considerable evidence to show that the other-directed personality was not just an aspect of the business world; its characteristics were widely dispersed throughout middle-class life. One source of this may have been Dr. Benjamin Spock's influential advice on raising children. Spock's popular manual, *The Common Sense Book of Baby and Child Care*, sold an average of one million copies a year between its first appearance in 1946 and 1960. Although Spock never endorsed the anarchic permissiveness attributed to him by later critics, he did insist that parents should foster in their children qualities and skills that would enhance their chances in what Riesman called the "popularity market." Reisman charged that this made the middle-class mother a "chauffeur and booking agent," determined to "cultivate all the currently essential talents, especially the gregarious ones. It is inconceivable to some that a child might prefer his own company or that of just another child."

ALIENATION IN THE ARTS Many of the best novels and plays of the postwar period reinforced Riesman's image of modern American society as a "lonely crowd" of individuals, hollow at the core, groping for a sense of belonging and affection. Arthur Miller's play *Death of a Salesman* (1949) powerfully explored this theme. Willy Loman, an aging, confused traveling salesman in decline, centers his life and that of his family on the notion of material success through personal popularity, only to be abruptly told by his boss that he is in fact a failure. Loman repeatedly insists that it is "not what you say, it's how you say it—because personality always wins the day," and he tries to raise his sons, Biff and Happy, in his own image, encouraging them to be athletic, outgoing, popular, and ambitious. As he instructs them: "Be liked and you will never want." Happy followed his father's advice but was anything but happy: "Sometimes I sit in my apartment—all alone. And I think of the rent I'm paying. And it's crazy. But then, it's what I always wanted. My own apartment, a car, and plenty of women. And still, goddammit, I'm lonely."

Such vacant loneliness is the play's recurring theme. Willy, for all his puffery about being well-liked, admits that he is "terribly lonely." He has no real friends; even his relations with his family

In Arthur Miller's Death of a Salesman, *Willy Loman (center, played by Lee J. Cobb) destroys his life and family with the credo "Be liked and you will never want."*

are neither honest nor intimate. "He never knew who he was," Biff sighs. Indeed, when Willy finally realizes that he has been leading a counterfeit existence, he yearns for a life in which "a man is not a piece of fruit," but eventually he is so haunted and dumbfounded by his predicament that he decides he can endow his life with meaning only by ending it.

Death of a Salesman and many other postwar plays written by Arthur Miller, Edward Albee, and Tennessee Williams portray a central theme of American literature and art during the postwar era: the sense of alienation experienced by sensitive individuals in the midst of an oppressive mass culture. In the aftermath of the horrors of World War II and the Holocaust, and in the midst of the nuclear terror, many of the country's foremost writers, painters, and poets refused to embrace the prevailing celebration of modern American life and values. The novelist Philip Roth observed in 1961: "The American writer in the middle of the twentieth century has his hands full in trying to understand, and then describe, and then make credible much of American reality. It stupefies, it sickens, it infuriates, and finally it is even a kind of embarrassment to one's own meager imagination." Roth's gloomy assessment was typical of the revulsion felt by other writers and artists, many of whom were determined to lay bare the conceits and illusions of their times.

While millions were reading heartwarming religious epics such as *The Cardinal* (1950), *The Robe* (1953), and *Exodus*

(1957), literary critics were praising the more unsettling and sobering novels of James Baldwin, Saul Bellow, John Cheever, Ralph Ellison, Joseph Heller, James Jones, Norman Mailer, Joyce Carol Oates, J.D. Salinger, William Styron, John Updike, and Eudora Welty. There were few happy endings here—and even fewer celebrations of contemporary American life. J.D. Salinger's *Catcher in the Rye* (1951) was a troubling exploration of a young man's search for meaning and self in a smothering society. Holden Caulfield finally decides that rebellion against conformity is useless. "If you want to stay alive," he concludes, "you have to say that stuff, like 'Glad to meet you' to people you are not at all glad to meet."

This brooding sense of resigned alienation dominated the most powerful imaginative literature in the two decades after 1945. The characters in novels such as Jones's *From Here to Eternity*, Ellison's *Invisible Man*, Bellow's *Dangling Man* and *Seize the Day*, Styron's *Lie Down in Darkness*, and Updike's *Rabbit, Run*, among many others, tended to be like Willy Loman—restless, tormented, impotent individuals who are unable to fasten on a satisfying self-image and therefore can find neither contentment nor respect in an overpowering or impersonal world.

PAINTING   The artist Edward Hopper (1882–1967) adopted a similar outlook in his paintings. From the start of his career at the turn of the century, Hopper explored the theme of desolate loneliness in urban-industrial American life. But his concern grew more acute in the postwar era. Virtually all of his paintings depict isolated individuals, melancholy, anonymous, motionless. A woman undressing for bed, a diner in an all-night restaurant, a housewife in a doorway, a businessman at his desk, a lone passerby in the street—these are the characters in Hopper's world. The silence of his scenes is deafening, the monotony striking, the alienation absorbing.

A younger group of painters centered in New York City were convinced that postwar society was so chaotic that it denied any attempt at literal representation. As Jackson Pollock maintained, "the modern painter cannot express this age—the airplane, the atomic bomb, the radio—in the old form of the Renaissance or of any past culture. Each age finds its own technique." The technique Pollock adopted came to be called Abstract Expressionism, and during the late 1940s and 1950s it dominated not only the American art scene but the international field as well. In addition to Pollock, its adherents included Robert Motherwell, William de Kooning, Arshile Gorky, Clyfford Still, Adolph Gottlieb, and

Office in a Small City *(1953). In his paintings, Edward Hopper captured the sense of the individual's isolation and alienation within the urban-industrial world of the postwar era.*

Mark Rothko. "Abstract art," Motherwell declared, "is an effort to close the void that modern men feel."

In practice this meant that the *act* of painting was as important as the final result, and that art no longer had to represent one's visual surroundings. Instead it could unapologetically represent the painter's personal thoughts and actions. Wyoming-born Pollock, for example, placed his huge canvases flat on the floor, and then walked around each side, pouring and dripping his paints, all in an effort to "literally be *in* the painting." Such action paintings, with their commanding size, bold form, powerful color contrasts, and rough texture, conveyed the whole spectrum of aesthetic qualities: they were vibrant, frenzied, meditative, disorienting, provocative. Needless to say, many among the general public found them simply provoking. One wit observed that "I suspect any picture I think I could have made myself."

THE BEATS   The desire to liberate self-expression and reject middle-class conventions also animated a small but highly visible and controversial group of young writers, poets, painters, and musicians known as the Beats. These angry young men—Jack Kerouac, Allen Ginsberg, Gary Snyder, William Burroughs, and

Gregory Corso, among others—were alienated by the mundane horrors of middle-class life. The Beats were not lost in despair, however; they strenuously embraced life. But it was life on their own terms, and their terms were shocking to most observers. The Beats grew out of the bohemian underground in New York's Greenwich Village. Kerouac was a handsome, athletic, working-class kid from Lowell, Massachusetts, who went to Columbia University on a football scholarship. Ginsberg also studied at Columbia, where a perplexed dean directed him to undergo psychotherapy. The moody poet chose William Burroughs as his therapist. Burroughs graduated from Harvard in 1936, then studied medicine in Vienna. Later he would become a heroin addict, kill his wife while trying to shoot an apple off her head, and write the influential experimental novel *Naked Lunch* (1959). This fervent threesome found its hero in Neal Cassady, a twenty-year-old ex-convict who arrived in New York from Denver hoping to enroll at Columbia. He was in their view a mythic cowboy turned "cool" hipster, utterly free and rootless because he defied both maturity and reason. Soon this quartet attracted others in quest of *real* life, and the Beat culture was born.

Essentially apolitical throughout the 1950s, the Beats sought personal rather than social solutions to their hopes and anxieties. As Kerouac insisted, they were not beat in the sense of beaten; they were "mad to live, mad to talk, mad to be saved." Their road to salvation lay in hallucinogenic drugs and alcohol, relentless sex, a penchant for jazz and the street life of urban ghettos, an affinity for Buddhism, and a restless, vagabond spirit that took them speeding back and forth across the country between San Francisco and New York.

This existential mania for intense experience and frantic motion provided the subject matter for the Beats' writing. Ginsberg's long prose-poem *Howl* (1956) featured an explicit sensuality as well as an impressionistic attempt to catch the color, movement, and dynamism of modern life. In this it bore a marked resemblance to Walt Whitman's *Leaves of Grass*. But *Howl* lacked Whitman's celebratory tone; its mood was bitter and critical. Ginsberg howled at the "Robot apartments! invincible suburbs! skeleton treasuries! blind capitals! demonic industries!" Kerouac published his autobiographical novel *On the Road* a year later. In frenzied prose it portrayed the Beats' life of "bursting ecstasies" and maniacal traveling. At one point Dean Moriarty (Neal Cassady) has the following exchange with Sal Paradise (Kerouac): "We gotta go and never stop going till we get there." "Where we going, man?" "I don't know, but we gotta go."

Howl and *On the Road* provoked angry sarcasm from many reviewers, but the books enjoyed a brisk sale, especially among young people. *On the Road* made the bestseller list, and soon the term "beat generation" or "beatnik" was being applied to almost any young rebel who openly dissented from the comfortable ethos of middle-class life. Defiant young actors such as James Dean and Marlon Brando were added to the pantheon of Beat "anti-heroes." In *The Wild One* (1954) a waitress asks Brando what he is rebelling against. He replies: "Whattaya got?" A young folk-singer from Minnesota named Bob Dylan was directly inspired by *Howl* and *On the Road*. In this sense the anarchic gaiety of the Beats played an important role in preparing the way for the more widespread youth revolt of the 1960s.

A Paradoxical Era

For all their color and vitality, the Beats had little impact on the prevailing patterns of postwar social and cultural life. The same held for most of the other critics who attacked the smug conformity and excessive materialism they saw pervading their society. The public had become understandably weary of larger social or political concerns in the aftermath of the Depression and the war. Instead Americans eagerly focused their efforts on personal and family goals and took great pride in their material achievements.

Yet those achievements, considerable as they were, eventually created a new set of problems. The benefits of abundance were by no means equally distributed, and millions of Americans still lived hidden in poverty. For those more fortunate, unprecedented affluence and security fostered greater leisure and independence, which in turn provided opportunities for pursuing more diverse notions of what the good life entailed. Yet the conformist mentality of the Cold War era discouraged experimentation. By the mid-1960s, however, tensions between innovation and convention would erupt into open conflict. Ironically, many members of the baby boom generation would become the leaders of the 1960s rebellion against the corporate and consumer cultures. Even more ironically, the person who would warn Americans of the 1960s about the mounting dangers of the burgeoning "military-industrial complex" was the president who had long symbolized its growth—Dwight D. Eisenhower.

FURTHER READING

There are a number of excellent overviews of social and cultural trends in the postwar era. Among the best are William H. Chafe's *The Unfinished Journey* (rev. ed., 1991),° William E. Leuchtenburg's *A Troubled Feast* (1982),° and William L. O'Neill's *American High: The Years of Confidence, 1945–1960* (1989).° For fascinating insights into the cultural life of the 1950s, see Douglas T. Miller and Marion Nowak's *The Fifties* (1977) and Jeffrey Hart's *When the Going Was Good: American Life in the Fifties* (1982).

The baby-boom generation and its impact are vividly described in Landon Jones's *Great Expectations: America and the Baby Boom Generation* (1980).° On the cultural effects of unprecedented prosperity see John K. Galbraith's *The Affluent Society* (1958)° and David Potter's *People of Plenty* (1954).° The emergence and impact of the television industry is discussed in Erik Barnouw's *Tube of Plenty* (1982).°

For an overview of the resurgence of religion in the 1950s, see George Marsden's *Religion and American Culture* (1990).° The most comprehensive account of suburban development is Kenneth Jackson's award-winning study *The Crabgrass Frontier* (1985).° Herbert Gans's *The Levittowners* (1957)° represented a pathbreaking sociological study of suburban life. In addition to Betty Friedan's *Feminine Mystique* (1963),° another good source of information about the status of women during and after the war years is Susan M. Hartmann's *The Homefront and Beyond: American Women in the 1940s* (1982).° The automobile's relationship to suburbanization is addressed in John B. Rae's *The Road and the Car in American Life* (1971). The middle class ideal of family life in the 1950s is examined in Elaine Tyler May's *Homeward Bound: American Families in the Cold War Era* (1990).°

A lively discussion of movies of the 1950s can be found in Peter Biskind's *Seeing Is Believing* (1983).° The origins and growth of rock and roll music are surveyed in Carl Belz's *The Story of Rock* (1972).° The colorful Beats are brought to life in John Tytell's *Naked Angels: The Lives and Literature of the Beat Generation* (1976).° Thoughtful interpretive surveys of postwar American literature include Marcus Klein's *After Alienation: The American Novel at Mid-Century* (1978),° and Malcolm Bradbury's *The Modern American Novel* (1984).° Developments in American art since World War II are assessed in *The New American Art* (1965) edited by Richard Kostelanetz and Serge Guibaut's *How New York Stole the Idea of Modern Art* (1983).°

° These books are available in paperback editions.

32

CONFLICT AND DEADLOCK: THE EISENHOWER YEARS

"TIME FOR A CHANGE"

By 1952 the Truman administration had piled up a heavy burden of political liabilities. Its bold stand in Korea had brought a bloody stalemate abroad, renewed wage and price controls at home, reckless charges of subversion and disloyalty, and exposure of corrupt lobbyists and influence peddlers who rigged favors in Washington. The disclosure of government corruption led Truman to fire nearly 250 employees of the Bureau of Internal Revenue. But doubts lingered that Truman would ever finish the house-cleaning.

EISENHOWER'S POLITICAL RISE   It was, in a slogan of the day, "time for a change," and Republicans saw public sentiment turning their way as the 1952 election approached. The Republican field quickly narrowed to two men, Ohio senator Robert A. Taft and General Dwight D. Eisenhower. The party wheelhorses turned instinctively to Taft, "Mr. Republican," long a faithful party worker. For all his experience and ability, however, Taft was a dull public figure. Eisenhower the war hero, on the other hand, had the popular appeal that Taft lacked, and his captivating and unpretentious manner inspired widespread support.

Despite his roots in rural Kansas Republican conservatism, Eisenhower had initially supported Roosevelt and the New Deal, and he admired the president's wartime leadership. But during the Truman years Eisenhower reverted to the political party of his youth. In January 1952 he affirmed that he was a Republican

Dwight D. Eisenhower (right) *and Richard M. Nixon* (left), *the Republican standardbearers for 1952.*

and in the following months permitted his name to be entered in party primaries. Bumper stickers across the land announced simply, "I like Ike," and the immensely popular Eisenhower won the nomination on the first ballot. He then balanced the ticket by choosing as his running mate a youthful Californian, the thirty-nine-year-old Senator Richard M. Nixon, who had built a career on strenuous opposition to "subversives."

THE 1952 ELECTION   The Twenty-second Amendment, ratified in 1951, forbade any president to seek a third term. The amendment exempted the incumbent, but weary of the war, harassed by charges of subversion and corruption in his administration, and with his popularity declining, Truman chose to withdraw. In a wide open Democratic race, Truman supported Illinois governor Adlai E. Stevenson, who aroused the convention delegates with an eloquent speech welcoming them to Chicago. On the third ballot the convention drafted Stevenson.

The campaign matched two of the most magnetic personalities ever pitted in a presidential contest. Both men attracted new followings among people previously apathetic to politics, but the race was uneven from the start. Eisenhower, though a political novice, was a world figure who had been in the public eye for a decade. Stevenson was hardly known outside Illinois.

The genial Eisenhower, who disliked politics and politicians, opened a domestic crusade to clean up "the mess in Washington." To this he added a promise, late in the campaign, that as president-elect he would go to Korea to secure "an early and honorable" peace. Stevenson offered a lofty eloquence spiced with a quick wit, but his resolve to "talk sense" and "tell the truth to the American people" came across as a bit too aloof, a shade too intellectual. The Republicans hastened to cast him in the role of an "egghead," in contrast to Eisenhower, the folksy man of the people, the man of decision and action. And Eisenhower's running mate, Richard Nixon, savagely—and clumsily —tried to tar Stevenson with the brush of being "soft" on communism. He branded the Democratic candidate as "Adlai the appeaser" who earned "a Ph.D. from Dean Acheson's College of Cowardly Communist Containment." Can such a man, Nixon asked the voters, be "trusted to lead our crusade against communism?" Stevenson replied: "If the Republicans will stop telling lies about us, we will stop telling the truth about them."

But Stevenson's humor and intellect were no match for Eisenhower's popularity. The war hero triumphed in a landslide of 34 million votes to 27 million. The election marked a turning point in Republican fortunes in the South: for the first time since the heyday of the Whigs in the 1840s the South was moving toward a two-party system. Stevenson carried only eight southern states plus West Virginia; Eisenhower picked up five states in the outer South: Florida, Oklahoma, Tennessee, Texas, and Virginia. The "nonpolitical" Eisenhower had made it respectable, even fashionable, to vote Republican in the South. Elsewhere, too, the general made inroads in the New Deal coalition, attracting supporters among the ethnic and religious minorities in the major cities.

The voters, it turned out, liked Ike better than they liked his party. Democrats retained most of the governorships, lost control of the House by only eight votes, and broke even in the Senate. The congressional elections two years later would weaken the Republican grip on Congress, and Eisenhower would have to work with a Democratic Congress until he left office.

IKE   Born in Denison, Texas, in 1890, Dwight David Eisenhower grew up in Abilene, Kansas. After finishing West Point he spent nearly his entire adult life in the military service. As a major-general he took command of American forces in the European theater and directed the invasion of North Africa in November 1941. In 1944 he assumed the post of supreme commander of allied forces in preparation for the invasion of the continent. After the war, by then a five-star general, he became chief of staff and supreme commander of NATO forces, with a brief interlude in between as president of Columbia University.

Eisenhower's inauguration brought a change in style to the White House. The contrast in character between the feisty Truman and the fatherly Ike was reinforced by a contrast in philosophy and approach to the presidency. Eisenhower's military experience developed in him an instinct for methodical staff work. He met with the cabinet and the National Security Council nearly every week, and relied heavily on them for advice. His chief assistant, former New Hampshire governor Sherman Adams, decreed that any paperwork destined for the Oval Office be digested into single-page summaries.

Such procedures, it seemed, tended to isolate the president from conflicting viewpoints and to reduce the policy choices available to him. The public image of Ike confirmed that view, but it endeared him all the more to the people as a man who rose above politics. It was hard not to like the buoyant and modest war hero. Ike was warm, sincere, and unpretentious, an ardent golfer and bridge player, a common man who read little but western novels, uninformed on the currents of intellectual and artistic life, and given to simple maxims: "Everybody ought to be happy every day. Play hard, have fun doing it, and despise wickedness." As one diplomat observed: "He was the nation's number one Boy Scout."

Yet those who were close to Ike have presented another side to the man. When provoked he could release a fiery temper and scalding profanity. The scrambled syntax in which he answered reporters' questions was sometimes intentional evasion. He once told his press secretary before a news conference: "Don't worry, Jim. If that comes up, I'll just confuse them."

"DYNAMIC CONSERVATISM" AT HOME   Like Ulysses Grant, however, Eisenhower betrayed a weakness for hobnobbing with rich men. His cabinet, a journalist quipped, consisted of "eight millionaires and a plumber." The plumber, Secretary of Labor Martin Durkin, was gone in eight months, charging that the administration had reneged on a promise to change the Taft-Hartley Act. The president of General Motors became secretary of defense, and two auto distributors were appointed secretary of the interior and postmaster-general. The New Dealers, Adlai Stevenson wryly remarked, "have all left Washington to make way for the car dealers."

Eisenhower called his domestic program "dynamic conservatism," which meant being "conservative when it comes to money and liberal when it comes to human beings." Budget cutting was a high priority. Eisenhower warned repeatedly against the dangers of "creeping socialism," huge bureaucracies, and budget deficits. His administration abolished the Reconstruction Finance Corporation, ended wage and price controls, and reduced farm price subsidies. But though Eisenhower chipped away at New Deal programs, his presidency in the end served rather to legitimate the New Deal by keeping its basic structure and premises intact during an era of prosperity. In a letter to his brother in 1954, he observed: "Should any political party attempt to abolish social security and eliminate labor laws and farm programs, you would not hear of that party again in our political history." He added that those conservative Republicans who sought to dismantle the New Deal in its entirety were "stupid." Essentially Eisenhower sought to leave the basic structure of the New Deal intact and to prevent its costs from rising. This led Republican Senator Barry Goldwater to grouse that Ike was promoting a "Dime Store New Deal."

In some ways, moreover, the administration not only maintained the New Deal but extended its reach, especially after 1954 when it had the help of Democratic Congresses. Amendments to the Social Security Act in 1954 and 1956 brought coverage to millions in categories formerly excluded: professional people, domestic and clerical workers, farm workers, and members of the armed forces. The federal minimum wage rose in 1955 from 75 cents to $1 an hour. Federal expenditures for public health rose steadily in the Eisenhower years, and the president went so far as to endorse federal participation in health insurance, but Congress twice refused to act. Low-income housing continued to be built, although on a much-reduced scale. Some farm-related aid programs were actually expanded during the Eisenhower years.

Despite Eisenhower's general disapproval of public power programs, he continued to support public works for which he saw a legitimate need. Indeed, two such programs left major monuments to his presidency: the St. Lawrence Seaway and the Interstate Highways. The St. Lawrence Seaway, opened in 1959 as a joint venture with Canada, made it possible for ocean-going ships to reach the Great Lakes. The Federal Highway Act of 1956 authorized the federal government to put up 90 percent of the cost of building 42,500 miles of limited-access interstate highways to serve the needs of commerce and defense, as well as private convenience. The states provided the remaining 10 percent. It was only afterward that people realized that the huge national commitment to the automobile might have come at the expense of America's railroad system, already in a state of advanced decay.

CONCLUDING AN ARMISTICE   America's new position in the postwar world continued to absorb Eisenhower's attention. The most pressing problem when he entered office was the continuing, painful deadlock in the Korean peace talks. The main stumbling block was the North Korean and Red Chinese insistence that all prisoners be returned regardless of their wishes. To break the deadlock, Eisenhower took a bold stand. In mid-May 1953 he stepped up aerial bombardment of North Korea, then had Secretary of State John Foster Dulles warn the Chinese of his willingness to use atomic bombs. Whether for that reason or others, negotiations then moved quickly toward an armistice along the established battle line just above the Thirty-eighth Parallel, and toward a complicated arrangement for prisoner exchange that allowed captives to decide whether to accept or refuse repatriation.

On July 26, 1953, Eisenhower announced the conclusion of the armistice. No one knows if he actually would have forced the issue with atomic weapons. Perhaps the more decisive factors in bringing about a settlement were the size of Chinese Communist losses, which they increasingly found unacceptable, and the new spirit of uncertainty and caution felt by Russian Communists after the death of Josef Stalin on March 5, 1953—six weeks after Ike's inauguration.

CONCLUDING A WITCH-HUNT   The Korean armistice helped to end another dismal episode: the meteoric career of Senator Joseph R. McCarthy, which had flourished amid the anxieties of wartime. Convinced that the government was thoroughly infested with communists and spies, the Wisconsin senator launched a splenetic crusade to root them out. In the process he and his aides lied, falsified evidence, and bullied or blackmailed witnesses. Eventually the logic of McCarthy's unscrupulous tactics led to his self-destruction, but not before he had left still more careers and reputations in ruins. The Republicans thought their victory in 1952 would curb his recklessness, but McCarthy actually grew more outlandish in his charges and his investigative methods. And many Americans caught up in the anticommunist hysteria viewed him as a heroic knight doing battle against the forces of darkness.

McCarthy finally overreached himself when, as chairman of the Senate's Government Operations Committee, he ordered closed hearings to investigate charges of Soviet espionage at the Army Signal Center in Fort Monmouth, New Jersey, and then tried to peddle the absurdity that the United States Army itself was "soft" on communism. From April 22 to June 17, 1954, the televised hearings displayed McCarthy at his capricious worst, scowling at critics, bullying witnesses, dragging out lengthy ir-relevancies, repeatedly calling "point of order." He became the perfect foil for the army's gentle but unflappable counsel, Jo-seph Welch, whose rapier wit repeatedly drew blood. When McCarthy tried to smear one of Welch's young associates, the counsel went into a cold rage: "Until this moment, Senator, I think I never really gauged your cruelty or your reckless-ness. . . . Have you no sense of decency, sir, at long last?" When the audience, including press corps photographers, burst into applause, the confused and skulking senator was reduced to whispering, "What did I do?"

Perhaps McCarthy never found out, but at that point the house he had thrown together began to crash around his ears. He de-scended into new depths of scurrility, now directing charges at

The Army-McCarthy Hearings, June 1954. *Joseph Welch (head in hand) listens dejectedly after McCarthy's attempt to smear one of Welch's associates.*

his own colleagues, calling one senator "senile" and another "a living miracle . . . the only man who has lived so long with neither brains nor guts." On December 2, 1954, the Senate voted 67 to 22 to "condemn" McCarthy for contempt of the Senate. McCarthy was finished and increasingly took to alcohol. Three years later, at the age of forty-eight, he was dead. For all his attacks and inquiries, he had never uncovered one Communist in government.

The witch-hunt was over. McCarthyism, Ike joked, had become McCarthywasm, though not for those whose reputations and careers had been wrecked. To the end Eisenhower kept his resolve not to "get down in the gutter with that guy" and sully the dignity of the presidency. He did work resolutely against McCarthy behind the scenes, but some scholars consider his "hidden hand" approach to have been ineffective at best and cowardly at worst. Eisenhower shared, nevertheless, the widely held conviction that espionage posed a real danger to national security. He denied clemency to Julius and Ethel Rosenberg, who had been convicted of passing atomic secrets to the Russians, on the grounds that they "may have condemned to death tens of millions of innocent people." Although few if any scientists believed that the design principles of the bomb were a secret, the Rosenburgs were electrocuted at Sing-Sing Prison in June 1953.

INTERNAL SECURITY   Even earlier, Eisenhower stiffened the government security program. In 1953 he issued an executive order broadening the basis for firing government workers by replacing Truman's criterion of "disloyalty" with the new category of "security risk." Under the new edict federal workers could lose their jobs because of dubious associations or personal habits that might make them careless or vulnerable to blackmail. In December 1953 the Atomic Energy Commission removed the security clearance of physicist J. Robert Oppenheimer, the "father of the atomic bomb," on the grounds that he had expressed qualms about the hydrogen bomb in 1949–1950 and had associated with Communists or former Communists in the past. Lacking evidence of any disloyalty or betrayal, the AEC nevertheless branded him a "security risk" because of "fundamental defects in his character."

The Supreme Court, however, modified some of the more extreme expressions of this new Red Scare. In September 1953 Eisenhower appointed as chief justice former governor Earl Warren of California, a decision the president later pronounced the "biggest damnfool mistake I ever made." Warren, who had seemed safely conservative while in electoral politics, led an active Court on issues of civil rights and civil liberties. The Warren Court (1953–1969), under the chief justice's influence, became an important agency of social and political change on through the 1960s. In connection with security programs and loyalty requirements, the Court veered back in the direction of traditional individual rights. A 1957 opinion construed the Smith Act of 1940, aimed at conspirators against the government, to apply only to those advocating revolutionary action. This, added to other decisions setting rigid standards for evidence, rendered the Smith Act a dead letter.

DULLES AND FOREIGN POLICY The Eisenhower administration promised new foreign policy departures under the direction of Secretary of State John Foster Dulles. Grandson of one secretary of state and nephew of another, Dulles pursued a lifetime career as an international lawyer and sometime diplomat. Son of a minister and himself an earnest Presbyterian layman, Dulles, in the words of the British ambassador, resembled those old zealots of the wars of religion who "saw the world as an arena in which the forces of good and evil were continuously at war." Tall, spare, and stooped, he gave the appearance of dour sternness and Calvinist righteousness. But he was also a man of immense energy, intelligence, and experience. As Eisenhower once said of Dulles, "There's only one man I know who has seen *more* of the world, and talked with more people and *knows* more than he does—and that's me."

The foreign policy planks of the 1952 Republican platform, which Dulles wrote, showed both the moralist and the tactician at work. Truman's policy of containment was needlessly defensive, Dulles thought. This conviction meshed nicely with the conventional wisdom of the right wing that Yalta was perhaps a betrayal, at best a blunder. The 1952 platform, therefore, promised to "repudiate all commitments . . . such as those of Yalta which aid Communist enslavement" and to end "the negative, futile and immoral policy of 'containment' which abandons countless human beings to a despotism and godless terrorism." A new policy of liberation, the platform promised, would help generate independence movements within the communist bloc.

The policy verged perilously close to proclaiming a holy war, but Dulles stressed that he did not intend forcible liberation. Soon it became apparent that it was less a policy than a web of rhetoric to catch ethnic voters whose homelands had fallen captive to the Russians. This became evident when the administration did nothing but deplore a Russian crackdown on rebellious East German workers in June 1953. For three years more Dulles assumed that his rhetoric was undermining the Communist hold on Eastern Europe—until ruthless Russian suppression of the 1956 uprising in Hungary underscored the danger of stirring futile hopes among captive peoples.

Insofar as American interventions occurred abroad, they were covert operations by the Central Intelligence Agency in countries outside the Soviet sphere. Under Eisenhower, Allen Dulles, brother of the secretary of state, rose from second in command to chief of the CIA. A veteran of the wartime Office of Strategic Services, he had already helped enhance the CIA's capacity for cloak-and-dagger operations. In two cases early in the Eisenhower years this capability was actually used to overthrow governments believed hostile to American interests: in Iran (1953) and in Guatemala (1954).

BRINKSMANSHIP   For all his talk of liberation, Dulles made no significant departure from the containment strategy created under Acheson and Truman. Instead he institutionalized containment in the rigid mold of his Cold War rhetoric and extended it into the military strategy of deterrence. Dulles betrayed a fatal affinity for colorful phrases. In addition to "liberation" and "roll back," he added two major new contributions while in office: "massive retaliation" and "going to the brink."

"Massive retaliation" was an effort to get, in the slogan soon current, "more bang for the buck." Budgetary considerations lay at the root of the administration's military plans, for Eisenhower and his cabinet shared the fear that in the effort to build a superior war power the country could spend itself into bankruptcy. During 1953 the Joint Chiefs of Staff designed a new military posture. The heart of their New Look was the assumption that nuclear weapons could be used in limited-war situations, allowing reductions in conventional forces and thus budgetary savings. No longer would "the Communists nibble us to death all over the world in little wars," Vice-President Nixon explained in March 1954.

By this time both the United States and Russia had exploded hydrogen bombs. With the new policy of deterrence, what Winston Churchill called a "balance of terror" had replaced the old "balance of power." The threat of nuclear holocaust was terrifying, but the notion that the United States would risk such a disaster in response to local wars had little credibility.

Dulles's policy of "brinksmanship" depended for its strategic effect on those very fears of nuclear disaster. Dulles argued in 1956 that in following a tough policy of confrontation with communism, one sometimes had to "go to the brink" of war: "The ability to get to the verge without getting into war is the necessary art. If you cannot master it, you inevitably get into war. . . . We walked to the brink and we looked it in the face." The first occasion on which a firm stand had halted further aggression had been America's threat in 1953 to break the Korean stalemate by using atomic weapons. The second had come in 1954, when aircraft carriers moved into the South China Sea "both to deter any Red Chinese attack against [French] Indochina and to provide weapons for instant retaliation."

INDOCHINA: THE BACKGROUND TO WAR   Like the rest of the old colonial world of Asia and Africa, Indochina experienced a wave of nationalism in the years after World War II, damaging both the power and prestige of the colonial powers. By the early 1950s most of British Asia was independent or on the way: India, Pakistan, Ceylon (now Sri Lanka), Burma (now Mynamar), and the Malay States (now Malaysia). The Dutch and French, however, were less willing to give up their colonies and thus created a dilemma for American policy-makers. Americans sympathized with colonial nationalists who sometimes invoked the example of 1776, but Americans also wanted Dutch and French help against the spread of communism. The Truman administration felt obliged to comply with their pleas for aid in reconquering areas that had passed from Japanese occupation into the hands of local patriots.

French Indochina, created in the nineteenth century out of the old kingdoms of Cambodia, Laos, and Vietnam, offered a variation on Third World nationalism. During World War II, opposition to the Japanese occupation of Indochina was led by the Vietminh (Vietnamese League for Independence), nationalists who fell under the influence of Communists led by the magnetic rebel, Ho Chi Minh. At the end of the war the Vietminh controlled part of northern Vietnam, and on September 2, 1945, Ho Chi Minh proclaimed a Democratic Republic of Vietnam, with its capital in Hanoi. American officers were on the reviewing stand in Hanoi and American planes flew over the celebration. Ho had received secret American help against the Japanese during the war, but his bids for further aid after the war went unanswered. Vietnam took low priority in American diplomatic concerns, which at the time were focused on restoring Western Europe and containing the spread of communism there.

Ho Chi Minh.

In March 1946 the French government, preoccupied with domestic politics, recognized Ho's new government as a "free state" within the French colonial union. Before the year was out, however, Ho opposed French efforts to establish another regime in the southern provinces, and this clash soon expanded into the First Indochina War. This was a troubling development for the American government. On the one hand, the United States resented France's determination to restore colonial rule. Yet Truman was even more determined to see France become a bulwark against communism in Europe. As a State Department report concluded in 1948, the United States had an "immediate and vital interest" in supporting the French government in order to further "our aims in Europe," and that goal must "take precedence over active steps looking toward the realization of our objectives in Indochina." As a result the American government acquiesced in France's efforts to crush Vietnamese nationalism.

The Vietminh movement thereafter became more completely dominated by Ho Chi Minh and his Communist associates, and more dependent on Russia and Red China for help. In 1950, with the outbreak of fighting in Korea, the struggle in Vietnam took on the appearance of a battleground in the Cold War. When the Korean War ended, American aid to the French in Vietnam, begun by the Truman administration, escalated dramatically. By the end of 1953 the Eisenhower administration was paying about two-thirds of the cost of the French war effort, or about $1 billion annually.

But even with lavish American aid the French were unable to suppress the well-organized and tenacious Vietminh. And in 1954 the United States found itself at the edge of the "brink" to which Dulles later referred. A major French force had been sent to Dien Bien Phu in the northwest corner of Vietnam, near the Laos border, in the hope of luring Vietminh guerrillas into the open and grinding them up with superior firepower. The French instead found themselves surrounded by a superior force that laid siege to their stronghold.

In March 1954 the French government requested an American air strike to relieve the pressure on Dien Bien Phu. Eisenhower seemed to endorse forceful action when he advanced his "domino theory" at a news conference on April 7, 1954. He implied that if Indochina fell to the Communists, the rest of Asia would be next. But Eisenhower opposed direct American military action unless the British lent support. When they refused, Eisenhower backed away from unilateral action, explaining that it would be a "tragic error to go in alone as a partner of France."

THE GENEVA ACCORDS AND U.S. POLICY America's decision not to intervene sealed the fate of the besieged French garrison at Dien Bien Phu. On May 7, 1954, the Vietminh launched massive attacks and finally overwhelmed the courageous, but vastly outnumbered, French resistance. It was the very eve of the day an international conference at Geneva took up the question of Indochina. Six weeks later, as French forces continued to meet defeats in Vietnam, a new French government promised an early settlement. On July 20 representatives of France, Britain, Russia, the People's Republic of China, and the Vietminh reached agreement on the Geneva Accords, and the next day produced their Final Declaration which proposed to neutralize Laos and Cambodia and divided Vietnam at the Seventeenth Parallel. The Vietminh would take power in the north and the French would remain south of the line until elections in 1956 should reunify Vietnam. American and South Vietnamese representatives refused either to join in the accord or to sign the Final Declaration.

Dulles then launched an effort to set up mutual defense arrangements for Southeast Asia. On September 8, 1954, at a meeting in Manila, the United States joined seven other countries in an agreement the press quickly labeled the Southeast Asia Treaty Organization (SEATO). The impression that it paralleled NATO was false, for the Manila Defense Accord was neither a common defense organization like NATO nor was it primarily Asian. The signers agreed that in case of an attack on

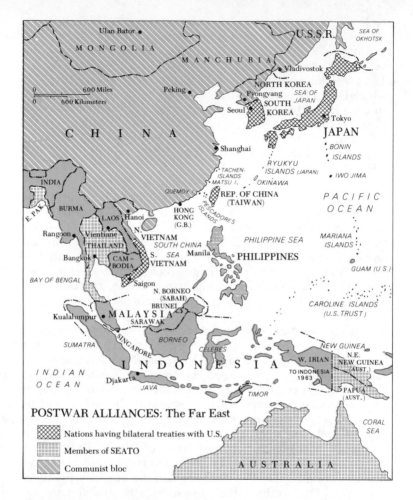

POSTWAR ALLIANCES: The Far East

Nations having bilateral treaties with U.S.

Members of SEATO

Communist bloc

one, the others would act according to their "constitutional practices," and in case of threats or subversion they would "consult immediately." The members included only three Asian countries—the Philippines, Thailand, and Pakistan—together with Britain, France, Australia, New Zealand, and the United States. India and Indonesia, the two most populous countries in the region, refused to join. A special protocol added to the treaty extended coverage to Indochina. The treaty reflected what Dulles's critics called "pactomania," which by the end of the Eisenhower administration had contracted the United States to defend forty-three other countries.

Eisenhower announced that though the United States "had not itself been party to or bound by the decision taken at the

[Geneva] Conference," any renewal of Communist aggression in Vietnam "would be viewed by us as a matter of grave concern." Ho Chi Minh and his government in Hanoi quickly sought to consolidate control throughout the north. In the hinterlands local Communists held kangaroo courts that tried and executed landowners and confiscated their lands. Residents of the north who wished to leave for southern Vietnam did so with American aid. Over 900,000 refugees, most of them Catholics, relocated to the south, causing staggering logistical problems for the struggling new government there.

Power in the south gravitated to a new premier: Ngo Dinh Diem, a Catholic nationalist who had opposed both the French and the Vietminh. Diem took office during the Geneva talks after returning from exile at a Catholic seminary in New Jersey. In October 1954 Eisenhower offered to assist Diem "in developing and maintaining a strong, viable state, capable of resisting attempted subversion or aggression through military means." In return the United States expected Diem to carry out "needed reforms." American aid was forthcoming in the form of CIA and military cadres charged with training Diem's armed forces and police.

Instead of instituting comprehensive reforms, however, Diem tightened his grip on the country, suppressing opposition on both right and left, offering little or no land distribution, and permitting widespread corruption. In 1956 he refused to join in the elections to reunify Vietnam, and the United States endorsed his decision. But Diem's efforts to eliminate all opposition only played into the hands of the Communists, who found more and more recruits among the discontented. By 1957 guerrilla forces in the south, known as the Vietcong, had begun attacks on the government, and in 1960 the resistance formed its own political arm, the National Liberation Front. As guerrilla warfare gradually disrupted the country, Eisenhower was helpless to do anything but "sink or swim with Ngo Dinh Diem."

CIVIL RIGHTS IN THE FIFTIES

If the Eisenhower presidency seems an interlude of relative tranquility between two decades of domestic and foreign strife, it should be remembered that those years also saw the onset of a revolution in race relations. Eisenhower entered office committed to civil rights in principle, and he did push the issue in areas of federal authority. During his first three years, public

Segregation began to be tested in the courts by the NAACP in the late 1930s.

services in Washington, D.C., were desegregated, as were navy yards and veterans hospitals. Beyond that, however, two aspects of the president's philosophy inhibited vigorous action: his preference for state or local rather than federal action, and his doubt that law could really be effective in such matters. "I don't believe you can change the hearts of men with laws or decisions," he stressed. For the time, then, leadership in the civil rights field came from the judiciary more than from the executive or legislative branches of the government.

THE *BROWN* DECISION   In the 1930s the NAACP had resolved to test the "separate but equal" doctrine which had upheld racial segregation since the *Plessy* decision in 1896. But it was not until the 1950s that challenges to segregation in the public schools were rising through the appellate courts. Five such cases, from Kansas, Delaware, South Carolina, Virginia, and the District of Columbia—usually cited by reference to the first, *Brown v.*

Board of Education of Topeka, Kansas—came to the Supreme Court for joint argument in 1952. Chief Justice Earl Warren wrote the opinion, finally handed down on May 17, 1954, in which a unanimous Court declared that "in the field of public education the doctrine of 'separate but equal' has no place." In support of its opinion the Court cited current sociological and psychological findings. A year later, after further argument, the Court directed that compliance with the *Brown* ruling should move "with all deliberate speed."

The white South's first response was relatively calm, deceptively so as it happened. Eisenhower refused to take any part in leading white southerners toward compliance. Privately he remarked: "I am convinced that the Supreme Court decision *set back* progress in the South *at least fifteen years*. The fellow who tries to tell me you can do these things by *force* is just plain *nuts*." While token integration began as early as 1954 in the border states, hostility mounted in the Deep South and Virginia, led by the newly formed White Citizens' Councils. Before the end of 1955 moderate sentiment in the South gave way to surly reaction. Democratic Sen. James Eastland of Mississippi growled that the South would neither "abide by nor obey this legislative decision by a political court."

Virginia's Senator Harry F. Byrd supplied a rallying cry for the growing opposition to the *Brown* decision: "Massive Resistance." State legislatures passed pupil assignment laws and adopted other dodges, all futile, to interpose their power between the courts and the schools. In March 1956, 101 southern members of Congress signed a "Southern Manifesto" that denounced the Court's decision as "a clear abuse of judicial power." At the end of 1956, in six southern states not a single black child attended school with whites.

THE MONTGOMERY BUS BOYCOTT   At the end of 1955 the drive for civil rights took a new turn in Montgomery, Alabama, "the cradle of the Confederacy." There, on December 1, 1955, Rosa Parks, a black seamstress weary at the end of a long day, was arrested for refusing to give up her seat on a city bus to a white man. The next night black community leaders met in the Dexter Avenue Baptist Church to organize the Montgomery Improvement Association and launch a massive bus boycott.

The movement found a courageous leader in Dexter Avenue's twenty-six-year-old pastor, Martin Luther King, Jr., who spoke in the sonorous cadences familiar to the Bible Belt. Born in Atlanta, the grandson of a slave and the son of a minister, King was endowed with intelligence, energy, courage, and charisma. After attending Morehouse College in Atlanta and then receiving a seminary degree, he earned a Ph.D. in philosophy from Boston College before accepting a call to preach in Montgomery. He brought to the infant civil rights movement a message of nonviolent, passive resistance compounded from the Gospels, the writings of Thoreau, and the example of Mahatma Gandhi in India. "We must use the weapon of love," he stressed. "We must realize so many people are taught to hate us that they are not totally responsible for their hate." To his antagonists he pledged: "We will soon wear you down by our capacity to suffer, and in winning our freedom we will so appeal to your heart and conscience that we will win you in the process." Although racists bombed his home and repeatedly threatened him and his family, King remained steadfast to his nonviolent principles.

The bus boycott achieved a remarkable solidarity. For months blacks in Montgomery got to and from home, work, and school by forming car pools, hitchhiking, or simply walking. The boycotters finally won the case they had initiated in the federal courts against bus segregation, and on December 20, 1956, the Supreme Court affirmed that "the separate but equal doctrine can no longer be safely followed as a correct statement of the

Martin Luther King, Jr., here facing arrest for leading a civil rights march, advocated nonviolent resistance to racial segregation.

law." The next day King and other blacks boarded the buses, but they still had a long way to travel before the Jim Crow system could be laid finally to rest. To keep alive the spirit of the bus boycott, King and a group of associates in 1957 organized the Southern Christian Leadership Conference (SCLC).

Despite Eisenhower's reluctance to take the lead in desegregating schools, he had no problem with supporting the right to vote for all citizens. In 1956 Eisenhower proposed legislation that became the Civil Rights Act of 1957, the first civil rights law passed since Reconstruction. It finally got through the Senate, after a year's delay, with the help of Democratic Majority Leader Lyndon B. Johnson, who won southern acceptance by watering down the act. Still, it established for a period of two years the Civil Rights Commission, which was later extended indefinitely, and a new Civil Rights Division in the Justice Department, which could seek injunctions to prevent interference with the right to vote. The SCLC promptly announced a campaign to register 2 million black voters in the South.

LITTLE ROCK   There had been sporadic violence in resistance to civil rights efforts, but in September 1957, a state governor for the first time stood in outright defiance of the law. Arkansas governor Orval Faubus called out the National Guard to prevent nine black students from entering Little Rock's Central High School under federal court order. A conference between the president and the governor proved fruitless, but on court order Faubus withdrew the Guard. When the students tried to re-enter the school, a hysterical mob outside forced their removal for their own safety. At that point Eisenhower, who two months before could not "imagine any set of circumstances that would ever induce me to send federal troops," ordered a thousand paratroopers to Little Rock to protect the students, and mobilized the National Guard. The soldiers stayed through the school year. Thereafter, massive resistance for the most part was confined to the deep South where five states, from South Carolina west through Louisiana, still held out against even token integration.

A LANDSLIDE FOR IKE   President Eisenhower suffered a "moderately severe" heart attack in September 1955, but he recovered quickly, and in February 1956 the president announced his decision to run again. In August the Republican convention renominated Eisenhower by acclamation and again named Nixon as the vice-presidential candidate. The party platform endorsed Eisenhower's "modern Republicanism."

The Democrats turned again to Stevenson, with a platform that evaded the civil rights issue and otherwise stuck to party staples: less "favoritism" to big business, repeal of the Taft-Hartley Act, increased aid to farmers, and tax relief for those in low-income brackets.

Neither candidate generated much excitement during the 1956 campaign. The Democrats did what they could with the issue of the president's health, but focused their fire on the heir apparent, Richard Nixon, a "man of many masks." Stevenson aroused little enthusiasm for two controversial proposals: to drop conscription and rely on an all-volunteer army, and to ban H-bomb tests by international agreement. Both involved military questions that put Stevenson at a disadvantage by pitting his judgment against that of a successful general. Voters handed Eisenhower a landslide victory. He lost one border state, Missouri, but in carrying Louisiana became the first Republican to win a Deep South state since Reconstruction; nationally, he carried all but seven states.

A SEASON OF TROUBLES

CRISIS IN THE MIDDLE EAST   To forestall Russian penetration into the Middle East, the Eisenhower-Dulles foreign policy sought to cultivate Arab friendship, departing from the Truman-Acheson focus on Israel and from the support of British and French economic interests. In 1955 Dulles completed his line of alliances across the "northern tier" of the Middle East. Under American sponsorship, Britain joined Turkey, Iraq, Iran, and Pakistan in the Middle East Treaty Organization (METO), or Baghdad Pact, as the treaty was commonly called. By linking the easternmost NATO state (Turkey) to the westernmost SEATO state (Pakistan), METO had a certain superficial logic. But after Iraq, the only Arab member, withdrew in 1959 it became clear that METO had been impotent from the start. Below the northern tier, moreover, the Arab states remained aloof from the organization. These were the states of the Arab League (Egypt, Jordan, Syria, Lebanon, and Saudi Arabia), which had warred on Israel in 1948–1949 and remained committed to its destruction.

The most fateful developments in the region turned on the rise of Egyptian general Gamal Abdel Nasser, who overthrew King Farouk in 1952. Nasser's nationalist regime soon pressed for the withdrawal of British forces guarding the Suez Canal, the crucial link between the Mediterranean Sea and the Indian Ocean. Ei-

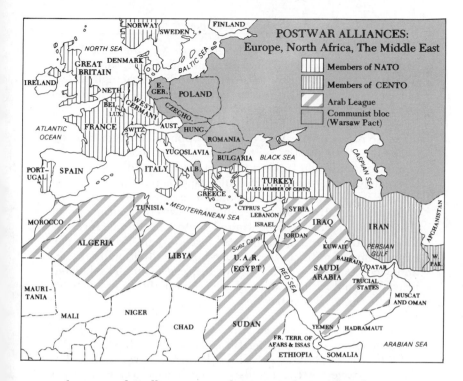

POSTWAR ALLIANCES:
Europe, North Africa, The Middle East

||||| Members of NATO

Members of CENTO

Arab League

Communist bloc
(Warsaw Pact)

senhower and Dulles supported Nasser's demand, and in 1954 an Anglo-Egyptian treaty provided for British withdrawal within twenty months. Ownership of the canal, however, remained with the Anglo-French Suez Canal Company.

Nasser, like other leaders of the Third World, remained unaligned in the Cold War and sought to play both sides off against each other. The United States in turn courted Egyptian support by offering the prospect of American assistance in building a great hydroelectric plant at Aswan on the Nile River. From the outset the administration's proposal was opposed by Jewish constituencies concerned with Egyptian threats to Israel, and by southern congressmen who feared the competition from Egyptian cotton. When Nasser then increased trade with the Soviet bloc and recognized Red China, Dulles abruptly canceled the loan offer in July 1956.

The outcome was far from a triumph of American diplomacy. The chief victims, it turned out, were Anglo-French interests in the Suez. Unable to retaliate against the United States, Nasser nationalized the Anglo-French Suez Canal Company and earmarked its revenues for the Aswan project, thereby enhancing his prestige in the Arab world. The British and French reacted strongly. While negotiations dragged, on October 29, 1956, Israeli forces invaded the Gaza Strip and Sinai peninsula. Ostensibly their aim was to root out Arab guerrillas but actually it was to synchronize with the British and French, who jointly began bombing Egyptian air bases and on November 3 occupied Port Said. The British and French claimed that their actions were meant to protect the canal against the opposing belligerents.

The Suez War put the United States in a quandary. Either the administration could support its Western allies and see the troublesome Nasser crushed, or it could stand on the United Nations Charter and champion Arab nationalism against imperialistic aggression. The latter course was adopted, with the unusual result that Russia sided with the United States' position. Once the threat of American embargoes had forced Anglo-French-Israeli capitulation, the Russians capitalized on the situation by threatening to use missiles against the Western aggressors. This belated bravado won for Russia some of the credit in the Arab world for what the United States had done.

REPRESSION IN HUNGARY   All the while, Soviet Premier Nikita Khrushchev was subjugating Hungary. On October 23, 1956, fighting against Hungary's Stalinist leadership broke out in Budapest, followed by the installation of a moderate Communist as head of the government. Seemingly content with these developments, the Russians withdrew their forces from Budapest on October 28, but Hungary's announcement three days later that it would withdraw from the Warsaw Pact brought back the Russian tanks. They installed a more compliant leader, and two years later, the Soviets executed the leader of Hungary's moderates. It was a tragic ending to a liberation movement that, at the outset, promised the sort of moderation that might have vindicated George Kennan's policy of "containment," if not Dulles's notion of "liberation."

SPUTNIK   On October 4, 1957, the Soviets launched the first man-made satellite, called *sputnik*, an acronym for the Russian phrase "fellow traveler of earth." Americans, until then complacent about their technical superiority, suddenly discovered an apparent "missile gap." If the Russians were so advanced in rocketry, then perhaps they could hit American cities just as Nazi rockets had hit London in 1944–1945. All along Eisenhower knew that the "gap" was more illusory than real, but he could not reveal that high-altitude American U-2 spy planes were gathering this information. Even so, American missile development floundered, with a tangle of agencies and committees engaged in waste and duplication. The launching of Explorer I, the first American satellite, on January 31, 1958, did not quiet the public outcry.

Russia's success with Sputnik frightened the United States and provoked efforts to enlarge defense spending, to offer NATO allies intermediate range ballistic missiles (IRBMs) pending development of long-range intercontinental ballistic missiles (ICBMs), to set up a new agency to coordinate space efforts, and to establish a crash program in science education. The "sputnik syndrome," compounded by a sharp recession through the winter of 1957–1958, loosened the purse strings of frugal congressmen, who added to the new budget more than Eisenhower wanted for both defense and domestic programs. In July 1958 Congress created the National Aeronautics and Space Agency (NASA) to coordinate research and development in the space program. Before the end of the year NASA had a program to put a manned craft in orbit, but the first manned flight, by Commander Alan B. Shepard, Jr., did not take place until May 5, 1961. Finally, in September 1958 Congress enacted the National Defense Education Act, which authorized federal grants especially for training in mathematics, science, and modern languages, as well as for student loans and fellowships.

CORRUPT PRACTICES   During the first two years of Eisenhower's second term, public confidence in his performance, as registered by opinion polls, dropped sharply from 79 percent to 49 percent. Emotional issues such as civil rights and defense policy had compounded his troubles. The president's image was further tarnished when congressional investigations revealed that the administration, which had promised to clean up "the mess in Washington," was itself touched by scandals, one of which involved the White House chief of staff, who had taken gifts of a fur coat and an Oriental rug from a businessman in exchange for favors. In September 1958 the president reluctantly accepted his aide's resignation.

Republicans also faced the growing opposition of farmers, angry with cuts in price supports, and organized labor, angry because many Republicans had made "right-to-work" (or open-shop) laws a campaign issue in 1958. The Democrats came out of the midterm elections with nearly two-to-one majorities in Congress: 282 to 154 in the House, 64 to 34 in the Senate. Eisenhower would be the first president to face three successive Congresses controlled by the opposition party. The president thus could manage few new departures in domestic policy, but he did oversee the admission of the first states not contiguous to the continental forty-eight. Alaska became the forty-ninth state on January 3, 1959, and Hawaii the fiftieth on August 21, 1959.

FESTERING PROBLEMS ABROAD   In July 1958 the Middle East flared up again. By this time the president had secured from Congress authority for what came to be called the Eisenhower Doctrine, which promised to extend economic and military aid to Middle East nations, and to use armed forces if necessary to assist any such nation against military aggression from any Communist country.

Egypt's President Nasser meanwhile had emerged from the Suez crisis with heightened prestige, and in February 1958 he created the United Arab Republic (UAR) by merger (a short-lived one) with Syria. Then on July 14, a leftist coup in Iraq, supposedly inspired by Nasser and the Russians, threw out the pro-Western government. Lebanon, already unsettled by internal conflict, appealed to the United States for support against a similar fate. Eisenhower immediately ordered 5,000 marines into Lebanon, where they limited themselves to the capital, Beirut, and its airfield. He proposed to go no farther because, he said later, if the government was not strong enough to hold out with such protection, then "we probably should not be there." Once the situation stabilized, and the Lebanese factions reached a compromise, American forces withdrew.

The problem of Berlin continued to fester with little chance of a resolution for either side. Premier Khrushchev called it a bone in his throat. West Berlin provided a "showplace" of Western democracy and prosperity in the middle of Communist East Germany, a listening post for Western intelligence, and a funnel through which news and propaganda from the West penetrated what Winston Churchill had called "the iron curtain." Although East Germany had sealed its western frontiers, refugees could still pass from East to West Berlin. On November 10, 1958, Khrushchev threatened to transfer Soviet obligations in the occupation to East Germany. After the deadline he set, May 27, 1959, Western occupation authorities would have to deal with the East German government, in effect recognizing it, or face the possibility of another blockade.

But Eisenhower refused to budge from his position on Berlin. At the same time he refused to engage in saber-rattling or even to cancel existing plans to reduce the size of the army. Khrushchev, it turned out, was no more eager for confrontation than Eisenhower. Khrushchev's deadline passed almost unnoticed. In September 1959, Premier Khrushchev visited the United States, going to New York, Washington, Los Angeles, San Francisco, and Iowa, and dropping in on Eisenhower at Camp David. In talks there Khrushchev endorsed "peaceful coexistence," and Eisenhower admitted that the Berlin situation was "abnormal." They agreed to hold a summit meeting in the spring.

THE U-2 SUMMIT   The summit meeting, however, blew up in Eisenhower's face. On May 1, 1960, a Soviet rocket brought down an American U-2 spy plane on a mission over the Soviet Union. On May 11, after a period of international jousting with Khrushchev, Eisenhower finally took personal responsibility for the incident—an unprecedented action for a head of state—and justified the action on grounds of national security. At a summit meeting in Paris five days later, Khrushchev called on the president to repudiate the U-2 flights, which had been going on for more than three years, and "pass severe judgment on those responsible." When Eisenhower refused, Khrushchev left the meeting.

CASTRO'S CUBA   The greatest thorn in Eisenhower's side was the Cuban regime of Fidel Castro, which took power on January 1, 1959, after three years of guerrilla warfare against a right-wing dictator. In their struggle Castro's forces had the support of many Americans who hoped for a new day of democratic government in Cuba. But these hopes were dashed when American television reported trials and executions conducted by the victorious Castro. Staged like a Roman holiday before crowds of howling spectators, the trials offered little in the way of legal procedure or proof. Castro, moreover, opposed the widespread foreign control of the Cuban economy. When he began programs of land reform and nationalization of foreign-owned property, relations with the United States worsened. Some observers believed, however, that by rejecting Castro's requests for loans and other help, the American government lost a chance to influence the direction of the revolution. Some thought too that by acting on the assumption that Communists already had the upper hand in his movement the administration may have ensured that fact.

Castro, on the other hand, eagerly accepted the Communist embrace. In February 1960 he entered a trade agreement to swap Cuban sugar for Soviet oil and machinery. One of Eisenhower's last acts as president was to suspend diplomatic relations with Cuba on January 3, 1961. The president also secretly au-

Fidel Castro (center) became Cuba's premier in 1959 after three years of guerrilla warfare against the Batista regime.

thorized the CIA to begin training a force of Cuban refugees (some of them former Castro stalwarts) for a new revolution. But the final decision on its use would rest with the next president, John F. Kennedy.

ASSESSING THE EISENHOWER YEARS

The Eisenhower years have not drawn much acclaim from journalists and historians. One observer called Ike's administration "the time of the great postponement," during which the president left domestic and foreign policies "about where he found them in 1953." Yet even these critics granted that Eisenhower had succeeded in ending the war in Korea and settling the dust raised by McCarthy. If Eisenhower had failed to end the Cold War and in fact had institutionalized it as a global confrontation, he had sensed the limits of American power and kept its application to low-risk situations. He also tried to restrain the arms race. If he took few initiatives in addressing the social problems that would erupt in the 1960s, he sustained the major innovations of the New Deal. If he tolerated unemployment of as much as 7 percent at times, inflation remained minimal during his two terms.

Eisenhower's farewell address to the American people showed his remarkable foresight in his own area of special expertise, the military. Like Washington, Eisenhower couched his wisdom largely in the form of warnings: that America's "leadership and prestige depend, not merely upon our unmatched material strength, but on how we use our power in the interests of world peace and human betterment"; that the temptation to find easy answers should take into account "the need to maintain balance in and among national problems"; and above all that Americans "must avoid the impulse to live only for today, plundering, for our own ease and convenience, the precious resources of tomorrow."

As a soldier, Eisenhower highlighted perhaps better than anyone else could have the dangers of a military establishment in a time of peace. "In the councils of government we must guard against the acquisition of unwarranted influence, whether sought or unsought, by the military-industrial complex. The potential for the disastrous rise of misplaced power exists and will persist." His great disappointment as he lay down his responsibilities, Eisenhower concluded, was his inability to affirm "that a lasting peace is in sight," only that "war has been avoided."

FURTHER READING

The best overview of the Eisenhower period is Charles C. Alexander's *Holding the Line: The Eisenhower Era, 1951–1962* (1975).° For the manner in which Eisenhower conducted foreign policy, see in particular Robert A. Divine's *Eisenhower and the Cold War* (1981).° On the conservatism of the 1950s, see George H. Nash's *The Conservative Intellectual Movement in America: Since 1945* (1976).°

For the buildup of American involvement in Indochina, consult Lloyd Gardner's *Approaching Vietnam: From World War II through Dienbienphu* (1988)° and George C. Herring's *America's Longest War: The United States and Vietnam, 1950–1975* (1979).° How the Eisenhower Doctrine came to be implemented is traced in Stephen Ambrose's *Rise to Globalism: American Foreign Policy, 1938–1980* (1981).°

Two introductions to the impact wrought by the Warren Supreme Court are Alexander Bickel's *The Supreme Court and the Idea of Progress* (1970)° and Paul Murphy's *The Constitution in Crisis Times* (1972).°

° These books are available in paperback editions.

Also helpful is Archibald Cox's *The Warren Court: Constitutional Decision as an Instrument of Reform* (1968).° A masterful study of the important Warren Court decision on school desegregation is Richard Kluger's *Simple Justice: The History of Brown v. Board of Education and Black America's Struggle for Equality* (1975).°

For the story of Montgomery, see David L. Lewis's *King: A Critical Biography* (1970)° and Juan Williams's *Eyes on the Prize: America's Civil Rights Years, 1954–1965* (1987).° William H. Chafe's *Civilities and Civil Rights: Greensboro, North Carolina, and the Black Struggle for Freedom* (1980)° examines how one community dragged its feet on the Brown implementation order.

33

NEW FRONTIERS:
KENNEDY AND JOHNSON

For those pundits who considered the social and political climate of the 1950s dull, the following decade would provide a striking contrast. The 1960s were years of extraordinary turbulence and innovation in public affairs—as well as sudden tragedy and trauma. Many social ills that had been festering for decades suddenly forced their way onto the national agenda during the 1960s. At the same time, the deeply entrenched assumptions of Cold War ideology led the country into the longest, most controversial, and least successful war in the nation's history.

THE NEW FRONTIER

KENNEDY VS. NIXON   In 1960, however, there was little sense of dramatic change on the horizon. The presidential election that year pitted two candidates—Richard M. Nixon and John F. Kennedy—who initially seemed to symbolize the becalmed politics of the 1950s. Though better known than Kennedy because of his eight years as Eisenhower's vice-president, Nixon had also developed the reputation of a cunning chameleon, the "Tricky Dick" who concealed his duplicity behind a series of masks. "Nixon doesn't know who he is," Kennedy told an aide, "and so each time he makes a speech he has to decide which Nixon he is, and that will be very exhausting."

But Nixon could not be so easily dismissed. He possessed ability, tenacious energy, and a compulsive love for politics, the more combative the better. Born in suburban Los Angeles in 1913, he grew up amid a Quaker family struggling to make ends meet. Acquaintances remembered young Richard Nixon as an introverted and diligent fellow. "He wasn't a little boy that you wanted to pick up and hug," recalled one family friend.

After law school and service in the Pacific during World War II, Richard Nixon jumped into the political arena in 1946 as a Republican and surprised observers by unseating a popular congressman in southern California. He arrived in Washington eager to reverse the tide of New Deal liberalism. "I was elected to smash the labor bosses," he explained. Four years later he won election to the Senate. In his campaigns, Nixon unleashed scurrilous personal attacks on his opponents, employing half-truths, lies, and rumors, and shrewdly manipulating the growing anticommunist hysteria. Yet Nixon became both a respected and effective member of Congress, and by 1950 he was the most requested Republican speaker in the country. His rapid rise to political stardom led to his being offered the vice-presidential nomination in 1952 and 1956. He was an active, highly visible vice-president.

Kennedy lacked such experience and exposure. Despite an abundance of assets, including a widely publicized record of heroism in World War II, a glamorous young wife, a Harvard education, and a large, wealthy family, the handsome 43-year-old Kennedy lacked national prominence and political distinction. Kennedy's record in the Senate was mediocre. Author of a Pulitzer Prize-winning study of political leaders who had "made the tough decisions," entitled *Profiles in Courage* (1956), Kennedy, said the Washington pundits, had shown more profile than courage during the McCarthy episode of the early 1950s and had a weak record on civil rights. Eleanor Roosevelt declined to endorse Kennedy in 1960, noting that presidential authority should not be vested in "someone who understands what courage is and admires it, but has not quite the independence to have it."

During his campaign for the Democratic nomination, Kennedy had shown that he had the energy to match his grace and ambition. As the first Catholic to run for the presidency since Al Smith, he strove to dispel the impression that his religion was a major political liability. By the time of the convention in August 1960, he had traveled over 65,000 miles, visited 25 states, and made over 350 speeches. Hubert Humphrey, the buoyant liberal senator from Minnesota, was knocked out of the race in the West Virginia primary. In his acceptance speech Kennedy found the stirring rhetoric that would stamp the rest of his campaign and his presidency: "We stand today on the edge of a New Frontier

John F. Kennedy's forthrightness in the debates with Richard Nixon impressed viewers and voters.

—the frontier of unknown opportunities and perils—a frontier of unfulfilled hopes and threats."

The turning point in the presidential campaign came when Richard Nixon agreed to debate his less prominent opponent on television. During the first of four debates, some 70 million viewers saw Nixon, still weak from a recent illness, perspiring heavily and sporting a five o'clock shadow. He looked haggard, uneasy, and even sinister before the camera. Kennedy, on the other hand, projected a cool poise that made him seem equal, if not superior, in his fitness for the office. Kennedy's popularity immediately shot up in the polls. Reporters discovered that he had "charisma" and noted the giddy young people who now greeted his arrival at campaign stops. In the words of a bemused southern senator, Kennedy combined "the best qualities of Elvis Presley and Franklin D. Roosevelt."

When the votes were counted, Kennedy and his running-mate, Lyndon B. Johnson of Texas, had won the closest presidential election since 1888. The winning margin was only 118,574 votes out of the 68 million cast. Kennedy's wide lead in the electoral vote, 303 to 219, belied the paper-thin margin in several key states, especially Illinois, where Chicago Mayor Richard Daley's Democratic machine appeared to have lived up to its legendary campaign motto: "In Chicago we tell our people to vote early and to vote often."

THE NEW ADMINISTRATION Kennedy was the nation's youngest president, and his cabinet appointments put an accent on youth and "Eastern Establishment" figures. A self-described "idealist without illusions," Kennedy sought to attract the "best and the brightest" minds available, men who would inject a tough, dispassionate, pragmatic, and vigorous outlook into governmental affairs. To that end he asked Robert McNamara, one of the "whiz kids" who had reorganized the Ford Motor Company with his "systems analysis" techniques, to bring his managerial magic to bear on the Department of Defense. Kennedy appointed Harvard professor McGeorge Bundy, whom he called "the second smartest man I know," as special assistant for national security affairs, and chose as his secretary of state Dean Rusk, a career diplomat and former Rhodes Scholar from Davidson College. When critics attacked the appointment of Kennedy's thirty-five-year-old brother Robert as attorney-general, the president quipped, "I don't see what's wrong with giving Bobby a little experience before he goes into law practice."

The inaugural ceremonies of January 20, 1961, set the tone of elegance and youthful vigor that would come to be called the "Kennedy style." After Robert Frost paid tribute to the administration in verse, Kennedy dazzled listeners with his uplifting rhetoric. "Let every nation know," he proclaimed, "that we shall pay any price, bear any burden, meet any hardship, support any friend, oppose any foe, to assure the survival and success of liberty. And so, my fellow Americans: ask not what your country can do for you—ask what you can do for your country." Spines tingled, Kennedy, one journalist wrote, was the first president to be Prince Charming.

THE KENNEDY RECORD But for all of his idealistic and energetic rhetoric, Kennedy had a difficult time launching his New Frontier domestic program. Elected by a razor-thin margin, he enjoyed no popular mandate. Moreover, Congress, although overwhelmingly Democratic, remained in the grip of a conservative coalition that blocked Kennedy's effort to increase federal aid to education, provide health insurance for the aged, and create a new Department of Urban Affairs.

Administration proposals, nevertheless, did win some notable victories in Congress. They included a new Housing Act that appropriated nearly $5 billion for urban renewal over four years, a raised minimum wage, and increased Social Security benefits. Just two months into his administration Kennedy launched the celebrated Peace Corps to supply volunteers for educational and technical service in underdeveloped countries. Kennedy also won support for an accelerated program to land Americans on the moon before the end of the decade. Congress readily approved a series of broad foreign aid programs to help Latin American nations, dubbed the "Alliance for Progress." Another important Kennedy initiative was a bold tax-reduction bill intended to accelerate economic growth. Although it was not passed until 1964, after Kennedy's death, it provided a surprisingly potent boost to the economy. Perhaps Kennedy's most significant legislative accomplishment was the Trade Expansion Act of 1962, which eventually led to tariff cuts averaging 35 percent between the United States and the European Common Market.

CIVIL RIGHTS   The most important development in American domestic life during the Kennedy years occurred in the area of civil rights. Kennedy was initially reluctant to challenge conservative southern Democrats on the race issue. He also was never as personally committed to civil rights as Hubert Humphrey or his brother Bobby. Despite a few dramatic gestures of support toward black leaders, John Kennedy only belatedly grasped the moral and emotional significance of the most widespread reform movement of the decade. Eventually, however, his conscience was pricked by the grass-roots civil rights movement so ably led by Martin Luther King, Jr.

After the Montgomery bus boycott of 1955, King's philosophy of "militant nonviolence" inspired thousands to challenge Jim Crow practices with direct action. At the same time, lawsuits to desegregate the schools activated thousands of parents and young people. The momentum generated the first genuine mass movement in the history of black Americans when four black college students sat down and demanded service at a "whites only" Woolworth's lunch counter in Greensboro, North Carolina, on February 1, 1960. Within a week the "sit-in" movement had spread to six more towns in the state, and within a month to towns in six more states.

In April 1960 the student participants, black and white, formed the Student Nonviolent Coordinating Committee (SNCC), which worked with King's Southern Christian Leadership Conference (SCLC) to spread the movement. The "sit-ins" at restaurants became "kneel-ins" at churches and "wade-ins" at segregated public pools. And even when struck with clubs, poked with cattle prods, or burned with lighted cigarettes, the protesters refused to retaliate. Not a few paid for such courage and commitment with their lives.

Sit-in at the Woolworth's Lunch Counter in Greensboro, North Carolinia, February 2, 1960. *The four protesters, students at North Carolina A&T College, were (from left) Joesph McNeil, Franklin McCain, Billy Smith, and Clarence Henderson.*

In May 1961 the Congress of Racial Equality (CORE) sent a group of black and white "freedom riders" on buses to test a federal ruling that had banned segregation on buses, trains, and their depots. In Alabama, mobs attacked the young travelers, burned one of the buses, and assaulted Justice Department observers, but the demonstrators persisted, drawing national attention and generating new support for their cause. The following year Gov. Ross Barnett of Mississippi, who believed that God made the Negro "different to punish him," defied a court order and refused to allow James H. Meredith to enroll at the University of Mississippi. Attorney-General Robert Kennedy thereupon dispatched federal marshals to enforce the law, but they were prevented by a violent white mob. Federal troops had to intervene, and Meredith was finally registered at "Ole Miss," but only after two deaths and many injuries.

Everywhere, it seemed, black activists and white supporters

were challenging deeply entrenched patterns of segregation and prejudice. In April 1963 Martin Luther King launched a series of demonstrations in Birmingham, Alabama, where Police Commissioner Eugene "Bull" Connor proved the perfect foil for King's tactic of nonviolent civil disobedience. Connor's policemen used dogs, tear gas, electric cattle prods, and fire hoses on the protesters while millions of outraged Americans watched the confrontation on television.

King, who was arrested and jailed during the demonstrations, then wrote his "Letter from a Birmingham Jail," a stirring defense of his nonviolent strategy that became a classic of the civil rights movement. "One who breaks an unjust law," he stressed, "must do so openly, lovingly, and with a willingness to accept the penalty." He also signaled a shift in his strategy for social change. Heretofore King had emphasized the need to educate southern whites about the injustice of segregation and other patterns of discrimination. Now he focused more on gaining federal enforcement and new legislation by provoking racists to display their violent hatreds in public. As King admitted in his "Letter," he sought through organized nonviolent protest to "create such a crisis and foster such a tension that a community which has constantly refused to negotiate is forced to confront the issue."

Still, southern traditionalists remained steadfast. In the fall of 1963, Governor George Wallace dramatically stood in the doorway of a building at the University of Alabama to block the enrollment of several black students, but he stepped aside in the face of insistent federal marshals. Later the same night NAACP official Medgar Evers was shot to death as he returned home in Jackson, Mississippi.

The high point of the integrationist phase of the civil rights movement occurred on August 28, 1963, when over 200,000 blacks and whites marched down the Mall in Washington, D.C., toward the Lincoln Memorial singing "We Shall Overcome." The March on Washington was the largest civil rights demonstration in American history. Standing in front of Lincoln's statue, King delivered one of the memorable public speeches of the century: "Even though we face the difficulties of today and tomorrow, I still have a dream. It is a dream chiefly rooted in the American dream . . . one day . . . the sons of former slaves and the sons of former slave-owners will be able to sit together at the table of brotherhood." That the time for such racial harmony had not yet arrived, however, became clear a little over two weeks later when a bomb exploded in a Birmingham church killing four black girls who had arrived early for Sunday school.

Eugene "Bull" Connor's police unleash attack dogs on civil rights demonstrators in Birmingham, Alabama, May 1963.

Yet King's dream—shared and promoted by thousands of other activists—survived. The intransigence and violence that civil rights workers encountered won converts to their cause all across the country. Persuaded by his brother Robert and by the pressure of events, President Kennedy finally decided that enforcement of existing statutes was not enough; new legislation was needed to deal with the race question. In June 1963 he told the nation that racial discrimination "has no place in American life or law," and he then endorsed an ambitious civil rights bill intended to end discrimination in public facilities, desegregate the public schools, and protect black voters. But southern conservatives quickly blocked the bill in Congress.

THE WARREN COURT   The Supreme Court under Chief Justice Earl Warren continued to be one of the strongest and most controversial influences on American domestic life during the 1960s. Its *Brown* decision of 1954 exerted a steady pressure for change in the traditional patterns of race relations, North and South. During the Kennedy-Johnson years, the Court's stand on civil liberties proved equally controversial. In 1962 the Court had ruled that a school prayer adopted by the New York State Board of Regents violated the constitutional prohibition against an established religion. In *Gideon v. Wainwright* (1963) the Court required that every felony defendant be provided a lawyer regardless of the defendant's ability to pay. Three years later, in *Miranda v. Arizona*, the Court confirmed the obligation of police to inform arrested suspects of their rights before questioning.

FOREIGN FRONTIERS

EARLY SETBACKS   Kennedy's record in foreign affairs was mixed, though more spectacularly so than his domestic record. Upon taking office he discovered that there was in the works a CIA operation designed to prepare 1,500 anti-Castro Cubans for an invasion of their homeland. The Joint Chiefs of Staff endorsed the plan; diplomatic advisers reported that the invasion would inspire Cubans on the island to rebel against Castro. The scheme, poorly planned and poorly executed, had about as much chance of succeeding as John Brown's raid on Harper's Ferry a little over a century earlier. When the invasion force landed at Cuba's Bay of Pigs on April 19, 1961, it was subdued in three days and 1,200 men were captured. A *New York Times* columnist lamented that the United States "looked like fools to our friends, rascals to our enemies, and incompetents to the rest."

Two months after the Bay of Pigs disaster Kennedy met Soviet Premier Khrushchev in Vienna, Austria. It was a tense confrontation during which Khrushchev tried to bully the young and inexperienced Kennedy. He threatened to limit Western access to Berlin, the divided city located deep within East Germany. Kennedy was shaken by the aggressive Soviet stand, but he returned home determined to demonstrate American resolve—and his own courage. He called up Army Reserve and National Guard units and asked Congress for another $3.2 billion in defense funds. The Soviets responded by erecting the Berlin Wall, which cut off movement between East and West Berlin and became a symbol of the chill in relations between the Soviet Union and the United States.

THE MISSILE CRISIS   A year later Khrushchev posed another serious challenge, this time just ninety miles south of Florida. Khrushchev granted Castro's request for Russian nuclear missiles in Cuba to protect the island from future American-sponsored invasions. While such missiles would hardly alter the military balance, they would come from a direction not covered by American radar systems and arrive too quickly for warning. More important to Kennedy was the psychological effect of American acquiescence to a Soviet presence on its doorstep. Khrushchev's purpose was apparently to demonstrate his toughness to both Chinese and Russian critics of his earlier advocacy of peaceful coexistence. But he misjudged the American response.

On October 14, 1962, American intelligence flights discovered that Russian missile sites were under construction in Cuba. The administration immediately decided that they had to be removed; the only question was how. In a series of secret meetings, the Executive Committee of the National Security Council debated between a "surgical" air strike and a blockade of Cuba. They opted for a blockade, but since this would technically represent an act of war, they called it a "quarantine" rather than a blockade. It offered the advantage of forcing the Soviets to shoot first, if it came to that, and it left open further options of stronger action. Monday, October 22, began one of the most anxious weeks in world history. On that day the president announced to Congress and then to the public the discovery of the missile sites in Cuba; he also announced the quarantine.

Tensions grew as Khrushchev blustered that Kennedy had pushed humankind "to the abyss of a world nuclear-missile war." Soviet ships, he declared, would ignore the quarantine. But on Wednesday, October 24, five Soviet supply ships stopped short of the American ships. Two days later an agent of the Russian embassy privately approached a television journalist with a proposal for an agreement: Russia would withdraw the missiles in return for a public pledge by the United States not to invade Cuba. Secretary of State Rusk sent back word that the administration was interested, but told the journalist: "Remember, when you report this, that eyeball to eyeball, they blinked first." On Sunday, October 28, Khrushchev agreed to remove the missiles and added a conciliatory invitation "to continue the exchange of views on the prohibition of atomic and thermonuclear weapons, general disarmament, and other problems relating to the relaxation of international tension."

In the aftermath of the crisis, the United States took several symbolic steps to relax tensions: an agreement to sell surplus wheat to the Soviets, the installation of a "hot line" telephone between Washington and Moscow to provide instant contact between the heads of government, and the removal of obsolete American missiles from Turkey, Italy, and Britain. The United States also negotiated a treaty with Russian and British representatives to stop nuclear testing in the atmosphere. The treaty, ratified in September 1963, did not provide for on-site inspection, nor did it ban underground testing, which continued, but it promised to end the dangerous pollution of the atmosphere with radioactivity. The test-ban treaty was an important move toward greater international cooperation on nuclear proliferation. Kennedy quoted the Chinese sage Confucius to suggest the treaty's significance: "A journey of a thousand miles begins with one step."

KENNEDY AND VIETNAM   As tensions with the Soviet Union were easing, a crisis was growing in Southeast Asia that would become within a decade the greatest American foreign policy debacle ever. During John Kennedy's "thousand days" in office the turmoil of Indochina never preoccupied the public mind for any extended period, but it dominated international diplomatic debates from the time the administration entered office.

The Geneva Accords of 1954 had declared the landlocked kingdom of Laos a neutral country but thereafter a complex power struggle erupted between the Communist Pathet Lao and the Royal Laotian Army. There matters stood when Eisenhower left office and told Kennedy: "You might have to go in there and fight it out." The chairman of the Joint Chiefs of Staff argued in favor of a stand against the Pathet Lao, even at the cost of direct intervention. After a lengthy consideration of alternatives, the Kennedy administration decided to back the formation of a neutralist coalition which would preclude American military involvement in Laos, yet prevent a Pathet Lao victory. The Soviets, who were extending aid to the Pathet Lao, indicated a readiness to negotiate, and in May 1961 talks began in Geneva. After more than a year of tangled negotiations, the three factions in Laos agreed to a neutral coalition.

Meanwhile, North Vietnam kept open the Ho Chi Minh Trail through eastern Laos, over which it supplied its Vietcong allies fighting in South Vietnam. There the situation worsened under the leadership of Premier Ngo Dinh Diem, despite encouraging reports from the military commander of the American "advisers" in South Vietnam. At the time the problem was less the scattered guerrilla attacks than Diem's failure to deliver social and economic reforms and to rally popular support. His repressive tactics, directed not only against Communists but also against Buddhists and other critics, played into the hands of his enemies.

In 1961 White House assistant Walt Rostow and General Maxwell Taylor became the first in a long train of presidential emissaries to South Vietnam's capital, Saigon. They proposed a major increase in the American military presence, but Kennedy refused, and instead continued to dispatch more military advisers. When he took office there had been 2,000 American troops in South Vietnam; by the end of 1963 there were 16,000, none of whom had been committed to battle. But the Diem regime continued to be its own worst enemy. By mid-1963 growing Buddhist demonstrations made the public discontent in South Vietnam more plainly visible. The spectacle of Buddhist monks immolating themselves on Saigon streets in protest of Diem's iron-fisted rule shocked Americans but brought from Diem's sister-in-law only sarcasm about "barbecued monks."

By the fall of 1963 the Kennedy administration had decided that Diem was a lost cause. When dissident Vietnamese generals proposed a coup d'état, American ambassador Henry Cabot Lodge assured them that Washington would not stand in the way. On November 1 they seized the government and murdered Diem. Yet the generals provided no more stability than earlier regimes, as successive coups set South Vietnam spinning from one military leader to the other.

KENNEDY'S ASSASSINATION   Kennedy seemed to be facing up to the intractability of the situation in Vietnam by the fall of 1963. In September he spoke of the South Vietnamese: "In the final analysis it's their war. They're the ones who have to win it or lose it. We can help them as advisers but they have to win it." Some of his aides later argued that Kennedy would never have allowed a dramatic escalation of American military involvement in Vietnam. Others strongly disagreed.

The answer of course will never be known, for on November 22, 1963, while on a campaign swing through downtown Dallas, Kennedy was shot twice in the throat and head and died almost immediately. A few hours later Dallas police arrested Lee Harvey Oswald, a twenty-four-year-old ex-Marine drifter who had worked in the Texas Book Depository, the building from which the shots were fired at Kennedy. Investigators had several other reasons to suspect Oswald: he had recently returned from a prolonged stay in the Soviet Union, in recent years he had also visited Cuba, and his family had ties to a Mafia member who had made threats to kill Kennedy. Yet before Oswald could be thoroughly interrogated, he too was killed. Two days after Oswald's arrest, as television cameras covered his transfer to another jail, Jack Ruby, a Dallas nightclub owner, stepped from the crowd of onlookers and fatally shot Oswald in the abdomen.

Oswald's death ignited a controversy over the assassination

Kennedy's vice-president, Lyndon B. Johnson, takes the presidential oath as Air Force One *returns from Dallas with Jacqueline Kennedy (right), the presidential party, and the body of the assassinated president.*

that still simmers today. In December 1963 President Johnson appointed a commission to investigate Kennedy's murder. Headed by Chief Justice Earl Warren, it concluded that Oswald had acted alone. Yet many people were (and are) not convinced, and since 1963 dozens of conspiracy theories have been hatched. Some blame the CIA or the Mafia, others point at Fidel Castro, whom the CIA had once tried to assassinate. Still others insist that Cuban exiles in Miami, angered by Kennedy's failure to rescue their comrades during the Bay of Pigs fiasco, were behind the assassination. In 1979 a House committee reported that more than one person had fired shots at Kennedy in Dallas, but FBI scientists discredited the theory. Books and movies setting forth various conspiracy theories have kept the controversy alive. Whatever the actual story of the assassination, Kennedy's tragic death enshrined him in the public imagination as a martyred leader cut down in the prime of his career.

LYNDON JOHNSON AND THE GREAT SOCIETY

Lyndon Johnson took the oath as president of the United States on board the plane that took John Kennedy's body back to Washington from Dallas. At age fifty-five, Johnson had spent twenty-six years on the Washington scene and had served nearly a decade as Senate Democratic leader, where he had displayed the greatest gift for compromise since Henry Clay. Johnson brought to the White House a marked change of style from his predecessor. A truly self-made man who through gritty determination and shrewd manipulation had worked his way out of a hardscrabble rural Texas background to become one of Washington's most powerful figures, he had none of the Kennedy elegance or charisma. Johnson yearned for both political power and public affection. The first southern president since Woodrow Wilson, he harbored a sense of being the perpetual "outsider" despite his long experience with power. And indeed he was so regarded by Kennedy "insiders."

Those who viewed Johnson as a stereotypical southern conservative ignored his long-standing admiration for Franklin Roosevelt, the depth of his concern for poor people, and his heartfelt commitment to the cause of civil rights. The day after the assassination he told an aide: "I am a Roosevelt New Dealer. As a matter of fact . . . Kennedy was a little too conservative to suit my taste." In foreign affairs Johnson was, like Woodrow Wilson, a novice. But in the domestic arena during the 1950s he was unsurpassed in his ability to shepherd legislation through the gauntlet of special interest lobbyists and Congress. He once bragged that "Ike couldn't pass the Lord's Prayer in Congress without me." Now he resolved to surpass Kennedy at his own game—in civil rights, in aid to the poor, in promoting freedom abroad.

POLITICS AND POVERTY   Quite naturally, Johnson established domestic politics as his first priority. He exploited the nation's grief after the assassination by declaring that Kennedy's cabinet and advisers would stay on and that the slain leader's legislative program, stymied in several congressional committees, would now be passed. The logjam in the Congress that had blocked Kennedy's program broke under Johnson's forceful leadership, and a torrent of legislation poured through.

At the top of Johnson's agenda were the stalled measures for tax reduction and civil rights. He then added to his "must" list a bold new idea which bore the LBJ brand: "This Administration today, here and now, declares unconditional war on poverty in America." The particulars were to come later, the product of an administration task force already at work before Johnson took office.

Americans had suddenly rediscovered poverty in the early 1960s when the social critic Michael Harrington published a powerful exposé entitled *The Other America* (1962). Brandishing an impressive array of statistics as well as convincing theories of social psychology, Harrington argued that while most Americans had been celebrating their rising affluence during the postwar era, some 40 to 50 million people were mired in a "culture of poverty" hidden from view and passed on from one generation to the other. Unlike the upwardly mobile immigrant poor at the turn of the century, they were impervious to hope. "To be impoverished," he asserted, "is to be an internal alien, to grow up in a culture that is radically different from the one that dominates the society."

President Kennedy read a review of *The Other America* in 1963 and asked his advisers to investigate the problem and suggest a plan of attack. Upon taking office Johnson announced that he wanted an anti-poverty package that was "big and bold that would hit the nation with real impact." Money for the program would come from the economic growth generated by the tax reduction of more than $10 billion passed in February 1964.

The administration's task force on poverty had its Economic Opportunity Bill ready to submit in March 1964. It incorporated a wide range of programs: a Job Corps for inner-city youths, a Head Start program for disadvantaged pre-schoolers, work-study jobs for college students, grants to farmers and rural business, loans to those willing to hire the chronic unemployed, the Volunteers in Service to America (VISTA, a "domestic Peace Corps"), and the Community Action Program, which would provide "maximum feasible participation" of the poor in directing programs designed for their benefit. Speaking at Ann Arbor, Michigan, in May 1964, Johnson called for a "Great Society" resting on "abundance and liberty for all. The Great Society demands an end to poverty and racial injustice, to which we are fully committed in our time." In theory it was liberalism triumphant; in practice its considerable achievements were accompanied by administrative bungling, corruption, and misguided idealism.

THE 1964 ELECTION   As the 1964 election approached, Johnson was conceded the Democratic nomination from the start. He chose as his running mate Hubert H. Humphrey of Minnesota, the prominent liberal senator with the seemingly permanent smile and inexhaustible supply of optimism and energy.

In the Republican party, conservatives charged that the party was falling into the hands of an eastern establishment that had given in to the same internationalism and big-government policies as liberal Democrats. Ever since 1940, so the theory went, the party had nominated "me-too" candidates who merely promised to run more efficiently the programs that Democrats promoted. Offer the voters "a choice, not an echo," they reasoned, and a truly conservative majority would assert itself.

By 1960 Arizona's Senator Barry Goldwater, a millionaire department-store owner from Phoenix, had begun to emerge as the leader of the Republican Right. A movement to draft Goldwater began as early as 1961, mobilizing conservative activists to capture party caucuses and contest primaries. In 1964 they took an early lead, and after Goldwater swept the all-important California primary, his forces controlled the Republican convention. "I would remind you," Goldwater told the delegates, "that extremism in the defense of liberty is no vice."

Goldwater was certainly an extremist. By the end of the campaign he had displayed an unusual gift for frightening voters. Accusing the administration of waging a "no-win" war in Vietnam, he urged wholesale bombing of North Vietnam and left the impression of being trigger-happy. He also savaged Johnson's War on Poverty and the New Deal tradition. At one stop he called LBJ the "Santa Claus of the free lunch." In Tennessee he proposed the sale of TVA; in St. Petersburg, Florida, a major retirement community, he questioned the value of Social Security. He had voted against both the nuclear test ban and the Civil Rights Act. Republican campaign buttons claimed: "In your heart, you know he's right." Democrats responded: "In your guts, you know he's nuts."

Johnson, on the other hand, appealed to the middle of the political spectrum. In contrast to Goldwater's bellicose rhetoric on Vietnam, he made a pledge that won great applause at the time and much comment later: "We are not about to send American boys nine or ten thousand miles from home to do what Asian boys ought to be doing for themselves."

The election was a landslide. Johnson polled 61 percent of the total vote; Goldwater carried only Arizona and five states in the Deep South. Johnson won the electoral vote by a whopping 482 to 52. In the Senate the Democrats increased their majority by two (68 to 32) and in the House by thirty-seven (295 to 140).

LANDMARK LEGISLATION Johnson took advantage of his new mandate to launch his Great Society program. It would, he promised, end poverty, renovate the decaying central cities, provide every young American with the chance to attend college, protect the health of the elderly, enhance the cultural life of the nation, clean up the air and water, and make the highways safer.

To accomplish such goals the Johnson administration pushed an array of new legislation through the Congress at a pace unseen since Roosevelt's Hundred Days. "Hurry, boys, hurry," Johnson told aides. "Get that legislation up to Capitol Hill and out. Eighteen months from now ol' Landslide Lyndon will be lame-duck Lyndon." Priority went to health insurance and aid to education, proposals that had languished since President Truman advanced them in 1945. The proposal for a comprehensive plan of medical insurance had long been stalled by the American Medical Association's ardent opposition. But now that Johnson had the votes, the AMA joined Republicans in boarding the bandwagon for a bill serving those over age sixty-five. The act not only created the Medicare insurance program for the aged, but added another program, Medicaid, which provided states with federal grants that would help cover medical payments for the indigent.

Five days after he submitted his Medicare program, Johnson sent to Congress his proposal for $1.5 billion in Federal aid to elementary and secondary education. Such proposals had been ignored since the 1940s, blocked alternately by issues of segregation or separation of church and state. Now Johnson and congressional leaders devised a means of extending aid to "poverty-impacted" school districts regardless of their public or parochial character.

The momentum generated by the passage of these measures had already begun to carry others along, and it continued through the following year. Altogether the tide of Great Society legislation carried 435 bills through the Congress. Among them was the Appalachian Regional Development Act of 1966, which allocated $1.1 billion for programs to enhance the standard of living of those in remote mountain coves. The Housing and Urban Development Act of 1965 provided for construction of 240,000 housing units and $2.9 billion for urban renewal. Rent supplements for low-income families followed in 1966, and in that year there began a new Department of Housing and Urban Development, headed by Robert C. Weaver, the first black cabinet member. Johnson had, in the words of one Washington reporter, "brought to harvest a generation's backlog of ideas and social legislation."

The Great Society programs included several genuine success stories. The Highway Safety Act and the Traffic Safety Act established safety standards for automobile manufacturers and highway design, and the scholarships provided for college students under the Higher Education Act were quite popular. Many Great

Society initiatives aimed at improving the health, nutrition, and education of poor Americans, young and old, made headway against these intractable problems. So, too, did efforts to clean up air and water pollution. But several ambitious programs were hastily designed and ill-conceived, others were vastly under-funded, and many were mismanaged. Medicare, for example, re-moved any incentives for hospitals to control costs, and medical bills skyrocketed. Often funds appropriated for various pro-grams never made it through the tangled bureaucracy to the needy. Widely publicized cases of welfare fraud placed a power-ful weapon in the hands of those opposed to liberal social pro-grams. By 1966 middle-class resentment over the cost and waste of the Great Society programs helped generate a strong conser-vative backlash.

FROM CIVIL RIGHTS TO BLACK POWER

VOTING RIGHTS   Among the successes of the Great Society were several key pieces of civil rights legislation. After Kennedy's death, President Johnson called for passage of the long-stalled civil rights bill as a memorial to the fallen leader. On July 2 John-son signed the Civil Rights Act of 1964, the most far-reaching civil rights measure ever enacted by the Congress. It outlawed

Martin Luther King, Jr. (second from left), and other civil rights leaders at the head of the March on Washington for Jobs and Freedom, August 28, 1963.

racial discrimination in hotels, restaurants, and other public accommodations. In addition, the attorney-general could now bring suits for school desegregation, relieving parents of a painful necessity.

Perhaps equally important, the Civil Rights Act gave new momentum to activists in the cause. Early in 1965 Martin Luther King, the recipient of the Nobel Peace Prize the year before, announced a voter-registration drive aimed at the 3 million eligible blacks in the South. On March 7 civil rights protesters began a march for voting rights from Selma, Alabama, to Montgomery, only to be violently dispersed by state troopers and a mounted posse. A federal judge then agreed to allow the march, and President Johnson provided federal protection. By March 25, when the demonstrators reached Montgomery, they numbered 35,000, and King delivered a rousing address from the steps of the state capitol.

Several days before the march President Johnson went before Congress with a moving plea for voting rights legislation. Johnson's speech reached its climax when he slowly intoned the words of the movement hymn: "And we shall overcome." The resulting Voting Rights Act of 1965, passed to ensure all the right to vote, authorized the attorney-general to dispatch federal examiners to register voters. In states or counties where fewer than half the adults had voted in 1964, the act suspended literacy tests and other devices commonly used to defraud citizens of the vote. By the end of the year some 250,000 blacks were newly registered.

"BLACK POWER" In the midst of success, however, the civil rights movement began to fragment. On August 11, 1965, less than a week after the passage of the Voting Rights Act, the predominantly black Watts area of Los Angeles exploded in a frenzy of riots and looting. When the uprising ended, there were 34 dead, almost 4,000 rioters in jail, and property damage exceeding $35 million. Liberal commentators were stunned, since the riots occurred in the wake of the greatest legislative victories for black Americans since the first Reconstruction.

But events did not stand still to await white liberal comprehension. The Watts upheaval marked the beginning of four "long hot summers" of racial conflagration. Riots in the summer of 1966 erupted in Chicago and Cleveland, along with forty other American cities. The following summer Newark and Detroit burst into flames. Detroit provided the most graphic example of urban violence, as tanks rolled through the streets and soldiers from the 101st Airborne used machine guns to root out snipers in the tenements.

In retrospect it was understandable that the civil rights movement would begin to focus on the plight of urban blacks. By the middle 1960s about 70 percent of America's black population lived in metropolitan areas, most of them in central-city ghettos that had been bypassed by the postwar prosperity. It seems clear, also in retrospect, that the nonviolent tactics that had worked in the rural South would not work in the northern cities. In the North, racial problems resulted from segregated residential patterns not amenable to changes in law, and northern white ethnic groups did not have the cultural heritage that southern whites shared with blacks. A special Commission on Civil Disorders noted that, unlike earlier race riots that had been started by whites, the urban upheavals of the middle 1960s were initiated by blacks themselves in an effort to destroy what they could not stomach and what civil rights legislation seemed unable to change.

In the midst of such violence, a new philosophy of racial separatism began to emerge. By 1966 "Black Power" had become the rallying cry of young activists. Radical members of SNCC had become estranged from Martin Luther King's theories of nonviolence. When Stokely Carmichael, a twenty-five-year-old graduate of Howard University, became head of SNCC in May 1966, he adopted a separatist philosophy of black power, and whites were ousted from the organization. "We reject an American dream defined by white people and must work to construct an American reality defined by Afro-Americans," said a SNCC position paper. H. Rap Brown, who succeeded Carmichael as head of SNCC in 1967, even urged blacks to "get you some guns" and "kill the honkies." Meanwhile Carmichael had moved on to the Black Panther party, a self-professed group of urban black revolutionaries founded in Oakland, California, in 1966 and headed by Huey P. Newton and Eldridge Cleaver. Under their leadership, the Black Panthers echoed the separatist demands of Marcus Garvey and terrified the public by wearing bandeleros and carrying rifles. Eventually the Panthers fragmented in spasms of violence, much of which the FBI and local police officials helped to provoke.

Perhaps the most articulate spokesman for black power was one of the earliest, Malcolm X (formerly Malcolm Little, with the "X" denoting his lost African surname). Malcolm had risen from a ghetto childhood of narcotics and crime to become the chief disciple of Elijah Muhammad, the Black Muslim prophet who re-

*Malcolm X, influential
spokesman for the Black
Muslim movement.*

jected Christianity as "the religion of white devils" and encouraged black culture and black pride. "Yes, I'm an extremist," Malcolm acknowledged in 1964. "You show me a black man who isn't an extremist and I'll show you one who needs psychiatric attention." By 1964 Malcolm had broken with Elijah Muhammad and founded his own organization, which was committed to the establishment of alliances between American blacks and the nonwhite peoples of the world. He also had begun to abandon his earlier separatist agenda and violent tactics. But just after the publication of his *Autobiography* in 1965, Malcolm was gunned down in Harlem by Black Muslim assassins. With him went the most effective voice for urban black militancy.

"Black Power" was a slogan more than a philosophy, a reflection more of futility than of hope. The conclusion of the 1967 Commission on Civil Disorders was harsh but accurate: "Black Power rhetoric and ideology actually expresses a lack of power. . . . Powerless to make any fundamental changes in the life of the masses . . . many advocates of Black Power have retreated into an unreal world, where they see an outnumbered and poverty-stricken minority organizing itself independently of whites and creating sufficient power to force white Americans to grant its demands." The shrill tone and violent acts associated with the Black Power movement shattered the unity of black activism and helped provoke a powerful blacklash among whites. As Representative Gerald Ford asked, "Are we going to abdicate law and order . . . in favor of a social theory that the man who heaves a brick through a window or tosses a firebomb into your car is simply the misunderstood and underprivileged product of a broken home?"

THE TRAGEDY OF VIETNAM

As violence was escalating in America's inner cities, the war in Vietnam reached new levels of intensity and destruction. At the time of President Kennedy's death there were 16,000 American military advisers in Vietnam. Lyndon Johnson inherited a commitment to prevent a Communist takeover in South Vietnam along with a reluctance to assume the military burden for fighting the war. One president after another had done just enough to avoid being charged with having "lost" Vietnam. Johnson did the same, fearing that any other course would undermine his influence and endanger his Great Society programs in Congress. But this path took him and the United States inexorably deeper into intervention in Asia.

ESCALATION   The official sanction for America's "escalation"—a Defense Department term coined in the Vietnam era—was the Tonkin Gulf Resolution, voted by Congress on August 7, 1964. Johnson reported in a national television address that two American destroyers had been attacked by North Vietnamese vessels on August 2 and 4 in the Gulf of Tonkin off the coast of North Vietnam. Although he described the attacks as unprovoked, in truth the destroyers had been monitoring South Vietnamese raids against two North Vietnamese islands—raids planned by American advisers. The Tonkin Gulf Resolution authorized the president to "take all necessary measures to repel any armed attack against the forces of the United States and to prevent further aggression."

Three months after Johnson's landslide victory over Goldwater, he and his advisers made the crucial decisions that shaped American policy in Vietnam for the next four years. On February 5, 1965, Vietcong guerrillas killed 8 and wounded 126 Americans at Pleiku. Further attacks on Americans later that week led Johnson to order operation "Rolling Thunder," the first sustained American bombings of North Vietnam, which were intended to stop the flow of soldiers and supplies into the south. Six months later a task force concluded that the bombing had little effect on the supplies pouring down the "Ho Chi Minh Trail" from North Vietnam through Laos. Still, the bombing continued.

VIETNAM, 1966

☐ Major U.S. bases

0   200 Miles

0   200 Kilometers

In March 1965 the new American army commander in Vietnam, Gen. William C. Westmoreland, requested and got the first installment of combat troops, ostensibly to defend American airfields. By the end of 1965 there were 184,000 American troops in Vietnam; in 1966 the troop level reached 385,000. And as combat operations increased, so did the list of American casualties, announced each week on the nightly news along with the "body count" of alleged enemy dead. "Westy's War," although fought with helicopter gunships, chemical defoliants, and napalm, became like the trench warfare of World War I—a grinding war of attrition.

THE CONTEXT FOR POLICY Johnson's decision to "Americanize" the war, so ill-starred in retrospect, was entirely consistent with the foreign policy principles pursued by all American presidents after World War II. The version of the containment theory articulated in the Truman Doctrine, endorsed by Eisenhower and Dulles throughout the 1950s, and reaffirmed by Kennedy, pledged United States opposition to the advance of communism anywhere in the world. "Why are we in Vietnam?" Johnson asked rhetorically at Johns Hopkins University in 1965. "We are there because we have a promise to keep. . . . To leave Vietnam to its fate would shake the confidence of all these people in the value of American commitment." Secretary of State Dean Rusk repeated this rationale before countless congressional committees, warning that Thailand, Burma, and the rest of Southeast Asia would fall to communism if American forces withdrew. American military intervention in Vietnam was thus no aberration, but a logical culmination of the assumptions widely shared by the foreign policy establishment and leaders of both political parties since the early days of the Cold War.

Nor did the United States blindly "stumble into a quagmire" in Vietnam, as some commentators maintained. Johnson insisted from the start that American military involvement must not reach levels that would provoke the Chinese or Soviets into direct intervention. He therefore exercised a tight rein over the bombing campaign, once boasting that "they can't even bomb an outhouse without my approval." Such a restrictive policy meant, in effect, that military victory in any traditional sense of the term was never possible. "It was startling to me to find out," the new secretary of defense, Clark Clifford, recalled in 1968, "that we had no military plan to end the war." America's goal was not to win the war in a conventional sense by capturing enemy territory, but to prevent the North Vietnamese and Vietcong from winning. This meant that America would have to maintain a military presence as long as the enemy retained the will to fight.

As it turned out, American public support for the war eroded faster than the will of the North Vietnamese leaders to tolerate casualties. Opposition to the war broke out on college campuses with the escalation of 1965. And in January 1966 Senator J. William Fulbright of Arkansas, chairman of the Senate Foreign Relations Committee, began congressional investigations into American policy. George Kennan, the founding father of the containment doctrine, told Fulbright's committee that the doctrine was appropriate for Europe, but not Southeast Asia. By 1967 opposition to the war had become so pronounced that antiwar demonstrations in New York and at the Pentagon attracted massive support. Nightly television accounts of the fighting— Vietnam was the first war to receive extended television coverage, and hence has been dubbed the "living room war" —brought the horrors of guerrilla warfare into American dens. As Secretary of Defense McNamara admitted, "The picture of the world's greatest superpower killing or injuring 1,000 non-combatants a week, while trying to pound a tiny backward nation into submission on an issue whose merits are hotly disputed, is not a pretty one."

In a war of political will, North Vietnam had the advantage. Johnson and his advisers never came to appreciate the tenacity of North Vietnam's commitment to unify Vietnam and expel the United States. Ho Chi Minh had warned the French in the 1940s that "You can kill ten of my men for every one I kill of yours, but even at those odds, you will lose and I will win." He knew that in a battle of attrition, the Vietnamese Communists had the advantage, for they were willing to sacrifice all for their cause. Indeed, just as General Westmoreland was assuring Johnson and the American public that his forces in early 1968 were on the verge of gaining the upper hand, the Communists again displayed their resilience.

THE TURNING POINT On January 31, 1968, the first day of the Vietnamese New Year (Tet), the Vietcong and North Vietnamese defied a holiday truce to launch a wave of surprise assaults on American and South Vietnamese forces throughout South Vietnam. The old capital city of Hué fell to the Communists, and

During the 1968 Tet offensive Viet Cong units temporarily took the grounds of the American embassy in Saigon. Here, American military police lead a captured Viet Cong guerrilla away from the embassy.

Vietcong units temporarily occupied the grounds of the American embassy in Saigon. Within a few days, however, American and South Vietnamese forces organized a devastating counterattack. General Westmoreland justifiably proclaimed the Tet offensive a major defeat for the Vietcong. But while Vietcong casualties were enormous, the psychological impact of the offensive on the American public was more telling. Time and Newsweek soon ran antiwar editorials urging American withdrawal. Walter Cronkite, the dean of American television journalists, confided to his viewers that he no longer believed the war was winnable. "If I've lost Walter," Johnson was reported to say, "then it's over. I've lost Mr. Average Citizen." Polls showed that Johnson's popularity declined to 35 percent, lower than any president since Truman's darkest days. In 1968 the United States was spending $322,000 on every enemy killed in Vietnam; the poverty programs at home received only $53 per person.

During 1968 Johnson grew increasingly isolated. The secretary of defense reported that a task force of prominent soldiers and civilians saw no prospect for a military victory. Robert Kennedy was considering a run for the presidency in order to challenge Johnson's Vietnam policy. And Senator Eugene McCarthy of Minnesota had already decided to oppose Johnson in the Democratic primaries. With antiwar students rallying to his candidacy, McCarthy polled 42 percent of the vote to Johnson's 48 percent in New Hampshire's March primary. Though voters had to write in Johnson's name to vote for the president, it was still a remarkable showing for a little-known senator, and each presidential primary now promised to become a referendum on Johnson's Vietnam policy.

Despite Johnson's troubles in the conduct of foreign policy, he remained a master at reading the political omens. On March 31 he announced a limited halt to the bombing of North Vietnam and fresh initiatives for a negotiated cease-fire. Then he added a dramatic postscript: "I have concluded that I should not permit the Presidency to become involved in the partisan divisions that are developing in this political year. Accordingly, I shall not seek, and I will not accept, the nomination of my party for another term as your President." Although American troops would remain in Vietnam for five more years and the casualties would mount, the quest for military victory had ended. Now the question was how the most powerful nation in the world could extricate itself from Vietnam with a minimum of damage to its prestige. It would not be easy. When direct negotiations with the

North Vietnamese finally began in Paris in May 1968 they immediately bogged down over North Vietnam's demand for an American bombing halt as a precondition for further discussion.

SIXTIES CRESCENDO

A TRAUMATIC YEAR History seemed to move at a fearful pace throughout the 1960s, but 1968 was a year of extreme turbulence even for that decade. On April 4, only four days after Johnson's announced withdrawal from the presidential race, Martin Luther King was gunned down while standing on the balcony of a motel in Memphis, Tennessee. The assassin had expressed hostility toward blacks, but debate still continues over whether he was a pawn in an organized conspiracy. King's death set off an outpouring of grief among whites and blacks. It also set off riots in over sixty American cities, with the most serious occurring in Chicago and Washington, D.C.

Two months later, on June 6, Robert Kennedy was shot in the head by a young Palestinian, who resented Kennedy's strong support of Israel. Kennedy died at the end of the day on which he had convincingly defeated Eugene McCarthy in the California primary, thereby assuming leadership of the antiwar forces in the race for the Democratic nomination for president.

CHICAGO AND MIAMI In August 1968 Democratic delegates gathered inside the convention hall at Chicago to nominate Vice-President Hubert Humphrey, while 24,000 police and National Guardsmen and a small army of television reporters stood watch over several thousand diverse protesters herded together miles away in a public park. The Democratic party's liberal tradition was clearly in disarray, a fact that gave heart to the Republicans who gathered in Miami to nominate Richard Nixon.

Nixon's nomination represented a remarkable political comeback. His narrow loss to Kennedy in 1960 had been followed by a disastrous defeat in the California gubernatorial race two years later. In what he labeled his "last press conference," he bitterly lashed out at reporters, claiming that they had cost him the race. "You won't have Nixon to kick around any more," he defiantly pledged. Yet Nixon displayed his remarkable resilience by returning to national politics in 1964, when he crisscrossed the nation in support of Goldwater's candidacy. For the next several years he remained active, and in 1968 Nixon was ready to take advantage of Johnson's crumbling popularity. He offered a vision of stability and order that a majority of Americans—soon to be called "the silent majority"—wanted desperately.

But others were ready as well to challenge the Democratic party regulars. George Wallace, the Democratic governor of Alabama, became a third candidate in the campaign on the American Independent party ticket. Wallace had made his political reputation as a brazen defender of segregation, but in his campaign for national office in 1968 he moderated his position on the race issue. And he appealed even more candidly than Nixon to the fears generated by antiwar protesters, the welfare system, and the growth of the federal government. Wallace insisted that "liberals, intellectuals, and long-hairs have run the country for too long" and he pledged that when he took over in Washington, he would "throw all these phonies and their briefcases into the Potomac." Wallace's platform was compelling in its simplicity: Rioters would be shot, the war in Vietnam would be won, states' rights and law and order would be restored, open-housing laws would be repealed, and welfare cheats would be jailed.

Wallace's reactionary candidacy generated considerable appeal outside his native South, especially in white working-class communities where resentment against Johnson's Great Society liberalism was rife. Although never a possible winner, Wallace's campaign had to be taken seriously: it held the possibility of denying Humphrey or Nixon an electoral majority and thereby throwing the choice into the House of Representatives, which would have provided an appropriate climax to a chaotic year.

NIXON AGAIN   It did not happen that way. Nixon enjoyed an enormous early lead in the polls, which narrowed as the election approached. Wallace's campaign was hurt by his outspoken running mate, retired Air Force General Curtis LeMay, who spoke approvingly of using nuclear weapons in Vietnam. In October 1968, Humphrey, tainted by his ties to LBJ and the party bosses, announced that he would stop bombing North Vietnam "as an acceptable risk for peace." Eugene McCarthy, who had been strangely silent during the campaign and had even spent some time cloistered in a monastery, eventually endorsed Humphrey.

Nixon and his running mate, Governor Spiro Agnew of Maryland, eked out a narrow victory by roughly 800,000 votes, a margin of about one percentage point. The electoral vote was more decisive, 301 to 191. Wallace won 10 million votes, 13.5 percent of the total, the best showing by a third-party candidate

Richard Nixon (right) and Spiro Agnew, victors in the 1968 election.

since Robert La Follette in 1924. All but one of Wallace's 46 electoral votes were from the Deep South. Nixon swept all but four of the states west of the Mississippi, while Humphrey's support came almost exclusively from the Northeast.

So at the end of a turbulent year, near the end of a traumatic decade, power passed peacefully to a president who was associated with the superficial stability of the 1950s. A nation that had seemed on the verge of consuming itself in spasms of violence looked to Richard Nixon to provide what he had promised in the campaign: "peace with honor" in Vietnam and a middle ground on which a majority of Americans, silent or otherwise, could come together.

FURTHER READING

Herbert Parmet traces the influence of Kennedy in two volumes, *Jack: The Struggle of John Fitzgerald Kennedy* (1980) and *JFK: The Presidency of John Fitzgerald Kennedy* (1983). A provocative and compelling account of Kennedy's private conduct and public life is Thomas C. Reeves's *A Question of Character: A Life of John F. Kennedy* (1991).° Fa-

° These books are available in paperback editions.

vorable memoirs from White House staffers include Arthur M. Schlesinger, Jr.'s *A Thousand Days: John F. Kennedy in the White House* (1965)° and Theodore C. Sorenson's *Kennedy* (1965). Less favorable assessments come from Henry Fairlie's *The Kennedy Promise* (1973) and Bruce Miroff's *Pragmatic Illusions: The Presidential Politics of John F. Kennedy* (1976).

Lyndon Johnson's own *The Vantage Point: Perspectives on the Presidency, 1963–1969* (1971),° can be balanced with Doris Kearns's *Lyndon Johnson and the American Dream* (1976).° Two recent—and quite different—biographies are Robert Caro's *Means of Ascent: The Years of Lyndon Johnson* (1990)° and Robert Dallek's *When Politics Was King: Lyndon Johnson and His Times* (1991).° Very helpful for background on the formation of social policy is James T. Patterson's *America's Struggle against Poverty, 1900–1980* (1981).°

On foreign policy, see Richard Walton's *Cold War and Counter-revolution: The Foreign Policy of John F. Kennedy* (1972).° Policy in Vietnam has received voluminous treatment from all political perspectives. Three of the most popular critical accounts of the struggle are Chester L. Cooper's *The Lost Crusade* (1970), Frances Fitzgerald's *Fire in the Lake: The Vietnamese and the Americans in Vietnam* (1972),° and David Halberstam's *The Best and the Brightest* (1972).° Works that see American policy in a favorable light include Norman Podhoretz's *Why We Were in Vietnam* (1982) and Guenter Lewy's *America in Vietnam* (1979).° John M. Newman's *JFK and Vietnam* (1992) argues that Kennedy would never have committed large numbers of combat troops in Vietnam.

Many scholars have dealt with various aspects of the civil rights movement and race relations of the 1960s. See especially Carl Brauer's *John F. Kennedy and the Second Reconstruction* (1977).° Two biographies of Martin Luther King, Jr., are helpful: David Garrow's *Bearing the Cross* (1986) and David Lewis's *King: A Critical Biography* (1970).° Other personalities in the civil rights movement are studied in Charles F. Kellogg's *NAACP* (1967), August Meier and Elliott Rudwick's *CORE* (1973),° and Howard Zinn's *SNCC: The New Abolitionists* (1964). For legal turns the civil rights movement took during the 1960s, see J. Harvie Wilkinson's *From Brown to Bakke: The Supreme Court and School Integration, 1954–1978* (1978). William Chafe's *From Civilities to Civil Rights: Greensboro, North Carolina, and the Black Struggle for Freedom* (1980)° details the original sit-ins. For race relations subsequent to the Civil Rights Act, consult Theodore Draper's *The Rediscovery of Black Nationalism* (1970). The demographic forces behind changing race relations are superbly surveyed in Nicholas Lemann's *The Promised Land: The Great Migration and How It Changed America* (1991).°

For the tumultuous events of the 1968 campaign, start with Theodore H. White's *The Making of the President, 1968* (1969).° Less favorable to Nixon is Joe McGinnis's *The Selling of the President* (1969).° Arthur M. Schlesinger, Jr.'s *Robert Kennedy and His Times* (1978)° and Marshall Frady's *Wallace* (1976)° report the campaign from the viewpoint of other candidates.

34 ✑

REBELLION AND REACTION
IN THE SEVENTIES

THE ROOTS OF REBELLION

By the 1960s the postwar baby boomers were maturing. Now young adults, they differed from their elders in that they had experienced neither economic depression nor a major war. They had been nurtured by the homogenizing effects of television and a flourishing consumer culture. Record numbers of these young people were attending American colleges and universities during the 1960s: college enrollment quadrupled between 1945 and 1970. At the same time, many universities had become sprawling institutions increasingly dependent upon research contracts from giant corporations and the federal government. As these "multiversities" grew more bureaucratic and hierarchical, they unknowingly invited resistance from many among a generation of students wary of involvement in what Eisenhower had called the "military-industrial complex."

The success of the Greensboro sit-ins in 1960 not only precipitated a decade of civil rights activism; it also signaled an end to the supposed apathy that had enveloped college campuses and social life during the 1950s. Although primarily concerned with the rights and status of black people, the sit-ins, marches, protests, principles, and sacrifices associated with the civil rights movement provided inspiring models for other estranged and excluded groups demanding justice, freedom, and equality.

During 1960–1961 a small but significant number of white students joined the sit-in movement. They and many others were also inspired by President Kennedy's direct appeals to their youthful idealism. Thousands enrolled in the Peace Corps and VISTA. But as it became clear that politics mixed with principle in the president's position on civil rights, and later, as criticism of escalating American involvement in Vietnam mounted, more and more young people grew disillusioned with the government as well as other institutional bastions of the status quo. By the mid-1960s, a full-fledged youth revolt erupted on many campuses, and rebellious students began to flow into two distinct, yet frequently overlapping, movements: the New Left and the counterculture.

THE NEW LEFT   The explicitly political strain of the youth revolt coalesced when Tom Hayden and Al Haber, two student radicals at the University of Michigan, formed the Students for a Democratic Society (SDS) in 1960. Hayden had been inspired during his college years by Jack Kerouac's *On the Road* and Jean Jacques Rousseau's notion of participatory democracy. Two years later, Hayden drafted what became known as the Port Huron Statement: "We are the people of this generation, bred in at least moderate comfort, housed in universities, looking uncomfortably to the world we inherit." Hayden's earnest manifesto focused on the absence of individual freedom in modern American life. The country, he insisted, was dominated by huge organizational structures—governments, corporations, universities—all of which conspired to oppress and alienate the individual. Inspired by the example of black activism in the South, Hayden declared that students had the power to restore "participatory democracy" to American life by wresting "control of the educational process from the administrative bureaucracy" and then forging links with other dissident movements. He and others soon adopted the term "New Left" to distinguish their efforts at grass-roots democracy from the Old Left of the 1930s, which had espoused an orthodox Marxism and had embraced Stalinism.

In the fall of 1964, students at the University of California at Berkeley took Hayden's program to heart. When Clark Kerr, the university chancellor, announced in October 1964 that sidewalk solicitations for political causes would no longer be allowed, several hundred students staged a sit-in. Soon thereafter over 2,000 more joined in, including even the conservative student members of Youth for Goldwater. After a tense standoff the administration relented. Student groups then formed the Free Speech Movement (FSM).

Led by Mario Savio, a philosophy major and compelling public speaker, the FSM was initially a protest in behalf of student rights. But it quickly escalated into a more general criticism of the modern university and what Savio called the "depersonalized, unresponsive bureaucracy" infecting all of American life. In December 1964 Savio made an impassioned speech on the steps of the main administration building in which he asserted that there comes "a time when the operation of a machine becomes so odious, makes you so sick at heart, that you can't take part—you can't even passively take part, and you've got to put your bodies upon the gears and upon the wheels, upon the levers, upon all the apparatus and you've got to make it stop." When he finished, hundreds of students rushed into the building and organized a sit-in. In the early morning hours 600 policemen moved in and arrested the protesters.

The program and tactics of the FSM and the SDS soon spread to universities throughout the country, but their focus changed as escalating American involvement in Vietnam brought a dramatic expansion of the military draft, and millions of young American men faced the grim prospect of participating in an increasingly unpopular war. In fact, however, Vietnam, like virtually every other American war, was a poor man's fight. In 1965–1966, thanks to deferments and exemptions, college graduates made up only 2 percent of all military inductees. Yet, several thousand male collegians would flee to Canada or Sweden to escape the draft while hundreds of thousands engaged in various protests of a war they considered to be immoral.

In the spring of 1967, 500,000 marchers of all ages converged on New York's Central Park, chanting "Hey, hey, LBJ, how many kids did you kill today?" Dozens of young men ceremoniously burned their draft cards, and the so-called resistance phase of the antiwar movement was born. Thereafter a coalition of protest groups around the country sponsored draft-card burning rallies and sit-ins, which led to numerous arrests. Meanwhile, some SDS leaders were growing even more militant. Inspired by the rhetoric and revolutionary violence of Black Power spokesmen such as Stokely Carmichael, Rap Brown, and Huey Newton, Tom Hayden abandoned his earlier commitment to participatory democracy and passive civil disobedience. "If necessary," he now could "shoot to kill." Not only did SDS embrace violence, it also grew more centralized and authoritarian. Rousseau was now replaced by Lenin as the organization's prophet, and capitalist imperialism replaced university bureaucracy as the primary foe.

During that eventful spring, spreading campus unrest reached a climax with the disruption of Columbia University. There on April 23, 1968, Mark Rudd, leader of the campus SDS chapter, and a small group of radicals led a protest of the university's insensitive decision to disrupt a neighboring black community in order to build a new gymnasium. During the following week more buildings were commandeered, faculty and administrative offices were ransacked, and classes were cancelled. University officials finally called in New York City police. While arresting the protesters, the police injured a number of innocent bystanders. Their excessive force angered many heretofore unaligned students, who staged a strike that shut down the university for the remainder of the semester. Antiwar militants were buoyed by the whole affair, and that same spring similar clashes between students, administrators, and eventually police occurred at Harvard, Cornell, and San Francisco State.

At the August 1968 Democratic convention in Chicago, the polarization of American society reached a tragic and bizarre climax. While inside the tightly-guarded convention hall Democrats were nominating Lyndon Johnson's faithful vice-president, Hubert Humphrey, on Chicago's streets there gathered the whole spectrum of antiwar dissenters, from the earnest supporters of Eugene McCarthy, through the Resistance and the SDS, to the nihilistic Yippies (the Youth International Party). The Yippies were especially determined to provoke anarchy in

The violence at the 1968 Democratic National Convention in Chicago seared the nation.

the streets of Chicago. Abbie Hoffman, one of their leaders, explained that their "conception of revolution is that it's fun."

Yet even the boorish behavior of the Yippies and other anarchic protesters did not justify the unrestrained response of Chicago's arch-conservative Mayor Richard Daley and his army of 12,000 policemen. As a national television audience watched, many of the police went berserk, clubbing and gassing demonstrators as well as bystanders caught up in the chaotic scene. The spectacle lasted three days and generated a wave of anger among many middle-class Americans, anger which Richard Nixon and the Republicans shrewdly exploited at their convention in Miami. At the same time, the Chicago riots helped to fragment the anti-war movement.

By 1968 SDS was breaking up into rival factions, the most extreme of which was the Weathermen, a term derived from Bob Dylan's lyrics: "You don't need a weatherman to know which way the wind is blowing." These hardened young activists, mesmerized by the chic radicalism of Third World guerrillas such as Cuba's Ché Guevara, decided that revolutionary terrorism was the only appropriate strategy. During 1969 and 1970 the Weathermen went on a rampage of violence and disruption, firebombing university and government buildings and killing innocent people—as well as several of themselves. Government forces responded in kind, arresting most of the Weathermen and sending the rest underground.

The mercurial Tom Hayden finally broke with the group, declaring that it was "not the conscience of its generation, but more like its id." By 1971 the New Left was dead as a political movement. In large measure it had committed suicide by abandoning the democratic and pacifist principles that had originally inspired participants and given the movement its moral legitimacy. The larger antiwar movement also began to fade. There would be a final wave of student protests against the Nixon administration in 1970-71, but then campus unrest virtually disappeared as American troops returned home from Vietnam and the draft ended.

If the social mood was changing during the Nixon years, still a large segment of the public persisted in the quest for personal fulfillment *and* social justice. The burgeoning environmental and consumer movements attested to the continuity of Sixties idealism. A *New York Times* survey of college campuses in 1969 revealed that many students were transferring their attention from the antiwar movement to the environment. This ecological conscience would blossom in the 1970s into one of the most compelling items on the nation's social agenda.

THE COUNTERCULTURE The numbing events of 1968 led other disaffected activists away from radical politics altogether and toward another manifestation of the Sixties youth revolt: the "counterculture." Long hair, blue jeans, tie-dyed shirts, sandals, mind-altering drugs, rock music, and group living arrangements were more important than revolutionary ideology or mass protest to the "hippies," the direct descendants of the Beats of the 1950s and the romantic utopians of the 1840s. These advocates of the counterculture were, like their New Left peers, primarily affluent, well-educated young whites alienated by the Vietnam War, racism, political and parental demands, runaway technology, and a crass corporate mentality that equated goodness with goods. Disillusioned with organized political action, they eagerly embraced the tantalizing credo announced by the Harvard professor Timothy Leary, "Turn on to the scene, tune in to what's happening, and drop out."

For some the counterculture primarily entailed the study and practice of Oriental mysticism. For others it focused on the use of hallucinogenic drugs such as LSD. Collective living in urban enclaves such as San Francisco's Haight-Ashbury district or New York's East Village was the rage for a time among the hippies, until conditions grew so crowded and violent that residents migrated elsewhere.

Rural communes also attracted many of the bourgeois rebels. During the 1960s and early 1970s thousands of young and inexperienced romantics flocked to the countryside, eager to be liberated from parental and institutional restraints, to live in harmony with nature, and to coexist in an atmosphere of love and openness. But only a handful of these utopian homesteads survived more than a few months.

Huge outdoor rock music concerts were also a popular source of community for the hippies. The largest of these was the Woodstock Music Festival, held in August 1969 on a 600-acre farm near the tiny rural town of Bethel, New York. For three days over 400,000 young people reveled in good music and cheap marijuana. According to one journalist, the country had never "seen a society so free of repression." But the Woodstock karma was short-lived. When promoters tried to repeat the scene four months later, this time at a Rolling Stones concert in Altamont, California, members of the motorcycle gang Hell's Angels beat to death a black man in front of the stage. Just as the Chicago

The Woodstock festival drew nearly half a million people to a New York farm in August 1969.

WOODSTOCK

3 DAYS OF PEACE
AND MUSIC...AND LOVE

Convention marked the end of the New Left as a vital political force, the violence at Altamont sharply diminished the appeal of the counterculture.

FEMINISM   The logic and lure of liberation that spread during the Sixties helped accelerate a powerful women's rights crusade. Like the New Left, the new feminism drew much of its inspiration and initial tactics from the civil rights movement. Its aim was to challenge the cult of domesticity that had become so firmly entrenched during the 1950s.

The mainstream of the women's movement was led by Betty Friedan. Her influential book, *The Feminine Mystique* (1963), launched a new phase of female protest on a national level. Friedan, a Smith College graduate, had married in 1947 and during the 1950s raised three children in a New York suburb. In 1957 she conducted a poll of her fellow Smith alumnae and discovered that despite the rhetoric about the happy suburban housewife during the Fifties, many were in fact miserable. This revelation led to more research, which culminated in the publication of *The Feminine Mystique*.

Betty Friedan, author of The
Feminine Mystique.

Women, Friedan wrote, had actually lost ground during the
years after World War II, when many left wartime assembly lines
and settled down in suburbia to care for the kids. They were encouraged to do so by advertisers and women's magazines that
promoted the "feminine mystique" of blissful domesticity. In
Friedan's view, the American middle-class home had become "a
comfortable concentration camp" where women saw their individual potential suffocated in an atmosphere of mindless consumption and affluent banality.

An immediate bestseller, *The Feminine Mystique* raised the
consciousness of many women who had long suffered from a feeling of being trapped in a rut. In 1966 Friedan and a small group
of spirited activists founded the National Organization for
Women (NOW), whose membership grew rapidly. NOW spearheaded efforts to end job discrimination on the basis of sex, to
legalize abortion, and to obtain federal and state support
for child-care centers.

Pressured by NOW, Congress and the Supreme Court in the
early 1970s advanced the cause of sexual equality. Under Title
IX of the Educational Amendments Act of 1972, colleges were
required to institute "affirmative action" programs to ensure
equal opportunity for women in such areas as admissions, faculty
and staff hiring, and athletics. In the same year Congress overwhelmingly approved the Equal Rights Amendment (ERA), and
the Supreme Court, in *Roe v. Wade*, struck down state laws forbidding abortions during the first three months of pregnancy on
the grounds of a constitutional right of privacy. Meanwhile,
many bastions of male education, including Yale and Princeton,

led a new movement for coeducation that swept the nation. "If the 1960s belonged to blacks," said one feminist, "the next ten years are ours."

By the end of the 1970s, however, sharp divisions between moderate and radical feminists, as well as the failure of the movement to broaden its appeal much beyond the confines of the white middle class, caused reform efforts to stagnate. In 1982 the ERA died several states short of ratification. And the very success of NOW's efforts to liberalize abortion laws helped generate a powerful reaction, especially among Catholics and fundamentalist Protestants, who mounted a potent "right to life" crusade.

But the success of the women's movement seemed likely to endure despite setbacks. For in fact women were not another minority group pursuing the traditional path of liberal reform. They were a majority: they constituted 51 percent of the population. Their growing political power and expanding presence in the work force combined to constitute one of the most dramatic developments of the era. By 1976 over half the married women in America and nine of ten women college graduates were employed outside the home, a development that one economist called "the single most outstanding phenomenon of this century." Many career women did not regard themselves as feminists; some took jobs because they and their families needed the money to survive or to achieve higher levels of material comfort. Whatever their motives, women were changing traditional sex roles and childbearing practices to accommodate the two-career family, which had replaced the established pattern of male breadwinner and female housekeeper as the new American norm.

MINORITIES The activism that fired the student revolt, the civil rights movement, and the women's rights crusade soon spread to include ethnic minorities, the poor, homosexuals, and the elderly. The nation's fastest growing minority group, the Hispanics, began in the 1960s to organize for political and economic action under the effective leadership of Cesar Chavez, who almost single-handedly founded the United Farm Workers (UFW) in California, then launched a series of strikes for an increase in the wages and benefits of migrant workers. By 1970 the UFW had won recognition from California's grape growers and national visibility for the plight of Hispanic farm laborers through well-publicized boycotts of table grapes and lettuce.

American Indians—many of whom now called themselves Native Americans—also emerged as a new political force in the late 1960s. Two conditions combined to make Indian rights a priority: first, white Americans felt a persistent sense of guilt for the destructive policies of their ancestors toward a people who had, after all, been here first; second, the plight of the Indian minority was more desperate than that of any other minority group in the country. Indian unemployment was ten times the national rate, their life expectancy was twenty years lower than the national average, and the suicide rate was one hundred times higher than that for whites. If blacks in the 1960s had extracted a deserved promise of compensation for past injustices from whites, Indians felt that they had an even more compelling claim on white consciences.

At first the Indian militants adopted the tactics of civil rights and black power activists. In 1968 the American Indian Movement (AIM) was founded on the promise of advancing "red power." The leaders of AIM occupied Alcatraz Island in San Francisco Bay in 1969, claiming the site "by right of discovery." And in 1972 an Indian sit-in at the Bureau of Indian Affairs in Washington attracted national attention to their cause. Soon Indian protesters discovered a more effective tactic than direct action and sit-ins. They went into Federal courts armed with copies of old treaties and demanded that these become the basis for restitution. In Alaska, Maine, and Massachusetts they won significant settlements that provided legal recognition of their tribal rights and financial compensation at levels that upgraded the standard of living on several reservations.

GAY RIGHTS   The liberationist impulses of the sixties encouraged homosexuals to organize and assert their own right to equal treatment and common dignity. On June 17, 1969, New York City police raided the Stonewall Inn, a gay bar in the heart of Greenwich Village. Efforts to close down homosexual gathering places were then commonplace around the country. But this time the patrons fought back and the struggle spilled into the streets, and hundreds of other gays and their supporters joined the fracas against the police. Rioting lasted throughout the weekend, and when it ended gays had forged a new sense of solidarity and a new organization called the Gay Liberation Front. "Gay is good for all of us," proclaimed one member of the GLF. "The artificial categories 'heterosexual' and 'homosexual' have been laid on us by a sexist society. As gays we demand an end to the gender programming which starts when we are born."

As news of the Stonewall riots spread across the country, the gay rights movement assumed national proportions. One of its main tactics was to encourage people to "come out" and make public their homosexuality. This was by no means an easy decision, for professing gays faced social ostracism, physical abuse, exclusion from the military and civil service, and discrimination in the workplace. Yet despite the risks, thousands of homosexuals did "come out." By 1973 almost 800 gay and lesbian organizations had been formed across the country, and every major city had a visible gay community and cultural life. One commentator noticed "an explosion of things gay." There were gay churches, synagogues, health clinics, community centers, restaurants, and a host of other social and business entities. Homosexuals started their own newspapers and gained election to public offices. In 1974 gay activists convinced the American Psychiatric Association to remove its classification of homosexuality as a "mental disorder" from its official diagnostic manual. The following year the U. S. Civil Service Commission lifted its ban on the employment of homosexuals.

But as was the case with the civil rights crusade and the women's movement, the campaign for gay rights soon suffered from internal divisions and a conservative backlash. Gay activists engaged in increasingly fractious disputes over tactics and objectives. Lesbian leaders, for instance, accused male homosexuals of being chauvinists insensitive to issues peculiar to women. One woman radical saw no common ground between the two groups: "Lesbians are feminists, not homosexuals." Even more threatening to the gay community during the seventies was the nationwide counterattack launched by conservative moralists and Christian fundamentalists. In Miami, Florida, St. Paul, Minnesota, and Wichita, Kansas, they successfully repealed new laws banning discrimination against homosexuals. True equality had yet to be achieved. By the end of the decade the gay movement had lost its initial momentum and was struggling to salvage many of its hard-won gains, just as an even more ominous threat emerged on the horizon in the form of AIDS.

Nixon and Vietnam

The numerous liberation movements of the 1960s fundamentally changed the tone and texture of American social life. But by the early 1970s there were signs that the pendulum of national mood was swinging back toward conservatism. The election of Richard Nixon and Spiro Agnew in 1968 and the rise of George Wallace as a serious political force on the radical Right reflected the emergence of the "silent majority"—those white working-class and middle-class citizens who were determined to regain control of a society they felt had become awash in permissiveness and special pleading.

Large as the gap was between the "silent majority" and the varied forces of dissent, they agreed on one thing: that the Vietnam War remained the dominant event of the time. Until the war was ended and all American troops were returned home, the nation would find it difficult to achieve the equilibrium that the new president had promised. In his State of the Union message of 1970, President Nixon called on Americans to pursue "the lift of a driving dream," a memorable phrase that reporters asked him to define. "Well, before we can get the lift of a driving dream," Nixon explained, "we have to get rid of the nightmares we inherited. One of the nightmares is a war without end."

GRADUAL WITHDRAWAL The Nixon administration promised a new course in Vietnam. Nixon and his special assistant for national security affairs, Henry Kissinger, claimed to have a secret plan to achieve "peace with honor." But peace was long in coming and not very honorable when it came.

The administration's new strategy in Vietnam moved along three separate fronts. The first front was at the deadlocked Paris peace talks, where American negotiators demanded the withdrawal of North Vietnamese forces from South Vietnam and the preservation of the American-supported regime of President Nguyen Van Thieu. The North Vietnamese and Vietcong negotiators, however, insisted on retaining a military presence in the south and reunifying the Vietnamese people under a government dominated by the Communists. There was no common ground on which to come together.

At the same time, Nixon tried to defuse domestic unrest generated by the war. To this end he sought to "Vietnamize" the conflict by turning over most of the combat missions to Vietnamese units and sharply reducing the number of American ground forces. To assuage the South Vietnamese he provided more equipment and training for their troops. From a peak of 540,000 in 1969, American combat units were withdrawn at a gradual and steady pace. By 1973 only 50,000 American troops remained in Vietnam. In December 1969 Nixon had also established a lottery system that clarified the likelihood of being drafted—only those with low lottery numbers would have to go. Nixon was more successful in achieving the goal of reducing antiwar activity than at forcing concessions from the North Vietnamese in Paris.

While reducing the number of American combat troops in Vietnam, Nixon and Kissinger secretly expanded the air war in an effort to persuade the enemy to come to terms. On March 18, 1969, American planes began "Operation Menu," a fourteen-month-long bombing of Communist sanctuaries in Cambodia. Over 100,000 tons of bombs were dropped, four times the tonnage dropped on Japan during World War II. Congress did not learn of these raids until April 1970, when Nixon announced what he called an "incursion" by United States troops into supposedly "neutral" Cambodia to "clean out" North Vietnamese staging areas.

DIVISIONS AT HOME   News of the Cambodia "incursion" came on the heels of another incident that rekindled public indignation against the war. Late in 1969 the story of the My Lai massacre broke. During the next two years the public learned the gruesome tale of Army Lieutenant William Calley, who ordered the murder of over 200 Vietnamese civilians in My Lai village in March 1968. Twenty-five officers were charged with complicity in the massacre and subsequent cover up, but only Calley was convicted of murder. Nixon shortly thereafter granted him parole.

The loudest public outcry against Nixon's Indochina policy occurred in the wake of the Cambodian "incursion." Campuses across the country witnessed a new wave of protests in May 1970. At Kent State University the Ohio National Guard was called in to quell rioting during which the campus ROTC build-

"Son. . . !" "Dad . . . !" *The Vietnam War caused vehement divisions between "hawks" and "doves," old and young, even parents and children.*

ing was burned. Pelted by rocks and verbal taunts, the inexperienced guardsmen panicked and opened fire on the
demonstrators, killing four. Eleven days later, on May 15, Mississippi highway patrolmen riddled a dormitory at Jackson State
College with bullets, killing two black students.

Although an official investigation of the Kent State episode
condemned the "casual and indiscriminate shooting," polls indicated that the American public supported the actions by the
National Guard; students had "got what they were asking for."

The following year, in June 1971, the *New York Times* began
publishing excerpts from a secret Defense Department study.
The so-called *Pentagon Papers*, leaked to the press by a former
Pentagon official, Daniel Ellsberg, confirmed what many critics
of the war had long suspected: Congress and the people had not
received the full story on the Gulf of Tonkin incident of 1964.
Contingency plans for American entry into the war were being
drawn up even while Johnson was promising the American people that combat troops would never be sent to Vietnam. The
Nixon administration attempted to block publication of the *Pentagon Papers*, arguing that publication would endanger national
security and prolong the war. By a vote of 6 to 3 the Supreme
Court ruled against the government. Newspapers throughout
the country began publication the next day.

WAR WITHOUT END   Although Nixon's decision in the spring of
1970 to use American forces to root out Communist bases in
Cambodia did bring a tactical victory, it also served to widen a
war he had promised to end. Moreover, his hopes that the South
Vietnamese units replacing American forces could hold their
own against the North Vietnamese were dashed when they suffered repeated defeats in 1971 and 1972. Disorganized, poorly
led, and lacking tenacity, the South Vietnamese soldiers had
to call upon American airpower to fend off North Vietnamese
offensives.

The deteriorating ground war along with mounting social divisions at home and the approach of the 1972 presidential elections combined to produce a shift in the American negotiating
position in Paris. In the summer of 1972 Henry Kissinger
dropped his insistence on the removal of all North Vietnamese
troops from the south before the withdrawal of American troops.
On October 26, only a week before the American presidential
election, he announced: "Peace is at hand." But the Thieu regime in South Vietnam objected to the plan for a cease-fire, understandably fearful that the continued presence of North

Vietnamese troops in the south virtually guaranteed an eventual Communist victory. Hanoi then stiffened its position by demanding that Thieu resign.

The talks broke off on December 16, and Nixon told his military advisers that only a massive show of American airpower would make the North Vietnamese more cooperative at the negotiating table. Two days later the United States unleashed furious B-52 raids on Hanoi and Haiphong. The so-called "Christmas bombings" aroused world-wide protest, but Henry Kissinger claimed Nixon's "jugular diplomacy" worked, for the talks in Paris soon resumed. On January 27, 1973, the United States signed an "agreement on ending the war and restoring peace in Vietnam." The agreement showed that despite the Christmas bombings, the North Vietnamese never altered their basic stance: they kept troops in the south and remained committed to the reunification of Vietnam under one government. What had changed since the previous fall was the willingness of the South Vietnamese to accept these terms, albeit reluctantly, on the basis of Nixon's promise that the United States would respond "with full force" to any violation of the agreement.

On March 29, 1973, the last American combat troops left Vietnam, leaving behind several thousand who were declared "missing in action." On that same day the last of several hundred American prisoners-of-war, most of them downed pilots, were released from Hanoi. Within a period of months, however, the war between north and south resumed, and the military superiority and greater political unity of the Communist forces soon became evident. In Cambodia and Laos, where fighting had been more sporadic, Communist victory also seemed inevitable. In March 1975 the North Vietnamese launched a full-scale armored invasion against the south. President Thieu appealed to Washington for assistance, but the Democratic majority in Congress refused, and on April 30 Americans watched on television as North Vietnamese tanks rolled into Saigon, soon to be named Ho Chi Minh City. The scene at the American embassy in Saigon, where thousands of terrified Vietnamese fought to board the last American helicopters, provided a poignant and tragic ending to America's greatest foreign policy disaster.

The longest war in American history was over, leaving in its wake a bitter legacy. The war described as a noble crusade in behalf of democratic ideals instead suggested that democracy was not easily transferrable to Third World regions, which lacked any historical experience with liberal values and representative government. The war designed to serve as a showcase for American

As Saigon falls to the North Vietnamese, mobs scale the fourteen-foot wall of the U.S. Embassy to reach helicopters for evacuation, May 1, 1975.

military power instead eroded respect for the military so thoroughly that many young Americans came to regard military service as inherently corrupting and ignoble. The war, fought to show the world that the United States was united in its convictions, instead divided Americans more drastically than any event since the Civil War. The Vietnam war cost the nation some 57,000 deaths and $150 billion. Little wonder that the dominant reaction to the war's end was the urge to "put Vietnam behind us" and revert to a non-interventionist foreign policy.

NIXON AND MIDDLE AMERICA

Richard Nixon had been elected in 1968 as the representative of "Middle America," those citizens fed up with the liberal politics and social radicalism of the 1960s. The Nixon cabinet and White House staff reflected the values of this "silent majority." The chief figures were John Mitchell, the gruff attorney-general who had made his fortune as a lawyer in Nixon's old firm, and H. R. Haldeman and John Ehrlichman, advisors on domestic policy whose major experience before their association with the

Nixon campaign had been in advertising. The cabinet was all white, all male, all Republican. "There are no blooded patricians in the lot," said *Time* magazine, "just strivers who have acted out the middle-class dream."

DOMESTIC AFFAIRS   Confronting a Congress controlled by Democrats, Richard Nixon focused his energies on foreign policy, where presidential initiatives were less restricted and where he, in tandem with Kissinger, achieved several stunning breakthroughs. The domestic front became a holding action in which Nixon, like Eisenhower before him, found it difficult to stop the march of liberal programs.

Despite the efforts of the Nixon administration, the civil rights legislation enacted during the Johnson years continued to take effect. Administration officials launched a concerted effort in 1970 to block congressional renewal of the Voting Rights Act and to delay implementation of court orders requiring the desegregation of school districts in Mississippi. Congress then extended the Voting Rights Act over Nixon's veto, and the Supreme Court, in the first decision made under the new Chief Justice Warren Burger—a Nixon appointee—ordered the integration of the Mississippi schools. More schools were desegregated during Nixon's first term than in all the Kennedy-Johnson years combined.

Nixon's attempts to block desegregation efforts in urban areas also failed. The Burger Court ruled unanimously in *Swann v. Charlotte-Mecklenburg Board of Education* (1971) that cities must bus students out of their neighborhoods if necessary to achieve integration. Protest over desegregation now began to manifest itself more in the North than in the South, as white families in Boston, Denver, and other cities denounced the destruction of "the neighborhood school." Busing opponents won a limited victory when the Supreme Court ruled in 1974 that requiring the transfer of students from the inner city to the suburbs was unconstitutional. This ruling, along with the *Bakke v. Board of Regents of California* (1978) decision, which restricted the use of quotas to achieve racial balance in university classrooms, marked the transition of desegregation from an issue of simple justice to a more tangled thicket of conflicting group and individual rights.

It also reflected the growing conservatism of the Supreme Court, a trend encouraged and engineered by Nixon. The litany of liberal decisions during the 1960s had made the Warren Court a prime target for mostly middle-class Americans who resented what they regarded as the federal government's excessive protection of the "undeserving." Fate and the aging of the justices on the Warren Court gave Nixon the chance to make four new appointments. Only one, William Rehnquist, would consistently support Nixon's conservative interpretation of the Constitution, but overall the tenor of the Court did shift toward a more moderate stance.

Nixon also fervently desired to reverse the welfare state policies of his Democratic predecessors and decentralize responsibility for social programs. To that end he proposed, and got from Congress in 1972, a five-year revenue-sharing plan that would distribute $30 billion of federal revenues to the states for use as they saw fit. But the administration never succeeded in developing a comprehensive domestic agenda acceptable to Congress. Frustrated by the Democratic majority on Capitol Hill, Nixon sent Vice-President Spiro Agnew on a national speaking tour in the fall of 1969 to assault the opposition. Agnew described war protesters as "anarchists and ideological eunuchs," the liberal news media as "an effete corps of impudent snobs" and "nattering nabobs of negativism."

But while Agnew turned phrases, the Democratic Congress moved forward with new legislation: the right of eighteen-year-olds to vote in national elections (1970) and, under the Twenty-sixth Amendment (1971), in state and local elections as well; increases in Social Security benefits tied to the inflation rate; a rise in food-stamp funding; the Occupational Safety and Health Act (1970), and the Federal Election Campaign Act (1972).

During Nixon's first term Americans in large numbers began to lobby for government action to improve and protect the natural environment. In April 1970 hundreds of thousands of activists rallied across the country in support of the first "Earth Day." In response, Congress established new programs to control water pollution and passed the Clean Air Act (1970) over Nixon's veto. Congress also created the Environmental Protection Agency (EPA) to oversee federal guidelines for air pollution, toxic wastes, and water quality. The EPA began requiring developers to perform environmental impact studies before new construction could begin. The agency also set fuel efficiency standards for automobiles and required manufacturers to reduce the level of carbon monoxide emissions from car engines.

ECONOMIC MALAISE The major domestic development during the Nixon years was a floundering economy. The inflation rate began to rise in 1967, when it was at 3 percent. By 1973 it reached 9 percent; a year later it was at 12 percent, and it remained in double digits for most of the 1970s. Unemployment, at a low of 3.3 percent when Nixon took office, climbed to 6 percent by the end of 1970 and threatened to keep rising. Somehow the American economy was undergoing a recession and inflation at the same time. Economists coined the term "stagflation" to describe the syndrome that defied the orthodox laws of economics.

The economic malaise had at least three deep-rooted causes. First, the Johnson administration had attempted to pay for both the Great Society and the war in Vietnam without a major tax increase, thus generating larger deficits, a major expansion of the money supply, and rapid price inflation. Second, and more important, by the late 1960s American goods faced stiff competition in international markets from West Germany, Japan, and other emerging industrial powers. This sharply reduced the export of American goods and generated a growing trade deficit.

Third, the American economy had grown heavily dependent on cheap sources of energy. Just as domestic petroleum reserves began to dwindle and dependence on foreign sources increased, the Organization of Petroleum Exporting Countries (OPEC), centered in the Middle East, combined to use their oil as a political and economic weapon. In 1973, when the United States sent massive aid to Israel during the Yom Kippur War, OPEC announced that it would not sell oil to nations supporting Israel and that it was raising its prices by 400 percent. American motorists thereafter faced long lines at gas stations, schools and offices closed down, factories cut production, and the inflation rate soared.

Another condition leading to stagflation was the flood of new workers—mainly baby boomers and women—entering the labor market. From 1965 to 1980 the work force grew by 40 percent, or almost 30 million workers, a figure greater than the total labor force of France or West Germany. The number of new jobs created could not keep up, leaving many unemployed. At the same time, worker productivity declined, pushing up prices in the face of rising demand.

Stagflation posed a new set of economic problems, but the Nixon administration responded erratically and ineffectively with old remedies. First, it tried to reduce the federal deficit by raising taxes and cutting the budget. When the Democratic Congress refused to cooperate with this approach, the White House encouraged the Federal Reserve Board to reduce the money supply by raising interest rates. But the move backfired as the stock market immediately collapsed, plunging the economy into the "Nixon recession."

A sense of desperation then infected the White House. In 1969, when asked about wage and price controls, Nixon had been unequivocal: "Controls. Oh, my God, no! . . . We'll never go to controls." On August 15, 1971, however, he reversed himself. He froze all wages and prices for ninety days, but still the economy floundered. By 1973 the wage and price guidelines were made voluntary, and therefore almost entirely ineffective. Stagflation continued, and it would plague the economy for the rest of the decade.

NIXON TRIUMPHANT

CHINA If the economy's ailments proved more than Nixon could remedy, in foreign policy his administration managed to improve American relations with the major powers of the Communist world—China and the Soviet Union—and to shift fundamentally the pattern of the Cold War. In July 1971 Henry Kissinger made a secret trip to Peking to explore the possibility of American recognition of China. Seven months later, in February 1972, Nixon arrived in Peking and made recognition an official and public fact. The irony of the event was overwhelming. Richard Nixon, the former anticommunist crusader who had condemned the

President Nixon and the chairman of the Chinese Communist party, Mao Tse-tung, February 1972.

State Department for "losing" China in 1949, accomplished a diplomatic feat his more liberal predecessors could not.

DÉTENTE   China sought the breakthrough in relations with the United States because its rivalry with the Soviet Union, with which it shares a long border, had become increasingly bitter. Soviet leaders, troubled by the Sino-American agreements, were also anxious for an easing of tensions now that they had, as the result of a huge arms buildup following the Cuban missile crisis, achieved virtual parity with the United States in nuclear weapons. Once again the president surprised the world by announcing that he would visit Moscow in May 1972 for discussions with Leonid Brezhnev, the Soviet premier.

What became known as "détente" with the Soviets offered the promise of a more orderly and restrained competition between the two superpowers. Nixon and Brezhnev signed the Strategic Arms Limitation Talks (SALT) agreement, which set ceilings for each nation on the number of intercontinental ballistic missiles (ICBMs) and sharp limits to the construction of antiballistic missile systems (ABMs). In effect the Soviets were allowed to retain a greater number of missiles with greater destructive power while the United States retained a lead in the total number of warheads. No limitations were placed on new weapons systems, though each side agreed to work toward a permanent freeze on all nuclear weapons.

SHUTTLE DIPLOMACY   The Nixon-Kissinger initiatives in the Middle East were less dramatic and conclusive than the China or Russia agreements, but did show that America recognized Arab power in the region and its own dependence on the oil from Islamic states fundamentally opposed to Israel. After Israel recovered from the initial shock of the Arab attacks that triggered the Yom Kippur War of 1973, it recaptured the Golan Heights and seized additional Syrian territory. Kissinger initiated the negotiations leading to a cease-fire and exerted pressure to prevent Israel from taking more Arab territory. American reliance on Arab oil led to closer ties with Egypt and its president, Anwar el-Sadat, and more restrained support for Israel. Kissinger, whose "shuttle diplomacy" among the capitals of the Middle East won acclaim from all sides, failed to find a comprehensive peace formula for the troubled region and ignored altogether the problem of establishing a homeland for Palestinian refugees. But his efforts did lay groundwork for the subsequent accord between Israel and Egypt in 1977.

THE 1972 ELECTION Nixon's foreign policy achievements allowed him to stage the campaign of 1972 as a triumphal procession. The main threat to his reelection came from George Wallace, who had the potential as a third-party candidate to deprive the Republicans of conservative votes and thereby throw the election to the Democrats or the Democratic-controlled Congress. But on May 15, 1972, Wallace was shot and left permanently paralyzed below the waist by a white midwesterner and was forced to withdraw from the campaign.

Meanwhile the Democrats were further ensuring Nixon's victory by nominating Senator George S. McGovern of South Dakota, a former college history professor and crusading liberal whose antiwar and social welfare positions were associated with the turbulence of the 1960s. At the Democratic convention party reforms helped McGovern's nomination by increasing the representation of women, blacks, and minorities, but these reforms alienated the party regulars. Chicago's Mayor Richard Daley was actually ousted from the convention, and the AFL-CIO refused to endorse the Democratic candidate.

Nixon won the greatest victory of any Republican presidential candidate in history, winning 520 electoral votes to only 17 for McGovern. During the course of the campaign McGovern complained about the "dirty tricks" of the Nixon administration, most especially the curious incident during the summer of 1972 in which burglars were caught breaking into the Democratic National Committee headquarters in the Watergate apartment complex in Washington. McGovern's accusations seemed shrill and biased at the time, the lamentations of an obvious loser. Nixon and his staff made plans for "four more years" as the investigation of the fateful Watergate break-in unfolded.

WATERGATE

Under the relentless prodding of Judge John J. Sirica, one of the Watergate burglars began to tell the full story of the Nixon administration's complicity in the episode. James W. McCord, a former CIA agent and security chief for the Committee to Reelect the President (CREEP), was the first of many informers and penitents in a melodrama that unfolded over the next two years. It ended in the first resignation of a president in American history, the conviction and imprisonment of twenty-five officials of the Nixon administration, including four cabinet members, and the most serious constitutional crisis since the impeachment trial of President Andrew Johnson.

UNCOVERING THE COVER-UP   The trail of evidence pursued by Judge Sirica, a grand jury and several special prosecutors, and a televised Senate investigation headed by Samuel J. Ervin, Jr., of North Carolina, led directly to the White House. No evidence surfaced that Nixon had ordered the break-in or that he had been aware of plans to burglarize the Democratic National Committee. But from the start Nixon participated in the cover-up, using his presidential powers to discredit and block the investigation. Perhaps most alarming was the discovery that the Watergate burglary was merely one small part of a larger pattern of corruption and criminality sanctioned by the Nixon White House. Since 1970, Nixon had ordered intelligence agencies to spy on his most outspoken opponents, open their mail, and even burglarize their homes in an effort to uncover compromisng information.

The cover-up unraveled further in April 1973 when L. Patrick Gray, acting director of the FBI, resigned after confessing that he had destroyed several incriminating documents. On April 30 Ehrlichman and Haldeman resigned, together with Attorney-General Richard Kleindienst. A few days later Nixon nervously assured the public in a television address: "I'm not a crook." But new evidence suggested otherwise. John Dean, whom Nixon had

Sen. Sam Ervin (D-N.C.), chairman of the Senate Watergate Committee, swears in the ex-White House counsel John Dean, whose testimony linked President Nixon to the coverup.

dismissed as presidential counsel, testified before the Ervin Committee and a rapt television audience that Nixon had approved the cover-up. In another "bombshell" disclosure, a White House aide told the committee that Nixon had installed a taping system in the White House and that many of the conversations about Watergate had been recorded.

A year-long battle for the "Nixon tapes" then began. The Harvard law professor Archibald Cox, whom Nixon had appointed as a special prosecutor to handle the Watergate case, took the president to court in October 1973 to obtain the tapes. Nixon, pleading "executive privilege," refused to release them and ordered Cox fired. In what became known as the "Saturday Night Massacre," the new attorney-general, Elliot Richardson, and his deputy resigned rather than execute the order. Cox's replacement as special prosecutor, Leon Jaworski, proved no more pliable than Cox, and he also took the president to court. On July 24, 1974, the Supreme Court ruled unanimously that the president must surrender the tapes. A few days later the House Judiciary Committee voted to recommend three articles of impeachment: obstruction of justice through the payment of "hush money" to witnesses and the withholding of evidence; using federal agencies to deprive citizens of their constitutional rights; and de-

Having resigned his office, Richard Nixon waves farewell outside the White House, August 9, 1974.

fiance of Congress by withholding the tapes. Before the House of Representatives could meet to vote on impeachment, however, Nixon handed over the complete set of White House tapes. On August 9, 1974, fully aware that the evidence on the tapes implicated him in the cover-up, Richard Nixon resigned from office.

EFFECTS OF WATERGATE   Vice-President Spiro Agnew did not succeed Nixon because Agnew himself had been forced to resign in October 1973 when it became known that he had accepted bribes from contractors before and during his term as vice-president. The vice-president at the time of Nixon's resignation was Gerald Ford, the former minority leader in the House, whom Nixon had appointed with congressional approval, under the provisions of the Twenty-fifth Amendment (1967). Ford insisted that he had no intention of pardoning Nixon, who was still liable for criminal prosecution. But a month after Nixon's resignation the new president issued the pardon, explaining that it was necessary to end the national obsession with the Watergate scandals. Many suspected that Nixon and Ford had made a deal, though there was no evidence to confirm the speculation.

If there was a silver lining in Watergate's dark cloud, it was the vigor and resiliency of the institutions that had brought a president down—the press, Congress, the courts, and an aroused public opinion. The Watergate revelations provoked Congress to pass several pieces of legislation designed to curb executive power in the future. The War Powers Act (1973) required presidents to consult with Congress before sending American troops into combat abroad and to withdraw troops after sixty days unless Congress specifically approved their stay. In an effort to correct abuses of campaign funds, Congress enacted legislation in 1974 that set new ceilings on contributions and expenditures. And in reaction to the Nixon claim of "executive privilege," Congress strengthened the 1966 Freedom of Information Act to require prompt responses to requests for information from government files and to place on government agencies the burden of proof for classifying information.

The nation had weathered a profound constitutional crisis, but the aftershock of the Watergate episode produced a deep sense of disillusionment with the so-called "imperial presidency." Coming on the heels of the erosion of public confidence generated by the Vietnam War, the Watergate affair renewed public cynicism toward a government that had systematically lied to the people and violated their civil liberties. Said one bumper sticker of the day: "Don't vote. It only encourages them." Restoring credibility and respect became the primary challenge facing Nixon's successors. Unfortunately, a new array of economic and foreign crises would make that task doubly difficult.

AN UNELECTED PRESIDENT

While the Watergate crisis dominated the Washington scene, major domestic and foreign problems received little executive attention. The perplexing combination of inflation and recession worsened, as did the oil crisis. At the same time, Henry Kissinger, who assumed virtually complete control over the management of foreign policy, watched helplessly as the South Vietnamese forces began to crumble before North Vietnamese attacks, attempted with limited success to establish a framework for peace in the Middle East, and supported a CIA role in overthrowing the popularly elected Marxist president of Chile.

THE FORD YEARS   Gerald Ford inherited these simmering problems, as well as the burden of being an unelected president. An amiable, honest man, Ford enjoyed widespread popular support for only a short time. "I am a Ford, not a Lincoln," he candidly recognized upon becoming vice-president. His pardon of Nixon on September 8, 1974, generated a storm of criticism. And as president he soon adopted the posture he had developed as a conservative minority leader in the House: a nay-saying leader of the opposition who believed that the federal government exercised too much power over domestic affairs. In his fifteen months as president, Ford vetoed thirty-nine bills, thereby outstripping Herbert Hoover's veto record in less than half the time. By resisting congressional pressure to reduce taxes and increase federal spending, he succeeded in plummeting the economy into the deepest recession since the Great Depression. Unemployment jumped to 9 percent in 1975, and the federal deficit hit a record $60 billion the next year. Ford rejected wage and price controls to curb inflation, preferring voluntary restraints.

In foreign policy, Ford retained Henry Kissinger as secretary of state and attempted to pursue Nixon's goals of stability in the Middle East, rapprochement with China, and détente with the Soviet Union. Late in 1974 Ford met with Russia's Leonid Brezhnev and accepted the framework for another arms-control agreement that was to serve as the basis for SALT II. Meanwhile Kissinger's tireless shuttling between Cairo and Tel Aviv produced an agreement: Israel promised to return to Egypt most of the Sinai territory captured in the 1967 war, and the two nations agreed to rely on negotiations rather than force to settle future disagreements.

These limited but significant achievements should have enhanced Ford's image, but they were drowned in the sea of criticism and carping that followed the collapse of South Vietnam in May 1975. Not only had a decade of American effort in Vietnam proven futile, but the Khmer Rouge, the Cambodian Communist movement, had also won a resounding victory, plunging that country into a fanatical bloodbath. And the OPEC oil cartel was threatening another boycott while other Third World nations denounced the United States as a depraved imperialistic power.

THE 1976 ELECTION   In the midst of such turmoil, the Democrats could hardly wait for the 1976 election. At the Republican convention Ford managed to thwart a powerful challenge for the nomination from the former California governor and Hollywood actor, Ronald Reagan. The Democrats chose an obscure former naval officer turned peanut farmer who had served one term as governor of Georgia. Jimmy Carter capitalized on the post-Watergate cynicism by promising never to "tell a lie to the American people" and by citing his independence from traditional Washington power politics.

To the surprise of many pundits Carter revived the New Deal coalition of southern whites, blacks, urban labor, and ethnic groups to win the election, 41 million votes to Ford's 39 million. Polls showed that the Carter victory benefited from a heavy turnout of blacks in the South, where he swept every state but Virginia. Minnesota Senator Walter F. Mondale, Carter's liberal running mate and a favorite among blue-collar workers and the urban poor, also gave the ticket a big boost. The real story of the election, however, was the low voter turnout. Almost half of America's eligible voters, apparently alienated by Watergate and the lackluster candidates, chose to sit out the election.

THE CARTER INTERREGNUM

EARLY SUCCESSES   During the first two years of his term, Carter enjoyed several successes. His administration appointed more blacks, Hispanics, and women than any before and offered amnesty to the thousands of young men who had fled the country rather than serve in Vietnam, closing one of the remaining open wounds of that traumatic event. He reformed the civil service to provide rewards for meritorious performance, and he created new cabinet-level Departments of Energy and Education. Carter also pushed significant environmental legislation through Congress, including a bill to regulate strip mining, and a "superfund" to clean up chemical waste sites.

His success was short-lived. Carter's political predicament emerged during the debate over energy policy. Borrowing a phrase from the turn-of-the-century philosopher William James, the president declared that solving the energy problem must become "the moral equivalent of war" for the nation, and he presented the Congress with what he called "a comprehensive energy program" that would ensure victory. Carter's energy bill called for the creation of a cabinet-level Department of Energy, tax incentives and penalties to encourage conservation and new oil and gas production as well as solar power and synthetic fuels, and the increased development of nuclear power as a "last resort." Yet the energy bill passed in August 1978 was a gutted version of the original. It focused primarily on new oil and gas production rather than conservation. Carter and his aides lacked the experience and the flexibility to maneuver his proposals around congressional obstacles.

In the summer of 1979, when renewed violence in the Middle East produced a second fuel shortage, motorists were forced to wait in long lines again for limited supplies of gasoline that they regarded as excessively expensive. Soon they directed their frustration at the White House. Opinion polls showed Carter with an approval rating of 26 percent, lower than Nixon during the worst moments of the Watergate crisis. Faced with such vanishing support, Carter solicited advice from an array of national leaders during an extraordinary retreat at Camp David, Maryland. He emerged ten days later and proclaimed that the nation required "a rebirth of the American spirit." He also announced a "new and positive energy program." It fell on skeptical ears. A Phoenix newspaper editorialized: "The nation did not tune in Carter to hear a sermon. It wanted answers. It did not get them." Congress only partially funded the major feature of his new program—synthetic energy research.

Several of Carter's early foreign policy initiatives also got caught in political crossfires. Soon after his inauguration Carter vowed that "the soul of our foreign policy" should be the defense of human rights abroad. But the human rights campaign drew sniping from several sides: those who feared it sacrificed a detached appraisal of national interest for high-level moralizing, and those who pointed to the administration's inconsistency in applying the standard.

Similarly, Carter's successful negotiation of treaties to turn over control of the Panama Canal to the Panamanian government in twenty years generated intense criticism. Even though administration spokesmen reminded Americans that Theodore Roosevelt himself had admitted "stealing" the Canal Zone for American use, many political conservatives flayed Carter's judicious decision all the same. Republican Ronald Reagan manipulated historical fact by claiming that the Canal Zone was sovereign American soil purchased "fair and square." Carter argued that the limitations on American influence in Latin America, and the deep resentment toward American colonialism in Panama, left the United States with no choice. The Senate ratified the treaties by a paper-thin margin (68 to 32, two votes more than the required two-thirds). The Canal Zone would revert in stages to Panama by 1999.

THE CAMP DAVID ACCORDS   Carter's crowning diplomatic achievement was the arrangement of a peace agreement between Israel and Egypt. In September 1978 Carter invited Egypt's President

Egyptian President Anwar Sadat (left), Jimmy Carter, and Israeli Prime Minister Menachem Begin at the announcement of the Camp David accords, September 1978.

Anwar el-Sadat and Israeli Prime Minister Menachem Begin to Camp David for two weeks of difficult negotiations. The first part of the eventual agreement required Israel to return all land in the Sinai in exchange for Egyptian recognition of Israel's sovereignty. But the second part of the agreement, calling for Israel to negotiate with Sadat a resolution to the Palestinian refugee dilemma, began to unravel soon after the Camp David summit. Still, Carter and Secretary of State Cyrus Vance had orchestrated a dramatic display of high-level diplomacy that, whatever its limitations, made an all-out war between Israel and the Arab world less likely. It also represented a significant first step toward a comprehensive settlement of the region's volatile tensions.

MOUNTING TROUBLES Carter's crowning failure was his management of the economy. In effect he inherited a bad situation and left it worse. Carter employed the same economic policies as Nixon and Ford to fight stagflation, but he reversed the order of the federal "cure," preferring to fight unemployment first with a tax cut and increased public spending. Unemployment declined slightly, from 8 to 7 percent in 1977, but inflation soared; at 5 percent when he took office, it reached 10 percent in 1978 and kept rising. During one month in 1980 it measured an annual rate of 18 percent. Like previous presidents, Carter then reversed himself to fight the other side of the economic malaise. By midterm he was delaying tax reductions and vetoing government spending programs that he had proposed in his first year. The result, however, was the worst of all possible worlds—a deepened recession with unemployment at 7.5 percent in 1980, mortgage rates at 15 percent, interest rates at an all-time high of 20 percent, and a runaway inflation averaging between 12 and 13 percent.

The conclusion of the SALT II treaty with the Soviets in June 1979 put Carter's leadership to the test just as the mounting economic problems made him the subject of biting editorial cartoons. To quell his conservative critics, who charged that SALT II would give the Soviets a decided advantage in the number and destructive power of land-based missiles, Carter announced that the United States would build the new MX missile system

But the SALT II treaty became moot in December 1979 when the Soviet army invaded Afghanistan in order to extend "fraternal assistance" to the faltering Communist government there, which was being challenged by Muslim rebels. While continuing the MX missile program, Carter immediately shelved SALT II, suspended grain shipments to the Soviet Union, and began a campaign for an international boycott of the 1980 Olympics, which were to be held that summer in Moscow. Zbigniew Brzezinski, Carter's hard-line national security advisor, won out over Cyrus Vance in the behind-the-scenes shuffling for influence and persuaded the president that the Soviet invasion of Afghanistan was only the first step in a Soviet scheme to dominate the oil-rich Persian Gulf. Calling the Soviet invasion "the gravest threat to world peace since World War II," Carter threatened that the United States would oppose by force any further Soviet advances in the Middle East.

IRAN   Then the Iranian crisis exploded in a year-long barrage of unwelcome events that epitomized the inability of the United States to control world events. The crisis began in January 1979 with the overthrow of the shah of Iran, long a staunch American ally and right-wing dictator. The revolutionaries who toppled the shah rallied around Ayatollah Ruhollah Khomeini, a fundamentalist Muslim leader who symbolized the Islamic values the shah had tried to replace with Western ways. Khomeini's hatred of the United States dated back to 1953 when the CIA had sponsored the overthrow of Iran's Prime Minister Mohammed Mossadegh, an ardent nationalist who sought to rid his country of western influence and interests. The 1953 coup had restored the shah's regime to power. Late in October 1979, Carter allowed the exiled shah to enter the United States in order to undergo cancer treatment. A few days later, on November 4, a frenzied mob stormed the American embassy in Teheran and seized the staff. Khomeini applauded the mob action and demanded the shah's return along with all his wealth in exchange for the release of the fifty-three American hostages. In the meantime the Iranian militants staged daily demonstrations, burning the American flag and effigies of Carter for the benefit of worldwide news and television coverage.

Carter was furious, but his options were limited. He appealed to the United Nations, protesting what was a clear violation of diplomatic immunity and international law. But Khomeini scoffed at U.N. requests for the release of hostages. Carter then froze all Iranian assets in the United States and appealed to American allies for a trade embargo of Iran. The trade restrictions were only partially effective—even America's most loyal European allies did not want to lose access to Iranian oil—so a frustrated Carter, hounded by a public and press demanding "action," authorized a rescue attempt by American commandos in April 1980. The raid, however, was aborted in the Iranian des-

The year-long Iranian hostage crisis damaged America's prestige and President Carter's chances for reelection.

ert because of helicopter malfunctions, and it ended with eight fatalities when another American helicopter collided with a transport plane. Carter's presidency died with them. Secretary of State Vance resigned in protest against the risky venture. Meanwhile, nightly television coverage of the taunting Iranian rebels generated a near obsession with the seeming impotence of the United States and the fate of the hostages. The crisis ended after 444 days of captivity when Carter, in his last act as president, released several billion dollars of Iranian assets to ransom the kidnapped hostages.

The turbulent and often tragic events of the 1970s—the conquest of South Vietnam, the Watergate scandal and Nixon's resignation, the energy shortage and stagflation, the Iranian hostage episode—provoked among Americans what Carter labeled a "crisis of confidence." By 1980 American power and prestige seemed to be on the decline, the economy remained in a shambles, and the rights revolution launched in the sixties, with the questions it raised for the family and other basic social and political institutions, had provoked a backlash of resentment among "middle America." With theatrical timing, Ronald Reagan emerged to tap the growing reservoir of public frustration and transform his political career into a crusade to make "America stand tall again." He told his supporters that there was "a hunger in this land for a spiritual revival, a return to a belief in moral absolutes." The United States, he declared, remained the "greatest country in the world. We have the talent, we have the drive, we have the imagination. Now all we need is the leadership."

FURTHER READING

Engaging overviews of the cultural trends of the 1960s include William L. O'Neill's *Coming Apart* (1972)° and Godfrey Hodgson's *America in Our Time* (1976).° The scholarly literature on the New Left and the antiwar movement continues to grow. A good starting point is Irwin Unger's *The Movement: A History of the American New Left* (1974).° On the evolution and eventual destruction of the Students for a Democratic Society, see Allen J. Matusow's *The Unraveling of America* (1984).° The story of the pivotal confrontation at Columbia is told in James Kunen's *The Strawberry Statement* (1968). See also David Caute's *Year of the Barricades: A Journey Through 1968* (1988) and Todd Gitlin's *The Sixties* (1988).° For a fascinating analysis of the role of the media in the street politics of the 1960s, see Gitlin's *The Whole World Is Watching* (1980).°

Two influential assessments of the counterculture are Theodore Roszak's *The Making of a Counterculture* (1969) and Charles Reich's *The Greening of America* (1970).° The relationship of hallucinogenic drugs to the counterculture is a feature of Tom Wolfe's *The Electric Kool-Aid Acid Test* (1969).°

There is a wealth of good books dealing with the women's liberation movement. Among the most powerful accounts are those by participants. See Shulamith Firestone's *The Dialectic of Sex* (1972); Betty Friedan's *It Changed My Life: Writings on the Women's Movement* (1985)°; Kate Millett's *Sexual Politics* (1971)°; and *Sisterhood Is Powerful* (1970),° edited by Robin Morgan. Sara Evans explained the ambivalent relationship with the civil rights movement in *Personal Politics: The Roots of Women's Liberation in the Civil Rights Movement and the New Left* (1980).°

The organizing efforts of Cesar Chavez are detailed in Ronald Taylor's *Chavez and the Farm Workers* (1975).° See also Feliciano Rivera's *The Chicanos* (1972). The struggles of native Americans for recognition and power are sympathetically described in Stan Steiner's *The New Indians* (1968).

A good start for the events of the Nixon years is the former president's memoirs, *RN: The Memoirs of Richard Nixon* (1978).° Studies of Nixon at the time of his resurgence to power include Garry Wills's *Nixon Agonistes* (1970).° Scholarly accounts of Nixon include Stephen E. Ambrose's *Nixon*, 2 vols. (1986, 1989)° and Herbert Parmet's *Richard Nixon and His America* (1990).°

° These books are available in paperback editions.

Stanley Kutler's *The Wars of Watergate* (1990)° captures all the details of the Watergate scandal. The works of the two *Washington Post* reporters involved, Robert Woodward and Carl Bernstein, recount their role in the events; follow *All the President's Men* (1974)° with *The Final Days* (1976).°

For the way the Republicans handled affairs abroad, consult Tad Szulc's *The Illusion of Power: Foreign Policy in the Nixon Years* (1978). On Henry Kissinger, see Seymour M. Hersh's *The Price of Power: Kissinger in the Nixon White House* (1983).°

The loss of Vietnam and the end of American involvement are traced in A. E. Goodman's *The Lost Peace: America's Search for a Negotiated Settlement of the Vietnam War* (1978) and Gareth Porter's *A Peace Denied: The United States, Vietnam and the Paris Agreement* (1975). William Shawcross's *Sideshow: Kissinger, Nixon, and the Destruction of Cambodia* (1978)° deals with the broadening of the war. Larry Berman's *Planning a Tragedy: The Americanization of the War in Vietnam* (1982)° assesses the final impact of American involvement.

Two key works dealing with cultural trends during the seventies are Peter N. Carroll's *It Seemed Like Nothing Happened* (1982) and Christopher Lasch's *The Culture of Narcissism* (1979).° For additional views of politics during the 1970s, consult Henry S. Parmet's *The Democrats: The Years after FDR* (1976),° particularly for the McGovern campaign of 1972. Gerald Ford's memoir, *A Time to Heal: The Autobiography of Gerald R. Ford* (1979), is illuminating on the post-Watergate years. See also Richard Reeve's *A Ford, Not a Lincoln* (1975).

To examine the rise of Jimmy Carter, consult Betty Glad's *Jimmy Carter: In Search of the Great White House* (1980) and James T. Wooten's *Dasher: The Roots and the Rise of Jimmy Carter* (1978). A work critical of the Carter administration is Haynes Johnson's *In the Absence of Power: Governing America* (1980). Gaddis Smith's *Morality, Reason, and Power* (1986) provides an overview of American diplomacy in the Carter years. Zbigniew Brzezinski's *Power and Principle: Memories of the National Security Advisor, 1977–1981* (1983) and Cyrus Vance's *Hard Choices: Critical Years in America's Foreign Policy* (1983) lend insight to the Carter approach to foreign policy.

Background on how the Middle East came to dominate much of American policy is found in William B. Quandt's *Decade of Decision: American Policy toward the Arab-Israeli Conflict, 1967-1976* (1977).° What followed in the Camp David Accords is handled best by Jimmy Carter in *Keeping Faith: The Memoirs of a President* (1982).° Background on the SALT controversy is provided in Harold B. Moulton's *From Superiority to Parity: The United States and the Strategic Arms Race, 1961–1972* (1973). On Iranian-American relations, see James Bill's *The Eagle and the Lion: The Tragedy of American-Iranian Relations* (1987).°

For an overview of politics in the Carter-Reagan years, see Walter Karp's *Liberty Under Siege* (1988).

35

A NEW GILDED AGE

The Reagan Restoration

THE MAKING OF A PRESIDENT   As the 1980 election approached, the Republicans eagerly anticipated the contest with a struggling Jimmy Carter. Their candidate, Ronald Reagan, had initially appeared as an even more improbable presidential possibility than Carter had four years earlier. Born in 1911, Reagan was the model midwestern boy growing up in Dixon, Illinois. After graduating from tiny Eureka College, Reagan worked as a cheery radio announcer and sportscaster before heading to Hollywood in 1937.

A disciple of New Deal politics, Reagan adopted FDR's confident rhetoric and engaging smile, and he employed both during World War II when he made uplifting patriotic movies. But after the war his movie career stagnated. In the 1950s General Electric hired him to host its weekly television program and to serve as its spokesman to civic groups across the country. As he and his second wife, starlet Nancy Davis, toured the small towns of middle America, puffing the same uplifting speech for GE, Reagan abandoned his New Deal liberalism. He grew enamored of corporate executives and the Republican party's premise that too much government stifled free enterprise.

In 1964 Reagan entered the political limelight when he delivered a rousing speech on behalf of Barry Goldwater at the Republican convention. During two terms as governor of California (1967–1975) he displayed a fervid commitment to conservative principles as well as a political realism capable of compromise. Nevertheless, by the middle 1970s Reagan's brand of free enterprise conservatism still appeared too extreme for a national audience.

THE MOVE TO REAGAN   By the eve of the 1980 election, however, Reagan had become the beneficiary of three developments that made his conservative vision of America much more than a harmless flirtation with nostalgia. First, the 1980 Census revealed that the American population (226,505,000) was aging, and was moving in large numbers from the liberal Northeast to the conservative "Sunbelt" states of the South and West. This dual development meant that demographic forces were carrying the electorate toward Reagan's position.

Second, in the 1970s the country experienced a major revival of evangelical religion not unlike the Great Awakenings of the eighteenth and early nineteenth centuries. No longer a local or provincial phenomenon, Christian evangelicals and fundamentalists owned their own television and radio stations and operated their own schools and universities. The Reverend Jerry Falwell's "Moral Majority" expressed the political sentiments of countless other fundamentalist groups: free enterprise should remain free, big government should be made little, abortion should be outlawed, evolution should be replaced in schoolbooks by the biblical story of creation, and Soviet expansion should be opposed as a form of pagan totalitarianism. The moralistic zeal and financial resources of the religious right made them effective opponents of liberal political candidates and programs. As defenders of traditional and local values—prayer in schools, families in which women stayed home to care for children, tough criminal laws—the religious right rallied to Reagan, who, ironically, himself rarely attended church.

A third, and related, factor contributing to the conservative resurgence was a well-organized and well-financed backlash against the feminist movement. Like all the liberationist crusades spawned during the 1960s, the feminist movement developed internal fissures over policies and tactics and provoked a conservative reaction. During the 1970s women opposed to the social goals of feminism formed counterorganizations with names such as "Women Who Want to Be Women," "Happiness of Womanhood," and "Females Opposed to Equality."

Spearheading such efforts was Phyllis Schlafly, a right-wing Republican activist from Illinois. She orchestrated the campaign to defeat the Equal Rights Amendment and thereafter served as the galvanizing force behind a growing antifeminist movement. She characterized feminists as a "bunch of bitter women seeking a constitutional cure for their personal problems," women who had rejected their God-given roles as wives and mothers. Feminists, she charged, were "anti-family, anti-children, and pro-abortion."

Many of Schlafly's supporters in the anti-ERA campaign also participated in a mushrooming anti-abortion or "pro-life" movement. By 1980 the National Right to Life committee, created by the National Conference of Catholic Bishops, boasted 11 million members representing all religious denominations. Their intensity of commitment made them a powerful political force in their own right, and the Reagan campaign was quick to highlight its own support for traditional family values, gender roles, and the rights of the unborn.

By 1980 Reagan also benefited from the deep popular disenchantment with Carter, whose campaign was burdened by the frustrations of the Iranian hostage crisis, a desperately sick economy, and the party divisions created by Senator Edward M. Kennedy's luckless quest for the Democratic nomination. Like Ford before him, Carter proved to be a sincere but lackluster leader who faced an almost insurmountable set of domestic and international problems. He was expected to cure the economic recession and inflation at a time when all industrial economies were shaken by a shortage of oil and confidence. He was expected to reassert America's global power at a time of waning respect for America's international authority. And he was expected to do this, as well as buoy the national spirit, through a set of political institutions in which many Americans had lost faith. In short, Carter was virtually predestined to fail at an impossible task.

By 1980 voters seemed eager to embrace Reagan's cheery promises of a new era of less government, lower taxes, renewed prosperity, waning inflation, and revived military strength and national pride. His "supply-side" economic proposals, soon dubbed "Reaganomics" by supporters and "voodoo economics" by critics, suggested that stagflation resulted from governmental intrusions into the marketplace and from excessive taxes that weakened the incentive to work, save, and reinvest. For a long-suffering nation, it was, in theory, an alluring economic panacea.

On election day Reagan swept to a decisive victory, with 489 electoral votes to 49 for Carter, who carried only six states. The popular vote proved equally lopsided: 44 million (51 percent) to 35 million (41 percent), with 7 percent going to John Anderson, a moderate Republican who had bolted the party after Reagan's nomination and ran on an independent ticket.

In addition to affirming Reagan's conservative agenda, the

election reflected the triumph of what one political scientist called the "largest mass movement of our time"—nonvoting. Almost as striking as Reagan's one-sided victory was the fact that his vote total represented only 28 percent of the potential electorate. Only 53 percent of eligible voters cast ballots in the 1980 election.

Where had all the voters gone? Political analysts noted that most of the non-voters were working-class Democrats in the major urban centers. Voter turnout was lowest in poor inner-city neighborhoods such as New York's Bedford-Stuyvesant district, which had a 19 percent voter participation rate. Turnout was highest, by contrast, in the affluent suburbs of large cities, areas where the Republican party was experiencing a dramatic surge in popularity. Such trends meant that American office-holders were being selected during the 1970s by an electorate increasingly dominated by middle- and upper-class white voters.

Explanations for the high levels of voter apathy among working-class Americans vary. Some argued that they reflected the continuing sense of disillusionment with government itself growing out of the Watergate affair. Others noted that the widespread perception that the Democratic party had turned its back on its traditional blocs of support among common folk had influenced voting behavior. Democratic leaders no longer spoke eloquently on behalf of those at the bottom of America's social scale. By embracing a fiscal conservatism indistinguishable from the Republicans, as Carter had done, Democrats lost their appeal among blue-collar workers and ghetto dwellers. When viewed in this light, Ronald Reagan's victory represented less a resounding victory for conservative Republicans than a self-inflicted defeat by a fractured Democratic party. But for the moment, at least, such results were masked by the Republicans' euphoric victory celebrations. Flush with a sense of power and destiny, Ronald Reagan headed toward Washington with a blueprint for dismantling the welfare state.

INAUGURATION The installation of the sixty-nine-year-old Reagan, the first professional actor to become chief executive, was a festival of opulence and show-biz spectacle as far removed as one could imagine from Jimmy Carter's Jeffersonian simplicity. Conspicuous consumption roared back in style. Even conservative senator Barry Goldwater lamented the "ostentatious" show. Yet many of the Reaganites claimed that the public wanted such pomp and luster returned to the White House. A Washington so-

President Ronald Reagan, "the great communicator."

cialite gushed that Reagan's election meant that "you didn't have to be ashamed of what you have anymore."

REAGANOMICS   Ronald Reagan brought to Washington not only conspicuous consumption but also the most conservative economic philosophy since Calvin Coolidge, whose picture soon replaced Harry Truman's in the Cabinet Room. "Government is not the solution to our problem," Reagan insisted; "Government is the problem." The new president also brought his polished skills as a public speaker and experienced television performer, which served him well in presenting his views to the American people. And unlike Carter, he seemed to know exactly what ailed the economy and how to restore America's prestige in the world.

Reagan first abandoned price controls on oil, then he ended the wheat embargo on the Soviet Union. But he focused most of his energies on dramatically increasing defense spending, sharply reducing social spending, and passing a sweeping tax reform proposal. Despite loud protests from liberal groups and politicians, Congress passed the entire Reagan economic package by the summer of 1981. Enough Democrats—mostly sympathetic southern conservatives dubbed "boll weevils"—supported the measures to pass them by overwhelming majorities. On August 1, 1981, Reagan signed the Economic Recovery Tax Act, which cut personal income taxes by 25 percent, lowered the maximum rate from 70 to 50 percent for 1982, cut the capital gains tax by a third, and offered a broad array of other tax concessions.

The new legislation embodied an idea that went back to Alexander Hamilton: more money in the hands of the affluent would benefit society at large, since the wealthy would engage in productive investment. A closer parallel was Treasury Secretary Andrew Mellon's tax reduction program of the 1920s under Harding and Coolidge. The difference was that the Reagan tax cuts were accompanied by massive increases in defense spending that generated ever-mounting deficits. Reagan's advisers insisted that such unbalanced budgets were only temporary; once their new tax plan began to take effect, the economy would take off and government revenues would soar as personal incomes and corporate profits skyrocketed. But it did not work out that way. By the summer of 1983 a major recovery was underway, but the deficits grew ever larger, so much so that the president, who in 1980 had pledged to have a balanced federal budget by 1983, had in fact run up debts larger than those of all his predecessors combined.

BUDGET CUTS In trying to slash expenditures, Reagan's budget director pushed through $35 billion in budget cuts in educational and cultural programs, housing, food stamps, and school lunches in 1981. Reagan assured critics that despite these cuts he was committed to maintaining the "safety net" of government services for the "truly needy." This meant that aid would remain available only to those who could not work because of disability or child care. New Deal welfare programs had had the same purpose, but the Roosevelt administration had also provided federal jobs for those who could work. This was not a part of "Reaganomics." Cuts in programs to the disadvantaged, when added to the sluggish economy, helped raise the percentage of persons living under the poverty level from 11.7 in 1979 to 15.3 in 1983.

American bankers and investors feared that the rising government debt would send interest rates soaring, a fear expressed in sagging bond and stock markets. A business slump and rising unemployment carried through most of 1982. That same year the federal deficit doubled. Aides finally convinced Reagan that to reassure the public about deficits and the threat of inflation the government needed "revenue enhancements," a euphemism for tax increases. With Reagan's support, Congress passed a new tax bill in 1982 that would raise almost $100 billion.

During the mid-term elections, Reagan rarely mentioned the new tax bill. Instead he focused his campaign speeches on the glories of supply-side economics and rosy economic forecasts. He urged voters to "stay the course" and appealed for more time to let his economic program take effect. But the economic slump persisted through 1982, with unemployment standing at 10.4 percent.

CONFLICTS OF INTEREST   Like Harding and Coolidge in the 1920s, Reagan, during his first term, named people to government positions who frequently were unsympathetic to the regulatory functions for which they were responsible, rendering such regulation less than effective. The most visible early example was Interior Secretary James Watt, who castigated environmentalists for hindering the commercial use of timber and mineral resources. He was finally forced out of office by the uproar over an offensive joke he made about affirmative action appointments.

The Reagan administration also paralleled the Harding administration by finding itself embroiled in charges of conflict of interest, ethical misconduct, and actual criminal behavior. Public outcry forced the administrator of the Environmental Protection Agency to resign for granting favors to industrial polluters, her former clients. The president's deputy chief-of-staff obtained a "sweetheart" loan from a person who was subsequently given a governmental post. Once he left the White House in 1985, he set up a lucrative consulting business that traded upon his connections with high government officials, as another former presidential aide had done earlier. Both men were later indicted.

Although some 200 other Reagan appointees were also accused of unethical or illegal activities, the president himself remained untouched by any hint of impropriety. His personal charisma and distinct managerial style helped shield him from the political fall-out associated with the growing scandals and conflicts of interest among his aides and cronies. Public affection for him as a person remained his most enduring asset. This led one member of Congress to label the Reagan White House the "Teflon Presidency," where the buck never stopped because the blame never stuck.

As in the 1920s, organized labor encountered severe setbacks during the Reagan years. Presidential appointments to the National Labor Relations Board tended to favor management, and in 1981 Reagan fired members of the Professional Air Traffic Controllers (PATCO) who had participated in an illegal strike. Even more importantly, Reagan's smashing electoral victories in 1980 and 1984 broke the political power of the AFL-CIO. His criticism of unions seemed to reflect a general trend in public opinion. Although a record number of new jobs were created during the 1980s, union membership steadily dropped. By 1987 unions represented only 17 percent of the nation's full-time workers, down from 24 percent in 1979.

Reagan also went on the offensive against feminism. He ardently opposed the Equal Rights Amendment, abortion on demand, and the legal guarantee of equal pay for jobs of comparable worth. He did name Sandra Day O'Connor as the first woman justice to the Supreme Court, but critics labeled it a token gesture rather than a reflection of any genuine commitment to gender equality.

Blacks and other minorities shared a similar aggravation at the administration's limited support for affirmative action programs in employment. Reagan cut funds for civil rights enforcement and the Equal Employment Opportunity Commission, and initially opposed renewal of the Voting Rights Act of 1965, but was overruled by Congress.

THE DEFENSE BUILD-UP Reagan's conduct of foreign policy was governed by the idea that trouble in the world stemmed mainly from Moscow. At one of his first news conferences he charged that the Soviets were "prepared to commit any crime, to lie, to

The massive demonstration against nuclear weapons, New York City, June 12, 1982.

cheat," and do anything necessary to promote world communism. He and Secretary of Defense Caspar Weinberger embarked on a major build-up of nuclear and conventional weapons to close the gap that they claimed had developed between Soviet and American military forces.

Reagan also recovered the rhetoric of Harry Truman, John Foster Dulles, and the Kennedy inaugural to express American resolve in the face of "Communist aggression anywhere in the world." Détente deteriorated even further when the Soviets imposed martial law in Poland during the winter of 1981. The crackdown came after Polish workers, united under the banner of an independent union called Solidarity, challenged the Communist monopoly of power. As with Hungary in 1956 and Czechoslovakia in 1968, there was little the United States could do except register protest and impose economic sanctions against Poland's Communist government.

THE AMERICAS Reagan's ruling passion, however, was Central America, where he detected the most serious Communist threat. The tiny nation of El Salvador, caught up since 1980 in a brutal struggle between communist-supported revolutionaries and right-wing extremists, received American commitments of economic and military assistance. Reagan stopped short of sending American troops, but he did increase the number of military advisers and the amount of financial aid to the Salvadoran government. He also abandoned Carter's strident criticism of right-wing militants whose "death-squads" engaged in systematic terror and murder. Critics argued that American involvement ensured that the revolutionary forces would emerge as the victorious representatives of Salvadoran nationalism. Supporters countered by warning that American failure to act would allow for a repeat of Communist victories in Nicaragua, and that Honduras, Guatemala, and then all of Central America would eventually enter the Communist camp. By 1984, however, the American-backed government of President José Napoleón Duarte brought a modicum of stability to El Salvador.

Even more troubling was the situation in Nicaragua. The Reagan State Department claimed that the Cuban-sponsored Sandinista government in Nicaragua, which had only recently taken control of the country after ousting a corrupt dictator, was funneling Soviet and Cuban arms to Salvadoran leftist rebels. In response the administration ordered the CIA to train and supply guerrilla bands of disgruntled Nicaraguans, tagged "Contras," who staged attacks on Sandinista bases and officials from sanctuaries in Honduras. In supporting these "freedom fighters," Reagan sought not only to impede the traffic in arms to Salvadoran rebels but also to overthrow the Communist Sandinistas.

Critics of Reagan's anti-Sandinista policy questioned the motives and ethics of the Contras, accusing them of being mostly right-wing fanatics who indiscriminately killed civilians as well as Sandinista soldiers. They also feared that the United States might eventually commit its own combat forces, thus threatening another Vietnam-like intervention. Reagan replied to such criticism by warning that if the Communists prevailed in Central America, "our credibility would collapse, our alliances would crumble, and the safety of our homeland would be jeopardized."

THE MIDDLE EAST   The Middle East remained a tinderbox of geopolitical conflict throughout the Reagan years. No peaceable end seemed possible to the bloody Iran-Iraq war, which had erupted in 1980, entangled as it was with the passions of Islamic fundamentalism. In 1984 both sides began to attack oil tankers in the Persian Gulf, a major source of the world's oil. Although the Reagan administration harbored no affection for either nation, it viewed Iranian fundamentalism as the greater threat and funneled aid to Iraq, a policy that produced unforeseen and grave consequences.

American statesmen continued to see Israel as the strongest ally in the region, all the while seeking to encourage moderate Arab groups. Israel's aim in the area was to secure peaceful borders, America's to prevent Russian involvement through its ally Syria. But both objectives were thwarted by the continuing chaos in Lebanon, where ethnic and religious tensions erupted into an anarchy of warring groups. The capital, Beirut, became a battleground of rival Muslim and Christian factions, the Palestine Liberation Organization (PLO) army, Syrian invaders cast as peacekeepers, and Israelis responding to PLO attacks.

In June 1982 Israeli forces pushed the PLO out of southern Lebanon all the way north to Beirut. The United States neither endorsed nor condemned the invasion, but sent a special ambassador to negotiate a settlement. That August, Israel began heavy shelling of PLO strongholds in Beirut, and horrified American reactions led to hurried attempts to negotiate a cease-fire. The combatants finally agreed to allow French, Italian, and American troops to supervise the withdrawal of PLO troops from Beirut. Reagan's new Secretary of State, George Shultz, sought to build a broad international settlement, with a homeland for the Palestinians and a guarantee of Israel's borders by its Arab neighbors.

A terrorist bomb attack devastated U.S. Marine headquarters near Beirut International Airport, October 23, 1983—241 Marines were killed, and 80 wounded, in the attack.

It was an admirable goal, but one defeated by age-old hostilities. Israeli troops moved back into Beirut, and while they looked the other way, Lebanese Christian militiamen took revenge for the murder of their president by slaughtering women and children left in Palestinian refugee camps.

French, Italian, and American forces thereupon moved into Beirut as "peacekeepers," but in such small numbers as to become targets themselves. On October 23, 1983, an Islamic suicide bomber drove a truck laden with explosives into the U. S. Marine quarters at Beirut airport. The explosion left 230 Americans dead. Reagan declared that a continued American presence in the city was essential, but he soon began preparations for the withdrawal of the exposed American troops. On February 7, 1984, he announced that the Marines would be redeployed on warships offshore. The Israelis pulled back to southern Lebanon while the Syrians remained in eastern Lebanon and imposed a tenuous peace upon the faction-ridden country.

GRENADA   In a fortunate turn for the Reagan administration, the chance for an easy triumph closer to home eclipsed news of the debacle in Lebanon. On the Caribbean island of Grenada, the smallest independent nation in the Western Hemisphere, a leftist government had admitted Cuban workers to build a new airfield and had signed military agreements with several Communist-bloc countries. In October 1983 an even more radical military council seized power.

Appeals from the governments of neighboring islands led Reagan in October 1983 to order 1,900 American Army paratroopers and Marines to invade the island, depose the radical regime, and evacuate a group of American students at Grenada's medical school. Grenadan troops and Cuban workers were easily subdued—although later reports suggested shockingly poor coordination of American forces.

The U.N. General Assembly condemned the action, and many Latin Americans saw it as a revival of gunboat diplomacy, but most Grenadans and their neighbors acclaimed the action, and it was immensely popular in the United States. Although it was a lopsided affair, the attack on the island made Reagan look decisive, and it served notice on Latin American revolutionaries that the president might use force elsewhere in the region.

REAGAN'S SECOND TERM

ELECTION OF 1984   The Reagan luck, running low in 1982, returned in force two years later. Countervailing policies of fiscal stimulus (tax cuts and heavy defense spending) and monetary restraint (high interest rates) brought at least in the short run an economic recovery with little inflation. Critics argued that the return of prosperity was more the result of the cyclical swings inherent in the economy and the dramatic fall in energy costs following the collapse of the OPEC cartel.

As the presidential election approached, however, Reagan and the Republicans shrewdly took full credit for the economic recovery. The slogan at the convention was "America is Back." And for many Americans the slogan rang true. It did seem that Reagan had brought new strength and vitality, luster and dignity, to the White House and the nation. The Democratic nominee, the former Minnesota senator and vice-president, Walter Mondale, faced an uphill struggle. But he quickly won the endorsement of several major organizations—the AFL-CIO, National Organization for Women, and the NAACP. And he won a lot of media attention by choosing as his running mate a woman, New York Representative Geraldine Ferraro. This attention soon focused, however, on her husband's dubious business finances, which made it awkward for the Democrats to use the administration's own "sleaze factor" as an issue.

Mondale further complicated his campaign by a fit of frankness in his acceptance speech. "Mr. Reagan will raise taxes, and so will I," he told the convention. "He won't tell you. I just did." Reagan in turn vowed never to approve a tax increase, and chided his opponent's candid stand. Thereafter, Mondale never caught up. Reagan's skill and confidence at campaigning outshone him, and the economic recovery made it difficult for Mondale to attract interest, much less generate enthusiasm. In the end, Reagan won almost 59 percent of the popular vote and lost only Minnesota and the District of Columbia. His coattails however, were not as long as in 1980. Republicans had a net gain of only fifteen seats in the House, leaving them still greatly outnumbered by Democrats, 253 to 182. They also lost two Senate seats, leaving their margin only 53 to 47.

THE LANDSLIDE SYNDROME Reagan's overwhelming victory brought him to a testing time between his heretofore charmed political life and the malevolent fate that seems to pursue presidents who win such lopsided electoral victories. The most recent victims of this fate had been Richard Nixon, who met his Watergate soon after winning a landslide reelection, and Lyndon Johnson, who got stuck in the Vietnam quagmire after his 1964 victory.

Reagan entered his second term with a goodly share of political time bombs ticking away around the world from Nicaragua to Afghanistan. At home the ethical and criminal violations of his subordinates continued to make headlines, and strains began to appear between the political conservatives in the party and the social conservatives who dominated evangelical religious groups.

Still, the Reagan luck held out. OPEC continued to lower oil prices, sending inflation down and the stock market up. In his 1985 State of the Union message, the president clarified what had come to be called the Reagan Doctrine in foreign affairs. America, he proclaimed, would support anticommunist forces around the world seeking to "defy Soviet-supported aggression." In effect, he was challenging the isolationism provoked by the nation's humbling experience in Vietnam and implying that America would not hesitate to intervene in world hot spots. Turning to domestic policy, the president dared Congress to raise taxes. His veto pen was ready.

TAX REFORM   Through much of 1985 Reagan was back again on the campaign trail, this time drumming up support for a tax simplification plan. After a vigorous debate that lasted nearly two years, Congress passed, and in September 1986 the president finally signed, a comprehensive Tax Reform Act. The new measure would by 1988 reduce the number of tax brackets from fourteen to two, and reduce rates from the maximum of 50 percent to 15 and 28 percent—the lowest since Coolidge. Tax shelters were also sharply curtailed.

ARMS CONTROL   Meanwhile Reagan, for all his bluff talk about Russia's being "an evil empire," seemed determined to reach an arms control agreement with the Soviet Union. In Geneva in November 1985 he met with Mikhail Gorbachev, the charismatic and innovative new leader of the Soviet Union. The two signed several cultural and scientific agreements and issued a statement on arms limitations talks, but no treaty was in the offing. A major stumbling block was Reagan's refusal to consider any restrictions on his pursuit of the Strategic Defense Initiative (SDI, often called "Star Wars,"), which he had announced in 1983. Its ob-

Soviet Premier Mikhail Gorbachev (left) and U.S. President Ronald Reagan during a light moment at the Geneva summit, November 1985.

jective was to shield the United States from nuclear attack by creating a space-based defense system using futuristic computers, laser beams, and more exotic technology. Critics, many of them scientists, argued that the system was a pipedream— expensive, far-fetched, and a violation of the Anti-Ballistic Missile Treaty of 1972.

Nearly a year after the Geneva summit, on sudden notice and with limited preparation, Gorbachev and Reagan met in Iceland for two days to discuss arms reduction. Early reports predicted a major breakthrough, as the two leaders discussed the possibility of a total ban on nuclear weapons, but the talks collapsed in disagreement over SDI. After the Iceland meeting the two nations reduced the scope of their discussions in order to break the impasse. Talks now focused on eliminating short-range nuclear weapons from Europe.

THE IRAN-CONTRA AFFAIR   The year 1986 opened with a terrible tragedy on January 28 when the space shuttle *Challenger* exploded minutes after liftoff, killing its crew members as a horrified nation watched on television. Investigations later revealed evidence of startling failures at NASA to heed warnings about cold-weather launches. Yet such revelations did little to affect Reagan's continuing popularity. In fact, the president's prestige shot up in April when he ordered a daring air raid on Libya, a country responsible for many of the terrorist killings, kidnappings, and hijackings that had become commonplace in the Middle East. The administration also drew praise for its support of the ouster of two corrupt dictators: Ferdinand Marcos of the Philippines and Haiti's "Baby Doc" Duvalier.

During the fall of 1986, however, Reagan's popularity balloon suddenly popped. The administration suffered a double blow on November 4, 1986. In the mid-term elections the Democrats regained control of the Senate by 55 to 45. For his final two years in office, Reagan would face an opposition Congress. What was worse, on Election Day, reports surfaced that the United States, with Israeli assistance, had been secretly selling arms to Iran in hope of securing the release of American hostages held in Lebanon by extremist Islamic groups with close ties to Iran. Such action contradicted Reagan's repeated public insistence that his administration would never negotiate with terrorists. It angered America's allies and many Americans who vividly remembered the 1979 Iranian takeover of the American Embassy.

Yet there was more to the story. Over the next several months, a series of revelations reminiscent of the Watergate affair dis-

Lt.-Col. Oliver North testifying before the congressional committee investigating the Iran-Contra affair, July 1987.

closed a more complicated and even more incredible series of covert activities carried out by administration officials. At the center of what came to be dubbed "Irangate" was the much-decorated Marine Lieutenant-Colonel Oliver North. An aide to the National Security Council who specialized in counter-terrorism, North had been running secret operations from the basement of the White House involving numerous governmental, private, and foreign individuals. His most far-fetched scheme sought to use the profits gained from the secret sale of arms to Iran to subsidize the Contra rebels fighting in Nicaragua, at a time when Congress had voted to ban such aid.

North's activities, it turned out, had been approved by National Security Adviser Robert McFarlane, his successor Admiral John Poindexter, and CIA Director William Casey. Secretary of State George Shultz and Secretary of Defense Caspar Weinberger both had criticized the sale of arms to Iran, but their objections were ignored. Later, on three occasions, Shultz threatened to resign because no one was trying to stop the "pathetic" scheme. As information about the secret, illegal dealings surfaced in the press, McFarlane attempted suicide, Poindexter resigned, North was fired, and Casey, who denied any connection, left the CIA for health reasons. Casey died shortly thereafter from a brain tumor.

The White House, meanwhile, assumed a siege mentality as the president's popularity plummeted. Under increasing criticism and amid growing doubts of his own credibility and ability,

Reagan appointed both an independent counsel and a three-man commission, led by former Republican senator John Tower, to investigate the spreading scandal.

The Tower Commission issued a devastating report early in 1987 which placed much of the responsibility for the bungled Iran-Contra affair on Reagan's loose management style. The report portrayed Reagan as uninformed and forgetful, a leader detached from the inner workings of his own administration.

Worse was yet to come. During the spring and summer of 1987, a joint House-Senate investigating committee began holding televised hearings into the Iran-Contra affair. The sessions dominated public attention for months and revealed a tangled web of inept financial and diplomatic transactions, the shredding of incriminating government documents, crass profiteering, and misguided patriotism. North's four-day appearance before the committee in a uniform festooned with medals was a bravura performance composed of patriotic rhetoric, self-righteous preaching and skillful evasion. For a few days his defense of his actions won over the hearts of many Americans, and he became the poster boy of the American Right. But his sudden popularity could not obscure the clumsiness and utter naïveté of the Iran-Contra affair. The hearings confirmed Reagan's insistence that he had not known about the diversion of funds to the Contras, but testimony also contradicted his earlier claim that the sale of arms to Iran was intended to open up new diplomatic channels rather than buy the freedom of American hostages.

The Iran-Contra affair left support for the Nicaraguan Contras badly eroded in the Congress, and it undermined much of Reagan's popularity. One Democratic senator said that the president had "become a kindly old relative that you don't have to pay much attention to. He's just run his course." The investigations of the independent counsel led to six indictments in 1988. A Washington jury found Oliver North guilty of three relatively minor charges but innocent of nine more serious counts, apparently reflecting the jury's reasoning that he had acted as an agent of higher-ups. His conviction was later overturned on appeal. Of those involved in the affair, only John Poindexter got a jail sentence—six months for his conviction on five felony counts of obstructing and lying to Congress. By the summer of 1992 the investigation was still uncovering information on the extent of the Reagan administration's involvement with the Iran-Contra affair, and former Secretary of Defense Weinberger was indicted for perjury and for withholding information from Congress.

TURMOIL IN CENTRAL AMERICA   The Iran-Contra affair showed the lengths to which members of the administration would go to support the Nicaraguan Contras. Fearing heightened Soviet and American involvement in Central America, neighboring countries pressed during the mid-1980s for a negotiated settlement to the fighting in Nicaragua. In 1987 Costa Rican President Oscar Arias received the Nobel Peace prize for designing an ambitious new regional peace plan signed by five Central American presidents on August 7. But by the end of the year, the plan had yet to be implemented. In January 1988 Daniel Ortega, the Nicaraguan president, pledged to negotiate directly with the Contra rebels.

In the spring of 1988 these negotiations produced a cease-fire agreement, ending nearly seven years of fighting in Nicaragua. Secretary of State Shultz called the pact an "important step forward," but it surprised and disappointed hardliners within the Reagan administration who saw in it a Contra surrender. The Contra leaders themselves, aware of the eroding support for their cause in the United States Congress, saw the truce as their only chance for tangible concessions such as amnesty for political prisoners, the return of the Contras from exile, and "unrestricted freedom of expression."

Meanwhile, in neighboring El Salvador, the administration's attempt to shore up the centrist government of José Napoleón Duarte through economic and military aid was dealt a body blow when the far-right ARENA party scored an upset victory at the polls during the spring. Further embarrassment to the administration's Latin American policies occurred when a federal grand jury in Miami indicted Panama's military ruler, General Manuel Antonio Noriega, for drug trafficking. After Noriega refused to resign, the Reagan administration applied economic sanctions in the hope of provoking a domestic rebellion, only to see Noriega turn to Cuba for military aid and tighten his iron-fisted control of the country. Everywhere in Central America, it seemed in 1988, events conspired to highlight the limits of American power and the ineptness of administration initiatives.

THE ECONOMY   During the 1980s, all kinds of debt—personal, corporate, and governmental—increased dramatically. Whereas in the 1960s, Americans on average saved 10 percent of their income, in 1987 it was less than 4 percent. The Reagan budget deficits also reached record levels. Between 1981 and 1987 the federal debt totaled $1.4 trillion, a figure half again larger than the entire debt for the previous two centuries. This statistic led some economists to refer to the nation's "charge card" economic recovery. Caught up in the exhilarating momentum of such prolonged prosperity and what had become a roaring bull market, however, few observers recognized the cost of such carefree spending.

A seeming epidemic of greed and self-absorbed materialism had spread through the country. Wall Street witnessed a rash of arrests and convictions for trading in securities on inside information unavailable to the public. Television ministries were embarrassed by revelations of sexual misconduct and intramural power plays. And more government officials, including Attorney General Edwin Meese, became entangled in the web of corruption. Commentators talked of a compulsive materialism energizing those young, upwardly mobile urban professionals dubbed "Yuppies." Caught up in the race for money, goods, and status, these post–World War II baby boomers in the fast lane captured the tone and mood of affluent life in the 1980s.

Then, on October 19, 1987, the bill collector suddenly arrived at the nation's doorstep. On that "Black Monday," Wall Street, already buffeted by sharp declines the previous week, experienced a tidal wave of selling reminiscent of the 1929 crash, as the Dow Jones Industrial Average plummeted 508 points, or an astounding 22.6 percent. The market plunge was almost double the record 12.8 percent fall on October 28, 1929. Almost $560 billion in paper value disappeared, an amount larger than the gross national product of France. With cyclonic suddenness the nation's financial mood went from boom to gloom during the fall of 1987. Several smaller brokerage houses went under amid the speculative whirlpool, thousands of investment bankers and stock brokers were fired, and consumer confidence took a beating. Wall Street's selling frenzy reverberated throughout the capitalist world, sending stock prices plummeting in Tokyo, London, Paris, and Toronto.

What caused such a goring of the bull market? The reasons were complex and long in developing. Some analysts argued that the runaway market of the 1980s had become artificially high, driven by greed and hope rather than by any relation to the economy's actual performance. Others blamed new computerized trading programs that distorted market activity and misled individual investors. But most agreed that the fundamental problem was the nation's spiraling indebtedness and chronically high trade deficits. Americans were consuming more than they were producing, importing the difference, and paying for it with borrowed money and a dollar sharply declining in value. Foreign investors had lost confidence in Reaganomics and were no longer willing to finance America's spending binge. As the editors of *Business Week* declared, "The Message of the Crash is clear: Americans have spent too much, borrowed too much, and imported too much. Now it has to stop."

In the aftermath of the calamitous selling spree on Black Monday, President Reagan, tried to reassure the nation that there was no need for panic. He insisted that the "underlying economy remains sound," an unsettling echo of Herbert Hoover's equally sunny assurances in 1929. Few observers actually feared a depression of the magnitude of the 1930s; there were too many safeguards built into the system to allow that. But there was real concern of an impending recession, and within a few weeks the White House began to take some action. Reagan agreed to work with Congress in developing a deficit-reduction package, and for the first time indicated that he was willing to include increased taxes in such a package. But the eventual compromise plan was so modest that it did little to restore investor confidence. As one Republican senator lamented, "There is a total lack of courage among those of us in the Congress to do what we all know has to be done."

AN HISTORIC TREATY In the midst of a shaky, unpredictable economic situation, the main prospect for positive achievement before the end of Reagan's second term seemed to lie in arms reduction agreements with the Soviet government. Under Mikhail Gorbachev the Soviets promoted renewed détente in order to free their energies to address pressing domestic problems. The log-jam impeding the arms negotiations suddenly broke in February 1987, when Gorbachev announced that he was willing to deal separately on a medium-range missile treaty. After nine more months of strenuous, highly technical negotiations, Reagan and Gorbachev met amid much fanfare in Washington on December 9, 1987, and signed a treaty to eliminate intermediate-range (300–3,000 miles) nuclear forces (INF). It was an epochal event, not only because it marked the first time that the two nations had agreed to destroy a whole class of weapons systems but because it represented a key first step toward the eventual end of the arms race altogether. Under the terms of the treaty, the United States would destroy 859 missiles, and the Russians would eliminate 1,752. Provision was also made for on-site inspections by each side to verify compliance. Still, this winnowing of weapons would represent only 4 percent of the total number of nuclear missiles on both sides. Arms control advocates thus looked toward a second and more comprehensive treaty eliminating long-range strategic missiles.

But virtually all Kremlin watchers were heartened by continuing evidence that General Secretary Gorbachev was successfully liberalizing Soviet domestic life and aggressively improving East-West foreign relations. The Soviets suddenly began stressing cooperation with the West in dealing with "hot spots" around the world. They urged the Palestine Liberation Organization to recognize Israel's right to exist and advocated a greater role for the U.N. in the volatile Persian Gulf. Perhaps the most dramatic symbol of a thawing Cold War was the phased withdrawal of 115,000 Soviet troops from Afghanistan, which began in May 1988.

THE REAGAN LEGACY   Looking back over 1987, Nancy Reagan described the year as "Terrible. Next year has got to be better." She was wrong. As the Reagan presidency neared its end, its public image continued to be rocked by dissension and scandal within the administration itself. Continuing allegations of shady financial dealings involving Attorney General Edwin Meese, perhaps the president's closest friend and political confidante, led to a year-long investigation by an independent counsel and repeated calls for Meese's resignation by Democrats and Republicans alike. In July 1988, the independent counsel issued a report that accused Meese of three separate legal violations but did not call for criminal indictments. The besieged attorney-general, claiming he had been exonerated, thereupon resigned.

As Ronald Reagan prepared to leave office, his legacy remained problematic. Would he be remembered as the architect of revitalized military spending, lower tax rates, sharply reduced inflation and unemployment, a prolonged economic recovery, and an unprecedented arms-reduction treaty? Or would history find an administration rife with corruption and policies that had weakened American credibility abroad and bequeathed an economic time bomb to the 1990s?

Only time would tell, but the herd of aspiring Democratic candidates for the 1988 election thought they knew the answer. Said Jesse Jackson, "We must fundamentally reject the lie of Reaganomics." He and other aspirants knew that history was on their side. Few two-term presidents had left office with greater popularity than when they entered it. Thus the stage was set for a tempestuous campaign year.

THE 1988 ELECTION Scenting victory in November, a gaggle of eight Democratic presidential candidates entered a wild scramble for their party's nomination. However, as the primary season progressed, it soon became a two-man race between Massachusetts governor Michael Dukakis and Jesse Jackson, the charismatic black civil rights activist who had been one of Martin Luther King, Jr.'s chief lieutenants. Dukakis eventually won out, and managed a difficult reconciliation with the Jackson forces that left the Democrats unified and confident as the fall campaign began. As in 1960, they envisioned a popular president and his tired presidency giving way to a cool, poised politician from Massachusetts.

The son of Greek immigrants, noted for his personal frugality and keen managerial skills, Dukakis trumpeted his success in balancing the Massachusetts state budget every year of his administration. For all his emphasis on management savvy, however, he also adopted liberal positions on several explosive issues: he opposed the death penalty and called for compulsory health insurance, gun control legislation, and an end to nuclear power plants. But he insisted that the election was not really about such issues: "This election is not about ideology; it's about competence."

The Republicans nominated Reagan's two-term vice-president George Bush, who after a bumpy start had easily cast aside his rivals in the primaries. As Reagan's hand-picked heir, Bush claimed credit for the administration's successes, but like all dutiful vice-presidents, he also faced the challenge of defining and asserting his own political identity. Although he was a veteran government official, having served as a Texas congressman, envoy to China, ambassador to the U.N., and head of the C.I.A., Bush projected none of Reagan's charisma, charm, or rhetorical skills. Cartoonists caricatured the patrician vice-president, the son of a rich Connecticut senator, schooled at Andover and Yale, as a well-heeled "wimp," and one Democrat described him as a man born "with a silver foot in his mouth." Early polls showed Dukakis with a surprisingly wide lead.

Yet at the Republican Convention Bush delivered a forceful address that sharply enhanced his stature. Although pledging to continue the Reagan agenda, he also recognized that "things aren't perfect" in America, an admission his boss rarely acknowledged. Bush promised to use the White House to fight bigotry, illiteracy, and homelessness. The most memorable line was a defiant statement on taxes: "Congress will push me to raise taxes, and I'll say no, and they'll push, and I'll say no, and they'll

George Bush (right) *at the 1988 Republican National Convention with his newly chosen running mate, Dan Quayle.*

push again. And all I can say to them is, read my lips: *no new taxes."*

Bush's convention performance gave his heretofore sluggish campaign a jump-start. The Republicans also enjoyed two real advantages. In 1988 the United States basked in peace and prosperity, and the Republican party benefited from its continuing demographic advantages. During the 1980s, population growth was most rapid in the Republican-dominated Sunbelt states. And throughout the nation, population during the decade had continued to shift from Democratic cities to Republican suburbs. In addition, the leftward tilt of the Democratic party in 1984 had led many moderate and conservative Democrats as well as the growing number of "independents" to vote for Reagan.

In a campaign given over to mud-slinging, the Bush campaign leaders fastened on an effective strategy: they attacked Dukakis as a camouflaged liberal in the mold of McGovern, Carter, and Mondale who would increase federal spending, raise taxes, gut the defense program, refuse to intervene against Communist aggression abroad, and oppose the pledge of allegiance to the flag. Perhaps the most inflammatory—and scurrilous—Republican tactic against Dukakis was an advertisement that preyed upon the prejudices and anxieties of middle-class whites by showing the picture of a convicted black murderer who brutally raped a woman after he had been let out of a Massachusetts prison on a weekend furlough. Dukakis chose not to respond to the Republican attacks. Studiously informed on the issues, he had a Jimmy Carter-like trust in the force of sweet reason. Dukakis was, in Bush's words, "the Iceman," cool, rational, in control of his emotions, blind to the emotional power that trivial issues could exert.

The Republican onslaught took its toll against the less organized, less focused Dukakis campaign. Dukakis took ten states plus the District of Columbia, with clusters in the Northeast, Midwest, and Northwest. Bush carried the rest, with a margin of about 54 percent to 46 percent in the popular vote and 426 to 111 in the electoral college—one Democratic elector voted for Lloyd Bentsen, the Texas senator Dukakis had chosen as his running mate.

The Bush Years

Although Bush's inaugural address lacked specific calls to action, it did invite national unity and bipartisan harmony. The American people had a purpose, he said, "to make kinder the face of the nation and gentler the face of the world." The new president acknowledged the sufferings of the homeless, "the children who have nothing," the addicted, the unwed mothers, but pleaded: "We have a deficit to bring down. We have more will than wallet, but will is what we need." In short, he looked to voluntary associations and individuals, not government, to take the lead on such issues.

During eight years as vice-president, Bush had loyally embraced the Reaganism he had once called "voodoo economics." His own administration, one commentator now said, would be "déjà voodoo." But there would be subtle differences. Whereas Reagan had hung Coolidge's portrait in place of Truman's on a White House wall, Bush now installed one of Theodore Roosevelt. The symbolism suggested two things. An eastern patrician with a Western patina, like Teddy Roosevelt, "Poppy" Bush would preside over an administration drawn mostly from the upper crust or career public servants. And in foreign policy he would go much further than TR in wielding the big stick. The parallels vanished, though, in Bush's lack of interest in domestic policy, noted by *Time* magazine when it named the president its "Men of the Year" for 1990, attributing to him a double image: "a foreign policy profile that was a study in resoluteness and mastery, the other a domestic visage just as strongly marked by wavering and confusion."

THE BAILOUT AND THE BUDGET   The Reagan administration left some issues that demanded immediate attention from the Bush White House. In February 1989 Bush tackled the most pressing of these, the savings and loan crisis. One effect of the Reagan administration's efforts to eliminate "unnecessary" federal regulations in the economic sector was a debacle in the savings and loan industry. To enable savings and loan institutions (also called S&Ls or "thrifts") to compete with commercial banks, Reagan pushed through a congressional bill that allowed them to invest depositors' funds in commercial real estate and junk bonds as well as in the traditional single-family housing market.

The result was catastrophic. Knowing that the federal government insured deposits up to $100,000, incompetent or corrupt lenders engaged in a frenzy of speculative high-risk investments and free-wheeling personal expenditures. By 1989 hundreds of thrifts had failed, and Bush responded with a rescue plan to close or sell ailing thrifts, and bail out the depositors. Congress responded the following August by consolidating the insurance fund for savings and loan deposits with the fund covering banks, the Federal Deposit Insurance Corporation (FDIC). A new agency, the Resolution Trust Corporation (RTC), was created to sell off failed thrifts—or at least their assets. At the time, the cost to taxpayers of the bailout was put at $300 billion over thirty years, although in July 1990 the General Accounting Office estimated the cost at $500 billion.

The biggest hangover from the binge years of the 1980s was the national debt, which stood at $2.6 trillion by the time Bush was elected, nearly three times its 1980 level. Bush's taboo on tax increases (meaning, mainly, income taxes) made it more difficult to reduce the deficit or trim the debt.

By early 1990, according to one political writer, the country faced "a horrendous fiscal mess." Bipartisan budget talks between administration and congressional leaders, begun in May, were characterized by "rancorous partisanship [and] deep divisions within the two parties." Eventually, on June 26, Bush issued a statement: "It seems clear to me that both the size of the deficit problem and the need for a package that can be enacted" required a number of measures, including "tax revenue increases." A budget plan wasn't announced until September 30, 1990, but with midterm elections coming in November, the political timing was about the worst possible for reasoned dialogue

in Congress, and a majority of both parties ended up voting
against the budget bill. Congress finally reacted to mounting
public anger at the continued indecision and approved a settlement with the Bush administration in October, although most
Republicans still opposed it. Through a combination of tax hikes
and spending cuts, the measure promised to reduce the budget
deficit by $43.1 billion in 1991 and by $331.4 billion in 1991–
1995.

SOCIAL CRISES Perhaps the most discussed and feared social crisis
was the spread of AIDS (Acquired Immune Deficiency Syndrome), a new—and fatal—disease that initially struck homosexuals and intravenous drug users, but soon appeared among
the larger population as well. Those infected with the Human
Immunodeficiency Virus (HIV) became susceptible to infections
and cancers that developed into AIDS and eventually proved
fatal. People contracted HIV by coming into contact with the
blood, semen, vaginal secretions, or breast milk of an infected
person. By June 1991, AIDS had claimed over 110,000 American lives, and nearly 1.5 million Americans were carrying the
deadly virus. Almost 90 percent of the AIDS cases were men,

A quilt commemorating the deaths of many thousands of Americans from
AIDS, displayed before the White House in October 1988.

and infections were disproportionately common among intravenous drug-users, African-Americans, and Hispanic-Americans. But during the nineties the number of women with the virus increased dramatically and was projected to pass the rate of men by the year 2000, and the number of cases traced to heterosexual contact was also on the rise. The disease gained greater visibility through the highly publicized disclosures that several Hollywood celebrities and athletic stars had contracted the virus. To address the epidemic, Reagan's surgeon general launched a controversial public education program that included encouraging "safe sex" through the use of condoms. With no prospect for an early cure and with skyrocketing treatment costs, AIDS became during the 1990s one of the nation's most horrifying—and frustrating—dilemmas.

The issue of what constitutes free speech aroused emotions when the Supreme Court ruled by a 5–4 vote in June 1989 that burning an American flag as a form of protest was protected as free speech under the First Amendment of the Constitution. Bush lead the Right in a call for a constitutional amendment to permit laws against desecrating the flag. Congress instead overwhelmingly passed legislation to make it a crime to desecrate the flag by burning or defacing it. When the high court struck down that law too, in 1990, the call for an amendment was renewed, but Congress again declined to tinker with the Bill of Rights on the eve of its 200th anniversary.

There was more symbolism than substance in the Bush administration's plans to deal with the deadly matter of drug abuse. During the 1980s, cocaine addiction had spread through sizable segments of American society, luring those with money to spend and, in its smokeable form, known as crack, those with little money to spare. Bush vowed to make drug abuse his number-one domestic priority, and appointed William J. Bennett, former education secretary, as "drug czar" or head of a new Office of National Drug Control Policy, with cabinet status but no department.

Bush's war on drugs was planned along three fronts: more stringent law enforcement, drug testing in the workplace, and heightened efforts to cut off the supply of drugs coming from Colombia and Peru. Although drug-related arrests increased 20 percent from 1988 to 1989, "crack" cocaine remained readily available and immensely popular. In 1989 some 375,000 American babies were born addicted to cocaine or heroin. Equally sobering was the connection between the drug subculture and the street gangs terrorizing inner cities across the country. Like Reagan before him, Bush chose to focus on arrests and interdiction, which failed to address the basic question: why were so many young people attracted by illegal drugs?

The answer involved many factors, but the disproportionate incidence of drug and alcohol abuse among poor people pointed to the culture of poverty as a primary culprit. The United States had clearly lost its thirty-year war on poverty. Statistics illuminate the tragic realities of what sociologists called America's hidden "underclass." In 1992 10 percent of whites were classified as "poor," compared to 26 percent of Hispanics and 30 percent of blacks. One quarter of all African-American men were in jail or on probation or parole. The greatest cause of death among young black men was a bullet. More than 60 percent of all black children were born to unwed mothers (five times the rate for whites) and 23 percent of Hispanic families were headed by single women. Everyone agreed that education was a necessary lever to catapult people out of such desperate circumstances, but few members of the underclass made it through the school system. Almost 40 percent of black male high school dropouts were unemployed. Only 4 percent of black males and 6 percent of black females attended college.

Most members of the American underclass subsisted on government welfare checks and lived in run-down, crime-ridden government housing projects and deteriorating ghettos, what one black minister called America's "brand of apartheid." A government official observed that these inner-city dwellers made up a "caste of people almost totally dependent on the state, with little hope of breaking free." Those living amid such squalor and stunted hopes constituted both a tragic refutation of the American dream of upward mobility and a ticking time bomb of anger and frustration waiting to explode.

"THE COLD WAR IS NOW BEHIND US" Replacing the portrait of Coolidge with Teddy Roosevelt's signified Bush's affinity with TR's "big stick" diplomacy—his conviction that America's manifest destiny was to become a world power. Bush entered the White House with more foreign policy experience than most presidents, and he found the spotlight of the world stage more congenial than wrestling with the intractable problems of the inner cities or the deficit. Within two years of his inauguration, George Bush would lead the United States into two wars, a record unequaled by any of his predecessors. Throughout most of 1989, however, he merely had to sit back and observe the dissolution of one totalitarian or authoritarian regime after another.

For the first time in years, democracy was suddenly on the march in a sequence of mostly bloodless revolutions that took the world by surprise.

Although in China a suddenly risen democracy movement came to a tragic end in June 1989, when government forces mounted a deadly assault on demonstrators in Peking's Tiananmen Square, Eastern Europe had an entirely different experience. Mikhail Gorbachev set events in motion by responding to Soviet economic problems with policies of *perestroika* (restructuring) and *glasnost* (openness), a loosening of central economic planning and censorship. His foreign policy sought rapprochement with the West, to encourage trade and relieve the Soviet economy of burdensome military costs.

Gorbachev backed off from Soviet imperial ambitions. Early in 1989, Soviet troops left Afghanistan, after nine years bogged down in civil war there. Then in July, in Paris, Gorbachev repudiated the "Brezhnev doctrine," which had asserted the right of the Soviet Union to intervene in the internal affairs of Communist countries. The days when Soviet tanks would roll through Warsaw and Prague were over, and hard-line leaders in the East-bloc countries found themselves beset by demands for reform. With opposition strength building, the old regimes fell in rapid

West Germans chipping away at the Berlin Wall on November 11, 1989, two days after all crossings between East and West Germany were opened.

order, and with surprisingly little bloodshed. Communist party rule ended first in Poland and Hungary, then in hard-line Czechoslovakia and in Bulgaria. In Romania, the year of peaceful revolution ended in a bloodbath when the Romanian people in December were joined by the army in a bloody uprising against the brutal dictator Nicolae Ceausescu. He and his wife were captured, tried, and then executed on Christmas Day. But lacking experienced opposition leaders, a problem in all the Eastern European countries, the new government fell under the control of members of the old Communist establishment.

The most spectacular event in the collapse of the Soviet empire in Eastern Europe came on November 9, when the chief symbol of the Cold War—the Berlin Wall—fell, and the East German government succumbed to popular pressures for change. With the borders to the West fully open, the Communist government of East Germany collapsed, a freely elected government followed, and on October 3, 1990, the five states of East Germany were united with the West. The reunified German nation remained in NATO, and the Warsaw Pact alliance was dissolved.

In late May 1990, Gorbachev visited Washington, where on June 1 he and Bush signed more than a dozen documents. These included an agreement to reduce long-range nuclear weapons to a limit of 1,600 delivery rockets and 6,000 warheads; another agreement requiring both countries to give up the manufacture of chemical weapons; and a treaty that would loosen trade restrictions between the countries. A few days later, speaking at Stanford University, Gorbachev said: "The Cold War is now behind us. Let us not wrangle over who won it."

The democratic movement reached other parts of the world. During 1990, the Communist party of Mongolia—a country strategically located on the borders of the Soviet Union and China—voted to give up its monopoly on power, and in Nicaragua, where the ruling Sandinista party avowed Maxism, President Daniel Ortega was defeated in a presidential election in February. Even in isolated Albania, the ruling party yielded to demands for a free election in 1991.

Democratic change overtook authoritarian regimes of a different stripe as well. In Chile, Augusto Pinochet, who had become military dictator in a bloody coup of 1973, yielded to a popular vote against continuing him in office, and was defeated in presidential elections in 1989. In South Africa, to which Congress had applied trade sanctions in protest of its apartheid (racial segregation) policies since 1986, a new prime minister,

THE POST COLD WAR WEST

0   400 Miles

0   400 Kilometers

SWEDEN

FINLAND

COMMONWEALTH
OF INDEPENDENT
STATES

NORWAY

St. Petersburg

ESTONIA

DENMARK

BALTIC SEA

LATVIA

☆Moscow

LITHUANIA

Gdansk

Berlin ☆

BELARUS

GERMANY

POLAND ☆
Warsaw

☥Bonn

☆
Prague

CZECHOSLOVAKIA

UKRAINE

Vienna ☆
AUSTRIA

☆Budapest

SWITZERLAND

HUNGARY

MOLDOVA

SLOVENIA

CROATIA

RUMANIA

ITALY

Belgrade ☆
BOSNIA ?
AND   ☪YUGOSLAVIA
HERZEGOVINA

Bucharest
☆

BLACK SEA

☆Rome

ADRIATIC SEA

BULGARIA

MACEDONIA

ALBANIA

GREECE

TURKEY

Frederik W. DeKlerk, came to office in August 1989. In early
1990 he released black nationalist Nelson Mandela from twenty-
seven years in prison and announced plans gradually to abandon
apartheid. By early 1992 DeKlerk had pushed through a constitution ending apartheid and setting up procedures for the full
integration of blacks into government and society.

The reform impulse that Gorbachev helped unleash in the
East-bloc countries began to grow beyond his control at home.
Gorbachev proved unusually adept at political restructuring.
While yielding to the Communist monopoly of government, he
built a new presidential system that gave him, if anything, increased powers. His skills, however, did not extend to an anti-
quated economy that resisted change. The revival of old ethnic

allegiances added to the instability. Although Russia proper included slightly over half the Soviet Union's population, it was only one of fifteen constituent republics, most of which began to seek autonomy, if not independence. Along the fringes of the Russian republic, to the west and south, lay a jigsaw puzzle of about a hundred nationalities and languages.

Gorbachev's popularity in the Soviet Union shrank as it grew abroad. It especially eroded among the Communist hard-liners who saw in his reforms the unraveling of their bureaucratic and political empire. On August 18, 1991, a cabal of political and military leaders suddenly tried to seize the reins of power. They accosted Gorbachev at his vacation retreat in the Crimea and demanded that he sign a decree proclaiming a state of emergency and transferring his powers to them. He replied: "Go to hell," whereupon he was placed under house arrest. Twelve hours later the Soviet news agency reported to the world that Gorbachev was "ill" and had temporarily transferred his powers to his vice-president and an eight-member emergency committee. Political parties were suspended, newspapers were silenced, a curfew was announced, and street demonstrations were banned. Tanks and armored vehicles surrounded strategic installations and government buildings in Moscow. The new leadership promised to end the "chaos and anarchy" they claimed was bedeviling the country.

But the coup was doomed from the start. Poorly planned and clumsily implemented, it lacked effective coordination. The plotters failed to arrest popular leaders such as Boris Yeltsin, the populist president of the Russian republic, and they neglected to close the airports or cut off telephone and television communications. Most important, the putschists failed to recognize the strength of the democratic idealism unleashed by Gorbachev's reforms. Upon learning of the attempted overthrow, tens of thousands of Muscovites poured into the streets outside Yeltsin's headquarters to act as human shields against efforts to arrest him. Three were killed in the process.

On August 20 President Bush, after a day of indecision, responded favorably to Yeltsin's request for support and convinced world leaders to join him in refusing to recognize the legitimacy of the new government. Siberian coal miners went on strike to oppose the coup. The next day word began to seep out that the plotters had given up and were fleeing. Several committed suicide, and a newly released Gorbachev ordered the others arrested. But his freedom did not bring a restoration of his power. By courageously clambering atop a menacing tank and publicly

Mikhail Gorbachev and Boris Yeltsin before the Soviet parliament in the days following the failed coup of late August 1991.

defying the conspirators, Yeltsin had emerged as the most popular political figure in the country. Gorbachev reclaimed the title of president, but was forced to resign as head of the Communist party and admit that he had made a grave mistake in appointing the men who had turned against him.

What began as a reactionary coup turned into a powerful accelerant for stunning new changes in the Soviet Union. No sooner had the plotters been arrested than most of the fifteen republics proclaimed their independence, with the Baltic republics of Latvia, Lithuania, and Estonia regaining the status of independent nations. The Communist party apparatus was dismantled, prompting celebrating crowds to topple statues of Lenin and other Communist heroes.

By December 1991, the Soviet Union dissolved into a new—and fragile—Commonwealth of Independent States made up of twelve autonomous republics. Held together by little other than historic ties and contiguous borders, the federated republics soon suffered outbreaks of ethnic tensions and separatist movements. For his part, Mikhail Gorbachev found himself out of a job. With the Communist party dissolved, the Soviet Union dismantled, and continuing economic woes raising objections to his leadership, Gorbachev resigned as president at the end of 1991 and was replaced by Yeltsin, who was now a national hero. The democratic reforms he had set in motion to save the

Union of Soviet Socialist Republics proved inadequate to the task.

The aborted coup accelerated Soviet and American efforts to reduce the stockpiles of nuclear weapons. In late September 1991 President Bush stunned the world by announcing that the United States would destroy all its tactical nuclear weapons on land and at sea in Europe and Asia, take its long-range bombers off twenty-four-hour alert status, and initiate discussions with the Soviet Union for the purpose of instituting sharp cuts in ICBMs with multiple warheads. Bush explained that the prospect of a Soviet invasion of Western Europe was "no longer a realistic threat," and this presented an unprecedented opportunity for reducing the threat of nuclear holocaust. President Gorbachev responded by announcing reciprocal Soviet cutbacks. As Joint Chiefs of Staff Chairman Colin Powell remarked, the Cold War "has vaporized before our eyes."

The dilution of the Russian military threat led the Defense Department in 1992 to withdraw large numbers of military personnel from bases in Asia and Europe. The Pentagon also announced a plan to shrink the armed forces by 500,000 troops over the next five years. In June 1992 Bush and Yeltsin announced their intention to reduce their combined arsenals of nuclear weapons from about 22,500 to no more than 7,000 by the year 2003. All land-based multiple-warhead missiles would be destroyed.

Drastic cuts in military spending pushed defense contractors into the sharpest cutbacks since World War II. "The world is becoming a friendlier place," noted one industry analyst, and American defense and aerospace firms faced a painful period of adjustment.

PANAMA   Despite the hopes of many, the end of the Cold War did not spell the end of international tensions and conflicts. Indeed, before the end of 1989, American troops were engaged in battle in Panama, where General Manuel Noriega, as chief of the Panamanian Defense Forces since 1983, was head of the government in fact if not in title. Years earlier Noriega had worked secretly with the CIA, providing information about developments in Central America. At the same time, however, he got involved in the lucrative—and illegal—drug trade. In February 1988, federal grand juries in Miami and Tampa, Florida, indicted him and fifteen others on charges of international drug smuggling, gun running, and laundering the money through Panamanian banks.

In December 1989 Panama's National Assembly named Noriega head of the government and proclaimed that Panama "is declared to be in a state of war" with the United States. The next day, December 16, 1989, four off-duty American servicemen were stopped at a roadblock and one marine was shot and killed. President Bush responded by ordering an invasion of Panama with the purpose of capturing Noriega for trial on the American indictments and installing a government headed by opposition leaders who had been chosen in an election nullified by Noriega earlier that year.

The 12,000 American military personnel in Panama were quickly joined by 12,000 more, and in the early morning of December 20, five military task forces struck at strategic targets in the country. They quickly disabled and seized the headquarters of the Panamanian Defense Forces, but Noriega vanished. Hit-and-run attacks by the Panamanian Defense Forces continued, but resistance collapsed when Noriega took refuge in the Vatican embassy on Christmas Eve. After intense negotiations among American, Vatican, and Panamanian diplomats, Noriega surrendered to American forces a week later. Twenty-three American servicemen were killed in the action, and estimates of Panamanians killed and wounded ranged up to 4,000, including many civilians caught in the crossfire. Noriega was detained in a U.S. federal jail well over a year after his surrender, before his trial began in late 1991. He was convicted in April 1992 on eight counts of racketeering and drug distribution.

THE GULF WAR Months after Panama had moved to the background of public attention, another former American client, Saddam Hussein, dictator of Iraq, focused attention on the Middle East when his army suddenly fell upon his tiny, wealthy neighbor Kuwait on August 2, 1990. A decade earlier, when Saddam attacked Iran hoping to exploit its revolutionary turmoil for territorial concessions, the United States and most Arab countries "tilted" toward Iraq as a regional buffer against Iran, which was then holding American diplomats hostage. From 1985 to 1990, Iraq received about $500 million worth of American technology—advanced computers, lasers, and specialized machine tools related to the development of missiles.

Saddam's war against Iran meanwhile bogged down in a bloody stalemate, until the U.N. finally arranged a truce on August 8, 1988. The very next day the neighboring oil-rich enclave of Kuwait raised its production of oil contrary to agreements with the Organization of Petroleum Exporting Countries (OPEC). The resultant drop in oil prices offended Saddam, deep in debt and heavily dependent on oil revenues. Complaining of "economic aggression" against Iraq, he demanded that Kuwait reduce its production and, with Saudi Arabia, cancel Iraqi debts of $30 million. He also revived boundary disputes that had simmered since the post–World War I settlement that had created the current map of the Gulf region. Saddam seemed to nurture hopes of unifying the Arab lands and dominating the region's oil resources.

As tensions heightened, American officials remained focused on events in Europe and on Iraq's value as a counterweight to Iran. A meeting on July 25, 1990, between Saddam Hussein and the American ambassador to Iraq, April Glaspie, failed to resolve the mounting crisis. A text of the meeting later released by Iraq pictured Glaspie as deferential and conciliatory, assuring Saddam that the United States would not get involved in a dispute between Arab neighbors. Glaspie, a career expert on the Middle East and fluent in Arabic, later testified to Congress: "I told him orally we would defend our vital interests, we would support our friends in the Gulf, we would defend their sovereignty and integrity." The main American mistake, she said, was not to "realize he was stupid." On August 2, the Iraqi army occupied Kuwait.

Saddam did not expect the firestorm of world indignation he ignited. The U.N. Security Council quickly voted 14–0 to condemn the invasion and demand withdrawal. On August 3, Secretary of State James Baker and Soviet foreign minister Edouard Shevardnadze issued a joint statement of condemnation. On August 6, the Security Council endorsed Resolution 661, an embargo on trade with Iraq, by a vote of 13–0, with Cuba and Yemen abstaining. Such unanimity, of course, would have been unlikely during the Cold War.

On August 2 President Bush condemned Iraq's "naked aggression" and said he was not ruling any options out. On August 3 the president called the "integrity of Saudi Arabia" a vital American interest. Two days later he vowed to reporters: "This aggression will not stand." Asked how it would be undone, he replied: "Just wait, watch, and learn." On August 6–7, the United States dispatched planes and troops to Saudi Arabia on a "wholly defensive" mission—to protect Saudi Arabia. British forces soon joined in, as did Arab troops from Egypt, Morocco, Syria, Oman, the United Arab Emirates, and Qatar. On August 22, Bush began to order the mobilization of American reserve forces for the operation dubbed "Desert Shield." Later in September, after meeting with Gorbachev in Helsinki, Bush told Congress that dictators could no longer find comfort in East-West divisions, and proclaimed a "New World Order," which he

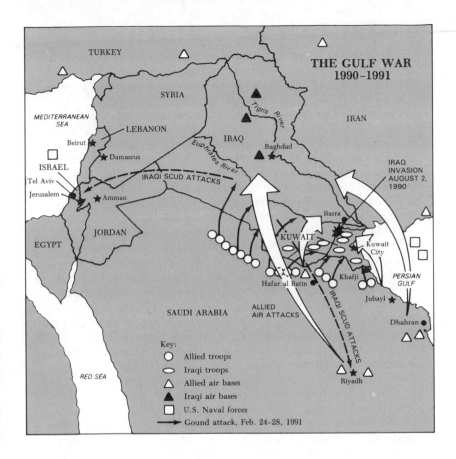

THE GULF WAR
1990–1991

TURKEY

SYRIA

MEDITERRANEAN
SEA

LEBANON

Beirut

Damascus

ISRAEL

Tel Aviv

Jerusalem

Amman

JORDAN

EGYPT

Tigris River

Euphrates River

IRAQ

Baghdad

IRAQI SCUD ATTACKS

IRAN

IRAQ
INVASION
AUGUST 2,
1990

Basra

KUWAIT

Kuwait
City

Khafji

PERSIAN
GULF

Hafar al Batin

SAUDI ARABIA

ALLIED
AIR ATTACKS

IRAQI SCUD ATTACKS

Jubayl

Dhahran

Riyadh

RED SEA

Key:
○ Allied troops
◡ Iraqi troops
△ Allied air bases
▲ Iraqi air bases
□ U.S. Naval forces
→ Gound attack, Feb. 24-28, 1991

described as "a world where the strong respect the rights of the weak."

Very early on the Pentagon was putting together plans for offensive military action. Although Colin Powell, chairman of the Joint Chiefs of Staff, favored sticking with the U.N. trade embargo against Iraq, which he believed would work over time, Bush declared it politically unfeasible. On October 1, large majorities in both houses of Congress approved the actions taken to that point. On November 8, Bush announced that he was doubling American forces in the Middle East from about 200,000 to 400,000, to build up "an adequate offensive military capability." Bush asserted that he already had authority to take such action under the Security Council resolutions.

The Congress erupted in debate, with many arguing that the embargo should have a chance to work, and that it would be ill-advised to go to war without formal congressional support.

Bush's position was strengthened on November 29 by U.N. Resolution 678, which authorized the use of force to dislodge Iraq from Kuwait, and set a deadline for Iraqi withdrawal of January 15, 1991.

A flurry of peace efforts sent diplomats scurrying all over, but without result. Saddam refused to yield, and declined even to meet with Secretary of State James Baker until three days before the U.N. deadline. On January 10 Congress began to debate a resolution authorizing the use of U.S. armed forces. The outcome was uncertain to the end, but on January 12 the resolution for the use of force passed the House by 250–183, and the Senate by 52–47.

By January 1991, a twenty-eight-nation allied force was committed to Operation Desert Shield. Some nations sent only planes, ships, or support forces, but sixteen committed ground combat forces, ten of these Islamic countries. Desert Shield became Operation Desert Storm when the first missiles and planes began to hit Iraq at about 2:30 A.M., January 17, Baghdad time, or about 6:30 P.M., January 16, Washington time. The Persian Gulf War, the "mother of all battles" in Saddam Hussein's words, was intense but short, ending with an allied cease-fire just six weeks later, and leaving consequences to be played out far into the future.

War has long been a popular spectator sport, alas, in the age of television literally so, and Americans derived their impressions of the Gulf conflict largely from that source. According to the polls, a great majority of Americans approved of the practice already followed in Grenada and Panama—a reaction to the "Vietnam syndrome"—of forming reporters into pools to be fed information primarily through official briefings. Commanding General H. Norman Schwarzkopf proved both telegenic and deft at handling questions. He became an instant public hero. Reporters could venture into the field only with military escorts who controlled what and whom they saw. Those reporters who ventured out on their own were quickly reined in.

The greatest wonder of the briefings was the television footage of "smart bombs"—missiles guided by laser beams precisely to their targets. One missile penetrated the center of the roof on Baghdad's telephone and communications center, and others could be seen going down the air shafts and into the doors of other strategic targets. Only later did it emerge that just 7 percent of the tonnage dropped had been "smart bombs," or about 6,520 tons out of 88,500. B-52s carrying conventional bombs from as far away as Britain and Spain delivered a heavy battering

H. Norman Schwarzkopf, commanding general of the allied force committed to Desert Storm.

to Saddam's elite Republican Guard, many of them lined up along the Kuwait border behind the less trained and less experienced conscripts on the front lines.

With the allies in control of the air from the beginning, Saddam's only recourse was to fire off lumbering Soviet-made SCUD missiles, which he aimed from the first day into Israel with the hope of provoking Israeli retaliation and undermining the coalition against him. But the resulting damage and casualties were light, and the Israelis showed remarkable restraint in the face of the continuing attacks. The Israelis gained a measure of protection from Patriot missiles installed and operated by American crews; the Patriots destroyed or altered the course of many incoming SCUDs, although, it turned out, not nearly as many as the military initially reported. The Iraqis responded also with desperation moves, which did more damage to the environment than to enemy forces: releasing oil into the Persian Gulf from tankers and loading platforms in Kuwait—and setting fire to hundreds of Kuwaiti oil wells.

Saddam's key strategy of digging in and prolonging the war into a costly land struggle, as he did in his war with Iran, never had a chance. He concentrated his forces in Kuwait—into a bag, as Schwarzkopf put it—and expected an allied attack northward into Kuwait and a landing on the coast. But the Iraqis were outflanked when 200,000 allied troops, largely American, British, and French, vanished with much of their heavy armor and turned up on the undefended border with Saudi Arabia 100–200 miles to the west. The allied ground assault began on February 24, and lasted only four days. Republican Guard tanks were smashed in the largest armored battle, probably, since the Battle of the Bulge. Thousands of Iraqi soldiers surrendered, and there was a quick breakthrough into Kuwait. Iraqi soldiers and civilians fleeing Kuwait, in some cases with hostages rounded up in large numbers, were caught in a traffic jam that provided what one naval pilot dubbed a "turkey shoot."

On February 28, President Bush called for a cease-fire, the Iraqis accepted, and the shooting ended. American fatalities were 137. The lowest estimates of Iraqi fatalities, civilian and military, were around 100,000. The coalition forces occupied about one-fifth of Iraq. In late March, after a quick survey, a U.N. official reported: "Bombing had wrought near apocalyptic results upon the infrastructure of what had been, until January 1991, a rather highly urbanized and mechanized society." The U.N. Children's Fund director called for a crash program of immunization to ward off epidemics. For all the destruction, Saddam Hussein remained in power.

Conditions in Iraq worsened when the Gulf War dissolved into civil war, in both the south and the north. Iraq was in fact something of an artificial entity, cobbled together by the British after World War I out of three provinces of the former Ottoman Empire and named by them what in Arabic meant "well-rooted country." In the south, a large minority of Arabs belonging to the Shi'ite sect of Islam—the prevailing group in Iran—rose in rebellion; in the north a larger minority of Kurds—Sunni Muslims, but a people of distinct identity and language since ancient times —sought release from Saddam's despotic rule. Although they had been promised an independent Kurdistan after World War I, they remained minorities in five different countries.

Although the Bush administration would have preferred a palace coup against Saddam Hussein, it now held forth a policy of not interfering in the internal affairs of Iraq. One unidentified official said that the president wanted to sign a cease-fire and "get the hell out of there." As a presidential spokesman explained, "It is good for the stability of the region that [Iraq] maintain its territorial integrity." And so with American troops already returning home to crowds of flag-waving celebrants, Iraqi forces held in reserve or newly escaped from the allied trap put down first the Shi'ite rebellion in the south, and then the Kurds in the north. American troops on the southern shore of the Euphrates had to stand by and watch as the rebels were brutally suppressed.

The Middle East, as it had for centuries, resisted any quick fix. The Persian Gulf War was far from a reprise of Vietnam, but it ended with what conceivably could turn into a longer hangover. There was an understanding—details to be worked out—that the United States would maintain a military presence in the Persia Gulf. Secretary of State Baker succeeded in organizing a conference to address the tough problems between Israel and its Arab neighbors, but any settlement remained far off. It was, ironically, an American missionary who said to one of the British planners carving up the former Ottoman territory after World War I: "You are flying in the face of four millenniums of history." The words retain their haunting quality.

THE HOME FRONT

The euphoria generated by the Allied victory in the Gulf War was as short-lived as the war itself. George Bush's popularity peaked during Operation Desert Storm and then began a steep decline. Gallup polls showed his public approval rating plummeting from 89 percent in March 1991 to 37 percent in May 1992. Most analysts agreed that the free fall in the president's performance ratings resulted primarily from his passive response to the recessionary economy. But other social events and issues also contributed to his declining fortunes.

SUPREME COURT MELODRAMA In mid-1991 Supreme Court Justice Thurgood Marshall, the first black to serve on the nation's highest court, announced his retirement after twenty-four years of service. To succeed him Bush nominated Clarence Thomas, a black federal judge who had been raised in poverty in the segregated South and educated in Catholic schools. After graduating from Yale Law School, he had worked as an aide for a Republican senator before serving as chairman of the Equal Employment Opportunity Commission (EEOC) in the Reagan administration. In 1991 Thomas was appointed to the U.S. Court of Appeals, and after serving in that capacity for only sixteen months, he was nominated for the Supreme Court.

Although the American Bar Association concluded that Thomas's scant experience as a lawyer and judge made him one of the least-qualified Supreme Court nominees in recent years, Bush claimed that he was the "best person" for the position. What made him especially attractive to the Bush administration was his conservative political and judicial philosophy. In

Anita Hill testifying before the Senate Judiciary Committee hearings on the confirmation of Clarence Thomas as Supreme Court Justice.

speeches, articles, and legal opinions, Thomas had criticized the minimum wage, questioned the constitutionality of abortion, assailed school busing and affirmative action hiring programs, and preached the virtues of black self-reliance. He once said that all civil rights leaders ever do is "bitch, bitch, moan, and whine."

Such volatile opinions ensured that Thomas's Senate confirmation hearings in October 1991 would be incendiary, but the real explosion occurred when Anita Hill, a black female law professor, charged that Thomas had sexually harassed her when she worked for him at the EEOC. Hill's soft-spoken, graphic testimony transformed the televised Judiciary Committee proceedings into a titillating spectacle and an intensely personal drama that raised the issue of sexual harassment to national prominence before reducing it to its most intractable level: her word against his.

After the all-male Senate panel finished an often savage and occasionally absurd cross-examination of Hill, Judge Thomas appeared before the committee and adamantly denied the charges against him. In a searing speech, he angrily characterized the hearings as a "high-tech lynching for uppity blacks" and implied that Hill had fabricated the charges at the behest of civil rights groups determined to thwart his confirmation. "I would have preferred an assassin's bullet to this kind of living hell," he said the next day, but he would "rather die than withdraw."

After days of anguished testimony from both parties, the only certainties were that either Hill or Thomas was a monumental liar, that both of them had been permanently scarred, and that the confirmation process had been transformed into a sleazy political circus. The Senate vote to confirm Thomas by a 52-to-48 margin reflected the hearing's residue of doubt.

Until the galvanizing effects of Anita Hill's treatment at the Thomas hearings, feminism as an organized political movement had been in disarray. As early as 1975 Betty Friedan had broken away from NOW, the organization she had started, claiming that radical feminist leaders had abandoned its original core constituency. By 1992 many claimed that NOW had reached a dead end. The prominent *Washington Post* columnist and novelist Sally Quinn charged that "many women have come to see the feminist movement as anti-male, anti-child, anti-family, anti-feminine. And therefore it has nothing to do with us."

In the ambiguous aftermath of the Thomas hearings, many women were furious about the way Republican senators and Bush staffers had treated Hill. "We will no longer beg for our rights from men in power," warned Patricia Ireland, the executive vice-president for the National Organization for Women. "We will replace them and take power for ourselves."

Indeed, an unprecedented number of women candidates ran for national and local offices in 1992, and fund-raising efforts for female candidates reached new highs. Concern about protecting the legality of abortion gave added momentum to the surge of women candidates. Equally important was a sense of frustration with the male-dominated political status quo. "There's a feeling we should give women a chance," explained one political scientist. "They can't do much worse than the men." The Thomas confirmation struggle thus promised to widen the gender gap for a Republican party already less popular with women than with men. "The war with Anita Hill," said one political commentator, "was not a war Bush needed."

THE "GREAT COMPRESSION" The most devastating development for the Bush administration and the nation during the early nineties was a prolonged economic recession that began in July 1990. It was the first economic setback in more than eight years and the longest, if not the deepest, since the Great Depression. Said one economist: "This is more than just a recession in the conventional sense. What has happened has put the fear of God into people." Indeed, the economies of nineteen states were technically in a state of "depression" rather than recession. By early 1992, over 2 million jobs had dried up. During 1991, 25 million workers—about 20 percent of the labor force—were unemployed at some time. What made this recession unusual was that its victims included large numbers of white-collar workers. In December alone General Motors, Xerox, and IBM cut 100,000 employees from their payrolls. The nationwide shrinkage of the work force led analysts to label the trend the "Great Compression."

Economists amassed sophisticated—and often contradictory —explanations of the slump, but most agreed that the economy was plagued by excess public and private indebtedness and excess capacity. Between 1980 and 1992, public-sector debt quadrupled and household debt tripled. The boom years of the "Reagan recovery" had saddled the nation with massive bills to pay, and the S&L crisis led not only to unprecedented bankruptcies but also to stricter lending guidelines that sharply curtailed the credit supply. The federal deficit under George Bush was almost 7 percent of the Gross Domestic Product (GDP), over twice as high as it had been under Reagan. With soaring expenditures on defense and social entitlement programs, a $150 billion annual deficit had become a $450 billion shortfall during 1991.

A Senate committee analysis of the stagnant economy included a chilling fact: George Bush was the only president under whom "the average standard of living has actually declined." Critics with a historical bent compared Bush to Herbert Hoover. Both presidents initially denied that there was a major problem with the economy and then assured the nation that it would be short and self-correcting. In December 1991 Bush confessed that he had not "been able to sort out exactly why there has been this degree of pessimism." Such a comment confirmed for many the impression that he was so preoccupied with managing foreign affairs that he had lost touch with developments in his own country.

A long-term cause of the economic downturn was a low rate of investment compared to America's major trading partners. While Japan was investing 31 percent of its Gross Domestic Product (GDP) on new machinery, equipment, and production technologies, the United States was spending only 15 percent of its GDP on domestic investment.

Whatever the reasons for the recession, the cure remained elusive. Although the Federal Reserve Board instituted a series of reductions in interest rates, the economy remained in the doldrums well into 1992. Throughout 1991 and most of 1992 the Democratic-led Congress and the president squabbled over what kind of recovery package would best serve the national economy. As a result little was done to stimulate new growth or reduce the hemorrhaging deficits. With his domestic policies in disarray, George Bush tried a clumsy balancing act, acknowledging on one hand that "people are hurting" while on the other urging Americans that "this is a good time to buy a car."

1992: AN UNUSUAL ELECTION YEAR Such lame responses did not bode well for the president's re-election prospects. "People are worried," reported the editor of *U.S. News and World Report* in January 1992, "and the president is part of the worries because he has seemed so out of touch." Bush, he added, "is a Velcro president, not a Teflon president. Blame sticks to him for the massive deficits of the Reagan years and for his indifference, delays and fumbling as president."

But there was plenty of blame to spread around. Revelations in October 1991 that over 300 members of the House of Representatives had bounced over 8,000 checks free of charge at their private bank recalled to mind Mark Twain's insistence that there was no such thing as a "distinctively native American criminal class, except Congress." The ensuing scandal reinforced public contempt for politicians of both parties. Voters in the fall 1991 special congressional elections swept both Democratic and Republican incumbents out of office. A wave of anti-tax, anti-recession, and anti-government sentiment washed across the landscape of American politics.

By early 1992 the once unassailable Bush found himself under assault by members of his own party. Patrick Buchanan, who had been an aide to presidents Nixon and Reagan and was a prominent conservative columnist and acerbic television commentator, launched a pugnacious campaign to challenge Bush for the Republican nomination. "George Bush is the biggest spender in American history," he railed. "He's the biggest taxer in American history. And he's walked away from the principles of the Republican Party." Buchanan's platform was a blend of pre–World War II Republican isolationism and social and fiscal conservatism. It called for an end to foreign aid programs, the withdrawal of American ground forces from Europe, and the curbing of immigration from less developed countries. His "America First" campaign also betrayed elements of anti-Semitism and ethnic prejudice.

Buchanan's two-fisted rhetoric and conservative credentials attracted thousands of young activists—primarily white, male, and angry—who were convinced that George Bush's unprincipled pragmatism had betrayed the Reagan legacy. They fanned out across the hills of New Hampshire, and in the February 1992 state primary, Buchanan won 37 percent of the vote and thereafter consistently received 20–30 percent support in the remaining primaries. Although Buchanan had no chance of winning the nomination, he refused to drop out of the race. His persistent support testified to Bush's fragile hold on his own party.

The Democrats relished the Republican infighting, but they had their own problems to confront. Many saw their hopes for retrieving the White House dimmed when Mario Cuomo, the governor of New York and the only Democratic hopeful with a truly national following, refused to become a candidate. His decision left Bill Clinton, a four-term governor of Arkansas and a consummate politician, as the Democratic front-runner in a field of mediocre aspirants.

On the surface Clinton's credentials were impressive. He was a graduate of Georgetown University, had won a Rhodes scholarship to Oxford, and then earned a law degree from Yale, where he met and married the brightest woman in the class, Hilary Rodham. By 1979, at age 32, he was back in Arkansas as the youngest governor in the country. Except for one two-year term, he has served as governor ever since and in the process developed a reputation for innovation, especially in the field of education reform. As a dynamic young leader within the national Democratic party, he headed the effort to win back the middle-class white voters who had fled to the Republicans during the eighties. Democrats had grown so liberal, he argued, that they had alienated their key constituencies. Unlike Jimmy Carter, he "never viewed government as the enemy. I think it has to be reformed so that the taxpayers feel it serves them." A self-professed moderate, he stressed the need for a leaner, yet activist government approach whereby people receiving government welfare support would also take greater responsibility for their lives. Clinton also promised to cut the defense budget, provide tax relief for the middle class, revamp the college student loan program, and provide a massive economic aid package to the former republics of the Soviet Union. He was less precise about the funding for such ambitious initiatives. Handsome, witty, in-

Democratic presidential nominee Bill Clinton and his running-mate Al Gore on the campaign trail.

telligent, and a compelling speaker, he reminded many of John F. Kennedy.

But underneath the veneer of Clinton's savvy political career —he had been planning for the presidency since age sixteen— were several flaws. Under his leadership, the state of Arkansas remained near the bottom of national rankings in per capita income, student test scores, child welfare, health insurance coverage, and industrial pollution. He also made extensive use of polls to shape his stance on issues, to pander to special interest groups, and to flip-flop on controversial issues, leading critics to label him "Slick Willie." Said one former opponent: "He'll be what people want him to be. He'll do or say what it will take to get elected." Even more enticing to the media were reports that he was an adulterer and that he had manipulated the ROTC program to avoid the draft during the Vietnam war. Clinton's denials of both allegations could not dispel a lingering distrust of the Democratic front-runner.

THE PEROT WILD CARD As Bush and Clinton staggered through the primaries, a new force appeared on the political horizon in the form of the independent candidacy of H. Ross Perot, a "rags-to-riches" Texas billionaire known for his candor and "can-do" spirit. The Perot campaign was fueled by voter rage at a political system grown corrupt, calcified, and mired in gridlock.

While appearing on a nationally televised call-in talk show in February 1992, Perot was asked if he would run for president. He would do so, he replied, only if volunteers were able to organize petition drives to have his name placed on the ballot in all fifty states. The immediate response was overwhelming. In the next two weeks Perot's corporate headquarters received over 2 million phone calls from people eager to help his campaign bid. By May, Perot was outpolling both Bush and Clinton in national surveys.

Republicans responded to the Perot candidacy by tarring him with the liberal label because of his opposition to the Gulf War and his support for gun-control laws, a woman's right to abortion, and a state income tax in Texas. Perot tried to deflect such efforts by reminding listeners of the obvious failure of both parties to govern the country effectively and efficiently. But like FDR, Perot promised people action without specifics, and for many people, it seems, that was enough.

No sooner had Perot established himself as a maverick presidential pretender than he stunned the nation by announcing his withdrawal from the race on July 16. His eroding support in the polls and the revitalization of the Democratic party convinced him that he could not win, and, as he explained it, he did not want to play the role of "spoiler" by stalemating the electoral college vote and allowing the House of Representatives to decide the election. Yet insiders claimed that Perot had developed a distaste for the political campaigning necessary to win a national contest. "I'm not having fun anymore," he confided to an aide.

THE DEMOCRATIC CONVENTION   While Perot was quitting the race in Dallas, the Democratic party convention in New York City was nominating the first baby-boomer ticket: forty-five-year-old Bill Clinton and his running mate, Al Gore, a dynamic young senator from Tennessee known for his expertise in environmental policy. Clinton accepted the nomination "in the name of all the people who do the work, pay the taxes, raise the kids and play by the rules—the hardworking Americans who make up our forgotten middle class." In his sharply partisan acceptance speech, Clinton claimed that the Democratic party had shed its popular image of spendthrift liberalism and special-interest favoritism and now provided the only true voice for change in the presidential contest. "It is time for us to realize that there is not a government program for every problem." He called for a "new covenant" between the American people and the federal government that would include welfare reform, college loans in exchange for national service, reformed health-care programs, higher taxes on the rich, and reduced military spending.

In the aftermath of the Democratic convention, national polls showed Clinton with a substantial lead, and panicky Republicans expressed mounting fears that their control of the White House was in real jeopardy. Some urged Bush to dump Vice-President Dan Quayle, whose mediocre abilities and frequent gaffes had made him the butt of repeated jokes. A few prominent conservative columnists even urged Bush himself to withdraw. "All three of the key ingredients for victory are missing as of now," lamented a key Bush campaign adviser in August. "We have no coordinated negative campaign, we have no positive campaign whatsoever, and we have no agenda for governing." The president, however, seemed unfazed. He reminded skeptics of Michael Dukakis's early lead in the 1988 contest and assured them that the Republican ticket would emerge triumphant again in November. "I will do what I have to do to get re-elected," he told his followers.

THE SOCIAL FABRIC IN THE 1990s

AGE, GENDER, RACE   At the same time that American military forces were converging on the Persian Gulf during Operation Desert Shield, an army of census workers were roaming the streets and byways of the United States, counting heads and accumulating data about the American people. The preliminary results of the 1990 census revealed several dramatic changes in the country's demographic profile. During the 1980s the nation's population grew by 10 percent, or some 23 million people, boosting the total to almost 250 million. The median age of the quarter-billion Americans rose from thirty to thirty-three, and the much-discussed baby-boom generation—the 43 million people born between 1946 and 1964—entered middle age.

Because of its disproportionate size, the baby-boom generation magnifies changes in American society as it moves through the life cycle. As one demographer noted, it resembles a "pig in a python." Political analysts suggested that this generation's maturation and preoccupation with practical concerns such as raising families and buying houses helped explain the surge of political conservatism during the 1980s. Surveys revealed that baby boomers wanted stronger family and religious ties in the eighties and promoted a greater respect for authority. Yet having come to maturity during the turbulent sixties and early seventies, the baby boomers also displayed more tolerance of social and cultural diversity than their parents.

The census revealed that the fastest-growing age groups, however, were the oldest ones. Americans in their nineties more than doubled during the 1980s, and those over a hundred grew by 77 percent. In 1991, over 57,000 Americans were centenarians. This "graying of America" was both a blessing and a burden. It demonstrated that Americans were healthier than ever, and helped erode the cultural stigma attached to the aged and aging, but it also posed a stiff challenge to public officials. How was the nation to care for so many old people? Corporations found their pension costs soaring. In 1967 the ratio of General Motors workers to pensioners—what demographers call the dependency ratio—was 10 to 1. In 1990 it was approaching 1 to 1. "We're building one hell of a burden for our future workers," warned a personnel manager. The same burden was straining the social security system. To finance an ever-growing group of retirees, American workers had to contribute an ever-higher portion of their paycheck to the social security system. During the 1980s, social security payroll taxes increased 24 percent.

The 1990 census described a nation on the move, as the "Sunbelt" states of the South and West continued to lure residents from the Midwest and Northeast. Fully 90 percent of the nation's total population growth during the 1980s came in southern or western states. California gained more people than any other state during the eighties, boosting its total to 29.8 million, 5 million more than in 1980. Texas and Florida each added more than 3 million new residents, while West Virginia, Iowa, and the District of Columbia experienced a net loss of residents. The Northeast became the least populous region of the country. These population shifts forced a massive redistricting of the House of Representatives, with Florida and California gaining three more seats each and Texas two, while states such as New York lost seats.

As they moved during the 1980s, Americans tended to settle in larger communities. Almost 90 percent of the decade's population growth occurred in metropolitan areas. The number of cities with 100,000 people or more increased by 29 to a total of 195, with 18 of the new metropolises in California alone. In 1990 some 78 percent of the population lived in a metropolitan urban area and, for the first time, a majority of Americans lived in cities of a million or more people. "We are a country not only of city dwellers," said a Census Bureau analyst, "but of large-city dwellers, a country of metropolitan-dwellers." This move to the cities largely reflected trends in the job market, as the economy continued to shift from manufacturing to professional service industries, particularly those specializing in telecommunications and information-processing.

The 1990 census also showed that women continued to enter the work force in large numbers. Indeed, one of the most significant sociological developments in American life since 1970 was the accelerated entry of women into the world of work outside the home. In 1970, 38 percent of the work force was female; in 1990 the figure was almost 50 percent. Women workers accounted for 60 percent of labor force growth since 1980, and fully 58 percent of all adult women were gainfully employed. A third of the new medical doctors during the eighties were women (4 percent in 1970); 40 percent of new lawyers were female (8.4 percent in 1970); and 22.6 percent of new dentists were women (less than 1 percent in 1970). Such advances in the professions indicated that women were also better educated than ever. During the 1980s the educational gap between men and women continued to narrow. Among people aged forty-five to fifty-four, the share of men with college degrees was ten points higher than the share of women. But among people aged twenty-five to thirty-four the difference was less than 1 percent.

The decline of the traditional family unit—two parents with children—continued during the 1980s. The proportion of the nation's households in that category declined from 31 percent in 1980 to 26 percent in 1990. And more people were living alone than ever before, largely as a result of high divorce rates or a growing practice of delaying marriage until well into the twenties. One out of every four households in 1990 was made up of a person living alone, a 26 percent increase over 1980. The number of single mothers increased 35 percent during the decade. The rate was much higher for African-Americans: in 1990 less than 38 percent of black children lived with both parents, down from 67 percent in 1960.

Young blacks burdened by the absence of one or both parents also faced shrinking economic opportunities in the 1980s. The 1990 census documented a slight decline in the proportion of Americans living in poverty, but a substantially heightened inequality in the distribution of income. Roughly 13 percent of the American people in 1990 were living at or below the official poverty level, pegged at $12,675 in annual income for a family of four. The urban poor were particularly victimized by a developing underclass culture, with young black males suffering the most.

THE NEW IMMIGRANTS   The Census Bureau reports also revealed that the racial and ethnic composition of the country changed more during the 1980s than at any other time in the twentieth century, with nearly one in every four Americans claiming African, Asian, Hispanic, or Native American ancestry. Among an overall population of 250 million, blacks represented 12 percent of the total, Hispanics 9 percent, Asians about 3 percent, and Native Americans almost 1 percent. The rate of increase among those four groups was twice as fast as it had been during the 1970s.

The primary cause of this dramatic change in the nation's ethnic mix was a surge of immigration. During the 1980's, legal immigration into the United Staes totaled almost 6 million people, 30 percent higher than the previous decade and more than in any other decade except 1901–1910. If the hundreds of thousands of illegal aliens, mostly Mexicans and Haitians, were added

RESIDENT POPULATION DISTRIBUTION FOR THE UNITED STATES BY RACE AND HISPANIC ORIGIN: 1990 AND 1980

	1990 Number	%	1980 Number	%	% Change
Total population	248,709,873	100.0	226,545,805	100.0	9.8
White	199,686,070	80.3	188,371,622	83.1	6.0
Black	29,986,060	12.1	26,495,020	11.7	13.2
American Indian, Eskimo or Aleut	1,959,234	0.8	1,420,400	0.6	37.9
Asian or Pacific Islander	7,273,662	2.9	3,500,439	1.5	107.8
Other race	9,804,847	3.9	6,758,319	3.0	45.1
Hispanic origin	22,354,059	9.0	14,608,673	6.4	53.0

Source: Bureau of the Census, 1991.

to the totals, the figure would surpass the 8.8 million newcomers of the first decade of the century. In 1990, the United States welcomed more than twice as many immigrants as all other countries in the world put together. The magnetic attraction of the United States to foreigners during the 1980s was vividly revealed in 1987 when the Immigration Service opened a special "visa lottery" for citizens in those countries historically shortchanged by annual immigration quotas. Officials allotted 10,000 such visas and assumed that would meet the demand, but 1.4 million people applied.

Even more significant than the overall number of newcomers were their places of origin. For the first time in the nation's history, the majority of immigrants came not from Europe but from other pats of the world. The percentage of European immigrants to the United States declined from 53 percent of the total in the 1950s to 12 percent in the 1980s. Asian-Americans were the fastest-growing segment of the population in the eighties, with numbers increasing by 80 percent, a rate seven times as great as the general population. Among the legal immigrants during the decade, Mexicans made up the largest share, averaging about 60,000 a year. The second-highest number came from the Philippines (46,000), and immigrants from mainland China, Taiwan, and Hong Kong totaled 45,000 annually. The next largest groups were Vietnamese and Koreans, followed by Dominicans, Asian Indians, Jamaicans, Iranians, Cubans, Cambodians, and Laotians.

Heightening the social impact of these new immigrants was their tendency to cluster in a handful of states and cities. Most of them gravitated to New York, Illinois, and New Jersey, as well as Florida, Texas, Hawaii, California, and other Sunbelt states. By 1990, California harbored 64 percent of the Asian-Americans in the country, and 34 percent of the Hispanics. The population of Miami, Florida, was 64 percent Hispanic, and San Antonio, Texas, boasted 55 percent. Los Angeles contained 2 million Mexican-Americans, more than any other city except Mexico City itself. Preferring their own ethnic enclaves and bringing with them distinctive languages, cuisine, clothes, dress, and folkways, the immigrants from Asia, Latin America, and the Caribbean quickly became an insistent cultural presence. "It's fascinating," remarked New York governor Mario Cuomo, himself the son of Italian immigrants. "For those of us who have been in the city for fifty years, it's wonderful to see the faces on the street now. Our diversity level has gone up." When asked to assess the overall impact of the new immigration trends, he replied: "Plus, plus, plus."

IMMIGRANTS ADMITTED BY
TOP 15 COUNTRIES OF BIRTH
IN FISCAL YEAR 1990

Country of Birth	1990
Total	**656,111**
Mexico	56,549
Philippines	54,907
Vietnam	48,662
Dominican Republic	32,064
Korea	29,548
China (mainland)	28,746
India	28,679
Soviet Union	25,350
Jamaica	18,828
Iran	18,031
Taiwan	13,839
United Kingdom	13,730
Canada	13,717
Poland	13,334
Haiti	11,862
Other	248,265

Source: U.S. Immigration and Naturalization Service, 1991.

But increasing diversity brought with it increasing tensions. African-America leaders worried that the newcomers were gaining an economic foothold at the expense of poor blacks, and many native whites resented the influx of newcomers into their communities. When a Miami radio talk-show host invited listeners to share their feelings about continuing Cuban immigration into south Florida, one suggested that they "be shot before they land." In Texas, Louisiana, and Florida, angry white fishermen joined with local chapters of the Ku Klux Klan in harassing and assaulting Vietnamese shrimpers. A group of laid-off Detroit auto workers vented their frustration against imported Japanese cars by beating to death an Asian passerby who, it turned out, was a Chinese-American. California witnessed a violent gang war between Hispanic and Cambodian residents, two immigrant groups with little in common except the desire to build a new life in the same neighborhood.

Such clashes recall earlier chapters in American immigrant history, a story marked from the start by ambivalence about the nation's tradition of inclusiveness. With rhetoric reminiscent of the nativist movement a century earlier, critics of the new tide of immigration charged that America was being "overrun" with foreigners; they questioned whether Hispanics and Asians could be "assimilated" into American culture. "We should start reducing quotas before we become a Third World country," argued David Duke, a former Klan member elected as Republican state legislator in Louisiana. Others made the same ethnocentric point. "As whites see their power and control over their lives declining," asked Dr. John Taton, co-founder of a nativist group called US English, "will they simply go quietly into the night? Or will there be an explosion?" Tanton vowed to fight, and he led a campaign for the repeal of bilingual education programs and for a federal law mandating English as the official national language. In 1986 California voters passed a referendum ending bilingual education. Florida soon followed suit.

The bitter irony of this new nativism was that it targeted recent immigrants for bringing with them to the United States virtues long prized by Americans—hope, energy, persistence, and an aggressive work ethic. Like most of the predecessors who braved tremendous hardships to make their way to America, they toiled long and hard for a slice of the American dream, and most economic studies concluded that their presence was beneficial to the nation. They created more wealth than they consumed, and many of them compiled an astonishing record of achievement. The median household income of Asian-Americans, for example, exceeded every other group, including native whites, and Asian-Americans were disproportionately represented in the nation's most prestigious colleges and universities. Although constituting only 1.6 percent of the total population in 1985, Asian-Americans made up over 11 percent of Harvard's freshman class and almost 20 percent at Berkeley and the California Institute of Technology. Yet the very success of the new immigrants contributed to the resentment they encountered from other groups.

THE FABRIC FRAYED   During the 1990s racial distrust and bitterness remained America's most intractable problem. Festering tensions boiled over in the spring of 1992 when a California jury acquitted four Los Angeles policemen charged with savagely beating a black suspect. A bystander had fortuitously captured the incident on a video camera and its gruesome contents were widely broadcast across the nation. To most observers the videotape offered compelling evidence of police brutality. Yet the sub-

In May 1992 riots erupted in south-central Los Angeles and other American cities when a jury acquitted four white Los Angeles policemen on charges of police brutality in the beating of a black motorist, Rodney King.

urban jurors, none of whom was black, stunned the nation by deciding in favor of the policemen. "Nobody," observed Los Angeles Mayor Tom Bradley, "could have anticipated this verdict."

The unexpected verdict ignited a huge riot in predominantly black-populated south-central Los Angeles. While hundreds of fires raged and businesses were ransacked, a television camera crew captured a white driver being dragged from his truck and bludgeoned. The police were agonizingly slow to respond, prompting California's governor to dispatch over 6,000 National Guard troops to Los Angeles. The conflagration resulted in 54 deaths, 2,400 injuries, 17,000 arrests, the destruction of some 10,000 businesses, and the loss of over 50,000 jobs in an area already plagued by high unemployment. Other ugly incidents occurred in Atlanta, San Francisco, Las Vegas, and Madison, Wisconsin.

Although the National Guard and police were able to restore an uneasy calm in Los Angeles, racial and ethnic unrest continued to simmer. The burning, looting, and indiscriminate attacks on whites recalled to mind the race riots of 1965. But there were

ominous differences. Whereas the earlier Watts riot had involved blacks against whites, the 1992 mayhem included worri-
some new developments: blacks targeting blacks, Latinos
attacking whites, blacks and Latinos preying upon Koreans and
other Asian-Americans, and well-organized and well-armed
gangs of thugs and youths eager to take advantage of the turmoil.

In the aftermath of the riots, social scientists and politicians
struggled to understand the infinitely complicated causes of
inner-city unrest and violence. They all agreed that old answers
were no longer sufficient.

Amid such a volatile atmosphere of mounting ethnic strife and
political confrontation, some observers worried that the social
fabric was being stretched to the breaking point. The nation
seemed awash in "special-interest groups," highly organized,
well-financed, and politically savvy organizations designed to
promote single issues: corporate tax breaks, gun ownership,
prayer in schools, abortion, animal rights, and environmental-
ism, to name just a few. It was becoming increasingly difficult to
recognize the common good. Said a prominent law professor:
"We are witnessing a gradual decline in the legal and social significance of community interests."

Many critics of this eroding sense of commonality blamed the
influx of foreigners. Yet as a 1991 editorial in the *Los Angeles
Times* pointed out, the immigrants of the eighties were not primarily responsible for the fragmentation of cultural consensus:
immigrants arrived in a country that was already losing its sense
of collective unity. "Conformity is no longer the norm because
there is nothing to conform to, no single national norm of culture, behavior, religion. In these circumstances, to blame immigrants for being different is to miss the point." Indeed, the most
potent challenge facing Americans during the 1990s came not
from abroad but from within: how could they find a "common
ground" of shared civic values that nourished both cultural pluralism and individual rights? How could Americans live up to
their national motto—*E pluribus unum,* One out of many? The
dream of pluralistic unity survives, and in its resilient imperative
Americans continued to find both challenge and hope.

FURTHER READING

For further insight into Reagan and his policies see the memoirs of
members of his administration, such as Donald Regan's *For the Record:
From Wall Street to Washington* (1988), Peggy Noonan's *What I Saw at
the Revolution: A Political Life in the Reagan Era* (1990), or Terrel Bell's
The Thirteenth Man: A Reagan Cabinet Memoir (1988).

Robert B. Reich's *The Next American Frontier* (1981)° examines the nation's recent industrial crisis. On Reaganomics, see David Stockman's *The Triumph of Politics: How the Reagan Revolution Failed* (1986) and Robert Lekachman's *Greed Is Not Enough: Reaganomics* (1982). On the issue of arms control, see Strobe Talbott's *Deadly Gambits: The Reagan Administration and the Stalemate in Nuclear Arms Control* (1984).°

For Reagan's foreign policy in Central America, see James Chace's *Endless War: How We Got Involved in Central America and What Can Be Done* (1984)° and Walter LaFeber's *Inevitable Revolutions: The United States in Central America* (rev. ed., 1984).° Broader views of Reagan's foreign policy are offered in Alexander M. Haig, Jr.'s *Caveat: Realism, Reagan, and Foreign Policy* (1984) and Caspar W. Weinberger's *Fighting for Peace: Seven Critical Years in the Pentagon* (1990).

Elizabeth Drew's *Campaign Journal: The Political Events of 1983–1984* (1985) covers the events of the election of 1984. Geraldine A. Ferraro and Linda B. Francke's *Ferraro: My Story* (1985)° is about America's first major female vice-presidential candidate.

On Reagan's second term, see Jane Mayer and Doyle McManus's *Landslide: The Unmaking of the President, 1984–1988* (1988) and Jane Hunter et al.'s *The Iran-Contra Connection* (1987). For a masterful work on the Iran-Contra affair, see Theodore Draper's *A Very Thin Line* (1991). Several books of essays collect varying assessments of the Reagan years. Among these are *The Reagan Revolution* (1988), edited by B. B. Kymlicka and Jean V. Matthews; *The Reagan Presidency: An Incomplete Revolution* (1990), edited by Dilys M. Hill et al.; and *Looking Back on the Reagan Presidency* (1990), edited by Larry Berman. The best overview thus far on the Reagan years is Lou Cannon's *The Role of a Lifetime* (1991).

On the 1988 campaign see Jack Germond and Jules Witcover's *Whose Broad Stripes and Bright Stars? The Trivial Pursuit of the Presidency, 1988* (1989) and Sidney Blumenthal's *The Last Campaign of the Cold War* (1990). Major issues in economic and social policy are addressed in Robert Reich's *The Work of Nations: Preparing Ourselves for Twenty-first Century Capitalism* (1991) and William Julius Wilson's *The Truly Disadvantaged: The Inner City, the Underclass, and Public Policy* (1987)°.

For analyses of the Persian Gulf war, see Stephen R. Graubard's *Mr. Bush's War: Adventures in the Politics of Illusion* (1992) and Harry Summers's *On Strategy II: A Critical Analysis of the Gulf War* (1992)°. On the antifeminist movement see Susan Faludi's *Backlash: The Undeclared War Against American Feminism* (1992)°.

° These books are available in paperback editions.

APPENDIX

THE DECLARATION OF
INDEPENDENCE

WHEN IN THE COURSE OF HUMAN EVENTS, it becomes necessary for one people to dissolve the political bands which have connected them with another, and to assume the Powers of the earth, the separate and equal station to which the Laws of Nature and of Nature's God entitle them, a decent respect to the opinions of mankind requires that they should declare the causes which impel them to the separation.

We hold these truths to be self-evident, that all men are created equal, that they are endowed by their Creator with certain unalienable rights, that among these are Life, Liberty, and the pursuit of Happiness. That to secure these rights, Governments are instituted among Men, deriving their just powers from the consent of the governed. That whenever any Form of Government becomes destructive of these ends, it is the Right of the People to alter or to abolish it, and to institute new Government, laying its foundation on such principles and organizing its powers in such form, as to them shall seem most likely to effect their Safety and Happiness. Prudence, indeed, will dictate that Governments long established should not be changed for light and transient causes; and accordingly all experience hath shown, that mankind are more disposed to suffer, while evils are sufferable, than to right themselves by abolishing the forms to which they are accustomed. But when a long train of abuses and usurpations, pursuing invariably the same Object evinces a design to reduce them under absolute Despotism, it is their right, it is their duty, to throw off such Government, and to provide new Guards for their future security.—Such has been the patient sufferance of these Colonies; and such is now the necessity which constrains them to alter their former Systems of Government. The history of the present King of Great Britain is a history of repeated injuries and usurpations, all having in direct object the establishment of an absolute Tyranny over these States. To prove this, let Facts be submitted to a candid world.

He has refused his Assent to Laws, the most wholesome and necessary for the public good.

He has forbidden his Governors to pass Laws of immediate and pressing importance, unless suspended in their operation till his Assent should be obtained; and when so suspended, he has utterly neglected to attend to them.

He has refused to pass other Laws for the accommodation of large districts of people, unless those people would relinquish the right of Representation in the Legislature, a right inestimable to them and for midable to tyrants only.

He has called together legislative bodies at places unusual, uncomfortable, and distant from the depository of their public Records, for the sole purpose of fatiguing them into compliance with his measures.

He has dissolved Representative Houses repeatedly, for opposing with manly firmness his invasions on the rights of the people.

He has refused for a long time, after such dissolutions, to cause others to be elected; whereby the Legislative powers, incapable of Annihilation, have returned to the People at large for their exercise; the State remaining in the mean time exposed to all dangers of invasion from without, and convulsions within.

He has endeavoured to prevent the population of these States; for that purpose obstructing the Laws of Naturalization of Foreigners; refusing to pass others to encourage their migrations hither, and raising the conditions of new Appropriations of Lands.

He has obstructed the Administration of Justice, by refusing his Assent to Laws for establishing Judiciary powers.

He has made Judges dependent on his Will alone, for the tenure of their offices, and the amount and payment of their salaries.

He has erected a multitude of New Offices, and sent hither swarms of Officers to harass our People, and eat out their substance.

He has kept among us, in times of peace, Standing Armies without the Consent of our legislature.

He has affected to render the Military independent of and superior to the Civil Power.

He has combined with others to subject us to a jurisdiction foreign to our constitution, and unacknowledged by our laws; giving his Assent to their Acts of pretended Legislation:

For quartering large bodies of armed troops among us:

For protecting them, by a mock Trial, from Punishment for any Murders which they should commit on the Inhabitants of these States:

For cutting off our Trade with all parts of the world:

For imposing taxes on us without our Consent:

For depriving us of many cases, of the benefits of Trial by jury:

For transporting us beyond Seas to be tried for pretended offences:

For abolishing the free System of English Laws in a neighbouring Province, establishing therein an Arbitrary government, and enlarging its Boundaries so as to render it at once an example and fit instrument for introducing the same absolute rule into these Colonies:

For taking away our Charters, abolishing our most valuable Laws, and altering fundamentally the Forms of our Governments:

For suspending our own Legislatures, and declaring themselves in vested with Power to legislate for us in all cases whatsoever.

He has abdicated Government here, by declaring us out of his Protection and waging War against us.

He has plundered our seas, ravaged our Coasts, burnt our towns, and destroyed the lives of our people.

He is at this time transporting large armies of foreign mercenaries to compleat the works of death, desolation, and tyranny, already begun with circumstances of Cruelty & perfidy scarcely paralleled in the most barbarous ages, and totally unworthy the Head of a civilized nation.

He has constrained our fellow Citizens taken Captive on the high Seas to bear Arms against their Country, to become the executioners of their friends and Brethren, or to fall themselves by their Hands.

He has excited domestic insurrections amongst us, and has endeavoured to bring on the inhabitants of our frontiers, the merciless Indian Savages, whose known rule of warfare, is an undistinguished destruction of all ages, sexes, and conditions.

In every stage of these Oppressions We have Petitioned for Redress in the most humble terms: Our repeated Petitions have been answered only by repeated injury. A Prince, whose character is thus marked by every act which may define a Tyrant, is unfit to be the ruler of a free people.

Nor have We been wanting in attention to our British brethren. We have warned them from time to time of attempts by their legislature to extend an unwarrantable jurisdiction over us. We have reminded them of the circumstances of our emigration and settlement here. We have appealed to their native justice and magnanimity, and we have conjured them by the ties of our common kindred to disavow these usurpations, which, would inevitably interrupt our connections and correspondence. They too must have been deaf to the voice of justice and of consanguinity. We must, therefore, acquiesce in the necessity, which denounces our Separation, and hold them, as we hold the rest of mankind, Enemies in War, in Peace Friends.

WE, THEREFORE, the Representatives of the UNITED STATES OF AMERICA, in General Congress, Assembled, appealing to the Supreme Judge of the world for the rectitude of our intentions, do, in the Name, and by Authority of the good People of these Colonies, solemnly publish and declare, That these United Colonies are, and of Right ought to be FREE AND INDEPENDENT STATES; that they are Absolved from all Allegiance to the British Crown, and that all political connection between them and the State of Great Britain, is and ought to be totally dissolved; and that as Free and Independent States, they have full Power to levy War, conclude Peace, contract Alliances, establish Commerce, and to do all other Acts and Things which Independent States may of right do. And for the support of this Declaration, with a firm reliance on the Protection of Divine Providence, we mutually pledge to each other our Lives, our Fortunes, and our sacred Honor.

The foregoing Declaration was, by order of Congress, engrossed, and signed by the following members:

John Hancock

NEW HAMPSHIRE
Josiah Bartlett
William Whipple
Matthew Thornton

MASSACHUSETTS BAY
Samuel Adams
John Adams
Robert Treat Paine
Elbridge Gerry

RHODE ISLAND
Stephen Hopkins
William Ellery

CONNECTICUT
Roger Sherman
Samuel Huntington
William Williams
Oliver Wolcott

NEW YORK
William Floyd
Philip Livingston
Francis Lewis
Lewis Morris

NEW JERSEY
Richard Stockton
John Witherspoon
Francis Hopkinson
John Hart
Abraham Clark

PENNSYLVANIA
Robert Morris
Benjamin Rush
Benjamin Franklin
John Morton
George Clymer
James Smith
George Taylor
James Wilson
George Ross

DELAWARE
Caesar Rodney
George Read
Thomas M'Kean

MARYLAND
Samuel Chase
William Paca
Thomas Stone
Charles Carroll, of
    Carrollton

VIRGINIA
George Wythe
Richard Henry Lee
Thomas Jefferson
Benjamin Harrison
Thomas Nelson, Jr.
Francis Lightfoot Lee
Carter Braxton

NORTH CAROLINA
William Hooper
Joseph Hewes
John Penn

SOUTH CAROLINA
Edward Rutledge
Thomas Heyward, Jr.
Thomas Lynch, Jr.
Arthur Middleton

GEORGIA
Button Gwinnett
Lyman Hall
George Walton

Resolved, That copies of the Declaration be sent to the several assemblies, conventions, and committees, or councils of safety, and to the several commanding officers of the continental troops; that it be proclaimed in each of the United States, at the head of the army.

ARTICLES OF CONFEDERATION

To ALL TO WHOM these Presents shall come, we the undersigned Delegates of the States affixed to our Names send greeting.

Whereas the Delegates of the United States of America in Congress assembled did on the fifteenth day of November in the Year of our Lord One Thousand Seven Hundred and Seventy-seven, and in the Second Year of the Independence of America agree to certain articles of Confederation and perpetual Union between the States of Newhampshire, Massachusetts-bay, Rhodeisland and Providence Plantations, Connecticut, New York, New Jersey, Pennsylvania, Delaware, Maryland, Virginia, North-Carolina, South-Carolina and Georgia in the Words following, viz.

Articles of Confederation and perpetual Union between the States of Newhampshire, Massachusetts-bay, Rhodeisland and Providence Plantations, Connecticut, New-York, New-Jersey, Pennsylvania, Delaware, Maryland, Virginia, North-Carolina, South-Carolina and Georgia.

ARTICLE I. The stile of this confederacy shall be "The United States of America."

ARTICLE II. Each State retains its sovereignty, freedom and independence, and every power, jurisdiction and right, which is not by this confederation expressly delegated to the United States, in Congress assembled.

ARTICLE III. The said States hereby severally enter into a firm league of friendship with each other, for their common defence, the security of their liberties, and their mutual and general welfare, binding themselves to assist each other, against all force offered to, or attacks made upon them, or any of them, on account of religion, sovereignty, trade or any other pretence whatever.

ARTICLE IV. The better to secure and perpetuate mutual friendship and intercourse among the people of the different States in this Union, the free inhabitants of each of these States, paupers, vagabonds and fugitives from justice excepted, shall be entitled to all privileges and immunities of free citizens in the several States; and the people of each State shall have free ingress and regress to and from any other State, and shall enjoy therein all the privileges of trade and commerce, subject to the same duties, impositions and restrictions as the inhabitants thereof respectively, provided that such restrictions shall not extend so far as to prevent the removal of property imported into any State, to any other State of which the owner is an inhabitant; provided also that no imposition, duties or restriction shall be laid by any State, on the property of the United States, or either of them.

If any person guilty of, or charged with treason, felony, or other high misdemeanor in any State, shall flee from justice, and be found in any of the United States, he shall upon demand of the Governor or Executive power, of the State from which he fled, be delivered up and removed to the State having jurisdiction of his offence.

Full faith and credit shall be given in each of these States to the records, acts and judicial proceedings of the courts and magistrates of every other State.

ARTICLE V. For the more convenient management of the general interests of the United States, delegates shall be annually appointed in such manner as the legislature of each State shall direct, to meet in Congress on the first Monday in November, in every year, with a power reserved to each State, to recall its delegates, or any of them, at any time within the year, and to send others in their stead, for the remainder of the year.

No State shall be represented in Congress by less than two, nor by more than seven members; and no person shall be capable of being a delegate for more than three years in any term of six years; nor shall any person, being a delegate, be capable of holding any office under the United States, for which he, or another for his benefit receives any salary, fees or emolument of any kind.

Each State shall maintain its own delegates in a meeting of the States, and while they act as members of the committee of the States.

In determining questions in the United States, in Congress assembled, each State shall have one vote.

Freedom of speech and debate in Congress shall not be impeached or questioned in any court, or place out of Congress, and the members of Congress shall be protected in their persons from arrests and imprisonments, during the time of their going to and from, and attendance on Congress, except for treason, felony, or breach of the peace.

ARTICLE VI. No State without the consent of the United States in Congress assembled, shall send any embassy to, or receive any embassy from, or enter into any conference, agreement, alliance or treaty with any king, prince or state; nor shall any person holding any office of profit or trust under the United States, or any of them, accept of any present, emolument, office or title of any kind whatever from any king, prince or foreign state; nor shall the United States in Congress assembled, or any of them, grant any title of nobility.

No two or more States shall enter into any treaty, confederation or alliance whatever between them, without the consent of the United States in Congress assembled, specifying accurately the purposes for which the same is to be entered into, and how long it shall continue.

No State shall lay any imposts or duties, which may interfere with any stipulations in treaties, entered into by the United States in Congress assembled, with any king, prince or state, in pursuance of any treaties already proposed by Congress, to the courts of France and Spain.

No vessels of war shall be kept up in time of peace by any State, except such number only, as shall be deemed necessary by the United States in Congress assembled, for the defence of such State, or its trade; nor shall any body of forces be kept up by any State, in time of peace, except such number only, as in the judgment of the United States, in Congress assembled, shall be deemed requisite to garrison the forts necessary for the defence of such State; but every State shall always keep up a well regulated and disciplined militia, sufficiently armed and accoutred, and shall provide and constantly have ready for use, in public stores, a due number of field pieces and tents, and a proper quantity of arms, ammunition and camp equipage.

No State shall engage in any war without the consent of the United States in Congress assembled, unless such State be actually invaded by enemies, or shall have received certain advice of a resolution being formed by some nation of Indians to invade such State, and the danger is so imminent as not to admit of a delay, till the United States in Congress assembled can be consulted: nor shall any State grant commissions to any ships or vessels of war, nor letters of marque or reprisal, except it be after a declaration of war by the United States in Congress assembled, and then only against the kingdom or state and the subjects thereof, against which war has been so declared, and under such regulations as shall be established by the United States in Congress assembled, unless such State be infested by pirates, in which case vessels of war may be fitted out for that occasion, and kept so long as the danger shall continue, or until the United States in Congress assembled shall determine otherwise.

ARTICLE VII. When land-forces are raised by any State of the common defence, all officers of or under the rank of colonel, shall be appointed by the Legislature of each State respectively by whom such forces shall be raised, or in such manner as such State shall direct, and all vacancies shall be filled up by the State which first made the appointment.

ARTICLE VIII. All charges of war, and all other expenses that shall be incurred for the common defence or general welfare, and allowed by the United States in Congress assembled, shall be defrayed out of a common treasury, which shall be supplied by the several States, in proportion to the value of all land within each State, granted to or surveyed for any person, as such land and the buildings and improvements thereon shall be estimated according to such mode as the United States in Congress assembled, shall from time to time direct and appoint.

The taxes for paying that proportion shall be laid and levied by the authority and direction of the Legislatures of the several States within the time agreed upon by the United States in Congress assembled.

ARTICLE IX. The United States in Congress assembled, shall have the sole and exclusive right and power of determining on peace and war, except in the cases mentioned in the sixth article—of sending and receiving ambassadors—entering into treaties and alliances, provided that no treaty of commerce shall be made whereby the legislative power of the respective States shall be restrained from imposing such imposts and duties on foreigners, as their own people are subjected to, or from prohibiting the exportation or importation of and species of goods or commodities whatsoever—of establishing rules for deciding in all cases, what captures on land or water shall be legal, and in what manner prizes taken by land or naval forces in the service of the United States shall be divided or appropriated—of granting letters of marque and reprisal in times of peace—appointing courts for the trial of piracies and felonies committed on the high seas and establishing courts for receiving and determining finally appeals in all cases of captures, provided that no member of Congress shall be appointed a judge of any of the said courts.

The United States in Congress assembled shall also be the last resort on appeal in all disputes and differences now subsisting or that hereafter may arise between two or more States concerning boundary, jurisdiction or any other cause whatever; which authority shall always be exercised in the manner following. Whenever the legislative or executive authority or lawful agent of any State in controversy with another shall present a petition to Congress, stating the matter in question and praying for a hearing, notice thereof shall be given by order of Congress to the legislative or executive authority of the other State in controversy, and a day assigned for the appearance of the parties by their lawful agents, who shall then be directed to appoint by joint consent, commissioners or judges to constitute a court for hearing and determining the matter in question: but if they cannot agree, Congress shall name three persons out of each of the United States, and from the list of such persons each party shall alternately strike out one, the petitioners beginning, until the number shall be reduced to thirteen; and from that number not less than seven, nor more than nine names as Congress shall direct, shall in the presence of Congress be drawn out by lot, and the persons whose names shall be so drawn or any five of them, shall be commissioners or judges, to hear and finally determine the controversy, so always as a major part of the judges who shall hear the cause shall agree in the determination: and if either party shall neglect to attend at the day appointed, without reasons, which Congress shall judge sufficient, or being present shall refuse to strike, the Congress shall proceed to nominate three persons out of each State, and the Secretary of Congress shall strike in behalf of such party absent or refusing; and the judgment and sentence of the court to be appointed, in the manner before prescribed, shall be final and conclusive; and if any of the parties shall refuse to submit to the authority of such court, or to appear or defend their claim or cause, the court shall nevertheless proceed to pronounce sentence, or judgment, which shall in like manner be final and decisive, the judgment or sentence and other proceedings being in either case transmitted to Congress, and lodged among the acts of Congress for the security of the parties concerned: provided that every commissioner, before he sits in judgment, shall take an oath to be administered by one of the judges of the supreme or superior court of the State where the case shall be tried, "well and truly to hear and determine the matter in question, according to the best of his judgment, without favour, affection or hope of reward:" provided also that no State shall be deprived of territory for the benefit of the United States.

All controversies concerning the private right of soil claimed under different grants of two or more States, whose jurisdiction as they may respect such lands, and the states which passed such grants are adjusted, the said grants or either of them being at the same time claimed to have originated antecedent to such settlement of jurisdiction, shall on the petition of either party to the Congress of the United States, be finally determined as near as may be in the same manner as is before prescribed for deciding disputes respecting territorial jurisdiction between different States.

The United States in Congress assembled shall also have the sole and exclusive right and power of regulating the alloy and value of coin struck by their own authority, or by that of the respective States—fixing the standard of weights and measures throughout the United States—regulating the trade and managing all affairs with the Indians, not members of any of the States, provided that the legislative right of any State within its own limits be not infringed or violated—establishing and regulating post-offices from one State to another, throughout all of the United States, and exacting such postage on the papers passing thro' the same as may be requisite to defray the expenses of the said office—appointing all officers of the land forces, in the service of the United States, excepting regimental officers—appointing all the officers of the naval forces, and commissioning all officers whatever in the service of the United States—making rules for the government and regulation of the said land and naval forces, and directing their operations.

The United States in Congress assembled shall have authority to appoint a committee, to sit in the recess of Congress, to be denominated "a Committee of the States," and to consist of one delegate from each State; and to appoint such other committees and civil officers as may be necessary for managing the general affairs of the United States under their direction—to appoint one of their number to preside, provided that no person be allowed to serve in the office of president more than one year in any term of three years; to ascertain the necessary sums of money to be raised for the service of the United States, and to appropriate and apply the same for defraying the public expenses—to borrow money, or emit bills on the credit of the United States, transmitting every half year to the respective States an account of the sums of money so borrowed or emitted,—to build and equip a navy—to agree upon the number of land forces, and to make requisitions from each State for its quota, in proportion to the number of white inhabitants in such

State; which requisition shall be binding, and thereupon the Legislature of each State shall appoint the regimental officers, raise the men and cloath, arm and equip them in a soldier like manner, at the expense of the United States; and the officers and men so cloathed, armed and equipped shall march to the place appointed, and within the time agreed on by the United States in Congress assembled: but if the United States in Congress assembled shall, on consideration of circumstances judge proper that any State should not raise men, or should raise a smaller number of men than the quota thereof, such extra number shall be raised, officered, cloathed, armed and equipped in the same manner as the quota of such State, unless the legislature of such State shall judge that such extra number cannot be safely spared out of the same, in which case they shall raise officer, cloath, arm and equip as many of such extra number as they judge can be safely spared. And the officers and men so cloathed, armed and equipped, shall march to the place appointed, and within the time agreed on by the United States in Congress assembled.

The United States in Congress assembled shall never engage in a war, nor grant letters of marque and reprisal in time of peace, nor enter into any treaties or alliances, nor coin money, nor regulate the value thereof, nor ascertain the sums and expenses necessary for the defence and welfare of the United States, or any of them, nor emit bills, nor borrow money on the credit of the United States, nor appropriate money, nor agree upon the number of vessels to be built or purchased, or the number of land or sea forces to be raised, nor appoint a commander in chief of the army or navy, unless nine States assent to the same: nor shall a question on any other point, except for adjourning from day to day be determined, unless by the votes of a majority of the United States in Congress assembled.

The Congress of the United States shall have power to adjourn to any time within the year, and to any place within the United States, so that no period of adjournment be for a longer duration than the space of six months, and shall publish the journal of their proceedings monthly, except such parts thereof relating to treaties, alliances or military operations, as in their judgment require secrecy; and the yeas and nays of the delegates of each State on any question shall be entered on the Journal, when it is desired by any delegate; and the delegates of a State, or any of them, at his or their request shall be furnished with a transcript of the said journal, except such parts as are above excepted, to lay before the Legislatures of the several States.

ARTICLE X. The committee of the States, or any nine of them, shall be authorized to execute, in the recess of Congress, such of the powers of Congress as the United States in Congress assembled, by the consent of nine States, shall from time to time think expedient to vest them with; provided that no power be delegated to the said committee, for the exercise of which, by the articles of confederation, the voice of nine States in the Congress of the United States assembled is requisite.

ARTICLE XI. Canada acceding to this confederation, and joining in the measures of the United States, shall be admitted into, and entitled to all the advantages of this Union: but no other colony shall be admitted into the same, unless such admission be agreed to by nine States.

ARTICLE XII. All bills of credit emitted, monies borrowed and debts contracted by, or under the authority of Congress, before the assembling of the United States, in pursuance of the present confederation, shall be deemed and considered as a charge against the United States, for payment and satisfaction whereof the said United States, and the public faith are hereby solemnly pledged.

ARTICLE XIII. Every State shall abide by the determinations of the United States in Congress assembled, on all questions which by this confederation are submitted to them. And the articles of this confederation shall be inviolably observed by every State, and the Union shall be perpetual; nor shall any alteration at any time hereafter be made in any of them; unless such alteration be agreed to in a Congress of the United States, and be afterwards confirmed by the Legislatures of every State.

And whereas it has pleased the Great Governor of the world to incline the hearts of the Legislatures we respectively represent in Congress, to approve of, and to authorize us to ratify the said articles of confederation and perpetual union. Know ye that we the undersigned delegates, by virtue of the power and authority to us given for that purpose, do by these presents, in the name and in behalf of our respective constituents, fully and entirely ratify and confirm each and every of the said articles of confederation and perpetual union, and all and singular the matters and things therein contained: and we do further solemnly plight and engage the faith of our respective constituents, that they shall abide by the determinations of the United States in Congress assembled, on all questions, which by the said confederation are submitted to them. And that the articles thereof shall be inviolably observed by the States we respectively represent, and that the Union shall be perpetual.

In witness thereof we have hereunto set our hands in Congress. Done at Philadelphia in the State of Pennsylvania the ninth day of July in the year of our Lord one thousand seven hundred and seventy-eight, and in the third year of the independence of America.

THE CONSTITUTION OF
THE UNITED STATES

WE THE PEOPLE OF THE UNITED STATES, in order to form a more perfect Union, establish Justice, insure domestic Tranquility, provide for the common defence, promote the general Welfare, and secure the Blessings of Liberty to ourselves and our Posterity, do ordain and establish this Constitution for the United States of America.

ARTICLE. I.

Section. 1. All legislative Powers herein granted shall be vested in a Congress of the United States, which shall consist of a Senate and House of Representatives.

Section. 2. The House of Representatives shall be composed of Members chosen every second Year by the People of the several States, and the Electors in each State shall have the Qualifications requisite for Electors of the most numerous Branch of the State Legislature.

No Person shall be a Representative who shall not have attained to the Age of twenty five Years, and been seven Years a Citizen of the United States, and who shall not, when elected, be an Inhabitant of that State in which he shall be chosen.

Representatives and direct Taxes shall be apportioned among the several States which may be included within this Union, according to their respective Numbers, which shall be determined by adding to the whole Number of free Persons, including those bound to Service for a Term of Years, and excluding Indians not taxed, three fifths of all other Persons. The actual Enumeration shall be made within three Years after the first Meeting of the Congress of the United States, and within every subsequent Term of ten Years, in such Manner as they shall by Law direct. The Number of Representatives shall not exceed one for every thirty Thousand, but each State shall have at Least one Representative; and until such enumeration shall be made, the State of New Hampshire shall be entitled to chuse three, Massachusetts eight, Rhode-Island and Providence Plantations one, Connecticut five, New-York six, New Jersey four, Pennsylvania eight, Delaware one, Maryland six, Virginia ten, North Carolina five, South Carolina five, and Georgia three.

When vacancies happen in the Representation from any state, the Executive Authority thereof shall issue Writs of Election to fill such Vacancies.

The House of Representatives shall chuse their Speaker and other Officers; and shall have the sole Power of Impeachment.

Section. 3. The Senate of the United States shall be composed of two Senators from each State, chosen by the legislature thereof, for six Years; and each Senator shall have one Vote.

Immediately after they shall be assembled in Consequence of the first Election, they shall be divided as equally as may be into three Classes. The Seats of the Senators of the first Class shall be vacated at the Expiration of the second Year, of the second Class at the Expiration of the fourth Year, and of the third Class at the Expiration of the sixth Year, so that one third maybe chosen every second Year; and if Vacancies happen by Resignation, or otherwise, during the Recess of the Legislature of any State, the Executive thereof may make temporary Appointments until the next Meeting of the Legislature, which shall then fill such Vacancies.

No Person shall be a Senator who shall not have attained to the Age of thirty Years, and been nine Years a Citizen of the United States, and who shall not, when elected, be an Inhabitant of that State for which he shall be chosen.

The Vice President of the United States shall be President of the Senate, but shall have no Vote, unless they be equally divided.

The Senate shall chuse their other Officers, and also a President pro tempore, in the Absence of the Vice President, or when he shall exercise the Office of President of the United States.

The Senate shall have the sole Power to try all Impeachments. When sitting for that Purpose, they shall be on Oath or Affirmation. When the President of the United States is tried, the Chief Justice shall preside: And no Person shall be convicted without the Concurrence of two thirds of the Members present.

Judgment in Cases of Impeachment shall not extend further than to removal from Office, and disqualification to hold and enjoy any Office of honor, Trust or Profit under the United States: but the Party convicted shall nevertheless be liable and subject to Indictment, Trial, Judgment and Punishment, according to Law.

Section. 4. The Times, Places and Manner of holding Elections for Senators and Representatives, shall be prescribed in each State by the Legislature thereof; but the Congress may at any time by Law make or alter such Regulations, except as to the Places of chusing Senators.

The Congress shall assemble at least once in every Year, and such Meeting shall be on the first Monday in December, unless they shall by Law appoint a different Day.

Section. 5. Each House shall be the Judge of the Elections, Returns and Qualifications of its own Members, and a Majority of each shall constitute a Quorum to do Business; but a smaller Number may adjourn from day to day, and may be authorized to compel the Attendance of absent Members, in such Manner, and under such Penalties as each House may provide.

Each House may determine the Rules of its Proceedings, punish its Members for disorderly Behaviour, and, with the Concurrence of two thirds, expel a Member.

Each House shall keep a Journal of its Proceedings, and from time to time publish the same, excepting such Parts as may in their Judgment require Secrecy; and the Yeas and Nays of the Members of either House on any question shall, at the Desire of one fifth of those Present, be entered on the Journal.

Neither House, during the Session of Congress, shall, without the Consent of the other, adjourn for more than three days, not to any other Place than that in which the two Houses shall be sitting.

Section. 6. The Senators and Representatives shall receive a Compensation for their Services, to be ascertained by Law, and paid out of the Treasury of the United States. They shall in all Cases, except Treason, Felony and Breach of the Peace, be privileged from Arrest during their Attendance at the Session of their respective Houses, and in going to and returning from the same; and for any Speech or Debate in either House, they shall not be questioned in any other Place.

No Senator or Representative shall, during the Time for which he was elected, be appointed to any civil Office under the Authority of the United States, which shall have been created, or the Emoluments whereof shall have been encreased during such time; and no Person holding any Office under the United States, shall be a Member of either House during his Continuance in Office.

Section. 7. All Bills for raising Revenue shall originate in the House of Representatives; but the Senate may propose or concur with Amendments as on other Bills.

Every Bill which shall have passed the House of Representatives and the Senate shall, before it become a Law, be presented to the President of the United States; If he approve he shall sign it, but if not he shall return it, with his Objections to that House in which it shall have originated, who shall enter the Objections at large on their Journal, and proceed to reconsider it. If after such Reconsideration two thirds of that House shall agree to pass the Bill, it shall be sent, together with the Objections, to the other House, by which it shall likewise be reconsidered, and if approved by two thirds of that House, it shall become a Law. But in all such Cases the Votes of both Houses shall be determined by yeas and Nays, and the Names of the Persons voting for and against the Bill shall be entered on the Journal of each House respectively. If any Bill shall not be returned by the President within ten Days (Sundays excepted) after it shall have been presented to him, the Same shall be a Law, in like Manner as if he had signed it, unless the Congress by their Adjournment prevent its Return, in which Case it shall not be a Law.

Every Order, Resolution, or Vote to which the Concurrence of the Senate and House of Representatives may be necessary (except on a question of Adjournment) shall be presented to the President of the United States; and before the Same shall take Effect, shall be approved by him, or being disapproved by him, shall be repassed by two thirds of the Senate and House of Representatives, according to the Rules and Limitations prescribed in the Case of a Bill.

Section. 8. The Congress shall have Power To lay and collect Taxes, Duties, Imposts and Excises, to pay the Debts and provide for the common Defence and general Welfare of the United States; but all Duties, Imposts and Excises shall be uniform throughout the United States;

To borrow Money on the credit of the United States;

To regulate Commerce with foreign Nations, and among the several States, and with the Indian Tribes;

To establish an uniform Rule of Naturalization, and uniform Laws on the subject of Bankruptcies throughout the United States;

To coin Money, regulate the Value thereof, and of foreign Coin, and fix the Standard of Weights and Measures;

To provide for the Punishment of counterfeiting the Securities and current Coin of the United States;

To establish Post Offices and Post Roads;

To promote the Progress of Science and useful Arts, by securing for limited Times to Authors and Inventors the exclusive Right to their respective Writings and Discoveries;

To constitute Tribunals inferior to the supreme Court;

To define and punish Piracies and Felonies committed on the high Seas, and Offences against the Law of Nations;

To declare War, grant Letters of Marque and Reprisal, and make Rules concerning Captures on land and Water;

To raise and support Armies, but no Appropriation of Money to that Use shall be for a longer Term than two Years;

To provide and maintain a Navy;

To make Rules for the Government and Regulation of the land and naval Forces;

To provide for calling forth the Militia to execute the Laws of the Union, suppress Insurrections and repel Invasions;

To provide for organizing, arming, and disciplining, the Militia, and for governing such Part of them as may be employed in the Service of the United States, reserving to the States respectively, the Appointment of the Officers, and the Authority of training the Militia according to the discipline prescribed by Congress.

To exercise exclusive Legislation in all Cases whatsoever, over such District (not exceeding ten Miles square) as may, by Cession of Particular States, and the Acceptance of Congress, become the Seat of the Government of the United States, and to exercise like Authority over all Places purchased by the Consent of the Legislature of the State in which the Same shall be, for the Erection of Forts, Magazines, Arsenals, dock-Yards, and other needful Buildings;—And

To make all Laws which shall be necessary and proper for carrying into

Execution the foregoing Powers, and all other Powers vested by this Constitution in the Government of the United States, or in any Department or Officer thereof.

Section. 9. The Migration or Importation of such Persons as any of the States now existing shall think proper to admit, shall not be prohibited by the Congress prior to the Year one thousand eight hundred and eight, but a Tax or duty may be imposed on such Importation, not exceeding ten dollars for each Person.

The Privilege of the Writ of Habeas Corpus shall not be suspended, unless when in Cases of Rebellion or Invasion the public Safety may require it.

No Bill of Attainder or ex post facto Law shall be passed.

No Capitation, or other direct, Tax shall be laid, unless in Proportion to the Census or Enumeration herein before directed to be taken.

No Tax or Duty shall be laid on Articles exported from any State.

No Preference shall be given by any Regulation of Commerce or Revenue to the Ports of one State over those of another: nor shall Vessels bound to, or from, one State, be obliged to enter, clear, or pay Duties in another.

No Money shall be drawn from the Treasury, but in Consequence of Appropriations made by Law; and a regular Statement and Account of the Receipts and Expenditures of all public Money shall be published from time to time.

No Title of Nobility shall be granted by the United States: And no Person holding any Office of Profit or trust under them, shall, without the Consent of the Congress, accept of any present, Emolument, Office, or Title, of any kind whatever, from any King, prince, or foreign State.

Section 10. No State shall enter into any Treaty, Alliance, or Confederation; grant Letters of Marque and Reprisal; coin Money; emit Bills of Credit; make any Thing but gold and silver Coin a Tender in Payment of Debts; pass any Bill of Attainder, ex post facto Law, or Law impairing the Obligation of Contracts, or grant any Title of Nobility.

No State shall, without the Consent of the Congress, lay any Imposts or Duties on Imports or Exports, except what may be absolutely necessary for executing it's inspection Laws: and the net Produce of all Duties and Imposts, laid by any State on Imports or Exports, shall be for the Use of the Treasury of the United States; and all such Laws shall be subject to the Revision and Controul of the Congress.

No State shall, without the Consent of Congress, lay any Duty of Tonnage, keep Troops, or Ships of War in time of Peace, enter into any Agreement or Compact with another State, or with a foreign Power, or engage in War, unless actually invaded, or in such imminent Danger as will not admit of delay.

ARTICLE. II.

Section. 1. The executive Power shall be vested in a President of the United States of America. He shall hold his Office during the term of four Years, and, together with the Vice President, chosen for the same Term, be elected, as follows

Each State shall appoint, in such Manner as the Legislature thereof may direct, a Number of Electors, equal to the whole Number of Senators and Representatives to which the State may be entitled in the Congress: but no Senator or Representative, or Person holding an Office of Trust or Profit under the United States, shall be appointed an Elector.

The Electors shall meet in their respective States, and vote by Ballot for two Persons, of whom one at least shall not be an Inhabitant of the same State with themselves. And they shall make a List of all the Persons voted for, and of the Number of Votes for each; which List they shall sign and certify, and transmit sealed to the Seat of the Government of the United States, directed to the President of the Senate. The President of the Senate shall, in the Presence of the Senate and House of Representatives, open all the Certificates, and the Votes shall then be counted. The Person having the greatest Number of Votes shall be the President, if such Number be a Majority of the whole Number of Electors appointed; and if there be more than one who have such Majority, and have an equal Number of Votes, then the House of Representatives shall immediately chuse by Ballot one of them for President; and if no Person have a Majority, then from the five highest on the List the said House shall in like Manner chuse the President. But in chusing the President, the Votes shall be taken by States, the Representation from each State having one Vote; A quorum for this Purpose shall consist of a Member or Members from two thirds of the States, and a Majority of all the States shall be necessary to a Choice. In every Case, after the Choice of the President, the Person having the greatest Number of Votes of the Electors shall be the Vice President. But if there should remain two or more who have equal Votes, the Senate shall chuse from them by Ballot the Vice President.

The Congress may determine the Time of chusing the Electors, and the Day on which they shall give their Votes; which Day shall be the same throughout the United States.

No Person except a natural born Citizen, or a Citizen of the United States, at the time of the Adoption of this Constitution, shall be eligible to the Office of President; neither shall any Person be eligible to that Office who shall not have attained to the Age of thirty five Years, and been fourteen Years a Resident within the United States.

In Case of the Removal of the President from Office, or of his Death, Resignation, or Inability to discharge the Powers and Duties of the said Office, the Same shall devolve on the Vice President, and the Congress may by Law provide for the Case of Removal, Death, Resignation or Inability, both of the President and Vice President, declaring what Officer shall then act as President, and such Officer shall act accordingly, until the Disability be removed, or a President shall be elected.

The President shall, at stated Times, receive for his Services, a Compensation, which shall neither be encreased or diminished during the Period for which he shall have been elected, and he shall not receive within that Period any other Emolument from the United States, or any of them.

Before he enters on the Execution of his Office, he shall take the following Oath or Affirmation:—"I do solemnly swear (or affirm) that I will faithfully execute the Office of President of the United States, and will to the best of my Ability, preserve, protect and defend the Constitution of the United States."

Section. 2. The President shall be Commander in Chief of the Army and Navy of the United States, and of the Militia of the several States, when called into the actual Service of the United States; he may require the Opinion, in writing, of the principal Officer in each of the executive Departments, upon any Subject relating to the Duties of their respective Offices, and he shall have Power to grant Reprieves and Pardons for Offences against the United States, except in Cases of Impeachment.

He shall have Power, by and with the Advice and Consent of the Senate, to make Treaties, provided two thirds of the Senators present concur; and he shall nominate, and by and with the Advice and Consent of the Senate, shall appoint Ambassadors, other public Ministers and Consuls, Judges of the supreme Court, and all other Officers of the United States, whose Appointments are not herein otherwise provided for, and which shall be established by Law; but the Congress may by Law vest the Appointment of such inferior Officers, as they think proper, in the President alone, in the Courts of Law, or in the Heads of Departments.

The President shall have Power to fill up all Vacancies that may happen during the Recess of the Senate, by granting Commissions which shall expire at the End of their next Session.

Section. 3. He shall from time to time give to the Congress Information of the State of the Union, and recommend to their Consideration such Measures as he shall judge necessary and expedient; he may, on extraordinary Occasions, convene both Houses, or either of them, and in Case of Disagreement between them, with Respect to the Time of Adjournment, he may adjourn them to such Time as he shall think proper; he shall receive Ambassadors and other public Ministers; he shall take Care that the Laws be faithfully executed, and shall Commission all the Officers of the United States.

Section. 4. The President, Vice President and all civil Officers of the United States, shall be removed from Office on Impeachment for, and Conviction of, Treason, Bribery, or other high Crimes and Misdemeanors.

Article. III.

Section. 1. The judicial Power of the United States, shall be vested in one supreme Court, and in such inferior Courts as the Congress may from time to time ordain and establish. The Judges, both of the supreme and inferior Courts, shall hold their Offices during good Behavior, and shall, at stated Times, receive for their Services, a Compensation, which shall not be diminished during their Continuance in Office.

Section. 2. The judicial Power shall extend to all Cases, in Law and Equity, arising under this Constitution, the Laws of the United States, and Treaties made, or which shall be made, under their Authority;—to all Cases affecting Ambassadors, other public Ministers and Consuls;—to all Cases of admiralty and maritime Jurisdiction;—the Controversies to which the United States shall be a Party;—to Controversies between two or more States;—between a State and Citizens of another State;—between Citizens of different States;—between Citizens of the same State claiming Lands under Grants of different States, and between a State, or the Citizens thereof, and foreign States, Citizens or Subjects.

In all cases affecting Ambassadors, other public Ministers and Consuls, and those in which a State shall be Party, the supreme Court shall have original Jurisdiction. In all the other Cases before mentioned, the supreme Court shall have appellate Jurisdiction, both as to Law and Fact, with such Exceptions, and under such Regulations as the Congress shall make.

The Trial of all Crimes, except in Cases of Impeachment, shall be by Jury; and such Trial shall be held in the State where the said Crimes shall have been committed; but when not committed within any State, the Trial shall be at such Place or Places as the Congress may by Law have directed.

Section. 3. Treason against the United States, shall consist only in levying War against them, or in adhering to their Enemies, giving them Aid and Comfort. No Person shall be convicted of Treason unless on the Testimony of two Witnesses to the same overt Act, or on Confession in open Court.

The Congress shall have Power to declare the Punishment of Treason, but no Attainder of Treason shall work Corruption of Blood, or Forfeiture except during the Life of the Person attainted.

Article. IV.

Section. 1. Full Faith and Credit shall be given in each State to the public Acts, Records, and judicial Proceedings of every other State. And the Congress may by general Laws prescribe the Manner in which such Acts, Records and Proceedings shall be proved, and the Effect thereof.

Section. 2. The Citizens of each State shall be entitled to all Privileges and Immunities of Citizens in the several States.

A Person charged in any State with Treason, Felony, or other Crime, who shall flee from Justice, and be found in another State, shall on Demand of the executive Authority of the State from which he fled, be delivered up, to be removed to the State having Jurisdiction of the Crime.

No Person held to Service or Labour in one State, under the Laws thereof, escaping into another, shall, in Consequence of any Law or Regulation therein, be discharged from such Service or Labour, but shall be delivered up on Claim of the Party to whom such Service or Labour may be due.

Section. 3. New States may be admitted by the Congress into this Union; but no new State shall be formed or erected within the Jurisdiction of any other State; nor any State be formed by the Junction of two or more States, or Parts of States, without the consent of the Legislatures of the States concerned as well as of the Congress.

The Congress shall have Power to dispose of and make all needful Rules and Regulations respecting the Territory or other Property belonging to the United States; and nothing in this Constitution shall be so construed as to Prejudice any Claims of the United States, or of any particular States.

Section. 4. The United States shall guarantee to every State in this Union a Republican Form of Government, and shall protect each of them against Invasion; and on Application of the Legislature, or of the Executive (when the Legislature cannot be convened) against domestic Violence.

ARTICLE. V.

The Congress, whenever two thirds of both Houses shall deem it necessary, shall propose Amendments to this Constitution, or, on the Application of the Legislatures of two thirds of the several States, shall call a Convention for proposing Amendments, which, in either Case, shall be valid to all Intents and Purposes, as Part of this Constitution, when ratified by the Legislatures of three fourths of the several States, or by Conventions in three fourths thereof, as the one or the other Mode of Ratification may be proposed by the Congress; Provided that no Amendment which may be made prior to the Year One thousand eight hundred and eight shall in any Manner affect the first and fourth Clauses in the Ninth Section of the first Article; and that no State, without its Consent, shall be deprived of its equal Suffrage in the Senate.

ARTICLE. VI.

All Debts contracted and Engagements entered into, before the Adoption of this Constitution, shall be as valid against the United States under this Constitution, as under the Confederation.

This Constitution, and the Laws of the United States which shall be made in Pursuance thereof; and all Treaties made, or which shall be made, under the Authority of the United States, shall be the supreme Law of the Land; and the Judges in every State shall be bound thereby, any Thing in the Constitution or Laws of any State to the Contrary notwithstanding.

The Senators and Representatives before mentioned, and the Members of the several State Legislatures, and all executive and judicial Officers, both of the United States and of the several States, shall be bound by Oath or Affirmation, to support this Constitution; but no religious Test shall ever be required as a Qualification to any Office or public Trust under the United States.

ARTICLE. VII.

The Ratification of the Conventions of nine States, shall be sufficient for the Establishment of this Constitution between the States so ratifying the Same.

Done in Convention by the Unanimous Consent of the States present the Seventeenth Day of September in the Year of our Lord one thousand seven hundred and Eighty seven and of the Independence of the United States of America the Twelfth. In witness thereof We have hereunto subscribed our Names,

G⁰. WASHINGTON—Presd ᵗ.
and deputy from Virginia.

New Hampshire	John Langdon Nicholas Gilman		Geo: Read Gunning Bedford jun John Dickinson Richard Bassett Jaco: Broom
Massachusetts	Nathaniel Gorham Rufus King	Delaware	
Connecticut	W ᵐ Sam ˡ Johnson Roger Sherman		
New York: . . .	Alexander Hamilton	Maryland	James M ᶜHenry Dan of S ᵗ Tho ˢ Jenifer Dan ˡ Carroll
New Jersey	Wil: Livingston David A. Brearley. W ᵐ Paterson. Jona: Dayton	Virginia	John Blair— James Madison Jr.
Pennsylvania	B Franklin Thomas Mifflin Rob ᵗ Morris Geo. Clymer Tho ˢ FitzSimons Jared Ingersoll James Wilson Gouv Morris	North Carolina	W ᵐ Blount Rich ᵈ Dobbs Spaight. Hu Williamson
		South Carolina	J. Rutledge Charles Cotesworth Pinckney Charles Pinckney Pierce Butler.
		Georgia	William Few Abr Baldwin

AMENDMENTS TO THE CONSTITUTION

ARTICLES IN ADDITION TO, and Amendment of the Constitution of the United States of America, proposed by Congress, and ratified by the Legislatures of the several States, pursuant to the fifth Article of the original Constitution.

AMENDMENT I.

Congress shall make no law respecting an establishment of religion, or prohibiting the free exercise thereof; or abridging the freedom of speech, or of the press; or the right of the people peaceably to assemble, and to petition the Government for a redress of grievances.

AMENDMENT II.

A well regulated Militia, being necessary to the security of a free State, the right of the people to keep and bear Arms, shall not be infringed.

AMENDMENT III.

No Soldier shall, in time of peace be quartered in any house, without the consent of the Owner, nor in time of war, but in a manner to be prescribed by law.

AMENDMENT IV.

The right of the people to be secure in their persons, houses, papers, and effects, against unreasonable searches and seizures, shall not be violated, and no Warrants shall issue, but upon probable cause, supported by Oath or affirmation, and particularly describing the place to be searched, and the persons or things to be seized.

AMENDMENT V.

No person shall be held to answer for a capital, or otherwise infamous crime, unless on a presentment or indictment of a Grand Jury, except in cases arising in the land or naval forces, or in the Militia, when in actual service in time of War or public danger; nor shall any person be subject for the same offence to be twice put in jeopardy of life or limb; nor shall be compelled in any criminal case to be a witness against himself, nor be deprived of life, liberty, or property, without due process of law; nor shall private property be taken for public use, without just compensation.

AMENDMENT VI.

In all criminal prosecutions, the accused shall enjoy the right to a speedy and public trial, by an impartial jury of the State and district wherein the crime shall have been committed, which district shall have been previously ascertained by law, and to be informed of the nature and cause of the accusation; to be confronted with the witnesses against him; to have compulsory process for obtaining witnesses in his favor, and to have the Assistance of Counsel for his defence.

AMENDMENT VII.

In Suits at common law, where the value in controversy shall exceed twenty dollars, the right of trial by jury shall be preserved, and no fact tried by a jury, shall be otherwise re-examined in any Court of the United States, than according to the rules of the common law.

AMENDMENT VIII.

Excessive bail shall not be required, nor excessive fines imposed, nor cruel and unusual punishments inflicted.

AMENDMENT IX.

The enumeration in the Constitution, of certain rights, shall not be construed to deny or disparage others retained by the people.

AMENDMENT X.

The powers not delegated to the United States by the Constitution, nor prohibited by it to the States, are reserved to the States respectively, or to the people. [The first ten amendments went into effect December 15, 1791.]

AMENDMENT XI.

The Judicial power of the United States shall not be construed to extend to any suit in law or equity, commenced or prosecuted against one of the United States by Citizens of another State, or by Citizens or Subjects of any Foreign State. [January 8, 1798.]

AMENDMENT XII.

The Electors shall meet in their respective states, and vote by ballot for President and Vice-President, one of whom, at least, shall not be an inhabitant of the same state with themselves; they shall name in their ballots the person voted for as President, and in distinct ballots the person voted for as Vice-President, and they shall make distinct lists of all persons voted for as President, and of all persons voted for as Vice President, and of the number of votes for each, which lists they shall sign and certify, and transmit sealed to the seat of the government of the United States, directed to the President of the Senate;—The President of the Senate shall, in the presence of the Senate and House of Representatives, open all the certificates and the votes shall then be counted;—The person having the greatest number of votes for

President, shall be the President, if such number be a majority of the whole number of Electors appointed; and if no person have such majority, then from the persons having the highest numbers not exceeding three on the list of those voted for as President, the House of Representatives shall choose immediately, by ballot, the President. But in choosing the President, the votes shall be taken by states, the representation from each state having one vote; a quorum for this purpose shall consist of a member or members from two-thirds of the states, and a majority of all the states shall be necessary to a choice. And if the House of Representatives shall not choose a President whenever the right of choice shall devolve upon them, before the fourth day of March next following, then the Vice-President shall act as President, as in the case of the death or other constitutional disability of the President.—The person having the greatest number of votes as Vice-President, shall be the Vice-President, if such number be a majority of the whole number of Electors appointed, and if no person have a majority, then from the two highest numbers on the list, the Senate shall choose the Vice-President; a quorum for the purpose shall consist of two-thirds of the whole number of Senators, and a majority of the whole number shall be necessary to a choice. But no person constitutionally ineligible to the office of President shall be eligible to that of Vice-President of the United States. [September 25, 1804.]

AMENDMENT XIII.

Section 1. Neither slavery nor involuntary servitude, except as a punishment for crime whereof the party shall have been duly convicted, shall exist within the United States, or any place subject to their jurisdiction.

Section 2. Congress shall have power to enforce this article by appropriate legislation. [December 18, 1865.]

AMENDMENT XIV.

Section 1. All persons born or naturalized in the United States, and subject to the jurisdiction thereof, are citizens of the United States and of the State wherein they reside. No State shall make or enforce any law which shall abridge the privileges or immunities of citizens of the United States; nor shall any State deprive any person of life, liberty, or property, without due process of law; nor deny to any person within its jurisdiction the equal protection of the laws.

Section 2. Representatives shall be apportioned among the several States according to their respective numbers, counting the whole number of persons in each State, excluding Indians not taxed. But when the right to vote at any election for the choice of electors for President and Vice President of the United States, Representatives in Congress, the Executive and Judicial officers of a State, or the members of the Legislature thereof, is denied to any of the male inhabitants of such State, being twenty-one years of age, and citizens of the United States, or in any way abridged, except for participation in rebellion, or other crime, the basis of representation therein shall be reduced in the proportion which the number of such male citizens shall bear to the whole number of male citizens twenty-one years of age in such State.

Section 3. No person shall be a Senator or Representative in Congress, or elector of President and Vice President, or hold any office, civil or military, under the United States, or under any State, who, having previously taken an oath, as a member of Congress, or as an officer of the United States, or as a member of any State legislature, or as an executive or judicial officer of any State, to support the Constitution of the United States, shall have engaged in insurrection or rebellion against the same, or given aid or comfort to the enemeis thereof. But Congress may by a vote of two-thirds of each House, remove such disability.

Section 4. The validity of the public debt of the United States, authorized by law, including debts incurred for payment of pensions and bounties for services in suppressing insurrection or rebellion, shall not be questioned. But neither the United States nor any State shall assume or pay any debt or obligation incurred in aid of insurrection or rebellion against the United States, or any claim for the loss or emancipation of any slave; but all such debts, obligations and claims shall be held illegal and void.

Section 5. The Congress shall have power to enforce, by appropriate legislation, the provisions of this article. [July 28, 1868.]

Amendment XV.

Section 1. The right of citizens of the United States to vote shall not be denied or abridged by the United States or by any State on account of race, color, or previous condition of servitude—

Section 2. The Congress shall have power to enforce this article by appropriate legislation.—[March 30, 1870.]

Amendment XVI.

The Congress shall have power to lay and collect taxes on incomes, from whatever source derived, without apportionment among the several States, and without regard to any census or enumeration. [February 25, 1913.]

Amendment XVII.

The Senate of the United States shall be composed of two senators from each State, elected by the people thereof, for six years; and each Senator shall have one vote. The electors in each State shall have the qualifications requisite for electors of the most numerous branch of the State legislature.

When vacancies happen in the representation of any State in the Senate, the executive authority of such State shall issue writs of election to fill such vacancies: *Provided,* That the legislature of any State may empower the executive thereof to make temporary appointments until the people fill the vacancies by election as the legislature may direct.

This amendment shall not be so construed as to affect the election or term of any senator chosen before it becomes valid as part of the Constitution. [May 31, 1913.]

Amendment XVIII.

After one year from the ratification of this article, the manufacture, sale, or transportation of intoxicating liquors within, the importation thereof into, or the exportation thereof from the United States and all territory subject to the jurisdiction thereof for beverage purposes is hereby prohibited.

The Congress and the several States shall have concurrent power to enforce this article by appropriate legislation.

This article shall be inoperative unless it shall have been ratified as an amendment to the Constitution by the legislatures of the several States, as provided in the Constitution, within seven years from the date of the submission thereof to the States by Congress. [January 29, 1919.]

Amendment XIX.

The right of citizens of the United States to vote shall not be denied or abridged by the United States or by any State on account of sex.

The Congress shall have power by appropriate legislation to enforce the provisions of this article. [August 26, 1920.]

Amendment XX.

Section 1. The terms of the President and Vice-President shall end at noon on the twentieth day of January, and the terms of Senators and Representatives at noon on the third day of January, of the years in which such terms would have ended if this article had not been ratified; and the terms of their successors shall then begin.

Section 2. The Congress shall assemble at least once in every year, and such meeting shall begin at noon on the third day of January, unless they shall by law appoint a different day.

Section 3. If, at the time fixed for the beginning of the term of the President, the President-elect shall have died, the Vice-President-elect shall become President. If a President shall not have been chosen before the time fixed for the beginning of his term, or if the President-elect shall have failed to qualify, then the Vice-President-elect shall act as President until a President shall have qualified; and the Congress may by law provide for the case wherein neither a President-elect nor a Vice-President-elect shall have qualified, declaring who shall then act as President, or the manner in which one who is to act shall be selected, and such person shall act accordingly until a President or Vice-President shall have qualified.

Section 4. The Congress may by law provide for the case of the death of any of the persons from whom the House of Representatives may choose a President whenever the right of choice shall have devolved upon them, and for the case of the death of any of the persons from whom the Senate may choose a Vice-President whenever the right of choice shall have devolved upon them.

Section 5. Sections 1 and 2 shall take effect on the 15th day of October following the ratification of this article.

Section 6. This article shall be inoperative unless it shall have been ratified as an amendment to the Constitution by the legislatures of three-fourths of the several States within seven years from the date of its submission. [February 6, 1933.]

Amendment XXI.

Section 1. The eighteenth article of amendment to the Constitution of the United States is hereby repealed.

Section 2. The transportation or importation into any State, Territory or possession of the United States for delivery or use therein of intoxicating liquors, in violation of the laws thereof, is hereby prohibited.

Section 3. This article shall be inoperative unless it shall have been ratified as an amendment to the Constitution by convention in the several States, as provided in the Constitution, within seven years from the date of the submission thereof to the States by the Congress. [December 5, 1933.]

Amendment XXII.

Section 1. No person shall be elected to the office of the President more than twice, and no person who has held the office of President, or acted as President, for more than two years of a term to which some other person was elected President shall be elected to the office of the President more than once. But this Article shall not apply to any person holding the office of President when this Article was proposed by the Congress, and shall not prevent any person who may be holding the office of President, or acting as President, during the term within which this Article becomes operative from holding the office of President or acting as President during the remainder of such term.

Section 2. This article shall be inoperative unless it shall have been ratified as an amendment to the Constitution by the legislatures of three-fourths of the several states within seven years from the date of its submission to the States by the Congress. [February 27, 1951.]

AMENDMENT XXIII.

Section 1. The District constituting the seat of government of the United States shall appoint in such manner as the Congress may direct:

A number of electors of President and Vice-President equal to the whole number of Senators and Representatives in Congress to which the District would be entitled if it were a State, but in no event more than the least populous State; they shall be in addition to those appointed by the States, but they shall be considered, for the purposes of the election of President and Vice-President, to be electors appointed by a State; and they shall meet in the District and perform such duties as provided by the twelfth article of amendment.

Section 2. The Congress shall have the power to enforce this article by appropriate legislation. [March 29, 1961.]

AMENDMENT XXIV.

Section 1. The right of citizens of the United States to vote in any primary or other election for President or Vice President, for electors for President or Vice President, or for Senator or Representative in Congress, shall not be denied or abridged by the United States or any State by reason of failure to pay any poll tax or other tax.

Section 2. The Congress shall have power to enforce this article by appropriate legislation. [January 23, 1964.]

AMENDMENT XXV.

Section 1. In case of the removal of the President from office or of his death or resignation, the Vice President shall become President.

Section 2. Whenever there is a vacancy in the office of Vice President, the President shall nominate a Vice President who shall take office upon confirmation by a majority vote of both Houses of Congress.

Section 3. Whenever the President transmits to the President pro tempore of the Senate and the Speaker of the House of Representatives his written declaration that he is unable to discharge the powers and duties of his office, and until he transmits to them a written declaration to the contrary, such powers and duties shall be discharged by the Vice President as Acting President.

Section 4. Whenever the Vice President and a majority of either the principal officers of the executive departments or of such other body as Congress may by law provide, transmit to the President pro tempore of the Senate and the Speaker of the House of Representatives their written declaration that the President is unable to discharge the powers and duties of his office, the Vice President shall immediately assume the powers and duties of the office as Acting President.

Thereafter, when the President transmits to the President pro tempore of the Senate and the Speaker of the House of Representatives his written declaration that no inability exists, he shall resume the powers and duties of his office unless the Vice President and a majority of either the principal officers of the executive departments or of such other body as Congress may by law provide, transmit within four days to the President pro tempore of the Senate and the Speaker of the House of Representatives their written declaration that the President is unable to discharge the powers and duties of his office. Thereupon Congress shall decide the issue, assembling within forty-eight hours for that purpose if not in session. If the Congress, within twenty-one days after receipt of the latter written declaration, or, if Congress is not in session, within twenty-one days after Congress is required to assemble, determines by two-thirds vote of both Houses that the President is unable to discharge the powers and duties of his office, the Vice President shall continue to discharge the same as Acting President; otherwise, the President shall resume the powers and duties of his office. [February 10, 1967.]

AMENDMENT XXVI.

Section 1. The right of citizens of the United States, who are eighteen years of age or older, to vote shall not be denied or abridged by the United States or by any State on account of age.

Section 2. The Congress shall have power to enforce this article by appropriate legislation [June 30, 1971.]

PRESIDENTIAL ELECTIONS

Year	Number of States	Candidates	Parties	Popular Vote	% of Popular Vote	Electoral Vote	% Voter Participation
1789	11	GEORGE WASHINGTON	No party designations			69	
		John Adams				34	
		Other candidates				35	
1792	15	GEORGE WASHINGTON	No party designations			132	
		John Adams				77	
		George Clinton				50	
		Other candidates				5	
1796	16	JOHN ADAMS	Federalist			71	
		Thomas Jefferson	Democratic-Republican			68	
		Thomas Pinckney	Federalist			59	
		Aaron Burr	Democratic-Republican			30	
		Other candidates				48	
1800	16	THOMAS JEFFERSON	Democratic-Republican			73	
		Aaron Burr	Democratic-Republican			73	
		John Adams	Federalist			65	
		Charles C. Pinckney	Federalist			64	
		John Jay	Federalist			1	

Year	Number of States	Candidates	Parties	Popular Vote	% of Popular Vote	Electoral Vote	% Voter Participation
1804	17	THOMAS JEFFERSON	Democratic-Republican			162	
		Charles C. Pinckney	Federalist			14	
1808	17	JAMES MADISON	Democratic-Republican			122	
		Charles C. Pinckney	Federalist			47	
		George Clinton	Democratic-Republican			6	
1812	18	JAMES MADISON	Democratic-Republican			128	
		DeWitt Clinton	Federalist			89	
1816	19	JAMES MONROE	Democratic-Republican			183	
		Rufus King	Federalist			34	
1820	24	JAMES MONROE	Democratic-Republican			231	
		John Quincy Adams	Independent			1	
1824	24	JOHN QUINCY ADAMS	Democratic-Republican	108,740	30.5	84	26.9
		Andrew Jackson	Democratic-Republican	153,544	43.1	99	
		Henry Clay	Democratic-Republican	47,136	13.2	37	
		William H. Crawford	Democratic-Republican	46,618	13.1	41	
1828	24	ANDREW JACKSON	Democratic	647,286	56.0	178	57.6
		John Quincy Adams	National-Republican	508,064	44.0	83	

Year	Number of States	Candidates	Parties	Popular Vote	% of Popular Vote	Electoral Vote	% Voter Participation
1832	24	ANDREW JACKSON	Democratic	688,242	54.5	219	55.4
		Henry Clay	National-Republican	473,462	37.5	49	
		William Wirt	Anti-Masonic	101,051	8.0	7	
		John Floyd	Democratic			11	
1836	26	MARTIN VAN BUREN	Democratic	765,483	50.9	170	57.8
		William H. Harrison	Whig			73	
		Hugh L. White	Whig	739,795	49.1	26	
		Daniel Webster	Whig			14	
		W. P. Mangum	Whig			11	
1840	26	WILLIAM H. HARRISON	Whig	1,274,624	53.1	234	80.2
		Martin Van Buren	Democratic	1,127,781	46.9	60	
1844	26	JAMES K. POLK	Democratic	1,338,464	49.6	170	78.9
		Henry Clay	Whig	1,300,097	48.1	105	
		James G. Birney	Liberty	62,300	2.3		
1848	30	ZACHARY TAYLOR	Whig	1,360,967	47.4	163	72.7
		Lewis Cass	Democratic	1,222,342	42.5	127	
		Martin Van Buren	Free Soil	291,263	10.1		
1852	31	FRANKLIN PIERCE	Democratic	1,601,117	50.9	254	69.6
		Winfield Scott	Whig	1,385,453	44.1	42	
		John P. Hale	Free Soil	155,825	5.0		
1856	31	JAMES BUCHANAN	Democratic	1,832,955	45.3	174	78.9
		John C. Frémont	Republican	1,339,932	33.1	114	
		Millard Fillmore	American	871,731	21.6	8	

Year	Number of States	Candidates	Parties	Popular Vote	% of Popular Vote	Electoral Vote	% Voter Participation
1860	33	**ABRAHAM LINCOLN**	Republican	1,865,593	39.8	180	81.2
		Stephen A. Douglas	Democratic	1,382,713	29.5	12	
		John C. Breckinridge	Democratic	848,356	18.1	72	
		John Bell	Constitutional Union	592,906	12.6	39	
1864	36	**ABRAHAM LINCOLN**	Republican	2,206,938	55.0	212	73.8
		George B. McClellan	Democratic	1,803,787	45.0	21	
1868	37	**ULYSSES S. GRANT**	Republican	3,013,421	52.7	214	78.1
		Horatio Seymour	Democratic	2,706,829	47.3	80	
1872	37	**ULYSSES S. GRANT**	Republican	3,596,745	55.6	286	71.3
		Horace Greeley	Democratic	2,843,446	43.9		
1876	38	**RUTHERFORD B. HAYES**	Republican	4,036,572	48.0	185	81.8
		Samuel J. Tilden	Democratic	4,284,020	51.0	184	
1880	38	**JAMES A. GARFIELD**	Republican	4,453,295	48.5	214	79.4
		Winfield S. Hancock	Democratic	4,414,082	48.1	155	
		James B. Weaver	Greenback-Labor	308,578	3.4		
1884	38	**GROVER CLEVELAND**	Democratic	4,879,507	48.5	219	77.5
		James G. Blaine	Republican	4,850,293	48.2	182	
		Benjamin F. Butler	Greenback-Labor	175,370	1.8		
		John P. St. John	Prohibition	150,369	1.5		
1888	38	**BENJAMIN HARRISON**	Republican	5,477,129	47.9	233	79.3
		Grover Cleveland	Democratic	5,537,857	48.6	168	
		Clinton B. Fisk	Prohibition	249,506	2.2		
		Anson J. Streeter	Union Labor	146,935	1.3		

Year	Number of States	Candidates	Parties	Popular Vote	% of Popular Vote	Electoral Vote	% Voter Participation
1892	44	GROVER CLEVELAND	Democratic	5,555,426	46.1	277	74.7
		Benjamin Harrison	Republican	5,182,690	43.0	145	
		James B. Weaver	People's	1,029,846	8.5	22	
		John Bidwell	Prohibition	264,133	2.2		
1896	45	WILLIAM McKINLEY	Republican	7,102,246	51.1	271	79.3
		William J. Bryan	Democratic	6,492,559	47.7	176	
1900	45	WILLIAM McKINLEY	Republican	7,218,491	51.7	292	73.2
		William J. Bryan	Democratic; Populist	6,356,734	45.5	155	
		John C. Wooley	Prohibition	208,914	1.5		
1904	45	THEODORE ROOSEVELT	Republican	7,628,461	57.4	336	65.2
		Alton B. Parker	Democratic	5,084,223	37.6	140	
		Eugene V. Debs	Socialist	402,283	3.0		
		Silas C. Swallow	Prohibition	258,536	1.9		
1908	46	WILLIAM H. TAFT	Republican	7,675,320	51.6	321	65.4
		William J. Bryan	Democratic	6,412,294	43.1	162	
		Eugene V. Debs	Socialist	420,793	2.8		
		Eugene W. Chafin	Prohibition	253,840	1.7		
1912	48	WOODROW WILSON	Democratic	6,296,547	41.9	435	58.8
		Theodore Roosevelt	Progressive	4,118,571	27.4	88	
		William H. Taft	Republican	3,486,720	23.2	8	
		Eugene V. Debs	Socialist	900,672	6.0		
		Eugene W. Chafin	Prohibition	206,275	1.4		

Year		Candidate	Party	Popular Vote	%	Electoral Vote	%
1916	48	WOODROW WILSON	Democratic	9,127,695	49.4	277	61.6
		Charles E. Hughes	Republican	8,533,507	46.2	254	
		A. L. Benson	Socialist	585,113	3.2		
		J. Frank Hanly	Prohibition	220,506	1.2		
1920	48	WARREN G. HARDING	Republican	16,143,407	60.4	404	49.2
		James M. Cox	Democratic	9,130,328	34.2	127	
		Eugene V. Debs	Socialist	919,799	3.4		
		P.P. Christensen	Farmer-Labor	265,411	1.0		
1924	48	CALVIN COOLIDGE	Republican	15,718,211	54.0	382	48.9
		John W. Davis	Democratic	8,385,283	28.8	136	
		Robert M. La Follette	Progressive	4,831,289	16.6	13	
1928	48	HERBERT C. HOOVER	Republican	21,391,993	58.2	444	56.9
		Alfred E. Smith	Democratic	15,016,169	40.9	87	
1932	48	FRANKLIN D. ROOSEVELT	Democratic	22,809,638	57.4	472	56.9
		Herbert C. Hoover	Republican	15,758,901	39.7	59	
		Norman Thomas	Socialist	881,951	2.2		
1936	48	FRANKLIN D. ROOSEVELT	Democratic	27,752,869	60.8	523	61.0
		Alfred M. Landon	Republican	16,674,665	36.5	8	
		William Lemke	Union	882,479	1.9		
1940	48	FRANKLIN D. ROOSEVELT	Democratic	27,307,819	54.8	449	62.5
		Wendell L. Willkie	Republican	22,321,018	44.8	82	

Year	Number of States	Candidates	Parties	Popular Vote	% of Popular Vote	Electoral Vote	% Voter Participation
1944	48	FRANKLIN D. ROOSEVELT	Democratic	25,606,585	53.5	432	55.9
		Thomas E. Dewey	Republican	22,014,745	46.0	99	
1948	48	HARRY S. TRUMAN	Democratic	24,179,345	49.6	303	53.0
		Thomas E. Dewey	Republican	21,991,291	45.1	189	
		J. Strom Thurmond	States' Rights	1,176,125	2.4	39	
		Henry A. Wallace	Progressive	1,157,326	2.4		
1952	48	DWIGHT D. EISENHOWER	Republican	33,936,234	55.1	442	63.3
		Adlai E. Stevenson	Democratic	27,314,992	44.4	89	
1956	48	DWIGHT D. EISENHOWER	Republican	35,590,472	57.6	457	60.6
		Adlai E. Stevenson	Democratic	26,022,752	42.1	73	
1960	50	JOHN F. KENNEDY	Democratic	34,226,731	49.7	303	64.0
		Richard M. Nixon	Republican	34,108,157	49.5	219	
1964	50	LYNDON B. JOHNSON	Democratic	43,129,566	61.1	486	61.7
		Barry M. Goldwater	Republican	27,178,188	38.5	52	
1968	50	RICHARD M. NIXON	Republican	31,785,480	43.4	301	60.6
		Hubert H. Humphrey	Democratic	31,275,166	42.7	191	
		George C. Wallace	American Independent	9,906,473	13.5	46	

Year	Number of States	Candidates	Party	Popular Vote	Percentage of Popular Vote	Electoral Vote	Percentage of Voter Participation
1972	50	RICHARD M. NIXON	Republican	47,169,911	60.7	520	55.5
		George S. McGovern	Democratic	29,170,383	37.5	17	
		John G. Schmitz	American	1,099,482	1.4		
1976	50	JIMMY CARTER	Democratic	40,830,763	50.1	297	54.3
		Gerald R. Ford	Republican	39,147,793	48.0	240	
1980	50	RONALD REAGAN	Republican	43,901,812	50.7	489	53.0
		Jimmy Carter	Democratic	35,483,820	41.0	49	
		John B. Anderson	Independent	5,719,722	6.6		
		Ed Clark	Libertarian	921,188	1.1		
1984	50	RONALD REAGAN	Republican	54,451,521	58.4	525	52.9
		Walter F. Mondale	Democratic	37,565,334	41.6	13	
1988	50	GEORGE H. BUSH	Republican	47,917,341	54.0	426	48.6
		Michael Dukakis	Democratic	41,013,030	46.0	112	
1992	50	BILL CLINTON	Democratic	43,728,375	43.0	370	54.0
		George H. Bush	Republican	38,167,416	38.0	168	
		H. Ross Perot	Independent	19,237,247	19.0	0	

Candidates receiving less than 1 percent of the popular vote have been omitted. Thus the percentage of popular vote given for any election year may not total 100 percent.

Before the passage of the Twelfth Amendment in 1804, the Electoral College voted for two presidential candidates; the runner-up became vice-president.

ADMISSION OF STATES

Order of Admission	State	Date of Admission	Order of Admission	State	Date of Admission
1	Delaware	December 7, 1787	26	Michigan	January 26, 1837
2	Pennsylvania	December 12, 1787	27	Florida	March 3, 1845
3	New Jersey	December 18, 1787	28	Texas	December 29, 1845
4	Georgia	January 2, 1788	29	Iowa	December 28, 1846
5	Connecticut	January 9, 1788	30	Wisconsin	May 29, 1848
6	Massachusetts	February 7, 1788	31	California	September 9, 1850
7	Maryland	April 28, 1788	32	Minnesota	May 11, 1858
8	South Carolina	May 23, 1788	33	Oregon	February 14, 1859
9	New Hampshire	June 21, 1788	34	Kansas	January 29, 1861
10	Virginia	June 25, 1788	35	West Virginia	June 30, 1863
11	New York	July 26, 1788	36	Nevada	October 31, 1864
12	North Carolina	November 21, 1789	37	Nebraska	March 1, 1867
13	Rhode Island	May 29, 1790	38	Colorado	August 1, 1876
14	Vermont	March 4, 1791	39	North Dakota	November 2, 1889
15	Kentucky	June 1, 1792	40	South Dakota	November 2, 1889
16	Tennessee	June 1, 1796	41	Montana	November 8, 1889
17	Ohio	March 1, 1803	42	Washington	November 11, 1889
18	Louisiana	April 30, 1812	43	Idaho	July 3, 1890
19	Indiana	December 11, 1816	44	Wyoming	July 10, 1890
20	Mississippi	December 10, 1817	45	Utah	January 4, 1896
21	Illinois	December 3, 1818	46	Oklahoma	November 16, 1907
22	Alabama	December 14, 1819	47	New Mexico	January 6, 1912
23	Maine	March 15, 1820	48	Arizona	February 14, 1912
24	Missouri	August 10, 1821	49	Alaska	January 3, 1959
25	Arkansas	June 15, 1836	50	Hawaii	August 21, 1959

POPULATION OF THE UNITED STATES

Year	Number of States	Population	% Increase	Population per Square Mile
1790	13	3,929,214		4.5
1800	16	5,308,483	35.1	6.1
1810	17	7,239,881	36.4	4.3
1820	23	9,638,453	33.1	5.5
1830	24	12,866,020	33.5	7.4
1840	26	17,069,453	32.7	9.8
1850	31	23,191,876	35.9	7.9
1860	33	31,443,321	35.6	10.6
1870	37	39,818,449	26.6	13.4
1880	38	50,155,783	26.0	16.9
1890	44	62,947,714	25.5	21.1
1900	45	75,994,575	20.7	25.6
1910	46	91,972,266	21.0	31.0
1920	48	105,710,620	14.9	35.6
1930	48	122,775,046	16.1	41.2
1940	48	131,669,275	7.2	44.2
1950	48	150,697,361	14.5	50.7
1960	50	179,323,175	19.0	50.6
1970	50	203,235,298	13.3	57.5
1980	50	226,504,825	11.4	64.0
1985	50	237,839,000	5.0	67.2
1990	50	250,122,000	5.2	70.6

IMMIGRATION TO THE UNITED STATES, FISCAL YEARS 1820–1990

Year	Number	Year	Number	Year	Number	Year	Number
1820–1989	55,457,531	1871–80	2,812,191	1921–30	4,107,209	1971–80	4,493,314
1820	8,385	1871	321,350	1921	805,228	1971	370,478
1821–30	143,439	1872	404,806	1922	309,556	1972	384,685
1821	9,127	1873	459,803	1923	522,919	1973	400,063
1822	6,911	1874	313,339	1924	706,896	1974	394,861
1823	6,354	1875	227,498	1925	294,314	1975	386,194
1824	7,912	1876	169,986	1926	304,488	1976	398,613
1825	10,199	1877	141,857	1927	335,175	1976. TQ	103,676
1826	10,837	1878	138,469	1928	307,255	1977	462,315
1827	18,875	1879	177,826	1929	279,678	1978	601,442
1828	27,382	1880	457,257	1930	241,700	1979	460,348
1829	22,520	1881–90	5,246,613	1931–40	528,431	1980	530,639
1830	23,322	1881	669,431	1931	97,139	1981–90	7,338,062
1831–40	599,125	1882	788,992	1932	35,576	1981	596,600
1831	22,633	1883	603,322	1933	23,068	1982	594,131
1832	60,482	1884	518,592	1934	29,470	1983	559,763
1833	58,640	1885	395,346	1935	34,956	1984	543,903
1834	65,365	1886	334,203	1936	36,329	1985	570,009
1835	45,374	1887	490,109	1937	50,244	1986	601,708
1836	76,242	1888	546,889	1938	67,895	1987	601,516
1837	79,340	1889	444,427	1939	82,998	1988	643,025
1838	38,914	1890	455,302	1940	70,756	1989	1,090,924
1839	68,069	1891–1900	3,687,564	1941–50	1,035,039	1990	1,536,483
1840	84,066	1891	560,319	1941	51,776		
1841–50	1,713,251	1892	579,663	1942	28,781		
1841	80,289	1893	439,730	1943	23,725		
1842	104,565	1894	285,631	1944	28,551		
		1895	258,536	1945	38,119		
		1896	343,267	1946	108,721		

Year	Number	Year	Number	Year	Number
1843	52,496	1897	230,832	1947	147,292
1844	78,615	1898	229,299	1948	170,570
1845	114,371	1899	311,715	1949	188,317
1846	154,416	1900	448,572	1950	249,187
1847	234,968	1901–10	8,795,386	1951–60	2,515,479
1848	226,527	1901	487,918	1951	205,717
1849	297,024	1902	648,743	1952	265,520
1850	369,980	1903	857,046	1953	170,434
1851–60	2,598,214	1904	812,870	1954	208,177
1851	379,466	1905	1,026,499	1955	237,790
1852	371,603	1906	1,100,735	1956	321,625
1853	368,645	1907	1,285,349	1957	326,867
1854	427,833	1908	782,870	1958	253,265
1855	200,877	1909	751,786	1959	260,686
1856	200,436	1910	1,041,570	1960	265,398
1857	251,306	1911–20	5,735,811	1961–70	3,321,677
1858	123,126	1911	878,587	1961	271,344
1859	121,282	1912	838,172	1962	283,763
1860	153,640	1913	1,197,892	1963	306,260
1861–70	2,314,824	1914	1,218,480	1964	292,248
1861	91,918	1915	326,700	1965	296,697
1862	91,985	1916	298,826	1966	323,040
1863	176,282	1917	295,403	1967	361,972
1864	193,418	1918	110,618	1968	454,448
1865	248,120	1919	141,132	1969	358,579
1866	318,568	1920	430,001	1970	373,326
1867	315,722				
1868	138,840				
1869	352,768				
1870	387,203				

Source: U.S. Immigration and Naturalization Service, 1991.

IMMIGRATION BY REGION AND SELECTED COUNTRY OF LAST RESIDENCE, FISCAL YEARS 1820–1989

Region and Country of Last Residence[1]	1820	1821–30	1831–40	1841–50	1851–60	1861–70	1871–80	1881–90
All countries	8,385	143,439	599,125	1,713,251	2,598,214	2,314,824	2,812,191	5,246,613
Europe	7,690	98,797	495,681	1,597,442	2,452,577	2,065,141	2,271,925	4,735,484
Austria-Hungary	—[2]	—[2]	—[2]	—[2]	—[2]	7,800	72,969	353,719
Austria	—[2]	—[2]	—[2]	—[2]	—[2]	[3]7,124	63,009	226,038
Hungary	—[2]	—[2]	—[2]	—[2]	—[2]	[3]484	9,960	127,681
Belgium	1	27	22	5,074	4,738	6,734	7,221	20,177
Czechoslovakia	—[4]	—[4]	—[4]	—[4]	—[4]	—[4]	—[4]	—[4]
Denmark	20	169	1,063	539	3,749	17,094	31,771	88,132
France	371	8,497	45,575	77,262	76,358	35,986	72,206	50,464
Germany	968	6,761	152,454	434,626	951,667	787,468	718,182	1,452,970
Greece	—	20	49	16	31	72	210	2,308
Ireland[5]	3,614	50,724	207,381	780,719	914,119	435,778	436,871	655,482
Italy	30	409	2,253	1,870	9,231	11,725	55,759	307,309
Netherlands	49	1,078	1,412	8,251	10,789	9,102	16,541	53,701
Norway-Sweden	3	91	1,201	13,903	20,931	109,298	211,245	568,362
Norway	—[6]	—[6]	—[6]	—[6]	—[6]	—[6]	95,323	176,586
Sweden	—[6]	—[6]	—[6]	—[6]	—[6]	—[6]	115,922	391,776
Poland	5	16	369	105	1,164	2,027	12,970	51,806
Portugal	35	145	829	550	1,055	2,658	14,082	16,978
Romania	—[7]	—[7]	—[7]	—[7]	—[7]	—[7]	11	6,348
Soviet Union	14	75	277	551	457	2,512	39,284	213,282
Spain	139	2,477	2,125	2,209	9,298	6,697	5,266	4,419
Switzerland	31	3,226	4,821	4,644	25,011	23,286	28,293	81,988
United Kingdom[5,8]	2,410	25,079	75,810	267,044	423,974	606,896	548,043	807,357
Yugoslavia	—[9]	—[9]	—[9]	—[9]	—[9]	—	—[9]	—[9]
Other Europe	—	3	40	79	5	8	1,001	682

Asia	6	30	55	141	41,538	64,759	124,160	69,942
China[10]	1	2	8	35	41,397	64,301	123,201	61,711
Hong Kong	—[11]	—[11]	—[11]	—[11]	—[11]	—[11]	—[11]	—[11]
India	—[12]	8	39	36	43	69	163	269
Iran	—[12]	—[12]	—[12]	—[12]	—[12]	—[12]	—[12]	—[12]
Israel	—[13]	—[13]	—[13]	—[13]	—[13]	—[13]	—[13]	—[13]
Japan	—[14]	—[14]	—[14]	—[14]	—[14]	186	149	2,270
Korea	—[15]	—[15]	—[15]	—[15]	—[15]	—[15]	—[15]	—[15]
Philippines	—[16]	—[16]	—[16]	—[16]	—[16]	—[16]	—[16]	—[16]
Turkey	1	20	7	59	83	131	404	3,782
Vietnam	—[11]	—[11]	—[11]	—[11]	—[11]	—[11]	—[11]	—[11]
Other Asia	3	—	1	11	15	72	243	1,910
America	387	11,564	33,424	62,469	74,720	166,607	404,044	426,967
Canada & Newfoundland[17,18]	209	2,277	13,624	41,723	59,309	153,878	383,640	393,304
Mexico[18]	1	4,817	6,599	3,271	3,078	2,191	5,162	1,913[19]
Caribbean	164	3,834	12,301	13,528	10,660	9,046	13,957	29,042
Cuba	—[12]	—[12]	—[12]	—[12]	—[12]	—[12]	—[12]	—[12]
Dominican Republic	—[20]	—[20]	—[20]	—[20]	—[20]	—[20]	—[20]	—[20]
Haiti	—[20]	—[20]	—[20]	—[20]	—[20]	—[20]	—[20]	—[20]
Jamaica	—[21]	—[21]	—[21]	—[21]	—[21]	—[21]	—[21]	—[21]
Other Caribbean	164	3,834	12,301	13,528	10,660	9,046	13,957	29,042
Central America	2	105	44	368	449	95	157	404
El Salvador	—[20]	—[20]	—[20]	—[20]	—[20]	—[20]	—[20]	—[20]
Other Central America	2	105	44	368	449	95	157	404
South America	11	531	856	3,579	1,224	1,397	1,128	2,304
Argentina	—[20]	—[20]	—[20]	—[20]	—[20]	—[20]	—[20]	—[20]
Colombia	—[20]	—[20]	—[20]	—[20]	—[20]	—[20]	—[20]	—[20]
Ecuador	—[20]	—[20]	—[20]	—[20]	—[20]	—[20]	—[20]	—[20]
Other South America	11	531	856	3,579	1,224	1,397	1,128	2,304
Other America	—[22]	—[22]	—[22]	—[22]	—[22]	—[22]	—[22]	—[22]
Africa	1	16	54	55	210	312	358	857
Oceania	1	2	9	29	158	214	10,914	12,574
Not specified[22]	300	33,030	69,902	53,115	29,011	17,791	790	789

Source: U.S. Immigration and Naturalization Service, 1991.

Region and Country of Last Residence[1]	1891–1900	1901–10	1911–20	1921–30	1931–40	1941–50	1951–60	1961–70
All countries	3,687,564	8,795,386	5,735,811	4,107,209	528,431	1,035,039	2,515,479	3,321,677
Europe	3,555,352	8,056,040	4,321,887	2,463,194	347,566	621,147	1,325,727	1,123,492
Austria-Hungary	592,707[2,3]	2,145,266[2,3]	896,342[2,3]	63,548	11,424	28,329	103,743	26,022
Austria	234,081[3]	668,209[3]	453,649	32,868	3,563[3,4]	24,860[3,4]	67,106	20,621
Hungary	181,288[3]	808,511[3]	442,693	30,680	7,861	3,469	36,637	5,401
Belgium	18,167	41,635	33,746	15,846	4,817	12,189	18,575	9,192
Czechoslovakia	—[4]	—[4]	3,426[4]	102,194	14,393	8,347	918	3,273
Denmark	50,231	65,285	41,983	32,430	2,559	5,393	10,984	9,201
France	30,770	73,379	61,897	49,610	12,623	38,809	51,121	45,237
Germany	505,152[2,3]	341,498[2,3]	143,945[2,3]	412,202	114,058[3,4]	226,578[3,4]	477,765	190,796
Greece	15,979	167,519	184,201	51,084	9,119	8,973	47,608	85,969
Ireland[5]	388,416	339,065	146,181	211,234	10,973	19,789	48,362	32,966
Italy	651,893	2,045,877	1,109,524	455,315	68,028	57,661	185,491	214,111
Netherlands	26,758	48,262	43,718	26,948	7,150	14,860	52,277	30,606
Norway-Sweden	321,281	440,039	161,469	165,780	8,700	20,765	44,632	32,600
Norway	95,015	190,505	66,395	68,531	4,740	10,100	22,935	15,484
Sweden	226,266	249,534	95,074	97,249	3,960	10,665	21,697	17,116
Poland	96,720[2,3]	—[2,3]	4,813[2,3]	227,734	17,026	7,571	9,985	53,539
Portugal	27,508	69,149	89,732	29,994	3,329	7,423	19,588	76,065
Romania	12,750	53,008	13,311	67,646	3,871	1,076	1,039	2,531
Soviet Union	505,290[2,3]	1,597,306[2,3]	921,201[2,3]	61,742	1,370	571	671	2,465
Spain	8,731	27,935	68,611	28,958	3,258	2,898	7,894	44,659
Switzerland	31,179	34,922	23,091	29,676	5,512	10,547	17,675	18,453
United Kingdom[5,8]	271,538	525,950	341,408	339,570	31,572	139,306	202,824	213,822
Yugoslavia	—[9]	—[9]	1,888[9]	49,064	5,835	1,576	8,225	20,381
Other Europe	282	39,945	31,400	42,619	11,949	8,486	16,350	11,604

Region and Country								
Asia	74,862	323,543	247,236	112,059	16,595	37,028	153,249	427,642
China[10]	14,799	20,605	21,278	29,907	4,928	16,709	9,657	34,764
Hong Kong	—[11]	—[11]	—[11]	—[11]	—[11]	—[11]	15,541[11]	75,007
India	—	4,713	2,082	1,886	496	1,761	1,973	27,189
Iran	—[12]	—[12]	—[12]	241[12]	195	1,380	3,388	10,339
Israel	—[13]	—[13]	—[13]	—[13]	—[13]	476[13]	25,476	29,602
Japan	25,942	129,797	83,837	33,462	1,948	1,555	46,250	39,988
Korea	—[15]	—[15]	—[15]	—[15]	—[15]	107[15]	6,231	34,526
Philippines	—[16]	—[16]	—[16]	—[16]	528[16]	4,691	19,307	98,376
Turkey	30,425	157,369	134,066	33,824	1,065	798	3,519	10,142
Vietnam	—[11]	—[11]	—[11]	—[11]	—[11]	—[11]	335[11]	4,340
Other Asia	3,628	11,059	5,973	12,739	7,435	9,551	21,572	63,369
America	38,975	361,888	1,143,671	1,516,716	160,037	354,804	996,944	1,716,374
Canada & Newfoundland[17,18]	3,311	179,226	742,185	924,515	108,527	171,718	377,952	413,310
Mexico[18]	971[19]	49,642	219,004	459,287	22,319	60,589	299,811	453,937
Caribbean	33,066	107,548	123,424	74,899	15,502	49,725	123,091	470,213
Cuba	—[12]	—[12]	—[12]	15,901[12]	9,571	26,313	78,948	208,536
Dominican Republic	—[20]	—[20]	—[20]	—[20]	1,150[20]	5,627	9,897	93,292
Haiti	—[20]	—[20]	—[20]	—[20]	191[20]	911	4,442	34,499
Jamaica	—[21]	—[21]	—[21]	—[21]	—[21]	—[21]	8,869[21]	74,906
Other Caribbean	33,066	107,548	123,424	58,998	4,590	16,874	20,935[21]	58,980
Central America	549	8,192	17,159	15,769	5,861	21,665	44,751	101,330
El Salvador	—[20]	—[20]	—[20]	—[20]	673[20]	5,132	5,895	14,992
Other Central America	549	8,192	17,159	15,769	5,188	16,533	38,856	86,338
South America	1,075	17,280	41,899	42,215	7,803	21,831	91,628	257,954
Argentina	—[20]	—[20]	—[20]	—[20]	1,349[20]	3,338	19,486	49,721
Colombia	—[20]	—[20]	—[20]	—[20]	1,223[20]	3,858	18,048	72,028
Ecuador	—[20]	—[20]	—[20]	—[20]	337[20]	2,417	9,841	36,780
Other South America	1,075	17,280	41,899	42,215	4,894	12,218	44,253	99,425
Other America	—[22]	—[22]	—[22]	31[22]	25	29,276	59,711	19,630
Africa	350	7,368	8,443	6,286	1,750	7,367	14,092	28,954
Oceania	3,965	13,024	13,427	8,726	2,483	14,551	12,976	25,122
Not specified[22]	14,063	33,523[25]	1,147	228	—	142	12,491	93

Region and Country of Last Residence[1]	1971–80	1981–89	1984	1985	1986	1987	1988	1989	Total 170 Years 1820–1989
All countries	4,493,314	5,801,579	543,903	570,009	601,708	601,516	643,025	1,090,924	55,457,531
Europe	800,368	637,524	69,879	69,526	69,224	67,967	71,854	94,338	36,977,034
Austria-Hungary	16,028	20,152	2,846	2,521	2,604	2,401	3,200	3,586	4,338,049
Austria	9,478	14,566	2,351	1,930	2,039	1,769	2,493	2,845	1,825,172[a]
Hungary	6,550	5,586	495	591	565	632	707	741	1,666,801[a]
Belgium	5,329	6,239	787	775	843	859	706	705	209,729
Czechoslovakia	6,023	6,649	693	684	588	715	744	526	145,223
Denmark	4,439	4,696	512	465	544	515	561	617	369,738
France	25,069	28,088	3,335	3,530	3,876	3,809	3,637	4,101	783,322
Germany	74,414	79,809	9,375	10,028	9,853	9,923	9,748	10,419	7,071,313
Greece	92,369	34,490	3,311	3,487	3,497	4,087	4,690	4,588	700,017
Ireland[5]	11,490	22,229	1,096	1,288	1,757	3,032	5,121	6,983	4,715,393
Italy	129,368	51,008	6,328	6,351	5,711	4,666	5,332	11,089	5,356,862
Netherlands	10,492	10,723	1,313	1,235	1,263	1,303	1,152	1,253	372,717
Norway-Sweden	10,472	13,252	1,455	1,557	1,564	1,540	1,669	1,809	2,144,024
Norway	3,941	3,612	403	386	367	372	446	556	800,672[a]
Sweden	6,531	9,640	1,052	1,171	1,197	1,168	1,223	1,253	1,283,097[6]
Poland	37,234	64,888	7,229	7,409	6,540	5,818	7,298	13,279	587,972
Portugal	101,710	36,365	3,800	3,811	3,804	4,009	3,290	3,861	497,195
Romania	12,393	27,361	2,956	3,764	3,809	2,741	2,915	3,535	201,345
Soviet Union	38,961	42,898	3,349	1,532	1,001	1,139	1,408	4,570	3,428,927
Spain	39,141	17,689	2,168	2,278	2,232	2,056	1,972	2,179	282,404
Switzerland	8,235	7,561	795	980	923	964	920	1,072	358,151
United Kingdom[5,8]	137,374	140,119	16,516	15,591	16,129	15,889	14,667	16,961	5,100,096
Yugoslavia	30,540	15,984	1,404	1,521	1,915	1,793	2,039	2,464	133,493
Other Europe	9,287	7,324	611	719	771	708	785	741	181,064

Asia	5,697,301	296,420	254,745	248,293	258,546	255,164	247,775	2,416,278	1,588,178
China[10]	873,737	39,284	34,300	32,669	32,389	33,095	29,109	306,108	124,326
Hong Kong	287,863[11]	15,257	11,817	8,785	9,930	10,795	12,290	83,848	113,467
India	426,907	28,599	25,312	26,394	24,808	24,536	23,617	221,977	164,134
Iran	161,946[12]	13,027	9,846	10,323	12,031	12,327	11,131	101,267	45,136
Israel	131,634[13]	5,494	4,444	4,753	5,124	4,279	4,136	38,367	37,713
Japan	455,813[14]	5,454	5,085	4,711	4,444	4,552	4,517	40,654	49,775
Korea	611,284[15]	33,016	34,151	35,397	35,164	34,791	32,537	302,782	267,638
Philippines	955,374[16]	66,119	61,017	58,315	61,492	53,137	46,985	477,485	354,987
Turkey	409,122	2,538	2,200	2,080	1,975	1,690	1,652	20,028	13,399
Vietnam	443,522[21]	13,174	12,856	13,073	15,010	20,367	25,803	266,027	172,820
Other Asia	940,099	74,458	53,717	51,793	56,179	55,595	55,998	557,735	244,783
America	12,017,021	672,639	294,906	265,026	254,078	225,519	208,111	2,564,698	1,982,735
Canada & Newfoundland[17,18]	4,270,943	18,294	15,821	16,741	16,060	16,354	15,659	132,296	169,939
Mexico[18]	3,208,543	405,660	95,170	72,511	66,753	61,290	57,820	975,657	640,294
Caribbean	2,590,542	87,597	110,949	100,615	98,527	79,374	68,368	759,416	741,126
Cuba	739,274[12]	9,523	16,610	27,363	30,787	17,115	5,699	135,142	264,863
Dominican Republic	468,000[20]	26,744	27,195	24,947	26,216	23,861	23,207	209,899	148,135
Haiti	214,888[20]	13,341	34,858	14,643	12,356	9,872	9,554	118,510	56,335
Jamaica	405,833[31]	23,572	20,474	22,430	18,916	18,277	18,997	184,481	137,577
Other Caribbean	762,547	14,417	11,812	11,232	10,252	10,249	10,911	111,384	134,640
Central America	673,385	101,273	31,311	30,366	30,086	28,447	27,626	321,845	134,640
El Salvador	195,066[20]	57,628	12,043	10,627	10,881	10,093	8,753	133,938	34,436
Other Central America	478,319	43,645	19,268	19,739	19,205	18,354	18,873	187,907	100,204
South America	1,163,482	59,812	41,646	44,782	42,650	40,052	38,636	375,026	295,741
Argentina	125,157[20]	3,766	2,556	2,192	2,318	1,925	2,287	21,374	29,897
Colombia	271,570[20]	14,918	10,153	11,482	11,213	11,801	10,897	99,066	77,347
Ecuador	143,293[20]	7,587	4,736	4,656	4,518	4,601	4,244	43,841	50,077
Other South America	623,454	33,541	24,201	26,452	24,601	21,724	21,208	210,745	138,420
Other America	110,126	3	9	11	2	2	2	458	995
Africa	301,348	22,485	17,124	15,730	15,500	15,236	13,594	144,096	80,779
Oceania	197,818	4,956	4,324	4,437	4,352	4,552	4,249	38,401	41,242
Not specified[22]	267,009	86	72	63	8	12	295	582	12

[1]Data for years prior to 1906 relate to country whence alien came; data from 1906–79 and 1984–89 are for country of last permanent residence; and data for 1980–83 refer to country of birth. Because of changes in boundaries, changes in lists of countries, and lack of data for specified countries for various periods, data for certain countries, especially for the total period 1820–1989, are not comparable throughout. Data for specified countries are included with countries to which they belonged prior to World War I.

[2]Data for Austria and Hungary not reported until 1861.

[3]Data for Austria and Hungary not reported separately for all years during the period.

[4]No data available for Czechoslovakia until 1920.

[5]Prior to 1926, data for Northern Ireland included in Ireland.

[6]Data for Norway and Sweden not reported separately until 1871.

[7]No data available for Romania until 1880.

[8]Since 1925, data for United Kingdom refer to England, Scotland, Wales, and Northern Ireland.

[9]In 1920, a separate enumeration was made for the Kingdom of Serbs, Croats, and Slovenes. Since 1922, the Serb, Croat, and Slovene Kingdom recorded as Yugoslavia.

[10]Beginning in 1957, China includes Taiwan.

[11]Data not reported separately until 1952.

[12]Data not reported separately until 1925.

[13]Data not reported separately until 1949.

[14]No data available for Japan until 1861.

[15]Data not reported separately until 1948.

[16]Prior to 1934, Philippines recorded as insular travel.

[17]Prior to 1920, Canada and Newfoundland recorded as British North America. From 1820 to 1898, figures include all British North America possessions.

[18]Land arrivals not completely enumerated until 1908.

[19]No data available for Mexico from 1886 to 1893.

[20]Data not reported separately until 1932.

[21]Data for Jamaica not collected until 1953. In prior years, consolidated under British West Indies, which is included in "Other Caribbean."

[22]Included in countries "Not specified" until 1925.

[23]From 1899 to 1919, data for Poland included in Austria-Hungary, Germany, and the Soviet Union.

[24]From 1938 to 1945, data for Austria included in Germany.

[25]Includes 32,897 persons returning in 1906 to their homes in the United States.

—represents zero.

NOTE: From 1820 to 1867, figures represent alien passengers arrived at seaports; from 1868 to 1891 and 1895 to 1897, immigrant aliens arrived; from 1892 to 1894 and 1898 to 1989, immigrant aliens admitted for permanent residence. From 1892 to 1903, aliens entering by cabin class were not counted as immigrants. Land arrivals were not completely enumerated until 1908. For this table, fiscal year 1843 covers 9 months ending September 1843; fiscal years 1832 and 1850 cover 15 months ending December 31 of the respective years; and fiscal year 1868 covers 6 months ending June 30, 1868.

PRESIDENTS, VICE-PRESIDENTS, AND SECRETARIES OF STATE

President	Vice-President	Secretary of State
1. George Washington, Federalist 1789	John Adams, Federalist 1789	T. Jefferson 1789 E. Randolph 1794 T. Pickering 1795
2. John Adams, Federalist 1798	Thomas Jefferson, Dem.-Rep. 1797	T. Pickering 1797 John Marshall 1800
3. Thomas Jefferson, Dem.-Rep. 1801	Aaron Burr, Dem.-Rep. 1801 George Clinton, Dem.-Rep. 1805	James Madison 1801
4. James Madison, Dem.-Rep. 1809	George Clinton, Dem.-Rep. 1809 Elbridge Gerry, Dem.-Rep. 1813	Robert Smith 1809 James Monroe 1811
5. James Monroe, Dem.-Rep. 1817	D. D. Tompkins, Dem.-Rep. 1817	J. Q. Adams 1817
6. John Quincy Adams, Dem.-Rep. 1825	John C. Calhoun, Dem.-Rep. 1825	Henry Clay 1825
7. Andrew Jackson, Democratic 1829	John C. Calhoun, Democratic 1829 Martin Van Buren, Democratic 1833	M. Van Buren 1829 E. Livingston 1831 Louis McLane 1833 John Forsyth 1834
8. Martin Van Buren, Democratic 1837	Richard M. Johnson, Democratic 1837	John Forsyth 1837
9. William H. Harrison, Whig 1841	John Tyler, Whig 1841	Daniel Webster 1841

President	Vice-President	Secretary of State
10. John Tyler, Whig and Democratic 1841		Daniel Webster 1841 Hugh S. Legare 1843 Abel P. Upshur 1843 John C. Calhoun 1844
11. James K. Polk, Democratic 1845	George M. Dallas, Democratic 1845	James Buchanan 1845
12. Zachary Taylor, Whig 1849	Millard Fillmore, Whig 1848	John M. Clayton 1849
13. Millard Fillmore, Whig 1850		Daniel Webster 1850 Edward Everett 1852
14. Franklin Pierce, Democratic 1853	William R. D. King, Democratic 1853	W. L. Marcy 1853
15. James Buchanan, Democratic 1857	John C. Breckinridge, Democratic 1857	Lewis Cass 1857 J. S. Black 1860
16. Abraham Lincoln, Republican 1861	Hannibal Hamlin, Republican 1861 Andrew Johnson, Unionist 1865	W. H. Seward 1861
17. Andrew Johnson, Unionist 1865		W. H. Seward 1865

President	*Vice-President*	*Secretary of State*
18. Ulysses S. Grant, Republican 1869	Schuyler Colfax, Republican 1869 Henry Wilson, Republican 1873	E. B. Washburne 1869 H. Fish 1869
19. Rutherford B. Hayes, Republican 1877	William A. Wheeler, Republican 1877	W. M. Evarts 1877
20. James A. Garfield, Republican 1881	Chester A. Arthur, Republican 1881	J. G. Blaine 1881
21. Chester A. Arthur, Republican 1881		F. T. Frelinghuysen 1881
22. Grover Cleveland, Democratic 1885	T. A. Hendricks, Democratic 1885	T. F. Bayard 1885
23. Benjamin Harrison, Republican 1889	Levi P. Morton, Republican 1889	J. G. Blaine 1889 J. W. Foster 1892
24. Grover Cleveland, Democratic 1893	Adlai E. Stevenson, Democratic 1893	W. Q. Gresham 1893 R. Olney 1895
25. William McKinley, Republican 1897	Garret A. Hobart, Republican 1897 Theodore Roosevelt, Republican 1901	J. Sherman 1897 W. R. Day 1897 J. Hay 1898
26. Theodore Roosevelt, Republican 1901	Chas. W. Fairbanks, Republican 1905	J. Hay 1901 E. Root 1905 R. Bacon 1909
27. William H. Taft, Republican 1909	James S. Sherman, Republican 1909	P. C. Knox 1909

President	Vice-President	Secretary of State
28. Woodrow Wilson, Democratic 1913	Thomas R. Marshall, Democratic 1913	W. J. Bryan 1913 R. Lansing 1915 B. Colby 1920
29. Warren G. Harding, Republican 1921	Calvin Coolidge, Republican 1921	C. E. Hughes 1921
30. Calvin Coolidge, Republican 1923	Charles G. Dawes, Republican 1925	C. E. Hughes 1923 F. B. Kellogg 1925
31. Herbert Hoover, Republican 1929	Charles Curtis, Republican 1929	H. L. Stimson 1929
32. Franklin D. Roosevelt, Democratic 1933	John Nance Garner, Democratic 1933 Henry A. Wallace, Democratic 1941 Harry S. Truman, Democratic 1945	C. Hull 1933 E. R. Stettinius, Jr. 1944
33. Harry S. Truman, Democratic 1945	Alben W. Barkley, Democratic 1949	J. F. Byrnes 1945 G. C. Marshall 1947 D. G. Acheson 1949
34. Dwight D. Eisenhower, Republican 1953	Richard M. Nixon, Republican 1953	J. F. Dulles 1953 C. A. Herter 1959
35. John F. Kennedy, Democratic 1961	Lyndon B. Johnson, Democratic 1961	D. Rusk 1961
36. Lyndon B. Johnson, Democratic 1963	Hubert H. Humphrey, Democratic 1965	D. Rusk 1963

President	Vice-President	Secretary of State
37. Richard M. Nixon, Republican 1969	Spiro T. Agnew, Republican 1969 Gerald R. Ford, Republican 1973	W. P. Rogers 1969 H. A. Kissinger 1973
38. Gerald R. Ford, Republican 1974	Nelson Rockefeller, Republican 1974	H. A. Kissinger 1974
39. Jimmy Carter, Democratic 1977	Walter Mondale, Democratic 1977	C. Vance 1977 E. Muskie 1980
40. Ronald Reagan, Republican 1981	George Bush, Republican 1981	A. Haig 1981 G. Schultz 1982
41. George Bush, Republican 1989	J. Danforth Quayle, Republican 1989	J. A. Baker 1989
42. Bill Clinton, Democrat 1993	Albert Gore, Jr. Democrat 1993	

CHRONOLOGY OF
SIGNIFICANT EVENTS

16,000–14,000 B.C.	Likely period for first crossing of land bridge from Old World to New World
5000 B.C.	Hunting and gathering established as a way of life in New World
2000–1500 B.C.	Permanent towns appear in Mexico
800 B.C.–A.D. 600	Adena-Hopewell culture (northeast United States)
400 B.C.-present	Pueblo-Hohokam culture (southwest United States)
A.D. 300–900	Mayan culture
600–1500	Mississippian culture (southeast United States)
1000	Leif Ericsson sights Newfoundland
1215	Magna Carta adopted in England
1300–1519	Aztec culture
1300–1598	Inca culture
1440	Gutenberg invents movable type
1477	Marco Polo's *Travels* published
1492–1504	Columbus's four voyages to New World
1493	Pope declares demarcation line
1517	Martin Luther launches Protestant Reformation
1519	Cortés conquers Aztec empire
1536	John Calvin publishes *The Institutes*
1558–1603	Reign of Queen Elizabeth I
1565	Town of St. Augustine founded by the Spanish

1587	Sir Walter Raleigh's "lost colony" at Roanoke
1588	Defeat of the Spanish Armada by the English
1603–1625	Reign of James I, first of England's Stuart kings
1606	Virginia Company chartered
1607	Jamestown founded
1614	Dutch trading post set up on Manhattan Island
1616	Tobacco becomes an export staple for Virginia
1619	Virginia's General Assembly first convenes
1619	First Africans brought to English America
1620	*Mayflower* lands at Plymouth
1625	Population of English colonies in America at 2,000
1625–1649	Reign of Charles I in England
1630	Gov. John Winthrop leads the Puritan migration to Massachusetts Bay
1634	First settlement in Maryland
1636	Harvard College founded
1638	Anne Hutchinson banished from Massachusetts in Antinomian controversy
1642–1649	English Civil War
1649–1660	The Commonwealth and Protectorate in England
1651	William Bradford completes *Of Plymouth Plantation*
1660	English monarchy restored under Charles II
1662	Half-Way Covenant adopted by New England Congregational churches
1664	Dutch New Netherland colony becomes English New York
1675	King Philip's War
1676	Bacon's Rebellion
1681	Pennsylvania founded
1685–1688	Reign of James II
1687	Newton's *Principia* published
1688	England's Glorious Revolution
1689	John Locke's *Two Treatises on Civil Government* published
1689–1697	King William's War (War of the League of Augsburg)

1692	Salem witch trials
1700	Population of English colonies in America at 250,000
1702–1713	Queen Anne's War (War of the Spanish Succession)
1704	First enduring newspaper published in America
1732	Georgia founded
1732–1757	Benjamin Franklin publishes *Poor Richard's Almanack*
1734	Great Awakening begins in colonies
1735	Trial of John Peter Zenger
1740–1748	King George's War (War of the Austrian Succession)
1754–1763	French and Indian War (Seven Years' War)
1763	Proclamation of 1763
1764	The Sugar Act
1764	The Currency Act
1765	The Stamp Act
1766	Declaratory Act
1767	Townshend Act
1768	John Dickinson publishes *Letters of a Pennsylvania Farmer*
1768	Samuel Adams's Massachusetts Circular Letter
1769	Virginia Resolves
1770	Boston Massacre
1773	Boston Tea Party
1774	Coercive Acts
1774	First Continental Congress
1775	Battles of Lexington and Concord
1775	Second Continental Congress
1775	Battle of Bunker Hill
1776	Thomas Paine's *Common Sense*
1776	Declaration of Independence
1777	American victory at Saratoga
1777	Congress adopts the Articles of Confederation
1778	Franco-American alliance set
1781	Battle of Yorktown
1782	Crèvecoeur's *Letters from an American Farmer*
1783	Peace of Paris
1784	*Empress of China* sails for Canton

1787 Shays's Rebellion
1787 The Constitutional Convention meets and submits the Constitution to states for ratification
1787 Northwest Ordinance
1788 Hamilton, Madison, and Jay publish *The Federalist*
1788 The Constitution ratified by the states
1789 George Washington elected president
1789 Bill of Rights submitted to the states
1790–1791 Hamilton's *Reports*
1790 Samuel Slater's cotton mill set up in Rhode Island
1793 Eli Whitney invents the cotton gin
1794 Whiskey Rebellion
1794 Jay Treaty
1795 Pinckney Treaty
1795 North Carolina opens first state university
1796 John Adams elected president
1797 XYZ Affair
1797–1810 Revivalism on the frontier
1798–1800 Undeclared war with France
1798 Alien and Sedition Acts
1798 Kentucky and Virginia Resolutions
1800 Thomas Jefferson elected president
1803 *Marbury v. Madison*
1803 Louisiana Purchase
1803–1806 Lewis and Clark expedition
1807 Embargo Act
1809 Non-Intercourse Act
1811 Battle of Tippecanoe
1811 National Road started
1812 Congress declares war on Great Britain
1814 Hartford Convention
1815 Battle of New Orleans
1815 Peace of Ghent
1817–1825 Construction of the Erie Canal
1819 *McCulloch v. Maryland*
1819 Adams-Onis Treaty
1820 Washington Irving's *The Sketch Book*
1820 Missouri Compromise
1820 Significant Irish immigration begins
1821 Boston opens first public secondary school
1821–1822 Santa Fe Trail opened

1822	Cotton mills opened in Lowell, Massachusetts
1823	Monroe Doctrine
1826	James Fenimore Cooper's *The Last of the Mohicans*
1828	Andrew Jackson elected president
1828	Calhoun's *South Carolina Exposition and Protest*
1829–1837	Battle over recharter of the Bank of the United States
1830	Webster-Hayne debate
1830	Indian Removal Act
1830–1847	The Mormon trek west
1830–1860	Hudson River school of painting
1831	*Cherokee Nation v. Georgia*
1831	William Lloyd Garrison begins publication of *The Liberator*
1831	Nat Turner's rebellion
1832	South Carolina Ordinance of Nullification
1833	Chicago founded
1836	Siege of the Alamo
1836	Texas declares its independence
1836–1850	Transcendentalism spreads in New England
1836	Ralph Waldo Emerson's *Nature*
1837	Panic of 1837
1837	*Charles River Bridge v. Warren Bridge*
1840	Edgar Allan Poe's *Tales of the Grotesque and Arabesque*
1842	Webster-Ashburton Treaty
1844	Samuel F. B. Morse invents the telegraph
1844–1846	Dispute with Great Britain over Oregon Territory
1845	United States annexes Texas
1846	Americans declare California an independent republic
1846	United States declares war on Mexico
1846	Wilmot Proviso
1846	Potato famine in Ireland
1848	Gold discovered in California
1848	Treaty of Guadalupe Hidalgo
1848	Seneca Falls convention on women's rights
1850	Compromise of 1850
1850	Nathaniel Hawthorne's *The Scarlet Letter*
1850	Clayton-Bulwer Treaty

1851	Herman Melville's *Moby-Dick*
1852	Harriet Beecher Stowe's *Uncle Tom's Cabin*
1853	Gadsden Purchase
1854	Perry's reopening of Japan
1854	Henry David Thoreau's *Walden*
1854	Ostend Manifesto
1854	Kansas-Nebraska Act
1855	Walt Whitman's *Leaves of Grass*
1856	"Bleeding Kansas"
1857	Dred Scott decision
1858	Lincoln-Douglas debates
1859	John Brown's Raid
1859	Charles Darwin's *Origin of Species*
1860	Abraham Lincoln elected president
1860–1861	Southern states secede from the Union
1861	The Civil War breaks out
1861	First Battle of Bull Run
1861–1890	Indian wars in the West
1862	Battle of Antietam
1862	Battle of Shiloh
1862	The Homestead Act
1863	Battle of Gettysburg
1863	New York City Draft Riots
1863	Lincoln issues the Emancipation Proclamation
1864	Sherman's March to the Sea
1865	Lee surrenders to Grant at Appomattox Courthouse
1865	Freedmen's Bureau established
1865	Assassination of President Lincoln
1866–1868	Fourteenth Amendment passed and ratified
1867	First Reconstruction Act
1867–1877	Congressional Reconstruction of the South
1867	United States purchases Alaska
1868	Impeachment of President Andrew Johnson
1869	Completion of first transcontinental railroad
1869	National Woman Suffrage Association founded
1870	Standard Oil Company of Ohio established by John D. Rockefeller
1873	Crédit-Mobilier Scandal
1876	Battle of the Little Big Horn
1876	Telephone invented by Alexander Graham Bell

1877	*Munr̄ v. Illinois*
1878	Bland-Allison Act
1879	Terence Powderly becomes president of Knights of Labor
1879	Incandescent bulb invented by Thomas Edison
1881	Helen Hunt Jackson's *A Century of Dishonor*
1882	Chinese Exclusion Act
1883	Pendleton Act
1883	Brooklyn Bridge completed
1884	Mark Twain's *The Adventures of Huckleberry Finn*
1885	Josiah Strong publishes *Our Country*
1886	Haymarket Riot
1886	American Federation of Labor founded
1887	Interstate Commerce Act
1887–1889	National Farmers' Alliance founded
1888	Edward Bellamy's *Looking Backward*
1889	Hull House founded by Jane Addams
1890	Battle of Wounded Knee
1890	Sherman Anti-Trust Act
1890	Jacob Riis's *How the Other Half Lives*
1892	Homestead Massacre
1892	Populist party founded
1893	Panic of 1893
1893	Stephen Crane's *Maggie: A Girl of the Streets*
1893	Chicago World's Fair
1894	Pullman Strike
1895	Booker T. Washington's Atlanta Exposition Speech
1896	*Plessy v. Ferguson*
1898	Spanish-American War
1899–1900	"Open Door" Notes
1899	Thorstein Veblen's *The Theory of the Leisure Class*
1900	Theodore Dreiser's *Sister Carrie*
1900–1917	"Ash Can" school of painting
1901–1917	Progressive movement
1903	Orville and Wilbur Wright's first flight
1903	William E. B. DuBois's *Souls of Black Folk*
1904	*Northern Securities Company v. U.S.*
1904–1905	Roosevelt corollary to Monroe Doctrine

1905	Roosevelt mediates end to Russo-Japanese War
1906	Upton Sinclair's *The Jungle*
1906–1914	Construction of the Panama Canal
1908	Gentlemen's Agreement with Japan
1909	First Model T automobile produced by Henry Ford
1909	National Association for the Advancement of Colored People founded
1909–1910	Ballinger/Pinchot dispute
1910	President Taft's "dollar diplomacy" in Nicaragua
1912	Woodrow Wilson elected president
1913	Underwood-Simmons Tariff Act
1913	Federal Reserve Act
1913–1917	Revolt in Mexico and U.S. intervention
1914	Clayton Anti-Trust Act
1914	Outbreak of World War I
1915	German submarine sinks *Lusitania*
1915	Albert Einstein's general theory of relativity
1917	Russian Revolution
1917	United States enters the war against Germany
1918	Wilson announces Fourteen Points
1919	Treaty of Versailles signed
1919	Boston Police Strike
1919	Volstead Act (Prohibition)
1919	Sherwood Anderson's *Winesburg, Ohio*
1919–1920	United States rejects treaty over League of Nations
1919–1920	Red Scare
1920–1930	Harlem Renaissance
1921	Marcus Garvey's African Zionist Movement
1922	T. S. Eliot's *The Waste Land*
1922	Washington Conference on Disarmament
1924	Harding administration scandals
1924	McNary-Haugen Bill
1925	Scopes trial
1925	F. Scott Fitzgerald's *The Great Gatsby*
1926	Ernest Hemingway's *The Sun Also Rises*
1927	Charles Lindbergh's solo flight to Paris
1927	Sacco and Vanzetti executed
1927	Babe Ruth hits 60 home runs
1928	Kellogg-Briand Peace Pact

1929	William Faulkner's *The Sound and the Fury*
1929	Stock market crash
1929–1933	Great Depression
1932	Bonus Army march on Washington
1932	Franklin Delano Roosevelt elected president
1933	Emergency Banking Act
1933	Unemployment Relief Act
1933	Agricultural Adjustment Act
1933	Tennessee Valley Authority Act
1933	National Industrial Recovery Act
1933	Hitler comes to power in Germany
1935–1936	Second New Deal
1935	National Labor Relations Act
1935	Social Security Act
1935	*Schechter v. United States*
1936	Spanish Civil War
1937	Supreme Court "packing" fight
1938	Munich Conference
1939	Germany annexes Czechoslovakia and invades Poland
1939	John Steinbeck's *The Grapes of Wrath*
1940	Battle of Britain
1940	Richard Wright's *Native Son*
1941	Lend-Lease aid to Allies
1941	Atlantic Charter
1941	Japanese attack on Pearl Harbor
1941	United States enters World War II
1944	Allied invasion of Normandy
1945	Atomic bombs dropped on Hiroshima and Nagasaki
1945	Germany surrenders; Japan surrenders
1945	Yalta Conference
1945	Potsdam Conference
1946	Benjamin Spock's *Baby and Child Care*
1947	Taft-Hartley Labor-Management Relations Act
1947	Truman Doctrine
1947	Marshall Plan
1947	Jackie Robinson becomes first black in major-league baseball
1949	North Atlantic Treaty Organization (NATO) founded
1949	Arthur Miller's *Death of a Salesman*
1950	Internal Security Act

1950–1953	Korean War
1950–1954	McCarthyism
1950	David Riesman's *The Lonely Crowd*
1952	Ralph Ellison's *Invisible Man*
1952	Norman Vincent Peale's *The Power of Positive Thinking*
1954	*Brown v. Board of Education of Topeka*
1954	Geneva Conference on Indochina
1955	Montgomery bus boycott
1955	Dr. Jonas Salk's polio vaccine
1956	Suez crisis
1956	Alan Ginsberg's *Howl*
1957	Dispute over integration in Little Rock, Arkansas
1957	Eisenhower Doctrine
1957	Jack Kerouac's *On the Road*
1957	USSR launches Sputnik satellite
1959	Fidel Castro leads revolution in Cuba
1960	U-2 incident
1960	"Sit-in" movement begins in Greensboro, N.C.
1960	Students for a Democratic Society founded
1961	Bay of Pigs invasion
1962	Cuban missile crisis
1962	Michael Harrington's *The Other America*
1962	Rachel Carson's *Silent Spring*
1963	Nuclear Test Ban Treaty
1963	Assassination of President John F. Kennedy
1963	March on Washington for civil rights
1963	Betty Friedan's *The Feminine Mystique*
1964	Gulf of Tonkin Resolution
1964, 1965	Civil Rights Acts
1965	President Lyndon Johnson's Great Society
1965	U.S. troop buildup begins in Vietnam
1965	Ralph Nader's *Unsafe at Any Speed*
1966	National Organization for Women founded
1967	Arab-Israeli War
1968	Tet Offensive in Vietnam
1968	Martin Luther King assassinated
1968	Robert Kennedy assassinated
1968	Violence at Democratic National Convention in Chicago
1969	Woodstock Festival for Music and Peace
1969	My Lai massacre

1969	Neil Armstrong becomes first man on moon
1970	Violence at Kent State and Jackson State Universities
1972	Earth Day demonstrations
1972	President Nixon visits China
1972–1974	Watergate scandal
1973	Vietnam Peace Agreement
1973–1974	Arab oil embargo
1975	Fall of South Vietnam
1978	Camp David accords between Egypt and Israel
1979	Three Mile Island nuclear accident
1979	SALT II Agreement
1979–1981	Iranian hostage crisis
1983	American marines killed in Lebanon
1986	Tax Reform Act
1986	Iran-Contra affair
1987	Scandals in politics and evangelical movement
1987	Congressional hearings on Iran-Contra affair
1987	Controversy over air traffic safety
1987	"Black Monday" on Wall Street
1987	INF treaty with Soviet Union
1988–1989	S&L crisis and bailout
1989	End of Communist Party rule in East-bloc nations
1989	Fall of the Berlin Wall
1989–1990	U.S. military action in Panama
1990–1991	Persian Gulf crisis
1991	U.S. military action against Iraq
1991	Failed coup in the Soviet Union
1992	Los Angeles riots
1992	Bill Clinton elected president

ILLUSTRATION CREDITS

Note: The number preceding each credit is the page number on which the illustration is located.

CHAPTER 1 3 / Milwaukee Public Museum. 7 / British Museum. 10 / The British Library. 13 / The Warder Collection. 16 / Library of Congress. 18 / Library of Congress. 24 / American Antiquarian Society. 26 / The Warder Collection. 32 / New York Public Library. 34 / Historical Society of Pennsylvania.

CHAPTER 2 43 / The Worcester Art Museum. 45 / Metropolitan Museum of Art. 47 / American Antiquarian Society. 49 / The Abby Aldridge Rockefeller Folk Art Center, Williamsburg, Virginia. 58 / From Ralph Gardiner, *England's Grievance Discovered*, 1655. 64 / Harvard University. 67 / Yale University Art Gallery.

CHAPTER 3 74 / Winterthur Museum. 75 / National Maritime Museum, London. 81 / The Library Company of Philadelphia. 90 / National Army Museum, London.

CHAPTER 4 94 / Courtauld Institute of Art. 99 / Historical Society of Pennsylvania. 104 / Library of Congress. 108 / Library of Congress. 109 / New York Public Library. 115 / National Gallery of Art. 117 / American Antiquarian Society.

CHAPTER 5 125 / New York Public Library. 137 / The British Library. 144 / Massachusetts Historical Society. 145 / National Gallery of Art. 147 / Museum of Art, Rhode Island School of Design. 149 / Yale University Art Gallery.

CHAPTER 6 158 / Boston Athenaeum. 163 / Library of Congress. 169 / Independence National Historical Park Collection.

CHAPTER 7 176 / Museum of the City of New York. 178 / The Smithsonian Institution. 184 / White House Collection. 187 / Frick Art Reference Library. 189 / The Warder Collection. 193 / American Antiquarian Society. 195 / Henry E. Huntington Library and Art Gallery.

CHAPTER 8 203 / Library of Congress. 205 / The Cincinnati Historical Society. 212 / New-York Historical Society. 215 / Historical Society of Pennsylvania. 218 / Museum of Natural History. 223 / Library of Congress. 227 / The Warder Collection.

CHAPTER 9 231 / Maryland Historical Society. 233 / The Smithsonian Institution. 241 / Metropolitan Museum of Art. 246 / New York State Bureau of Historic Sites. 249 / New-York Historical Society.
CHAPTER 10 253 / Library of Congress. 255 / National Archives. 258 / Boston Art Commission. 262 / American Antiquarian Society. 266 / Boatmen's National Bank of St. Louis. 268 / New-York Historical Society. 271 / Library of Congress. 273 / Library of Congress. 276 / Library of Congress.
CHAPTER 11 280 / Amon Carter Museum. 287 / New York State Historical Association. 290 / Merrimack Valley Textile Museum. 294 / New York Public Library. 299 / Maryland Historical Society. 302 / Historical Society of Pennsylvania.
CHAPTER 12 309 / Library of Congress. 315 / The Warder Collection. 317 / The Essex Institute. 319 / National Archives. 324 / Library of Congress. 327 / Schlesinger Library, Radcliffe College. 329 / The Warder Collection.
CHAPTER 13 341 / Library of Congress. 345 / Library of Congress. 348 / Library of Congress. 353 / Chicago Historical Society.
CHAPTER 14 360 / New-York Historical Society. 362 / Library of Congress. 368 / New York Public Library. 370 / Chicago Historical Society. 372 / Library of Congress. 374 / Metropolitan Museum of Art. 377 / (left) Library of Congress; (right) New-York Historical Society.
CHAPTER 15 389 / Metropolitan Museum of Art. 393 / New-York Historical Society. 396 / Library of Congress. 402 / (left) Missouri Historical Society; (right) National Archives. 407 / The Warder Collection. 410 / Chicago Historical Society. 412 / New York Public Library.
CHAPTER 16 421 / Chicago Historical Society. 432 / Library of Congress. 438 / National Archives. 442 / Library of Congress. 448 / Library of Congress.
CHAPTER 17 455 / Library of Congress. 457 / Library of Congress. 459 / (left) Library of Congress; (right) National Archives. 461 / Library of Congress. 465 / Chicago Historical Society. 469 / Library of Congress. 471 / Library of Congress. 474 / Library of Congress.
CHAPTER 18 481 / The Warder Collection. 483 / Brown Brothers. 489 / (left) Library of Congress; (right) The Warder Collection. 495 / (top) The Smithsonian Institute; (bottom) The Smithsonian Institute. 499 / Solomon D. Butcher Collection, Nebraska State Historical Society.
CHAPTER 19 505 / Union Pacific Railroad Museum Collection. 508 / U.S. Department of the Interior, National Park Service, Edison National Historic Site. 509 / The Warder Collection. 512 / Carnegie Library, Pittsburgh. 514 / The Pierpont Morgan Library. 517 / Carnegie Library, Pittsburgh. 521 / The Warder Collection. 524 / The Archives of Labor and Urban Affairs, Wayne State University.
CHAPTER 20 532 / Library of Congress. 534 / Museum of the City of New York. 536 / (top) New York Public Library; (bottom) New York Public Library. 541 / California Historical Society Library. 543 / Library of Congress. 549 / Mark Twain Memorial, Hartford, Connecticut. 552 / The Salvation Army. 554 / New York Public Library. 556 / Schlesinger Library, Radcliffe College.
CHAPTER 21 560 / Library of Congress. 565 / The Warder Collection. 568 /

The Warder Collection. 574 / Library of Congress. 578 / Library of Congress. 584 / Library of Congress. CHAPTER 22 590 / Public Archives of Hawaii. 595 / Library of Congress. 599 / National Archives. 602 / Library of Congress. 603 / National Archives. 606 / Library of Congress. 611 / Library of Congress. CHAPTER 23 620 / National Archives. 623 / Library of Congress. 627 / The Warder Collection. 633 / Library of Congress. 637 / The Warder Collection. 638 / Historical Pictures Services, Chicago. 640 / Brandeis University. CHAPTER 24 645 / The Warder Collection. 647 / Library of Congress. 652 / The *New York Times*. 654 / United Press International Photo. 658 / National Archives. 660 / National Archives. 663 / National Archives. 666 / National Archives. 672 / Library of Congress. 675 / The Bettmann Archives, Inc. CHAPTER 25 680 / UPI/Bettmann Newsphotos. 682 / Looking Back at Tennessee Collection, Tennessee State Library and Archives, Courtesy of Mrs. Frances Robinson Gabbert. 684 / Chicago Historical Society. 687 / Library of Congress. 688 / State Historical Society of Wisconsin. 690 / The Warder Collection. 695 / Ramsey Archive. 697 / National Archives. 698 / AP/Wide World Photos. 700 / University of Virginia. CHAPTER 26 704 / Library of Congress. 709 / Library of Congress. 712 / National Archives. 715 / Library of Congress. 719 / International News/ Herbert Hoover Presidential Library. 723 / Museum of History and Industry, Seattle. CHAPTER 27 730 / Wide World Photos. 736 / Library of Congress. 742 / UPI/ Bettmann Newsphotos. 745 / Library of Congress. 747 / UPI/Bettmann Newsphotos. 752 / *Life* magazine, © 1965, Time, Inc. 754 / National Archives. CHAPTER 28 764 / Wide World Photos. 771 / The *Daily Mail*, London. 779 / (top) National Archives; (bottom) National Archives. CHAPTER 29 786 / National Archives. 787 / National Archives. 789 / National Archives. 796 / Library of Congress. 802 / National Archives. 805 / National Archives. 808 / National Archives. CHAPTER 30 813 / University of Louisville Photographic Archives. 815 / New York Public Library. 823 / The *Hartford Courant*. 825 / UPI/Bettmann Newsphotos. 827 / United Press International Photo. 832 / Roche in the *Buffalo Courier Express*. 835 / United Press International Photo. CHAPTER 31 840 / Culver Pictures, Inc. 843 / Photo by J. R. Eyerman, *Life* magazine, © 1953 by Time, Inc. 846 / The Warder Collection. 826 / Photo by Dan Weiner, courtesy Sandra Weiner. 851 / Culver Pictures, Inc. 853 / Metropolitan Museum of Art, George A. Hearn Fund, 1953. CHAPTER 32 858 / UPI/Bettmann Newsphotos. 863 / UPI/Bettmann Newsphotos. 868 / The Warder Collection. 872 / Standard Oil of New Jersey Collection, University of Louisville. 874 / © Charles Moore, Black Star. 882 / AP/Wide World Photos. CHAPTER 33 887 / National Archives. 890 / National Archives. 892 / National Archives. 897 / Wide World Photos. 902 / National Archives. 905 / UPI/Bettmann Newsphotos. 909 / AP/Wide World Photos. 913 / UPI/ Bettmann Newsphotos. CHAPTER 34 918 / R. Malloch, Magnum Photos. 921 / Library of Congress.

922 / The Warder Collection. 927 / Conrad in the *Los Angeles Times.* 930 / Wide World Photos. 934 / United Press International Photo. 937 / United Press International Photo. 938 / Wide World Photos. 943 / Wide World Photos. 946 / United Press International Photo. CHAPTER 35   953 / United Press International Photo. 956 / UPI/Bettmann Newsphotos. 959 / AP/Wide World Photos. 962 / Reuters/Bettman Newsphotos. 964 / UPI/Bettmann Newsphotos. 971 / © Tom Sobolik, Black Star. 974 / © Rick Gerharter, Black Star. 977 / © Anthony Suau, Black Star. 981 / AP/Wide World Photos. 987 / © David Turnley, Black Star. 990 / Jose Lopez/NYT Pictures. 995 / Reuters/Bettmann. 1004 / Reuters/Bettmann.

INDEX

ABC powers (Argentina, Brazil, and
    Chile), 646
abortion laws, 922, 923
abortion rights, 951, 991
Absalom! Absalom! (Faulkner), 700
Abstract Expressionism, 852–53
Acadia, 84
Acheson, Dean, 829–30, 833, 834, 866,
    876
Act for the Impartial Administration of
    Justice (1774), 108–9
Adams, Abigail, 118, 145–46, 160, 177,
    194, 322–23
Adams, Henry, 476, 559
Adams, John, 103, 118, 127, 138,
    139–40, 146, 150, 152–53, 163
    as ambassador to Great Britain, 158
    background of, 194
    Boston Massacre and, 104–5
    domestic discontent and, 197
    foreign policy under, 194–97
    judicial appointments of, 200, 204
    political philosophy of, 194
    in presidential elections, 193–94, 199,
        200
    as vice-president, 175, 177
Adams, John Quincy, 152, 210, 296,
    332, 351
    abolitionism and, 379
    party affiliation of, 270
    presidency of, 246–48
    in presidential elections, 244, 245–46
    as secretary of state, 234, 236, 242, 243
Adams, Samuel, 102–3, 105, 107–8,
    112, 118, 150, 171
Adams, Sherman, 860
Adamson Act (1916), 641
Addams, Jane, 554, 653
Administrative Reorganization Act
    (1939), 755
Adventures of Huckleberry Finn, The
    (Twain), 548
Adventures of Tom Sawyer, The (Twain),
    548
advertising, 841

affirmative action programs, 956
Affluent Society, The (Galbraith), 849
Afghanistan, Soviet invasion of (1979),
    944–45, 961, 969, 977
African-Americans, *see* blacks
age groups, fastest-growing, 998
Agnew, Spiro, 912, 925, 932, 939
Agricultural Adjustment Act (1933),
    734–38
Agricultural Adjustment Act (1938),
    737, 748
agriculture:
    in colonial period, 41, 44–46, 84
    crop rotation in, 45
    exchanges between New and Old
        Worlds and, 7–8
    in Great Depression, 734–38
    growth of (early 1800s), 278–80, 288
    in 1920s, 715–17
    in New West, 498–500
    in pre-Columbian civilizations, 7–8, 41
    in South, 44–46, 361–62, 483–84
    technological improvements in, 500
Agriculture Department, U.S., 626, 627
Aguinaldo, Emilio, 598, 602, 603
AIDS (Acquired Immune Deficiency
    Syndrome), 925, 974–75
Aiken, Conrad, 694
air conditioning, 842
airplanes, 712
Alabama, 260, 468, 487
Alabama, University of, 891
Alamance, battle of (1771), 106
Alamo, battle of (1836), 344–45
Alaska, 880, 924
    gold rush in, 530, 586
    purchase of, 588–89
    Russian claim to, 242, 340
Albania, 766, 978
Albee, Edward, 851
Albion's Seed (Fischer), 39
Alcatraz Island, 924
alcohol consumption, *see* prohibition
    movement
Alcott, Bronson, 314

Algeciras, Act of (1906), 613
Alger, Horatio, 513, 533
Algeria, 206, 227–28, 791
Algerian pirates, 196
Algonquian Indians, 80–84
Alien and Sedition Acts (1798), 197–98
Allen, Ethan, 105, 114
Alliance for Progress, 889
Altamont concert (1969), 920–21
Altgeld, John Peter, 525
Amalgamated Association of Iron and
    Steel Workers, 523
Amalgamated Clothing Workers, 751
American and Foreign Anti-Slavery
    Society, 376
American Anti-Imperialist League, 603
American Anti-Slavery Society, 375,
    376, 377
American Bar Association, 989
American Birth Control League, 687
American Civil Liberties Union (ACLU),
    681
American Colonization Society, 373
American Crisis, The (Paine), 123
American Federation of Labor (AFL),
    661, 751
    formation of, 521–23
American Federation of Labor-Congress
    of Industrial Organizations
    (AFL-CIO), 841, 936, 955, 960
American First Committee, 771
American Historical Association, 500
American Indian Movement (AIM), 924
American Individualism (Hoover), 714
American Liberty League, 741
American Medical Association (AMA),
    901
American party, 299–300, 397, 401
American Political Ideas (Fiske), 592
American Protective Association (APA),
    540
American Psychiatric Association, 925
American Railway Union, 524–25, 526
American Revolution, 112–39
    arts and, 148–49
    Boston Tea Party and, 107–8
    causes of, assessed, 119
    civilians during, 126–27
    as civil war, 124
    fighting in, 112–13, 114–16, 119
    financing of, 125–26
    French aid in, 130, 131, 136–37, 138,
        535
    ideologists of, 139–40
    independence issue in, 118
    Indians in, 128, 132–33, 156
    loyalists and, 112, 124, 128, 132–34,
        135, 139, 140, 143, 157–58
    mercenaries (Hessians) in, 116, 121,
        123
    militiamen in, 124–25
    naval warfare in, 136
    outbreak of, 112–13
    Peace of Paris and, 138–39
    political revolution concurrent with,
        139–42

public opinion and, 123–24
religion and, 146–48
social revolution effected by, 142–48
tax policies and, 96–102, 103–4, 105,
    107–10, 142
trade and commerce in, 116, 126–27,
    131, 156–57
Whig ideology and, 133, 135, 139–40
women in, 145–46
American Society for the Promotion of
    Temperance, 325
American Steel and Wire Company, 498
American Temperance Union, 325
American Tobacco Company, 482, 624
American Unitarian Association, 307
American Woman Suffrage Association,
    555
Amherst, Jeffrey, 90
Amish, 34
Anaconda strategy, 423
anarchism, 678–79
Anderson, Robert, 413, 417, 449
Anderson, Sherwood, 685–86, 694, 695
André, John, 135
Andrews, Samuel, 509
Andros, Sir Edmond, 75, 76
Angel Island, 540–41
Anglican Church (Church of England),
    23, 55, 69, 70, 146, 148
    in colonies, 29, 39, 50–51
    founding of, 12–13
    repudiated by Puritans, 20–22, 25
Anglo-French Suez Canal Company, 877
Annapolis Convention (1786), 162
Anschluss, 765
Anthony, Susan B., 328, 329, 555, 556
anthropology, 693
antiballistic missile systems (ABMs), 935,
    963
Anti-Ballistic Missile Treaty (1972), 963
Antietam (Sharpsburg), battle of (1892),
    429–31
Antifederalists, Constitution opposed by,
    169–70, 171
Anti-Masonic party, 266, 270, 271
Anti-Saloon League, 621, 683
antislavery movements, 333, 363
    African colony proposed by, 373
    blacks in, 376–78
    Fugitive Slave Law and, 397
    in Great Britain, 346
    martyrs for, 379
    party affiliations and, 379, 401
    radicalization of, 374–75, 408–9
    split in, 375–76
    women's role in, 328, 376
antitrust laws:
    Taft's enforcement of, 630
    T. Roosevelt's enforcement of, 622–23
    Wilson's program for, 637–38
Apache Indians, 494
Appalachia, 39, 40
Appalachian Regional Development Act
    (1966), 901
Appomattox, surrender at (1865), 449
Arabic, 653

Arab League, 876
Arapaho Indians, 493–94
Arbella, 23
architecture:
  Georgian, 50
  Jefferson and, 184
  New England, 40
Ardennes Forest, battle in (1944), 801
ARENA, 966
Arena, 617
Argentina, 646
Arias, Oscar, 966
Arizona, 395, 492
Arkansas, 417, 736, 875
Arkansas Territory, 238
Armstrong, Louis, 686
Army nurse corps, 660
Army Signal Center, 863
Arnold, Benedict, 114, 128, 135
Arrowrock Dam, 498
Arthur, Chester A., 540, 563, 564–66
Articles of Confederation (1781), 152, 153
  amendment process for, 168–69
  drafting and ratification of, 141–42
  proposed revision of, 161, 162, 165
  weak central government in, 161–62
  see also Confederation of the United States
arts, Revolution-era nationalism and, 148–49
  see also architecture; literature
Asbury, Francis, 309
Ashburton, Alexander Baring, 1st baron of, 336
Ashley-Cooper, Sir Anthony, earl of Shaftesbury, 29, 30
Asian Americans, 1000–1003
Asian Indians, 1001
As I Lay Dying (Faulkner), 700
Astor, John Jacob, 303
Aswan Dam, 877
asylum reformers, 325, 326–27
Atchison, Topeka and Santa Fe railroad, 505–6
Atlanta, 1004
  siege and burning of (1864), 446–47
Atlanta Compromise, 489
Atlantic, battle of the (1943), 794–95
Atlantic Charter (1941), 774
Atlantic Constitution, 480
Atlantic Monthly, 549
atomic bombs, 807–9, 818–19, 862
Atomic Energy Commission, U.N., 819, 864
Attucks, Crispus, 104
Auburn Penitentiary, 326
Auschwitz, death camp at, 806
Austin, Stephen F., 343
Australia, 797, 870
  in World War II, 781, 782
Austria, 89, 214, 538, 724, 765, 803
Austria-Hungary, in World War I, 648, 663, 665, 666, 670, 673
Autobiography (Carnegie), 511
Autobiography (Malcolm X), 905

automobiles, 531, 713–14, 843
Aztec Indians:
  culture of, 2
  subjugation of, 9–11

Babbit (Lewis), 711
baby-boom generation, 813, 839–40, 842, 915, 997–98
Bacon, Nathaniel, 83
Bacon's Rebellion (1676), 82–84
Baer, George F., 624
Baghdad Pact, 876
Bagot, Charles, 234
Baker, James, 984, 986, 989
Bakke v. Board of Regents of California, 931
Baldwin, James, 852
Ball, Lucille, 840
Ballinger, Richard A., 629
Ballinger-Pinchot controversy (1910), 629
Baltic republics, 981
Baltimore, Md., 537
Bankhead-Jones Farm Tenant Act (1937), 753
banking holidays, 731
Bank of North America, 153
Bank of the United States (national bank), 180–81, 228, 232
  constitutionality of, 180–81, 240–42
  controversy over rechartering of (1832), 264–65
  controversy over rechartering of (1842), 335
  expiration of (1811), 219
  government deposits removed from (1833), 267–69
  in Panic of 1819, 237–38
  reinstatement of (1816), 229–30
banks, banking:
  failure of, in Great Depression, 721
  F. D. Roosevelt's reforms in, 731–32
  in Great Depression, 724
  regulation of, 434
  Wilson's reforms in, 636–37
Baptists, 34, 56, 69, 70, 147, 308–9
  in split over slavery, 380, 397
Barbados, 29, 30
Barbary pirates, 206, 227
barbed-wire, 497–98
Barnett, Ross, 889
Barton, Clara, 422, 433
Baruch, Bernard, 659, 820
Bataan Peninsula, 781
"Battle Hymn of the Republic" (Howe), 422
Bay of Pigs invasion (1961), 893, 897
Beard, Charles A., 170, 771
Beauregard, Pierre G. T., 417, 419–20
Beecher, Catherine, 327, 376
Beecher, Henry Ward, 552
Beecher, Lyman, 300, 308
Begin, Menachem, 943, 944
Beirut airport, terrorist attack at (1983), 959

Belgium, 714, 760, 801, 822
  in World War II, 770
Bell, Alexander Graham, 507
Bell, John, 411
Bellow, Saul, 734, 852
Bell Telephone Association, 507
Benedict, Ruth, 693
Bennett, James Gordon, 320
Bennett, William J., 975
Benton, Thomas Hart, 222, 259, 352
  slavery issue and, 384, 390
  western settlement promoted by, 256
Bentsen, Lloyd, 972
Berkeley, John, Lord, 32
Berkeley, William, 83
Berlin, 803, 880–81, 893
Berlin, Irving, 538
Berlin Airlift (1948–1949), 821
Berlin Decree (1806), 214, 217
Berlin Wall, 893, 977, 978
Bessemer, Sir Henry, 511–12
Beveridge, Albert J., 591, 603
Bible:
  Puritan use of, 55
  translation of, 82
Biddle, Nicholas, 238, 265–66, 267, 268
Bill for the More General Diffusion of
    Knowledge, 150
bills of rights:
  English, 76
  in state constitutions, 141, 163, 177
  in U.S. Constitution, 171, 172, 177, 975
  for western territories, 155
Birmingham, Ala., 531
Birney, James G., 379
birthrate, 813
Bismarck Sea, battle of the (1943), 797
Black, Hugo, 750
Black Boy (Wright), 698
Black Friday (1869), 473
Black Hawk War, 261–62
Black Monday (1987), 967, 968
Black Muslims, 904–5
Black Panther party, 904
Black Power, 690, 903–6
blacks:
  AIDS and, 975
  in American Revolution, 144–45
  in antebellum southern society,
    366–73
  in cabinet, 901
  in Carter administration, 941
  in Civil War, 423, 433–34
  disfranchisement of, 485–87, 641
  in Great Depression, 739
  Hoover's policies toward, 720
  immigration of, 1000–1001, 1002
  literature of, 689
  New Negro spirit among, 689–91
  northward migration of, 659–60, 689,
    788, 844
  political influence of, 689
  Reconstruction and, 456–57, 458,
    460, 464–66, 467, 478
  as single parents, 999

stereotypes and caricatures of,
    359–60, 380
suffrage for, 456, 458, 462, 464, 471,
    639, 902–3
Truman's policies toward, 824
as underclass, 976, 999–1000
violence against, 423, 460, 468, 675,
    659–60, 824, 1003–5
as voters, protection of, 469
voting patterns of, 747
  in West, 496, 579
  in World War I, 659–60, 666
  in World War II, 787–88
Blackwell, Elizabeth, 329
Blaine, James G., 476, 561, 563
  in presidential elections, 564, 566–68,
    571
Bland-Allison Act (1878), 563–64, 572,
    576
Blithedale Romance, The (Hawthorne),
    332
Blitzkrieg, 770
blockades:
  in Civil War, 417, 423
  of Cuba, 894
  in Napoleonic Wars, 214, 217, 226
Boa Dai, emperor of Vietnam, 829
Board of Customs Commissioners, 105
Board of Trade (Lords Commissioners of
    Trade and Plantations), 73, 77, 78,
    88
Bohemian-Americans, 538
Bolshevik Revolution (1917), 656, 663,
    665, 667, 676
bonds, junk, 973
Bonus Expeditionary Force, 725–26, 728
Boone, Daniel, 95, 191
Booth, John Wilkes, 454
Boston, Mass., 531, 537
  in colonial era, 62, 74, 87
  religious rationalism in, 307–8
  in Revolutionary War, 126, 127
  siege of (1775–1776), 114–16
  size and population of, 87
  tax protests in, 107–8, 110
Boston Associates, 287
Boston Gazette, 98–99
Boston Manufacturing Company, 287
Boston Massacre (1770), 103–5
Boston Police Strike (1919), 674
Boston Port Act (1774), 108, 110
Boston Tea Party (1773), 107–8
Boulder (Hoover) Dam, 498
Bourbons, 484–86
Bowie, James, 344, 345
Boxer Rebellion (1900), 605
boycotts:
  of British goods, 100, 103, 111
  of Montgomery bus system, 873–75,
    889
Brackenridge, Hugh Henry, 148
Bradford, William, 21
Bradley, Omar, 832–33
Bradley, Tom, 1004
Bragg, Braxton, 357, 442, 444

Brandeis, Louis D., 621, 634, 635, 638, 640, 743, 750
Brando, Marlon, 855
Braun, Eva, 805
Brazil, 9, 646
Breckinridge, John C., 410, 411
Brest-Litovsk, Treaty of (1918), 667
Brezhnev, Leonid, 935, 940
Brezhnev doctrine, 977
Briand, Aristide, 761
Bridger, Jim, 338
brinksmanship, 866–67
Britain, battle of, 770
British Columbia, 588–89
Brook Farm, 332–33
Brooklyn, N.Y., 122
Brooklyn Eagle, 656
Brooks, Preston S. "Bully," 400, 458
Brotherhood of Sleeping Car Porters, 787
Brown, H. Rap, 904, 917
Brown, John, 399–400
    execution of, 408
    Harper's Ferry raided by, 407–9, 410
Brownson, Orestes, 314
Brown University (College of Rhode Island), 70
Brown v. Board of Education of Topeka, Kansas, 872–73, 892
Bruce, Blanche K., 466
Brussels Pact (1948), 822
Bryan, William Jennings, 602, 619, 632, 635, 644
    in presidential elections, 583–85, 616, 625, 627–28
    in Scopes trial, 681–83
    as secretary of war, 652, 653
    U.S. neutrality and, 653
Brzezinski, Zbigniew, 945
Buchanan, James:
    in presidential elections, 401–2
    secession and, 413–14
    slavery issue and, 404
Buchanan, Patrick, 993–94
budget deficits, 954, 966, 973–74
Buena Vista, battle of (1847), 354–55, 386
Buffalo, N.Y., 538
Buffalo Evening Telegraph, 567
Bulgaria, 774, 818, 978
    in World War I, 666
Bulge, battle of the (1944), 801, 988
Bull Run, first battle of (1861), 419–20
Bull Run, second battle of (1862), 428–29
Bunau-Varilla, Philippe, 610
Bundy, McGeorge, 888
Bunker Hill, battle of (1775), 114–15
Bunting v. Oregon, 621
Bunyan, John, 617
Bureau of Corporations, 624, 634, 637, 638
Bureau of Immigration, 535
Bureau of Indian Affairs (BIA), 924
Bureau of Internal Revenue, 434, 857

Bureau of Mines, 630
Bureau of Reclamation, 498
Bureau of Refugees, Freedmen, and Abandoned Lands, 453
Burford, Anne Gorsuch, 955
Burger, Warren, 931
Burgoyne, John, 114, 127, 128–29
Burke, Edmund, 77, 110, 111
Burma, 775, 781, 867
Burns, Anthony, 397
Burnside, Ambrose E., 431, 438, 441
Burr, Aaron:
    conspiracy of, 212–13
    Hamilton's duel with, 210
    in presidential elections, 193, 199, 200
    treason charges against, 211–13
Burroughs, William, 853, 854
buses, racial segregation on, 873–75, 889
Bush, George:
    domestic policy of, 972, 973, 974–76, 989–93
    foreign policy of, 972–73, 976–89
    income tax increases by, 970–71, 973
    1990–1992 recession and, 991–93
    Panama invasion and, 982–83
    Persian Gulf War and, 983–89
    popularity of, 989
    presidency of, 972–89
    in presidential elections, 970–72, 993–97
    S&L bailout and budget reduction problems of, 973–74
    Soviet Union dissolution and, 977–82
    Supreme Court nominations of, 989, 991
    symbolism of, 972, 975
business:
    Coolidge's support of, 710
    entrepreneurship in, 508–15
    Harding's support of, 704–7
    philosophical rationale for, 511–13
    politicians' alliance with, 561
    post–World War II culture of, 844–45
    see also antitrust laws; regulation, governmental; trusts; *specific industries*
busing, 931
Butler, Andrew P., 400
Byrd, Harry F., 873
Byrd, William, 42, 50
Byrnes, James F., 818

Cable, George Washington, 488, 547
cable cars, 531
Cabot, John, 9
Cadore, Jean Baptiste Nompère de Champagny, duc de, 217
Cairo, declaration of (1943), 795
Calhoun, Floride, 254
Calhoun, John C., 219, 387, 388, 397
    economic policies of, 230
    ideological transformation of, 247–48
    Mexican War and, 383

Calhoun, John C. *(continued)*
  in nullification crisis, 255–56, 257,
    258–61
  in presidential elections, 244–45,
    247–48
  as secretary of state, 346
  as secretary of war, 234, 235, 236, 243
  slavery issue of, 380, 384, 386, 387
  Van Buren's rivalry with, 253, 254, 259
California, 242
  dust bowl migration to, 697, 736
  gold rush in, 285, 298, 387, 492
  immigrants in, 1001–1003, 1005
  population growth of, 998
  as republic, 353
  settlement of, 340–43
  slavery issue in, 387, 391
  statehood for, 387, 391
  U.S. acquisition of, 348, 353
California, University of, at Berkeley,
    916, 1003
California Institute of Technology, 1003
Calley, William, 927
Call of the Wild (London), 550
Calvert, Cecilius, 2nd Lord Baltimore,
    19–20, 45
Calvert, George, 1st Lord Baltimore, 19
Calvin, John, 12
Calvinism, 12, 13, 55, 69, 306, 308
Cambodia, 867, 869, 927, 928, 929, 941
  immigrants from, 1001, 1002
Camden, S.C., 133
Camp David Accords (1978), 943–44
Canada, 586, 589, 818, 822
  colonial wars and, 89–91, 93
  as source of Indian troubles, 188
  War of 1812 and, 217, 219, 220–22
canals:
  proliferation of (early 1800s), 282–83
  state funding of, 282
Cane (Toomer), 689
Cannibals All! or, Slaves Without Masters
    (Fitzhugh), 380
Canning, George, 243
Cannon, Joe, 624
Capone, Al, 683–84
Caribbean immigrants, 1001
Carmichael, Stokely, 904, 917
Carnegie, Andrew, 511–13, 523, 603
Carnegie Endowment for International
    Peace, 833
Carolina colony, 29–31
carpetbaggers, 466–67
Carranza, Venustiano, 645–47
Carroll, John, 148
Carson, Christopher "Kit," 342, 353
Carter, Jimmy, 971, 972, 994
  domestic policies of, 941–42, 944
  economic policies of, 944, 953
  foreign policy of, 942–46
  hostage crisis and, 945–46
  Middle East policy of, 942, 943–44
  in presidential elections, 941, 949, 952
Carteret, Sir George, 32
Cartier, Jacques, 14
Cartwright, Peter, 309

Casablanca, conference at (1943), 791
Casey, William, 964
Cass, Lewis, 385
Cassady, Neal, 854
Castle Garden, 293, 535
Castro, Fidel, 881–82, 893, 897
Catcher in the Rye (Salinger), 852
Catholic church, 148, 340, 341, 592
  immigrant ties with, 295, 296, 297
  nativist attacks on, 299–300
  Reformation challenges to, 12–13
  social doctrine of, 553
  Spanish conquests and, 11
Catholics:
  as English sovereigns, 75–76
  Maryland as refuge for, 19
Cato's Letters (Trenchard and Gordon),
    97
Catt, Carrie Chapman, 556, 653, 687–88
cattle industry, 499
  barbed-wire introduced into, 497–98
  open-range phase of, 496–97
Caulfield, Holden, 852
Cayuga Indians, 133
Ceausescu, Nicolae, 978
"Celebrated Jumping Frog of Calaveras
    County, The" (Twain), 547
Celtic immigrants, 39, 535
census of 1990, 997–1003
Central Federated Union of New York,
    661
Central Intelligence Agency (CIA), 816,
    836, 866, 897
  in Chile, 940
  in Cuba invasion, 882, 893
  in Nicaragua, 957
  in Panama, 982
Central Pacific railroad, 504, 506, 505
Century of Dishonor, A (Jackson), 496
Ceylon (Sri Lanka), 867
Challenger, 963
Chamberlain, Joshua, 449
Chambers, Whittaker, 834
Champlain, Samuel de, 14, 84
Chancellorsville, battle of (1863),
    438–40, 444
Chandler, Zachariah, 436
Channing, William Ellery, 307
Chaplin, Charlie, 712
Charles I, king of England, colonization
    and, 23
Charles II, king of England, 29, 86
  colonial administration under, 72, 73,
    74
  colonization advanced by, 31, 32, 33
Charleston, S.C., 62, 126, 133
  founding of, 30
Chase, Salmon P., 463
Chattanooga, battle of (1863), 442–44
Chauncey, Charles, 69
Chavez, Cesar, 923
Cheever, John, 734, 852
chemical waste sites, 942
Cherokee Indians, 156, 191, 218, 262–64
Cherokee Nation v. Georgia, 263–64
Chesapeake, 215, 226

Chesnut, Mary Boykin, 364–65, 373
Cheves, Langdon, 237–38
Cheyenne Indians, 493, 494
Chiang Kai-shek, 763, 795, 804, 828
Chicago, Ill., 292, 538, 539, 659, 675,
  686, 903, 918–19
  Haymarket Affair in (1886), 520–21
Chicago Defender, 659
Chickamauga, battle of (1863), 442, 443
Chickasaw Indians, 158, 191, 218
child labor, 738, 754
  Progressive campaign against, 621, 641
Children's Bureau, 630
Chile, 646, 978
China, Imperial:
  Boxer Rebellion in, 605
  demise of, 762
  dollar diplomacy with, 647–48
  Japanese influence in, 611–12
  Open Door policy and, 604–6, 611, 612
  U.S. trade with, 394
China, Nationalist:
  Japanese intervention in, 762–63, 765,
    768
  Open Door policy and, 760
  Soviet intervention in, 761
  in World War I, 759
  in World War II, 773, 775, 777, 795,
    797, 804, 828
  see also Taiwan
China, People's Republic of, 894
  creation of, 828–29
  democracy movement in, 977
  Egypt's recognition of, 877
  Korean War and, 831–33, 862
  rapprochement with, 934–35
  Vietnam and, 867, 869
Chinese-Americans, 298, 504–5, 540–41,
  612, 1001, 1002
Chinese Eastern Railway, 761
Chinese Exclusion Act, 540–41
Chiricahua Apache Indians, 494
Chivington, J. M., 493
Choctaw Indians, 158, 191, 218
Christian Century, 843
"Christmas bombings," 929
Churchill, Winston, 770, 783, 802, 818,
  820, 866, 880
  World War II strategies and, 774,
    790–91, 795
Church of Jesus Christ of Latter Day
  Saints (Mormons), 311–13, 492
Cincinnati, Ohio, 292, 538
Cincinnati Enquirer, 413
cities:
  colonial, 61–63
  government and policies in, 532–33
  growth of (late 1800s), 530–32
  immigrants in, 533, 538–39
  industrialization as impetus to, 292
  reform efforts in, 554–55
  in Revolutionary War, 126, 127
  tenements in, 532
  transportation in, 531
  in World War I, 659–60
city-manager plan, 619

"Civil Disobedience" (Thoreau), 316
Civilian Conservation Corps (CCC),
  733–34, 790
Civil Rights Act (1886), 459–60
Civil Rights Act (1957), 875
Civil Rights Act (1964), 902–3
Civil Rights Commission, 875
civil rights movements, 824–26, 871–75,
  889–92, 956
  Black Power and, 903–6
  boycotts in, 873–75
  L. B. Johnson and, 898, 899
  legislative victories of, 903, 931
  nonviolence and, 874
  in World War II, 787–88
civil service, 565
  reform in, 941–42
Civil Service Commission, U.S., 565, 925
Civil War, English, *see* English Civil War
Civil War, Spanish (1936–1939), 767–68
Civil War, U.S., 416–49
  black soldiers in, 433–34
  blockade in, 417, 423
  border states in, 417–19
  casualties in, 420, 429
  civil liberties suspended in, 417,
    436–38
  Confederate command structure in,
    428
  conscription in, 422–23
  Eastern Theater of, 424, 426–32,
    438–42
  financing of, 435
  as first "modern" war, 420–23
  government and politics in, 434–38
  military advantages in, 416
  military governors in, 451–52
  naval warfare in, 423–24
  outbreak of hostilities in, 416–17,
    419–20
  presidential transition and
    (1860–1861), 413–14, 416–17
  quick victory attempted in, 419–20
  romantic view of, 416, 420
  as social revolution, 434
  surrender in, 448–49
  Union command structure in, 426,
    428, 431, 438, 444
  veterans of, 569
  as war on slavery, 432–34
  Western Theater of, 424–26, 432,
    440–41, 442–44
  see also Reconstruction; secession of
    South
Civil Works Administration (CWA), 733
Clark, George Rogers, 132, 208
Clark, William, 208
Clark Memorandum (1928), 762
Clay, Henry, 219, 253–54, 290, 352,
  373, 387, 388–90, 405
  economic policies of, 230, 247, 254,
    260, 265, 335, 347
  party affiliations of, 270
  in presidential elections, 244, 245,
    246, 248, 267, 335
  slavery policies of, 239

Clayton, Henry D., 638
Clayton Antitrust Act (1914), 638–39
Clean Air Act (1970), 932
Cleaver, Eldridge, 904
Clemenceau, Georges, 663, 668, 669, 670
Clemens, Samuel Langhorne (Mark Twain), 547–48, 559
Clermont, 281
Cleveland, Grover, 540, 583, 584
    foreign policy of, 590–91
    in presidential elections, 567–68, 570–71, 582
    Pullman Strike and, 525
Cleveland, Ohio, 538, 903
Clifford, Clark, 908
Clinton, Bill, 994–97
Clinton, De Witt, 282
Clinton, George, 171
Clinton, Sir Henry, 114, 115, 131, 133
clipper ships, 285
clothing, in twenties, 686
coal industry, 482, 516
coal strike (1902), 623–24
Cobb, Lee J., 851
Cobbett, William, 324
cocaine, 975
Coercive Acts (Intolerable Acts) (1774), 109, 110
Cold Harbor, battle of (1864), 445
Cold War, 816–23, 828–36, 839, 969
    Berlin and, 821–22, 893
    brinksmanship in, 866–67
    containment policy in, 865–66
    Cuban missile crisis and, 893–95
    détente and, 934–35
    end of, 976–82
    Indochina and, 867–71
    Red Scares in, 815, 833–35, 862–64
    U-2 incident and, 881
Coleridge, Samuel Taylor, 314
College of William and Mary, 70
colleges and universities:
    coeducational, 311, 323
    denominational, 322
    federal aid to, 434
    graduate studies at, 542–43
    moral revolution at (1920s), 685
    professors at, 542
    racial segregation and, 311, 889, 891
    state-run, 150, 322
    student activism at, 915–20, 927–28
    for women, 323, 542
Colombia, 610, 975
colonial governments:
    assemblies' powers in, 79–80
    courts in, 78, 105
    English administration and, 72–77, 78
    English models for, 79
    governors' powers in, 78–79
    reorganized as provincial congresses, 112, 140–41
    representative assemblies established in, 24–25
colonial period:
    agriculture in, 41, 44–46, 84

border disputes in, 105
boycott of British goods in, 100, 103, 111
British folkways in, 39–40
cities in, 61–63
colonial unity in, 109
education in, 65, 70
Enlightenment in, 64–65
Great Awakening in, 66–70
land policies in, 45, 51
marriage in, 44, 54
population growth in, 41–42
postal service in, 62
religion in, 50–51, 54–55, 66–70; see also Puritans; Quakers
rural areas in, 105–6
slavery in, 19, 39, 46–49
social hierarchy in, 43–44, 56, 61, 83
soldiers in, 93–94
taxation in, 76, 96–102, 103–4, 105, 107–10
trade and commerce in, 14, 16, 30–31, 35, 41, 52–54, 72–74
women's status in, 27, 44
colonial wars, 86–91
    see also French and Indian War
colonization, Dutch, 27, 28, 31–32
colonization, English, 16–36
    administration of, 35–36
    arguments for, 16
    concentrated settlements in, 36
    English Civil War and, 28–29, 33
    of Middle Colonies, 19–20
    of New England, 20–28
    Restoration and, 29
    of South, 15–19
colonization, French, 14, 35, 36, 84–88
    see also Spanish Empire
Colorado, 492
Colored Farmers Alliance, 579
Columbia, S.C., burning of (1865), 448
Columbia University (King's College), 70, 860, 918
Columbus, Christopher, 4–6
Comanche Indians, 493–94
Command of the Army Act (1867), 461, 463
Commerce and Labor, U.S. Department of, 624
Commission on Civil Disorders, 904–5
commission system, 619
Committee for Industrial Organization (CIO), 751
Committee of European Economic Cooperation (CEEC), 821
Committee on Civil Rights, 824
Committee on Public Information, 661
Committee on Un-American Activities, House, 755, 833, 834
committees of correspondence, 107
Committee to Defend America by Aiding the Allies, 771
Committee to Re-elect the President (CREEP), 936
Commodity Credit Corporation (CCC), 735

common ground, culture and, 1005
Common Law, The (Holmes), 546
Common Sense (Paine), 116–17
Common Sense Book of Baby and Child Care, The (Spock), 850
Commonwealth and Protectorate, 72
Commonwealth of Independent States, 981
Commonwealth v. Hunt, 301
Communist party, disintegration of, 981
Communists, American, 726
  during Great Depression, 696–97, 730
  Red Scares and, 676–77, 717, 815, 833–35, 862–64
  Wallace supported by, 827
Community Action Program, 899
Compromise of 1850, 387–94
Compromise of 1877, 477, 478
Comstock Lode, 492
Conciliatory Resolution (1775), 111
Concord, battle of (1775), 113
condoms, safe sex and, 975
Conestoga Indians, 105
Confederate States of America (Confederacy):
  defeat of, 444–49
  finances of, 435
  foreign recognition sought by, 423, 429, 433, 435–36
  formation of, 412
  political discontent in, 437–38
  see also Civil War, U.S.
Confederation Congress, 153
  close of business of, 172–73
  drafting of Constitution and, 162
  land policies of, 154–55
  Peace of Paris negotiated by, 152
  powers of, 152–53
Confederation of the United States:
  diplomacy of, 157–59
  land policies of, 153–56
  trade and commerce in, 156–57, 159, 161
Congregational church, 66, 69, 70, 147, 307–8
Congress, U.S.:
  election mechanisms for, 164, 166–67
  first meeting of (1789), 175–77
  powers of, 168
  war powers of, 831
  see also Confederation Congress; House of Representatives, U.S.; Senate, U.S.
Congress of Industrial Organizations (CIO), 751–52, 814, 815
Congress of Racial Equality (CORE), 890
Congress of Verona (1822), 243
Conkling, Roscoe, 563, 564–65, 567
Connecticut, 140–41, 146, 147, 249
  in adoption of Constitution, 165, 172
Connecticut Anti-Slavery Society, 376
Connecticut colony:
  charter of, 28, 29, 78, 141
  first settlements in, 27–28
  government of, 28, 75, 78
  Indians in, 81

"Connecticut Compromise" (1787), 165
Connor, Eugene "Bull," 891
conquistadores, 9–11
conscription, *see* draft
conservation movement, *see* environmental movement
"Conservative" (Democratic) parties, 469–70
Constellation, 196
Constitution, 196
Constitution, U.S., 162–73
  amendment process of, 168–69
  broad vs. strict construction of, 180–81, 207–8, 213, 216, 228
  internal improvements and, 232
  judical review principle and, 168, 241
  ratification of, 169–73
  separation of powers in, 166–69
  slavery issues and, 165–66, 206, 239–40, 414
  state compact theory and, 198, 257
  see also Articles of Confederation
constitutional amendments, U.S.:
  Bill of Rights, 171, 172, 177, 975
  proposed Equal Rights Amendment, 688, 922, 956
  proposed slavery-protecting amendment, 414
  1st, 975
  10th, 168
  13th, 434, 456, 478
  14th, 460, 462, 478, 488, 691
  15th, 464, 478, 486–87, 691
  16th, 630, 636
  17th, 630
  18th (prohibition), 169, 621, 683, 702, 729
  19th (women's suffrage), 639, 687–88, 702
  20th, 731
  21st (repeal of prohibition), 169, 732
  22nd, 816, 858
  25th, 939
  26th, 932
Constitutional Convention (1787), 162–69, 178
  call for, 162
  delegates to, 162–63
  political philosophy of, 163–64
  representation issue in, 164–65
  slavery issue in, 165–66
constitutions of states, 140–41, 162, 166, 177, 403–4
consumer culture, 840–42
consumer movement, 919
consumption ethic, 711
containment policy, 819–20, 865–66, 878, 907–8
Continental Congress:
  currency issued by, 114
  first (1774), 110–11
  independence proclaimed by, 117–19
  peace initiatives and, 131
  Revolutionary fighting directed by, 125–26, 131, 134

Continental Congress (continued)
    as revolutionary government, 114,
        115, 141–42
Continental System, 214
Contract Labor Law (1864), 519, 534
Contra rebels, 957–58, 964–66
Convention of 1800, 197
Convention of 1818, 234–35
convicts:
    leasing of, 485
    sent to America, 38–39, 46
Cooke, Jay, 435, 475
Coolidge, Calvin, 689, 715, 718, 720,
        953, 954, 955, 972, 976
    in Boston Police Strike, 674–75
    business and, 707, 710–11
    farm policy of, 715, 716–17
    foreign policy of, 761
    as vice president, 703, 708–9
coolies, 298, 504–5
Cooper, James Fenimore, 316
cooperatives, 577, 579, 716
Copernicus, Nicolaus, 63
Copley, John Singleton, 149
copper, 492
Copperheads, 436
Coral Sea, 797
    battle of the (1942), 782
corn, 715
Cornell, Alonzo, 563
Cornell University, 918
Cornwallis, Charles, Lord, 128, 133,
        135–37, 149
Corregidor, 781
corruption, 562–71
Corso, Gregory, 854
Cortés, Hernando, 9–10
Cosmopolitan, 713
Costa Rica, 966
cotton, 574–75, 715
Cotton, John, 55
cotton exports, 237
cotton gin, 278–79
cotton prices, panics and, 272
cotton production, 269–70
    antebellum, growth in, 278–79, 361,
        363
    in postbellum economy, 482, 483, 484
Coughlin, Charles E., 743, 748
Council of National Defense, 658
counterculture, in sixties, 920–21
country music, 737
Country of the Pointed Firs, The (Jewett),
        547
cowboys, 496–98
Cox, Archibald, 938
Cox, James, 704
Coxey, Jacob S., 582
crack cocaine, 975
Crack in the Picture Window, The (Keats),
        849
Crandall, Prudence, 378
Crane, Stephen, 549–50
Crawford, William H., 234
    in presidential elections, 244–46
credit card, 841

Crédit Mobilier Company, 473, 506
Creek Indians, 156, 158, 191, 196, 218,
        222, 235
Creel, George, 661
Creole, 335
crime, 62
    organized, 683–84
Crittenden, John J., 414
Crocker, Charles, 504, 505
Crockett, Davy, 344, 345
Croly, Herbert, 634
Cromwell, Oliver, 29
    colonial administration under, 72
Cronkite, Walter, 910
crop lien system, 484
Cruikshank, Robert, 253
Cuba, 91, 960, 966, 984
    Castro's rise to power in, 881–82
    CIA and, 882, 893
    immigrants from, 1001, 1002
    missile crisis and, 893–95
    Ostend Manifesto and, 394
    see also Spanish-American War
Cuban Revolutionary party, 593
Cudahy, Michael, 295
Cudahy Packing Company, 295
Cullen, Countee, 689
culture:
    American, emergence of, 148–49
    broader definition of, 693
    in 1990s, 997–1005
Cumberland Gap, 95
Cumberland (National) Road, 232, 233,
        254, 281
Cumberland Road Bill (1882), 233
Cuomo, Mario, 994, 1001
currency:
    in colonial period, 53–54, 106, 114
    under Confederacy, 435
    under Confederation, 159
    devaluation of (1933–1934), 732
    European, 724
    greenbacks, 475, 577
    as issue in 1896 elections, 573
    national banknotes as, 180
    shortage of, 230
    Wilson's reforms of, 636–37
    see also gold; gold standard; silver
        coinage
Currency Act (1764), 96–97, 105
Custer, George A., 494
Customs Commissioners, 102
Czechoslovakia, 670, 821, 957, 978
    German occupation of, 765
Czolgosz, Leon, 607

Daley, Richard, 887, 919, 936
Dangling Man (Bellows), 852
Daniels, Josephus, 653
Darrow, Clarence, 682
Dartmouth College v. Woodward, 240
Dartmouth University, 70
Darwin, Charles, 512, 544, 681, 693
Daugherty, Harry M., 705, 707
Davenport, James, 69
Davenport, John, 28

Davis, Henry Winter, 452
Davis, Jefferson, 262, 354, 416, 417, 419, 444
  capture of, 448
  Civil War strategy of, 423
  political dissent and, 437–38
  as president of Confederacy, 412
  as U.S. secretary of war, 395
Davis, John W., 710, 741
Dawes, William, 112
Dawes Severalty Act (1887), 496
D-Day, 795–96
Dean, James, 855
Dean, John, 937–38
Dearborn, Henry, 220–21
death camps, 806
Death of a Salesman (Miller), 850–51
Debs, Eugene V., 524–25, 527, 628, 635, 662, 708
debt, national, 973
  after Civil War, 472–73
  Hamiltonian program and, 179–80
debts, Latin American, as excuse for intervention, 611
Decatur, Stephen, 206, 227–28
Declaration of American Rights (1774), 110–11
Declaration of Independence (1776), 118, 144, 306, 328
Declaration of Sentiments (1848), 328
Declaration of the Causes and Necessity of Taking Up Arms (1775), 115, 116
Declaration of the Rights and Grievances of the Colonies (1765), 100
Declaratory Act (1766), 101
Deere, John, 279
Deism, 306–7
DeKlerk, Frederik W., 979
de Kooning, William, 852
Delaware, 39, 143, 147
  adoption of Constitution and, 172
  Civil War and, 417
  slavery in, 434
Delaware colony, 29, 34
Delaware River, crossing of (1776), 123
DeLeon, Daniel, 526
de Lôme, Depuy, 594
democracy, Puritanism and, 55
Democratic party, 275, 918
  Bourbons and, 484, 485–86
  conservatives in, 469–70
  cultural analysis of, 561–62
  farmers' influence in, 579, 581
  Great Depression-era division of, 754–55
  labor's influence in, 302
  in 1980s, 971
  origins of, 267
  during Republican dominance (1869–1913), 560
  Southern resurgence of, 469–70
  split over slavery, 348, 397, 404, 405, 407, 409–10
  War vs. Peace wings of, 436
  see also elections and campaigns

Democratic Tariff of 1857, 405
Denmark, 657, 770, 822
Denver, Colo., 531
departments, U.S. governmental, origin of, 153, 177
Dependent Pension Act (1890), 572
Dependent Pension bill (1887), 569
Depression, Great, 728, 729–30
  bank failures in, 731–32
  Hoover's efforts against, 722–25
  literary trends in, 696–700
  renewed economic slump in, 752–53
  unemployment in, 721
  World War II as end of, 783
  see also New Deal
depressions:
  of 1890, 582
  after Revolution, 157, 159
Desert Shield, Operation, 984–86
Desert Storm, Operation, 986–88, 989
détente, 935
Detroit, Mich., 903–4, 1002
Dewey, George, 597–98, 602
Dewey, John, 546–47
Dewey, Thomas E., 801, 825–27
Dial, 314, 329
Diaz, Porfirio, 644–45
Dickens, Charles, 454
Dickinson, Emily, 317
Dickinson, John, 102, 115, 141, 162
Diem, Ngo Dinh, 871, 895–96
Dien Bien Phu, battle of (1954), 869
Dies, Martin, 755
Dingley Tariff (1897), 586
disarmament, after World War I, 759–61
disease:
  European, Indians susceptible to, 8–9, 11
  of immigrants, 293
  Spanish flu, 673–74
  susceptibility to, in Europe vs. colonies, 43
Distribution Act (1836), 269
District of Columbia, 998
Division of Forestry, 627
divorce, 145, 146, 999
Dix, Dorothea Lynde, 326–27
Dixiecrats, 826, 827
Doeg Indians, 83–84
dollar diplomacy, 647–48
Dominican Republic, 611, 761
  immigrants from, 1001
  U.S. intervention in (1916–1924), 648
Donnelly, Ignatius, 581
Douglas, Stephen A.:
  Compromise of 1850 and, 390
  death of, 436
  in Kansas-Nebraska crisis, 395–97
  popular sovereignty espoused by, 385
  in presidential elections, 401, 409, 411
  in senatorial elections (1858), 404
Douglass, Frederick, 378, 453
draft:
  in Civil War, 422–23
  in Vietnam War, 926, 941
  in World War I, 657–58

draft-card burning, 917
Drake, Sir Francis, 15
Dred Scott v. Sanford, 402–3
Dreiser, Theodore, 533, 550
drug abuse, 975–76
drugs, 920, 966, 982–83
Duane, William J., 267
Duarte, José Napoleón, 957, 966
Dubinksy, David, 751
Du Bois, W. E. B., 490, 690
Dukakis, Michael, 970–72, 997
Duke, David, 1003
Duke, James Buchanan "Buck," 482
Duke, Washington, 481–82
Dulles, Allen, 866
Dulles, John Foster, 862, 865–67,
    876–77, 878, 907
Durham, N.C., 531
Durkin, Martin, 860
Dust Bowl, 697, 735
    migrants of, 735–36
Dutch East India Company, 31
Dutch Reformed Church, 59, 70
Duvalier, Jean-Claude "Baby Doc," 963
Dylan, Bob, 855, 919
dynamic conservatism, 861
Dynamic Sociology (Ward), 545

Earhart, Amelia, 713
Eastern European countries, 978,
    979–80
East India Company, 107–8
East Indies, Dutch, 775, 777
Eastland, James, 873
East Village, New York, 920
Eaton, John H., 254
Eaton, Peggy, 254
*Economic Interpretation of the
    Constitution, An* (Beard), 170
Economic Opportunity Bill (1964), 899
Economic Recovery Tax Act (1981),
    953–54
economics, in social criticism, 550–51
economy:
    Bush and, 991–93
    Hamiltonian program for, 178–82,
        198–99, 205, 230
    nationalism and, 229–32
    in 1920s, 714–15, 720–21
    in 1970s, 932–33, 944
    in 1980s, 999
    post-Civil War, 503–28
    post-World War II growth in, 838–39
    Reagan and, 953–54, 966–68
    transportation improvements and,
        280–86
    World War I demobilization and,
        674–75
    World War II management of, 783–85
    see also agriculture; Bank of the United
        States; banks, banking; business;
        debt, national; Depression, Great;
        depressions; manufacturing;
        recessions; trade and commerce;
        specific acts and panics
Edison, Thomas Alva, 507–8

Edison Electric Illuminating Company,
    507
education:
    in colonial period, 65, 70
    federal aid to, 901
    in late 1800s, 541–43
    professionalism and, 543
    progressive, 546–47
    public, 149–50, 154, 303, 321–22,
        467, 541–42, 976
    Revolution-era nationalism and,
        149–50
    segregation in, 378, 872–73, 875,
        889, 890, 891, 931
    in South, 485
    of women, 542, 922–23, 976, 999
    see also colleges and universities
Education, U.S. Department of, 942
Edwards, Jonathan, 66–67, 68, 150, 211
efficiency, 618–19
Egypt, 773, 791, 876, 880, 935,
    940–41, 943–44, 984
    in Suez crisis, 878, 880
Ehrlichman, John, 930, 937
Einstein, Albert, 692, 693, 807
Eisenhower, Dwight D., 726, 824, 833,
    835, 855
    background of, 859–60
    cabinet of, 860–61
    civil rights movement and, 871–72,
        882
    corruption under, 879–80
    domestic policy of, 861–62, 882
    farewell address of, 883
    foreign policy of, 865–66, 876–79,
        880–82
    Korean War and, 862
    Middle East policy of, 876–78, 880
    on military-industrial complex, 883
    in presidential elections, 857–59,
        875–76
    religion promoted by, 847
    security program of, 864–65
    Soviet relations and, 880–81
    Vietnam and, 868–71, 895, 907
    in World War II, 791, 795, 801, 803
Eisenhower Doctrine, 880
Elbe River, 805
elections and campaigns:
    congressional, mechanisms for, 164,
        166–67
    conventions introduced into, 266–67
    decided in House of Representatives,
        200, 245, 477
    funding of, 939
    nomination process in, 244–45,
        266–67
    popular vs. electoral vote in, 348, 393,
        477, 571
    running mates introduced into, 245
    senatorial popular vote instituted in,
        618
    of 1789, 175
    of 1792, 185
    of 1796, 193–94
    of 1800, 198–200

...ctrification, 739–40
...hant Butte Dam, 498
...s, 531
...n, 82
...S., 694
...beth I, queen of England, 12–13,
     15, 16
Elkins Act (1903), 624
Ellis, Samuel, 535
Ellis Island, 535–38, 540
Ellison, Ralph, 734, 852
Ellison, William, 367
Ellsberg, Daniel, 928
El Salvador, 957, 966
Emancipation Proclamation, 432–34
  black military service and, 433–34
embargo, against Japan, 776, 777
Embargo Act (1807), 216
Emergency Banking Relief Act (1933),
     731
Emergency Immigration Act (1921), 679
Emerson, Ralph Waldo, 323, 357, 383
  reform movements and, 330, 332, 392,
     408
  in Transcendental Movement, 314–16
Employment Service, U.S., 661
Energy, U.S. Department of, 942
energy bill (1978), 942
energy crisis, 933
Enforcement Acts (1870–1871), 469
England, *see* Great Britain
English-Americans, 39–40, 298, 538
English Civil War (1642–1646), 72
  colonization and, 28–29, 33
Enlightenment, 63–65, 140, 313
  America receptive to, 64–65
Enola Gay, 808
Enterprise, 782
environment, 41, 491, 932
environmental movement, 919–20, 942,
     955
  T. Roosevelt's concern for, 626–27
Environmental Protection Agency (EPA),
     932, 955
Episcopal church, 148
  see also Anglican church
Equal Employment Opportunity
     Commission (EEOC), 956, 989,
     990
Equal Rights Amendment (ERA), 688,
     922, 923, 950, 951, 956
Equal Rights ("Locofocos") party, 302
Erie Canal, 269
Erie Railroad, 506, 514
Ervin, Samuel J., Jr., 937, 938
Espionage Act (1917), 662
Essay on Human Understanding (Locke),
     64
Essex, 214
Estonia, 981
Ethiopia, 765, 767
European immigrants, 1001
European Recovery Program, 821
Evans, Oliver, 287
Evers, Medgar, 891
evolution, bans on teaching of, 681–83

    ...–63
    ...64
  ..., 566–68
  ...88, 570–71
  ...1890, 573
of 1892, 581–82
of 1894, 582
of 1896, 583–86
of 1898, 606
of 1900, 606–7, 616
of 1904, 625
of 1908, 627–28
of 1912, 630–31, 632–35, 642
of 1914, 640
of 1916, 654–55
of 1918, 667–68
of 1920, 703–4
of 1924, 710
of 1928, 718–19
of 1930, 724
of 1932, 728–31
of 1934, 741
of 1936, 746–49
of 1938, 755
of 1940, 772–73
of 1942, 789
of 1944, 800–801
of 1946, 814–15
of 1948, 824, 825–27
of 1952, 857–59
of 1956, 875–76
of 1958, 879
of 1960, 885–87
of 1964, 899–900, 949
of 1968, 911–13, 918–19
of 1972, 928, 936–37
of 1976, 941
of 1980, 949–52
of 1982, 954–55
of 1984, 960–61, 971
of 1986, 963
of 1988, 970–72
of 1992, 993–97
see also suffrage; women's suffrage
     movement
electricity, 507

...on, 712
...13), 636–37, 639
...93
...06, 724
...7, 732
...37–39,
...734
...)
...991

executive branch, *see* president, presidency
executive privilege, 213, 939
Exodusters, 578
Explorer I, 879
Export Control Act (1940), 775

factories, 289–92
Fair Deal, 823–25, 827
Fair Employment Practices Committee (FEPC), 812
Fair Labor Standards Act (1938), 753–54
Fall, Albert B., 705, 707
Fallen Timbers, battle of (1794), 188
Fall River system, 291–92
Falwell, Jerry, 950
family system, 291–92
family unit, traditional, 999
Farewell to Arms, A (Hemingway), 696
Farm Bloc, 716
Farm Credit Administration (FCA), 732
farmers:
  currency issues and, 159, 160, 572, 575, 577
  economic hardships of (1870–1898), 574–75
  in Granger movement, 576–77
  in Great Depression, 725
  loans for, 640–41
  problems of, 573–76
  Progressive movement and, 616, 639
  standard of living of, 288
  see also agriculture; planters
Farmers' Alliance, 577–78, 735
Farm Security Administration (FSA), 753
Farm Tenant Act (1937), 753, 754
Farouk, king of Egypt, 876
Farragut, David, 424
Faubus, Orval, 875
Faulkner, William, 699–700, 738
Federal Art Project, 734
Federal Bureau of Investigation (FBI), 846, 897, 904
Federal Bureau of Labor Statistics, 521
Federal Communications Commission, 712
federal deficit, 940, 992
Federal Deposit Insurance Corporation (FDIC), 732, 973
Federal Election Campaign Act (1972), 932
Federal Emergency Relief Administration (FERA), 733–34
Federal Farm Loan Act (1916), 640
Federal Highway Act (1956), 861–62
Federal Home Loan Bank Act (1932), 724
Federal Housing Administration, 843
Federalist, The, 170–71, 178
Federalist party, 186, 191
  decline of, 210, 226, 234
  origins of, 183
  Republican, 228
  see also elections and campaigns
Federalists, Constitution advocated by, 169–70, 171, 172, 177, 178

Federal Radio Commis[...]
Federal Reserve Act (19[...]
Federal Reserve Board, [...]
Federal Reserve System, [...]
Federal Securities Act (19[...]
Federal Theatre Project, 73[...]
Federal Trade Commission, [...] 706, 732
Federal Writers' Project, 698,[...]
Feminine Mystique, The (Frieda[...] 921–22
feminism, 921–23, 950–51, 956,[...]
Ferdinand II, king of Aragon, 4, 6
Ferdinand VII, king of Spain, 243
Ferguson, Mariam "Ma," 681
Ferguson, Patrick, 133–34
Ferraro, Geraldine, 960–61
fifties, *see* postwar era
Fillmore, Millard, 394
  background of, 390
  in presidential elections, 393, 401
  slavery issue and, 390–92
Finland, 818
Finney, Charles Grandison, 310–11, 331
fires, in colonial cities, 62
fireside chats, 731, 741, 773
Fischer, David Hackett, 39
Fish, Hamilton, 472
fisheries, in New England, 51–52
fishing rights, 235
Fisk, Jim, 473
Fiske, John, 592
Fitzgerald, F. Scott, 678, 685, 686, 695, 696
Fitzgerald, Zelda, 695
Fitzhugh, George, 380
Five-Power Naval Treaty (1921), 760, 765
Fletcher v. Peck, 240
Florida, 982
  British acquisition of (1763), 91
  immigrants in, 1001–1003
  population growth of, 998
  real-estate boom in, 720
  returned to Spain (1783), 138
  Spanish colonization of, 35
  statehood for, 237
  U.S. acquisition of, 235–37, 259
Florida, Spanish, 35, 138, 156, 190, 208, 211, 217, 219, 224–25, 235–37
Flying Cloud, 285
Flynn, Elizabeth Gurley, 528
Foch, Ferdinand, 670
folk art, 700–701
Food Administration, 658, 714
Foraker Act (1900), 604
Foran Act (1885), 521
Force Bill (1833), 260–61
Ford, Gerald R., 905–6, 951
  foreign affairs and, 940
  Nixon pardoned by, 939, 940
  in presidential elections, 941
  veto record of, 940
Ford, Henry, 714
Ford Motor Company, 713

Fordney-McCumber Tariff (1922), 706
Foreign Affairs, 819
Forest Reserve Act (1891), 627
Formosa, *see* Taiwan
Fort Detroit, 132
Fort Donelson, 424
Fort Henry, 424
Fort Jackson, Treaty of (1814), 222
Fort McHenry, 223–24
Fort Moultrie, 413–14
Fort Niagara, 132, 133
Fort Riley, 673
Fort Sumter, 413
    fall of (1861), 417
Fort Ticonderoga, 114
Fortune, 700, 838
Four Freedoms, 773
Four-Power Treaty (1921), 760
Fourteen Points, 665–66, 774
Fox, George, 33
France, 80, 95, 127, 211, 342–43,
    760–61, 820, 821, 829, 870, 958,
    959
    breakdown of U.S. relations with
        (1797–1801), 194–97
    Citizen Genêt and, 186
    colonies' alliance with (1778), 130
    colonization by, 14, 35, 36, 84–88, 93
    Imperial China and, 604–5
    in Indochina, 867–69
    Louisiana purchased from, 206–8
    in Moroccan crisis (1905–1906), 613
    in NATO, 822
    in Persian Gulf War, 987
    in Revolutionary War, 130, 132,
        136–37, 138, 535
    in Suez War, 878
    Texas and, 346
    in U.S. Civil War, 423, 433, 435
    Vichy government in, 775, 791
    in World War I, 648, 657, 663–64,
        668, 669, 670
    World War I debt of, 759
    in World War II, 765, 769, 770, 775,
        791, 794, 795–96, 803
    XYZ Affair and, 195–96
    see also Napoleonic Wars
Franciscans, missionary work of, 340,
    341
Franco, Francisco, 765
Frankfurter, Felix, 538, 743
Franklin, battle of (1864), 447
Franklin, Benjamin, 68, 106, 108, 117,
    136, 184, 307
    adoption of Constitution and, 162, 173
    as emissary to France, 91, 138
    Enlightenment epitomized by, 64–65
    Plan of Union of, 88
    as postmaster, 116
Franz Ferdinand, archduke of Austria,
    648
Frederick II (the Great), king of Prussia,
    89
Fredericksburg, battle of (1862), 431–32
Freedmen's Bureau Bill (1866), 460
Freedom of Information Act (1966), 939

Freeman, Elizabeth, 144
Freeport Doctrine, 406
Free Soil party, 386
Free Speech Movement (FSM), 916–17
Frémont, John Charles, 342, 353
    in presidential elections, 401
French and Indian War (Seven Years'
    War) (1754–1763), 86, 87–91,
    207
    legacy of, 93–95
French Revolution, 185–86, 293
Freneau, Philip, 148
Freud, Sigmund, 685–86
Frick, Henry Clay, 523, 625
Friedan, Betty, 921–22, 991
From Here to Eternity (Jones), 852
frontier:
    closing of, 500–501
    migration to, 337–43
    religious revivals on, 308–13
    see also Manifest Destiny; West, New;
        specific territories
Frost, Robert, 888
Fuel Administration, 658–59
Fugitive Slave Act (1850), 392
    protests against, 397
Fulbright, J. William, 908
Fuller, Margaret, 314, 329–30, 332
Fulton, Robert, 241, 281
Fundamental Constitutions of Carolina,
    30
fundamentalism, 681–83, 950
Fundamental Orders of Connecticut, 28
fur trade, 31, 41, 82, 340
    French colonists in, 84

Gadsden, Christopher, 148
Gadsden Purchase (1853), 356, 395
Gage, Thomas, 109, 112, 114, 116
Galbraith, John K., 849
Gallatin, Albert, 204, 205–6, 219
Galveston, Tex., 537, 618
Gandhi, Mohandas K., 316, 874
Garfield, James A., 478
    assassination of, 564
    presidency of, 564
Garner, John Nance, 728, 769
Garrison, William Lloyd, 374–75, 378,
    386
    in radical wing of antislavery
        movement, 408
Garvey, Marcus, 690, 904
Gaspee, H.M.S., 106
gasoline production, 942
Gates, Horatio, 133
Gates, John W. "Bet-a-Million," 498
Gay Liberation Front, 924
Gay rights, 924–25
General Accounting Office, 973
General Motors, 992, 998
General Federation of Women's Clubs,
    556
General Intelligence Division, 676
General Motors, 751
Genêt, Edmond Charles, 186
Geneva Accords (1954), 869–71, 895

Geneva Summit (1985), 962, 963
"Gentleman's Agreement" (1907), 612
gentry, in southern colonies, 50
George, Henry, 550–51
George I, king of England, 77
George II, king of England, 34, 77, 91
George III, king of England, 93–95, 108,
    115–16, 158, 240
  accession of, 91
  military strategies and, 130, 133
Georgia, 143, 155, 156, 260, 262,
    263–64, 468, 487
  adoption of Constitution and, 172
  Civil War fighting in, 442, 443,
    446–48
  slavery in, 144
Georgia, University of, 150
Georgia colony, founding of, 35
German-Americans, 293, 295, 297–98,
    521, 535, 671, 788
  in colonial period, 59–60
German Democratic Republic (East
    Germany), 822, 866, 880, 893,
    977, 978
German Federal Republic (West
    Germany), 822, 823, 933, 977
German scholarship, 543, 546
Germany, Imperial:
  Imperial China and, 604–5
  in Moroccan crisis (1905–1906), 613
  Pacific possessions of, 589
  in World War I, 648–50, 651–53,
    655–57, 663–64, 665–66, 669,
    673, 674
Germany, Nazi:
  collapse of, 805
  Hitler's rise to power in, 764
  in prelude to World War II, 765–66
  see also World War II
Germany, occupied, governance of, 803,
    818, 821–22
Germany, Weimar, 666, 759
Geronimo, chief of Chiricahua Apaches,
    494
Gerry, Elbridge, 162–63, 166, 171, 195
Gettysburg, battle of (1863), 441–42
Ghent, Treaty of (1814), 225, 234
ghettos, 539, 976
Gibbons, Thomas, 242
Gibbons v. Ogden, 242
GI Bill of Rights (1944), 813
Gideon v. Wainwright, 893
Gilbert Islands, 781, 797–800
Gilded Age, The (Twain and Warner), 559
Ginsberg, Allen, 853, 854
Gladden, Washington, 553
glasnost (openness), 977
Glaspie, April, 984
Glass-Steagall Act (1932), 724
Glass-Steagall Banking Act (1933), 732
Glidden, Joseph, 497–98
Glorious Revolution (1688), 79, 86
  colonies affected by, 76–77
gold, 492, 586
gold rushes, 285, 298, 492, 530, 586

gold standard, 582–86, 625, 724, 732
Goldwater, Barry, 861, 900, 906, 949,
    952
Gompers, Samuel, 518, 603, 639,
    674–75
  union philosophy and tactics of,
    521–23
Good Neighbor policy, 761–62
Goodyear, Charles, 288
Gorbachev, Mikhail, 962, 963, 968–69,
    977, 984
  failed political/military coup against,
    980–81
  Soviet Union dissolution and, 977–82
Gordon, Thomas, 97
Gore, Albert, Jr., 995, 996
Gorges, Sir Ferdinando, 28
Gorky, Arshile, 852
"Gospel of Wealth, The" (Carnegie),
    512–13
Gottlieb, Adolph, 852
Gould, Jay, 473, 506, 520, 570
government:
  growth of, in Progressive era, 624
  limited role for, 544, 563, 569
  New Deal's transformation of, 756
  Social Darwinists' view of, 544
  see also reform movements
Government Operations Committee, 863
Graduation Act (1854), 280
Grady, Henry W., 480
Graham, Sylvester, 324
Grand Army of the Republic, 569
Grand Canyon, 627
grandfather clause, 487, 691
Grand State Alliance, 578
Granger Movement, 576–77, 579
Grant, Ulysses S., 350–51, 357, 413, 704
  in Chattanooga campaign, 442–44
  economic policy of, 472–73, 475
  in Kentucky and Tennessee campaigns,
    417, 424–25
  Lee pursued by, 444–46, 448–49
  in presidential elections, 471–72, 564
  in Reconstruction, 461, 463
  scandals and corruption under,
    472–74, 476
  in Vicksburg campaign, 440–41
Grapes of Wrath, The (Steinbeck), 697,
    735
Grasse, François Joseph Paul de, 136–37
Graves, Thomas, 136
Gray, L. Patrick, 937
Graying of America, 998
Grayson, William J., 380
Great Awakening, 66–70, 306
Great Britain (England), 207, 342–43,
    394, 553, 588, 589, 820, 821, 870
  in arms control negotiations, 759, 760
  border disputes with, 234–35, 274
  colonial administration by, 78–80
  French conflicts with, 80, 86, 87–91
  French Revolution and, 185, 186
  immigrants from, 39–40, 298, 538
  Imperial China and, 604–5

industry in, 286
intrigues with Indians by, 157, 219,
220, 235–36
Jay's Treaty with, 186–88, 195
in Middle East, 876–78
Monroe Doctrine and, 243, 244
in Napoleonic Wars, 214–17
in NATO, 822
Oregon country claims of, 243, 350
Panama Canal and, 609
in Persian Gulf War, 986–87
power of king vs. Parliament in, 79
Reformation in, 12–13
slave trade and, 335–36, 375
Spanish conflicts with, 14–15, 16
Texas statehood and, 346
trade with, 127, 237, 363
in U.S. Civil War, 423, 433, 435–36
U.S. missiles in, 894
U.S. trade with, 156–57, 234–35, 237,
269–70, 272
in World War I, 648, 650, 651, 657,
664, 668, 670, 674
World War I debt of, 759
see also American Revolution; colonial
period; colonial wars;
colonization, English; War of
1812; World War I; World War II
Great Compression, 991–93
"Great Compromise" (1787), 165
Great Depression, *see* Depression, Great
Great Gatsby, The (Fitzgerald), 695
Great Migration, 689
Great Northern railroad, 623, 660
Great Plains, 491
Great Railroad Strike (1877), 516–18,
563
Great Society program, 878–90, 899,
912, 933
Greece, 773, 774, 820, 822–23
in World War I, 665
Greek-Americans, 538
Greeley, Horace, 320, 474, 475
Green, William, 751
Greenback party, 577
Greene, Nathanael, 124–25, 134–35
Greenland, Viking settlement on, 1
Green Mountain Boys, 105, 114
Greenville, Treaty of (1795), 188, 191
Grenada, invasion of (1983), 959–60,
986
Grenville, George, 96–97, 100, 101
Grimké, Angelina, 376
Grimké, Sarah, 376
Gross Domestic Product (GDP), 992
Grundy, Felix, 219
Guadalcanal, battle of (1942), 797
Guadalupe Hidalgo, Treaty of (1848), 356
Guam, 778, 781
Guantanamo Bay, U.S. naval base at, 604
Guatemala, 866, 957
Guevara, Ché, 919
Guinn v. United States, 691
Guiteau, Charles, 564
Gullah blacks, 371

habeas corpus, suspensions of, 417,
436–37
Habeas Corpus Act (1863), 436–37
Haber, Al, 916
Haight-Ashbury, San Francisco, 920
Haiti, 963
U.S. intervention in (1915–1934),
648, 762
Haitian-Americans, 1000–1001
Haldeman, H. R., 930, 937
Half-Breeds, 563
Half-Way Covenant, 57
Halleck, Henry, 426, 428
Halpin, Maria, 567
Hamilton, Alexander, 148, 162, 192, 954
in adoption of Constitution, 163, 164,
166, 170, 171, 172
death of, 210
foreign policy of, 195
land policy of, 191
as military officer, 137, 196–97
political philosophy of, 182, 183, 184
presidential elections and, 193–94,
199, 200
as secretary of treasury, 177, 178–82,
188–90, 198–99, 205, 230
Hancock, John, 108, 112, 118
Hanna, Mark, 585, 586, 600, 607
Harding, Warren G., 673, 715, 954, 955
appointments of, 704–7
big business and, 704–7
corruption and, 707–8
death of, 708
foreign policy of, 758, 760
"Ohio Gang" of, 705, 707
in presidential election, 703–4
shortcoming of, 703–4, 705, 708
Harlem Renaissance, 689
Harlem Shadows (McKay), 689
Harper's Ferry, 429–30
Brown's attack on (1859), 407–9, 410
Harper's Monthly, 549
Harper's Weekly, 420
Harriman, E. H., 625
Harrington, Michael, 898–99
Harris, Joel Chandler, 547
Harris, Townsend, 395
Harris Convention (1858), 395
Harrison, Benjamin, 571–73, 709
foreign policy under, 590
in presidential elections, 571, 582
Harrison, William Henry:
as governor of Indiana Territory, 218,
222
presidency of, 335
in presidential elections, 271, 274–75
Hartford Convention (1814), 225–26
Harvard College (University), 70, 152,
918, 1003
Haugen, Gilbert N., 716
Havana, Cuba, 91
Hawaii, 880, 1001
annexation of, 589–91, 602
in World War II, 777–80, 782
Hawkins, Sir John, 15

Hawley-Smoot Tariff (1930), 720, 723
Hawthorne, Nathaniel, 284–85, 317–18, 332, 421
Hay, John, 600, 605, 609–10
Hayden, Tom, 916, 917, 919
Hayes, Lucy, 562
Hayes, Rutherford B., 563
    background of, 562
    on Indian wars, 496
    in presidential elections, 476–78
Hay-Herrán Treaty (1903), 610
Haymarket Affair (1886), 520–21
Hayne, Robert Y., 256–57, 259
Haynes, Lemuel, 147
Hay-Pauncefote Treaty (1901), 609
Haywood, William D. "Big Bill," 527–28
Head Start, 899
health insurance, 901
Hearst, William Randolph, 593, 594, 746
Heisenberg, Werner, 692
Heller, Joseph, 852
Hell's Angels, 920
Hemingway, Ernest, 548, 695–96
Henry, Patrick, 97, 99–100, 110, 144, 148, 184
    Constitution opposed by, 171, 172, 176
Henry VII, king of England, 9
Henry VIII, king of England, 12
Hepburn, Peter, 625
Hepburn Act (1906), 625–26
Herbert, Victor, 295
heroin, 975
Herrán, Thomas, 610
Hessians, 116, 121, 123
Higher Education Act (1965), 901
highways, 844, 861–62
Highway Safety Act (1966), 901
Hill, Anita, 990–91
Hill, A. P., 428
Hill, D. H., 428
Hill, Joe, 528
Hillman, Sidney, 750–51
hippies, 920
Hireling and the Slave, The (Grayson), 380
Hirohito, emperor of Japan, 777, 807, 809
Hiroshima, nuclear bombing (1945), 808–9
Hispanic-Americans, 679, 923, 941, 975, 976, 1000–1003
Hiss, Alger, 833–34
history, study of, 545–46
History of the American Revolution (Ramsey), 148
Hitler, Adolf, 755
    death of, 805
    in rise to power, 764
    see also World War II
Ho Chi Minh, 829, 867, 871, 909
Ho Chi Minh Trail, 895, 906
Hodgkins, Sarah, 126
Hoe, Richard, 320
Hoe Rotary Press, 320
Hoffman, Abbie, 919

Holmes, Oliver Wendell, Jr., 546, 662, 729
Holmes, Oliver Wendell, Sr., 317
Holocaust, 806
Home Owner's Loan Act (1933), 732
Home Owner's Loan Corporation (HOLC), 732
Homestead Act (1862), 434, 498, 499
Homestead Steel Strike (1892), 523
Homestead Works, 523
Honduras, 957, 958
Hong Kong, 778, 781, 1001
Hood, John B., 446–47
Hooker, Joseph E., 438–40, 441, 443, 444
Hooker, Thomas, 28
Hoover, Herbert, 658–59, 705, 707, 708, 709, 714, 771, 940, 992
    foreign policy of, 759, 762, 763
    Great Depression and, 721–25
    in presidential elections, 718–19, 728
Hoover, J. Edgar, 676, 846
Hoover (Boulder) Dam, 498
Hope, Bob, 538
Hopkins, Harry L., 733, 753
Hopkins, Mark, 504
Hopper, Edward, 852
Hornet, 782
Horsehoe Bend, battle of (1814), 222
House, Edward M., 635, 652, 665
House Beautiful, 845
House of Representatives, U.S., 177, 179
    A. Johnson impeached by, 462–63
    Committee on Un-American Activities of, 755, 833, 834
    Constitutional Convention and, 166–67
    presidential elections decided by, 200, 245, 477
housing, 539, 840
    federal aid for, 901
Housing Act (1961), 888
Housing and Urban Development, U.S. Department of, 901
Housing and Urban Development Act (1965), 901
Housing Authority, U.S., 753
Houston, Sam, 345
Houston, Tex., 531
Howard University, 720
Howe, Elias, 288
Howe, Julia Ward, 422, 555
Howe, Sir William, 114, 116
    in New York and New Jersey campaigns, 121–23, 127–28
    resignation of, 131
Howells, William Dean, 549
Howl (Ginsberg), 854, 855
Hudson, Henry, 31
Hué, 909
Huerta, Victoriano, 645, 646
Hughes, Charles Evans, 619, 654, 705, 760
Hughes, Langston, 689
Huguenots, 29, 85
Hull, Cordell, 769, 776, 777

Hull, William, 220
Hull House, 554, 555
Humphrey, Hubert H., 826, 886, 889
  in presidential elections, 899, 911–13, 918
Hungarian-Americans, 538
Hungary, 673, 774, 818, 866, 957, 978
  uprising in (1956), 878
Hunt, Harriet, 329
Huntington, Collis P., 504
Huron Indians, 84
Hurston, Zora Neal, 689
Hussein, Saddam, 983–88
Hutchinson, Anne, 26–27
Hutchinson, Thomas, 104, 106, 107–8
hydroelectric power, 482
hydrogen bomb, 829, 866

IBM, 992
Iceland, 774, 822
Iceland Summit (1986), 963
Ickes, Harold L., 738, 742, 753
Idaho, 572
Illinois, 261, 1001
  French settlers in, 84
"I Love Lucy," 840
immigrants:
  "Americanizing" of, 541
  negative perception of, 562
  in 1980s and 1990s, 1000–1003, 1005
  see also specific ethnic groups
immigration:
  through Angel Island, 540–41
  through Castle Garden, 293
  through Ellis Island, 535–38, 540
  in late 1800s, 533–41
  in mid 1800s, 292–301
  new ethnic sources of, 535, 1000–1003
  restrictions on, 540–41, 677, 679
  see also nativism
Immigration Service, 1001
impeachment, 167, 938
imperialism:
  naval power in, 591–92
  Open Door Policy and, 604–6, 611, 612, 760
  opposition to, 602
  in Pacific, 588–91
  philosophical justifications for, 592
  as quest for markets, 600, 603
  see also Spanish-American War
Inca Indians:
  conquest of, 10
  culture of, 2
income tax, 654, 706, 720
  in New Deal, 745–46
Independent Treasury, 273–74
India, 867
  British conquest of, 91, 93
Indiana, 188
Indiana Territory, 218
Indian Peace Commission, 493
Indian Removal Act (1830), 261
Indian reservations, 84

Indians, American, 284, 1000
  British intrigues with, 157, 219, 220, 235–36
  in colonial wars, 80–84
  in early contacts with whites, 6–8, 9–11
  European diseases and, 8–9, 11, 340
  in fur trade, 41, 82
  in Jamestown and Virginia colony, 17, 19
  Mexican subjugation of, 340–41
  in Middle Colonies, 59
  in Native American movement, 923–24
  Northwest Territory claims of, 154
  Pacific Northwest exploration and, 208
  at Plymouth colony, 21
  pre-Columbian, 1–3, 41
  Quakers' friendship with, 34
  removal of, 41, 261–64
  reservation policy toward, 496, 924
  in Revolutionary War, 129, 132–33, 156
  as slaves, 30–31, 48–49, 341
  Spanish intrigues with, 156, 157, 158–59, 219
  Spanish subjugation of, 6, 9–11, 340
  trade with, 14, 17
  westward expansion of colonists and, 156
  Roger Williams aided by, 25–26
  see also specific tribes
Indian wars:
  in colonial period, 80–84, 95, 105
  in Great Plains, 492–96
  in Northwest Territory, 188
  in Old Southwest, 222
  see also French and Indian War
Indochina, French, 775, 776
Indochina War (1946–1954), 829, 867–71
  see also Vietnam War
Industrial Workers of the World (IWW; Wobblies), 526–28, 662
industry:
  cities and, 292
  growth of (early 1800s), 278, 286–92
  post-World War I reconversion of, 674
  see also manufacturing; *specific industries*
inflation:
  in 1970s, 932–33, 940, 944
  silver coinage and, 575, 586
  after World War II, 814
Influence of Sea Power upon History, 1660–1783, The (Mahan), 591
In re Debs (1894), 525
instrumentalism, 546–47
intercontinental ballistic missiles (ICBMs), 879, 935, 982
intermediate range ballistic missiles (IRBMs), 879
intermediate range nuclear forces (INF) treaty (1987), 968–69
International Court of Justice, 817
International Harvester, 520–21

International Ladies Garment Workers, 751
Interstate Commerce Act (1887), 570
Interstate Commerce Commission (ICC), 570, 620, 625–26, 639, 706
Intolerable Acts (Coercive Acts) (1774), 109, 110
Invisible Man (Ellison), 852
Iowa, 491, 998
Iran:
    CIA activities in, 866
    hostage crisis in (1979–1981), 945–46, 983
    immigrants from, 1001
    in Persian Gulf War, 984, 988
    in pro-Western pacts, 876
Iran-Contra affair, 964–66
Iran-Iraq war, 958, 983
Iraq, 876, 880, 958
    in Persian Gulf War, 983–89
Ireland, Patricia, 991
Irish-Americans, 39, 293–97, 538, 568, 671
    in labor force, 300
    in politics, 296
iron curtain, 880
Iroquois Indians, 156
    French relations with, 84, 86
    Middle Colonies' relations with, 31, 84
Irving, Washington, 291, 316
Isabella of Castile, queen of Spain, 4, 6
Ishii, Viscount Kikujiro, 759
Islam, 988
isolationism, World War I participation and, 764, 768–69
Israel, 823, 935, 940–41, 943–44, 963, 969
    Lebanon invaded by (1982), 958–59
    in Persian Gulf War, 987, 989
    in Suez War, 878
Italian-Americans, 538, 671, 788
Italy, 670, 820, 822, 894, 958, 959
    Ethiopia invaded by (1934), 765, 767
    Mussolini's rise to power in, 763–64
    treaties with, 760
    in World War I, 648, 649, 663, 665, 668
    in World War II, 767, 773, 791, 794, 818
Iwo Jima, battle of (1945), 806

Jackson, Andrew, 272, 303, 345, 346, 359
    appointments of, 252–55
    assessment of, 275–76
    Eaton affair and, 254
    federal surplus and, 269
    in Florida campaign, 235–37, 259
    inauguration of, 252
    Indian policy of, 261–64, 492
    internal improvements and, 254–55
    in national bank controversy, 264–65
    in nullification crisis, 258–61, 335
    in presidential elections, 244, 245, 246, 248–50
    Truman compared with, 812

    in War of 1812, 222, 224–25, 226
    Whig coalition against, 270–71
Jackson, Frankie "Half Pint," 695
Jackson, Helen Hunt, 496
Jackson, Jesse, 969, 970
Jackson, Rachel, 254
Jackson, "Shoeless Joe," 675
Jackson, Thomas "Stonewall," 357, 420, 426, 429, 431, 439–40
Jackson State College, 928
Jamaica, immigrants from, 1001
James, Henry, 530, 549
James, William, 546, 549, 603, 942
James I, king of England, 16, 20, 21
James II, king of England (duke of York), 75–76, 86
    colonization and, 32
    overthrow of, 76
Jamestown, 17–19, 46
    burning of (1676), 83
    representative assembly established in, 19
    site chosen for, 17
Japan, 668, 933
    Imperial China and, 604, 605–6
    pre-World War II treaties with, 612, 759–60
    reopening of, 394
    Russian war with (1904–1905), 611–12
    U.S. immigration restrictions and, 612
    in World War I, 648–49
    in World War II, 775–80, 790, 795, 797–800, 803, 818, 828, 829, 867
Japanese-Americans, 540, 612
    wartime internment of, 788–89
Java, 781
Jaworski, Leon, 938
Jay, John, 153, 159, 160, 170, 171, 192, 195
    as chief justice, 177
    land policy of, 191
    as secretary for foreign affairs, 176
    treaties negotiated by, 138, 186–88, 194, 199
Jay's Treaty (1795), 186–88, 194–95, 199
jazz, 686, 695
Jeffers, Robinson, 694
Jefferson, Thomas, 50, 110, 111, 118, 146, 150, 154, 160, 185, 186, 202–16, 233, 275–76, 278, 289, 306, 307, 328, 359
    Alien and Sedition Acts opposed by, 198
    Burr Conspiracy and, 212–13
    cabinet and appointments of, 204
    Constitutional Convention and, 162, 163
    Declaration of Independence by, 118, 144
    economic policies of, 205–6
    exploration of West and, 208–9
    foreign policy under, 206–9, 214–16, 243
    Hamiltonian program and, 180, 181

inaugurations of, 202–3, 210
internal improvements under, 231–32
land policy of, 191
political philosophy of, 182, 183–85
in presidential elections, 193–94,
    199–200
presidential style of, 203
religion and, 147
as secretary of state, 177
slavery and, 144–45, 239, 240, 380
Jesuits, missionary work by, 14
Jewett, Sarah Orne, 547
Jewish immigrants, 535
Jews, 297, 298, 538
    Israel and, 823
    Nazi persecution of, 764, 806
Jim Crow system, 487–89, 639, 875, 889
Job Corps, 899
Johns Hopkins University, 908
Johnson, Andrew, 436, 437, 471, 588,
    936
    background of, 454
    congressional conflicts with, 458–62
    impeachment and trial of, 462–63
    Reconstruction plan of, 454–56
Johnson, Hiram, 619
Johnson, Hugh S., 738
Johnson, James Weldon, 689
Johnson, Lyndon B., 887, 918
    background of, 734
    civil rights and, 875, 898, 899, 902–3,
        931
    inauguration of, 897
    in presidential elections, 899–900, 912
    presidential style of, 898
    tax program of, 898
    Vietnam War and, 906, 910
    war on poverty of, 898–99, 900–902
Johnson, Richard M., 219
Johnson Debt Default Act (1934), 759,
    773
Johnston, Albert Sidney, 424, 425, 426
Johnston, Joseph E., 420, 427–28, 444
    Sherman's pursuit of, 444, 448
Joint Chiefs of Staff, 816, 832, 866, 893,
    895
Joint Committee on Reconstruction, 457,
    460
Joliet, Louis, 84
Jolson, Al, 538
Jones, James, 852
Jones, John Paul, 136
Jordan, 876
Joseph, chief of Nez Perce, 494
journalism:
    censorship of, 197–98
    yellow, 593, 594
J. Pierpont Morgan and Company, 513
Judiciary Act (1801), 200, 204
Julian, George W., 436, 457
Jungle, The (Sinclair), 626
Justice, U.S. Department of, 177

Kamikaze planes, 800, 806–7
Kansas, 491, 579
Kansas City, Mo., 530–31

Kansas-Nebraska Act (1854), 395–402
    violence in Kansas and, 398–400
    violence on Senate floor and, 400
Kansas Pacific Railroad, 497
Kansas Territory:
    constitutional (Lecompton) convention
        in (1857), 403–4
    violence in, 398–400
Kant, Immanuel, 314
Kearny, Stephen, 353
Keating-Owen Child Labor Act (1916),
    641
Keats, John, 849
Kelley, Florence, 621
Kelley, Oliver H., 576–77
Kellogg, Frank B., 761
Kellogg-Briand Pact (1928), 761, 763
Kennan, George F., 819, 820, 878, 908
Kennedy, Edward M., 951
Kennedy, Jacqueline, 897
Kennedy, John F., 898, 899, 995
    assassination of, 896–97
    background of, 886
    Bay of Pigs invasion and, 882, 893
    cabinet of, 888
    civil rights movement and, 889–92
    Cuban missile crisis and, 893–95
    domestic programs of, 888, 892
    inauguration of, 888
    in presidential elections, 885–87
    Vietnam and, 895–96, 907
Kennedy, Robert F., 888, 889, 890, 892,
    910
    assassination of, 911
Kent State University, 927–28
Kentucky, 156, 158, 192
    Civil War fighting in, 424
    slavery in, 366, 434
    Unionist vs. Confederate sentiments,
        417–18
Kentucky Resolution (1798), 198
Kerouac, Jack, 853, 854–55, 916
Kerr, Clark, 916
Key, Francis Scott, 224
Keystone Studios, 711–12
Khmer Rouge, 941
Khomeini, Ayatollah Ruhollah, 945
Khrushchev, Nikita, 878, 880–81,
    893–95
King, Martin Luther, Jr., 316, 891, 903,
    904, 970
    assassination of, 911
    Montgomery bus boycott led by,
        873–75, 889
King, Rodney, 1003–4
King, Rufus, 233
King, Susie, 433
King George's War (War of the Austrian
    Succession) (1744–1784), 86
King Philip's War (1675–1678), 82
Kings Mountain, battle of (1780), 133–34
King William's War (War of the League
    of Augsburg) (1689–1697), 86
Kiowa Indians, 493–94
Kissinger, Henry, 931, 934, 935, 940
    Vietnam and, 926, 927, 928

Kleindienst, Richard, 937
Knights of Labor, 519–20, 521, 522
Know-Nothing party, 299–300, 397, 401
Knox, Henry, 177, 196
Konoye, Fumimaro, 776, 777
Korea, 795
    division of, 829–30
    Russo-Japanese rivalry over, 611–12
Korean-Americans, 612, 1001
Korean War, 829–33, 839, 867
    armistice in, 862
Krutch, Joseph Wood, 848
Ku Klux Klan (KKK), 468–69, 1002, 1003
    revived after World War I, 679–81
Kuomintang, 762–63, 828
Kurds, 988
Kurile Islands, 804
Kuwait, 983–88
Kwantung Army, 763
Kyoto, 808

labor:
    disorganization of, 516
    Great Railroad Strike and, 516–18, 563
    immigrant, 300–301, 515, 519, 535
    ten- and eight-hour days won by, 518, 621, 641
    women and, 785–86
    working conditions of, 515–16, 621
    see also child labor
labor laws:
    in Great Depression, 738–39, 751
    after World War II, 815–16, 879
labor unions, 516–28, 639
    coal strike and (1902), 623–24
    decline of, under Reagan, 956
    emergence of, 301–3, 518–20
    Great Depression-era growth of, 751–52
    in politics, 302–3
    reforms sought by, 303
    secrecy in, 519
    socialism and, 525–28
    violence attributed to, 520–21, 523
    women in, 660–61
    World War I demobilization and, 661, 674–75, 677, 717
    World War I expansion of, 661
    after World War II, 814–16
    World War II restrictions on, 790
Labrador, 235
Lafayette, Marie Joseph, marquis de, 136
La Follette, Robert M. "Fighting Bob," 619, 630, 653, 710, 913
Lake Champlain, battle of (1814), 222, 224
Lamar, Mirabeau Bonaparte, 346
Land Act of 1796, 191–92
Land Act of 1800, 192
Landon, Alfred M., 748
Land Ordinance (1784), 154
Land Ordinance (1785), 154
land policies:
    in colonial era, 45, 51
    of Confederation, 153–56

    in early 1800s, 280
    nullification doctrine and, 256
    during Reconstruction, 453, 458
    Revolution and, 143
    settlement vs. revenue as goal of, 191–92
Lange, Dorothea, 789
Lansing, Robert, 652, 653, 760
Lansing-Ishii Agreement (1917), 760
Laos, 867, 869, 929, 1001
La Salle, Robert Cavalier, sieur de, 14, 84
Las Vegas, Nev., 1004
Lathrop, Julia, 555
Latin America, 1001
    Alliance for Progress programs for, 889
    Good Neighbor policy and, 761–62
    Reagan's policy in, 957–58, 964–66
    see also specific countries
Latin immigrants, 535, 539
Latvia, 981
Laurens, Henry, 138
Lawrence, 221
Lawrence, James, 226
Lazarus, Emma, 535
League of Nations, 668, 758, 763, 764
Leary, Timothy, 920
Lease, Mary Elizabeth, 579–80
Leaves of Grass (Whitman), 320, 854
Lebanon, 876, 880, 958–59
Lecompton Constitution, 403–4
Lee, Henry "Light-Horse Harry," 189, 418
Lee, Richard Henry, 117–18, 171
Lee, Robert E., 357, 408, 428, 431
    in Bull Run and Antietam offensive, 428–31
    Chancellorsville victory of, 438–40
    Confederate cause chosen by, 418
    Gettysburg assault led by, 441–42
    Grant's pursuit of, 444–46, 448–49
LeMay, Curtis, 912
Lemke, William, 748
Lend-Lease Bill (1941), 773
Lenin, V. I., 526, 663, 667, 676, 917, 981
Leningrad, 774
Leopard, 215
Leo XIII, Pope, 553
Lesbians, 925
"Letter from a Birmingham Jail" (King), 891
Letters of a Pennsylvania Farmer (Dickinson), 102
Levitt, William, 843
Lewis, John L., 750, 751, 790
Lewis, Meriwether, 208
Lewis, Sinclair, 685, 711
Lexington, 782
Lexington, British assault on (1775), 112–13
Leyte Gulf, battle of (1944), 800
Liberator, The, 374–75
Liberia, 373
Liberty Loan Act (1917), 657
Liberty party, 348, 379, 386
Libya, 773, 791, 963

licensing laws, 543
Lie Down in Darkness (Styron), 852
Life, 845
Life on the Mississippi (Twain), 548
light bulb, 507
Light in August (Faulkner), 700
Liliuokalani, queen of Hawaii, 590
Lincoln, Abraham, 262, 419, 456
  able general sought by, 428, 431, 438,
    444
  assassination of, 449, 454
  background of, 405–6
  civil liberties suspended by, 417,
    436–37
  Emancipation Proclamation of, 432–34
  Grant admired by, 426
  inauguration of, 416
  Mexican War opposed by, 351
  peninsular campaign and, 426–27
  in presidential elections, 410–11
  Reconstruction policy of, 451–54
  in senatorial election (1858), 405–7
  slavery issue and, 384, 406–7, 408, 416
Lincoln, Benjamin, 160
Lincoln, Mary Todd, 449
Lindbergh, Charles A., Jr., 712–13, 771
Lindsay, Vachel, 694
literacy rate, 321
literature:
  flowering of (early 1800s), 316–20
  in Great Depression, 696–700
  in late 1800s, 547–51
  local color movement in, 547–49
  modernist, 693–96
  naturalism in, 549–50
  in postwar era (1945–60), 850–52,
    853–55
  realism in, 549–50
  southern, 698–700
  Transcendentalism and, 314–16
Lithuania, 538, 981
Little Big Horn River, battle of (1874),
  494
Little Rock, Ark., 875
Livingston, Robert R., 153, 207, 241, 281
Lloyd, Henry Demarest, 551, 617
Lloyd George, David, 668, 670
local colorists, 547
Lochner v. New York, 621
Locke, John, 30, 64, 69, 76, 97, 118,
  119, 162
"Locofocos" (Equal Rights party), 302
Lodge, Henry Cabot, 540, 591, 599,
  668, 671–72, 707, 896
  on elective courses, 542
Log College, 67, 70
London, Jack, 550
London Company:
  charter of, 16
  Jamestown established by, 17–19
Lonely Crowd, The (Riesman), 849
Long, Huey P., Jr., 741–42, 743, 748
Longfellow, Henry Wadsworth, 316–17
Longstreet, James A., 428, 429, 441, 467
Longview, Tex., 675
Longworth, Alice Roosevelt, 705

Look Homeward, Angel (Wolfe), 699
Lookout Mountain, battle of (1863),
  443–44
Los Alamos, N. Mex., 807
Los Angeles, Calif., 530, 737, 1001
  riots in (1965), 903
  riots in (1992), 1003–5
Los Angeles Times, 528, 1005
lost generation, 678
Louisiana, 158, 238
  French in, 84
  immigrants in, 1002, 1003
  racial segregation in, 488
Louisiana Purchase (1803), 206–8
  boundaries of, 235
  explorations of, 208–10
  slavery in, 238–40
Louisiana Territory, 190
  French colonization of, 89
Louisville, Ky., 292
Louis XIV, king of France, 84, 86
Louis XVI, king of France, 185
Lovejoy, Elijah P., 379
"Love Song of J. Alfred Prufrock, The"
  (Eliot), 694
Lowell, Amy, 694
Lowell, James Russell, 317, 451
Lowell system, 289–92
Loyalists (Tories), 112, 124, 128,
  132–34, 135, 139, 140, 143,
  157–58
LSD, 920
Lublin Committee, 803–4
Ludendorff, Erich, 665
lumber industry, 45, 482
Lusitania, 652–53
Luther, Martin, 12
Lutherans, 297
Luxembourg, 801, 822
lynchings, 488, 691
Lyon, Mary, 323

MacArthur, Douglas:
  bonus marchers dispersed by, 726
  in Korean War, 829–30, 831–32
  in World War II, 776, 781, 797, 800,
    809
McAuliffe, Anthony C., 801
McCarran Internal Security Act (1950),
  835
McCarthy, Eugene, 910, 911, 912, 918
McCarthy, Joseph R., 834–35, 862–64
McClellan, George B., 357, 417
  in peninsular campaign, 426–28
  in presidential elections, 437
McClure's Magazine, 617
McCord, James W., 936
McCormick, Cyrus Hall, 287–88, 361
McCoy, Joseph G., 497
McCulloch v. Maryland, 240–42, 264
McDowell, Irvin, 419–20, 426
McFarlane, Robert, 964
McGovern, George S., 936, 971
machine politics, 561
McKay, Claude, 689
McKinley, William, 573, 608, 705

McKinley, William (continued)
  assassination of, 606
  in presidential elections, 583–86, 606
  Spanish-American War and, 594–96, 597, 600–602, 603
McKinley Tariff (1890), 572–73, 590
McLane, Louis, 267
McNamara, Robert, 888, 908–9
McNary, Charles L., 716
McNary-Haugen bill, 716–17, 718
Macon, Nathaniel, 217
McTeague (Norris), 549
Macune, Charles W., 578
Madero, Francisco I., 645
Madison, Dolley, 223
Madison, James, 161, 186, 192, 228, 243
  in adoption of Constitution, 162, 163, 164, 165, 167, 170, 171, 183
  Alien and Sedition Acts opposed by, 198
  Bill of Rights and, 177
  economic policies of, 179–80, 232
  land policy of, 191
  in presidential elections, 216
  as secretary of state, 204
  slavery and, 239, 373
Mafia, 896, 897
Maggie: A Girl of the Streets (Crane), 549–50
Maginot Line, 770
Mahan, Alfred Thayer, 591–92, 613
Mailer, Norman, 852
Maine, 82, 147, 226, 924
  disputes over border of, 274, 336
Maine, 594
Maine colony, 28
Main Street (Lewis), 685
maize, 7–8, 21
Malaya, British, 775
Malay Peninsula, 778
Malaysia, 867
Malay States, 867
Malcolm X, 904–5
Manassas, see Bull Run, first battle of;
  Bull Run, second battle of
Manchuria, 761, 763, 804
  Russian interests in, 605, 612
Manchuria Incident (1932), 763
Mandan Sioux Indians, 208
Mandela, Nelson, 979
Manhattan Project, 807
Manifest Destiny, 491, 588, 592
  as election issue, 348
  New Mexico and, 338
  Oregon country and, 338–40, 349–50
  origin of term, 337
  see also imperialism
Manila, 91
Manila Bay, capture of (1898), 597–98
Mann, Horace, 321
manufacturing, 181–82, 191, 591, 999
  protection of, 247–48
  in South, 362–63
  technological advances in, 507
  see also industry; tariffs; textile manufactures

Mao Tse-tung, 828
Marbury v. Madison, 204–5, 240, 403
March on Washington (1963), 891, 903
Marco Polo Bridge, battle at (1937), 765, 768
Marcos, Ferdinand, 963
Mariana islands, 800
Maria Theresa, empress of Austria, 89
Marine Corps, U.S., founding of, 116
Marion, Francis, 134
Marne, second battle of the (1918), 663–64
Marquette, Père Jacques, 14, 84
marriage:
  in colonial period, 44, 54
  among slaves, 48
Marshall, George C., 790, 820, 835
Marshall, John, 195, 373
  appointed chief justice, 200
  in Burr trial, 213
  federal power enhanced by, 240–42
  implied powers doctrine and, 240–42
  Indian affairs and, 263–64
  judicial review affirmed by, 204–5
  at presidential inaugurations, 202
Marshall, Thurgood, 989
Marshall Plan, 820–21
Martin, Luther, 163, 171
Martineau, Harriet, 284
Mary, queen of Scots, 15
Mary I, queen of England, 76, 77
Maryland, 143, 147, 161
  adoption of Constitution and, 172
  Civil War and, 417, 429
Maryland colony, 31, 45
  Anglican church in, 50
  charter of, 19–20
  first settlement in, 19–20
  Indians in, 83
  population growth in, 29
Mason, George, 163, 166, 167, 177
Mason, John, 28
Massachusetts, 141, 147, 159–60, 186, 249, 924
  adoption of Constitution and, 172
  asylum reform in, 326–27
  public education in, 150, 321
Massachusetts Circular Letters, 103
Massachusetts colony (Massachusetts Bay Colony), 22–25, 39, 54–55, 56, 57–58, 74, 100, 103
  charter of, 23, 24–25, 29, 57, 74, 78, 141
  in colonial wars, 87
  education in, 65
  government of, 24–25, 74–76, 78
  Plymouth colony united with, 76
  religion in, 66–67, 68
Massachusetts Government Act (1774), 109, 131
Masters, Edgar Lee, 694
Mather, Increase, 54
Maya Indians, 1–2
Mayflower, 21
Mayflower Compact (1620), 21, 23
Mayhew, Jonathan, 69

Maysville Road Bill (1830), 254–55
Mead, Margaret, 693
Meade, George C., 357, 441, 442, 444
Meany, George, 841
Meat Inspection Act (1906), 626
meat-packing industry, regulation of, 626
   see also cattle industry
Medicaid, 901
Medicare, 901, 902
medicine, women in, 329
Medicine Creek Lodge, conference at
   (1867), 493–94
Meese, Edwin, 969, 967
Mellon, Andrew W., 705–6, 707, 719,
   722, 954
Melville, Herman, 318–19, 333, 351
Memphis, Tenn., 460, 686
Mencken, H. L., 681, 709, 698–99
Mennonites, 34, 59–60
mental illness, reformers and, 326–27
Menu, Operation, 927
mercantilism, 157
Meredith, James H., 890
Merrimack, 424
Merrimack Manufacturing Company,
   289
Methodist Episcopal Church, 380
Methodists, 69, 147–48, 309–10, 338
   in split over slavery, 380, 397
Meuse-Argonne offensive (1918),
   664–65
Mexican-Americans, 659, 1000–1001
Mexican War (1845–1848), 350–57
   California annexation and, 353
   legacies of, 383, 385
   Mexican campaign in, 354–55
   opposition to, 316, 351
Mexico:
   California as territory of, 343
   Gadsden Purchase from, 395
   insurrection in (1911–1917), 644–47
   pre-Columbian civilizations in, 1–3
   Texas as territory of, 343–44
   U.S. economic interests in, 762
Miami, Fla., 925
Miami Indians, 188
Michigan, University of, 916
Micronesia, 759
Middle Colonies, 59–61
   ethnic mixture in, 59–60
   see also specific colonies
Middle East:
   Carter's policy in, 942, 943–44,
      945–46
   Eisenhower's policy in, 876–78, 880
   Kissinger's shuttle diplomacy in, 935
   Persian Gulf War in, 983–89
   Reagan's Marine deployment in,
      958–59
Middle East Treaty Organization
   (METO), 876
Midway, 778, 797
   battle of (1942), 782
Milan Decree (1807), 214, 217
Military Reconstruction Act (1867),
   461–62

Millay, Edna St. Vincent, 694
Miller, Arthur, 842, 850–51
Milwaukee, Wis., 538
minimum wage, 888
mining:
   copper, 492
   gold rushes in, 492, 530, 586
   labor and, 516
   regulation of, 942
   silver, 492
Minneapolis, Minn., 530–31
Minnesota, 579
minorities, 923–24
   see also specific minorities
Mint Act (1792), 181, 575
Minuit, Peter, 31
Minute Men, 112–13
Miranda v. Arizona, 893
missionaries:
   French colonization and, 14
   Spanish colonization and, 11, 340
   U.S. imperialism and, 592, 600–601
missions, Franciscan, 340, 341
Mississippi, 260, 931
   blacks disfranchised in, 487
   Civil War fighting in, 425–26, 440–41
   women's rights in, 328
Mississippi, University of, 890
Mississippi River, 158–59
Missouri, 736
   statehood for, 237
   Unionist vs. Confederate sentiments in,
      417, 418
Missouri, 809
Missouri Compromise (1820), 238–40,
   361, 385
   constitutionality of, 403
   repeal of, 396–97
Missouri-Pacific railroad, 520
Mitchell, John, 930
Moby Dick (Melville), 319
Model T, 713–14
Mohammed Reza Pahlavi, shah of Iran,
   945
Mohawk Indians, 31
Molly Maguires, 516
Molotov, V. M., 817–18, 821
Mondale, Walter F., 941, 960–61, 971
Mongolia, 978
Mongolia, Outer, 804
Mongrel Tariff (1883), 566
Monitor, 424
Monmouth Court House, 131
Monroe, Harriet, 694
Monroe, James, 123, 240, 373
   background of, 232–33
   foreign policy under, 234–37, 243–44
   in presidential elections, 233
Monroe Doctrine, 605, 669, 835
   Clark Memorandum and, 762
   formulation of, 243–44
   Kellogg-Briand Pact and, 761
   Roosevelt Corollary to, 611
Montana, 492
Montcalm, Louis Joseph de, 90
Monterey, Calif., 340

Montesquieu, Charles de Secondat, baron de La Brède et de, 162
Montezuma II, emperor of Aztecs, 2, 10
Montgomery Improvement Assocation, 873
Montréal, 90
Moral Majority, 950
Moravian Indians, 105–6
Moravians, 34
Morgan, J. P., 507, 513–15, 623, 625, 629
Morgan, J. P., Jr., 746
Morgenthau, Henry, Jr., 753
Mormons, 311–13, 492
Morocco, 206, 791, 984
Morocco crisis (1905–1906), 613
Morrill Land Grant Act (1862), 434
Morrill Tariff (1861), 434
Morris, Gouverneur, 160, 163
Morris, Robert, 126, 153, 179
Morristown, winter headquarters at (1776–1777), 123, 126
Morse, Samuel F., 288
Morton, Jelly Roll, 686
Moscow, 774
Mossadegh, Mohammed, 945
Motherwell, Robert, 852, 853
Mott, Lucretia, 328
movies, 711–12
muckrakers, 617
Mugwumps, 566–67, 569, 616–17
Muhammed, Elijah, 904–5
Mukden Incident (1931), 763
Muller v. Oregon, 621
Mulligan, James, 476
Munich, conference at (1938), 765
Munn v. Illinois, 577
Mussolini, Benito, 765, 770, 794
  death of, 805
  see also World War II
MX missiles, 944
My Lai massacre (1968), 927
Mynamar, 867

Nagasaki, nuclear bombing of (1945), 808, 809
Naked Lunch (Burroughs), 854
Napoleon I, emperor of France, 185, 197, 207, 226
  victories and defeats of, 279
  wartime trade disruptions and, 214
Napoleon III, emperor of France, 435
Napoleonic Wars, 243, 293
  trade in, 205–6, 214–17, 219, 225–26, 227–28, 335
Narragansett Indians, 26, 81
Narrative of the Life of Frederick Douglass (Douglass), 378
Nash, Beverly, 464
Nashville, 610
Nashville, battle of (1864), 447
Nasser, Gamal Abdel, 876–77, 878, 880
National Aeronautics and Space Agency (NASA), 879, 963
National American Woman Suffrage Assocation, 556, 687

National Association for the Advancement of Colored People (NAACP), 690–91, 788, 960
National Banking Act (1862), 434
National Bell Telephone Company, 507
National Broadcasting Company (NBC), 841
National Child Labor Committee, 621
National City Bank, 721
National Conference of Catholic Bishops, 951
National Consumers League, 556–57, 621
National Defense Act (1916), 653
National Defense Education Act (1958), 879
National Greenback party, 476
National Industrial Recovery Act (NIRA), (1933), 738–39, 743
nationalism:
  conquest of Florida and, 235
  economy and, 229–32, 233
  emergence of, 229–32, 233
  in Revolutionary era, 148–49
National Labor Relations Act (1935), 744
National Labor Relations Board, 744, 955
National Labor Union, 518
national military establishment, 816, 836
National Organization for Women (NOW), 922, 923, 960, 991
National Recovery Administration (NRA), 738–39, 741, 756
National Right to Life committee, 951
National (Cumberland) Road, 232, 233, 254, 281
National Security Act (1947), 816
National Security Agency, 836
National Security Council (NSC), 816, 829, 836, 860, 894, 964
National Suffrage Association, 687
National Trades' Union, 301
National Typographical Union, 303
National Union for Social Justice, 743
"National Union" ticket, 437
National Woman Suffrage Association, 555
National Youth Administration (NYA), 734, 789–90
Native Son (Wright), 698
nativism, 299–300, 539–40, 561, 562, 1003
  of Klan, 679–81
  after World War I, 678–79
naturalism, 549–50
Naturalization Act (1798), 197
natural selection, 544–45
Nauvoo, Ill., 312
Naval Construction Act (1916), 654
Naval War of 1812, The (T. Roosevelt), 607
Navigation Act (1651), 72
Navigation Act (1660), 73
Navigation Act (Plantation Duty Act) (1673), 73
Navigation Act (Staple Act) (1663), 73
navigation acts, British enforcement of, 73–74, 77, 96

Navy, Continental, 116, 136
Navy, U.S., 206, 219–20
  building for, 759
  economic importance of, 591–92
  world tour of (1907), 613
Navy, U.S. Department of the, 196
Nazi (National Socialist) party, 764
Nebraska, 491, 579
Nebraska Territory, 395
Negroes, *see* blacks
Nelson, Horatio, Lord, 214
Neo-orthodoxy, 848
Netherlands, 14–15, 59, 72, 127, 130,
    171, 185, 760, 770, 822, 867
  colonization by, 27, 28, 31–32
  Puritans flight to, 20–21
Neutrality Act (1935), 767
Neutrality Act (1939), 767, 769
Neutrality laws, 767
Nevada, 492
New Amsterdam, 31, 32
Newark, N.J., 903
New Deal, 731–56, 774
  agricultural recovery programs in,
    734–38
  Eisenhower and, 861
  industrial recovery program in,
    738–39
  labor legislation in, 738
  labor unions and, 750–52
  legacy of, 754–56
  monetary system reformed in, 731–32
  opposition to, 741, 746, 755, 789–90
  regional planning in, 739–40
  relief measures in, 733–34
  renewed depression during, 753–54
  Second, 741–46, 750
  Supreme Court opposition to, 737,
    739, 743, 749–50
  as trial-and-error effort, 731
  Truman and, 812
  see also Roosevelt, Franklin D.
New England, 146
  in American revolution, 156
  colonial life in, 40, 51–58
  colonization of, 20–28
  dialect in, 40
  Dominion of, 74–76
  religion in, 54–55; *see also* Puritans
  secession considered in, 210, 226
  see also specific colonies and states
New England Anti-Slavery Society, 375
New England Emigrant Aid Society,
    398–99
New England Women's Club, 556
Newfoundland, 1, 235
New Freedom, 633, 634–35, 637
New Frontier domestic program, 888
New Guinea, 782, 797
New Hampshire, 147
  adoption of Constitution and, 172
New Hampshire colony, 28, 82
  in border dispute, 105
New Harmony, 332
New Haven colony, 28, 29
New Jersey, 147, 535, 632, 1001

  adoption of Constitution and, 172
  Revolutionary fighting in, 123, 131
New Jersey colony, 29, 33
  ethnic groups in, 33, 39
  founding of, 33
  government of, 75
New Jersey plan, 165, 168
Newlands, Francis G., 498
Newlands Reclamation Act (1901), 498
New Left, 916–20
New Mexico, 492
New Mexico Territory:
  slavery issue in, 390, 391
  U.S. acquisition of, 348, 354, 395
New Nationalism, 633–34
New Netherland colony, 28, 29, 31–32
New Orleans, La., 841, 537, 686
  battle of (1815), 224–25
  as port, 282
  racial riots in (1866), 460
Newport, R.I., 62
newspapers:
  in colonial period, 62–63
  proliferation of (1800s), 320
Newsweek, 841, 910
Newton, Huey P., 904, 917
Newton, Sir Isaac, 63, 69, 307, 691–93
Newtown (Elmira), battle of (1779),
    132–33
New York, 143, 156, 220, 242, 249, 269,
    292, 1001
  adoption of Constitution and, 172
  Revolutionary fighting in, 114, 129
  secession scheme and, 210
New York, N.Y., 476, 507, 531, 567,
    920, 924
  arts in, 852, 854
  as capital, 172, 175
  in colonial era, 62
  as economic center, 283
  immigration through, 293, 535–38
  Revolutionary War and, 123, 124, 126,
    131
New York Central railroad, 506
New York colony, 29, 59
  in border disputes, 105
  ethnic groups in, 59
  government in, 75
  New Netherland as predecessor of,
    31–32
  patroonships in, 31, 59
  Quartering Act and, 101–2
New York Consumers League, 556–57
New York Herald, 320
New York Journal, 593, 594
New York Sun, 320, 625, 645–46
New York Times, 686, 893, 919, 928
New York Tribune, 296, 320, 329, 585
New York Weekly Journal, 63
New York World, 593
New Zealand, 870
Nez Perce Indians, 494
Nicaragua, 961, 978
  Reagan's policy in, 957–58, 964–66
  U.S. interventions in, 648, 761–62
Nicaraguan National Guard, 762

Niebuhr, Reinhold, 848
Nietzsche, Friedrich, 550
Nile River, 877
Nimitz, Chester, 782, 797–800
Nine-Power Treaty (1921), 760, 761, 763
Nixon, Richard M., 866, 919, 961, 993
    background of, 734, 885–86
    cabinet and staff of, 930–31
    domestic policy of, 930–34
    foreign policy of, 934–35
    Hiss affair and, 834
    in presidential elections, 858, 859,
        875, 876, 885–87, 919, 925,
        911–13
    resignation of, 939
    Vietnam War and, 925–30
    Watergate and, 936–40
Nixon tapes, 938–39
Nobel Peace prize, 613, 903, 966
Non-Intercourse Act (1809), 216
Noriega, Manuel Antonio, 966, 982–83
Normandy landing (1944), 794, 795–96
Norris, Frank, 549
Norris, George W., 739–40
Norris v. Alabama, 691
Norsemen (Vikings), 1
North, Frederick, Lord, 107–9, 111,
    130, 138
North, Oliver, 964, 965
North Atlantic Treaty Organization
    (NATO), 822–23, 860, 876, 879,
    978
North Carolina, 134, 135, 143, 147,
    155, 156, 262, 264, 417, 487
    adoption of Constitution and, 172
North Carolina, University of, 150
North Carolina colony, 49
    discontent in, 99
North Dakota, 492
Northern Pacific railroad, 514, 623
Northern Securities Company, 623
Northwest Ordinance (1787), 155, 239
Northwest Territory (Old Northwest)
    Indian problems in, 188
    land policy for, 154–55, 239
    slavery banned from, 155, 239, 255
Norway, 538, 657, 770, 822
Norwegian-Americans, 298
Notes on Virginia (Jefferson), 144–45,
    184, 380
Nova Scotia, 84
Noyes, John Humphrey, 331–32
nuclear weapons, 893–95
    agreements on, 894–95, 935, 940,
        944, 968–69, 982
    atomic bombs, 807–8, 818–19, 862
    Japanese cities destroyed by, 807–9
nullification doctrine, 255–61, 259
    Jackson's proclamation on, 260
    Jackson's rift with Calhoun over,
        258–59
    South Carolina Ordinance and,
        259–60, 261
    Webster-Haynes debate on, 256–58
Nullification Proclamation (1832), 260
Nye, Gerald P., 767

Oates, Joyce Carol, 852
Oberlin College, 311, 323
Occupational Safety and Health Act
    (1970), 932
O'Connor, Sandra Day, 956
Office of National Drug Control Policy,
    975
Office of Price Administration (OPA),
    784, 814
Office of Scientific Research and
    Development, 783
Of Plymouth Plantation (Bradford), 21
Ogden, Aaron, 242
Ohio, 156, 188
    public education in, 322
    statehood for, 206, 232
Ohio Life Insurance and Trust Company,
    404
oil, imported, 933, 935
oil industry, 482, 714, 942
    Rockefeller's dominance of, 509–11
Okies, 736–37
Okinawa, battle of (1945), 806–7
Oklahoma, 487, 492, 691
    Dust Bowl exodus from, 697, 735–36
    Indian lands in, 494
Olive Branch Petition (1775), 115–16
Oliver, James, 500
Oliver, King, 686
Olmec Indians, 1
Olmsted, Frederick Law, 531
Olney, Richard, 525
Omaha, Neb., 530–31
Oman, 984
Oneida Community, 331–32
On the Origin of Species (Darwin), 544
On the Road (Kerouac), 854–55, 916
Open Door Policy, 604–6, 611, 612, 760
Opium War (1839–1842), 394
Oppenheimer, J. Robert, 807, 864
Orders in Council (1793), 186
Orders of Council (1806 and 1807), 214,
    217
Ordinance of 1784, 154
Ordinance of Secession (1860), 411
Oregon, 618
Oregon country:
    claims to, 242–43, 347, 348, 349–50
    exploration and settlement of, 208–9,
        338–40
    slavery excluded from, 385
Organization of Petroleum Exporting
    Countries (OPEC), 933, 941, 960,
    961, 983
Oriskany, N.Y., ambush at (1777), 128
Orlando, Vittorio, 668
orphans, sent to America, 46
Ortega Saavedra, Daniel, 966, 978
Osceola, chief of Seminoles, 262
Ostend Manifesto (1854), 394
O'Sullivan, John Louis, 337
Oswald, Lee Harvey, 896, 897
Other America, The (Harrington),
    898–99
Otis, Harrison Gray, 226
Otis, James, 98, 103

Otis Elevator Company, 531
Ottawa Indians, 84, 90–91, 95
Ottoman Empire, 988, 989
*Our Country: Its Possible Future and Its
    Present Crisis* (Strong), 592
Overlord, Operation, 796
Owen, Robert, 332, 526

Paine, Thomas, 116–17, 123
painting, in post-World War II era,
    852–53
Pakenham, Sir Edwin, 225
Pakistan, 870, 876, 867
Palestine, 823
Palestine Liberation Organization (PLO),
    958, 969
Palestinians, 935, 944, 958–59
Palmer, A. Mitchell, 676
Pamunkey Indians, 17
Panama, 609–10, 966
    invasion of (1989), 982–83, 986
Panama Canal, 609–10
Panama Canal Treaty (1978), 943
Panamanian Defense Forces, 982, 983
Pan-American Conference (1933), 762
Panics:
    of 1819, 234, 237–38, 264
    of 1837, 270, 272–73, 283, 285, 303
    of 1857, 404–5
    of 1873, 475, 517
    of 1893, 514
    of 1907, 636
Paragon, 241
Paris, Pact of (Kellogg-Briand Pact)
    (1928), 761, 763
Paris, Peace of (1763), 91, 93
Paris, Peace of (1783), 152, 157, 190–91
Paris, Treaty of (1898), 600–602
Paris peace conference (1919), 667–70
Paris peace talks (1968–1973), 926, 927,
    928–29
parity, 716–17
Parker, Alton B., 625
Parker, John, 112–13
Parker, Theodore, 296, 314
Parks, Rosa, 873
Parliament, English:
    American Revolution and, 116, 118,
        130–31, 138
    colonial authority of, 79
    power of king vs., 79
    taxation of colonies and, 96–97,
        100–102, 105, 108–9, 110–11
party system, 204
    establishment of, 183–85
    mass parties and, 275
    third parties introduced into, 266
    Washington's criticism of, 192
Patent Office, U.S., 506
Paterson, William, 165
Pathet Lao, 895
Patriot missiles, 987
patroonships, 31, 59
Patton, George S., Jr., 726, 794
Paul, Alice, 687–88
Paxton Boys, 105, 106

Peabody, Elizabeth, 314
Peabody, Sophia, 314
Peace Corps, 888–89
Peale, Charles Willson, 149
Peale, Norman Vincent, 847–48
Pea Ridge, battle of (1862), 418
Pearl Harbor, Hawaii, 589, 782
    Japanese attack on (1941), 777–80,
        816
Peking, Tiananmen Square
    demonstrations in, 977
Pendleton, George H., 472, 565
Pendleton Civil Service Act (1883), 565,
    569
Penn, William, 65, 297
    Pennsylvania colony founded by,
        33–34
Pennsylvania, 143, 146, 150, 156
    adoption of Constitution and, 172
    Civil War fighting in, 441–42
    Revolutionary fighting in, 123
    tax revolts in, 188–90
Pennsylvania, University of (Philadelphia
    Academy), 70
Pennsylvania Chronicle (Dickinson), 102
Pennsylvania colony, 29, 39, 105–6
    education in, 65
    religion and, 67–68
Pennsylvania Journal, 99
Pennsylvania Railroad, 518
Pentagon Papers, 928
People's party, 573
Pequot Indians, 28
Pequot War (1637), 81
perestroika (restructuring), 977
Perot, H. Ross, 995–96
Perry, Matthew, C., 394, 604
Perry, Oliver H., 221
Pershing, John J., 647, 657
Persian Gulf, 945, 958, 969
    war in (1991), 983–89
Peru, 1, 975
Petersburg, siege of (1864–1865),
    445–46, 448–49
Ph.D. revolution, 543
Philadelphia, 206
Philadelphia, Pa., 127, 531, 537
    in colonial era, 62, 67–68, 106, 110
    occupation of, 131
    Revolutionary fighting in, 126, 128
    as U.S. capital, 180
Philadelphia Hospital, 326
Philadelphia-Lancaster Turnpike, 281
Philadelphia railroad, 514
Philip II, king of Spain, 15
Philippine Government Act (1902),
    603–4
Philippines, 91, 612, 830, 870, 963
    American annexation of, 600–603,
        606–7
    immigrants from, 1001
    Spanish-American War in, 596–98
    World War II fighting in, 776, 778, 797,
        800
Philippine Sea, battle of the (1944), 800
phonograph, 507

"Phony War" (1939–1940), 769
physics, 691–93
Picasso, Pablo, 693
Pickering, Timothy, 195, 210, 226
Pickett, George E., 357, 441
Pierce, Franklin:
    foreign policy of, 393, 394
    in presidential elections, 393–94, 401
    slavery issue and, 397
Pike, Frederick, 281
Pilgrims, 20
Pilgrim's Progress (Bunyan), 617
Pinchback, Pinckney B. S., 466
Pinchot, Gifford, 627, 629
Pinckney, Charles, 200
Pinckney, Charles Cotesworth, 195, 196, 210
Pinckney, Thomas, 191, 193, 194
Pinckney Treaty (1795), 190–91, 235
Pinkerton agents, 520, 523
Pinochet, Augusto, 978
pirates, Barbary, 206, 227
Pitcairn, John, 112, 113
Pitt, William, 89, 91, 100–101, 111
Pittsburgh, Pa., 292, 538
Pizarro, Francisco, 10
Planck, Max, 692
Plan of Union (1754), 88
Plantation Duty Act (1673), 73
Platt Amendment (1901), 604, 762
Plessy v. Ferguson, 488, 872
pluralistic unity, 1005
Plymouth colony, 20–22, 25, 54
    government of, 21–22
    Indians in, 21, 82
    united with Massachusetts, 76
Pocahontas, 18
Poe, Edgar Allan, 318
"Poem on the Rising Glory of America, A" (Freneau and Brackenridge), 148
poetry:
    of beat generation, 854, 855
    of 1800s, 316–17, 319–20
    in Revolutionary era, 148
Poetry: A Magazine of Verse, 694
Poindexter, John, 964, 965
Point Four, 828
Poland, 670, 803–4, 817, 957, 978
    German conquest of (1939), 769
police, in colonial cities, 62
Polish-Americans, 538
Polish Committee of National Liberation, 817
Polk, James K.:
    Mexican War and, 350–57
    in presidential elections, 347–48
    slavery issue and, 383–85
    westward expansion under, 383–86, 387
Pollock, Jackson, 852, 853
Polo, Marco, 4
Ponce de Leon, Juan, 11
Pontiac, chief of Ottawas, 90–91, 95, 105
Pope, John, 428–29

popular art, 700–701
population growth:
    in colonial period, 41–42
    in 1980s, 971, 997, 998–99
    postwar baby boom and, 813, 839–40, 842
    see also immigration
populism, 636
    progressivism as successor of, 615–16
Populist (People's) party, 716, 735
    black vote sought by, 486
    in elections of 1892, 581–82
    in elections of 1896, 585
    Farmers' Alliances as antecedents of, 579
Port Huron Statement, 916
Port Royal, 84
Portsmouth, Treaty of (1905), 612
Portugal, 243, 760, 822
    New World explorations of, 9
positive thinking, 847–48
postal service, in colonial period, 62
Post Office Department, U.S., 116
postwar era (1945–60)
    arts in, 850–55
    civil rights in, 871–75
    consumer culture in, 840–42
    economy and business in, 838–39, 844–45, 849–50
    loneliness of, 849–50
    religious revival in, 846–48
    suburbs in, 842–44
    women in, 845–46
Potsdam Conference (1945), 808
Potsdam Declaration (1945), 808
Pottawatomie Massacre (1856), 399, 400
Pound, Ezra, 694
poverty:
    under Bush, 976, 999–1000
    in colonial cities, 62
    under Reagan, 954, 999–1000
    in Revolutionary War, 127
    in South, 359, 366
    war on (1960s), 898–99
Powderly, Terence V., 519–20, 521
Powell, Colin, 982, 985
Power of Positive Thinking, The (Peale), 847
Powhatan, chief of Pamunkey, 17, 18, 19, 81
pragmatism, 546
Preemption Act (1830), 280
Presbyterian church, 61, 67, 69, 148, 380
Prescott, Samuel, 112
president, presidency:
    powers of, 167
    weakness of (1869–1913), 560
Presidential Succession Act (1947), 816
press, freedom of, 62–63, 197, 198
    see also newspapers
Preston, Levi, 119
Price, The (Miller), 842
price controls, 785
Princeton, battle of (1776), 123
Princeton University, 70, 631, 632

prison reforms, 325–26
Proclamation of Amnesty (1865), 455
Proclamation of Amnesty and
  Reconstruction (1863), 452
Professional Air Traffic Controllers, 955
professionalism, 543
professional service industries, 999
Profiles in Courage (Kennedy), 886
Progress and Poverty (George), 550–51
Progressive party, 631, 826, 827
progressivism, 615–42
  antecedents to, 616–17
  conservatism of, 615
  democracy sought by, 618
  efficiency gospel of, 618–19
  Harding's dismantling of, 704–7
  muckraking in, 617
  post-World War I transformation of,
    702–3
  regulatory efforts of, 619–20
  social justice espoused by, 620–21
  of T. Roosevelt, 615, 622–24
  of Wilson, 632, 640–41
prohibition movement:
  bootlegging and, 683–84
  constitutional amendment and, 621,
    683, 702
  early temperance movements and,
    324–25
  in elections of 1928, 718
Prohibitory Act (1775), 131
Promise of American Life, The (Croly),
    633–34
Protestant Council of New York City, 847
Protestantism, 12–13, 14, 15, 365, 737
  missionaries of, 592
  social gospel movement in, 552–53
  see also religion; *specific churches*
Providence, R.I.:
  founding of, 26
  unrest in, 106
Prussia, 89
public works, 723
Public Works Administration (PWA), 738
Puerto Rico, U.S. annexation of, 600, 604
Pulitzer, Joseph, 593
Pullman Palace Car Company, 524
Pullman Strike (1894), 523–25
Pure Food and Drug Act (1906), 626
Puritans, 29, 51, 52, 76, 147
  Anglican church repudiated by, 13
  blows to hegemony of, 69
  education emphasized by, 65
  Indian troubles and, 81, 82
  lifestyle of, 54–55
  Massachusetts Bay Colony established
    by, 22–25, 39
  theology of, 55
  Transcendentalism and, 314
  see also Separatists

Qatar, 984
Quaker Oats Company, 297
Quakers (Society of Friends), 39, 56, 147
  Pennsylvania founded by, 33–34
  schools established by, 65

quantum theory, 692
Quartering Act (1765), 97, 101–2, 105
Quartering Act (1774), 109
Quayle, Dan, 971, 997
Québec, 84
  battle of (1759), 89–90
Quebec Act (1774), 109–10
Queen Anne's War (War of the Spanish
  Succession) (1701–1713), 86
Quinn, Sally, 991

Rabbit, Run (Updike), 852
racial riots, 460
  in 1960s, 903–4, 1004–5
  in 1990s, 1004–5
  after World War I, 675
  in World War I, 659–60
  in World War II, 788
racism, *see* blacks; nativism
Radical Republicans, *see* Republicans,
  Radical
radio, 712
radioactivity, 692
railroads:
  cattle and beef transported on, 497
  decay of, 862
  early, 283–85
  financing of, 506
  New West shaped by, 499
  oil industry and, 509, 510
  racial segregation in, 487–88
  regulation of, 557, 569–70, 620,
    625–26
  strikes against, 516–18, 520
railroads, transcontinental:
  construction of, 503–6
  dispute over route for, 395–96
  Republican support for, 434
Rainbow, 285
Raleigh, Sir Walter, 15–16
Ramsey, David, 148
Randolph, A. Philip, 747, 787, 825
Randolph, Edmund, 177
Randolph, John, 210, 211, 219, 253, 367
Randolph, Peyton, 110
Rankin, Jeanette, 778
rationing, 785
Reading Railroad, 514, 624
Reagan, Nancy, 949, 969
Reagan, Ronald, 943, 946–47, 993
  appointees of, 955
  background of, 949
  economic program of, 953–54
  feminists opposed by, 956
  foreign policy of, 956–57, 962–63,
    964–66, 968–69
  inauguration of, 952–53
  labor setbacks under, 955–56
  minorities and, 955
  popularity of, 955
  in presidential elections, 941, 949–52,
    960, 961
  savings and loan industry and, 973
  scandals under, 955, 964–66, 969
Reagan Doctrine, 961
Reaganomics, 953–54

realism, 545–51
reaper, 287–88
recessions:
  of 1957–1958, 879
  of 1970s, 933, 934, 940
  of 1990–1992, 991–93
  see also panics
Reconstruction:
  black politicians in, 464–66
  carpetbaggers and scalawags in, 466–67
  civil rights legislation in, 462, 464, 467
  collapse of Republican control in, 469
  corruption and abuses in, 467–68
  end of, 478
  Johnson's plan for, 454–56
  land policy in, 453, 458
  Lincoln's program for, 451–54
  military rule in, 462, 464
  pardons in, 452, 455
  Radicals' program for, 452–53, 457–59, 473–75
  repressive Black Codes in, 456–57, 459
  southern intransigence in, 456–57
  state governments reorganized in, 456
  Wade-Davis plan for, 452–53
  white terror in, 468–69
  see also South
Reconstruction Finance Corporation (RFC), 724, 725, 861
Red Badge of Courage, The (Crane), 549, 550
Red River War (1874–1875), 494
Red Scares:
  in Cold War, 815, 833–35, 862–64
  after World War I, 676–77, 717
Reformation, 12–13
reform movements, 375, 562, 563, 565, 567
  dietary, 328
  for prisons and asylums, 325–27
  Transcendentalism and, 323
  utopian, 330–33
  women's role in, 327
  see also antislavery movements; labor laws; progressivism;prohibition movement; women's rights movement; women's suffrage movement
regulation, governmental:
  business support for, 615
  Harding's reduction of, 706–7
  progressivism and, 619–20
  of railroads, 557, 569–70, 620, 625–26
  see also antitrust laws; Interstate Commerce Commission; labor laws; Sherman Antitrust Act
Regulators, 106
Rehnquist, William, 932
religion:
  church-state separation and, 25–27, 55
  deism and, 63
  Enlightenment and, 63–64, 66
  freedom of, 76, 79

fundamentalist movement in, 681–83, 950
  government support of, 847
  Great Awakening and, 66–70
  literature on, 851
  postwar revival of, 846–48
  schools and, 892–93
  Second Awakening and, 308–13
  among slaves, 48, 371–72
  Unitarian and Univeralist movements, 307–8
  see also Anglican church; Bible; Catholic church; missionaries; Protestantism; Puritans; Quakers
religious persecution:
  of Puritans, 23–24
  of Quakers, 56
  of Separatists, 25–27
religious tolerance, 25–27, 30, 57, 59–60
reparations, after World War I, 669–70, 759, 803
Reparations Commission, 759, 803
Report of Public Credit, First (1790), 179–80
Report on Public Credit, Second (1790), 181
Report on the Condition of the Indian Tribes, 493
Republican party, 406
  antislavery stance of, 401
  in Civil War, 434
  cultural analysis of, 561
  domination of (1869–1913), 559–60
  in 1980s, 971
  origins of, 398, 401
  see also elections and campaigns
Republicans, Democratic, see Democratic party
Republicans, Jeffersonian, 183–85, 188, 191, 219, 230
  Alien and Sedition Acts opposed by, 197–98
  divisions among, 210–11, 234
  dominance of, 209–10
  Federalist views adopted by, 228, 229
  Tertium Quid dissenters in, 210–11
  see also elections and campaigns
Republicans, Liberal, 474
Republicans, National:
  in election of 1832, 265, 267
  in formation of Whig coalition, 270
  origins of, 247
Republicans, Old, 272
Republicans, Radical, 455
  accomplishments of, 467–68
  black suffrage and, 458
  electoral success of, 460–62
  Johnson's removal sought by, 462–63
  presidential candidates of, 471
  Reconstruction program of, 452–53, 457–59, 473–75
  in southern politics, 466–68, 470
Rerum novarum (Leo XIII), 553
Resistance, 918
Resolution Trust Corporation (RTC), 973

Restoration, English, 29, 72, 86
Resumption Act (1875), 475
Revels, Hiram, 466
Revenue Act (1916), 654
Revenue Act (1926), 706
Revenue Act (1935), 746
Revere, Paul, 104, 112, 159
Revolutionary War, *see* American
    Revolution
Rhett, Robert Barnwell, 392
Rhineland, 765
Rhode Island, 140–41
    adoption of Constitution and, 162, 172
Rhode Island colony, 106
    charter of, 27, 29, 78, 141
    first settlements in, 26, 27
    government of, 27, 75, 78
    Indians in, 82
    religious toleration in, 27
Rhode Island system, 291–92
rice production, 31, 45
Richardson, Elliot, 938
Richmond Times, 488
Ridgway, Matthew, 832
Riesman, David, 849–50
right-to-work laws, 879
Ripley, George, 314, 332
river transportation, 281–83
    federal funding for, 231
    Gibbons v. Ogden and, 242
    state funding for, 282
    steamboats in, 241, 242, 281, 282
    see also canals
roads:
    federal funding for, 231–32, 233,
        254–55
    movement for improvement of,
        280–81
Roanoke Island, colony on, 16
roaring twenties, 685–86
    moral values in, 685–86
    women's fashions in, 686
Rockefeller, John D., 509, 545, 721
    organizational innovations of, 510
Rockingham, Charles Watson-Wentworth,
    marquis of, 100–101, 138
Rockne, Knute, 538
Roe v. Wade, 922
Rogers, Will, 668, 710
Rolfe, John, 18, 19
Rolling Stones, 920
Rolling Thunder, Operation, 906
Romania, 978
Romanticism, 313–16
Rome, battle of (1944), 794
Rommel, Erwin, 773
Roosevelt, Eleanor, 729, 747–48, 886
Roosevelt, Franklin D., 714, 816, 817,
        828, 898
    at Allied conferences, 791, 802, 804
    atomic bomb and, 807
    background of, 728–29
    court-packing plan of, 749–50
    declining health and death of, 804,
        805
    fireside chats of, 731, 741, 773

Hundred Days of, 731–32
    inaugural addresses of, 731, 749
    in presidential elections, 704, 728–31,
        748–49, 772–73, 800–801
    Prohibition and, 729
    U.S. neutrality and, 767, 768, 769
    World War II and, 770, 777, 778, 800
    see also New Deal
Roosevelt, Theodore, 309–10, 627, 628,
        671, 729, 756, 972, 976
    background of, 606–9
    coal strike and, 623–24
    conservation movement and, 626–27
    as imperialist, 591
    Monroe Doctrine extended by, 611
    Moroccan crisis and, 613
    New Nationalism of, 630
    in presidential elections, 606–7, 625,
        630–31, 633–35
    progressivism of, 615, 622–24
    regulatory legislation sought by,
        625–26
    in Rough Riders, 598–99
    in Spanish-American War, 594, 595
    Taft criticized by, 629–30
    as trustbuster, 622–23, 625
    U.S.-Japanese relations and, 612
    World War I and, 652
Roosevelt Corollary, 611
Roosevelt Dam, 498
Root, Elihu, 612
Root-Takahira Agreement (1908), 612
Rosecrans, William, 442–43
Rosenberg, Ethel, 834, 864
Rosenberg, Julius, 834, 864
"Rosie the Riveter," 845
Rostow, Walt, 895
Roth, Philip, 851
Rothko, Mark, 853
Roughing It (Twain), 547
Rough Riders, 598–99
Rousseau, Jean Jacques, 916, 917
Royal Air Force (RAF), 795
Royal Proclamation (1763), 95
rubber, 288
Ruby, Jack, 896
Rudd, Mark, 918
Ruffin, Edmund, 392
Rumania, 670, 774, 818
    in World War I, 665
Rural Electrification Administration
        (REA), 740
Rush, Benjamin, 150
Rush, Richard, 234
Rush-Bagot Agreement (1817), 234
Rusk, Dean, 888, 894, 908
Russell, Jane, 847
Russia, Imperial, 89, 214, 538
    Imperial China and, 604–5
    North American claims of, 242, 340,
        588–89
    in World War I, 648, 656, 663, 665,
        666
    see also Soviet Union
Russian-Americans, 538
Russian Republic, 656, 663, 980–81

Russian Revolution (1917), 656, 663, 665, 666–67, 676
Russo-Japanese War (1904–1905), 611–12, 613, 804
Rutgers University (Queen's College), 70
Rutledge, John, 165

Saar Basin, 765
Sacajawea, 208
Sacco, Nicola, 678–79
Sackville-West, Sir Lionel, 571
Sadat, Anwar el-, 935, 943, 944
Saigon, 910, 929
St. John de Crèvecoeur, J. Hector, 39–40
St. Lawrence Seaway, 861
St. Louis, Mo., 238, 292, 538, 659
St. Mary's, Md., 19–20
St. Paul, Minn., 530–31, 925
Salem, Mass.:
    Williams's pastorate in, 25
    witchcraft hysteria, in, 57–58
Salinger, J. D., 852
Salvation Army, 553
Samoa, 589
Sandburg, Carl, 694
San Diego, Calif., 340, 341, 737
Sandino, César Augusto, 340, 341, 540–41, 737, 761–62, 1004
San Francisco, Calif., 340, 341, 530, 540–41, 737, 920, 924,1004
    United Nations Charter Conference in (1945), 817
San Francisco State University, 918
Sanger, Margaret, 687
Santa Anna, Antonio López de, 344–45, 354–55
Santa Fe, N.Mex., trade expeditions to, 338
Santa Fe Railroad, 530
Santo Domingo, 207
Saratoga, battle of (1777), 128–29
Sartoris (Faulkner), 699–700
Sassamon, 82
satellites, 878–79
"Saturday Night Massacre," 938
Saudi Arabia, 876
    in Persian Gulf War, 984, 987–88
Savannah, Ga., 126, 133
savings, 841
savings and loan industry, bailout of, 973
Savio, Mario, 917
scalawags, 466–67
Scarlet Letter, The (Hawthorne), 318
Schechter Poultry Corporation v. United States, 743
Schenck v. United States, 662
Schlafly, Phyllis, 950–51
Schmacher, Ferdinand, 927
school prayer, 892–93
Schurz, Carl, 474
Schwarzkopf, H. Norman, 986, 987
science, 288–89, 691–93
Scopes, John T., 681–83
Scotland, 15
Scott, Dred, 402–3
Scott, Winfield, 219, 260, 423

in Civil War, 418
in Mexican War, 352, 354, 355–56, 357
in presidential elections, 393
Scotch-Irish Americans, 39, 61
Scottsboro case, 691
SCUD missiles, 987
Seattle, Wash., 530, 674
Sea Wolf, The (London), 550
secession of South, 411–14
    Buchanan's response to, 413
    compromise efforts in, 414
    Lincoln's response to, 413
    movement for, 392
    see also Civil War, U.S.
Sedition Act (1798), 197
Sedition Act (1918), 662
segregation, 487–89, 824, 826, 912
    of buses and trains, 873–75, 889
    in housing, 904
    of schools, 378, 871–72, 875, 889, 890, 891, 931
    see also blacks; civil rights movement
Seize the Day (Bellow), 852
Selective Service Act (1917), 657–58
Seminole Indians, 235, 262
Senate, U.S.
    A. Johnson acquitted by, 463
    Constitutional Convention and, 167
    violence on floor of (1856), 400
Seneca Indians, 133
Sennett, Mack, 711–12
Separatists, 13, 20–22
    in Rhode Island, 25–27
Serra, Junipero, 340
Servicemen's Readjustment Act (1944), 813
settlement houses, 554–55, 620
Sevastopol, 774
Seven Days' battles (1862), 428
Seven Pines, battle of (1862), 428
Seventeen, 842
Seven Years' War (French and Indian War) (1754–1763), 86, 87–91, 207
    legacy of, 93–95
Seward, William H., 389
    in foreign affairs, 588–89
    slavery issue and, 408
sewing machines, 288
sex:
    frankness about, in 1920s, 685–86
    Oneida Community and, 331–32
    premarital, 686
    Puritan views on, 54
    safe, 975
sexual harassment, 990–91
Seymour, Horatio, 472
Shakers, 330–31
Shame of the Cities, The (Steffens), 617
Shantung Peninsula, 759
sharecropping, 483–84
Share Our Wealth program, 742
Sharpsburg (Antietam), battle of (1862), 429–31
Shaw, Anna Howard, 556

Shawnee Indians, 218
Shays, Daniel, 160
Shays's Rebellion (1787), 159–60, 161
Shelburne, Sir William Petty, earl of, 138
Shepard, Alan B., Jr., 879
Sheridan, Philip H.:
  in Civil War, 449
  in Indian wars, 494
Sherman, John, 560, 563, 571, 572
Sherman, Roger, 163, 165, 166
Sherman, William Tecumseh, 426, 443
  Johnston pursued by, 444, 446
  in march to sea, 446–48
  in Vicksburg campaign, 440
Sherman Antitrust Act (1890), 511, 619, 622, 623
Sherman Silver Purchase Act (1890), 572, 576, 583
Shevardnadze, Edouard, 984
Shi'ite Muslims, 988
Shiloh, battle of (1862), 425–26
Shipping Board, U.S., 658
Shultz, George P., 958, 964, 966
shuttle diplomacy, 935
Siberia, 775
Sicily, invasion of (1943), 794
"Significance of the Frontier in American History, The" (Turner), 500–501
silent majority, 926
silver coinage, 564, 572, 575, 581, 582–86
silver mining, 492
Simmons, William J., 679–80
Simpson, "Sockless" Jerry, 580, 585
Sinclair, Upton, 626
Singapore, 781
Singer, Isaac Merritt, 288
"Sinners in the Hands of an Angry God" (Edwards), 67, 68
Sino-Japanese War (1894–1895), 604
Sioux Indians, 494
Sirica, John J., 936, 937
Sister Carrie (Dreiser), 533, 550
sit-ins, 915, 916, 917, 924
Slater, Samuel, 286
slave codes, 369
slavery:
  banned from Old Northwest, 155, 239, 255
  in colonial period, 19, 39, 46–49
  Compromise of 1850 and, 387–94
  Consititution on, 165–66, 206, 239–40, 414
  cotton and, 279
  Dred Scott decision and, 402–3
  in Mexican Cession, 383–87
  Mexican War and, 383
  myths about, 359–60
  profitability of, 363, 366, 367
  religion and, 379–81
  southern defenses of, 379–81
  southern middle-class and, 365–66
  Texas statehood and, 346
  Wilmot Proviso and, 383–84
  see also antislavery movements; blacks;

emancipation; Emancipation Proclamation; Fugitive Slave Act; Kansas-Nebraska Act; Missouri Compromise
slaves:
  in American Revolution, 144–45
  as contrabands of war, 432
  emancipation of, 432–34
  escaped, 378, 392, 398, 432
  ethnic diversity of, 46–47
  families of, 372–73
  female, sexual exploitation of, 373
  freed, 366–67, 367
  Indians as, 30–31, 48–49
  infant mortality rate of, 369
  insurrections of, 47, 369
  owners' relationship with, 371
  on plantations, 368–71
  prices of, 366–68
  religion of, 48, 371–72
slave trade:
  domestic, 367–68
  foreign, outlawing of, 206, 335–36, 368
  with West Indies, 11
Slavic immigrants, 535, 538, 539
Slovak-Americans, 538
Smalls, Robert, 433
smart bombs, 986
Smith, Adam, 156–57
Smith, Alfred E., 718, 741
Smith, Emma, 312
Smith, Francis, 112
Smith, Hyrum, 313
Smith, John, 17–18, 43, 81
Smith, Joseph, Jr., 311–13
Smith Act (1940), 865
Smith College, 542
Smith-Connally War Labor Disputes Act (1943), 790
Smith-Hughes Act (1917), 641
Smith-Lever Act (1914), 641
Smith v. Allwright, 788
smuggling, 102, 105, 106, 107, 157
Snyder, Gary, 853
social criticism, 550–51
Social Darwinism, 544–45, 628
Social Democratic party, 526
social gospel, 551–53
socialism, progressivism spurred by, 617
Socialist Labor party, 526
Socialist party, 676
  presidential candidates of, 526, 628, 635, 730
Social Security, 750, 752, 813, 888, 932, 998
Social Security Act (1935), 744–46, 861
Sociology for the South; or, The Failure of a Free Society (Fitzhugh), 380
Soil Conservation and Domestic Allotment Act (1936), 737
Solidarity, 957
Solomon Islands, 797, 800
Somoza, Anastasio, 762
Sons of Liberty, 102–3
Soulé, Pierre, 394

Sound and the Fury, The (Faulkner), 699,
 700
South:
 agriculture in, 44–46, 361–62,
  483–84
 American Revolution and, 133–37
 blacks disfranchised in, 485–87, 641
 Bourbons of, 484–86
 in colonial period, 40, 44–51
 cotton production in, 278–79
 decline of Democratic dominance of,
  859
 dialects in, 40
 economic growth of, in postbellum era,
  481–82
 education in, 321
 gentry in, 50
 literature of, 698–700
 manufactures and industry in, 362–63
 middle class in, 365–66
 mythology of, 359–60
 New, 480–90
 planters and plantations in, 364–65
 poor whites in, 359, 366
 religion in, 50–51
 Republican groups established in, 464
 segregation in, 487–89, 873–75, 889,
  890–91, 931
 Union blockade of, 417, 423
 western territories and, 155–56
South Africa, 586, 978–79
South Carolina, 133–34, 135, 147, 156,
  468, 618
 adoption of Constitution and, 172
 Civil War fighting in, 448
 nullification crisis in, 255–61
 slavery in, 47, 367
South Carolina colony, 31
 slavery in, 47
 social structure in, 50
South Carolina Exposition and Protest
  (1828), 248, 256, 257
South Carolina Ordinance (1832), 259–60
South Dakota, 492, 579, 618
Southeast Asia Treaty Organization
  (SEATO), 869, 876
Southern Baptist Convention, 380
Southern Christian Leadership
  Conference (SCLC), 875, 889
Southern Manifesto (1956), 873
Southern Pacific Railroad, 505–6, 530
Southern Power Company, 482
Southern Railway, 514
South Improvement Company, 509
South Manchurian Railway, 763
Soviet Union, 676, 869, 966
 Afghanistan invaded by (1979),
  944–45
 China and, 761, 763
 containment strategy and, 819–20
 Cuba and, 893–95
 détente with, 934, 935
 disintegration of, 977–82
 in Eastern Europe, 791, 792, 817–19,
  878
 Hungary invaded by (1956), 878

Korean War and, 829, 831
 Middle East and, 877, 878
 Nazi nonaggression pact with, 766
 nuclear arsenal of, 829, 866, 893–95
 space program of, 878–79
 in Spanish Civil War, 768
 U.S. defense buildup and, 956–57
 U.S. recognition of, 764–65
 U.S. treaties with, 935, 940, 968–69
 in World War I, 663
 in World War II, 774, 775, 795,
  801–3, 809–10
 see also Russia, Imperial; Russian
  Republic; Russian Revolution
space programs:
 American, 878–79, 889, 963
 Soviet, 878–79
Spain, Spanish Empire, 14–15, 16, 17, 35,
  36, 126, 185, 186, 340, 343, 823
 cattle industry and, 497
 challenges to, 13–15
 in Cuba, 394; *see also* Spanish-
  American War
 in discovery and conquest of America,
  4, 9–12
 Florida as territory of, 35, 138, 156,
  190–91, 208, 211, 217, 219,
  224–25, 235–37
 Havana and Manila lost by, 91
 intrigues with Indians of, 157, 158–59,
  191
 in Napoleonic Wars, 214, 243
 in Persian Gulf War, 986–87
 Pinckney Treaty with, 190–91, 235
 post-Revolution relations with, 158–59
Spanish-American War (1898), 592–604,
  608, 609
 annexation debate in, 600–603
 Cuban campaign in, 598–600
 Cuban insurrection leading to, 592–93
 governments established in
  acquisitions from, 603–6
 Maine incident and, 594
 Manila Bay taken in, 597–98
 Philippine insurrection and, 596–98,
  602
 war declaration and, 596
 yellow journalism and war frenzy in,
  593, 594
Spanish Civil War (1936–1939), 767–68
Spanish flu, 673–74
Specie Circular (1836), 269
speech, freedom of, 197–98, 975
Spencer, Herbert, 512, 544–45
Spindletop gusher, 714
Spock, Benjamin, 850
spoils system, 252–55, 562, 563,
  564–65, 616
Spoon River Anthology, 694
Spotsylvania Court House, battle of
  (1864), 444–45
Spotted Tail, chief of Sioux, 494
Sputnik, 878–79
Squanto, 21
Sri Lanka (Ceylon), 867
stagflation, 933–34

Stalin, Joseph, 697, 755, 791, 795, 802, 817, 819, 828, 862
Stalwarts, 563, 564, 565
Stamp Act (1765), 97
  colonial protests against, 98–100
  repeal of, 100–101, 138
Stamp Act Congress (1765), 100, 148
Standard Oil Company, 509–11, 617, 624
Stanford, Leland, 504
Stanley, Ann Lee, 330
Stanton, Edwin M., 436, 462, 463
Stanton, Elizabeth Cady, 328, 555, 556
Staple Act (1663), 73 *Star of the West,* 413
Starr, Ellen, 554
"Star Spangled Banner, The" (Key), 224
Star Wars (Strategic Defense Initiative), 962–63
State, U.S Department of, 177
state compact theory, 198, 257
states' rights, Webster-Hayne debate on, 256–58
  see also nullification doctrine
States' Rights Democrats, 826, 827
Statue of Liberty, 535
Staunton, Va., 619
steam engines, 286, 287
steamships, 285
steel industry, 482, 511–12, 514–15
Steel Workers Organizing Committee, 751
Steffens, Lincoln, 617
Stein, Gertrude, 694–95
Steinbeck, John, 697, 735
Steinway pianos, 297
Steinweg, Heinrich, 297
Stephens, Alexander H., 412, 438, 456
Stephens, Uriah S., 519
Steuben, Baron Friedrich von, 131
Stevens, Thaddeus, 436, 457–58, 471
Stevenson, Adlai E., 846, 858–59, 860–61, 876
Stewart, Alexander T., 295
Still, Clyfford, 852
Stimson, Henry L., 761, 808
stock market, 720–21, 967
Stone, Lucy, 555
Stonewall Inn, 924
Story, Joseph, 252
Stowe, Harriet Beecher, 392
Strategic Arms Limitation Talks (SALT), 935, 940, 944
Strategic Defense Initiative (SDI; Star Wars), 962–63
Strauss, Levi, 298
streetcars, 482, 531
Strong, George Templeton, 296
Strong, Josiah, 592
Stuart, J. E. B., 408, 428, 429, 441
Student Nonviolent Coordinating Committee (SNCC), 889, 904
Students for a Democratic Society (SDS), 916, 917–18, 919
Stuyvesant, Peter, 32
Styron, William, 852
submarines, 652–53, 655–56

sub-treasury plan, 735
suburbs, 842–44, 849
Sudetenland, 765
Suez Canal, 876–78
Suez War (1956), 878, 880
Suffolk Resolves (1774), 110
suffrage:
  for blacks, 456, 458, 462, 464, 471, 639, 902–3
  in colonial America, 79
  property holding and, 143
  taxpaying qualifications for, 248
  see also women's suffrage movement
Sugar Act (Revenue Act) (1764), 96, 97, 98, 105
sugar cane production:
  in Hawaii, 589–90
  tariffs and bounties in, 589–90
Sugar Trust, 623
Sumner, Charles, 436, 457, 458
  bludgeoned on Senate floor, 400
  slavery issue and, 386
Sumner, William Graham, 545, 628
Sumter, Thomas, 134
Sun Also Rises, The (Hemingway), 696
Sunbelt, 842
Sunni Muslims, 988
Sun Yat-sen, 763
Supreme Court, U.S., 165, 167, 177
  under Burger, 931
  civil rights decisions of, 871–72, 874–75
  Civil War and, 417
  F. D. Roosevelt court-packing plan for, 749–50
  free speech and, 975
  government secrecy and, 928
  Indian affairs and, 263–64
  judicial nationalism and, 240–42
  judicial review principle affirmed by, 204–5
  New Deal programs and, 737, 739, 743, 749–50
  powers of, 168
  Reconstruction issues and, 462
  slavery issues and, 402–3, 406
  Thomas nomination for, 989–91
  under Warren, 864–65, 892, 931–32
  Watergate and, 938
Supreme Headquarters, Allied Expeditionary Forces (SHAEF), 795–96
Surratt, Mary, 454
Susquehannock Indians, 83–84
Sutter, John A., 341

Taft, Helen "Nellie," 628
Taft, Robert A., 814, 857
Taft, William Howard, 540, 612
  accomplishments of, 630
  background of, 628
  as chief justice, 628, 634–35, 705
  Philippine government organized by, 603
  in presidential elections, 627, 630–31, 633–35

Taft-Hartley Act (1947), 815–16, 827, 860, 876
Taft-Katsura Agreement (1905), 612
Taiwan (Formosa; Republic of China), 604, 777, 797, 830, 832
  immigrants from, 1001
  Nationalists' flight to, 828–29
Talleyrand, Charles Maurice de, 195, 196, 197, 207
Tallmadge, James, Jr., 238
Talmage, De Witt, 552
Tammany Hall, 567
Taney, Robert B., 402, 403
Taney, Roger, 267
Tappan, Arthur, 375
Tappan, Lewis, 375
Tarawa, battle of (1943), 797
tariffs, 178–79, 559
  of Abominations (1828), 255–56
  on agricultural goods, 247
  Cleveland's annual message on, 571
  Dingley (1897), 586
  economic nationalism and, 230–31
  of 1816, 231
  of 1824, 247
  of 1832, 259
  of 1833, 269
  farmers disadvantaged by, 575
  on finished goods, 247
  Fordney-McCumber (1922), 706
  in Hamiltonian program, 181–82, 188–90
  Hawley-Smoot (1930), 720, 723
  McKinley (1890), 572–73
  Mongrel (1883), 566
  Morrill (1861), 434
  protection of manufactures as goal of, 159
  Southern opposition to, 255–56, 259, 260–61
  Taft's attempted reduction of, 628–29
  Underwood-Simmons (1913), 636
  Walker (1846), 348
Tarleton, Banastre, 133
Taton, John, 1003
taxation:
  under Articles of Confederation, 142
  under Bush, 970–71, 973
  in Civil War financing, 435
  colonial unrest and, 76, 96–102, 103–4, 105, 107–10, 142
  in elections of 1800, 198
  "external" vs. "internal," 101, 102
  Grenville's program of, 96–100
  in Hamiltonian program, 181, 183
  on increasing land value, 550–51
  under L. B. Johnson, 898
  under Reagan, 962
  Shays's rebellion and, 159–60
  for Social Security, 744–45
  Townshend's program of, 101–5
  on whiskey, 205
  see also income tax
Tax Reform Act (1986), 962
Taylor, Frederick W., 618
Taylor, John, 211

Taylor, Maxwell, 895
Taylor, Zachary, 471
  death of, 390
  in Mexican War, 350, 351, 352, 354–55
  in presidential elections, 385–86
  slavery issue and, 386, 388–90
tea, Chinese, 285
Tea Act (1773), 107–8
Teapot Dome scandal, 707
technology, importance of, 288–89
Tecumseh, chief of Shawnees, 218, 222
Teheran meeting (1943), 795
telegraph, 288
telephone, 507
television, 840–41
Teller Amendment (1898), 596
  see also prohibition movement
tenant farmers, 483–84
tenement houses, dumbell, 539
Tennent, Gilbert, 67
Tennent, William, 67, 70
Tennessee, 156, 158, 192, 417, 681–83
  Civil War fighting in, 442–44, 447
Tennessee Valley Authority (TVA), 739–40
Tenure of Office Act (1867), 461–62
territories, under Confederation, 154–56
terrorism, 959, 963
test-ban treaty (1963), 894–95
Tet offensive (1968), 909–10
Texas, 681, 736
  annexation of, 348–49, 350
  boundaries of, 391
  elections of 1844 and, 347–48, 349
  immigrants in, 1001, 1002
  independence from Mexico declared by, 344
  as Mexican territory, 343–44
  population growth of, 998
  as republic, 344–46
  settlement of, 343–44
  statehood of, 349
Texas and New Mexico Act (1850), 391
Texas v. White, 462
textile manufactures:
  growth of (early 1800s), 286–87
  Lowell and family systems in, 291–92
  in South, 482
Thailand, 870
Thames, battle of the (1813), 222
Thanksgiving, origins of, 21
Theory of the Leisure Class, The (Veblen), 551
Thieu, Nguyen Van, 926, 928–29
third parties, 211, 266
This Side of Paradise (Fitzgerald), 685, 695
Thomas, Clarence, 989–91
Thomas, George H., 442–44, 447
Thomas, Norman, 730
Thomson, Charles, 110, 153
Thoreau, Henry David, 314–16, 874
thrift institutions, bailout of, 973
Thurmond, J. Strom, 826, 827

Tiananmen Square demonstrations, 977
Tilden, Samuel J., 476–77, 562
Time, 910, 931, 972–73
Tippecanoe, battle of (1811), 218–19
Title IX of the Educational Amendments
  Act (1972), 922
Tituba, 57
tobacco:
  clergy paid in, 51
  in colonial period, 20
  in postbellum economy, 481–82
  Rolfe's experiments with, 18
Tocqueville, Alexis de, 140, 308, 810
Tojo, Hideki, 777, 797, 800
Toleration Act (1689), 76
Tonkin Gulf Resolution (1964), 906
Toomer, Jean, 689
Tories (Loyalists), 112, 124, 128, 132–34,
  135, 139, 140, 143, 157–58
To Secure These Rights, 824
Tower, John, 965
Tower Commission, 965
Townsend, Francis E., 742–43, 748
Townshend, Charles, 101–2
Townshend Acts (1767), 101–2
  modification and repeat of, 105, 131
townships, in New England, 51
trade and commerce:
  with Asia, 285, 394
  in colonial period, 14, 16, 30–31, 35,
    41, 52–54, 72–74
  in Confederation, 156–57, 159, 161
  in French Revolution, 186, 195, 196
  with Great Britain, 156–57, 234–35,
    237, 269–70, 272
  Hamiltonian program and, 181–82
  illegal drugs, 982–83
  imperialism and, 591, 605
  with Indians, 14, 17
  as motive for English colonization, 16
  Napoleonic Wars and, 205–6, 214–17,
    219, 225–26, 227–28, 335
  in 1970s, 933
  pirates and, 206, 227–28
  in Revolutionary era, 116, 126–27,
    131, 156–57
  with South Africa, 978
  in Texas, 346
  urban growth and, 292
  westward migration and, 285, 338
  after World war II, 889
  see also blockades; fur trade; tariffs;
    specific foreign powers
trade-association movement, 715
trade deficits, 967–68
Trade Expansion Act (1962), 889
Trafalgar, battle of (1805), 214
Traffic Safety Act (1966), 901
Transcendentalism, 314–16, 323
Transcontinental Treaty (1819), 237, 242
transportation:
  in early 1800s, 280–86
  in early 1900s, 712–14
  federal improvement of, 231–32,
    285–86
  ocean, 285

racial segregation in, 487–88, 873–75,
  889
urban, 531
see also canals; railroads; river
  transportation; roads
Travis, William B., 344, 345
treason, 213
Treasury, U.S. Department of, 177
  Hamilton's program for, 178–82
Treatise on Domestic Economy, A
  (Beecher), 327
Treaty of Alliance (1778), 130, 197
Treaty of Amity and Commerce (1778),
  130
Trenchard, John, 97
Trenton, battle of (1776), 123
Triangle Shirtwaist Company, 621
Tripartite Pact (1940), 775
Tripoli, 206, 228
Truman, Harry S, 866, 868, 876, 954,
  972
  atomic bomb and, 807–8
  background of, 811–12
  domestic program of, 812, 813–16,
    823–25, 827
  foreign policy of, 828
  Israel and, 823
  military reform under, 816
  in presidential elections, 801, 824,
    825–27
  Red Scare and, 833
  Roosevelt compared with, 811
Truman Doctrine, 820, 833, 835–36,
  907–8
Trumbull, John, 149
trusts:
  in oil industry, 510–11
  T. R. Roosevelt's policies on, 622–23
  see also antitrust laws; Sherman
    Antitrust Act
Truth, Sojourner, 377–78
Tubman, Harriet, 378, 433
Tunis, 206, 228
Tunisia, battle of (1943), 791
Turkey, 819–20, 822–23, 876, 894
  in World War I, 649, 666
Turner, Frederick Jackson, 500–501, 591
Turner, Nat, 369, 375
turnpikes, 281
TV Guide, 840
Twain, Mark (Samuel Langhorne
  Clemens), 547–48, 559, 993
Tweed Ring, 476
Twenties, *see* roaring twenties
Twice Told-Tales (Hawthorne), 318
Two Treatises on Government (Locke),
  76–77
Tydings-McDuffie Act (1934), 604
Tyler, John, 260, 274–75, 335–36, 349,
  414

U-2 incident, 881
U-boats, 652–53, 655–56
Uncle Tom's Cabin (Stowe), 392
Underground Railroad, 378, 392
Underwood-Simmons Tariff (1913), 636

unemployment:
  under Bush, 976, 992
  in Great Depression, 721, 731
  in 1970s, 933, 940, 944
  under Reagan, 955
unemployment insurance, 744–45
Union Leagues, 464, 466
Union of Russian Workers, 676
Union Pacific Railroad, 473, 504, 506,
  520, 623
Union Theological Seminary, 848
Unitarianism, 307–8
United Arab Emirates, 984
United Arab Republic (UAR), 880
United Automobile Workers, 751
United Farm Workers (UFW), 923
United Mine Workers (UMW), 623–24,
  750
United Nations (U.N.), 823, 960, 969,
  983
  creation of, 802, 803, 816–17
  Korean War and, 830–33
  Persian Gulf War and, 984–86, 988
  Resolution 661 of, 984
  Resolution 678 of, 986
United Negro Improvement Association,
  690
United States, 196
United States Steel, 751
United States v. Butler, 737
United States v. E. C. Knight and
  Company, 623
United States v. Northern Securities
  Company, 623
United Steelworkers of America, 751
Universalism, 308
Updike, John, 852
US English, 1003
U.S. News and World Report, 993
Utah, 313
Utah Act (1850), 391

Valley Forge, winter headquarters at
  (1777–1778), 128
Van Buren, Martin, 246, 346
  background of, 271–72
  Calhoun's rivalry with, 253, 254, 259
  economic policies of, 272–73, 303
  in presidential elections, 267, 271,
    274–75, 347, 386
Vance, Cyrus, 944, 945, 946
Vanderbilt, Cornelius, 506
Van Rensselaer, Stephen, 220
Vanzetti, Bartolomeo, 678–79
Varick, Mary, 176
Vassar College, 323, 542
Veblen, Thorstein, 551
V-E Day, 806
Vera Cruz, battle of (1847), 355
Vera Cruz incident (1914), 647
Vermont, 143, 192
  Revolutionary fighting in, 128
Vermont colony, 105
Verrazzano, Giovanni da, 14
Versailles Peace Conference (1919), 765
Versailles Treaty (1919), 667–73
  Hitler's violation of, 764, 765
  League of Nations formed by, 668
  reparations in, 669–70
  U.S. rejection of, 670–73
Vesey, Denmark, 255
Vespucci, Amerigo, 6–7
veterans:
  of Civil War, 569
  of World War I, bonuses for, 725–26
Veterans Bureau, 707
Victor Emmanuel III, king of Italy, 794
Vienna Conference (1961), 893
Vietcong, 871, 906, 908, 909, 926
Vietminh, 867–69
Vietnam, Democratic Republic of,
  867–69
Vietnamese-Americans, 1001, 1002
Vietnam War, 906–11, 925–30
  bombing of North in, 906, 910, 929
  Cambodian bombing in, 927
  casualties in, 907, 930
  conscription in, 926, 941
  Diem leadership and, 895–96
  escalation of, 906–7
  as issue in presidential elections, 911
  opposition to, 917, 918, 926
  origins of, 895–96
  peace talks in, 926, 927, 928–29
  social and economic costs of, 910
  Tet offensive in, 909–10
  U.S. withdrawal from, 926–30, 941
  Vietnamization of, 926
  see also Indochina War
Vikings (Norsemen), 1
Villa, Pancho, 646–47
Vincennes, battle of (1778), 132
Virginia, 133, 146–47, 155, 161, 417,
  487
  adoption of Constitution and, 172
  American Revolution and, 133,
    135–37
  Civil War fighting in, 424, 426–32,
    438–40, 444–46
Virginia, 424
Virginia, University of, 322
Virginia Bill of Rights, 163, 177
Virginia colony, 87
  Anglican church in, 50–51
  charter of, 17–18
  first permanent settlement in, 16–19
  government of, 19, 79
  Indians in, 81–84
  land policies in, 45
  population growth in, 29, 42
  slavery in, 19, 46
  social structure in, 39, 40, 50
  in tax protests, 99–100, 103, 107, 110
  tobacco production in, 44–46
Virginia Company, 16, 21, 45
  see also London Company
Virginia Declaration of Rights (1776),
  146–47
Virginia plan, 164–66, 168
Virginia Resolution (1798), 198
Virginia Statute of Religious Freedom
  (1786), 147

Volunteers in Service to America
    (VISTA), 899, 916
voter participation, 561
Voting Rights Act (1965), 903, 931, 956

Wabash Railroad v. Illinois, 570
Wade, Benjamin, 436, 452, 455, 457
Wade-Davis Bill (1864), 452–53
Wade-Davis Manifesto, 453
wage controls, 785
Wagner, Robert G., 725, 744
Wagner Act (1935), 744, 751
Wagner Labor Relations Acts, 750
Wagner-Steagall National Housing Act
    (1937), 753
Wake Island, 602, 781
Wald, Lillian, 554
Walden, or Life in the Woods (Thoreau),
    316
Walker, David, 374
*Walker's Appeal . . . to the Colored
    Citizens of the World* (Walker), 374
Walker Tariff (1846), 348
Wallace, George, 891, 912–13, 926
Wallace, Henry A., 705, 735, 772, 801,
    814, 826
Wall Street, 720–21, 967
Wall Street Journal, 710
Walpole, Horace, 101
Walpole, Robert, 77
Wampanoag Indians, 82
war bonds, 434–35, 784
Ward, Lester Frank, 545
Warehouse Act (1916), 641
War Hawks, 219
War Industries Board (WIB), 659, 673
Warner, Charles Dudley, 559
War of 1812, 217–28
    aftermath of, 226–28, 229, 278,
        286–87, 362
    Baltimore attacked in, 223 24
    Indian troubles and, 217–18
    New Orleans battle in, 224–25
    northern front in, 220–22
    peace treaty in, 225
    preparations for, 219–20
    southern front in, 222
    trade disruptions leading to, 217–19
    Washington, D.C. captured in, 223
War of the Austrian Succession (King
    George's War) (1744–1784), 86
War of the League of Augsburg (King
    William's War) (1689–1697), 86
War of the Spanish Succession (Queen
    Anne's War) (1701–1713), 86
War Powers Act (1973), 939
War Production Board (WPB), 783
War Refugees Board, 806
War Relocation Camps, 788–89
Warren, Earl, 864–65, 873, 892, 897
Warren, Joseph, 114
Warsaw, 803
Warsaw Pact alliance, 978
Warsaw Treaty Organization, 823, 878
Washington (state), 492
Washington, Booker T., 489–90

Washington, D.C.:
    capture and burning of (1814), 223
    design and construction of, 202
    march on (1963), 891, 903
    Peace Conference in (1861), 414
Washington, George, 110, 126, 160, 196
    as commander-in-chief of Continental
        Army, 114, 116, 124, 125, 133,
        136–37, 161
    as commander of U.S. Army, 189, 190,
        196
    at Constitutional Convention, 162,
        163, 164, 173
    elections and inaugurations of, 175,
        185
    Farewell Address of, 192–93, 836
    foreign policy under, 186–88
    in French and Indian War, 87, 88
    frontier campaigns and, 132–33
    Hamilton and, 180–81, 182, 183
    in New York and New Jersey
        campaigns, 121–23
    portraits of, 149, 176
    presidential etiquette set by, 176
    slavery and, 144, 367
    in Valley Forge, 131
Washington, Martha, 176
Washington Armaments Conference
    (1921), 760
Washington Post, 592, 991
"Waste Land, The" (Eliot), 694
Watergate scandal, 936–40, 952, 961
Watson, Tom, 580
Watt, James (Interior secretary), 955
Watt, James (inventor), 286
Watts, Los Angeles, 903, 1004–5
Wayne, Anthony, 188, 191
Wealth Against Commonwealth (Lloyd),
    551, 617
Wealth of Nations, The (Smith), 156–57
Wealth Tax Act (1939), 746
Weathermen, 919
Weaver, James B., 581, 582
Weaver, Robert C., 901
Webster, Daniel, 240, 352, 373, 388–89
    economic policies of, 230, 248, 265,
        273–74
    on nullification doctrine, 256–58
    party affiliatons of, 270
    in presidential elections, 271
    as secretary of state, 335
Webster, Noah, 161
Webster-Ashburton Treaty (1842), 337
Weinberger, Caspar, 957, 964, 965
Welch, Joseph, 863
welfare state, emergence of, 557
Welles, Orson, 734
Wellesley College, 542
Welsh-Americans, 538
Welty, Eudora, 852
West, Benjamin, 149
West, New, 490–501
    agriculture in, 498–500
    cattle and cowboys in, 496–98
    Indians in, 492–96
    mining in, 492

Western Federation of Miners, 526–27
Western Union, 507
West Florida colony, U.S. acquisition of, 208
West India Company, 31
West Indies, 185, 187, 188, 214
trade with, 157, 158, 235
Westinghouse, George, 508
Westinghouse Electric Company, 508
Westmoreland, William C., 907, 909, 910
Westo Indians, 30
West Virginia, 417, 998
Weyler, Valeriano "Butcher," 593
whaling industry, 52
wheat, 288, 498–99, 500, 574–75, 715
Wheeler, Burton K., 773
Wheelwright, John, 28
Whig party, 275, 320
as coalition against Jackson, 270
economic policies of, 273–74, 335
Mexican War and, 351, 352
split over slavery, 397, 401
see also elections and campaigns
Whigs, British, 94–95
Whigs, Revolutionary, 133, 135, 139–40
Whiskey Rebellion (1794), 188–90, 199
White, Hugh Lawson, 271
White, John, 16
White, William Allen, 615–16, 653, 704
White Citizens' Councils, 873
Whitefield, George, 67–68
White Plains, N.Y., 131
Whitman, Walt, 319–20, 357, 854
Whitney, Eli, 278–79
Whittier, John Greenleaf, 317
Wichita, Kans., 925
Wilderness, battle of the (1864), 444
Wilderness Road, 95, 281
Wild One, The, 855
Wilhelm II, kaiser of Germany, 612, 613, 666
Wilkinson, Eliza, 166
Willard, Emma, 323
Willard, Samuel, 58
William III, king of England, 76, 77, 86
Williams, Roger, 25–26, 27
Williams, Tennessee, 851
Williams, William Carlos, 694
Willkie, Wendell L., 772
Wilmot, David, 383–84
Wilmot Proviso (1846), 383–84
Wilson, Allen B., 288
Wilson, Henry, 457
Wilson, James, 111, 163
Wilson, Woodrow, 540, 559, 703, 756, 898
antitrust program of, 637–39
background of, 631–32
banking and currency reform under, 636–37
Caribbean interventions and, 647–48
Fourteen Points of, 665–66
League of Nations championed by, 668, 670–73
Mexican insurrection and, 644–47
neutrality and mediation efforts of, 652–53, 655–56
in presidential elections, 632–35, 655, 702
progressivism of, 640–41
social justice issues and, 639
stroke and paralysis of, 671
tariff reform under, 635, 636
Versailles Treaty and, 667–73
women's suffrage and, 639, 687
Winesburg, Ohio (Anderson), 694
Winthrop, John, 23–24, 27, 43, 44, 150, 306
Wirt, William, 267
Wisconsin, 261, 1004
witchcraft, 57–58
Wobbelin concentration camp, 805
Wobblies (Industrial Workers of the World), 526–28, 662
Wolfe, James, 89–90
Wolfe, Thomas, 699
Woman in the Nineteenth Century (Fuller), 330
women:
in agrarian movement, 577–78
AIDS and, 975
in antislavery movement, 376
in Civil War, 422
clothing and undergarments for, 686
in colonial period, 27, 44
domestic duties of, 845–46
education of, 321, 322–23, 542, 922–23, 976, 999
employment of, 289–91, 660–61, 688–89, 785–86, 941, 999
ignored by Constitutional Convention, 166
in labor unions, 516–17
in 1920s, 686
in 1940s and 1950s, 845–46
in politics, 991
religion and, 310
as single mothers, 999
slaves, sexual exploitation of, 373
in social reform, 554–55
in West, 339–40, 499–500
working conditions of, 621
Women Accepted for Volunteer Emergency Service (WAVES), 785
Women's Army Corps (WAC), 785
Women's Christian Temperance Union, 621, 683
women's clubs, 556–57
women's rights movement:
emergence of, 327–30
resurgence of (1960s-1970s), 921–23
suffrage victory and, 687–88
women's suffrage movement, 555–57, 639, 661, 686–89
Nineteenth Amendment and, 639
splits in, 555–56
state referenda and, 655
Women's Trade Union League, 660
Woodstock Music Festival (1969), 920, 921
Worcester v. Georgia, 264

working class, *see* labor; labor unions
Working Men's parties, 302
work programs, 734
Work Projects Administration (WPA), 734, 789
World War I, 767
  Americans' sympathies in, 650
  civil liberties curtailed in, 661–62
  debt from, 759
  economic planning in, 735
  economic readjustment after, 674
  European alliances in, 648–49
  German-Mexican alliance in, 656
  labor movement in, 661
  labor unrest after, 674–75
  mobilization for, 658–61, 663
  neutral rights issue in, 652–53
  opposition to, 662
  outbreak of, 648–49
  Paris Conference in, *see* Versailles Treaty
  propaganda in, 650, 657, 662
  racial riots after, 675
  Red Scare after, 676–77, 717
  reparations after, 669–70, 759
  U.S. entry into, 656–62
  U.S. neutrality in, 650–51
  U.S. preparedness for, 653–54
  U.S. troops in, 664–65
  veterans of, bonuses for, 725–26
World War II:
  air warfare in, 770, 777, 795
  alliances and pacts in, 765, 775
  Allied advances in, 791, 794, 796, 801–2
  Allied conferences in, 790–91, 795, 802
  Allied military strategy in, 790–91, 794–95, 797–800
  Atlantic shipping and, 782–83, 790
  atomic bomb in, 807–9
  blacks in, 787–88
  casualties of, 778, 806–7, 808–9
  debate over U.S. involvement in, 771–72, 778
  demobilization after, 813–14
  economic conversion in, 783–85
  European developments leading to, 763–66, 767–68, 769–70
  European theatre in, 770–71, 794, 796, 801–6
  financing of, 784
  foreign assets frozen in, 774, 775
  German advances in, 765–66, 770, 773, 775, 801
  Italian advances in, 773
  Italian expansionism and, 765, 767
  Italian front in, 794
  Japanese aggression leading to, 762–63, 765, 768–69
  Japanese strategy in, 782
  lend-lease program and, 773
  North African campaign in, 773, 791
  Pacific theatre in, 775–80, 781–82, 797–800, 806–9, 818, 829–30
  Pearl Harbor attack in, 777–80
  "Phony War" and, 769
  reparations after, 803
  Russian front in, 775
  submarine warfare in, 774, 782–83, 790
  U.S. aid in, 773, 775, 777
  U.S. declaration of war in, 778
  U.S. defense spending in, 770
  U.S. mobilization for, 783–90
  women's role in, 785–86
Worth, Jonathan, 478
Wright, Orville, 712
Wright, Richard, 697–98
Wright, Wilbur, 712
Wylie, Elinor, 694
Wyoming, 572

Xerox, 992
XYZ Affair (1797), 195–96

Yale College (University), 70, 545
Yalta Conference (1945), 802, 804–5, 817, 818
Yalta Declaration of Liberated Europe (1945), 804
Yamamoto, Isoruku, 782
Yancey, William Lowndes, 392, 409
yellow journalism, 593, 594
Yellowstone National Park, 627
Yeltsin, Boris, 980–82
Yemen, 984
Yippies (Youth International Party), 918–19
Yom Kippur War (1973), 933, 935
Yorktown, 782
Yorktown, battle of (1781), 135–37
Young, Brigham, 313
Young Men's Christian Association, 553
Young Women's Christian Association, 556
Youth for Goldwater, 916
Yugoslavia, 670, 774
Yuppies, 967

Zenger, John Peter, 63
Zimmermann, Arthur, 656
Zimmermann Telegram, 656